파고다

토익 Ⓡⓒ

종합서

파고다 토익 RC 종합서

초판 1쇄 인쇄 2022년 6월 15일
초판 1쇄 발행 2022년 6월 22일
초판 2쇄 발행 2025년 1월 8일

지 은 이 | 파고다교육그룹 언어교육연구소
펴 낸 이 | 박경실
펴 낸 곳 | **PAGODA Books** 파고다북스
출판등록 | 2005년 5월 27일 제 300-2005-90호
주   소 | 06614 서울특별시 서초구 강남대로 419, 19층(서초동, 파고다타워)
전   화 | (02) 6940-4070
팩   스 | (02) 536-0660
홈페이지 | www.pagodabook.com

저작권자 | ⓒ 2022 파고다아카데미

ISBN 978-89-6281-886-4 (13740)

파고다북스   www.pagodabook.com
파고다 어학원   www.pagoda21.com
파고다 인강   www.pagodastar.com
테스트 클리닉   www.testclinic.com

┃ 낙장 및 파본은 구매처에서 교환해 드립니다.

파고다 토익 프로그램

독학자를 위한 다양하고 풍부한 학습 자료

세상 간편한 등업 신청으로 각종 학습 자료가 쏟아지는

파고다 토익 공식 온라인 카페
http://cafe.naver.com/pagodatoeicbooks

교재 Q&A

교재 학습 자료
나의 학습 코칭
정기 토익 분석 자료
기출 분석 자료
예상 적중 특강
논란 종결 총평

온라인 모의고사 2회분
받아쓰기 훈련 자료
단어 암기장
단어 시험지
MP3 기본 버전
MP3 추가 버전(1.2배속 등)
추가 연습 문제 등 각종 추가 자료

매회 업데이트! 토익 학습 센터

시험 전 적중 문제, 특강 제공
시험 직후 실시간 정답, 총평 특강, 분석 자료집 제공

토익에 풀! 빠져 풀TV

파고다 대표 강사진과 전문 연구원들의 다양한 무료 강의를 들으실 수 있습니다.

파고다 토익 기본 완성 RC

토익 리딩 기초 입문서
토익 초보 학습자들이 단기간에 쉽게 접근할 수 있도록 토익의 필수 개념을 집약한 입문서

600+

파고다 토익 실력 완성 RC

토익 개념&실전 종합서
토익의 기본 개념을 확실히 다질 수 있는 풍부한 문제 유형과 실전형 연습 문제를 담은 훈련서

700+

파고다 토익 고득점 완성 RC

최상위권 토익 만점 전략서
기본기를 충분히 다진 토익 중상위권들의 고득점 완성을 위해 핵심 스킬만을 뽑아낸 토익 전략서

800+

파고다 토익 입문서 RC
기초와 최신 경향 문제 완벽 적응 입문서
개념-집중 훈련-실전 훈련의 반복을 통해 기초와 실전에서 유용한 전략을 동시에 익히는 입문서

파고다 토익 종합서 RC
중상위권이 고득점으로 가는 도움 닫기 종합서
고득점 도약을 향한 한 끗 차이의 간격을 좁히는 종합서

이제는 인강도 밀착 관리!

체계적인 학습 관리와 목표 달성까지 가능한

파고다 토익 인생 점수반
www.pagodastar.com

성적 달성만 해도 100% 환급
인생 점수 달성하면 최대 300% 환급

최단 기간 목표 달성 보장
X10배속 토익

현강으로 직접 듣는 1타 강사의 노하우

파고다 토익 점수 보장반
www.pagoda21.com

1개월 만에 2명 중 1명은 900점 달성!
파고다는 오직 결과로 증명합니다.

파고다 토익 적중 실전 RC

최신 경향 실전 모의고사 10회분
끊임없이 변화하는 토익 트렌드에 대처하기 위해
적중률 높은 문제만을 엄선한 토익 실전서

900+   VOCA+

파고다 토익 실전 1000제 LC+RC

LC+RC 실전 모의고사 5회분(1000제)
문제 구성, 난이도, 시험지 사이즈까지 동일한 최신
경향 모의고사와 200% 이해력 상승시키는 해설서
구성의 실전서

파고다 토익 VOCA

LC, RC 목표 점수별 필수 어휘 30일 완성
600+, 700+, 800+, 900+ 목표 점수별,
우선 순위별 필수 어휘 1500

목차

PART 5

이 책의 구성과 특징

PART 5   GRAMMAR 토익 실력자들에게 꼭 필요한 핵심 토익 문법과 문제 유형을 학습한다.
          문장의 구조와 틀을 이해하고 각 문제를 푸는 방법을 익힌다.

PART 5   VOCA Part 5, 6, 필수 동사, 명사, 형용사, 부사 어휘를 핵심 어휘 문제로 풀어본다.

PART 6   Part 5에서 학습한 어법 적용 문제, 어휘 문제, 글의 흐름상 빈칸에 알맞은 문장을 삽입하는 문제에도
          충분히 대비한다.

PART 7   문제 유형별 해결 전략을 학습한다.

OVERVIEW

학습을 시작하기 전에 각 PART의 이해도를 높이기 위해 낱낱이 파헤쳐 본다.

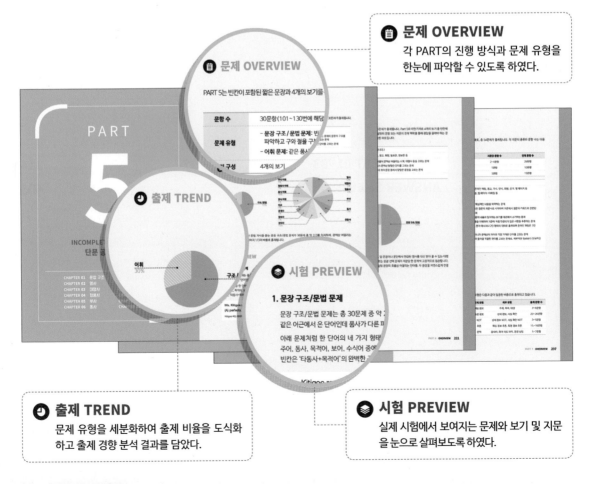

📑 문제 OVERVIEW
각 PART의 진행 방식과 문제 유형을
한눈에 파악할 수 있도록 하였다.

⏱ 출제 TREND
문제 유형을 세분화하여 출제 비율을 도식화
하고 출제 경향 분석 결과를 담았다.

📚 시험 PREVIEW
실제 시험에서 보여지는 문제와 보기 및 지문
을 눈으로 살펴보도록 하였다.

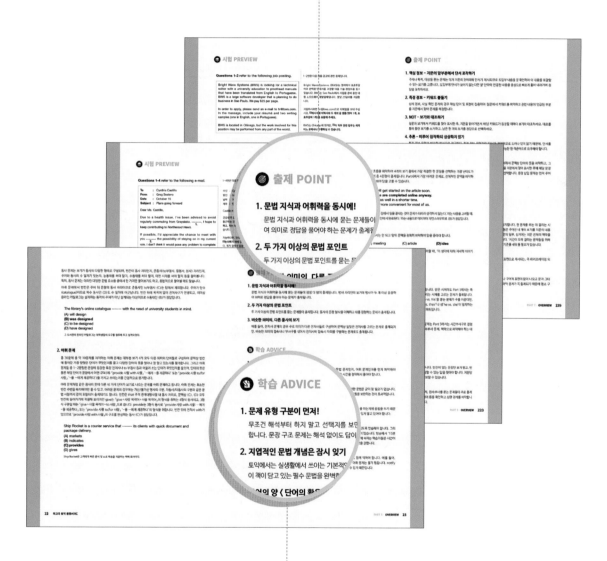

학습 ADVICE

각 PART 학습을 위해 꼭 알아두어야
하는 사항을 정리하였다.

이 책의 구성과 특징

각 PART의 실전 전략형 핵심 개념과 예문을 살펴보고, 그 외 알아두면 좋을 표현까지 정리하여 제시하였다.

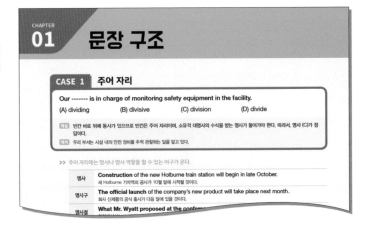

CASE 집중훈련

핵심 개념을 제대로 이해했는지 문제를 통해 확인한다. 실전 감각을 높이기 위한 단계로, 파트별 최대 빈출 문제로 구성하여 집중적인 독해 훈련을 돕고자 하였다.

PART 5: 8문제
PART 6: 8문제
PART 7: 16~20문제

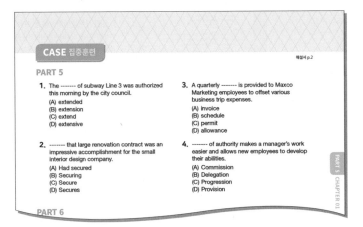

CASE 실전훈련

각 CHAPTER의 총체적인 내용을 아우르는 다양한 유형의 문제를 풀어보면서 독해 실력을 확인한다.

PART 5: 12문제
PART 6: 16문제
PART 7: 22문제

CASE 실전훈련 해설서 p.8

1. All staff members must obtain ------- from their directors for extended absences after November 1.
(A) authorization
(B) authoritative
(C) authorizing
(D) authorize

2. Please ------- expense records, since reimbursement will not be processed without proof of purchase.
(A) keeping
(B) kept
(C) keeps
(D) keep

3. The product team at Goodman Electronics ------- a smartphone with a better battery life.
(A) developing
(B) develop

7. Elias Craig Shipping's partnership with Chapman Constructions expires in three months, and ------- no renewal proposals have been reviewed.
(A) as yet
(B) apart from
(C) so that
(D) only if

8. Copywriters at Prose Advertising are skilled at adhering ------- to clients' needs to produce ideas that appeal to the target audience.
(A) closely
(B) officially
(C) moderately
(D) discreetly

ACTUAL TEST

토익 시험 전 실전 감각을 최종 점검하는 시간을 가질 수 있도록 실제 정기 토익 시험과 가장 유사한 형태의 실전 모의고사 3회분을 제공하였다.

ACTUAL TEST 01 해설서 p.170

READING TEST

In the Reading test, you will read a variety of texts and answer several different types of reading comprehension questions. The entire Reading test will last 75 minutes. There are three parts, and directions are given for each part. You are encouraged to answer as many questions as possible within the time allowed.

You must mark your answers on the separate answer sheet. Do not write your answers in your test book.

PART 5

Directions: A word or phrase is missing in each of the sentences below. Four answer choices are given below each sentence. Select the best answer to complete the sentence. Then mark the letter (A), (B), (C), or (D) on your answer sheet.

101. The cafeteria will be closed on Wednesday for renovations, ------- please make other arrangements for lunch.
(A) which
(B) why
(C) if
(D) so

105. To our -------, a new system for monitoring waste has been implemented in seven cities.
(A) knowledge
(B) skill
(C) ability
(D) competence

해설서

교재에 수록된 모든 문제의 해석은 물론, 정답의 근거를 자세히 설명하였다. 또한 문제 풀이에 필요한 어휘와 키워드 및 패러프레이징 표현을 함께 수록하여 정답 적중률을 한층 더 높이도록 구성하였다.

PART 5

CHAPTER 01 문장 구조

CASE 집중훈련 본서 p.25
1. (B) 2. (B) 3. (D) 4. (B) 5. (D) 6. (B)
7. (C) 8. (A)

1. 주어 자리
The **extension** of subway Line 3 was authorized this morning by the city council.
오늘 아침 시의회에서 지하철 3호선 연장이 승인되었다.
해설 빈칸은 정관사 the의 한정을 받으며 주어 역할을 하는 명사 자리이므로 (B)가 정답이다.
어휘 authorize 승인하다 | city council 시의회

2. 주어 자리
Securing that large renovation contract was an impressive accomplishment for the small interior design company.
그 대형 보수 계약을 따낸 것은 작은 인테리어 디자인 회사에 있어서 놀라운 업적이었다.
해설 빈칸은 that large renovation contract를 목적어로 취하면서 문장의 주어 역할을 하는 자리이다. 동명사는 '~하는 것/~하기'의 의미로 명사의 역할을 하면서 타동사인 동명사로 쓰일 경우 목적어를 수반할 수 있으므로 (B)가 정답이다.
어휘 secure 따내다, 확보하다 | impressive 인상적인 | accomplishment 업적
✦ Key point

해설 문맥상 '권한의 위임이 관리자의 일을 더 쉽게 만든다'는 내용이 자연스러우므로 (B)가 정답이다. delegation은 '위임'이란 뜻 외에, '대표단'이란 의미도 있다.
어휘 authority 권한 | allow ~할 수 있도록 하다, 허락하다 | ability 능력

5-8번은 다음 광고에 관한 문제입니다.

이동하고 싶으신가요? 오늘 DLB Management로 연락하세요. 당신의 업무 공간을 내놓는 시기를 선택하는 것이 중요하다는 걸 기억하세요. 경험이 많은 사업가에게조차, 언제 파는 게 결정하는 건 어려울 수 있습니다. 5요즘은, 시장이 빠르게 변화하고, 복잡하며, 글로벌합니다. 많은 지역 부동산 중개인들은 당신에게 필요한 지식을 제공하는 국제 네트워크에 접근하지 못합니다. 6다행히, DLB Management의 에이전트들은 가능합니다. 저희 에이전트들은 국제 비즈니스 관계에 대해 7특별히 교육을 받습니다. 저희 웹사이트, dlbmgmt.com을 방문하셔서 저희 전문가 8중 한 명과 상담일정을 잡아보세요.

어휘
move on ~으로 가다, 이동하다 | get in touch with ~와 연락하다 | management 경영, 관리 | timing 시기(선택), 타이밍 | list 목록에 포함시키다 | crucial 중요한 | experienced 경험이 많은 | business owner 사업주 | determine 결정하다 | realtor 부동산 중개인 | have access to ~에 접근할 수 있다 | knowledge 지식 | agent 대리인, 에이전트 | train 교육하다 | schedule 일정을 잡다 | consultation 상담 | expert 전문가

5. 어휘 - 동사
해설 빈칸은 주어인 동명사구 determining의 목적어인 'when + to부정사' 구조의 to부정사를 완성하는 동사 자리이다. 빈칸 앞 문장의 '업무 공간을 내놓는 시기 선택은 중요하다'는 내용을 고려할 때, 문맥상 '언제 팔지 결정하는 건 어려울 수 있다'는 내용으로 이어져야 자연스러우므로 (D)가 정답이다.
✦ Key word

11

토익이란?

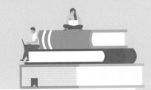

TOEIC(Test Of English for International Communication)은 영어가 모국어가 아닌 사람들을 대상으로 일상생활 또는 국제 업무 등에 필요한 실용 영어 능력을 평가하는 시험입니다.

상대방과 '의사소통할 수 있는 능력(Communication ability)'을 평가하는 데 중점을 두고 있으므로 영어에 대한 '지식'이 아니라 영어의 실용적이고 기능적인 '사용법'을 묻는 문항들이 출제됩니다.

TOEIC은 1979년 미국 ETS(Educational Testing Service)에 의해 개발된 이래 전 세계 160개 이상의 국가 14,000여 개의 기관에서 승진 또는 해외 파견 인원 선발 등의 목적으로 널리 활용하고 있으며 우리나라에는 1982년 도입되었습니다. 해마다 전 세계적으로 약 700만 명 이상이 응시하고 있습니다.

▶ 토익 시험의 구성

	파트	시험 형태		문항 수	시간	배점
듣기 (LC)	1	사진 묘사		6	45분	495점
	2	질의응답		25		
	3	짧은 대화		39		
	4	짧은 담화		30		
읽기 (RC)	5	문장 빈칸 채우기		30	75분	495점
	6	지문 빈칸 채우기		16		
	7	독해	단일 지문	29		
			이중 지문	10		
			삼중 지문	15		
계				200	120분	990점

1979 첫 토익

2006 NEW 토익

2016 신토익

Present

토익 시험 접수와 성적 확인

토익 시험은 TOEIC 위원회 웹사이트(www.toeic.co.kr)에서 접수할 수 있습니다. 본인이 원하는 날짜와 장소를 지정하고 필수 기재 항목을 기재한 후 본인 사진을 업로드하면 간단하게 끝납니다.

보통은 두 달 후에 있는 시험일까지 접수 가능합니다. 각 시험일의 정기 접수는 시험일로부터 2주 전까지 마감되지만, 시험일의 3일 전까지 추가 접수할 수 있는 특별 접수 기간이 있습니다. 그러나 특별 추가 접수 기간에는 응시료가 4,400원 더 비싸며, 희망하는 시험장을 선택할 수 없는 경우도 발생할 수 있습니다.

성적은 시험일로부터 12~15일 후에 인터넷이나 ARS(060-800-0515)를 통해 확인할 수 있습니다.

성적표는 우편이나 온라인으로 발급받을 수 있습니다. 우편으로 발급받을 경우는 성적 발표 후 대략 일주일이 소요되며, 온라인 발급을 선택하면 유효 기간 내에 홈페이지에서 본인이 직접 1회에 한해 무료 출력할 수 있습니다. 토익 성적은 시험일로부터 2년간 유효합니다.

시험 당일 준비물

시험 당일 준비물은 규정 신분증, 연필, 지우개입니다. 허용되는 규정 신분증은 토익 공식 웹사이트에서 확인하기 바랍니다. 필기구는 연필이나 샤프펜만 가능하고 볼펜이나 컴퓨터용 사인펜은 사용할 수 없습니다. 수험표는 출력해 가지 않아도 됩니다.

시험 진행 안내

시험 진행 일정은 시험 당일 고사장 사정에 따라 약간씩 다를 수 있지만 대부분 아래와 같이 진행됩니다.

▶ 시험 시간이 오전일 경우

AM 9:30~9:45	AM 9:45~9:50	AM 9:50~10:05	AM 10:05~10:10	AM 10:10~10:55	AM 10:55~12:10
15분	5분	15분	5분	45분	75분
답안지 작성에 관한 Orientation	수험자 휴식 시간	신분증 확인 (감독 교사)	문제지 배부, 파본 확인	듣기 평가(LC)	읽기 평가(RC) 2차 신분증 확인

* 주의: 오전 9시 50분 입실 통제

▶ 시험 시간이 오후일 경우

PM 2:30~2:45	PM 2:45~2:50	PM 2:50~3:05	PM 3:05~3:10	PM 3:10~3:55	PM 3:55~5:10
15분	5분	15분	5분	45분	75분
답안지 작성에 관한 Orientation	수험자 휴식 시간	신분증 확인 (감독 교사)	문제지 배부, 파본 확인	듣기 평가(LC)	읽기 평가(RC) 2차 신분증 확인

* 주의: 오후 2시 50분 입실 통제

파트별 토익 소개

PART 5

INCOMPLETE SENTENCES
단문 공란 메우기

PART 5는 빈칸이 포함된 짧은 문장과 4개의 보기를 주고 빈칸에 들어갈 가장 알맞은 보기를 고르는 문제로, 총 30문제가 출제된다. 크게 문장 구조/문법 문제와 어휘 문제로 문제 유형이 나뉜다.

문항 수	30문항(101~130번에 해당합니다.)
문제 유형	**- 문장 구조 / 문법 문제:** 빈칸의 자리를 파악하여 보기 중 알맞은 품사나 형태를 고르는 문제와 문장의 구조를 파악하고 구와 절을 구분하여 빈칸에 알맞은 접속사나 전치사, 또는 부사 등을 고르는 문제 **- 어휘 문제:** 같은 품사의 4개 어휘 중에서 정확한 용례를 파악하여 빈칸에 알맞은 단어를 고르는 문제
보기 구성	4개의 보기

▶ **시험지에 인쇄되어 있는 모양**

어형 문제
>>

101. If our request for new computer equipment receives ------, we are going to purchase 10 extra monitors.

(A) approval (B) approved
(C) approve (D) approves

어휘 문제
>>

102. After being employed at a Tokyo-based technology firm for two decades, Ms. Mayne ------ to Vancouver to start her own IT company.

(A) visited (B) returned
(C) happened (D) compared

문법 문제
>>

103. ------ the demand for the PFS-2x smartphone, production will be tripled next quarter.

(A) Even if (B) Just as
(C) As a result of (D) Moreover

정답 **101.**(A) **102.**(B) **103.**(C)

PART 6

TEXT COMPLETION
장문 공란 메우기

Part 6는 4개의 지문에 각각 4개의 문항이 나와 총 16문제가 출제되며, Part 5와 같은 문제이나, 맥락을 파악해 정답을 골라야 한다. 편지, 이메일 등의 다양한 지문이 출제되며, 크게 문장 구조/문법을 묻는 문제, 어휘 문제, 문장 선택 문제로 문제 유형이 나뉜다.

문항 수	4개 지문, 16문항(131~146번에 해당합니다.)
지문 유형	설명서, 편지, 이메일, 기사, 공지, 지시문, 광고, 회람, 발표문, 정보문 등
문제 유형	- **문장 구조 / 문법 문제:** 문장 구조, 문맥상 어울리는 시제 등을 고르는 문제 - **어휘 문제:** 같은 품사의 네 개 어휘 중에서 문맥상 알맞은 단어를 고르는 문제 - **문장 선택 문제:** 앞, 뒤 문맥을 파악하여 네 개의 문장 중에서 알맞은 문장을 고르는 문제
보기 구성	4개의 보기

▶ 시험지에 인쇄되어 있는 모양

Questions 131-134 refer to the following e-mail.

To: sford@etnnet.com
From: customersupprt@interhostptimes.ca
Date: July 1
Re: Your Subscription

Congratulations on becoming a reader of *International Hospitality Times*. --131.-- the plan you have subscribed to, you will not only have unlimited access to our online content, but you will also receive our hard copy edition each month. If you wish to --132.-- your subscription preferences, contact our Customer Support Center at +28 07896 325422. Most --133.-- may also make updates to their accounts on our Web site at www.interhosptimes.ca. Please note that due to compatibility issues, it may not be possible for customers in certain countries to access their accounts online. --134.--. Your business is greatly appreciated.

International Hospitality Times

문법 문제
▶▶
131. (A) Besides
(B) As if
(C) Under
(D) Prior to

어형 문제
▶▶
133. (A) subscribe
(B) subscriptions
(C) subscribers
(D) subscribing

어휘 문제
▶▶
132. (A) purchase
(B) modify
(C) collect
(D) inform

문장 삽입 문제
▶▶
134. (A) We have branches in over 30 countries around the globe.
(B) We provide online content that includes Web extras and archives.

정답 **131.**(C) **132.**(B) **133.**(C) **134.**(C)

PART 7

READING COMPREHENSION
독해

Part 7은 단일·이중·삼중 지문을 읽고 그에 딸린 2~5개의 문제를 푸는 형태로, 총 15개 지문, 54문제가 출제되어 RC 전체 문항의 절반 이상을 차지한다. 같은 의미의 패러프레이징된 표현에 주의하고, 문맥을 파악하는 연습을 한다. 키워드 파악은 문제 해결의 기본이다.

문항 수	54문항(147~200번에 해당합니다.)
지문 유형	- **단일 지문**: 이메일, 편지, 문자 메시지, 온라인 채팅, 광고, 기사, 양식, 회람, 공지, 웹 페이지 등 - **이중 지문**: 이메일/이메일, 기사/이메일, 웹 페이지/이메일 등 - **삼중 지문**: 다양한 세 지문들의 조합
문제 유형	- **핵심 정보**: 주제 또는 제목과 같이 가장 핵심적인 내용을 파악하는 문제 - **특정 정보**: 세부 사항을 묻는 문제로, 모든 질문이 의문사로 시작하며 지문에서 질문의 키워드와 관련된 부분을 읽고 정답을 찾는 문제 - **NOT**: 지문을 읽는 동안 보기 중에서 지문의 내용과 일치하는 보기를 대조해서 소거하는 문제 - **추론**: 지문의 내용을 바탕으로 전체 흐름을 이해하며 지문에 직접 언급되지 않은 사항을 추론하는 문제 - **화자 의도 파악**: 화자의 의도를 묻는 문제로, 문자 메시지나 2인 형태의 대화로 출제되며 온라인 채팅은 3인 이상의 대화 형태로 출제 - **동의어**: 주어진 단어의 사전적 의미가 아니라 문맥상의 의미와 가장 가까운 단어를 고르는 문제 - **문장 삽입**: 지문의 흐름상 주어진 문장이 들어갈 적절한 위치를 고르는 문제로, 세부적인 정보보다 전체적인 문맥 파악이 중요한 문제
보기 구성	4개의 보기

▶ **시험지에 인쇄되어 있는 모양**

Questions 151-152 refer to the following text message chain.

Naijia Kuti

My bus to Ibadan was canceled due to engine problems, and all other buses to that city are full. I don't know if I can give my presentation at the history conference. What should I do?
　　　　　　12:02 P.M.

Adebiyi Achebe

12:04 P.M.　Not to worry. I'll come pick you up in my car.

Naijia Kuti

I appreciate it! My seminar starts at 5 P.M. As long as we depart from Lagos by 1:30, I'll be able to make it on time.
　　　　　　12:05 P.M.

Adebiyi Achebe

12:07 P.M.　Where should I go?

Naijia Kuti

In front of La Pointe Restaurant, near Terminal Rodoviario. Call me when you're getting close.　12:08 P.M.

화자 의도 파악 문제

151. At 12:04 P.M., what does Mr. Achebe most likely mean when he writes, "Not to worry"?
(A) He has a solution to Ms. Kuti's problem.
(B) He can reschedule a presentation.
(C) He knows another bus will arrive soon.
(D) He is happy to cover Ms. Kuti's shift.

세부사항 문제

152. What is implied about Ms. Kuti?
(A) She has a meeting at a restaurant.
(B) She is going to be late for a seminar.
(C) She plans to pick up a client at 1:30 P.M.
(D) She is within driving distance of a conference.

정답 **151.**(A) **152.**(D)

Questions 158-160 refer to the following Web page.

http://www.sdayrealestate.com/listing18293

Looking for a new home for your family? This house, located on 18293 Winding Grove, was remodeled last month. It features 2,500 square feet of floor space, with 5,000 square feet devoted to a gorgeous backyard. Also included is a 625 square feet garage that can comfortably fit two mid-sized vehicles —[1]—. Located just a five-minute drive from the Fairweather Metro Station, this property allows for easy access to the downtown area, while providing plenty of room for you and your family. —[2]—. A serene lake is just 100–feet walk away from the house. —[3]—. A 15 percent down payment is required to secure the property. —[4]—. For more detailed information or to arrange a showing, please email Jerry@sdayrealestate.com.

 세부사항 문제

158. How large is the parking space?
(A) 100 square feet
(B) 625 square feet
(C) 2,500 square feet
(D) 5,000 square feet

 사실확인 문제

159. What is NOT stated as an advantage of the property?
(A) It has a spacious design.
(B) It has been recently renovated.
(C) It is in a quiet neighborhood.
(D) It is near public transportation.

 문장 삽입 문제

160. In which of the positions marked [1], [2], [3], and [4] does the following sentence best belong?

"A smaller amount may be accepted, depending on the buyer's financial situation."

(A) [1]
(B) [2]
(C) [3]
(D) [4]

정답 **158.**(B) **159.**(C) **160.**(D)

17

학습 플랜

4주 플랜

DAY 1	DAY 2	DAY 3	DAY 4	DAY 5
CHAPTER 01 문장 구조	CHAPTER 02 명사	CHAPTER 03 대명사	CHAPTER 04 형용사	CHAPTER 05 부사

DAY 6	DAY 7	DAY 8	DAY 9	DAY 10
PART 5 CHAPTER 01-05 다시 보기 - 틀린 문제 다시 보기 - 중요 어휘 체크해서 암기 하기	CHAPTER 06 동사	CHAPTER 07 준동사	CHAPTER 08 전치사	CHAPTER 09 접속사

DAY 11	DAY 12	DAY 13	DAY 14	DAY 15
CHAPTER 10 관계사	PART 5 CHAPTER 06-10 다시 보기 - 틀린 문제 다시 보기 - 중요 어휘 체크해서 암기 하기	CHAPTER 11 특수 구문	CHAPTER 12 어휘	CHAPTER 13 파트 6 문제 유형

DAY 16	DAY 17	DAY 18	DAY 19	DAY 20

CHAPTER 14
파트 7 문제 유형
	PART 5 특수 구문&어휘
	PART 6&7 다시 보기
	- 틀린 문제 다시 보기
	- 중요 어휘 체크해서 암기
	  하기
		PART 5-7 전체 다시 보기
		- 틀린 문제 다시 보기
		- 중요 어휘 체크해서 암기
		  하기
			ACTUAL TEST	ACTUAL TEST 다시 보기
				- 틀린 문제 다시 보기
				- 중요 어휘 체크해서 암기
				  하기

8주 플랜

DAY 1	DAY 2	DAY 3	DAY 4	DAY 5
CHAPTER 01 문장 구조	CHAPTER 01 다시 보기 - 집중 훈련 및 실전 훈련 다시 풀어 보기 - 중요 어휘 체크해서 암기 하기	CHAPTER 02 명사	CHAPTER 02 다시 보기 - 집중 훈련 및 실전 훈련 다시 풀어 보기 - 중요 어휘 체크해서 암기 하기	CHAPTER 03 대명사

DAY 6	DAY 7	DAY 8	DAY 9	DAY 10
CHAPTER 03 다시 보기 - 집중 훈련 및 실전 훈련 다시 풀어 보기 - 중요 어휘 체크해서 암기 하기	CHAPTER 04 형용사	CHAPTER 04 다시 보기 - 집중 훈련 및 실전 훈련 다시 풀어 보기 - 중요 어휘 체크해서 암기 하기	CHAPTER 05 부사	CHAPTER 05 다시 보기 - 집중 훈련 및 실전 훈련 다시 풀어 보기 - 중요 어휘 체크해서 암기 하기

DAY 11	DAY 12	DAY 13	DAY 14	DAY 15
PART 5 CHAPTER 01-05 전체 다시 보기 - 틀린 문제 다시 보기 - 중요 어휘 체크해서 암기 하기	CHAPTER 06 동사	CHAPTER 06 다시 보기 - 집중 훈련 및 실전 훈련 다시 풀어 보기 - 중요 어휘 체크해서 암기 하기	CHAPTER 07 준동사	CHAPTER 07 다시 보기 - 집중 훈련 및 실전 훈련 다시 풀어 보기 - 중요 어휘 체크해서 암기 하기

DAY 16	DAY 17	DAY 18	DAY 19	DAY 20
CHAPTER 08 전치사	CHAPTER 08 다시 보기 - 집중 훈련 및 실전 훈련 다시 풀어 보기 - 중요 어휘 체크해서 암기 하기	CHAPTER 09 접속사	CHAPTER 09 다시 보기 - 집중 훈련 및 실전 훈련 다시 풀어 보기 - 중요 어휘 체크해서 암기 하기	CHAPTER 10 관계사

DAY 21	DAY 22	DAY 23	DAY 24	DAY 25
CHAPTER 10 다시 보기 - 집중 훈련 및 실전 훈련 다시 풀어 보기 - 중요 어휘 체크해서 암기 하기	PART 5 CHAPTER 06-10 전체 다시 보기 - 틀린 문제 다시 보기 - 중요 어휘 체크해서 암기 하기	CHAPTER 11 특수 구문	CHAPTER 11 다시 보기 - 집중 훈련 및 실전 훈련 다시 풀어 보기 - 중요 어휘 체크해서 암기 하기	CHAPTER 12 어휘

DAY 26	DAY 27	DAY 28	DAY 29	DAY 30
CHAPTER 12 다시 보기 - 집중 훈련 및 실전 훈련 다시 풀어 보기 - 중요 어휘 체크해서 암기 하기	CHAPTER 13 파트 6 문제 유형	CHAPTER 13 다시 보기 - 집중 훈련 및 실전 훈련 다시 풀어 보기 - 중요 어휘 체크해서 암기 하기	CHAPTER 14 파트 7 문제 유형	CHAPTER 14 다시 보기 - 집중 훈련 및 실전 훈련 다시 풀어 보기 - 중요 어휘 체크해서 암기 하기

DAY 31	DAY 32	DAY 33	DAY 34	DAY 35
PART 5 특수 구문&어휘 PART 6&7 전체 다시 보기 - 틀린 문제 다시 보기 - 중요 어휘 체크해서 암기 하기	PART 5 CHAPTER 01-05 전체 다시 보기 - 틀린 문제 다시 보기 - 중요 어휘 체크해서 암기 하기	PART 5 CHAPTER 06-10 전체 다시 보기 - 틀린 문제 다시 보기 - 중요 어휘 체크해서 암기 하기	PART 5 특수 구문&어휘 PART 6&7 전체 다시 보기 - 틀린 문제 다시 보기 - 중요 어휘 체크해서 암기 하기	PART 5 전체 다시 보기 - 틀린 문제 다시 보기 - 중요 어휘 체크해서 암기 하기

DAY 36	DAY 37	DAY 38	DAY 39	DAY 40
PART 6&7 전체 다시 보기 - 틀린 문제 다시 보기 - 중요 어휘 체크해서 암기 하기	ACTUAL TEST	ACTUAL TEST 다시 보기 - 틀린 문제 다시 보기 - 중요 어휘 체크해서 암기 하기	PART 5&6 전체 다시 보기 - 틀린 문제 다시 보기 - 중요 어휘 체크해서 암기 하기	PART 7&ACTUAL TEST 전체 다시 보기 - 틀린 문제 다시 보기 - 중요 어휘 체크해서 암기 하기

PART

5

INCOMPLETE SENTENCES
단문 공란 메우기

📋 문제 OVERVIEW

PART 5는 빈칸이 포함된 짧은 문장과 4개의 보기를 주고 빈칸에 들어갈 가장 알맞은 보기를 고르는 형태로, 총 30문제가 출제됩니다.

문항 수	30문항(101~130번에 해당합니다.)
문제 유형	- **문장 구조 / 문법 문제:** 빈칸의 자리를 파악하여 보기 중 알맞은 품사나 형태를 고르는 문제와 문장의 구조를 파악하고 구와 절을 구분하여 빈칸에 알맞은 접속사나 전치사, 또는 부사 등을 고르는 문제 - **어휘 문제:** 같은 품사의 4개 어휘 중에서 정확한 용례를 파악하여 빈칸에 알맞은 단어를 고르는 문제
보기 구성	4개의 보기

🕐 출제 TREND

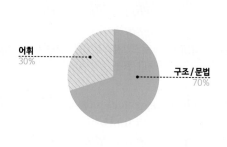

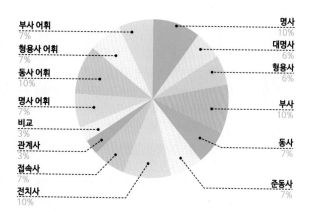

문장 구조의 이해와 특정한 문법 지식을 묻는 문장 구조/문법 문제가 30문제 중 약 2/3를 차지하며, 문맥상 어울리는 단어를 묻는 어휘 문제가 나머지 1/3의 비율로 출제됩니다.

📚 시험 PREVIEW

1. 문장 구조/문법 문제

문장 구조/문법 문제는 총 30문제 중 약 20문제를 차지합니다. 명사, 형용사, 부사 등의 품사 자리 문제는 보기가 모두 같은 어근에서 온 단어인데 품사가 다른 파생어들로 구성된 것이 특징입니다.

아래 문제처럼 한 단어의 네 가지 형태가 보기로 나오는 문제를 품사 자리 문제라고 합니다. 이러한 문제는 빈칸이 주어, 동사, 목적어, 보어, 수식어 중에 어떤 자리인지를 파악해서 보기 중 알맞은 품사나 형태를 답으로 고르면 됩니다. 빈칸은 '타동사+목적어'의 완벽한 구조 뒤에서 동사를 수식하는 부사 자리이므로 (B)가 정답입니다.

Ms. Kitigoe recalled her speech ------- even two weeks after giving it at the conference.

(A) perfects   **(B) perfectly**   (C) perfecting   (D) perfected

Kitigoe 씨는 회의에서 연설한 지 2주가 지나서도 자신의 연설을 완벽하게 기억해 냈다.

동사 문제는 보기가 동사의 다양한 형태로 구성되며, 빈칸이 동사 자리인지, 준동사(to부정사, 동명사, 분사) 자리인지, 주어와 동사의 수 일치가 맞는지, 능동태를 써야 할지, 수동태를 써야 할지, 어떤 시제를 써야 할지 등을 물어봅니다. 특히, 동사 문제는 이러한 다양한 문법 요소들 중에서 한 가지만 물어보기도 하고, 종합적으로 물어볼 때도 많습니다.

아래 문제에서 빈칸은 주어 뒤 문장의 동사 자리이므로 준동사인 to부정사 (C)는 답에서 제외합니다. 주어가 단수(catalogue)이므로 복수 동사인 (D)도 수 일치에 어긋납니다. 빈칸 뒤에 목적어 없이 전치사구가 연결되고, 의미상 온라인 카탈로그는 설계하는 동작의 주체가 아닌 설계되는 대상이므로 수동태인 (B)가 정답입니다.

The library's online catalogue ------- with the need of university students in mind.

(A) will design
(B) was designed
(C) to be designed
(D) have designed

그 도서관의 온라인 카탈로그는 대학생들의 요구를 염두에 두고 설계되었다.

2. 어휘 문제

총 30문제 중 약 10문제를 차지하는 어휘 문제는 대부분 보기 4개 모두 다른 의미의 단어들로 구성하여 문맥상 빈칸에 들어갈 가장 알맞은 단어가 무엇인지를 묻고 다양한 단어의 뜻을 얼마나 잘 알고 있는지를 평가합니다. 그리고 어휘 문제들 중 1~2문항은 문장에 등장한 특정 전치사나 to 부정사 등과 어울려 쓰는 단어가 무엇인지를 물며, 단어의 뜻은 물론 해당 단어가 문장에서 어떤 규칙(예: 「provide 사람 with 사물」 '…에게 ~을 제공하다' 또는 「provide 사물 to/for 사람」 '~을 …에게 제공하다')을 가지고 쓰이는지를 간접적으로 평가합니다.

아래 문제처럼 같은 품사의 뜻이 다른 네 가지 단어가 보기로 나오는 문제를 어휘 문제라고 합니다. 어휘 문제는 최소한 빈칸 주변을 해석해야만 풀 수 있고, 어려운 문제의 경우에는 가산/불가산 명사의 구분, 자동사/타동사의 구분과 같은 문법 사항까지 같이 포함되어 출제되기도 합니다. 빈칸은 that 주격 관계대명사절 내 동사 자리로, 문맥상 (C), (D) 모두 빈칸에 들어가기에 적절해 보이지만 give는 「give+사람 목적어+사물 목적어」의 형식을 취하는 4형식 동사이고, 3형식 구문일 때는 「give+사물 목적어+to 사람」으로 씁니다. provide는 3형식 동사로 「provide 사람 with 사물: …에게 ~을 제공하다」 또는 「provide 사물 to/for 사람」 '~을 …에게 제공하다'의 형식을 취합니다. 빈칸 뒤에 전치사 with가 있으므로 「provide 사람 with 사물」의 구조를 완성하는 동사 (C)가 정답입니다.

Ship Rocket is a courier service that ------- its clients with quick document and package delivery.

(A) markets
(B) indicates
(C) provides
(D) gives

Ship Rocket은 고객에게 빠른 문서 및 소포 배송을 제공하는 택배 회사이다.

◎ 출제 POINT

1. 문법 지식과 어휘력을 동시에!

문법 지식과 어휘력을 동시에 묻는 문제들이 점점 더 많이 출제됩니다. 명사 자리인데 보기에 명사가 두 개 이상 등장하여 의미로 정답을 풀어야 하는 문제가 출제됩니다.

2. 두 가지 이상의 문법 포인트

두 가지 이상의 문법 포인트를 묻는 문제들이 출제됩니다. 동사의 문장 형식을 이해하고 태를 결정하는 문제가 출제됩니다.

3. 비슷한 의미의, 다른 품사의 보기

예를 들어, 전치사 문제의 경우 주로 의미가 다른 전치사들로 구성하여 문맥상 알맞은 전치사를 고르는 문제로 출제되지만, 비슷한 의미의 접속사나 부사구를 섞어서 전치사와 접속사 자리를 구별하는 문제로도 출제됩니다.

◎ 학습 ADVICE

1. 문제 유형 구분이 먼저!

무조건 해석부터 하지 말고 선택지를 보면서 문장 구조 문제인지, 문법 문제인지, 어휘 문제인지를 먼저 파악해야 합니다. 문장 구조 문제는 해석 없이도 답이 나오는 문제가 많으므로 최대한 시간을 절약해서 풀어야 합니다.

2. 지엽적인 문법 개념은 잠시 잊기

토익에서는 실생활에서 쓰이는 기본적인 문법을 물어보기 때문에 지엽적이거나 난해한 문법은 굳이 알 필요가 없습니다. 이 책이 담고 있는 필수 문법을 완벽히 숙지하고 문제를 많이 풀면서 추가적인 문법 사항들을 보완하는 것이 효과적입니다.

3. 단어의 양 < 단어의 활용성

토익 시험은 얼마나 많은 단어를 암기하고 있는지가 아니라 주요 단어를 얼마나 잘 활용할 줄 아는지에 중점을 두기 때문에, 단어를 많이 외우는 것도 중요하지만 한 단어가 가지고 있는 다양한 의미와 품사를 깊이 있게 알고 있어야 합니다.

4. 시간과의 싸움

많은 시간을 요구하는 PART 6 & 7을 위해 PART 5의 풀이 시간을 10분 이내로 단축할 수 있도록 연습해야 합니다. 그리고 보통 RC를 PART 5 → 6 → 7 순서로 문제를 풀어서 PART 7을 끝까지 못 푸는 학생들이 많습니다. 방송에서 '15분 남았다, 5분 남았다' 하면 긴 글은 눈에 잘 들어오지 않기 때문에, 지문 읽는 속도가 느린 편에 속하는 학습자들은 시간이 촉박해지면서 느끼는 심리적 부담감을 덜 수 있도록 PART 7 → 6 → 5 순서로 문제를 풀 것을 권합니다.

5. 어휘의 품사, 파생어, 용법까지 함께 공부하기

고득점을 얻기 위해서는 단어의 뜻만 외우기보다는 그 단어의 품사, 파생어, 용법도 함께 익혀야 합니다. 예를 들어, announce와 notify를 똑같이 '알리다'로 외워두면 두 단어가 같이 보기에 나오는 어휘 문제는 풀기 힘듭니다. notify 뒤에는 목적어로 사람이 나온다는 사실을 알고 있어야 두 동사의 쓰임새를 구별할 수 있기 때문입니다.

문장 구조

CASE 1 주어 자리

Our ------- is in charge of monitoring safety equipment in the facility.

(A) dividing　　　　(B) divisive　　　　(C) division　　　　(D) divide

> **해설** 빈칸 바로 뒤에 동사가 있으므로 빈칸은 주어 자리이며, 소유격 대명사의 수식을 받는 명사가 들어가야 한다. 따라서, 명사 (C)가 정답이다.
>
> **해석** 우리 부서는 시설 내의 안전 장비를 추적 관찰하는 일을 맡고 있다.

>> 주어 자리에는 명사나 명사 역할을 할 수 있는 어구가 온다.

명사	**Construction** of the new Holburne train station will begin in late October. 새 Holburne 기차역의 공사가 10월 말에 시작될 것이다.
명사구	**The official launch** of the company's new product will take place next month. 회사 신제품의 공식 출시가 다음 달에 있을 것이다.
명사절	**What Mr. Wyatt proposed at the conference** confused the audience. 학회에서 Wyatt 씨가 제안한 것이 청중을 혼란스럽게 했다.
대명사	**All** of our senior managers have graduate degrees in finance. 우리의 선임 관리자들 모두가 재무 석사 학위를 소지하고 있다.
동명사구	**Preventing accidents in advance** is the best way to minimize workplace injuries. 미리 사고를 예방하는 것이 작업장 부상을 최소화하는 최선의 방법이다.
to부정사구	**To maintain positive relations with the VIP guests** is extremely important for all employees. VIP 손님들과 긍정적인 관계를 유지하는 것이 전 직원들에게 매우 중요하다.

❶ 동사, 형용사, 부사는 주어나 목적어 자리에 올 수 없다.

>> 가주어 It - 진주어 to부정사 / that절 구문

주어 자리에 to부정사나 that절이 와서 문장이 길어지면, 이를 뒤로 보내고 주어 자리에 대신 가주어 It을 쓴다.

To respond quickly to internal problems is essential.
→ **It** is essential **to respond quickly to internal problems**. 내부 문제에 빠르게 대응하는 것이 매우 중요하다.

That the new regulations for vehicle registration will take effect before February 1 is unlikely.
→ **It** is unlikely **that the new regulations for vehicle registration will take effect before February 1**.
차량 등록을 위한 새 규정이 2월 1일 이전에는 시행될 것 같지 않다.

알면 3초! >> 주어와 동사의 자리가 바뀌는 문장이 있다.

Brooks Auto has been recalling its TX301 model because there ------- several car accidents due to its faulty brakes.

(A) being　　　　(B) to be　　　　(C) was　　　　(D) were

일반적으로 영어는 평서문일 때 주어-동사의 어순을 취하지만 주어-동사의 어순이 바뀔 때가 있는데, 하나는 도치 구문이고, 다른 하나는 There 구문이다. 뒤에서 다룰 도치 구문은 강조할 말을 문장 맨 앞으로 빼면, 주어와 동사의 자리를 바꿔 쓴다는 건데, 이는 평서문이 의문문으로 변화하는 것과 비슷한 과정을 거친다. 그런데, 원래부터 주어-동사의 어순을 바꿔 쓰는 문장이 있으니 '존재(~이 있다)'를 나타내는 「There+동사+주어」 구문이다. 동사 자리에는 보통 be동사가 오며, 이때 동사는 뒤에 오는 주어(명사)에 수를 일치시키므로, 복수 주어 accidents에 수가 일치되는 복수 be동사의 과거형 (D)가 정답이다.

> **해석** Brooks 자동차는 결함이 있는 브레이크로 인해 여러 건의 자동차 사고가 있었기 때문에 TX301 모델을 리콜하고 있다.

PART 5

1. The ------- of subway Line 3 was authorized this morning by the city council.
(A) extended
(B) extension
(C) extend
(D) extensive

2. ------- that large renovation contract was an impressive accomplishment for the small interior design company.
(A) Had secured
(B) Securing
(C) Secure
(D) Secures

3. A quarterly ------- is provided to Maxco Marketing employees to offset various business trip expenses.
(A) invoice
(B) schedule
(C) permit
(D) allowance

4. ------- of authority makes a manager's work easier and allows new employees to develop their abilities.
(A) Commission
(B) Delegation
(C) Progression
(D) Provision

PART 6

Questions 5-8 refer to the following advertisement.

Are you interested in moving on? Get in touch with DLB Management today. Remember, the timing of listing your office space is crucial. Even for experienced business owners, determining when to ------- may be difficult. -------. Many local realtors do not have access to international networks that 5.   6. can provide you with the necessary knowledge. -------, the agents of DLB Management do! Our 7. agents are trained ------- in international business relations. Visit our Web site, dlbmgmt.com, to 8. schedule a consultation with one of our experts.

5. (A) contact
(B) ship
(C) join
(D) sell

6. (A) The promotional event will last until the end of this week.
(B) Nowadays, the market is fast-paced, complicated, and global.
(C) The training will be offered at various locations.
(D) DLB Management has been operating for over half a decade.

7. (A) In addition
(B) In case
(C) Luckily
(D) After

8. (A) specifically
(B) specifications
(C) specific
(D) specify

CASE 2 동사 자리

None of the coaches ------- that the team would win the state championship.

(A) expecting   (B) expected   (C) expectation   (D) expectedly

콕 찍어 포인트 ⋯ 보기에 동사와 준동사가 있다면 빈칸이 동사 자리인지 먼저 확인한다.

해설 빈칸은 문장의 주어 None of the coaches와 목적어인 that 명사절 사이에 오는 동사 자리이므로 동사의 과거형 (B)가 정답이다.

해석 어느 코치도 그 팀이 주 선수권 대회에서 우승하리라고는 예상하지 못했다.

≫ 하나의 문장에는 반드시 하나의 동사가 있어야 한다. 단, 접속사, 관계사가 쓰일 경우 동사가 두 개 이상일 수 있다.

기본 문장	In addition to a base salary, sales associates **will receive** monthly commissions. 기본급 외에도, 영업사원들은 월별 수수료를 받을 것이다.
등위 접속사 문장	Ms. Baker **is** in a meeting, **but** she **can respond** to urgent e-mails. Baker 씨가 미팅 중이긴 하지만 그녀는 긴급한 이메일들에 답할 수 있다.
부사절 접속사 문장	**While** your room **is being prepared**, please **check in** at the reception desk. 객실이 준비되는 동안 프런트에서 체크인 하십시오.
명사절 접속사 문장	Joanna Mitchell **has claimed that** creativity **is** the most important characteristic for a software developer to have. Joanna Mitchell은 창의성이 소프트웨어 개발자가 가져야 할 가장 중요한 특성이라고 주장했다.
관계사 문장	Employees **who are interested** in registering for the conference **should contact** Ms. Lee. 학회 신청에 관심이 있는 직원들은 Lee 씨에게 연락해야 합니다.

≫ 동사 자리에는 「(조동사) + 동사 원형」이나 수, 태, 시제에 따라 다양한 형태의 동사가 온다.

동사 원형 (명령문)	Please **welcome** Mr. Roberts to the Sales Division. to welcome (X), welcoming (X) Roberts 씨의 영업부 합류를 환영해주십시오. → 명령문은 주어 없이 동사 원형으로 시작하거나 이 문장처럼 「Please V」의 형태를 쓰기도 한다.
조동사 + 동사 원형	According to Gloria Claughton's research, mobile advertisements **do not** necessarily **increase** sales. Gloria Claughton의 연구에 따르면, 모바일 광고가 반드시 매출을 올리는 것은 아니다. → 조동사 뒤에는 동사 원형이 오고, 그 사이에 부정어 not이나 그 밖의 부사가 올 수 있다.
be + -ing / p.p.	Ms. Phillips **was told** to call back during the afternoon. 수동형 Phillips 씨는 오후에 회신해 달라고 들었다. → be동사 뒤에 동사가 올 경우 현재분사나 과거분사로 바꿔 쓰며, 현재분사일 때는 능동 진행형 「be + -ing」를, 과거분사일 때는 수동형 「be + p.p.」를 나타낸다.
have / has / had + p.p.	The employees **have asked** the CEO to upgrade the company restrooms. 완료형 직원들은 CEO에게 회사 화장실을 업그레이드해 달라고 요청했다. → 조동사 have/has/had 뒤에 동사가 올 경우 과거분사로 바꾸어 완료형(have/has/had + p.p.)을 나타낸다.

 알면 3초!   **≫** to부정사, 동명사, 분사는 동사 자리에 올 수 없다.

After reviewing the report, ------- your supervisor with any further questions you may have.

(A) contact   (B) contacts   (C) contacting   (D) to contact

빈칸이 조동사 뒤에 위치해 있거나 명령문의 동사 자리라면 주저 없이 동사 원형을 고르면 된다. 물론, 조동사와 동사 원형 사이에 부사가 들어가 주의를 흐리게 하거나, 주어 없이 동사 원형으로 시작되는 명령문 앞에 공손함을 나타내는 please를 붙이거나 긴 부사절이 와서 동사 원형을 그냥 써도 되나 싶기도 하지만, 준동사라 일컫는 to부정사, 동명사, 분사가 동사 자리에 들어갈 수 없다는 점을 상기한다면 보기의 절반 이상을 지워낼 수 있다. 빈칸은 부사구 뒤 명령문의 동사 자리이므로 동사 원형 (A)가 정답이다.

해석 보고서를 검토해 보시고, 추가적인 질문이 있으시면 당신의 상관에게 연락하세요.

PART 5

1. The cost estimate for the construction project ------- any extra charges for wage increases and additional materials.

(A) excludes
(B) exclusive
(C) excluding
(D) to exclude

2. To secure the wire rack to the wall, ------- the screws enclosed in the package.

(A) use
(B) useful
(C) using
(D) used

3. Because of budget restrictions, Ms. Chen ------- the suggestion to hold the anniversary party at the hotel.

(A) misled
(B) inquired
(C) rejected
(D) recalculated

4. A minor alteration in the building blueprint ------- the construction company over 10,000 dollars.

(A) saved
(B) protected
(C) improved
(D) prevented

PART 6

Questions 5-8 refer to the following e-mail.

To: All staff
From: thad.butler@Butler-Hanna.com
Date: June 30
Subject: A record Q2

I know many of you are planning to take some time off next month. But before you head out to the beach, I want to express my gratitude.

------- the second quarter of the year ending, I want to thank the whole team at Butler-Hanna for all the extraordinary work. Throughout the spring, we ------- on our goal of upgrading our security software in response to new challenges. Consequently, we are positioned for ------- in the coming year. -------. Indeed, the favorable reviews we've gotten have caused a spike in sales, and Q3 is likely to be our best one ever.

Thanks, everyone! Keep up the good work and enjoy your summer.

5. (A) With
(B) Until
(C) During
(D) Then

6. (A) concentrated
(B) must concentrate
(C) been concentrated
(D) concentrating

7. (A) effort
(B) success
(C) consideration
(D) management

8. (A) The acquisition should help us reach these new sales targets.
(B) Check your e-mail for further updates regarding bonuses next week.
(C) Our improved products have attracted customers and driven growth.
(D) In the fall, we will be moving our headquarters.

CASE 3 목적어 자리

> We are sorry for the shipping delay and will provide ------- as needed.
>
> (A) compensate　　(B) compensating　　(C) compensated　　(D) compensation

해설 빈칸은 타동사 provide의 목적어 자리이다. 접속사 and로 연결된 두 문장의 관계를 고려할 때, 문맥상 '배송 지연에 사과드리며, 보상하겠다'는 의미가 되어야 자연스러우므로 명사 (D)가 정답이다.

해석 배송 지연에 대해 사과드리며, 필요한 경우 보상해 드리겠습니다.

>> 목적어 자리에는 명사나 명사 역할을 할 수 있는 어구가 온다.

명사	Mr. Trevor will review **your report** again before making a decision. 동사의 목적어 Trevor 씨는 결정을 내리기 전에 당신의 보고서를 다시 검토할 것이다. In response to **your request**, I have sent an e-mail to **the CEO**. 전치사의 목적어 당신의 요청에 응하여, 저는 CEO에게 이메일을 보냈습니다.
명사절	The executive manager stated **that he expected all employees to work cooperatively after the merger**. 동사의 목적어 그 임원은 합병 후에 전 직원이 협력해서 일하기를 기대했다고 밝혔다.
대명사	If your order is incorrect, you can send **us** an e-mail within two weeks to correct it. 동사의 목적어 주문이 잘못된 경우, 수정을 위해 2주 내에 저희에게 이메일을 보내시면 됩니다. Ms. Drake requested the product launch to be delayed, but her boss wants to talk with **her** first. 전치사의 목적어 Drake 씨는 제품 출시를 연기해달라고 요청했지만 상사는 그녀와 먼저 얘기 나누기를 원한다.
동명사구	A clerk's duties include **confirming** the customers' order with them. 동사의 목적어 점원의 직무는 고객들의 주문을 확인하는 일을 포함한다. New Horizons is committed to **providing** excellent service. 전치사의 목적어 New Horizons는 훌륭한 서비스를 제공하는 데 전념하고 있다.
to부정사구	Due to the rising maintenance costs, the CEO finally decided **to raise** its service fees. 동사의 목적어 유지비 상승으로 인해, CEO는 결국 서비스 요금을 인상하기로 결정했다. → to부정사는 전치사의 목적어로 쓸 수 없다.

>> 가목적어 It – 진목적어 to부정사 / that절 구문

「동사＋목적어＋목적격 보어」 구문을 취하는 5형식 동사의 목적어 자리에 to부정사나 that절이 올 때는 이를 목적격 보어 뒤로 보내고 대신 목적어 자리에 가목적어 it을 쓴다.

Employees should make **to work hard** a habit.
= Employees should make **it** a habit **to work hard**. 직원들은 열심히 일하는 것을 습관화해야 한다.

Director Fisher made **that it is his intent to hire only the best interns** clear.
= Director Fisher made **it** clear **that it is his intent to hire only the best interns**.
　Fisher 이사는 최고의 인턴들만을 채용하겠다는 그의 의도를 명확히 했다.

알면 3초!　>> 명사와 동사의 형태가 동일한 단어에 주의한다.

The owner of the Blue Oak Restaurant was pleased to receive ------- reviews in the local newspaper.

(A) positive　　　(B) positivity　　　(C) positively　　　(D) positiveness

단어 중에는 명사와 동사의 형태가 동일하여 문장에서 어떤 품사로 쓰였는지 구별해야 할 때가 있다. 위의 단어 review를 예로 들면, 동사로 '검토하다, 논평하다'란 의미도 있지만, 명사로 '검토, 논평'의 의미로도 쓰인다. 따라서 이런 단어들은 문맥과 함께 문장에서 위치를 확인하여 어떤 품사로 쓰였는지 구별할 수 있어야 이를 꾸며주는 품사를 결정할 수 있다. 위 문제에서는 review가 명사로 쓰였으니 빈칸은 명사를 수식하는 형용사 자리로 (A)가 정답이다.

해석 Blue Oak 레스토랑의 주인은 지역 신문에서 긍정적인 평가를 받고 기뻐했다.

PART 5

1. Culturally sensitive marketing is an important factor influencing the ------- of our international product sales.
(A) succeed
(B) successfully
(C) success
(D) successful

2. Because of transportation ------- due to the heavy snowstorm, some packages will be delivered a few days later than scheduled.
(A) delays
(B) to delay
(C) is delayed
(D) had delayed

3. Welt Insurance Company provides options that offer full ------- of most medical procedures.
(A) reductions
(B) guarantees
(C) coverage
(D) standard

4. The Nightingale Gallery is hosting a ------- next month to showcase the artwork of painter Elizabeth Helsing.
(A) reception
(B) formality
(C) location
(D) society

PART 6

Questions 5-8 refer to the following notice.

In order to maintain premium levels of ------- for our tenants, the meeting rooms on the third floor
5.
will be undergoing renovations next week, from August 17 until August 21. ------- renovations are
6.
underway, the meeting rooms will be unavailable. Tenants are advised to use the meeting rooms on
the fourth floor instead.

We ------- for any inconvenience caused, and we ask for your understanding. -------.
7.   8.

The Coatesville Properties Group

5. (A) comfortable
(B) comfort
(C) comforted
(D) comforting

6. (A) While
(B) During
(C) Throughout
(D) However

7. (A) compromise
(B) influence
(C) concur
(D) apologize

8. (A) Please refrain from holding meetings until next week.
(B) If you have a problem with your invoice, please inquire directly.
(C) The fourth-floor meeting rooms should be avoided whenever possible.
(D) Any questions or concerns can be sent directly to our head office.

보어 자리

Several issues have become ------- and need to be addressed promptly.

(A) apparent   (B) appear   (C) apparently   (D) appearance

> **해설** 동사 become 뒤에는 주격 보어로 명사나 형용사가 올 수 있는데, 문맥상 '몇 가지 문제가 명백해졌기에 신속하게 처리되어야 한다'는 의미가 되어야 자연스러우므로 주어를 서술하는 형용사 (A)가 정답이다.
>
> **해석** 몇 가지 문제가 명백해졌으므로 신속하게 처리되어야 한다.

>> 보어 자리에는 주어/목적어와 동격인 명사나 주어/목적어를 서술하는 형용사가 온다.

명사	**The company** has quickly become **a threat** to its competitors. The company = a threat 그 회사는 금세 경쟁사들에게 위협이 되었다. The CEO named **Mr. Ling the new marketing director** of the company. Mr. Ling = the new marketing director CEO는 Ling 씨를 회사의 새 마케팅 이사로 임명했다. → 주어와 주격 보어, 목적어와 목적격 보어가 동격 관계일 때는 보어 자리에 명사를 쓴다.
형용사	**Most items** in this store are **available** online at a cheaper price. Most items → available 이 상점에 있는 대부분의 물품들은 온라인에서 더 저렴한 가격으로 이용할 수 있다. Many users found **the new interface confusing**. the new interface → confusing 많은 고객들은 새 인터페이스가 혼동하기 쉽다는 것을 알았다. → 주어나 목적어의 상태를 나타낼 때는 보어 자리에 형용사를 쓴다.

>> 주격 보어를 취하는 동사: 「주어 + 동사 + 주격 보어」

be ~이다 become ~이 되다 seem/appear ~처럼 보이다 remain/stay ~인 채로 있다 feel ~하게 느끼다
prove ~로 판명되다

Some people have complained that our application **is** overly **complicated**.
몇몇 사람들은 우리의 애플리케이션이 지나치게 복잡하다고 불평했다.

>> 목적격 보어를 취하는 동사: 「주어 + 동사 + 목적어 + 목적격 보어」

make 만들다 find 알게 되다 keep 유지하다 consider 여기다 call 부르다 name 임명하다 leave (~한 상태로) 두다

These windows are designed to **keep** residents **warm** during the winter.
이 창은 겨울 동안 주민들을 따뜻하게 해 주도록 고안되었다.

 알면 3초!   >> 부사는 보어 자리에 올 수 없다.

Overseas travel is likely to become more ------- as many airlines are planning to increase fares by up to 15 percent.

(A) expensive   (B) expense   (C) expenses   (D) expensively

'해외 여행이 비싸지는(become expensive) 거랑 비싸게 되는(become expensively) 거랑 뭐가 달라요?'라는 질문을 받을 때가 많다. 보어 자리에 올 수 있는 품사를 머릿속에 담아두지 않은 채 우리말로 해석해서 풀려고만 하면 부사도 말이 될 때가 많기 때문에 벌어지는 일이다. 위에 정리한 2형식 동사나 5형식 동사가 보어를 가지며, 보어 자리에 형용사나 분사가 올 때는 주어나 목적어를 서술해주고, 명사가 올 때는 주어나 목적어와 동격 관계를 이룬다. 하지만, 부사는 보어 자리에 올 수 없다! 위의 문장에서 빈칸은 주격 보어를 취하는 become 동사 뒤에 나와 주어를 서술하는 자리이므로 형용사 (A)가 정답이다.

> **해석** 많은 항공사들이 15퍼센트까지 운임을 올릴 계획을 하고 있기 때문에 해외여행은 더 비싸질 것 같다.

PART 5

1. Mr. Rader's innovative renovation of Vaduz Fine Arts Museum is -------.

(A) commends
(B) commendable
(C) commend
(D) commending

2. The programmers are ------- that the software update will be available for download before the end of the week.

(A) hope
(B) hoped
(C) hopefully
(D) hopeful

3. The Chief Financial Officer at Cosmo Electronics remains ------- to the proposed changes to the company's investment policy.

(A) interfered
(B) eager
(C) anxious
(D) opposed

4. Many plumbing companies provide advice on making kitchens and bathrooms ------- water efficient.

(A) about
(B) neither
(C) more
(D) a few

PART 6

Questions 5-8 refer to the following information.

Congratulations on purchasing your brand-new Jumbo Series mountain bike. Although our bicycles are ------- to survive harsh conditions on- or off- road, your product is protected by a free one-year
5.
warranty. -------. To get free repairs under the warranty, visit an authorized Jumbo Series shop. The
6.
dealer will inspect your bike and discuss the ------- that will be required. You can ------- mail faulty
7.   8.
parts directly to our factory for replacement.

5. (A) designing
(B) design
(C) designed
(D) designer

6. (A) The tires are made from eco-friendly materials.
(B) You have been automatically registered for this coverage.
(C) A sales professional will be happy to assist you.
(D) Our bicycles may no longer be purchased online.

7. (A) promotion
(B) budget
(C) exercise
(D) work

8. (A) also
(B) then
(C) once
(D) before

Managers need to remember that accounts should be checked ------- for errors.

(A) regular   (B) regularly   (C) regulate   (D) regulation

해설   빈칸은 수동태 동사구(should be checked)와 전치사구(for errors) 사이에서, 전치사구와 함께 수동태 동사구를 수식하는 자리이므로 부사 (B)가 정답이다.

해석   관리자들은 계좌에 오류가 있는지 정기적으로 점검해야 한다는 것을 기억해야 한다.

>> 수식어는 문장을 완성하기 위한 필수 요소가 아니다.

(As a token of our appreciation), **please accept this coupon**, (which will give you 80 percent off on all
     (전치사구)   문장의 최소 완성 단위   (관계사절)

our products) (with free delivery).
           (전치사구)

감사의 표시로, 전 제품에 대해 80퍼센트 할인과 무료 배송을 제공할 이 쿠폰을 받아 주시기 바랍니다.

>> 부사, 전치사구, to부정사구(부사절 용법일 경우만 해당), 분사 구문, 관계사절, 부사절은 수식어이다.

부사	Ms. Bennet's assistant (**simply**) wanted a few interns to finish their data entry project. Bennet 씨의 보조원은 데이터 입력 프로젝트를 끝내는 데 단지 인턴 몇 명만을 원했다.
전치사구	The invitation (**for next month's online seminar**) will be sent out to all clients tomorrow. 다음 달 온라인 세미나를 위한 초대장이 내일 모든 고객들에게 발송될 것이다.
to부정사구	Customer service employees will make an effort (**to respond to customers' inquiries within 24 hours**). 고객 서비스 직원들은 24시간 내에 고객 문의에 답하기 위해 노력해야 할 것이다. (**To apply for this internship,**) applicants should have no more than a year of experience. 이 인턴십에 지원하려면, 지원자들은 단 1년의 경력만 있으면 된다.
분사 구문	(**Preferred by elderly customers,**) our services have a notable market presence. 연세가 드신 고객들에 의해 선호되는 저희 서비스는 상당한 시장 입지를 가지고 있습니다.
관계사절	There has been extremely heavy rain, (**which has caused many flight cancelations**). 엄청난 폭우가 내렸고, 이는 다수의 항공기 결항으로 이어졌다.
부사절	We will purchase new furniture (**once the CEO approves the request**). CEO가 요청을 승인하는 대로 우리는 새 가구를 구매할 것이다.

알면 3초!   >> 문장의 필수 요소와 수식어를 구분해서 파악하는 연습을 하자.

A revised proposal for Goodwill Bank ------- that it increase its interest rates as other local banks have done.

(A) to suggest   (B) suggesting   (C) suggestion   (D) suggests

A revised proposal (for Goodwill Finance Bank) **suggests** that it increase its interest rates (as other local banks have done).
    주어   (전치사구)   동사   목적어   (부사절)

문장의 빈칸을 완성하는 Part 5 문제의 경우 빈칸이 전체 문장의 주어 자리인지, 관계사절의 주어 자리인지 또는 전체 문장의 목적어 자리인지, to부정사구의 목적어 자리인지 등을 파악할 수 있으려면 하나의 문장을 이루고 있는 각종 요소들을 전체적으로 이해해야 한다. 이들이 유기적으로 얽혀 있기 때문에 처음 공부할 때는 등장하는 용어조차 이해하기 쉽지 않다. 하지만 인내심을 가지고 끝까지 완독하면서 문제 풀이와 문장 구조 훈련을 병행한다면 독해력을 더 빠르게 향상할 수 있다. 오늘부터라도 문장의 필수 요소(주어, 동사, 목적어, 보어)와 수식어를 파악하는 연습을 하자. 위 문장의 빈칸은 that 이하의 목적어를 받는 동사 자리이므로 (D)가 정답이다.

해석   Goodwill 은행을 위한 수정안은 그 은행이 지역의 다른 은행들이 해왔던 것처럼 이자율을 올릴 것을 제안한다.

PART 5

1. The finance manager was attentive ------- the main presentations delivered by the regional supervisors during the annual business meeting.
(A) throughout
(B) although
(C) later
(D) underneath

2. The in-room wall safes in each of the suites ensure that the guests' valuables can be stored -------.
(A) secured
(B) secure
(C) securely
(D) security

3. The staff at the Mountain Chalet ------- shapes the snow removed from walkways into sculptures.
(A) creatively
(B) creative
(C) creating
(D) create

4. A new action plan is under consideration to ------- our services more aggressively in Latin America.
(A) invest
(B) market
(C) compete
(D) perform

PART 6

Questions 5-8 refer to the following e-mail.

To: sallychen@gchemtech.com
From: bferguson@lwmail.com
Date: March 17
Subject: Meeting
Attachment: Ferguson_CV, Recommendation

Dear Ms. Chen,

Thanks for taking the time to meet and talk about the open position in the Human Resources Department at GloboChem Technologies. I ------- discussing the details of the job with you. And after
5.
much deliberation, I've decided to officially apply for the job. -------.
6.
As my CV reflects, my ------- experience at Holdenfield Beverages, where I routinely led training
7.
workshops, should make me a great fit for the position. Mary Timony, who wrote the attached letter, oversaw my department for four years when I worked there and is someone I consider a close personal friend. She speaks ------- of your firm and first recommended it to me.
8.

If there's anything else I should provide, let me know, and I'll be happy to send it along.

Best,
Brenda Ferguson

5. (A) will appreciate
(B) appreciates
(C) appreciated
(D) am appreciating

6. (A) Accordingly, I've included my curriculum vitae and a professional reference.
(B) I would like to recommend my colleague, Mary Timony, for the position.
(C) I should also thank you for your tour of the building.
(D) So, it would be very helpful to me if you filled out the attached form.

7. (A) past
(B) considerate
(C) average
(D) expensive

8. (A) favored
(B) favorable
(C) favorably
(D) favorite

1. All staff members must obtain ------- from their directors for extended absences after November 1.
   (A) authorization
   (B) authoritative
   (C) authorizing
   (D) authorize

2. Please ------- expense records, since reimbursement will not be processed without proof of purchase.
   (A) keeping
   (B) kept
   (C) keeps
   (D) keep

3. The product team at Goodman Electronics ------- a smartphone with a better battery life.
   (A) developing
   (B) develop
   (C) development
   (D) developed

4. The capability to adapt ------- is one of the most critical qualities in a company for the 21st century.
   (A) effectiveness
   (B) effective
   (C) effectively
   (D) effect

5. Full sponsorships for undergraduate students ------- one year after the government announced the controversial plan.
   (A) had raised
   (B) raise
   (C) raised
   (D) were raised

6. Investors are keenly ------- the foreign market for lucrative business opportunities.
   (A) inviting
   (B) exploring
   (C) sending
   (D) executing

7. Elias Craig Shipping's partnership with Chapman Constructions expires in three months, and ------- no renewal proposals have been reviewed.
   (A) as yet
   (B) apart from
   (C) so that
   (D) only if

8. Copywriters at Prose Advertising are skilled at adhering ------- to clients' needs to produce ideas that appeal to the target audience.
   (A) closely
   (B) officially
   (C) moderately
   (D) discreetly

Questions 9-12 refer to the following article.

BERVILLE (17 November) — Minton Enviro-Technologies (MET), a Hong Kong-based start-up specializing in green energy technologies, recently deployed the first of its new wind turbines in Cambodia. The Fengche, which was granted a patent last year, is reported to be one of the most efficient windmills available. MET hopes to power remote areas of Asia --------- taking advantage of the abundant winds.
9.

According to Mr. Kenson Wong, MET's Chief of Technology, "We take power for granted here, and it's incredible how -------- it is to our lives. In many areas of Asia, people have to learn to get by without
10.
power. At MET, we think this is unacceptable, and this is how the Fengche was born. We know that these villages do not have much money. --------. Additionally, the Fengche can -------- some much-
11.   12.
needed light at night."

MET hopes to spend the next year producing Fengches to deploy around Asia.

9. (A) since
(B) then
(C) that
(D) by

10. (A) contingent
(B) necessary
(C) intriguing
(D) credible

11. (A) The windmills were designed using common materials.
(B) The windmills will need to be replaced after a few years.
(C) The windmills can also serve decorative purposes.
(D) The windmills may pose a danger to native bird species.

12. (A) provided
(B) provide
(C) has provided
(D) was providing

CASE 6 명사 자리

Proper ID is always required for ------- to the facility.

(A) accessing   (B) access   (C) accessed   (D) accessible

콕 찍어 포인트 ⋯ access는 타동사로 '~을 이용하다, 접근하다'와 불가산 명사로 '이용 (권한), 접근 (권한)'의 의미를 갖는다.

해설   빈칸은 전치사 for의 목적어 역할을 하는 명사 자리이다. 빈칸 뒤에 목적어가 아닌 전치사 to가 있으므로 명사 (B)가 정답이다.

해석   그 시설에 접근하려면 항상 올바른 ID가 요구된다.

>> 명사는 문장에서 주어, 목적어, 보어의 역할을 한다.

주어	**Remodeling** of the old library will begin in early June. 오래된 도서관의 리모델링이 6월 초에 시작될 것이다.
동사의 목적어	The corporate mission at Magna Energy Solutions actively supports **sustainability**. Magna Energy Solutions의 기업 사명은 지속 가능성을 적극적으로 지지한다.
전치사의 목적어	Shipping was delayed as a result of **an error** regarding the customer's credit card information. 고객의 신용카드 정보에 관한 오류로 인해 배송이 지연되었다.
보어	Trip Global is a **travel service** that provides its clients with affordable vacation packages. Trip Global은 고객들에게 알맞은 가격의 휴가 패키지를 제공하는 여행서비스 업체이다.

 알면 3초!   >> to부정사, 동명사, 현재분사 뒤에도 목적어로서 명사가 온다.

Ms. Bernal was pleased to get ------- that her firm soon will appear on the Top Ten Canadian Companies list.

(A) notifies   (B) notify   (C) notifying   (D) notification

명사는 본동사나 전치사의 목적어뿐만 아니라 to부정사, 동명사, 현재분사의 목적어 역할도 한다. 목적어를 필요로 하는 타동사에 명사가 따라붙는 것처럼, 타동사에서 변형된 to부정사, 동명사, 현재분사도 마찬가지로 목적어로서 명사를 수반한다는 점을 기억하면, 위 문제는 빈칸 앞의 'to get'만 보고도 get의 목적어로서 명사가 들어갈 자리임을 알 수 있다. 따라서 명사 (D)가 정답이다. that절 이하의 통보를 받게 되어 기뻤다는 내용으로 명사 notification과 that절이 동격 관계를 갖는 문장 구조이다.

해석   Bernal 씨는 그녀의 회사가 곧 상위 10개의 캐나다 기업 목록에 나올 것이라는 통보를 받고 기뻐했다.

PART 5

1. BJ's Steak is scheduled to open its first south-suburban ------- later this month.

(A) location
(B) locate
(C) located
(D) locating

2. Experts remain optimistic about the continuing ------- of the Indian stock market.

(A) stability
(B) stable
(C) stabilize
(D) stabilized

3. The Galt Corp. building control system combines security and excellent ------- of use.

(A) easy
(B) ease
(C) eased
(D) easily

4. To receive -------, make sure to carefully review the terms before signing the acknowledgement form.

(A) to renew
(B) renew
(C) renewed
(D) renewals

PART 6

Questions 5-8 refer to the following notice.

Effective the first of October, Hammersmith and Sons management is implementing some ------- to our time-off procedure. This decision was deemed necessary after analyzing the results from a recent survey about staff -------. It showed that a significant number of team members were planning to be away on the same days during the upcoming holiday season.

As this time of year usually attracts a high number of customers, it would be ------- for a large portion of our staff to be gone at the same time. So for the next few months, management will require that all leave request forms be filled out at least one month in advance. -------.

5. (A) adjusts
(B) adjusted
(C) adjusting
(D) adjustments

6. (A) promptness
(B) deadlines
(C) vacations
(D) advantages

7. (A) inconvenient
(B) concise
(C) recurring
(D) false

8. (A) As a courtesy, we ask that all staff members fill out the survey forms by October 1.
(B) More customers than usual are expected due to the recent advertising campaign.
(C) Priority will be given in the order the requests are received.
(D) The management team is pleased to say that these are our highest-ever sales figures.

명사와 한정사

Please submit a short ------- of the item you wish to sell on our online platform.

(A) described   (B) describing   (C) description   (D) descriptive

해설   빈칸은 타동사 submit의 목적어로서 관사(a)와 형용사(short)의 수식을 받는 명사 자리이므로 (C)가 정답이다.

해석   당사의 온라인 플랫폼에서 판매하고자 하는 품목에 대한 간단한 설명을 제출해 주십시오.

>> 명사 앞에는 관사나 소유격 등의 한정사 또는 형용사가 온다.

관사 + 명사	XYZ, Inc. has shown **a commitment** to its customer service quality. XYZ 사는 고객 서비스 품질에 대한 헌신을 보여 주었다.
관사 + 형용사 + 명사	XYZ, Inc. has shown **a firm commitment** to its customer service quality. XYZ 사는 고객 서비스 품질에 대한 확고한 헌신을 보여 주었다.
소유격 + 명사	Lux-Corp's improved sales resulted from **its initiative** to optimize its delivery system. Lux-Corp의 개선된 매출은 배송 시스템을 최적화하려는 그들의 계획에 기인한 것이다.
소유격 + 형용사 + 명사	Lux-Corp's improved sales resulted from **its recent initiative** to optimize its delivery system. Lux-Corp의 개선된 매출은 배송 시스템을 최적화하려는 그들의 최근 계획에 기인한 것이다.

알면 3초!   **>>** 전치사 앞에 빈칸이 있다면 명사가 정답이다.

Cirque Outdoor has just announced a superb ------- of functional winter coats from Switzerland.

(A) selectively   (B) selective   (C) selection   (D) select

알맞은 품사를 고르는 문제에서 전치사 앞에 빈칸이 올 경우에는 명사가 정답이다. 전치사의 기능상 앞뒤로는 명사의 연결이 일반적이며, 특히 of 앞에 빈칸을 주고 명사를 고르게 하는 경향이 두드러지므로 이때는 명사를 정답 1순위에 두고 쓱 확인해서 답을 고른다. '엄선한, 다양한'을 뜻하는 관용 표현 a selection of에, 그 정도를 강조하는 형용사 superb가 들어간 형태로 형용사의 수식을 받는 명사 자리 문제이긴 하나 시간에 쫓긴다면 'of 앞 빈칸 → 명사'로 풀어도 좋다. 따라서 명사 (C)가 정답이다.

해석   Cirque Outdoor는 스위스산의 매우 엄선한 기능성 겨울 코트를 막 발표했다.

CASE 집중훈련

PART 5

1. Employees are required to add a personal ------- to Mr. Dale's birthday card.

(A) note
(B) noting
(C) noted
(D) notes

2. Ms. Osuyah has scheduled internal training sessions for all staff due to the ------- about the new system.

(A) confuse
(B) confusion
(C) confused
(D) confusing

3. Ms. Kitahara is so renowned that customers must wait five days for an ------- with her.

(A) appointing
(B) appointed
(C) appoint
(D) appointment

4. Gage Athletics will debut a new line of winter parkas beginning ------- fall.

(A) into
(B) until
(C) this
(D) precisely

PART 6

Questions 5-8 refer to the following e-mail.

To: Production team
From: Tiffany Herzberger
Date: Wednesday, 24 August
Subject: Sailing reshoots

Hi everyone,

Please remember that we need to reshoot the sailing scenes this Sunday at the Dolphin Cove location. Shooting at sea can create many complications, and the footage we shot last month was not up to the standards of the rest of the film. -------, I would like to begin shooting at sunrise, so we
5.
can get our filming done well before we break for lunch. -------.
6.

I also need to ------- the fact that no mobile phones are allowed on set, unless you have express
7.
permission. Checking text messages or taking pictures can be a -------.
8.

Tiffany Herzberger

Palatial Estates Studios

5. (A) Unless
(B) If possible
(C) Rather
(D) Either way

6. (A) However, it's possible it will last the whole day.
(B) Nonetheless, we managed to do an excellent job.
(C) Fortunately, this error only appeared in a few shots.
(D) The new location will not present as many challenges.

7. (A) stress
(B) prevent
(C) dispute
(D) request

8. (A) distract
(B) distracting
(C) distraction
(D) distractions

가산 명사 vs. 불가산 명사

You're supposed to have a ------- to camp in this park.

(A) permit   (B) permitted   (C) permitting   (D) permission

콕 찍어 포인트 ··· ① 가산 명사는 반드시 관사(a[n], the)와 같은 한정사와 함께 쓰거나 복수형으로 쓴다.
② permit vs. permission: permit은 '허가증'을 뜻하는 가산 명사이며, permission은 '허가 (행위)'를 뜻하는 불가산 명사이다.

해설 빈칸은 동사 have의 목적어 자리로 명사가 와야 하며, 빈칸 앞에 부정관사(a[n])가 있으므로 '허가증'을 뜻하는 가산 명사 (A)가 정답이다. permission은 '허가 (행위)'를 뜻하는 불가산 명사이므로 부정관사를 동반할 수 없다.

해석 당신은 이 공원에서 캠핑할 수 있는 허가증이 있어야 한다.

≫ 가산 명사는 단수형일 때 반드시 앞에 한정사를 동반하며, 한정사가 없다면 복수형이 정답이다.

     Applicant (X)
Applicants for the research project should sign up online.
연구 프로젝트 지원자들은 온라인으로 지원해야 한다.

≫ 불가산 명사는 부정관사 a(n) 함께 쓸 수 없고, 끝에 복수형 '-(e)s'를 붙일 수 없다.

The annual engineering conference will offer numerous resources for new graduates seeking **employment.** an employment (X), employments (X)
연례 공학 컨퍼런스는 직장을 구하려는 새 졸업생들에게 많은 자원을 제공할 것이다.

비슷한 의미의 가산 명사 vs. 불가산 명사

가산 명사		불가산 명사	
approach	접근 방식	access	접근, 접속
description	설명	information	정보
guide	안내인, 안내서	guidance	안내
permit	허가증	permission	허가
product	제품	merchandise	상품
survey	(설문) 조사	research	(연구) 조사

어근이 같은 가산 명사 vs. 불가산 명사

가산 명사		불가산 명사	
account	계좌, 계정, 고객	accounting	회계(학)
fund	자금	funding	자금 조달, 재정 지원
plan	계획	planning	계획 수립, 기획
process	과정, 절차	processing	처리
ticket	표	ticketing	발권
seat	좌석	seating	좌석 배치

알면 3초!   ≫ 불가산 명사가 들어간 관용 표현을 외운다.

Thanks to our updated multi-viewing system, you can now stream our live broadcasting from the device of your -------.

(A) choosing   (B) choose   (C) choices   (D) choice

지금처럼 빈칸 앞에 형태상 어느 명사든지 받을 수 있는 소유격이 왔고, 보기 중에 복수 가산 명사 형태인 (C)와 단수 가산 or 불가산 명사 형태인 (D)가 모두 등장했을 때, 해석을 해서 가장 그럴 듯해 보이는 형태를 고르지 말고 'of one's choice(~가 선택한)'라는 관용 표현을 미리 외우고 기계적으로 답을 고른다. 따라서 답은 (D)이다. 'until further notice(추후 공지가 있을 때까지), have access to(~에 접근할 수 있다)' 등 토익 빈출 표현에는 불가산 명사를 쓰는 경우를 흔히 볼 수 있고, 이런 유형의 문제를 의미 차이에서 오는 '불가산 명사 vs. 가산 명사' 문제로 바라볼 것이 아니라, 그저 '하나의 덩어리 표현을 알고 있는지가 출제 포인트였구나'로 생각을 전환하자. 그러니 토익에 자주 등장하는 관용 표현들은 그냥 외운다.

해석 업데이트된 저희 다중 시청 시스템 덕분에, 이제 여러분이 선택하신 기기로 저희 방송을 생중계로 받아볼 수 있습니다.

CASE 집중훈련

PART 5

1. The study reveals that ------- in Eastville has sharply fallen over the last 12 months.

(A) employed
(B) employs
(C) employers
(D) employment

2. North Shore Grill's head chef always allows diners to make menu -------.

(A) substitute
(B) substituted
(C) substituting
(D) substitutions

3. The HR Department gives financial ------- to new hires from overseas.

(A) support
(B) supports
(C) supported
(D) supporting

4. Due to a lack of production staff on the factory floor, Niobe Furniture will be unable to accept orders ------- further notice.

(A) until
(B) besides
(C) about
(D) through

PART 6

Questions 5-8 refer to the following article.

WILMINGTON (4 March) — Rochester Wood Farm revealed its annual Fruit Tree Showcase this morning. According to Rochester employee Olga Smith, this ------- event highlights the company's most current efforts in fruit tree farming. Many of these efforts result from customer questionnaires created to gain an understanding of common difficulties. -------. This year, the company's fruit tree farms have turned out strong breeds, such as the High Gate Peach Tree. These trees can withstand extended droughts without compromising their growth. "Growers in dry ------- will appreciate the High Gates in particular," noted Smith. "And ------- might also be interested in our new R8 plum trees, which also do well in similar conditions."

5. (A) daily
(B) weekly
(C) monthly
(D) yearly

6. (A) The company seeks out the most profitable sectors in fruit tree farming.
(B) The company interviews experts from around the country.
(C) Their extensive research produces some of the most exquisite fruit trees on the market.
(D) The research and development department then works to create solutions that address these challenges.

7. (A) region
(B) regional
(C) regions
(D) regionally

8. (A) he
(B) she
(C) we
(D) they

CASE 9 사람 명사 vs. 사물/추상 명사

------- for the job as head teacher will be interviewed next week.

(A) Apply   (B) Applying   (C) Applications   (D) Applicants

콕 찍어 포인트 ··· application vs. applicant: application은 '지원(서)'를 의미하는 사물 명사이며, applicant는 '지원자'를 의미하는 사람 명사이다.

해설 빈칸은 문장의 주어 자리이므로 동사 (A)는 소거한다. 문맥상 '지원자들이 면접을 볼 것이다'라는 내용이 되어야 적절하므로 빈칸에는 사람 명사가 필요하다. 따라서, (D)가 정답이다.

해석 부장 교사에 지원한 지원자들은 다음 주에 면접을 볼 것이다.

≫ 사람 명사와 사물/추상 명사의 구별 문제는 해석해서 푼다.

~ supervision 관리 (X)

Staff members must report to their immediate **supervisors** before clocking out for the day.
직원들은 하루 일을 마치기 전에 직속 상관에게 보고해야 한다.
→ 동사가 report to(~에게 보고하다)이며, 보고의 대상은 사람이므로 supervisors(상관)가 정답이다.

~ chemist 화학자 (X)

All of our lab assistants have graduate degrees in **chemistry**.
우리 연구 보조원들 전원이 화학 분야의 석사 학위를 보유하고 있다.
→ 연구원들이 화학 분야의 석사 학위를 가지고 있다는 의미이므로 사물/추상 명사인 chemistry(화학)가 정답이다.

빈출 사람 명사 vs. 사물/추상 명사

사람 명사		사물/추상 명사	
assistant	보조원	assistance	도움, 지원
applicant	지원자	application	지원, 지원서
attendant	종업원, 안내원 *cf.* attendee 참석자	attendance	참석, 참석자 수
consultant	상담가, 자문위원	consulting	자문
contributor	기부자, 기고자	contribution	기여, 공헌
correspondent	기자, 통신원	correspondence	서신
delegate	대표자	delegation	위임
employee	직원 *cf.* employer 고용주	employment	고용
journalist	기자	journal	신문, 학술지
professional	전문가	profession	직업
resident	주민, 거주자	residence	주거, 주택
supervisor	감독자, 상사	supervision	감독

알면 3초!   ≫ 사람 명사는 단수일 때 반드시 한정사를 동반하거나 복수형으로 쓴다.

If the package has been damaged by the carrier, do not acknowledge ------- of the shipment, and call customer service to arrange for a refund.

(A) receive   (B) receiving   (C) receipt   (D) recipient

보기 중에 사물/추상 명사인 (C) receipt(가산 명사: 영수증, 불가산 명사: 수령, 인수)와 사람 명사인 (D) recipient(가산 명사: 수령인)가 제시될 경우 앞에서 언급한 것처럼 해석을 통해 답을 고를 수도 있지만, 사람 명사는 가산 명사라서 단수일 때 반드시 관사, 소유격 등의 한정사를 동반하거나 복수형으로 쓴다는 점을 알고 있다면, 위 문제에서처럼 빈칸 앞에 한정사가 없을 때는 단수 형태의 사람 명사는 해석 없이도 답에서 제외시킬 수 있으므로 (C)가 정답이다.

해석 배송업체에 의해 패키지가 손상된 경우, 배송 사실을 인정하지 말고 고객 서비스 부서에 연락하여 환불을 받으세요.

CASE 집중훈련

PART 5

1. Congratulations to our new committee for the fantastic work on the Richmond -------.
(A) accounted
(B) accountant
(C) account
(D) accountable

2. Bugz Begone's specialty is the safe and effective ------- of pests and critters from your home.
(A) eliminate
(B) eliminated
(C) eliminator
(D) elimination

3. We honor ------- from the university at an annual ceremony at the end of each academic year.
(A) retire
(B) retirement
(C) retiree
(D) retirees

4. An outgoing disposition and background in computer technology are mandatory for the position of sales ------- at Kirlian Electronics.
(A) association
(B) associating
(C) associated
(D) associate

PART 6

Questions 5-8 refer to the following article.

BOSTON (August 25) — Torrance and Posner Group yesterday unveiled a new accounting platform it plans to market to small business customers. The system is designed to be a powerful and easy-to-use one-stop bookkeeping solution. In real time, it seamlessly tracks company-wide revenue ------- the total amount spent on payroll and other expenses. -------. All of this data is organized
5.   6.
in an intuitive manner and can be accessed from a wide range of devices. ------- think it will save
7.
employees time and ------- overspending caused by a lack of information.
8.

5. (A) as far as
(B) as well as
(C) among
(D) during

6. (A) The updated version includes a smart phone application.
(B) Local and federal taxes are also taken into account.
(C) The software is intended for use by trained accountants only.
(D) Installing the system may take longer than usual.

7. (A) Developing
(B) Development
(C) Develop
(D) Developers

8. (A) inform
(B) enforce
(C) prevent
(D) analyze

CASE 10   복합명사

The Low Ridge Mall is promoting its annual holiday ------- event this month.

(A) sell   (B) sells   (C) sold   (D) sales

콕 찍어 포인트 ⋯ 두 개 이상의 명사가 결합하여 하나의 단어처럼 쓰이는 것을 복합명사라 하며, 대개 앞의 명사(들)은 마지막 명사의 종류를 나타내므로, 명사의 성질이나 상태 등을 나타내는 형용사와는 그 쓰임새를 구별할 수 있어야 한다.

해설 빈칸은 its annual holiday와 함께 문장의 목적어인 event를 수식하는 자리이므로 holiday, event와 함께 복합명사를 이루는 명사 (D)가 정답이다.

해석 Low Ridge Mall에서는 이번 달 연례 연휴 할인 판매 행사를 홍보하고 있다.

>> 두 개 이상의 명사가 결합된 복합명사는 한 단어로 외운다.

The high cost of comprehensive employee **health** insurance poses a financial burden to small-sized businesses.
(health 위에 healthy (X))

직원 종합 건강 보험의 높은 요금은 소규모 업체들에 재정 부담을 야기한다.

→ health insurance는 '건강 보험'을 의미하는 복합명사이다.

Catering services are available for all events hosted at the Plaza Motel.
(Catering 위에 Catered (X))

Plaza 모텔에서 주최되는 모든 행사에 출장 연회 서비스가 이용 가능하다.

→ catering service는 '출장 연회 서비스'를 의미하는 복합명사이다.

빈출 복합명사

application form	신청서, 지원서	performance evaluation	성과 평가
attendance record	출석 기록	replacement product	교체품
clearance sale	점포 정리 세일	retirement celebration	은퇴식
enrollment fee	등록비	safety regulations	안전 수칙
expiration date	만료일	safety precautions	안전 예방 조치
interest rate	이자율	safety procedures	안전 절차
job opening	공석	sales figure	매출액
keynote address[speech]	기조 연설	savings account	보통 예금 계좌
meal preference	선호하는 메뉴	tourist attraction	관광 명소
office supplies	사무용품	water usage	물 사용(량)

3SECS 알면 3초!   >> 보기에 한 단어에서 파생된 의미가 다른 두 개 이상의 명사가 제시되면 해석해서 푼다.

Chef Bakkalapulo plans to offer several unique dessert ------- at his restaurant in Boston.

(A) creativity   (B) create   (C) creative   (D) creations

보기는 모두 동사 'create'의 파생어이다. 빈칸이 앞의 형용사 several, unique의 수식을 받으면서 명사 dessert와 복합명사를 이루는 명사 자리인 걸 파악해도 보기에 명사가 (A), (D) 두 개이므로 바로 답을 고를 수는 없을 것이다. 이때에는 어휘를 해석해서 정답을 찾아야 한다. 명사에서 '명사 자리 파악 → 주어진 두 개의 명사 중 의미상 어울리는 명사 선택'의 과정을 거쳐야 하는 문제들이 자주 등장하고 있으니 참고해두자. creativity는 '창의성'을, creation 은 '창작(물), 창작품'을 의미한다는 점에서 문맥상 (D)가 정답이다.

해석 Bakkalapulo 요리사는 Boston에 있는 그의 레스토랑에서 몇 가지 독특한 디저트 창작물을 제공할 계획이다.

PART 5

1. Our database ------- policy has been upgraded in order to maintain the confidentiality of client records.

(A) secure
(B) securely
(C) security
(D) secured

2. Visit our nearest community center and register today for the information technology -------.

(A) workshop
(B) ticket
(C) action
(D) picture

3. Alternative sources of ------- energy have been a hot topic at this congress.

(A) renew
(B) renews
(C) renewal
(D) renewable

4. If you have finished entering items to purchase, press 'SUBMIT' to calculate total and shipping -------.

(A) charges
(B) guidelines
(C) rights
(D) concerns

PART 6

Questions 5-8 refer to the following e-mail.

To: Beatrice Dalton <b_dalton1984@lmmail.com>
From: Anthony Vanderfell <anthonyv@wfservices.com>
Date: April 1
Subject: Consumer Research

Dear Ms. Beatrice Dalton,

I work for a major market research company called WF Services. We are ------- distributing questionnaires to athletes and physical education teachers so that we can better understand their consumer behavior for both online and offline shopping. We want to examine the elements that affect ------- habits. You ------- because you are a subscriber to *Boynton Fitness Enthusiast*. -------. Should you take part, we will provide you with a $50 coupon for a meal at a restaurant in your area. If you'd like to participate, reply to this e-mail, and I will send the questionnaire form to you.

Thanks for your time.

Anthony Vanderfell,
Marketing Outreach Specialist

5. (A) instantly
(B) currently
(C) collaboratively
(D) progressively

6. (A) buying
(B) medical
(C) legal
(D) lending

7. (A) are selecting
(B) will be selected
(C) select
(D) have been selected

8. (A) This will, unfortunately, be the last print issue of the magazine.
(B) The list of participating locations is printed on the back.
(C) We give advice to top companies in a variety of fields.
(D) The questionnaire should take no more than 15 minutes.

1. About 50 percent of our streaming service's
------- reside overseas.

(A) subscribe
(B) subscribing
(C) subscribers
(D) subscriptions

2. Urban scholars predict more population
------- in the Sun Belt due to its well-developed
infrastructure.

(A) to grow
(B) grown
(C) grower
(D) growth

3. While Cherryville Growers is a well-known
------- of fruit and vegetables, its market share
is lower than its main competitor's.

(A) produce
(B) producer
(C) productive
(D) production

4. Ms. Wu at the facility ------- office announced
to us that the fire alarm system will be
inspected at 10:00 A.M. today.

(A) manage
(B) management
(C) manager
(D) manageable

5. Glenwood Electronics expects to finish the
fiscal year with a budget ------- of 800,000
dollars.

(A) restriction
(B) surplus
(C) commencement
(D) association

6. The Legend's third album, Come on Now, sold
well on the ------- of the band's hit single.

(A) talent
(B) strength
(C) time
(D) money

7. Potential candidates must complete and
submit a personal ------- before their interview.

(A) statement
(B) background
(C) identity
(D) transcription

8. The Office of Public Roads has employed
supplementary ------- so that motorways are
quickly removed of any icy buildup.

(A) representatives
(B) commuters
(C) contractors
(D) shareholders

Questions 9-12 refer to the following memo.

To: Sales Team 4
From: Marcus Stone, Product Manager
Date: February 3
Subject: Quarter 4 Results

Let me preface this e-mail by congratulating the entire team on the fantastic results in quarter four. ------- I saw the breakdown of sales by product, I was astounded. I would like to propose that we
9.
meet on Monday to ------- some of the findings in detail.
10.

In particular, I want to focus on the sharp increase in home automation equipment. -------. What
11.
spurred the sudden interest among the public? Are our competitors also seeing similar trends?

I think we should do a ------- between our results and our competitors' to see where we should focus
12.
on for this year. I'll prepare the agenda and send it through tomorrow.

9. (A) Yet
(B) During
(C) When
(D) Since

10. (A) confound
(B) analyze
(C) suggest
(D) generate

11. (A) The meeting should take no longer than 20 minutes.
(B) Some suggestions should be made to improve our brand.
(C) I have revised the schedule accordingly.
(D) Last year, it was an underperforming category.

12. (A) comparison
(B) comparability
(C) comparable
(D) compare

CASE 11 주격 대명사

Remember to email Mr. Falk to ask if ------- is available on Thursday for a photo shoot.

(A) his   (B) him   (C) he   (D) himself

> 해설   빈칸은 if 종속절의 주어 자리이므로 주격 대명사 (C)가 정답이다.
> 해석   그가 목요일에 사진 촬영을 할 수 있는지 물어보려면 Falk 씨에게 이메일 보내는 걸 잊지 마세요.

>> 주격은 주어 자리에 온다.

Once Mr. Lane received Ms. Kim's application, **he sent** her a confirmation e-mail.
주격   동사

Lane 씨가 Kim 씨의 신청서를 받자마자, 그는 그녀에게 확인 이메일을 보냈다.

>> 대명사가 가리키는 명사에 인칭, 수, 성을 일치시킨다.

Once **Mr. Lane** received **Ms. Kim**'s application, **he** sent **her** a confirmation e-mail.
남성   여성

⏱ 알면 3초!   >> 관계대명사절의 격을 묻는다.

The employee manual contains solutions to any problems ------- may encounter with a client.

(A) you   (B) yours   (C) yourself   (D) your own

문장에 주어(The employee manual)와 본동사(contains)가 이미 존재함에도 빈칸 뒤에 또 다른 동사(may encounter)가 등장하므로, 빈칸 앞에 목적격 관계대명사 that이 생략되어 있고, 빈칸에는 선행사 problems를 수식하는 관계대명사절 내 주어 자리임을 알아차릴 수 있다면 쉽게 풀리는 문제이다. '당신이 부딪힐 수 있는 문제들에 대한 해결책들(solutions to any problems (that) you may encounter)을 포함하고 있다'라는 의미가 되어야 자연스러우므로 주격 대명사 (A)가 정답이다.

> 해석   직원 수칙은 여러분이 고객과 부딪힐 수 있는 문제들에 대한 해결책들을 포함하고 있다.

PART 5

1. Customers have plenty of time to take advantage of the store discount, as ------- lasts until the end of the year.

(A) we
(B) she
(C) it
(D) they

2. Mr. Barton promised Ms. Alvarez that ------- can complete the assignment with the assistance of his team members.

(A) himself
(B) him
(C) his
(D) he

3. Ms. Kimura was busy this morning, so ------- needs to be informed about the policy changes that were announced.

(A) her
(B) she
(C) hers
(D) herself

4. Here at Parker's Learning Institute, ------- help underprivileged children master subjects they struggle to understand.

(A) we
(B) us
(C) our
(D) ourselves

PART 6

Questions 5-8 refer to the following Web page.

www.earlwin.edu/connect

All students and faculty are invited to try the new Earlwin Connect App, a resource that will put all relevant campus information, from event and class schedules to cafeteria menus, at your fingerprints. To start using the app, students and faculty first need to sign up for an Earlwin Connect account. -------. Send a text message reading "set up" to (555) 462-9201, or write "set up" in the subject header to connectapp@earlwin.edu. A few minutes thereafter, ------- will be sent an ID and temporary password. After receiving this, access the Connect app through your smart device, and enter the appropriate credentials when prompted.

In the interest of protecting our network, the one-time password ------- after one day, so make sure to use it promptly. To clear up ------- that come up during the registration procedure, call IT at (555) 462-2000.

5. (A) Our online portal will undergo routine maintenance.
(B) To protect student privacy, some scheduling information has been removed.
(C) Setup will require the latest version of Campus Messenger.
(D) The process consists of several simple steps.

6. (A) she
(B) you
(C) I
(D) they

7. (A) has expired
(B) would have expired
(C) expiring
(D) expires

8. (A) appeals
(B) discussions
(C) issues
(D) criticisms

CASE 12 소유격 대명사

The aviation safety inspector has certified ------- newly hired aircraft mechanics.

(A) our   (B) us   (C) ours   (D) ourselves

해설   빈칸은 명사구 'newly hired aircraft mechanics'를 수식하는 자리이므로 소유격 대명사 (A)가 정답이다.

해석   항공 안전 검사관은 우리의 새로 채용된 항공기 정비공들에게 자격을 부여했다.

>> 소유격 대명사는 명사 앞에 온다.

The cleaning crew members have been mindful of **our regulations**. 소유격 + 명사
청소부 직원들은 우리의 규정에 유념했다.

>> 소유격 대명사와 명사 사이에 들어갈 수 있는 수식어(복합명사, 형용사, 부사)에 주의한다.

The cleaning crew members have been mindful of **our safety regulations**. 소유격 + 복합명사
청소부 직원들은 우리의 안전 규정에 유념했다.

The cleaning crew members have been mindful of **our quite strict regulations**. 소유격 + 부사 + 형용사 + 명사
청소부 직원들은 우리의 상당히 엄격한 규정에 유념했다.

 알면 3초!   >> 「one's own + 명사(= 명사 + of one's own)」는 소유의 의미를 강조한다.

Both the Brighten Hotel and the Altamont Inn are conveniently located and have ------- own café.

(A) they   (B) their   (C) all   (D) another

빈칸 뒤 own은 동사(소유하다)뿐 아니라 소유격 뒤에서 소유의 의미를 강조하는 형용사(~ 자신의)로도 쓰인다는 점을 기억한다. 빈칸 이하가 have의 목적어에 해당하므로 빈칸은 명사 café를 수식하는 자리이며, 소유의 의미를 강조하는 형용사 own이 있음을 고려할 때, 관용 표현 「one's own + 명사(~만의 명사)」를 완성하는 소유격 (B)가 정답이다. have their own café는 have a café of their own과 같은 표현이다.

해석   Brighten 호텔과 Altamont 여관 둘 다 편리한 위치에 있으며 그들만의 카페를 소유하고 있다.

PART 5

1. This economic forecast relies on the assumption that all firms will be minimizing ------- costs.
(A) they
(B) them
(C) their
(D) themselves

2. Ms. Raina dealt with ------- clients' requests promptly and with professionalism.
(A) she
(B) her
(C) herself
(D) hers

3. There are numerous power tools available for ------- citizens to borrow for a nominal fee.
(A) you
(B) ours
(C) they
(D) our

4. Included in the lease agreement to Whittingham Apartments is exclusive use of our ------- designed rooftop.
(A) attractive
(B) attraction
(C) attractor
(D) attractively

PART 6

Questions 5-8 refer to the following e-mail.

To: Veronica Humphrey <v.humphrey@corpsol.com>
From: Darla Weimer <darla.w@xcoindustries.com>
Date: June 2
Subject: May 20 Seminar

Dear Ms. Humphrey,

This e-mail is to show our ------- for the seminar Benjamin Morey gave on May 20 at our office
                                5.
building. Several staff members ------- concerns about the need for this type of seminar. These very
                                   6.
staff members were the most enthusiastic participants in the seminar, and they also asked if we
could host similar events in the future. Attendees were asked to fill out a feedback survey ------- to
                                                                                             7.
evaluate the usefulness of the seminar. The majority of responses were positive; nearly 85 percent of
the attendees indicated that they were more confident in their public speaking abilities now. -------. If
                                                                                                8.
you are interested in going over the results in person, please contact me.

Sincerely,

Darla Weimer

5. (A) appreciation
(B) appreciates
(C) appreciated
(D) appreciative

6. (A) were to be raised
(B) had raised
(C) is raising
(D) raise

7. (A) frequently
(B) rather
(C) because
(D) afterwards

8. (A) A small number of attendees stated they wanted more hands-on activities.
(B) A different seminar on time management will be provided from time to time.
(C) A billing statement will be sent to your e-mail address soon.
(D) The seminar has been postponed to next week.

CASE 13 목적격 대명사와 소유대명사

The new healthcare program will allow ------- to learn patient care techniques more efficiently.

(A) we   (B) our   (C) ourselves   (D) us

> **해설** 빈칸은 타동사 allow의 목적어 자리이며 문맥상 '새 의료 관리 프로그램이 우리에게 환자 치료 기법을 더 효율적으로 배우는 것을 가능하게 할 것이다'라는 의미가 되어야 자연스러우므로 목적격 대명사 (D)가 정답이다.

> **해석** 새 의료 관리 프로그램은 우리가 환자 치료 기법을 더 효율적으로 배우게 해 줄 것이다.

>> 목적격은 타동사나 전치사의 목적어 자리에 온다.

If your meal is unsatisfactory, you can **send us** an e-mail regarding your dining experience.

타동사 + 목적격

If your meal is unsatisfactory, you can send an e-mail **to us** regarding your dining experience.

전치사 + 목적격

식사에 만족하지 않으면, 식사 경험에 대해 저희에게 이메일을 보낼 수 있습니다.

>> 소유대명사는 「소유격 + 명사」를 의미하며, 명사가 쓰이는 자리(주어, 목적어, 보어)에 온다.

Mr. Lawson has filed **his tax return**, but Ms. Peters has still not done **hers**. ↳ hers = her tax return
Lawson 씨는 소득세 신고서를 제출했지만, Peters 씨는 아직 자신의 것을 하지 못했다.

⏱ 알면 3초!   >> 목적격 대명사와 소유대명사의 구별은 해석해서 푼다.

Although Mr. Howard submitted his proposal much later than Ms. Mason, the manager chose his idea instead of -------.

(A) she   (B) her   (C) herself   (D) hers

빈칸이 전치사 of의 목적어 자리이긴 하지만 무작정 목적격을 골라선 안 된다. 보기 중에 목적격 외에, 주어, 목적어, 보어 자리에 모두 올 수 있는 소유대명사가 있다면 반드시 해석을 해서 문맥상 어울리는 답을 골라야 한다. 문맥상 'Howard 씨가 Mason 씨보다 제안서를 훨씬 늦게 내기는 했지만, 매니저는 그녀의 아이디어보다 그의 아이디어를 선택했다'는 의미가 되어야 자연스러우며, 'her idea = hers'이므로 소유대명사 (D)가 정답이다.

> **해석** Howard 씨가 Mason 씨보다 제안서를 훨씬 늦게 내긴 했지만, 매니저는 그녀의 것보다 그의 아이디어를 선택했다.

PART 5

1. Mr. Howard promised to send ------- a confirmation e-mail by 5 this afternoon.

(A) our
(B) we
(C) us
(D) ourselves

2. There are several books on public speaking at our store that will help ------- to improve your communication skills.

(A) your
(B) you
(C) yourself
(D) yourselves

3. An employee of ------- will be attending the global trade conference in Germany.

(A) I
(B) me
(C) my
(D) mine

4. Your duties as a project manager are essentially the same as -------.

(A) he
(B) him
(C) himself
(D) his

PART 6

Questions 5-8 refer to the following memo.

To: All Kitchen Staff
From: Rachel Wong, Human Resources Manager
Date: February 11
Subject: New health regulations

As of March 1, we will be required to ------- new rules regarding keeping hot food on our premises. **5.** We have purchased some food thermometers to keep in the kitchen. -------. As you record **6.** temperatures, throw out any food that falls below the given guidelines. Also, we were warned in our last check-up to print out the updated health guidelines. The old one is no longer ------- for our **7.** restaurant. If you have any ------- regarding anything that was shared, please let me know. **8.**

5. (A) protest
(B) remain
(C) standardize
(D) accommodate

6. (A) Verifiers spend years studying for their professions.
(B) Use them to periodically record temperatures.
(C) The certification process can be seen on the Web site.
(D) A video will explain the inconsistencies.

7. (A) applicable
(B) posted
(C) examined
(D) determined

8. (A) query
(B) queried
(C) queries
(D) to query

CASE 14 재귀대명사

Students are expected to discuss among ------- while the instructor monitors and provides feedback.

(A) them   (B) theirs   (C) themselves   (D) they

> **해설** 빈칸은 전치사 among의 목적어 자리이므로 (D)는 소거한다. 문맥상 '학생들이 그들끼리 토론할 것으로 예상된다'는 의미가 되어야 자연스러우므로 빈칸에 들어갈 대명사는 문장의 주어 Students를 가리켜야 한다. 따라서, (C)가 정답이다. 'among themselves[yourselves, ourselves]'는 '그들[너희, 우리] 끼리'라는 의미의 관용 표현이기도 하다.

> **해석** 학생들은 강사가 모니터링하고 피드백을 제공하는 동안 그들끼리 토론할 것으로 예상된다.

>> 행위의 주체와 대상 즉, 동사의 주어와 목적어가 동일할 때 목적어 자리에 재귀대명사를 쓴다.

During the meeting, **Mr. Walter** proved **himself** to be knowledgeable. 주어 = 목적어 → 재귀대명사
회의 중에, Walter 씨는 자신이 박식하다는 것을 증명했다.

>> '직접'이란 뜻으로 주어, 목적어를 강조할 때 재귀대명사를 쓴다.

The interior designer (himself) supervised the remodeling of the kitchen.
The interior designer supervised the remodeling of the kitchen (himself).
그 인테리어 디자이너가 직접 주방 리모델링을 감독했다.
→ 이때 재귀대명사는 강조하는 말 뒤나 문장 끝에 쓰며, 문장의 필수 성분이 아니므로 생략할 수 있다.

 알면 3초!   >> 관용 표현 'by oneself = on one's own (혼자서)'를 외운다.

Professor Ko will deliver the lecture by ------- since her teaching assistant has called in sick.

(A) herself   (B) her   (C) hers   (D) she

빈칸은 전치사 by의 목적어 자리로 목적격 대명사(her), 소유대명사(hers), 재귀대명사(herself) 모두 보기에 들어갈 수 있으므로 해석이 필요한 문제이지만, by 뒤의 대명사 선택 문제는 대부분 재귀대명사의 관용 표현 'by oneself(혼자서)'를 묻는다는 점에서 재귀대명사를 정답 1순위로 놓고, 해당 절을 빠르게 해석해서 문맥상 이상이 없으면 바로 정답으로 체크하고 넘어간다. 'Ko 교수가 혼자서 강의를 할 것이다'로 자연스럽게 해석되므로 재귀대명사 (A)가 정답이다.

> **해석** 조교가 병가를 냈기 때문에 Ko 교수가 혼자서 강의를 할 것이다.

PART 5

1. Katrina Ling, Director of International Sales, chose to conduct the interview -------.

(A) she
(B) herself
(C) hers
(D) her

2. When visiting ABC Cosmetics' booth at the convention, remember to help ------- to a free sample.

(A) yourself
(B) you
(C) yours
(D) your

3. Vice President Harley has an impressive background in finance and so has appointed ------- to fill the vacant finance director position.

(A) he
(B) him
(C) himself
(D) his

4. Ms. Kimura assured the executives that she would complete the budget report ------- by the end of the day.

(A) ourselves
(B) themselves
(C) myself
(D) herself

PART 6

Questions 5-8 refer to the following e-mail.

To: All Employees <listserv@wiztech.com>
From: Lance Hughes <lhuges@wiztech.com>
Date: September 15
Subject: Breakfast reimbursement

Greetings everyone,

I ------- to share some exciting news with all employees. Starting next month, WizTech will now
5.
be reimbursing all employees for breakfast meals. This is a part of our new employee well-being program, and our first step is to ensure that our employees are getting a nutritious breakfast every day. To ------- for the reimbursement, you will need to keep the receipt for your purchase and file
6.
your expenses at the end of the month. The money will come out of your team budget. -------. If you
7.
have any questions about our new program, please feel free to reach out to ------- or anyone else
8.
from the human resources team.

Thank you,

Lance

5. (A) like
(B) had liked
(C) liked
(D) would like

6. (A) consider
(B) qualify
(C) obtain
(D) suggest

7. (A) Detailed nutritional information can be found using the Internet.
(B) As a rule, please try to keep purchases below $20.
(C) Many employees currently do not eat breakfast.
(D) A new restaurant has opened up in the building opposite us.

8. (A) myself
(B) yourself
(C) you
(D) them

TAC, Inc.'s current sales revenues are remarkably similar to ------- of last year.

(A) that　　　　　　(B) those　　　　　　(C) these　　　　　　(D) them

콕 찍어 포인트 ··· **목적격 대명사나 지시대명사 this/these는 뒤에 전치사구, 분사구, 관계절 등의 수식어를 취할 수 없다.**

해설 TAC 사의 현재 매출액이 작년의 매출액과 매우 유사하다는 의미로, 빈칸에는 앞에 나온 복합명사 sales revenues를 대신하는 자리이며 복수이므로 (B)가 정답이다.

해석 TAC 사의 현재 매출액이 작년의 그것들과 매우 유사하다.

>> 앞에 나온 명사를 반복할 때, 지시대명사 that은 단수 명사, those는 복수 명사를 대신한다.

The **opinions** expressed in this newspaper column are **those** of the authors. those = opinions
이 신문 칼럼에 게재된 의견들은 저자들의 것이다.

→ 이때 that/those는 it, them, this/these 등과는 달리 뒤에 전치사구 등의 수식어구를 동반할 수 있다.

>> those는 'who 관계대명사절, 분사구, 전치사구' 등의 수식을 받아 '~하는/~인 사람들'이라는 의미로 쓰인다.

Once all applicants have arrived, **those** (**who** are) **applying** for the marketing position will be interviewed first.
모든 지원자들이 도착하는 대로, 마케팅 직책에 지원하는 사람들이 먼저 면접을 볼 것이다.

→ 이때는 지시대명사의 단수형인 that이나 인칭대명사 they, them 등을 those 대신 쓸 수 없다.

3초 알면 3초! 　　**>>** 「those who + 복수 동사」와 「anyone who + 단수 동사」의 수 일치에 주의한다.

------- who is interested in joining the biotechnology study should email Ms. Labelle at Liddell Medical Institute.

(A) Those　　　　　(B) Others　　　　　(C) Anyone　　　　　(D) Them

빈칸은 주격 관계대명사 who의 선행사 자리로, 먼저 보기 중에서 관계대명사절의 수식을 받을 수 없는 대명사 (B), (D)를 소거한 후, 'Those who(~하는 사람들)'가 맞는지, 'Anyone who(~하는 사람은 누구나)'가 맞는지를 결정한다. 이때 those는 복수 동사로, anyone은 단수 동사로 수를 일치시킨다는 점을 알고 있다면, who 뒤의 동사만 확인해도 해석 없이 문제를 풀 수 있다. who 뒤의 동사가 단수(is)이므로 (C)가 정답이다.

해석 생명 공학 연구에 동참하는 데 관심 있는 사람은 누구나 Liddell 의료기관의 Labelle 씨에게 이메일을 보내면 된다.

CASE 집중훈련

PART 5

1. If the conference time changes, ------- who register early will be informed by phone.
(A) they
(B) those
(C) them
(D) whose

2. ------- who are interested in participating in the clinical trial should contact Prof. Lee from the Molly Medical Research Institute.
(A) Anyone
(B) Yours
(C) One another
(D) Those

3. Vault Systems will ------- its installation fee for anyone who purchases an air purifier this week.
(A) vacate
(B) retreat
(C) restrict
(D) waive

4. Customers enrolled in our mailing list may receive rewards, such as gift cards, if they ------- a certain number of points.
(A) act
(B) acquire
(C) promote
(D) perceive

PART 6

Questions 5-8 refer to the following article.

How Tax Cuts Work

Tax cuts for the wealthy are often ------- as a quick fix to a stagnant economy. At its core, tax cuts for the wealthy are intended to increase spending by the recipients. -------.
5.   **6.**

A slow economy occurs when uncertainty about the future causes people to stop spending money. When people stop spending money, many stores ------- a decline in their revenues. This leads to the closing of stores, as well as the loss of jobs.
7.

The ------- behind a tax cut is to increase spending by the wealthy. If the wealthy spend more money
8.
in the economy, it will generate more revenue for businesses, leading to more jobs. Thus, tax cuts can reverse the effects of a slow economy.

5. (A) promotional
(B) promoted
(C) promote
(D) promotion

6. (A) There are many hidden downsides to tax cuts.
(B) Tax cuts can stimulate slow economies into action.
(C) Jobs are often lost during an economic downturn.
(D) The recent tax cuts have failed to work as planned.

7. (A) subsidize
(B) advocate
(C) mandate
(D) experience

8. (A) rationale
(B) conception
(C) participation
(D) generation

CASE 16   부정대명사 one

Our children are the main ------- who use the computer for games.

(A) thing   (B) ones   (C) here   (D) except

콕 찍어 포인트 ⋯ **부정대명사 one(s)는 문장 내 '(앞서 언급된 명사와 같은 종류/성격의) 것[사람]'을 가리킨다.**

[해설] 빈칸은 the main의 수식을 받는 명사 자리이다. 문맥상 '주로 게임을 위해 컴퓨터를 사용하는 아이들'이라는 의미가 되어야 자연스러우므로 앞서 언급된 children을 가리키는 부정대명사 (B)가 정답이다.

[해석] 우리 아이들은 주로 게임을 위해 컴퓨터를 사용한다.

>> one은 '정해지지 않은 어떤 하나(한 개, 한 명)'를 의미한다.

Buy one, get one 50 percent off!
하나를 사시면, 하나를 50퍼센트 할인해 드려요!

GT Automobile has become one of the largest carmakers in the world. one of 복수 명사 '~ 중 하나'
GT 자동차는 세계에서 가장 큰 자동차 제조업체 중 하나가 되었다.

>> one(s)은 앞뒤에 수식어를 동반하여 '(앞서 언급된 명사와 같은 종류 / 성격의) 것(들)'을 나타낸다.

The vending machine was replaced with a new **one**, because **it** malfunctioned so often.
그 자판기가 너무 자주 오작동해서 새것으로 교체되었다.
→ it은 앞서 언급된 바로 그 명사(the vending machine)를 지칭한다는 점에서 one과 차이가 있다. 반면, a new one에서 oen은 불특정한 자판기를 가리키게 된다.

알면 3초!   **>>** 부정대명사 'another, the other(s), others, one another'의 의미와 용법을 구별한다.

Using banking applications has become the most convenient way to make monetary transfers from one account to -------.

(A) other   (B) another   (C) the others   (D) one another

another	앞서 언급한 것 이외의 '또 다른 하나'	others	정해지지 않은 수 중에서 '나머지 일부'
the other	정해진 수 중에서 '나머지 하나'	one another	셋 이상에서 '서로'
the others	정해진 수 중에서 '나머지 전부'		

'한 계좌에서 다른 계좌로'라는 의미이므로 another account를 나타내는 부정대명사 (B)가 정답이다. 정해지지 않은 대상들 중 'one ~ another ~(하나는 ~, 다른 하나는 ~)', 'some ~ others ~(일부는 ~, 다른 일부는 ~)'가 주로 대구를 이룬다.

[해석] 은행 애플리케이션을 사용하는 것이 한 계좌에서 다른 계좌로 자금을 이체하는 가장 편리한 방법이 되었다.

PART 5

1. Dr. Hanks will personally call ------- who was chosen to participate in the clinical trial for the allergy medication.

(A) everywhere
(B) some
(C) everyone
(D) several

2. All of the applicants are so well-qualified that ------- the CEO hires will be a good fit with the department.

(A) anyone
(B) other
(C) several
(D) someone

3. The Kubeo Pro X200 laser printer is the most expensive ------- in the store at the moment.

(A) another
(B) one
(C) each
(D) all

4. We were previously unable to purchase additional computers for the office because our usual supplier has ------- in stock.

(A) lastly
(B) mainly
(C) any
(D) none

PART 6

Questions 5-8 refer to the following e-mail.

To: Yvonne Reeves <yreeves@gkbank.com>
From: Ian Day <iday@greenshoesoft.com>
Date: 14 July
Re: Error during update

Dear Ms. Reeves,

Thank you for submitting your inquiry regarding the software malfunction that you have been experiencing. I apologize for the delay in getting back to you. ------- the issue has taken us longer than usual due to its complexity. This has been compounded by the fact that ------- of our senior engineers is currently on leave. Regarding your inquiry, we have determined why you have been unable to update your client's information. -------. Next time you log in, you should see a ------- asking you to update. Following the on-screen instructions will correctly apply the update.

I apologize once again for the inconvenience.

Sincerely,

Ian Day
Customer Service, GreenShoe Software Group

5. (A) Diagnose
(B) Diagnosis
(C) Diagnosing
(D) Diagnosed

6. (A) some
(B) many
(C) another
(D) one

7. (A) Updating the software is mandatory due to the potential for security breaches.
(B) You should sign up using your work e-mail to receive the full benefits.
(C) The issue is complicated to explain, but fortunately it has been resolved.
(D) Our team will be updating with any new information we receive.

8. (A) ticket
(B) prompt
(C) credential
(D) category

CASE 17 수량을 나타내는 부정대명사

The new rule is for ------- of the team to follow, with no exceptions.

(A) either   (B) every   (C) both   (D) all

콕 찍어 포인트 … all은 대명사, 한정사, 부사로 쓸 수 있는 반면, every는 한정사의 역할만 한다.

해설 빈칸은 전치사 for의 목적어 역할을 하는 명사 자리이다. 문맥상 '팀원 모두가 따라야 하는 것'이라는 의미가 되어야 자연스러우므로 (D)가 정답이다.

해석 새로운 규칙은 예외 없이 팀원 모두가 따라야 하는 것이다.

≫ 「부정대명사 + of the [소유격] + 명사」의 패턴으로 명사의 수량을 나타낸다.

> one / each + of the[소유격] + 가산 복수 명사 + 단수 동사 ~중 하나/각각
>
> either / neither + of the[소유격] + 가산 복수 명사 + 단수 동사 둘 중 어느 것이든 ~이다/어느 쪽도 ~아니다
>
> both / several / many / few / a few + of the[소유격] + 가산 복수 명사 + 복수 동사 ~ 중 둘 다/몇몇/다수/거의 없음/약간
>
> much / little / a little + of the[소유격] + 불가산 명사 + 단수 동사 ~ 중 많이/거의 없음/약간
>
> some / any / half / most / all + of the[소유격] + 가산 복수 명사[불가산 명사] + 복수 동사[단수 동사] ~ 중 일부/아무것/절반/대부분/모두
>
> none + of the[소유격] + 가산 복수 명사 + 단수 동사[복수 동사] ~ 중 아무도/어떤 것도 …가 아니다

Unfortunately, **neither of the two applicants has** the qualifications for the position.
안타깝게도, 두 지원자 모두 그 직책에 자격이 없다.

 알면 3초!   ≫ 부정대명사도 단독으로 쓸 수 있으므로 해석과 함께 명사나 동사의 수를 확인한다.

Although Alaska and the Caribbean are very different destinations, ------- are popular places to take a cruise.

(A) all   (B) both   (C) none   (D) few

부정대명사도 대명사이므로 단독으로 주어나 목적어 자리에 쓸 수 있다. 문맥상 알맞은 부정대명사를 골라야 하는 문제는 해석을 통해 명사나 동사의 단수, 복수를 확인해야 한다. 문맥상 '알래스카와 카리브해가 매우 다른 곳이긴 해도, 둘 다 인기 있는 장소이다'라는 의미가 되어야 자연스러우므로 두 곳을 가리키는 (B)가 정답이다.

해석 비록 알래스카와 카리브해는 매우 다른 목적지이지만, 둘 다 유람선을 타기에 인기 있는 장소이다.

CASE 집중훈련

PART 5

1. ------- of the two invoices sent to the accounting office was accepted on account of inadequate billing details.

(A) Another
(B) Neither
(C) Whatever
(D) Those

2. Though Zoom Fitness Center offers a cash discount, most of ------- members choose to pay with a credit card.

(A) her
(B) whose
(C) this
(D) its

3. J&J Global Blog has ------- of the largest number of subscribers in Korean news media.

(A) one
(B) still
(C) those
(D) already

4. Even though most supermarkets in the area offer delivery services, ------- provide the extensive list of grocery items that we do.

(A) all
(B) any
(C) either
(D) few

PART 6

Questions 5-8 refer to the following notice.

Lincoln City Transportation Authority Policy Update

Have you ever wanted to bring a bike with you when using Lincoln City Public Transit? Thanks to recent upgrades, all of our buses now have the ----5---- to accommodate your bike. Before boarding the bus, inform your driver. Keep in mind that a special ticket ----6---- for you and your bicycle. Book a place for your bike ----7----. Each bus can only fit two bikes. Confirm that your bike is properly loaded before boarding. ----8---- You are solely responsible for your personal property when riding with us.

---

5. (A) network
(B) stock
(C) profits
(D) equipment

6. (A) is required
(B) was required
(C) requiring
(D) require

7. (A) again
(B) instead
(C) early
(D) often

8. (A) Payment can be made with your transit card.
(B) We also recommend using a secure lock.
(C) The bus schedule is posted at the station.
(D) Folding bikes are more popular nowadays.

1. Mr. Tanaka was awarded Employee of the Year for ------- contribution to the advertising campaign.

(A) he
(B) his
(C) him
(D) himself

2. Mr. Salazar showed his appreciation that ------- of his many colleagues filled in for him while he was on holiday.

(A) anyone
(B) both
(C) every
(D) all

3. Mr. Cole was not available to work on Wednesday due to personal reasons, so Ms. Hanson substituted for -------.

(A) himself
(B) his
(C) his own
(D) him

4. Ms. Nichols will respond to all e-mails ------- while Mr. Morris is on vacation.

(A) she
(B) hers
(C) herself
(D) her

5. Palmer mayor Patricia Craig thanked ------- of the volunteers with a delicate handshake.

(A) their
(B) each
(C) every
(D) either

6. Instead of throwing away expired ingredients and food waste, Green Eating composts ------- at our local farm.

(A) ones
(B) them
(C) it
(D) its

7. Dr. Moreno will experiment with different types of plastic that are less environmentally damaging than ------- used today.

(A) greater
(B) those
(C) what
(D) current

8. ------- of the photos submitted by Mr. Wang were sold at the art fair.

(A) None
(B) Nothing
(C) Nobody
(D) No one

Questions 9-12 refer to the following invitation.

The Glen Park Center for Innovation invites you to its ------- networking event on May 12. This
year's event will be an especially good opportunity for people who are interested in running their
own businesses to meet and discuss ------- ideas with like-minded people from the area. We have
invited successful business owners from the area to talk about some of their experiences in running
a business. ------- should bring business cards with them, as networking can make or break your
business in the early stages. The cost of a ticket for the event is $50, and this price includes parking
space as well as refreshments. -------.

---

9. (A) fortunate
(B) tentative
(C) annual
(D) complimentary

10. (A) them
(B) themselves
(C) their
(D) they

11. (A) Applicants
(B) Nominees
(C) Organizers
(D) Attendees

12. (A) Tickets are limited, so make sure you
purchase yours early.
(B) Business owners should bring samples of
their work.
(C) The event may be canceled next year
based on attendance numbers.
(D) A university degree is a good qualification
to have for entrepreneurs.

형용사

CASE 18 | 명사를 수식하는 형용사

Biographies of the province's most ------- artists are included in next month's *British Columbia Art Journal*.

(A) influencer   (B) influential   (C) influentially   (D) influence

콕 찍어 포인트 ···› 형용사의 최상급 most 앞에는 정관사 the 또는 소유격 대명사가 와야 한다.

[해설] 빈칸은 최상급 most의 수식을 받으며 명사 artists를 수식하는 형용사 자리이므로 (B)가 정답이다.

[해석] 이 지방의 가장 영향력 있는 예술가들의 약력이 다음 달 〈British Columbia Art Journal〉에 포함된다.

➤➤ 형용사는 명사를 수식하며, 명사를 앞에서 수식할 때 「관사/소유격 + (부사) + 형용사 + 명사」의 어순을 취한다.

↪ exception (X), exceptionally (X)

The scholarship is intended to recognize students who achieved **exceptional grades** this semester.
이 장학금은 이번 학기에 우수한 학점을 받은 학생들의 공로를 인정하기 위해 마련된 것이다.

➤➤ -able로 끝나는 형용사가 전치사구나 to부정사 등을 이끌어 수식어구가 길어질 때 명사를 뒤에서 수식한다.

↪ responsibility (X), responsibly (X)

Ms. Ronan is the **manager responsible** for running the South Port branch.
Ronan 씨는 South Port 지사를 운영하는 책임을 맡은 매니저이다.

⏱ 알면 3초!   ➤➤ 형용사 자리 문제는 일반 형용사를 답으로 선호한다.

The ------- government provided tax deductions to encourage foreign investment in the region.

(A) locality   (B) localize   (C) local   (D) localizing

명사 앞에 빈칸이 있고, 보기의 조합이 '일반 형용사, 분사 형용사 또는 명사'라면 수식을 받는 명사와 의미를 따져 볼 필요가 있다. 이때 일반 형용사를 정답 1순위로 놓고 해석해 보는 게 좋은데, 이러한 문제에서 일반 형용사의 정답률이 매우 높기 때문이다. 위 문제 역시 빈칸이 명사 government를 수식하는 자리이며, 보기 중 일반 형용사인 local을 제일 먼저 정답으로 고려했을 때, 지방 정부를 뜻하는 'local government'의 어구가 자연스러우므로 다른 보기들은 따져볼 필요 없이 (C)가 답이다. 하지만 의미를 살펴볼 필요가 있다면, 분사 형용사는 동사가 형용사의 기능을 하기 위해 능동의 현재분사(-ing)나 수동의 과거분사(-ed)로 변형된 것이라는 점에서 동사의 의미를 그대로 대입하여 현재분사는 능동의 의미(~하는), 과거분사는 수동의 의미(~된)로 해석해보고 일반 형용사의 뜻과 비교하여 문맥상 무엇이 더 적절한지 확인한다. 명사 앞의 빈칸은 복합명사의 정답 가능성이 있으므로 명사의 '종류'를 나타내는 명사가 맞는지, 명사의 '성질'이나 '상태'를 나타내는 형용사가 맞는지 확인한다.

[해석] 지방 정부는 지역 내 해외 투자를 장려하기 위해 세금 공제를 제공했다.

PART 5

1. Increasing employee productivity at Kruger Consulting will require a ------- modification of the current workflow.

(A) creative
(B) creation
(C) creativity
(D) creating

2. Ms. Fowler has a reputation for being overly aggressive in business deals, but her colleagues describe her as fairly ------- in other areas of her work.

(A) caution
(B) cautioning
(C) cautious
(D) cautiously

3. Please keep in mind that ------- materials are optional, but will be used in evaluating your application.

(A) supplements
(B) supplementing
(C) supplemented
(D) supplementary

4. Social media marketers spend an ------- amount of time browsing the Web every day.

(A) equal
(B) exciting
(C) unknown
(D) excessive

PART 6

Questions 5-8 refer to the following notice.

The Luton Football Club will be holding its annual 10-kilometre walk across Sandown Beach. The event will take place this weekend, and it is open to the public. ------- will receive a free t-shirt as well as some Luton Football Club goodies. The cost for registration is $15, and this should ------- through the Web site before the event. All proceeds will go towards the Christchurch earthquake relief fund. -------. Some rain is expected over the weekend, so be sure to wear ------- clothing. Get some exercise while supporting a good cause this weekend!

5. (A) Organizers
(B) Travelers
(C) Participants
(D) Volunteers

6. (A) have been paid
(B) have paid
(C) be paying
(D) be paid

7. (A) The walk will take the same route as last year.
(B) Sports players will have a large advantage.
(C) The news will run a piece on the benefits of exercising.
(D) The price for the event may increase next year.

8. (A) warm
(B) warmly
(C) warmth
(D) warmest

CASE 19 주어/목적어의 상태를 설명하는 형용사

The engineers feel that building an additional bridge would be more ------- than trying to dig a tunnel under the river.

(A) practical　　　　(B) practice　　　　(C) practically　　　　(D) practicality

콕 찍어 포인트 ┈ 보어 자리에는 형용사 또는 명사가 올 수 있는데, 형용사는 주어의 상태를 설명하고, 명사는 주어와 의미상 동격 관계를 갖는다.

해설 빈칸은 be동사 뒤의 보어 자리이며, 문맥상 '다리를 추가로 건설하는 것이 더 실용적일 것이다'라는 의미가 되어야 자연스러우므로 형용사 (A)가 정답이다.

해석 기술자들은 강 아래에 터널을 파는 것보다 다리를 추가로 건설하는 것이 더 실용적일 것이라고 생각한다.

≫ 형용사는 2형식 동사의 주격 보어 자리에 쓰여 주어의 상태를 설명한다.

be ~이다 become ~이 되다 remain / stay ~인 채로 있다	
seem / appear ~처럼 보이다 prove ~로 판명되다	+ 주격 보어(형용사)

The software upgrade **will be available** to the public on November 5.
그 소프트웨어 업그레이드는 11월 5일에 일반 대중이 이용할 수 있게 될 것이다.

≫ 형용사는 5형식 동사의 목적격 보어 자리에 쓰여 목적어의 상태를 설명한다.

make ~하게 하다 consider ~라고 여기다 find ~라고 생각하다	
keep 계속 ~하게 하다 leave ~인 채로 두다	+ 목적어 + 목적격 보어(형용사)

Many customers **have found** the new delivery service quite **useful**.
많은 고객들은 새로운 배달 서비스가 매우 유용하다는 것을 알았다.

 알면 3초!　　≫ 5형식 동사의 수동태에 주의한다.

A system update is necessary once a month to guarantee that the firm's data is kept -------.
(A) securing　　　　(B) security　　　　(C) securely　　　　(D) secure

얼핏 보면 that절의 동사가 수동태(is kept)이고, 그 뒤에 빈칸이 있어 동사를 수식하는 부사 자리겠구나 생각하기 쉬운데, 이 keep이란 동사, 쉽게 봐서는 안 된다. keep을 포함하여 「목적어+목적격 보어」를 이끄는 5형식 동사는 단순히 목적어를 취하는 3형식 타동사의 역할도 기본적으로 하고 있고, 3형식일 때와 5형식일 때의 의미 차이가 있기 때문에 이를 구별할 필요가 있다. 3형식의 keep은 '~을 보관하다'란 뜻으로 물리적으로 어딘가에 물건을 넣어둔다는 뜻이고 수동태일 때 뒤에 부사나 전명구 등의 수식어가 오는 데 비해, 5형식의 keep은 '특정한 상태를 계속 유지하다[유지하게 하다]'의 의미로 수동태일 때 뒤에 목적격 보어로 형용사가 나온다. 따라서 위 문제와 같이 보기에 부사와 형용사가 모두 등장한다면 의미를 구별하여 알맞은 품사를 골라야 한다. '데이터가 안전한 상태로 유지된다'는 의미가 적절하므로 5형식의 keep 문장이 수동태로 쓰인 것으로 판단하고 목적격 보어로 형용사 (D)를 답으로 고른다.

해석 회사의 데이터가 안전하게 유지되는 것을 보장하려면 한 달에 한 번 시스템 업데이트가 필요하다.

PART 5

1. The plant manager, Mr. Phuong revised the production record template because the language in it is too -------.
(A) repeating
(B) repetitive
(C) repetition
(D) repeat

2. Customer service employees should not be ------- of customers who call with complaints about our products.
(A) critical
(B) critically
(C) critic
(D) criticize

3. Luxury watch maker Feltam reported its profits remained ------- in the third quarter.
(A) ready
(B) often
(C) steady
(D) elementary

4. The Market Times ------- its readers informed about business and the economy with its in-depth reporting.
(A) gives
(B) stays
(C) buys
(D) keeps

PART 6

Questions 5-8 refer to the following article.

Business News

January 10 (Sacramento) — Zhang and Patel Corporation, the San Francisco-based construction firm, confirmed that they have won a $3-billion contract to complete work on the new Playa de las Americas beach resort in Ensenada, Mexico. -------. The ------- is predicted to take five years to
5.   6.
finish. According to Zhang Xiao-Jun, co-owner of Zhang and Patel, their company ------- a large
7.
financial incentive if it can be completed earlier.

"We are ------- that we can accomplish this goal," Zhang explained. "We were awarded similar
8.
incentives before, so it's definitely possible to do it again."

---

5. (A) San Francisco has several other famous construction companies.
(B) Zhang and Patel has grown significantly in recent years.
(C) The resort will house a luxury hotel, three restaurants, and an amusement park.
(D) Mexican officials toured the facility last week.

6. (A) project
(B) review
(C) acquisition
(D) contest

7. (A) gotten
(B) having gotten
(C) to get
(D) will get

8. (A) confident
(B) evident
(C) able
(D) fair

CASE 20 수량형용사

------- full-time employees take classes on weekends at Johnson County Community College.

(A) Many   (B) Every   (C) Much   (D) Almost

해설 빈칸은 문장의 주어인 복수 가산 명사 employees를 수식하는 자리로, 가산 단수 명사 또는 불가산 명사를 수식하는 Every와 불가산 명사를 수식하는 Much는 소거한다. 문맥상 '많은 정규직 직원들이 주말에 수업을 듣는다'라는 의미가 되어야 자연스러우므로 (A)가 정답이다.

해석 많은 정규직 직원들이 주말에 Johnson 전문 대학에서 수업을 듣는다.

>> 수량형용사는 수식하는 명사의 수와 종류를 결정한다.

a(n), one 하나의 each 각각의 every 모든 another 또 다른 either 둘 중 하나의 neither 둘 다 아닌	+ 가산 단수 명사
a few / several 몇몇의 few 거의 없는 quite a few 꽤 많은 a couple of 두어 개[사람]의 many / a number of / numerous 많은 various / a variety[range, selection] of 다양한 both 둘 다의	+ 가산 복수 명사
a little 약간의 little 거의 없는 less 더 적은 much / an amount of / a great[good] deal of 많은	+ 불가산 명사
all 모든 some 어떤 other 다른 more 더 많은 most 가장 많은, 대부분의 a lot of / lots of / plenty of 많은	+ 가산 복수 명사 + 불가산 명사
any 어떤 ~라도, 모든 no 어떤 ~도 없는	+ 모든 명사

↝ all (X)
Once a month, managers from **every** branch meet at the head office.
한 달에 한 번, 모든 지사의 매니저들이 본사에서 만난다.

↝ many (X)
Campaigns to reduce fuel consumption have not had **much** impact on the public.
연료 소비를 줄이기 위한 캠페인이 대중에게 많은 영향을 미치지 못했다.

↝ another (X)
The excellent service at Blazing-Burgers sets the restaurant apart from **other** competitors.
Blazing-Burgers의 우수한 서비스는 그 식당을 다른 경쟁 업체들과 차별화시킨다.

↝ all (X)
The contract states that the company will be responsible for **any** product that is defective.
이 계약서는 회사가 결함이 있는 어떤 제품이라도 책임을 질 것이라고 명시한다.

 알면 3초! >> every와 another 뒤에 숫자가 오면 복수 명사를 취한다.

All the team members are required to brief their supervisors on the progress of their work ------- two weeks.

(A) some   (B) several   (C) every   (D) most

수량형용사 every와 another 뒤에는 가산 단수 명사가 오는 것이 일반적이지만, 둘 이상의 숫자를 동반할 경우 복수 명사를 취하면서 그 의미를 달리한다. 「every + 숫자 + 복수 명사」는 '~마다(예: every three years 3년마다)'란 의미로 빈도를 나타내며, 「another + 숫자 + 복수 명사」는 '~더(예: another three people 3명 더)'란 의미로 추가를 나타낸다는 점을 구별해서 기억하자. 빈칸 뒤에 가산 복수 명사(weeks)가 와 있어 every를 맨 먼저 걸러내기 쉬운데, 「숫자 + 복수 명사」가 와 있고 '2주마다 업무 진행 사항을 보고해야 한다'는 의미가 적절하므로 (C)가 정답이다.

해석 모든 팀원들은 2주마다 그들의 업무 진행 사항에 대해 상관에게 보고해야 한다.

CASE 집중훈련

PART 5

1. Many advertisers distribute USB memories instead of ------- promotional items because of their portability.
(A) other
(B) every
(C) another
(D) each

2. This morning we received numerous ------- messages from viewers about yesterday's episode.
(A) credible
(B) accurate
(C) positive
(D) conditional

3. All product ------- must be forwarded to the customer support team.
(A) inquiry
(B) inquirer
(C) inquiries
(D) inquiringly

4. Kwik Logistics truck drivers are required to comply with all local traffic ------- while making long-distance deliveries.
(A) regulates
(B) regulations
(C) regulator
(D) regulating

PART 6

Questions 5-8 refer to the following letter.

Rebecca Judy
HR Department
IMF Design Solutions
Sunnyvale, CA 91967

Ms. Judy,

I'm writing this letter of recommendation on behalf of Chuck Bousculer, who has worked under me as a software engineer at LeetTech for the last seven years. As his manager, I was in charge of evaluating Mr. Bousculer's work regularly. He showed tremendous creativity and an aptitude for leadership. -------. This June, he led the development team in my absence, a role he performed very -------. I am positive that he would do well as a lead engineer at IMF Design Solutions. He is accomplished and ambitious, and always volunteers to take on added -------. I can say that I have ------- reservations about recommending him to your company.

Best,

Basil Cleese
LeetTech Software

5. (A) He will be available to join your company in July.
(B) He always excels when collaborating with other engineers.
(C) He has expressed interest in switching fields.
(D) He will enroll in a graduate program in the fall.

6. (A) competent
(B) competencies
(C) competently
(D) competence

7. (A) duties
(B) notes
(C) payments
(D) breaks

8. (A) no
(B) a few
(C) none
(D) another

CASE 21 혼동하기 쉬운 형용사

Local manufacturers are becoming heavily ------- on foreign semiconductor suppliers.

(A) reliable   (B) rely   (C) reliant   (D) relying

콕 찍어 포인트 ···> ① 2형식 동사 become은 형용사를 주격 보어로 취할 수 있다.
    ② reliable vs. reliant: reliable은 '믿을 수 있는, 신뢰할 수 있는'을, reliant는 '의존하는'을 의미한다.
    ③ 형용사 reliant는 전치사 on을 동반한다.

해설 빈칸은 동사 are becoming과 전치사 on 사이의 자리이다. 전치사 on을 동반하면서, 문맥상 '국내 제조업체들이 해외 반도체 공급업체에 크게 의존하고 있다'라는 의미가 되어야 자연스러우므로 (C)가 정답이다.

해석 국내 제조업체들은 해외 반도체 공급업체에 크게 의존하고 있다.

>> 형태는 비슷하지만 의미가 다른 형용사들이 제시될 때는 문맥에 어울리는 형용사를 골라야 한다.

confident '확신하는' (X)
Our employee database is kept strictly **confidential**.
우리의 직원 데이터베이스는 엄격히 기밀로 유지되고 있다.

reliant '의존하는' (X)
Successful candidates for this job must have a **reliable** internet connection and a personal mobile phone.
이 직책의 합격자들에게는 확실한 인터넷 접속과 개인 휴대폰이 있어야 한다.

유사한 형태의 빈출 형용사

considerate	사려 깊은	considerable	상당한, 많은
confident	확신하는	confidential	기밀의
comprehensive	종합적인	comprehensible	이해할 수 있는
favorite	매우 좋아하는	favorable	우호적인
forgetful	잘 잊어버리는	forgettable	쉽게 잊혀질
informative	유익한	informed	잘 아는
reliable	믿을 수 있는, 확실한	reliant	의존하는
respective	각각의	respectful	공손한
responsible	책임 있는	responsive	반응하는, 호응하는
sensitive	민감한	sensible	분별 있는
successful	성공적인	successive	연속적인
various	다양한	variable	변동이 심한

특정 전치사를 동반하는 빈출 형용사

be appreciative of	~에 감사하다	be exempt from	~로부터 면제되다
be attentive to	~에 주의를 기울이다	be faced with	~에 직면하다
be capable of	~을 할 수 있다	be familiar with	~에 익숙하다
be compatible with	~와 호환되다	be indicative of	~을 나타내다
be consistent with	~와 일치하다	be relevant to	~에 관련되다
be eligible for	~에 자격이 있다	be responsible for	~을 책임지다

 알면 3초!   >> 특정 전치사를 동반하는 빈출 형용사를 외운다.

Most survey respondents said they were ------- with the performance of their new vehicles.

(A) pleased   (B) pleasure   (C) pleasing   (D) pleasurable

'be pleased with(~에 만족해하다)'를 덩어리째 알고 있으면 바로 (A)를 고르고 다음 문제를 보고 있을 수 있다. 이처럼 특정 전치사나 to부정사, that절 등을 관용적으로 동반하는 형용사는 형용사 어휘 문제로 출제되거나 형용사 뒤에 빈칸을 주고 알맞은 전치사나 to부정사 등을 고르라는 문제로 출제되므로 빈출 형용사의 관용 표현을 미리 외워두자.

해석 대부분의 설문 응답자들은 그들의 새로운 차량의 성능에 만족해했다고 말했다.

PART 5

1. It is not an ------- list, but these are some of the many responsibilities of the managerial position at Bethlehem University Hospital.

(A) exhaustive
(B) exhausting
(C) exhausted
(D) exhaustion

2. Roh Agriculture negotiated an agreement with Yanjing Logistics and can now ship their merchandise internationally at very ------- prices.

(A) reasonable
(B) reasoning
(C) reasoned
(D) reason

3. Please be ----- and refrain from using mobile phones while driving to guarantee the safety of other road users.

(A) considerable
(B) consider
(C) consideration
(D) considerate

4. Since survey takers described Galaway Resort's present logo as -------, the company wants to design a new one.

(A) forgot
(B) forgetful
(C) forgettable
(D) forgetting

PART 6

Questions 5-8 refer to the following e-mail.

To: Esther Carter
From: Tabitha Palinski
Date: 7 June
Subject: Senior Software Engineer Application

Dear Ms. Carter,

Thank you for meeting with me this morning. I ------- our discussion very interesting. I'm still
5.
interested in the job as a senior software engineer. I would be very happy to come in for an additional
round of -------.
6.
I believe that I have the perfect skill set for the projects you mentioned. In the past 15 years, I have
contributed to several major successes for my employers, and I have acquired a ------- amount of
7.
experience. Few people in our industry have spent more time creating and refining high-end security
software for the manufacturing sector.

I have confirmed my schedule, as we agreed while discussing when I could begin work. ------- I hope
8.
to hear back from you at your earliest convenience.

5. (A) finding
(B) find
(C) will find
(D) found

6. (A) corrections
(B) interviews
(C) advancements
(D) elections

7. (A) considerate
(B) considerable
(C) considerably
(D) consider

8. (A) I appreciate your offer, and I will happily look it over.
(B) I think my background qualifies me for the job.
(C) I do, however, have a few more questions for you.
(D) I would be able to start any time after the 27th of the month.

1. Bukhara Restaurant serves ------- cuisine from northern India.

(A) authenticate
(B) authentic
(C) authenticity
(D) authentically

2. Nutri Health will be giving out complimentary supplement samples at local pharmacies on ------- Sunday in July.

(A) regular
(B) once
(C) several
(D) each

3. Though Ella Dunn's team helped design the company's new electric car, she alone came up with the ------- concept.

(A) original
(B) origin
(C) originality
(D) originally

4. The financial auditor suggests removing some ------- wording from the statements for the yearly report in order to remain objective and factual.

(A) description
(B) describing
(C) describe
(D) descriptive

5. According to the system, you are ------- for your annual dental appointment with Dr. Herrera.

(A) overdue
(B) engaged
(C) essential
(D) involved

6. Web Watch is the ------- provider of on-demand streaming media for a worldwide audience.

(A) arbitrary
(B) leading
(C) privileged
(D) assured

7. Because of the reduced number of patrons, it is no longer ------- for Lumen Art Gallery to open for admissions every day of the week.

(A) presumable
(B) payable
(C) profitable
(D) permissible

8. The ------- recipient of the promotion is the current manager of the Marketing Department.

(A) rotated
(B) particular
(C) likely
(D) closest

Questions 9-12 refer to the following information.

Business Minds Quarterly

Got a story to share?

Recently, we have received many e-mails from our readers asking how one would go about changing industries. Many ------- have been made vacant due to the prolonged economic downturn. -------, 9. 10. many professionals have found themselves out of a job. What this has opened up, however, is the opportunity to go down a new career path.

If you have recently changed industries and would like to share your story, we would love to hear from you. Simply tell us your story in less than 750 words, and in particular, state ------- skills helped 11. you the most. Send your story to editorial@businessquarterly.com. -------. If the deadline is missed, 12. we unfortunately cannot include your story.

9. (A) industries
   (B) professions
   (C) openings
   (D) positions

10. (A) As a result
    (B) In addition
    (C) Nonetheless
    (D) Ironically

11. (A) how
    (B) whose
    (C) why
    (D) which

12. (A) The article on job interview tips has also been requested.
    (B) All e-mails must be sent in by April 23.
    (C) We ask that you check your mailboxes frequently.
    (D) The next edition will debut this new design.

부사

CASE 22 부사 자리 1

Ms. Rani Meshawari has ------- led Jhodphur Textiles for over three decades.

(A) succeeded   (B) successes   (C) successfully   (D) success

> **해설** 빈칸은 현재 완료 동사(has led) 사이에 위치해 있으므로 동사를 수식하는 부사 (C)가 정답이다.
>
> **해석** Rani Meshawari 씨는 30년 넘게 Jhodphur 섬유를 성공적으로 이끌어왔다.

>> 부사는 동사를 수식하며 다양한 자리에 위치한다.

부사 + 동사(+ 목적어)	His supervisor **quickly ate his breakfast** and went out. 그의 감독관은 서둘러 아침을 먹고 밖으로 나갔다.
동사(+ 목적어) + 부사	The maintenance job **proceeded slowly** due to a scheduling conflict. 이 유지 보수 업무는 일정이 겹쳐서 느리게 진행되었다.
조동사 + 부사 + 동사	The new hires **will shortly be assigned** to their respective teams based on their performance appraisals. 신입 직원들은 업무 수행 평가에 근거하여 곧 각 팀에 배정될 것이다.
자동사 + 부사 + 전치사	Visitor numbers at the Natural History Museum **increased rapidly following** the opening of the new dinosaur exhibit. 자연사 박물관 방문객 수가 신규 공룡 전시 개장 이후 빠르게 증가했다.
be동사 + 부사 + 형용사	Proper hygiene and creativity **are equally important** to Sensation Salon's makeup artists. 적절한 위생과 창의성이 Sensation 살롱의 메이크업 아티스트들에게 똑같이 중요하다.
be동사 + 부사 + -ing	Prax Media **is desperately trying** to acquire Pixels Animation Studio. Prax 미디어는 Pixels 애니메이션 스튜디오를 필사적으로 매입하려 하고 있다.
be동사 + 부사 + p.p.	The product development must **be carefully reviewed** before it is passed onto the CEO. 제품 개발은 CEO에 의해 통과되기 전에 주의 깊게 검토되어야 한다.
have / has / had + 부사 + p.p.	Since Mr. Elliot was appointed CFO, morale at Braiden Electronics **has significantly improved**. Elliot 씨가 CFO로 임명된 이후로, Braiden 전자의 사기가 상당히 개선되었다.

>> 부사는 동사의 성질을 지닌 to부정사, 동명사, 분사를 수식한다.

부사 + to부정사	It is essential **to diligently review** all the terms of the contract before you sign it. 계약서에 서명하기 전에 모든 계약 조건을 부지런히 검토하는 것이 중요하다.
부사 + 동명사	Management emphasized the need to improve revenue by **gradually increasing** the marketing budget. 경영진은 마케팅 예산을 점차 늘림으로써 수익을 개선할 필요성에 대해 강조했다.
부사 + 분사	**Having thoroughly considered** every candidate, the executive manager decided to hire Sheryl Peppers. 모든 후보자를 면밀하게 고려한 뒤, 그 간부는 Sheryl Peppers를 고용하기로 결정했다.

⏱ 알면 3초!   **>>** 부사는 동사와 목적어 사이에 오지 못한다.

The HR Department decided that Friday's reception will require ------- seating.

(A) additionally   (B) additional   (C) additions   (D) addition

우선 빈칸 앞뒤의 단어가 어떤 품사와 역할을 하는지 확실히 해둘 필요가 있는데, require는 타동사, seating은 명사로서 목적어에 해당한다. 얼핏 부사가 동사를 수식하고, 동사 앞뒤에 올 수 있다고 해서 부사를 고르기 쉬운데, 동사와 목적어 사이에는 부사가 오지 못한다는 것을 알고 있다면 동사와 목적어 사이의 부사를 놓고 고민할 일은 없을 것이다. 따라서 여기서는 명사 목적어를 수식하는 형용사 (B)가 정답이다.

> **해석** 인사부는 금요일에 있을 환영회에 추가적인 좌석 배치가 필요하다고 결정했다.

CASE 집중훈련

PART 5

1. The inquiry revealed that the resort staff had handled the guest's complaints -------, and that their actions did not go against resort policy.

(A) appropriate
(B) more appropriate
(C) appropriateness
(D) appropriately

2. An agreement was ------- signed after a lengthy negotiation between two corporations.

(A) already
(B) constantly
(C) finally
(D) exactly

3. Residents of the town must be consulted ------- before making any changes to the current transportation system.

(A) individual
(B) individually
(C) individualism
(D) individualist

4. Motorists on the Brisbane Bridge are asked to drive ------- during September due to the continuing street repairs.

(A) cautiously
(B) cautiousness
(C) caution
(D) cautious

PART 6

Questions 5-8 refer to the following e-mail.

To: Collette Snead
From: Ayrton de Silva <asilva@sarbaevents.com>
Date: September 22
RE: Company Anniversary

Dear Ms. Snead,

We appreciate your interest in using Sarba for your party next month. I'd be happy to let you know some details about the spaces at our disposal.

------- Our ballroom, for example, can host a group of up to 150 and has a stage for live
5.
entertainment. This area is ------- for a company-wide gathering. The more exclusive rooftop lounge
6.
is suitable for formal -------. In addition, the Eastwood Pavilion has scenic views and fresh air with
7.
room for 50-70 party goers. We can ------- arrange for parking and/or ground transportation for
8.
guests in accordance with your needs and scheduling considerations as well.

Please reply directly if you'd like to know more. We are always open to suggestions.

Best,

Ayrton de Silva

5. (A) We are happy to e-mail you with the additional information.
(B) We would appreciate it if you took the time to fill out a brief survey.
(C) We provide custom settings suited to groups of varying sizes.
(D) We can book a musical group in a genre of your choice.

6. (A) accurate
(B) ideal
(C) concerned
(D) total

7. (A) locations
(B) occasions
(C) procedures
(D) styles

8. (A) easier
(B) ease
(C) easy
(D) easily

부사 자리 2

Unusually warm weather was ------- responsible for the high number of guests at Hillside's Autumn City Barbecue.

(A) large   (B) larger   (C) largely   (D) largest

> 해설 빈칸은 형용사 responsible을 수식하는 부사 자리이므로 (C)가 정답이다.

> 해석 Hillside's Autumn City Barbecue의 높은 방문자 수는 평소와 다른 따뜻한 날씨가 큰 원인이었다.

➤➤ 부사는 형용사, 부사, 전치사구를 수식하며 수식하는 형용사, 부사, 전치사구 바로 앞에 위치한다.

부사 + 형용사	Mr. Yong started work as an accounting assistant, but now he is a **nationally renowned** financial analyst. Yong 씨는 회계 보조원으로 일을 시작했지만, 이제는 전국적으로 유명한 금융 분석가이다.
부사 + 부사	You should consider all your options **very carefully**. 당신은 모든 선택지들을 매우 신중하게 고려해야 합니다.
부사 + 전치사구	Some of the machinery malfunctioned, **reportedly due to a software error**. 들리는 바에 의하면, 소프트웨어 오류로 인해 일부 장비가 고장 났다고 한다.

➤➤ 부사는 문장 전체를 수식하며 주로 문장 맨 앞에 위치한다.

부사 + 문장 전체	**Unfortunately, the sales director will not be present at the conference due to a family emergency.** 안타깝게도, 그 영업 이사는 급한 집안 일로 회의에 참석할 수 없을 것이다.

 알면 3초!   ➤➤ 부사 only, even은 명사나 대명사도 수식하여 그 의미를 강조한다.

Raban Photography's newly released line of cameras, ------- those with state-of-the-art optics, cost more or less the same as last year's models.

(A) allowing   (B) because   (C) instead   (D) even

'부사는 모든 문장 성분을 수식할 수 있다' 또는 '부사는 명사나 대명사를 수식할 수 있다'라는 말에 '일부는 맞고, 일부는 틀리다' 정도로 답하는 게 좋을 것이다. 앞에서도 정리했지만 부사는 거의 모든 품사를 수식하지만 명사나 대명사 수식은 일부 부사들에만 자격이 주어지며, 명사나 대명사의 의미를 강조/한정하는 역할을 한다. 이러한 부사들로는 'only/solely/just(오직), even(~조차), particularly/especially/specifically(특히)' 등이 있으며, 시험에서는 only와 even을 자주 묻는다. 따라서 이들 부사가 나오면 명사나 대명사를 수식할 수 있다는 점을 염두에 두고 해석해서 답을 결정하는 것이 좋다. 위 문장에서 even은 빈칸 뒤의 대명사 those를 수식하여 그 의미를 강조할 수 있으므로 정답은 (D)다.

> 해석 Raban 사진의 새로 출시된 카메라 라인은, 최첨단 광학이 탑재된 것들조차도, 작년 모델과 가격이 거의 동일했다.

CASE 집중훈련

PART 5

1. ------- films that have been released within the past year will be shown in the CineGlobe Film Festival.
(A) Once
(B) Few
(C) Only
(D) Either

2. We offer free tours of the ------- significant Gooseberry Porte to the public every Saturday.
(A) history
(B) historian
(C) historical
(D) historically

3. ------- the most important step in the hiring process is determining a fair pay and benefits package for the potential employee.
(A) While
(B) Perhaps
(C) Outside
(D) Each

4. Moving operations to another country is ------- a challenging undertaking, but it can increase revenue.
(A) understandable
(B) understood
(C) understandably
(D) understanding

PART 6

Questions 5-8 refer to the following notice.

Temporary water shutdown at the Cano Center

On Wednesday, June 27, maintenance workers are scheduled to turn off the water in Cano Center from 8 A.M. to 8 P.M. The building ------- for the whole day. While the water is off, the plumbing
5.
system will be overhauled. -------, all the sinks will be upgraded to more efficient models and older
6.
piping will be replaced.

------- leaving your offices and class rooms on Tuesday, check to make sure that all equipment and
7.
materials are stored properly to avoid creating obstructions for the plumbing staff. Also, remember to clear all food and personal belongings from the break rooms. -------. If you have any questions, call
8.
campus operations at 555-948-1982.

---

5. (A) has closed
(B) will be closed
(C) was closing
(D) would close

6. (A) Normally
(B) Specifically
(C) As a result
(D) Instead of

7. (A) Except
(B) Within
(C) Before
(D) Once

8. (A) Food should be labeled with the date it was stored.
(B) Office staff will be expected to work their regular hours.
(C) Make-up classes will be scheduled for June 30.
(D) All items left behind will be disposed of.

CASE 24 시간부사

We thought we had plenty of time to get tickets to the show, but they were ------- sold out by the time we tried to buy them.

(A) after   (B) already   (C) during   (D) first

> **해설** 빈칸은 수동태 동사구인 be p.p. 사이에서 동사를 수식하는 부사 자리이며, 문맥상 '우리가 표를 사려고 할 때는 이미 매진되었다'라는 의미가 되어야 자연스러우므로 (B)가 정답이다.
>
> **해석** 우리는 공연 표를 살 시간이 충분하다고 생각했지만, 우리가 표를 사려고 할 때는 이미 매진되었다.

>> already, still, yet

already 이미, 벌써	Despite its tight schedule, Purple Publishing has **already** finished editing the new manuscript. 빡빡한 일정에도 불구하고, Purple 출판사는 새 원고의 편집 업무를 이미 끝마쳤다. → already는 주로 현재 완료 시제와 어울리므로 have/has + p.p.가 단서가 될 수 있다.
still 여전히, 아직도	Despite decreasing sales figures, the management is **still** optimistic about reaching the yearly quota. 매출액의 감소에도 불구하고, 경영진은 여전히 연간 할당량에 도달하는 데 낙관적이다.
yet (긍정문) have/be yet to do 아직 ~하지 못하다 (부정문, 의문문) 아직	City inspectors have **yet** to determine the cause of the pipe explosions. 시 조사관들은 배관 폭발의 원인을 아직 알아내지 못했다. The board has not decided on the venue for the conference **yet**. 이사회는 학회 장소를 아직 결정하지 못했다.

>> soon, ago, once

soon (미래 시제/미래 표현과 함께) 곧, 머지않아	Although the stock prices have been unpredictable lately, the company's market value is expected to rise **soon**. 최근 주식 가격이 예측하기 힘들지만, 그 회사의 시장 가치가 곧 오를 것으로 예상된다. → soon은 주로 미래 시제나 미래를 나타내는 동사(expect, look forward to 등)와 어울린다.
ago (과거 시제와 함께) 전에	Ms. Welsh has been with the firm since it was established 10 years **ago**. Welsh 씨는 10년 전 그 회사가 설립된 이후로 그 회사에서 근무하고 있다. → ago는 '시간표현 + ago'의 형태로 과거 시점을 나타낸다.
once (과거 시제와 함께) 한때 cf. 한 번	Liam Franklin was **once** the HR manager of Corpus Inc. Liam Franklin은 한때 Corpus 사의 인사 관리자였다. cf. The company dance team meets for practice **once** a week. 회사 댄스팀은 연습을 위해 일주일에 한 번 만난다.

 알면 3초!   **>>** still은 not 앞에, yet은 not 뒤에 쓴다.

The work request was sent, but maintenance ------- has not responded.

(A) already   (B) still   (C) ever   (D) yet

'아직'이라는 뜻의 still과 yet이 보기 중에 함께 나온다면 어떻게 해야 할까? 부정문에서 still은 not 앞에, yet은 not 뒤에 쓴다는 규칙을 갖는다. 따라서 빈칸이 not 앞쪽에 있는지, 뒤쪽에 있는지를 확인해서 정답을 고르면 된다. not이 빈칸 뒤에 있으므로 정답은 (B)이다.

> **해석** 업무 요청서를 보냈지만 유지 보수 쪽에서는 여전히 답을 하지 않았다.

해설서 p.36

PART 5

1. There were ------- 100 people attending the seminar when Ms. Nunez invited 10 of the current interns.
(A) already
(B) in case
(C) just as
(D) all

2. The site for August's charity auction is yet to be -------.
(A) averted
(B) decided
(C) concluded
(D) attracted

3. Although Janice Langdon was going to leave Kyro Inc., she ------- has a seat on the board of directors.
(A) once
(B) also
(C) chiefly
(D) still

4. The companies listed in this directory are first grouped by category and ------- alphabetized.
(A) still
(B) mostly
(C) since
(D) then

PART 6

Questions 5-8 refer to the following article.

MONTPELIER — Chez Les Rois, the French restaurant in the Sunflower Resort, ------- its doors next week after a quarter of a century in operation. Owner and manager Jean Bisset retired late last year, sparking discussion about major changes. The eatery is due to undergo remodeling over the summer, and will reopen under new ownership with a new ------- according to a representative from the resort. -------. What the new restaurant will be called, though, is still ------- to be decided.
5.

6.

7.

8.

5. (A) had closed
(B) to close
(C) closed
(D) will be closing

6. (A) theme
(B) inventory
(C) location
(D) meal

7. (A) The entire menu will be vegetarian.
(B) Expenses have risen in recent years.
(C) Montpelier has a range of dining options.
(D) Other restaurants are located nearby.

8. (A) somewhat
(B) by
(C) yet
(D) without

CASE 25 빈도 부사와 부정부사

Marcel said he understood very ------- of the technical support representative's explanation.

(A) less (B) few (C) little (D) some

콕 찍어 포인트 … ① 부사 very는 형용사 또는 부사를 수식할 수 있다.

② little은 부사로서 '거의 ~하지 않다'를, 형용사로서 '작은, 어린'을, 대명사/한정사로서 '거의 없는'을 의미한다.

해설 빈칸은 부사 very의 수식을 받는 자리이다. 빈칸 앞뒤의 어구를 고려할 때, 문맥상 'Marcel이 기술 지원 담당자의 설명을 거의 이해하지 못했다'라는 의미가 되어야 자연스러우므로 부정의 의미를 담고 있으면서 동사를 수식하는 부사 (C)가 정답이다.

해석 Marcel은 기술 지원 담당자의 설명을 거의 이해하지 못했다고 말했다.

>> 빈도 부사는 주로 '조동사/be동사 뒤', '일반 동사 앞'에 위치한다.

sometimes / occasionally 때때로	We may **occasionally** send you e-mail newsletters about our sales and promotion. 저희는 때때로 세일과 프로모션에 관한 이메일 소식지를 보내 드릴 수 있습니다.
often / frequently 종종	Stockholders are **often** reluctant to trust companies that are not transparent about their finances. 주주들은 종종 재무가 투명하지 않은 기업들을 신뢰하는 데 주저한다.
usually / normally 보통	Tickets to this musical **normally** sell out in less than a day due to its popularity. 이 뮤지컬 티켓은 그 인기 때문에 보통 하루도 안 되어 매진된다.
always 항상	To avoid losing your belongings, please ensure you always **keep** your valuables with you. 소지품을 잃어버리지 않기 위해, 귀중품은 항상 소지하고 계시기 바랍니다.

>> 부정부사는 부정의 의미를 지니고 있어 다른 부정어와 함께 쓰지 않는다.

hardly / rarely / barely / scarcely / little / seldom 거의 ~않다	Since Ms. Prince became the director, there have **hardly ever** been any unnecessary meetings. ↳ hardly never (X), hardly ever 좀처럼 ~않다 (O) Prince 씨가 책임자가 되고 난 이후로 줄곧, 어떠한 불필요한 회의도 거의 없었다.
never 전혀 ~않다	A new position must be created since this job has **never** been needed before. ↳ never not (X) 이 일이 전에는 전혀 필요한 적이 없었어서 새로운 자리가 만들어져야 한다.

 알면 3초! **>> 부정부사는 강조를 위해 문장 맨 앞에 올 수 있다.**

------- should any confidential document be distributed by interoffice correspondence such as a messenger or an e-mail.

(A) Never (B) Appropriately (C) Although (D) Ever

hardly, rarely, barely, scarcely, little, seldom 거의 ~않다 never 전혀 ~않다	+ 동사 + 주어
no + 명사 어떤 ~도 …않다 not until ~할 때까지 …않다[~하고 나서야 …하다] not only ~, but (also) ~ ~뿐만 아니라	+ 조동사 + 주어 + 동사

부정문에서 부정의 의미를 확실히 전달하고 싶을 때 부정어를 문장 맨 앞으로 보내면 된다. 이때 부정어가 문장 맨 앞으로 오게 되면 주어와 동사의 어순이 바뀌는 규칙을 갖게 되며, 시험에서는 위 문제와 같이 문장 맨 앞에 빈칸을 주고 빈칸 뒤에 동사-주어로 어순이 바뀐 것을 단서로 삼아 부정어를 고르는 문제를 출제하거나 문장 맨 앞에 부정어가 온 것을 단서로 「동사+주어」 또는 「조동사+주어+동사」의 어순을 묻는 문제를 출제한다. 따라서 부정부사 (A)가 정답이다.

해석 어떠한 기밀서류도 메신저나 이메일과 같은 회사 내 연락망에 의해 절대 배포되어서는 안 된다.

CASE 집중훈련

PART 5

1. The IT Department should ------- be consulted when there is an increase in server errors.
(A) finally
(B) once
(C) always
(D) just

2. Mr. Lee couldn't be here today, but he ------- comes to all monthly meetings.
(A) hardly
(B) even
(C) usually
(D) formerly

3. Ms. Mavis noted that Mr. Kasim is ------- late for appointments.
(A) little
(B) far
(C) seldom
(D) well

4. Alan Yovich often played video games as a hobby but ------- thought he would make a fortune by joining a professional league.
(A) never
(B) while
(C) anyhow
(D) here

PART 6

Questions 5-8 refer to the following article.

DUBLIN (10 September) — Next week represents a new era for the footwear brand Ida. The franchise, which has stores across England, ------- its first Irish location on Wicklow Street. The
5.
two-story location is less than a block from the ------- Grafton Street Shopping Arcade and Trinity
6.
College. "There is tremendous foot traffic in the neighbourhood, with shoppers, students, and tourists," explained Justin Mann, an Ida executive here for the opening. -------. The renovated space
7.
on the top floors of the Kilpatrick Building has large windows with ------- of nearby parks, as well as
8.
a coffee shop and children's play area. Mann added, "The Dublin store is a great opportunity for us, and it will also add another major attraction to an already popular district."

5. (A) to open
(B) will open
(C) opening
(D) has opened

6. (A) enthusiastic
(B) demanding
(C) excessive
(D) prominent

7. (A) Rather, the company is planning a social media campaign to build publicity.
(B) Architects will be on hand to discuss the space's unique design.
(C) He added that Ida's sales will be helped by the area's popularity among locals and visitors to the city.
(D) A new semester at the university is scheduled to start next month.

8. (A) views
(B) patterns
(C) features
(D) displays

CASE 26 · 강조 부사

> On Monday, ------- at 10:00 A.M., the governor will cut the ribbon at the opening ceremony of the new train station.
>
> (A) preciseness   (B) precise   (C) precision   (D) precisely

콕 찍어 포인트 ··· ① 부사는 부사(구), 형용사, 동사, 전치사구, 문장 등을 수식하며, 문장 내 가장 다양한 위치에 올 수 있는 품사이다.
② 시간 표현과 주로 함께 쓰이는 부사들은 immediately, precisely, promptly 등이 있다.

해설   빈칸은 시간을 나타내는 at 전치사구를 수식하는 부사 자리이므로 (D)가 정답이다.

해석   월요일 오전 10시 정각에, 주지사는 새 기차역의 개통식에서 커팅식을 할 것이다.

>> 전치사구 앞에 올 수 있는 강조 부사

largely / primarily / mainly 주로	**largely** due to the efforts of the marketing team 주로 마케팅 팀의 노력 덕택에
particularly / especially 특히	**especially** in the winter 특히 겨울에는
promptly / precisely 정확히	**promptly** at 9 A.M. 오전 9시 정각에
exclusively / solely 오로지, ~만	**exclusively** for the company's clients 그 회사의 고객들만을 대상으로
currently 현재	**currently** out of stock 현재 재고가 없는
even 심지어, ~도	**even** before the conference 회의하기도 전에
well 훨씬	**well** below / above the price 그 가격 훨씬 밑으로 / 위로 **well** ahead of time 예정보다 훨씬 빨리 **well** in advance 훨씬 앞서

>> 「관사 + 명사」 형태의 명사구 앞에 올 수 있는 강조 부사

especially 특히	Customers love the snack served in the guest lounge, **especially** the cheese crackers. 고객들은 고객 휴게실에 제공되는 스낵, 특히 치즈 크래커를 매우 좋아한다.
only / just / simply 단지	Our hotel employs **only** the most courteous staff. 저희 호텔은 가장 공손한 직원들만을 채용합니다.
formerly / previously 이전에	There has been commercial development in Ashfield, which was **formerly** an agricultural area. Ashfield에 상업 개발이 있었는데, 이곳은 이전에 농업 지역이었다.
originally 원래	The hit movie, Kensington Family, was **originally** a short story written by Anna Williams. 히트 영화, 〈Kensington Family〉는 원래 Anna Williams가 쓴 단편소설이었다.
arguably / easily 아마도, 틀림없이 understandably 당연히	Of all the core values of most companies, integrity is **arguably** the most overlooked. 대다수 회사들의 핵심 가치 중, 분명 진실성이 가장 간과된다.
even 심지어, ~도	**Even** the most well-known entrepreneurs have faced difficulties running their companies. 가장 잘 알려진 기업가들조차도 회사를 운영하는 어려움에 직면해 있다.

 알면 3초!   **>> before / after와 함께 '~ 직전에 / 직후에'란 표현을 완성하는 다양한 강조 부사들을 익힌다.**

Hoping to remember as much as possible, the manager wrote down a lot of notes ------- after attending the seminar.

(A) immediate   (B) immediacy   (C) immediately   (D) immediateness

promptly / immediately / soon / shortly / just / right / directly	+ before / prior to ~ 직전에 + after / following ~ 직후에

전치사 'before / prior to(~ 전에)'나 'after / following(~ 후에)' 앞에 '바로, 즉시'라는 의미의 다양한 강조 부사가 와서 '~ 직전에 / 직후에'란 빈출 표현을 만들 수 있다. 위의 문제와 같이 품사 문제로 출제되든, 어휘 문제로 출제되든 위의 표현을 눈에 익혀두면 바로 답을 고를 수 있다. 위의 문장에서 빈칸 뒤의 after 이하를 꾸밀 수 있는 강조 부사 (B)가 정답이다.

해석   가능한 한 많이 기억되길 바라며, 매니저는 세미나 참석 직후에 메모를 많이 했다.

CASE 집중훈련

PART 5

1. The Human Resources Department requires employees to hand in their travel plans ------- after reserving tickets for a trip.
(A) rather
(B) soon
(C) very
(D) somewhat

2. ------- the assistant sales manager, Mr. Cochran has just been appointed Director of Marketing at GP Corp.
(A) Individually
(B) Formerly
(C) Genuinely
(D) Immediately

3. After your meeting is finished, please leave ------- five tables in the room and put the rest of them back into the storage room.
(A) quite
(B) rather
(C) just
(D) more

4. The management had ------- planned to open a new branch by the end of the year, but it was deemed too costly.
(A) comparably
(B) flawlessly
(C) originally
(D) notably

PART 6

Questions 5-8 refer to the following article.

Opening Your Own Marketing Agency

Opening a new marketing agency can be an exciting venture. However, such an undertaking comes with many obstacles. It is crucial to be aware of ---5.--- you need and then acts accordingly. First, you will need to get a business loan to cover startup costs. Current research indicates that you will need between $7,000 and $20,000. Next, you will need to hire a staff of skilled employees. These include a secretary, at least one marketing assistant, also, maybe ---6.--- a chief financial officer. Of course, you will also need a location to conduct business, as well as some office equipment. ---7.---. And don't leave out any required supplies such as copy machines, filing cabinets, etc., to keep business ---8.--- very well.

---

5. (A) when
(B) what
(C) that
(D) whose

6. (A) despite
(B) since
(C) even
(D) besides

7. (A) They can even work on this project with friends.
(B) Here are some criteria for choosing a good name for your Web site.
(C) However, your work should be completed in two weeks.
(D) Suitable offices can be a valuable resource.

8. (A) advising
(B) renovating
(C) accepting
(D) running

CASE 27 접속부사

Ms. Yoo was satisfied with the food samples; -------, she hired the caterer for the company event.

(A) in general   (B) just as   (C) in contrast   (D) as a result

> **해설** 빈칸 앞에 접속사를 대신하는 세미콜론(;)이 와 있으므로 빈칸은 접속부사 자리이다. 문맥상 '샘플에 만족하여 해당 업체를 고용했다' 는 내용이 자연스러우므로 결과를 나타내는 (D)가 정답이다.
>
> **해석** Yoo 씨는 식품 샘플에 만족했고, 그 결과, 그녀는 회사 행사를 위해 그 음식 공급 업체를 고용했다.

>> 접속부사 문제는 두 개의 절의 의미 관계를 파악하는 것이 관건이다.

시간	then/thereafter/afterward(s)/subsequently 그리고 나서 meanwhile/in the meantime 그동안
결과	therefore/thus/hence 그러므로 consequently/as a result 결과적으로
추가	moreover/furthermore/besides/also/in addition/additionally 게다가 likewise 마찬가지로
양보	nevertheless/nonetheless 그럼에도 불구하고 even so 그렇기는 하지만
대조	however 그러나 on the contrary/in contrast 반면에 rather 오히려
기타	or/otherwise 그렇지 않으면 if so 만약 그렇다면 instead 대신에 in fact 사실 for instance 예를 들어

The shipment will not be ready until next week; **therefore,** delivery may be delayed by up to ten business days.
배송품이 다음 주까지는 준비되지 않을 것이어서, 배송은 영업일로 최대 10일까지 지연될 수도 있다.

>> 주의해야 할 접속부사

otherwise [접속부사] 그렇지 않으면 [일반 부사] 달리	The supplier failed to notify us about the accounting error. **Otherwise**, we would have requested an updated invoice. 공급업체에서 회계 오류에 대해 우리에게 알리지 않았다. 그렇지 않으면, 우리가 업데이트된 청구서를 요청했을 것이다. Unless **otherwise** noted, all evening seminars for new employees last two hours. 달리 공지가 없다면, 신입 직원들을 위한 모든 저녁 세미나는 2시간 동안 진행된다.
however [접속부사] 그러나 [복합 관계부사] 아무리 ~할지라도	We have enough interns. **However**, we still need to assign each of them to an appropriate team. 우리에겐 인턴들이 충분합니다. 그러나, 우리는 그들 각각을 적합한 팀에 배정해야 합니다. ~→ However + 형용사/부사 '아무리 ~할지라도' **However** proficient they are in Mandarin, managers are required to take a language exam to qualify for a promotion. 매니저들은 아무리 표준 중국어에 능통하다 해도, 승진 자격을 갖추기 위해 어학 시험을 치러야 한다.
besides [접속부사] 게다가 [전치사] ~외에	I can't help you with that. **Besides**, I don't know how to use that accounting software. 제가 그 문제에 대해 당신을 도울 수 없습니다. 게다가, 저는 그 회계 소프트웨어의 사용법을 알지 못합니다. **Besides** lunch, snacks and beverages will also be provided. 점심 식사 외에, 간식과 음료도 제공될 것입니다.

 알면 3초!   >> 접속부사와 부사절 접속사를 혼동해서는 안 된다.

1. The hotel's main elevators will be closed ------- the worn cables are replaced.

(A) meanwhile   (B) yet   (C) still   (D) while

2. ------- attending the company's year-end party is optional, you should go if you can.

(A) Even   (B) Nevertheless   (C) Although   (D) For

접속부사와 부사절 접속사 둘 다 두 절을 이어주지만, 접속부사는 두 절을 의미상으로만 연결해 주고 접속사의 기능은 없기 때문에 1번 문제에서처럼 한 문장 내의 두 절을 이어주기 위해서는 의미상 알맞은 접속사를 동반하거나 접속사의 기능을 갖는 세미콜론을 함께 써야 한다는 점에서 형태만 보고도 접속부사는 답에서 제외시킨다. 따라서 1번 문제에서는 부사절 접속사 (D)가 정답이다. 또한 접속부사는 부사절 접속사처럼 부사절을 주절 앞이나 뒤에서 자유롭게 이끌 수 없고, 항상 두 절 사이에만 오기 때문에 2번 문제와 같이 문장 맨 앞에 빈칸이 온다면 이 때도 해석 없이 접속부사 (B)는 답에서 제외시킨다. 2번 문제에서도 부사절 접속사 (C)가 정답이다.

> **해석** 1. 호텔의 주요 엘리베이터는 마모된 케이블이 교체되는 동안 폐쇄될 것이다.
> 2. 회사 송년회 참석은 선택 사항이지만, 갈 수 있으면 가야 한다.

PART 5

1. Enrollment at private universities is declining, ------- public universities are enjoying steady growth.
(A) whereas
(B) otherwise
(C) moreover
(D) nevertheless

2. Although material costs for our line of personal computers have been increasing, we will ------- maintain the current prices.
(A) therefore
(B) instead
(C) nevertheless
(D) but

3. Over half of the committee must sign the agreement, ------- it will not be valid.
(A) still
(B) or
(C) moreover
(D) while

4. As our usual supplier did not have the materials we required available, we ordered from a local distributor -------.
(A) instead
(B) particularly
(C) throughout
(D) otherwise

PART 6

Questions 5-8 refer to the following advertisement.

Year-end Savings at Exham Sportswear

We urgently ------- you not to miss this opportunity to save big during our annual year-end event. Any piece of clothing ------- with a pink tag is half off, while those with yellow tags are discounted 20 percent. Almost all of our most popular apparel is available at unbeatable prices. Don't miss out!

-------, our first 100 customers in the store each Saturday will win $100 in in-store credit. -------. In-store credit may only be used at the store location where it was received, and will expire at the end of April. To learn more about this offer, check out our inventory, or join our rewards program, go to Exham-sports.co.uk. Or if you're in the neighborhood, just stop by your local store and ask one of our associates in person.

---

5. (A) advice
(B) advisable
(C) advise
(D) advising

6. (A) labeled
(B) worn
(C) manufactured
(D) welcomed

7. (A) Thus
(B) Additionally
(C) Similarly
(D) Nonetheless

8. (A) We have to make room for new inventory.
(B) This may be redeemed on our Web site.
(C) Some limitations do apply.
(D) The next sale this big isn't until July.

CASE 28 　주의해야 할 부사

Government officials worked ------- with scientists to create a plan to reduce pollution.

(A) close　　　　(B) closely　　　　(C) closing　　　　(D) closeness

콕 찍어 포인트 ⋯ 부사 close는 시공간적으로 '가까이'란 뜻이며, closely는 '긴밀히, 주의 깊게'를 의미한다.

[해설] 빈칸은 동사 worked와 전치사구 사이의 자리이다. 문맥상 '과학자들과 긴밀히 협력했다'라는 의미가 되어야 자연스러우므로 부사 (B)가 정답이다.

[해석] 정부 관계자들은 오염을 줄이기 위한 계획을 세우기 위해 과학자들과 긴밀히 협력했다.

›› '-ly'가 붙어서 의미가 바뀌는 부사

hard 열심히, 힘들게 **vs. hardly** 거의 ~않다	close 가까이 **vs. closely** 면밀히(= carefully)
near 가까이 **vs. nearly** 거의(= almost)	clear ~에서 떨어져 **vs. clearly** 분명히, 또렷하게
high 높이 **vs. highly** 매우(= very)	short 짧게 **vs. shortly** 곧, 얼마 안 되어(= soon)
late 늦게 **vs. lately** 최근에(= recently)	most 가장 **vs. mostly** 주로(= mainly)

↗ hardly (X)

Although the business consultant worked extremely **hard**, his request for time off was not granted.
엄청나게 열심히 일했음에도 불구하고, 그 비즈니스 컨설턴트의 휴가 요청은 승인되지 않았다.

›› 숫자나 양을 수식하는 부사

nearly/almost 거의　approximately/about/around/roughly 대략　a maximum of/up to 최대 a minimum of/at least 최소　more than/over 이상　less than/under 미만　just 딱　only 겨우	+ 숫자/양

↗ somewhat (X)

It takes **approximately** five business days to process your application.
신청서를 처리하는 데 영업일로 대략 5일이 걸립니다.

›› 동사를 수식할 수 없는 부사

so/very/fairly/quite 꽤　extremely/exceptionally/incredibly/overly 몹시, 극도로 relatively 비교적	+ 형용사/부사

↗ quite (X)

Although the documentary is educational, the instructor thinks students will **still** find it entertaining.
비록 그 다큐멘터리가 교육적이긴 하지만, 강사는 학생들이 그것을 여전히 재미있어 할 거라고 생각한다.

⏱ 3SECS 알면 3초!　›› enough는 부사로 쓰일 때 형용사 뒤에 온다.

Churubusco Inc.'s profits were high ------- for it to expand its operations and still increase its dividend to shareholders.

(A) forward　　　　(B) even　　　　(C) well　　　　(D) enough

enough + 명사 / be동사 + enough 충분한	enough (for A) to do (A가) ~하기에 충분한
일반 동사/형용사 + enough 충분히	more than enough 너무 많은

enough는 형용사뿐만 아니라 부사로도 쓰이는데, 형용사일 때는 일반 형용사와 마찬가지로 명사 앞이나 be동사 뒤에 위치하지만, 부사일 때는 일반 동사나 형용사를 뒤에서만 수식한다. 그 밖에 enough는 to부정사를 동반할 수 있으며, more than enough도 자주 쓰이는 관용 표현이니 꼭 기억해두자. 위 문장에서는 'enough for A to do'의 표현이 쓰이므로 정답은 (D)다.

[해석] Churubusco 사의 수익은 사업을 확장하면서도 주주들에 대한 배당을 늘릴 수 있을 만큼 충분히 높았다.

PART 5

1. Since the writer did not submit the article early ------, it could not be revised in time for the autumn issue.

(A) instead
(B) enough
(C) about
(D) before

2. Hansen Dining was hired to cater the office party because Ms. Marina spoke so ------- of their services.

(A) high
(B) higher
(C) highly
(D) highest

3. Jericho Fitness's beginner CrossFit courses have been in great demand -------.

(A) late
(B) latest
(C) lateness
(D) lately

4. Windsor Cleaning Company has been offering affordable service to local residents for ------- three decades.

(A) neared
(B) nearest
(C) nearby
(D) nearly

PART 6

Questions 5-8 refer to the following memo.

To: All Staff Members
From: Irene Turner, Personnel Manager
Date: September 5
Re: Physical Examinations

To support our continuing effort to promote health and fitness here at Wilbur Communications, we will be offering physical examinations for all staff members and their families at no charge. No one is required to ------- an examination. They are strictly -------. They will take place in Building A.

5.   6.

Please allow ------- 20 minutes per person per exam. Our first round of examinations will be held on

7.

Saturday, September 26. To schedule an appointment, please click the Personnel tab on our Web page. Please do not hesitate to schedule your physical examination. -------.

8.

5. (A) retain
(B) signify
(C) express
(D) undergo

6. (A) voluntary
(B) deliberate
(C) contrary
(D) standard

7. (A) approximate
(B) approximating
(C) approximation
(D) approximately

8. (A) The building closed last Friday.
(B) Gym memberships are another option.
(C) Available times may vary based on prior reservations.
(D) Your presence is mandatory.

1. Moravia Inc.'s recent merger ------- established the company as an industry leader.

(A) firmed
(B) firmer
(C) firmly
(D) firmest

2. The renowned business tycoon Brianna Warden's autobiography ------- explains the monetary struggles she surmounted at the beginning of her career.

(A) opens
(B) opened
(C) openness
(D) openly

3. Platforms 5 and 6 are ------- out of service for repair work at Gold Acres Station.

(A) periodically
(B) periodicals
(C) periodic
(D) periods

4. Travis Webb's seminar suggests new perspectives about farming irrigation systems and ------- includes recommendations for further research.

(A) although
(B) only
(C) despite
(D) also

5. Ms. Watts ------- uses an outside consultant, but he recently employed an internal auditor to evaluate the company.

(A) normally
(B) thoughtfully
(C) coincidentally
(D) subsequently

6. Momma's Little Bakery had to ------- stop its production for a week because its permits expired.

(A) temporarily
(B) presently
(C) closely
(D) potentially

7. With a week of extra showings, *The Midnight Song* will ------- play through July 28 at CMC Cinemas.

(A) largely
(B) now
(C) instantly
(D) continue

8. At Friday's show, one fortunate Sarolah Theater Group fan will be ------- selected via a raffle to dine with the troupe.

(A) apparently
(B) justly
(C) incorrectly
(D) randomly

Questions 9-12 refer to the following testimonial.

Alice Holt had been grappling with a problem every manager can relate to, which was how to handle ------- in a time-efficient manner. A colleague happened to refer Ms. Holt to a highly touted executive recruiter. "I knew I had to give recruiters a go. I was getting so many résumés that it was taking up my entire day going through -------. That was when I decided to give Mr. Sok from Buff Recruiters a call." Mr. Sok explained that he helps companies find the right employees faster. First, he ensures that he understands ------- the kind of employee a business is looking for. Then, he uses his network to get in touch with professionals with the corresponding skillset. -------. "In the end, business is all about the people," Ms. Holt says, "and with Buff Recruiters, I can build my very own dream team."

9. (A) recruitment
   (B) production
   (C) training
   (D) information

10. (A) it
    (B) that
    (C) those
    (D) them

11. (A) precise
    (B) preciseness
    (C) precisely
    (D) precision

12. (A) He is new to the industry, but he is enjoying it so far.
    (B) He hopes to one day be in charge of Buff Recruiters.
    (C) He has helped hundreds of businesses this way.
    (D) He also helps manage an art museum.

CASE 29 주어-동사의 수 일치

Ms. Munn ------- expected to arrive from her tour of the Singapore facility by 6:00 P.M.

(A) be   (B) is   (C) are   (D) were

> 해설   빈칸은 주어 뒤 수동태 동사 구문(be p.p.)을 완성하는 be동사 자리이다. 주어가 3인칭 단수 명사이므로 단수 동사 (B)가 정답이다.
>
> 해석   Munn 씨는 오후 6시까지 싱가포르 시설 견학에서 돌아올 예정이다.

>> 반드시 주어와 동사의 수를 일치시킨다.

가산 단수 명사	단수 동사	**The supervisor** comprehensively **reviews** all the expense reports before submitting them to the headquarters. 그 관리자는 본사에 제출하기 전에, 모든 경비 보고서를 종합적으로 검토한다.
불가산 명사		**Access** to the laboratory **is** strictly prohibited unless you hold an authorized pass. *(are (X))* 인가 받은 출입증을 소지하고 있지 않으면 연구소의 출입이 엄격히 금지된다.
동명사		**Making** an appointment **is** no longer required in our restaurant from the beginning of next week. 다음 주부터 저희 식당에서는 더 이상 자리 예약이 필수가 아닙니다. → 주어가 to부정사나 명사절일 때에도 단수 취급하여 단수 동사를 쓴다.
가산 복수 명사	복수 동사	**Returns** for all items **are** processed within five business days. 모든 물품에 대한 반품은 영업일로 5일 이내에 처리됩니다.
(Both) A and B		**(Both) Your phone and other electronic equipment need** to be turned off during the test. *(needs (X))* 전화기와 그 밖의 다른 전자 기기는 (둘 다) 시험 중에 꺼야 한다.

>> A or B, Either A or B, Neither A nor B, Not only A but (also) B / B as well as A는 **B**에 수를 일치시킨다.

Neither the director **nor the actors have** ever worked on a romantic comedy.
감독과 배우들 누구도 로맨틱 코미디물을 작업해 본 적이 없다.

>> 「There+동사+주어」 구문의 동사는 뒤에 오는 주어에 수를 일치시킨다.

(are (X))
There **is** an instruction **manual** that shows the assembly process of the equipment.
그 장비의 조립 과정을 보여주는 안내 매뉴얼이 있다.

 알면 3초!   **>>** 회사명 등의 고유명사 주어는 복수 형태라도 단수 취급한다.

Avery Brothers ------- that it will offer a 30-percent discount on all in-store purchases this month.

(A) advertiser   (B) advertise   (C) advertised   (D) advertisement

주어-동사의 수 일치를 확인해야 할 때 주어의 단·복수를 묻는 문제라면 먼저 동사의 단·복수를 확인하고, 마찬가지로 동사의 단·복수를 묻는 문제라면 주어의 단·복수를 먼저 확인해야 하는데, 이때 주의를 요할 때가 있다. 주어의 단·복수를 확인하는 방법으로 보통 주어의 생김새 즉, 주어에 -(e)s가 붙어 있으면 복수, 붙어 있지 않으면 단수로 간주하는 게 일반적이긴 하지만 고유명사는 단수로 취급한다. 위 문제와 같은 품사 어형 문제에서 빈칸을 동사 자리로 파악했다면, 우선 (A)와 (D)를 답에서 제외시키고 주어의 단·복수 여부를 확인할 텐데, 지금처럼 주어가 엄연히 -s를 품은 복수형이니 복수 동사도 정답 후보에 넣고 의미를 따져보려 애쓸 것이다. 하지만 회사 이름과 같은 고유명사는 형태가 어떻든 단수 취급하기 때문에 이 문제는 해석 없이도 (C)를 정답으로 골라낼 수 있다.

> 해석   Avery Brothers는 이번 달에 모든 매장에서 구매 시 30퍼센트 할인을 제공할 것이라고 광고했다.

PART 5

1. Kelter's most popular photocopier ------- a document compiling system.

(A) featuring
(B) was featured
(C) feature
(D) features

2. Visitors will be glad to know that Dartmoor Furniture now provides free delivery service, but this option ------- mean a later arrival date.

(A) builds
(B) has
(C) brings
(D) does

3. The revised spring issue ------- by the editor-in-chief before it is printed.

(A) reviewed
(B) to be reviewed
(C) must be reviewed
(D) are reviewed

4. During her two decades working at Shimmer Engineering & Construction, Ms. O'Driscoll ------- the crane at numerous construction sites.

(A) operate
(B) operation
(C) operated
(D) operating

PART 6

Questions 5-8 refer to the following article.

COPENHAGEN (10 JUNE) — At a press conference this morning, Schmitt Aeronautics announced the ------- of the energy company, Nimbus. A new technology created by Nimbus ------- seawater
5.   6.
into a powerful fuel called MNV which can be used to power aircrafts. The acquisition means Schmitt can count this cutting-edge technology ------- its assets. "Everyone is excited for the chance to
7.
collaborate with the Nimbus team," said Schmitt representative Torry Glass. "MNV will provide an alternative to costly and environment damaging petroleum-based fuels." -------. MNV is also just as
8.
powerful as current fuel sources, meaning that existing aircraft designs will not have to be altered to use the fuel source.

5. (A) purchase
(B) recovery
(C) establishment
(D) understanding

6. (A) to convert
(B) conversion
(C) has converted
(D) converts

7. (A) aside
(B) among
(C) away
(D) about

8. (A) Unfortunately, the technology is not likely to be ready for market until next year.
(B) MNV-powered vehicles produce considerably more pollution.
(C) The cost of switching to MNV systems is surprisingly low.
(D) At the moment, MNV can only be produced in small quantities.

The specifications for the power plant construction ------- a variety of equipment and materials.

(A) require   (B) requires   (C) requiring   (D) requirements

> **해설** 빈칸은 주어와 목적어 사이의 동사 자리로, 긴 수식어(for the power plant construction)를 걷어낼 수 있어야 주어-동사의 수 일치를 확인할 수 있다. 주어가 복수 명사(specifications)이므로 복수 동사 (A)가 정답이다.
>
> **해석** 발전소 건설을 위한 사양은 다양한 장비와 재료를 필요로 한다.

>> 수 일치에 영향을 주지 않는 수식어가 주어-동사 사이에 들어가 수 일치를 방해한다.

전치사구	**Regional managers** (from the company) **are** expected to make a speech at the event. 회사의 지역 관리자들이 행사에서 연설할 것으로 예상된다.
현재분사구	**Customers** (applying for a store loyalty card) **need** to go to the customer service center. 매장 고객카드를 신청하실 고객들께서는 고객 서비스 센터로 가셔야 합니다.
과거분사구	The **conclusions** (drawn by the analyst) **are** directly reported to the CEO. 그 분석가가 내린 결론들은 CEO에게 직접 보고된다. ↳ is (X)
관계사절	The **proposal** (that the employees submitted at the meeting) **was** repetitive. 회의 때 직원들이 제출한 안은 반복되는 것이 많았다. ↳ were (X)
동격	**Ms. Chang**, (the front-desk assistant), **answers** the phone every time it rings. 안내 데스크 직원인 Chang 씨는 전화가 울릴 때마다 받는다.

❶ 주어-동사 수 일치와 관련하여, 주어 뒤에 긴 수식어가 올 때 수식어의 명사와 주어를 혼동해선 안 된다.

알면 3초!   **>>** 주격 관계대명사절의 동사는 선행사에 수를 일치시킨다.

Royal Tableware which ------- in traditional dish making techniques, expanded its market into Latin America last year.

(A) specializes   (B) specialize   (C) are specializing   (D) specializing

단수 선행사	+ 주격 관계대명사(who/which/that)	+ 단수 동사
복수 선행사		+ 복수 동사

위의 문장은 원래 'Royal Tableware specializes in traditional dish making techniques.'와 'Royal Tableware expanded its market into Latin America last year.'의 두 문장이었으나, 중복되는 명사가 주어인 문장을 주격 관계대명사를 사용하여 수식어(관계대명사절)로 만들어 'Royal Tableware which specializes in traditional dish making techniques, expanded its market ~.'과 같이 하나의 문장으로 만든 것이다. 이때 중복되는 명사를 선행사라 하며, 이 선행사는 주격 관계대명사절의 주어에 해당하므로 주격 관계대명사절의 동사는 선행사에 수를 일치시키는 것이다. 참고로, 위의 두 문장은 모두 중복되는 명사가 주어에 해당하므로 둘 중 어느 것이든 주격 관계대명사절로 만들 수 있기 때문에 'Royal Tableware which expanded its market into Latin America last year, specializes in traditional dish making techniques.'로도 바꿔 쓸 수 있다. 따라서 단수 동사 (A)가 정답이다.

> **해석** 전통적인 접시 제조 기술을 전문으로 하는 Royal Tableware는 작년에 중남미로 시장을 확장했다.

CASE 집중훈련

PART 5

1. A ------- of business and community leaders will be discussing SDK Laboratory's plans to build their headquarters in the city.

(A) proposal
(B) support
(C) panel
(D) version

2. The stock market analyst, Daniel Glutzer, ------- predicted last week's economic upswing.

(A) correct
(B) correctly
(C) corrective
(D) correctness

3. An ------- to build a storage shed was presented to the homeowners' association.

(A) establishment
(B) incident
(C) accomplishment
(D) application

4. Mr. Perault, the ------- head accountant, has provided comprehensive documentation that his replacement should find beneficial.

(A) specific
(B) ended
(C) alike
(D) previous

PART 6

Questions 5-8 refer to the following customer review.

It was my first time ordering, and it was absolutely worth it. I have been trying to find a new fabric supplier for my clothing business. I have had bad experiences with suppliers in this area. -------, I didn't have high hopes for Systema. When I received my order, I was blown away by the results. The ------- were exactly what I ordered, and the delivery was surprisingly fast. Given the price Systema quoted, I wasn't sure if the quality would be acceptable. However, I sent out some samples to my clients. -------. Based on the excellent feedback, I will ------- be using Systema again for my business.

Cesar Bowers

5. (A) Thereafter
(B) Conversely
(C) However
(D) Therefore

6. (A) ramifications
(B) specifications
(C) applications
(D) qualifications

7. (A) The shipments may have faced unavoidable delays.
(B) I would like to make a few suggestions.
(C) They could all immediately tell the difference.
(D) A comparison would have been very useful.

8. (A) exclusively
(B) exclusive
(C) exclusiveness
(D) exclusivity

CASE 31 수량 표현의 수 일치

Every technician at Gelco Pharmaceuticals ------- to wash their hands before entering the laboratories.

(A) expect   (B) expecting   (C) is expected   (D) are expected

> **해설** 빈칸은 문장의 동사 자리이며, 주어가 「Every + 단수 명사」 형태의 단수 주어이므로 보기 중 단수 동사인 (C)가 정답이다.
>
> **해석** Gelco 제약회사의 모든 기술자들은 실험실에 들어가기 전에 손을 씻을 것으로 기대된다.

>> 항상 단수 동사를 취하는 수량 표현

Each / Every		단수 명사	
Everyone / Everybody / Everything			+ 단수 동사
One / Each	of the	복수 명사	
The number of			

are (X)

Each of the regional managers is required to take management courses before starting work.
각 지역 매니저는 근무 시작 전에 경영 과정을 이수해야 한다.

>> of 뒤의 명사에 수를 일치시키는 수량 표현

Much / A little / Little		불가산 명사	+ 단수 동사
Some / Part / Half / Most / Any / All /	of the		
The rest / 20 percent / Two-thirds		가산 복수 명사	+ 복수 동사
Many / A few / Few / Both / Several			

are (X)

Most of the information (on our products) **is** posted on our social media channels.
저희 제품에 대한 정보 대부분이 소셜 미디어 채널에 게시되어 있습니다.

>> 뒤에 오는 명사에 수를 일치시키는 수량 표현

An amount of	불가산 명사	+ 단수 동사
A lot of / Lots of / Plenty of		
A number of / A couple of	가산 복수 명사	+ 복수 동사

is (X)

A number of safety inspectors are coming next week to verify the factory's compliance with labor laws.
그 공장의 노동법 준수를 확인하기 위해 많은 안전 조사관들이 다음 주에 올 것이다.

⏱ 3SECS 알면 3초! >> 「A number of + 복수 명사」는 복수 동사, 「The number of + 복수 명사」는 단수 동사를 취한다.

The number of people using public transportation ------- sharply because of the rise in oil prices.

(A) has increased   (B) have increased   (C) increase   (D) increasing

A number of	복수 명사	+ 복수 동사
The number of		+ 단수 동사

관사의 차이로 의미와 해석이 완전히 달라지는 「A number of + 복수 명사」와 「The number of + 복수 명사」를 구별해 둘 필요가 있다. 「A number of + 복수 명사」는 '많은 복수 명사'로 해석되는 형용사 수량 표현으로서 주 명사가 '복수 명사'이기 때문에 이에 수를 일치시켜 복수 동사를 취하는 데 반하여, 「The number of + 복수 명사」는 '복수 명사의 수'로 해석되므로 'The number'에 수를 맞추어 단수 동사를 취한다. 따라서 단수 동사인 (A)가 정답이다.

> **해석** 유가 상승으로 대중교통을 이용하는 사람들의 수가 급격히 증가했다.

PART 5

1. The number of mobile phone ------- has decreased sharply in the past five years due to competition.

(A) manufacture
(B) manufactured
(C) manufacturing
(D) manufacturers

2. The Hawthorne Times is planning to interview the president of Morrilton Textile Company regarding ------- recent announcement that it will soon lay off up to 100 employees.

(A) few
(B) whose
(C) any
(D) its

3. ------- of Harriet Solomon's performances was filmed for a documentary about the dancer.

(A) All
(B) Each one
(C) Theirs
(D) Her own

4. The recent issue of *Politics Monthly Magazine* contains fifteen articles, ------- of which are about the upcoming election.

(A) several
(B) another
(C) nothing
(D) those

PART 6

Questions 5-8 refer to the following information.

The majority of the ------- to *Huber's Poetry Monthly* are seasoned writers who have worked closely
5.
with us for years. -------, we are always searching for new talent. In each issue, we do our best to
6.
introduce our readers to a new poet, but competition for space in the magazine is very intense.
Therefore, make sure to look carefully at the guidelines posted on www.huberpoetry.org/guidelines to
get a feel for the kind of work we hope to include in our publication. -------.
7.

Although we strive to reply to inquiries as quickly as possible, there will be times where you may
receive a slow response. Because of this, we must ask for you to be -------.
8.

5. (A) contributors
(B) contribution
(C) contributing
(D) contributes

6. (A) For example
(B) In this instance
(C) To put it another way
(D) With that said

7. (A) So, the publication will be selecting a new editor.
(B) This will make your submission more likely to be selected.
(C) Unfortunately, we cannot use your work in this month's issue.
(D) This is a good resource for finding magazines that publish beginning writers.

8. (A) accurate
(B) careful
(C) patient
(D) prompt

3형식 동사의 태

The IT Department has advised all employees that new software ------- next week.

(A) to install   (B) will install   (C) will be installed   (D) is installing

해설 타동사 install의 알맞은 형태를 묻는 문제로 빈칸은 that절의 동사 자리이며, 빈칸 뒤에 목적어가 없으므로 수동태 동사인 (C)가 정답이다.

해석 IT 부서는 모든 직원들에게 다음 주에 새 소프트웨어가 설치될 것이라고 알려주었다.

≫ 해석으로 태 구분: 주어가 동사 행위의 주체이면 능동태를, 동사 행위의 대상이면 수동태를 쓴다.

– 보통 능동태는 '주어가 동사하다'로, 수동태는 '주어가 동사되다'로 해석한다.

≫ 목적어의 유무로 태 구분: 동사 뒤에 목적어가 있으면 능동태를, 없으면 수동태를 쓴다.

	주어	3형식 동사	목적어
능동태	The fitness instructor 피트니스 강사가	**encouraged** 권장했다	the use of protein supplements. 단백질 보충제의 사용을
	주어	be + p.p.	수식어(by + 행위의 주체)
수동태	The use of protein supplements 단백질 보충제의 사용이	**was encouraged** 권장되었다	(by the fitness instructor). (피트니스 강사에 의해)

– 동사 뒤에 목적어 한 개를 갖는 동사를 '3형식 동사' 또는 '(완전) 타동사'라고 하며, 대부분의 동사가 여기에 속한다.
– 행위의 대상인 목적어가 주어 자리에 오면서 타동사를 「be + p.p.」의 형태로 바꿔 쓴 것을 수동태라고 한다.
– 수동태로 바꿔 쓸 때, 'by + 행위의 주체'는 종종 생략되기도 한다.

≫ 시제에 따른 수동태의 형태

단순 시제	진행 시제	완료 시제
be + p.p.	be being + p.p.	have / has / had been + p.p.

The company's HR manager will contact you in writing if your job application **is accepted**. 단순 시제
귀하의 입사 지원서가 수락되면 회사의 인사 관리자가 귀하에게 서면으로 연락할 것입니다.

Safety regulations for the factory's production line **are being revised** in response to the recent accident. 진행 시제
최근 사고에 대응하여 공장 생산 라인의 안전 규정이 수정되고 있다.

A thorough survey **has been conducted** to develop new marketing strategies. 완료 시제
새 마케팅 전략을 짜기 위해 철저한 조사가 실시되었다.

 알면 3초!   ≫ 주격 관계대명사절의 동사는 선행사에 태를 일치시킨다.

The drama series that ------- on channel 55 last month was more popular than expected.

(A) showing   (B) shows   (C) to show   (D) was shown

주어-동사 수 일치에서 배운 개념과 마찬가지로, 태 역시 주어와 동사의 관계를 고려하여 능·수동을 가리며 이를 '태 일치'로 부르기도 한다. 주어-동사의 태를 맞추기 위해, 주어가 동사의 행위를 직접 한 문장인지(→능동태), 주어가 동사의 행위를 당한 문장인지(→수동태)를 해석으로 확인할 수도 있고, 대부분의 동사가 3형식 타동사인 점을 이용하여 목적어가 있으면 능동태, 목적어가 없으면 수동태로 구분할 수도 있다는 사실도 배웠다. 이는 당연히 선행사가 의미상 주어가 되는 주격 관계대명사절에서도 그대로 적용되기 때문에 위와 같이 관계대명사절에 들어갈 알맞은 동사 형태를 고르는 문제가 나오면 먼저, 관계대명사절의 목적어의 유무로 능동태 동사인지, 수동태 동사인지를 가늠하고, 선행사를 주어로 가져와 선행사가 행위의 주체인지, 행위의 대상인지를 해석하여 문제 풀이를 완료한다. 위 문제에서 선행사에 해당하는 드라마 시리즈는 상영되는 대상이기 때문에 수동태인 (D)가 정답이다.

해석 지난달 55번 채널에서 방영된 드라마 시리즈는 기대 이상의 인기를 끌었다.

CASE 집중훈련

해설서 p.47

PART 5

1. Royale House will ------- to include a library that contains videos and audiobooks related to the solar system.
(A) be renovated
(B) renovate
(C) be renovating
(D) have renovated

2. Auditors' reports will be submitted only to the management and should not be ------- under any circumstances.
(A) publicity
(B) publicly
(C) publication
(D) publicized

3. Job opportunities for part-time editors ------- to be posted on Ottawa Publishing's Web site on April 10.
(A) have been anticipating
(B) are anticipated
(C) anticipate
(D) anticipates

4. Mr. Zhang will ------- the data transfer to the cloud with the service provider.
(A) be coordinating
(B) to coordinating
(C) be coordinated
(D) to coordinate

PART 6

Questions 5-8 refer to the following article.

SAN FRANCISCO (4 October) — Trifecta announced this morning the upcoming release of the new action camera, the T6 model, which will be produced in collaboration with Mayflower, Inc. The T6 model blends Trifecta's innovative designs with ------- materials by Mayflower, Inc. Mayflower **5.** developed the T6's touch screen using its original technique, a glasslike substance that ------- to be **6.** virtually unbreakable. Although this was originally intended for use in microscope lenses, an ability to withstand drops from great heights without shattering was ------- recognized by Mayflower's **7.** product development department as a quality that would make it perfect for use in other products. A representative for Trifecta, Vivian Washington, credited the research staff at Mayflower, Inc., with valuable contributions to the T6's development. -------. **8.**

5. (A) vulnerable
(B) formal
(C) superior
(D) productive

6. (A) will create
(B) was created
(C) having created
(D) had been creating

7. (A) immediate
(B) immediately
(C) immediateness
(D) immediacy

8. (A) Customers are responsible for making payments in full.
(B) Now Mayflower, Inc., is under new management.
(C) Both companies are very delighted with their partnership in the project.
(D) Consumers do not always want the latest high-tech gadget.

PART 5 · CHAPTER 06 동사 **97**

Crimson Inc. announced that its annual sales turnover ------- steady compared to that of last year.

(A) remaining   (B) has remained   (C) to remain   (D) was remained

해설   remain은 '계속 ~한 상태이다'라는 뜻의 자동사로서 수동태로 쓸 수 없으므로 (B)가 정답이다.

해석   Crimson 사는 연례 매출액이 작년 매출액과 비교하여 안정된 상태를 유지했다고 발표했다.

>> 목적어를 취하지 않는 자동사는 수동태로 쓸 수 없다.

	주어	1형식 동사	(수식어)
능동태	All products (ordered online) (온라인으로 주문한) 모든 제품들이	**will arrive** 도착할 것이다	(from our Pohang warehouse). (자사 포항 창고에서)
1형식 동사	arrive 도착하다 exist 존재하다 expire 만료되다 last 지속되다 proceed 진행하다 commence 시작하다 rise 오르다 occur/happen/take place 일어나다 work 일하다		

	주어	2형식 동사	보어
능동태	The market (for slim laptops) (얇은 노트북) 시장이	**has** (recently) **become** (최근에) 되었다	(very) **competitive**. (매우) 치열하게
2형식 동사	be ~이다 become ~이 되다 feel ~로 느끼다 look ~처럼 보이다 prove ~임이 드러나다 remain/stay/keep 여전히 ~이다 seem/appear ~인 것 같다		

- 동사 뒤에 목적어를 갖지 않는 동사를 '자동사'라고 한다.
- 동사 뒤에 부사나 전치사구 등의 수식어만 오는 동사를 '1형식 동사' 또는 '(완전) 자동사'라고 한다.
- 동사 뒤에 명사 보어나 형용사 보어가 오는 동사를 '2형식 동사' 또는 '(불완전) 자동사'라고 한다.

>> 「자동사 + 전치사」 형태의 구동사는 수동태로 쓸 수 있다.

	주어	구동사	목적어
능동태	The public relations team 홍보 팀이	**will carry out** 수행할 것이다	the customer survey. 고객 설문을
	주어	be p.p.	(수식어)
수동태	The customer survey 고객 설문이	**will be carried out** 수행될 것이다	(by the public relations team). (홍보팀에 의해)
구동사	account for ~을 설명하다 bring up ~을 (화제를) 꺼내다 call off ~을 취소하다 carry out ~을 수행하다 comment on ~을 논평하다 deal with ~을 다루다 go through ~을 조사하다 interfere with ~을 방해하다 narrow down ~을 좁히다, 줄이다 refer to ~을 참고하다 rely on ~을 의존하다 set up ~을 설치하다 take care of ~을 담당하다 turn down ~을 거절하다		

 알면 3초!   >> 상태나 소유를 나타내는 동사는 수동태로 쓸 수 없다.

A TF team which is ------- of representatives from relevant divisions will be organized.

(A) introduced   (B) consisted   (C) composed   (D) instituted

「자동사 + 전치사」 형태라고 해서 모두 수동태로 쓸 수 있는 건 아니다. 'consist of(~로 구성되다)'나 'belong to(~에 속하다)' 등의 '상태'를 나타내는 구동 사나 '소유'를 나타내는 동사인 have, own, possess 등은 수동태로 쓸 수 없기 때문에 위 문제에서 '~로 구성되다'라는 의미를 완성하기 위해서는 빈칸 앞의 is 없이 'consists of'만 쓰거나 같은 의미의 타동사 compose를 수동태로 바꿔 쓴 'is composed of'를 써야 한다. 따라서 위 문제의 정답은 (C)가 된다.

해석   관련 부서의 대표들로 구성된 TF 팀이 조직될 것이다.

PART 5

1. Balmer Industries has responded ------- to Komplet Automotive's offer to jointly develop a forecasting system.

(A) favorably
(B) favor
(C) favorable
(D) favoring

2. The board of directors will ------- next month to approve the two-year strategic business plan for international activities.

(A) confide
(B) acquire
(C) accompany
(D) convene

3. Ms. Kobayashi and her team worked ------- for weeks to land the profitable federal contract.

(A) immediately
(B) extremely
(C) diligently
(D) particularly

4. Stock prices for Oceania Airlines will go back up when investors feel ------- about the future.

(A) economical
(B) cautious
(C) valuable
(D) confident

PART 6

Questions 5-8 refer to the following notice.

On 21 June, the Middlesbrough Transportation Commission (MTC) will begin ------- on the long stretch of Highway 105 between Hammock Tunnel and the downtown area. This undertaking will include repaving and expanding the route to five driving lanes, up from its ------- four. The aim of the project is to make the roads safer and reduce heavy traffic during peak hours. The MTC always tries to ensure efficient transport throughout our region for everyone, and we recognize that this project will create some disruptions to regular service. The project is set to ------- in September. -------.

Check mtc-connect.co.uk for the latest updates.

5. (A) constructed
(B) constructive
(C) construction
(D) construct

6. (A) mutual
(B) connecting
(C) shorter
(D) current

7. (A) prepare
(B) leave
(C) conclude
(D) commence

8. (A) In the interim, the use of public transportation is recommended.
(B) In the meantime, find ways to lower operating expenses.
(C) During the period of June to September, the toll payment system will be upgraded.
(D) Many residents have complained about MTC's newest mobile app.

4형식 동사의 태

Everyone who signed up for the symposium on the Effects of Global Warming ------- a letter regarding the schedule.

(A) was sending　　　　(B) would send　　　　(C) sent　　　　(D) was sent

해설 문맥상 '모든 사람들이 편지를 받았다'는 내용이 나와야 하는데, 'send (…에게 ~을 보내다)'는 4형식 동사로 뒤에 두 개의 목적어를 갖는다. 능동태 문장이 수동태가 되면서 사람 목적어가 주어(Everyone)로 이동한 경우이므로 빈칸에는 수동태가 나와야 하기 때문에 (D)가 정답이다. 4형식 동사는 3형식 동사도 가능하므로 빈칸에 능동형이 들어가 뒤에 목적어를 취하는 구조도 가능하지만 등록한 사람들이 일정에 관한 편지를 보내는 것은 문맥에 맞지 않는다.

해석 지구 온난화의 영향에 관한 심포지엄에 등록한 모든 사람들은 일정에 관한 편지를 받았다.

>> 목적어가 두 개인 4형식 동사는 수동태 뒤에 목적어가 올 수 있다.

	주어	4형식 동사	간접 목적어	직접 목적어
능동태	The company 그 회사는	gives 준다	experienced applicants 경력직 지원자들에게	the chance to interview. 면접 볼 기회를
	주어	4형식 동사	목적어	(수식어)
수동태 1	Experienced applicants 경력직 지원자들은	are given 받는다	the chance to interview. 면접 볼 기회를	-
수동태 2	The chance to interview 면접 볼 기회가	is given 주어진다	-	(to experienced applicants). (경력직 지원자들에게)
4형식 동사	give 주다　offer 제공하다　award 수여하다　send 보내다　issue 발부하다　grant 승인하다　show 보여주다			

- 동사 뒤에 목적어 두 개를 갖는 동사를 '4형식 동사' 또는 '수여 동사'라고 한다.
- 4형식 동사 뒤의 첫 번째 목적어를 '간접 목적어', 두 번째 목적어를 '직접 목적어'라고 부른다.
- 간접 목적어에는 '사람'이, 직접 목적어에는 '사물'이 오며, '(사람)에게 (사물)을 주다'로 해석한다.
- 4형식 동사는 목적어가 두 개이므로 수동태 또한 두 가지 형태로 쓸 수 있다.
- 간접 목적어가 주어로 온 수동태는 동사 뒤에 직접 목적어가 남으므로 3형식 동사의 능동태 문장과 혼동하지 않도록 주의한다.

3초 알면 3초!　**>>** 3형식과 4형식을 넘나드는 '통지·인식의 동사'와 그 쓰임 패턴을 외워라.

We were ------- that the package is still being inspected by customs.

(A) instructed　　　　(B) informed　　　　(C) explained　　　　(D) announced

3형식 동사	주어	inform/notify 알리다, 통지하다　remind 상기시키다	사람 목적어	of 전치사구
4형식 동사		assure 장담하다　convince 확신시키다　warn 경고하다		that절
수동태	주어	be p.p.	of 전치사구/that절	

통지·인식의 동사는 3형식과 4형식의 특징을 모두 지니고 있어서 따로 정리해두는 수밖에 없다. 이들 동사는 ① 목적어로 '사람'이 온다는 점 ② 사람 목적어 뒤에는 of 전치사구나 that절이 연결된다는 점이 핵심으로, 위 문제의 경우 보기 모두 의미는 그럴 듯해 보이지만, 수동태 뒤에 that절을 목적어로 취할 수 있는 동사는 보기 중 (B) 뿐이다. 이처럼 이들의 특징이 다양하게 응용되어 출제되니 숙지해두자.

해석 우리는 그 소포가 아직도 세관에서 조사되고 있다고 들었다.

PART 5

1. Café Celeste ------- patrons a complimentary dessert now through the end of June.
(A) are offered
(B) will be offering
(C) offering
(D) to offer

2. Those without a permit will not be granted ------- to the employee parking lot.
(A) enters
(B) entered
(C) entry
(D) is entering

3. Please be ------- that every complaint from our clients will receive immediate attention.
(A) assure
(B) to assure
(C) assuring
(D) assured

4. The realtor will show Mr. Grant suitable ------- office spaces for the new accounting firm he is going to open.
(A) constant
(B) financial
(C) commercial
(D) conservative

PART 6

Questions 5-8 refer to the following e-mail.

To: Anna Badmaeva <ABadmaeva@starsupply.eu>
From: David Deehan <DDeehan@walkerengineering.co.uk>
Date: 28 August
Subject: Order

I'd like to request a change to Walker Engineering's ------- order. Fewer of our projects require fungus-proof surfacing these days, so we are using much less AF2713 fungicidal varnish. -------, I'm hoping to reduce the order quantity to just seven cans, starting next month. We also need an additional 10 cans of LX8757 heat-resistant coating each month.

At some point, we will wrap up all projects requiring the use of AF2713 varnish. But I ------- you sufficient notice in advance. Please send me an invoice that reflects the revisions. -------.

Thanks,

David Deehan
Walker Engineering

5. (A) first
(B) late
(C) duplicate
(D) standing

6. (A) Regardless
(B) Accordingly
(C) Unexpectedly
(D) However

7. (A) gave
(B) give
(C) will give
(D) have been given

8. (A) The company has done a number of projects in coastal areas.
(B) We are unsure of the exact amounts that will be required.
(C) You should have received it from my colleague yesterday.
(D) Our Accounting Department has requested it.

Pet owners ------- to keep their animals inside for the next week because of the extreme weather that has been forecast.

(A) advise　　　　　(B) advising　　　　　(C) are advised　　　　　(D) would advise

| 해설 | advise는 to부정사를 목적격 보어로 취하는 5형식 동사로 빈칸 뒤에 목적어 없이 to부정사가 바로 연결되므로 수동태 동사인 (C)가 정답이다. |
| 해석 | 애완동물 주인들은 예보된 극심한 날씨 때문에 다음 주에 동물들을 실내에 두도록 권고받는다. |

>> 명사나 형용사를 목적격 보어로 취하는 5형식 동사의 수동태

	주어	5형식 동사	목적어	목적격 보어
능동태	Business Insights Magazine Business Insights 잡지가	has named 거명했다	Thompson Corporation Thompson 사를	the city's best workplace. 시에서 가장 좋은 일터로
	주어	be p.p.	목적격 보어	(수식어)
수동태	Thompson Corporation Thompson 사가	has been named 거명되었다	the city's best workplace 시에서 가장 좋은 일터로	(by Business Insights Magazine). (Business Insights 잡지에 의해)
5형식 동사	appoint 임명하다 name 거명하다, 명명하다 call 부르다 elect 선출하다 make 만들다 find 알게 되다 keep 유지하다 leave (~한 상태로) 두다 consider 여기다			

- 동사+목적어 뒤에 명사 보어나 형용사 보어가 오는 동사를 '5형식 동사' 또는 '(불완전) 타동사'라고 한다.
- 5형식 동사가 쓰인 문장의 수동태는 동사 뒤에 명사나 형용사가 남으므로 능동태 문장과 혼동하지 않도록 주의한다.

>> 5형식 동사의 목적격 보어가 to부정사일 때의 수동태

	주어	5형식 동사	목적어	목적격 보어
능동태	BZ Buses BZ 버스는	encourages 권장한다	customers 고객들이	to book their tickets in advance. 티켓을 미리 예약하도록
	주어	be p.p.	목적격 보어	(수식어)
수동태	Customers 고객들은	are encouraged 권장된다	to book their tickets in advance 티켓을 미리 예약하도록	(by BZ Buses). (BZ 버스에 의해)
5형식 동사	요구	ask/request/invite 요청하다 require 요구하다 urge 촉구하다		
	제안	advise 충고하다 encourage 권장하다 convince 납득시키다 remind 상기시키다		
	지시	instruct 지시하다 force/obligate 강요하다 oblige ~하게 하다		
	기타	allow/permit 허락하다 cause 야기하다 enable 가능하게 하다 expect/project 기대하다, 예상하다		

알면 3초!　　>> to부정사를 목적격 보어로 취하는 5형식 동사의 수동태를 덩어리째 기억하라.

Those who are looking for jobs are ------- to be prepared for short interviews.

(A) recommended　　　(B) criticized　　　(C) monitored　　　(D) excused

공지나 회람, 계약서 등의 공문에서는 to부정사를 목적격 보어로 취하는 5형식 동사들이 능동태보다는 수동태로 훨씬 더 많이 쓰이는데, 이는 수동태 문장이 행위의 대상을 강조하면서 감정을 섞지 않고 단언적으로 전달하기에 더 좋은 방법이기 때문이다. 따라서 목적격 보어로 to부정사를 취하는 동사들의 종류뿐만 아니라 'be recommended to do(~하도록 권고되다)' 식으로 해당 동사들의 수동태를 덩어리째 익혀두는 것이 문제를 빨리 풀 수 있는 방법이다. 위 문제에서 '구직자들'은 '권고를 받는' 대상이므로 (A)가 정답이다.

| 해석 | 구직자들은 짧은 면접을 준비하도록 권장된다. |

PART 5

1. All factories currently operating in Texas are expected to ------- to the stringent safety guidelines issued by the government.

(A) conform
(B) conforms
(C) conforming
(D) be conformed

2. Defects in its newest line of audio devices caused Kisaki Electronics to adopt higher ------- for inspecting products.

(A) chances
(B) foundation
(C) features
(D) standards

3. The fire sprinkler system must be kept clean at ------- times.

(A) all
(B) ready
(C) one
(D) many

4. Dr. Ryo was ------- the sales director due to his impressive credentials.

(A) located
(B) appointed
(C) supplied
(D) determined

PART 6

Questions 5-8 refer to the following memo.

To: Robert Green
From: July Dench
Date: June 29
Subject: A token of gratitude

Hi Robert,

Please send my gratitude to everyone who got involved in our survey last month, especially to Ms. Indira Joseph. -------. First, she let me know that some questions were too vague to ask. I indeed was in a rush when I created the questionnaire. -------, she helped me to revise the entire wordings on her own initiative.

Ms. Joseph showed a great ------- and willingness to help us in ensuring that the questionnaire was perfect before it got distributed. Her diligence, efforts, and brightness allowed the survey ------- on time. I hope that I can have her in my team for the next projects. Anyway, please send my thanks to everyone.

Sincerely,

July Dench
Marketing Manager
F&N Consultant

5. (A) She brought important matters to my attention.
(B) The questionnaire was ready to be distributed.
(C) The respondents were already selected.
(D) I have prepared everything.

6. (A) In addition
(B) As a result
(C) Nonetheless
(D) All of a sudden

7. (A) occupation
(B) motivation
(C) foundation
(D) dedication

8. (A) conduct
(B) conducted
(C) to conduct
(D) to be conducted

CASE 36 시제의 기본 개념

> **A client walked in just as we ------- our team meeting.**
>
> (A) will start   (B) have started   (C) have been starting   (D) were starting
>
> **해설** 빈칸은 'just as(막 ～하는 바로 그 순간에)' 종속절의 동사 자리이다. 주절의 시제가 과거이며, 문맥상 '회의를 시작하려고 할 때 고객이 들어왔다'라는 의미가 되어야 자연스러우므로 과거 진행 시제인 (D)가 정답이다.
>
> **해석** 팀 회의를 막 시작하려고 할 때 고객이 들어왔다.

>> 시제의 의미

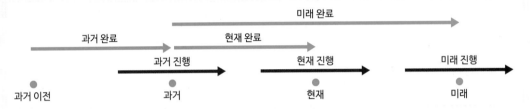

>> 시제의 종류

	단순	진행	완료
현재	**현재 시제** ～이다, ～한다 - 동사 원형(-e)s - 일반적인 사실, 반복되는 일	**현재 진행 시제** ～하고 있다, ～하는 중이다 - am/is/are + -ing - 현재 진행 중인 일	**현재 완료 시제** ～였다, ～했다 - have/has + p.p. - 과거의 일이 현재까지 영향을 미치는 일
과거	**과거 시제** ～였다, ～했다 - 동사 원형(-e)d - 과거에 일어난 일	**과거 진행 시제** ～하고 있었다, ～하는 중이었다 - was/were + -ing - 과거에 진행 중이었던 일	**과거 완료 시제** ～였다, ～했다 - had + p.p. - 과거 시점 이전에 일어난 일
미래	**미래 시제** ～일 것이다, ～할 것이다 - will + 동사 원형 - 미래에 일어날 일	**미래 진행 시제** ～하고 있을 것이다 - will be + -ing - 미래에 진행되고 있을 일	**미래 완료 시제** ～되었을 것이다, ～했을 것이다 - will have + p.p. - 미래의 어느 시점까지 계속/완료될 일

알면 3초! >> 조동사의 과거형이 쓰인 표현의 의미 차이를 구별하라.

> **Several employees complained that it ------- difficult to bear all the construction noise.**
>
> (A) would be   (B) will be   (C) was   (D) being

조동사 + 동사 원형 [→ 미래의 일에 대한 추측/기대]		조동사 + have p.p. [→ 과거의 일에 대한 추측/기대]	
would + 동사 원형	～일[할] 것이다	would have p.p.	～였을[했을] 텐데
should + 동사 원형	～해야 한다(충고/비판)	should have p.p.	～였어야[했어야] 했는데
must + 동사 원형	～해야 한다(필요/강한 권유)	must have p.p.	～였음에[했음에] 틀림없다
could + 동사 원형	～일[할] 수 있을 것이다	could have p.p.	～일[할] 수 있었을 텐데
might + 동사 원형	～일지도[할지도] 모른다	might have p.p.	～였을[했을] 수도 있는데

시제 문제에서 「조동사 + 동사 원형」이나 「조동사 + have p.p.」 형태의 보기를 접할 때가 많으니, 기본적인 의미 차이를 구별해두자. 위의 문제의 경우, 불평한 시점이 과거이며(complained), 그 시점에 공사 소음을 견디기 힘들었다는 의미이므로 과거 시제인 (C)가 답이 되는 건 알겠는데, 혹자는 '(A)의 would는 will의 과거형인데 이건 뭐가 다르지? 해석을 어떻게 해야 될까?'와 같은 질문을 할 수 있고, 대다수의 교재에서도 이런 걸 굳이 해석해서 답이 아니라고 얘기해 주지 않는다. 그러니 위의 표를 일단 외워두자.

해석 몇몇 직원들은 모든 공사 소음을 견디기 힘들다고 불평했다.

PART 5

1. Mega Construction's safety managers meet monthly with employees to make sure that regulations ------- properly.
(A) would have followed
(B) are being followed
(C) to be followed
(D) had been followed

2. The annual pass ------- admission to the amusement park and one free snack per day.
(A) covering
(B) is covered
(C) cover
(D) covers

3. The mobile app developed by Weylan Solutions has been ------- to meet your company's needs.
(A) customize
(B) customizes
(C) customized
(D) customizing

4. The sales contracts the Legal Department had asked for ------- by express mail last Friday.
(A) arrival
(B) arriving
(C) arrives
(D) arrived

PART 6

Questions 5-8 refer to the following article.

HOBART— The Fourth Annual Hobart Literary Conference starts 10 July and ------- until the 21st. **5.** The Conference this year will offer more than just work by Australian nationals. We will also be featuring ------- from Europe and North America. Due to popular demand, we will be bringing back **6.** panel discussions with star authors and top editors this year. Be sure to get your pass for this ------- event early. It is expected to sell out far in advance. -------. Citizens of Hobart are eligible for **7.** **8.** discounted passes. To get your pass, call our hotline at 491-555-110, or visit our Web site: www. hobartliteraryfestival.au.

5. (A) continue
(B) continued
(C) was continued
(D) will continue

6. (A) fashions
(B) crafts
(C) novels
(D) films

7. (A) expedited
(B) enclosed
(C) encouraging
(D) exciting

8. (A) Tickets go on sale on Monday, 1 June.
(B) The venue's capacity has been expanded.
(C) Interviews are conducted by Teri Schultz.
(D) The evening's closing event was well-attended.

CASE 37 단순 시제의 시간 표현

Colmar Industries has announced that it ------- employees to work from home up to 3 days per week from now on.

(A) will allow   (B) will be allowed   (C) had allowed   (D) allowing

해설 빈칸은 that절 내의 주어 it과 목적어 employees 사이의 동사 자리이다. that절 내에 미래 시점을 나타내는 표현 'from now on(앞으로)'이 있으므로 능동태 미래 시제인 (A)가 정답이다.

해석 Colmar 산업은 앞으로 직원들이 주 3일까지 재택근무를 할 수 있도록 하겠다고 밝혔다.

>> 현재 시제와 어울리는 시간 표현

regularly / routinely / periodically 정기적으로   usually / normally / typically / ordinarily / generally / commonly 보통, 일반적으로   always 항상   often / frequently 자주   every / each + 시간 ~마다

will hold (X)
The supervisor **holds** a weekly staff meeting **every Tuesday**.
관리자는 매주 화요일에 주간 직원 회의를 연다.

were (X)
Safety inspections at the manufacturing facility **are normally conducted** by city officials.
제조 시설의 안전 검사는 보통 시 공무원들에 의해 수행된다.

>> 과거 시제와 어울리는 시간 표현

yesterday 어제   recently 최근에   시간 + ago ~ 전에   last + 시점 지난 ~에   previously / formerly 이전에   once 한때   originally 원래

implements (X), will implement (X),
The management **implemented** a policy to conserve energy **yesterday**.
경영진은 에너지 절약을 위한 규정을 어제 시행했다.

>> 미래 시제와 어울리는 시간 표현

tomorrow 내일   soon, shortly 곧, 머지 않아   next + 시점 다음 ~에   starting / beginning / as of + 미래 시점 ~부터

has attended (X)
The director of international sales **will attend** a conference in Tokyo **next week**.
해외 영업 이사는 다음 주 Tokyo에서 있을 회의에 참석할 것이다.

알면 3초!   >> 현재 시제나 현재 진행 시제로도 미래를 나타낼 수 있다.

The contract with our current vendor for bottled water delivery ------- in 90 days.

(A) expire   (B) expires   (C) had expired   (D) could have expired

계약서가 90일 후에 만료될 거라는 내용으로 (A)는 주어(contract)와 수 일치에 어긋나고, (C)나 (D)는 문맥상 어울리지 않으니 답에서 제외시킨다. 답이 될 수 있는 건 (B)뿐인데 왜 미래 시제는 정작 보기에 없을까? 일반적인 사실이나 반복되는 행위를 나타낼 때 쓰는 현재 시제는 계약서나 일정, 보증 기간, 할인 등 이미 정해 놓은 미래의 일을 나타낼 때도 쓸 수 있다. 마찬가지로 현재 진행 시제 역시 가까운 미래의 예정된 계획을 나타낼 때 자주 쓰이므로 보기 중에 미래 시제가 보이지 않는다면 현재 시제나 현재 진행 시제를 자신 있게 답으로 고른다.

해석 생수 배달을 위한 현 판매상과의 계약은 90일 후 만료된다.

해설서 p.53

PART 5

1. The sales report will be discussed at the ------- weekly meeting.

(A) usually
(B) next
(C) near
(D) soon

2. Mr. Routhier will ------- have the opportunity to visit the office in San Jose.

(A) soon
(B) even
(C) simply
(D) yet

3. Paulson Law Firm started as a small, six-person firm and ------- provides services to prominent celebrities and politicians across the country.

(A) along
(B) before
(C) last
(D) now

4. The monthly payments charged by Amazing Prime Videos are ------- updated depending on changes in taxes and inflation.

(A) periodically
(B) particularly
(C) recently
(D) formerly

PART 6

Questions 5-8 refer to the following article.

Mondale-Sterling Teams Up with Area Health Providers

Hamilton (11 August) — Last week, Mondale-Sterling President Gerard Mondale, ------- an alliance
5.
with Hamilton Hospital System. As the North Island's top heating and air conditioning contractor, the firm is well-equipped to do the work necessary to optimize heating and cooling systems to run with greater efficiency and lower energy consumption. The upgrades, which feature new -------,
6.
sensors, and smart thermostats, will reduce power bills by eliminating as much as 50 percent of the cost generated by inefficient heating and cooling, says Mondale. "We're happy to provide these improvements at a third of the ------- price. Mondale-Sterling is excited to prove the capabilities of
7.
our new VulcanMax system and do some good for the city at the same time." -------.
8.

---

5. (A) announcing
(B) announced
(C) will announce
(D) announce

6. (A) windows
(B) beds
(C) vehicles
(D) fans

7. (A) affordable
(B) usual
(C) frequent
(D) higher

8. (A) To learn more about Mondale-Sterling's HVAC services, visit MondaleSterling.co.nz.
(B) Some hospital systems have not been upgraded in 25 years.
(C) The hospital network plans to replace its air conditioners next.
(D) If you qualify, please apply in person at the Waikato District Health Board.

완료 시제의 시간 표현

It appears that lately, more people ------- to commute to work by public transportation than in previous years.

(A) would have chosen   (B) have been choosing

(C) will have been chosen   (D) are to choose

콕 찍어 포인트 ··· 부사 lately는 현재 완료 (진행) 시제와 함께 쓰인다.

[해설] 빈칸은 진주어를 이끄는 that 명사절 내 주어 more people의 동사 자리이다. that절 내에 현재 완료 (진행) 시제와 어울려 쓰이는 lately가 있으므로 (B)가 정답이다.

[해석] 예년과 비교해서 최근에 더 많은 사람들이 대중교통으로 통근하는 것을 선택하고 있는 것으로 보인다.

>> 현재 완료 시제와 어울리는 시간 표현

완료: 과거의 행위가 현재 완료된 일 (~했다)

> just 막, 방금   already 이미, 벌써   recently / lately 최근에   not yet 아직 ~아닌

❗ recently는 현재 완료와 과거 시제에 모두 쓸 수 있으나, lately는 현재 완료 시제에만 쓴다.

The branch manager **has already submitted** this year's sales report.
지점장은 이미 올해 매출 보고서를 제출했다.

계속: 과거의 행위가 현재까지 계속되는 일 (~해왔다)

> for / over / during / in the last[past] + 기간 지난 ~ 동안   since + 과거 시점 / 과거 시제의 절 ~ 이후로
> until now, so far 지금까지

The start-up **has expanded** its business **over the last nine months**.
그 신생 업체가 지난 9개월 간 사업을 확장해 왔다.

경험: 과거부터 현재까지의 경험 (~해 본 적이 있다)

> never 결코 ~아닌   ever 한 번이라도   before 이전에

We **have never experienced** such outstanding service anywhere.
우리는 이렇게 훌륭한 서비스를 어디에서도 받아 본 적이 없다.

 알면 3초!   **>> since 문장의 시제를 공식처럼 암기하라.**

Accidents at the Gonyang Apartment construction site have been substantially reduced since the revised safety regulation procedures -------.

(A) have been implemented   (B) were implemented

(C) had implemented   (D) will be implementing

주어 + 현재 완료(have/has + p.p.)	+ since + 과거 시점 (전치사 since)
	+ since + 주어 + 과거 동사 (접속사 since)

'~ 이후로'란 뜻으로 쓰인 since 앞뒤의 시제를 고르는 문제를 자주 접하게 될 텐데, 여기서 since 앞뒤의 시제란 since를 기준으로 주절의 시제 또는 since절의 시제를 말한다. since는 전치사와 접속사의 기능을 모두 가지고 있어 의미상(~ 이후로) since가 전치사로 쓰일 땐 뒤에 '과거 시점'이, 접속사로 쓰일 땐 뒤에 '과거 동사'가 오는 패턴을 갖는다. 이때 주절의 시제 역시 since의 의미에 영향을 받아 현재 완료 시제를 쓰게 되는데, 바로 이 규칙을 문제로 내는 것이다. 빈칸이 올 수 있는 자리는 ① 주절의 시제 ② since절의 시제 ③ since 총 세 군데로 이 공식을 기억하여 응용해서 풀면 된다. 위 문장에서 빈칸은 since절의 시제로 나왔고, since는 접속사로 쓰였기에 과거 동사 (B)가 정답이다.

[해석] Gonyang 아파트 건설 현장에서의 사고들은 개정된 안전 규정 절차들이 시행된 이후로 상당히 줄었다.

CASE 집중훈련

PART 5

1. A local burger BBX ------- announced that it will no longer serve French fries with its burgers.
(A) entirely
(B) kindly
(C) recently
(D) fully

2. Excessive spending by government officials has decreased ------- new policies were introduced last year.
(A) since
(B) amid
(C) during
(D) before

3. Crosston's economy has been improving recently thanks to an ------- of new businesses.
(A) induction
(B) intention
(C) incline
(D) influx

4. Over the last three decades, Mr. Drake ------- quickly up the corporate ladder at an international consulting firm.
(A) climb
(B) climbing
(C) will climb
(D) has climbed

PART 6

Questions 5-8 refer to the following e-mail.

From: Management
Date: February 12
Subject: Chris Searle
To: All Staff

Everyone,

I want to inform you all that Chris Searle ------- our offer to become the new director of mergers and acquisitions. His first day in the office is scheduled to be March 19. Mr. Searle has two decades of experience in strategic corporate actions, the last five mainly in the banking -------. His first task will be to advise our board of directors on a possible acquisition of Quad City Mutual. A welcome party is being planned on his first day. -------. Please e-mail me if you'd like to -------.

5. (A) having accepted
(B) was accepted
(C) has accepted
(D) will accept

6. (A) sector
(B) résumé
(C) account
(D) code

7. (A) I would like to finalize the date this week.
(B) Mr. Searle would appreciate your insight on the matter.
(C) It will take place at Barney's Grill starting at 6 P.M.
(D) Another round of consultations will be held then.

8. (A) confirm
(B) volunteer
(C) apply
(D) attend

Mr. Nasseri ------- his students to be at the testing site by 8 A.M., even though the test did not begin until 9 A.M.

(A) had asked　　　(B) was asked　　　(C) will have asked　　　(D) is being asked

해설　문맥상 '오전 9시에 와도 됐을 시험에 오전 8시까지 와달라고 요청했었다'는 의미가 되어야 한다. 기준 시점이 과거이고(did not begin), 빈칸을 포함한 절은 기준이 되는 과거 시점 이전에 일어난 일이므로 과거 완료 시제인 (A)가 정답이다.

해석　Nasseri 씨는 시험이 오전 9시가 넘어서야 시작되었음에도 불구하고, 학생들에게 오전 8시까지 시험장에 와달라고 요청했었다.

》》 문장이 주절과 종속절로 이루어져 있을 때 한쪽 절의 시제를 기준으로 해석을 통해 나머지 절의 시제를 파악한다.

Big Beds **had conducted** a survey **before** they <u>decided</u> to launch a new product.
　　　　　　　 기준 시점: 과거 완료　　　　　　　　　　　　　 will decide (X)
　　　　　　　　　　　　　　　　　　　　　　 기준 시점 이후에 일어난 일: 과거

Big Beds는 신제품을 출시하기로 결정하기 전에 설문 조사를 실시했다.

》》 과거 완료가 쓰이는 문장에는 항상 비교의 기준이 되는 과거 시점이 언급된다.

The results of the clinical trials **were made public after** the research center **had approved** the release.
　　　　　　　　　　　　 기준 시점: 과거　　　　　　　　　　　　　 approves (X)
　　　　　　　　　　　　　　　　　　　　　　　　 기준 시점 이전에 일어난 일: 과거 완료

임상 실험의 결과는 연구소에서 발표를 승인한 후에 공개되었다.

 알면 3초! 　》》 by the time 문장의 시제를 공식처럼 암기하라.

By the time the merger -------, Roxy Co. had suffered from profit loss for a long time.
(A) announce　　　(B) is announced　　　(C) was announced　　　(D) had been announced

by the time + 주어 + 과거 동사, 주어 + 과거 완료(had p.p.) ~했을 때쯤, (이미) ~했었다

by the time + 주어 + 현재 동사, 주어 + 미래 완료(will have p.p.) ~할 때쯤이면, (이미) ~했을 것이다

완료 시제는 우리에게 없는 시제라서 이해하기 만만치가 않다. 완료 시제 중에서 가장 많이 쓰이고 출제되는 건 단연 현재 완료 시제라서 이 시제의 특징과 시간 표현을 기억하기도 버겁기만 한데, 과거 완료며, 미래 완료라니… 그나마 다행인 건 과거 완료나 미래 완료 시제는 그 쓰임이 매우 제한적이라서 문장에 특정한 패턴이 주어지는 형태로 출제되는 게 일반적이다. 그중 시간 접속사인 by the time(~할 때쯤)이 등장하는 문장이 대표적이며, by the time이 이끄는 부사절의 동사가 과거 시제면 주절은 과거 완료를, by the time이 이끄는 부사절의 동사가 현재 시제면 주절은 미래 완료를 쓰는 규칙을 가지고 있으므로 by the time 시제 문제가 나오면 일일이 문맥을 따져 풀기보다는 서로의 시제를 단서로 삼아 공식처럼 암기해둔다. 위 문제에서도 주절에 과거 완료 시제가 쓰였으므로 빈칸에는 과거 시제 (C)가 나와야 한다.

해석　합병이 발표되었을 때쯤 Roxy 사는 (이미) 오랫동안 수익 감소를 겪고 있었다.

CASE 집중훈련

PART 5

1. Excelsior Dentistry allows a 10-minute grace period for late arrivals after which the patient -------.
(A) be rescheduled
(B) rescheduled
(C) is rescheduled
(D) had been rescheduled

2. After acquiring OneClick Money, Milton Ltd. ------- a broad selection of online financial services.
(A) offer
(B) offered
(C) offering
(D) to offer

3. All job applicants are required to state what key skills they ------- before their interviews.
(A) possess
(B) had possessed
(C) possessing
(D) will possess

4. By the end of this quarter, the plant in Texas ------- at least 10,000 air conditioning units.
(A) will be built
(B) will have built
(C) has built
(D) has been built

PART 6

Questions 5-8 refer to the following e-mail.

To: Omar Radcliffe <oradcliffe@yelcot.com>
From: LY Sports Equipment <orders@lysportsequipment.com>
Date: 2 October
Subject: Order #3862

Dear Mr. Radcliffe,

Thank you for your order of the Louisville basketball goal with adjustable pole. We did not ------- this
                                                                                        5.
basketball goal becoming such a popular item and selling out so quickly. Unfortunately, we are unable
to fulfill your order right now. However, our factory has promised us speedy delivery of additional goals.
We ------- your item to ship in about three weeks. You will receive an e-mail ------- the truck is on its
      6.   7.
way. -------. If you decide to cancel your order, we will be happy to issue you a full refund.
      8.

Sincerely,

LY Sports Equipment

5. (A) foresee
(B) measure
(C) allocate
(D) detain

6. (A) expected
(B) expect
(C) have expected
(D) will be expected

7. (A) so that
(B) as well as
(C) even if
(D) as soon as

8. (A) In fact, basketball goals come in a variety of sizes.
(B) Shipping costs have been steadily growing.
(C) Our catalog features an extensive line of products.
(D) Please accept our apologies for the inconvenience.

CASE 40 　시제 일치의 예외

Beijing Airlines will hold a press conference ------- the management decides whether or not to merge with Shanghai Airlines.

(A) such as   (B) once   (C) otherwise   (D) so that

> **해설** 빈칸은 두 문장을 연결하는 접속사 자리이다. 주절이 미래일 때 시간/조건의 접속사가 이끄는 부사절에서는 현재 시제가 미래 시제를 대신한다는 점에서 once를 넣어서 해석해 본다. '경영진이 상하이 항공과의 합병 여부를 결정하는 대로 기자회견을 열 것이다'라는 의미가 완성되므로 (B)가 정답이다.
>
> **해석** 베이징 항공은 경영진이 상하이 항공과의 합병 여부를 결정하는 대로 기자회견을 열 것이다.

>> 시간/조건 접속사가 이끄는 부사절에서는 미래 시제 대신 현재 시제를 쓴다.

시간 접속사	when ~할 때 　as soon as ~하자마자 　while ~하는 동안 　until ~할 때까지 　before ~하기 전에 after ~한 후에 　by the time ~할 때쯤
조건 접속사	if, provided[providing] (that) ~이라면 　once 일단 ~하면 　in case ~할 경우에 대비하여 as[so] long as, as far as ~하는 한 　unless ~하지 않는 한

❶ 시간 / 조건절의 현재 동사는 주절의 시제가 미래임을 나타내는 단서이며, 그 반대의 경우도 마찬가지이다.

As soon as we **find** a proper instructor for the seminar, further details **will be provided**.
적합한 세미나 강사를 찾는대로 더 자세한 정보를 알려드리겠습니다.

The lease with The Lawson Group **will be continued if** updates to the existing warehouses **are made**.
기존 창고들이 업데이트된다면 Lawson 사와의 임대 계약이 지속될 것이다.

>> 요구/요청/제안/주장/명령 동사나 판단의 형용사 뒤에 오는 that절에는 시제와 상관 없이 「(should)＋동사 원형」을 쓴다.

요구 / 요청 / 제안 / 주장 / 명령 동사	판단 형용사
ask, request 요청하다 　require, demand 요구하다 suggest, propose 제안하다 　recommend, advise 권고하다 insist 주장하다 　urge 촉구하다 　order 명령하다	necessary 필요한 　important 중요한 essential, crucial, vital, imperative 필수적인

⌐ was submitted (X)
The chairman **requested that** the budget proposal (should) **be submitted** by next Monday.
회장은 다음 주 월요일까지 예산안을 제출할 것을 요청했다.

⌐ is kept (X)
It is **imperative that** clients' personal information (should) **be kept** confidential.
고객들의 개인 정보가 기밀로 유지되어야 하는 것은 필수이다.

 알면 3초!   >> 시간·조건의 부사절에는 현재 완료 시제도 쓸 수 있다.

After we have reviewed the details of your contract, we ------- you to arrange a meeting.

(A) was contacting   (B) has contacted   (C) contact   (D) will contact

주절의 시제를 결정해야 하는 문제에서 시간·조건절의 시제가 현재 동사면 주절의 시제는 미래 시제를 선택하는 것이 일반적인 요령이긴 한데, 지금처럼 시간·조건절의 시제가 현재 완료면 어떻게 하겠는가? 시제를 일치시키라고 했으니 주절도 현재 완료 시제를 쓰겠는가? Nope! 시간·조건절에서는 현재가 미래를 대신하는 것처럼, 현재 완료가 미래 완료를 대신한다! 이건 단지 어감상의 차이 즉, 시간·조건절에서 그냥 하는 것(→현재)과 하는 것을 완료하는 것(→현재 완료)을 나타내기 위한 차이일 뿐이므로 위의 문장은 'After we review the details ~'로 바꿔 써도 아무런 문제가 없다. 그러니 시간·조건절의 시제가 현재뿐만 아니라 현재 완료 동사여도 주절은 미래 시제여야 하고, 반대로 시간·조건절의 시제를 묻는 경우에도 주절의 시제가 미래라면, 시간·조건절에는 현재 동사뿐만 아니라 현재 완료 동사도 쓸 수 있다는 점을 꼭 기억해두자. 따라서 이 문제의 정답은 (D)가 된다.

> **해석** 저희가 귀하의 계약서 세부 사항의 검토를 완료한 후에, 회의를 잡기 위해 연락드리겠습니다.

해설서 p.57

PART 5

1. As soon as the warehouse -------- for fire hazards, you may resume your normal business operations.

(A) is examining
(B) examining
(C) was examined
(D) is examined

2. After the trial period -------, users have the option of paying for the software or deleting it from their servers.

(A) expires
(B) will be expiring
(C) is expiring
(D) expired

3. If an employee ------- to take a leave of absence, they must first speak to their manager.

(A) wish
(B) wishes
(C) will wish
(D) was wishing

4. To validate yesterday's results, Dr. Kim is asking that the test ------- today by a different research laboratory.

(A) be repeated
(B) is repeating
(C) will have repeated
(D) had been repeating

PART 6

Questions 5-8 refer to the following e-mail.

To: laura.lewis@tnet.com
From: WeightLossManagementHelp@wlm.net
Date: November 28
Re: Updates

To our customers:

We are pleased to announce that our weight loss management company has more than tripled its number of clients this year. Due to this increase, we will be ------- some updates to our policies, **5.** including a change in procedure for membership renewal options. We will be adding an automatic payment feature.

-------. However, you can go ahead and sign into your membership account now to read ------- **6.** **7.** information about these updates on our Membership Renewal page. When you enter our Home Page, you ------- to type your initials at the bottom of the log in box verifying that you agree to the **8.** new updates.

We appreciate you trusting us to help you in your weight loss journey, and good luck reaching your goals.

Weight Loss Management Help

5. (A) fulfilling
(B) convincing
(C) implementing
(D) prolonging

6. (A) We will issue a violation notice addressed to you.
(B) To rate your recent experience, click on the Feedback link.
(C) Clients report that this is a successful diet plan.
(D) The changes will go into effect on December 16.

7. (A) detailed
(B) designed
(C) devoted
(D) decided

8. (A) have been required
(B) were required
(C) will be required
(D) have required

1. The Center for National Health's recent report ------- that the amended rules and regulations have been successful.

(A) concluding
(B) concludes
(C) to conclude
(D) in conclusion

2. Gershwin Theater Group ------- its latest musical *The Midnight Sky* on December 10.

(A) debuting
(B) has been debuted
(C) is debuted
(D) will debut

3. The floor plan of the apartment complex ------- to be in accordance with all the codes stipulated in the building regulation.

(A) finding
(B) will find
(C) had found
(D) was found

4. Camping gear from Norseland Outdoors are manufactured with an innovative synthetic ------- that resists harsh weather conditions.

(A) substantial
(B) substantive
(C) substances
(D) substance

5. When Ms. Patterson checked her credit card statement, she ------- a discrepancy in the billed cost.

(A) noticed
(B) initiated
(C) reviewed
(D) deferred

6. At present, Costsave Supermarket ------- to implement a long-awaited home delivery service through their Web site.

(A) working
(B) has worked
(C) is working
(D) will be working

7. For the last two years, Vunder Partners has persistently ------- the lowest commission rates on commercial real estate.

(A) implied
(B) displayed
(C) offered
(D) discovered

8. Ms. Berretta amended the company's hiring policy to ------- new recruits higher base salaries.

(A) question
(B) grant
(C) relieve
(D) strengthen

Questions 9-12 refer to the following notice.

As part of our city's ongoing green initiative, the Greenbriar International Food Festival will be completely plastic-free this year. Therefore, all --------- will only be offered on paper plates. This also
9.
applies to cutlery, where it is expected that guests bring their own or utilize the wooden utensils provided.

The Greenbriar International Food Festival will be held at the Highland Fields on Saturday, May 16, from 9 A.M. to 4 P.M. If you are a vendor this year, we ask that you --------- at least an hour early in
10.
order to prepare your stalls. ---------.
11.

We would like to extend our thanks to the city council for providing us with the necessary funds and --------- for the event. We hope you bring the whole family to this year's festival!
12.

9. (A) consumables
(B) possessions
(C) entertainment
(D) collectibles

10. (A) have arrived
(B) be arriving
(C) arrive
(D) can arrive

11. (A) To become a vendor, you must fill out the application form.
(B) If you require help with transporting your goods, please let us know.
(C) We hope the green initiatives lead to more household recycling.
(D) Last year's festival featured foods from a diverse range of countries.

12. (A) permits
(B) permittance
(C) permitted
(D) permittee

준동사

CASE 41 to부정사의 특징

Costello Corp. is purchasing an overseas manufacturing facility to ------- its production costs.

(A) reduction   (B) reduce   (C) reduced   (D) reduces

해설 빈칸 앞에 to가 있고 뒤에는 명사구가 연결되어 있으므로 to부정사 자리이다. 빈칸은 to부정사를 완성하는 동사 원형의 자리이므로 (B)가 정답이다.

해석 Costello 사는 생산 비용을 줄이기 위해 해외 제조 시설을 매입하고 있다.

>> 「to + 동사 원형」을 to부정사라 하며 명사, 형용사, 부사 역할을 한다.

명사	The management **hopes to decrease** the turnover rate for this position. 경영진은 이 직책의 이직률을 줄이기를 바라고 있다. ↳동사 hope의 목적어 자리
형용사	There are online Spanish courses that help you to improve your **ability to speak** fluently. 여러분이 유창하게 말할 능력을 향상시켜 줄 온라인 스페인어 과정들이 있습니다.　　명사 ability 수식
부사	Mr. Kim suggested focusing on developing additional products **to remain** competitive. Kim 씨는 경쟁력을 유지하기 위해 추가적인 제품 개발에 집중하자고 제안했다.　'~하기 위해'라는 뜻의 부사 자리

>> to부정사도 동사처럼 다양한 형태를 갖는다.

기본형	We are happy **to offer** you a 20 percent discount. to + 동사 원형 당신께 20퍼센트 할인을 제공하게 되어 기쁩니다.
수동형	The keynote speaker for the expo is **to be announced**. to + be p.p. 엑스포의 기조 연설자가 발표될 예정이다.
완료형	It was uncomfortable for the customers **to have waited** for so long in the cold. to + have p.p. 고객들이 추위 속에서 너무 오래 기다려온 것은 불편한 일이었다.
부정형	The HR department decided **not to start** the new trainee program until next year. not + to + 동사 원형 인사부는 내년까지 새 연수생 프로그램을 시작하지 않기로 결정했다.

>> to부정사의 의미상 주어는 to 앞에 「for + 목적격」으로 나타낸다.

It is important **for interns** to report any problems to their immediate supervisor.
인턴들은 어떠한 문제든 그들의 직속 상사에게 보고하는 것이 중요하다.

알면 3초!　　>> 준동사는 단독으로 동사 자리에 올 수 없다.

The Degas' Island Restaurant requests that reservations for a table ------- at least a week in advance.

(A) make   (B) be made   (C) to make   (D) making

동사가 정답인 문제에서 정말 많이 등장하는 오답 보기가 바로 to부정사, 동명사, 분사와 같은 준동사 패밀리이다. 이렇게 준동사를 보기에 자주 등장시키는 가장 큰 이유는 '준동사는 동사 자리에 들어갈 수 없다'는 문법적 규칙을 묻는 데 있다. 이들을 '준동사'라고 부르니, 'to부정사인 (C)나 동명사/현재분사인 (D)도 동사 자리에 들어갈 수 있는 거 아닌가?'라고 착각하기 쉬운데, 준동사로 부르는 건 동사의 성질을 가지고 있어서이지, 동사를 대신할 수 있다는 말이 아니다. 그러니, 동사 자리 문제의 보기로 to부정사나 동명사, 분사가 등장한다면 오답 1순위로 소거하자. 위 문제에서 빈칸은 that절 내 동사 자리이며, '예약'은 '손님들에 의해 만들어지는' 것이기에 수동태를 써야 하고 요구/요청/제안/주장/명령의 동사가 뒤에 that절을 취하면 that절의 should는 생략되므로 (B)가 정답이다.

해석 Degas' Island 레스토랑은 적어도 일주일 전에 테이블을 예약할 것을 요청한다.

PART 5

1. Bellefontaine District Council officials have drafted a proposal ------- additional businesses to the newly opened office complex.

(A) attracts
(B) attracted
(C) will attract
(D) to attract

2. The chef will demonstrate how to ------- some of his most popular meals, and then audience members will be given samples to taste.

(A) preparation
(B) prepared
(C) prepare
(D) preparing

3. Teowool Travel Services will match the price from any other major ticketing agencies to ------- that they remain competitive.

(A) offer
(B) exemplify
(C) manage
(D) ensure

4. In order ------- Dr. Garth to contact you regarding your next therapy session, he will need your e-mail address.

(A) to
(B) of
(C) for
(D) with

PART 6

Questions 5-8 refer to the following notice.

Traffic Advisory for June 21: Notification of Upcoming Disruptions

This notice is to notify all members of the public that areas of Hollow Glade will be closed off today. Whitwell Street and Binhamy Road will be closed from 9 A.M. to 4 P.M. ------- damages from last week's storm.
5.

Additionally, areas directly below the university on Bowden Dale may be highly congested on June 25. This is due to a ------- event held by the university, which will run for the entire day. Residents are
6.
advised to take the alternative route via Cotswold Cross.

Gipsy Street leading to Southview Gate will be closed on June 30 and June 31 from 9 A.M. The Farmer's Association will be hosting their annual farmer's market ------- the day. -------.
7.   8.

5. (A) repaired
(B) repair
(C) repairing
(D) to repair

6. (A) preferred
(B) special
(C) contrasting
(D) definite

7. (A) by
(B) before
(C) for
(D) toward

8. (A) The street is expected to reopen around 4 P.M.
(B) The invites will be sent out shortly.
(C) We are accepting proposals for the new land lot.
(D) You can request a monthly breakdown by e-mailing us.

to부정사의 역할 1

Falcon Financial Services intends ------- three more banking centers in the Chicago area this year.

(A) open   (B) opens   (C) opening   (D) to open

해설 '의도하다, 계획하다'라는 뜻의 intends는 to부정사를 목적어로 취하는 동사이므로 (D)가 정답이다.

해석 Falcon 금융 서비스는 올해 시카고 지역에 3개의 은행 업무 센터를 더 열 계획이다.

>> to부정사는 명사 역할을 하여 주어와 목적어 자리에 온다.

주어	가주어 It – 진주어 to부정사 구문 **To submit a budget plan by next Monday** is impossible. ❶ to부정사 주어는 단수 취급한다. = **It** is impossible **to submit a budget plan by next Monday**. 다음주 월요일까지 예산 계획을 제출하는 것은 불가능하다.
목적어	가목적어 It – 진목적어 to부정사 구문 The store owner considers for employees **to make an effort at all times** important. = The store owner considers **it** important for employees **to make an effort at all times**. 상점 주인은 직원들이 항상 애쓰는 모습을 보이는 것이 중요하다고 생각한다. → to부정사가 5형식 동사 'consider, make, find, think 등'의 목적어 자리에 올 때는 가목적어 it을 쓰고 진목적어를 목적격 보어 뒤로 보낸다.

>> to부정사를 목적어로 취하는 동사 「3V + to부정사」

희망	want/wish/hope 바라다 would like 하고 싶다 expect 기대하다	
의도	intend 의도하다 plan 계획하다 aim 목표로 하다	
의지	try/strive 노력하다 promise/pledge 약속하다	+ to부정사
결정	decide/choose 결정하다 agree 동의하다	~하기를
부정	refuse/decline 거절하다 fail ~하지 못하다 hesitate 주저하다	
기타	need ~할 필요가 있다 manage 용케도 ~하다 afford ~할 여유가 있다	

The articles for the magazine **need to be reviewed** by Friday.
잡지 기사들은 금요일까지 검토되어야 한다.

 알면 3초!   >> to부정사를 목적어로 취하는 동사 vs. 동명사를 목적어로 취하는 동사

The design team has been working overtime since the supervisor ------- to extend the deadline.

(A) avoided   (B) disposed   (C) refused   (D) sustained

해석상으로는 (A)와 (C) 모두 그럴듯해 보이지만 avoid는 동명사를, refuse는 to부정사를 목적어로 취하는 대표적인 동사이고 빈칸 뒤에 to부정사가 와 있으니 (C)를 답으로 고르는 문제이다. 특정 동사 뒤에 to부정사가 오는지, 동명사가 오는지를 묻는 문제뿐만 아니라 반대로, 빈칸 뒤에 to부정사나 동명사를 제시하고 이들을 목적어로 취하는 동사를 구별하라는 어휘 문제도 출제되고 있다.

해석 디자인 팀은 상사가 마감 기한 연장을 거절했기 때문에 초과 근무를 해오고 있다.

CASE 집중훈련

PART 5

1. Ms. Bowen would like ------- a training session about the new accounting software within this month.
(A) organizing
(B) to organize
(C) having organized
(D) organization

2. Trolley Consulting has failed to ------- positive relationships with its clients.
(A) maintain
(B) maintaining
(C) maintained
(D) maintenance

3. The Medical Doctors Association announced that maintaining indoor humidity at 50 percent will undoubtedly diminish the time it takes ------- from respiratory illnesses.
(A) be recovered
(B) to recover
(C) having recovered
(D) will be recovering

4. Mr. Woodworth emphasized that it is important to ------- explicit policies regarding telecommuting.
(A) establish
(B) estimate
(C) flourish
(D) correspond

PART 6

Questions 5-8 refer to the following press article.

CARDIFF (1 February) — Major Canadian sports apparel retailer Doonesbury ------- to make its presence known in the UK. This afternoon, the company told investors that 10 Doonesbury locations will be opened across England and Wales, with a Cardiff-based store opening first next month. -------. Doonesbury's ------- involves opening sprawling suburban outlet stores which offer a wide variety of outdoor and sports apparel, as well as an industry-leading price match guarantee. "The board is ------- to bring our business to UK customers and to share our incredible brands and customer service," explained the firm's Vice President, Christina Maddow.

5. (A) planned
(B) to plan
(C) is planning
(D) could plan

6. (A) The rest will open within the next six months.
(B) Doonesbury plans to upgrade each existing store.
(C) A well-known athlete will be visiting soon.
(D) A proposed downtown location did not offer enough space.

7. (A) requirement
(B) transaction
(C) strategy
(D) occasion

8. (A) shocked
(B) eager
(C) patient
(D) amazed

CASE 43 to부정사의 역할 2

The training seminar for newly hired staff members is to ------- with a keynote speech from the CEO at 2:00 P.M.

(A) commencing　　(B) commenced　　(C) commences　　(D) commence

해설 '~할 예정이다'라는 의미의 「be to V」 용법을 사용해야 하므로 to부정사를 완성하는 동사 원형 (D)가 정답이다.

해석 새로 채용된 직원들을 위한 교육 세미나가 오후 2시 CEO의 기조연설로 시작될 예정이다.

>> be동사 뒤에 to부정사가 올 때 다양한 의미를 갖는다.

	「be to V」 용법
보어	The purpose of this seminar **is to help** employees learn about filing taxes. ~하는 것이다 이 세미나의 목적은 직원들이 세금 신고에 관해 배우도록 돕는 것이다. The office move **is to begin** on April 1 and **to be finished** by April 8. ~할 예정이다 사무실 이동은 4월 1일에 시작해서 4월 8일에 완료될 예정이다. The total amount of this month's mortgage **is to be paid** by the end of the month. ~해야 한다 이달 융자금의 총액이 월말까지 지불되어야 한다.

>> to부정사를 목적격 보어로 취하는 5형식 동사 「5V + 목적어 + to부정사」

요구	ask/request/invite 요청하다　require 요구하다　urge 촉구하다	
제안	advise 충고하다　encourage 권장하다　convince 납득시키다　remind 상기시키다	+ 목적어 + to부정사
지시	instruct 지시하다　force/obligate 강요하다　oblige ~하게 하다	~가　~하도록
기타	allow 허락하다　cause 야기하다　enable 가능하게 하다　expect 기대하다	

The upcoming business trip will not **allow** Ms. Chan **to attend** the conference.
곧 있을 출장은 Chan 씨가 학회에 참석할 수 없도록 할 것이다.

>> to부정사는 형용사 역할을 하여 명사를 후치 수식한다.

	to부정사의 수식을 받는 명사 「명사 + to부정사」		
명사 수식	ability to do ~할 능력 attempt to do ~하려는 시도 chance/opportunity to do ~할 기회 decision to do ~하려는 결정	desire to do ~하려는 열정 effort to do ~하려는 노력 failure to do ~하지 못함 proposal to do ~하자는 제안서	plan to do ~하려는 계획 right to do ~할 권리 time to do ~할 시간 way to do ~하는 방법

Customer service representatives will make an **effort to respond** to customers' inquiries within 48 hours.
고객 서비스 담당자들은 48시간 이내에 고객의 문의에 답하기 위한 노력을 기울일 것이다.

알면 3초!　>> to부정사를 목적격 보어로 취하는 동사의 수동태에 주의한다.

Technicians are expected ------- with all of the laboratory's safety regulations.

(A) compliances　　(B) complies　　(C) to comply　　(D) complying

빈칸 앞의 are expected만 보고 (C)를 선택할 수 있어야 한다. 위에 정리한 'to부정사를 목적격 보어로 취하는 동사'는 잘 외우면서, 이들의 목적어가 주어 자리로 간 수동태 구문 「be p.p. + to부정사」는 새로운 개념으로 여기는 웃지 못할 일이 벌어지곤 하는데, 「동사 + 목적어 + 목적격 보어」의 5형식은 수동태 구문 「목적어 + be p.p. + 목적격 보어」로도 곧잘 쓰이기 때문에 목적격 보어 자리에 오는 to부정사가 be p.p. 뒤에 바로 붙어 나올 수 있다는 점을 염두에 두어야 한다. (**expect** technicians **to comply** → Technicians **are expected to comply**)

해석 기술자들은 실험실의 모든 안전 규정을 따르도록 준수해야 합니다.

PART 5

1. Marriage counselor Jordan Mitchell advises people ------- a partner who has similar life goals.

(A) find
(B) to find
(C) finding
(D) to have found

2. The security system in the plant allows managers to ------- the manufacturing processes via cameras.

(A) monitors
(B) monitor
(C) monitoring
(D) monitored

3. Vella Beverage's board of directors cited the numerous customer complaints as the main reason for the decision ------- production of all sugary drinks marketed to children.

(A) was discontinuing
(B) have discontinued
(C) to discontinue
(D) will discontinue

4. The first viewer ------- this number and accurately identify the creator of this artwork will win a free trip for two to the Metropolitan Museum of Art.

(A) for calling
(B) call
(C) is called
(D) to call

PART 6

Questions 5-8 refer to the following article.

RICHMOND (July 13) — Portsmith, Inc., announced yesterday the completion of updates to its Epicurious app. Epicurious provides users with the opportunity ------- nearby restaurants, access coupons, and read customer reviews. When users sign in to Epicurious, they will see a map with pinpointed locations of all eating establishments within a five-mile radius. They can search by cuisine type and price ------- and can sort restaurants by ratings to find a good one. -------, with the most recent update, Epicurious will send users alerts about coupons and scheduled promotions. -------.

5. (A) locating
(B) locates
(C) to locate
(D) would have located

6. (A) way
(B) control
(C) source
(D) range

7. (A) And now
(B) In fact
(C) Even so
(D) As though

8. (A) Details will not be disclosed until after the contract is signed.
(B) The app market is also extremely popular these days.
(C) Therefore, there is no reason to lose out on all the excitement.
(D) Thus, this feature is not available any more.

Employees are reminded to keep office doors closed ------- entry by unauthorized personnel.

(A) prevent   (B) preventing   (C) prevented   (D) to prevent

콕 찍어 포인트 ⋯ to부정사는 문장 내에서 명사, 형용사, 부사 역할을 할 수 있다.

해설 빈칸은 명사구를 완전한 문장에 연결하는 자리이다. 문맥상 '허가받지 않은 직원들의 출입을 막기 위해'라는 의미가 되어야 자연스러우므로, 부사구를 완성하는 to부정사 (D)가 정답이다.

해석 직원들은 허가받지 않은 직원이 들어오는 것을 방지하기 위해 사무실 문을 닫아 두도록 당부 받는다.

➤➤ to부정사는 부사 역할을 하여 주로 '~하기 위해서'라는 목적의 의미를 나타낸다.

To apply for this grant, applicants should be at least 3 years into their PhD program.
이 보조금에 지원하려면, 지원자는 박사 과정에 적어도 3년은 있어야 한다.

➤➤ to부정사의 목적의 의미를 강조할 때는 in order to나 so as to를 쓴다.

All proceeds from the fundraiser will be used **(in order/so as) to support families in need**.
기금 모금 행사의 수익금 전액은 어려움에 처한 가정을 지원하기 위해 사용될 것이다.

➤➤ to부정사를 동반하는 형용사 「be + 형용사 + to부정사」

be due/scheduled to do ~할 예정이다	be about to do 막 ~하려고 하다	be supposed to do ~하기로 되어 있다
be likely to do ~할 것 같다	be ready to do ~할 준비가 되다	be hesitant to do ~하기를 망설이다
be pleased to do ~하게 되어 기쁘다	be eager to do ~하기를 열망하다	be reluctant to do ~하기를 꺼리다
be willing to do 기꺼이 ~하다	feel free to do 기꺼이 ~하다	be eligible to do ~할 자격이 있다
be able to do ~할 수 있다	be sure to do 반드시 ~하다	be available to do ~할 시간이 있다

Hello Smoothie **is pleased to announce** the opening of a new location.
Hello Smoothie는 새 지점의 개점을 발표하게 되어 기쁩니다.

➤➤ 「too + 형용사/부사 + to부정사」 구문 '너무 …해서 ~할 수 없는'

It is **too time-consuming to update** all product information on the Web site manually.
너무 시간 소모가 커서 웹사이트에 수작업으로 모든 제품 정보를 업데이트할 수 없다.

➤➤ 「형용사/부사 + enough + to부정사」 구문 '…하기에 충분히 ~한'

The new hiking shoes are **durable enough to withstand** harsh weather conditions.
새 등산화는 악천후를 견디기에 내구성이 충분히 강하다.

 알면 3초!   ➤➤ 빈칸이 문장 맨 앞에 올 때 'to부정사 vs. 분사 구문'은 해석으로 판별한다.

(To be / Being) eligible for the sales manager position, candidates must have a university degree in marketing.

(To be / Being) a sales manager, Mr. Simpson is in charge of the overall branch operations.

두 예문을 비교해보자. 빈칸이 문장 맨 앞에 와 있고, 보기에 to부정사와 분사가 모두 등장하는 경우, 분사 구문도 목적을 나타내는 to부정사처럼 문장 맨 앞에 위치할 수 있으니 무작정 to부정사를 고르면 안 된다. to부정사는 목적의 '~하기 위해서'로, 분사는 주절의 주어를 바로 꾸며주는 식으로 해석하여 문맥상 어울리는 형태를 고른다. 첫 번째 예문은 영업 매니저 직책을 갖기 위해 지원자들은 학위가 있어야 한다는 내용이므로 To be가 정답이며, 두 번째 예문은 영업 매니저인 Simpson 씨가 전반적인 지사 운영을 담당한다는 내용이므로 Being이 정답이다.

해석 영업 매니저 직책 요건에 부합하려면, 지원자들은 마케팅 학사 학위가 있어야 한다.
영업 매니저인 Simpson 씨는 전반적인 지사 운영을 담당한다.

PART 5

1. The institute requires its researchers to provide it with the written evidence needed ------- the financing of their projects.

(A) support
(B) supported
(C) will support
(D) to support

2. All authorized staff must enter a personal identification number ------- enter the laboratory.

(A) in light of
(B) always
(C) involving
(D) in order to

3. Given the present real estate market, Cristobal Investments is ------- to acquire new property.

(A) delinquent
(B) worthy
(C) hesitant
(D) ineffective

4. After evaluating each applicant interested in the sales representative position, we are ------- to inform you that you have been selected for the job.

(A) responsible
(B) concerned
(C) innovative
(D) pleased

PART 6

Questions 5-8 refer to the following e-mail.

To: All@TarkingtonAccounting.co.uk
From: Philippa Houston
Date: 16 December
Subject: Employee Manual Seminar

Tarkington Accounting has made some changes to its employee manual. -------. Though the majority of policies and procedures are unchanged, a few key adjustments have been made. The manual now features guidelines on online data storage, encrypted communications, and special expense reports. The process for requesting time off has also been -------. The new process should be more straightforward and fairer to everyone.

Each employee will be expected to attend a meeting to go over these guidelines. Meetings will be conducted from 5 P.M. to 6 P.M. every Tuesday and Thursday until the end of the month in Conference Room D. -------, employees will be expected to sign a document certifying that they've gotten a copy of the manual and understand its contents. Make arrangements with your department head ------- one of these meetings.

Philippa Houston,
Human Resources Team

5. (A) The new design changes will be implemented on 1 January.
(B) These are the first alterations to be made in 5 years.
(C) Our in-house counsel created the new rules.
(D) We appreciate your cooperation in this matter.

6. (A) waived
(B) informed
(C) updated
(D) debated

7. (A) Afterwards
(B) In contrast
(C) To sum up
(D) As it turns out

8. (A) in attendance at
(B) while attending
(C) who attended
(D) to attend

원형 부정사를 취하는 동사 help

Ms. Barton's architectural model helped the board ------- how the theater should look after the planned remodeling.

(A) imagined   (B) imagine   (C) imagination   (D) imaginative

콕 찍어 포인트 ··· 동사 help가 5형식 문장에서 쓰일 때, 목적격 보어 자리에는 to부정사 또는 원형 부정사가 올 수 있다.

해설 빈칸은 동사 help와 목적어 the board 뒤의 목적격 보어 자리이다. 빈칸 뒤의 how 명사절을 목적어로 취할 수 있는 원형 부정사 (B)가 정답이다.

해석 Barton 씨의 건축 모형은 위원회로 하여금 예정된 리모델링 후 극장이 어떤 모습일지 상상할 수 있게 도와주었다.

>> 동사 help는 목적격 보어 자리에 to부정사와 원형 부정사를 모두 쓸 수 있다.

「help + 목적어 + (to) do」 구문 '~가 …하는 것을 돕다'

Company training programs **help** new hires **(to) improve** their communication skills.
회사 교육 프로그램은 신입 직원들이 의사소통 기술을 개선하는 것을 돕는다.
→ 원형 부정사란 to가 없는 부정사로, 형태는 동사 원형과 같다.

>> 동사 help는 목적어 자리에 to부정사와 원형 부정사를 모두 쓸 수 있다.

「help + (to) do」 구문 '~하는 것을 돕다'

Flexible work hours will **help (to) reduce** traffic congestion, particularly in metropolitan areas.
탄력 근무제는 특히 대도시 지역에서 교통 혼잡을 감소시키는 데 도움이 될 것이다.

---

3 SECS 알면 3초!   >> 동사 make도 목적격 보어로 원형 부정사를 취한다.

Akcu Studio can use photo manipulation techniques to make your images ------- more attractive.

(A) looked   (B) have looked   (C) looks   (D) look

「사역동사 make / let / have + A + 원형 부정사」 'A가 ~하게 하다'

동사 make는 3형식 동사로서 목적어를 바로 취할 수도 있고 5형식 동사로서 뒤에 「목적어 + 목적격 보어」의 어순을 갖기도 한다. 그런데 make의 역할을 이 정도만 알고 있다면 목적격 보어 자리에 동사 원형이 오는 예문은 낯설게 느껴질 것이다. 흔히 목적격 보어 자리에는 명사나 형용사가 오고, 명사가 올 때는 목적어와 동격, 형용사가 올 때는 목적어를 서술해 주는 기능을 한다고 하는데, 5형식 동사로 make가 오게 되면 목적격 보어 자리에 명사나 형용사 외에 원형 부정사 즉, 동사 원형도 올 수 있다. 이때의 make를 사역동사라 부르며 '목적어가 ~하게 하다'라는 의미를 갖는다. let이나 have 등도 목적격 보어 자리에 원형 부정사를 취하여 사역동사의 역할을 한다는 점도 함께 알아두자. 위 문제에서 make는 사역동사이고 빈칸은 목적격 보어 자리이므로 원형 부정사 (D)가 정답이다.

해석 Akcu 스튜디오는 귀하의 이미지를 더 매력적으로 보이게 하도록 사진 조작 기술을 사용할 수 있다.

PART 5

1. My manager highly recommended taking the training course on the new marketing automation system because it will help ------- work efficiency.

(A) improves
(B) improved
(C) improving
(D) improve

2. Many stores provide free gifts to customers who share their social media posts ------- they help build the company's online presence.

(A) despite
(B) because
(C) besides
(D) instead

3. According to the employee survey, flexible work hours help employees ------- relationships with their family.

(A) would strengthen
(B) strengthen
(C) strengthened
(D) will strengthen

4. Mr. Parker in the lost and found department is tired of his job helping people ------- their lost phones.

(A) support
(B) remind
(C) locate
(D) behave

PART 6

Questions 5-8 refer to the following e-mail.

To: Jody Triesch
From: Gerald Ko
Date: 11 November
Subject: Online biography
Attachment: summary

Jody,

When you get a chance, please write and upload a biography to our Web site regarding our new CEO, Ms. Heidecker. I included a summary detailing her many ------- at our company. If you require additional information about what she has done, I'd recommend speaking with Rebecca Stevens. 5. -------. If you can, make the biography ------- like a magazine profile. It would be great if we can 6. 7. get some news outlets or social media sites to use it for a story. More press will ------- improve our 8. chances of attracting other talented individuals to the company. Please send me a completed draft by the end of the business day on Wednesday.

Best,

Gerald Ko

5. (A) measurements
(B) commitments
(C) coworkers
(D) achievements

6. (A) Ms. Stevens and Ms. Heidecker have often worked together on various projects.
(B) I was very impressed with the new design for the Web site.
(C) I will be meeting with Ms. Heidecker this afternoon.
(D) The celebration will take place on Wednesday.

7. (A) to seem
(B) seeming
(C) seem
(D) seems

8. (A) before
(B) hopefully
(C) currently
(D) again

Since ------- Internet service providers, employees at CGC Inc. have reported significantly fewer technical difficulties.

(A) change　　　　(B) changed　　　　(C) changing　　　　(D) to change

해설　빈칸은 전치사 since의 목적어 자리이자, 빈칸 뒤의 명사구를 받을 수 있는 동사의 역할도 해야 한다. 따라서, 명사와 동사의 기능을 모두 갖는 동명사 (C)가 정답이다.

해석　인터넷 서비스 제공 업체를 바꾼 이후로, CGC 사의 직원들은 기술적 어려움이 현저히 줄어들었다고 보고했다.

>> 동명사는 「동사 원형 + -ing」의 형태로 명사 역할을 하여 주어, 목적어, 보어 자리에 온다.

주어	**Assisting** clients courteously **is** how we keep them satisfied. ❶ 동명사 주어는 단수 취급한다. 고객들을 공손하게 돕는 것이 우리가 그들을 계속 만족스럽게 하는 방법이다.
목적어	*타동사의 목적어* The digital content team **recommends enhancing** video quality to attract more viewers. 디지털 컨텐츠 팀은 더 많은 시청자들을 끌어 모으기 위해 영상 질을 개선할 것을 권한다. The security department is in the process **of establishing** its new safety guidelines. 보안 부서는 새 안전 지침을 마련하는 중이다. *전치사의 목적어*
보어	One of the roles of a director is helping resolve conflicts among employees. 이사의 역할 중 하나는 직원들 간의 갈등을 해결하는 것을 돕는 것이다.

>> 동명사도 동사처럼 다양한 형태를 갖는다.

기본형	The mobile app company increased its user engagement by **expanding** its customer base globally. *동사 원형 + -ing* 그 모바일 앱 회사는 고객 기반을 전 세계적으로 확대함으로써 사용자 참여도를 높였다.
수동형	Mr. Hall has a good chance of **being promoted**. *being p.p.* Hall 씨가 승진할 가능성이 높다.
완료형	Ms. Finley got an award for **having invented** a cutting edge 3-D printer. *having p.p.* Finley 씨는 최첨단 3D 프린터를 발명한 것으로 상을 받았다.

>> 동명사의 의미상 주어는 동명사 앞에 목적격이나 소유격으로 나타낸다.

The CEO objected to **you[your] becoming** a member of the board.
CEO는 당신이 이사회의 멤버가 되는 것에 반대했다.

 알면 3초!　　>> 동명사도 태와 시제를 구별해서 쓴다.

Mr. Walker was given a bonus after (appointing / **being appointed**) as sales director last month.
(**having sold** / being sold) 11 cars in just one week.

to부정사와 마찬가지로 동명사도 동사적 성질을 띠고 있어서 태와 시제를 반영하여 나타낼 수 있는데, 동명사와 의미상 주어가 능동 관계라면 기본형인 「동사 원형 + -ing」를 쓰고, 수동 관계라면 수동형인 being p.p.를 쓴다. 마찬가지로, 동명사의 시제가 본동사보다 더 이전에 일어난 일임을 보여줄 때는 완료형인 having p.p.를 쓴다. 이 원리를 적용하면, 첫 번째 예문은 appoint와 의미상 주어인 Walker 씨가 수동 관계(Walker 씨가 임명의 대상)이므로 being appointed가 답이 되고, 두 번째 예문은 차량을 판매한 행위가 보너스를 받은 시점 이전에 일어난 일이므로 완료형인 having sold가 답이 된다. 참고로 두 번째 예문은 단순히 Walker 씨가 11대의 차량을 판매한 주체라는 사실만 보여주는 거라면 having sold 대신 기본형인 selling을 써도 무방하다.

해석　Walker 씨는 지난달 영업 이사로 임명되고 나서 상여금을 받았다.
　　　　Walker 씨는 일주일 만에 열한 대의 차량을 판매한 뒤 상여금을 받았다.

PART 5

1. ------- sales meetings is one of the secretary's most important responsibilities.

(A) Schedule
(B) Scheduling
(C) Scheduled
(D) To Schedule

2. At Ivanhoe Rental Properties, all tenants are responsible for ------- their own apartments.

(A) maintain
(B) to maintain
(C) maintained
(D) maintaining

3. Because of her education at an award-winning culinary institute in Rome, Maria Espinoza is ------- skilled at preparing tasty pasta dishes.

(A) approximately
(B) hardly
(C) especially
(D) swiftly

4. The video *From Mansion to Inn* guides viewers in ------- old homes into successful bed and breakfasts.

(A) transporting
(B) watching
(C) debating
(D) developing

PART 6

Questions 5-8 refer to the following notice.

It is regrettable that the deal with LCK Ventures fell through. However, it is with great pleasure we ------- a new deal with Baratic Corporation. While Baratic is a company best known for providing
5.
funding for tech start-ups, the management team there saw the need for ------- in the firm's portfolio.
6.
With the funding, we can proceed with this year's plan to expand into new areas. ------- areas have
7.
been suggested as lucrative opportunities, and we will make a decision regarding the location of
our expansion shortly. -------. Detailed plans for the next quarter will be posted when the decision is
8.
finalized.

5. (A) revelation
(B) reveal
(C) revealing
(D) revealed

6. (A) retraction
(B) confirmation
(C) diversification
(D) conversion

7. (A) Introducing
(B) Several
(C) Prepare
(D) Throughout

8. (A) The northern parts of the city have looked promising.
(B) We have been forced to downsize in recent times.
(C) Suggestions are rarely accepted in such meetings.
(D) The tech industry has been underfunded recently.

CASE 47 동명사 vs. 명사

Investors are advised to read all enclosed information before ------- an account.

(A) open   (B) opening   (C) opened   (D) to open

콕 찍어 포인트 … 동명사는 명사 자리에 올 수 있으며, 타동사의 동명사는 동사처럼 목적어를 취할 수 있다.

해설 빈칸은 전치사 before의 목적어 자리이다. 빈칸 뒤에 목적어 an account가 있으므로 동명사 (B)가 정답이다.

해석 투자자들은 계좌를 개설하기 전에 동봉된 모든 정보를 읽어 보라고 권고받는다.

▶▶ 명사는 뒤에 목적어가 바로 올 수 없지만, 동명사는 뒤에 목적어를 취할 수 있다.

↗ renewal (X)
Thank you for **renewing your passport** in advance.
미리 당신의 여권을 갱신해주셔서 감사합니다.

▶▶ 명사는 형용사의 수식을 받고, 동명사는 부사의 수식을 받는다.

↗ thorough (X)
Install the printer after **thoroughly reviewing** the user manual.
사용설명서를 꼼꼼하게 검토한 뒤 프린터를 설치하십시오.

↗ unanimously (X)
cf. Legislators were able to reach **unanimous agreement** on the new tax law.
입법자들은 새 세법에 대해 만장일치로 합의에 이를 수 있었다.

▶▶ 명사 앞에는 관사(a / an / the)가 올 수 있지만, 동명사 앞에는 관사가 올 수 없다.

↗ approving (X)
The contract will not be signed without **the approval** of the owner.
계약은 소유주의 승인 없이는 체결되지 않을 것이다.

 알면 3초!   ▶▶ 동명사 vs. -ing형 명사

All employees must receive ------- training in the use of delicate equipment.

(A) adequate   (B) adequately   (C) adequacy   (D) adequateness

-ing형 명사

accounting 회계	clothing 의류	marketing 마케팅	restructuring 구조 조정	training 교육, 훈련
advertising 광고 (행위)	dining 식사	opening 공석, 개장	seating 좌석 (배치)	ticketing 발권
boarding 탑승	funding 자금 조달	planning 계획 수립	screening 검열	understanding 이해
catering 음식 공급	housing 주택 공급	pricing 가격 책정	staffing 직원 채용	
cleaning 청소	mailing 우편물 발송	processing 처리	spending 지출	

❶ -ing형 명사도 일반 명사와 마찬가지로 관사나 형용사의 수식을 받을 수 있다. (동명사와 구별)
❶ -ing형 명사는 주로 불가산 명사이고, 일반 명사는 주로 가산 명사이다. (일반 명사와 구별)

위에 정리된 공식대로라면 빈칸은 training을 수식하는 자리이고, training은 -ing 형태의 동명사일 테니, 동명사를 수식하는 부사를 선택하기 쉽지만, 아니다. 여기서 training은 '교육'이란 뜻의 명사로 쓰였고, 그래서 정답은 형용사 adequate이다. 분명 동명사처럼 보이지만 '-ing'로 끝나는 명사가 존재한다는 사실을 간과해서는 안 된다. 이 -ing형 명사는 대개 일반 명사에 -ing를 붙여서 '행위'나 '활동'의 의미를 가미한 것으로 이를 테면, fund는 '자금'을 뜻하지만, funding은 '자금 조달 (행위)'를 의미하는 것과 같은 논리이다. 따라서 토익에 등장하는 -ing형 명사를 최대한 익혀 두어야 동명사로 쓰였는지, -ing형 명사로 쓰였는지, 더 나아가 -ing형 명사가 답인지, 일반 명사가 답인지를 쉽게 구별할 수 있다.

해석 전 직원들은 정교한 장비를 사용할 때 반드시 적절한 교육을 받아야 한다.

PART 5

1. The HR Department decided that Friday's reception will require ------- seating.

(A) additionally
(B) additional
(C) additions
(D) addition

2. Felrafel Enterprises is interested in ------- new business models as part of an ongoing effort to expand its production lines.

(A) explore
(B) exploration
(C) exploring
(D) explored

3. After ------- the product specifications, Ms. Nunez decided not to upgrade the refrigeration system in her factory.

(A) assess
(B) assessing
(C) assessment
(D) assessed

4. The temporary ------- of schools in the area was unavoidable due to the inclement weather conditions.

(A) closed
(B) closable
(C) closing
(D) close

PART 6

Questions 5-8 refer to the following memo.

To: all@davidwallaceuniversity.edu
From: President Doug Benson
Date: January 2
Subject: Common spaces

I'm excited to announce that the refurbished Foster-Allen Hall will re-open this semester. In addition to hosting classes, the building will now include several common spaces for meetings or activities. All of these rooms are ---5--- from the Foster-Allen central lobby.

The spaces vary in size, holding anywhere from 10 to 25 guests, and they may be used by students and staff alike. ---6---. Patrick Lucas will be in charge of room reservations until February 15. ---7---, he will go back to work in the Admissions Department. We're currently interviewing candidates to serve as a permanent Campus Event Coordinator. This employee will be in charge of ---8--- reservations of the new rooms.

5. (A) adequate
(B) accessible
(C) allowable
(D) aligned

6. (A) Advance booking is required to use one of the spaces.
(B) Mr. Lucas will lead the opening session of the conference.
(C) The remodeling project has been postponed until the summer.
(D) More rooms have also been added to Butler Library.

7. (A) At that time
(B) In a word
(C) Moreover
(D) Similarly

8. (A) supervision
(B) supervise
(C) supervises
(D) supervising

CASE 48 　동명사 관용 표현

Please do not forget to switch off the air conditioner when you have finished ------- the conference room.

(A) to use　　　　(B) useful　　　　(C) using　　　　(D) use

> **해설** '~을 끝마치다'라는 의미의 타동사 finish는 동명사를 목적어로 취하므로 (C)가 정답이다. 빈칸 뒤에 오는 the conference room은 동명사 using의 목적어에 해당한다.
>
> **해석** 회의실 사용을 마치면 에어컨을 끄는 것을 잊지 마세요.

▶▶ 동명사를 목적어로 취하는 동사 「3V + 동명사」

제안	recommend 권하다, 추천하다 suggest 제안하다	
중단	stop 멈추다 quit 그만두다 discontinue 중단하다 finish 끝내다	**+ 동명사** ~하기를
회피	avoid 피하다 mind 꺼려하다 postpone/delay 미루다 deny 부인하다 give up 포기하다	
기타	consider 고려하다 enjoy 즐기다 appreciate 고마워하다 include 포함하다 keep 계속하다	

　　　　　　　　　　　　　　　　to honor (X)
Some board members **suggested honoring** the founder of the company at the annual reception.
일부 이사회 임원들은 연례 연회에서 회사 창업주를 기리자고 제안했다.

▶▶ 동명사 관용 표현

be busy (in) -ing ~하느라 바쁘다	have difficulty[a hard time] -ing ~하는 데 어려움을 겪다
be capable of -ing ~할 수 있다	keep (on) -ing 계속해서 ~하다
be worth -ing ~할 가치가 있다	on[upon] -ing ~하자마자
cannot help -ing ~하지 않을 수 없다	prevent[prohibit] A from -ing A가 ~하는 것을 막다
feel like -ing ~하고 싶다	refrain from -ing ~하는 것을 삼가다
go -ing ~하러 가다	spend 시간/돈 -ing ~하는 데 시간/돈을 쓰다

　　　　　　　　　　　　　　　　to design (X)
The senior architect **spent weeks designing** a plan to renovate the resort.
선임 건축가는 리조트 수리 계획을 디자인하는 데 몇 주를 보냈다.

알면 3초!　　▶▶ 전치사 to vs. to부정사의 to

Daily Stock Exchange Broadcasting is dedicated to ------- accurate investment information.

(A) providing　　　　(B) provide　　　　(C) provided　　　　(D) provision

「전치사 to + 명사 / 동명사」 관용 표현

be accustomed[used] to ~에 익숙하다	be committed[devoted, dedicated] to ~에 전념하다		
be entitled to ~할 자격이 있다	be opposed to ~에 반대하다	be attributed to ~에 기인하다	
consent to ~에 동의하다	lead to ~을 초래하다	object to ~에 반대하다	**+ 명사/동명사**
contribute to ~에 기여하다	look forward to ~을 고대하다	respond to ~에 대응하다	
according to ~에 따라	in addition to ~에 더하여	prior to ~ 전에	

to 뒤에 빈칸이 들어간 문제들은 보기에 꼭 동사 원형과 명사 또는 동명사가 주어진다. 빈칸 앞의 to가 전치사 to인지, to부정사의 to인지를 알고 있는지 묻는 것이다. 이 to가 전치사인지, to부정사의 to인지를 구별하기 위해 위의 전치사 to 관련 표현들을 외워두는 것이 좋다. 위 문제에서 be dedicated to 뒤에는 명사나 동명사가 나와야 하는데 빈칸 뒤에 오는 명사구를 목적어로 받아야 하므로 동명사 (A)가 정답이다.

> **해석** Daily 증권 거래 방송은 정확한 투자 정보를 제공하는 데 전념하고 있다.

PART 5

1. The designer suggested ------- the font to enhance the readability of the brochure.
(A) change
(B) changing
(C) to change
(D) changes

2. It would be better for Fabulous Footwear to discontinue ------- sandals and focus on ankle boots instead.
(A) produce
(B) would produce
(C) producing
(D) to produce

3. ------- arriving at the main building, all visitors must sign in at the reception desk and obtain an identification tag.
(A) Out of
(B) Within
(C) Upon
(D) Up to

4. The spike in interest in Pavilion Tech can be ------- to the variety of projects the company has undertaken over the past few months.
(A) amplified
(B) subtracted
(C) confirmed
(D) attributed

PART 6

Questions 5-8 refer to the following e-mail.

To: Ronald Kuba
From: Piper Keurig
Date: November 16
Subject: Tuesday's meeting

Dear Professor Kuba,

I appreciate you making time to discuss graduate programs in Biology. Your ------- were extremely helpful, and I'm now planning to write e-mails to several universities regarding paid teaching assistant positions before applying. I'll start with the schools you mentioned.
5.

Also, per your suggestion, I will ------- a membership in the Biological Sciences Graduates Society's (BSGS) online forum. -------. It's good to know that this type of resource is available on the Web.
6.
7.

Once again, thank you so much for your ------- advice.
8.

Gratefully,

Piper Keurig

5. (A) discoveries
(B) changes
(C) questionnaires
(D) insights

6. (A) determine
(B) consider
(C) promote
(D) anticipate

7. (A) This job opening will be filled very soon.
(B) I am not sure I will extend my membership next month.
(C) It will be helpful discussing issues with my fellow peers.
(D) I look forward to attending the lecture on her latest research.

8. (A) generous
(B) generosity
(C) generousness
(D) generously

CASE 49 현재분사 vs. 과거분사

The ------- budget cuts should help raise cash to fund construction of a new highway.

(A) propose   (B) proposing   (C) proposed   (D) proposal

콕 찍어 포인트 ⋯ 분사는 형용사처럼 명사를 수식할 수 있다. 현재분사는 능동(~한 상태를 유발하는)의 의미를, 과거분사는 수동(~한 상태가 된)의 의미를 갖는다.

해설 빈칸 뒤의 명사구인 예산 삭감은 사람들에 의해 제안을 받는 수동의 의미를 가지므로 과거분사 (C)가 정답이다.

해석 제안된 예산 삭감은 새로운 고속도로 건설 자금을 조달하는 데 도움이 될 것이다.

▶▶ 분사는 동사 원형에 -ing나 -ed를 붙여 형용사처럼 쓸 수 있도록 변형된 형태이다. 분사는 「동사 원형 + -ing」 형태의 현재분사와 「동사 원형 + -ed」 형태의 과거분사로 나뉜다.

현재분사	Please submit **documentation verifying** your vaccination status. → verified (X) 당신의 백신 접종 상태를 증명하는 서류를 제출하세요. [명사 뒤에서 수식] → 명사 '서류'는 증명의 주체이므로 능동의 현재분사(~하는, ~하고 있는)를 쓴다.
과거분사	→ revising (X) Please submit a **revised copy** of the brochure design by tomorrow. 수정된 소책자 디자인 사본을 내일까지 제출하세요. [명사 앞에서 수식] → 명사 '사본'은 수정의 대상이므로 수동의 과거분사(~된, ~되는)를 쓴다.

▶▶ 분사는 명사의 앞뒤에 와서 명사를 수식하거나 주어 / 목적어를 서술하는 주격 / 목적격 보어 역할을 한다. 명사를 수식 / 서술할 때, 명사와 분사의 관계가 능동이면 현재분사를, 수동이면 과거분사를 쓴다.

주격 보어	The **decision** to replace the manager of the cafeteria remains **unchanged**. → unchanging (X) 구내식당의 매니저를 교체하기 위한 결정이 계속 바뀌지 않고 있다. → 주어인 '결정'은 변경의 대상이므로 수동의 과거분사를 쓴다.
목적격 보어	→ informing (X) We need to keep our **customers informed** of any data leak. 우리는 고객들이 데이터 유출에 대한 정보를 계속해서 받도록 해야 한다. → 목적어인 '고객들'은 데이터 유출에 대한 통지의 대상이므로 수동의 과거분사를 쓴다.

▶▶ 명사를 수식/서술할 때, 자동사는 항상 현재분사를 쓴다.

Walker Wealth Management has stopped its marketing activity in order to focus on **existing customers** for the time being. → existed (X)
Walker 자산 운용은 당분간 기존 고객에 집중하기 위해 마케팅 활동을 중단했다.

 알면 3초!   ▶▶ 빈칸 뒤에 목적어가 있으면 현재분사, 목적어가 없으면 과거분사가 답이다.

A renowned Web site ------- people to make hotel reservations has attracted more than two million members.

(A) helps   (B) helping   (C) helped   (D) has helped

위 문제는 단문 구조로서 has attracted가 본동사로 와 있으므로 동사 helps와 has helped를 답에서 제외시키면 현재분사인 helping과 과거분사인 helped만이 남는다. 분사의 수식을 받는 명사와의 의미를 따져 능동이면 현재분사를, 수동이면 과거분사를 고르라는 문제인데, 명사와 분사의 의미만 따지면 웹사이트가 도움을 준다는 건지, 도움을 받는다는 건지 판단하기 어려워 문장을 다 해석하는 일이 생긴다. 대부분의 동사가 목적어를 동반하는 타동사라는 점, 그리고 이 타동사가 분사화 된다는 점에 착안하여 명사를 후치 수식할 때 뒤에 목적어가 있을 땐 현재분사, 뒤에 목적어 없이 부사나 전명구만이 와 있을 땐 과거분사를 쓴다는 공식을 도출할 수 있으니, 빈칸 뒤의 목적어 유무만 확인해도 현재분사를 쓸지, 과거분사를 쓸지 쉽게 판단할 수 있다. 따라서 빈칸 뒤의 목적어 people만 보고도 (B)를 답으로 고를 수 있는 것이다. 단, 자동사나 수여 동사(4V)의 분사는 주의가 필요한데, 목적어가 오지 못하는 자동사는 수동태로 쓸 수 없는 것과 마찬가지로 수동의 과거분사로도 쓸 수 없으며, 두 개의 목적어를 취하는 수여 동사(4V)는 수동태로 써도 남은 목적어가 뒤따라 오기 때문에 뒤에 목적어가 있더라도 과거분사를 쓸 수 있다.

해석 사람들이 호텔 예약하는 걸 도와주는 한 유명 웹사이트는 2백만 명 이상의 회원을 유치했다.

CASE 집중훈련

PART 5

1. Ms. Whitlock is examining the bids to choose the company best ------- for the project.
(A) qualify
(B) qualified
(C) qualifies
(D) qualification

2. Mobile Meals has customizable catering menus to satisfy all clients' ------- needs.
(A) entertain
(B) entertaining
(C) entertained
(D) entertains

3. The executives of Morton Fragrances sent an e-mail to the staff members ------- them for the exceptional sales revenue this quarter.
(A) commend
(B) commended
(C) commentary
(D) commending

4. Because of the ------- typhoon, ferry services will be suspended for the next two days.
(A) elaborated
(B) adjoining
(C) exposed
(D) impending

PART 6

Questions 5-8 refer to the following e-mail.

To: Product Design Team
From: Brandon Conner
Date: 12 July
Subject: Celebration dinner

Dear Team:

To celebrate the hard work from ------- in this team, I would like to propose a team dinner next week.
    5.
I have ------- for a fantastic Italian restaurant from Ms. Bell, the head of sales. She seems to know
    6.
all of the good restaurants in this area. I understand there are people with dietary restrictions. -------.
    7.
I would like to also invite Ellis Holt to join us. As you know, he will be joining our team next month.
------- will help him acclimatize to our team greatly.
    8.

Sincerely,

Brandon Conner, Head of Product Design
KD Manufacturing

5. (A) everybody
(B) other
(C) either
(D) one

6. (A) been recommending
(B) recommending
(C) recommended
(D) a recommendation

7. (A) I confirmed that it does cater to vegetarians and vegans.
(B) We can avoid working on weekends if we arrive a little earlier.
(C) The new project will be launched this quarter.
(D) Other teams have exceeded their monthly budgets already.

8. (A) Initiations
(B) Presentations
(C) Introductions
(D) Inductions

CASE 50 | 감정 동사의 현재분사 vs. 과거분사

The board members who interviewed Ms. Tan were very ------- by her extensive work experience.

(A) impress   (B) impression   (C) impressive   (D) impressed

해설 빈칸은 be동사 뒤의 주격 보어 자리이다. 주어가 The board members로 사람 명사이며, 이사진이 깊은 인상을 받은 상태가 되어야 문맥상 자연스러우므로 과거분사 (C)가 정답이다.

해석 Tan 씨를 면접 본 이사진은 그녀의 폭넓은 업무 경험에 매우 깊은 인상을 받았다.

≫ 수식/서술의 대상인 명사가 감정을 일으키면 현재분사, 감정을 느끼면 과거분사를 쓴다.

The shareholders found the **dividend** rather **disappointing**, contrary to expectations of big profits.
주주들은 큰 수익의 기대에 반하여 배당금이 다소 실망스럽다고 느꼈다. ↳ disappointed (X)
→ 배당금(dividend)은 실망스러운 감정을 일으키는 원인이므로 현재분사(disappointing)를 쓴다.

The **members** of the R&D Department were **disappointed** with the consumer feedback regarding their new idea. ↳ disappointing (X)
연구개발 부서의 직원들은 새 아이디어에 관한 고객 피드백에 실망했다.
→ 직원들(members)은 실망스러운 감정을 느끼는 대상이므로 과거분사(disappointed)를 쓴다.

≫ 감정을 나타내는 타동사 3V

기쁨/만족	실망/불만	놀람/혼란
amuse 즐겁게 하다	annoy 짜증나게 하다	alarm 놀라게 하다
encourage 격려하다	depress 좌절시키다	amaze 놀라게 하다
excite 흥미진진하게 만들다	disappoint 실망시키다	bewilder 당황하게 하다
fascinate 매료시키다	disturb 불안하게 하다	confuse 당황하게 하다
impress 감명을 주다	exhaust 지치게 하다	embarrass 당황하게 하다
interest 흥미를 끌다	frustrate 좌절시키다	distract 산만하게 하다
please 기쁘게 하다	worry 걱정시키다	overwhelm 압도하다
satisfy 만족시키다	tire 피곤하게 하다	surprise 놀라게 하다

 알면 3초!   ≫ 수식을 받는 명사가 사람이면 과거분사, 사물이면 현재분사가 답이다.

The HR team of Intec Combo has interviewed more than 100 applicants ------- in the advertised position.

(A) interested   (B) interest   (C) interesting   (D) interests

감정을 느끼는 건 사람이고 이때는 과거분사를 쓴다는 것만 기억해두면 사물 등 그 이외의 명사들에는 현재분사를 쓰면 된다. 이를 공식화해 두면, 흥미를 느끼는 지원자인지, 흥미를 유발시키는 지원자인지 일일이 따져 가며 시간을 들일 필요가 없다. 위와 같은 문제의 체크 포인트는 딱 두 가지이다. '빈칸 앞의 수식을 받는 명사가 사람인가, 사물인가? (감정 동사 체크)' 그리고 '빈칸 뒤에 목적어가 있는가, 없는가? (더블 체크)' 위 문제에서 빈칸 앞에 수식을 받는 명사가 사람 명사이므로 과거분사 (A)가 정답이다.

해석 Intec Combo의 인사팀은 광고된 자리에 관심이 있는 100명 이상의 지원자들을 면접했다.

해설서 p.71

PART 5

1. I am ------- to announce that our advertising campaign was a huge success.
(A) pleased
(B) please
(C) pleasing
(D) pleases

2. Analysis of the sales data revealed some ------- information about the spending habits of customers in their 20's.
(A) surprising
(B) surprise
(C) surprisingly
(D) surprised

3. Although the latest Blaze tablet PC has received largely positive reviews for its affordable price point, its sales have thus far been -------.
(A) disappoint
(B) disappointed
(C) disappointment
(D) disappointing

4. Sherman Inc. now provides assistance of tuition for personnel interested in the ------- of certification programs.
(A) ambition
(B) recognition
(C) completion
(D) obstruction

PART 6

Questions 5-8 refer to the following e-mail.

To: Christian Shelton
From: web@eatingbetter.com
Date: August 2
Subject: EatingBetter Foods

Dear Mr. Shelton,

We are ------- to introduce EatingBetter Foods, the world's foremost diet and exercise experts. We
    5.
cater to every individual's health goals and work hard to provide only the best nutritional and exercise advice. If you take a look at our Web site, you can see the full list of services we can provide. -------.
    6.
We are committed to bettering the lives of others through healthier eating and living, and we want to help transform your life today.

Contact us today at 030-555-9712 ------- a complimentary consultation. All ------- who sign up
    7.   8.
within the month will receive our grand opening discount of 30 percent off for two months.

Sincerely,

All of us at EatingBetter Foods

5. (A) thrill
(B) thriller
(C) thrilled
(D) thrilling

6. (A) EatingBetter Foods was born from a desire to improve the lives of others.
(B) They include eating plans as well as personalized workout programs.
(C) You can also request a list of our employees and their credentials.
(D) Those may come at additional cost.

7. (A) has been arranged
(B) arranging
(C) to be arranged
(D) to arrange

8. (A) customers
(B) apprentices
(C) athletes
(D) consultants

This year's production target was reduced because of the ------- funds available for raw materials.

(A) limit   (B) limiting   (C) limited   (D) limits

해설 빈칸은 관사와 명사 사이에 위치한 형용사 자리이고, limited는 '제한된'이라는 뜻의 과거분사형 형용사이므로 (C)가 정답이다.

해석 올해 생산 목표가 축소된 것은 원자재로 쓸 수 있는 자금이 한정돼 있었기 때문이다.

▶▶ 형용사로 굳어진 현재분사

challenging task 힘든 과제	lasting impression 지속적인 인상	outstanding professional 뛰어난 전문가
closing speech 폐회사	leading supplier 선두의 공급 업체	preceding year 지난해
demanding supervisor 까다로운 상사	missing luggage 분실된 짐	presiding officer 사회자, 감독관
existing facility 기존 시설	mounting pressure 증가하는 압력	promising candidate 유망한 후보자
following year 다음 해	on a rotating basis 교대로, 돌아가며	remaining paperwork 남은 서류 작업
growing demand 증가하는 수요	opening remarks 개회사	rewarding career 보람 있는 직업
inviting atmosphere 매력적인 분위기	opposing point of view 대립되는 견해	surrounding area 주변 지역

▶▶ 형용사로 굳어진 과거분사

accomplished writer 노련한 작가	dedicated employee 헌신적인 직원	limited time 제한 시간
attached document 첨부된 문서	designated area 지정 구역	preferred means 선호되는 수단
authorized dealer 인가된 딜러	detailed information 상세한 정보	qualified employee 자격을 갖춘 직원
completed form 작성된 서식	distinguished artist 저명한 예술가	renowned artist 유명한 예술가
complicated manual 복잡한 설명서	enclosed brochure 동봉된 책자	skilled employee 숙련된 직원
customized program 맞춤형 프로그램	experienced employee 경험 많은 직원	sophisticated equipment 정교한 장비
damaged goods 파손된 제품	informed decision 현명한 결정	written permission 서면 허가

▶▶ 형용사로 굳어진 분사는 능동/수동 관계를 따지기보다는 그 뜻을 미리 알아두고 그대로 적용한다.

The labor union complained that the current **work hours** were too **demanding** for employees.
노동 조합은 현재의 업무 시간이 직원들에게 너무 부담이 크다고 불평했다. ↳ demanded (X)

The art exhibition will feature sculpture by the **accomplished artist**, Nora Patel.
그 미술전은 기량이 뛰어난 예술가인 Nora Patel의 조각품을 특징으로 할 것이다. ↳ accomplishing (X)

 알면 3초!   ▶▶ 보기에 형용사와 분사가 주어진다면 대개 형용사가 답이다.

Of all the interviewees, Mr. Hernandez has the most ------- background in telecommunications business operations.

(A) impressive   (B) impressed   (C) impresses   (D) impressively

앞서 감정 동사의 분사를 선택하는 스킬처럼 '현재분사 vs. 과거분사'가 아닌, '분사 vs. 순수 형용사'를 선택하는 문제라면 어떻게 하겠는가? 보기의 뜻을 잘 모른다면 그나마 순수 형용사를 고르는 게 좋다. 분사는 동사에서 파생된 형태이기 때문에 대부분 동사의 의미를 그대로 가져와 -ing가 붙으면 능동의 의미를, -ed가 붙으면 수동의 의미를 갖는다. 이를 테면 '깊은 인상을 주다, 감명을 주다'란 뜻의 동사 impress가 과거분사 impressed로 쓰이면 '깊은 인상을 받은, 감명을 받은'으로 해석되는 것처럼 말이다. 그런데 순수 형용사는 동사(impress 인상을 주다)에서 파생된 형용사(impressive 인상적인)일 수도 있지만, 뜻이 가미되거나 모양만 비슷할 뿐 그 자체가 어원일 수도 있다. 즉, 이 순수 형용사는 분사와 비슷한 뜻일 수도, 아닐 수도 있기 때문에 단순 어형 문제에서는 분명 순수 형용사가 분사보다 답이 될 확률이 높다. 위 문제에서는 문맥상 '인상적인 경력'이라는 내용이 되어야 자연스러우므로 순수 형용사 (A)가 답이다.

해석 인터뷰 대상자 중에서 Hernandez 씨가 가장 인상적인 통신사업 운영 경력을 가지고 있다.

PART 5

1. The ------- e-mail is the summary of the order that we are currently processing for you.

(A) follow
(B) following
(C) follows
(D) followed

2. GL Optical Center will be open during the holiday season with ------- hours.

(A) limitation
(B) limiting
(C) limited
(D) limit

3. At Harrison Technical College only ------- instructors will be teaching your classes.

(A) complete
(B) renowned
(C) recent
(D) extended

4. According to the Department of Transportation, the addition of the new bus routes should reduce traffic congestion in the ------- area.

(A) surrounding
(B) surround
(C) surrounds
(D) surrounded

PART 6

Questions 5-8 refer to the following e-mail.

To: Accounting Staff
From: Donna Cutler
Date: December 1
Subject: Ronald Kaepernick

Hello everyone,

I have some bittersweet news to share with you all: Ronald Kaepernick will be leaving our company to join Douglass Financial as a senior analyst. His ------- day here will be next Wednesday, the 12th.
5.

For as long as he has been with us, Ronald has been a crucial part of the accounting team. For the last several years, he has excelled, leading some of our largest and most sensitive projects. While doing so, he ------- strong and lasting bonds with just about everyone he came in contact with at the
6.
company. His commitment to doing excellent work the right way helped us tremendously. -------.
7.

I'd like to wish Ronald the very best going forward and ------- success at his new company.
8.

Best,

Donna Cutler, Vice President

---

5. (A) latest
(B) last
(C) next
(D) nearest

6. (A) develops
(B) developed
(C) will develop
(D) must develop

7. (A) He earned a master's degree in mathematics at the University of Middleton.
(B) The interviews will take place in the East Conference Room, next Thursday.
(C) All of us will miss Ronald's sense of humor as well as his positive attitude.
(D) His work on the project led to record profits in the third quarter of this year.

8. (A) continue
(B) continuation
(C) continues
(D) continued

CASE 52 분사 구문

------- on the recent changes in the industry, the CEO promised the staff that there would still be plenty of career opportunities.

(A) Comment   (B) Commented   (C) Comments   (D) Commenting

콕 찍어 포인트 ··· 분사 구문은 부사절의 '접속사 + (주절과 동일한) 주어'를 생략하고 동사를 분사로 전환한 형태이다. 이때, 부사절의 동사와 주절의 주어와의 능동/수동의 의미 관계에 따라 분사 구문 내 현재/과거분사의 종류가 결정된다.

해설 빈칸은 on 전치사구와 주절을 연결하는 분사 자리이다. comment on[about]이 '~을 논평하다/언급하다'를 의미하며 주절의 주어가 논평한 주체인 사람 명사 CEO 임을 고려할 때, '최근 산업의 변화에 대해 언급하면서, 그 CEO는 ~'이라는 의미가 되어야 문맥상 자연스러우므로 현재분사 (D)가 정답이다.

해석 최근 산업의 변화에 대해 언급하면서, 그 CEO는 직원들에게 여전히 많은 직업 기회가 있을 것이라고 약속했다.

≫ 분사 구문은 부사절의 접속사와 주어를 생략하고 동사를 분사로 전환한 형태이다.

Mr. Samson was hired as assistant manager ~~because he~~ **proved** himself to be the most qualified candidate.
Samson 씨는 자신이 가장 자격을 갖춘 후보임을 증명했기 때문에 부매니저로 채용되었다.
→ 주절의 주어와 부사절의 주어가 같을 때, 부사절의 주어와 접속사를 생략하고 동사를 분사로 전환한다.

= Mr. Samson was hired as assistant manager, (**proving** / proved) himself to be the most qualified candidate.
→ 동사를 분사로 전환할 때, 주어와 능동 관계이면 현재분사를, 수동 관계이면 과거분사를 쓴다.

= Mr. Samson was hired as assistant manager, **having proved** himself to be the most qualified candidate.
→ 분사 구문이 주절의 시제보다 먼저 일어났음을 나타낼 때, 능동은 'having + p.p.', 수동은 'having been + p.p.'를 쓴다.

= **Having proved** himself to be the most qualified candidate, Mr. Samson was hired as assistant manager.
자신이 가장 자격을 갖춘 후보임을 증명한 Samson 씨는 부매니저로 채용되었다.
→ 분사 구문은 주절의 앞 또는 뒤에 올 수 있다.

≫ 주절과 부사절이 동시 상황을 보여줄 때도 분사 구문을 사용할 수 있다.

Velcra, Inc. announced its merger with Kip Co., ~~and it~~ **confirmed** rumors of its confidential corporate strategy.
Velcra 사는 Kip 사와의 합병을 발표했고, 그것은 기밀 경영 전략에 대한 소문을 확인해주었다.

└ Velcra, Inc. announced its merger with Kip Co., **confirming** rumors of its confidential corporate strategy.
Velcra 사는 Kip 사와의 합병을 발표하여 기밀 경영 전략에 대한 소문을 확인해주었다.

 알면 3초!   ≫ 분사 구문의 의미를 명확히 전달하고자 할 때는 접속사를 생략하지 않는다.

When ------- a purchase online, you should use a secure network at all times.

(A) make   (B) making   (C) made   (D) being made

분사 구문은 주절과 종속절의 주어가 같을 때, 종속절의 주어와 접속사를 함께 생략하고 동사를 알맞은 분사 형태로 바꾸는 것이라고 배웠다. 그런데 지금처럼 접속사는 남아 있고 주어만 생략된 형태의 분사 구문을 종종 접할 수 있다. 분사 구문을 사용하는 이유는 문장을 간결하게 나타내기 위함이지만, 모든 문장을 분사 구문화할 수 있다면 굳이 부사절 접속사가 왜 필요하겠는가. 따라서 분사 구문의 의미를 명확히 전달하고 싶을 때는 반복되는 주어만 날리고 접속사는 살려두기로 한 것이다. 이때도 동사를 분사로 바꿔 쓰며, 그 원리는 앞서 배운 내용과 동일하다. 위 문제에서 주절의 주어는 구매한 주체인 사람 명사이므로 빈칸에는 현재분사 (B)가 들어가야 한다.

해석 온라인으로 구매할 때, 언제나 안전한 네트워크를 이용해야 한다.

해설서 p.73

PART 5

1. Ms. Liam, a talk show host, recently secured an exclusive interview with a world-famous pop star, ------- it her most celebrated guest yet.
   (A) making
   (B) made
   (C) make
   (D) makes

2. When ------- used, Tia Skincare Device rejuvenates your face by toning and lifting your skin.
   (A) consist
   (B) consisting
   (C) consistent
   (D) consistently

3. Utilizing high-quality wood will lower the chance of warping, ------- increasing the structural integrity.
   (A) previously
   (B) over
   (C) more
   (D) consequently

4. Staff members who take public transportation to work will be eligible for travel reimbursement ------- Monday.
   (A) given
   (B) thereafter
   (C) starting on
   (D) instead of

PART 6

Questions 5-8 refer to the following advertisement.

Pedro Carter has made a name for himself when it comes to doing taxes. He became so inundated with requests for help on taxes that he took it upon himself to publish a book titled "Doing Taxes the Easy Way." Carter says he hopes the book demonstrates that tax season doesn't have to be frustrating or burdensome. "Taxes really aren't as complicated as they seem. Most people simply don't know the -------," said Carter. "Using my guide, you ------- with your taxes in a day. Plus, you'll
5.   6.
save yourself a lot of money by not hiring a tax expert every year." -------.
7.

Carter's book is expected to hit the stores in November. It will make the perfect gift for the holiday season. Head on down to your local bookstore and ------- your copy!
8.

5. (A) equipment
   (B) component
   (C) progress
   (D) process

6. (A) can be done
   (B) be done
   (C) doing
   (D) have been done

7. (A) Increased tax rates are due to a new policy.
   (B) Carter has recently stepped into a new role at his company.
   (C) A job in the accounting department may be available.
   (D) The book also includes sections on corporate taxes.

8. (A) note
   (B) purchase
   (C) suggest
   (D) mail

1. All visitors must show valid identification at the reception desk before ------- the office building.
   (A) entering
   (B) entered
   (C) enters
   (D) enter

2. The slides for Mr. Neal's board of directors meeting ------- in our team's annual strategy packet next week.
   (A) can include
   (B) has been included
   (C) to include
   (D) will be included

3. Arrow Assurance assigns office workspaces to employees ------- on their seniority.
   (A) depend
   (B) depends
   (C) depended
   (D) depending

4. ------- the contest past the due date, Ms. Chen was surprised to be admitted.
   (A) Had entered
   (B) Entered
   (C) Was entering
   (D) Having entered

5. It was ------- fitting for the company to invite its owner, Mr. Regal, to the reopening of its premises following the devastating earthquake.
   (A) strictly
   (B) extensively
   (C) entirely
   (D) cautiously

6. The Mikku Automatic Vacuum has many convenient features, but -------, it is easy to use.
   (A) as well
   (B) rather
   (C) inclusive
   (D) above all

7. By utilizing more energy-efficient processors, we could reduce our monthly power bills by ------- 6 percent in the long run.
   (A) rougher
   (B) roughly
   (C) roughest
   (D) rough

8. This experimental eye drop will provide much needed ------- from itchiness and dryness.
   (A) relieve
   (B) relieved
   (C) to relieve
   (D) relief

Questions 9-12 refer to the following press release.

AZWELL (August 3) — Chorevic announced today its ------- anticipated release of its StreetWiFi
                                                         9.
system at no charge for mobile phone users.

Compared to the abundant number of hotspots in the city, receiving WiFi service in the suburbs can
be challenging. Chorevic's new WiShare program works by ------- WiFi signals from nearby Chorevic
                                                           10.
routers. Using the combined signal, Chorevic mobile phones will have access to WiFi. -------. As
                                                                                      11.
more people change to Chorevic routers, the network will continue to grow wider. The company
expects its network ------- to lead all service providers in the coming months.
                     12.

For more information on the new WiShare program or about Chorevic's line of products, visit the Web
site at www.chorevicglobal.com.

---

9. (A) greater
(B) greatly
(C) great
(D) greatness

10. (A) pool
(B) pooled
(C) pooling
(D) to pool

11. (A) The previous system may not be
compatible with the most current one.
(B) The network can then span entire
neighborhoods.
(C) The technology used is a recent
advancement in the field.
(D) The average internet speed in the area has
increased exponentially.

12. (A) coverage
(B) analysis
(C) shelter
(D) coating

전치사

CASE 53 시간 전치사

We encourage our clients to review the terms and conditions ------- their registration for our gym membership.

(A) prior to   (B) in   (C) despite   (D) as of

> 해설   빈칸 뒤에 명사구가 있으므로 빈칸은 전치사 자리이며, '체육관에 회원가입을 하기 전에 이용약관을 살펴보라'는 의미가 되어야 문맥상 자연스러우므로 (A)가 정답이다.
>
> 해석   저희는 고객이 체육관에 회원가입을 하기 전에 이용약관을 검토하시기를 권합니다.

>> 「at / on / in + 때」

at + 시각/구체적인 때 ~에	**at** 5 P.M. / **at** noon / **at** the end of the month
on + 요일/날짜/특정한 날 ~에	**on** Monday / **on** July 5 / **on** his birthday
in + 월/계절/년도/아침/점심/저녁 ~에	**in** July / **in** summer / **in** 2022 / **in** the morning

The marketing director has informed all the managers that the new advertising campaign will be launched **on** Tuesday.
마케팅 이사는 모든 관리자들에게 화요일에 새 광고 캠페인이 시작될 것이라고 알렸다.

>> 「by / until / before / after / from / since + 시점」

by + 시점 ~까지(완료되는 동작)	submit the report **by** the end of the month
until + 시점 ~까지(지속되는 상태)	remain open **until** 5 P.M.
before(= prior to) + 시점 ~ 전에	**before** lunch / **before** signing the contract / one hour **prior to** the deadline
after(= following) + 시점 ~ 후에	**after** lunch / **after** signing the contract / two hours **following** the deadline
past + 시점 ~ 지나서	**past** noon
from(= beginning) + 시점 ~부터	**from** today / two months **from** today / **beginning** May 1
since + 과거 시점 ~ 이후로	**since** last May / **since** the product's launch

Bricks Retailers employees are entitled to negotiate their salary and benefits **after** their one-year anniversary at the company.
Bricks 소매 직원들은 회사에서 1년을 근무한 후에 급여와 혜택을 협상할 자격이 주어진다.

③SECS 알면 3초!   >> '~까지'를 의미할 때 by는 완료 의미의 동사와, until은 계속 의미의 동사와 함께 쓴다.

The HR Department asks all employees to make their summer vacation requests ------- 6:00 P.M. Friday.

(A) until   (B) on   (C) by   (D) in

빈칸 뒤에 시점을 취할 때 보기 중 by와 until이 모두 있다면? 둘 다 '~까지'로 해석되긴 하지만, by는 그 시점까지 완료되는 것을 의미할 때 쓰고, until은 그 시점까지 계속되는 것을 의미할 때 쓰기 때문에 by는 주로 complete, finish, deliver, return, submit 등 완료의 의미를 갖는 동사와, until은 last, remain, stay, continue, postpone 등 계속의 의미를 갖는 동사와 어울린다. 위 문제에서도 요청서를 작성하는 행위는 한 번 행하고 끝나는 완료의 개념이므로 빈칸 뒤 시점은 by가 이끄는 것이 옳으므로 (C)가 정답이다.

> 해석   인사부는 전 직원에게 금요일 저녁 6시까지 여름 휴가 신청서를 작성하라고 요청한다.

PART 5

1. Customers who visited La Belle Bakery ------- opening day received special cookies to celebrate.
(A) while
(B) in
(C) also
(D) on

2. All personnel must upload their work to the shared folder ------- leaving for the day.
(A) within
(B) around
(C) before
(D) from

3. The Accounting Department will pay employees only by direct deposit ------- October 1 onward.
(A) from
(B) now
(C) when
(D) during

4. The 13-inch laptop from IJM Electronics is currently out of stock and will not be available ------- November 7.
(A) since
(B) around
(C) within
(D) until

PART 6

Questions 5-8 refer to the following invitation.

To Whom It May Concern:

We at the World Peace Committee cordially invite you to attend our annual Global Introduction Day at the City Hall. Every year, we invite local communities to ------- their representatives to contribute
5.
toward this annual event. The representatives will be asked to share their ideas on how to build a global peace during the event. We would require all participants to join our discussion for at least two hours. -------.
6.

We would appreciate it if you could respond to us before May 31. We will share more ------- about
7.
the event once we have heard from all participants. The discussion agenda will be shared ------- or
8.
before June 4. We are really grateful for the time of every participant.

Sincerely,

Mario Hill, World Peace Committee Director

5. (A) send
(B) hire
(C) relocate
(D) offer

6. (A) Your community has confirmed that it will participate.
(B) The location has an adequate parking lot.
(C) The City Hall is chosen because it is free of charge.
(D) The discussion will only last for one day.

7. (A) details
(B) issues
(C) incentives
(D) traits

8. (A) on
(B) at
(C) in
(D) between

CASE 54 기간 전치사

For certified contractors, a building plan is usually authorized ------- two weeks from submission.

(A) within   (B) among   (C) soon   (D) through

> **해설** 빈칸은 기간 명사 two weeks를 이어주는 전치사 자리이다. 문맥상 '제출 후 2주 이내에 인가된다'라는 의미가 되어야 자연스러우므로 (A)가 정답이다.

> **해석** 공인 도급업자의 경우, 건축 계획은 보통 제출 후 2주 이내에 인가된다.

>> 「for / during / over / in / through / throughout / within / 기간 + to + 기간」

for + 숫자 / 기간 ~동안	**for** two weeks / **for** the last ten years
during + 기간 명사 ~동안	**during** the meeting / **during** the business hours
over + 기간 ~동안	**over** ten years
in + 숫자 / 기간 ~후에[만에]	**in** ten minutes
through + 시점 / 기간 ~내내, ~까지	**through** a concert
throughout + 기간 ~내내	**throughout** the year
within + 기간 ~이내에	**within** two weeks of purchase
기간 + to + 기간 ~부터 …까지	takes two **to** four weeks

Over the past 30 years, Axterp Construction Company has offered comprehensive services, with the up-to-date technology for constructing buildings.
지난 30년 동안, Axterp 건설사는 빌딩을 건설하기 위한 최신 기술과 함께 포괄적인 서비스를 제공해 왔다.

Though advertised as a winter resort, Spitzer Mountain Adventure reported steady reservations **throughout** the year.
겨울 휴양지로 광고되었지만, Spitzer Mountain Adventure는 연중 꾸준한 예약을 보고했다.

 알면 3초!   >> '~동안'을 의미할 때 for는 숫자를, during은 행사나 사건 등의 일반 명사를 이끈다.

Brittany's car dealership offers an extended warranty that is effective ------- eight years.

(A) on   (B) to   (C) for   (D) during

앞서 다룬 by vs. until과 마찬가지로, for vs. during 역시 해석은 같은데 쓰임새에 차이가 있어 전통적인 토익 이슈로 분류된다. 둘 다 기간 명사를 취하여 '~(하는) 동안'으로 해석되지만, for는 시간의 길이를 나타내기 위해 쓰기 때문에 보통 숫자 명사를 이끄는 데 비해, during은 행사나 사건 등의 기간을 나타내기 위해 쓰므로 meeting, visit, season 등 기간의 의미를 머금고 있는 일반 명사를 취한다. (예: during the conference, during the summer, during business hours) 위 문제에서 빈칸 뒤에 숫자를 포함한 기간 명사구가 연결되어 있으므로 (C)가 정답이다.

> **해석** Brittany's 자동차 대리점은 8년간 유효한 연장 보증을 제공한다.

해설서 p.78

1. *Design Enthusiast Magazine* features articles written by experts who have worked in the interior design industry ------- several years.

(A) among
(B) except
(C) for
(D) off

2. The newly renovated Shocker Stadium, scheduled to open ------- about five weeks, has 100,000 seat capacity.

(A) now
(B) just
(C) in
(D) as

3. Marie's Alpine Café has already opened three new branches ------- its first five years of operation.

(A) onto
(B) within
(C) before
(D) toward

4. The Home Improvement Emporium's employee manual states that all mobile devices must be turned off ------- work hours.

(A) during
(B) only
(C) soon
(D) just

Questions 5-8 refer to the following e-mail.

To: Carrie Ann Richardson
From: Rikard Eye Care Center
Date: February 15
Subject: Your eyesight

Dear Ms. Richardson,

Your eyesight is ------- to us. It is time for you to make an appointment for a checkup. Your last visit
   5.
with us was ------- 16 months ago. At Rikard Eye Care Center, we suggest that you get a ------- eye
   6.   7.
exam every 12 months. We look forward to seeing you and serving your eye care needs. -------.
                                                                                        8.

Sincerely,

Barbara Ong
Rikard Eye Care Center
4587 Jaunty Road, Suite B
Singapore 168938
Phone: 65 6323 0112

5. (A) uncertain
(B) important
(C) successive
(D) impartial

6. (A) from
(B) to
(C) out
(D) over

7. (A) routine
(B) resistant
(C) recent
(D) rigorous

8. (A) It has been a pleasure doing business with your agency.
(B) This is your last chance to change your mind.
(C) Please give us a call if you have any questions or concerns.
(D) Unfortunately, we are unable to accept new patients to our practice.

CASE 55 장소 전치사

> **An archive of resources for forensic analysts was recently retrieved ------- the organization's servers.**
>
> (A) at (B) except (C) into (D) from
>
> 해설 빈칸은 뒤에 오는 명사구 the organization's servers와 함께 전치사구를 이뤄, 앞에 있는 동사 was retrieved를 수식하는 전치사 자리이다. 장소를 나타내는 명사를 목적어로 취하여, 문맥상 '기관 서버에서 검색되었다'라는 의미가 되어야 자연스러우므로 출처를 나타내는 전치사 (D)가 정답이다.
>
> 해석 법의학 분석가들을 위한 자료 보관소가 최근에 기관 서버에서 검색되었다.

>> 「at / on / in / through / throughout / across + 장소」

at ~에(지점)	**at** the corner / **at** the bank	through ~을 지나	**through** the door
in ~ 안에(공간 안)	**in** Seoul / **in** the office	throughout ~ 전역에	**throughout** the country
on ~에(접촉면)	**on** the floor / **on** Main Street	across ~ 전역에	**across** Europe

The internal memo was sent to all executives **across** multiple regional offices.
그 내부 회람이 다수 지점 전역의 모든 간부들에게 보내졌다.

>> 「to / toward / from / into / across / between / among / within 등 + 방향 / 위치」

방향		위치	
from ~로부터(출발점)	past ~을 지나서	between (둘) 사이에	beside / next to / by ~ 옆에
to ~로(도착점)	opposite ~ 건너에	among (셋 이상) 사이에	near ~ 가까이에
toward(s) ~ 쪽으로, ~을 향해	across from ~ 건너에	within ~ 이내에, ~ 안에	around ~ 주위에
into ~ 안으로	across ~을 가로질러	in front of ~ 앞에	over / above ~ 위에
out of ~ 밖으로	along ~을 따라	behind ~ 뒤에	under / below ~ 아래에

Our staff members help clients work **toward** a certain financial goal, such as creating an emergency fund.
저희 직원들은 고객들이 긴급 자금 마련과 같이 특정한 재무 목표를 향해 노력하는 일을 돕습니다.

3SECS 알면 3초! >> 전치사 정답 1순위인 within에 주목하라.

The Wallistown Monument is ------- driving distance of the historic downtown area.

(A) within (B) next to (C) following (D) without

사실 전치사의 종류, 특히 출제되는 전치사란게 거기서 거기이긴 하지만, 기본 뜻만 대충 알고 있다면 막상 문제를 풀 때 '코에 걸면 코걸이, 귀에 걸면 귀걸이' 식의 해석이 되어 답을 고르기 애매한 경험을 할 수 있다. 이렇듯 모호함의 아이콘인 전치사는 여느 단어보다 그 의미와 쓰임새가 다양하고 우리말로 딱 떨어지게 정의되지 않는 경우가 많기 때문에 다양한 예문들을 익히면서 각각의 어감을 익히는 것이 중요하다. 이 within이란 전치사 역시 기간, 장소, 범위, 거리, 한계 등 다양한 종류의 명사를 이끌며, 전치사 중 가장 높은 정답률을 자랑하긴 하지만, (어찌된 영문인지) '~이내에'란 뜻만 꽉 잡고 있으면 문제 될 게 없다. 따라서 (D)가 정답이다.

해석 Wallistown 기념비는 역사적인 도심 구역에서 운전해서 갈 수 있는 거리 이내에 있다.

PART 5

1. The mission of our outreach program is to develop cooperation and understanding ------- groups.
(A) between
(B) after
(C) while
(D) under

2. The board of directors approved the installation of cell phone charging stations to be located ------- the student center.
(A) following
(B) toward
(C) notwithstanding
(D) throughout

3. Falkland Island is located near Norminton City, just a short drive ------- the Chesapeake Bay Bridge.
(A) across
(B) between
(C) outside
(D) about

4. Museum visitors can enjoy a spectacular view of the sunset ------- the west-facing windows.
(A) through
(B) into
(C) down
(D) besides

PART 6

Questions 5-8 refer to the following letter.

July 15

Gretchen Cunningham
12 Washington Street
San Antonio, TX 78213

Dear Ms. Cunningham,

Thank you for letting us know about your experience with the cruise ship Highgate Escape, which was scheduled to depart on July 12. We regret that this voyage ------- (5.). In keeping with our policy, we will provide compensation for the ------- (6.). We have sent a refund for your unused ticket in the amount of $750. We are also happy to cover the $500 you incurred in additional travel expenses resulting ------- (7.) the disruption. ------- (8.). Be aware that each transfer may take up to 72 hours to process.

Regards,

Terry Clare
Coleridge Cruises

---

5. (A) will be canceled
(B) had to cancel
(C) is canceling
(D) was canceled

6. (A) flaw
(B) inconvenience
(C) period
(D) activity

7. (A) in
(B) from
(C) without
(D) before

8. (A) Thank you for choosing Coleridge Cruises.
(B) Your understanding is greatly appreciated.
(C) Both amounts should already appear on your balance.
(D) We will look into the issue you mentioned.

CASE 56 | 비슷한 의미의 전치사

The city council authorized the airport expansion project ------- the concerns of several residents.

(A) despite   (B) due to   (C) beyond   (D) such as

> **해설** 빈칸 뒤의 명사구 the concerns of several residents를 목적어로 취할 전치사가 필요한 자리로, 문맥상 '주민들의 염려에도 불구하고 인가를 내줬다'라는 의미가 자연스러우므로 (A)가 정답이다.
>
> **해석** 시 의회는 몇몇 주민들의 염려에도 불구하고 공항 확장 프로젝트에 인가를 내줬다.

>> 비슷한 의미의 전치사들은 묶음으로 암기한다.

이유	due to/owing to/because of/on account of/thanks to ~ 때문에
양보	despite/in spite of/notwithstanding ~에도 불구하고
반대	against/contrary to/in opposition to ~에 반하여
제외	without ~없이 except (for)/excluding/barring/aside from/apart from ~을 제외하고
대체	instead of/in place of/in lieu of ~ 대신에
추가	including ~을 포함하여 in addition to/besides/plus/aside from/apart from ~ 외에도
동반	with/along with/together with/in conjunction with/in cooperation with/in association with ~와 함께
수단	by/through/with ~을 통해, ~로
주제	on/about/over/regarding/as to/as for/in[with] respect to/in[with] regard to ~에 관하여
관련	concerning/pertaining to/in relation to/in[with] reference to ~와 관련하여
고려	considering/given ~을 고려해 볼 때
비유	such as ~와 같은 like ~와 같이 unlike ~와 달리

The government authorized the construction of the dam **despite** the concerns of environmental activists.
정부는 환경운동가들의 염려에도 불구하고 댐 건설을 인가했다.

Besides a larger customer database, we also require a more efficient system for tracking returns.
우리는 더 큰 고객 데이터베이스 외에 수익을 추적하기 위한 더 효율적인 시스템 또한 필요하다.

 알면 3초!   >> 분사 형태의 전치사를 집어낸다.

Once we have all of the necessary documents ------- the application fee, we can begin processing your application.

(A) conveying   (B) including   (C) contracting   (D) leading

분사형(-ing/p.p.) 전치사	including ~을 포함하여 excluding ~을 제외하여 barring ~이 없다면 following ~ 후에 regarding ~에 관하여 concerning ~와 관련하여 considering ~을 고려하여 given ~을 고려하여

'신청 비용을 포함하여 모든 필요 서류를 수령하는 대로'라는 문맥으로 '~을 포함하여'라는 뜻의 전치사 (B)가 답이 되는 문제이다. 빈칸 앞의 부사절이 완전한 문장이므로 빈칸 이하는 수식어구로 볼 수 있으니 앞 문장을 의미상 잘 받쳐주는 단어를 고르면 되는데, 보기 중 유독 including만이 현재분사나 동명사 외에 전치사로도 쓰인다는 점이 불현듯 생각났다면 '~을 포함하여'를 먼저 해석에 대입해 보는 센스를 발휘해 보자. 그만큼 -ing나 -ed의 분사형 전치사는 외울 게 얼마 안 된다.

> **해석** 신청 비용을 포함하여 모든 필요 서류를 수령하는 대로, 귀하의 신청서 처리를 시작할 수 있습니다.

PART 5

1. Some managers may have heard ------- the database program that the company has been working on for the past year.
(A) about
(B) from
(C) before
(D) inside

2. ------- requiring a large capital investment, these projects will need a more highly trained workforce.
(A) However
(B) Besides
(C) Naturally
(D) After

3. Bleifer Solutions plays a vital role ------- ensuring our company has the best personnel for each project.
(A) yet
(B) most
(C) in
(D) since

4. ------- her exceptional computer skills, Katja Goldstein was made Head of IT at Parker Industries.
(A) Since
(B) Finding
(C) Regarding
(D) Given

PART 6

Questions 5-8 refer to the following advertisement.

La View Catering Services

Need food for a party or special event? -------. La View can help, whatever type of event you may be planning — from a large wedding to a small holiday party.
5.

We have a skilled staff that specializes in all types of wonderful cuisine. These include cakes and other desserts, Mexican food, Italian pastas, Chinese and Thai dishes, and traditional appetizers. ------- most other caters, our staff consists entirely of professionally trained chefs. This specialization
6.
allows us to provide you with food that is more delicious than any of our ------- can provide.
7.

You can be confident that La View Catering Services will get your party food delivered on time. We want you ------- back to focusing on your guests!
8.

5. (A) We provide professional catering services.
(B) Decorations are included.
(C) Prices will be fully compensated.
(D) La View is a privately owned company.

6. (A) Unlike
(B) After
(C) Altogether
(D) Instead

7. (A) developers
(B) attendees
(C) successors
(D) competitors

8. (A) to get
(B) and got
(C) who gets
(D) getting us

CASE 57 기타 전치사

------- her upcoming relocation to Hanoi, Ms. Wilson began learning Vietnamese.

(A) By   (B) After   (C) For   (D) From

콕 찍어 포인트 ··· 'to Hanoi'를 보고 'from A to B(A에서 B로)'를 떠올려 전치사 from을 선택하지 않도록 유의한다.

해설 전치사 to가 들어가는 표현은 다양하므로, 여러 가지 선택지가 가능할 경우 반드시 문맥상 자연스러운지 확인하도록 한다. 빈칸은 명사 relocation을 목적어로 하는 전치사 자리로, 문맥상 '곧 있을 하노이로의 이전을 위해'라는 의미가 되어야 자연스러우므로 목적을 나타내는 (C)가 정답이다.

해석 곧 있을 하노이로의 이전을 위해, Wilson 씨는 베트남어를 배우기 시작했다.

➤➤ 시험에 나오는 기타 주요 전치사의 다양한 쓰임을 익힌다.

for	[목적] ~을 위해, ~으로	people who travel **for** leisure
	[대상] ~을 대상으로, ~에 대해	a training session **for** new sales managers
	[용도] ~을 위해, ~용의	space **for** storage
of	[소유] ~의	effectiveness **of** work procedures
	[동작의 주체/대상] ~의	the arrival **of** the president
as	[자격] ~로서	work **as** sales manager
in	[증가/감소] ~의	increase[rise, growth] **in**, decrease[drop, decline] **in**
	[분야/업계] ~에서	**in** accounting, **in** the hospitality industry
	[색깔/언어] ~로	**in** green, **in** English
under	[계속] ~ 중인	**under** construction
	[영향력] ~ 아래에, ~하에	**under** the supervision[direction, guidance] of
at	[가격/비율/속도/온도] ~로	**at** the cost[rate] of / **at** 100 km an hour / **at** low temperatures
beyond	[기대] ~ 이상	**beyond** their expectation
	[한계] ~할 수 없는	**beyond** repair

Hopkins Library will be open **for** a special book-signing event on Saturday.
Hopkins 도서관은 토요일에 있을 특별 책 사인회 행사를 위해 문을 열 것이다.

Though her work experience was short, Margo Anderson made the most convincing arguments for hiring her **as** our systems analyst.
업무 경력이 짧긴 했지만, Margo Anderson은 그녀를 우리의 시스템 분석가로 채용하는 것에 대한 가장 설득력 있는 주장을 펼쳤다.

 알면 3초! ➤➤ 「by+-ing」는 '~함으로써'로 해석한다.

Ms. Cruz became a valued asset at BF Solutions ------- expanding its international customer base.

(A) as   (B) inside   (C) plus   (D) by

by+-ing ~함으로써   in+-ing ~하는 데 있어서   for+-ing ~하려는 용도로

보기로 열거된 각각의 전치사와 「동사+-ing」의 결합인 expanding의 뜻은 따로따로는 알겠는데 한데 붙여 쓰면 어떻게 해석할지 몰라 당황스러울 때가 있다. 이 점을 어찌 용케도 알았는지 빈칸 뒤에 -ing를 써서 의미상 어울리는 전치사를 고르라는 문제가 심심찮게 출제되는데, 별 수 있는가? 암기의 시간이다. 몇몇 전치사와 동명사(-ing)가 결합하여 하나의 관용 표현을 이룰 때가 있는데, 시험에서 가장 많이 묻는 표현이 「by+-ing」이며, 이때 by는 수단의 의미를 지녀 '~함으로써'란 의미를 갖는다. 빈칸 뒤에 expanding과 함께 '해외 고객층을 넓힘으로써 소중한 자산이 되었다'라는 의미를 만드는 전치사 (D)가 정답이다.

해석 Cruz 씨는 해외 고객층을 넓힘으로써 BF Solutions의 소중한 자산이 되었다.

PART 5

1. The prime minister commended HCO Hospital ------- its assistance in developing the nation's physical activity guidelines.

(A) for
B) by
(C) to
(D) on

2. Though her résumé was short, Theresa Lim made the most convincing arguments for hiring her ------- our sales manager.

(A) by
(B) at
(C) as
(D) yet

3. Executives should compare the company's financial as well as historical performance ------- industry norms.

(A) exclusive of
(B) superior to
(C) contrary
(D) against

4. In the last year, manufacturing at the Gilman facility has nearly tripled in -------.

(A) intensity
(B) release
(C) finance
(D) volume

PART 6

Questions 5-8 refer to the following advertisement.

Start the New Year by signing up at Dagabe Gym for our new --------: the Holiday Special. There's
                                                                                      5.
no better time to make a --------. For a low rate of $30 per month, you will gain access to our gym
                             6.
equipment and swimming pool -------- our new spa room. Get in shape this season with the help of
                                   7.
our many qualified trainers. --------. Find out more by visiting www.dagabe.com.au/newyear.
                                 8.

5. (A) plan
   (B) planned
   (C) planning
   (D) planner

6. (A) contract
   (B) stance
   (C) change
   (D) revision

7. (A) about
   (B) including
   (C) until
   (D) unless

8. (A) The gym may be closed for occasional cleaning.
   (B) We have hundreds of clients who have worked successfully with our trainers.
   (C) Any concerns about work safety should be raised.
   (D) A promotional event is currently in progress.

CASE 58　전치사 관용 표현

Our branch manager ------- with the auditors' request to show our financial records.

(A) continued　　　(B) complied　　　(C) coincided　　　(D) convinced

> **해설** 빈칸은 전치사 with와 어울리는 자동사 자리이다. comply with가 '~을 따르다/준수하다'를 뜻하는 관용 표현임을 고려할 때, 문맥상 '회계 감사관들의 요청을 따랐다[준수했다]'라는 의미가 되어야 자연스러우므로 (B)가 정답이다. coincide with는 '~와 동시에 일어나다/일치하다'라는 뜻이다.

> **해석** 우리 지점장은 우리의 회계 기록을 보여 달라는 회계 감사관들의 요청을 들어주었다.

>> 특정 전치사를 동반하는 관용 표현을 한 단어처럼 암기한다.

동사 + 전치사	adhere **to** ~을 준수하다 contribute **to** ~에 공헌하다 subscribe **to** ~을 구독하다	account **for** ~을 설명하다 allow **for** ~을 참작하다 make up **for** ~을 보상하다	deal **with** ~을 다루다 comply **with** ~을 준수하다 interfere **with** ~을 방해하다
명사 + 전치사	access **to** ~의 이용[접근] attention **to** ~에 대한 주의 solution **to** ~의 해결책	demand **for** ~에 대한 수요 request **for** ~에 대한 요구 respect **for** ~에 대한 존경	advance **in** ~의 진보 interest **in** ~에 대한 관심 experience **in** ~에 대한 경험
형용사 + 전치사	committed **to** ~에 헌신하는 entitled **to** ~에 자격이 있는 accustomed **to** ~에 익숙한	eligible **for** ~에 자격이 있는 ideal **for** ~에 적합한 responsible **for** ~을 담당하는	appreciative **of** ~에 감사하는 aware **of** ~을 알고 있는 capable **of** ~을 할 수 있는
전치사 + 단어/구	**at** once 즉시 **at** a discount 할인하여 **at** one's earliest convenience ~가 편한 시간에	**on** duty 근무 중인 **on** foot 걸어서 **on** a regular basis 규칙적으로	**in** advance 미리 **in** particular 특히 **in** a timely manner 시기적절하게

Renter's insurance helps tenants who sometimes deal **with** damaged property.
세입자 보험은 종종 손상된 부동산 문제를 처리하는 임차인들을 돕는다.

Children under 12 years old are eligible **for** free flu shots.
12세 미만의 어린이는 무료 독감 예방 주사를 맞을 수 있다.

※ 전치사 관용 표현 문제는 ① 관용 표현의 의미를 통으로 물어보거나, ② 주어진 전치사를 힌트로 삼아 이와 어울리는 단어를 고르거나,
　③ 특정 단어와 어울리는 전치사를 고르는 문제로 출제되므로 한 단어처럼 통째로 외워둔다.

 알면 3초!　　>> 두 단어 이상이 결합된 주요 구전치사를 암기한다.

Some of the client files became disorganized ------- being transferred to the new company server.

(A) for the reason that　　(B) contrary to　　(C) in exchange for　　(D) in the process of

두 단어 이상이 결합된 형태를 '구(phrase)'라고 부르듯이, in honor of(~을 기념하여), on behalf of(~을 대신하여), in exchange for(~와 교환하여), in the process of(~의 과정에서)처럼 두 단어 이상이 결합하여 하나의 전치사로 쓰이는 형태를 '구전치사(phrasal preposition)'라 부른다. 시험에서는 구전치사의 의미를 통으로 물어보거나, 이 덩어리 표현 중 전치사 자리를 비워두고 채우라는 식으로 출제되는데, 일일이 따져보거나 해석할 시간은 언제나 부족하기 때문에 구전치사 역시 낱개의 단어를 외우듯이 외우면 된다. 일부 고객 파일이 서버로의 전송 과정에서 흐트러진 것이므로 '~의 과정에서'의 의미를 갖는 (D)가 정답이다.

> **해석** 새로운 회사 서버로 전송되는 과정에서 일부 고객파일이 흐트러졌다.

PART 5

1. Farmers in cotton production and its by-products have suffered heavy losses ------- from high operating costs.

(A) concerning
(B) completing
(C) resulting
(D) expecting

2. For recruitment purposes, three years of relevant work experience is ------- to having a degree.

(A) significant
(B) equivalent
(C) reasonable
(D) appropriate

3. Ms. Tanaka was ------- resigning when the vice president asked her to manage the IT team at the new data center.

(A) forward
(B) about to
(C) close to
(D) nearby

4. Every branch of Third Dimension Custom Printing keeps at least 5,000 kilograms of raw materials in -------.

(A) shipment
(B) storage
(C) provision
(D) results

PART 6

Questions 5-8 refer to the following memo.

To: Accounting Staff, Prodio Bank
From: Isaac O'Reilly, Vice president
Date: June 15
Re: Announcement

Kindly join me in ------- Tom Harris to the bank. As a certified auditor, one of his main responsibilities will be to assist the bank's senior partners with tax cases to ensure that appropriate legal action is taken ------- state and federal laws. Tom has a great deal of experience, having worked on a large number of cases during his 11-year career. At his ------- bank, he has advised on a wide variety of clients on their growth strategies and restructuring plans. -------. His first day of work will be June 20.

5. (A) welcoming
(B) wishing
(C) giving
(D) looking

6. (A) subsequent to
(B) in accordance with
(C) in advance of
(D) regardless of

7. (A) permanent
(B) previous
(C) temporary
(D) approximate

8. (A) We have been using a simple system since May 12.
(B) Tom will bring firsthand knowledge in this field.
(C) Our bank will launch a new mobile banking service.
(D) A large financing program has recently been approved.

1. Restaurant visitors can enjoy a jazz performance every evening ------- 7 P.M.

(A) for
(B) in
(C) on
(D) at

2. Attendees are welcome to bring snacks and beverages and enjoy it ------- the training session.

(A) although
(B) even if
(C) during
(D) so that

3. Pixel Design Studio is situated ------- Moorcroft Street, near its junction with Arden Terrace.

(A) along
(B) adjacent
(C) under
(D) within

4. Vacancies at the Alkyna Hotel are generally affordable, ------- its quality and reputation.

(A) to consider
(B) consideration
(C) considering
(D) considered

5. Ms. Nguyen spoke ------- her entire division when receiving the Outstanding Design Award at the annual conference last month.

(A) on behalf of
(B) at a rate of
(C) in exchange for
(D) under the condition that

6. The strategic announcement of the Acaru XC70 automobile was propelled by a decline ------- sales of the XC60 model.

(A) than
(B) over
(C) in
(D) on

7. The Bard Theater Group invites the local residents ------- a free play at Fuller Amphitheater this weekend.

(A) out
(B) as
(C) to
(D) with

8. Mr. Joseph is the most qualified person in the accounting department ------- Ms. Sims.

(A) insofar
(B) after
(C) precede
(D) overall

Questions 9-12 refer to the following e-mail.

To: employees@eastgate.com
From: jwillis@eastgate.com
Date: 16 July
Subject: Professional development planning

Dear All Employees,

Starting on 11 August and continuing ------- until 8 September, in partnership with Strathfield
                                        9.
Collective, Eastgate will be providing professional development planning for all employees. You will
all have received an e-mail with a list of your assigned dates and times. Your team leaders will have
also received the e-mails. -------.
                            10.

The sessions will be run by Dr. Miranda Conner, a highly ------- consultant. She will guide you in
                                                          11.
improving your career -------. This is a great opportunity to try and branch out into different teams or
                        12.
roles. Dr. Conner will help write out your development plan to help you get there.

To ensure you get the most out of these sessions, please view the introduction video on www.
strathfield.com/about.

Sincerely,

Joe Willis, Human Resources

9. (A) through
   (B) about
   (C) against
   (D) between

10. (A) Additionally, suggestions for improving
       communication lines are welcome.
    (B) The previous meeting has already been
       canceled.
    (C) You may refer to the Web site for more
       details.
    (D) Therefore, you do not need to give advance
       notice.

11. (A) considered
    (B) consider
    (C) considering
    (D) consideration

12. (A) succession
    (B) precedence
    (C) progression
    (D) continuation

접속사

CASE 59 · 시간·조건의 부사절 접속사

The senior engineer told his staff that ------- they found a way to improve the connection speed, the project could not be considered completed.

(A) since   (B) until   (C) assuming   (D) considering

> 해설 빈칸은 that 명사절 내에서 두 개의 문장을 연결하는 부사절 접속사 자리이다. 두 문장의 관계를 고려할 때, 문맥상 '연결 속도를 향상시킬 방법을 찾기 전까지 프로젝트는 완료되지 않은 것으로 간주한다'라는 의미가 되어야 자연스러우므로 시간의 부사절 접속사 (B)가 정답이다.

> 해석 선임 엔지니어는 직원들에게 연결 속도를 향상시킬 방법을 찾기 전까지는 프로젝트가 완료된 것으로 간주할 수 없다고 말했다.

>> 시간·조건의 부사절 접속사

시간	when ~할 때 as soon as ~하자마자, ~하는 대로 before ~하기 전에 while ~하는 동안 since ~한 이후로	as ~할 때, ~하는 동시에 once ~하자마자, 일단 ~하면 after ~한 후에 until ~할 때까지 by the time ~할 때쯤에
조건	if, provided that, providing that 만약 ~라면 unless(= if not) 만약 ~가 아니라면 assuming (that), supposing (that) ~라고 가정하여 in case (that) ~인 경우에 대비하여	as[so] long as ~하는 한, ~하기만 하면 as[so] far as ~하는 한, ~에 관한 한 only if ~하는 경우에만 in the event that ~인 경우에

while (X)
Renovations will start **as soon as** the blueprint is finalized.
청사진이 확정되는 대로 수리공사가 시작될 것이다.
as soon as (X)
Use the fan **while** the air conditioner is being repaired.
에어컨이 수리되는 동안 선풍기를 이용하세요.

 알면 3초!   >> 관용 표현 「unless otherwise + 과거분사」 '달리 ~하지 않으면'

All ingredients in our products are organic unless otherwise -------.

(A) specifies   (B) specifying   (C) specified   (D) specifications

---

unless otherwise instructed[noted / indicated] 달리 안내[언급 / 표시]가 없으면

접속사 unless를 이용한 빈출 관용 표현 「unless otherwise+p.p.」 '달리[별도로] ~하지 않으면'을 외워두면, unless 자리나 과거분사 자리에 빈칸을 주고 알맞은 접속사나 어형을 묻는 문제 또는 부사 otherwise를 묻는 문제가 나올 때 쉽게 답을 고를 수 있을 뿐만 아니라, 독해에서 많이 등장하는 이 표현을 하나의 단어로 인식하여 빠르게 해석할 수 있다. 접속사 unless 뒤에 주어, 동사의 축약 형태로, 이때는 과거분사만이 가능하다는 점을 기억해 둔다. 따라서 위 문제에서도 과거분사 (C)가 정답이다.

> 해석 저희 제품의 모든 재료는 별도로 명시되어 있지 않으면 모두 유기농입니다.

PART 5

1. ------- he joined our group in January, Mr. Kang has worked to raise Chevoir's brand awareness in the global marketplace.
(A) Besides
(B) Since
(C) As much as
(D) Not only

2. This warranty is valid ------- the product is used in the country in which it was purchased.
(A) whenever
(B) within
(C) only if
(D) even though

3. Weekly meetings generally take place in the 19th floor conference room ------- otherwise noted on the company Web site.
(A) beyond
(B) because
(C) later
(D) unless

4. The corporation's profits over the next fiscal year will escalate, ------- the lucrative merger with Shrader Financial can be concluded before the end of the quarter.
(A) assuming that
(B) whereas
(C) whenever
(D) even if

PART 6

Questions 5-8 refer to the following letter.

March 14

Ms. Amy Blanche
4421 Council Street
Seattle, WA 98123

Dear Ms. Blanche,

This letter is in --------- to your inquiry on March 9. I understand that you will be working over the summer as a tour guide at Denali National Park and would like to obtain a fishing license without incurring an out-of-state resident fee. There is indeed a waiver for non-Alaskans who work or study here. ---------, you do qualify to receive a license at the standard rate. You --------- for an in-state license as long as you provide proof of employment. ---------. After we confirm your status with your employer, you will be eligible for a license at the in-state price.

Best regards,

Douglas Jefferson,
Wildlife Commission, Anchorage Office

5. (A) respond
(B) response
(C) responded
(D) responder

6. (A) However
(B) Accordingly
(C) Even
(D) Similarly

7. (A) applying
(B) may apply
(C) would have applied
(D) applied

8. (A) The fish this season are especially fresh.
(B) Unfortunately, the Anchorage Branch is closed for renovation at the moment.
(C) Simply bring your documents to the Wildlife Commission office.
(D) A fee of $25 must be paid to renew a license.

CASE 60 이유·양보의 부사절 접속사

------- heavy snow is so common in Kashkingrad, the city council approved a plan to connect all buildings downtown.

(A) Although   (B) Wherever   (C) Because   (D) Once

> **해설** 빈칸은 두 문장을 연결하는 접속사 자리이다. 문맥상 '폭설이 흔하기 때문에, 시내 모든 건물들을 연결하는 기획안에 승인했다'라는 의미가 나와야 자연스러우므로 이유를 나타내는 (C)가 정답이다.
>
> **해석** Kashkingrad에서는 폭설이 자주 오기 때문에, 시 의회에서는 시내 모든 건물들을 연결하는 기획안을 승인했다.

>> 이유·양보의 부사절 접속사

이유	because / as / since ~이기 때문에 now that (이제) ~이므로, ~이기 때문에 in that ~이므로, ~라는 점에서
양보	although / though / even though 비록 ~이긴 하지만 even if 설령 ~라 하더라도 while ~이긴 하지만
대조	while / whereas ~인 반면에, ~이긴 하지만

                                           ↪ althrough (X)

Ms. Carter was hired as HR manager **because** she proved herself to be the only honest candidate.
Carter 씨는 자신이 유일하게 정직한 후보자라는 것을 증명했기 때문에 인사 매니저로 채용되었다.

    ↪ Now that (X)

While Mr. Sato appreciated the job offer, he chose to start his own business.
Sato 씨는 일자리 제의에 감사히 여기긴 했지만, 자기 사업을 하기로 결정했다.

 알면 3초!   >> 의미에 따라 달라지는 since의 품사

Payroll systems will be offline from 6 A.M. to 8 A.M. next Thursday ------- routine maintenance.

(A) although   (B) since   (C) rather than   (D) due to

The prices on the list may not be accurate **since** manufacturers often change their price.
                                     접속사
제조업체들이 자주 가격을 변경하기 때문에 목록에 나와 있는 가격은 정확하지 않을 수 있다.

→ since 뒤에 절이 연결되어 부사절 접속사로 쓰였으므로 '~때문에'와 '~한 이후로' 중 문맥상 적절한 것으로 해석한다.

Mr. Smith's grades have been showing signs of improvement **since** he began taking private lessons.
                                           접속사
Smith 씨는 개인 강습을 받기 시작한 이후로 등급이 개선될 조짐을 보이고 있다.

→ since가 시간(~한 이후로)을 나타낼 때, since 뒤에는 과거 시점/시제가, 주절에는 현재 완료 시제가 온다. 따라서 이를 힌트로 삼아 '~한 이후로'로 해석한다.

Our operating expenses have declined by 10 percent **since** last year.
                                           전치사
작년부터 운영비가 10퍼센트나 줄었다.

→ since 뒤가 절이 아닌 명사구이므로 '~ 이후로'로 해석한다.

She left home in 1993 and hasn't been seen **since**.
                                           부사
그녀는 1993년에 집을 떠났고 그 이후로 보이지 않았다.

→ since가 없어도 문장이 완전하므로 부사로 쓰였으며, '그 이후로'로 해석한다.

since는 접속사와 전치사의 기능을 모두 갖는 연결어 중 하나로, 의미에 따라 품사를 달리한다. since가 시간(~한 이후로)을 의미할 때는 부사절 접속사, 전치사, 부사가 모두 가능한 반면, 이유(~이기 때문에)를 의미할 때는 '부사절 접속사'로만 쓰인다는 점에 주의하고, 문제를 풀 때 이를 힌트로 삼을 수 있어야 한다. 위의 문제의 경우 빈칸 뒤에 절이 아닌 명사구(routine maintenance)가 연결되어 있으니 보기의 since는 '~ 이후로'란 뜻만 가능한 전치사임을 재빨리 눈치채야 한다. 따라서 '~ 때문에'를 의미하는 전치사 (D)가 정답이다.

> **해석** 급여 시스템은 정기 보수 작업 때문에 다음 주 목요일 오전 6시에서 8시까지 오프라인 상태가 될 것이다.

PART 5

1. ------- attendance at monthly book club meetings has been declining, the club leader decided that the group would select a different book.

(A) Because
(B) How
(C) Only if
(D) Until

2. Many stores are still demanding cash payments ------- there are now lots of other alternatives.

(A) even though
(B) for one thing
(C) similarly
(D) lastly

3. ------- Eagle Sporting Goods has found a more suitable commercial space, it will start negotiating the lease agreement.

(A) Gladly
(B) Although
(C) Now that
(D) In fact

4. Mr. Campanella will develop training courses for the new design software, since ------- employees are familiar with the program.

(A) all
(B) other
(C) few
(D) more

PART 6

Questions 5-8 refer to the following e-mail.

To: Nick Peralta <nperalta@theorymail.com>
From: Libbie Sweeney <lsweeney@bruno.us>
Date: 12 September
Subject: Orientation

Dear Mr. Peralta,

We are delighted that you have confirmed your position for this year's intake at Bruno Academy's apprenticeship program. As you may be aware, the program entails ------- classes from Monday to Wednesday, while Thursdays and Fridays can be spent at home studying. ------- you will not be required to sign in, it is expected that you will still be reachable by phone.

The classes ------- on 30 October at the Brighton Campus. Please check your mail in the coming days. -------. We look forward to seeing you soon!

Sincerely,

Libbie Sweeney
Recruitment Officer

5. (A) attending
(B) attendance
(C) attend
(D) to attend

6. (A) Despite
(B) However
(C) Although
(D) Nonetheless

7. (A) commencing
(B) will commence
(C) commenced
(D) commencement

8. (A) You will receive a detailed schedule and map.
(B) Your application must be signed before we can process it.
(C) New apprentices will receive their work phones.
(D) A new offer may be available soon.

목적·결과 및 기타 부사절 접속사

Ms. Bandy agreed to attend the conference in New York ------- Mr. Ciaramitaro could stay in Dallas and meet with clients.

(A) so that   (B) as if   (C) even though   (D) in case

콕 찍어 포인트 … **부사절 접속사 so that은 주로 조동사 can[could]와 함께 쓰여 목적의 의미를 전달한다.**

해설 빈칸은 두 개의 절을 연결하는 접속사 자리이다. 문맥상 'Ciaramitaro 씨가 Dallas에 머물면서 고객들을 만날 수 있도록 Bandy 씨가 회의 참석에 동의했다'라는 의미가 되어야 자연스러우므로 목적의 부사절 접속사 (A)가 정답이다.

해석 Bandy 씨는 Ciaramitaro 씨가 Dallas에 머물면서 고객들을 만날 수 있도록 뉴욕에서 열리는 회의에 참석하기로 했다.

>> 목적·결과 및 기타 부사절 접속사

목적	so that ~ can[may] ~할 수 있도록 in order that ~ can[may] ~하기 위해서
결과	so ~ that, such ~ that 너무 …해서 ~하다 *so ~ that 사이에는 형용사나 부사가 오며, such ~ that 사이에는 「a(n) + 형용사 + 명사」가 위치한다.
기타	as if[though] 마치 ~인 것처럼 given that, considering (that) ~을 고려하면 in that ~라는 점에서 except that ~인 것을 제외하고 whether or not ~이든 아니든, ~와 상관없이

Ms. Black wants to reserve the largest event hall **in case** more guests decide to attend.
Black 씨는 더 많은 손님이 참석을 결정할 경우에 대비해서 가장 넓은 행사장을 예약하기를 원한다.

 알면 3초!   >> 「------- 문장1, 문장2」 또는 「문장1 ------- 문장2」의 구조에서 빈칸은 부사절 접속사 자리이다.

------- education can improve your chances of getting a good job, it is not the only thing that employers consider.

(A) Mainly   (B) Although   (C) Alternatively   (D) Nevertheless

✓ 부사절은 주절을 수식하는 역할을 하며, 부사절 접속사는 부사절을 이끌어 주절과 연결해주는 접속사를 말한다.
✓ 부사절은 「부사절 접속사 + 주어 + 동사」의 형태로 완전한 문장을 이끈다.
✓ 부사절은 주절 앞이나 뒤에 모두 올 수 있다. 「부사절 접속사 + 부사절, 주절」 or 「주절 + 부사절 접속사 + 부사절」

접속사 문제 중에서 보기와 빈칸 앞뒤의 구조만 보고도 풀리는 문제가 종종 등장한다. 위의 문제에서도 Mainly와 Alternatively는 '-ly' 형태의 전형적인 부사이고, Nevertheless는 접속부사, Although는 양보의 의미(비록 ~이지만)를 갖는 부사절 접속사이다. 빈칸을 포함한 문장의 형태가 「------- + 주어(education) + 동사(can improve), 주어(it) + 동사(is)」이니 절과 절을 이어주는 부사절 접속사가 필요하기 때문에 (B)가 정답이다. 이처럼 보기에 제시된 단어들의 뜻을 정확히 모른다고 하더라도 이들이 접속사/부사/전치사 중 어디에 해당하는지를 가늠할 수 있고, '부사절 접속사는 문장과 문장을 이어주는 역할을 한다.'라는 개념만 잡혀 있다면 이러한 문제는 해석 없이도 풀 수 있다.

해석 비록 교육이 좋은 직업을 가질 수 있는 가능성을 높일 수는 있지만, 그것이 고용주들이 고려하는 유일한 것은 아니다.

PART 5

1. ------- the time allocated for this project is extremely short, it is important to prioritize speed at each phase of the project.
(A) Even if
(B) Because of
(C) Unless
(D) Considering

2. ------- the renovation of the lobby is incomplete, please use the garage entrance.
(A) Therefore
(B) As a result of
(C) In the event that
(D) Concerning

3. The spring sale last year was ------- profitable that it will take place again this April.
(A) first
(B) much
(C) so
(D) what

4. The intelligent guidance system is specially designed so that all workers can perform complex tasks -------.
(A) irreversibly
(B) efficiently
(C) vaguely
(D) especially

PART 6

Questions 5-8 refer to the following notice.

Starting 1 March, the long-awaited Metro Wheels will finally be ready for action. This shuttle service ------- to Jacobson senior citizens who are unable to walk unassisted. All Metro Wheel buses are
5.
equipped with wheelchair ramps and temperature-controlled interiors. -------. The shuttle service will
6.
run from Monday – Saturday, 8 A.M. – 6 P.M.

To schedule a trip, please contact the Metro Wheels guest center (555-3494) at least three days beforehand ------- we can make the proper arrangements. The Metro Wheels service is free, but
7.
financial ------- are encouraged. This can be done by submitting an online payment or placing cash
8.
into the jar located to the right of the bus driver.

5. (A) would have been provided
(B) was provided
(C) has been provided
(D) is being provided

6. (A) Residents tend to take public buses due to the cheap fares.
(B) We appreciate you using the Metro Wheels service today.
(C) Passengers can be dropped off anywhere within 20 kilometers of their departure point.
(D) The driver will make an announcement within the next 20 minutes.

7. (A) from there
(B) in which
(C) until then
(D) so that

8. (A) contributes
(B) contributions
(C) contributors
(D) contributing

부사절 접속사 vs. 전치사

The director announced a surprise inspection on Wednesday afternoon ------- the next day was scheduled for maintenance.

(A) despite　　　　(B) as well as　　　　(C) even though　　　　(D) due to

해설 빈칸은 두 개의 완전한 절을 연결하는 접속사 자리이다. 보기 중 완전한 절을 이어주는 접속사는 부사절 접속사 even though 뿐이므로 (C)가 정답이다.

해석 임원은 다음 날 정비가 예정되어 있음에도 불구하고 수요일 오후에 기습 점검을 발표했다.

>> 부사절 접속사 뒤에는 「주어＋동사」가 포함된 절이 오고, 전치사 뒤에는 명사(구)가 온다.

종류	부사절 접속사		의미	전치사	
시간	while		~ 동안	during	
	before		~ 전에	before/prior to	
	after		~ 후에	after/following	
	until		~까지	until/by	
	as soon as		~하자마자	on[upon] -ing	
조건	unless		~가 아니라면	barring/without/but for	
	in case (that)/in the event (that)	＋주어＋동사	~에 대비하여	in case of/in the event of	＋명사(구)
이유	because/as/since/now that/in that		~ 때문에	due to/owing to/because of/on account of/thanks to	
양보	although/though/even though		~이긴 하지만	despite/in spite of/notwithstanding	
목적	so that ~ can[may]/in order that ~ can[may]		~을 위해서	for/for the purpose of	
제외	except (that)		~을 제외하고	without/except (for)/excluding/barring/aside from/apart from	

↱ Prior to (X)
Before the conference begins, please check the schedule and venues for each guest speaker.
학회가 시작되기 전에, 각 초청 연사를 위한 일정과 장소를 확인해주세요.

③SECS 알면 3초!　　>> 접속사와 전치사로 둘 다 쓰이는 단어에 주의한다.

Visitors enjoy spending time in Williamsburg in Virginia, which has been restored to look ------- it did during the colonial period.

(A) for　　　　(B) out　　　　(C) as　　　　(D) down

부사절 접속사		전치사	
before/after,/until given that/considering (that) except that **since** ~이래로, ~때문에 **as** ~때문에, ~할 때, ~한 대로	＋주어＋동사	before/after/until given/considering except (for) **since** ~이래로 **as** ~로서	＋명사(구)

위의 단어들은 부사절 접속사와 전치사로 둘 다 쓰이며, 특히 since와 as는 접속사로 쓰일 때와 전치사로 쓰일 때 의미가 달라진다는 점에 유의한다. 이들이 보기에 등장하면, 먼저 빈칸 뒤의 문장 구조를 확인하여 빈칸에 들어갈 수 없는 보기들을 소거하고 나서 남은 보기들 중 의미상 어울리는 답을 고른다. 위의 문제에서 빈칸 뒤에 「주어＋동사」의 절이 나오고 '그곳이 식민지 시대 때처럼 복원되었다'라는 의미가 되어야 하므로 부사절 접속사 (C)가 정답이다.

해석 방문객들은 Virginia의 Williamsburg에서 시간 보내는 것을 좋아하는데, 그곳은 식민지 시대 때처럼 보이도록 복원되었다.

PART 5

1. ------- there has been a 70 percent increase in sales, four new managers have been hired to deal with urgent matters.
(A) Given that
(B) Beyond
(C) As long as
(D) Except for

2. Preventive maintenance of elevators in your building guarantees that minor problems can be resolved ------- they become major ones.
(A) before
(B) despite
(C) as a result
(D) on top of

3. ------- Wes Chamberlain has now retired, Yumiko Fujihara will take over as our sales representative.
(A) While
(B) Unless
(C) Though
(D) Since

4. California Recycling Systems announced to its workers that all types of aluminum materials ------- aerosol cans should first be processed with hydraulic presses.
(A) without
(B) except
(C) even though
(D) after all

PART 6

Questions 5-8 refer to the following memo.

To: Penasquitos Executives
From: Daniel Winokur, Executive Board Chairperson
Date: 15 May
Subject: Meeting

Penasquitos Industries will hold an executive board meeting at 5:00 P.M. on Thursday, May 22 at our main office. -------.
5.

The first task on our schedule ------- the list of operating expenses for next quarter. Since many of
6.
these are -------, the confirmation process should not take too long. ------- that confirmation, we'll
7.   8.
have a serious talk about the proposed relocation of our headquarters.

---

5. (A) Please enroll in the course as soon as possible.
(B) The construction project was concluded last week.
(C) You also have the option of participating via our videoconferencing system.
(D) This matter will be addressed by the executive board in a timely manner.

6. (A) was approving
(B) will be to approve
(C) to approve
(D) had been approved

7. (A) whole
(B) available
(C) open
(D) routine

8. (A) Although
(B) After
(C) Considering
(D) Despite

PART 5 CHAPTER 09

부사절 접속사의 축약

It is important to carefully measure the dimensions of an office ------- determining how many desks can fit in the room.

(A) not only   (B) in fact   (C) when   (D) instead

해설 빈칸은 주절과 현재분사 구문을 연결하는 자리이므로 부사절 접속사 (C)가 정답이다.

해석 사무실에 몇 개의 책상이 들어갈 수 있는지를 결정하기 전에 사무실의 치수를 신중하게 측정하는 것이 중요하다.

>> 부사절 접속사 뒤에 분사, 형용사, 전치사구의 축약 형태가 올 수 있다.

1. 「부사절 접속사 + 현재분사(-ing) + 목적어」   *when they watch*

   Most people get excited **when watching** their favorite singer perform on stage.

   대다수의 사람들은 그들이 좋아하는 가수가 무대에서 공연할 때 흥분한다.

   → 능동태 문장의 축약: 주절과 동일한 부사절의 주어를 생략하면서, 일반 동사를 현재분사로 변경한다.

2. 「부사절 접속사 + 과거분사(p.p.) + 전치사구」   *when he/she is faced*

   The sales representative must respond quickly **when faced** with a customer complaint.

   영업 사원은 고객 불만에 직면할 때 재빠르게 대응해야 한다.

   → 수동태 문장의 축약: 주절과 동일한 부사절의 주어를 생략하면서, be동사도 함께 생략한다.

3. 「부사절 접속사 + 형용사」   *whenever it is possible*

   Please update me on the progress of the project **whenever possible**.

   가능할 때마다 제게 프로젝트의 진행 상태를 업데이트해 주세요.

   → 앞 문장 전체를 받는 가주어 it을 생략하면서, be동사도 함께 생략한다.

4. 「부사절 접속사 + 전치사구」   *while they are on duty*

   Employees should refrain from using their personal devices **while on duty**.

   직원들은 근무 중에 개인 기기의 사용을 삼가야 한다.

   → 주절과 동일한 부사절의 주어를 생략하면서, be동사도 함께 생략한다.

🕐 알면 3초!   >> 축약 형태와 연계하여 while과 during을 구별한다.

Technicians are required to adhere to all safety guidelines ------- working in the lab.

(A) during   (B) otherwise   (C) while   (D) since

while 뒤에는 절이 오고, during 뒤에는 명사(구)가 오는 접속사와 전치사의 차이만 알고서는 답을 고르기 애매한 문제이다. 이 문제를 쉽게 풀려면 두 개의 추가 정보를 알고 있어야 한다. 우선, 부사절 접속사 뒤에는 축약 형태로 분사나 전치사구가 바로 올 수 있지만, 전치사 뒤에는 분사나 전치사구를 바로 취하지 못한다는 점과, 일반 전치사는 동명사(-ing)를 목적어로 취할 수 있는 데 비해, during은 뒤에 오직 명사(구)만을 목적어로 취한다는 점이다. 위의 문제에서 빈칸 뒤의 working in the lab은 주절의 주어와 동일한 they가 생략되면서 work를 현재분사로 바꾼 축약 형태로 이해하고 접속사 (C)를 답으로 고를 수 있어야 한다.

해석 기술자들은 연구실에서 일하는 동안 모든 안전 규정을 준수하도록 요구된다.

PART 5

1. Senior employees are required to have regular meetings with interns while ------- their progress.

(A) processing
(B) assessing
(C) allocating
(D) engaging

2. Visitors must keep their phones on silent mode at all times ------- on the studio grounds.

(A) while
(B) toward
(C) clearly
(D) after

3. The deposit is ------- reimbursable as indicated so long as the following requirements are met.

(A) definitive
(B) define
(C) definite
(D) definitely

4. To avoid leakage, users should exercise ------- when replacing the toner cartridge.

(A) cautioned
(B) caution
(C) cautious
(D) cautiously

PART 6

Questions 5-8 refer to the following press release.

FOR IMMEDIATE RELEASE
CONTACT: Shirley Frazier, (188) 555-7996

(March 5) — Merrill Transportation is proud to announce that the bridge connecting the norther parts of Tulare to city center will be officially opening. Tulare residents are encouraged ------- in the opening ceremony at 12:30 P.M. to 2:30 P.M. on March 11. The event will also unveil the recently ------- bus lanes. The bridge was designed by Brightwater Limited and is expected to reduce congestion. -------, it will reduce travel times by up to 30 minutes. The construction project is finally complete after having been in progress for three years. -------. We hope to see everybody at the ceremony.

5. (A) to participate
(B) participating
(C) the participation of
(D) they participated

6. (A) adding
(B) additive
(C) added
(D) addition

7. (A) However
(B) Despite
(C) In fact
(D) Previously

8. (A) An analysis of the city revealed some surprising trends.
(B) Electric vehicles may lead the way in the near future.
(C) There were several delays relating to worker strikes.
(D) A new plan has been released to the public.

등위 접속사

Many employees do not like evaluations, ------- HR Director Alyssa Dinonikis thinks they are a useful way to improve productivity.

(A) as　　　　　　(B) but　　　　　　(C) for　　　　　　(D) nor

해설 빈칸은 두 개의 완전한 문장을 연결하는 접속사 자리이다. 두 문장의 내용이 서로 상반된다는 점을 고려할 때, 문맥상 '직원들은 평가를 좋아하지 않지만, 인사 임원은 그것이 유용한 방법이라고 생각한다'라는 의미로 이어져야 자연스러우므로 역접을 나타내는 등위 접속사 (B)가 정답이다.

해석 많은 직원들이 평가를 좋아하지 않지만, 인사 임원 Alyssa Dinonikis는 그것이 생산성을 향상시키는 유용한 방법이라고 생각한다.

>> 문맥에 알맞은 등위 접속사를 묻는다.

and 그리고	or 또는	but 그러나	yet 그러나	so 그래서	for 왜냐하면

~~but (X)~~
Breakfast will be catered by Duffle Bakery **and** March Kitchen.
아침 식사는 Duffle 제과점과 March 식당에 의해 제공될 것이다.

>> 등위 접속사는 동일한 문장 성분을 연결하며 반복되는 부분은 생략될 수 있다.

단어 – 단어	Participation in the mentoring program is **welcome but** (it is) completely **optional**. [형용사–형용사] 멘토링 프로그램 참여는 환영하지만 전적으로 선택적이다.
구 – 구	The assembly line **has stopped but** (it) **will resume** once the new workers arrive. [동사구–동사구] 조립 라인이 멈췄지만, 새 근로자들이 도착하는 대로 재개될 것이다.
절 – 절	**Protective gear is generally required at construction sites, but some exceptions may be made.** [절–절] 안전 장비는 일반적으로 건설 현장에서 필수이지만, 몇몇 예외가 있을 수 있다.

>> 등위 접속사 so와 for는 절과 절만 연결할 수 있다.

Mr. Carter extended the deadline, so we would have enough time to prepare the contract.
[절–절] Carter 씨가 마감일을 연장해 줘서, 우리가 그 계약을 준비할 충분한 시간이 있을 것이다.

---

③SECS 알면 3초!　　>> 등위 접속사와 접속부사는 첫 문장 맨 앞에 올 수 없다.

------- gas prices have risen, KM Logistics did not increase its delivery fees.

(A) Despite　　　　(B) Although　　　　(C) But　　　　(D) Nevertheless

Although gas prices have risen, KM Logistics did not increase its delivery fees.
= Gas prices have risen, **but** KM Logistics did not increase its delivery fees.
= Gas prices have risen; **nevertheless,** KM Logistics did not increase its delivery fees.
= **Despite** the rise in gas prices, KM Logistics did not increase its delivery fees.

위의 문제는 빈칸의 위치를 보자마자 등위 접속사 (C)와 접속부사 (D)를 소거하고, 빈칸 뒤의 「주어 + 동사」를 보고 전치사 (A)도 소거하여 (B)를 답으로 고를 수 있어야 한다. 비슷한 의미의 접속사 vs. 전치사 구별은 앞에서 설명한 것으로 대신하기로 하고, 핵심은 '등위 접속사와 접속부사는 문두에 올 수 없다'는 것이다. 등위 접속사는 앞선 내용을 대등하게 연결해주는 역할을 갖는다는 점에서, 접속부사는 두 문장 사이에서 의미만을 이어주는 부사이고 실제적으로 두 절을 연결하는 형태는 and나 세미콜론(;)이므로 이러한 형태가 없다면 쓰일 수 없다. 따라서 지금처럼 Part 5 문제에서 빈칸이 맨 앞에 와 있다면 이 둘은 기계적으로 답에서 제외시킬 수 있어야 한다.

해석 연료비가 오르긴 했지만, KM 택배는 배송료를 올리지 않았다.

PART 5

1. Both full-time and part-time business programs have advantages, ------- prospective students should weigh each option carefully against the other.

(A) or
(B) so
(C) as well
(D) yet

2. Many personal trainers find working with trainees to be a rewarding ------- of the job, but the overall satisfaction is relatively low.

(A) overview
(B) aspect
(C) tone
(D) session

3. The new sleeping bags by Wildling Provisions have more space than the previous designs, ------- they are not comfortable.

(A) for
(B) how
(C) unless
(D) but

4. Pontchartrain Supermarket has expanded -------, and its Baton Rouge location now has a baked goods section as well as a pharmacy.

(A) closely
(B) rightfully
(C) considerably
(D) willingly

PART 6

Questions 5-8 refer to the following information.

The Pelmont Education Association (PEA) is ---5--- to mark the 20th year of its annual fundraiser.

This event will allow educators, ---6---, and interested residents to come together and recognize the progress PEA has made in improving local educational programs. ---7---. Dinner, catered by Lavantino's, will begin promptly at 6:00 P.M.

There will be a raffle at 8:30 P.M. Guests are permitted to stick around and mingle until the event ---8--- at 10:30 P.M.

5. (A) proud
(B) essential
(C) concerned
(D) talented

6. (A) donate
(B) donated
(C) donation
(D) donors

7. (A) PEA's main office will not be open next week due to renovations.
(B) PEA is not accepting membership applications at this time.
(C) The celebration will take place on Friday, April 8.
(D) Last year's event attracted a small number of guests.

8. (A) compliments
(B) connects
(C) commences
(D) concludes

Sports fans taking public transportation should either take the green line subway -------
bus 101 to get to the stadium.

(A) and　　　　　(B) but　　　　　(C) both　　　　　(D) or

콕 찍어 포인트 ⋯ 「either A or B」는 'A나 B 둘 중 하나'를 의미한다.

> **해설** 빈칸은 동사 take의 목적어인 명사구 2개를 연결하는 자리이다. 빈칸 앞에 either가 있기에 상관 접속사의 관용 표현 「either A or B(A나 B 둘 중 하나)」를 완성하는 (D)가 정답이다.

> **해석** 대중교통을 이용하는 스포츠 팬들은 경기장에 가려면 지하철 녹색라인을 타거나 101번 버스를 타야 한다.

>> 두 단어 이상이 짝을 이루는 상관 접속사는 서로의 짝을 찾는 문제로 출제된다.

both A and B	A와 B 둘 다	not A but B	A가 아니라 B
either A or B	A나 B 둘 중 하나	B, but not A	A가 아니라 B
neither A nor B	A와 B 둘 다 아닌	between A and B	A와 B 사이에
not only A but (also) B	A뿐만 아니라 B도	whether A or B	A인지 B인지, A이든 B이든
B as well as A	A뿐만 아니라 B도	A rather than B	B보다는 A

nor (X)

Either complete the test online **or** take it in person.
시험을 온라인으로 치르시거나 직접 보시면 됩니다.

→ Either를 보고 or를 정답으로 선택한다.

either (X)

After discussing the new benefits package, **both** management **and** employees reached an agreement.
새 복리 후생 제도에 대해 논의하고 나서, 경영진과 직원들 모두 합의를 보았다.

→ and를 보고 both를 정답으로 선택한다.

 알면 3초!　　>> 상관 접속사로 연결된 주어의 수 일치에 주의한다.

As neither the conference rooms nor the auditorium ------- due to the renovations, regular staff meetings will
not be held this month.

(A) available　　　　(B) availability　　　　(C) is available　　　　(D) are available

등위 접속사	A and B		복수 동사
상관 접속사	both A and B		복수 동사
	either A or B, neither A nor B, not only A but (also) B,　B as well as A, not A but B(= B, but not A)		B에 수 일치

사실 토익의 수 일치 문제는 동사의 태나 시제와 결부되어 출제되는 것이 일반적이지만, 위 문제와 같이 주어가 상관 접속사로 연결되어 있고 주어−동사의 수 일치를 결정해야 하는 문제로 출제될 경우, 공식처럼 암기해 두지 않으면 틀리기 십상이므로 위의 등위·상관 접속사 수 일치 공식을 암기해두자. 상관 접속사 「neither A nor B」는 B에 수를 일치시키며 B의 주어가 단수(the auditorium)로 쓰였으므로 (C)가 정답이다.

> **해석** 회의실과 강당 둘 다 수리 때문에 이용할 수 없어서, 정기 직원 회의가 이달에는 열리지 않을 것이다.

PART 5

1. Mountainview Hotel offers ------- valet parking and complimentary breakfasts to all VIP guests.
(A) in addition
(B) both
(C) in that
(D) also

2. Greenery Architecture specializes in sustainable design that is affordable ------- environmentally friendly.
(A) at last
(B) after all
(C) accordingly
(D) as well as

3. ------- laying off employees, the CEO decided to reduce executive travel privileges.
(A) Either
(B) Rather than
(C) Lately
(D) Just as

4. The Hannam Library is seeking volunteers between the hours of 9 ------- 6 for its summer program.
(A) so
(B) or
(C) yet
(D) and

PART 6

Questions 5-8 refer to the following e-mail.

To: Jessie Reyes
From: Wade Morton
Date: 24 November
Subject: Party Catering

Jessie,

I have decided to go with Benson Caterers for our end-of-year party. This means that all of the necessary plans ------- the party are now confirmed.
5.

Our technical support team ------- with setting up the cameras, monitors, and sound system at the
6.
venue. However, we will still need another team to co-ordinate the food, beverages, and gift bags. Additionally, we will need a team to clean up after the -------. I heard that the product design team
7.
will stay late. -------. I will receive confirmation and let you know. Just in case, we should make
8.
alternative plans.

Thanks.

Wade

5. (A) for
(B) to
(C) by
(D) in

6. (A) have helped
(B) to help
(C) will help
(D) helped

7. (A) ceremony
(B) setback
(C) operation
(D) component

8. (A) Teams will arrive at different times accordingly.
(B) We should ask them to volunteer to do that.
(C) Communications with other teams are slow this time of year.
(D) The venue might be too small for everyone.

명사절 접속사의 역할

Planners have yet to indicate ------- on the island the resort will be built.

(A) why   (B) what   (C) which   (D) where

해설 빈칸은 동사 indicate의 목적어 역할을 하면서 빈칸 뒤의 완전한 절 '(on the island) the resort will be built'을 이어주는 명사절 접속사 자리이다. 의문사 where, why가 완전한 절을 이끄는데, 문맥상 '리조트가 섬 어디에 지어질지 장소를 밝히지 않았다'라는 의미가 되어야 자연스러우므로 (D)가 정답이다. what과 which도 명사절 접속사이지만 뒤에 불완전한 절을 이끈다.

해석 계획자들은 그 리조트가 그 섬의 어디에 지어질지 아직 밝히지 않았다.

>> 명사절 접속사는 주어, 목적어, 보어 역할을 하며, 명사절 접속사 that, what, whether/if 외에, 의문사와 복합 관계대명사도 명사절을 이끈다.

종류	역할	예문
명사절 접속사 (that / what / whether / if) / 의문사 / 복합 관계대명사	주어	**Whether the company will merge with XYZ Corp.** <u>will be</u> discussed during the meeting. 회사가 XYZ 사와 합병할 것인지는 회의에서 논의될 것이다. **Whoever sells the most number of vehicles** <u>will be</u> named Employee of the Year. 가장 많은 차량을 판매한 사람은 누구든지 올해의 직원으로 지명될 것이다.
	타동사의 목적어	The attendees <u>reported</u> **that the workshop had been a huge disappointment**. 참가자들은 그 워크숍이 큰 실망을 주었다고 말했다. The CEO has to <u>decide</u> **who will be promoted to Director of Marketing** today. CEO는 오늘 누가 마케팅 책임자로 승진할 것인지를 결정해야 한다. Once the Director of Operations has reviewed Embrace Inc.'s documents, she will <u>determine</u> **whose proposal will be chosen**. 운영 책임자가 Embrace 사의 서류 검토를 완료하는 대로, 그녀는 누구의 제안서가 채택될 것인지 결정할 것이다. You can <u>request</u> **whatever you need for your office** on this Web site. 사무실에 필요한 것은 무엇이든 이 웹사이트에서 요청할 수 있습니다.
	전치사의 목적어	This is a guide <u>on</u> **how we can use the new groupware**. 이것은 새 그룹웨어를 어떻게 사용할 수 있는지에 대한 안내서이다.
	보어	The entertainment section <u>is</u> **what most readers of the monthly magazine read first**. 연예 섹션은 대부분의 월간지 독자들이 가장 먼저 읽는 부분이다.

 알면 3초!   >> 명사절 접속사 that 뒤에는 완전한 문장이 오고, what 뒤에는 불완전한 문장이 온다.

Our annual financial report indicates ------- we should reduce the overall operating costs.

(A) since   (B) what   (C) as   (D) that

문제를 풀다 보면 보기 중에 that과 what이 같이 등장하는 경우를 심심찮게 볼 수 있는데, 이때는 바로 해석을 하기 전에 먼저 that과 what 중 하나가 정답이 될 확률이 높다는 점을 인지하고 명사절 접속사 즉, 명사의 역할을 하는 접속사의 관점에서 「that+완전한 문장」, 「what+불완전한 문장」의 공식을 본능적으로 떠올려야 한다. 위의 문제에서, 빈칸 뒤에 본동사 indicates의 목적어로 주어(we), 동사(should reduce), 목적어(the overall operating costs)를 모두 갖춘 완전한 절이 오니 (B)를 탈락시킨다. 'that 이하를 보여준다'라고 자연스럽게 해석되므로 (D)를 답으로 선택하면 된다.

해석 연간 재무 보고서는 우리가 전체적인 운영비를 절감해야 한다는 것을 보여준다.

PART 5

1. The goal of probationary period is to figure out ------- the skills and performances of the employee matches their résumé.

(A) even if
(B) whether
(C) now that
(D) neither

2. ------- needs to be determined is the date for the company's upcoming charity fundraiser.

(A) That
(B) Whose
(C) Which
(D) What

3. Mr. Heath was ------- that his landscape photographs were used on the company's official Web site.

(A) welcomed
(B) objected
(C) flattered
(D) completed

4. Sterlington Supermarket sent an e-mail to its frequent customers ------- that it now provides free same-day shipping.

(A) adjusting
(B) preserving
(C) confirming
(D) arranging

PART 6

Questions 5-8 refer to the following e-mail.

To: TeriKim@globobiz.com
From: Frieda.Juarez@DBZTech.com
Date: October 30
Subject: RE: software issue

Ms. Kim,

I apologize for the inconvenience caused by your department's inability to access the groupware file system. Others have been making the same complaint. It is helpful to know that you ------- to change your login information.
5.

We're still investigating the source of this trouble. -------, it is caused by a faulty server or an incompatible older version of the software. -------. Our team is looking into the matter, and it is likely that the issue will be sorted out ------- the next 24 hours. When it is, I'll send an e-mail to all of you.
6.   7.   8.

Best,

Frieda Juarez
Digital Solutions Analyst

5. (A) attempting
(B) to attempt
(C) attempted
(D) attempt

6. (A) Specifically
(B) Moreover
(C) Ordinarily
(D) Accordingly

7. (A) Take a moment to verify that you have downloaded the latest software update.
(B) File sharing allows for greater collaboration between departments.
(C) Your login information doesn't appear to work at the moment.
(D) IT professionals will train each department individually.

8. (A) within
(B) or else
(C) at most
(D) entirely

Please be advised ------- your order needs to be re-submitted due to a computer error on our side.

(A) as　　　　　　(B) how　　　　　　(C) that　　　　　　(D) whether

콕 찍어 포인트 ⋯ **명사절 접속사 that vs. whether:** that은 '~하는 것'을, whether는 '~인지 아닌지'를 의미한다.

해설 빈칸은 수동태 동사구와 절을 연결하는 자리이다. 동사 advise가 직접 목적어에 that절을 취하는 4형식 동사이므로 수동태가 되어도 뒤에 절 형태의 목적어가 올 수 있다. 문맥상 '고객님의 주문서가 다시 제출되어야 함을 알려드린다'라는 의미가 되어야 자연스러우므로 (C)가 정답이다.

해석 고객님의 주문서가 저희 측의 전산 오류로 인해 다시 제출될 필요가 있음을 알려드립니다.

>> 「명사절 접속사 that + 완전한 문장」 vs. 「명사절 접속사 what + 불완전한 문장」

The record shows **(that)** Mr. Simpson paid a delivery fee for the order.
↳ what (X)

이 기록은 Simpson 씨가 주문품의 배송비를 지불했다는 것을 보여준다.

→ 타동사의 목적어절을 이끄는 that은 생략할 수 있다.

The workshop will explain **what** new employees should do. 워크숍은 신입 직원들이 해야 하는 것을 설명할 것이다.
↳ that (X), what = the thing which

→ what은 동사 do의 목적어가 없는 불완전한 절을 이끈다

>> 「명사절 접속사 that + 완전한 문장」 vs. 「관계대명사 that + 불완전한 절」

The customers insist **that they only buy ingredients that have been classified** as organic.

고객들은 유기농으로 분류된 재료들만을 구매한다고 주장한다.

→ 앞의 that은 본동사 insist의 목적어로 완전한 절을 이끄는 명사절 접속사이며, 뒤의 that은 불완전한 절을 이끌어 앞의 선행 명사 (ingredients)를 수식하는 관계대명사이다.

>> 전치사 뒤에는 that절이 올 수 없다. (단, except that / in that은 예외)

The company will hire interns regardless of **whether applicants have previous work experience**.
↳ that (X)

회사는 지원자들의 이전 업무 경력의 여부에 관계없이 인턴들을 채용할 것이다.

>> 명사절 접속사 that이 주어 절을 이끌어 주어가 길어질 때, 가주어 It-진주어 that절 구문 「It ~ that절」로 바꿔 쓴다.

That employees always follow safety guidelines is important. 직원들은 항상 안전 가이드라인을 따르는 것이 중요하다.
↳ **It** is important **that employees always follow safety guidelines**.

 알면 3초! >> 「명사 + that절」과 「형용사 + that절」의 관용 표현을 익힌다.

Please be aware ------- the changed regulations for vehicle inspection will take effect on December 1.
(A) of　　　　　　(B) that　　　　　　(C) as　　　　　　(D) regarding

명사 + that절(동격의 that)	형용사 + that절
the fact that ~라는 사실	be aware that ~인 것을 인식하다
the evidence that ~라는 증거	be certain[confident] that ~인 것을 확신하다
the idea that ~라는 생각	be concerned[worried/afraid] that ~인 것을 걱정하다
the report that ~라는 보도	be pleased[glad] that ~인 것에 대해 기뻐하다
the conclusion that ~라는 결론	be disappointed that ~인 것에 대해 실망하다

형용사 aware 뒤에 절이 연결되어 있는 형태로, aware가 「of + 명사(구)」나 that절을 관용적으로 이끄는 형용사임을 알고 있다면 고민하지 않고 (B)를 정답으로 고를 수 있다.

해석 변경된 차량 점검 규정은 12월 1일부터 효력이 발생한다는 점을 알고 계시기 바랍니다.

PART 5

1. The manager requests ------- all interns submit their monthly progress reports by 3 P.M. on April 30.
(A) what
(B) or
(C) that
(D) if

2. The fact ------- celebrity endorsements can cause both positive and negative publicity is an important aspect of advertising.
(A) because
(B) that
(C) which
(D) for

3. Ms. Poole e-mailed yesterday afternoon for ------- that the job application she sent on Friday had been accepted.
(A) confirm
(B) confirmed
(C) confirming
(D) confirmation

4. The organizers are ------- that the weather will clear up for the festival.
(A) hopeful
(B) hope
(C) hopefully
(D) hopes

PART 6

Questions 5-8 refer to the following letter.

5 May

Frances Moon
BBD Construction
Goose Bay, Labrador

Ms. Moon,

We are pleased to announce that the Goose Bay School System ------- your company for the construction of the new wing of Tommy Prince Elementary School. Your crew may enter the ------- effective 1 July.

As we discussed in the bidding process, BBD Construction will be liable for any incidental damage or injuries that occur on school property. I've included the School District's master plans, which contain our up-to-date schedule. -------, the document includes the contact information of other key stakeholders in the project. Give me a call directly if you have questions or concerns. -------.

Best Regards,

Virginia Jayne, Superintendent
Goose Bay School District

5. (A) would select
(B) had selected
(C) was selecting
(D) has selected

6. (A) time
(B) site
(C) data
(D) contest

7. (A) Additionally
(B) Yet
(C) Nonetheless
(D) Again

8. (A) I will do my best to address them in a timely manner.
(B) This must be filled out before the project can begin.
(C) We will let you know within a month.
(D) Once again, thank you for choosing our company.

명사절을 이끄는 접속사 whether

Ms. Elliot contacted the customer to ask ------- there is a freight elevator in their building.

(A) whether   (B) so   (C) for   (D) about

> 해설   빈칸은 동사 ask와 절 사이의 자리이므로, 절을 ask의 목적어인 명사절로 만들어주는 명사절 접속사 (A)가 정답이다.

> 해석   Elliot 씨는 건물 안에 화물용 엘리베이터가 있는지의 여부를 묻기 위해 고객에게 연락했다.

>> 「whether + 완전한 문장 + (or not)」, 「whether (or not) + 완전한 문장」 '~인지 (아닌지)'

After the meeting on Tuesday, the city council will determine **whether** the factory should be closed (or not).
화요일 회의 후에 시 의회는 공장을 폐쇄할지를 결정할 것이다.   = whether (or not) the factory should be closed

>> 「whether A or B」 'A인지 (아니면) B인지'

We have not determined **whether** the annual company gala will be on company grounds or in River Park.
우리는 연례 회사 행사를 회사 부지에서 할지, (아니면) River 공원에서 할지 결정하지 못했다.

cf. **Whether** you wish to work in IT or finance, there are hundreds of classes that will help you achieve your goals.   부사절 접속사 whether 'A이든 B이든 (상관없이)'
당신이 IT 분야에서 일하기를 바라든, 재무 분야에서 일하기를 바라든, 당신의 목표를 달성하는 데 도움을 줄 수백 개의 수업이 있다.

>> 「whether + to부정사」 '~할지 (말지)'

The office administrator will decide **whether** to order printers from Office Warehouse or Supplies R Us.
사무 관리자는 프린터를 Office Warehouse에서 주문할지 (아니면) Supplies R Us에서 주문할지 결정할 것이다.

⏱ 알면 3초!   **>> 명사절 접속사 whether vs. if의 차이를 구별한다.**

Canterra employees can choose ------- to work from home or at the office.

(A) that   (B) whether   (C) about   (D) if

명사절 접속사 whether와 if
- ✓ whether와 if가 명사절 접속사로 쓰일 때 둘 다 같은 의미(~인지 아닌지)로 쓰인다.
- ✓ whether는 주어, 목적어, 보어 자리에 모두 쓰일 수 있지만, if는 타동사의 목적어로만 쓰인다.
- ✓ whether는 전치사 뒤에 올 수 있지만, if는 전치사 뒤에 올 수 없다.
- ✓ whether는 뒤에 to부정사가 올 수 있지만, if는 뒤에 to부정사가 올 수 없다.
- ✓ whether는 or not과 함께 쓰이지만, if는 or not과 함께 쓰이지 못한다.

부사절 접속사 whether와 if
- ✓ whether(~이든 아니든 (상관없이))와 if(만약 ~라면)가 부사절 접속사로 쓰일 때 둘은 다른 의미로 쓰인다.

명사절 접속사 whether와 if는 둘 다 '~인지 아닌지'로 해석되며 뒤에 완전한 문장이 오지만, if는 whether에 비해 사용에 제약이 많으므로 둘의 차이를 구별해 둘 필요가 있다. 위의 문제에서 빈칸 뒤에 to부정사가 나오므로 if는 쓰일 수 없고 또한 뒤에 or가 있으므로 대구를 이루는 (B)가 정답이다.

> 해석   Canterra의 직원들은 집에서 일할지, 사무실에서 일할지를 선택할 수 있다.

CASE 집중훈련

PART 5

1. Please tell us ------- you would like to use a credit card or pay cash once you have chosen the item you would like to purchase.
   (A) so that
   (B) whether
   (C) in order to
   (D) whereas

2. The CEO has reviewed Mr. Reilly's qualifications and will decide ------- to appoint him as the new marketing director.
   (A) about
   (B) after
   (C) that
   (D) whether

3. The HR department is still having a discussion about ------- it is necessary to increase the number of monthly staff training sessions.
   (A) which
   (B) whether
   (C) what
   (D) while

4. Panther Manufacturing has not decided ------- or not to upgrade its safety equipment at its factory.
   (A) whether
   (B) neither
   (C) either
   (D) unless

PART 6

Questions 5-8 refer to the following advertisement.

Bank of Lenexa is looking for a new Business Development Manager. The manager ------- the business development activity in our Toledo branch. The position requires, among other things, organizing sales campaigns, meeting with prospects and existing clients, and evaluating the activities and results of New Accounts specialists. This work includes frequent handling of confidential client data, so the successful candidate must be ------- and careful with all materials. Applicants should have prior experience in personal banking, and preferably, a good knowledge of the SalesHorse prospect tracking software. -------, applicants with strong sales backgrounds in other industries are also encouraged to apply. For consideration, please e-mail your CV and a recent photograph to HR@Lenexabank.com. -------
   5.
   6.
   7.
   8.

5. (A) supervise
   (B) supervised
   (C) supervises
   (D) supervising

6. (A) discreet
   (B) polite
   (C) positive
   (D) eager

7. (A) Nonetheless
   (B) Accordingly
   (C) Specifically
   (D) Overall

8. (A) We have offered banking services in the Midwest for 75 years.
   (B) Make sure to mention reference number 504 in your message.
   (C) We plan to open another location in Garrington.
   (D) You should fill out an application at your local branch.

명사절을 이끄는 의문사

Ms. Yamauchi wanted us to tell her ------- of the five cities she should visit first.

(A) which   (B) those   (C) what   (D) where

콕 찍어 포인트 → ① 동사 tell은 4형식 문장에서 'tell + 간접 목적어(~에게) + 직접 목적어(…을/를): ~에게 …을 말하다'의 구조를 취한다.
② 의문사는 '의문사 + 주어 + 동사 ~'의 형태로 명사절을 이끌며, 문장 내에서 주어, 목적어, 보어 자리에 올 수 있다. which는 의문 대명사이자 의문 형용사이기 때문에 의문 형용사일 때는 명사절 내의 주어를 수식할 수 있다.

해설 빈칸은 동사 tell의 직접 목적어 자리이고, 빈칸 뒤에 「주어 + 동사」의 완전한 문장 구조가 이어지므로 완전한 절을 이끄는 명사절 접속사가 들어가는 것이 알맞다. 또한, 빈칸 뒤에 of the five cities가 있음을 고려할 때, '다섯 개의 도시 중 어느 곳'이라는 의미가 되어야 자연스러우므로 의문 대명사 (A)가 정답이다.

해석 Yamauchi 씨는 우리가 그녀에게 그녀가 다섯 도시 중 어느 곳을 먼저 방문해야 하는지를 말해주길 원했다.

>> 「의문 대명사 + 불완전한 문장」

Ms. Franklin was uncertain **who had placed the order for new printer cartridges**.
Franklin 씨는 새 프린터의 카트리지 주문을 누가 했는지 잘 몰랐다.

>> 「의문 형용사 + 명사 + 불완전한 문장」

Before deciding on a new project, we will review **whose idea is the most creative**.
새 프로젝트에 대해 결정하기 전에, 우리는 누구의 아이디어가 가장 독창적인지를 검토할 것이다.

>> 「의문 부사 + 완전한 문장」

The product development team will talk about **when they expect to finish the project**.
제품 개발팀은 그들이 프로젝트를 언제 완료할 것으로 예상하는지에 대해 논의할 것이다.

의문 대명사	의문 형용사	의문 부사
who 누가 ~하는지	which + 명사 어느 명사가 ~하는지	when 언제 ~하는지
what 무엇이[을] ~하는지	whose + 명사 누구의 명사가 ~하는지	where 어디서 ~하는지
which 어느 것이[을] ~하는지	what + 명사 무슨 명사가 ~하는지	how 어떻게 ~하는지
whom 누가를 ~하는지		why 왜 ~하는지

 알면 3초!   >> 의문사가 명사절을 이끌 때, 「의문사 + to부정사」의 형태로 바꿔 쓸 수 있다.

The event organizer has decided ------- to hold the party.

(A) whether   (B) what   (C) where   (D) which

빈칸 뒤에 to부정사가 있고, 앞서 「whether + to부정사」를 배웠다고 (A)를 고르고 넘어가면 안 된다. 파티를 열지 말지를 결정하는 행위는 앞으로 일어날 일이니 미래 시제와 어울리지(will decide whether to hold the party), 이미 결정했음을 나타내는 완료 시제(has decided)와는 어울리지 않는다. whether 명사절과 마찬가지로 의문사가 이끄는 명사절 역시 to부정사로 축약할 수 있다. 그러니, 보기가 다 to부정사로 축약해서 쓸 수 있음을 파악했다면, 귀찮아도 해석을 해봐야 한다. 의미상 파티를 '어디서' 열지를 결정했다고 해야 자연스러우니 정답은 (C)이며, 'The event organizer has decided where he or she would hold the party.'라는 원 문장에서 주절과 동일한 주어(he or she)를 생략하면서 미래 조동사(would)를 to부정사의 to로 축약한 문장으로 이해하면 된다. 단, why는 to부정사로 축약해서 쓰지 않는다는 점도 함께 알아둔다.

해석 행사 기획자는 파티를 어디서 열지 결정했다.

해설서 p.98

PART 5

1. LAC Auto executives met this afternoon to discuss ------- to increase sales of its new pickup trucks.

(A) how
(B) trial
(C) for
(D) later

2. The Internet survey asks ------- how they prefer to learn about upcoming community events.

(A) residence
(B) residents
(C) residential
(D) residencies

3. Ms. Patel asked us to explain to her ------- of the three mobile phones was most user-friendly.

(A) that
(B) what
(C) which
(D) such

4. Having only three days until the presidential race, eligible voters must soon decide ------- contender has the most attractive policies.

(A) who
(B) which
(C) on
(D) about

PART 6

Questions 5-8 refer to the following memo.

To: All workers
From: Landon Donovan, CEO, Advanced Technologies
Date: February 7
Subject: Acquisition of Sanvit Tech

As you may have read in our internal magazine, you must be aware that we are closing a deal to acquire Sanvit Tech, as the negotiations are already in the final phase. This deal will give us the ------- to further enhance our competitive edge over the market.
5.

I am sure that some of you might be questioning about ------- this acquisition may impact your
6.
position at this company. I can convince you that all of you ------- your position. -------. Thus, there is
7.   8.
no reason for you to worry about the upcoming changes.

5. (A) capability
(B) agreement
(C) qualification
(D) instrument

6. (A) that
(B) what
(C) how
(D) which

7. (A) retain
(B) will retain
(C) have retained
(D) would have retained

8. (A) Consequently, the staff meeting has been canceled.
(B) It is normal if you feel that way.
(C) Furthermore, you still have a job to do.
(D) We even plan to hire additional staff to help you out.

1. ------- summer arrives, stagnant bodies of water must be drained to repel mosquitoes.

(A) Before
(B) Because
(C) Although
(D) Whereas

2. ------- the director and the assistant director are authorized to make remuneration for the staff.

(A) Both
(B) Each
(C) Either
(D) Whomever

3. Exchanges on purchases will not be approved ------- a tax invoice or receipt is presented.

(A) considering
(B) despite
(C) although
(D) unless

4. ------- Marketing Insights hires a replacement for its chief financial officer, Kaitian Guan will assume the position.

(A) Until
(B) Concurrently
(C) Following
(D) Meantime

5. Ms. Boyd will make an announcement to the department members ------- the company-wide meeting will take place.

(A) when
(B) whose
(C) who
(D) what

6. The discount is no longer valid online, ------- other offers may be available at the physical store.

(A) if
(B) but
(C) again
(D) either

7. Chairman Silvia conveyed dissatisfaction that CPO Industries ------- market share compared to last year.

(A) lost
(B) loser
(C) lose
(D) losing

8. Mordring, Inc. carpeting may be coordinated with the conference room's wallpaper, obtainable in contrasting ------- complementary colors.

(A) yet
(B) still
(C) like
(D) or

Questions 9-12 refer to the following notice.

The Ellsworth City Library will be closed until further notice. Due to the -------- prevalence of storms in
the area recently, we are experiencing water leaks throughout the building. At this point, we have no
choice but to undergo -------. The plan is to repair the roof for any damages first. -------.

As the library will be unavailable to return books to, we have set up a book deposit box outside.
However, we will also be allowing patrons who already have checked out books to keep them -------
the library re-opens.

9. (A) have increased
(B) to increase
(C) increasing
(D) increase

10. (A) renovations
(B) samples
(C) explorations
(D) studies

11. (A) The library has been around for over 30
years.
(B) The library may also need new flooring.
(C) The library is fully run by volunteers.
(D) The library will be receiving new books
shortly.

12. (A) for
(B) when
(C) until
(D) between

관계사

CASE 70 관계대명사의 기본 개념

Hotel guests ------- want to extend their stays should confirm with the front desk by noon of the day prior to checkout.

(A) they   (B) which   (C) when   (D) who

> 해설 빈칸은 Hotel guests를 수식하는 형용사절을 이끄는 관계사 자리이다. 선행사가 사람이고 빈칸 뒤에 바로 동사가 나오므로 주격 관계대명사인 (D)가 정답이다.
>
> 해석 숙박 연장을 원하시는 호텔 투숙객들은 체크아웃 전 정오까지 프런트에 확인하시기를 바랍니다.

>> 관계대명사는 「접속사＋대명사」의 역할을 하며, 선행사를 수식하는 관계대명사절을 이끈다.

A free copy of Mr. Murphy's latest book is available to **anybody** if he/she pledges to make a small donation to the Make a Wish Foundation. (= who pledges to make a small donation ~ Foundation)
Murphy 씨가 최근 펴낸 책은 Make a Wish 재단에 소액 기부를 약속하면 누구나 무료로 구할 수 있다.

>> 관계대명사는 선행사의 종류와 격에 따라 구별해 쓰며, 관계대명사 뒤에는 불완전한 문장이 온다.

	사람 선행사	사물 선행사	선행사 없음	관계대명사절	해석
주격	who/that	which/that	what	＋동사	~한 선행사
목적격	who(m)/that	which/that	what	＋주어＋동사	주어가 동사한 선행사
소유격	whose	whose	-	＋명사＋동사	명사가 동사한 선행사

>> 관계대명사의 격은 관계대명사절 내의 빠진 문장 성분에 의해 결정된다.

주격	**[선행사＋주격 관계대명사＋동사]** 주어가 빠진 불완전한 문장 which (X) The **engineer who[that] is** currently in charge of the research will resign next week. 현재 연구를 담당하고 있는 엔지니어가 다음 주에 사임할 것이다. → 주격 관계대명사절의 동사는 선행사에 수와 태를 일치시킨다.
목적격	**[선행사＋목적격 관계대명사＋주어＋동사]** 목적어가 빠진 불완전한 문장 The **film festival which[that] the HR team has organized** will take place on Friday. 인사 팀이 조직한 회사 축제가 금요일에 열릴 것이다.
소유격	**[선행사＋소유격 관계대명사＋명사＋동사]** 무관사 명사로 시작되는 완전한 문장 Mr. Hill will give a lecture at the **conference whose attendees are** mostly graduate students. Hill 씨는 참석자들이 대부분 대학원생인 학회에서 강연할 것이다.

 알면 3초!   >> 관계대명사 that은 콤마 뒤에 쓰지 않는다.

To visit the headquarters of Harington Corporation, please take Highway 11 south to Exit 3, ------- is next to the Eliot Building.

(A) that   (B) where   (C) which   (D) who

'관계사 문제네! 선행사가 Exit 3(3번 출구)이고 빈칸 뒤의 관계대명사절의 주어에 해당하네!'까지 파악이 되어 주격 관계대명사를 고르려고 하니 (A), (C), (D)가 다 주격 관계대명사인 경우, 선행사가 사물이니 (D)는 소거해도 that과 which가 둘 다 남는다. 이때, '선행사에 콤마가 찍혀 있다면 that은 오답'이라는 것을 기억하자. 이럴 때는 which나 who만 가능하며 이를 계속적 용법이라 부른다. 따라서 (C)가 정답이다.

> 해석 Harington 사의 본사를 방문하시려면, 남쪽으로 11번 고속도로를 타시다가 Eliot 건물 옆의 3번 출구로 나오시면 됩니다.

PART 5

1. A meeting will be held for the delegates from the two academic research institutions, ------- will work collaboratively.

(A) who
(B) which
(C) whose
(D) what

2. First-time users are strongly encouraged to read the operation manual that ------- their product.

(A) accompany
(B) accompanying
(C) accompanies
(D) accompaniment

3. The sales director congratulated all employees whose ------- effort led to a 30 percent increase in annual revenue.

(A) collects
(C) collection
(C) collective
(D) collect

4. The user manual contains solutions to any problems you may ------- with the product.

(A) qualify
(B) encounter
(C) embrace
(D) reside

PART 6

Questions 5-8 refer to the following article.

DUBROVNIK — It was only four summers ago that Marko Gligorov started operating Boskarin Kolica, a food truck that serves gourmet street food in Dubrovnik's Old Town. Though the original operation was just Gligorov cooking and serving food by himself, it has grown substantially. -------.
5.

Before starting Boskarin Kolica, Gligorov worked at an ------- that regularly took all over Europe on
6.
a regular basis. He says he loved the work, but missed his home. "The travel was -------. I found
7.
myself in a new city almost every night, and realized I didn't want to keep doing that forever," said Gligorov.

That's why Gligorov decided to start his own venture, with the support of the city's Entrepreneurs for the Future Initiative. "I found there was plenty of ------- out there for people starting small businesses,"
8.
he said. "Without the guidance they gave me, I wouldn't have been able to do any of this.

Boskarin Kolica is open Tuesday-Sunday in Old Town. Find where the truck is today at BoskarinKolica. hr.

5. (A) He has no plans to open a permanent location for the restaurant.
(B) Lines outside the food truck are usually short.
(C) Gligorov moved to Dubrovink for culinary school.
(D) Now Boskarin Kolica employs two cooks and a social media manager.

6. (A) organized
(B) organizing
(C) organization
(D) organize

7. (A) satisfying
(B) occasional
(C) exhausting
(D) private

8. (A) assistance
(B) substitution
(C) concession
(D) ability

CASE 71   관계대명사 that vs. what

Ashraf Iftikhar marketed a device ------- he invented while studying to be an electrical engineer.

(A) what   (B) that   (C) though   (D) where

콕 찍어 포인트 ···› 목적격 관계대명사는 완전한 문장(주절)과 목적어가 빠진 불완전한 문장(관계대명사절)을 연결하는 역할을 하며, 문장 내에서 생략할 수 있다.

해설 빈칸은 완전한 문장과 「주어 + 동사」 사이의 자리이다. 동사 invented는 목적어를 필요로 하는 타동사라는 것을 고려할 때, 빈칸은 a device를 선행사로 하는 목적격 관계대명사 자리이므로 (B)가 정답이다.

해석 Ashraf Iftikhar는 전기 엔지니어가 되기 위해 공부하는 동안 그가 발명한 장치를 시장에 내놓았다.

>> 관계대명사 that은 불완전한 문장을 이끌며, 명사절 접속사 that은 완전한 문장을 이끈다.

North Airlines announced **the plan that** 관계대명사 that **will reduce the number of its nonstop flights** to Tokyo.
North 항공사는 Tokyo행 직항 노선의 수를 줄일 계획을 발표했다.

cf. North Airlines **announced that** 명사절 접속사 that **it will reduce the number of its nonstop flights** to Tokyo.
North 항공사는 Tokyo행 직항 노선의 수를 줄일 것이라고 발표했다.

>> 관계대명사 what은 주격이나 목적격 관계대명사로 쓰이며, 불완전한 문장을 이끈다.

What is important to us 주격 is that clients are happy with our products.
우리에게 중요한 것은 고객들이 우리 제품에 만족해하는 것이다.

The travel guides show **what travelers should do** 목적격 in case of an accident overseas.
여행 가이드는 해외에서 사고가 일어날 경우에 대비해 여행객들이 해야 하는 것을 보여준다.

>> 관계대명사 what은 선행사가 내재해 있어, 선행사 없이 명사절을 이끈다.

The manager reviewed **what** Mr. Lowry reported. that (X), what = the thing which
그 관리자는 Lowry 씨가 보고한 것을 검토했다.

cf. The manager reviewed **the findings that** Mr. Lowry reported. what (X)
그 관리자는 Lowry 씨가 보고한 조사 결과들을 검토했다.

→ 선행사를 포함하는 관계대명사 what은 '~하는 것'으로 해석되어, 선행사를 수식하는 관계대명사 that과 구별된다.

 알면 3초!   >> 관계대명사 that 앞에는 명사가 있고, what 앞에는 명사가 없다.

A ceremony will be held in honor of all athletes ------- played on the football team this year.
(A) their   (B) they   (C) what   (D) that

문제를 풀 때 자주 나오는 보기가 what과 that이다. 생김새도 비슷하고, 쓰임새도 비슷해서 혼동하기 쉽기 때문이다. 관계대명사 문제에서 앞에 명사가 있으면 that, 없으면 what이 정답이란 얘기를 종종 들었을 텐데, 이는 what에 선행사가 들어 있는 특징 때문이다. 선행사를 스스로 가지고 있으니 what을 쓰려면 앞에 선행하는 명사가 있으면 안 된다. 그러니 what과 that이 보기에 함께 등장한다면 빈칸 앞에 명사가 있는지 먼저 살펴보자. 위의 문제에서 빈칸은 앞의 완전한 문장과 뒤의 불완전한 문장을 연결하는 역할을 하며, 앞에 선행하는 명사(athletes)가 있으므로 (D)가 정답이다.

해석 올해 축구팀에서 뛰었던 모든 선수들을 기리기 위해 기념식이 열릴 것이다.

PART 5

1. ------- is particularly remarkable about Mega Express Market is its one-day delivery option.
(A) Why
(B) That
(C) Which
(D) What

2. The HR department requests ------- all employees submit their monthly expense reports by 2 P.M. on April 25.
(A) that
(B) what
(C) about
(D) if

3. The online employee training video explains ------- new employees need to know regarding workplace safety regulations.
(A) how
(B) where
(C) which
(D) what

4. If you need to improve your public speaking ability, a course at Toronto Business Academy may be ------- what you are looking for.
(A) exactly
(B) professionally
(C) necessarily
(D) helpfully

PART 6

Questions 5-8 refer to the following article.

Da Nang (February 12) — Bien Dong Enterprises has plans to open a world-class water park in the area. The firm ------- its proposal for the water park to local authorities on Friday. Officials are said to have been "favorably impressed" with the plans.
5.

The attractions at the park will include a special pool with waves to challenge even the most advanced surfers. But for less adventurous visitors, there is also a pleasant water slide that flows ------- down to an enormous swimming area. There will also be a large aquarium devoted to providing a ------- learning experience about the area's marine life. "We want to give visitors a chance to immerse themselves in the wonders of the ocean," says Chief Planner Dao Viet Ha. The park will be located on Hon Kho Lon Island, just a short boat ride from Hoi An City. -------.
6. **7.** **8.**

5. (A) submitted
(B) to submit
(C) had submitted
(D) will submit

6. (A) slowed
(B) slowing
(C) slows
(D) slowly

7. (A) confirmed
(B) revised
(C) realistic
(D) possible

8. (A) Bien Dong Enterprises has launched a number of successful projects in the past.
(B) Dao was previously the director of an oceanography institute in Nha Trang.
(C) It has a stunning view of the ocean on all sides.
(D) Surfing has gained popularity in Vietnam as tourism has increased.

전치사 + 관계대명사

The Greenich Bank offers all loan applicants remote consultations during ------- details of each applicant's financial history are discussed online.

(A) which   (B) where   (C) while   (D) whose

> 해설   빈칸은 사물 선행사(remote consultations)를 수식하며 전치사 during의 목적어 역할을 할 수 있는 목적격 관계대명사 (A)가 정답이다. 전치사 뒤의 목적어 자리에는 관계부사 (B), 부사절 접속사 (C)는 올 수 없다.
>
> 해석   Greenich 은행은 모든 대출 신청자들에게 원격 상담을 제공하는데, 그동안 각 신청자의 재정 기록에 대한 정보가 온라인에서 논의된다.

>> 선행사가 관계대명사절 내 전치사의 목적어에 해당할 때는 「전치사 + 목적격 관계대명사」 형태로 쓴다.

The community center offers **a facility and** residents can enjoy fitness activities **in the facility**.
   ⌐ The community center offers **a facility in which** residents can enjoy fitness activities.
     주민 센터는 주민들이 체력 단련 활동을 즐길 수 있는 시설을 제공한다.

>> 「전치사 + 목적격 관계대명사」 뒤에는 완전한 문장이 온다.

To initiate a file download, click on one of the links below and select the folder **in which you would like to save the file**.
파일 다운로드를 시작하려면, 아래의 링크 중 하나를 클릭하여 파일을 저장하고 싶은 폴더를 선택하세요.
→ 선행사가 관계대명사절의 전치사구에 해당하므로 「전치사 + 목적격 관계대명사」 뒤에는 완전한 문장이 온다.

>> 전치사 뒤에는 관계대명사 that을 쓸 수 없다.

                            ↱ on that (X)
The government will provide the land **on which** the crops will be grown.
정부는 농작물을 경작할 땅을 제공할 것이다.

>> 선행사의 일부나 전체를 나타낼 때는 「일부/전체의 수량 표현 + of + 목적격 관계대명사」 형태로 쓴다.

                                             ↱ all of whom (X)
Digital Players, Inc. carries a wide range of **computer games, all of which** can be downloaded online.
Digital Players 사는 다양한 컴퓨터 게임을 취급하는데, 이들 모두를 온라인에서 다운로드할 수 있다.
→ 일반 목적격 관계대명사와 마찬가지로 선행사가 사람이면 whom을, 사물이면 which를 쓴다.

알면 3초!   >> 목적격 관계대명사 앞에 오는 전치사는 선행사와 관계대명사절의 동사로 결정한다.

The date ------- which members may purchase tickets for the new exhibition has been pushed back.

(A) as   (B) from   (C) into   (D) about

알맞은 전치사를 고르는 문제로 딱히 힌트가 보이지 않아 해석을 잘 해보고 골라야 한다. 전치사를 넣을 빈칸 뒤에 관계대명사절이 연결되어 있다면, 빈칸 앞 명사가 선행사가 되어 관계대명사절의 전치사구에 해당한다는 것이다. 그렇다면 'Members may purchase tickets for the new exhibition ------- the date'로 바꿔서 보기들을 대입해 봐야 한다. '회원들이 티켓을 구매할 수 있는데, 그 날짜부터(from) 구매할 수 있다는 거군!'이라고 해석해 봤더니 의미가 통한다면 (B)를 찍고 다음 문제로 넘어가는 거고, 여전히 다른 보기와 헷갈린다면 그때 나머지 보기도 마저 넣어서 해석해 봐야 한다.

> 해석   회원들이 새 전시회 입장권의 구매를 시작할 수 있는 날짜가 미루어졌다.

PART 5

1. Mr. Garfield needs more training for the new project, ------- he will be in charge of data management.
(A) in which
(B) along with
(C) not only
(D) instead of

2. Résumés and cover letters may be submitted via the company's recruitment website, in ------- case the documents should be uploaded as a single file.
(A) what
(B) which
(C) that
(D) whose

3. Ten photographs, five of ------- were over 100 years old, were recently found on the property.
(A) what
(B) which
(C) them
(D) these

4. Lately, Greenville Hospital has received a number of large donations, ------- are from members of former patients and local charities.
(A) considering that
(B) the reason for
(C) most of which
(D) due to them

PART 6

Questions 5-8 refer to the following article.

Birdie's Lends a Hand

(24 June) — Birdie's, the leading supplier of bottled water in Arlington, has made a bold promise. Partnering with the United Aid Organization (UAO), Birdie's will be providing clean water to impoverished countries in Asia. CEO Sinead Legge ------- last year to traveling in Asia to gain a better understanding of the conditions these countries face. -------. Ms. Legge then spent time meeting with employees from UAO, ------- they agreed on the best strategy to help these regions. Ms. Legge has also challenged her ------- to do the same. "We are in a position to lend a hand," she says, "So what are we waiting for?"

5. (A) will dedicate
(B) to dedicate
(C) dedicated
(D) dedicate

6. (A) Ms. Legge has considered stepping down from her role.
(B) UAO has offices set up in various locations across Asia.
(C) What she saw compelled her to take action.
(D) Other regions can also be considered in the future.

7. (A) where
(B) that
(C) upon
(D) why

8. (A) shares
(B) components
(C) activities
(D) competitors

The city council released a list of local businesses ------- considers to be the most beneficial to the community.

(A) its own   (B) itself   (C) its   (D) it

해설   빈칸 앞이 완전한 문장이고 뒤에 연결사와 주어 없이 동사 considers로 시작하는 것으로 보아, 빈칸 이하의 절은 선행사 local businesses를 수식하는 문장으로서 목적격 관계대명사가 생략된 관계사절이고 빈칸은 관계사절의 주어 자리이다. 따라서, 동사 considers 앞에서 주어가 될 수 있는 it이 The city council을 받으면서 '시 의회(it)가 가장 유익하다고 여기는 지역 기업체 목록'이라고 보는 것이 적합하므로 (D)가 정답이다.

해석   시 의회는 그것이 지역 사회에 가장 유익하다고 여기는 지역 기업체 목록을 공개했다.

>> 「주격 관계대명사 + be동사」는 생략할 수 있다. → 「선행사 + 분사 / 형용사」

Employees (who are) interested in relocating branches should contact Ms. Lee.
지점 이전에 관심이 있는 직원들은 Lee 씨에게 연락해야 한다.
→ 「주격 관계대명사 + be동사」가 생략된 경우 선행사 바로 뒤에 분사나 형용사가 온다.

>> 목적격 관계대명사는 생략할 수 있다. → 「선행사 + 주어 + 동사」

The **fitness center (which) PEX Ltd. has been renovating** will open to employees next month.
PEX 사가 개조하고 있는 체육관이 다음 달에 직원들에게 개방될 것이다.
→ 목적격 관계대명사가 생략된 경우 선행사 바로 뒤에 「주어 + 동사」가 온다.

>> 전치사 뒤에 오는 목적격 관계대명사는 생략할 수 없다.

Full-time employees are required to provide the date **on which** they are available to meet with the CEO.
상근직 직원들은 CEO와 만나기 위해 시간이 되는 날짜를 알려주어야 한다.

 알면 3초!   >> 문장의 본동사와 관계대명사절의 동사를 구별한다.

Please use the copier sparingly, since the toner cartridges it requires ------- temporarily unavailable.

(A) being   (B) what   (C) are   (D) which

목적격 관계대명사가 생략될 수 있다는 사실을 모르면, 위와 같은 문제에서, since절의 주어가 toner cartridges인 건 알겠는데, 동사가 requires인 건지, 그러면 it은 왜 들어가 있는 건지, 어떻게 해석해야 할지 등 머릿속이 복잡해지기 쉽다. 출제자는 이를 노려 목적격 관계대명사가 생략되어 있는 문장을 제시하여 관계대명사절의 주어나 동사를 찾으라거나 지금처럼 문장의 본동사를 찾으라는 문제를 출제한다. 앞서 배웠듯이 목적격 관계대명사절의 기본 구조는 「선행사 + 목적격 관계대명사 + 주어 + 동사」로 '주어가 동사한 선행사'로 해석하며, 목적격 관계대명사는 생략할 수 있으므로 「선행사 + 주어 + 동사」도 가능하다. 위 문제에서 since 뒤의 문장 구조가 「명사(the toner cartridges, 선행사) + 주어(it = the copier) + 동사(requires)」이니 목적격 관계대명사가 생략되었음을 간파했다면 requires는 관계대명사절의 동사이므로 since절의 본동사가 빠져 있다는 것을 알 수 있다. 보기 중 본동사로 가능한 형태는 (C)뿐이며, 빈칸에 are가 들어가야 문장이 완벽해진다.

해석   복사기에 필요한 토너 카트리지가 당분간 구입할 수 없는 상태이므로 복사기를 아껴 써주시기 바랍니다.

해설서 p.105

PART 5

1. To appeal to a younger audience, Channel 12 has created more shows ------- for children.

(A) improvised
(B) classical
(C) disagreeable
(D) appropriate

2. The HR manager could not start the employee orientation because the conference room ------- usually used was no longer available.

(A) he
(B) that
(C) was
(D) whose

3. The revised manuscript contains information Mr. Rogers -------.

(A) correct
(B) to correct
(C) has been corrected
(D) will correct

4. There is sensitive information ------- to all aspects of the company and its clients in a secure server at the company's headquarters.

(A) relevance
(B) relevant
(C) relevantly
(D) relevancy

PART 6

Questions 5-8 refer to the following information.

Chastain Electronics guarantees that its products will ------- as advertised for at least two years from
the purchase date. -------. This warranty applies only to items ------- at Chastain Electronics stores
and other licensed retailers. Items that are found to be damaged may be mailed back to our address
for repair or exchange. Please be aware that, whenever possible, items that are being returned due
to ------- should be mailed to us in the original box.

5. (A) value
(B) practice
(C) function
(D) expect

6. (A) Chastain Electronics stores are located in four countries.
(B) A digital receipt was sent to you at that time.
(C) Item samples are available in our stores.
(D) Under specific cases, this period may be extended for some products.

7. (A) sold
(B) sale
(C) were sold
(D) to sell

8. (A) distraction
(B) urgency
(C) defect
(D) charge

복합 관계대명사

Ms. Romaneski was directed to choose ------- she decided was the safest delivery method.

(A) whichever (B) some (C) whoever (D) rest

콕 찍어 포인트 ··· ① 접속사 없이 한 문장에 두 개 이상의 동사가 올 수 없다.
② 문장에서 명사절 또는 부사절을 이끌 수 있는 복합 관계대명사는 그 자체에 선행사를 포함하고 있다. 명사절일 때에는 문장의 주어 또는 목적어 자리에 올 수 있으며, whoever는 'anyone who ~(~하는 사람이면 누구든지)'로, whatever/whichever는 'anything that ~(~하는 것은 무엇이든지)'을 의미한다.

해설 빈칸은 동사 choose의 목적어인 명사 자리이다. 빈칸 뒤에 동사가 2개(decided, was) 등장함을 고려할 때, 빈칸은 문장을 명사절로 만들어주는 접속사 자리이다. 첫 번째 동사는 '주어(she) + 동사(decided)'의 형태를 갖추어 문장 내 삽입된 절임을 알 수 있으며, 두 번째 동사 was에 해당하는 주어가 없으므로 빈칸에는 주어 및 명사절 접속사 역할을 하는 복합 관계대명사가 나와야 하므로 (A)가 정답이다.

해석 Romaneski 씨는 그녀가 결정한 가장 안전한 배송 방법이 무엇이든 선택하라는 지시를 받았다.

>> 복합 관계대명사 = 「선행사 + 관계대명사」

whoever = anyone who ~하는 사람은 누구든지	whatever = anything that ~하는 것은 무엇이든지	whichever = anything that ~하는 것은 어떤 것이든지

↗ Anyone (X)
Whoever is interested in getting an employee discount for the new product should speak to their manager.
신제품에 대한 직원 할인을 받는 데 관심이 있는 분은 누구든지 자신의 매니저에게 얘기하셔야 합니다.
→ Whoever는 선행사를 포함한 관계대명사로 Anyone who와 바꿔 쓸 수 있다.

>> 「복합 관계대명사 + 불완전한 문장」 vs. 「복합 관계부사 + 완전한 문장」

복합 관계대명사	복합 관계부사
whoever/whatever/whichever + 불완전한 문장	whenever/wherever/however + 완전한 문장

↗ whenever (X)
You can bring **whatever you need for the flight** in this carry-on bag.
이 휴대용 가방 안에 비행에 필요한 것은 무엇이든 가져오실 수 있습니다.
→ 문장의 목적어 자리에 온 whatever는 불완전한 문장(동사 need의 목적어가 빠짐)을 이끌어 문장의 목적어 역할을 한다.

 알면 3초! >> '복합 관계대명사 vs. 의문사' 또는 '복합 관계대명사 vs. 복합 관계대명사'는 해석을 통해 판단한다.

------- gets the best evaluation will be promoted to Branch Manager.

(A) Who (B) Wherever (C) Anyone (D) Whoever

우선 해석을 하기 전에 각 보기가 문법적으로 빈칸이 위치한 문장 맨 앞에 올 수 있는지 살펴본다. (A)는 의문 대명사이자, 주격·목적격 관계대명사에 해당하며, (B)는 복합 관계부사, (C)는 일반 대명사, (D)는 복합 관계대명사에 해당한다. 빈칸 뒤에 주어가 빠진 불완전한 절이 오고(gets the best evaluation), 그 뒤로 동사(will be promoted)가 연결된 형태이므로 '빈칸은 불완전한 절을 이끌어서 문장의 주어 역할을 해야 하는구나'라는 생각에 이르러야 한다. 그렇다면 우리가 배운 대로, 절을 이끌어 문장의 주어로 쓰일 수 있는 명사절 접속사를 떠올려야 하고 보기에서 명사절 접속사에 해당하지 않는 대명사 (C)와(대명사는 접속사의 기능이 없다!) 완전한 절을 이끄는 복합 관계부사 (B)를 소거할 수 있어야 한다. 남은 의문 대명사 (A)와 복합 관계대명사 (D)는 해석을 통해 답을 명확히 가릴 수 있고, 의미상 '~한 사람은 누구든지'라는 Whoever가 나와야 하므로 (D)를 답으로 고른다. 이처럼 문법적인 판단으로 답이 될 수 없는 보기를 재빨리 소거하고, '복합 관계대명사 vs. 의문사' 또는 '복합 관계대명사 vs. 복합 관계대명사'만 남으면 해석을 통해 답을 결정한다.

해석 가장 좋은 평가를 받는 사람은 누구든지 지점 매니저로 승진할 것이다.

PART 5

1. We only have a few reference sources, so remember to quickly return ------- ones you signed out.

(A) whichever
(B) wherever
(C) whose
(D) what

2. Please e-mail me the transcript of the meeting with Mr. Torres ------- it is possible for you.

(A) whatever
(B) likewise
(C) containing
(D) whenever

3. ------- accesses company files on public computers should make sure to delete them when finished.

(A) Whatever
(B) Whoever
(C) Everyone
(D) Anything

4. The e-mail sent by the director stated that employees may discuss ------- they like at the upcoming all-hands meeting.

(A) those
(B) most
(C) it
(D) whatever

PART 6

Questions 5-8 refer to the following memo.

To: All maintenance personnel
From: Ricardo Strauss
Date: Tuesday, January 8
Subject: Vehicle inspection

Everyone,

As discussed at yesterday's Maintenance Department meeting, the management team ------- a
            5.
detailed inspection of all runway vehicles. Their aim is to determine ------- transport and luggage-
                                                        6.
handling vehicles need to be replaced.

We would appreciate your assistance on this -------. Be sure to indicate any mechanical defects or
                                      7.
persistent issues you have encountered when operating the vehicles. Please do this by submitting
form RV100 to your supervisor. -------. You only need to include the vehicle's model number and a
                          8.
short summary explaining the problem. As always, thank you for your hard work.

5. (A) will be conducting
(B) should conduct
(C) was conducting
(D) will have conducted

6. (A) each
(B) which
(C) some
(D) whom

7. (A) trial
(B) matter
(C) type
(D) location

8. (A) The meeting schedule has not been finalized yet.
(B) Please let us know if anyone is interested in becoming a maintenance worker.
(C) It is unnecessary to provide comprehensive details.
(D) The cause of the problem is still being determined.

CASE 75 관계부사

Don't miss this year's Culinary Trade Show, ------- a variety of innovative professional cooking devices will be presented.

(A) where   (B) also   (C) then   (D) if

꼭 찍어 포인트 ··· 관계부사 where는 「접속사 + 장소부사구」 역할을 하며, 문장에서 수식어 역할을 하는 부사구를 대신하기 때문에 관계부사 뒤에는 완전한 문장이 온다.

해설 빈칸은 콤마와 함께 완전한 두 문장을 연결하는 자리이다. 문맥상 '요리 무역 박람회에서 전문 조리 기구가 선보일 것이다'라는 의미로 이어져야 자연스러우므로 「접속사 + 장소부사구 (and + at this year's Culinary Trade Show」를 지칭하는 관계부사 (A)가 정답이다.

해석 다양한 혁신적인 전문 조리 기구가 선보일 올해의 요리 무역 박람회를 놓치지 마세요.

>> 관계부사는 「접속사 + 부사」의 역할을 하며, 「전치사 + 관계대명사」로 바꿔 쓸 수 있다.

Every August, the city's community center holds **a job fair and** many companies interview college students for job openings **there**.

└ Every August, the city's community center holds a job fair **where** many companies interview college students for job openings.   = at which

매년 8월, 시 지역 주민 센터는 취업 박람회를 개최하는데, 그곳에서 많은 기업들이 채용을 위해 대학생들을 면접한다.

	선행사	관계부사	전치사 + 관계대명사	해석 (선행사를 가리키며)
장소	장소 명사	where	in/on/at/to which	그곳에서
시간	시간 명사	when	in/on/at/during which	그때
이유	the reason	why	for which	그것 때문에
방법	the way*	how*	in which	그 방법으로

* 선행사 the way와 관계부사 how는 둘 중 하나만 쓸 수 있다. (*the way how X)

>> 관계부사 뒤에는 완전한 문장이 온다.

Due to the continuous increase in rent, TRC Pharmacy will inevitably move to another location **where rent is more affordable**.
            완전한 문장

지속적인 임대료 상승으로 인해, TRC 약국은 불가피하게 임대료가 보다 저렴한 다른 곳으로 이전할 것이다.

→ 선행사가 관계부사절의 부사에 해당하므로 관계부사 뒤에는 완전한 문장이 온다.

 알면 3초!   >> 알맞은 관계부사를 골라야 할 때 선행사를 먼저 확인한다.

The Hill Bank offers all loan applicants one-on-one interviews ------- details of each applicant's financial history are discussed.

(A) which   (B) when   (C) why   (D) what

관계대명사 (A)와 (D)는 뒤에 불완전한 문장이 온다고 했는데, 빈칸 뒤에 수동태인 완전한 문장으로 연결되어 있으니 두 개의 보기를 소거한다. (B)와 (C)는 방금 배웠듯, 관계부사로도 쓰인다는 걸 알았으니 해석을 해봐야 한다. 보기에 두 개 이상의 관계부사가 들어 있다면 제일 먼저 선행사를 끌어와 빈칸 뒤의 내용과 어울리는지 확인한다. (사실 대부분의 관계부사 문제는 선행사로 명확한 장소나 시간을 제시하여 선행사가 장소면 where, 시간이면 when, 이런 식으로 나오는데, 그 보다는 난이도가 높은 문제이긴 하다.) 어쨌든 interview '때' 어떤 정보가 논의된다는 게 맞는지, interview '때문에' 어떤 정보가 논의된다는 게 맞는지 따져보면 답은 (B)로 분명해진다!

해석 Hill 은행은 모든 대출 신청자들에게 각 신청자의 재무 기록에 대한 정보가 논의되는 일대일 면담을 제공한다.

PART 5

1. Every year, the university holds a free seminar ------- mental health professionals discuss topics on clinical depression.

(A) where
(B) there
(C) it
(D) which

2. Calwell Financial Services puts all new employees through a training period during ------- exams for several professional licenses are taken.

(A) when
(B) what
(C) which
(D) where

3. The CEO of Blitz International moved to Hong Kong, ------- he founded a data analytics company called Nomad Analysis.

(A) what
(B) where
(C) which
(D) while

4. The Temple Tower Building, ------- which OBW Logistics has resided for the last nine years, will undergo renovations this June.

(A) down
(B) from
(C) until
(D) in

PART 6

Questions 5-8 refer to the following information.

At Carver Auto, we take pride in our vehicles' durability, and that's why every one of them comes with a full 50,000-mile guarantee, which ------- for just a few dollars more. But just in case your car or truck is ever in need of repair, make sure to fill out the form below and send it in to our headquarters.
5.
All repairs must be performed by an approved Carver Auto mechanic. -------, you will be responsible for the full cost of the repairs. Make sure to enclose a detailed invoice with your claim ------- verify the mechanic's certification.
6.
7.

A refund will be sent in the form of a check. -------. To expedite the process, you can fax or email the paperwork to us.
8.

5. (A) extend
(B) extendable
(C) had been extended
(D) may be extended

6. (A) Therefore
(B) Otherwise
(C) Likewise
(D) Instead

7. (A) in order to
(B) in reference to
(C) in response to
(D) in addition to

8. (A) Carver Auto's vehicles are rated number one for reliability.
(B) Thanks again for your purchase, and drive safely.
(C) It will take 2 to 4 weeks to receive your reimbursement.
(D) To find a certified dealer, please visit our Web site.

복합 관계부사

At Berglioni's Restaurant, reservations are required ------- there is a convention at the hotel nearby.

(A) whatever　　　　(B) whenever　　　　(C) whoever　　　　(D) however

콕 찍어 포인트 ··· 복합 관계대명사 whatever '~하는 무엇이든지', whoever '~하는 누구든지'는 불완전한 절을 이끈다.

해설 빈칸은 두 개의 완전한 문장을 연결하는 접속사 자리이다. 복합 관계부사 whenever이 완전한 절을 이어줄 수 있음을 고려할 때, 빈칸 뒤가 완전한 절이고 문맥상 'Berglioni's 레스토랑은 근처의 호텔에서 컨벤션이 있을 때면 언제나 예약을 해야 한다'라는 의미가 되어야 자연스러우므로 (B)가 정답이다.

해석 Berglioni's 레스토랑은 근처의 호텔에서 컨벤션이 있을 때면 언제나 예약을 해야 한다.

≫ 복합 관계부사는 「관계부사＋-ever」의 형태로 부사절을 이끈다.

whenever = no matter when	wherever = no matter where	however = no matter how
언제 ~하더라도[하든]	어디서 ~하더라도[하든]	아무리 ~하더라도, 어떻게 ~하든

↪ whatever (X)
Please call the customer service line **whenever you have a technical issue**.
기술적 문제가 있을 때는 언제든 고객서비스 전화로 연락해 주십시오.　　　완전한 문장

≫ 복합 관계부사 however는 바로 뒤에 형용사나 부사가 먼저 온다.

whenever / wherever + 주어 + 동사	+ 주절
however + 형용사/부사 + 주어 + 동사	

↪ whenever (X)
However often singers may stand in front of large crowds, they still experience some stage fright.
가수들은 많은 군중 앞에 서는 일이 아무리 자주 있다고 해도, 여전히 어느 정도의 무대 공포증을 경험한다.

 알면 3초!　　≫ 복합 관계대명사는 명사절과 부사절을 모두 이끈다.

------- finds a solution to this problem will be given a special reward by the CEO.
(A) That　　　　(B) Whom　　　　(C) Whoever　　　　(D) Anybody

복합 관계대명사	명사절	부사절
whoever	~하는 사람은 누구든지(= anyone who)	누가 ~하든지(= no matter who)
whatever	~하는 것은 무엇이든지(= anything that)	무엇을 ~하든지(= no matter what)
whichever	~하는 것은 어느 것이든지(= anything that)	어느 것을 ~하든지(= no matter which)

복합 관계대명사는 명사절을 이끈다. 그런데 복합 관계부사와 마찬가지로 복합 관계대명사는 부사절을 이끌기도 한다. 둘 다 불완전한 문장을 이끌며, 의미상의 차이는 거의 일어나지 않지만, 명사절을 이끄는 명사절 접속사로 쓰일 때와 부사절을 이끄는 부사절 접속사로 쓰일 때의 형태상의 차이를 아래에 다시 써본다. 위 문제에서 빈칸은 사람을 나타내고 명사절을 이끄므로 복합 관계대명사 (C)가 정답이다.

Whoever finds a solution to this problem will be given a special reward by the CEO.
　　명사절 = 주어　　　　　　　　　동사

Whoever finds a solution to this problem, they will be given a special reward by the CEO.
　　　　부사절　　　　　　　　주어　　동사

위 문제에서 빈칸은 사람을 나타내고 부사절을 이끄므로 복합 관계대명사 (C)가 정답이다.

해석 이 문제에 대한 해결책을 찾는 사람은 누구든지 CEO로부터 특별한 보상을 받을 것이다.

PART 5

1. ------- carefully the accountant goes through the figures, there is always a possibility of an error being made.
(A) Hardly
(B) However
(C) Cautiously
(D) Fairly

2. ------- a national holiday falls on a Saturday, Finley Ltd. allows its employees to take an extra day off the following week.
(A) Despite
(B) Whenever
(C) Nearly
(D) By

3. Whenever customers are lined up outside the restaurant, we must offer them free beverages -------.
(A) actively
(B) initially
(C) promptly
(D) greatly

4. ------- inconvenient it may be, visitors to the Wakeville College Dormitories must provide an acceptable form of identification.
(A) No matter how
(B) Notwithstanding
(C) In order that
(D) Nonetheless

PART 6

Questions 5-8 refer to the following e-mail.

To: Blackwell Orchestra <orchestra@bwcommunity.com>
From: Gladys Phelps <gphelps@bwcommunity.com>
Date: 25 March
Subject: Performance Date

Dear members,

I have just received confirmation for our annual summer performance. The ------- will be the Opera
5.
House, and we are scheduled to perform on 19 June. ------- will be performing the same program
6.
as we did when we visited Bennett in December last year. The reason for using the same program is because we haven't had much time to rehearse together due to the holiday season. I will be going overseas in April -------. In my opinion, it will be easier if we perform something we are already
7.
familiar with. I have uploaded the score again in case you lost your copy. -------. I will bring some
8.
copies in case you don't bring yours. I hope to see everyone there.

Sincerely,

Gladys Phelps, Conductor

5. (A) venue
(B) situation
(C) plan
(D) deal

6. (A) I
(B) They
(C) We
(D) It

7. (A) since
(B) therefore
(C) as well
(D) however

8. (A) The program is likely to change before then.
(B) You may purchase a copy directly from me if needed.
(C) New members are also welcome to join us.
(D) We'll have our first rehearsal next Monday at our usual time.

1. The directors will gather on Tuesday to see ------- will be appointed Chief Finance Officer.

(A) who
(B) when
(C) which
(D) whose

2. Having a subway station ------- is within walking distance from your home is a practical choice.

(A) where
(B) that
(C) it
(D) here

3. Ida Manning is a renowned tapestry artist ------- products are unparalleled in their exquisite designs and impeccable quality.

(A) as
(B) whose
(C) her
(D) how

4. Artists who care about ------- in the quality of their work paint with Worchester brand brushes.

(A) consistent
(B) consisting
(C) consistently
(D) consistency

5. ParkPlace Industries' employees ------- have signed the new employment contracts may work from their homes once a week.

(A) those
(B) anyone
(C) they
(D) who

6. Mr. Barry is printing the documents ------- prepared for this week's meeting.

(A) he
(B) his
(C) him
(D) himself

7. In their application, prospective students should state only those portions of their education ------- that pertain to the degree they are pursuing.

(A) attitudes
(B) history
(C) appointments
(D) institution

8. A critical ------- of the new electrical vehicle was the high price point, which discouraged many potential buyers.

(A) opportunity
(B) shortcoming
(C) dependency
(D) exaggeration

Questions 9-12 refer to the following article.

GENOA (September 21) — Lincoln County Zoo will finally be re-opening its doors to the public on Saturday, September 25. The zoo, which has been closed for renovations since February, will offer upgraded facilities for guests. The renovations saw the addition of a safari zone as well as a children's area. -------.
        9.

Lincoln County mayor Rose Erickson will be cutting the ceremonial ribbon at 9 A.M., followed by an opening speech. -------, the opening ceremony is expected to run for one hour. The mayor,
                   10.
------- was the catalyst behind the renovation project, previously spoke about the need for Lincoln
  11.
County to attract more tourists. Additionally, the zoo is also being seen as providing ------- learning
                                                                                        12.
experiences to children. Erickson notes that learning more about animals will pave the way for greater animal conversation efforts in the future.

9. (A) Some membership passes may not be valid upon reopening.
(B) There may be ongoing construction for the next few months.
(C) The plans for the next phase of renovations will be released shortly.
(D) The latter is conveniently located next to a new café.

10. (A) Prior to
(B) In all
(C) Sometime
(D) Consequently

11. (A) who
(B) her
(C) that
(D) she

12. (A) signify
(B) significantly
(C) significant
(D) significance

특수 구문

CASE 77 원급 비교

Last year, our department made ------- as much money as it had made in the entire decade before.

(A) nearby   (B) nearest   (C) nearly   (D) nearer

> **콕 찍어 포인트** ⋯ 수치, 양을 나타내는 표현 앞에 주로 사용되는 부사는 nearly/almost(거의), about/around/approximately(대략), just(딱, 단지), only(오직) 등이 있다.
>
> **해설** 빈칸은 원급 비교 구문 「as + 형용사/부사의 원급 + as」의 앞 자리이다. '이전 10년 동안 벌었던 것과 거의 같은 돈'이라는 의미가 되어야 자연스러우므로 (C)가 정답이다.
>
> **해석** 작년에 우리 부서는 이전 10년 동안 벌었던 것과 거의 같은 돈을 벌었다.

>> 원급 비교 구문: 두 비교 대상이 동등할 때 원급 비교를 쓴다.

as + 형용사/부사의 원급 + as …만큼 ~한/하게

Fortunately, the trip to Shanghai was **as exciting as** I expected.
다행히도 Shanghai 여행은 내가 기대했던 만큼 재미있었다.

as + 형용사/부사의 원급 + as possible 가능한 한 ~한/하게

The ad campaign for the new computer should be changed **as dramatically as possible** to attract customer attention.
고객들의 관심을 끌려면 새 컴퓨터의 광고 캠페인이 가능한 한 인상적으로 변경되어야 한다.

as many/few + 복수 가산 명사 + as …만큼이나 많은/적은

The management should listen to **as many opinions as** possible to make a democratic decision.
경영진은 민주적인 결정을 내리기 위해 되도록 많은 의견을 들어야 한다.

as much/little + 불가산 명사 + as …만큼이나 많은/적은

Our company aims to provide **as much information as** possible on legal issues.
우리 회사는 법적인 문제에 대해 가능한 한 많은 정보를 제공하는 것을 목표로 한다.

>> 원급 강조 부사

very/so/extremely/quite/too 매우, 아주, 대단히

↗ more helpful (X)
The assistant has been **quite helpful** with organizing the project files.
그 보조원은 프로젝트 파일을 정리하는 데 대단히 도움이 되었다.

 알면 3초!   >> 원급의 품사(형용사 vs. 부사)는 「as ~ as」를 빼고 문장 구조를 확인한다.

No previous suppliers were as ------- to our requests as SEM Corp.

(A) response   (B) respond   (C) responsive   (D) responsively

원급 비교 구문 「as ~ as」 사이에 들어갈 알맞은 품사를 묻는 문제는 비교 구문의 단골 문제로, 「as ~ as」 사이에 원급 형용사나 부사가 들어간다는 건 알고 있다. 「as ~ as」는 문장 성분에 아무런 영향을 주지 않는, 그저 비교 구문을 만들기 위해 들어가는 장식품에 불과하기 때문에 「as ~ as」를 벗겨내고 앞의 동사가 무엇인지 살핀다. 앞의 동사가 일반 동사라면 동사를 수식하는 부사 자리이고, be동사 등의 2형식 동사라면 보어 역할의 형용사 자리이다. 위 문제에서 빈칸은 be동사의 보어 역할을 하는 형용사 자리이므로 (C)가 정답이다.

해석 이전의 어떤 공급업체들도 SEM 만큼 우리의 요청에 응하지 않았다.

CASE 집중훈련

PART 5

1. Marlena Stewart's newest article is a ------- and revealing analysis of stock market trends.

(A) most thoughtful
(B) thoughtfully
(C) thoughtful
(D) thought

2. No previous client was as ------- to our feedback as Mr. Newman.

(A) respond
(B) responds
(C) responsive
(D) responsively

3. Advertising on ------- social media platforms as possible can be expensive, but it is the most effective in reaching a younger demographic.

(A) as many
(B) as much
(C) quite many
(D) quite much

4. Few of the dehumidifiers tested for their capacity turned out to be as impressive ------- their manufacturers claimed.

(A) what
(B) like
(C) as
(D) of

PART 6

Questions 5-8 refer to the following customer review.

I recently had the opportunity to try out Mr. Westbrook's Computer Repair Service. My computer had stopped working, and with not much money left for this month, I desperately needed it fixed as ------- as possible. When I walked into his shop, Mr. Westbrook greeted me warmly. ------- I didn't book ahead of time, Mr. Westbrook immediately diagnosed and explained the problem. He then proceeded to get my computer up and running again within my budget, and he even went out of his way to clear out some dust and even remove some viruses from my computer! -------.

It's no wonder everybody recommends Mr. Westbrook for computer problems. He provides ------- service, and I would certainly recommend him to everybody.

Sander Evans, Christchurch

5. (A) cheapen
(B) cheapness
(C) cheaply
(D) cheapest

6. (A) Previously
(B) Consequently
(C) Meanwhile
(D) Although

7. (A) There were many customers in the store.
(B) I bought some new parts.
(C) You should book ahead of time.
(D) It runs even faster than before.

8. (A) excessive
(B) unparalleled
(C) provisional
(D) questionable

CASE 78 비교급 비교

Students with specific career goals tend to study ------- than those who are undecided.

(A) serious   (B) seriousness   (C) most serious   (D) more seriously

해설 빈칸은 동사 study를 수식하는 부사 자리이다. 빈칸 뒤에 than이 있음을 고려할 때, 빈칸은 비교급 구문을 완성하는 (D)가 정답이다.

해석 구체적인 진로 목표를 가진 학생들은 결정하지 못한 학생들보다 더 진지하게 공부하는 경향이 있다.

>> 비교급 비교 구문: 두 비교 대상이 차이가 있을 때 비교급 비교를 쓴다.

형용사/부사의 비교급+than …보다 더 ~한/하게

Now that Mr. Kirby's online store is **more profitable than** last year, he is planning to expand his business.
Kirby 씨의 온라인 상점이 작년보다 더 많은 수익을 남겼기 때문에, 그는 사업을 확장할 계획이다.

형용사의 비교급+명사+than …보다 더 ~한

Our company guarantees that we offer **more durable products than** our competitors.
우리 회사는 경쟁 업체들보다 더 내구성 있는 제품을 제공하는 것을 보증한다.

the+비교급 ~, the+비교급… ~하면 할수록, 더 …하다

The more information we gather about our competitors, **the more useful** our research findings will be.
우리의 경쟁업체들에 관한 정보를 더 많이 모을수록 연구 결과는 더 유용할 것이다.

the+비교급+of the two 둘 중에서 더 ~한/하게

The government decided to give support and funding to **the smaller of the two companies**.
정부는 두 회사 중 더 작은 쪽에 지원과 자금을 조달하기로 결정했다.

>> 비교급 강조 부사

much/far/even/still/a lot 훨씬	significantly/considerably/noticeably/markedly 상당히

Because the product was **much more profitable than** he expected, Mr. Colby decided to invest more in product development.
그 제품이 예상보다 훨씬 더 수익성이 있었기 때문에 Colby 씨는 제품 개발에 더 많이 투자하기로 결정했다.

 알면 3초!   >> 문맥상 비교 대상이 명확할 경우 than 이하는 생략할 수 있다.

With the help of state-of-the-art equipment, the manager is expecting the workers to work much -------.

(A) more efficient   (B) most efficiently   (C) efficient   (D) more efficiently

위 문제는 보기가 원급, 비교급, 최상급 형용사/부사로 구성되어 있고 빈칸 앞의 much가 비교급 강조 부사이며 동사 work를 수식하는 부사 자리이므로 부사의 비교급 형태인 (D)를 답으로 고르는 문제였다. 그런데, 비교 구문이라면 비교 대상을 나타내는 'than'을 힌트로 삼지 않는가? 그런데 '비교 문장에 than이 없어도 되나?' 싶을 것이다. 결론적으로 '~보다'라는 의미의 than은 문맥상 비교 대상이 명확하거나 '현재(now)'일 경우 than이 없어도 비교급을 쓸 수 있다. 위 문제도 '최첨단 장비의 도움으로 직원들이 훨씬 더 효율적으로 일할 것'이라는 내용이므로 비교 대상은 최첨단 장비가 없을 때임을 쉽게 알 수 있다.

해석 최첨단 장비의 도움으로, 매니저는 직원들이 훨씬 더 효율적으로 일할 것으로 기대하고 있다.

PART 5

1. According to new figures, the statewide production of tomatoes is ------- than expected.

(A) light
(B) lightly
(C) lighter
(D) lightest

2. The new Robomark washing machines are ------- more efficient than the existing models, saving you money on both electricity and water.

(A) significance
(B) significantly
(C) significant
(D) signification

3. The updated banking app makes it much ------- for customers to track their spending.

(A) simply
(B) simple
(C) simplify
(D) simpler

4. Salespeople at Crater Publishing offer their textbooks for ------- prices than the competition.

(A) neater
(B) lower
(C) narrower
(D) easier

PART 6

Questions 5-8 refer to the following advertisement.

If you'd like to see India's beautiful countryside, the best way to do it is from a train. And if you're planning to go far and wide, you should use the Indian Rail Passport (IRP). This single ticket will allow you unlimited trips on most of the nation's major train lines. So the farther you -------, the more you will save. -------. Tickets should be ordered through the IRP Web site before departing from your own country and will be available for use as soon as you arrive in India. The IRP will remain ------- for six weeks. The price of the ticket ------- includes a deluxe commemorative map and exclusive discount coupons.

5. (A) travel
(B) traveling
(C) traveled
(D) traveler

6. (A) Only certain travel agencies provide individual tours.
(B) During summer months, the trains are often crowded.
(C) Air travel is a more expensive option.
(D) This special pass is only offered to international tourists.

7. (A) valid
(B) regular
(C) convenient
(D) open

8. (A) apart from
(B) as well as
(C) also
(D) before

최상급 비교

Our regional sales office in Jakarta just reported that it had its ------- quarter ever after the latest advertising campaign.

(A) good   (B) better   (C) best   (D) well

> **콕 찍어 포인트** ··· 부사 ever '이제까지'는 최상급 문장에서 「최상급 + ever」의 형태로 쓰여 그 의미를 강조한다.
>
> [해설] 빈칸은 명사 quarter를 수식하는 형용사 자리로, 뒤에 부사 ever가 있으니, 최상급 강조 구문을 완성하는 최상급 형용사 (C)가 정답이다.
>
> [해석] Jakarta에 있는 우리 지역 영업소는 방금 최근 광고 캠페인이 끝난 후 사상 최고의 분기를 보냈다고 보고했다.

>> 최상급 비교 구문: 셋 이상의 비교 대상 중 하나가 가장 우월할 때 최상급 비교를 쓴다.

the/소유격 + 최상급 + 명사 + of/among + 전체 명사 ~중에서 가장 …한

The audience ratings received by the movie were **the highest of all films released that same weekend**.
그 영화의 관람객 수가 같은 주말에 개봉된 모든 영화들 중 가장 높았다.

the/소유격 + 최상급 + 명사 + 장소/범위 ~에서 가장 …한

The XYZ Pro was previously regarded as **the fastest laptop on the market**.
이전에는 XYZ Pro가 시장에서 가장 빠른 노트북으로 여겨졌다.

the/소유격 + 최상급 + 명사 + 주어 + have (ever) p.p. 지금까지 …한 것 중 가장 ~한

The AI dishwasher was **the most user-friendly model we have ever tested**.
그 AI 식기세척기는 우리가 시험해 본 것들 중 가장 사용자 친화적인 모델이었다.

one of/among + the/소유격 + 최상급 + 복수 명사 가장 …한 것들 중 하나

Greeting customers at the gate is **one of your most important duties**.
문 앞에서 손님을 맞이하는 일이 당신의 가장 중요한 직무 중 하나입니다.

the/소유격 + 서수 + 최상급 + 명사 … 번째로 ~한

Singapore is the home of **the second largest port** in the world. 싱가포르는 세계에서 두 번째로 큰 항만 시설의 본거지이다.

the/소유격 + single + 최상급 단연 가장 ~한

The results of these clinical trials are **the single most important** factor in determining the effectiveness of the product. 이러한 임상 실험의 결과가 제품의 유효성을 결정하는 데 있어 가장 중요한 요인이다.

the/소유격 + 최상급 + 명사 + possible/available 가능한 한 가장 ~한/이용 가능한 것 중 가장 …한

In order to provide **the best service possible**, County Bank is extending its business hours.
County 은행은 가능한 한 최고의 서비스를 제공하기 위해 영업 시간을 연장할 것이다.

>> 최상급 강조 부사

even/simply/by far/single/ever/possible 단연코

The tastiest burger ever to be served in this restaurant includes whole wheat buns and truffle mushrooms. 이 식당에서 제공되는 단연코 가장 맛있는 버거에는 통밀빵과 송로 버섯이 들어간다.

 알면 3초!   >> 최상급 뒤에 오는 명사의 의미가 명확할 경우 명사는 생략할 수 있다.

Among the nine candidates Ms. Brook has interviewed, Mr. Sanders is the ------- highly qualified.

(A) much   (B) such   (C) so   (D) most

최상급 구문에서 형용사의 최상급 뒤에 명사가 없는 경우, 명사가 생략되었다고 생각한다. 최상급 뒤에 오는 명사의 의미가 명백할 때 즉, 비교 대상이 이미 언급되어 있어서 또 쓸 필요가 없을 때 생략이 가능하다. 위의 문제에서 최상급 표현 'the most highly qualified'가 나와야 하며 qualified가 수식하는 명사가 생략되어 있는데, 문맥상 '9명의 후보자들 중 Sanders 씨가 가장 자질이 뛰어난 후보자'란 뜻이니 qualified 뒤에 앞서 등장한 candidate가 생략된 것으로 이해하면 된다. much는 비교급 강조 부사이므로 뒤에 more highly qualified의 형태가 되어야 하고 앞에 정관사 the는 쓰지 않는다. 따라서, (D)가 정답이다.

[해석] Brook 씨가 면접 봤던 아홉 명의 지원자들 중에서, Sanders 씨가 가장 자질이 뛰어났다.

PART 5

1. The success of the project will bring new life to the city park, which was once one of Millville's ------- recreation spots.

(A) popularity of
(B) as popular as
(C) popular than
(D) most popular

2. Among the likely candidates for the job, Ms. Wang is the most -------.

(A) conditional
(B) requisite
(C) secured
(D) qualified

3. Ms. Yun plans to purchase the ------- shade of green curtains for the employees' offices.

(A) bright
(B) brightest
(C) brightens
(D) brightness

4. At Midian Investments, ------- the most successful stock market brokers must attend weekly training seminars.

(A) even
(B) other
(C) yet
(D) aside

PART 6

Questions 5-8 refer to the following e-mail.

To: All Employees
From: Daniel Harris
Date: 9 August
Subject: Congatulatory Event

Dear Employees,

It is with pleasure today that we can ------- Flora Norton as our new President of Sales. Ms. Norton
5.
has been with our company for 15 years, and her track record speaks for itself. Some of Jensza's most successful projects have been the result of Ms. Norton's hard work. -------. Therefore, it is with
6.
pleasure that we extend our congratulations to Ms. Norton.

We would like to hold a ceremony at 3:00 P.M. on 15 August in Conference Hall A to congratulate Ms. Norton on her ------- promotion. We hope everyone joins us. We will also be hearing from Ms.
7.
Norton herself about her ------- for Jensza during her tenure.
8.

Best regards,

Daniel Harris
Human Resources Team

5. (A) consider
(B) surprise
(C) announce
(D) retire

6. (A) The most notable was her work on the StateCom deal.
(B) Next year will mark her 16th year at Jensza.
(C) Overseas projects are a priority for next year.
(D) Our Web site lists many of our recent accomplishments.

7. (A) impressed
(B) impressively
(C) impress
(D) impressive

8. (A) vision
(B) advancement
(C) character
(D) concept

비교 구문 관용 표현

Doshi Automotive's latest SUV, despite being significantly cheaper, looks more or ------- identical to top-of-the-line models.

(A) less   (B) like   (C) still   (D) higher

> 해설   more or less는 '거의'란 뜻의 관용 표현으로 '최고급 모델들과 거의 똑같아 보인다'라는 의미이므로 (A)가 정답이다.
>
> 해석   Doshi 자동차의 최신 SUV는 상당히 저렴하지만, 최고급 모델들과 거의 똑같아 보인다.

>> 원급, 비교급, 최상급을 이용한 관용 표현

the same (+명사) as ~와 같은	no longer, not any longer 더 이상 ~하지 않다
all the more 더욱 더	more than doubled/tripled 두 배/세 배 이상
rather than ~보다는	would rather A than B B하느니 차라리 A하다
other than ~ 이외에	비교급+than any other 다른 어떤 …보다 더 ~한
more than ~ 이상	비교급+than ever 그 어느 때보다 더 ~한
less than ~ 미만	비교급+than expected/planned 예상했던/계획했던 것보다 더 ~한
more or less 거의, 대략	most probably/likely 아마도(가장 가능성이 큰)
no later than 늦어도 ~까지	at most 기껏해야
no more than 겨우, ~일 뿐	at least 적어도, 최소한
no sooner than, sooner or later 조만간	at the latest 아무리 늦어도

Please submit the report **no later than** July 10.
이 보고서를 늦어도 7월 10일까지 제출해 주세요.

The sales event is **most probably** the reason for the increase in customers.
그 할인 행사는 아마 고객이 증가한 가장 큰 이유일 것이다.

⏱ 알면 3초!   **>> 비교 대상 앞에 than 대신 to를 쓰는 비교급에 주의한다.**

The recently released version of the accounting software is far superior ------- the last version.

(A) to   (B) of   (C) than   (D) even

---

prior to ~ 이전에, ~보다 먼저   superior to ~보다 우월한   inferior to ~보다 열등한   prefer A to B A를 B보다 선호하다

비교 대상 앞에 than이 아닌, to를 쓰는 비교급 표현이 있다. 문법에서는 이를 라틴계 비교급이라고 하는데, 「형용사-er + than」 또는 「more + 형용사 +than」이 일반적인 비교급 형태인 데 비해, 이 라틴계 비교급은 「-or+to」의 형태를 갖는다는 점에 차이가 있다. 토익에 등장하는 라틴계 비교급 표현은 몇 개 안 되니 외워두면 편하다. 위의 문제에서 superior은 전치사 to를 필요로 하는 비교급 표현이므로 (A)가 정답이다.

> 해석   최근에 출시된 버전의 회계 소프트웨어가 지난 버전보다 훨씬 더 우수하다.

PART 5

1. During the monsoon season, staff members are permitted to work ------- rather than commuting to headquarters.
(A) remotely
(B) closely
(C) fundamentally
(D) carefully

2. The Greene Art Museum is ------- spectacular when you realize that it was constructed over hundreds of years ago.
(A) so much as
(B) all the more
(C) by far
(D) at most

3. It is necessary that every job applicant submit their résumé ------- June 30.
(A) rather than
(B) more than
(C) no longer
(D) no later than

4. Given the steady increase in the popularity of healthy foods, Cheap-O Burgers is ------- the number one restaurant in the country.
(A) another
(B) no longer
(C) anymore
(D) not enough

PART 6

Questions 5-8 refer to the following notice.

The Sanderson Office Supplies Web site is currently ------- due to maintenance. The new and improved site can be used after 6 P. M. this evening. ------- providing heightened security to protect your data, the online store will include features to make ordering from Sanderson simpler than ever before. These include more user-friendly navigation tools and item recommendations ------- on your past orders. -------. The updates should provide easier transactions in the future.

5. (A) related
(B) disinterested
(C) inaccessible
(D) completed

6. (A) Furthermore
(B) Compared with
(C) Despite
(D) Other than

7. (A) taken
(B) based
(C) agreed
(D) intended

8. (A) Qualifying orders must be placed before 6 P.M.
(B) New items often sell quickly on the site.
(C) We appreciate your patience during this time.
(D) Thank you for your participation.

CASE 81 가정법

> If they had managed their time more carefully, Dan and Laura ------- the project far ahead of schedule.
>
> (A) completed (B) had completed (C) could have completed (D) will complete

콕 찍어 포인트 ··· 가정법 과거 완료 시제의 문장 구조는 다음과 같다: 「If + 주어1 + had p.p., 주어2 + 조동사 + have p.p.」

해설 빈칸은 주절의 동사 자리이다. If 종속절의 시제가 과거 완료이므로, 가정법 과거 완료 시제를 완성하는 (C)가 정답이다.

해석 그들이 시간을 좀 더 신중하게 관리했더라면, Dan과 Laura는 예정보다 훨씬 일찍 프로젝트를 끝낼 수 있었을 것이다.

» if절과 주절의 동사 시제를 짝지어 가정법 형태를 기억한다.

가정법 과거: 현재 사실을 반대로 가정할 때

> If + 주어 + **과거 동사**, 주어 + **would / should / could / might + 동사 원형** (지금) 만약 ~한다면, …일 텐데

Braxton, Inc. warned that it **would reevaluate** its business relations with our company if we **did not abide by** its decision to work with our competitor.
Braxton 사는 경쟁업체와 일하기로 한 결정을 따르지 않으면 우리 회사와의 사업 관계를 재평가하겠다고 경고했다.

가정법 과거 완료: 과거 사실을 반대로 가정할 때

> If + 주어 + **과거 완료(had p.p.)**, 주어 + **would / should / could / might + have p.p.** (과거에) 만약 ~했더라면, …했을 텐데

If he **had received** the blueprint earlier, Mr. Hoffman **could have begun** the construction before the end of May. Hoffman 씨가 청사진을 더 일찍 받았더라면 5월 말 전에 공사를 시작할 수 있었을 것이다.

가정법 미래: 미래에 실현 가능성이 낮은 일을 가정하거나 정중한 요청이나 제안을 할 때

| If + 주어 + **should + 동사 원형**, | **명령문** (미래에) 혹시 ~한다면, …해라 |
| | 주어 + **will / shall / can / may + 동사 원형** (미래에) 혹시 ~한다면, …할 것이다 |

If you **should have** any questions, **please** feel free to call our sales representative.
문의 사항이 있으실 때는 언제든 저희 영업 담당자에게 전화하시기 바랍니다.

가정법 현재: 미래에 있을 법한 일을 단순히 가정할 때 (= 조건문)

> If + 주어 + **현재 동사**, 주어 + **will / can + 동사 원형** 만약 ~하면, …할 것이다

If you **are not satisfied** with the quality of our customer service, we **will** promptly **address** the issue.
저희 고객 서비스의 질에 만족하지 못하신다면 즉시 그 문제를 해결하겠습니다.

 알면 3초! **»** 문장 맨 앞에 Had나 Should가 오면 if가 생략된 가정법 문장임을 알아챈다.

> Had we been aware of the guests' complaints during their stay at our hotel, we ------- to move them to another room.
>
> (A) would have offered (B) has offered (C) is being offered (D) would have been offered

문장이 Had나 Should로 시작하거나 문장 맨 앞에 빈칸이 주어지고 보기 중에 Had나 Should가 있다면 가정법 문장이 도치된 것일 수 있다. 가정법 문장은 if가 생략되고 조동사가 주어 앞으로 오는 도치가 일어날 수 있으며 시험에서는 주로 가정법 과거 완료나 가정법 미래의 도치가 출제되는데, 위 문제와 같이 Had나 Should로 시작되는 문장을 보고 주절의 시제를 맞추거나 동사 형태가 had p.p.(가정법 과거 완료)나 동사 원형(가정법 미래)인 것을 보고 if가 생략된 도치 문장으로 짐작하여 Had나 Should를 고르는 문제가 출제된다. 위의 문제는 If절의 If를 생략하고 Had로 시작하는 가정법 과거 완료 구문이므로 빈칸에는 「조동사의 과거형+have p.p.」 형태의 (A)가 나와야 한다. offer가 여기서는 'offer to V(~하겠다고 제안하다)'의 문형으로 수동태인 (D)를 고르지 않게 주의해야 한다.

해석 저희 호텔의 투숙 기간 동안에 손님들의 불만 사항들을 알았더라면, 저희는 다른 방으로 옮겨드리겠다는 제안을 했을 텐데요.

PART 5

1. Mr. Gruber would have attended the meeting if his flight ------- as scheduled.
(A) arrive
(B) arrives
(C) will arrive
(D) had arrived

2. If Ms. Chung had remained with the company longer, she ------- the company's strategic business plan.
(A) revises
(B) will revise
(C) had been revising
(D) could have revised

3. Had hotel reservations ------- sooner, we might have been able to eat at the hotel buffet tonight.
(A) made
(B) making
(C) been made
(D) was made

4. ------- the quality of our products not meet your expectations, contact our customer service center to notify us of any issues.
(A) Besides
(B) Should
(C) Anywhere
(D) Whatever

PART 6

Questions 5-8 refer to the following advertisement.

Highpoint Cleaners, located at 58 Polinar Place, ------- in graffiti removal around the city of
                                                    5.
Oklahoma. We do not use traditional chemicals or water blasters other companies use to remove
graffiti. Instead, we use a new technique that uses dry ice to blast away any graffiti. -------, we offer
                                                                                        6.
the cleanest, safest, and most environmental-friendly graffiti removal solution. -------. If you find a
                                                                                 7.
cheaper price than us, we will match it. Still not convinced? Give us a call, and we will provide a free
------- of our service. Once you see it, we guarantee you will be convinced.
  8.

5. (A) specializes
(B) had specialized
(C) will specialize
(D) specializing

6. (A) Additionally
(B) Whereas
(C) Therefore
(D) However

7. (A) We suggest trying to clean graffiti using a cleaning solution.
(B) We have been in business for over ten years.
(C) We have recently partnered with the local council.
(D) We are confident we have the lowest prices.

8. (A) exhibition
(B) consultation
(C) demonstration
(D) acquisition

CASE 82 도치

------- is the Marketing Department's budget proposal for the upcoming year.

(A) Attach　　　　(B) Attachment　　　　(C) Attaching　　　　(D) Attached

해설 | 빈칸 뒤에 「be동사 + 주어」 형태로 어순이 바뀌어 있는 점으로 보아 주격 보어가 문장 맨 앞에 오는 도치 구문임을 알 수 있으므로 (D)가 정답이다.

해석 | 내년도 마케팅부의 예산안이 첨부되어 있습니다.

>> 부정어가 문장의 맨 앞에 오는 경우 도치가 일어난다.

hardly / rarely / barely / scarcely / little / seldom 거의 ~않다	
never 결코 ~않다	+ 동사 + 주어
no + 명사 어떤 ~도 ···않다	+ 조동사 + 주어 + 동사
not until ~할 때까지 ···않다[~하고 나서야 ···하다]	
not only ~뿐만 아니라	

Never have we experienced such outstanding service at this restaurant.
이 식당의 훌륭한 서비스는 어디에서도 경험해 본 적이 없습니다.

>> only 부사구[절]가 문장의 맨 앞에 오는 경우 도치가 일어난다.

Only with this ID card **can employees enter** the office.
이 신분증 카드가 있어야만 직원들이 사무실로 들어갈 수 있다.

>> 보어가 문장의 맨 앞에 오는 경우 도치가 일어난다.

Enclosed / Attached / Included + is[are] + 주어 주어가 동봉/첨부/포함되어 있다

Enclosed are the documents requested for the meeting.
회의를 위해 요청하신 서류들이 동봉되어 있습니다.

 알면 3초!　　>> 앞의 내용을 간단히 so나 neither로 대신할 때도 도치가 일어난다.

The advertising director cannot participate in the board meeting on Thursday, and ------- can the marketing director.

(A) neither　　　　(B) however　　　　(C) so　　　　(D) also

도치는 보통 강조하고 싶은 어구를 문장 앞으로 빼낼 때 일어나는데, 이때 주어와 동사의 자리가 바뀌거나 조동사가 주어 앞으로 오는 현상이 일반적이다. 부정어, only, be동사의 보어를 문두로 보내는 도치 구문이 대표적인데, 이 외에도 앞의 내용을 받아 '~도 역시 ··· 하다' 또는 '~도 역시 ··· 하지 않다'를 의미할 때 사용되는 so나 neither가 문장을 이끌 때도 「so + (조)동사 + 주어」, 「neither + (조)동사 + 주어」 형태의 도치가 일어난다. 위 문제에서 '광고 책임자는 이사회에 참석할 수 없다(cannot)'고 하고 빈칸 문장에서도 '마케팅 책임자 역시 참석할 수 없다'(라는 의미가 되어야 자연스러우므로 「neither + (조)동사 + 주어」의 '~도 역시 ···하지 않다')'라는 의미를 만드는 (A)가 정답이다.

해석 | 광고 책임자는 목요일에 이사회에 참석할 수 없고, 마케팅 책임자 역시 참석할 수 없다.

PART 5

1. ------- should any personal data about clients or coworkers be shared outside the company through any social media platform.
(A) Never
(B) Although
(C) Properly
(D) Ever

2. Only recently has the company's marketing director ------- the proposed changes for the new advertising campaign.
(A) assessing
(B) assessed
(C) assesses
(D) will assess

3. As the number of visitors visiting the Wakeville Gallery increases, ------- does the need for curators.
(A) then
(B) so
(C) again
(D) however

4. ------- among the qualifications the company is seeking is the ability to fluently communicate in several different languages.
(A) Feasible
(B) Capable
(C) Appropriate
(D) Primary

PART 6

Questions 5-8 refer to the following e-mail.

To: aharmon@coolmail.com.au
From: ddrake@diamondrealty.co.au
Date: 11 January
Subject: 505 Lyndale Avenue

Thanks for inquiring about the availability of the unit at 101 Lyndale Avenue. I just looked it up in our online system this morning, and --5.----, the property has already been purchased.

If you let me know the specifications of what you're in the market for, I --6.---- you in identifying other suitable options. Simply let me know what your preferences are in regards to location, floor space, and your available budget via e-mail. --7.----.

You can also register for --8.----. By doing so, you will get a text message as soon as a new property listing is posted.

Regards,

Daniel Drake
Head Realtor, Diamond Realty

5. (A) apparently
(B) significantly
(C) mainly
(D) shortly

6. (A) help
(B) am helping
(C) can help
(D) have been helping

7. (A) It will be the topic of the upcoming real estate convention.
(B) Please note that I will require your signature on the document.
(C) This will allow me to find an apartment that meets your needs.
(D) The open house will be held on August 8 at 8:00 P.M.

8. (A) payments
(B) alerts
(C) rewards
(D) inquiries

1. The grape-flavored beverage received -------
ratings in the focus group than the orange-
flavored one.

(A) highly
(B) higher
(C) highest
(D) highness

2. Selecting an ideal location is the ------- aspect
to consider when expanding overseas.

(A) as important as
(B) importantly
(C) more importantly
(D) most important

3. This year's materials science conference will
showcase more innovations in sustainable
fabrics ------- in previous years.

(A) more
(B) there
(C) than
(D) now

4. No one can clean and organize your office as
------- as Marty Cleaners.

(A) more efficient
(B) efficiency
(C) efficiently
(D) more efficiently

5. The yearly bake sale has been pushed back
------- uncertain weather conditions.

(A) because of
(B) afterward
(C) suddenly
(D) unwillingly

6. Senior employees ------- work on Mondays
except when they show up to meet with
executives.

(A) seldom
(B) rather
(C) almost
(D) perhaps

7. Students may borrow books and media from
libraries ------- their own university's if they are
unavailable.

(A) other than
(B) with
(C) live in
(D) whenever

8. Should anyone require a ------- with Mr. Cruz,
make sure to do so after the board meeting.

(A) consultation
(B) consideration
(C) connection
(D) contemplation

Questions 9-12 refer to the following e-mail.

To: Ellen Park <e.park@commercemail.com>
From: Adam Harrison <aharrison@duskshine.net>
Date: September 28
Subject: Welcome
Attachment: Pre-employment documents

Greetings, Ms. Park,

Welcome to Duskshine Finance! We are very pleased to be bringing you on board.

Before we get you started, there are a few documents we will need you to complete. In the attachment documents, you will find an Offer of Employment as well as a Health Questionnaire. Please have a look and e-mail them back to us -------- your start date. Also, please feel free -------
9.   10.
with any questions.

--------. We have a very thorough onboarding process planned which covers your rights and benefits
11.
as an employee, your required duties, and appropriate -------- in the office. The latter will cover some
12.
of the cultural norms and expectations that our international recruits may be unaware of.

9. (A) at least
(B) before
(C) former
(D) previous

10. (A) is replying
(B) reply
(C) replied
(D) to reply

11. (A) Our facilities feature some of the most advanced tools in the industry.
(B) Your salary expectations have been taken into account.
(C) The recreation area is free for all of our employees to enjoy.
(D) As per our agreement, your start date has been set for October 12.

12. (A) conduct
(B) process
(C) system
(D) scheme

어휘

CASE 83 | 명사 어휘

For the ------- of our members, workout gear and towels are provided by our fitness club.

(A) precision   (B) purpose   (C) situation   (D) convenience

> 해설   주절의 내용을 고려할 때, 문맥상 '회원들의 편리함을 위해, 운동 장비 및 수건이 제공된다'라는 의미가 자연스러우므로 (D)가 정답이다.
>
> 해석   회원 편의를 위해, 운동 장비 및 수건은 저희 헬스클럽에서 제공합니다.

>> 빈칸 뒤 of 이하의 수식어는 언제나 명사 어휘 문제의 핵심 단서이다.

     ↗ range (X)

The new rollercoaster lifts riders to a **height of nearly 200 feet**.

새 롤러코스터는 탑승자들을 거의 200피트의 높이까지 들어 올린다.

>> 빈칸 앞 / 뒤에 명사가 있으면 복합명사를 완성하라는 문제이다.

     ↗ influence (X)

To lower **energy usage**, motion sensors were added to all escalators in the outlet mall.

에너지 사용을 낮추기 위해서 움직임 감지 센서가 아웃렛 몰 내의 모든 에스컬레이터에 추가되었다.

>> 빈칸이 주어 자리에 오면 문장 전체를 해석해서 푼다.

The west wing **renovation** will happen over the next two to three weeks.

서쪽 부속 건물 수리가 다음 2주에서 3주 동안 있을 것이다.

❶ 주어 자리에 오는 명사는 문장 전체를 해석해야 답을 찾을 수 있는 문제가 많다.

(3 SECS) 알면 3초!   >> 특정 전치사와 어울리는 명사 표현을 묻는다.

Ms. Calabrese earned the Carter Prize in ------- of her exceptional news reporting.

(A) suggestion   (B) impression   (C) collaboration   (D) recognition

「전치사+명사」 표현

above normal 평균 이상	in case of ~인 경우에, ~에 대비하여	in terms of ~에 관하여
above one's expectation ~의 기대를 넘어서는	in celebration of ~을 축하하여	in the event of ~인 경우에
as a result of ~의 결과로	in charge of ~을 책임지는	on arrival 도착하자마자
at all times 항상	in comparison with ~와 비교하여	on behalf of ~을 대신하여
at no cost 무료로	in compliance with ~을 준수하여	on the basis of ~을 기반으로
at one's convenience ~가 편할 때	in conjunction with ~와 함께	on the recommendation of ~의 추천으로
at the conclusion of ~가 끝날 때	in detail 상세하게	to one's surprise ~가 놀랍게도
below normal 평균 이하	in favor of ~을 찬성하여	under construction 공사 중인
beyond capacity 능력 밖으로	in honor of ~을 기념하여	under pressure 압력을 받는
by means of ~을 이용하여	in observance of ~을 기념하여	upon receipt of ~을 받자마자
in advance 미리	in recognition of ~을 인정하여	
in advance of ~보다 앞선	in response to ~에 응하여	

어휘 문제에서도 해석 없이 풀 수 있는 문제들이 종종 등장한다. 위의 문제를 무조건 해석해서 풀려고 하기 전에, 'in recognition of(~을 인정하여)'란 표현을 미리 알고 있었다면, 빈칸 앞/뒤에 연결된 전치사만 확인해도 '(D)가 답이 되겠구나' 하고 기쁨의 미소를 지을 수 있다. 「전치사+명사」 형태의 고정 표현들, 특히 토익에 자주 등장하는 실용 표현들은 되도록 많이 외워두는 것이 좋다.

> 해석   Calabrese 씨는 뛰어난 뉴스 보도를 인정받아 Carter상을 받았다.

PART 5

1. All subsidiaries are expected to conduct an in-house ------- and subsequently submit full reports on the findings before March.
(A) area
(B) audit
(C) purpose
(D) product

2. ------- of duties can reduce a supervisor's workload and enable other staff members to try new assignments.
(A) Permission
(B) Reputation
(C) Qualification
(D) Delegation

3. Ms. Van Tassel wants to see her team members take more ------- and follow through with their annual goals.
(A) initiation
(B) initiated
(C) initiative
(D) initiate

4. Please send the information requested to the address listed above at your earliest -------.
(A) option
(B) probability
(C) requirement
(D) convenience

PART 6

Questions 5-8 refer to the following advertisement.

At Dawson Beverages, we ------- only the freshest organically grown fruit go into our juices. It has
        5.
been our mission since our founding ten years ago. ------- then, we have partnered with trusted
         6.
farmers all around the country to ensure the same high quality juice every time. Our best sellers
include our avocado banana juice and our strawberry plum juice. -------.
         7.

Visit any one of our stores today to receive a special ------- of our new smoothie line. Offer is only
        8.
good until stocks last, so get yours today!

5. (A) guaranteeing
(B) had guaranteed
(C) to guarantee
(D) guarantee

6. (A) Upon
(B) Since
(C) After
(D) Previously

7. (A) These are seasonal products, so they won't be here forever.
(B) Keeping juices in the fridge will preserve their shelf life.
(C) The Web site details where our farmers are located.
(D) All fruits go through a thorough cleaning process.

8. (A) boost
(B) model
(C) sample
(D) imitation

동사 어휘

Friendwork Inc. has announced its plans to ------- rising competitor HeyyThere.

(A) depart   (B) converse   (C) acquire   (D) transfer

> 해설   빈칸은 명사 plans를 수식하는 to부정사구를 완성하는 동사 자리이다. 목적어인 'rising competitor'를 고려할 때 문맥상 '경쟁사를 인수할 계획을 발표했다'라는 의미가 되어야 자연스러우므로 (C)가 정답이다.
>
> 해석   Friendwork 사는 떠오르는 경쟁사인 HeyyThere를 인수할 계획을 발표했다.

>> 목적어는 언제나 동사 어휘 문제의 핵심 단서이다.

      applies (X)

The contract **covers the lease of the vehicles** and basic collision insurance.
계약서에는 차량 임대와 기본 충돌 보험이 포함된다.

>> 수동태 문장은 주어가 핵심 단서이다.

The **site** for August's charity auction is yet to be **decided**.
8월 자선 경매 장소가 아직 정해지지 않았다.

>> 접속사로 연결된 문장은 문장 전체를 해석해서 푼다.

The sales in the spring were not impressive, but they have **risen** in the early summer months.
봄철 매출은 인상적이지 않았지만, 초여름에는 매출이 올랐다.

>> to부정사구를 완성하는 문제는 문장 전체를 해석해서 푼다.

      perform (X)

A new action plan is under consideration to **market** our services more aggressively in Latin America.
중남미에서 우리의 서비스를 더 적극적으로 광고하기 위해 새로운 사업 계획이 고려 중이다.

3SECS 알면 3초!   >> 특정 전치사와 어울리는 동사를 묻는다.

Peter Simpson, the renowned electronics designer, recently ------- with Eder Electronics in order to design a new refrigerator.

(A) substituted   (B) collaborated   (C) employed   (D) proceeded

「자동사＋전치사」 표현

to	adhere to ~을 준수하다 agree to ~에 동의하다 apologize to ~에게 사과하다 apply to ~에 적용되다 belong to ~에 속하다	contribute to ~에 기여하다 fall to ~로 떨어지다 object to ~에 반대하다 point to ~을 지적하다 refer to ~을 참조하다	respond to ~에 반응하다 speak to ~에게 얘기하다 subscribe to ~을 구독하다 succeed to ~을 계승하다 talk to ~에게 얘기하다
for	account for ~을 설명하다 care for ~을 돌보다	apologize for ~에 대해 사과하다 hope for ~을 바라다	apply for ~에 지원하다 leave for ~로 떠나다
with	collaborate with ~와 협력하다 compete with[against] ~와 경쟁하다	comply with ~을 준수하다 deal with ~을 다루다	interfere with ~을 방해하다 proceed with ~을 진행하다
on	collaborate on ~에 대해 협력하다 comment on ~에 대해 논평하다	focus[concentrate] on ~에 집중하다 insist on ~을 주장하다	remark on ~에 대해 언급하다 work on ~에 애쓰다

빈칸 앞 또는 뒤에 전치사가 있다면 보기 중 해당 전치사와 어울리는 동사가 있는지 먼저 확인한다. 주어진 동사가 타동사인지, 자동사인지, 어떤 전치사와 함께 쓰이는지를 모르고, 의미로만 풀려 하면 이 문제처럼 (B)와 (C)를 두고 고민하기 쉽다. (C)는 '고용하다'란 의미의 타동사로 빈칸 뒤에는 목적어가 와야 하며 (B)는 전치사 with(~와 함께 협력하다)나 on(~에 대해 협력하다)과 함께 쓰는 자동사이다. 따라서, (B)가 정답이다.

> 해석   저명한 가전 디자이너 Peter Simpson은 최근 새로운 냉장고를 고안하기 위해 Eder 전자와 협력했다.

PART 5

1. This accommodation also provides area information and a coupon to ------- a discount at the outlet mall.
(A) obtain
(B) descend
(C) develop
(D) advertise

2. Monsoi Toy Company amended the contract with its shipper, so complaints about late deliveries should ------- in the near future.
(A) compress
(B) diminish
(C) prioritize
(D) anticipate

3. Mayflower Foundation ------- to donate 3,000 books to a local library in honor of National Literacy Week.
(A) pledged
(B) warranted
(C) believed
(D) explained

4. Following the introduction of a new menu at Shin-U Restaurant a month ago, the number of customers has almost -------.
(A) supported
(B) predicted
(C) controlled
(D) tripled

PART 6

Questions 5-8 refer to the following e-mail.

To: All JCI Members
From: Richard White
Date: Friday, July 11
Subject: Relocation of the workshop

Dear JCI Members,

I am writing to inform you that the annual JCI Workshop this year will ------- due to uncontrollable
                   5.
occasions. We will move the workshop from the JCI California's Main Hall to the JCI's Headquarters
in New York. As it will surely ------- much time for the workshop to be completed, you can take this
                 6.
opportunity to browse around the city of New York and visit various places as well. -------. You can
                                  7.
walk down the street and enjoy delicious foods from the street merchants. The nearby attractions are
------- for a morning or night walk, too. We recommend you to bring extra clothes and shoes.
 8.
I'm looking forward to meeting you next month.

Yours,

Richard White, Workshop Manager
JCI

5. (A) be relocated
(B) relocating
(C) to relocate
(D) relocates

6. (A) convey
(B) consume
(C) converge
(D) conceal

7. (A) They are attracting new businesses.
(B) They are reserved for local residents.
(C) They are truly breathtaking.
(D) They are required to supply a meal and beverages.

8. (A) supposed
(B) operated
(C) perfect
(D) modest

CASE 85 형용사 어휘

The Filmmakers Association urges viewers not to blindly accept ------- reviews about a movie.

(A) opposing   (B) productive   (C) biased   (D) complete

> **해설** 빈칸은 명사 reviews를 수식하되 빈칸 앞 문맥과 잘 어울릴 수 있는 형용사 자리로, '편향된 비평을 맹목적으로 받아들이지 말라'라는 의미를 만드는 (C)가 정답이다.
>
> **해석** 영화 제작자 협회는 관객들에게 영화에 대한 편향된 비평을 맹목적으로 받아들이지 말라고 충고한다.

>> 빈칸 뒤의 명사나 빈칸 앞의 부사는 언제나 형용사 어휘 문제의 핵심 단서이다.

All **qualified candidates** for the IT manager position must provide valid certifications and complete an aptitude test. IT 관리자 직책에 자격을 갖춘 모든 지원자들은 유효한 증명서를 제공하고 적성 검사를 완료해야 한다.

valuable (X)

>> 빈칸이 be동사 뒤에 오면 주어가 핵심 단서이며 문장 전체를 해석해서 푼다.

For restaurant owners hoping to increase their net revenue, social media **marketing tips** on this Web site should be **helpful**. 순수익을 끌어올리기를 바라는 레스토랑 소유주들에게 이 웹사이트의 소셜 미디어 마케팅 팁이 도움이 될 것이다.

prompt (X)

>> 정답의 확실한 근거는 수식어에 있는 경우가 많다.

available (X)

To bring in fresh ideas, the Harrisburg City Council is organizing an **external search for an innovative architect**. 참신한 아이디어를 유치하기 위해, Harrisburg 시 의회는 혁신적인 건축가를 구하는 데 외부 탐색을 준비하고 있다.

알면 3초!   **>>** 특정 전치사와 어울리는 형용사를 묻는다.

Mr. Sanchez will be ------- for presenting the weekly reports while the President is away on a business trip.

(A) responsible   (B) capable   (C) exemplary   (D) thorough

「형용사＋전치사」 표현

to	accessible to ~이 이용할 수 있는 accustomed to ~에 익숙한 beneficial to ~에게 도움이 되는 comparable to ~에 필적한 courteous to ~을 정중히 대하는	entitled to ~에 대해 자격이 있는 equivalent to ~와 동등한 native to ~ 출신[원산지]인 open to ~에 개방되어 있는 payable to ~에게 청구하는	relevant to ~와 관련이 있는 responsive to ~에 반응하는 similar to ~와 비슷한 subject to ~의 대상이 되는 vital to ~에 필수적인
of	appreciative of ~에 감사하는 aware of ~을 알고 있는 capable of ~을 할 수 있는	considerate of ~을 배려하는 critical of ~에 비판적인 indicative of ~을 나타내는	representative of ~을 대표하는 sure of ~에 확신을 가지는 unaware of ~을 모르고 있는
for	adequate for ~에 적합한 available for ~에게 이용 가능한 eligible for ~에 대한 자격이 있는 famous for ~으로 유명한	grateful for ~으로 감사하는 ideal for ~에 이상적인 known for ~으로 유명한 necessary for ~에 필요한	ready for ~할 준비가 된 renowned for ~으로 유명한 responsible for ~을 책임지는 suitable for ~에 적합한
with	compatible with ~와 호환 가능한 complete with ~이 완비된 compliant with ~에 순응하는	concerned with ~와 관련이 있는 consistent with ~와 일치하는 content with ~에 만족하는	familiar with ~에 익숙한 satisfied with ~에 만족한 unfamiliar with ~에 익숙하지 않은

해석으로만 접근하려고 하면, Sanchez 씨가 발표를 담당한다는(responsible) 건지, 발표를 할 수 있다는(capable) 건지, 발표에 모범적이라는(exemplary) 건지, 발표에 빈틈이 없다는(thorough) 건지 뭘 답으로 골라야 할지 당황하기 쉽다. 이런 유형의 문제는 정답과 함께 쓰는 전치사를 힌트로 제공하고, 이 전치사와 어울리는 형용사를 고르라는 게 일반적이다. 형용사 responsible은 전치사 for를 동반하여 '~을 책임지는'을 뜻하며, capable은 전치사 of를 동반하여 '~을 할 수 있는'을 뜻한다. 따라서 전치사 for를 동반하는 (A)가 정답이다. 특정 형용사가 동반하는 전치사가 있다면 꼭 한 단어처럼 외워두어야 한다.

해석 Sanchez 씨는 사장님이 출장을 가 계신 동안 주간 보고를 발표하는 일을 담당할 것이다.

해설서 p.122

PART 5

1. Due to privacy reasons, the clients' current ------- address cannot be displayed until their consent is given.
(A) global
(B) arrival
(C) essential
(D) postal

2. Many people are opening bank accounts with the Yolo Bank following its ------- offer to grant account holders fixed interest.
(A) diminished
(B) invaluable
(C) unconditional
(D) farthest

3. The CEO was ------- of the proposed new product ranges but he gave in after an impressive presentation by the sales team.
(A) proud
(B) capable
(C) skeptical
(D) aware

4. Nina Tom won her 4th ------- businesswoman-of-the-year award after her company earned $30,000 more in profits ahead of Emmy Baker's company, her closest competitor.
(A) constant
(B) following
(C) consecutive
(D) repeated

PART 6

Questions 5-8 refer to the following letter.

Dear Principal Rubinstein,

Thank you for expressing interest in having your school visit our museum. In response to your questions, the minimum age for entry into our museum is seven years old. ------- 5. Additionally, here is a list of some of the ------- 6. activities we offer here at the museum. Please note that some of these ------- 7. may be unavailable due to weather conditions. In particular, our most popular attractions, namely the observatory deck and the botanical garden, may be closed off.

Please keep ------- 8. updated about what your plans are by next week. We are looking forward to seeing you all soon!

Sincerely,

Paul Costello, Coordinator
Eagle Harbor Museum

5. (A) The museum holds many events during the holidays.
(B) This may tentatively change depending on the weather.
(C) Younger students may enter at no additional cost.
(D) This is a rule that is enforced strictly.

6. (A) fiscal
(B) academic
(C) psychological
(D) mundane

7. (A) questions
(B) exhibits
(C) sequences
(D) experiments

8. (A) us
(B) them
(C) one
(D) you

CASE 86 부사 어휘

> The Johannesburg Daily News is broadcast ------- on television and their Web site.
>
> (A) collectively (B) instinctively (C) mutually (D) simultaneously

해설 빈칸은 수동태 동사구와 전치사구 사이의 부사 자리이다. 문맥상 '텔레비전과 웹사이트에서 동시에 방송된다'라는 의미가 되어야 자연스러우므로 (D)가 정답이다.

해석 Johannesburg Daily News는 텔레비전과 웹사이트에서 동시에 방송된다.

>> 동사를 핵심 단서로 삼는다.

excessively (X)

Mr. Strazinski listened intently to each presenter's lecture. Strazinski 씨는 각 발표자의 강연을 열심히 들었다.

>> 형용사, 부사, 구를 핵심 단서로 삼는다.

expertly (X)

The data provided in Mining Technology News is generally quite reliable.
Mining Technology News에 제공되는 정보는 일반적으로 상당히 신뢰할 만하다.

>> 문장 전체를 해석해서 푼다.

likewise (X)

Doctor Ruyter will not be able to present the opening speech but will instead give the closing one on Wednesday. Ruyter 박사는 개회사를 할 수 없지만 대신 수요일에 폐회사를 할 것이다.

>> 증가, 감소, 확장, 개선, 변화를 의미하는 동사와 어울리는 부사는 따로 있다.

증가하다	increase / rise / grow		considerably / significantly / substantially 상당히
감소하다	decrease / decline / fall / reduce		dramatically / sharply / markedly / drastically / rapidly 급격히
확장하다	expand	+	abruptly / suddenly 갑자기
개선하다	improve		gradually / steadily / incrementally 점진적으로
변하다	change		slightly / modestly / moderately / somewhat / marginally 약간, 조금

AEB Marketing's research showed that time spent on social networking sites increased significantly last year. AEB Marketing의 연구는 작년에 소셜 네트워킹 사이트에 소비된 시간이 크게 증가했다는 것을 보여주었다.

 알면 3초! >> 부사적 관용 표현

> Grafton Brothers Legal Firm's office is ------- from the Halifax Train Station.
>
> (A) across (B) nearly (C) gone (D) about

부사적 관용 표현

across from ~의 바로 맞은편에	ever since ~ 이후로 줄곧	shortly after / before ~ 직후에/직전에
around the clock 24시간 내내, 하루 종일	from around the world 전 세계로부터	such as 예를 들어, ~와 같은
as a token of ~의 표시로	from now on 앞으로는, 지금부터 계속	to the contrary 그 반대를 보여주는
as[so] long as ~하는 한, ~하기만 하면	in a timely manner 적시에	under no circumstances 어떤 경우에도
as of ~부로, ~일자로	in the foreseeable future 가까운 미래에	until further notice 추후 통보가 있을 때까지
as soon as possible 가능한 한 빨리	on a regular basis 정기적으로	up to ~까지
at least 적어도, 최소한	on one's own 혼자서	when it comes to ~에 관한 한
at once 즉시	other than ~ 외에, ~이 아닌	with the help of ~의 도움으로
based on ~에 근거하여	rather than ~보다는 차라리	

부사적 표현을 완성하는 단어를 고르라는 문제에서는 빈칸 앞/뒤에 보기에 나열된 특정 단어와 어울리는 단어[구]가 보인다면, 그 보기를 빈칸에 우선 대입해서 해석해본다. 내가 'across from(~의 바로 맞은편에)'이란 표현을 알고 있는데, 빈칸 뒤에 from이 있고 보기에 across가 보이니 across from이 문맥상 자연스러운지만 확인하고 넘어가면 되므로, 그만큼 시간을 절약할 수 있다. 두 단어 이상의 덩어리 표현을 익히는 데 따로 시간을 할애할 필요가 없다.

해석 Grafton Brothers 법률 회사 사무실은 Halifax 기차역 바로 맞은 편에 있다.

PART 5

1. This vending machine will deliver reliable quality service to the user as long as maintenance checks are performed -------.

(A) regularly
(B) widely
(C) recently
(D) brightly

2. Adams said that he ------- remembered his first visit to India to perform in a charity concert.

(A) curiously
(B) fondly
(C) punctually
(D) equally

3. Despite adopting different marketing approaches, both Comms Global & PM Wireless have ------- gained thousands of new subscribers.

(A) moreover
(B) namely
(C) nevertheless
(D) similarly

4. Flexible work hours would ------- improve the efficiency of our managerial staff.

(A) persuasively
(B) significantly
(C) primarily
(D) willingly

PART 6

Questions 5-8 refer to the following letter.

Dear readers,

This letter is to ------- you of a modification to our magazine's policy on pausing weekly delivery
5.
when you travel, or on other occasions when unread issues might otherwise pile up.

If you give us 7 days notice, we can suspend delivery for up to 30 days without an additional fee.
-------.
6.

Don't forget that your subscription also gives you unlimited access to our in-depth online news
-------. Just register for digital credentials by entering your account information on WeeklyInquirer.
7.
com/Digitalsubscription to receive access on up to 5 devices at once.

To ------- suspend print delivery, email us at customerservice@weeklyinquirer.com or call us at 555-
8.
991-2313.

5. (A) profile
(B) inform
(C) call
(D) deliver

6. (A) Subsequently, regular delivery will resume.
(B) The discount will be applied to your digital account.
(C) Our quality reporting is made possible by readers like you.
(D) This decision was reached due to increasing costs.

7. (A) covers
(B) coverable
(C) covered
(D) coverage

8. (A) alternately
(B) better
(C) partially
(D) temporarily

해설서 p.125

1. Medellin Industries grew ------- in its first five years of operations, increasing its annual growth rate by 50 percent.
   - (A) deeply
   - (B) rapidly
   - (C) approximately
   - (D) obscurely

2. Six vendors submitted construction bid ------- for the new hospital building.
   - (A) proposals
   - (B) authorities
   - (C) foundations
   - (D) predictions

3. Once orders are placed on our Website, they are ------- within 24 hours.
   - (A) refined
   - (B) engaged
   - (C) revealed
   - (D) fulfilled

4. This afternoon's presentation will ------- best practices for communicating with our clients to see how we can improve our services.
   - (A) pursue
   - (B) conduct
   - (C) examine
   - (D) engage

5. Mr. Medina will not be able to attend the seminar this afternoon because she is ------- in traffic.
   - (A) stood
   - (B) stuck
   - (C) called
   - (D) pulled

6. Blue Lode Solutions remunerates its software developers with some of the most ------- salaries in all of Comobabi.
   - (A) marginal
   - (B) analogous
   - (C) contingent
   - (D) competitive

7. Stabilo Corporation compensates high-earning sales representatives with weekend ------- at the finest hotels.
   - (A) occupants
   - (B) places
   - (C) stays
   - (D) terms

8. Although the government supports first-time home buyers, it may take time before ------- changes to policies are passed.
   - (A) ordinary
   - (B) undeniable
   - (C) meaningful
   - (D) experienced

Questions 9-12 refer to the following article.

GRENVILLE (23 April) — American fashion giant StackRack ------- plans on its expansion into the
9.
United Kingdom. StackRack's spokesperson Ivan Palmer recently made public the plans for its
expansion into Europe, with Grenville being its first location.

-------. The initial launch will offer its impressive clothing range, which has created media buzz for its
10.
simple yet ------- designs. Following the initial launch, the company hopes to also open up its iconic
11.
lounge and spa, although the company could not specify the time frame. ------- is due to start in
12.
September.

---

9. (A) compromised
   (B) revealed
   (C) handled
   (D) questioned

10. (A) StackRack is optimistic that the location
        will be successful.
    (B) StackRack's expansion strategy has been
        deemed risky.
    (C) StackRack has also recently entered the
        Asia market.
    (D) StackRack has elected to open the new
        location in phases.

11. (A) fashion
    (B) fashions
    (C) fashionable
    (D) fashioned

12. (A) Agreement
    (B) Development
    (C) Formation
    (D) Negotiation

PART

6

TEXT COMPLETION
장문 공란 메우기

📋 문제 OVERVIEW

Part 6은 4개의 지문과 각 지문에 4개의 문항이 나와 총 16문제가 출제됩니다. Part 5와 마찬가지로 4개의 보기 중 빈칸에 들어갈 가장 알맞은 보기를 고르는 형태이긴 하지만, 빈칸 앞뒤의 문장 또는 지문의 전체 맥락을 통해 정답을 골라야 하는 문제가 많이 등장하기 때문에 글의 흐름을 파악하는 것이 중요한 파트입니다.

문항 수	4개 지문, 16문항(131~146번에 해당합니다.)
지문 유형	설명서, 편지, 이메일, 기사, 공지, 지시문, 광고, 회람, 발표문, 정보문 등
문제 유형	– 문장 구조 / 문법 문제: 문장의 구조와 더불어 문맥상 어울리는 시제, 대명사 등을 고르는 문제 – 어휘 문제: 같은 품사의 네 개 어휘 중에서 문맥상 알맞은 단어를 고르는 문제 – 문장 선택 문제: 앞뒤 문맥을 파악하여 네 개의 문장 중에 알맞은 문장을 고르는 문제
보기 구성	4개의 보기

⏱ 출제 TREND

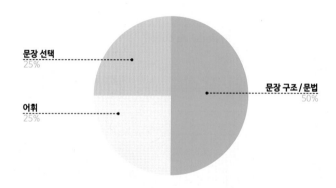

문장 구조 / 문법 문제에서는 주로 문맥상 어울리는 시제, 앞 문장이나 문단에서 언급된 명사를 대신 받아 줄 수 있는 대명사 문제가 가장 많이 출제되며, 문맥상 알맞은 문장을 고르는 문장 선택 문제가 지문당 한 문제씩 고정적으로 등장합니다. 어휘 문제 역시 해당 문장에만 어울리는 단어가 아니라 앞뒤 문장의 흐름상 어울리는 단어를, 두 문장을 자연스럽게 연결해 주는 접속부사를 고르는 문제가 많이 출제됩니다.

Questions 1-4 refer to the following e-mail.

1-4번은 다음 이메일에 관한 문제입니다.

To	:	Cynthia Castillo
From	:	Greg Sestero
Date	:	October 15
Subject	:	Plans going forward

Dear Ms. Castillo,

Due to a health issue, I've been advised to avoid regularly commuting from Grayslake. -------, I hope to keep contributing to *Northwood News*.

1.

If possible, I'd appreciate the chance to meet with you ------- the possibility of staying on in my current role. I don't think it would pose any problem to complete my work from home. -------. Besides, when it is absolutely necessary, I can still make the trip to the Highland Park office.

2.   **3.**

I would love to talk about this ------- in detail as soon as possible.

4.

Best,
Greg Sestero

수신 : Cynthia Castillo
발신 : Greg Sestero
날짜 : 10월 15일
제목 : 향후 계획

Castillo 씨께,

건강상의 문제 때문에, 저는 Grayslake에서 정기적으로 통근하는 것을 피하라고 권고받았습니다. **1**그럼에도 불구하고, 저는 계속해서 〈Northwood News〉에 기고하고 싶습니다.

가능하다면, 현재의 제 역할을 계속하는 것이 가능한지를 **2**논의하기 위해 당신을 만날 기회를 주시면 감사하겠습니다. 제가 집에서 일을 끝내는 것이 문제가 되리라 생각하지 않습니다. **3**어쨌거나 제 현재 업무는 대부분 온라인에서 완료됩니다. 게다가 꼭 필요할 때, 저는 여전히 Highland 공원 사무실로 갈 수 있습니다.

가능한 한 빨리 이 **4**생각에 대해 자세히 이야기하고 싶습니다.

마음을 담아,
Greg Sestero

1. 어휘 문제

Part 5 어휘 문제와 달리 Part 6의 어휘 문제는 빈칸이 들어 있는 그 문장만 봐서는 안 되고 앞뒤 문맥을 정확히 파악하여 답을 골라야 합니다. 어휘 문제는 네 개의 보기 중 의미상 가장 적절한 어휘를 고르는 문제입니다. 전후 문맥을 파악하여 풀어야 하므로 PART 5의 어휘 문제들보다 어려운 편입니다. 보통 5~6문항이 출제됩니다.

(A) And so   (B) In the end   **(C) Nonetheless**   (D) Consequently

(접속부사) 빈칸 앞 문장의 '건강상의 문제로 통근을 피하라고 권고받았다'라는 내용과 빈칸 뒷부분의 '계속해서 회사에 기여하고 싶다'라는 내용을 고려할 때, 문맥상 '통근하지 않음에도 불구하고 계속해서 회사에는 기여하겠다'라는 내용으로 이어져야 자연스러우므로 (C)가 정답입니다.

2. 문장 구조 / 문법 문제

한 단어의 네 가지 형태가 나오는 문제를 품사 자리 문제라고 합니다. 빈칸의 자리를 파악하여 네 개의 선택지 중에서 빈칸에 들어갈 적절한 품사 및 형태를 묻는 문제인데, 전체 16문항 중 3~4문항 정도가 출제됩니다. 동사 시제 문제는 문맥을 파악하는 까다로운 문제로 출제됩니다. 문법 문제는 구와 절, 즉 문장 구조를 파악하는 문제입니다. Part 6에서는 출제 빈도가 낮은 편이지만 Part 5보다 상당히 어려운 문제들이 출제됩니다. 전체 16문항 중 1~2문항 정도가 출제됩니다.

(A) to discuss   (B) are discussing   (C) have discussed   (D) discuss

(to부정사) 문장 내에 이미 동사 would appreciate가 있으므로 빈칸은 준동사 자리입니다. 문맥상 '가능성에 대해 논의하기 위해서 만나고 싶다'라는 의미가 되어야 자연스러우므로, 부사적 용법으로 쓰여 목적을 나타내는 to부정사 (A)가 정답입니다.

3. 문장 선택 문제

문장 선택 문제는 전반적인 지문의 흐름을 파악하여 4개의 보기 중에서 가장 적절한 한 문장을 선택하는 가장 난이도가 높은 문제입니다. 지문마다 한 문제씩 총 4문항이 출제됩니다. Part 6에서 가장 어려운 문제로, 전체적인 문맥을 파악하고, 접속부사나 시제 등을 종합적으로 봐야 답을 고를 수 있습니다.

(A) With your permission, I will get started on the article soon.
(B) Most of my current tasks are completed online anyway.
(C) I think it can be done just as well in a shorter time.
(D) The Grayslake location is more convenient for most of us.

(문장 선택) 빈칸 앞 문장의 '통근하지 않고 집에서 일을 끝내는 것이 문제가 되리라 생각하지 않는다.'라는 내용을 고려할 때, 문제 되지 않는 이유로 '업무 대부분이 온라인에서 완료된다.'라는 내용으로 이어져야 자연스러우므로 (B)가 정답입니다.

4. 어휘 문제

1번과 같은 어휘 문제로, 한 문장만 봐서는 안 되고 앞뒤 문맥을 정확히 파악하여 답을 골라야 합니다.

(A) deadline   (B) meeting   (C) article   **(D) idea**

(어휘 명사) 첫 번째 단락의 '통근하지 않고 재택근무를 하고 싶다'는 내용을 고려할 때, '이 생각에 대해 자세히 이야기하고 싶다'는 내용이 되어야 자연스러우므로 (D)가 정답입니다.

출제 POINT

1. 지문을 이해하는 독해 능력 평가

Part 6은 기본 문법 지식을 토대로 지문 내용을 얼마나 잘 이해하는지를 평가합니다. 같은 시제라도 Part 5에서는 특정 시제와 어울리는 시간부사구가 출제된다면, Part 6에서는 글의 흐름상 어울리는 시제를 고르는 문제가 출제됩니다. 대명사 문제도 Part 5에서는 문장의 자리에 어울리는 대명사의 격 'he vs. him vs. his'을 묻는 문제가 주를 이룬다면, Part 6에서는 대명사가 가리키는 명사를 파악해서 이를 받아줄 수 있는 수 'its vs. their'나 성 'he vs. she'이 일치하는 대명사를 묻는 문제가 출제됩니다. 기본 문법 지식과 독해 능력을 함께 평가하는 파트입니다.

2. 맥락 파악

앞뒤 문맥을 통해 시제를 결정하는 문제의 출제 비중이 높습니다. 시제를 묻는 문제는 Part 5에서는 시간부사구로 결정하지만, Part 6에서는 맥락으로 파악합니다. 두 문장을 자연스럽게 이어주는 접속부사 문제, 맥락으로 파악해야 하는 대명사의 인칭 문제, 수 일치 문제, 그리고 어휘 문제가 출제됩니다.

학습 ADVICE

1. 순차적으로 읽기

빈칸이 있는 문장만 보고 문제를 풀면 출제자가 만들어 놓은 함정에 빠지기 쉽습니다. 빈칸이 있는 문장만 보지 말고, 반드시 처음부터 읽어 가면서 글의 '맥락'을 파악하고 전체의 글을 논리적으로 완성할 수 있는 답을 찾아야 합니다. 지문당 2분, 총 8분 이내에 Part 6을 끝내야 Part 7에서 문제당 1분씩의 할애 시간을 확보할 수 있습니다.

2. 정독으로 정면승부

단순히 문장 구조나 문법을 묻는 문제도 출제되지만, 맥락과 연결되는 어휘나 시제, 접속부사를 묻는 문제들이 주로 출제된다는 것에 유의해야 합니다. 문장 선택 문제는 빈칸 앞뒤 문장의 대명사나 연결어 등을 확인하고 상관 관계를 파악합니다. 지문의 길이가 짧기 때문에 정독해서 읽으면 오히려 더 쉽게 해결할 수 있습니다.

파트 6 문제 유형

CASE 87 | 문맥에 맞는 대명사

[announcement]

We have received reports that some of our subscribers have not received this month's issue. If you have not received one yet, you may be one of them. Contact us via e-mail, and you will receive this month's issue by next week. If you find this arrangement to be unacceptable, then please give us a call immediately. Otherwise, ------- response may be delayed.

We apologize for the inconvenience. We understand we regrettably let down our loyal subscribers. We will strive to provide a better service in the future.

Thank you, and we thank you for your understanding.

(A) many   (B) your   (C) our   (D) no

해설 빈칸에는 명사 response를 수식할 수 있는 적절한 형용사나 소유격 대명사가 들어가야 한다. 빈칸 앞의 내용을 보면, 간행물 발행 주체(we)가 이번 달 호를 아직 받지 못한 구독자(you)에게 보내는 안내문임을 알 수 있고, 다음 주까지 이번 호를 받을 수 있게 해 주겠다면서, 이러한 조치를 'you'가 수용할 수 없다면, 'we'에게 즉시 연락하라는 내용이므로, 이어지는 문장은 '그렇지 않으면, 저희의(our) 응대가 늦어질 수도 있다'라는 의미가 되어야 자연스럽다. 따라서, 'we'의 소유격 대명사인 (C)가 정답이다.

해석 [안내문]

저희 일부 구독자께서 이번 달 간행본을 수령하지 못했다는 보고를 받았습니다. 아직 받아보지 못하셨다면, 귀하께서 그분들 중 한 분에 해당하실지도 모릅니다. 저희에게 이메일로 연락해 주시면, 다음 주까지 이번 달 호를 받으실 수 있습니다. 만약 이러한 조치를 받아들이실 수 없다면, 저희에게 바로 전화해 주시기 바랍니다. 그렇지 않으면, 저희의 응대가 늦어질 수 있습니다.

불편을 끼쳐드려 죄송합니다. 유감스럽게도 저희 오랜 구독자분들께 실망을 안겨드렸습니다. 앞으로 더 나은 서비스를 제공해 드리도록 노력하겠습니다.

감사드리며, 양해 바랍니다.

어휘 report 보고 | subscriber 구독자 | issue (잡지 등 정기 간행물의) 호 | via ~로 | arrangement 처리 방식 | immediately 즉시, 바로 | apologize 사과하다 | inconvenience 불편 | understand 이해하다 | regrettably 유감스럽게도, 애석하게도 | loyal 충실한 | strive 분투하다, 노력하다 | provide 제공하다 | in the future 미래에

>> Point

문맥상 앞에서 언급한 명사를 대신하는 대명사를 고르는 유형은 앞에 나온 어떤 명사를 가리키는지를 해석을 통해 찾은 다음, 선택지를 빈칸에 넣어서 문맥이 자연스럽게 연결되는지 확인한다.

>> Key word

We have received reports that some of our subscribers have not received this month's issue. If you have not received one yet, you may be one of them. Contact us via e-mail, and you will receive this month's issue by next week. **If you find this arrangement to be unacceptable, then please give us a call immediately. Otherwise, our response may be delayed.**

CASE 집중훈련

PART 5

1. After a ------- review in the online food blog, profits at Gigi's Café increased last week.
(A) provisional
(B) restricted
(C) rising
(D) favorable

2. All factory floor workers must print and keep a copy of workplace safety tips close at hand for quick -------.
(A) implication
(B) procedure
(C) reference
(D) assembly

3. -------, both domestic and international travel to industry conventions are discouraged due to budget cuts.
(A) Systematically
(B) Regrettably
(C) Consistently
(D) Unsuccessfully

4. While each of the accountants ------- well during their final interviews, Ga-In Lee stood out from everyone else.
(A) admitted
(B) treated
(C) performed
(D) handled

PART 6

Questions 5-8 refer to the following memo.

To: Residents of 15 Quarry Oval
From: Willie Ingram, Facilities Manager
Date: March 16

Dear Residents,

On March 23 and 24, our crew ------- necessary adjustments that were requested by several residents residing here. Chief among those is the installation of an electronic security system at the entrance. ------- will drastically increase security by limiting who can enter the building. As part of the installation, we will be installing a card-reader at the main entrance as well as automatically locking electronic doors. -------. The backdoor will be available, but it is quite narrow. Therefore, please do not plan for any large ------- on either day. Once installations are complete, we will be issuing all residents two cards that will grant entrance into the building.

Sincerely,

Willie Ingram

---

5. (A) was making
(B) can be made
(C) to make
(D) will be making

6. (A) Those
(B) Who
(C) This
(D) Some

7. (A) The main entrance will be closed off for the duration.
(B) The schedule may fall behind due to the weather.
(C) Additional repairs may be made, but some may incur costs.
(D) Windows should be carefully looked after.

8. (A) renditions
(B) deliveries
(C) commitments
(D) releases

[e-mail]

To: Shawna Wallace, Contracting Manager
From: Homer Greer
Date: 21 August
Subject: Expansion strategy

Dear Ms. Wallace,

We have recently come to the decision that due to falling sales of our beverages, Twoser Refresh will not be expanding overseas this year. -------, we will be refining our products and re-thinking our marketing campaign. As you know, we agreed on a joint venture together. We would like to put that on hold for now.

We'd like to review some of the research you conducted for us last year. Specifically, I recall that your company conducted some product testing sessions. That data could be extremely valuable to us. If you could send us the feedback gathered from those, we'd like to start by analyzing those. Could you e-mail those to us?

I would appreciate it if we could get that information at your earliest convenience.

Thank you,

Homer Greer

(A) Otherwise　　　(B) Whereas　　　(C) Instead　　　(D) Therefore

> **해설** 빈칸은 두 문장을 연결하는 접속부사 자리이다. 빈칸 앞 문장의 '올해 해외 진출을 하지 않기로 했다'는 내용과 빈칸 뒷부분의 '제품을 개선하고 마케팅 캠페인에 대해 재고해 볼 예정'이라는 내용을 고려할 때, 해외 진출 대신 제품과 마케팅을 검토한다는 내용으로 연결되어야 문맥상 자연스러우므로 (C)가 정답이다.

> **해석** [이메일]
> 수신: Shawna Wallace, 계약 담당자
> 발신: Homer Greer
> 날짜: 8월 21일
> 제목: 확장 전략
>
> Wallace 씨께,
>
> 음료 매출 하락으로 인해 Twoser Refresh에서는 올해 해외 진출에 나서지 않기로 하는 결정을 최근 내렸습니다. 대신에, 제품을 개선하고 마케팅 캠페인에 대해 재고해 볼 예정입니다. 아시다시피, 저희는 함께 합작 투자를 하는데 합의했습니다. 당분간은 그것을 보류했으면 합니다.
>
> 저희는 작년에 귀사에서 실시한 몇 가지 조사를 검토해 보려 합니다. 구체적으로는, 귀사에서 제품 테스트 세션을 몇 번 시행했던 걸로 기억합니다. 그 자료가 저희에게 매우 유용할 수 있을 것 같습니다. 거기서 수집한 피드백을 저희에게 보내주신다면, 자료 분석부터 시작해 보려 합니다. 자료를 이메일로 보내주실 수 있으신가요?
>
> 가급적 빨리 저희가 정보를 받아볼 수 있다면 감사하겠습니다.
>
> 감사합니다.
>
> Homer Greer

> **어휘** contract 계약하다 | expansion 확장 | strategy 전략 | recently 최근 | falling 하락하는 | sales 매출 | beverage 음료 | expand 확장하다 | overseas 해외로 | refine 개선하다 | product 제품 | re-think 재고하다 | marketing campaign 마케팅 캠페인 | agree on ~에 합의[동의]하다 | joint venture 합작 투자

>> Point

접속부사, 접속사, 부사 등 두 문장을 연결하기에 자연스러운 연결어를 고르는 유형에서는 문맥상 앞뒤 문장을 논리적으로 이어줄 수 있는 보기를 선택하면 된다.

>> Key word

We have recently come to the decision that due to falling sales of our beverages, **Twoser Refresh will not be expanding overseas this year. Instead, we will be refining our products and re-thinking our marketing campaign.**

CASE 집중훈련

PART 5

1. Education experts predict that AI programs that are designed to personalize students' learning progress will continue increasing in -------.
(A) popularity
(B) balance
(C) character
(D) exchange

2. Following the resignation of Ms. Tsang, the department ------- a search for a new director of operations.
(A) launched
(B) evaluated
(C) related
(D) influenced

3. The new division of We Build For You mainly ------- on roofing supplies and installations for both residential and commercial properties.
(A) catches
(B) belongs
(C) cooperates
(D) focuses

4. National Public Transport will convert its subway trains to be completely automated ------- the technology improves the reliability of the system.
(A) only if
(B) no longer
(C) moreover
(D) prior to

PART 6

Questions 5-8 refer to the following article.

CANTERBURY (February 15) — What started out as a family tradition has turned into a yearly event at Glasgow University. Today, ------- can enjoy a massive 50-meter hyacinth garden that runs along
5.
the main entrance to the university. -------. Nobody knows, -------, why the tradition of planting
6.   7.
hyacinths caught on with the community. What we do know is that it has been an ongoing tradition for at least 70 years.

-------, the tradition looks to be enjoying consistent popularity. Throughout the year, students at the
8.
university volunteer to take care of the garden by providing water, soil, and clearing out pests. The hyacinths will be around for many generations to enjoy.

5. (A) visiting
(B) visit
(C) visits
(D) visitors

6. (A) It may be the biggest hyacinth garden in the world.
(B) Other flower species may be easier to manage.
(C) Hyacinths typically bloom around mid-spring.
(D) Due to their popularity, hyacinths fetch a high price.

7. (A) precise
(B) precisely
(C) precision
(D) preciseness

8. (A) Fortunately
(B) Regrettably
(C) Similarly
(D) Otherwise

[notice]

The local council ------- methods to optimize the use of its current funds. The goal is to invest the saved money into some major projects that will transform the city. Over the past year, the council has evaluated several possibilities. Once the council has confirmed its available budget going into next year, it plans to engage in more detailed discussions. A vote will be taken shortly after. All citizens are invited to have their say in what the city needs most. The council hosts a town hall meeting every month.

(A) has been trialing　　　(B) trial　　　(C) trialing　　　(D) will have trialed

해설 빈칸은 주어와 목적어 사이의 동사 자리이다. 빈칸 뒤에 '지난 한 해 동안, 의회에서는 여러 가능성들을 평가해왔다'는 현재 완료 시제의 문장이 있음을 고려할 때, 빈칸에는 '의회에서 현재 자금의 활용을 최적화하는 방법을 (과거부터 지금까지) 시험해왔다'라는 의미를 전달하는 현재 완료 진행 시제가 와야 문맥상 자연스러우므로 (A)가 정답이다.

해석 [공지]
지방 의회에서는 현재 자금의 활용을 최적화하는 방법을 시험해 왔습니다. 목표는 저축해 놓은 자금을 도시를 탈바꿈할 주요 프로젝트에 투자하는 것입니다. 지난 한 해 동안, 의회에서는 여러 가능성들을 살펴봤습니다. 의회에서 내년도 가용 예산을 확정하면, 보다 상세한 논의를 진행할 계획입니다. 조만간 투표가 실시됩니다. 모든 시민은 시에 가장 필요한 것에 대한 발언권을 가질 수 있습니다. 의회에서는 매달 시청 회의를 주재합니다.

어휘 local council 지방 의회 | method 방법 | optimize 최적화하다 | use 사용 | current 현재의 | fund 자금 | goal 목표 | invest 투자하다 | save 저축하다 | major 주요한 | transform 변화시키다 | evaluate 평가하다 | several 몇몇의 | once 일단 ~하면 | confirm 확정하다 | available 이용 가능한 | budget 예산 | engage in ~에 참여[관여]하다 | citizen 시민 | say 발언권 | town hall 시청

>> Point

앞뒤 문장의 흐름을 논리적으로 이어주기에 알맞은 시제를 고르는 유형에서는 앞뒤 문장에 제시된 사건의 진행 순서를 파악하여 시제를 결정해야 한다.

>> Key word

The local council has been trialing methods to optimize the use of its current funds. The goal is to invest the saved money into some major projects that will transform the city. **Over the past year, the council has evaluated** several possibilities.

CASE 집중훈련

PART 5

1. Dr. Cheng designed detailed charts to record the factory's energy needs ------.
(A) broadly
(B) relatively
(C) precisely
(D) dominantly

2. Even though admission to the Kenville Nature Museum is free, tourists are encouraged to ------- to the exhibition fund.
(A) apply
(B) donate
(C) dedicate
(D) support

3. Passengers aboard Pacific Air aircrafts will appreciate traveling alongside an ------- group of flight attendants.
(A) expert
(B) endless
(C) idle
(D) initial

4. Haldane Industry released some ------- forecast in its latest financial report.
(A) supporting
(B) optimistic
(C) collective
(D) activated

PART 6

Questions 5-8 refer to the following letter.

17 October

Dear Employees:

The merger with Gamst Partners has officially gone through. Today is the first day of our new combined company, Kristin & Gamst. -------. Following the merger, we ------- to aggressively expand
    5.   6.
overseas using our pooled resources. With Gamst Partners' expertise in tax law and our knowledge of contract law, our chances of success are very high.

The biggest change taking place following the merger will be the ------- of the new management
                                                                    7.
team. This is something that was already pre-negotiated with Gamst Partners, and we are excited to fill you in on the details. The company will be convening in the Conference Hall across the street at 2 P.M. this afternoon, where we will celebrate the occasion. -------, we will reveal what we have
                                                                          8.
planned for this coming year. We hope to see you there.

Sincerely,

Damon Sandoval
Human Resources Manager
Kristin Corporation

5. (A) Corporate legal services are in high demand today.
(B) Employees should email their representatives with any questions.
(C) Kristen & Gamst is now one of the country's largest law firms.
(D) The area is rife with competition, so any advantage is welcome.

6. (A) planned
(B) have been planning
(C) planning
(D) are planning

7. (A) accumulation
(B) extraction
(C) speculation
(D) announcement

8. (A) Additionally
(B) For instance
(C) On that note
(D) In contrast

CASE 90 문맥에 맞는 문장

[notice]

Lab Equipment Sterilization Rules

Our lab uses plasticware equipment in an effort to reduce waste and lower costs. On the other hand, unlike glass, plastic equipment requires more effort during the cleaning process. This means that you must carefully follow certain guidelines when cleaning lab tools made of plastic. For instance, to properly wash a plasticware container, you need to avoid treating it with a strong alkaline cleaner or abrasive scrubbing pad, which can leave scratches. -------. Although most of our plasticware equipment is just as reusable as glass, some older tubes and dishes made of lower grade material have a strict expiration date. If you see one of these pieces, do not use it. It has a high likelihood of containing contaminants. Instead, place it in the green recycling bins, not the blue ones for standard waste.

(A) New protective goggles have been ordered for lab staff.
(B) These need to be washed at the end of each session.
(C) In all cases, check the lab's safety guide first.
(D) Glassware is preferable in the majority of cases.

해설 빈칸 앞 문장들에서 '플라스틱으로 만들어진 실험실 도구를 세척할 때 특정 지침을 주의 깊게 따라야 한다'고 하며 이어서 예를 들어 설명하고 있음을 고려할 때, 문맥상 플라스틱 도구 세척 지침과 관련된 내용으로 이어져야 자연스러우므로 (C)가 정답이다.

해석 [공지]

실험실 장비 소독 규칙

저희 실험실은 쓰레기를 줄이고 비용을 낮추려는 노력으로 플라스틱 장비를 사용합니다. 반면, 유리와 달리, 플라스틱 장비는 세척 과정에서 더 많은 노력을 요합니다. 이는 플라스틱으로 만들어진 실험실 도구를 세척할 때, 특정 지침을 주의 깊게 따라야 함을 의미합니다. 예를 들어, 플라스틱 용기를 제대로 씻으려면, 강한 알칼리성 세제나 스크래치를 남길 수 있는 연마성 수세미로 닦는 것을 피해야 합니다. 모든 경우에, 실험실 안전 가이드를 먼저 확인하십시오. 저희 플라스틱 장비의 대부분은 유리처럼 재사용이 가능하지만, 낮은 등급의 재료로 만들어진 일부 오래된 통과 접시들은 사용 기한이 엄격합니다. 이들 제품 중 하나를 보실 경우, 사용하지 마십시오. 오염 물질을 함유하고 있을 가능성이 매우 높습니다. 대신, 일반 쓰레기용의 파란색 통이 아닌, 녹색 재활용 쓰레기통에 넣어주세요.

(A) 연구실 직원들을 위한 새로운 보호 고글이 주문되었습니다.
(B) 이것들은 각 세션이 끝날 때마다 세탁해야 합니다.
(C) 모든 경우에, 실험실 안전 가이드를 먼저 확인하십시오.
(D) 대부분의 경우 유리 제품이 더 좋습니다.

어휘 lab 실험실 | equipment 장비, 용품 | plasticware 플라스틱 용기 | in an effort to ~하려는 노력으로 | reduce 줄이다 | waste 쓰레기, 폐기물 | lower 낮추다; 낮은 | cost 비용, 경비 | require 필요로 하다, 요구하다 | tool 도구, 연장 | properly 제대로, 적절히 | container 용기 | alkaline 알칼리성의 | abrasive 연마재의, 거친 | scrubbing pad 수세미 | scratch 스크래치, 긁힌 자국 | reusable 다시 사용할 수 있는 | tube 통, 튜브 | strict 엄격한 | expiration 만료, 만기 | likelihood (어떤 일이 있을) 가능성 | contain 함유하다 | contaminant 오염 물질 | place 놓다 | recycling 재활용 | bin (휴지)통 | standard 일반적인, 보통의

>> Point

빈칸 앞뒤 문장과 자연스럽게 어울리는 문장을 고르는 유형은 대개 빈칸 앞에서 결정적인 단서가 제시될 때가 많으므로, 앞에 언급된 내용을 파악한 후 관련이 없는 보기들을 소거하면서 가장 어울릴만한 보기를 넣어 앞뒤 문장과의 연결이 자연스러운지 확인한다. 오답 보기는 주로 지문에 등장한 단어를 이용하거나 지문의 내용을 보고 연상하기 쉬운 상황을 기술한다는 점에 주의한다.

>> Key word

This means that **you must carefully follow certain guidelines when cleaning lab tools made of plastic. For instance**, to properly wash a plasticware container, you need to avoid treating it with a strong alkaline cleaner or abrasive scrubbing pad, which can leave scratches. **In all cases, check the lab's safety guide first**.

PART 5

1. COMED Corporation ------- its dress code only for staff that work in the laboratory.

(A) enforces
(B) instructs
(C) conforms
(D) measures

2. To determine which caterer would be the most affordable, Gretchen Kim requested bids from ------- services.

(A) numerous
(B) detailed
(C) measured
(D) obvious

3. Lassiter Hardware generally does not offer refunds, but for certain items it will make an -------.

(A) opportunity
(B) assurance
(C) objective
(D) exception

4. The merger agreement draft must be completed this week so that the lawyers will have the opportunity to review it -------.

(A) thoroughly
(B) purposely
(C) importantly
(D) commonly

PART 6

Questions 5-8 refer to the following notice.

Update on UD Dress Code

Based on the results of our latest employee survey, Ubiquitous Designs has recognized that employees would like more of their fashion ------- to be accommodated by the current dress code policy.
5.

Therefore, starting next month, we will be making the following adjustments to the policy. -------.
6.
Additionally, employees will be allowed to wear open-toed shoes ------- around the office. Finally,
7.
Casual Fridays have been much requested, so we are happy to announce that they will be coming into effect alongside the other changes.

We hope you are happy with the ------- changes. If you have any questions, you can reach out to the
8.
human resources team.

---

5. (A) preferred
(B) preferences
(C) prefer
(D) preferring

6. (A) Jewelry, including necklaces and bracelets, will now be allowed.
(B) Dresses have undergone many changes recently.
(C) The dress code was last updated two years ago.
(D) Employees are issued two sets of uniforms upon employment.

7. (A) freely
(B) forcefully
(C) abruptly
(D) reluctantly

8. (A) employee
(B) corporation
(C) workplace
(D) career

CASE 실전훈련

Questions 1-4 refer to the following job posting.

H2Go Games seeks talented writers to join our game development team. H2Go Games has been a leader in the gaming industry, and our latest games are now considered ------- games of the last
1.
decade. With the release of the new Gamma2 game system, we are looking to provide the same great gaming experience. Our writers do this by ------- immersive worlds and creating deep storylines
2.
that draw gamers into our world. We are looking for people who have a knack for storytelling and have experience in the video game industry. -------, we value vision far more than industry
3.
experience. We offer a competitive salary, flexible hours, and a great work culture with plenty of room for career development. -------. Apply today at www.h2gogames.com/recruit.
4.

1. (A) iconic
(B) classical
(C) reserved
(D) official

2. (A) design
(B) designed
(C) designing
(D) to design

3. (A) However
(B) Contrary to
(C) Otherwise
(D) Since

4. (A) The interview will consist of three sections.
(B) See for yourself why our employee satisfaction scores are so high.
(C) Be sure to include a portfolio of your past work.
(D) H2Go Games aims to be the market leader in five years.

Questions 5-8 refer to the following press release.

GULF HILLS — DMP Media --------- its new internship program at its Jackson office two months ago. Since then, the company has provided valuable work --------- to over 50 students, many of whom are pursuing careers in media.

The program began thanks to the efforts of its CEO, Jana Thomas, who thought Jackson students needed more opportunities. ---------. The internship program provides high school students with minor roles at its office including some deskwork, editing, and writing emails.

To --------- for a spot in the program, high school students should fill out the form on DMP Media's Web site (www.dmpmedia.com/intern). Internships are for three months but may be extended.

5. (A) has launched
   (B) launched
   (C) will launch
   (D) is launching

6. (A) suggestion
   (B) experience
   (C) presence
   (D) subject

7. (A) Students often lack the time to commit to work responsibilities.
   (B) A new office is expected to open in the area next year.
   (C) Due to legal requirements, positions are usually unpaid.
   (D) The company also hopes to give back to the community.

8. (A) request
   (B) satisfy
   (C) apply
   (D) interest

Questions 9-12 refer to the following article.

BIGLER (12 October) — From next year, electric vehicles from Arbiter Collective ---9.--- powered by Minassi batteries. Minassi has previously worked with other ---10.--- companies, but it has signed an exclusive agreement with Arbiter Collective. The ---11.--- arose after Minassi's CEO, Ross Norman, became interested in focusing his business more on local companies. ---12.---. "Once I sat down with Arbiter Collective's team, I knew that they were perfect for us. We have the same goals in mind, and we are willing to work hard to get there," said Mr. Norman. Arbiter Collective was not available for comment.

9. (A) have been
(B) will be
(C) are
(D) were

10. (A) materials
(B) industrial
(C) automotive
(D) utilities

11. (A) order
(B) acquisition
(C) partnership
(D) linkage

12. (A) The costs of exporting batteries had risen sharply.
(B) The batteries were shown to be the most efficient on the market.
(C) The vehicles are expected to increase in price.
(D) The industry had been stagnant in recent years.

Questions 13-16 refer to the following e-mail.

To: kreed@sporacle.co.uk
From: omurphy@callaghantours.com
Date: 17 September
Subject: Proposal

Dear Ms. Reed,

Thank you for finding time to meet with us last week. -------- the rate you can provide us, we would
love to hire Sporacle Partners to handle our designing needs. The concept pictures you showed us
were -------- and clearly tailored for our market needs. --------.

We will also need approval from the CEO. As he was absent from our meeting, we would like to
show him the same samples you showed us. Would it be possible to e-mail a copy at your earliest
convenience?

Finally, I would like to -------- a detail regarding the timeline. We were split between launch the
advertising campaign in December or January. However, we would like to hold off until February
because we are making some last-minute changes to our product line.

Thank you, and I look forward to hearing from you.

Orlando Murphy

13. (A) In conjunction
    (B) Depending on
    (C) Subsequently
    (D) By contrast

14. (A) articulation
    (B) articulating
    (C) to articulate
    (D) articulate

15. (A) I'm sure they will strongly appeal to our
        younger demographic.
    (B) The invoice will have to be updated before
        being approved.
    (C) My contact details are included on my
        business card.
    (D) A new product is likely to cost a lot of
        money.

16. (A) devise
    (B) clarify
    (C) integrate
    (D) accept

PART

7

READING COMPREHENSION
독해

📋 문제 OVERVIEW

Part 7은 지문을 읽고 그에 딸린 2~5개의 문제를 푸는 형태로, 총 54문제가 출제됩니다. 각 지문의 종류와 문항 수는 다음과 같습니다.

지문의 종류	지문 수	지문당 문항 수	전체 문항 수
단일 지문	10개	2~4문항	29문항
이중 지문	2개	5문항	10문항
삼중 지문	3개	5문항	15문항

문항 수	54문항(147~200번에 해당합니다.)
지문 유형	– **단일 지문:** 이메일, 편지, 문자 메시지, 온라인 채팅, 광고, 기사, 양식, 회람, 공지, 웹 페이지 등 – **이중 지문:** 이메일-이메일, 기사-이메일, 웹 페이지-이메일 등 – **삼중 지문:** 다양한 세 지문들의 조합
질문 유형	– **핵심 정보:** 주제 또는 목적과 같이 가장 핵심적인 내용을 파악하는 문제 – **특정 정보:** 세부 사항을 묻는 문제로, 모든 질문이 의문사로 시작하며 지문에서 질문의 키워드와 관련된 부분을 읽고 정답을 찾는 문제 – **NOT:** 지문을 읽는 동안 보기 중에서 지문의 내용과 일치하는 보기를 대조해서 소거하는 문제 – **추론:** 지문의 내용을 바탕으로 전체 흐름을 이해하며 지문에 직접 언급되지 않은 사항을 추론하는 문제 – **화자 의도:** 화자의 의도를 묻는 문제로, 문자 메시지나 2인 형태의 대화로 출제되며 온라인 채팅은 3인 이상의 대화 형태로 출제 – **동의어:** 주어진 단어의 사전적 의미가 아니라 문맥상의 의미와 가장 가까운 단어를 고르는 문제 – **문장 삽입:** 지문의 흐름상 주어진 문장이 들어갈 적절한 위치를 고르는 문제로, 세부적인 정보보다 전체적인 문맥 파악이 중요한 문제
보기 구성	4개의 보기

🕐 출제 TREND

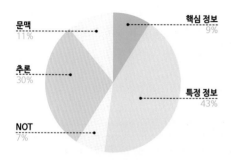

문맥 11%
추론 30%
NOT 7%
핵심 정보 9%
특정 정보 43%

각 유형은 다음과 같이 일정한 비중으로 출제되고 있습니다.

문제 유형	세부 유형	출제 문항 수
핵심 정보	주제, 목적, 대상	3~6문항
특정 정보	상세 정보, 사실 확인	23~26문항
NOT	상세 정보 NOT, 사실 확인 NOT	3~5문항
추론	핵심 정보 추론, 특정 정보 추론	15~18문항
문맥	동의어, 화자 의도 파악, 문장 삽입	5~7문항

🔷 시험 PREVIEW

Questions 1-2 refer to the following job posting.

Bright Wave Systems (BWS) is looking for a technical editor with a university education to proofread manuals that have been translated from English to Portuguese. BWS is a large software developer that is planning to do business in Sao Paulo. We pay $25 per page.

In order to apply, please send an e-mail to hr@bws.com. In the message, include your résumé and two writing samples (one in English, one in Portuguese).

BWS is located in Chicago, but the work involved for this position may be performed from any part of the world.

1-2번은 다음 채용 공고에 관한 문제입니다.

Bright Wave Systems (BWS)는 영어에서 포르투갈어로 번역된 안내서를 교정할 대졸 기술 편집자를 찾고 있습니다. BWS는 Sao Paulo에서 사업을 준비 중인 대형 소프트웨어 개발업체입니다. 장당 25달러를 지급합니다.

지원하시려면 hr@bws.com으로 이메일을 보내 주십시오. **1**메시지에 이력서와 두 개의 글 샘플(영어 1개, 포르투갈어 1개)을 포함해 주세요.

BWS는 Chicago에 있지만, **2**이 직무 관련 업무는 세계 어느 곳에서나 수행하실 수 있습니다.

1. 특정 정보(상세 정보)

What is needed from applicants?

(A) Materials written in two languages
(B) Reference letters from former employers
(C) An official university transcript
(D) A bank account number

두 번째 단락에서 이력서와 두 개의 글 샘플을 포함하라(include your résumé and two writing samples)고 했으므로 (A)가 정답이에요.

+ Paraphrasing
your résumé and two writing samples → Materials,
English, Portuguese → two languages

2. 특정 정보(사실 확인)

What is indicated about the technical editor job?

(A) It requires occasional international travel.
(B) It can lead to a permanent position.
(C) It can be done remotely.
(D) It requires a one-year commitment.

세 번째 단락에서 이 직책에 관련된 일을 세계 어느 곳에서나 수행할 수 있다(the work involved for this position may be performed from any part of the world)고 했으므로 (C)가 정답이에요.

+ Paraphrasing
be performed from any part of the world → be done remotely

◎ 출제 POINT

1. 핵심 정보 – 지문의 앞부분에서 단서 포착하기

주제나 목적, 대상을 묻는 문제는 대개 지문의 첫머리에 단서가 제시되므로 도입부 내용을 잘 확인하여 이 내용을 포괄할
수 있는 보기를 고릅니다. 도입부에 단서가 보이지 않는다면 앞 단락에 언급된 내용을 중심으로 빠르게 훑어 내려가며 정
답을 포착하세요.

2. 특정 정보 – 키워드 붙들기

상세 정보, 사실 확인 문제의 경우 핵심 단어 및 표현에 집중하여 질문에서 키워드를 파악하고 관련 내용이 언급된 부분
을 지문에서 찾아 문제를 해결합니다.

3. NOT – 보기와 대조하기

질문과 보기에서 키워드를 찾아 표시한 후, 지문을 읽어가면서 해당 키워드가 등장할 때마다 보기와 대조하세요. 대조를
통해 틀린 보기를 소거하고, 남은 한 개의 보기를 정답으로 선택하세요.

4. 추론 – 미루어 짐작하되 상상하지 않기

특정 정보 유형과 비슷한 방식으로 접근하되, 특정 정보 유형처럼 단서가 직접적으로 드러나 있지 않기 때문에, 단서를
토대로 미루어 짐작할 수 있는 보기를 정답으로 골라야 합니다. 주어진 단서를 가능한 한 객관적으로 유추해야 합니다.

5. 문맥 – 앞뒤 문장의 연결성 고려하기

동의어 문제의 경우 주어진 단어를 지문에서 찾아 표시한 후에 해당 문장을 해석해서 문맥상 단어의 뜻을 파악하고, 그
뜻과 바꿔 쓸 수 있는 보기를 선택합니다. 화자 의도 파악 유형 역시 주어진 문장을 지문에서 찾아 표시한 후에 해당 문장
의 앞뒤의 맥락을 토대로 화자가 왜 그렇게 말했는지를 적절하게 기술한 보기를 선택합니다. 문장 삽입 문제는 먼저 주어
진 문장을 정확히 이해해 두어야 지문을 두세 번 읽지 않고 풀 수 있습니다.

◎ 학습 ADVICE

1. 나름의 기준 세우기

Part 7은 15개의 지문에 총 54문제가 출제되어 RC 전체 문항의 절반 이상을 차지합니다. 한 문제를 푸는 데 걸리는 시
간도 평균 1분 내외로 다른 파트에 비해 많은 시간을 요구합니다. 특히 NOT 유형은 주어진 네 개의 보기를 지문의 내용
과 일일이 대조하여 답을 골라야 하고, 화자 의도 파악이나 문장 삽입 유형은 지문의 일부, 심지어는 지문 전체의 맥락을
파악해야 할 때도 있어서 문제를 푸는 데 적게는 1분, 많게는 3분 이상도 걸립니다. '시간이 오래 걸리는 문제들을 위해
핵심 정보 유형과 특정 정보 유형의 문제들은 30초 이내에 풀자.'와 같은 나름의 기준을 세워 둘 필요가 있습니다.

2. 패러프레이징에 유념하기

Part 3&4와 마찬가지로 지문에 등장한 내용이 문제에서는 비슷한 의미의 다른 표현으로 제시되는, 즉 패러프레이징 되
어 나오기 때문에 지문을 정확하게 해석할 수 있는 능력을 길러야 합니다.

3. 구어체 표현 익히기

Part 7에서 문자 메시지나 온라인 채팅은 난이도가 비교적 높지 않습니다. 그러나 구어체 표현이 많이 나오고 문자 그대
로의 사전적인 의미가 아닌 문맥상 그 안에 담겨 있는 숨은 뜻을 찾는 화자 의도 파악 문제가 꼭 출제되기 때문에 평소 구
어체 표현을 숙지하고 대화의 흐름을 파악하는 연습을 해야 합니다.

파트 7 문제 유형

CASE 91 | 주제/목적/대상

[article]

Around the Company

If you see Ryan Newmyer around the office, make sure to congratulate him. With Samantha Lee transferring to the Operations Department, he will now move up to become a Senior Buyer.

Ryan has won our trust in the 18 months he's been with the Purchasing Department. This summer, he won the Rising Star Award for his exceptional contributions. His commitment to the company is truly impressive, and he has motivated others to work harder. His inventive strategies helped bring the cost of materials down, which led to an unexpected drop in the department's expenditures this quarter. Nice work, Ryan. Keep it up!

Q. Why was the article written?

(A) To describe an awards ceremony
(B) To explain a revised budget proposal process
(C) To introduce a new product line
(D) To announce an upcoming promotion

1단계 문제 유형 파악하기

Why was the article written? 이 기사는 왜 작성되었는가?
→ 기사를 쓴 '목적'을 묻는 문제

2단계 첫 번째 단락 읽기

If you see Ryan Newmyer around the office, make sure to congratulate him. **With Samantha Lee transferring to the Operations Department, he will now move up to become a Senior Buyer.**
→ Ryan이 수석 바이어로 승진할 것이라는 내용으로 시작하는 기사

3단계 주제 문장의 맥락과 일치하는 보기 고르기

(A) To describe an awards ceremony 시상식을 설명하려고
(B) To explain a revised budget proposal process 수정된 예산 제안 과정을 설명하려고
(C) To introduce a new product line 새 제품군을 소개하려고
(D) To announce an upcoming promotion 곧 있을 승진을 발표하려고

[기사]

회사 소식

만약 여러분이 사무실에서 Ryan Newmyer를 보게 되신다면 축하해 주십시오. Samantha Lee가 운영 부서로 이동하면서 그가 이제 수석 바이어로 승진하게 되었습니다.

Ryan은 구매 부서에서 일한 18개월 동안 우리의 신뢰를 얻었습니다. 올여름 뛰어나게 우수한 기여에 대해 신예 스타상을 받기도 했습니다. 회사를 향한 그의 헌신은 정말로 인상적이며, 그는 다른 직원들이 더 열심히 일하도록 동기부여를 했습니다. 그의 창의적인 전략은 자재 비용 절감을 도왔고, 이는 이번 분기 부서의 지출 비용을 예상치 못하게 감소시켰습니다. 훌륭해요, Ryan. 계속 열심히 하세요!

어휘 congratulate 축하하다 | transfer 이동하다 | operation 운영 | buyer 구매자, 바이어 | trust 신뢰 | purchasing department 구매 부서 | exceptional 이례적일 정도로 우수한 | contribution 기여 | commitment 전념, 헌신 | impressive 인상적인 | motivate 동기 부여를 하다 | inventive 창의적인, 독창적인 | strategy 전략 | cost 비용 | material 재료, 자재 | unexpected 예상치 못한 | drop 감소, 축소 | expenditure 지출, 비용 | quarter 분기

>> Point

지문에 딸린 문제의 순서와 지문에 등장하는 단서의 순서는 대부분 일치하며 주제/목적/대상 문제의 단서는 주로 지문의 앞부분에 등장하므로 첫 단락에서 정답의 단서를 찾는다.

간혹 지문 전체의 내용을 토대로 주제를 파악해야 할 때가 있는데, 이때는 앞에서부터 빠르게 읽어 내려가면서 보기와 매칭시켜 가며 풀거나 다른 문제들을 먼저 푼 뒤에 지문의 내용이 전체적으로 파악되면 마지막에 풀어도 좋다.

주제 문장을 패러프레이징하거나, 지문 전체의 내용을 요약한 보기를 선택한다.

>> 빈출 문제 유형

What is the main topic of the article?
이 기사의 주제는 무엇인가?

What does the letter mainly discuss?
편지에서 주로 논의하는 것은?

What is the purpose of the Web page?
이 웹 페이지의 목적은 무엇인가?

Why was the notice written?
이 공지는 왜 쓰였는가?

Who is the advertisement intended for?
이 광고는 누구를 대상으로 하는가?

Questions 1-3 refer to the following article.

LONDON (5 NOVEMBER) — Birkstein Media has officially acquired Juniper Studios. Juniper currently produces eight television shows across multiple networks. —[1]—. The studio was recently awarded the Tremon Prize for excellence in TV production. —[2]—.

"We are thrilled to have Juniper Studios join the Birkstein family and to work together to produce shows that everyone can enjoy," commented Birkstein CEO Robert Segor in a statement. Bill Lorrie founded Juniper 25 years ago with his colleague, Gail Bonds. —[3]—. After growing the company into the powerhouse it is today, Lorrie decided that it was time to move on. "I've done everything that I can to help this company. And for it to take the next step, I believe that this is the right move." —[4]—.

---

1. What is the purpose of the article?

(A) To announce the acquisition of a firm
(B) To discuss a television schedule
(C) To promote a new show
(D) To reveal the winner of an award

2. What is indicated about Juniper Studios?

(A) It was started by two business partners.
(B) It mainly produces documentaries.
(C) It created eight shows in 25 years.
(D) It moved to a new location.

3. In which of the positions marked [1], [2], [3], and [4] does the following sentence best belong?

"They attract a large volume of viewers in their respective genres."

(A) [1]
(B) [2]
(C) [3]
(D) [4]

Questions 4-6 refer to the following e-mail.

To	Team C
From	Amanda Yazzy
Date	October 15
Subject	Company-Issued Phone Upgrades

Resolute Insurance takes pride in equipping everyone in its Claims Department with company-issued smartphones. According to our documents, those of you receiving this e-mail are due for an upgrade by the end of November. —[1]—. As per company policy, your team's phones need to retire after 24 months of service time.

Please send a text message to my colleague Timothy Sullivan at (555) 891-2855 about your availability to exchange your phone for a new model. Make sure to reach out to him before the end of business tomorrow if you want to receive yours in the first week of November. —[2]—. He will set a time for your upgrade.

In the interest of making the process run smoothly, please delete any personal data and make a backup ahead of your appointed time. —[3]—. It should take about 30 minutes to file your forms, turn in your current phone, and set up your new device. —[4]—.

4. Who is the e-mail intended for?

(A) Resolute Insurance claims staff
(B) Employees who were recently hired
(C) IT specialists in Ms. Yazzy's team
(D) Workers who need phone repairs

5. What is mentioned about the procedure for turning in a smartphone?

(A) Appointments must be made with Mr. Sullivan.
(B) Employees will need to get their manager's approval.
(C) Arrangements must be made by October 16.
(D) Information that is not backed up will be deleted.

6. In which of the positions marked [1], [2], [3], and [4] does the following sentence best belong?

"Also, make sure to read through and sign the company smartphone terms and conditions paperwork attached."

(A) [1]
(B) [2]
(C) [3]
(D) [4]

Major News for the Lakewood Opera House

Leia Mansoori, Staff Writer

LAKEWOOD (15 December) — Last year, the Lakewood Opera House was forced to shut down, leaving the town without a proper space for live musical performances. The neighboring and popular Buzz Jazz Diner also closed its doors at the same time. But now, Patrick Crosby looks to bring them back to the spotlight.

Mr. Crosby has enjoyed a long and successful career in the music industry. After gaining recognition as a skilled musician, he focused his attention on conducting about seven years ago. Originally from Chicago, he noticed the abandoned Lakewood Opera House while visiting some friends. Right then, he decided to raise money to acquire the lot and restore the four-decade-old building. Despite a few mishaps, the revamped center will soon be filling its auditorium with visitors.

On 5 January, the remodeled center will host its very first performance, *Letters from Louis*, conducted by Austin Summers with special guest violinist Mina Song making her concert debut. This show will run for three weeks.

On 26 December, the newly renovated Buzz Jazz Diner will also be open to the public. Customers will be able to listen to live music while enjoying various dishes, including newly added vegetarian items. "Music is an important part of life, and I'm glad that I can reintroduce some of it back into this community," stated Mr. Crosby.

Events at the Lakewood Opera House

Currently on Stage: *Letters From Louis*

Due to popular demand, this performance will run for one extra week! Make sure to get your tickets now. Come find out why everyone has been talking about this amazing production. Tickets still start at $10.

Next Up: *Growing Up My Way*

The inspirational story based on the life of renowned actress Margaret Yeldon is told through opera in *Growing Up My Way*. Yeldon wrote and arranged this autobiographical piece, which has received critical acclaim. Conducted by Patrick Crosby, this production will surely leave you holding your breath and wanting more. *Growing Up My Way* opens on February 22 with shows every night. Tickets range from $15 to $50.

Find out more on our Web site at www.lakewoodoperahouse.com/events.

7. Why was the article written?

(A) To provide information on a local music festival

(B) To highlight the accomplishments of a retiring artist

(C) To review some recent musical performances

(D) To report on the reopening of local establishments

8. What is implied about the Buzz Jazz Diner?

(A) It offers affordable prices.

(B) It has a recording studio.

(C) It employs a reputable chef.

(D) It expanded its menu.

9. What aspect of *Letters From Louis* was changed?

(A) The number of shows

(B) The performance's director

(C) The sound equipment

(D) The cost of admission

10. Who is Margaret Yeldon?

(A) An opera singer

(B) A music composer

(C) A student of Mr. Crosby

(D) A manager at a talent agency

11. What is true about the conductor of *Growing Up My Way*?

(A) He is a native of Lakewood.

(B) He owns the Lakewood Opera House.

(C) He taught Mina Song.

(D) He co-wrote the production.

Questions 12-16 refer to the following Web page, e-mail, and survey.

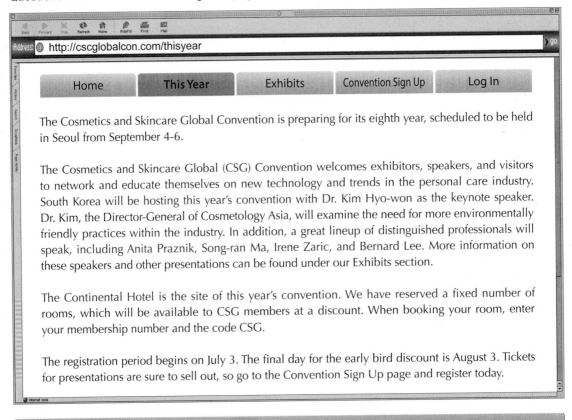

| Home | This Year | Exhibits | Convention Sign Up | Log In |

Address: http://cscglobalcon.com/thisyear

The Cosmetics and Skincare Global Convention is preparing for its eighth year, scheduled to be held in Seoul from September 4-6.

The Cosmetics and Skincare Global (CSG) Convention welcomes exhibitors, speakers, and visitors to network and educate themselves on new technology and trends in the personal care industry. South Korea will be hosting this year's convention with Dr. Kim Hyo-won as the keynote speaker. Dr. Kim, the Director-General of Cosmetology Asia, will examine the need for more environmentally friendly practices within the industry. In addition, a great lineup of distinguished professionals will speak, including Anita Praznik, Song-ran Ma, Irene Zaric, and Bernard Lee. More information on these speakers and other presentations can be found under our Exhibits section.

The Continental Hotel is the site of this year's convention. We have reserved a fixed number of rooms, which will be available to CSG members at a discount. When booking your room, enter your membership number and the code CSG.

The registration period begins on July 3. The final day for the early bird discount is August 3. Tickets for presentations are sure to sell out, so go to the Convention Sign Up page and register today.

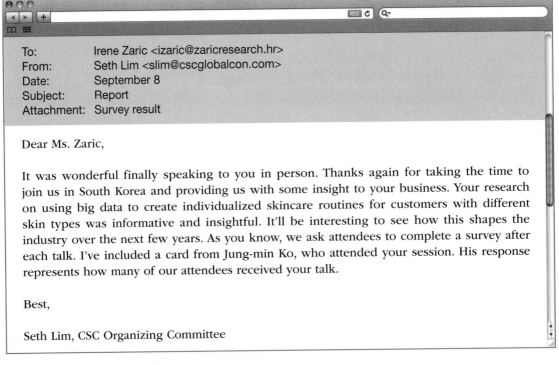

To:	Irene Zaric <izaric@zaricresearch.hr>
From:	Seth Lim <slim@cscglobalcon.com>
Date:	September 8
Subject:	Report
Attachment:	Survey result

Dear Ms. Zaric,

It was wonderful finally speaking to you in person. Thanks again for taking the time to join us in South Korea and providing us with some insight to your business. Your research on using big data to create individualized skincare routines for customers with different skin types was informative and insightful. It'll be interesting to see how this shapes the industry over the next few years. As you know, we ask attendees to complete a survey after each talk. I've included a card from Jung-min Ko, who attended your session. His response represents how many of our attendees received your talk.

Best,

Seth Lim, CSC Organizing Committee

Cosmetic and Skincare Global Convention Survey

	Excellent	Fair	Poor
Venue	X		
Exhibitors	X		
Preparations			X
Accommodations	X		

Remarks: Checking in to the convention was a headache. Even though I had my confirmation sheet, my details were not in the system. This situation was eventually resolved, but it caused me to miss the keynote speech. The rest of the event, however, went smoothly. One presentation in particular stood out—the one about data analysis. It was very interesting, and I now have newfound appreciation for technology in the skincare industry.

Jung-min Ko

12. What is indicated about the convention?

(A) Eligible attendees can receive a reduced rate on their accommodation.
(B) It takes place at the same venue every year.
(C) All participants need to register by 3 August.
(D) Only industry professionals are invited to attend.

13. What is the purpose of the e-mail?

(A) To sign up for a conference discussion
(B) To provide comments on a session
(C) To request completion of a survey
(D) To suggest topics for a presentation

14. In the e-mail, the word "shapes" in paragraph 1, line 4, is closest in meaning to

(A) contours
(B) produces
(C) influences
(D) fashions

15. What is suggested about Mr. Ko?

(A) He was unable to attend Dr. Kim's presentation.
(B) He was impressed with check-in process.
(C) He wishes that some talks were longer.
(D) He thinks the event location was inconvenient.

16. Which speaker did Mr. Ko particularly like?

(A) Anita Praznik
(B) Song-ran Ma
(C) Irene Zaric
(D) Bernard Lee

CASE 92 상세 정보

[e-mail]

To: Melvin Lu; Jonah Pape; Sherrill Acevedo; Alexa Packard
From: Verna Ortega
Date: Monday, 19 July
Subject: Mentoring program
Attachment: Mentor meetings

Dear Colleagues,

Congratulations on accepting your job offer from Shalksy Data. We are very excited to bring you onboard, and we hope you enjoy your tenure here.

Something we pride ourselves over is our keen interest in the personal and professional development of our staff. From your first day here, we will show you everything you will need to excel at your role as well as provide pathways up the corporate ladder. For this reason, we have a mentor program, where an experienced data analyst will act as your mentor for your first two months. Your mentor will guide you through your first days here and help you out with any problems you encounter. While you will normally be messaging your mentor every day, there will be a face-to-face meeting once a week. These meetings give you the opportunity to discuss in depth any difficulties you are facing and get your mentor's advice. For more information on these meetings, please see the attached document.

Congratulations once again on your employment.

Sincerely,

Verna Ortega, Human Resources

Q. What are the recipients of the e-mail expected to do?

(A) Respond to the e-mail in a timely manner
(B) Work closely with a senior employee for two months
(C) Provide feedback on the onboarding process
(D) Choose from a list of prearranged courses

해석 [이메일]

수신: Melvin Lu; Jonah Pape; Sherrill Acevedo; Alexa Packard
발신: Verna Ortega
날짜: 7월 19일, 월요일
제목: 멘토링 프로그램
첨부: 멘토 회의

동료 여러분께,

Shalksy Data의 채용 제안 수락을 축하드립니다. 여러분을 맞이하게 되어 매우 기쁘며, 이곳에서의 근무를 즐기시길 바랍니다.

저희는 직원의 개인적, 직업적 성장에 대한 깊은 관심을 가지고 있는데 대해 자부심을 갖고 있습니다. 입사 첫날부터 저희는 여러분이 각자의 역할에서 두각을 드러내는데 필요한 모든 것을 보여드릴 뿐만 아니라 승진 계단을 올라가는 길을 제시해 드릴 것입니다. 이러한 이유로 저희는 멘토 프로그램을 운영하며, 첫 두 달간 경험 많으신 데이터 분석가가 여러분의 멘토 역할을 맡게 됩니다. 여러분의 멘토는 입사 초반에 여러분을 이끌어주며, 여러분이 겪게 되는 모든 문제들을 도와줄 것입니다. 보통은 매일 멘토와 메시지를 주고받으면서, 일주일에 한 번씩 대면 회의를 갖게 됩니다. 이 회의는 여러분이 겪는 힘든 점에 대해 깊이 있게 논의하며 멘토의 조언을 얻을 수 있는 기회가 됩니다. 회의에 대한 더 자세한 내용은 첨부 문서를 확인해 주세요.

다시 한번 입사를 축하드립니다.

감사합니다.

Verna Ortega, 인사팀

어휘 colleague 동료 | accept 수락하다 | job offer 채용 제안 | bring ~ onboard ~를 합류시키다 | enjoy 즐기다 | tenure 재직 | pride oneself over ~에 대해 자랑스럽게 여기다 | keen 깊은, 열렬한 | interest 관심 | personal 개인적인 | professional 직업적인 | development 성장, 발전 | staff 직원 | excel at ~에 뛰어나다 | role 역할 | provide 제공하다 | pathway 진로 | corporate ladder 기업의 계층 서열 | reason 이유 | experienced 경험이 풍부한 | data analyst 데이터 분석가 | act as ~의 역할을 맡다 | guide through 안내해 주다 | encounter 맞닥뜨리다 | normally 보통 | message 메시지를 보내다 | face-to-face 대면의 | opportunity 기회 | discuss 논의하다 | in depth 깊이 있게 | difficulty 어려움 | face 직면하다 | advice 조언 | attach 첨부하다 | employment 취업, 고용

>> Point

질문의 의문사와 키워드를 확인한다.

의문사와 키워드를 기억한 상태에서 지문을 빠르게 훑어가며 해당 정보가 언급된 부분을 찾는다.

질문의 단서를 그대로 쓰거나 패러프레이징한 보기를 선택한다.

>> 빈출 문제 유형

What does Ms. Erikson want to do on May 28?
Erikson 씨가 5월 28일에 무엇을 하길 원하는가?

What does Ms. Keenum think about the plans?
Keenum 씨가 이 계획에 대해 어떻게 생각하는가?

When should customers pay Handy Paintings for their services?
고객들은 Handy Paintings에 서비스 요금을 언제 지불해야 하는가?

Where was Ms. Winters when she sent the text message?
문자 메시지를 보냈을 때 Winters 씨는 어디에 있었는가?

Why are employees asked to contact Mr. Dieng?
직원들은 왜 Dieng 씨에게 연락하라고 요구받는가?

What is NOT a new policy?
새로운 정책의 아닌 것은?

Questions 1-2 refer to the following advertisement.

Kitsap Solution

Kitsap Solution is proud to have offered the very best home repair service in the country for many years. During this time, we have continuously expanded our list of services to include any repairs you may need, including plumbing problems, leaky ceilings, and faulty wiring. With our award-winning team of professionals coupled with the lowest rates you will find in the industry, choosing Kitsap Solution for any home repair you may need is a no-brainer! Call our team and have your issue diagnosed for free today. And don't worry about paying for anything until we have fully diagnosed the issue because we will always provide a full quote before we start on any work.

---

1. What does Kitsap Solution provide?

(A) Fitness consultation
(B) Technology repairs
(C) Architectural designs
(D) Home improvement

2. What is stated about Kitsap Solution?

(A) It started operations last year.
(B) It will provide quotes free of charge.
(C) It has won awards for its staff's performance.
(D) It can only begin work upon receiving payment.

Questions 3-5 refer to the following Web page.

Learn New Skills Online Using LifeCoach!

- Sign up now and learn new skills to boost your career—no prior experience or university degrees necessary!
- Access our selection of hundreds of courses including programming, graphic design, and market research
- Receive personalized feedback on assignments from our team of expert instructors
- View your progress and achievements you've earned

Take your career to the next level for only $16.99 a month. Sign up today and take advantage of our limited offer of 50% off for your first three months. If you wish to find out more about what we can offer you, please do not hesitate to contact our customer service line at 0800-555-1352.

Sign up now and let LifeCoach transform your career!

3. What is suggested about LifeCoach?

(A) It is a relatively new company.
(B) It does not require prior knowledge.
(C) It has partnered with many companies.
(D) It will offer in-person classes.

4. What are users of LifeCoach able to do?

(A) Select an instructor of their choice
(B) Compare their progress with other users
(C) View graded evaluations or assessments
(D) Upgrade their subscription

5. According to the Web page, why would a customer contact the customer service line?

(A) To request information
(B) To cancel a subscription
(C) To receive a catalog
(D) To dispute a charge

Questions 6-10 refer to the following online form and e-mail.

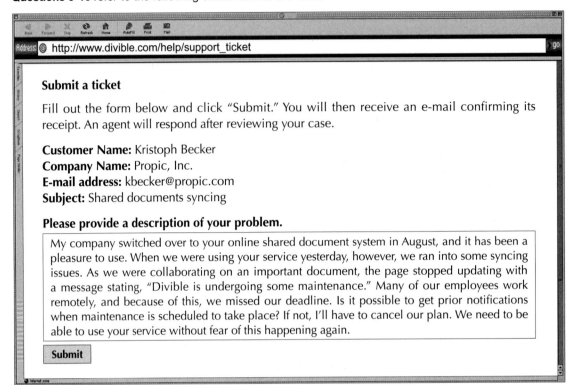

http://www.divible.com/help/support_ticket

Submit a ticket

Fill out the form below and click "Submit." You will then receive an e-mail confirming its receipt. An agent will respond after reviewing your case.

Customer Name: Kristoph Becker
Company Name: Propic, Inc.
E-mail address: kbecker@propic.com
Subject: Shared documents syncing

Please provide a description of your problem.

My company switched over to your online shared document system in August, and it has been a pleasure to use. When we were using your service yesterday, however, we ran into some syncing issues. As we were collaborating on an important document, the page stopped updating with a message stating, "Divible is undergoing some maintenance." Many of our employees work remotely, and because of this, we missed our deadline. Is it possible to get prior notifications when maintenance is scheduled to take place? If not, I'll have to cancel our plan. We need to be able to use your service without fear of this happening again.

Submit

To	Kristoph Becker <kbecker@propic.com>
From	Divible Help Desk <help@divible.com>
Date	4 December
Subject	Support ticket 1249058 – Shared documents syncing

Dear Mr. Becker,

On behalf of the company, I apologize for the inconvenience you experienced last Tuesday. The problem was a result of a power outage at our server facility. This, of course, was unexpected. Therefore we could not inform customers ahead of time. Normally, the emergency power system would have turned on automatically, but it failed this time.

After considering your feedback, our executives have agreed to rephrase our dialog box from "undergoing some maintenance" to "facing technical problems." This should clarify to users that the issue was unanticipated and not previously planned. I would like to mention that when we do perform maintenance checks and upgrades, our servers rarely go offline.

Again, we sincerely apologize about the disruption in our service and the troubles it caused your team. Your feedback and support is very important to us. As a token of our appreciation, we have credited your business account for this month's fees.

Best regards,

Vernon Enunwa, Divible Help Team

6. What does Mr. Becker request on the online form?

(A) A visit from an IT technician
(B) A new method to upload documents
(C) A maintenance schedule
(D) A payment refund

7. What is suggested about Mr. Becker?

(A) He works on documents online.
(B) He was hired by Propic in August.
(C) He applied for a job at Divible.
(D) He has a deadline every Tuesday.

8. What is Mr. Becker's complaint regarding Divible's shared document system?

(A) It cannot open some of his files.
(B) It is not reliable.
(C) It is inaccessible by employees working remotely.
(D) It is difficult to navigate.

9. What does Mr. Enunwa say Divible will change?

(A) Its user manual
(B) Its failure alert
(C) Its membership benefits
(D) Its power source

10. What is indicated about Propic, Inc.?

(A) It upgraded its subscription option.
(B) It subscribes to a monthly plan with Divible.
(C) It inspects its servers every day.
(D) It employs workers from around the world.

Freddington Artists on Display in Community Project
By Shelby de Mello

Freddington (3 September) — At its Small Business Convention in the Freddington Civic Center yesterday, the Freddington Chamber of Commerce announced a new campaign to promote local businesses via public art. Called Drawing Inspiration, this initiative matches area artists with business owners in the community to redesign storefronts in the city.

Interested business owners are welcome to fill out an application that includes their business's involvement in the community along with any record that proves that their store has been in operation at its current location for more than three years. Artists who want to get involved with the campaign must submit a detailed application about their connection to Freddington, along with samples of their own artwork.

Please send all application to Kathleen Osmough at kosmough@freddingtoncoc.org no later than October 1. Freddington will compensate artists for necessary supplies of up to $100.

To:	Kathleen Osmough
From:	Tae-kyung Lim
Date:	October 7
Subject:	Drawing Inspiration Request
Attachment:	Sketch_ver. 2

Dear Ms. Osmough,

Thank you for taking the time to meet with me this week at Mali Bakery to discuss ideas for the Drawing Inspiration redesign project. The bakery was a favorite of mine growing up, and I still visit the place regularly whenever I have a craving for their famous apple pie. Actually, I go there so often that the owner even put up one of my paintings on the bakery wall.

Per your recommendation, I have modified the color pattern to match the interior of Mali Bakery. Please take a look and let me know if you'd like to see any other changes.

Regards,

Tae-kyung Lim

Reimbursement Form for Freddington Chamber of Commerce

Please fill out the form and provide itemized documentation of the purchase. Processing will take no longer than one week.

Date: October 8
Name: Tae-kyung Lim
Purpose: Drawing Inspiration
Details: Materials needed for the Drawing Inspiration project. All goods were purchased at Freddington's Art Box. Invoice has been attached.

ITEM	Price per Item	Number of Items	Total Price
Canary yellow acrylic paint, 32 oz	$25.99	1	$25.99
Mustard yellow acrylic paint, 18 oz	$15.99	1	$15.99
Painting knife set	$9.99	1	$9.99
Acrylic varnish spray, 11 oz	$10.99	2	$21.98
	Grand Total (tax incl.)		$76.53
Approved by: K. Osmough	**Date Approved:** 15 October		

11. According to the article, where will artists display their work?

(A) At the Chamber of Commerce
(B) In public parks
(C) At the Freddington Civic Center
(D) At local businesses

12. What is the purpose of the e-mail?

(A) To receive confirmation of a design
(B) To schedule a meeting place
(C) To request a budget increase
(D) To accept a job offer

13. What is indicated about the supplies Mr. Lim purchased?

(A) They were purchased online.
(B) They are not available in Freddington.
(C) Their approval has not been confirmed.
(D) Their cost will be fully reimbursed.

14. What needs to be included with the form?

(A) A photo of the finished project
(B) A sales receipt
(C) A business address
(D) A bank account number

15. What is most likely true about Mali Bakery?

(A) It will use a new logo designed by Mr. Lim.
(B) Its interior is yellow.
(C) It opened three years ago.
(D) It raises money for local artists.

[memo]

To: All Assembly Plant Employees
From: Darius Mountebank
Date: 22 February
Subject: Outstanding Worker Leave

Starting in the second quarter of this year, Emmerich Industries will institute the Outstanding Worker Leave (OWL) program. This initiative will award select employees with an extra week of paid leave if they have regularly shown exceptional dedication, leadership, or ingenuity. Outstanding work could include, but would not be limited to: remarkable productivity, a record of resolving difficult reliability issues, or the implementation of time-saving procedures.

OWL nominations will be made anonymously, must be supported by a testimonial from at least one colleague within the nominee's department, and are to be submitted by March 31. All staff are eligible for nominations and may be nominated multiple times. Final selections will be made by the plant managers and announced at the spring company meeting. OWL may be used within a year. Any OWL not redeemed within 12 months will expire.

Q. What is NOT indicated about nominations?

    (A) There are no restrictions on who can be nominated.
    (B) They expire after 12 months.
    (C) They will be considered by management.
    (D) They must include a recommendation.

1단계 질문의 키워드 확인하기

What is NOT indicated about nominations? 후보 지명에 관하여 언급되지 않은 것은?

2단계 질문의 키워드와 관련된 내용 포착하기

OWL nominations will be made anonymously, **must be supported by a testimonial from at least one colleague within the nominee's department, (→D)** and are to be submitted by March 31. **All staff are eligible for nominations and may be nominated multiple times. (→A) Final selections will be made by the plant managers and announced at the spring company meeting. (→C)**

OWL 후보 지명은 익명으로 이루어지며, 지명된 사람의 부서 내 동료 최소 한 명의 추천을 받아야 하며, (→D) 3월 31일까지 제출되어야 합니다. 전 직원은 후보로 추천될 수 있으며 여러 번 추천 받을 수 있습니다. (→A) 공장 관리자들이 최종 선택을 하며 춘계 회사 회의에서 발표됩니다. (→C)

3단계 질문의 키워드와 관련된 내용을 보기와 하나씩 대조하기

(A) There are no restrictions on who can be nominated. 누가 지명될 수 있는지에 관해 제한이 없다.
(B) They expire after 12 months. 12개월 후에 만료된다.
(C) They will be considered by management. 경영진이 검토할 것이다.
(D) They must include a recommendation. 추천서를 포함해야 한다.

[회람]

수신: 조립 공장 전 직원
발신: Darius Mountebank
날짜: 2월 22일
제목: 우수사원 휴가

올해 2분기부터 Emmerich 산업은 우수사원 휴가 (OWL) 프로그램을 도입합니다. 이 계획은 특별한 헌신, 리더십 또는 독창성을 꾸준히 보인, 엄선된 직원들에게 추가 일주일의 유급 휴가를 수여합니다. 우수 업무에는 주목할 만한 생산성, 어려운 안정성 문제 해결 기록 또는 시간 절약 절차의 실행이 포함될 수 있지만, 이에 국한되지는 않습니다.

OWL 후보 지명은 익명으로 이루어지며, 지명된 사람의 부서 내 동료 최소 한 명의 추천을 받아야 하며, 3월 31일까지 제출되어야 합니다. 전 직원은 후보로 추천될 수 있으며 여러 번 추천 받을 수 있습니다. 공장 관리자들이 최종 선택을 하며 춘계 회사 회의에서 발표됩니다. OWL은 1년 내에 사용될 수 있습니다. 12개월 이내에 사용되지 않은 OWL은 만료됩니다.

어휘 **outstanding** 뛰어난 | **leave** 휴가 | **institute** 도입하다 | **initiative** 계획 | **award** 수여하다 | **select** 엄선된 | **paid leave** 유급 휴가 | **regularly** 정기적으로 | **exceptional** 이례적인, 우수한 | **dedication** 헌신 | **ingenuity** 독창성 | **limited** 국한된 | **remarkable** 놀라운, 주목할 만한 | **productivity** 생산성 | **resolve** 해결하다 | **reliability** 신뢰성, 안정성 | **issue** 문제, 사안 | **implementation** 시행 | **time-saving** 시간을 절약하는 | **procedure** 절차 | **nomination** 후보 지명 | **anonymously** 익명으로 | **testimonial** 추천서 | **nominee** 지명된 사람 | **eligible for** ~에 자격이 있는 | **selection** 선택 | **redeem** 현금[상품]으로 바꾸다

>> Point

질문에 등장한 키워드(보통 질문의 'about' 뒤의 명사)를 확인한다.

지문에서 질문의 키워드와 관련된 내용을 포착한다.

각 보기와 지문 내용을 대조해 가며 정답을 골라낸다.

>> 빈출 문제 유형

What is true about the new accounting office? 새 회계사무소에 관하여 사실인 것은?

What is stated about phone numbers? 전화번호에 관하여 언급된 것은?

What is mentioned about the Garden to Table event? Garden to Table 행사에 관하여 언급된 것은?

What is NOT stated about the new parking permit stickers? 새로운 주차 허가 스티커에 관하여 언급되지 않은 것은?

Questions 1-3 refer to the following invoice.

Gryseld Allied Workforce

Client:
Tresa Maddox
49 Austin Hill
Glenmora, Louisiana 71433

Invoice number: 197-914

Description: The driveway shows signs of severe damage evidenced by the abundance of potholes. Recommendation is to dig up the driveway and drain the water out first. Then it should be redone using asphalt. The driveway includes a brick path to the front door which measures 16 x 10 feet. Total cost will include the cost to replace this path.

We provide a 10 percent discount to all first-time clients.

Costs for services and materials:

Description	Amount
Dig up and drain driveway	$2,400
Install new driveway	$1,750
Material costs (asphalt, bricks)	$950
Labor costs	$1,200
Total charge	$6,300 - 10% = $5,670 A 25% down payment of $1,417.50 is required ahead of work.

All jobs require a 25 percent down payment before any work can begin. The amount can be paid via credit card.

---

1. The word "evidenced" in paragraph 1, line 1, is closest in meaning to

(A) contradicted
(B) tested
(C) promoted
(D) reflected

2. What is indicated about the path?

(A) It is rarely used.
(B) It leads to a house.
(C) It is due for a repair.
(D) It was recently put in.

3. What is implied about Ms. Maddox?

(A) She is hiring the company for the first time.
(B) She intends on paying using a check.
(C) She expected a lower cost for the work.
(D) She has recently moved into the area.

Questions 4-6 refer to the following memo.

MEMO

To: Branch Managers
From: Dalia Kay, Chief Financial Officer
Date: 29 April
Subject: Quarterly Report

This is a friendly reminder that your quarterly reports must be submitted by 4 May. Every branch manager has a duty to fill out the report as per his or her employment conditions, and it is a responsibility we place special emphasis on. This is because we have a legal obligation to show that our branches are conforming to the health and safety standards as prescribed by the province. However, the reports also reflect which of our food items are selling well. This is typically how we determine whether we need to adjust our menus. The reports are compiled at the end of every quarter, and we present the results at our shareholder meetings.

The template for the report has been attached to this e-mail for your convenience. As a reminder, we have made a change to how the reports are to be filled out. We are now requiring that you provide your operating revenue as well as your net income. This will help us determine what effect the upcoming tax change will have on our bottom line.

---

4. What is a purpose of the memo?
(A) To introduce managers to a new system
(B) To remind managers of a deadline
(C) To mention the future outlook of the company
(D) To send over a new employment contract

5. What is NOT mentioned as a possible use of the report?
(A) Comparing with competing companies
(B) Planning necessary changes
(C) Sharing with current and future investors
(D) Complying with required standards

6. According to the memo, how do this year's reports differ from those of previous quarters?
(A) Additional financial information will be required.
(B) They will need to be audited by an independent agency.
(C) They will need to be submitted through a new system.
(D) Expenses should be categorized according to function.

Questions 7-11 refer to the following e-mail and agenda.

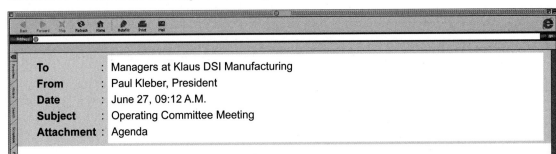

To : Managers at Klaus DSI Manufacturing
From : Paul Kleber, President
Date : June 27, 09:12 A.M.
Subject : Operating Committee Meeting
Attachment : Agenda

Good morning, everyone.

Adjustments have been made to the operating committee meeting that is scheduled for today at 3 P.M. You can find the updated agenda attached to this e-mail.

We will not be hearing a summary on the Stockholm Conference that took place this week because Michael Becker, our mechanical engineer who was in attendance, was unable to get on a flight back due to inclement weather. He will be arriving in Berlin tomorrow evening. His report on the conference will be given at our next meeting.

In Mr. Becker's slot, we have added two other speakers. To start, executive director Julian Hodges will give us a demonstration of our latest 3D printers. We expect it to be our most efficient model yet. Then, one of our department heads will introduce the accomplishments of senior manager Edetta Greco, who is eligible for a promotion to an executive position. We will take a moment to evaluate her performance and vote on her status.

If you have anything you would like to add to the minutes, please speak with my assistant, Chadwick Peters, by noon today, and we will see if we can include it.

Paul Kleber, President

Klaus DSI Manufacturing

Operating Committee Meeting Agenda
June 27, 3:00 P.M. — 5:30 P.M.

3:00 P.M. — 3:20 P.M.	Mr. Chadwick Peters (Pension Policy and Meeting Room Maintenance)
3:20 P.M. — 3:50 P.M.	Ms. Gemma Schneider (Client Communications)
3:50 P.M. — 4:20 P.M.	Ms. Lina Jacobs (Research, Development, and Innovation)
4:20 P.M. — 5:15 P.M.	Mr. Bailey Hodges (Demonstration) Mr. Ian Thys (Introduction, Evaluation, and Vote)
5:15 P.M. — 5:30 P.M.	Mr. Paul Kleber (Final Remarks)

7. What is the purpose of the e-mail?

(A) To explain revisions to an agenda
(B) To inform staff members of a conference
(C) To notify employees about a worker's promotion
(D) To disclose the location of a presentation

8. What does the e-mail state about Mr. Becker?

(A) He will not be attending a meeting.
(B) He has submitted his vote online.
(C) He is on holiday.
(D) He is eligible for a promotion.

9. Who will talk about Ms. Greco's accomplishments?

(A) Mr. Hodges
(B) Ms. Jacobs
(C) Mr. Thys
(D) Ms. Schneider

10. What is likely one of Mr. Peters's responsibilities?

(A) Developing innovative products
(B) Manufacturing printers
(C) Communicating with clients
(D) Maintaining office spaces

11. Who will give the closing remarks?

(A) The chairman of the board
(B) The company president
(C) A mechanical engineer
(D) An administrative assistant

Questions 12-16 refer to the following e-mails and Web page.

To	Rima Albert <r.albert@lbjdesigns.com>
From	Tracey Emerson <t.emerson@iccity.com>
Date	June 28
Subject	Internet options

Dear Ms. Albert:

Thank you for inquiring about recommendations for which internet plan is right for your design company. In order to provide the best possible recommendations, I would need to know answers to the following questions:

1. How flexible is your budget, and does your budget include the installation fees? Different companies may offer different rates depending on how long the contract is. In general, the longer the better.

2. How stable do you require your connection to be? Stable connections are hard to find and are normally more expensive.

3. What are the main activities of your company that would require extensive internet use? General office use such as e-mailing and web browsing does not require a fast connection, but accessing, for example, digital media might.

4. How important is uploading to your company? Companies offer fast download speeds but often neglect upload speed because it is not a commonly requested feature.

5. Do you anticipate expanding your internet usage in the future?

Please get back to me at your earliest convenience, and I will be happy to make a recommendation.

Sincerely,

Tracey Emerson

To:	Tracey Emerson <t.emerson@iccity.com>
From:	Rima Albert <r.albert@lbjdesigns.com>
Date:	June 29
Subject:	RE: Internet options

Dear Ms. Emerson,

Right now, our internet needs for both upload and download are high. As we are a design company working with many international companies, we upload and download media files every single hour. Stability is also a big factor for us as we have many of our meetings online these days. We would like to experience minimal disruptions. As for our office, I believe we are committed to renewing our lease indefinitely.

I discussed the budget issue with my boss yesterday, and he has said that cost is not a priority for us, so long as we can get our job done more efficiently. Therefore, I don't think we have to worry about this aspect. I hope these answers will help you find the best package for us.

Rima Albert

Based on our latest investigation last week into the various internet options available, we have compiled our picks for the best internet service providers:

Company	Specialty	Comments
Limitless Networks	Household	Low cost but connection can be spotty
Spark	Home office	Cheap and good for general use
WorldNet	Enterprise	Expensive but no installation costs
TrustPower	Enterprise	Very high cost but extremely reliable

12. What most likely is Ms. Emerson's job?

(A) Newspaper reporter
(B) Customer service
(C) Technical consultant
(D) Civil engineer

13. What does Ms. Emerson indicate about internet plans?

(A) Longer contracts usually result in lower prices.
(B) Internet prices have been on the rise in recent years.
(C) Traffic to international sites may incur additional costs.
(D) Installation fees are normally waived by the internet service provider.

14. Which of Ms. Emerson's questions does Ms. Albert fail to answer?

(A) Number 1
(B) Number 2
(C) Number 3
(D) Number 5

15. According to the second e-mail, what is suggested about the design company?

(A) It has recently relocated offices.
(B) It has seen an upsurge in business this year.
(C) It primarily deals with advertisements.
(D) It requires fast upload and download speeds.

16. What company will Ms. Emerson most likely recommend?

(A) Limitless Networks
(B) Spark
(C) WorldNet
(D) TrustPower

[brochure]

STA Solutions

Offering our expertise to local residences for over two decades

Our services include:
- A wireless security system that can be linked to any device with an Internet connection
- 24/7 customer service support in various languages
- Three-year warranty on all of our products

❷ Rates begin at $40/month for the starter security system package. A comprehensive package is also available. Contact us today to sign up for a free one-month trial!

Testimonials

"Ever since installing the security system at my apartment, I haven't been worried about leaving my place. The customer service associates were really helpful in assisting me when I encountered some technical issues."
- Shawn Workman

"STA Solutions is your answer for a secure home. I constantly travel overseas for business, so the wireless security system is perfect for me. I can easily monitor my house from wherever I am."
- Leila Wong

❶ **Q. What is implied about STA Solutions?**

❸ (A) It only offers services to local businesses.
(B) It provides various security system packages.
(C) It is operated by former security officers.
(D) It has more than one location.

1단계 질문의 키워드 확인하기

What is implied about STA Solutions? STA Solutions에 관하여 알 수 있는 것은?

2단계 질문의 키워드와 관련된 내용을 보기와 매칭하기

Rates begin at $40/month for the starter security system package. A comprehensive package is also available. Contact us today to sign up for a free one-month trial!
요금은 보안 시스템 첫 개시 패키지 상품에 대해 월 40달러로 시작합니다. 종합 패키지 상품도 이용할 수 있습니다. 오늘 연락하여 무료 1개월 체험판을 신청하세요!

3단계 지문의 단서와 일치하는 보기 선택하기

(A) It only offers services to local businesses. 지역 업체들에게만 서비스를 제공한다.
(B) It provides various security system packages. 다양한 보안 시스템 패키지 상품을 제공한다.
(C) It is operated by former security officers. 전직 보안직원들에 의해 운영된다.
(D) It has more than one location. 한 곳 이상의 지점이 있다.

[책자]

STA Solutions

20년 이상 지역 주택들에 전문 기술 제공

저희 서비스는 다음을 포함합니다:

– 인터넷이 연결된 모든 장치에 연결할 수 있는 무선 보안 시스템
– 다양한 언어로 상시 고객 서비스 지원
– 모든 자사 제품에 대한 3년 품질 보증

요금은 보안 시스템 첫 개시 패키지 상품에 대해 월 40달러로 시작합니다. 종합 패키지 상품도 이용할 수 있습니다. 오늘 연락하여 무료 1개월 체험판을 신청하세요!

추천 후기

"저희 아파트에 보안 시스템을 설치한 이후부터, 저는 집을 떠나는 것에 대해 걱정하지 않습니다. 고객 서비스 직원들이 제가 기술적인 문제에 맞닥뜨렸을 때 저를 도와주는 데 큰 도움이 되었습니다."
– Shawn Workman

"STA Solutions는 안전한 가정을 위한 해답입니다. 저는 사업차 해외 출장을 계속 다니기 때문에, 무선 보안 시스템이 제게 아주 좋습니다. 제가 어디에 있든 용이하게 저희 집을 감시할 수 있습니다."
– Leila Wong

expertise 전문 기술 | **residence** 주택, 거주지 | **wireless** 무선의 | **security** 보안 | **link** 연결하다, 접속하다 | **device** 장치 | **connection** 연결 | **24/7** 하루 24시간 1주 7일 동안, 언제나 | **warranty** 품질 보증서 | **rate** 요금 | **starter** 처음으로 ~하는 사람 | **package** 패키지, 일괄 상품 | **comprehensive** 종합적인 | **sign up for** 신청하다 | **trial** 시험 | **testimonial** 추천의 글 | **install** 설치하다 | **leave** 떠나다 | **customer service associate** 고객 서비스 직원 | **helpful** 도움이 되는 | **encounter** 맞닥뜨리다, 부딪치다 | **issue** 사안, 문제 | **secure** 안전한 | **constantly** 끊임없이 | **easily** 쉽게, 용이하게 | **monitor** 감시하다

>> Point

질문의 키워드를 확인하고, 키워드가 없는 전체 추론 문제인 경우에는 보기들을 먼저 확인한다.

지문에서 질문의 키워드와 관련된 내용을 보기와 매칭시키며, 지문의 단서를 토대로 추론할 수 있는 내용의 보기를 선택한다.

암시/추론 문제의 정답은 항상 보기에 그대로 주어지지 않고 패러프레이징되어 있다.

>> 빈출 문제 유형

What is implied about the writers?
작가들에 관하여 알 수 있는 것은?

What is suggested about Elio Marketing?
Elio 마케팅에 관하여 암시되는 것은?

What can be inferred about Ms. Pei?
Pei 씨에 관하여 유추되는 것은?

Who most likely is Ms. Winston?
Winston 씨는 누구이겠는가?

Where would the notice most likely appear?
공지는 어디서 볼 수 있겠는가?

해설서 p.145

Questions 1-3 refer to the following e-mail.

To	RobinSimeon@simeonmoss.com
From	VLatowski@simeonmoss.com
Date	August 22
Subject	Update
Attachment	Latowski_file

Dear Robin,

I'm sending this e-mail to keep you informed about my upcoming plans. As I've mentioned, I will be at the Stockholm Conference for one week beginning this Thursday. —[1]—. I'm sending over a list of clients I'm working with and their contact information along with summaries of their cases and upcoming court dates. —[2]—. I understand that you, as a senior partner in the firm, have your hands full, so I've asked an associate to look after these clients during my absence.

Natalia Dubrovsky and I have worked in conjunction on contracts and acquisitions for most of the past year, so she is familiar with the clients and will know what to do to keep things on track. We met for breakfast at Diane's Bakery this morning to discuss the details. —[3]—. As I've directed, Natalia will reach out to clients who require urgent advice over the phone. Additionally, though I will not have reliable Wi-Fi service at my hotel, I will be in touch for daily updates throughout the time I am away. —[4]—.

Best,
Virginia Latowski

---

1. Where most likely does Ms. Latowski work?

(A) At a law firm
(B) At a real estate agency
(C) At a hotel
(D) At a bakery

2. What does Ms. Latowski write that Ms. Dubrovsky will do?

(A) Organize a breakfast meeting
(B) Make some phone calls
(C) Book a hotel room
(D) Fix an Internet connection

3. In which of the positions marked [1], [2], [3], and [4] does the following sentence best belong?

"While we were there, we finalized the list of clients and went over her upcoming responsibilities."

(A) [1]
(B) [2]
(C) [3]
(D) [4]

Questions 4-7 refer to the following article.

Norfolk Unlimited

BERRINGTON (3 December) — Norfolk Unlimited has agreed to take over as the official supporter of the Berrington Bears Women's Hockey Team. Norfolk will assume the role previously filled by Colt Active. Colt Active chose not to back the team after their previous contract expired in November of this year. Since then, Colt Active has discontinued its line of hockey sticks and skates, shifting its resources to promote equipment for leisure activities.

According to Norfolk's Public Relations Director Terry Greene, the company will provide high-end carbon sticks. Additionally, Norfolk has agreed to supply the team with improved protective clothing. "As far as the cost of renting a rink for practice, we will still have to rely on revenue generated by attendance at our games," said head coach Ellen Smythe.

Ms. Smythe, with the help of the team's equipment director, put together the deal with Norfolk Unlimited. Ms. Smythe majored in physical therapy at the University of Malton and was employed by various professional hockey teams, designing treatment plans to help injured athletes. During that time, she developed the skills necessary to become a coach, and eventually, took over the Berrington Bears. Regarding the deal, she said, "I'm excited about this opportunity. This is going to be a productive relationship, both for us and for Norfolk Unlimited."

4. What is the article mainly discussing?

(A) A new sponsor for a team
(B) A revision to a tournament schedule
(C) The results of a recent competition
(D) The retirement of a head coach

5. What is suggested about Colt Active?

(A) It was purchased by Norfolk Unlimited.
(B) It stopped selling certain sports gear.
(C) It has shut down several stores.
(D) It changed management recently.

6. Which part of the Berrington Bear's budget is funded by people's attendance at games?

(A) Overseas travel
(B) Protective equipment
(C) Training facilities
(D) Player salaries

7. What most likely was Ms. Smythe's previous job?

(A) Accounting specialist
(B) Physical therapist
(C) Equipment director
(D) Event planner

Questions 8-12 refer to the following e-mail and article.

To: Jose Romero <jromero@centennialtech.org>
From: Lynne Osborne <losborne@centennialtech.org>
Date: May 20
Re: Anniversary Celebration

Dear Mr. Romero,

Thank you for letting us know about the company-wide event next week. I absolutely love the idea of having the key members of the company give speeches. I am honored to have received an invitation to speak, and I would love to accept.

Upon reviewing the schedule, it appears as though I will be speaking at 2:00 P.M. However, the timing might be too tight as I will only be able to get there by 2:15 P.M. I see that Ms. Cox is scheduled to speak after me. Would it be possible to switch my position with Ms. Cox's position so that I speak after her? I will then be able to fit it into my schedule.

I would like to commend you for putting together this fantastic event. Please let me know your answer, and I will make the necessary preparations.

Sincerely,

Lynne Osborne

Centennial Tech Anniversary

CLEARMONT (May 29) — Centennial Tech, a fast-growing company headquartered in Clearmont, held their one-year anniversary celebration on May 27. The company had a fantastic first year as a public company and has helped put Clearmont on the map. They have recently expanded operations to cover most of the southwest and have plans to go international in the very near future.

The anniversary event had many of the employees in attendance, with numbers approaching 500. The night included fine food as well as speeches from company founders including Warren Miller, the CEO; Linda Cox, the COO; Lynne Osborne, the CFO; and Harry Ford, the CTO. The night was rounded off with a performance by The Four Men Quartet.

8. Why did Ms. Osborne write to Mr. Romero?

(A) To request a schedule change
(B) To inquire about an event
(C) To decline an invitation
(D) To review a document

9. In the e-mail, the word "commend" in paragraph 3, line 1, is closest in meaning to

(A) control
(B) tolerate
(C) recognize
(D) applaud

10. What is indicated about Ms. Osborne?

(A) She has worked overseas.
(B) She does not live in Clearmont.
(C) She helped start the company.
(D) She works in human resources.

11. According to the article, what happened on May 27?

(A) A performance took place.
(B) A change in management was announced.
(C) A magazine was published.
(D) A company announced plans to expand internationally.

12. What is suggested about the anniversary event?

(A) Ms. Osborne delivered a speech.
(B) Mr. Miller stepped down from his post.
(C) Ms. Cox was suffering from an illness.
(D) Mr. Ford had to leave early.

Questions 13-17 refer to the following e-mail, ticket, and schedule.

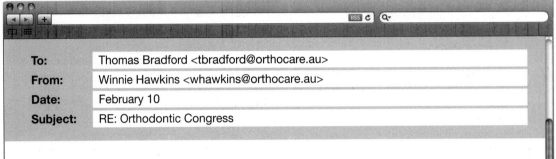

To:	Thomas Bradford <tbradford@orthocare.au>
From:	Winnie Hawkins <whawkins@orthocare.au>
Date:	February 10
Subject:	RE: Orthodontic Congress

Dear Dr. Bradford,

Thank you for the e-mail. I too am excited about attending this year's orthodontic congress. I would have enjoyed traveling there together but sadly, I have an appointment scheduled until 4 P.M. on February 22. Therefore, I'll be missing all the events scheduled on the first day. I will be in town that night and the following three days however.

Perhaps you have time for dinner on one of these nights? Ozan Demirel mentioned that the two of you were researching new 3D digital technologies, and I'm interested in hearing more about these tools.

I look forward to hearing from you soon.

Regards,

Winnie Hawkins, DDS

JOW Air		Frequent Flyer #: 029580059
Date		**FLIGHT**
February 22		MLA401
Passenger	**Class**	**Seat**
Thomas Bradford	Economy Plus	Unassigned
Origin	**Return Trip**	**Miles Earned**
Queensland	N/A	0 mi
Destination	**Meal**	**Boarding Time**
Melbourne	Vegetarian	5:00 A.M.
Reservation made on February 11		

Townsville Airport Departure Schedule Queensland to Melbourne				
Flight Number	Gate	Departure Time	Arrival Time	Duration
MLA 401	24	05:25	07:20	1 hr 55 min
JOW 723	41	08:00	10:00	2 hours
MLA 258	12	11:15	13:25	2 hr 10 min
JOW 194	38	12:45	14:50	2 hr 5 min
MLA 326	12	14:25	16:15	1 hr 50 min
JOW 590	41	18:45	21:00	2 hr 15 min

Mileage will not be issued for tickets purchased with frequent flyer miles. Passengers in our frequent flyer program may enjoy exclusive priority boarding. Meals are served on all flights, and menus can be found at http://www.jowair.com/mealplan.

13. Who most likely is Ozan Demirel?

(A) An engineer
(B) An office assistant
(C) A congress representative
(D) A dentist

14. What does the ticket indicate about Dr. Bradford's trip?

(A) He can choose where to sit.
(B) He has been upgraded to business class.
(C) He will experience a two-hour layover.
(D) He will not be served a meal.

15. Based on her availability, what plane will Dr. Hawkins most likely take?

(A) MLA 401
(B) MLA 258
(C) JOW 194
(D) JOW 590

16. What is suggested about Dr. Bradford?

(A) He purchased his ticket using airline miles.
(B) He booked his ticket through a travel agent.
(C) He has family in Melbourne.
(D) He will be traveling with one of his colleagues.

17. According to the schedule, what is true about the airplane routes?

(A) They arrive at the same destination.
(B) They take the same amount of time.
(C) They depart from the same gate.
(D) They are operated by the same airline.

CASE 95 동의어

[article]

Lawton Annual Bake Sale

LAWTON (Mar. 17) — Lawton will be holding its annual bake sale next month. This year, we are raising funds to help our farmers during the prolonged drought this season. All profits will go towards this cause.

We are now accepting applications for bakers who want to enter the pie contest. Bakers are free to make any kind of pie they wish. However, as it is a vegetarian-friendly event, bakers should not use any meat-based products.

The bake sale will run all day on April 23, from 9 A.M. to 4 P.M. At 2 P.M., we will have a panel of three judges who will judge the pie contest. The prize for the best-tasting pie will be a brand new Xpedient smartphone, sponsored by Xpedient.

Any attendees are encouraged to bring their whole families. We will have all kinds of baked goods, and there will also be a raffle for a furniture set. It's for a good cause, so come on down and show your support.

Q. The word "run" in paragraph 3, line 1, is closest in meaning to

(A) generate
(B) charge
(C) experience
(D) proceed

1단계 제시어 확인하기
The word "run" in paragraph 3, line 1, is closest in meaning to

2단계 제시어가 속한 문장을 해석하여 문맥상 의미 확인하기
The bake sale will **run** all day on April 23, from 9 A.M. to 4 P.M.
'(해당 기간 동안) 진행되다, 계속되다'의 의미로 사용
베이크 세일은 4월 23일 오전 9시부터 오후 4시까지 하루 종일 진행됩니다.

3단계 제시어와 바꿔 써도 의미가 통하는 보기 선택하기
(A) generate 창출하다
(B) charge 청구하다
(C) experience 경험하다
(D) proceed 진행되다

[기사]

Lawton 연례 베이크 세일

LAWTON (3월 17일) — Lawton 시는 다음 달에 연례 베이크 세일을 개최할 예정입니다. 올해에는, 이번 시즌 오랫동안 지속된 가뭄을 겪은 농민을 돕기 위해 기금을 마련합니다. 모든 수익은 이러한 대의에 쓰일 것입니다.

현재 파이 경연 대회에 참가를 희망하는 제빵사들의 신청을 받고 있습니다. 제빵사는 자신이 원하는 종류의 파이를 자유롭게 만들 수 있습니다. 하지만 채식주의 행사이기에, 제빵사는 고기가 들어간 제품을 사용하면 안 됩니다.

베이크 세일은 4월 23일 오전 9시부터 오후 4시까지 하루 종일 진행됩니다. 오후 2시에는 파이 경연 대회를 심사할 심사 위원 3명을 모실 것입니다. 최고의 맛 파이 상은 Xpedient 신상 스마트폰으로, Xpedient에서 후원합니다.

참석자는 누구나 가족 전체를 데려오도록 장려됩니다. 온갖 종류의 구움 과자가 있을 것이며, 가구 세트가 걸린 경품 행사도 있을 것입니다. 대의를 위한 일이니, 오셔서 응원을 보내 주시길 바랍니다.

annual 연례의 | **bake sale** 베이크 세일(자선 기금 목적으로 가정에서 빵류를 직접 구워 판매하는 행사) | **raise** (자금을) 모으다 | **fund** 자금, 기금 | **prolonged** 오래 지속된, 장기적인 | **drought** 가뭄 | **profit** 수익 | **go towards** ~에 쓰이다 | **cause** 대의(명분) | **baker** 제빵사, 빵 굽는 사람 | **pie** 파이 | **contest** 경연 대회 | **vegetarian** 채식주의(자)의 | **-friendly** ~ 친화적인 | **panel** 패널, 자문단 | **judge** 심사 위원; 심사하다 | **brand new** 신품의 | **raffle** 추첨 | **furniture** 가구

>> Point

제시어가 쓰인 위치를 확인하여 해석해보고 어떤 의미로 쓰였는지 파악한다.

보기 중 주어진 단어와 바꿔 써도 의미가 통하는 보기를 선택한다.

제시어의 동의어가 오답으로 제시되기도 하므로 사전적 의미가 아닌, 문맥 속 의미를 파악해야 한다.

>> 빈출 문제 유형

In the e-mail, the word "fixed" in paragraph 1, line 1, is closest in meaning to
이메일에서, 첫 번째 단락, 첫 번째 줄의 단어 "fixed"와 의미상 가장 가까운 것은

Questions 1-4 refer to the following article.

The Long Distance Marks Director Comeback

OHIO (November 21) — Dianne Bush's latest play, *The Long Distance*, has proved to be popular with the young crowd. The Cincinnati Theater, whose capacity reaches 1,500 seats, was packed with fans, eager to see the performance before the end of its run.

The play features two familiar names in Randall Parker and Beatrice Riley, both of whom featured in Bush's previous play. However, Bush has also emphasized her desire to bring in new actors into her productions. To this end, the audience was treated to two newcomers in Jeanette Griffith and Gustavo Graves.

The premise of the play captivated audiences, particularly the young, because of its relatable premise. "The play definitely resonated with the young crowd because it's a heartwarming love story," said theater manager Kathryn Harmon. "It's a love story that accurately depicts the highs and lows of a relationship."

"The play didn't debut to a big audience, but word of mouth soon spread. But the sudden spike in popularity? That was surprising for us," continued Ms. Harmon. "We did not anticipate the buzz the play generated."

Bush has experienced a downturn in her career as a playwright following lukewarm receptions of her last two plays. After taking the past year off to re-focus, *The Long Distance* has pushed her back up into the upper echelon of playwrights.

1. What is stated about the Cincinnati Theater?
   (A) It is the oldest theater in Ohio.
   (B) It is often Bush's theater of choice.
   (C) It is located in the center of the city.
   (D) It can seat 1,500 audience members.

2. What is indicated about Mr. Parker?
   (A) He was in Bush's previous play.
   (B) He received an award last year.
   (C) He prefers working with experienced actors.
   (D) He plays the lead role in the play.

3. The word "captivated" in paragraph 3, line 1, is closest in meaning to
   (A) assigned
   (B) conditioned
   (C) trapped
   (D) charmed

4. What surprised Ms. Harmon?
   (A) The size of the theater
   (B) The reaction of the actors
   (C) The increase in demand
   (D) The sound of the audience

Questions 5-8 refer to the following information.

Marietta Jam House

An order from Marietta Jam House may take up to seven days. If this process sounds excessively long, it is because of our policy to only send fresh jam. The fruit that goes into your jam is not picked until your order has been placed and our system has processed it.

Once we receive your order, we send our workers to pick only the ripest fruit for your order. Then, it is thoroughly washed and then transported to factory. There, it is placed into our jamming machine, where we add a bit of sugar as well as pectin. After leaving it cooking for over 12 hours, it is bottled and then sent out. As a guarantee of our quality, our factory manager is busy at work throughout this entire process. He is making sure the fruit is ripe, tasting the jam once made, and ensuring that it is well-packaged and headed to your location.

As a special offer to our Monthly Jam Club members, we are launching a new service called Jam of the Month, where we send out a special, not-for-sale jam to you every month for just $50 a year.

Note that our jams are highly seasonal. Although some jams are available year-round, most are contingent on what season it is. For a full list of jams and when they are available, call us at 705-555-9715 to receive a free catalog. Alternatively, access the digital version by heading over to www.mariettajam.com/jams.

---

5. What is the reason for Marietta Jam House's long delivery times?

(A) The need to maintain freshness
(B) The lack of workers available
(C) The unreliability of delivery services
(D) The remoteness of the factory

6. What is NOT mentioned as a task completed by the factory manager?

(A) Maintaining hygiene standards
(B) Sampling the taste of the jam
(C) Inspecting the fruit being used
(D) Verifying the packaging for adequacy

7. What service is offered exclusively to club members?

(A) Special discounts
(B) Overnight deliveries
(C) Customizable sizes
(D) Exclusive jams

8. The word "contingent" in paragraph 4, line 2, is closest in meaning to

(A) subjective
(B) ingrained
(C) dependent
(D) invariable

Questions 9-13 refer to the following e-mail and report.

To	g.mack@calmelon.com
From	t.fisher@calmelon.com
Date	19 April
Subject	RE: Venue for dinner

Dear Mr. Mack:

As you know, I confirmed that the Wayford Inn has experienced a major leak in the kitchen. I think it's unlikely the issue will be resolved before Friday, 23 April. Therefore, I think it's best we bring our clients elsewhere. I've taken the liberty to look around at other venues. Here is my suggestion.

The Grand Harbor, which is located on the same street as the Wayford Inn, is our only viable option. They have an upper floor that can be reserved to accommodate our party. I do have some reservations about their service though. I would have liked to choose an establishment that is known for hosting large events. However, we'll have to make do with what is available.

I do agree with your comment that it was unacceptable for Wayford to, once again, not be upfront about their issues. Given our past experiences with them, I don't think we should consider them again. I even asked if we could just use their function hall and bring our own food. However, they were not willing to help us. I will be requesting a refund of our deposit as soon as possible, and letting them know we will not be working with them again.

Regards,

Tricia Fisher

Harrell Brothers
Commercial Plumbing

Client: Wayford Inn 163 Tavistock Strand Parnell, Illinois 61842	Notes: Water supply infrastructure seems sound. The building was checked last year and was found to be in good standing.

Incident Report

We were called in on Monday, 19 April, by the head chef, who noted that the water pressure in the kitchen was too low. He could also hear a dripping sound. Two plumbers were dispatched on Tuesday, 20 April. The problem was identified to be a burst pipe. The leaked water also caused extensive damage to the walls. The pipe has been temporarily patched. This is only a temporary solution as we will need to fully replace the pipe. The parts should be arriving early next week. Wayford is advised to close its premises until the repairs are done.

I am also putting in a recommendation for the wiring to be checked by an electrician.

9. In the e-mail, the word "help" in paragraph 3, line 4, is closest in meaning to

(A) accommodate
(B) consult
(C) benefit
(D) advise

10. According to Ms. Fisher, why is the Grand Harbor acceptable?

(A) It has experience hosting functions.
(B) It is conveniently located.
(C) It has received good reviews.
(D) It offers the lowest rates.

11. What does Ms. Fisher suggest about the Wayford Inn?

(A) It needs to hire more staff.
(B) It had not planned to host her dinner party.
(C) It is overdue for a change in management.
(D) It has not been providing adequate service.

12. According to the report, what is wrong with the kitchen at the Wayford Inn?

(A) Water has been contaminated.
(B) A pipe needs to be replaced.
(C) The equipment needs new wiring.
(D) The walls have evidence of mold.

13. What is indicated about the Wayford Inn?

(A) It is the oldest restaurant in Parnell.
(B) It will hire its function hall out to Ms. Fisher.
(C) It is unable to host the dinner on 23 April.
(D) It recently renovated its premises.

Questions 14-18 refer to the following Web page, form, and e-mail.

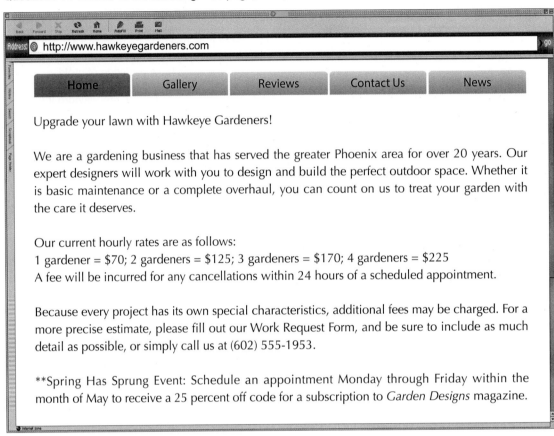

http://www.hawkeyegardeners.com

| Home | Gallery | Reviews | Contact Us | News |

Upgrade your lawn with Hawkeye Gardeners!

We are a gardening business that has served the greater Phoenix area for over 20 years. Our expert designers will work with you to design and build the perfect outdoor space. Whether it is basic maintenance or a complete overhaul, you can count on us to treat your garden with the care it deserves.

Our current hourly rates are as follows:
1 gardener = $70; 2 gardeners = $125; 3 gardeners = $170; 4 gardeners = $225
A fee will be incurred for any cancellations within 24 hours of a scheduled appointment.

Because every project has its own special characteristics, additional fees may be charged. For a more precise estimate, please fill out our Work Request Form, and be sure to include as much detail as possible, or simply call us at (602) 555-1953.

**Spring Has Sprung Event: Schedule an appointment Monday through Friday within the month of May to receive a 25 percent off code for a subscription to *Garden Designs* magazine.

Hawkeye Gardeners
Work Request Form

Today's Date:	Tuesday, April 28
Customer Name:	Hunter Blue
Contact Information:	E-mail: hblue@inet.com Phone: (602) 555-7438
Work Site Address:	1855 Elmwood Avenue, Tempe, AZ 85283
Work Request Date:	Monday, May 18
Work to be Done:	Pruning and general care of the flowers in our 10 flowerbeds (including orchids, lavenders, and lilacs, and others), 15 eucalyptus trees, 7 Chinese Elm trees, and various bushes and shrubs on our property.
Notes:	We are looking for a gardener to come and maintain the landscape around our shopping mall. It's quite a big project, so I think we need at least 3 people to help prune. Our current gardener recently retired so we're looking for a replacement. I initially wrote down May 18 as a potential start date, but I would prefer something earlier—so long as I qualify for the promotion that's listed on your online page.

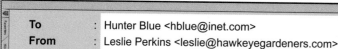

To	: Hunter Blue <hblue@inet.com>
From	: Leslie Perkins <leslie@hawkeyegardeners.com>
Date	: April 29
Subject	: Mall Landscaping Job
Attachment	: Estimate #91824.xls

Dear Mr. Blue,

Thank you for contacting Hawkeye Gardeners!

We recently worked on a similar-sized project at a nearby apartment complex, and judging from that experience, three people would not be enough to complete the job. Attached to this e-mail you will find a quotation sheet which includes all labor costs, including four gardeners, machinery, and other maintenance work. Please be advised that a removal fee has not been included in the estimate but will be charged if necessary.

Upon checking our schedule, we have an opening exactly one week prior to the date you requested on the form, which means you will still be able to participate in our spring event.

Please call us at (602) 555-2359 if you would like to continue with our services, or if you have any questions about the estimate. Thank you for your time and we look forward to hearing from you soon.

Best,

Leslie Perkins
Hawkeye Gardeners

14. On the Web page, the word "treat" in paragraph 1, line 3, is closest in meaning to

(A) look upon
(B) satisfy
(C) pay
(D) deal with

15. What does Mr. Blue mention about the garden?

(A) It has not been maintained before.
(B) It will require special machinery.
(C) It will take multiple days to complete.
(D) It includes a variety of plants.

16. If Mr. Blue uses Hawkeye Gardeners, what is the standard hourly payment that he will most likely pay?

(A) $70
(B) $125
(C) $170
(D) $225

17. What is suggested about Mr. Blue?

(A) He wants to set up an appointment for a weekday.
(B) He recently retired from his job at a shopping mall.
(C) He has planted many gardens before.
(D) He prefers to hire an experienced gardening company.

18. According to Ms. Perkins, what can her company do?

(A) Work on a garden earlier than expected
(B) Provide pictures of previous work
(C) Exclude a removal fee
(D) Install some flowerbeds

[memo]

Urgent Message

To: All Employees
From: Management
Date: May 5

❷ As many of you already know, since yesterday afternoon, we have been experiencing telecommunications difficulties. Currently, this is affecting phone service in the entire building. —[1]—. Construction at the complex across the street may have cut one of our cables. —[2]—. Whatever the cause, we are currently without phone service.

❸ We are in contact with representatives from GC&E Communications. They're still looking for the source of the problem and are promising to restore service soon. —[3]—. We will provide frequent updates on the company Web site, so visit the bulletin board regularly. We're sorry for any difficulties this may have caused. —[4]—.

Q. In which of the positions marked [1], [2], [3], and [4] does the following sentence best belong?

❶ "At the moment, however, we can't say for sure when that will take place."

(A) [1]
(B) [2]
(C) [3]
(D) [4]

1단계 주어진 문장 확인하기
"At the moment, however, we can't say for sure when that will take place."

2단계 주어진 문장이 들어갈 자리에 유념하며 지문 읽기
As many of you already know, since yesterday afternoon, we have been experiencing telecommunications difficulties. Currently, this is affecting phone service in the entire building. —[1]—. Construction at the complex across the street may have cut one of our cables. —[2]—. Whatever the cause, we are currently without phone service.

3단계 적합한 위치에 문장을 넣어서 문맥 확인하기
We are in contact with representatives from GC&E Communications. **They're still looking for the source of the problem and are promising to restore service soon. At the moment, however, we can't say for sure when that will take place. We will provide frequent updates on the company Web site, so visit the bulletin board regularly.** We're sorry for any difficulties this may have caused. —[4]—.

[회람]

긴급 메시지

수신: 전 직원
발신: 관리부
날짜: 5월 5일

많은 분들이 이미 알고 계시듯, 우리 회사는 어제 오후부터 통신에 문제가 있습니다. 현재, 이 문제는 건물 전체의 전화 서비스에 영향을 주고 있습니다. —[1]—. 길 건너편 복합 건물에서 진행하는 공사가 우리 건물 전선 중 하나를 끊었을지도 모릅니다. —[2]—. 원인이 무엇이든 우리 회사는 현재 전화 서비스를 이용하지 못하고 있습니다.

저희는 GC&E 통신사의 대리인들과 연락하고 있습니다. 그분들은 여전히 문제의 원인을 찾고 있으며 서비스를 곧 복구하겠다고 약속하고 있습니다. —[3]—. 회사 웹사이트에 자주 업데이트를 할 예정이니, 게시판을 정기적으로 봐주시기 바랍니다. 이 일이 초래한 곤란에 사과드립니다. —[4]—.

[1], [2], [3], [4]로 표시된 곳 중, 다음 문장이 들어갈 위치로 가장 적절한 것은?

"그러나 지금은 언제 그 일이 일어날지 확실히 말씀드릴 수 없습니다."

어휘 **urgent** 긴급한 | **management** 경영, 관리 | **experience** 경험하다 | **telecommunication** 전기 통신 | **difficulty** 어려움 | **currently** 현재, 지금 | **affect** 영향을 주다 | **entire** 전체의 | **construction** 공사, 건설 | **complex** 건물 단지 | **cable** 전선 | **cause** 원인 | **representative** (회사의) 대리인 | **source** 근원, 원천 | **restore** 복구하다 | **frequent** 빈번한, 잦은 | **bulletin board** 게시판 | **regularly** 정기적으로

>> Point

주어진 문장을 읽고, 키워드를 확인한다.

지문에서 키워드와 관련된 내용을 포착하여 주어진 문장을 넣어서 문맥을 살핀다. 이때 앞뒤 문장과 밀접한 관계를 갖는 he/she/it/they/each 등의 지시어와 additionally, therefore, however 등의 연결어구를 단서로 삼는다.

주어진 문장을 넣었을 때 문맥상 앞뒤 문장과 가장 어울리는 위치를 정답으로 선택한다.

>> 빈출 문제 유형

In which of the positions marked [1], [2], [3], and [4] does the following sentence best belong?

"For instance, she offers free repairs on bikes to young aspiring cyclists."

[1], [2], [3], [4]로 표시된 곳 중, 다음 문장이 들어갈 위치로 가장 적절한 것은?

"예를 들어, 그녀는 젊은 예비 사이클 선수들에게 자전거 무료 수리를 제공합니다."

Questions 1-3 refer to the following announcement.

Attention All Umi Employees

—[1]—. Umi Sushi is proud to be announcing the opening of our fourth Umi Sushi location. Due to growing customer demand for our food, particularly in the newly-developed suburbs of Auckland, management has made the decision to open a location at Whangaparaoa. —[2]—. During the opening months, Monique Jacobs will be designated as the head chef. Ms. Jacobs will have a busy time training new staff members, so please assist her as much as you can.

The location is due to open on 8 October. —[3]—. More information about this event can be found on our Web site at www.umisushi.co.nz. —[4]—.

---

1. What is the purpose of the announcement?

(A) To suggest a name change
(B) To request assistance from staff
(C) To provide an update on a company
(D) To demand feedback on a product

2. What is indicated about the location?

(A) It has undergone renovations.
(B) It is located in Auckland.
(C) It has new staff members.
(D) It is owned by Ms. Jacobs.

3. In which of the positions marked [1], [2], [3], and [4] does the following sentence best belong?

"There will be a ceremony to commemorate the opening."

(A) [1]
(B) [2]
(C) [3]
(D) [4]

Questions 4-6 refer to the following e-mail.

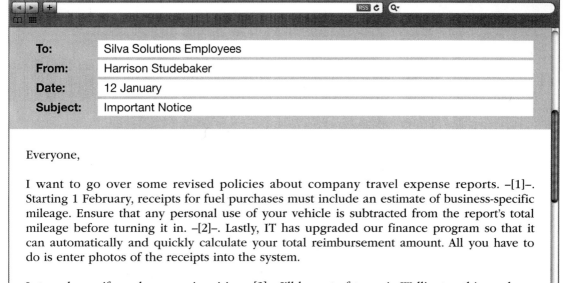

To: Silva Solutions Employees
From: Harrison Studebaker
Date: 12 January
Subject: Important Notice

Everyone,

I want to go over some revised policies about company travel expense reports. –[1]–. Starting 1 February, receipts for fuel purchases must include an estimate of business-specific mileage. Ensure that any personal use of your vehicle is subtracted from the report's total mileage before turning it in. –[2]–. Lastly, IT has upgraded our finance program so that it can automatically and quickly calculate your total reimbursement amount. All you have to do is enter photos of the receipts into the system.

Let me know if you have any inquiries. –[3]–. I'll be out of town in Wellington this week, so please keep in mind I may not respond to your messages right away. –[4]–.

Best,

Harrison Studebaker
President, Silva Solutions

4. What is indicated about Silva Solutions?

(A) It will implement updated policies for reporting business trip expenses.
(B) It has decreased the budget allotted to gasoline purchases.
(C) It will be recruiting new IT employees.
(D) It has multiple office locations in the area.

5. Why is the finance program mentioned?

(A) To apologize for its constant errors
(B) To point out one of its special features
(C) To urge staff to download it
(D) To remind personnel that it will be upgraded soon

6. In which of the positions marked [1], [2], [3], and [4] does the following sentence best belong?

"By adhering to these guidelines, we will be able to reimburse you in a timely manner."

(A) [1]
(B) [2]
(C) [3]
(D) [4]

Questions 7-10 refer to the following e-mail.

To:	kburns@fissionmail.com
From:	mwillis@nwpublishings.co.nz
Date:	7 August
Subject:	Possibility for interview

Dear Mr. Burns,

My name is May Willis, and I'm working on the biography of the late author Leroy Mendez. We have been given the rights by his widow to work on his life story. —[1]—. From what she has told us so far, you had a very significant influence on Mr. Mendez's decision to become a writer. —[2]—. From my research into this topic, I couldn't find much information on this, as Mr. Mendez largely led a private life.

Therefore, I would like to ask whether you would be open to me stopping by and asking you a few questions. —[3]—. If you could get back to me whenever you're able to, that would be great.

As for the biography, we want to include as many anecdotes as possible. Some of his close friends and relatives will write some sections of the book. This invitation is also open to you if you have a great anecdote to share. —[4]—. In case you are interested, our deadline for the book is 31 October.

Sincerely,

May Willis
Head Writer

7. Why did Ms. Willis contact Mr. Burns?

(A) To recommend a biographer
(B) To schedule a seminar
(C) To verify an agreement
(D) To request an interview

8. What is indicated about Ms. Willis's research?

(A) It was conducted in one day.
(B) It was inconclusive.
(C) It was gathered by a team.
(D) It was deemed inaccurate.

9. What is mentioned about the biography?

(A) It will be published in October.
(B) It will include a foreword by Mr. Burns.
(C) It will be made into a movie.
(D) It will be authored by many people.

10. In which of the positions marked [1], [2], [3], and [4] does the following sentence best belong?

"If you prefer, we could speak over the phone instead."

(A) [1]
(B) [2]
(C) [3]
(D) [4]

Questions 11-14 refer to the following brochure.

Feilong Business Movers
(FBM)

—[1]—. Do you plan on expanding your company's presence into the Chinese market? In order to do so, you must have extensive knowledge about the legal and cultural aspects of running a business in China. FBM's team of professionals can ensure that your move into this country will be smooth and successful. —[2]—.

Legal Documentation
Perhaps the most important aspect of working abroad is making sure all the necessary documentation is prepared. Obtaining the necessary visa and permits can prove to be overwhelming. Not to mention, local governments are constantly revising the procedures for foreigners in the country. Fortunately, our legal specialists attend seminars every year to stay up-to-date on the latest law changes. With us, paperwork will be the last thing on your mind. —[3]—.

Property Management
FBM has a department dedicated to dealing with real estate in China. A designated employee will help you find an office space that matches your needs. Also, our facility managers will offer you advice on the best unit for storing your excess items.

Culture Training
In addition, FBM will help you get acclimated to your new surroundings. Language courses and etiquette training are available for those who are interested. These classes are designed to help you and other relevant employees get adjusted to the country. —[4]—.

---

11. Whom was the brochure written for?

(A) Growing global firms
(B) Moving companies in China
(C) Chinese government workers
(D) Property owners

12. According to the brochure, which FBM employees receive annual training?

(A) Legal experts
(B) File clerks
(C) Real estate agents
(D) Language teachers

13. According to the brochure, what advice does a FMB facility manager provide?

(A) How to organize a work area
(B) How to install lights
(C) What office furniture to purchase
(D) Which storage unit to use

14. In which of the positions marked [1], [2], [3], and [4] does the following sentence best belong?

"To find out more about the services we provide, read below."

(A) [1]
(B) [2]
(C) [3]
(D) [4]

Questions 15-18 refer to the following Web page.

Management at EXJ Industries wants our team members to thrive. —[1]—. Our advising initiative ensures that each employee has someone to confide in and offer input when they run into difficulty. —[2]—.

The advisor-advisee relationship is beneficial for everyone involved. Advisees learn from their seasoned coworkers. Advisors gain the trust of their colleagues, while honing their communication skills. After all, a firm grows more when it has a better informed and more cohesive workforce. —[3]—.

Below is a list of the advising programs that are currently ongoing: —[4]—.

New Hire Advising: All new hires receive an advisor at their branch who has experience within their field. Advisors do not work directly with advisees, nor do employees have to necessarily meet on set schedule. However, many do appreciate the relationship, with some becoming productive partnerships lasting for decades.

Inter-Office Advising: A chance to learn from peers at other EXJ locations. Open to team members with any level of experience.

International Advising: When staff members are relocated to an overseas office, they are assigned local advisors who know the region. These relationships last for six months or less.

Career-matching Advising: This year-long program begins in January. Team members at select locations are paired with interns, who will get a chance to learn about various departments.

If you want to know about any of these programs, call Stewart Browning at 555-931-2394.

15. What is suggested about EXJ Industries?

(A) It plans to move its headquarters.
(B) It recently hired a large number of employees.
(C) It has locations in multiple countries.
(D) It was founded within the last ten years.

16. What does the Web page suggest about the advising initiative?

(A) It is a new program at EXJ Industries.
(B) It is available only to employees at certain branches.
(C) It is beneficial for the entire company.
(D) It is mandatory for all employees.

17. What is indicated about the current advising initiative?

(A) They last for up to six months.
(B) They are only offered in a limited number of departments.
(C) There are choices for employees with any experience level.
(D) There is only one program with availability.

18. In which of the positions marked [1], [2], [3], and [4] does the following sentence best belong?

"Advisors not only offer professional advice, but can also build strong personal bonds that go beyond the workplace."

(A) [1]
(B) [2]
(C) [3]
(D) [4]

[text message chain]

Jaime Torres [11:59 A.M.]

We can't go through with the meeting after lunch. Mr. Gregory is still not in the office.

Tomas Sullivan [12:02 P.M.]

We can't delay this meeting. We have to finalize and send the blueprints by tonight.

Jaime Torres [12:05 P.M.]

He's not answering his phone. His flight must have been delayed.

Tomas Sullivan [12:09 P.M.]

I'm speaking with Patricia Bryant. She's saying she will be reviewing all of the blueprints tomorrow afternoon. The latest we can send them in is actually tomorrow morning.

Jaime Torres [12:13 P.M.]

I don't like the idea of sending it last minute. We also don't want to give off the impression that we cannot meet deadlines at this juncture.

Tomas Sullivan [12:14 P.M.]

I'm with you. So what's the alternative if we cannot get through to Mr. Gregory?

Jaime Torres [12:16 P.M.]

Let me try to call Ms. Freeman. She also went on the same business trip as Mr. Gregory.

Q. At 12:14 P.M., what does Mr. Sullivan imply when he writes, "I'm with you"?

(A) He wants somebody to apologize to the client for the delay.
(B) He thinks he should request an extension on a deadline.
(C) He is concerned that Mr. Gregory will not return by today.
(D) He would like to send the blueprints by today.

1단계 주어진 인용 문장의 위치 확인하기

At 12:14 P.M., what does Mr. Sullivan imply when he writes, "I'm with you"?
오후 12시 14분에, Sullivan 씨가 "저도 그래요"라고 할 때 그가 암시한 것은?

2단계 주변 대화 내용을 확인하여 인용 문장의 의미 파악하기

Tomas Sullivan [12:09 P.M.]
I'm speaking with Patricia Bryant. She's saying she will be reviewing all of the blueprints tomorrow afternoon. **The latest we can send it in is actually tomorrow morning.**
제가 Patricia Bryant와 이야기 중이에요. 내일 오후에 전체 설계도를 검토할 예정이라고 하시네요. 저희가 보낼 수 있는 가장 늦은 때는 사실상 내일 오전이에요.

Jaime Torres [12:13 P.M.]
I don't like the idea of sending it last minute. We also don't want to give off the impression that we cannot meet deadlines at this juncture.
전 막판에 보내고 싶지는 않아요. 이 시점에서 마감일을 못 지킨다는 인상을 주고 싶지도 않고요.

Tomas Sullivan [12:14 P.M.]
I'm with you.
저도 그래요.

3단계 인용 문장의 의도를 가장 잘 나타낸 보기 선택하기

(A) He wants somebody to apologize to the client for the delay. 그는 지연된 것에 대해 누군가가 고객에게 사과하기를 원한다.
(B) He thinks he should request an extension on a deadline. 마감일 연장을 요청해야 한다고 생각한다.
(C) He is concerned that Mr. Gregory will not return by today. Gregory 씨가 오늘까지 복귀하지 않을까 봐 염려된다.
(D) He would like to send the blueprints by today. 오늘까지 설계도를 보내고 싶어 한다.

해석 [문자 메시지]

Jaime Torres [오전 11시 59분]
점심 이후에 회의를 진행할 수 없어요. Gregory 씨가 아직 사무실에 안 계세요.

Tomas Sullivan [오후 12시 02분]
이 회의를 미룰 수 없어요. 오늘 밤까지 설계도를 마무리해서 보내야 해요.

Jaime Torres [오후 12시 05분]
그분이 전화를 안 받으세요. 틀림없이 비행기가 연착됐을 거예요.

Tomas Sullivan [오후 12시 09분]
제가 Patricia Bryant와 이야기 중이에요. 내일 오후에 전체 설계도를 검토할 예정이라고 하시네요. 저희가 보낼 수 있는 가장 늦은 때는 사실상 내일 오전이에요.

Jaime Torres [오후 12시 13분]
전 막판에 보내고 싶지는 않아요. 이 시점에서 마감일을 못 지킨다는 인상을 주고 싶지도 않고요.

Tomas Sullivan [오후 12시 14분]
저도 그래요. 그러면 Gregory 씨와 연락이 안 될 경우 대안이 뭐예요?

Jaime Torres [오후 12시 16분]
제가 Freeman 씨에게 전화해 볼게요. 그분도 Gregory 씨와 같은 출장을 갔어요.

어휘 **go through with** (절차상 필요한) ~을 거치다[하다] | **delay** 미루다 | **finalize** 마무리 짓다 | **send** 보내다 | **blueprint** 설계도 | **answer** 대답하다, 응답하다 | **flight** 비행 | **latest** 가장 늦은 | **last minute** 막판에 | **give off** 풍기다, 내다 | **impression** 인상 | **meet a deadline** 기한[마감]에 맞추다 | **juncture** 시점, 단계 | **alternative** 대안 | **get through to** 전화로 ~와 연락이 닿다 | **business trip** 출장

>> Point

질문에 등장한 인용 문장과 그 위치를 확인한다.

지문에서 인용 문장의 주변 대화 내용을 확인하여, 그 문맥상의 의미를 파악한다.

인용 문장의 의도를 가장 잘 나타낸 보기를 선택한다.

>> 빈출 문제 유형

At 9:34 A.M., what does Ms. Bardet mean when she writes, "That's your call"?
오전 9시 34분에, Bardet 씨가 "당신이 결정하면 돼요"라고 할 때 그녀가 암시한 것은?

Questions 1-2 refer to the following text message chain.

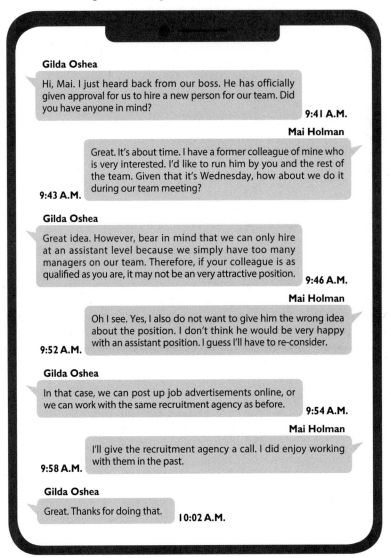

Gilda Oshea

Hi, Mai. I just heard back from our boss. He has officially given approval for us to hire a new person for our team. Did you have anyone in mind?

9:41 A.M.

Mai Holman

Great. It's about time. I have a former colleague of mine who is very interested. I'd like to run him by you and the rest of the team. Given that it's Wednesday, how about we do it during our team meeting?

9:43 A.M.

Gilda Oshea

Great idea. However, bear in mind that we can only hire at an assistant level because we simply have too many managers on our team. Therefore, if your colleague is as qualified as you are, it may not be an very attractive position.

9:46 A.M.

Mai Holman

Oh I see. Yes, I also do not want to give him the wrong idea about the position. I don't think he would be very happy with an assistant position. I guess I'll have to re-consider.

9:52 A.M.

Gilda Oshea

In that case, we can post up job advertisements online, or we can work with the same recruitment agency as before.

9:54 A.M.

Mai Holman

I'll give the recruitment agency a call. I did enjoy working with them in the past.

9:58 A.M.

Gilda Oshea

Great. Thanks for doing that.

10:02 A.M.

1. What is suggested about Ms. Oshea and Ms. Holman?

(A) They meet every Wednesday.
(B) They work for a talent agency.
(C) They have a dinner appointment.
(D) They commute to work together.

2. At 9:52 A.M., what does Ms. Holman mean when she writes "I guess I'll have to re-consider"?

(A) She will speak to the human resources team.
(B) She will organize a meeting with the boss.
(C) She will not recommend a job to a colleague.
(D) She will not attend the next company meeting.

Questions 3-4 refer to the following text message chain.

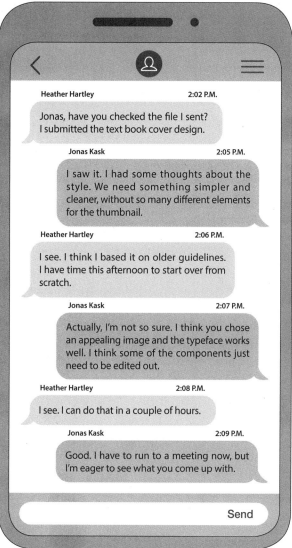

Heather Hartley   2:02 P.M.

Jonas, have you checked the file I sent? I submitted the text book cover design.

Jonas Kask   2:05 P.M.

I saw it. I had some thoughts about the style. We need something simpler and cleaner, without so many different elements for the thumbnail.

Heather Hartley   2:06 P.M.

I see. I think I based it on older guidelines. I have time this afternoon to start over from scratch.

Jonas Kask   2:07 P.M.

Actually, I'm not so sure. I think you chose an appealing image and the typeface works well. I think some of the components just need to be edited out.

Heather Hartley   2:08 P.M.

I see. I can do that in a couple of hours.

Jonas Kask   2:09 P.M.

Good. I have to run to a meeting now, but I'm eager to see what you come up with.

Send

3. What mistake did Ms. Hartley make?

(A) She used an inappropriate image.
(B) The style she used was too complex.
(C) She did not spend enough time on a project.
(D) The cover was formatted incorrectly.

4. At 2:07 P.M., what does Mr. Kask most likely mean when he writes, "Actually, I'm not so sure"?

(A) Ms. Hartley should not submit a design.
(B) Ms. Hartley does not have to change her schedule.
(C) Ms. Hartley does not have to completely redo her design.
(D) Ms. Hartley should not reschedule a meeting.

Questions 5-8 refer to the following online chat discussion.

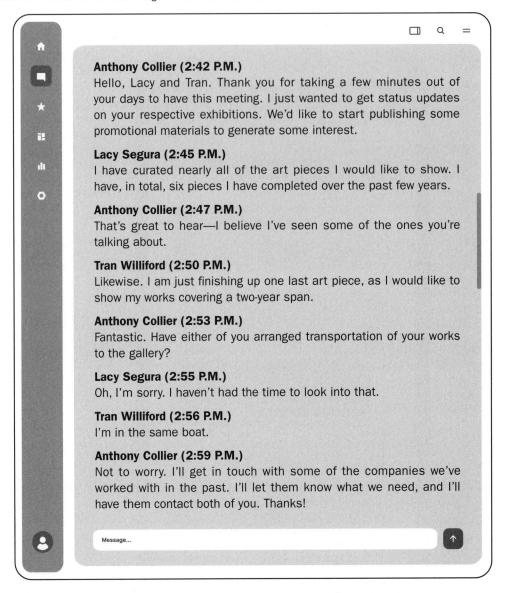

Anthony Collier (2:42 P.M.)
Hello, Lacy and Tran. Thank you for taking a few minutes out of your days to have this meeting. I just wanted to get status updates on your respective exhibitions. We'd like to start publishing some promotional materials to generate some interest.

Lacy Segura (2:45 P.M.)
I have curated nearly all of the art pieces I would like to show. I have, in total, six pieces I have completed over the past few years.

Anthony Collier (2:47 P.M.)
That's great to hear—I believe I've seen some of the ones you're talking about.

Tran Williford (2:50 P.M.)
Likewise. I am just finishing up one last art piece, as I would like to show my works covering a two-year span.

Anthony Collier (2:53 P.M.)
Fantastic. Have either of you arranged transportation of your works to the gallery?

Lacy Segura (2:55 P.M.)
Oh, I'm sorry. I haven't had the time to look into that.

Tran Williford (2:56 P.M.)
I'm in the same boat.

Anthony Collier (2:59 P.M.)
Not to worry. I'll get in touch with some of the companies we've worked with in the past. I'll let them know what we need, and I'll have them contact both of you. Thanks!

Message...

5. Who most likely is Mr. Collier?

(A) A logistics worker
(B) A school teacher
(C) A professional athlete
(D) An art curator

6. What is indicated about Ms. Segura and Mr. Williford's art pieces?

(A) They were influenced by modern art.
(B) They have been exhibited previously.
(C) They were completed in recent years.
(D) They will be delivered in the next four days.

7. At 2:56 P.M., what does Mr. Williford most likely mean when he writes, "I'm in the same boat"?

(A) He is currently traveling overseas.
(B) He takes responsibility for the mistake.
(C) He is disappointed in Ms. Segura.
(D) He has not arranged transportation.

8. What will Mr. Collier most likely do next?

(A) Speak to a shipping company
(B) Transport some artworks
(C) Publish some advertisements
(D) Remind the artists of the deadline

Questions 9-12 refer to the following online chat discussion.

Wednesday, October 12

Penelope Everdeen (7:16 P.M.)
This is a reminder that on Friday afternoon contractors from Tranchford will be coming here to Alton, Inc. to excavate a portion of the parking lot and replace some pipes. My staff will block off the whole lot, so remember that you and your teams will need to arrange alternative forms of transportation or park at a garage nearby.

Mohamed Khoury (7:17 P.M.)
Kenneth Davis from Salford Industries plans to drive in to attend a presentation at 5:00 P.M. on Friday. What about him? Should he reach out to building management?

Lucinda Dubuque (7:18 P.M.)
I was just watching the weather report and there's a high chance of severe winds. Is the excavation still possible?

Penelope Everdeen (7:19 P.M.)
That's right. You can give Mr. Davis my contact information. I'll give him the address of the lot on Baker Street and reserve a spot.

Penelope Everdeen (7:20 P.M.)
And yes. Tranchford makes sure their teams work through thick and thin to finish on time.

Beatrice Ianucci (7:21 P.M.)
Also, keep in mind that we do have the option of letting staff members work remotely on Friday. Just have everyone log on to the company messenger software.

Penelope Everdeen (7:23 P.M.)
Great point. Have a good night, everyone.

SEND

PART 7 CHAPTER 14

9. Who most likely is Ms. Everdeen?
(A) An excavating crew member
(B) A building supervisor
(C) A commercial plumber
(D) An out-of-town client

10. Why will Mr. Davis contact Ms. Everdeen?
(A) To recommend alternative transportation
(B) To give directions to an office
(C) To arrange for parking assistance
(D) To reschedule a presentation

11. What is most likely to happen on October 14?
(A) Alton, Inc. will be closed for the day.
(B) Mr. Davis will have dinner with Mr. Khoury.
(C) Some Alton, Inc. employees will work from home.
(D) Ms. Ianucci will set up some software.

12. At 7:20 P.M., what does Ms. Everdeen mean when she writes, "their teams work through thick and thin"?
(A) Tranchford is well-known for its competent workers.
(B) Alton, Inc. staff must be on time, even in severe weather.
(C) The weather report may not be correct.
(D) An outdoor work schedule will not be altered.

Questions 13-16 refer to the following online chat discussion.

Kirsten Holland   2:37 P.M.

Has anyone been up on the fourth floor this afternoon? It doesn't feel like the cooling system is working up there.

Beverly Alvarado   2:38 P.M.

I have. It's definitely getting hot and stuffy.

Kirsten Holland   2:40 P.M.

Yeah, it looks like some of the capacitors went down during the thunderstorm last night. We're lucky the forecast isn't too hot this weekend because we don't have the parts to fix them. In any case, I'm going to contact a professional repair team.

Beverly Alvarado   2:41 P.M.

I don't think the guests who paid a premium for their rooms are going to be happy. Remember, the big conference is tomorrow—we're completely sold out. Don't we have some portable AC units in the maintenance office?

Jamal Salamanca   2:42 P.M.

We cannot afford a batch of bad reviews.

Kirsten Holland   2:43 P.M.

Only at other locations. If Mr. Salamanca would authorize it, I could drive the truck up to the Toledo branch. They should be able to spare five or six of them. I wouldn't be back until 9:30 or 10:00 P.M., though.

Jamal Salamanca   2:44 P.M.

Kirsten, I'm giving you permission to use the company credit card to buy electric fans for all the guest rooms likely to be affected immediately. Check to see how many you need and look for a cost-effective model. Make sure to get an itemized receipt.

Kristen Holland   2:45 P.M.

OK, I'm on it.

Jamal Salamanca   2:46 P.M.

If the local appliance store doesn't have them, drive over to the Henderson Valley Mall.

Message...

13. What issue are the writers mainly discussing?

(A) High temperatures are expected over the weekend.
(B) Replacing capacitors is too costly.
(C) The climate control system is broken.
(D) The company vehicle is in need of repairs.

14. At 2:43 P.M., what does Ms. Holland mean when she writes, "Only at other locations"?

(A) Local guests are unlikely to complain.
(B) No portable units are stored on-site.
(C) The hotel does not have a maintenance office.
(D) She does not think that any action needs to be taken.

15. Why most likely does Mr. Salamanca decide against using the units in Toledo?

(A) They will need to be returned too soon.
(B) They are available at a local store.
(C) They cannot be transported effectively.
(D) They will take too long to arrive.

16. What will most likely happen next?

(A) Ms. Salamanca will compare some prices.
(B) Ms. Holland will make a purchase.
(C) A maintenance team will look for some replace parts.
(D) The electric fans will be dropped off at the hotel.

[draft e-mail and attachment]

To: All Employees
From: Daniel Shepard
Date: November 24
Subject: Parking Facility
Attachment: Parking_spaces.doc

Dear staff,

Puth Financial has a long-standing contract with Comstock Parking Facility to secure a fixed number of parking spaces for employee vehicles. These designated spaces must be renewed every year.

Attached is a table of the spaces that are currently in use. If you are the owner of one of these, I ask that you contact me at dshepard@puthfinancials.com by December 1 to advise whether you will still be needing it. In addition, those of you who want to change the location of your space should let me know as soon as possible. Keep in mind that your request may be denied. For those who do not get back to me in time, your space will become available and given to the next employee on the wait list. Employees who wish to be on the wait list should contact me by the end of this week.

The updated list of parking spaces for next year will be available on December 12. The new parking permit decals will also be distributed then. Please pick them up from the HR office at your earliest convenience. Make sure to place the stickers on the lower right side of the front windshield of your vehicle. Security guards at the facility will inspect all vehicles for the new permits beginning January 1.

I appreciate your cooperation.

Daniel Shepard

Comstock Parking Facility

➢ Zone 1 is located on the west side of the building and is closest to the main entrance.
➢ Parking spots 55 to 60 are for electric vehicles only.

Zone	Parking Spot	Employee Name
1	20	Joe Bean
1	21	Akemi Davidson
1	22	Patricia Wells
2	57	Kevin Houlihan
2	58	Daniel Shephard
2	59	Nancy Jackson
3	1	Rick Duke
3	2	Adrian Stein

Q. What should Ms. Jackson do by December 1?

(A) Contact Mr. Shepard.
(B) Upload an updated list of spaces.
(C) Sign up for a wait list.
(D) Put a sticker on her windshield.

What should Ms. Jackson do by December 1? Jackson 씨는 12월 1일까지 무엇을 해야 하는가?

(A) Contact Mr. Shepard Shepard 씨에게 연락한다
(B) Upload an updated list of spaces 업데이트된 공간 목록을 업로드한다
(C) Sign up for a wait list 대기자 명단을 신청한다
(D) Put a sticker on her windshield 차 앞 유리에 스티커를 붙인다

2단계 첫 번째 단서 확인

2	59	Nancy Jackson

3-1단계 두 번째 단서 확인

Attached is a table of the spaces that are currently in use. If you are the owner of one of these, I ask that you contact me at dshepard@puthfinancials.com **by December 1** to advise whether you will still be needing it. 첨부된 것은 현재 사용 중인 공간 도표입니다. 공간 중 하나를 점유하고 계시다면 저에게 12월 1일까지 dshepard@puthfinancials.com으로 연락하셔서 공간을 계속 사용할지 여부를 알려주시길 요청 드립니다.

3-2단계 두 번째 단서 확인

FROM: Daniel Shepard

해석 [이메일 초고와 첨부 파일]

수신: 전 직원
발신: Daniel Shepard
날짜: 11월 24일
제목: 주차 시설
첨부: 주차_공간.doc

직원분들께,

Puth 금융은 일정 수의 직원 차량용 주차 공간 확보를 위해 Comstock 주차 시설과 오랫동안 계약을 맺고 있습니다. 이 지정 공간은 매년 갱신되어야 합니다.

첨부된 것은 현재 사용 중인 공간 도표입니다. 공간 중 하나를 점유하고 계시다면 저에게 12월 1일까지 dshepard@puthfinancials.com으로 연락하셔서 공간을 계속 사용할지 여부를 알려 주시길 요청 드립니다. 또한, 주차 공간의 위치를 변경하길 원하는 분은 저에게 가급적 빨리 알려 주셔야 합니다. 요청이 거부될 수 있는 점 유의해 주십시오. 제때에 저에게 연락하지 않은 분들의 경우, 그 공간은 비어지게 되고 대기 명단에 있는 다음 직원에게 넘어갈 것입니다. 대기 명단에 오르기를 원하는 직원들은 이번 주 말까지 저에게 연락해 주셔야 합니다.

내년 분의 업데이트된 주차 공간 목록은 12월 12일에 확인하실 수 있습니다. 새로운 주차 허가 스티커 또한 그때 배포될 것입니다. 되도록 빨리 인사과 사무실에서 가져가시기 바랍니다. 반드시 차량 전면 유리 우측 하단에 스티커를 부착하십시오. 시설 경비원이 1월 1일부터 전 차량의 신규 허가증을 검사할 것입니다.

협조해 주셔서 감사합니다.

Daniel Shepard

어휘 parking facility 주차 시설 | long-standing 오래된 | contract 계약 | secure (특히 힘들게) 얻어 내다, 획득[확보]하다 | designated 지정된 | be in use 사용되고 있다 | location 위치 | in time (~에) 시간 맞춰[늦지 않게] | decal 스티커 | windshield 바람막이 창 | inspect 검사하다 | cooperation 협조

해석

Comstock 주차 시설

➢ 1구역은 건물 서쪽에 위치해 있으며 정문에서 가장 가깝습니다.
➢ 55~60번 주차 공간은 전기 자동차 전용입니다.

구역	주차 공간	사원명
1	20	Joe Bean
1	21	Akemi Davidson
1	22	Patricia Wells
2	57	Kevin Houlihan
2	58	Daniel Shephard
2	59	Nancy Jackson
3	1	Rick Duke
3	2	Adrian Stein

어휘 located ~에 위치한 | parking spot 주차 공간 | electric vehicle 전기차

>> Point

질문의 키워드를 확인하여 먼저 봐야 할 지문을 결정한다.

먼저 봐야 할 지문에서 첫 번째 단서를 잡고, 연관성을 고려하여 추가로 필요한 두 번째 단서를 다른 지문에서 찾는다.

둘 이상의 단서를 종합하여 보기와 매칭시킨다.

Questions 1-5 refer to the following e-mail and employee manual.

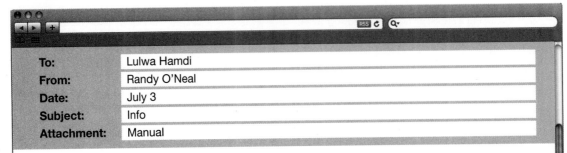

To:	Lulwa Hamdi
From:	Randy O'Neal
Date:	July 3
Subject:	Info
Attachment:	Manual

Hello Ms. Hamdi,

Welcome to AttoTech Industries. I am certain that you'll find your work environment to be pleasant.

I have attached information regarding the company's rules and guidelines. Please take a moment to look them over. In addition, due to limited parking spaces, we encourage employees here to participate in our carpool program. To join, visit the Facilities Department's office anytime between 9 A.M. and 7 P.M.

Also, please remember to make the proper travel arrangements for your trip to visit the other branches. Your first stop will be to the main office next Monday. After that, you will head to our other locations before returning to your branch at the end of the month. For assistance, contact Ned Ewing at newing@attotech.ca.

If you have any questions, do not hesitate to contact me.

Best,

Randy O'Neal

AttoTech Industries

Policy and Procedure Manual

Electronic Device Policy

The use of electronics depends on the location of your office. The main office in Toronto and our Detroit location require employees to use company issued devices during working hours. Employees at our Syracuse and Ontario locations are required to turn in their devices before each shift. In the case of emergency, landline phones are available throughout the facility.

Transportation

AttoTech strives to be an eco-friendly company. Therefore, we offer various incentives to employees depending on how they commute to work.

Those who work in Toronto are eligible for discounted transit passes, which can be used on subways and buses throughout the city. To make a purchase, please visit your Facilities Department.

Employees who choose to bus, bike, or even walk to our Syracuse and Ontario branches can receive monetary rewards based on how far they commute. Additionally, they will be granted access to company vehicles for work-related trips. To sign up, contact the HR Department.

The Detroit branch promotes a carpool initiative. Drivers are given a space near the entrance, plus a stipend for gas. For more information, speak with a representative in the Facilities Department.

1. What is a purpose of the e-mail?

   (A) To provide a corporate file
   (B) To announce a training workshop
   (C) To review a holiday schedule
   (D) To explain a revised procedure

2. In the e-mail, the word "find" in paragraph 1, line 1, is closest in meaning to

   (A) discover
   (B) locate
   (C) expose
   (D) gain

3. What is indicated about Ms. Hamdi?

   (A) She will be traveling throughout July.
   (B) She edited a company manual.
   (C) She was interviewed by Mr. Ewing.
   (D) She rides the subway to work.

4. Where does Ms. Hamdi most likely work?

   (A) In Toronto
   (B) In Syracuse
   (C) In Ontario
   (D) In Detroit

5. According to the manual, what do all AttoTech branches have in common?

   (A) Workers must follow certain electronic device policies.
   (B) Company vehicles are available for rent.
   (C) Mobile phones must be stored away before working.
   (D) Staff members can only use public transportation to access them.

Firstrate Realtors • 715 Leigh Crest • Christchurch NZ 1250

9 October

Geneva Boone
6 Overdale Street
Fendalton NZ 1279

Dear Mr. Webb,

This notice is to let you know that your lease at 127 Andover Point is due to expire on 31 December.

If you would like to renew the lease, please note the following amendment. While we would love to give you the same rate, we have been forced to increase our rent prices. I am sure you are aware of the increasing price of goods here. Accordingly, our monthly rate for our standard five-year lease is now $3,000. This will be the new rate going into next year on 1 January.

If you are interested in renewing your lease, please let us know and we will prepare the relevant paperwork. In the case that you wish to end your tenancy, please also let me know at your earliest convenience. Thank you very much.

Morris Green

To:	Morris Green <m.green@firstrate.co.nz>
From:	Simon Webb <s.webb@hayleys.co.nz>
Date:	14 October
Subject:	Lease agreement

Dear Mr. Green,

First off, I would like to thank Firstrate so much for being such excellent landlords over the past five years. I completely understand Firstrate's decision to increase prices. We have had to increase prices of our home appliances across our locations to keep up with the rising costs of goods. Despite this, our stores, and especially our location at Andover Point, recorded our highest sales since our inception. We have actually been looking into opening up a second location around this area as our home appliances have been selling so well.

To bring us back on topic, we have decided to accept the lease at the new price. Although the price is higher than we would have liked to pay, Andover Point is our flagship location, so we feel it is more valuable to keep our premises there. If you could send the new lease over, we will be happy to sign it.

Thank you once again for everything.

Simon Webb

6. According to the letter, on what date will the rent increase at 127 Andover Point?

(A) 1 January
(B) 9 October
(C) 14 October
(D) 31 December

7. What do both Mr. Green and Mr. Webb agree on?

(A) That costs for things have risen over the years
(B) That advertising has become overly expensive
(C) That commercial properties have fallen in supply
(D) That the area is saturated with new businesses

8. According to the e-mail, what type of business is in the Andover Point office space?

(A) A commercial realtor
(B) A market research firm
(C) A home appliances store
(D) An equipment manufacturer

9. What does the e-mail indicate about Mr. Webb's business?

(A) It has been featured in the newspaper.
(B) It has been in business for five years.
(C) It is a subsidiary of another company.
(D) It is considering expanding overseas.

10. How does Mr. Webb comply with the request from Firstrate Realtors?

(A) By locating another real estate agent to compare prices
(B) By suggesting a new location to expand into
(C) By conducting a survey on property prices
(D) By agreeing to renew the lease at the new price

The Juniper Group

Make sure your advertisements are reaching the audience you want through The Juniper Group, your one-stop shop for all of your internet marketing needs. Headquartered in Amsterdam, we have been in business for over 10 years, and our track record speaks for itself. We offer a range of services including social media marketing, search engine optimization, and much more. Browse through some of our previous work at junipergroup.com, or just give us a call at 137-555-9485. Based on your needs, we'll provide the full list of services we can offer. Sign up now and if you are a first-time customer, we'll knock 10 percent off your price.

To	jbarton@sbmerch.com
From	services@junipergroup.com
Date	April 21
Subject	RE: Updates

Dear Ms. Barton,

I am sincerely sorry for the delay in getting back to you. We have been out of our minds due to moving offices, so things have fallen behind. I want to reassure you that we have received your payment, and we will be fulfilling your order as soon as possible.

I also want you to know that this is not at all our usual standards, and I hope this doesn't mar your first experience with us. I will do all I can to make the rest of your experience with us impeccable.

Best regards,

Lora Wong

Hiring Now

The Juniper Group is seeking talented interns to join our crew in Amsterdam. This is an in-house paid internship with the possibility to lead to a full-time position. As an intern, you will provide administrative support for our employees. You will also be responsible for ensuring smooth communications between our clients and our team via e-mail. The ideal candidate should be service-oriented and a frequent user of — or be familiar with — social media. Interested applicants can contact Lora Wong at 137-555-9485 or inquire directly at lwong@junipergroup.com.

11. What aspect of The Juniper Group's business does the brochure emphasize?

(A) Their important clients
(B) Their growing revenue
(C) Their low prices
(D) Their high reputation

12. According to the brochure, what is suggested about The Juniper Group?

(A) It is an international company.
(B) It features samples of its work online.
(C) It produces newspaper advertisements.
(D) It requires customers to pay a deposit.

13. According to the e-mail, why has communication from Ms. Wong been slow?

(A) The company has relocated offices.
(B) The company has had a staff shortage.
(C) The company has had too much work.
(D) The company has been closed.

14. What is most likely true about Ms. Barton's advertisement order?

(A) It is advertising a new business.
(B) It has been highly successful.
(C) It was removed due to a mistake.
(D) It was bought at a discounted rate.

15. What is a responsibility of an intern?

(A) Assisting employees at company headquarters
(B) Traveling overseas to meet clients face-to-face
(C) Creating online marketing campaigns
(D) Conducting international market research

Sponsoring to Get Ahead

In today's advertisement-saturated world, businesses are looking for different ways to stand out and get their message across to their customers. Sponsorships offer just that: a way to stand out to their demographic. So how do sponsorships work?

Commercial sponsorships refer to cash paid by companies to support a specific event, activity, or organization. This is often done so that companies can show their support on particular causes, or to help out their communities.

While sponsorships may appear to be a drain on a company's resources, they can confer many benefits. Importantly, the company gains favor with the public. In instances where a company sponsors a charity event, the public may view the company in a positive light. This may lead to increased business for the company as more people may buy their products. Additionally, people may be more likely to recommend their products to other people.

Sponsorships can be a valuable tool for many companies to benefit their communities while also increasing their profits.

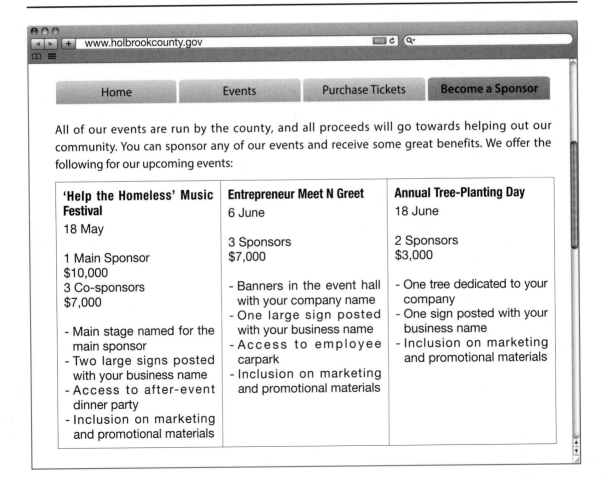

www.holbrookcounty.gov

| Home | Events | Purchase Tickets | **Become a Sponsor** |

All of our events are run by the county, and all proceeds will go towards helping out our community. You can sponsor any of our events and receive some great benefits. We offer the following for our upcoming events:

'Help the Homeless' Music Festival	**Entrepreneur Meet N Greet**	**Annual Tree-Planting Day**
18 May	6 June	18 June
1 Main Sponsor $10,000 3 Co-sponsors $7,000	3 Sponsors $7,000	2 Sponsors $3,000
- Main stage named for the main sponsor - Two large signs posted with your business name - Access to after-event dinner party - Inclusion on marketing and promotional materials	- Banners in the event hall with your company name - One large sign posted with your business name - Access to employee carpark - Inclusion on marketing and promotional materials	- One tree dedicated to your company - One sign posted with your business name - Inclusion on marketing and promotional materials

'HELP THE HOMELESS' MUSIC FESTIVAL
Schedule of Events
Saturday, April 29

Please consult the attached map for directions to the stages. Each hall has a maximum capacity and will operate on a 'first come, first serve' basis. Please remember that we had to turn away some attendees last year, so make sure to arrive early.

Time	Event	Location
4:30 P.M.	Piano recital by Yeonwoo Kim	"DreamIns" Theater
4:30 P.M.	Rock group "Yellow Glasses"	"A&E Partners" Stage
7:00 P.M.	Headliner R&B Singer "Hugo Monte"	"Reach Services" Main Stage
10:00 P.M.	Jazz group "Kilo Davis"	"Pylo Vendors" Stage
10:00 P.M.	R&B Singer "Shona Veronica"	"DreamIns" Theater
11:30 P.M.	Closing Speech	"Reach Services" Main Stage

*****Note**: Weather permitting, Hugo Monte may perform at "DreamIns" Theater.

16. According to the article, what is the main benefit for a company sponsoring an event?

(A) An increase in the number of qualified applicants
(B) An improvement to the company's social standing
(C) A reduction in the tax expense for the company
(D) A greater opportunity to expand into locations

17. What is indicated on the Web page?

(A) A sponsor may be eligible for a discount.
(B) Sponsoring the music festival will also provide free tickets.
(C) All sponsors receive a sign bearing their name.
(D) The tree dedication is limited to a single sponsor.

18. Which company listed on the schedule is the main sponsor for the music festival?

(A) DreamIns
(B) Reach Services
(C) A&E Partners
(D) Pylo Vendors

19. What advice from the article did the companies follow?

(A) They allied with other companies to sponsor events together.
(B) They got involved in the planning of events prior to sponsorship.
(C) They requested additional privileges for the sponsorship.
(D) They sponsored a charitable event to help better their image.

20. What can be concluded from the schedule?

(A) The closing speech may run over time.
(B) Parking space is not included as part of the ticket.
(C) The festival generally exceeds capacity.
(D) Hugo Monte performed at the festival last year.

Questions 1-2 refer to the following online chat discussion.

Bart Townsley (11:08 A.M.)
    Thank you for contacting Ashberg Power Tools. My name is Bart. How can I assist you?

Larry Davis (11:09 A.M.)
    Hello, Bart. I sent back an item eight weeks ago, but the order status on my account page still says "incomplete."

Bart Townsley (11:09 A.M.)
    I'll be happy to check on that for you. Could you give me the tracking number or invoice number?

Larry Davis (11:10 A.M.)
    It was invoice #1039583, and the tracking number is #IG3145.

Bart Townsley (11:10 A.M.)
    Thank you. Please be patient as I check our computer. Just one moment please.

Bart Townsley (11:13 A.M.)
    We received the returned item, and your United credit card was credited, even though it still says "incomplete." I will just manually update that status now to "refunded." Sometimes our computer program takes a few days to update on its own.

Larry Davis (11:16 A.M.)
    Thank you so much. I'll check my credit card statement to make sure the credit was processed.

Bart Townsley (11:17 A.M.)
    Needless to say. You will receive a transcript of this chat session in your e-mail inbox. Please don't hesitate to contact us again if you have any other questions or problems.

Larry Davis (11:18 A.M.)
    I appreciate your help!

SEND

---

1. Why did Mr. Davis contact Ashberg Power Tools?

(A) To inquire about a refund policy
(B) To check the status of a return
(C) To review a copy of a credit card statement
(D) To report an item missing from an order

2. At 11:17 A.M., what does Mr. Townsley most likely mean when he writes, "Needless to say"?

(A) He will contact Mr. Davis at a later time.
(B) He realizes that Mr. Davis is frustrated.
(C) He understands Mr. Davis's response.
(D) He is pleased to help Mr. Davis.

Questions 3-5 refer to the following news bulletin.

Evansville Ballet News

Season Tickets Now on Sale
Order your season tickets now at www.evansvilleballet.com/seasontickets.
April 3-11: *The Tea Dance* (1 1/2 hours with 1 intermission)
June 5-13: *Mirage* (2 1/2 hours with 1 intermission)
August 13-21: *Titan's Curse* (1 hour with no intermission)
October 29 - November 7: *Peter Pan* (3 hours with 2 intermissions)
Performances will be held at the Tatiana Theater starting promptly at 7:00 P. M.

Dancers-in-Residence Series
Our rotating dancers-in-residence program strives to bring new talent from around the world, as an addition to the performances of our regular troupe. They've received many awards and much international recognition. Join us for a special series of 1 P. M. matinee performances by these dancers and help us celebrate the next generation of talent coming into the field of ballet. Each performance will feature an assortment of ballet favorites selected and performed by one of our dancers-in-residence.

April 3: Elaine Thomas
June 5: Luis Ruiz
August 13: Daniela Hedenheim
October 29: Olga Cieminski

3. Which ballet will be performed without a break?
   (A) *The Tea Dance*
   (B) *Mirage*
   (C) *Peter Pan*
   (D) *Titan's Curse*

4. What is probably true about the dancers-in-residence?
   (A) They are all well-known around the globe.
   (B) They have previously performed in Evansville.
   (C) They are older than the regular dancers.
   (D) They are professionally trained as actors.

5. Who most likely will perform in *Mirage*?
   (A) Ms. Thomas
   (B) Ms. Hedenheim
   (C) Mr. Ruiz
   (D) Ms. Cieminski

HANOI, Vietnam, 13 October — Blue Games just released a statement today that the studio is currently preparing for the launch of its latest project, Street Footballers, in December. —[1]—. Around 300 lucky professional players will get the chance to try the beta version next week. —[2]—. Street Footballers itself takes the format of street football matches, in which players will play in a group of five. —[3]—. Players will be able to join an online match and group with other players. They will automatically be grouped by the system. There are limitless possibilities for players in building their avatars. —[4]—. Players could also buy a wide range of sporting goods in our offline store.

6. What most likely is Street Footballers?

(A) A sporting event
(B) A training program
(C) A video game
(D) A TV show

7. What is NOT mentioned about Street Footballers?

(A) Players can join an online match.
(B) Players can trade their items.
(C) Players can create characters.
(D) Players can purchase merchandise.

8. In which of the positions marked [1], [2], [3], and [4] does the following sentence best belong?

"They will provide comments to the developer before the game is officially launched."

(A) [1]
(B) [2]
(C) [3]
(D) [4]

GREENVIEW PARK

CALL FOR PROPOSALS

Greenview Park is currently looking for a reputable cleaning service vendor for the park daily maintenance. Businesses may submit their proposals starting from September 29 to October 31 to the Park Management Office, 33 Timlin Avenue. We will not accept any late submission.

Every proposal must include the vendor's business license, history, qualifications, and advantages. Four copies of the proposal are required. The proposal shall also include at least two reference letters from the vendor's clients within the past six months. Any questions should be directed to Ms. Jessica Roberts at the address above. They must be submitted in writing and will be responded to accordingly.

Proposals will be assessed by the Park's Committee. The five shortlisted vendors will have to present their proposal in front of the Committee on November 4. The successful company will be advised via mail. The final decision will be made based on the suitability and expertise of the vendor.

9. What will happen after October 31?

(A) Maintenance will be performed.
(B) Projects will be reassigned.
(C) Proposals will be evaluated.
(D) A team will be assembled.

10. What is NOT required for proposal submission?

(A) Sample images
(B) Two letters of reference
(C) Copies of the proposal
(D) Description of their strengths

11. What is indicated about the Park's Committee?

(A) It will consider submitted proposals.
(B) It posts a planned project online.
(C) It focuses on taking care of lawns.
(D) It is planning to operate a visitors' center.

12. What is suggested about Ms. Roberts?

(A) She will change her career soon.
(B) She has excellent administration skills.
(C) She e-mailed a company representative.
(D) She will provide responses to businesses.

Questions 13-17 refer to the following e-mails.

To	customersupport@topride.com
From	cgupta@fivestar.com
Date	Tuesday, July 28, 11:17 A.M.
Subject	Inquiry for Assistance

Dear Customer Support Manager,

I am writing to inform you that I have been failing to make a booking through your Web page. It seems that your booking page is broken because I could not load it over and over again.

My relatives and I are planning to fly to New Mexico in two weeks for a 7-day trip, and we would need a car for rent for our time there. I would love to have a car that can contain six people with a spacious trunk for six large backpacks and costs no more than $120 a day.

I have experience in using your service last year and I noticed that you offered extra services back then, including a set of umbrellas. Do you still offer such extra service? Or do you have any other services that I could benefit from?

I'm looking forward to hearing from you soon.

Chandra Gupta

To	cgupta@fivestar.com
From	ianrich@topride.com
Date	Tuesday, July 28, 2:25 P.M.
Subject	Re: Inquiry for Assistance

Dear Mr. Gupta,

I would like to apologize for the poor experience that you had when trying to access our Web site. I have forwarded your concern to the IT team and they say that it will be fixed in a couple of hours. Please retry to make the booking at around 5 P.M.

In regard with your requirements, my suggestion would be HR-V Uniq. The car meets all of your requirements perfectly. Regarding the extra service that you referred to in your e-mail, it is available at an additional fee. I am also more than pleased to let you know that you can get 15% discount if you stay at one of the hotels that take part in our Business Reference Program.

Should you have any further inquiries, you can talk to one of our customer service representative by calling at 555-374-7774. You may also download our recently launched app for your booking needs.

I hope my responses satisfy you well.

Ian Richardson, Customer Support Manager

Top Ride

13. What does the first e-mail indicate about Mr. Gupta?

(A) He resides in New Mexico.
(B) He has never used Top Ride's service before.
(C) He just bought a new vehicle.
(D) He requires a car to rent for one week.

14. What is true about the HR-V Uniq?

(A) It is too expensive for Mr. Gupta.
(B) It may contain up to six people.
(C) It is the best-seller at Top Ride.
(D) It does not have a wide trunk.

15. What does Mr. Richardson offer Mr. Gupta?

(A) A set of free umbrellas
(B) A guidebook for his trip
(C) A discount program for a hotel booking
(D) A loyalty program for a car rental reservation

16. In the second e-mail, the word "meets" in paragraph 2, line 1, is closet in meaning to

(A) satisfies
(B) locates
(C) provides
(D) notifies

17. What does the second e-mail indicate about Top Ride?

(A) It is the best car rental service in New Mexico.
(B) It has a fixed maintenance schedule for its Web site.
(C) It expanded its services to several other cities recently.
(D) It has added a new way to make reservations.

DeLillo Tower Complex

EAST ORANGE (March 11) — O'Malley Properties (OP) may be forced to halt construction of its ambitious DeLillo Tower Complex. A source within the city council has expressed major concerns about the possible environmental impact construction could have on the rest of the community. The terms of OP's contract require that, in addition to using solar panels to achieve a net-zero energy rating, they must also improve nearby public parks and green spaces. Concerned that the company could fall short on both counts,

council members are threatening to freeze OP's construction permit.

Backers of the project are uncomfortable with this development. The mayor's chief of staff, Mark Carlsen said, "This project promises to serve as a magnet for attracting other commercial enterprises to the downtown East Orange. We need to come to an agreement so that OP can move forward. Our legislators need to remember OP's unimpeachable record in designing and constructing beautiful buildings that become community landmarks."

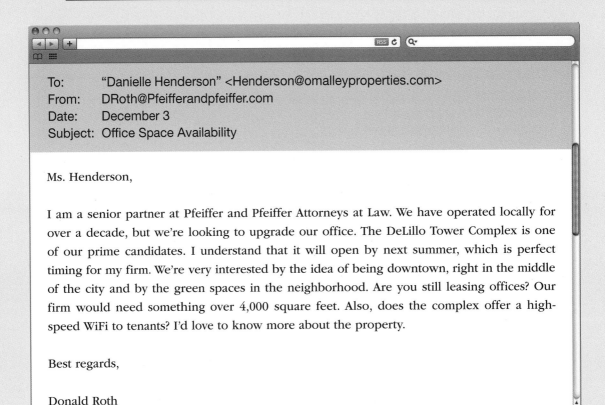

To: "Danielle Henderson" <Henderson@omalleyproperties.com>
From: DRoth@Pfeifferandpfeiffer.com
Date: December 3
Subject: Office Space Availability

Ms. Henderson,

I am a senior partner at Pfeiffer and Pfeiffer Attorneys at Law. We have operated locally for over a decade, but we're looking to upgrade our office. The DeLillo Tower Complex is one of our prime candidates. I understand that it will open by next summer, which is perfect timing for my firm. We're very interested by the idea of being downtown, right in the middle of the city and by the green spaces in the neighborhood. Are you still leasing offices? Our firm would need something over 4,000 square feet. Also, does the complex offer a high-speed WiFi to tenants? I'd love to know more about the property.

Best regards,

Donald Roth

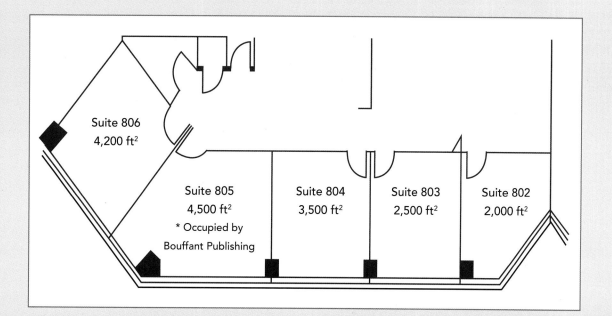

Suite 806
4,200 ft²

Suite 805
4,500 ft²
* Occupied by
Bouffant Publishing

Suite 804
3,500 ft²

Suite 803
2,500 ft²

Suite 802
2,000 ft²

18. What is the main purpose of the article?

(A) To profile a local property developer
(B) To report on a new city regulation
(C) To discuss the progress of a project
(D) To discuss green construction methods

19. What positive feature of the DeLillo Tower Complex does Mr. Carlsen mention?

(A) The expected value of its architecture
(B) Its energy efficiency
(C) The amount of commercial space available
(D) Its central location

20. What is suggested about OP in Mr. Roth's e-mail?

(A) It has been in business for over 10 years.
(B) It plans to relocate to East Orange.
(C) It resolved a potential conflict.
(D) It only provides retail spaces.

21. What information about the complex does Mr. Roth request from Ms. Henderson?

(A) The businesses located within the complex
(B) The opening date of the complex
(C) The availability of an Internet connection
(D) The distance to nearby parks

22. Which location would Pfeiffer and Pfeiffer Attorneys at Law most likely choose to rent?

(A) Suite 802
(B) Suite 803
(C) Suite 804
(D) Suite 806

ACTUAL TEST

ACTUAL TEST 01 해설서 p.170

READING TEST

In the Reading test, you will read a variety of texts and answer several different types of reading comprehension questions. The entire Reading test will last 75 minutes. There are three parts, and directions are given for each part. You are encouraged to answer as many questions as possible within the time allowed.

You must mark your answers on the separate answer sheet. Do not write your answers in your test book.

PART 5

Directions: A word or phrase is missing in each of the sentences below. Four answer choices are given below each sentence. Select the best answer to complete the sentence. Then mark the letter (A), (B), (C), or (D) on your answer sheet.

101. The cafeteria will be closed on Wednesday for renovations, ------- please make other arrangements for lunch.

(A) which
(B) why
(C) if
(D) so

102. Mr. Cech earned the trust of his clients when he delivered his ------- two days ahead of schedule.

(A) reportable
(B) reported
(C) report
(D) reporter

103. McCullough Corporation is often ------- as a company that hires employees of all ages.

(A) permitted
(B) perceived
(C) inclined
(D) regulated

104. The Maitre Hotel chain employs a strict set of regulations to ensure a ------- guest experience.

(A) consisting
(B) consist
(C) consistently
(D) consistent

105. To our -------, a new system for monitoring waste has been implemented in seven cities.

(A) knowledge
(B) skill
(C) ability
(D) competence

106. Since we installed an energy saving central air conditioner, expect ------- utility fee to be reduced.

(A) you
(B) your
(C) yours
(D) yourself

107. The Filmmakers Association urges viewers not to blindly accept ------- reviews about a movie.

(A) opposing
(B) productive
(C) biased
(D) complete

108. Monthly maintenance costs ------- depending on the location and size of the apartment unit rented.

(A) continue
(B) vary
(C) repeat
(D) repair

109. ------- he has experience and expertise in the field, Mr. Walker is an ideal candidate for the position.

(A) If so
(B) Rather than
(C) Owing to
(D) Given that

110. Marketing Department staff must be ------- with regard to client meeting starting times.

(A) immediate
(B) punctual
(C) accessible
(D) periodic

111. Ms. Park is evaluating the ------- of the partnership agreement with Sauber GmbH.

(A) effort
(B) grip
(C) turn
(D) scope

112. Mr. Jalah has submitted a ------- estimate of the expenses of opening a new store location.

(A) conserving
(B) conservative
(C) conserves
(D) conserved

113. While growth was ------- slow in the early years, it gave Pavicen Construction a chance to thoroughly learn the business.

(A) admit
(B) admission
(C) admitting
(D) admittedly

114. Last month, the council ------- 76 fines to companies that violated the regulation.

(A) constructed
(B) viewed
(C) issued
(D) acted

115. When you remove a price tag label, great care should be taken to avoid leaving a ------- residue.

(A) sticky
(B) stuck
(C) stickiest
(D) stick

116. Warren Brothers employees are entitled to negotiate their salary figure ------- six months of working at the company.

(A) toward
(B) after
(C) into
(D) between

117. With its production facilities in Mexico and Argentina nearing -------, RK Automobiles is now concentrating its efforts on entering the local market.

(A) completely
(B) completion
(C) completed
(D) complete

118. According to the consumer research held two years ago and ------- this year, younger customers are more likely to make purchases online rather than at physical stores.

(A) recent
(B) later
(C) yet
(D) again

119. The feature about Maarsden Corp. was -------- Marilyn Carter's best article of the year.

(A) easily
(B) easiest
(C) easier
(D) easy

120. Companies should improve their products' quality ------- committing more resources to the marketing of poor-quality products to gain a bigger market share.

(A) according to
(B) instead of
(C) in regard to
(D) as to

GO ON TO THE NEXT PAGE

121. Marder Studios creates ------- short films that are often intended to highlight the pros and cons of business strategies.

(A) primary
(B) compelling
(C) persistent
(D) concerned

122. ------- the two models of wireless earphones feature different options, they look nearly identical.

(A) But
(B) Although
(C) Neither
(D) Yet

123. Please provide your receipts ------- your travel reimbursement forms by September 15.

(A) most of all
(B) in addition
(C) in the event
(D) as well as

124. Next to the Shinhwa Resort is an extravagant entertainment area, complete ------- a golf course and temperature-regulated outdoor spa.

(A) beyond
(B) for
(C) of
(D) with

125. Many people find the wait before receiving the results from their physical checkup almost -------.

(A) unyielding
(B) outstanding
(C) unbearable
(D) insufficient

126. Frank Harwood created a cash flow chart technique, which is now used by many ------- investors all over the world.

(A) also
(B) extra
(C) other
(D) else

127. The entire team at FM Finance is ready to provide any assistance, and we hope our cooperation will be ------- beneficial for now and in the long run.

(A) punctually
(B) mutually
(C) respectively
(D) precisely

128. The president's address will be recorded in its ------- and uploaded to our Web site for staff who could not attend the meeting.

(A) system
(B) entirety
(C) estimation
(D) recognition

129. The total cost of the manufacturing process should be ------- before proposing the production of a new item.

(A) calculates
(B) calculation
(C) calculating
(D) calculated

130. Many wholesalers of fresh fruit ------- base their operations near the growers' orchards.

(A) persuasively
(B) personably
(C) purposely
(D) proficiently

PART 6

Directions: Read the texts that follow. A word, phrase, or sentence is missing in some of the sentences. Four answer choices are given below each of these sentences. Select the best answer to complete the text. Then mark the letter (A), (B), (C), or (D) on your answer sheet.

Questions 131-134 refer to the following notice.

Save your weekend plans next week because Norman Sparks will be in town. Mr. Sparks has been making headlines for his --------, which earned him the award for Best Debut of the Year. He will
131.
be holding a concert at the Voci Arena as part of his fundraiser to help kids in need. The concert will take place next weekend, March 22. We hope everyone comes out to -------- a good cause.
132.
Additionally, every ticket purchased will enter you into -------- raffle where you can meet Mr. Sparks
133.
backstage in person. --------. You'll also have a chance to chat with him. This is a once-in-a-lifetime
134.
opportunity, so make sure you don't miss out! Head on over to www.vociarena.com/events for more details.

131. (A) movie
(B) song
(C) poem
(D) play

132. (A) support
(B) organize
(C) consider
(D) create

133. (A) each
(B) another
(C) every
(D) a

134. (A) The arena is expected to be packed.
(B) A new concert date may be announced.
(C) The award ceremony will be next week.
(D) There will be some autographed goodies.

GO ON TO THE NEXT PAGE

To: All Grunsfield Spa Employees
From: Vicki Farmer
Date: September 7
Subject: Latest report

You will --------- hear some upsetting news. According to the latest surveys, customers rate our
                135.
reputation to be quite negative. In fact, there are online groups dedicated to talking about --------
                                                                                              136.
experiences with us. Rather than feeling sad, we should take this as an opportunity. --------. I want us
                                                                                      137.
to divide into teams and maybe interview some disgruntled customers. I know we have other work
going on that is taking up a lot of your time. --------, this is more important. It should take priority over
                                               138.
everything else.

135. (A) sometimes
     (B) previously
     (C) now
     (D) later

136. (A) my
     (B) our
     (C) its
     (D) their

137. (A) Our revenues have gone down in
         recent years.
     (B) I need some ideas for what our next
         project should be.
     (C) We can consider inviting other teams
         to get their opinions.
     (D) Let's do some research to find out how
         we can do better.

138. (A) Supposedly
     (B) However
     (C) Despite
     (D) In contrast

Questions 139-142 refer to the following e-mail.

To: TBW Readers
From: customerservice@tbw.com
Date: 31 March
Subject: Interruption

At Tavermont Business Weekly (TBW), we ------- to providing our readers with high-quality content.
                                   139.
However, it appears that we have been unable to meet those standards lately. I'm sure you noticed

that there were many editing errors in our most recent issue. -------. Because of this, April's issue will
                                                              140.
not be released on its usual date next week. This is a ------- situation. We have plans in place to fully
                                                        141.
address the problem. -------, we believe that the final result will be a significant improvement in the
                     142.
quality of our publication. We are very sorry about the delay, and appreciate your understanding.

Thank you,

Calvin Lo
Customer Service Manager, TBW

---

139. (A) would have dedicated
(B) will be dedicating
(C) dedicating
(D) are dedicated

140. (A) Sadly, we were unable to issue you a full refund.
(B) Lamentably, we have been forced to raise subscription fees.
(C) Regrettably, we have been dealing with some major personnel issues.
(D) Unfortunately, your subscription payment was not processed correctly.

141. (A) temporary
(B) favorable
(C) quick
(D) planned

142. (A) Ever since then
(B) In the event that
(C) As a matter of fact
(D) On one side

GO ON TO THE NEXT PAGE

Questions 143-146 refer to the following article.

Fernbrook Co. to Partner with Kangley Logistics

Fernbrook, England — Fernbrook Co., an up-and-coming business dealing primarily in computer parts, ------- a partnership with Kangley Logistics. Under this partnership, it is expected that Kangley Logistics will handle all of Fernbrook Co.'s international shipping orders.
143.

"This is a momentous decision for us because we feel that Kangley Logistics is the perfect ------- for us," said Fernbrook Co. owner Frankie Watson. "Our international orders have been picking up a lot.
144.
It's great that we have Kangley Logistics on our side now. -------."
145.

Mr. Watson also praised Kangley Logistics on how ------- their distribution centre is. "You can just tell when you walk into their centre that they know what they're doing. Everything was meticulously
146.
arranged, and their employees knew the answers to all of the questions we had. There's a reason why everybody recommends Kangley Logistics."

143. (A) may announce
(B) can announce
(C) will be announced
(D) has announced

144. (A) deal
(B) ally
(C) ship
(D) contract

145. (A) We are looking to start selling overseas.
(B) Shipping domestically is not a problem.
(C) The order has not yet been made.
(D) They are experts in overseas shipping.

146. (A) systematic
(B) hygienic
(C) creative
(D) cumbersome

PART 7

Directions: In this part, you will read a selection of texts, such as magazine and newspaper articles, letters, and instant messages. Each text or set of texts is followed by several questions. Select the best answer for each question and mark the letter (A), (B), (C), or (D) on your answer sheet.

Questions 147-148 refer to the following notice.

Sun King Suites Appreciates Your Business

To make your stay more enjoyable, we provide a free light rail pass that can be used at all stations in the Old Town neighborhood. The light rail system connects to many of the city's most popular landmarks, including the history museum, the Presidential Palace, and MPX Mall. Even though these locations are accessible on foot, the light rail system will provide greater convenience, especially during the hot summer months. The light rail system, favored by both tourists and locals alike, also connects to Central Station, where you can catch regional trains.

A complete timetable is available on the hotel's Web site. Loyalty club members are eligible for discounts at each of the sites mentioned above. Ask at the front desk for details.

147. What is being offered?

(A) A ticket to the Presidential Palace
(B) Special rates for regional trains
(C) A new loyalty club membership
(D) Free transportation

148. What is implied about the Sun King Suites?

(A) It is well-reviewed by business travelers.
(B) It is near the Old Town neighborhood.
(C) It is a favorite among tourists.
(D) It is a famous local landmark.

GO ON TO THE NEXT PAGE

Mondegreen Martial Arts Gym

Stay fit by adding our proven workout regimen to your daily routine.

From now until November 30, all six-month membership packages are 33 percent off.

Also, for each additional person to join the gym on your recommendation, earn extra 10 percent off your membership package.

Advantages of being a member include:
- Personal instruction from our skilled trainers
- Classes for every level: from beginner to master
- On-site showers and sauna
- Exercise equipment available 24/7

149. According to the advertisement, why should someone join the gym?

(A) To exercise in an outdoor setting
(B) To become a martial arts instructor
(C) To build a professional network
(D) To create healthy habits

150. How can customers get a discount?

(A) By signing up for beginner level classes
(B) By referring another customer
(C) By purchasing a year-long membership
(D) By joining the gym in December

Questions 151-152 refer to the following e-mail.

To	Schmieg Business Development Team
From	Jason Herrera
Date	February 13
Subject	Ms. Wu

Dear employees,

Schmieg Industries is proud to announce that our Head of Business Development, Yabin Wu, has been nominated for Business Digest's Businesswoman of the Year. This should come as no surprise given her accomplishments in turning Schmieg into an international firm. Five years ago, Schmieg served 3,000 customers. Five years later, with Ms. Wu at the helm the entire time, we are now serving 50,000 customers. Therefore, we would like to take this time to celebrate her accomplishment.

We have reserved the restaurant, Chandelier Room, for this Friday. Please let me know if you are attending so that we can get an accurate head count. Also, if you see Ms. Wu in the office, be sure to congratulate her on her excellent accomplishment.

Kind regards,

Jason Herrera, Human Resources
Schmieg Industries

151. Why did Mr. Herrera send the e-mail?
(A) To announce the departure of an employee
(B) To celebrate an employee's achievement
(C) To provide an update on a recent decision
(D) To inform staff of a change in leadership

152. What is suggested about Ms. Wu?
(A) She has been with the company for five years.
(B) She has recently changed roles within the company.
(C) She was initially hired by Mr. Herrera.
(D) She has worked overseas for some time.

GO ON TO THE NEXT PAGE

Questions 153-154 refer to the following text message chain.

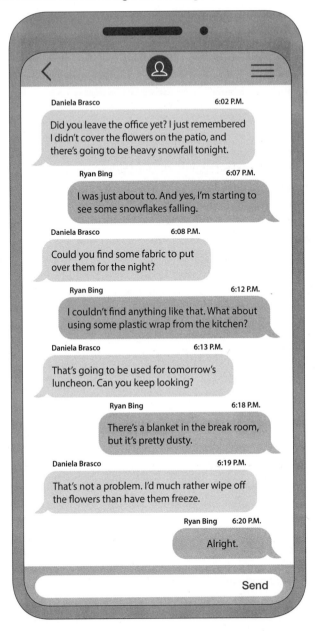

Daniela Brasco   6:02 P.M.

Did you leave the office yet? I just remembered I didn't cover the flowers on the patio, and there's going to be heavy snowfall tonight.

Ryan Bing   6:07 P.M.

I was just about to. And yes, I'm starting to see some snowflakes falling.

Daniela Brasco   6:08 P.M.

Could you find some fabric to put over them for the night?

Ryan Bing   6:12 P.M.

I couldn't find anything like that. What about using some plastic wrap from the kitchen?

Daniela Brasco   6:13 P.M.

That's going to be used for tomorrow's luncheon. Can you keep looking?

Ryan Bing   6:18 P.M.

There's a blanket in the break room, but it's pretty dusty.

Daniela Brasco   6:19 P.M.

That's not a problem. I'd much rather wipe off the flowers than have them freeze.

Ryan Bing   6:20 P.M.

Alright.

Send

---

153. What does Ms. Brasco ask Ms. Bing to do?

(A) Move some patio furniture
(B) Organize the break room
(C) Protect some plants
(D) Watch a weather report

154. At 6:19 P.M. what does Ms. Brasco most likely mean when she writes, "That's not a problem"?

(A) She will purchase some gardening tools.
(B) She does not mind some dust.
(C) She wants Mr. Bing to host a luncheon.
(D) She is fine with Mr. Bing using a vacation day.

MANCHESTER, 15 July — Manchester's own Cinco Corporation has agreed to a merger with the Eindhoven-based AJX Electronik. —[1]—. Cinco produces and sells high-end televisions. For most of the past decade, Cinco has purchased LED panels from AJX, whose components are widely considered to be the industry standard. —[2]—. High demand for AJX LED panels from other manufacturers occasionally created shortages, forcing Cinco to make compromises on the design of some products. —[3]—. Wout Van Der Poel, the AJX CEO, asserted that AJX would now be able to open a second manufacturing plant in Utrecht. —[4]—. "There's no doubt in my mind; this deal is a true win-win," stated Van Der Poel.

155. What is the purpose of the article?

(A) To discuss problems with an acquisition
(B) To reveal a new model of high-resolution TV
(C) To provide a timeline for a future factory opening
(D) To announce the conclusion of an agreement

156. What does the article suggest will happen?

(A) TV prices will continue to increase.
(B) LED panels will feature in more products.
(C) LED panels will be made at a new site.
(D) TV production will be increased.

157. In which of the positions marked [1], [2], [3] and [4] does the following sentence best belong?

"But the change guarantees Cinco's exclusive access."

(A) [1]
(B) [2]
(C) [3]
(D) [4]

SAN JOSE (14 September) — This morning JBXL, headquartered here in San Jose, revealed that it has reached an agreement to purchase Pingguo Corp. The television and home audio maker says the deal will allow JBXL to expand to a new continent as well as build its presence in the portable projector market. Pingguo products have sold well in the company's native Taiwan, where they are one of the most popular home theater solutions.

"Pingguo, despite being a relatively new company, has some of the most cutting-edge manufacturing techniques in the world and will help us to get a foothold in Taiwan," CEO Hope Chun told reporters gathered for the announcement, "And I want to assure everyone at JBXL and Pingguo that we only intend to grow our operations on both sides of the Pacific," she added in response to rumors that the merger would lead to a loss of jobs.

"Purchasing Pingguo is essential in our strategy to become a global leader in television, home audio, and projector sales," explained Chun. "We aim to enter new markets through collaborations with leading manufacturers and designers who share our commitment to great products."

158. Why did JBXL acquire Pingguo Corp.?

(A) JBXL was looking for a less expensive supplier.
(B) Pingguo had been a major competitor.
(C) Pingguo has a lengthy track record of success.
(D) JBXL wanted to enter a new region.

159. What is true about the products Pingguo Corp. manufactures?

(A) They are assembled in San Jose.
(B) They are often used to film movies.
(C) They will release new models soon.
(D) They can be carried easily.

160. According to the article, what will JBXL most likely do in the future?

(A) Relocate its main office to Taiwan
(B) Cut the number of staff in San Jose
(C) Nominate a new executive officer
(D) Partner with more companies like Pingguo

Questions 161-163 refer to the following employment agreement.

Florence Hotel Group

EMPLOYMENT CONTRACT

1. Agreement between Florence Hotel Group and Jordan Abbas

2. Employment Period Beginning: March 1

3. Duties: The position consists of the following responsibilities:
   - Processing reservations over the phone
   - Greeting and building rapport with guests
   - Scheduling bus and taxi services for visitors
   - Addressing complaints regarding hotel amenities
   - Recommending local tourist attractions and sites
   - Reporting daily earnings to the shift manager

4. Other Duties: The employee will be required to partake in mandatory training sessions during the three-month probationary period.

5. Remuneration: The employee shall receive an annual salary, payable in monthly installments in the amount of $38,000 per year. Performance evaluations are held during the fourth quarter of the year. Salary is subject to increases based on the results of the assessment.

6. Standard Annual Leave: In accordance with the company's standard annual leave (SAL) policy, employees are entitled to 20 paid vacation days, 5 sick days, and 10 public holidays every year. Staff members who need to take more than 5 days off due to medical reasons must refer to the company's extended leave of absence policy, as this kind of case is not covered by the SAL policy.

---

161. What most likely will be Mr. Abbas's job title?

(A) Tour guide
(B) Corporate trainer
(C) Housekeeping staff
(D) Front-desk assistant

162. When will Mr. Abbas's salary most likely be adjusted?

(A) During the fourth quarter
(B) At the end of the three-month probationary period
(C) Next March
(D) Next January

163. What is NOT covered by Florence Hotel Group's SAL policy?

(A) Public holidays
(B) Extended time off
(C) Sick leave
(D) Personal vacations

GO ON TO THE NEXT PAGE

November 27

Timothy Ng
3543 Rue Levy
Montreal, Quebec

Dear Mr. Ng,

I appreciate your comments from the letter you sent us on November 25. On behalf of Bello Ristorante, I want to apologize for your unpleasant experience at our restaurant during your graduation party on November 21. —[1]—. Unfortunately, the food came out slower than usual that day as two of our cooks called in sick. I'm deeply sorry for the inconvenience we caused you. I want to thank you for taking the time to voice your frustration. Customer satisfaction is of upmost importance to us. I am, however, relieved that you enjoyed the meal. —[2]—.

Because we appreciate your patronage, I have sent you a voucher for a free entrée. —[3]—. This voucher is valid at Bello Ristorante or at our sister restaurant, Garden Opera at 22 Greenhouse Avenue. The Garden Opera has fewer seating areas than Bello Ristorante has, but is more intimate. Not to mention, Garden Opera has been featured in several culinary magazines for its unique menu. In addition, the all-natural décor of the restaurant offers a dining experience you can't get anywhere else. —[4]—.

I would like to apologize again and appreciate you taking the time to write us. If there's anything else I can do, please do not hesitate to contact me.

Sincerely,

Esther Lyons

Esther Lyons, General Manager

ENCLOSURE

164. Why did Mr. Ng originally contact Ms. Lyons?

(A) To schedule a reservation
(B) To complain about a service
(C) To inquire about a menu
(D) To support a new ownership

165. When did Mr. Ng visit Bello Ristorante?

(A) On November 21
(B) On November 22
(C) On November 25
(D) On November 27

166. What does Ms. Lyons NOT mention about Garden Opera?

(A) It does not have as many seats as Bello Ristorante.
(B) It mainly sells vegetarian dishes.
(C) It has all-natural decorations.
(D) It has been featured in publications.

167. In which of the positions marked [1], [2], [3], and [4] does the following sentence best belong?

"It must be redeemed within one year."

(A) [1]
(B) [2]
(C) [3]
(D) [4]

GO ON TO THE NEXT PAGE

Questions 168-171 refer to the following text message chain.

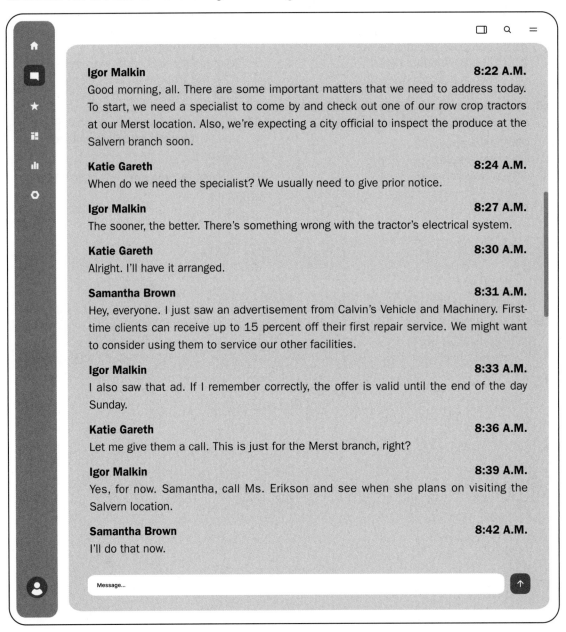

Igor Malkin   8:22 A.M.

Good morning, all. There are some important matters that we need to address today. To start, we need a specialist to come by and check out one of our row crop tractors at our Merst location. Also, we're expecting a city official to inspect the produce at the Salvern branch soon.

Katie Gareth   8:24 A.M.

When do we need the specialist? We usually need to give prior notice.

Igor Malkin   8:27 A.M.

The sooner, the better. There's something wrong with the tractor's electrical system.

Katie Gareth   8:30 A.M.

Alright. I'll have it arranged.

Samantha Brown   8:31 A.M.

Hey, everyone. I just saw an advertisement from Calvin's Vehicle and Machinery. First-time clients can receive up to 15 percent off their first repair service. We might want to consider using them to service our other facilities.

Igor Malkin   8:33 A.M.

I also saw that ad. If I remember correctly, the offer is valid until the end of the day Sunday.

Katie Gareth   8:36 A.M.

Let me give them a call. This is just for the Merst branch, right?

Igor Malkin   8:39 A.M.

Yes, for now. Samantha, call Ms. Erikson and see when she plans on visiting the Salvern location.

Samantha Brown   8:42 A.M.

I'll do that now.

Message...

168. What is implied about the business for which the writers work?

(A) It recently opened a new location.
(B) It upgraded its inventory system.
(C) It sells machine parts.
(D) It operates farms.

169. At 8:30 A.M., what does Ms. Gareth most likely mean when she writes, "I'll have it arranged"?

(A) She will contact a mechanic.
(B) She will visit the Salvern branch.
(C) She will prepare an agreement form.
(D) She will e-mail some clients.

170. What is indicated about Calvin's Vehicle and Machinery?

(A) It is holding a limited-time offer.
(B) It is closed on Sundays.
(C) It has been operating for 15 years.
(D) It provides international shipping.

171. Who most likely is Ms. Erikson?

(A) A city inspector
(B) A supermarket owner
(C) A sales associate
(D) A vehicle designer

GO ON TO THE NEXT PAGE

To	All
From	Robert Upton
Date	May 25
Subject	IBA Convention
Attachment	Convention Timetable

Everyone,

This year's convention of the International Baristas' Association will be held here in Kona during the last week of August. I am honored to share that I've been invited by Jake Hu, the chief organizer, to put on two seminars. It is an achievement to be recognized by such a decorated barista, who is also the director of the award-winning documentary series on Hawaii's unique coffee traditions, *Finding Black Gold*. Most of all, this is an amazing chance for Upton's Café to market its world-class quality to a wider audience.

The first seminar will be about cupping techniques for evaluating beans. As our chief roaster, Cindy Hong, excels at this, I've asked her to co-lead the workshop. The second seminar is supposed to explain the difficulty of building and maintaining a loyal customer base. As assistant manager, Jim Plunkett has always done fine work organizing events to engage the public, so I've asked for his help in this.

If you can make time in your schedule, it would be a great idea to come to at least one session. However, the coffee shop needs a full staff throughout the convention, as business will be quite strong. To keep track of this, could all team members let me know which sessions they'd like to attend at least two weeks before the convention starts on August 23? I've attached the full timetable for reference.

Best regards,

Robert Upton

172. What is the purpose of the e-mail?

(A) To reveal details about an award
(B) To discuss participation in an event
(C) To publicize an upcoming promotion
(D) To announce changes to employee leave

173. What is indicated about Mr. Hu?

(A) He is based in Hawaii.
(B) He is delivering the keynote speech.
(C) He has directed multiple films.
(D) He will come to Upton's Café in August.

174. What is suggested about Ms. Hong and Mr. Plunkett?

(A) They are proficient at their jobs.
(B) They have experience leading workshops.
(C) They are coffee roasting experts.
(D) They are the two longest-serving employees.

175. What are staff members asked to do?

(A) Book tickets for a convention
(B) Submit some information
(C) Fill out an attached form
(D) Work extra additional hours

GO ON TO THE NEXT PAGE

Questions 176-180 refer to the following letter and order.

Emperor Entertainment
1797 Edsel Road, Los Angeles, CA, 90017

February 19

Ms. Isabelle Frankel
Tuttgarter Platz 33
Berlin, Germany

Dear Ms. Frankel,

We have deposited the royalties you have accrued for *Walking to the Moon*. An e-mail was sent to you breaking down the number of sales as well as the royalty payments you will be receiving for the physical and digital copies of your album.

We are pleased to inform you that Emperor Entertainment was named Record Label of the Year by the American Music Committee last December. We owe this to the great artists who have worked with us since we were established eight years ago.

To show our appreciation, every artist under the Emperor Entertainment label will be given an artist discount of half off all merchandise from our online store. Enter code LOY983 during checkout.

Please get in touch with me if I may assist you in any way.

Best wishes,

Marshall Benson

Marshall Benson

---

https://www.emperorent.com/confirmationpage

YOUR ORDER HAS BEEN PLACED!

Receive a free poster on all purchases over $50 during the month of February.

Paid By:	Pamela Coutee
Confirmation E-mail:	pam.coutee@allmail.com
Process Date:	February 23
Shipping Address:	Pamela Coutee 3927 Mesa Drive Las Vegas, NV 89101

1. Turning Point Hooded Sweatshirt (M)	$60.00
2. Signed copy of *Sounds of the Night* by Henry James	$50.00
COUPON (LOY983)	-$55.00
TOTAL	$55.00

*Payment by card ending in 3247

Some items may not be available due to low inventory. You will be notified if any changes are made to your order.

176. Why was the letter sent?

(A) To recommend some music
(B) To invite Ms. Frankel to a celebration
(C) To announce changes to an agreement
(D) To inform Ms. Frankel of a deposit

177. What was sent in a separate message to Ms. Frankel?

(A) An updated logo for an album
(B) A gift certificate
(C) An explanation of sales figures
(D) A tour calendar

178. What does Mr. Benson mention about Emperor Entertainment?

(A) It will hold a concert for its eighth anniversary.
(B) It recruited a new band in December.
(C) It will begin producing movies.
(D) It received recognition.

179. What is implied about Ms. Coutee?

(A) She produced *Sounds of the Night*.
(B) She is an Emperor Entertainment artist.
(C) She went to college with Ms. Frankel.
(D) She has bought merchandise from Emperor Entertainment before.

180. What is indicated about the order?

(A) It includes several clothing items.
(B) It comes with a complimentary poster.
(C) It will be paid for in installments.
(D) It will be delivered overnight.

GO ON TO THE NEXT PAGE

Questions 181-185 refer to the following e-mail and information.

To	cs@travelbuddy.com
From	agruskin@kmail.com
Date	September 3
Subject	Upcoming trip

Hi,

I'm organizing a family trip to Central America either in December or January, and I'm interested in your tour packages. There will be a total of eight people (all adults). We're looking to go somewhere warm and near the water (we're also interested in snorkeling). It is important, however, that we book an accommodation that provides steady wireless service. I will need to lead some very important conference calls while on vacation, and I need to have a stable connection.

I eagerly await your response.

Sincerely,

Abraham Gruskin

	Package Code
Travel Buddy Tour Package Brochure All packages include lodging at 4-star hotels and above with conference centers, 24/7 wireless internet, and award-winning restaurants.	
Costa Rica: December 14-22 Go from the mountain to the beach in this Costa Rican excursion. This journey will take you up to Volcán Irazu 3,432 meters above sea level. Spend some time at the nearby national park. We'll then head towards water and stay in the small village of Manuel Antonio, just a stone's throw away from the beach.	325
Mexico: December 22-31 Enjoy Playa Del Carmen the way it was meant to: relaxing on the white-sand beaches and swimming in turquoise waters. Don't forget to take a day trip to the ancient Mayan site Chichén Itzá, which is ideal for those wanting to learn about old structures.	166
Belize: December 28-January 3 Experience nature at its best in San Ignacio. The surrounding jungle is home to various wildlife, waterfalls, and caves, making it the perfect trip for those who are looking for a more exciting experience. Then, move to Caye Caulker, an island off the coast of Belize for some much needed rest and relaxation at one of the most beautiful beaches that the Caribbean has to offer.	290
Panama: January 5-15 If you're looking for fun in the sun, look no further. Join us in Bocas del Toro and experience one of the Caribbean's best. Snorkel in the crystal clear waters, and see coral reefs up close, or just relax on the beach and get your tan on. And if you enjoy socializing, Bocas del Toro offers some of the best nightlife experiences in Panama. This package is perfect for groups without children.	789

181. What is implied about Mr. Gruskin?

  (A) He will be working during his trip.
  (B) He is relocating to Central America to start a business.
  (C) He has booked tour packages with Travel Buddy before.
  (D) He used to be a professional swimmer.

182. In the e-mail, the word "lead" in paragraph 1, line 5, is closest in meaning to

  (A) manage
  (B) surpass
  (C) influence
  (D) cause

183. What is one thing that all of the tours have in common?

  (A) They involve some time at the beach.
  (B) They are intended for athletes.
  (C) They are created for families with children.
  (D) They last for exactly one week.

184. What tour location is best for people interested in architecture?

  (A) Costa Rica
  (B) Mexico
  (C) Belize
  (D) Panama

185. What tour will Mr. Gruskin most likely select?

  (A) 325
  (B) 166
  (C) 290
  (D) 789

GO ON TO THE NEXT PAGE

TO ALL PATRONS

Upon receiving the third evaluation from city building inspectors last week, the Shelby County Park Association (SCPA) has no choice but to shut down the Wayne Park Conservatory on 11 April. While we were able to preserve the vast majority of the plants in our indoor collection, the 21 January earthquake seems to have done irreparable damage to the structure itself. Sadly, our organization does not have sufficient funds to cover the restoration of this 100-year-old landmark. However, Unity Arboretum in nearby Wellington has graciously offered to accept many of our most beloved plants. They will have a new home in the newly renovated section of Unity Arboretum, set to open on 25 May. The SCPA is currently seeking people to volunteer on 13 April for either of the following duties: transporting plants or organizing the storage rooms. A variety of plants will also be auctioned off to interested individuals and organizations.

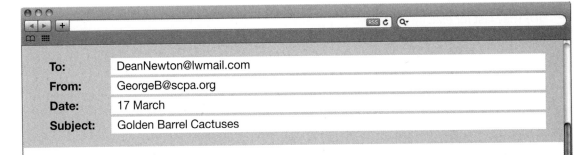

To:	DeanNewton@lwmail.com
From:	GeorgeB@scpa.org
Date:	17 March
Subject:	Golden Barrel Cactuses

Mr. Newton,

We appreciate your message. Our recent decision still grieves us, but we're happy that most of our plants will find a new home.

As to your inquiry, our golden barrel cactuses will be available for purchase. You can view these plants and other items during the auction period (8-11 April). To make an offer on an item, though, you'll have to log in to www.scpa.org/auction_event. The recipients of the items will be announced on 15 April. There will be plenty of decorative items to liven up your living room.

As for your offer to help with relocating plants, please text Mikhail Gabbert at 555-984-1987. He is in charge of coordinating our volunteer efforts.

Best Regards,

George Blanche
Shelby County Park Association, Vice President

Unity Arboretum Layout

Rothman Woods

Elegant walkways lined with spectacular landscaping

Juniper Greenhouse (reopening May 25)

Fern Room	Woodward Botanical Center	Palm House	Aroid Collection

Hillside Gardens

Best location for spring blooms and local plant species

Stevenson Orchid Center

Featuring rare specimens from around the world

186. What is the purpose of the notice?

(A) To discuss plant care tips
(B) To publicize a new park
(C) To solicit funds for a charity
(D) To announce a closing

187. What is suggested about Mr. Newton?

(A) He is interested in donating a number of items.
(B) He is looking for something to decorate his home.
(C) He owns a large collection of cactuses.
(D) He is a member of the Shelby County Park Association.

188. When will Mr. Newton most likely volunteer at the Wayne Park Conservatory?

(A) On April 8
(B) On April 11
(C) On April 13
(D) On April 15

189. According to the e-mail, what can patrons do on the association's Web site?

(A) Register as a volunteer
(B) Sign up for a newsletter
(C) Bid on an item
(D) Post an article

190. Where will some objects from the Wayne Park Conservatory be housed?

(A) In Rothman Woods
(B) In Juniper Greenhouse
(C) In Hillside Gardens
(D) In Stevenson Orchid Center

GO ON TO THE NEXT PAGE

Questions 191-195 refer to the following text message, schedule, and e-mail.

To: Terrell Elway
From: Lupita Monroe
Time: 02:14 P.M., July 10

- -

Terrell,

Chester's World notified us that they won't be able to perform at Music on the Rocks next month. This means that there is an opening on the Littleton Stage at 4:45 P.M. If you'd like to take this spot, please contact me immediately. The promotional posters must be printed tomorrow afternoon.

Music on the Rocks
Performance Lineup: Sunday, 15 August

	12:00 P.M.	2:15 P.M.	4:45 P.M.	6:00 P.M.
Copperton Stage		Jubilee Crew		The Counters
Littleton Stage	Marsha Payne		The Writing	Angelus
Brandly Stage	Vince Clip	Social System	Reignmen	

The first 100 guests through the gate will be given a 20 percent off voucher for any souvenirs purchased. All attendees will receive a complimentary T-shirt upon entry. Outside food and drinks are strictly prohibited. It is recommended that you bring extra layers of clothing, as the venue is located at a high altitude. The show will go on rain or shine. For more information about the performers and the venue, please visit www.musicontherocks.com.

```
TO          :  lupitam@musicontherocks.com
FROM        :  chadwick@lockstudios.com
DATE        :  28 August
SUBJECT     :  Pictures
ATTACHMENT  :  Mountain photo
```

Hello Lupita,

Thank you for the opportunity to shoot the concert! I'm currently going through the pictures, but I have attached one that caught my eye. This picture was taken just as the Jubilee Crew was walking onto the stage. I really like this shot because it shows the entire crowd as well as the Pike mountain range in the background. I think you should consider using it on the homepage of your Web site. As I continue to look through the photos, I'll set aside a few that I think will look good in next month's issue of *Music Today*.

Talk to you soon.

Chadwick Lock
Lock Studios

191. According to the text message, what will happen on July 11?

(A) Chester's World will go on tour.
(B) Ms. Monroe will sing at a concert.
(C) A performance stage will be built.
(D) An advertisement will be printed.

192. What is the name of Mr. Elway's band?

(A) The Writing
(B) Reignmen
(C) The Counters
(D) Angelus

193. What is indicated on the schedule?

(A) Food will be provided by the venue.
(B) Souvenirs can be purchased online.
(C) Free merchandise will be given to attendees.
(D) The concert will be postponed in the event of rain.

194. What is suggested about Mr. Lock's photos?

(A) They will be available for purchase on a Web site.
(B) They will be featured in a publication.
(C) They were signed by the performers.
(D) They were taken on the Pike mountain range.

195. When did Mr. Lock take the photo he attached to the e-mail?

(A) At 12:00 P.M.
(B) At 2:15 P.M.
(C) At 4:45 P.M.
(D) At 6:00 P.M.

GO ON TO THE NEXT PAGE

Questions 196-200 refer to the following Web page, e-mail, and article.

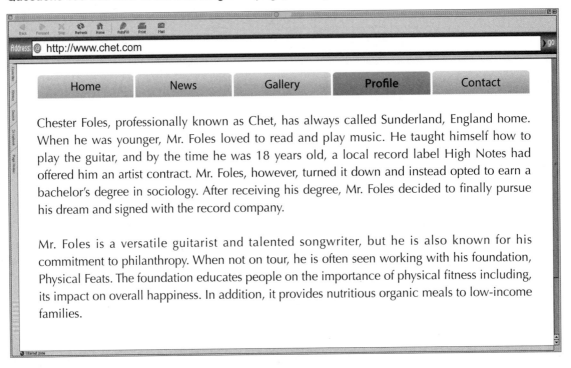

Home | News | Gallery | **Profile** | Contact

Chester Foles, professionally known as Chet, has always called Sunderland, England home. When he was younger, Mr. Foles loved to read and play music. He taught himself how to play the guitar, and by the time he was 18 years old, a local record label High Notes had offered him an artist contract. Mr. Foles, however, turned it down and instead opted to earn a bachelor's degree in sociology. After receiving his degree, Mr. Foles decided to finally pursue his dream and signed with the record company.

Mr. Foles is a versatile guitarist and talented songwriter, but he is also known for his commitment to philanthropy. When not on tour, he is often seen working with his foundation, Physical Feats. The foundation educates people on the importance of physical fitness including, its impact on overall happiness. In addition, it provides nutritious organic meals to low-income families.

TO	Olga Mazur <omazur@raltut.com>
FROM	Kenny Uma <kuma@raltut.com>
DATE	July 22
SUBJECT	New endorser

Dear Olga,

As we discussed, I was looking for a candidate to become our celebrity spokesperson as we enter the UK market. I came across Chester Foles, a musician from Sunderland, England, and I think he fits our profile. His non-profit organization focuses on well-being, which has a natural connection to our products at Raltut. You can find more information on him at his Web site, www.chet.com. If you think he would be a good fit, I will contact his team to gauge their level of interest.

I also spent some time on the phone with Ms. Sakic this afternoon. She mentioned that the marketing campaign has been put on hold. She said that as long as we find an endorser by November, we will be fine.

Sincerely,

Kenny

Raltut Crosses the Pond

Sunderland (3 September) — Raltut, the American organic snack manufacturer, has made its way into the UK marketplace with Sunderland-raised artist Chester "Chet" Foles as the new face of the company. A teaser video was released on Tuesday, giving viewers a glimpse of Mr. Foles and some of the products that will be launched. The advertising campaign will kick off in stages starting next week.

The organic snack company, based in Boulder, Colorado, has been enjoying success ever since new CEO Rhonda Faulk took over. After expanding into Japan nearly a decade ago, the company is now looking to repeat its success on the other side of the world.

---

196. According to the Web page, what did Mr. Foles receive before joining a record label?

(A) Singing lessons
(B) Exercise equipment
(C) A new guitar
(D) An undergraduate degree

197. Why does Mr. Uma consider Mr. Foles a suitable celebrity endorser?

(A) Raltut makes musical instruments.
(B) Raltut is headquartered in Sunderland.
(C) His singing abilities are widely recognized.
(D) His foundation promotes healthy eating.

198. What does the e-mail suggest about Ms. Sakic?

(A) She is Mr. Foles's manager.
(B) She is a colleague of Mr. Uma and Ms. Mazur.
(C) She is the current endorser of Raltut.
(D) She has visited Mr. Foles's Web page.

199. What is indicated about Mr. Foles?

(A) He has invested money in Raltut.
(B) He joined a campaign earlier than planned.
(C) He will be donating all of his proceeds.
(D) He recently released a new album.

200. What information about Raltut is included in the article?

(A) How long it has been in business
(B) Where it is located
(C) Who founded the company
(D) Which of its products is most popular

Stop! This is the end of the test. If you finish before time is called, you may go back to Part 5, 6, and 7 and check your work.

ACTUAL TEST 02 해설서 p.190

101. Liberty Fashion makes their ------- of summer clothing with the highest quality fabric.

(A) result
(B) addition
(C) line
(D) usage

102. A group of marine scientists will be brought ------- to try to increase tuna farm yields.

(A) among
(B) since
(C) together
(D) any

103. After the parade ------- Huber Park, the town will conduct its tree lighting ceremony.

(A) spins
(B) rolls
(C) circles
(D) loosens

104. Keitel's Cleaners provides clients with discrete document disposal service at an ------- price.

(A) affordability
(B) affording
(C) affordable
(D) affords

105. The high cost of comprehensive employee health ------- poses a financial burden to small-sized businesses.

(A) insure
(B) insures
(C) insurance
(D) insured

106. After selling five hundred thousand shares in a month, Kopac Mining is now ------- Warsaw's fastest-growing companies.

(A) over
(B) into
(C) against
(D) among

107. A built-in red light serves as an ------- to users when the cord is left plugged in.

(A) example
(B) allowance
(C) administration
(D) alert

108. Employees traveling for business will share accommodations ------- they request prior approval for a private room.

(A) still
(B) however
(C) unless
(D) likewise

109. In July, a shopping mall will be opening in the vicinity, offering convenient eating options with a ------- atmosphere.

(A) charmingly
(B) charming
(C) charmer
(D) charm

110. The Johannesburg Daily News is broadcast ------- on television and their Web site.

(A) collectively
(B) instinctively
(C) mutually
(D) simultaneously

111. The wardrobe for the cast of the musical *The Emperor Dragonfly* has been ------- labeled.

(A) clear
(B) clearly
(C) clearing
(D) clearest

112. The company contracted by the city council has used a stone wall to create a strict ------- for the town.

(A) boundary
(B) building
(C) origin
(D) inventory

113. Traffic on Summit Boulevard ------ comes to a standstill when major sports competitions are held at Jefferson Stadium.

(A) over
(B) yet
(C) evenly
(D) nearly

114. Markham Supermarket delivers groceries at no charge ------- a 10-kilometer radius.

(A) nearby
(B) within
(C) during
(D) except

115. Shwester Medical Group never ------- patient data to other parties without the individual's official permission.

(A) handles
(B) discloses
(C) recovers
(D) gathers

116. Researchers at DRI Medical announced outcomes much like those published -------.

(A) further
(B) elsewhere
(C) wherever
(D) furthermore

117. Ms. Yamato's budget estimate is ------- too low now, given the alterations to the building plans.

(A) certainty
(B) certain
(C) certainly
(D) certainties

118. Ms. Lang suggested sending a text message to clients ------- after their monthly payment is received.

(A) more immediate
(B) immediate
(C) most immediately
(D) immediately

119. Due to increasing demands for sustainability, the solar energy market is ------- to grow over the next few years.

(A) projector
(B) projected
(C) projection
(D) projecting

120. The renovated wing of the museum will feature a more spacious food court, a second gift shop, more exhibit halls, and ------- parking.

(A) permissible
(B) positive
(C) improved
(D) heavy

GO ON TO THE NEXT PAGE

121. ------- increased admission fees, every show of Alexia Montez's new musical for the entire summer season has sold out.

(A) Despite
(B) Prior to
(C) During
(D) Except for

122. The high amount of risk linked with investing in the stock market ------- justifies a thorough studying of the company's performance using financial statements.

(A) initially
(B) concisely
(C) surely
(D) extensively

123. The marketing team recently surveyed customers to ensure our products work as -------.

(A) intentional
(B) to intend
(C) intend
(D) intended

124. Ms. Bernal was pleased to get a ------- that her firm soon will appear on the Top Ten Canadian Companies list.

(A) notifies
(B) notify
(C) notifying
(D) notification

125. When writing your self-evaluation report, make sure to record only the significant accomplishments and disregard ------- details.

(A) insufficient
(B) constricted
(C) compulsory
(D) incidental

126. Academic dissertations must be handed in by this Thursday and should include an outline and a one-page -------.

(A) abstract
(B) denotation
(C) knowledge
(D) expedition

127. *Travel Africa Magazine* hails Mangaluru Hotel as surprisingly inexpensive considering its exceptional ------- and central location.

(A) testimonies
(B) subsidies
(C) remedies
(D) amenities

128. Please explain your concern with the accommodation ------- we can address it promptly.

(A) so that
(B) still
(C) or
(D) for example

129. Mr. Hwang is ------- that a replacement for a receptionist can be found by Monday.

(A) remote
(B) doubtful
(C) hesitant
(D) exemplary

130. Ms. Bryant will be invited to interview for the open position first because she has the best -------.

(A) permits
(B) portions
(C) credentials
(D) agreements

PART 6

Directions: Read the texts that follow. A word, phrase, or sentence is missing in some of the sentences. Four answer choices are given below each of these sentences. Select the best answer to complete the text. Then mark the letter (A), (B), (C), or (D) on your answer sheet.

Questions 131-134 refer to the following article.

JAKARTA (5 November) – Lorenzen Group, a leader in the international ------- industry, announced
                                                                     131.
a major update to its Web site this morning. The Web site, LorenzenLook.com, ------- in partnership
                                                                               132.
with Morales Design and launched late Tuesday evening. LorenzenLook.com now gives customers
a chance to browse ------- all of the company's clothing, from previews of next season's offerings to
                     133.
discounted casual wear. Customers using the site will have exclusive access to discounts and the
ability to order certain items early. -------. This will make it easy for Lorenzen's online customers to
                                      134.
learn about the best deals before anyone else.

131. (A) financial
(B) sports
(C) fashion
(D) technology

132. (A) is being redesigned
(B) was redesigned
(C) will be redesigned
(D) is redesigned

133. (A) with
(B) after
(C) middle
(D) through

134. (A) The sale is scheduled to last for the next two weeks.
(B) LorenzenLook.com even sends reminders when these offers become available.
(C) The winter collection has been widely praised by members of the media.
(D) Loyalty club members can use their points at most major retailers.

GO ON TO THE NEXT PAGE

Questions 135-138 refer to the following memo.

MEMO

To: All Starzone Staff
From: Sara Jordan
Date: July 12
Subject: Customer Data Update

Please note that as of July 24, new regulations on the storage of customer data will come into ------- . All information ------- from customers must be stored securely using the new protection
135.   136.
methods. Customer data should also be kept anonymous whenever possible so that even if a breach
does take place, no identifying information is leaked. ------- . We have sent an e-mail with the new
137.
instructions and regulations, so please take some time this weekend to read through it carefully. If
you are unclear about the ------- , please e-mail us back with any questions.
138.

Thank you.

Sara Jordan
IT Team

---

135. (A) effective
　　　(B) effect
　　　(C) effectively
　　　(D) effected

136. (A) presented
　　　(B) sorted
　　　(C) requested
　　　(D) collected

137. (A) While this is unlikely, we should still be
　　　　prepared.
　　　(B) A new suggestion can be made if you
　　　　desire.
　　　(C) Lawmakers continue to debate this
　　　　topic.
　　　(D) A vote will be taking place next week.

138. (A) changes
　　　(B) formats
　　　(C) events
　　　(D) sites

To: All Sales Staff
From: Ray Tran
Date: September 1
Subject: New Prospect Tracking Software
Attachment: timetable.doc

Starting on September 15, Bakersfield Insurance Company ------- from using a personal computer-based prospect tracking system to a new smartphone application called ProTrac. With this ------- application, our sales consultants will have the ability to access all client and prospect information and update it as needed from any location. They can also use it to create new account profiles.

Sales staff will be required to track all of their activity using the application, and data will be reviewed by branch managers for employees' quarterly evaluations.

Training classes will be offered in the second week of September. -------. If you cannot make it to your designated time -------, please contact me.

Best Regards,

Ray Tran

---

139. (A) has switched
(B) would switch
(C) switched
(D) is going to switch

140. (A) traditional
(B) convenient
(C) temporary
(D) regular

141. (A) This was the best way to cut costs.
(B) Refer to the attached file for more information.
(C) Please submit it by the end of the week.
(D) Results so far have been excellent.

142. (A) restriction
(B) slot
(C) consequence
(D) evaluation

Questions 143-146 refer to the following announcement.

LEXINGTON (13 February) — With the winter season ------- reaching its end, Expediters Inc. will
                                                         143.
be releasing a free newsletter filled with great travel deals and advice. In the newsletter, we have
included ------- on the hottest places to visit this year as well as some hidden gems located in the
         144.
city.

To receive our free newsletter, all you have to do is sign up on our Web site and answer a few basic
questions. -------. Users who sign up and complete the questions ------- the newsletter via e-mail.
           145.   146.
The newsletter will also have special coupons that will provide discounts for your travels.

143. (A) suddenly
     (B) immediately
     (C) quickly
     (D) often

144. (A) suggestions
     (B) imitations
     (C) invitations
     (D) criticisms

145. (A) International travel may not be a
         popular choice.
     (B) The newsletter is sponsored by
         TravelGate.
     (C) We will be updating our Web site in the
         future.
     (D) The survey will be anonymous and
         securely stored.

146. (A) will receive
     (B) had received
     (C) receiving
     (D) will have received

PART 7

Directions: In this part, you will read a selection of texts, such as magazine and newspaper articles, letters, and instant messages. Each text or set of texts is followed by several questions. Select the best answer for each question and mark the letter (A), (B), (C), or (D) on your answer sheet.

Questions 147-148 refer to the following notice.

**Huntington-Wells University
Library Services**

November 7
All Guests

Our printing policies have been revised. Please note the following:

· Guests with a HWU library card are now allotted 50 print credits per week.
· Printing in color is available for 3 print credits per page.
· Credits will no longer transfer over to the following week.
· All computers now print double-sided by default.
· Staff will no longer change paper for custom printing projects.

Please direct comments and questions to the Reference Desk on the 2nd Floor.

We appreciate your cooperation.

Huntington-Wells University Library Services

147. Where would the notice most likely be posted?

(A) In a dormitory room
(B) In a computer lab
(C) In a product manual
(D) In a class catalog

148. What is one purpose of the notice?

(A) To provide some updated guidelines
(B) To encourage participation in a survey
(C) To announce the purchase of some new printers
(D) To report on the progress of a construction project

GO ON TO THE NEXT PAGE

How to build your brand-new Trappa Chair (MZDA 323) from Wronken Home Store

1. Place chair body on a flat surface with chair back facing down and armrests facing up.
2. Using the tool provided, connect the chair back to the aluminum seat frame with the shorter bolts, taking care not to overtighten.
3. Insert legs into the slots at the bottom of the seat frame, ensuring that each slides into its appropriate slot (note: the front left leg is labeled "Wronken" in yellow lettering).
4. Tighten the longer bolts to secure the legs.
5. Place the chair upright and put the seat cushion on the frame.

149. According to the instructions, what part should the builder attach to the chair back?

(A) The arms
(B) The legs
(C) The seat frame
(D) The cushion

150. What is marked on one of the parts?

(A) A brand name
(B) A company logo
(C) An item price
(D) A model number

Hello Angie,

Please review my schedule below. David booked me a hotel room near the beach in Hammersted — I can't wait to get out of the city! I just finished making the slide show for the workshop I'm leading at Hammersted Convention Hall. I'll be back in the office on Monday. If you can, keep my schedule clear for the beginning of the week as I need some time to work on the blueprints for Dr. Anderson.

Brent O'Keefe's Schedule Friday, May 1	
8:15 A.M.	Progress update with Jana Abernathy from the Development Team
9:30 A.M.	New design presentation for Hamilton project, Todd Chen
10:45 A.M.	Employee evaluation with Joaquin Berry
2:00 P.M.	Summary of Q2 budget, Sven Torbjorn
4:00 P.M.	Leave office
7:00 P.M.	Check into a hotel in Hammersted

Brent

151. What will Mr. O'Keefe do in Hammersted?

(A) Take a tour
(B) Conduct a seminar
(C) Create some blueprints
(D) Enroll in a swimming class

152. Who most likely will introduce a new idea?

(A) Ms. Abernathy
(B) Mr. Chen
(C) Mr. Berry
(D) Ms. Torbjorn

GO ON TO THE NEXT PAGE

Questions 153-154 refer to the following text message chain.

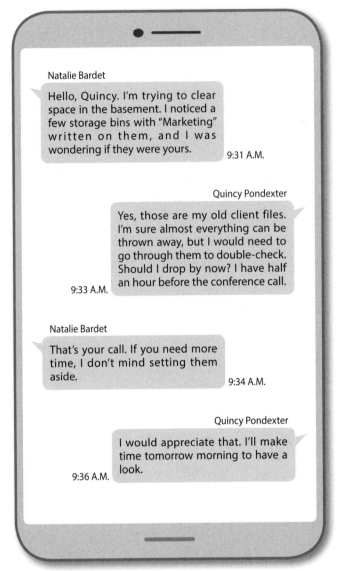

Natalie Bardet

Hello, Quincy. I'm trying to clear space in the basement. I noticed a few storage bins with "Marketing" written on them, and I was wondering if they were yours.
9:31 A.M.

Quincy Pondexter

Yes, those are my old client files. I'm sure almost everything can be thrown away, but I would need to go through them to double-check. Should I drop by now? I have half an hour before the conference call.
9:33 A.M.

Natalie Bardet

That's your call. If you need more time, I don't mind setting them aside.
9:34 A.M.

Quincy Pondexter

I would appreciate that. I'll make time tomorrow morning to have a look.
9:36 A.M.

153. Why did Ms. Bardet contact Mr. Pondexter?

(A) To request assistance with clearing out a basement
(B) To check if he needs additional storage space
(C) To find out the location of a room key
(D) To see if some documents belong to him

154. At 9:34 A.M., what does Ms. Bardet mean when she writes, "That's your call"?

(A) She can organize some client records for Mr. Pondexter.
(B) Mr. Pondexter can select which bins to use.
(C) She can set up equipment for a conference call.
(D) Mr. Pondexter can decide when to inspect some files.

Questions 155-157 refer to the following Web page.

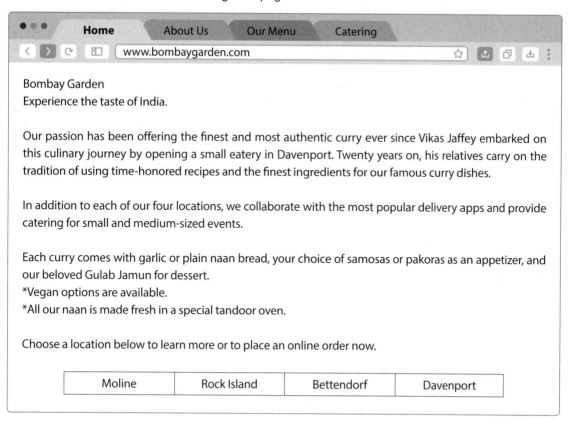

155. What is true about the Bombay Garden location in Davenport?

(A) It was the first to open.
(B) It does not offer catering.
(C) It has a new owner.
(D) It is being expanded.

156. What is indicated about Bombay Garden's curry dishes?

(A) They are imported from India.
(B) They are made from family recipes.
(C) They are inexpensively priced.
(D) They are made in a special oven.

157. What is NOT included with an order of curry?

(A) A beverage
(B) An appetizer
(C) A dessert
(D) Naan bread

GO ON TO THE NEXT PAGE

Dear Guest,

We would like to welcome you to your stay at the Ridgemont Resort. —[1]—. We are honored to have you as a guest. Due to the high number of guests we generally have, we would like to share some rules we expect our guests here to adhere to.

The facilities at our resort, such as the pool and gym, are open for all to use at no additional charge. —[2]—. However, we ask that excessive noise be avoided so as not to disturb other guests. Additionally, there is a botanical garden located near the back entrance of the resort. —[3]—. While it is open, please refrain from veering off the path. Finally, if you are staying with children under the age of 12, we ask that they be supervised at all times. —[4]—. Thank you, and we hope you enjoy your stay.

158. What is the purpose of the note?

(A) To promote a new service
(B) To clarify a price
(C) To recommend some activities
(D) To inform guests of some rules

159. What is NOT indicated about the Ridgemont Resort?

(A) It is normally busy with guests.
(B) It is located by a lake.
(C) It has a back entrance.
(D) It offers facilities that are free to use.

160. In which of the positions marked [1], [2], [3], and [4] does the following sentence best belong?

"If you have any other questions, please call the front desk at 555-1837."

(A) [1]
(B) [2]
(C) [3]
(D) [4]

Turning Old to New

Sandra Lim

Bristol (10 October) — In a joint press conference yesterday, the mayor announced a three-way collaboration to build smart charging stations in a number of locations in the metro area by making use of outdated telephone booths. Each station will serve a number of functions: allowing electric bicycle, scooter, and smartphone charging, providing tourist information, and offering coupons to nearby shops and restaurants, while being an access point for high-speed WiFi. Registered users will be able to use this service for 30 minutes at a time without charge.

The collaboration will feature the Irish technology firm O'Rourke Enterprises, regional architecture company JFC Designs, as well as Newport-based Shenk Communications. O'Rourke and JFC will partner on technology, design, and construction, while Shenk Communications will provide internet connectivity. Advertising and subscription fees will ensure the project will have a minimum cost to taxpayers.

The stations will debut over the next several months, with 25 stations due to go into service in December, and another 75 expected by next summer. O'Rourke has experience with comparable projects in Europe. Its smart charging stations in Dublin, launched 3 years ago, fuel 5,000 vehicles daily, and have helped thousands top up depleted smartphone batteries.

161. What is mentioned about the project?

(A) It will utilize obsolete telephone booths.
(B) It will be paid for with an increased tax.
(C) It has been scheduled to conclude in December.
(D) It has increased the number of visitors to the area.

162. What does the article NOT indicate will be a feature of the stations?

(A) Local information
(B) Unlimited Internet Service
(C) Restaurant vouchers
(D) Cellphone charging

163. What is indicated about O'Rourke Enterprises?

(A) It has been acquired by JFC Designs.
(B) It has built similar stations in the past.
(C) Its internet services are widely used.
(D) Its headquarters is in Bristol.

GO ON TO THE NEXT PAGE

Questions 164-167 refer to the following online chat discussion.

Crispin Adams (3:04 P.M.)
Good afternoon. Shelly McSteel's producer just submitted a new mix of the last few tracks, and they sound great. It's time to put this record out!

Devon Carter (3:05 P.M.)
Fantastic news. When are the fans going to be able to buy it?

Crispin Adams (3:07 P.M.)
In late spring. Third week of May. First, we need the Legal Department to authorize some samples, hire a graphic designer for the cover art, and arrange interviews with the press. Oh, and we need some promotional photos. Let's get those done soon.

Devon Carter (3:08 P.M.)
Absolutely. I remember she wanted to do a photo shoot in Great Basin Park.

Crispin Adams (3:09 P.M.)
Mina, would you be able to take some shots of Ms. McSteel next week in Great Basin Park?

Mina Doan (3:10 P.M.)
Definitely. Just let me know where she wants to meet exactly. Thursday would be good.

Devon Carter (3:12 P.M.)
She just messaged me. Sounds like Friday is the best day for her.

Crispin Adams (3:13 P.M.)
Mina, do you mind scheduling around Ms. McSteel? And Devon, please keep Ms. McSteel updated.

Devon Carter (3:14 P.M.)
Certainly. I'll call her when we're done.

Mina Doan (3:15 P.M.)
I can make it work.

Crispin Adams (3:16 P.M.)
OK. That should do it. Thanks, everyone.

SEND

164. What will happen in May?

(A) An interview will be conducted.
(B) An album will be released.
(C) A song will be recorded.
(D) An exhibition will be opened.

165. Who most likely is Ms. Doan?

(A) A graphic artist
(B) A journalist
(C) A photographer
(D) A singer

166. What will Mr. Carter most likely do next?

(A) Edit a new album
(B) Conduct an interview
(C) Call the Legal Department
(D) Confirm some arrangements

167. At 3:15 P.M. what does Ms. Doan mean when she writes, "I can make it work"?

(A) She will adjust a release date.
(B) She will be able to bring some equipment.
(C) She will adjust her schedule.
(D) She will listen to some tracks.

CHENNAI TIMES

(March 10) — Currently, two popular social media firms are engaged in a competition to acquire the most users in India. Social media giants, Instabook and Chidiya, have made it clear that they are vying for the top spot in the country. –[1]–.

Last summer, Instabook, the Silicon Valley-based tech business, finally launched its mobile app in India. –[2]–. It was already a leading firm, with tens of millions of users around the world. In contrast, Chidiya is mostly unknown outside the subcontinent but has attracted a huge user base in India. Chidiya's reach is already impressive, and it has become one of the nation's most trusted sources of information.

–[3]–. Social media firms, including Seoul-based Murmur, have been unhappy with restrictions the government has placed on content that can be shared, especially as these restrictions created changes in their global platforms. Consequently, Murmur closed its local offices and pulled its service from popular Indian app stores after only one year of activity in the country.

Chidiya, on the other hand, has an edge over other businesses. –[4]–. The firm is dedicated to checking the accuracy of content posted on its site. Chidiya has also adapted well to the needs of its ethnically-diverse users, providing eight different language options on its app. Additionally, the company appeals to younger users through pop music sponsorships and exclusive music releases. Instabook has reached more global users, but it will have a hard time overcoming an established brand like Chidiya.

Salmaan Reddy

168. What is the article mainly discussing?

(A) Innovative marketing techniques
(B) A rise in engineering positions
(C) Popular electronics in India
(D) A rivalry between some companies

169. What is indicated about Murmur?

(A) It briefly did business with Indian customers.
(B) It is popular among younger users.
(C) It was founded one year ago.
(D) It recently moved its headquarters to Silicon Valley.

170. What is NOT mentioned as a strength of Chidiya?

(A) It confirms the accuracy of online posts.
(B) It has branches in many countries.
(C) It offers a program in multiple languages.
(D) It provides access to exclusive music.

171. In which of the positions marked [1], [2], [3], and [4] does the following sentence best belong?

"Strict regulations have presented a major obstacle."

(A) [1]
(B) [2]
(C) [3]
(D) [4]

GO ON TO THE NEXT PAGE

Questions 172-175 refer to the following letter.

October 12

Ms. Carolyn Carter
Oasis Architecture
5 Kimberly Leys
Carleton, OH 33022

Dear Ms. Carter,

The School of Architecture and Planning at Carleton University would like to extend an invitation for you to be one of our speakers at the opening ceremony of our new building, the Osman Building. We would be honored to have you as a speaker as a distinguished alumnus of our school, as well as your contributions to the design of the building. Without your firm's assistance during the planning stages, the Osman Building would never have been possible.

The opening ceremony is due to take place on Saturday, October 24, with the event beginning at 10 A.M. We will start the day with speeches from invited guests and then commence with the ribbon-cutting ceremony. A local newspaper will be covering the event, so we will be having a photo shoot as well. There will also be a paid-for lunch catered by Papermoon Café. The day will be rounded out with a closing speech by Professor Suzanne Park, the Head of School.

We would be honored if you could join us for the ceremony on October 24. If you have any questions, I can be reached at 197-555-4682. If you could confirm your availability at your earliest convenience, that would be highly appreciated.

Sincerely,

Lance Luna
Senior Lecturer, School of Architecture and Planning
Carleton University

172. What is the purpose of the letter?

(A) To request assistance from Ms. Carter on a new project
(B) To invite Ms. Carter to attend an opening event
(C) To clarify a misunderstanding about Carleton University
(D) To inquire about the possibility of a partnership

173. What is indicated about Ms. Carter?

(A) She gives lectures on architecture.
(B) She attended Carleton University.
(C) She started her own business.
(D) She donates to the school regularly.

174 What is true about Oasis Architecture?

(A) It offers internships to students from Carleton University.
(B) It will soon relocate its head office.
(C) It has been featured in the newspaper.
(D) It consulted on the planning of the Osman Building.

175. What is NOT mentioned in the letter as part of the ceremony?

(A) A closing speech
(B) A photoshoot
(C) An afterparty
(D) Speeches from guests

GO ON TO THE NEXT PAGE

Questions 176-180 refer to the following Web page and e-mail.

Address: http://newdelhitexglobe.co.in

Millennium Rockets

We are now accepting bookings for shared spaces on our launches for the next year. With us, not only will you get the cheapest rates in the industry, but you'll also receive the best service. Check our schedule below and see if we can help you with your upcoming endeavors.

Launch Number	Launch Date	Orbit Height	Launch Site Satellite	Weight Limit
1	1st Quarter	3,800 km	India	250 kg
2	1st Quarter	37,000 km	China	50 kg
3	2nd Quarter	3,000 km	United States	50 kg
4	3rd Quarter	5,400 km	Russia	175 kg
5	3rd Quarter	37,000 km	China	250 kg
6	4th Quarter	3,000 km	Norway	175 kg

To	Garrett Hampton <ghampton@spinstitute.com>
From	Brenda Lowe <blowe@spinstitute.com>
Date	December 2
Subject	Satellite Launch Dates

Dear Mr. Hampton,

Based on your recommendation, I have received Millennium's launch schedule for the next year. While their dates are not set in stone, they have given rough launch dates. Based on our needs, only two of the satellites they are launching are high enough for our requirements. However, one of them launches in the first quarter, which may be too early for us. The other launches in the third quarter. I understand that we want to launch as soon as possible but launching in the first quarter may cause us to rush over details. Therefore, I would like to know whether delaying the launch date for the SKY satellite is at all on the cards.

My preferred option would be to delay our launch until the third quarter so that we can mitigate any risks possible. This will give us enough time to finetune our components so that our broadcasts are correctly received by the satellite dishes. Please let me know if the above plan is viable, and I will communicate with Millennium accordingly.

Sincerely,

Brenda Lowe, SP Institute, SKY Project Team

176. From which country will Millennium Rockets launch a rocket during the second quarter?

(A) India
(B) Norway
(C) the United States
(D) China

177. What is the purpose of the e-mail?

(A) To postpone an existing plan
(B) To request additional funding
(C) To suggest a new product
(D) To explain a company's policy

178. What launch number does Ms. Lowe recommend they prepare for?

(A) Launch 2
(B) Launch 3
(C) Launch 4
(D) Launch 5

179. What does the e-mail imply is the function of the SKY satellite?

(A) Television programming
(B) Weather forecasting
(C) Airplane communications
(D) Space exploration

180. In the e-mail, the word "mitigate" in paragraph 2, line 2, is closest in meaning to

(A) burden
(B) reduce
(C) satisfy
(D) divide

GO ON TO THE NEXT PAGE

Questions 181-185 refer to the following e-mail and schedule.

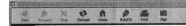

To	: Epic Industries Department Managers
From	: Justin Sherman
Date	: 2 December
Subject	: Meeting
Attachment	: finalized_schedule

Hello,

Please remember that there will be a managers' meeting tomorrow at 10 A.M. Attached is the finalized meeting schedule. You'll see that another item has been included in the initial schedule. Our sales manager, Phan Nguyen, will discuss the details of our latest product launch. His talk will run for about half an hour.

Prior to the meeting, please make sure that you have looked over the company's business plan for the next quarter. In addition, please prepare copies of your most recent budget report and estimated expenses for the following quarter.

Please contact me if you have any questions.

Justin Sherman

Epic Industries Managers' Meeting

Place: 5th Floor Meeting Room
Date: 3 December
Time: 10 A.M.

Speaker	Subject	Details
Phan Nguyen	Car Navigator	• Analyze the sales figures of the mobile application
Patrick Bell	Company Expenses	• Review projected costs and current budgets
Justin Sherman	Progress Updates	• Present any issues that have emerged • Review timeline and ability to complete projects on time
Amber Vessel	Marketing Strategies	• Discussion of the best platforms to advertise apps on
Michelle Finney, Co-founder of Work Together, Inc.	Expanding Your Demographic	• How to capture people outside your target market

181. In the e-mail, what does Mr. Sherman imply about the meeting?

(A) It will take longer than expected.
(B) It will include a catered meal.
(C) It will be attended by some investors.
(D) It will be led by a newly hired manager.

182. What item on the agenda is new?

(A) Car Navigator
(B) Progress Updates
(C) Marketing Strategies
(D) Expanding Your Demographic

183. What does Mr. Sherman ask meeting attendees to prepare?

(A) Client contact information
(B) A revised schedule
(C) A list of qualified candidates
(D) Updated financial files

184. What does the schedule indicate about Ms. Finney?

(A) She is an expert in managing finances.
(B) She will take part in the meeting via videoconference.
(C) She formed her own company.
(D) She is a colleague of Mr. Sherman.

185. What does Epic Industries most likely sell?

(A) Compact vehicles
(B) Electronic devices
(C) Home appliances
(D) Software programs

GO ON TO THE NEXT PAGE

Questions 186-190 refer to the following proposal forms and e-mail.

Precision Painters PROPOSAL

Client:	Elio Marketing
Address:	39 Mt. Taylor Drive St. Heliers, Auckland, NZ 6022
Date:	6 February

Precision Painters will paint, coat, and finish all the walls indicated in the contract and applied per the manufacturer's specifications. Items on walls and shelves will be carefully placed in boxes and returned to their original positions after completion. Our work is guaranteed for one year (complete warranty details are on our Web site).

Service Charge: $7,450 + tax (includes the referral discount)
This amount is to be paid immediately upon completion of the project.

Prepared by:	Denise Nel
Delivered to:	
Date:	

PROPOSAL

CONTRACTOR	CLIENT:
Handy Painters	Elio Marketing
32 Robina Court	39 Mt. Taylor Drive
Burswood, Manukau, NZ 2105	St. Heliers, Auckland, NZ 6022

Work Scope
- Preparation and application of paint to all indicated sections.
- Hardware, accessories, and similar items on the surface to be painted must be removed by the client.
- Sheets and tape will be provided to cover desks.
 *Note: All work comes with a six-month warranty that covers all painted wall finishes.

Company Proposal
- Handy Painters proposes to complete the above work at the price of $6,350 including tax, paint, and labor fees.
- Payment is due within seven days of finishing the paint job.
- This proposal is valid for one month.

Submitted by: Janice Hart
Date: 9 February

Client Signature: _____
Date: _____

TO:	all@eliomarketing.com
FROM:	Renée Young, President
DATE:	1 March
SUBJECT:	Interior Painting

As many of you know, we'll be repainting our walls starting next Monday. It will take approximately one week for the job to be completed. As a result, we need to prepare a few things. First, you'll need to protect your belongings from being damaged by the paint. We will provide drapes to place over your desks. Don't worry about the pictures on the wall — the contractor will handle those. Since we won't be able to work in the office while the painters are here, I've rented a work space for next week (more details will be sent soon). Thank you for your understanding.

186. Who most likely is Ms. Nel?

(A) An employee of Precision Painters
(B) A supervisor at Elio Marketing
(C) A friend of Ms. Young
(D) A freelance painter

187. When should customers pay Handy Painters for their services?

(A) Within one week of the project's completion
(B) Upon getting the electronic billing statement
(C) One month after receiving the proposal
(D) The day of signing the proposal form

188. What do both companies offer to customers?

(A) Some protective equipment
(B) A service warranty
(C) Payment installment options
(D) A wide selection of paint colors

189. What does Ms. Young ask all employees to do?

(A) Work remotely on Monday
(B) Choose a proposal
(C) Remove items from the walls
(D) Cover their workstations

190. What is suggested about Elio Marketing?

(A) It recently moved into a new building.
(B) It has worked with Handy Painters before.
(C) It hired Precision Painters.
(D) It will be closed for one week.

GO ON TO THE NEXT PAGE

The Trinchera Innovation Trade Fair for Innovation Returns!
Saturday and Sunday, July 5-6
Trinchera Stadium

The Trinchera Innovation Trade Fair is back this year, and this year's iteration is sure to be the best one yet. For one, we have invited some very important guest speakers. While we are confirming our full list of speakers, we can confirm that Darnell Sutton, CEO of Pantomime, will be in attendance. As always, vendors who participated in last year's event will be eligible for a 25 percent discount.

The Trinchera Innovation Trade Fair is the best way for small businesses to showcase their products and services to the public. Like every year, only small-sized (less than 15 employees) enterprises will be allowed to purchase booths. This is in line with our goal to promote entrepreneurship in Trinchera. There will be a reception for all vendors the night before the event begins. This is a great opportunity for like-minded entrepreneurs to build networks and forge partnerships.

Trinchera Innovation Trade Fair Vendor Booth Application Form

Company Name: The Coolair Company
Contact Name: Anthony Porter
Date: May 29
E-mail: aporter@coolair.com

Attended Previous Year? ☑ Yes ☐ No
Preferred Exhibit Space? Please list up to four choices. We will try to prioritize your first choices.

First choice: 75A
Second choice: 67D
Third choice: 57C
Fourth choice: 73C

For a map of all booth spaces, please head on over to our Web site at www.trincheracouncil.com/ITF/map.

To:	Anthony Porter, The Coolair Company
From:	Kayla Abbott, Trinchera Innovation Trade Fair
Date:	June 12
Subject:	Application update

Dear Mr. Porter,

Thank you for participating in the Trinchera Innovation Trade Fair once again. Unfortunately, we regret to inform you that we were unable to reserve your top two booth choices as your application was delivered late. Therefore, we have reserved your third choice.

To maximize what you can get out of this event, I want to call your attention to the advertising during the speeches. We will be playing advertisements from our vendors in between speeches, and this can be a great way to attract attention to your business. If you would like full details on the pricing, please let me know.

Enjoy the rest of your week, and I hope to see you at the event.

Best regards,

Kayla Abbott
Event Coordinator

191. What does the advertisement suggest will remain unchanged about the event this year?

(A) The list of guests invited
(B) The venue of the event
(C) The price for booths
(D) The eligibility of vendors

192. What is indicated in the advertisement about the reception?

(A) It will require a ticket to attend.
(B) It will take place on July 4.
(C) It may be re-scheduled based on attendance.
(D) It includes a dinner meal.

193. What can be concluded about Mr. Porter?

(A) He is one of the organizers of the event.
(B) He recently moved to Trinchera.
(C) He will receive a discount on his booth.
(D) He has previously met Mr. Sutton.

194. Where will The Coolair Company display its products?

(A) 57C
(B) 67D
(C) 73C
(D) 75A

195. In the e-mail, what does Ms. Abbott encourage Mr. Porter to do?

(A) Apply for the event earlier
(B) Send a sample of his product
(C) Invite a partner to his booth
(D) Purchase advertising time

GO ON TO THE NEXT PAGE

TO	Joseph Han
FROM	Kelly Owens
DATE	May 13
SUBJECT	Suggestions

Dear Mr. Han,

Ever since the Customer Service Department moved into our office space, it has been too noisy to work. We understand that they need to speak with clients, but the noise has gotten so distracting that my team members are trying to find empty meeting rooms and other areas to complete their assignments. This has negatively affected productivity and created some animosity.

One solution would be to move our team into the third-floor meeting room — it's mostly used by our employees anyway. If that's inconvenient, we can set up several partitions to help block out the noise. Another option is to change our lunch schedule, so we are out of the office at different times. Also, some of the employees asked if it would be possible to work remotely. It could lead to cost savings and increased productivity.

Please respond at your earliest convenience.

Best,

Kelly Owens
Accounting Manager, Nirvana Corp.

---

memo

TO: Accounting and Customer Service
FROM: Joseph Han, Personnel Director
DATE: May 18
SUBJECT: Office issues

Gio Construction is in the process of transforming the unused media center on the second floor into a new office for the accounting team. The move will take place on June 8, when the work is finished.

In the meantime, the maintenance team has installed some dividers to separate the two departments. This should help reduce the sounds generated by both teams.

Also, I have noticed that the majority of the employees in this office tend to pack their lunch. While this is acceptable, please note that certain dishes produce strong odors and can make the room smell. So please keep this in mind when packing your lunch.

TO	jhan@nirvana.co.uk
FROM	fcristafno@gioconstruction.co.uk
DATE	14 June
SUBJECT	Office transformation

Hello Mr. Han,

We hope that your employees have been enjoying their new space. We provide a five-year guarantee with bi-yearly inspections. The first check will take place six months after the project completion date. If you encounter any problems before this, do not hesitate to call us. We'll send over an employee right away.

Thinking about making your office more attractive? Look into our Spruce Up service. At an affordable rate, one of our specialists will come by and provide tips on how to decorate your workspace. If this interests your company, please contact me at anytime.

Best regards,

Frank Cristafano
Client Relations Manager, Gio Construction

196. According to the first e-mail, how have some employees coped with a problem?

(A) By using high-quality headphones
(B) By staying at the office later
(C) By working away from their desks
(D) By recruiting additional personnel

197. Which of Ms. Owens's ideas did Mr. Han implement?

(A) Changing a scheduled lunch time
(B) Permitting staff to work at home
(C) Using a meeting room
(D) Placing partitions in an area

198. According to the memo, what is the issue with certain foods?

(A) They use expensive ingredients.
(B) They create an uncomfortable environment.
(C) They take a long time to prepare.
(D) They must be packaged in a specific way.

199. What is true about the new accounting office?

(A) It is the largest one in the company.
(B) It includes a security lock feature.
(C) It has used furniture.
(D) It will be inspected on December 8.

200. What does the Spruce Up service offer?

(A) Weekend office cleaning
(B) Computer system upgrades
(C) Regular equipment maintenance
(D) Interior decoration consultation

Stop! This is the end of the test. If you finish before time is called, you may go back to Part 5, 6, and 7 and check your work.

ACTUAL TEST 03 해설서 p.209

101. During his time as Vice President, Mr. Harper demonstrated many ------- traits.

(A) admire
(B) admiring
(C) admirable
(D) admiration

102. The owner of FamChem Pharmaceutical Company is proud of ------- business role in the industry.

(A) she
(B) her
(C) hers
(D) herself

103. Although it is rare to find fully ------- condominiums in Bridgeton, dining tables and chairs are occasionally provided.

(A) revised
(B) essential
(C) furnished
(D) composite

104. The remodeled Montaine Resort contains an ------- water park with many refreshment stands and shaded seating.

(A) imaginary
(B) effective
(C) active
(D) immense

105. For such a big company, the key ------- that determine profitability entail proper management of the human resource.

(A) exercises
(B) elements
(C) similarities
(D) recipes

106. Before the improved version can go into -------, the software has to be updated.

(A) produce
(B) product
(C) production
(D) producing

107. Sunday's heavy rainfall -------- disrupted power service at Sculper, Ltd.'s assembly plant.

(A) temporarily
(B) annually
(C) whenever
(D) anywhere

108. A sports-club member ------- wishes to cancel must give 30 days' notice without exception.

(A) whose
(B) who
(C) whoever
(D) to whom

109. The Accord Building features uniquely designed sand curtains, which can turn windows ------- clear to opaque at the press of a button.

(A) between
(B) starting
(C) from
(D) about

110. Jazz guitarist Mila Foreman enjoys performing in smaller venues because they give her a ------- with the entire audience.

(A) opinion
(B) signal
(C) connection
(D) observation

111. These economical insect repellants from Buzz Removal are ------- potent.

(A) unbelieved
(B) unbelieving
(C) unbelievably
(D) unbelievable

112. To bring in fresh ideas, the Harrisburg City Council is organizing an ------- search for an innovative architect.

(A) available
(B) exotic
(C) external
(D) absolute

113. Gemini Motors CEO confirmed that its new line of electric cars would be ready to ------- by February 22.

(A) commute
(B) launch
(C) ascend
(D) transmit

114. The Contemporary Art Museum is allocating its funds on ------- renovating the sculpture garden.

(A) extensive
(B) extending
(C) extensively
(D) extent

115. Unless otherwise indicated, all instructional videos on this Web page are the ------- property of Youngstown Clinic.

(A) perceptive
(B) evident
(C) confined
(D) exclusive

116. New company policies implemented last week ------- all visitors wear identification badges issued at the information desk upon arrival.

(A) insure
(B) coordinate
(C) mandate
(D) scrutinize

117. The e-mail was sent to all staff members ------- multiple branches.

(A) between
(B) with
(C) for
(D) across

118. *Industry Insider* magazine ------- its rising subscription rate to the quality of its editorial staff.

(A) permits
(B) responds
(C) believes
(D) credits

119. For the past three years, net cocoa ------- from the Cacao Coast has fallen due to drought.

(A) number
(B) output
(C) outcome
(D) total

120. Applicants must have at least three years of management experience to qualify ------- this position.

(A) by
(B) for
(C) from
(D) in

GO ON TO THE NEXT PAGE

121. Reyes Grocers recently ------- its organic produce section to offer a wider variety of fruits and vegetables.

(A) described
(B) announced
(C) indicated
(D) expanded

122. ------- heavy snow is so common in Kashkingrad, the city council approved a plan to connect all buildings downtown.

(A) Although
(B) Wherever
(C) Because
(D) Once

123. City residents may now choose to purchase electricity from a private company ------- the federal energy agency.

(A) other than
(B) come from
(C) connected
(D) whenever

124. The city government has voted unanimously to renovate some of the city's oldest ------- in the downtown area, including the West Street Postal Office.

(A) objectives
(B) neighborhoods
(C) structures
(D) inquiries

125. The house went back on the market since ------- of our clients' final offers was accepted by the owner.

(A) someone
(B) no one
(C) neither
(D) either

126. After receiving ------- reviews in literary magazines, Umberto Ello's latest novel was nominated for several awards.

(A) favorable
(B) tentative
(C) expanding
(D) few

127. In light of unexpected -------, the Ballet Focus Group was obligated to cancel its play last night at the King Edward's Hall.

(A) arrangements
(B) circumstances
(C) encounters
(D) representatives

128. Since Dr. Valdez is occupied with reviewing the employee assessments, she will attend this Friday's conference ------- no other executive is able to.

(A) only if
(B) so that
(C) as to
(D) rather than

129. ------- its effort to innovate its product and user experience, Gellar Electronics has hired a new Head of Design.

(A) In order to
(B) As part of
(C) Even though
(D) In case

130. Passengers for the Caledonia Resort's complimentary shuttle service must be at the lobby five minutes before the bus's ------- departure time.

(A) selective
(B) anticipated
(C) competent
(D) responsible

PART 6

Directions: Read the texts that follow. A word, phrase, or sentence is missing in some of the sentences. Four answer choices are given below each of these sentences. Select the best answer to complete the text. Then mark the letter (A), (B), (C), or (D) on your answer sheet.

Questions 131-134 refer to the following notice.

The third annual Bruger Partners family picnic will take place on September 12. Due to ------- high
131.
popularity among employees last year, we have decided to hold the event by Dazai Lake. The larger

------- means we will be able to accommodate all of our families and friends. Additionally, it will open
132.

up possibilities for more activities such as sports games and treasure hunts. As a bonus this year,

we have also secured the services of prominent singer Roy Mills. He ------- a short concert. Fans
133.

of his should bring any CDs or posters. -------. For detailed information about the event, check the
134.

company Web site.

131. (A) its
(B) their
(C) our
(D) your

132. (A) organization
(B) distance
(C) space
(D) scope

133. (A) perform
(B) will perform
(C) has performed
(D) performed

134. (A) This is a great chance to get them
autographed.
(B) He has recently returned from an
overseas trip.
(C) The event will have to be held indoors
if it rains.
(D) It may require booking in advance due
to limited slots.

GO ON TO THE NEXT PAGE

Questions 135-138 refer to the following information.

In today's business world, a strong leader can make all the difference. At Velimas Life Coaching (VLC), we have a simple mission. We want to ------- people into true leaders. At VLC, we provide leadership
135.
------- and coaching services to ensure you are equipped with the skills to become an effective
136.
leader. Our courses are taught by business leaders who have had successful careers of their own. -------, VLC also has an internship program designed to give you some valuable workplace
137.
experience. -------. This is a great way to test your leadership skills while also creating your own
138.
network.

135. (A) development
(B) develop
(C) developed
(D) developing

136. (A) procedures
(B) courses
(C) ambitions
(D) successes

137. (A) Meanwhile
(B) Supposedly
(C) However
(D) Additionally

138. (A) Our career coaches hail from all over the world.
(B) The course will only be available once a year.
(C) Many prestigious businesses participate every year.
(D) You may be eligible for a discount on tuition fees.

Questions 139-142 refer to the following advertisement.

Freeport Better Futures Project
Wednesday, 4 November to Friday, 6 November

Griswold County is just a 20-minute drive ------- Freeport, and they have been doing their part
                                            139.
in going green. The ------- from Griswold have come together and nearly reached their annual
                       140.
sustainability goal already. And they ------- to exceed this goal by year's end. Wondering what their
                                        141.
secret is? -------. The show will be airing next week on Channel One. We hope you tune in!
            142.

139. (A) across
     (B) along
     (C) from
     (D) over

140. (A) residents
     (B) residences
     (C) resides
     (D) residencies

141. (A) continue
     (B) suggest
     (C) refuse
     (D) intend

142. (A) Sign up for our newsletter and receive
         an exclusive discount.
     (B) Participate in a trip down to the county
         and experience it firsthand.
     (C) Find out in our exclusive television
         documentary covering the county.
     (D) Send in your questions to us by
         following the instructions.

GO ON TO THE NEXT PAGE

Questions 143-146 refer to the following book review.

Franchesca Thurman's latest book, *Kitchen Masterpieces*, is sure to appeal to those wanting to eat a little healthier this year. The book ------- with working adults in mind who may not have the time to go shopping every day. -------. Moreover, the book forgoes the ------- personal stories that typically accompany recipes found online in today's world, a trend Thurman is vehemently opposed to. Thurman insists that all recipes should be quick and easy to understand. *Kitchen Masterpieces* also contains recipes for the major ------- including Thurman's famous Christmas cookies. The book is expected to hit the shelves in February.

143. (A) is written
(B) will be written
(C) would have been written
(D) has written

144. (A) The book includes a section on affordable restaurants in the area.
(B) The recipes are not guaranteed to be vegan-friendly.
(C) The book will also be available in a digital format in the coming months.
(D) The recipes only use ingredients readily available in most kitchens.

145. (A) legitimate
(B) mundane
(C) convenient
(D) unbiased

146. (A) meetings
(B) celebrations
(C) situations
(D) holidays

Directions: In this part, you will read a selection of texts, such as magazine and newspaper articles, letters, and instant messages. Each text or set of texts is followed by several questions. Select the best answer for each question and mark the letter (A), (B), (C), or (D) on your answer sheet.

Questions 147-148 refer to the following article.

The Belwater Exhibition Center will host a career expo this weekend from 10 A.M. to 5 P.M. to recruit potential candidates for employment at the Rochester Resort.

With positions in various sectors available from front-desk representatives and concierges to security officers and cleaning staff, there is a wide range of available jobs. Admission to the event is complimentary, and those who pre-register through the Web site can have their résumés looked over before the expo.

Rita Logan, Chief Information Officer at Belwater, released a statement on behalf of the exhibition center expressing her delight in hosting the fair. Having started her career as an assistant event planner at Naworld Inn, she knows firsthand how a job in the hospitality industry can lead to some exciting opportunities.

"Jobs in this industry can be very satisfying and rewarding," mentioned Ms. Logan. "People who have any visible interest in a career in hospitality should attend the expo."

147. What is the purpose of the article?

(A) To announce a construction project
(B) To review a newly opened business
(C) To discuss the appointment of an executive
(D) To promote an upcoming event

148. What is indicated about Ms. Logan?

(A) She has experience working at a hotel.
(B) She will be looking over some résumés.
(C) She wants to change her job.
(D) She used to live near Rochester.

GO ON TO THE NEXT PAGE

Hyper Railways is on the Fast Track

Sherry Lee, Staff Writer

BEIJING (2 May) — Earlier this morning, Hyper Railways announced plans to extend its railroad network as well as upgrade its current tracks to accommodate longer and faster trains. —[1]—. Capable of reaching speeds of 400 km/h, passengers will be able to arrive at their destinations quicker than ever before. Included in this development is the creation of six new stations extending west to Xinjiang Province. —[2]—.

"Our main goal is to make it more convenient for customers to get to where they want using the newest technologies," stated CEO and founder Qiao Cai.

In addition, Hyper Railways unveiled a new rewards card, available from 1 October, that will offer discounts and other perks. Those who accrue enough reward points will have the option of choosing to upgrade their seats. However, note that these seats cannot be selected in advance. —[3]—. Individuals interested in signing up should check out their Web site at www.hyperrails.com/rewards. —[4]—.

149. What is mentioned about Hyper Railways?

(A) It aims to reduce travel times.
(B) It designed new train seats.
(C) It has created routes in different countries.
(D) It will relocate its head office to Xinjiang.

150. What will happen in October?

(A) Hyper Railways will host a job fair.
(B) A membership program will be launched.
(C) Passengers will be able to download a booking application.
(D) Mr. Cai will announce his retirement.

151. In which of the positions marked [1], [2], [3], and [4] does the following sentence best belong?

"They will be designated on the day of departure."

(A) [1]
(B) [2]
(C) [3]
(D) [4]

Questions 152-153 refer to the following Web page.

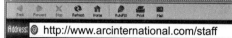

Address: @ http://www.arcinternational.com/staff   go

Daryl Anderson, Finance Coordinator

Mr. Anderson has been with ARC International for five years now. His decade of experience in the banking industry is crucial in helping us to manage our finances. This allows us to make better use of our donors' generous contributions and achieve ARC's mission of providing micro loans.

Before joining ARC, Mr. Anderson was at Astorium Capital for five years in Lagos, where he directly witnessed how accessible loan programs can promote economic growth. He advised Astorium Capital to wisely invest in the construction of several manufacturers' factories in La Paz and Quito. After briefly retiring, he committed himself to the nonprofit industry, which led to his decision to move to Boston to work for ARC International in order to help promote microloans and development for all.

152. Where was Mr. Anderson's previous job?

(A) In Lagos
(B) In La Paz
(C) In Quito
(D) In Boston

153. What is suggested about ARC International?

(A) It operates factories.
(B) It works with investment banks.
(C) It is a nonprofit company.
(D) It has locations in several countries.

GO ON TO THE NEXT PAGE

Questions 154-155 refer to the following text message chain.

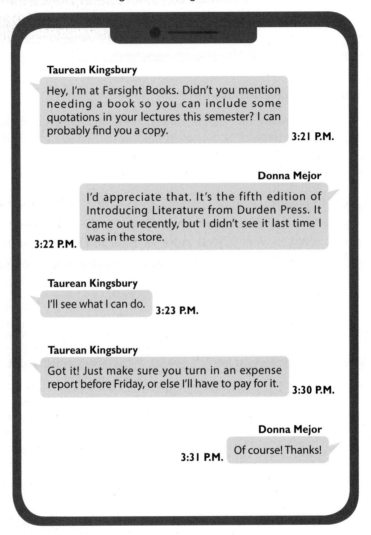

Taurean Kingsbury

Hey, I'm at Farsight Books. Didn't you mention needing a book so you can include some quotations in your lectures this semester? I can probably find you a copy.

3:21 P.M.

Donna Mejor

I'd appreciate that. It's the fifth edition of Introducing Literature from Durden Press. It came out recently, but I didn't see it last time I was in the store.

3:22 P.M.

Taurean Kingsbury

I'll see what I can do.

3:23 P.M.

Taurean Kingsbury

Got it! Just make sure you turn in an expense report before Friday, or else I'll have to pay for it.

3:30 P.M.

Donna Mejor

Of course! Thanks!

3:31 P.M.

154. What is implied about the book?

(A) It was edited by Ms. Mejor.
(B) It is not sold at Farsight Books.
(C) It will be referenced in lectures.
(D) It has been assigned for a course.

155. At 3:31 P.M., what does Ms. Mejor mean when she writes, "Of course"?

(A) She will submit a document on time.
(B) She will pay for the book.
(C) She will check if the book is available.
(D) She will make a purchase on Friday.

Questions 156-157 refer to the following Web page.

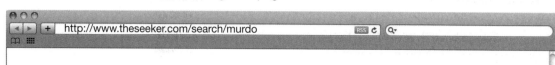

The Seeker

Luminosity Range, a company specializing in golf products, is opening a new location in Murdo. The company is now looking for a Facility Manager to manage its new location.

Roles and Responsibilities: The Facility Manager will oversee all aspects of the store to ensure smooth operations. Responsibilities include monitoring inventory and placing orders as required, resolving any customer-related issues, and submitting monthly reports.

Requirement: Must have a minimum of five proven years as a facility manager in a retail environment. Excellent attention to detail as well as punctuality is essential. Preferably, you will have a passion for golf and golf products.

About Luminosity Range: We were founded by a small team of passionate golfers who wanted to bring high-quality products to the market. We experienced unprecedented growth last year for such a young company, which is why we have started to expand aggressively. A career with us confers excellent benefits such as top salaries, generous vacation days, and opportunities for personal development.

156. What is suggested about Luminosity Range?

(A) It is an international business.
(B) It is hiring for multiple positions.
(C) It is a relatively new business.
(D) It manufactures all of its products.

157. What are Facility Manager applications NOT expected to have?

(A) A degree related to business
(B) The ability to submit documents on time
(C) Experience managing retail locations
(D) The ability to settle consumer complaints

GO ON TO THE NEXT PAGE

MUTUMOBO PROJECTIONS STRENGTHEN

This quarter is projected to be a strong one for the CTS brand after an increase in its soybean sales across West Africa. The last several years have seen declining yields due to flooding as well as unusually low temperatures. But even under these difficult conditions, CTS soybean crops have been able to set records at harvest time.

CTS was designed by Mutumobo Co. in Lagos, Nigeria. Although farmers have traditionally preferred to buy lower-cost brands, CTS's unique properties have become well-known throughout the continent. As a result, the company's stock has risen in anticipation of this quarter's sales report.

158. According to the article, what is one factor that affected soybean production?

(A) Excessive rainfall
(B) High temperatures
(C) Crop diseases
(D) New harvesting techniques

159. The word "set" in paragraph 1, line 4, is closest in meaning to

(A) prepare
(B) estimate
(C) achieve
(D) schedule

160. According to the article, what did Mutumobo Co. do?

(A) Hire a new executive
(B) Create a kind of soybean
(C) Open an R&D facility in Lagos
(D) Sell the CTS brand to another company

Questions 161-163 refer to the following press release.

For Immediate Release

Darnold Industries is the Latest Major Firm to Adopt the Award-Winning Services of TAMOS

Lagos (10 January) — Darnold Industries, a major clean energy company in Nigeria, will be installing a facial recognition system to bolster their security. The system, to be installed and maintained by Scottish firm TAMOS, will allow workers to gain access to the factory by having their faces scanned.

Darnold's President, Sandra McGee, commented that facial recognition is a leap forward compared to previous security solutions.

"By investing in TAMOS, I really think we're going to see a big improvement," said McGee. "Previously, we required employees to use photo ID passes to enter our factories. However, constantly making new IDs proved to be costly. Using these passes wasn't always safe either. For example, when workers lost their passes, security officers would have to take certain steps to remedy the situation. Ultimately, the IDs presented both budget and security issues."

TAMOS has been an innovative source of workplace security systems since it launched five years ago. The company, based in Edinburgh, is proud to provide its products to companies around the world. To find out more about their updated line of facial recognition systems, check out www.tamos.com.

---

161. What is suggested about Ms. McGee?

(A) She lost her employee pass several times.
(B) She is a cyber security expert.
(C) She is responsible for numerous plants.
(D) She usually works in Edinburgh.

162. Why does Ms. McGee prefer TAMOS's product over past products?

(A) It enables users to enter an access code.
(B) It requires a photo ID.
(C) It does not need frequent maintenance.
(D) It will save money in the long run.

163. What is implied about TAMOS?

(A) It moved its headquarters to Lagos.
(B) It has many international clients.
(C) It is planning to build a new factory.
(D) It was acquired by Darnold Industries.

GO ON TO THE NEXT PAGE ➤

Questions 164-167 refer to the following letter.

Timothy da Silva
276 Cedar Road
Dayton, Ohio 45406

Samantha Simmons
6061 Plainview Terrace
Beavercreek, OH 44831

Dear Ms. Simmons,

While looking through property records on the Montgomery County Web site, I found out that you currently own the complex that once served as home to the old Pinegrove Theater. From what I understand, the complex has been an empty shell since the theater closed years ago. —[1]—. I'd like to know whether it is for sale.

My business partner and I are looking to develop a retail property that would feature vintage clothing stores and dining options. We think that with some remodeling, your complex would be the ideal spot. To be clear, it is our intention to preserve the original character of the complex. —[2]—. Only slight improvements will be made.

There are other spaces in the downtown area that would attract more foot traffic, but residents do not have the same attachment to them. —[3]—. I know many people in the area who tell stories about how much they miss the theater and would like to see it come back to life as something new. —[4]—. I'm certain our plan would prove popular in Dayton.

Thanks for taking the time to consider this proposal. If you're interested in meeting about this, e-mail me at dasilva@silverchairdevelopment.com.

Best regards,

Timothy da Silva

Timothy da Silva

---

164. What is indicated about Montgomery County?

(A) It posts information about properties online.
(B) Its downtown area has a large clothing outlet.
(C) It recently introduced new building codes.
(D) Its main office is located across from a movie theater.

165. What is implied about the Pinegrove Theater complex?

(A) It can currently be accessed by visitors.
(B) It has recently been remodeled.
(C) It has been unoccupied for a while.
(D) It has been owned by several different landlords.

166. Why most likely is Mr. da Silva interested in Ms. Simmons's property?

(A) It is situated in the business district.
(B) Its purchase price is negotiable.
(C) Its amenities are brand-new.
(D) It is well-known to the locals.

167. In which of the positions marked [1], [2], [3], and [4] does the following sentence best belong?

"For example, the 1950's-style sign on the entry arch will be kept to maintain the place's old-fashioned appeal."

(A) [1]
(B) [2]
(C) [3]
(D) [4]

Questions 168-171 refer to the following memo.

MEMO

To: R&D Staff
From: Suha Mathur
Date: 16 February
Subject: New Product Meeting

I have booked Conference Room B for this Thursday, 19 February, at 9 A.M., so we can get started on the development of our latest nutrition bar, FiBur. During this meeting, we'll be going over everything from the ingredients to the wrapping design. In addition, we'll need to create a logo that will catch the attention of customers who are looking to have a post-workout snack at the gym.

In the afternoon, we'll split into small groups to further discuss how we can sell our products in other countries. I have e-mailed you a market research paper by the firm, Michak International. It has data on consumer trends that will surely help us. Pay special attention to the section regarding mobile technology and its uses going forward.

---

168. What type of business does Ms. Mathur most likely work for?

(A) A food manufacturer
(B) An advertising agency
(C) A sports stadium
(D) A graphic design company

169. What is probably true about FiBar?

(A) It will be made with organic ingredients.
(B) It was analyzed by Michak International.
(C) It comes in different flavors.
(D) It will be available in fitness clubs.

170. According to the memo, what will small groups do during the meeting?

(A) Discuss business expansion strategies
(B) Check some results from a questionnaire
(C) Participate in role-playing activities
(D) Test a new mobile technology

171. What are memo recipients expected to do?

(A) Note their lunch preference
(B) E-mail a client
(C) Review a research paper
(D) Sample a competitor's product

GO ON TO THE NEXT PAGE

Questions 172-175 refer to the following online chat discussion.

Meryl Lindholm   2:08 P.M.

Good afternoon, everyone. I'm honored to lead the team here at Klay & Field, but as this position as Head Editor came unexpected, I'll be relying on your expertise. First off, please share with me your plans to generate additional revenue from our intellectual property.

Aaron Salters   2:10 P.M.

We've been working on improving the quality of our audiobooks and can have some results for you to hear by next week.

Ray Walters   2:11 P.M.

This should be exciting. We're bringing in new voice talent and using higher fidelity audio. In addition, we'll upload the entire back archive to our Web site, so everything will be easily available for digital purchases.

Meryl Lindholm   2:14 P.M.

A welcome change, but we need to do something that will get the attention of new customers.

Julia Roglic   2:16 P.M.

I'm almost done with the beta version of a new smartphone app. For a monthly charge, it would allow customers to purchase unlimited access to our materials. A special algorithm would recommend new media to subscribers based on authors, genres, or subjects they've shown interest in.

Meryl Lindholm   2:17 P.M.

That could be promising. I'd like to be updated on its progress as much as possible.

Julia Roglic   2:18 P.M.

I can have a beta version up and running by Wednesday.

Meryl Lindholm   2:19 P.M.

Great. Do you mind showing me how to use it in person? Can we all meet in my office around this time on Thursday?

Message...

172. Where do the writers most likely work?

(A) At a news agency
(B) At a software developer
(C) At an accounting firm
(D) At a publishing company

173. What is currently being upgraded?

(A) The allocation of certain resources
(B) The size of an advertising budget
(C) The quality of some audio files
(D) The design of a Web site

174. At 2:17 P.M. What does Ms. Lindholm mean when she writes, "That could be promising"?

(A) She likes a program Ms. Roglic is designing.
(B) She is pleased with a report on revenue.
(C) She agrees that a change is necessary.
(D) She is excited about newly hired talent.

175. What will most likely happen on Thursday?

(A) A demonstration
(B) A sales meeting
(C) An HR workshop
(D) A product release

GO ON TO THE NEXT PAGE

VIDALIA SOLUTIONS

Vidalia Solutions has been the number one provider of moving services in the city of Lauderdale for over 20 years. Here are some of our services:
- Moving houses or offices
- Deep cleaning
- Long-term item storage
- Furniture and rubbish disposal

All services come with our money-back guarantee. If you're not fully satisfied with our service, you won't have to pay a cent.

And to kick off the year, we are offering a 30% discount on our storage service from now until February. To receive a free quote on any of our services, give us a call at 555-7375, or e-mail us at bookings@vidalia.com. Alternatively, we have a new app available that lets you conveniently book like never before. Get it today!

To:	bookings@vidalia.com
From:	jkang93@deltalook.com
Date:	January 8
Subject:	Request for estimate

Hello,

I recently came across your advertisement, and as chance would have it, you are offering a discount on the exact service I need! I am in the proces of moving to Lauderdale, but the new house isn't ready yet as it is being renovated. Therefore, I'm looking for some storage options for my furniture in the meantime. I saw that you offer long-term storage, but I was wondering what rates you offer for one month worth of storage. I will be in town on January 21 to finalize my housing contract, and I would like to arrange my furniture to be in storage by then as well. Please let me know what is possible, and I will get in touch.

Thank you,

Jisoo Kang

176. What is one purpose of the advertisement?

(A) To notify the public of price increases
(B) To publicize the launching of a new app
(C) To celebrate the receipt of an award
(D) To campaign for a policy change

177. What does the advertisement mention about Vidalia Solutions?

(A) It offers a promise on excellent service.
(B) It has additional locations in other cities.
(C) It also provides home renovation services.
(D) It is a publicly traded company.

178. What is indicated about Ms. Kang?

(A) She will be moving to Lauderdale.
(B) She is a first-time homebuyer.
(C) She works in real estate.
(D) She has previously used Vidalia Solutions.

179. What service does Ms. Kang most likely want to arrange?

(A) Home cleaning
(B) Moving items
(C) Rubbish disposal
(D) Furniture storage

180. According to the e-mail, what does Ms. Kang plan to do on January 21?

(A) Move offices
(B) Travel to Lauderdale
(C) Call Vidalia Solutions
(D) Confirm an appointment

GO ON TO THE NEXT PAGE

To get in touch with one of our staff, please fill in the form below. Please allow two to three days for processing.

Thank you for your interest in Korgale LLC.

Name	Lois Hayes
Phone	(143) 555-4992
E-mail	lhayes@hazymornings.com
Business Name	Hazy Mornings
Years active	7
Locations	2

Provide a short description of what you need:

We are looking to change suppliers. We are currently sourcing our tea from a supplier in Asia. However, we have been experiencing more and more issues with them. I would rather go with a more reliable and experienced supplier. Given our past experiences with you, I decided to contact you. I will be available to meet with a representative all of next week except Monday and Friday, as I have prior obligations.

What is your expected order size and frequency?

Ideally, I would like to put in orders once every two weeks. We used to go through one tin of your tea leaves every two weeks.

To: lhayes@hazymornings.com
From: shawndaniel@korgale.com
Date: August 17
Subject: Hazy Mornings

Dear Ms. Hayes,

Thank you for considering Korgale LLC as your supplier. We understand the frustrations felt from unreliable suppliers. Fortunately, we are in a position to help. I will get my colleague, Tanya Andrews, to contact you. She represents the greater Liane area. She is normally in the office 9:00 A.M. to 5:00 P.M. from Monday to Wednesday. However, please note that she will not be in the office this Wednesday. Since you last worked with us, we have added a wide variety of new products. I'll have Ms. Andrews set up a tea sampling session for you.

Ms. Andrews should be contacting you within the week. As part of our welcome back package, we would also like to offer you a reduced rate on your first order.

Thank you for your interest, and we look forward to working with Hazy Mornings again.

Best regards,

Shawn Daniel, Customer Relations
Korgale LLC

181. Why did Ms. Hayes fill out the form?

(A) To report an issue with a delivery
(B) To provide feedback on a service
(C) To inquire about an advertisement
(D) To request a meeting with a supplier

182. What is indicated about Hazy Mornings?

(A) It is currently opening up a new location.
(B) It switched suppliers last year.
(C) It has been featured on television.
(D) It used Korgale as its supplier in the past.

183. Who most likely is Ms. Andrews?

(A) An accountant
(B) A store manager
(C) A research analyst
(D) A sales representative

184. When will a tea tasting most likely take place at Hazy Mornings?

(A) On Monday
(B) On Tuesday
(C) On Wednesday
(D) On Thursday

185. What does Mr. Daniel offer to Hazy Mornings?

(A) Priority delivery
(B) A discounted price
(C) Industry contacts
(D) Exclusive products

GO ON TO THE NEXT PAGE

Questions 186-190 refer to the following Web page, online form, and e-mail.

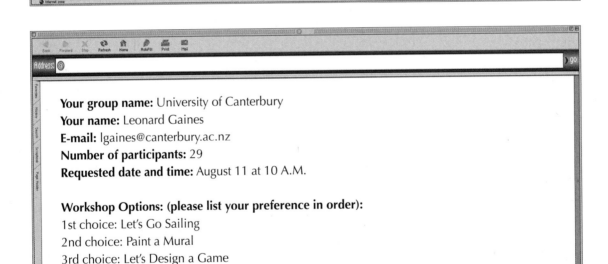

Building Connections provides fun and creative ways to promote team building at your organization. With an array of workshops suitable for a wide range of people, Building Connections can help make your teams communicate better and become more efficient. Each workshop lasts for three hours.

Workshop Options:
· Let's Go Sailing · Make your Own Pottery · Shoot a Short Film · Let's Design a Game · Paint a Mural (based on popular demand)

Workshop Pricing:

Number of participants	Per-person cost
Less than 10	$65
10-20	$60
21-30	$55
31 or more	$50

Your group name: University of Canterbury
Your name: Leonard Gaines
E-mail: lgaines@canterbury.ac.nz
Number of participants: 29
Requested date and time: August 11 at 10 A.M.

Workshop Options: (please list your preference in order):
1st choice: Let's Go Sailing
2nd choice: Paint a Mural
3rd choice: Let's Design a Game
4th choice: Shoot a Short Film

Please tell us about your group:
The university has recently gone through a major restructure. As a result, we've found ourselves in entirely new teams. I'd like for my team to get acquainted with one another, and I thought something practical would be a memorable event.

To	Leonard Gaines <lgaines@canterbury.ac.nz>
From	Maureen Crawford <mcrawford@buildingconnections.co.nz>
Date	August 5
Subject	ACCEPTED: Team building workshop request

Dear Mr. Gaines,

Thank you for transferring the full amount. As we have received the funds, you are now confirmed for August 11 at 10 A.M. Based on the forecasted weather, I have scheduled your group for your second preference.

The event will run for three hours. We do provide basic refreshments and beverages. However, if you would like a full catering service to be provided, we can arrange that. Please note that this will cost you extra. There is an area for the entire group to eat in, so please feel free to make use of that space.

We look forward to meeting you and your team next week. If anything changes, please let us know as soon as possible.

Best regards,

Maureen Crawford
Building Connections

186. What does the first Web page indicate about Building Connections?

(A) It is run by the local government.
(B) It can customize its workshops for customers.
(C) It uses participant feedback to make changes to its workshop content.
(D) It adds one new workshop every month.

187. What does the form suggest about the University of Canterbury?

(A) It placed its employees into new teams.
(B) It is the oldest university in the area.
(C) Its employees intend to take part in multiple workshops.
(D) It has had a change in leadership.

188. What will the per-person cost be for a workshop for the University of Canterbury?

(A) $50
(B) $55
(C) $60
(D) $65

189. For what workshop does Ms. Crawford confirm registration?

(A) Shoot a Short Film
(B) Let's Go Sailing
(C) Paint a Mural
(D) Let's Design a Game

190. What does the e-mail indicate about refreshments?

(A) They are sponsored by a local company.
(B) They are provided at no extra cost.
(C) They cannot be eaten on the premises.
(D) They are only provided for some of the workshops.

GO ON TO THE NEXT PAGE

Questions 191-195 refer to the following reservation receipt, regulations, and e-mail.

Hiro Rent-a-Car

Name of Renter: Nancy Ori
Pickup Date: 4 July, 10:00 A.M.
Return Date: 8 July, 06:00 P.M. (5 Days)
Rental Location: Nagasaki Airport

Hiro Rent-A-Car is a short shuttle bus ride away from the airport terminal. Please be sure to bring a copy of this receipt to the service counter as proof of your payment. Your vehicle will be ready for you as soon as you arrive.

PLEASE READ: Fuel levels for each vehicle will vary. Because of the number of vehicles we rent out and receive every day, it is impossible to keep all tanks full. We will, however, ensure that you are able to drive to the nearest gas station. It is the renter's responsibility to refuel the vehicle to the same level on the pickup date. If you are unable to return the car with the same amount of fuel, your credit card will be charged the cost of completely refilling the tank.

Hiro Rent-A-Car — Highway Toll Services

For those renting vehicles for more than a week, a toll sticker will be placed on your windshield. This sticker will save you time by allowing you to use the express toll booths in the far-right lanes of the toll collection area. The toll will be charged to the credit card on file.

Vehicles without stickers are required to stop at any of the booths in the left lanes to pay the toll in cash. Please be aware that vehicles that fail to pay will be ticketed and fined an amount of up to 10 times the original toll. Processing fees and court costs may also be incurred.

TO: Nancy Ori <nori@falcom.ca>
FROM: Hiro Rent-A-Car <help@hirocars.co.jp >
DATE: July 5
SUBJECT: Message Received

Dear Ms. Ori,

I received the message you sent today explaining the issue of accidentally passing through the express toll booth on Expressway 7 without paying the toll on your first day here. To settle this matter, you will need to visit the Metropolitan Expressway Public Corporation's Web site (www.mepc.com) and enter the license plate number of the rental vehicle and travel date. The toll will be calculated for you. Please double-check the information and confirm. Then, you will need to enter your payment information. If you settle the charge within five days of the incident, all additional fees will be waived.

Sincerely,

Hiro Rent-A-Car Help Center

191. What is indicated about Ms. Ori's rental agreement?

(A) A vehicle is already paid for in full.
(B) A GPS system will cost extra.
(C) It is for a fuel-efficient vehicle.
(D) It was prearranged by her company.

192. What information is emphasized in the reservation receipt?

(A) The rental duration cannot be extended on short notice.
(B) The daily average rate is calculated on the morning of the vehicle's return.
(C) Hiro Rent-A-Car limits the number of drivers to two.
(D) A certain amount of fuel must be left in the vehicle.

193. On what date did Ms. Ori travel on Expressway 7?

(A) July 4
(B) July 5
(C) July 6
(D) July 7

194. Why did Ms. Ori contact Hiro Rent-A-Car's Help Center?

(A) To detail a car accident
(B) To confirm a license plate number
(C) To schedule a new return date
(D) To resolve a missed payment

195. What is suggested about Ms. Ori?

(A) She used the far-right lane of a toll collection area.
(B) She cannot find an updated invoice.
(C) She was not issued a reservation receipt.
(D) She had to take an unexpected detour.

GO ON TO THE NEXT PAGE

C-Cellular Customer Service Representative Training Manual to Handle Calls

Currently: With Scripts

- Service representatives use a script to handle all customer issues.

- Service representatives transfer issues not addressed in the script to the supervising manager.

Moving Forward: Using a Manual

- Service representatives follow a manual to assist customers.

- Service representatives provide more personalized support for the customers.

Advantages
- ▶ Fewer transferred calls
- ▶ Quicker solutions
- ▶ Improved customer experience

TO:	C-Cellular Customer Service Department
FROM:	Renee Young, Training Director
DATE:	8 February
SUBJECT:	Initial testing guidelines

Dear Customer Service Department Managers,

We appreciate your patience while we update and improve our customer service hotline. We hope that you enjoyed the live Web-based training session as much as we did; despite the distance between us, it gave us an opportunity to resolve a lot of common concerns.

As mentioned earlier, we will be rolling out the new customer service manuals for a one-month pilot program beginning March 4. During this time, data regarding its efficacy will be collected so that we can readjust the process before implementation.

As for the pilot program, we would like the following numbers of representatives from each branch: 15 participants from Karachi and Lagos, and a minimum of seven each from both Dhaka and Edmonton. These employees will need to keep records of all the calls they take in addition to attending assessment meetings twice a week for fine-tuning purposes.

Regards,

Renee Young
Training Director, C-Cellular Operations

New Manual Pilot Program
Report for Week 3

While it seems that the durations of calls have become a bit longer, surveys have shown that our customer ratings have improved. As our representatives learn the new system, we believe call times will also decrease.

Branch	Representatives
Karachi	16
Lagos	15
Dhaka	5
Edmonton	7

196. According to the slide, why is C-Cellular changing its procedure?

(A) To increase the number of transferred calls
(B) To reduce call times for service representatives
(C) To improve efficacy of the training process
(D) To comply with updated government protocol

197. What is true about the training discussed in the e-mail?

(A) It will be prerecorded.
(B) It will last for one month.
(C) It was conducted on March 4.
(D) It was held remotely.

198. According to the e-mail, what are the pilot participants required to do?

(A) Demonstrate the new process to their coworkers
(B) Collaborate with a manager during calls
(C) Examine other C-Cellular call centers
(D) Log all of the calls they answer

199. Who most likely are the pilot participants?

(A) Customer service agents
(B) New service providers
(C) Supervising managers
(D) C-Cellular trainers

200. Which service center did not provide the required number of pilot participants?

(A) Karachi
(B) Lagos
(C) Dhaka
(D) Edmonton

Stop! This is the end of the test. If you finish before time is called, you may go back to Part 5, 6, and 7 and check your work.

ANSWER SHEET

파고다 토익 종합서 RC – ACTUAL TEST 01

READING (Part V-VII)

NO.	ANSWER A B C D	NO.	ANSWER A B C D	NO.	ANSWER A B C D	NO.	ANSWER A B C D	NO.	ANSWER A B C D
101	Ⓐ Ⓑ Ⓒ Ⓓ	121	Ⓐ Ⓑ Ⓒ Ⓓ	141	Ⓐ Ⓑ Ⓒ Ⓓ	161	Ⓐ Ⓑ Ⓒ Ⓓ	181	Ⓐ Ⓑ Ⓒ Ⓓ
102	Ⓐ Ⓑ Ⓒ Ⓓ	122	Ⓐ Ⓑ Ⓒ Ⓓ	142	Ⓐ Ⓑ Ⓒ Ⓓ	162	Ⓐ Ⓑ Ⓒ Ⓓ	182	Ⓐ Ⓑ Ⓒ Ⓓ
103	Ⓐ Ⓑ Ⓒ Ⓓ	123	Ⓐ Ⓑ Ⓒ Ⓓ	143	Ⓐ Ⓑ Ⓒ Ⓓ	163	Ⓐ Ⓑ Ⓒ Ⓓ	183	Ⓐ Ⓑ Ⓒ Ⓓ
104	Ⓐ Ⓑ Ⓒ Ⓓ	124	Ⓐ Ⓑ Ⓒ Ⓓ	144	Ⓐ Ⓑ Ⓒ Ⓓ	164	Ⓐ Ⓑ Ⓒ Ⓓ	184	Ⓐ Ⓑ Ⓒ Ⓓ
105	Ⓐ Ⓑ Ⓒ Ⓓ	125	Ⓐ Ⓑ Ⓒ Ⓓ	145	Ⓐ Ⓑ Ⓒ Ⓓ	165	Ⓐ Ⓑ Ⓒ Ⓓ	185	Ⓐ Ⓑ Ⓒ Ⓓ
106	Ⓐ Ⓑ Ⓒ Ⓓ	126	Ⓐ Ⓑ Ⓒ Ⓓ	146	Ⓐ Ⓑ Ⓒ Ⓓ	166	Ⓐ Ⓑ Ⓒ Ⓓ	186	Ⓐ Ⓑ Ⓒ Ⓓ
107	Ⓐ Ⓑ Ⓒ Ⓓ	127	Ⓐ Ⓑ Ⓒ Ⓓ	147	Ⓐ Ⓑ Ⓒ Ⓓ	167	Ⓐ Ⓑ Ⓒ Ⓓ	187	Ⓐ Ⓑ Ⓒ Ⓓ
108	Ⓐ Ⓑ Ⓒ Ⓓ	128	Ⓐ Ⓑ Ⓒ Ⓓ	148	Ⓐ Ⓑ Ⓒ Ⓓ	168	Ⓐ Ⓑ Ⓒ Ⓓ	188	Ⓐ Ⓑ Ⓒ Ⓓ
109	Ⓐ Ⓑ Ⓒ Ⓓ	129	Ⓐ Ⓑ Ⓒ Ⓓ	149	Ⓐ Ⓑ Ⓒ Ⓓ	169	Ⓐ Ⓑ Ⓒ Ⓓ	189	Ⓐ Ⓑ Ⓒ Ⓓ
110	Ⓐ Ⓑ Ⓒ Ⓓ	130	Ⓐ Ⓑ Ⓒ Ⓓ	150	Ⓐ Ⓑ Ⓒ Ⓓ	170	Ⓐ Ⓑ Ⓒ Ⓓ	190	Ⓐ Ⓑ Ⓒ Ⓓ
111	Ⓐ Ⓑ Ⓒ Ⓓ	131	Ⓐ Ⓑ Ⓒ Ⓓ	151	Ⓐ Ⓑ Ⓒ Ⓓ	171	Ⓐ Ⓑ Ⓒ Ⓓ	191	Ⓐ Ⓑ Ⓒ Ⓓ
112	Ⓐ Ⓑ Ⓒ Ⓓ	132	Ⓐ Ⓑ Ⓒ Ⓓ	152	Ⓐ Ⓑ Ⓒ Ⓓ	172	Ⓐ Ⓑ Ⓒ Ⓓ	192	Ⓐ Ⓑ Ⓒ Ⓓ
113	Ⓐ Ⓑ Ⓒ Ⓓ	133	Ⓐ Ⓑ Ⓒ Ⓓ	153	Ⓐ Ⓑ Ⓒ Ⓓ	173	Ⓐ Ⓑ Ⓒ Ⓓ	193	Ⓐ Ⓑ Ⓒ Ⓓ
114	Ⓐ Ⓑ Ⓒ Ⓓ	134	Ⓐ Ⓑ Ⓒ Ⓓ	154	Ⓐ Ⓑ Ⓒ Ⓓ	174	Ⓐ Ⓑ Ⓒ Ⓓ	194	Ⓐ Ⓑ Ⓒ Ⓓ
115	Ⓐ Ⓑ Ⓒ Ⓓ	135	Ⓐ Ⓑ Ⓒ Ⓓ	155	Ⓐ Ⓑ Ⓒ Ⓓ	175	Ⓐ Ⓑ Ⓒ Ⓓ	195	Ⓐ Ⓑ Ⓒ Ⓓ
116	Ⓐ Ⓑ Ⓒ Ⓓ	136	Ⓐ Ⓑ Ⓒ Ⓓ	156	Ⓐ Ⓑ Ⓒ Ⓓ	176	Ⓐ Ⓑ Ⓒ Ⓓ	196	Ⓐ Ⓑ Ⓒ Ⓓ
117	Ⓐ Ⓑ Ⓒ Ⓓ	137	Ⓐ Ⓑ Ⓒ Ⓓ	157	Ⓐ Ⓑ Ⓒ Ⓓ	177	Ⓐ Ⓑ Ⓒ Ⓓ	197	Ⓐ Ⓑ Ⓒ Ⓓ
118	Ⓐ Ⓑ Ⓒ Ⓓ	138	Ⓐ Ⓑ Ⓒ Ⓓ	158	Ⓐ Ⓑ Ⓒ Ⓓ	178	Ⓐ Ⓑ Ⓒ Ⓓ	198	Ⓐ Ⓑ Ⓒ Ⓓ
119	Ⓐ Ⓑ Ⓒ Ⓓ	139	Ⓐ Ⓑ Ⓒ Ⓓ	159	Ⓐ Ⓑ Ⓒ Ⓓ	179	Ⓐ Ⓑ Ⓒ Ⓓ	199	Ⓐ Ⓑ Ⓒ Ⓓ
120	Ⓐ Ⓑ Ⓒ Ⓓ	140	Ⓐ Ⓑ Ⓒ Ⓓ	160	Ⓐ Ⓑ Ⓒ Ⓓ	180	Ⓐ Ⓑ Ⓒ Ⓓ	200	Ⓐ Ⓑ Ⓒ Ⓓ

ANSWER SHEET

ANSWER SHEET

파고다 토익 종합서 RC – ACTUAL TEST 02

READING (Part V-VII)

NO.	ANSWER A B C D	NO.	ANSWER A B C D	NO.	ANSWER A B C D	NO.	ANSWER A B C D	NO.	ANSWER A B C D
101	Ⓐ Ⓑ Ⓒ Ⓓ	121	Ⓐ Ⓑ Ⓒ Ⓓ	141	Ⓐ Ⓑ Ⓒ Ⓓ	161	Ⓐ Ⓑ Ⓒ Ⓓ	181	Ⓐ Ⓑ Ⓒ Ⓓ
102	Ⓐ Ⓑ Ⓒ Ⓓ	122	Ⓐ Ⓑ Ⓒ Ⓓ	142	Ⓐ Ⓑ Ⓒ Ⓓ	162	Ⓐ Ⓑ Ⓒ Ⓓ	182	Ⓐ Ⓑ Ⓒ Ⓓ
103	Ⓐ Ⓑ Ⓒ Ⓓ	123	Ⓐ Ⓑ Ⓒ Ⓓ	143	Ⓐ Ⓑ Ⓒ Ⓓ	163	Ⓐ Ⓑ Ⓒ Ⓓ	183	Ⓐ Ⓑ Ⓒ Ⓓ
104	Ⓐ Ⓑ Ⓒ Ⓓ	124	Ⓐ Ⓑ Ⓒ Ⓓ	144	Ⓐ Ⓑ Ⓒ Ⓓ	164	Ⓐ Ⓑ Ⓒ Ⓓ	184	Ⓐ Ⓑ Ⓒ Ⓓ
105	Ⓐ Ⓑ Ⓒ Ⓓ	125	Ⓐ Ⓑ Ⓒ Ⓓ	145	Ⓐ Ⓑ Ⓒ Ⓓ	165	Ⓐ Ⓑ Ⓒ Ⓓ	185	Ⓐ Ⓑ Ⓒ Ⓓ
106	Ⓐ Ⓑ Ⓒ Ⓓ	126	Ⓐ Ⓑ Ⓒ Ⓓ	146	Ⓐ Ⓑ Ⓒ Ⓓ	166	Ⓐ Ⓑ Ⓒ Ⓓ	186	Ⓐ Ⓑ Ⓒ Ⓓ
107	Ⓐ Ⓑ Ⓒ Ⓓ	127	Ⓐ Ⓑ Ⓒ Ⓓ	147	Ⓐ Ⓑ Ⓒ Ⓓ	167	Ⓐ Ⓑ Ⓒ Ⓓ	187	Ⓐ Ⓑ Ⓒ Ⓓ
108	Ⓐ Ⓑ Ⓒ Ⓓ	128	Ⓐ Ⓑ Ⓒ Ⓓ	148	Ⓐ Ⓑ Ⓒ Ⓓ	168	Ⓐ Ⓑ Ⓒ Ⓓ	188	Ⓐ Ⓑ Ⓒ Ⓓ
109	Ⓐ Ⓑ Ⓒ Ⓓ	129	Ⓐ Ⓑ Ⓒ Ⓓ	149	Ⓐ Ⓑ Ⓒ Ⓓ	169	Ⓐ Ⓑ Ⓒ Ⓓ	189	Ⓐ Ⓑ Ⓒ Ⓓ
110	Ⓐ Ⓑ Ⓒ Ⓓ	130	Ⓐ Ⓑ Ⓒ Ⓓ	150	Ⓐ Ⓑ Ⓒ Ⓓ	170	Ⓐ Ⓑ Ⓒ Ⓓ	190	Ⓐ Ⓑ Ⓒ Ⓓ
111	Ⓐ Ⓑ Ⓒ Ⓓ	131	Ⓐ Ⓑ Ⓒ Ⓓ	151	Ⓐ Ⓑ Ⓒ Ⓓ	171	Ⓐ Ⓑ Ⓒ Ⓓ	191	Ⓐ Ⓑ Ⓒ Ⓓ
112	Ⓐ Ⓑ Ⓒ Ⓓ	132	Ⓐ Ⓑ Ⓒ Ⓓ	152	Ⓐ Ⓑ Ⓒ Ⓓ	172	Ⓐ Ⓑ Ⓒ Ⓓ	192	Ⓐ Ⓑ Ⓒ Ⓓ
113	Ⓐ Ⓑ Ⓒ Ⓓ	133	Ⓐ Ⓑ Ⓒ Ⓓ	153	Ⓐ Ⓑ Ⓒ Ⓓ	173	Ⓐ Ⓑ Ⓒ Ⓓ	193	Ⓐ Ⓑ Ⓒ Ⓓ
114	Ⓐ Ⓑ Ⓒ Ⓓ	134	Ⓐ Ⓑ Ⓒ Ⓓ	154	Ⓐ Ⓑ Ⓒ Ⓓ	174	Ⓐ Ⓑ Ⓒ Ⓓ	194	Ⓐ Ⓑ Ⓒ Ⓓ
115	Ⓐ Ⓑ Ⓒ Ⓓ	135	Ⓐ Ⓑ Ⓒ Ⓓ	155	Ⓐ Ⓑ Ⓒ Ⓓ	175	Ⓐ Ⓑ Ⓒ Ⓓ	195	Ⓐ Ⓑ Ⓒ Ⓓ
116	Ⓐ Ⓑ Ⓒ Ⓓ	136	Ⓐ Ⓑ Ⓒ Ⓓ	156	Ⓐ Ⓑ Ⓒ Ⓓ	176	Ⓐ Ⓑ Ⓒ Ⓓ	196	Ⓐ Ⓑ Ⓒ Ⓓ
117	Ⓐ Ⓑ Ⓒ Ⓓ	137	Ⓐ Ⓑ Ⓒ Ⓓ	157	Ⓐ Ⓑ Ⓒ Ⓓ	177	Ⓐ Ⓑ Ⓒ Ⓓ	197	Ⓐ Ⓑ Ⓒ Ⓓ
118	Ⓐ Ⓑ Ⓒ Ⓓ	138	Ⓐ Ⓑ Ⓒ Ⓓ	158	Ⓐ Ⓑ Ⓒ Ⓓ	178	Ⓐ Ⓑ Ⓒ Ⓓ	198	Ⓐ Ⓑ Ⓒ Ⓓ
119	Ⓐ Ⓑ Ⓒ Ⓓ	139	Ⓐ Ⓑ Ⓒ Ⓓ	159	Ⓐ Ⓑ Ⓒ Ⓓ	179	Ⓐ Ⓑ Ⓒ Ⓓ	199	Ⓐ Ⓑ Ⓒ Ⓓ
120	Ⓐ Ⓑ Ⓒ Ⓓ	140	Ⓐ Ⓑ Ⓒ Ⓓ	160	Ⓐ Ⓑ Ⓒ Ⓓ	180	Ⓐ Ⓑ Ⓒ Ⓓ	200	Ⓐ Ⓑ Ⓒ Ⓓ

ANSWER SHEET

ANSWER SHEET

READING (Part V-VII)

NO.	ANSWER A B C D	NO.	ANSWER A B C D	NO.	ANSWER A B C D	NO.	ANSWER A B C D	NO.	ANSWER A B C D
101	Ⓐ Ⓑ Ⓒ Ⓓ	121	Ⓐ Ⓑ Ⓒ Ⓓ	141	Ⓐ Ⓑ Ⓒ Ⓓ	161	Ⓐ Ⓑ Ⓒ Ⓓ	181	Ⓐ Ⓑ Ⓒ Ⓓ
102	Ⓐ Ⓑ Ⓒ Ⓓ	122	Ⓐ Ⓑ Ⓒ Ⓓ	142	Ⓐ Ⓑ Ⓒ Ⓓ	162	Ⓐ Ⓑ Ⓒ Ⓓ	182	Ⓐ Ⓑ Ⓒ Ⓓ
103	Ⓐ Ⓑ Ⓒ Ⓓ	123	Ⓐ Ⓑ Ⓒ Ⓓ	143	Ⓐ Ⓑ Ⓒ Ⓓ	163	Ⓐ Ⓑ Ⓒ Ⓓ	183	Ⓐ Ⓑ Ⓒ Ⓓ
104	Ⓐ Ⓑ Ⓒ Ⓓ	124	Ⓐ Ⓑ Ⓒ Ⓓ	144	Ⓐ Ⓑ Ⓒ Ⓓ	164	Ⓐ Ⓑ Ⓒ Ⓓ	184	Ⓐ Ⓑ Ⓒ Ⓓ
105	Ⓐ Ⓑ Ⓒ Ⓓ	125	Ⓐ Ⓑ Ⓒ Ⓓ	145	Ⓐ Ⓑ Ⓒ Ⓓ	165	Ⓐ Ⓑ Ⓒ Ⓓ	185	Ⓐ Ⓑ Ⓒ Ⓓ
106	Ⓐ Ⓑ Ⓒ Ⓓ	126	Ⓐ Ⓑ Ⓒ Ⓓ	146	Ⓐ Ⓑ Ⓒ Ⓓ	166	Ⓐ Ⓑ Ⓒ Ⓓ	186	Ⓐ Ⓑ Ⓒ Ⓓ
107	Ⓐ Ⓑ Ⓒ Ⓓ	127	Ⓐ Ⓑ Ⓒ Ⓓ	147	Ⓐ Ⓑ Ⓒ Ⓓ	167	Ⓐ Ⓑ Ⓒ Ⓓ	187	Ⓐ Ⓑ Ⓒ Ⓓ
108	Ⓐ Ⓑ Ⓒ Ⓓ	128	Ⓐ Ⓑ Ⓒ Ⓓ	148	Ⓐ Ⓑ Ⓒ Ⓓ	168	Ⓐ Ⓑ Ⓒ Ⓓ	188	Ⓐ Ⓑ Ⓒ Ⓓ
109	Ⓐ Ⓑ Ⓒ Ⓓ	129	Ⓐ Ⓑ Ⓒ Ⓓ	149	Ⓐ Ⓑ Ⓒ Ⓓ	169	Ⓐ Ⓑ Ⓒ Ⓓ	189	Ⓐ Ⓑ Ⓒ Ⓓ
110	Ⓐ Ⓑ Ⓒ Ⓓ	130	Ⓐ Ⓑ Ⓒ Ⓓ	150	Ⓐ Ⓑ Ⓒ Ⓓ	170	Ⓐ Ⓑ Ⓒ Ⓓ	190	Ⓐ Ⓑ Ⓒ Ⓓ
111	Ⓐ Ⓑ Ⓒ Ⓓ	131	Ⓐ Ⓑ Ⓒ Ⓓ	151	Ⓐ Ⓑ Ⓒ Ⓓ	171	Ⓐ Ⓑ Ⓒ Ⓓ	191	Ⓐ Ⓑ Ⓒ Ⓓ
112	Ⓐ Ⓑ Ⓒ Ⓓ	132	Ⓐ Ⓑ Ⓒ Ⓓ	152	Ⓐ Ⓑ Ⓒ Ⓓ	172	Ⓐ Ⓑ Ⓒ Ⓓ	192	Ⓐ Ⓑ Ⓒ Ⓓ
113	Ⓐ Ⓑ Ⓒ Ⓓ	133	Ⓐ Ⓑ Ⓒ Ⓓ	153	Ⓐ Ⓑ Ⓒ Ⓓ	173	Ⓐ Ⓑ Ⓒ Ⓓ	193	Ⓐ Ⓑ Ⓒ Ⓓ
114	Ⓐ Ⓑ Ⓒ Ⓓ	134	Ⓐ Ⓑ Ⓒ Ⓓ	154	Ⓐ Ⓑ Ⓒ Ⓓ	174	Ⓐ Ⓑ Ⓒ Ⓓ	194	Ⓐ Ⓑ Ⓒ Ⓓ
115	Ⓐ Ⓑ Ⓒ Ⓓ	135	Ⓐ Ⓑ Ⓒ Ⓓ	155	Ⓐ Ⓑ Ⓒ Ⓓ	175	Ⓐ Ⓑ Ⓒ Ⓓ	195	Ⓐ Ⓑ Ⓒ Ⓓ
116	Ⓐ Ⓑ Ⓒ Ⓓ	136	Ⓐ Ⓑ Ⓒ Ⓓ	156	Ⓐ Ⓑ Ⓒ Ⓓ	176	Ⓐ Ⓑ Ⓒ Ⓓ	196	Ⓐ Ⓑ Ⓒ Ⓓ
117	Ⓐ Ⓑ Ⓒ Ⓓ	137	Ⓐ Ⓑ Ⓒ Ⓓ	157	Ⓐ Ⓑ Ⓒ Ⓓ	177	Ⓐ Ⓑ Ⓒ Ⓓ	197	Ⓐ Ⓑ Ⓒ Ⓓ
118	Ⓐ Ⓑ Ⓒ Ⓓ	138	Ⓐ Ⓑ Ⓒ Ⓓ	158	Ⓐ Ⓑ Ⓒ Ⓓ	178	Ⓐ Ⓑ Ⓒ Ⓓ	198	Ⓐ Ⓑ Ⓒ Ⓓ
119	Ⓐ Ⓑ Ⓒ Ⓓ	139	Ⓐ Ⓑ Ⓒ Ⓓ	159	Ⓐ Ⓑ Ⓒ Ⓓ	179	Ⓐ Ⓑ Ⓒ Ⓓ	199	Ⓐ Ⓑ Ⓒ Ⓓ
120	Ⓐ Ⓑ Ⓒ Ⓓ	140	Ⓐ Ⓑ Ⓒ Ⓓ	160	Ⓐ Ⓑ Ⓒ Ⓓ	180	Ⓐ Ⓑ Ⓒ Ⓓ	200	Ⓐ Ⓑ Ⓒ Ⓓ

ANSWER SHEET

파고다 토익

RC

종합서 | 해설서

PAGODA Books

파고다 토익 RC

종합서 | 해설서

PART 5

CHAPTER 01 문장 구조

CASE 집중훈련
본서 p.25

1. (B) **2.** (B) **3.** (D) **4.** (B) **5.** (D) **6.** (B)
7. (C) **8.** (A)

---

1. 주어 자리

The **extension** of subway Line 3 was authorized this morning by the city council.
오늘 아침 시의회에서 지하철 3호선 연장이 승인되었다.

해설 빈칸은 정관사 the의 한정을 받으며 주어 역할을 하는 명사 자리이므로 (B)가 정답이다.

어휘 authorize 승인하다 | city council 시의회

---

2. 주어 자리

Securing that large renovation contract was an impressive accomplishment for the small interior design company.
그 대형 보수 계약을 따낸 것은 작은 인테리어 디자인 회사에 있어서 놀라운 업적이었다.

해설 빈칸은 that large renovation contract를 목적어로 취하면서 문장의 주어 역할을 하는 자리이다. 동명사는 '~하는 것/~하기'의 의미로 명사의 역할을 하면서 타동사가 동명사로 쓰일 경우 목적어를 수반할 수 있으므로 (B)가 정답이다.

어휘 secure 따내다, 확보하다 | impressive 인상적인 | accomplishment 업적

✛ Key point
동명사의 특징은 다음과 같다.
① '~하는 것/~하기'의 의미로 명사 자리에 쓰일 수 있다.
② 타동사가 동명사로 쓰일 경우, 목적어를 수반할 수 있다.
③ 명사와 달리, 앞에 관사나 한정사를 받을 수 없다.

---

3. 어휘 – 명사

A quarterly **allowance** is provided to Maxco Marketing employees to offset various business trip expenses.
Maxco 마케팅 직원들에게는 다양한 출장비를 상쇄하기 위한 분기별 수당이 지급된다.

해설 문맥상 출장비를 상쇄하기 위해 제공되는 것으로 적절한 것은 보기 중 '수당'이므로 (D)가 정답이다.

어휘 quarterly 분기별의 | offset 상쇄하다

---

4. 어휘 – 명사

Delegation of authority makes a manager's work easier and allows new employees to develop their abilities.
권한의 위임은 관리자의 일을 더 쉽게 만들고 신입 사원들이 그들의 능력을 개발할 수 있도록 한다.

해설 문맥상 '권한의 위임이 관리자의 일을 더 쉽게 만든다'는 내용이 자연스러우므로 (B)가 정답이다. delegation은 '위임'이란 뜻 외에, '대표단'이란 의미도 있다.

어휘 authority 권한 | allow ~할 수 있도록 하다, 허락하다 | ability 능력

5-8번은 다음 광고에 관한 문제입니다.

이동하고 싶으신가요? 오늘 DLB Management로 연락하세요. 당신의 업무 공간을 내놓는 시기를 선택하는 것이 중요하다는 걸 기억하세요. 경험이 많은 사업가들에게조차, 언제 **⑥팔지** 결정하는 건 어려울 수 있습니다. **⑥요즘은, 시장이 빠르게 변화하고, 복잡하며, 글로벌합니다.** 많은 지역 부동산 중개인들은 당신에게 필요한 지식을 제공하는 국제 네트워크에 접근하지 못합니다. **⑦다행히,** DLB Management의 에이전트들은 가능합니다! 저희 에이전트들은 국제 비즈니스 관계에 대해 **⑧특별히** 교육을 받습니다. 저희 웹사이트 dlbmgmt.com을 방문하셔서 저희 전문가 중 한 명과 상담일정을 잡아보세요.

어휘
move on ~로 옮기다, 이동하다 | get in touch with ~와 연락하다 | management 경영, 관리 | timing 시기(선택), 타이밍 | list 목록에 포함시키다 | crucial 중요한 | experienced 경험이 많은 | business owner 사업주 | determine 결정하다 | realtor 부동산 중개인 | have access to ~에 접근할 수 있다 | knowledge 지식 | agent 대리인, 에이전트 | train 교육하다 | schedule 일정을 잡다 | consultation 상담 | expert 전문가

---

5. 어휘 – 동사

해설 빈칸은 주어인 동명사구 determining의 목적어 「when + to부정사」 구조의 to부정사를 완성하는 동사 자리이다. 빈칸 앞 문장의 '업무 공간을 내놓는 시기 선택은 중요하다'라는 내용을 고려할 때, 문맥상 '언제 팔지 결정하는 건 어려울 수 있다'는 내용으로 이어져야 자연스러우므로 (D)가 정답이다.

✛ Key word
Remember, **the timing of listing your office space** is crucial. Even for experienced business owners, **determining when to sell** may be difficult.

---

6. 문장 선택

(A) 판촉 행사는 이번 주말까지 계속됩니다.
(B) 요즘은, 시장이 빠르게 변화하고, 복잡하며, 글로벌합니다.
(C) 훈련은 다양한 장소에서 실시됩니다.
(D) DLB 사는 5년 이상 운영되어 왔습니다.

해설 빈칸 뒷문장의 '많은 지역 부동산 중개인들은 국제 네트워크에 접근하지 못한다'는 내용을 고려할 때, '요즘 시장은 빠르고, 복잡하며, 글로벌하다'라는 내용이 앞에 들어가야 문맥상 자연스러우므로 (B)가 정답이다.

✛ Key word
Nowadays, the market is fast-paced, complicated, and global. Many local realtors do not have access to international networks that can provide you with the necessary knowledge.

---

7. 접속부사

해설 빈칸은 문장 도입부의 접속부사 자리이다. 앞 문장과 빈칸 뒷부분의 내용이 서로 상반된다는 점을 고려할 때, '많은 지역 부동산 중개인들은 국제 네트워크에 접근하지 못한다. (그러나) 다행히도, DLB Management 에이전트들은 접근할 수 있다'라는 의미로 연결되어야 문맥상 자연스러우므로 (C)가 정답이다.

✦ **Key word**
Many local realtors do not have access to international networks that can provide you with the necessary knowledge. **Luckily, the agents of DLB Management do**!

8. 부사 자리

해설 빈칸은 수동태 동사 구문과 전치사구 사이의 부사 자리이므로 (A)가 정답이다.

✦ **Key point**
수동태 동사 구문 뒤에는 수식어 역할을 하는 부사 또는 전치사구 등이 올 수 있다.

CASE 집중훈련
본서 p.27

1. (A) **2.** (A) **3.** (C) **4.** (A) **5.** (A) **6.** (A)
7. (B) **8.** (C)

---

1. 동사 자리

The cost estimate for the construction project **excludes** any extra charges for wage increases and additional materials.
공사 프로젝트를 위한 비용 견적에서 임금 인상과 추가 자재에 대한 어떠한 추가 청구액이라도 제외합니다.

해설 빈칸은 주어 The cost estimate와 목적어 any extra charges 사이에 들어갈 동사 자리이므로 (A)가 정답이다.

어휘 cost estimate 비용 견적 | wage 임금 | material 자재

2. 동사 자리

To secure the wire rack to the wall, **use** the screws enclosed in the package.
벽에 와이어 랙을 고정시키기 위해, 포장물에 동봉된 나사를 사용하세요.

해설 enclosed는 동사가 아닌 screws를 수식하는 과거분사로 해당 절에 아직 동사가 없는 것으로 보아 해당 절은 목적어 the screws를 이끄는 명령문 자리이다. 명령문은 동사 원형으로 시작하므로 (A)가 정답이다.

어휘 secure 고정시키다 | wire rack 와이어 랙, 철사로 만든 걸이 | screw 나사 | enclosed 동봉된

✦ **Key point**
명령문은 동사 원형으로 시작한다.

---

3. 어휘 – 동사

Because of budget restrictions, Ms. Chen **rejected** the suggestion to hold the anniversary party at the hotel.
예산 제한으로 인해, Chen 씨는 호텔에서 기념파티를 열자는 제안을 거절했다.

해설 빈칸은 주어와 목적어 사이의 동사 자리이다. Because of 전치사구와 주절의 관계를 고려할 때, '예산 제한으로 호텔에서 파티를 열자는 제안을 거절했다'라는 의미가 나와야 자연스러우므로 (C)가 정답이다.

어휘 budget 예산 | restriction 제한, 규제 | suggestion 제안 | hold 열다, 개최하다 | anniversary 기념일

✦ **Key word**
Because of budget restrictions, Ms. Chen **rejected** the suggestion to hold the anniversary party at the hotel.

---

4. 어휘 – 동사

A minor alteration in the building blueprint **saved** the construction company over 10,000 dollars.
건물 설계도에서의 작은 변경은 건설사로 하여금 만 달러 이상 절약하게 해주었다.

해설 빈칸은 주어와 목적어 사이의 동사 자리이다. 문맥상 '작은 변경은 건설사가 만 달러 이상을 절약하게 해주었다'라는 의미가 되어야 자연스러우므로 (A)가 정답이다.

어휘 minor 작은, 사소한 | alteration 변화, 변경, 개조 | blueprint 계획, 청사진 | construction 건설 | over ~ 이상; ~이 넘는

✦ **Key word**
A minor alteration in the building blueprint **saved** the construction company **over 10,000 dollars**.

5-8번은 다음 이메일에 관한 문제입니다.

수신: 전 직원
발신: thad.butler@Butler-Hanna.com
날짜: 6월 30일
제목: 기록적인 2분기

다음 달에 많은 분들이 휴가를 갈 계획인 것을 알고 있습니다. 그런데 여러분이 해변으로 떠나기 전에 감사 인사를 드리고 싶네요.

올해 2분기가 끝나감과 **⑤함께**, 저는 Butler-Hanna에 있는 전 팀에게 대단한 작업을 해주신 것에 대해 감사드리고 싶습니다. 우리는 봄철 내내 새로운 문제에 대한 대응책으로 자사의 보안 소프트웨어를 업그레이드하는 목표에 **⑥전념했습니다**. 그 결과, 우리는 내년에 **⑦성공할** 수 있는 자리를 잡았습니다. **⑧자사의 향상된 제품들은** 고객들을 끌어들였고 성장을 이끌었습니다. 실제로 우리가 받은 호평이 매출 급증을 일으켰고, 3분기에는 사상 최고가 될 것 같습니다.

여러분, 감사합니다! 계속 수고해 주시고 여름 잘 보내세요.

어휘
time off 휴식, 휴가 | head out to ~로 향하다 | express 표현하다 | gratitude 감사 | whole 전체의 | extraordinary 대단한 | in response to ~에 응하여 | challenge 도전 | consequently 결과적으로 | indeed 정말, 확실히 | favorable 호의적인 | cause 유발하다 | spike 급등 | keep up 계속하다

---

5. 전치사 자리

해설 빈칸은 명사구를 이어주는 전치사 자리이다. 문맥상 '올해 2분기가 끝나감과 함께, 저는 Butler-Hanna에 있는 전 팀에게 대단한 작업을 해주신 것에 대해 감사드리고 싶습니다.'라는 내용이 나와야 자연스러우므로 (A)가 정답이다. 추가적으로, 「with + 목적어 + 분사」는 동시동작을 나타내는 분사 구문의 일종이다.

✦ **Key word**
With the second quarter of the year ending, I want to thank the whole team at Butler-Hanna for all the extraordinary work.

---

6. 동사 자리

해설 빈칸은 주어 뒤의 동사 자리이다. 빈칸 앞 문장의 '대단한 작업을 해주신 것에 감사드리고 싶다'라는 내용과 빈칸 뒷문장의 '그 결과 내년에 성공할 수 있을 것 같다'라는 내용을 고려할 때, 문맥상 '봄철 내내 소프트웨어를 업그레이드하는 목표에 전념했다'라는 내용이 되어야 자연스러우므로 과거 시제 (A)가 정답이다. 추가로 이메일을 쓴 날짜는 6월 30일이므로 '봄철 내내'가 문장에서 과거 시점임을 유추할 수도 있다.

✛ Key word

With the second quarter of the year ending, I want to thank the whole team at Butler-Hanna for all the extraordinary work. Throughout the spring, we concentrated on our goal of upgrading our security software in response to new challenges. **Consequently, we are positioned for success in the coming year.**

7. 어휘 – 명사

해설 빈칸은 전치사 for의 목적어 역할을 하는 명사 자리이다. 빈칸 앞 부분의 '대단한 작업을 해준 것에 감사드리며 봄철 내내 소프트웨어를 업그레이드하는 목표에 전념했다'라는 내용을 고려할 때, 문맥상 '그 결과 내년에 성공할 수 있는 자리를 잡았다'라는 내용으로 이어져야 자연스러우므로 (B)가 정답이다.

✛ Key word

With the second quarter of the year ending, I want to **thank** the whole team at Butler-Hanna for **all the extraordinary work. Throughout the spring, we concentrated on our goal of upgrading our security software in response to new challenges. Consequently**, we are positioned for **success in the coming year.**

8. 문장 선택

(A) 이번 인수를 통해 새로운 매출 목표를 달성할 수 있을 것입니다.
(B) 다음 주 보너스에 대한 추가 업데이트는 이메일을 확인하세요.
(C) 자사의 향상된 제품들은 고객들을 끌어들였고 성장을 이끌었습니다.
(D) 가을에는 본사를 이전할 예정입니다.

해설 빈칸 뒷문장의 '호평이 매출 급증을 일으켰고 3분기에는 사상 최고가 될 것 같다'라는 내용을 고려할 때, 문맥상 '향상된 제품이 고객을 끌었고 성장을 이끌었다'라는 내용이 앞에 들어가야 자연스러우므로 (C)가 정답이다.

✛ Key word

Our improved products have attracted customers and driven growth. Indeed, **the favorable reviews we've gotten have caused a spike in sales, and Q3 is likely to be our best one ever.**

CASE 집중훈련   본서 p.29

1. (C) **2.** (A) **3.** (C) **4.** (A) **5.** (B) **6.** (A)
7. (D) **8.** (D)

---

1. 목적어 자리

Culturally sensitive marketing is an important factor influencing the **success** of our international product sales.

문화적인 부분에서의 세심한 마케팅은 국제 제품 판매의 성공에 영향을 미치는 중요한 요인이다.

해설 빈칸은 정관사(the) 뒤의 명사 자리이므로 (C)가 정답이다.

어휘 culturally 문화적으로, 문화와 관련된 | sensitive 세심한, 민감한 | factor 요인 | influence ~에 영향을 미치다 | international 국제적인

✛ Key point
명사 앞에는 관사(a, an), 정관사(the), 소유격 등의 한정사나 형용사가 올 수 있다.

---

2. 목적어 자리

Because of transportation **delays** due to the heavy snowstorm, some packages will be delivered a few days later than scheduled.

폭설로 인한 수송 지연으로, 일부 소포는 예정보다 며칠 늦게 배송될 것이다.

해설 빈칸은 구전치사 because of의 목적어 자리이다. 빈칸 앞에 명사가 있음을 고려할 때 문맥상 '폭설로 인한 수송 지연으로 인해'라는 의미가 되어야 자연스러우므로, transportation과 함께 복합명사를 이루는 명사 (A)가 정답이다.

어휘 transportation 수송 | package 상자, 소포 | deliver 배달하다 | later than scheduled 일정보다 늦게

✛ Key point
① because of는 구전치사이므로 뒤에 명사구가, because는 접속사이므로 뒤에 「주어＋동사」의 형태를 갖춘 절이 올 수 있다.
② 복합명사는 두 개 이상의 명사가 「명사＋명사」의 형태로 하나의 단어처럼 쓰인다.

---

3. 어휘 – 명사

Welt Insurance Company provides options that offer full **coverage** of most medical procedures.

Welt 보험사는 대부분의 의료 시술에 대한 완전 보장을 제공하는 옵션이 있다.

해설 문맥상 '보험사가 대부분의 의료 시술을 보장하는 옵션을 제공한다'는 내용이 적절하므로 (C)가 정답이다. coverage는 '(보험의) 보호, 보상 범위'라는 뜻이고, guarantee는 '(품질/사물의 손해/위험 따위에 대한) 보증'을 뜻한다.

어휘 medical procedure 의료 시술

---

4. 어휘 – 명사

The Nightingale Gallery is hosting a **reception** next month to showcase the artwork of painter Elizabeth Helsing.

Nightingale 갤러리는 화가 Elizabeth Helsing의 작품을 전시하기 위해 다음 달에 리셉션을 주최할 예정이다.

해설 동사 host(주최하다)와 호응을 이루려면 행사와 관련한 목적어가 필요하다. 문맥상 '갤러리에서 리셉션을 주최한다'는 내용이 자연스러우므로 (A)가 정답이다.

어휘 host 주최하다 | showcase 전시하다, 진열하다 | artwork 예술 작품

5-8번은 다음 공지에 관한 문제입니다.

입주민께 최고 수준의 **❺편안함**을 유지해 드리기 위해, 3층 회의실이 다음 주인 8월 17일부터 8월 21일까지 보수공사에 들어갑니다. 보수가 진행되는 **❻동안**, 회의실을 이용하실 수 없습니다. 대신 입주민께서는 4층 회의실을 이용해 주시길 권장드립니다.

불편을 끼쳐드린 점 **❼사과드리며**, 양해해 주시길 요청드립니다. **❽궁금하신 점이나 우려사항은 저희 관리사무소로 직접 연락주세요.**

Coatesville Properties 그룹

어휘

maintain 유지하다 | premium 고급의 | tenant 세입자, 입주민 | undergo 겪다 | renovation 개조, 보수 | underway 진행 중인 | unavailable 이용할 수 없는 | advise 조언하다, 알리다 | instead 대신 | inconvenience 불편 | cause 야기하다, 유발하다 | property 부동산, 재산

5. 목적어 자리

해설 빈칸은 전치사 of의 목적어 자리이다. 문맥상 '입주민께 최고 수준의 편안함을 제공해 드리기 위해'라는 의미가 되어야 자연스러우므로, 명사 (B)가 정답이다.

+ **Key point**
동사 comfort는 목적어가 필요하므로 동명사 comforting은 빈칸에 올 수 없다.

6. 부사절 접속사 자리

해설 빈칸은 두 개의 절을 연결하는 부사절 접속사 자리이다. '보수가 진행되는 동안, 회의실을 이용하실 수 없습니다'라는 의미가 되어야 자연스러우므로 동시동작인 '~하는 동안'을 의미하는 (A)가 정답이다.

+ **Key point**
접속사 while 뒤에는 절이, 전치사 during 뒤에는 명사구가 올 수 있으며, 둘 다 '~하는 동안'이라는 의미를 갖는다. Throughout도 '~내내'라는 뜻으로 기간 명사와 어울리는 전치사이다.

7. 어휘 – 동사

해설 문맥상 '불편에 사과드린다'는 의미가 되어야 자연스러우므로 (D)가 정답이다.

+ **Key word**
We apologize for any inconvenience caused, and we ask for your understanding.

8. 문장 선택

(A) 다음 주까지는 회의를 자제해 주세요.
(B) 송장에 문제가 있으면 직접 문의해 주세요.
(C) 4층 회의실은 가급적 피해야 합니다.
(D) 궁금하신 점이나 우려사항은 저희 관리사무소로 직접 연락주세요.

해설 빈칸 앞 문장의 '불편에 사과드리며, 양해해 주시길 요청드린다'는 내용을 고려할 때, 빈칸에는 '궁금하신 점이나 우려사항은 저희 본사로 직접 연락해 달라'는 내용이 들어가야 자연스러우므로 (D)가 정답이다.

+ **Key word**
We apologize for any inconvenience caused, and we ask for your understanding. **Any questions or concerns can be sent directly to our head office.**

CASE 집중훈련

1. (B) 2. (D) 3. (D) 4. (C) 5. (C) 6. (B)
7. (D) 8. (A)

1. 보어 자리

Mr. Rader's innovative renovation of Vaduz Fine Arts Museum is **commendable**.
Vaduz 미술관에 대한 Rader 씨의 혁신인인 개보수는 인정받을 만하다.

해설 빈칸은 be동사 뒤에서 주격 보어 역할을 하는 형용사 자리이다. '혁신적인 개보수는 인정받을 만하다'라는 의미가 되어야 자연스러우므로 형용사 (B)가 정답이다.

어휘 innovative 혁신적인 | renovation 개보수 | fine art 미술

+ **Key point**
형용사, 명사, 전치사구가 보어 역할을 할 수 있다. 일반적으로 형용사의 정답률이 가장 높다.

2. 보어 자리

The programmers are **hopeful** that the software update will be available for download before the end of the week.
프로그래머들은 주말 전에 소프트웨어 업데이트가 다운로드 가능할 것이라고 기대한다.

해설 빈칸은 be동사 뒤의 주격 보어 자리이다. 빈칸 뒤의 that절의 시제가 미래(will be)임을 고려할 때, '프로그래머들은 다운로드 가능할 것이라는 것에 희망적이다'라는 의미가 되어야 자연스러우므로 형용사 (D)가 정답이다.

어휘 programmer 프로그래머 | software 소프트웨어 | update 업데이트; 최신정보를 알려주다 | available 이용 가능한 | download 다운로드된 데이터; 다운로드하다

+ **Key point**
형용사 hopeful은 「be hopeful (that) + S + V(미래 시제)」 (S가 V할 것이라고 기대한다[희망에 차 있다])의 구조로 자주 사용된다.

3. 어휘 – 형용사

The Chief Financial Officer at Cosmo Electronics remains **opposed** to the proposed changes to the company's investment policy.
Cosmo 전자의 최고 재무 책임자는 회사의 투자 정책의 제안된 변경안을 여전히 반대하고 있다.

해설 빈칸은 문장의 보어 자리이다. 빈칸 뒤의 전치사 to에 유의해 문맥을 살펴보면, '정책 변경안에 반대하는 입장이다'라는 내용이 되어야 자연스러우므로 'opposed to'를 완성하는 (D)가 정답이다.

어휘 Chief Financial Officer (CFO) 재무 담당 최고 책임자 | remain 계속 ~이다 | proposed 제안된 | investment 투자 policy 정책

+ **Key point**
「형용사 + 전치사」의 짝을 기억해두자.
- opposed to 명사
- interfere with 명사
- anxious about 명사
cf. eager to 동사

PART 5 CHAPTER 01

4. 부사 자리

Many plumbing companies provide advice on making kitchens and bathrooms **more** water efficient.

많은 배관업체들이 주방과 욕실에서 물을 더 절약하는 것에 관한 조언을 제공한다.

해설 빈칸은 동사 make의 목적격 보어인 형용사 water efficient를 수식하는 부사 자리이다. 문맥상 '주방과 욕실에서 물을 더 절약하는 방법에 관한 조언'이라는 의미가 되어야 자연스러우므로 (C)가 정답이다.

어휘 plumbing 배관(작업) | provide 제공하다 | advice 조언 | water efficient 물을 절약하는

✚ Key point

동사 make는 5형식 문장에서 「make + 목적어 + 목적격 보어」 '~가 …하게 만들다'의 구조를 취한다.

5-8번은 다음 정보에 관한 문제입니다.

저희의 신상 Jumbo Series 산악 자전거 구입을 축하합니다. 저희 자전거는 도로 및 비포장 도로의 거친 환경에서 살아남도록 **⑤설계되긴** 하였으나, 당신이 구입한 상품은 1년 무료 보증에 의해 보호됩니다. **⑥당신은 이 보장프로그램에 자동으로 등록되셨습니다.** 보증기간 중에 무료 수리를 받으시려면, Jumbo Series 공인 매장을 방문해 주십시오. 직원이 당신의 자전거를 점검하고 필요한 **⑦작업**을 논의할 것입니다. **⑧또한** 당신은 교체가 필요한 결함부품을 저희 공장으로 바로 보내실 수 있습니다.

어휘
purchase 구매하다; 구매, 구입 | brand-new 아주 새로운, 신품의 | survive 살아남다 | harsh 혹독한, 거친 | condition 상태, 환경 | protect 보호하다 | warranty (품질)보증 | repair 수리; 수리하다 | authorized 인정받은, 공인된 | dealer 딜러, 중개인 | inspect 점검하다, 검사하다 | discuss 논의하다 | require 필요로 하다, 요구하다 | mail (우편으로) 보내다, 메일을 보내다; 우편물 | faulty 결함이 있는 | part 부분 | directly 즉시, 바로 | factory 공장 | replacement 대체

---

5. 과거분사

해설 빈칸은 although 종속절 내 be동사와 to부정사 구문 사이의 자리로, be동사에 대한 주격 보어 또는 be동사와 함께 수동태 구문을 이루는 과거분사 자리이다. 주어가 our bicycles이므로, 보기 중 주어와 의미상 동격 관계를 이루는 명사는 없으며, 문맥상 '자전거는 거친 환경에서 살아남도록 설계되었다'라는 내용이 자연스러우므로 수동태 구문을 완성하는 과거분사 (C)가 정답이다.

✚ Key point

문장의 be동사 뒤에는 주격 보어인 명사 또는 형용사, 수동태 동사 구문 「be + 과거분사」를 완성하는 과거분사가 올 수 있으며, 이 때 빈칸에 올 문장 성분은 문제의 보기 구성 및 문맥을 통해 파악한다.

6. 문장 선택

(A) 타이어는 친환경 소재로 제작되었습니다.
(B) 당신은 이 보장 프로그램에 자동으로 등록되셨습니다.
(C) 판매 전문가가 기꺼이 도와드리겠습니다.
(D) 저희의 자전거는 더 이상 온라인으로 구매할 수 없습니다.

해설 빈칸 앞 문장의 '당신의 제품은 1년간 무료 보증으로 보호받는다'는 내용을 고려할 때, '당신은 이 보장에 자동 등록되었다'는 내용으로 이어져야 자연스러우므로 (B)가 정답이다.

✚ Key word

Although our bicycles are designed to survive harsh conditions on- or off- road, **your product is protected by a free one-year warranty. You have**

---

been automatically registered for this coverage.

7. 어휘 – 명사

해설 빈칸은 동사 discuss의 목적어 자리이다. 접속사 and로 연결된 두 문장의 관계를 고려할 때, '직원이 당신의 자전거를 살펴보고 필요한 작업에 대해 이야기를 나눌 것'이라는 의미가 나와야 자연스러우므로 '필요한 수리작업'을 뜻하는 (D)가 정답이다.

✚ Key word

To get free repairs under the warranty, visit an authorized Jumbo Series shop. The **dealer will inspect your bike** and discuss the **work that will be required**.

8. 부사 자리

해설 빈칸은 동사를 수식하는 부사 자리이다. 빈칸 앞 문장의 '무료 보증으로 수리를 받으려면, 공인 매장에 방문해 제품의 점검 및 수리를 받으라'는 내용과 빈칸이 포함된 문장의 '결함부품을 공장으로 바로 보낼 수 있다'는 내용을 고려할 때, 빈칸 문장에서 수리를 받는 다른 방법을 제시하고 있으므로 추가의 의미를 갖는 부사 (A)가 정답이다.

✚ Key word

To get free repairs under the warranty, visit an authorized Jumbo Series shop. ~ You can also mail faulty parts directly to our factory for replacement.

CASE 집중훈련   본서 p.33

| 1. (A) | 2. (C) | 3. (A) | 4. (B) | 5. (C) | 6. (A) |
| 7. (A) | 8. (C) |

1. 전치사 자리

The finance manager was attentive **throughout** the main presentations delivered by the regional supervisors during the annual business meeting.

그 재무 관리자는 연례 비즈니스 회의에서 지역 관리자들이 한 주된 발표에 내내 귀를 기울였다.

해설 빈칸 뒤에 절이 아닌 명사구(the main presentations)가 연결되어 있어 빈칸은 전치사 자리이며 문맥상 '주된 발표에 내내 귀를 기울였다'는 의미가 자연스러우므로 '(특정 기간) 내내'라는 뜻의 (A)가 정답이다.

어휘 attentive 귀를 기울이는, 배려하는 | main 주된, 주요한 | presentation 발표 | deliver (발표 등을) 하다 | regional 지역의 | supervisor 관리자, 감독관 | annual 연례의

✚ Key word

The finance manager was attentive throughout the main presentations delivered by the regional supervisors during the annual business meeting.

---

2. 부사 자리

The in-room wall safes in each of the suites ensure that the guests' valuables can be stored **securely**.

각 스위트룸에 비치된 객실 내 벽 금고는 투숙객들의 귀중품이 안전하게 보관될 수 있도록 보장한다.

해설 빈칸은 문장의 목적어인 that절 내 수동태 동사 구문(can be stored) 뒤의 수식어 자리이므로 부사 (C)가 정답이다.

어휘 **wall** 벽 | **safe** 금고; 안전한 | **suite** 스위트룸 | **ensure** 보장하다, 반드시 ~하게 하다 | **valuables** 귀중품 | **store** 보관하다, 저장하다

+ **Key point**
수동태 동사 구문 뒤에는 수식어 역할을 하는 부사 또는 전치사구 등이 올 수 있다.

3. 부사 자리

The staff at the Mountain Chalet **creatively** shapes the snow removed from walkways into sculptures.
Mountain Chalet의 직원들은 보도에서 치운 눈을 창의적으로 조각품으로 만든다.

해설 빈칸은 주어 the staff와 동사 shapes 사이에서 동사를 수식하는 부사 자리이므로 (A)가 정답이다.

어휘 **shape** ~모양[형태]로 만들다 | **remove** 제거하다, 치우다 | **walkway** 통로, 보도 | **sculpture** 조각

+ **Key point**
주어와 동사 사이에는 동사를 수식하는 부사가 올 수 있다.

4. 어휘 - 동사

A new action plan is under consideration to **market** our services more aggressively in Latin America.
중남미에서 당사의 서비스를 보다 적극적으로 마케팅하기 위한 새로운 사업 계획이 검토되고 있다.

해설 빈칸은 our services를 목적어로 취하며 to부정사구를 완성하는 타동사 자리이다. 문맥상 '우리 서비스를 더 적극적으로 광고하기 위해'라는 의미가 나와야 자연스러우므로 (B)가 정답이다. 참고로 보기에서 invest는 주로 in과 잘 쓰여 'invest in(~에 투자하다)'를 의미하며, compete는 with/against와 잘 쓰여 'compete with/against(~와 [~에] 경쟁하다)'의 의미로 두 동사 모두 자동사로 쓰이므로 정답이 될 수 없다.

어휘 **action plan** 사업 계획, 조치 계획 | **under consideration** 고려 중인 | **aggressively** 적극적으로, 공격적으로

+ **Key word**
A **new** action **plan** is **under consideration to market our services more aggressively** in Latin America.

5-8번은 다음 이메일에 관한 문제입니다.

수신: sallychen@gchemtech.com
발신: bferguson@lwmail.com
날짜: 3월 17일
제목: 만남
첨부: Ferguson_이력서, 추천서

Chen 씨께,

GloboChem Technologies 인사팀 자리에 대해 이야기를 나누는 데 시간을 내주셔서 감사합니다. 당신과 직무의 세부내용에 대해 논의할 수 있어 ⑤**감사했습니다.** 그리고 많은 심사숙고 끝에, 저는 정식으로 그 직무에 지원하기로 결정했습니다. ⑥**이에, 제 이력서와 전문가 추천서를 함께 보내드립니다.**

제 이력서에 나와있는 것처럼, 제가 정기적으로 교육 워크숍을 진행했던 Holdenfield 음료회사에서의 저의 ⑦**과거** 경험은 저를 그 직무에 적임자로 만들어줄 것입니다. 첨부된 추천서를 작성해 준 Mary Timony는 제가 그곳에서 근무할 때 4년간 저의 부서를 관리했고, 제가 가장 가까운

친구라고 여기는 사람입니다. 그녀는 귀사에 대해 ⑧**호의적으로** 이야기하고, 처음 저에게 권해주었습니다.

그 외 제가 제출해야 할 것이 있으면, 알려주세요. 바로 보내드리겠습니다.

진심을 담아,
Brenda Ferguson

어휘 **CV** 이력서(Curriculum Vitae의 약어) | **recommendation** 추천(서) | **open position** 공석, 채용직 | **discuss** 논의하다 | **detail** 세부사항 | **deliberation** 숙고 | **officially** 공식적으로 | **apply for** 지원하다 | **reflect** 나타내다, 반영하다, 비추다 | **experience** 경험 | **beverage** 음료 | **routinely** 일상적으로 | **lead** 이끌다 | **training** 교육 | **workshop** 워크숍 | **fit** 어울림, 조화 | **attach** 첨부하다 | **oversee** 감독하다 | **department** 부서 | **consider** 고려하다 | **close** 가까운 | **personal** 개인적인 | **firm** 회사 | **recommend** 추천하다 | **provide** 제공하다

5. 동사의 시제

해설 빈칸은 주어와 목적어인 동명사 사이의 동사 자리이다. 현재 완료 시제인 빈칸 다음 문장과 접속사 and로 연결되어 있음을 고려할 때, '직무의 세부 사항에 대해 이야기를 나눠주셔서 감사했고, 많은 심사숙고 끝에 그 직무에 지원하기로 결정했다'는 내용이 나와야 자연스러우므로 현재 완료보다 앞선 과거 시제 (C)가 정답이다.

+ **Key word**
I **appreciated discussing the details of the job with you. And after much deliberation, I've decided** to officially apply for the job.

6. 문장 선택

(A) 이에, 제 이력서와 전문가 추천서를 함께 보내드립니다.
(B) 제 동료 Mary Timony를 그 자리에 추천하고 싶습니다.
(C) 그리고 건물 견학에 감사드립니다.
(D) 그러니, 첨부된 양식을 작성해 주시면 감사하겠습니다.

해설 빈칸 앞 문장의 '정식으로 직무에 지원하기로 결정했다'는 내용과 빈칸 뒤 문장의 '제 이력서에 나와있는 것처럼'의 내용을 고려할 때, 빈칸에는 이력서를 보냈다는 내용이 나와야 자연스러우므로 (A)가 정답이다.

+ **Key word**
And after much deliberation, **I've decided to officially apply for the job. Accordingly, I've included my curriculum vitae and a professional reference.**

7. 어휘 - 형용사

해설 빈칸은 명사 experience를 수식하는 형용사 자리이다. 문맥상 '정기적으로 교육을 진행한 과거 경험은 저를 그 직무의 적임자로 만들어줄 것'이라는 의미가 되어야 자연스러우므로 (A)가 정답이다.

+ **Key word**
As my CV reflects, **my past experience at Holdenfield Beverages, where I routinely led training workshops, should make me a great fit for the position.**

8. 부사 자리

해설 빈칸은 자동사 speak와 of 전치사구 사이의 자리이므로, 동사를 수식하는 부사 (C)가 정답이다.

+ **Key point**
동사를 수식할 수 있는 품사는 부사이다.

CASE 실전훈련

본서 p.34

1. (A) **2.** (D) **3.** (D) **4.** (C) **5.** (D) **6.** (B)
7. (A) **8.** (A) **9.** (D) **10.** (B) **11.** (A) **12.** (B)

1. 목적어 자리

All staff members must obtain **authorization** from their directors for extended absences after November 1.

전 직원은 11월 1일부터 휴가 연장을 위해 관리자들의 허가를 받아야 한다.

해설 빈칸은 동사 obtain의 목적어인 명사 자리이므로 (A)가 정답이다.

어휘 obtain 얻다 | director 관리자 | extended 길어진, 늘어난 | absence 결근, 결석

2. 동사 자리

Please **keep** expense records, since reimbursement will not be processed without proof of purchase.

구입 증빙 없이는 환급이 처리되지 않으니, 지출 기록을 가지고 계시기 바랍니다.

해설 please로 시작하는 명령문이므로, 동사 원형 (D)가 정답이다.

어휘 expense 비용, 지출 | record 기록 | reimbursement 상환, 환급 | process 처리하다 | proof 증명 | purchase 구입

3. 동사 자리 / 수 일치

The product team at Goodman Electronics **developed** a smartphone with a better battery life.

Goodman 전자의 제품팀은 배터리 수명이 개선된 스마트폰을 개발했다.

해설 빈칸은 주어와 목적어 사이의 동사 자리이다. 동사 자리에 들어갈 수 없는 (A), (C)는 탈락이 되며, 주어가 단수이므로 수 일치에 의해 (B)가 탈락된다. 따라서, 단수 동사의 과거형인 (D)가 정답이다.

어휘 product 제품 | electronics 전자 기기, 전자 공학 | battery life 배터리 수명

✛ Key point

가산 명사는 동사와 반드시 수 일치가 되어야 한다.

4. 부사 자리

The capability to adapt **effectively** is one of the most critical qualities in a company for the 21st century.

효과적으로 적응하는 능력은 21세기에 회사에서 가장 중요한 자질 중 하나이다.

해설 빈칸은 주어인 명사구와 be동사 사이의 자리이다. 문맥상 '효과적으로 적응하는 능력은 가장 중요한 자질'이라는 내용이 나와야 자연스럽고, 빈칸은 to부정사 adapt를 수식하는 부사 자리이므로 (C)가 정답이다.

어휘 capability 능력, 역량 | adapt 적응하다 | critical 대단히 중요한 | quality 자질

✛ Key point

동사 adapt는 자동사일 때는 '적응하다', 타동사일 때는 '적응시키다, 개조하다'라는 의미를 갖는다.

5. 동사의 태

Full sponsorships for undergraduate students **were**

raised one year after the government announced the controversial plan.

정부가 논란이 된 방안을 발표한 지 일 년 만에 학부생에 대한 전액 후원이 이루어졌다.

해설 빈칸은 주어 Full sponsorships에 대한 동사 자리이다. 타동사 raise는 목적어를 필요로 하나, 빈칸 뒤에 목적어에 해당하는 명사구가 없으며, 문맥상 '전액 후원이 이루어졌다'라는 수동의 의미가 되어야 자연스러우므로 수동태 동사 구문 (D)가 정답이다.

어휘 full 완전한 | sponsorship (재정적) 후원 | undergraduate student 학부생 | government 정부 | announce 발표하다 | controversial 논란이 많은 | plan 계획, 방안

6. 어휘 – 동사

Investors are keenly **exploring** the foreign market for lucrative business opportunities.

투자자들은 수익성 좋은 사업 기회를 위해 해외 시장을 열심히 탐색하고 있다.

해설 빈칸은 주어 Investors에 대해 현재 진행형의 동사 구문을 완성하는 현재분사 자리이다. 문맥상 '투자자들이 해외 시장을 열심히 탐색하고 있다'는 내용이 나와야 자연스러우므로 (B)가 정답이다.

✛ Key word

Investors are keenly **exploring the foreign market for lucrative business opportunities**.

7. 어휘 – 부사

Elias Craig Shipping's partnership with Chapman Constructions expires in three months, and **as yet** no renewal proposals have been reviewed.

Elias Craig Shipping이 Chapman Constructions와 맺은 제휴는 3달 후 만료됐는데, 아직까지 갱신 제안은 검토되지 않았다.

해설 빈칸은 등위 접속사 and 뒤에 오는 완전한 문장 사이의 수식어 자리이므로 부사구 (A)가 정답이다. apart from은 '~외에'라는 뜻의 전치사구이다. so that은 '~할 수 있도록'이라는 뜻의 목적을 나타내는 부사절 접속사이고, only if는 '오직 ~인 경우에'라는 뜻으로 절을 취하는 접속사이다.

어휘 shipping 운송 | partnership 제휴, 협력 | construction 건설 | expire 만료되다 | renewal 갱신, 연장 | proposal 제안 | review 검토하다

✛ Key point

① 부사구 as yet은 '아직까지, 그때까지'를 의미한다.
② 종속절 역할을 하는 부사절과 주절은 등위 접속사로 연결될 수 없다.

8. 어휘 – 부사

Copywriters at Prose Advertising are skilled at adhering **closely** to clients' needs to produce ideas that appeal to the target audience.

Prose 광고의 카피라이터들은 광고 타깃층의 마음을 끄는 아이디어를 만들어 내라는 고객의 요구를 충실히 지키는 일에 전문이다.

해설 빈칸은 adhering 동명사구를 수식하는 부사 자리이다. 문맥상 '광고 카피라이터들은 고객의 요구를 충실히 고수하는 데 전문'이라는 내용이 나와야 자연스러우므로 (A)가 정답이다.

어휘 copywriter 카피라이터 | advertising 광고 | skilled 숙련된, 전문적인 | adhere to ~를 고수하다 | appeal to ~의 마음을 끌다 | target audience 광고 타깃층

+ Key word

Copywriters at Prose Advertising are skilled at **adhering closely to clients' needs** to produce ideas that appeal to the target audience.

9-12번은 다음 기사에 관한 문제입니다.

BERVILLE (11월 17일) — 홍콩에 본사를 둔 친환경 에너지 기술 전문 스타트업 Minton Enviro-Technologies(MET)에서는 최근 자사의 신규 풍력발전 터빈을 캄보디아에 최초로 배치했습니다. 지난해 특허를 받은 Fengche는 시중에 나와있는 풍차 중 가장 효율적이라고 알려져 있습니다. MET에서는 풍부한 바람을 이용해**❾**해 아시아의 오지에 동력을 공급하게 되길 희망합니다.

MET의 기술본부장인 Kenson Wong 씨에 따르면, "이곳에서는 동력을 당연하게 여기는데, 그것이 우리 삶에 얼마나 **❿필수적**인지는 믿을 수 없을 정도입니다. 아시아의 많은 지역에서 사람들은 동력 없이 살아가는 법을 배워야 합니다. MET에서는 이를 용납할 수 없다고 여기며, 이것이 Fengche가 탄생한 배경입니다. 저희는 이들 마을에 자금이 충분하지 않다는 것을 알고 있습니다. **⓫풍차는 흔한 재료를 사용해 설계되었습니다.** 뿐만 아니라, Fengche는 밤에 매우 필요한 빛을 **⓬공급**할 수 있습니다."라고 말했습니다.

MET에서는 내년에 아시아 전역에 배치할 수 있을 만큼 Fengche를 생산하기를 희망합니다.

어휘
-based ~에 본사[근거지]를 둔 | specialize in ~를 전문으로 하다 | green energy 친환경[그린] 에너지 | recently 최근 | deploy 배치하다 | wind turbine 풍력 발전용 터빈 | grant 승인하다 | patent 특허 | report 알리다 | efficient 효율적인 | windmill 풍차 | available 구할 수 있는 | power 동력을 공급하다; 동력, 전기 | remote 먼, 외딴 | area 지역 | take advantage of ~를 이용[활용]하다 | abundant 풍부한 | take ~ for granted ~를 당연하게 생각하다 | incredible 믿을 수 없는 | get by 그럭저럭[간신히] 살아가다 | unacceptable 받아들일[용납할] 수 없는 | village 마을 | additionally 또한, 뿐만 아니라 | much-needed 매우 필요한 | spend (시간을) 보내다 | produce 생산하다, 제작하다

---

9. 전치사 자리

해설 빈칸은 동명사구인 명사구를 목적어로 취하는 전치사 자리이다. 문맥상 '풍부한 바람을 이용해 아시아의 오지에 동력을 공급하기를 바란다'는 의미가 되어야 자연스러우므로 수단, 방법을 나타내는 전치사 (D)가 정답이다.

+ Key point
전치사 by는 수단과 방법을, since는 시점을 나타낸다.

10. 어휘 – 형용사

해설 빈칸은 의문사 how가 이끄는 명사절에서 how의 수식을 받는 형용사 자리이다. 빈칸은 정도를 나타내는 형용사 자리로, 문맥상 how절 내 주어인 it이 가리키는 대상이 power임을 알 수 있으므로, '이곳에서는 동력을 당연하게 여기는데, 동력이 우리 삶에서 얼마나 필수적인지는 믿을 수 없을 정도'라는 의미가 되어야 자연스러우므로 (B)가 정답이다.

+ Key word
We take power for granted here, and it's incredible how necessary it is to our lives.

11. 문장 선택

(A) 풍차는 흔한 재료를 사용해 설계되었습니다.
(B) 풍차는 몇 년 후에 교체되어야 할 것입니다.

(C) 풍차는 장식적인 용도로도 사용할 수 있습니다.
(D) 풍차는 토종 조류에게 위험할 수 있습니다.

해설 빈칸 앞 문장의 '마을에 자금이 충분하지 않다는 것을 알고 있다'는 내용을 고려할 때, 풍차 설치에 많은 비용이 들지 않는다는 내용으로 이어져야 문맥상 자연스러우므로 '(구하기 쉬운) 흔한 재료를 사용해 설계되었다'는 의미를 전달하는 (A)가 정답이다.

+ Key word
We know that these villages **do not have much money.** The windmills were **designed using common materials.**

12. 동사 자리

해설 빈칸은 조동사 can 뒤의 동사 원형 자리이므로 (B)가 정답이다.

CHAPTER 02 명사

CASE 집중훈련
본서 p.37

1. (A) **2.** (A) **3.** (B) **4.** (D) **5.** (D) **6.** (C)
7. (A) **8.** (C)

1. 명사 자리

BJ's Steak is scheduled to open its first south-suburban **location** later this month.

BJ's Steak는 이번 달 말 남쪽 교외에 첫 번째 지점을 열기로 예정되어 있다.

해설 빈칸은 소유격 its 뒤에서 형용사 south-suburban의 수식을 받는 명사 자리이므로 (A)가 정답이다.

어휘 be scheduled to ~하기로 예정되어 있다 | suburban 교외의

+ Key point
locate는 '~을 찾다'라는 동사의 뜻도 있음을 꼭 기억해두어야 독해할 때 도움이 된다.

2. 명사 자리

Experts remain optimistic about the continuing **stability** of the Indian stock market.

전문가들은 인도 주식 시장의 지속적인 안정성에 관하여 낙관적인 입장을 취하고 있다.

해설 빈칸은 전치사 about의 목적어로 형용사 continuing의 수식을 받는 명사 자리이다. 문맥상 '~의 지속적인 안정성에 관하여'라는 의미를 완성해줄 명사인 (A)가 정답이다.

어휘 expert 전문가 | remain ~인 채로 남아 있다, 계속 ~이다 | optimistic 낙관적인 | continuing 지속적인 | stability 안정성 | stable 안정적인 | stabilize 안정시키다, 안정되다

3. 명사 자리

The Galt Corp. building control system combines security and excellent **ease** of use.

Galt 사의 건물 관리 시스템은 보안과 뛰어난 사용 편리성을 겸비한다.

해설 빈칸은 형용사 excellent의 수식을 받으며 명사 security와 함께 동사

combine의 목적어 역할을 하는 명사 자리이므로, 'combine A and B(A와 B를 겸비하다)'의 표현을 완성하는 (B)가 정답이다.

어휘 Corp. 기업(corporation의 약자) | combine 겸비하다, 결합하다 | security 보안, 경비

+ Key point
형용사의 수식을 받는 품사는 명사이다. ease는 '덜해지다[덜어주다]'의 동사로도 쓰인다.

----

4. 명사 자리

To receive **renewals**, make sure to carefully review the terms before signing the acknowledgement form.
갱신을 받으려면, 반드시 승인 양식에 서명하기 전 약관을 주의 깊게 살펴보시기 바랍니다.

해설 빈칸은 to부정사구를 이루고 있는 동사 receive의 목적어 자리이므로 명사 (D)가 정답이다.

어휘 make sure 반드시 ~하다 | carefully 주의 깊게, 신중하게 | review 검토하다 | terms 약관 | sign 서명하다 | acknowledgement 승인, 인정, 답신 | form 양식

5-8번은 다음 공지에 관한 문제입니다.

10월 1일부터 Hammersmith and Sons 경영진은 휴가 절차를 일부 **5변경** 시행합니다. 이번 결정은 직원 **6휴가**에 관한 최근의 설문조사 결과 분석 후 필요하다고 판단되었습니다. 상당수의 팀원들이 다가올 연휴 기간에 같은 날 자리를 비울 계획이었습니다.

연중 이 시기에는 보통 많은 고객들이 몰리기 때문에, 많은 직원이 동시에 자리를 비우면 **7불편할** 것입니다. 그래서 앞으로 몇 달간 경영진에서는 최소 한 달 전에 미리 휴가 신청서를 작성할 것을 요청 드립니다. **8신청서가 접수되는 순서대로 우선순위가 주어집니다.**

어휘
effective (규정 등이) 시행되는 | management 경영, 관리 | implement 시행하다 | time-off 일을 쉬는, 휴식의 | procedure 절차 | deem ~로 여기다 | analyze 분석하다 | significant 중요한 | away 자리에 없는 | attract 끌다 | portion (더 큰 것의) 부분 | leave request form 휴가 신청서 | fill out 작성하다 | in advance 미리, 사전에

---

5. 명사 자리

해설 빈칸은 동사 implement의 목적어인 명사 자리이므로 (D)가 정답이다.

6. 어휘 – 명사

해설 빈칸은 명사 staff와 함께 복합명사를 이루는 명사 자리이다. 빈칸 앞 문장의 '휴가 절차를 일부 변경 시행한다'는 내용을 고려할 때, 문맥상 '직원 휴가에 관한 설문조사 결과 분석 후'라는 내용으로 이어져야 자연스러우므로 (C)가 정답이다.

+ Key word
Effective the first of October, Hammersmith and Sons management is **implementing** some **adjustments to our time-off procedure. This decision** was deemed **necessary after analyzing** the **results from** a recent **survey about staff vacations**.

7. 어휘 – 형용사

해설 빈칸은 be동사의 보어 자리이다. 접속사 as로 연결된 두 절의 관계를 고려할 때, 문맥상 '고객이 많은 시기이기에, 많은 직원들이 동시에 자

리를 비우면 불편할 것'이라는 의미로 이어져야 자연스러우므로 (A)가 정답이다.

+ Key word
As this time of year usually **attracts a high number of customers**, it would be **inconvenient for a large portion of our staff** to be **gone at the same time**.

8. 문장 선택

(A) 의례적으로, 10월 1일까지 모든 직원은 설문지를 작성해 주시기 바랍니다.
(B) 최근의 광고 캠페인으로 인해 평소보다 더 많은 고객들이 예상되고 있습니다.
(C) 신청서가 접수되는 순서대로 우선순위가 주어집니다.
(D) 경영팀은 이것이 역대 최고 매출액이라고 말할 수 있게 되어 기쁩니다.

해설 빈칸 앞 문장의 '최소 한 달 전 휴가신청서를 작성해 달라'는 내용을 고려할 때, 신청서 접수 순서대로 우선 순위가 주어질 것'이라는 내용으로 이어져야 자연스러우므로 (C)가 정답이다.

+ Key word
So for the next few months, management will require that **all leave request forms be filled out at least one month in advance. Priority will be given in the order the requests are received.**

CASE 집중훈련
본서 p.39

1. (A) **2.** (B) **3.** (D) **4.** (C) **5.** (B) **6.** (A)
7. (A) **8.** (C)

1. 명사 자리

Employees are required to add a personal **note** to Mr. Dale's birthday card.
직원들은 Dale 씨의 생일카드에 개인적인 메모를 포함시키도록 요구된다.

해설 빈칸은 형용사 personal의 수식을 받는 명사 자리이다. 빈칸 앞에 부정관사 a가 있으므로 단수 명사인 (A)가 정답이다.

어휘 add 포함시키다, 더하다 | personal 개인의, 사적인

+ Key point
부정관사 a [n]는 가산 단수 명사를 동반한다.

----

2. 명사 자리

Ms. Osuyah has scheduled internal training sessions for all staff due to the **confusion** about the new system.
Osuyah 씨가 새로운 시스템에 관한 혼란으로 인해 전 직원을 위한 내부 교육 세션을 잡았다.

해설 빈칸은 전치사 due to의 목적어로 정관사 the의 한정을 받는 명사 자리이다. 문맥상 '새로운 시스템에 관한 혼란으로 인해'라는 의미가 되어야 자연스러우므로 (B)가 정답이다.

어휘 schedule 일정을 잡다 | internal 내부의 | all staff 전 직원 | confuse 혼란시키다 | confusion 혼란, 혼동

✦ Key point

명사를 수식하는 품사
- 관사 + 명사
- 소유격 + 명사
- 형용사 + (형용사) + 명사
- 관사 + 부사 + 형용사 + 명사

- -

3. 명사 자리

Ms. Kitahara is so renowned that customers must wait five days for an **appointment** with her.

Kitahara 씨는 너무 유명해서 고객들은 그녀와 약속을 잡으려면 5일을 기다려야 한다.

해설 빈칸은 관사 an 뒤의 명사 자리이므로 (D)가 정답이다.

어휘 renowned 유명한 ㅣ wait 기다리다

- -

4. 한정사

Gage Athletics will debut a new line of winter parkas beginning **this** fall.

Gage Athletics는 이번 가을부터 새로운 겨울 파카 라인을 선보일 것이다.

해설 빈칸은 명사 fall를 수식하는 한정사 자리이다. 한정사 this는 요일, 계절, 달 등과 같은 시간 명사와 함께 쓰여 시간부사구 '이번'을 의미하므로 (C)가 정답이다.

어휘 debut 선보이다 ㅣ parka 파카

✦ Key point

this는 시간을 나타내는 명사 앞에서 쓰여 '이번 ~'이란 뜻으로 시간부사구의 의미로 쓰인다.

- -

5-8번은 다음 이메일에 관한 문제입니다.

수신: 제작팀
발신: Tiffany Herzberger
날짜: 8월 24일 수요일
제목: 항해 재촬영

여러분, 안녕하세요.

이번 주 일요일 Dolphin Cove에서 항해 장면을 재촬영해야 하는 걸 기억하시기 바랍니다. 바다에서 촬영하면 많은 문제들이 생길 수 있는데, 우리가 지난달에 촬영한 장면이 영화 나머지 부분과 맞지 않았습니다. **⑤가능하다면,** 저는 점심시간 전에 촬영을 마칠 수 있도록 해 뜨는 시간에 촬영을 시작하고 싶습니다. **⑥하지만, 하루 종일 지속될 수도 있습니다.**

그리고 명확한 허가가 없으면, 촬영장에서 핸드폰을 쓸 수 없다는 걸 **⑦강조드립니다.** 문자메시지를 확인하거나 사진을 찍는 행위는 **⑧방해**가 될 수 있습니다.

Tiffany Herzberger

Palatial Estates Studios

어휘
reshoot 재촬영하다 ㅣ sailing 배타기, 출항 ㅣ scene 장면 ㅣ dolphin 돌고래 ㅣ cove 작은 만 ㅣ location 위치, 장소 ㅣ shoot 촬영하다 ㅣ complication 문제 ㅣ footage 장면, 화면 ㅣ up to the standard 기준에 부응하여 ㅣ rest 나머지 ㅣ sunrise 일출 ㅣ film 영화; 촬영하다 ㅣ allow 허용하다 ㅣ set 촬영장 ㅣ express 분명한, 급행의 ㅣ permission 허가 ㅣ check 확인하다 ㅣ text message 문자메시지

5. 어휘 - 부사

해설 빈칸 뒤에 콤마가 있으므로, 빈칸은 부사구 자리이다. 빈칸 뒤의 내용을 고려할 때, 문맥상 '가능하다면 점심시간 전에 촬영을 마칠 수 있게, 해 뜨는 시간에 촬영을 시작하고 싶다'는 내용으로 연결되어야 자연스러우므로 (B)가 정답이다.

✦ Key word

If possible, I would like to begin shooting at sunrise, so we can get our filming done well before we break for lunch.

6. 문장 선택

(A) 하지만, 하루 종일 지속될 수도 있습니다.
(B) 그럼에도 불구하고, 우리는 훌륭하게 해냈습니다.
(C) 다행히, 이 오류는 몇 번밖에 나타나지 않았습니다.
(D) 새로운 장소에서는 많은 문제가 발생하지 않을 것입니다.

해설 앞서 '점심시간 전에 촬영을 마칠 수 있도록 해 뜨는 시간에 촬영을 시작하고 싶다'고 했는데 역접의 However로 연결해 '하지만 종일 이어질 수도 있다'는 문맥이 되면 자연스러우므로 (A)가 정답이다.

✦ Key word

If possible, I would like to begin shooting at sunrise, **so we can get our filming done well before we break for lunch. However,** it's possible **it will last the whole day.**

7. 어휘 - 동사

해설 빈칸은 the fact that 동격의 명사절을 목적어로 하는 동사 자리이다. '명확한 허가 없이는 촬영장에서 핸드폰 사용이 금지된다는 사실을 강조한다'는 내용이 되어야 문맥상 자연스러우므로 (A)가 정답이다.

✦ Key word

I also **need to stress the fact that no mobile phones are allowed on set, unless you have express permission.**

8. 명사 자리

해설 빈칸은 관사 a 뒤의 단수 명사 자리이므로 (C)가 정답이다.

CASE 집중훈련 본서 p.41

1. (D) 2. (D) 3. (A) 4. (A) 5. (D) 6. (D)
7. (C) 8. (D)

---

1. 가산 명사 vs. 불가산 명사

The study reveals that **employment** in Eastville has sharply fallen over the last 12 months.

그 연구는 Eastville의 직원 채용이 지난 12개월 동안 가파르게 감소했다는 것을 보여준다.

해설 빈칸은 명사절인 that절 내에서 has fallen을 동사로 하는 주어 자리이다. 동사가 단수 동사이므로 단수 명사 또는 불가산 명사가 주어가 되어야 한다. 따라서 (D)가 정답이다.

어휘 reveal 보여주다 ㅣ employment 직원 채용 ㅣ sharply 가파르게 ㅣ fall 떨어지다

2. 가산 명사 vs. 불가산 명사

North Shore Grill's head chef always allows diners to make menu **substitutions**.

North Shore Grill의 수석 요리사는 항상 손님들이 메뉴 변경을 할 수 있게 해준다.

해설 빈칸은 동사 make의 목적어 자리이다. 이 문장처럼 복합명사가 나올 때, 복합명사의 문법적 기준은 뒷명사에 있다. 빈칸이 명사 menu의 수식을 받고 있으며 menu 앞에 관사가 없음을 고려할 때, 빈칸은 복수 명사 또는 불가산 명사 자리이다. 보기에서 (A) substitute는 가산 명사이고 (D) substitution은 가산, 불가산 모두 가능한 명사이므로 가산 복수 명사 (D)가 정답이다. 가산 명사 menu는 관사가 반드시 필요하기에, 동사 make를 5형식 동사로 생각해 make 뒤의 자리가 각각 목적어와 목적격 보어가 되는 구조는 불가능하다.

어휘 head chef 수석 요리사 l allow 허용하다, 허락하다 l diner 식당 손님

＋ Key point

명사 substitute vs. substitution: substitute은 가산 명사로 '대리인, 대용품'을, substitution은 가산/불가산 명사로 '대리, 대용'을 의미한다.

---

3. 가산 명사 vs. 불가산 명사

The HR Department gives financial **support** to new hires from overseas.

인사부는 해외에서 오는 신입 사원들에게 재정적 지원을 해준다.

해설 동사 gives의 목적어이면서 형용사 financial의 수식을 받는 자리이므로 명사인 (A)와 (B) 중에서 선택해야 하는데, 'support(지지, 지원)'는 셀 수 없는 명사이므로 (A)가 정답이다.

어휘 hire 신입 사원

---

4. 관용 표현

Due to a lack of production staff on the factory floor, Niobe Furniture will be unable to accept orders **until** further notice.

작업 현장의 생산 직원 부족으로, Niobe 가구는 추가 공지가 있을 때까지 주문을 받을 수 없을 것이다.

해설 빈칸 뒤의 further notice를 보고 'until further notice'의 표현을 묻는 문제임을 파악해야 한다. 따라서 (A)가 정답이다.

어휘 lack 부족, 결핍 l production 제작 l factory floor 작업 현장 l furniture 가구 l accept 받다, 수용하다 l order 주문 l notice 공지, 알림

5-8번은 다음 기사에 관한 문제입니다.

WILMINGTON (3월 4일) — Rochester Wood Farm은 오늘 오전 연례 '과일 나무 전시회'를 공개했다. Rochester 직원 Olga Smith의 말에 따르면, 이 **5**연례 행사는 과일 나무 농업 분야에서 회사의 가장 최근 노력을 돋보이게 한다. 이 노력 중 많은 부분은 흔한 어려움에 대한 이해를 얻기 위해 작성된 고객 설문이 원인이다. **6**그런 후에 연구개발부는 이러한 어려운 과제들을 해결하려는 솔루션을 만들기 위해 작업한다. 올해, 회사의 과일 나무 농장에는 High Gate 복숭아 나무와 같은 강한 품종이 나타났다. 이 나무들은 성장에 영향을 받지 않으면서도 오랜 가뭄에 견딜 수 있다. Smith는 "건조한 **7**지역의 재배자들은 특히 High Gates에 고마워할 거예요.", "그리고 **8**그들은 마찬가지로 비슷한 환경에서 잘 자라는 새 R8 자두나무에도 관심을 갖게 될 겁니다."라고 말했다.

어휘

reveal 공개하다, 드러내다 l highlight 강조하다 l effort 활동, 노력 l farming 농업, 농사 l result from ~에서 비롯되다 l questionnaire 설문(지) l gain 얻다 l understanding 이해 l common 일반적인, 흔한 l turn out 모습을 드러내다 l breed 품종 l withstand 견디다, 이겨내다 l extended 연장된, 늘어난 l drought 가뭄 l compromise 해치다, 절충하다 l grower 재배자 l appreciate 고맙게 여기다 l in particular 특히, 특별히

---

5. 어휘 - 형용사

해설 빈칸 앞 문장에서 해당 행사를 연례(annual) '과일 나무 전시회'라고 했으므로 annual과 같은 의미의 (D)가 정답이다.

＋ Key word

Rochester Wood Farm revealed **its annual Fruit Tree Showcase** this morning. According to Rochester employee Olga Smith, **this yearly event** highlights the company's most current efforts in fruit tree farming.

---

6. 문장 선택

(A) 회사는 과수 재배에서 가장 수익성이 높은 분야를 찾는다.
(B) 회사는 전국의 전문가들을 인터뷰한다.
(C) 그들의 광범위한 연구는 시장에서 가장 아름다운 과수들 중 일부를 만들어낸다.
(D) 그런 후에 연구개발부는 이러한 어려운 과제들에 초점을 맞춘 해결책을 만들기 위해 작업한다.

해설 빈칸 앞 문장의 '이 노력 중 많은 부분은 흔한 어려움에 대한 이해를 얻기 위해 작성된 고객 설문이 원인이다.'라는 내용과 빈칸 뒤 문장의 '올해, 회사의 과일 나무 농장에는 High Gate 복숭아 나무와 같은 강한 품종이 나타났다.'라는 내용을 고려할 때, 문맥상 '그런 후에 연구개발부는 이러한 어려운 과제들을 해결하려는 솔루션을 만들기 위해 작업한다.'는 내용이 두 문장 사이에 들어가야 자연스러우므로 (D)가 정답이다.

＋ Key word

Many of these efforts result from customer questionnaires created **to gain an understanding of common difficulties**. The research and development department then **works to create solutions that address these challenges**.

---

7. 단수 명사 vs. 복수 명사

해설 빈칸은 형용사 'dry(건조한)'의 수식을 받는 명사 자리로 (A)와 (C)가 정답 후보인데, region은 '장소, 지역'을 뜻하는 가산 명사로 빈칸 앞에 관사나 소유격 등의 한정사가 없으므로 복수 명사 (C)가 정답이다.

＋ Key point

1. 형용사의 수식을 받는 품사는 명사이다.
2. 단수 가산 명사는 반드시 부정관사(a [n])나 소유격 등의 한정사와 함께 써야 한다.

---

8. 대명사

해설 빈칸 앞 문장의 '건조한 지역의 재배자들은 특히 High Gates에 고마워할 거예요.'라는 내용을 고려할 때, 빈칸에 들어갈 대명사 주어는 'growers(재배자들)'를 받는 they이므로 (D)가 정답이다.

＋ Key word

"Growers in dry regions will appreciate the High Gates in particular," noted Smith. "And **they might**

---

also be interested in our new R8 plum trees, which also do well in similar conditions."

CASE 집중훈련
본서 p.43

1. (C)　2. (D)　3. (D)　4. (D)　5. (B)　6. (B)
7. (D)　8. (C)

---

1. 사람 명사 vs. 사물 / 추상 명사

Congratulations to our new committee for the fantastic work on the Richmond **account**.

Richmond 고객 대상으로 멋진 작업을 해준 새로운 위원회에 축하를 보낸다.

해설 빈칸은 정관사 the의 수식을 받으며, Richmond와 복합명사를 이루는 명사 자리로 문맥상 'Richmond 고객을 대상으로 한 멋진 작업'이라는 의미가 되어야 자연스러우므로 (C)가 정답이다. account는 '계좌, 계정'의 뜻 외에, '고객, 단골'의 의미도 있음에 유의한다.

어휘 congratulations to ~에게 축하를 보내다 | committee 위원회 | fantastic 멋진, 환상적인 | accountant 회계사 | account 고객, 단골 | accountable 책임이 있는

+ Key word

Congratulations to our new committee for **the fantastic work on the Richmond account**.

---

2. 사람 명사 vs. 사물 / 추상 명사

Bugz Begone's specialty is the safe and effective **elimination** of pests and critters from your home.

Bugz Begone의 전문분야는 귀댁에서 나오는 해충과 생물의 안전하고 효과적인 제거입니다.

해설 빈칸은 the safe and effective의 수식을 받는 명사 자리이다. '해충과 생물의 안전하고 효과적인 제거'라는 의미가 되어야 문맥상 자연스러우므로 (D)가 정답이다. eliminator(제거자)와 specialty가 동격 관계로는 어색하므로 사람 명사는 오답이다.

어휘 specialty 특색, 특징 | effective 효과적인 | pest 해충 | critter 생물

+ Key point

명사 eliminator vs. elimination: eliminator는 '제거자'를, elimination은 '제거'를 의미한다.

---

3. 단수 명사 vs. 복수 명사

We honor **retirees** from the university at an annual ceremony at the end of each academic year.

저희는 매 학년말에 연례 행사에서 대학교를 은퇴하신 분들께 영예를 드립니다.

해설 빈칸은 문장의 목적어인 명사 자리로, 동사인 (A)를 먼저 소거한다. (B)는 '은퇴, 퇴직'을 의미하는 사물/추상 명사이며, (C)와 (D)는 '은퇴자, 퇴직자'라는 뜻의 사람 명사인데, 동사 'honor(예우하다, 경의를 하다)'의 대상은 사람이므로 (B)도 소거한다. 사람 명사 retiree는 가산 명사로서 빈칸 앞에 관사가 없으므로 복수형 (D)가 정답이다.

어휘 honor 존경하다, 명예를 주다 | annual 연간의 | ceremony 의식 | academic year 학년

---

4. 사람 명사 vs. 사물 / 추상 명사

An outgoing disposition and background in computer technology are mandatory for the position of sales **associate** at Kirlian Electronics.

활발한 성격과 컴퓨터 공학에의 배경은 Kirlian 전자의 판매사원 직무에 필수적이다.

해설 빈칸은 전치사 of의 목적어이자, 빈칸 앞 명사 sales와 함께 복합명사를 완성하는 명사 자리이다. 문맥상 'Kirlian 전자의 판매사원 직무'라는 의미가 되어야 자연스러우므로 '판매사원'이라는 의미를 완성하는 (D)가 정답이다.

어휘 outgoing 외향적인, 사교적인 | disposition 성격, 성향 | background 배경 | mandatory 의무적인 | position (일)자리, 직위, 위치

+ Key word

An outgoing disposition and background in computer technology are mandatory for **the position of sales associate at Kirlian Electronics**.

5-8번은 다음 기사에 관한 문제입니다.

BOSTON (8월 25일) — Torrance and Posner 그룹은 어제 중소기업 고객들에게 판매할 신규 회계 플랫폼을 발표했다. 시스템은 강력하고 사용이 편리한 원스톱 부기 솔루션으로 설계된다. 급여 및 기타 비용에 사용된 지출 총액 **⑤뿐만 아니라** 회사 전체의 수익을 실시간으로 원활하게 추적한다. **⑥지방 및 연방 정부세 또한 고려된다.** 모든 자료는 보기 쉽게 정리되며, 다양한 종류의 기기에서 이용할 수 있다. **⑦개발자들은** 이것이 직원들의 시간을 절약해주고, 정보 부족으로 인한 초과 지출을 **⑧막아줄** 것으로 본다.

어휘
unveil 발표하다 | accounting 회계 | platform 플랫폼(사용기반이 되는 컴퓨터 시스템, 소프트웨어) | market 광고하다 | easy-to-use 사용하기 편리한 | one-stop 원스톱의, 한 자리에서 다 할 수 있는 | bookkeeping 부기 | solution 해결책 | seamlessly 매끄럽게, 원활하게 | track 추적하다 | company-wide 전사차원의, 회사 전반의 | revenue 수입 | payroll 급여 | expense 비용 | intuitive 사용 [이해]하기 쉬운 | device 기기, 장치 | overspending 초과 지출 | cause 야기하다 | lack 부족

---

5. 상관 접속사

해설 빈칸은 두 개의 명사구 사이의 자리이다. 빈칸 뒤의 명사구를 목적어로 취하는 전치사 또한 올 수 있으나, '급여 및 기타 비용에 사용된 지출 총액뿐만 아니라 회사 전체의 수익을 추적한다'는 내용이 되어야 문맥상 자연스러우므로 (B)가 정답이다.

+ Key point

'A as well as B'는 'B뿐만 아니라 A도'라는 부가의 의미로 사용되며, A와 B를 병렬시킨다.

---

6. 문장 선택

(A) 업데이트된 버전에는 스마트폰 애플리케이션이 포함되어 있다.
(B) 지방 및 연방 정부세 또한 고려된다.
(C) 이 소프트웨어는 숙련된 회계사들만 사용할 수 있다.
(D) 시스템 설치는 평소보다 시간이 더 걸릴 수 있다.

해설 빈칸 앞 문장의 '급여 및 기타 비용에 사용된 지출 총액뿐만 아니라, 회사 전체의 수익을 실시간으로 원활하게 추적한다'는 내용과 빈칸 뒷문장의 '모든 자료는 보기 쉽게 정리된다'는 내용을 고려할 때, 해당 프로그램에서 추적하는 수치 관련 자료와 관련된 내용이 들어가야 문맥상 자연스러우므로 (B)가 정답이다.

✦ Key word

In real time, it seamlessly tracks company-wide revenue as well as the total amount spent on payroll and other expenses. Local and federal taxes are also taken into account. All of this data is organized in an intuitive manner and can be accessed from a wide range of devices.

7. 사람 명사 vs. 사물 / 추상 명사

해설 빈칸은 문장의 주어인 명사 자리이다. 빈칸 뒤 동사 자리에 think가 있음을 고려할 때, 문맥상 '개발자들은 시스템이 직원들의 시간을 절약해 줄 것이라고 생각한다'는 내용이 되어야 자연스러우므로 사람 명사 (D)가 정답이다.

✦ Key point

명사 development vs. developer: development는 '개발, 발달'을, developer는 '개발자[회사]'를 의미한다.

8. 어휘 – 동사

해설 빈칸은 save와 함께 등위 접속사 and로 연결된 동사 자리이다. 문맥상 '시스템이 직원들의 시간을 절약해주고 초과 지출을 막아줄 것이라고 개발자들은 생각한다'는 내용이 되어야 자연스러우므로 (C)가 정답이다.

✦ Key word

Developers think it will save employees time and prevent overspending caused by a lack of information.

> ## CASE 집중훈련
> 본서 p.45
> **1.** (C) **2.** (A) **3.** (D) **4.** (A) **5.** (B) **6.** (A)
> **7.** (D) **8.** (D)

1. 복합명사

Our database **security** policy has been upgraded in order to maintain the confidentiality of client records.
우리 데이터베이스 보안 정책은 고객 정보의 비밀을 유지하기 위해 업그레이드 되어왔다.

해설 빈칸은 명사 policy와 함께 복합명사를 이루는 명사 자리이다. 문맥상 '보안 정책'이라는 의미가 되어야 자연스러우므로 'security policy(보안 정책)'라는 복합명사를 완성하는 명사 (C)가 정답이다.

어휘 policy 정책 ❘ maintain 유지하다 ❘ confidentiality 비밀

✦ Key point

토익에 자주 출제되는 복합명사 형태는 20개 남짓이므로 반드시 미리 암기해야 한다.

---

2. 어휘 – 명사

Visit our nearest community center and register today for the information technology **workshop**.
가까운 시민 회관을 방문해서 정보 기술 워크숍에 오늘 등록하세요.

해설 빈칸은 등록할 대상이 되는 행사 등을 나타내야 한다. 따라서 정보 기술 '워크숍'이라는 의미로 이어져야 자연스러우므로 (A)가 정답이다.

어휘 community center 시민 회관 ❘ register 등록하다

✦ Key word

Visit our nearest community center and **register today for the information technology workshop**.

---

3. 형용사 자리

Alternative sources of **renewable** energy have been a hot topic at this congress.
재생 가능 에너지의 대체원이 의회에서 관심이 많은 주제였다.

해설 빈칸은 명사 energy를 수식하는 형용사, 또는 복합명사를 이루는 명사 자리인데 (C)는 형태상 형용사로 보이지만 '갱신, 연장'이라는 명사라서 문법상 가능하지만 의미가 맞지 않고, 문맥상 '재생 가능 에너지의 대체원'이라는 의미가 자연스러우므로 (D)가 정답이다.

어휘 alternative 대체의 ❘ source 원천 ❘ congress 의회 ❘ renew 갱신하다 ❘ renewal 갱신, 연장 ❘ renewable 재생 가능한

✦ Key word

Alternative sources of renewable energy have been a hot topic at this congress.

---

4. 어휘 – 명사

If you have finished entering items to purchase, press 'SUBMIT' to calculate total and shipping **charges**.
구매할 물품들을 입력하는 것을 끝냈다면, 총액과 배송 요금을 계산하기 위해 '제출'을 누르세요.

해설 빈칸은 앞의 명사 shipping과 복합명사를 완성해줄 명사 자리이다. 문맥상 '총액과 배송 요금을 계산하기 위해 ~'라는 의미가 되어야 자연스러우므로 (A)가 정답이다.

어휘 finish 끝내다 ❘ enter 입력하다 ❘ purchase 구매하다 ❘ press 누르다 ❘ calculate 계산하다 ❘ shipping 배송, 운송 ❘ charge 요금 ❘ guideline 지침, 가이드라인 ❘ right 권리 ❘ concern 우려, 걱정거리

✦ Key word

If you have finished entering items to purchase, press 'SUBMIT' to calculate **total and shipping charges**.

> **5-8번은 다음 이메일에 관한 문제입니다.**
>
> 수신: Beatrice Dalton ⟨b_dalton1984@lmmail.com⟩
> 발신: Anthony Vanderfell ⟨anthonyv@wfservices.com⟩
> 날짜: 4월 1일
> 제목: 소비자 조사
>
> Beatrice Dalton 씨께,
>
> 저는 WF Services라는 주요 시장조사기관에서 근무하고 있습니다. 저희는 온라인과 오프라인 쇼핑 모두에서 소비자 행동을 더 잘 파악하기 위해 **5** 현재 운동선수와 체육교사에게 설문지를 배포하고 있습니다. 저희는 **6** 구매 습관에 영향을 미치는 요소들을 조사하고 싶습니다. 귀하는 ⟨Boynton Fitness Enthusiast⟩의 구독자셔서 **7** 선정되셨습니다. **8** 설문은 15분을 초과하지 않을 것입니다. 참여하신다면, 저희는 귀하의 지역 내 레스토랑에서 식사 시 이용하실 수 있는 50달러 쿠폰을 제공해 드립니다. 참여하고 싶으시면, 이 이메일에 회신해 주세요, 그러면 설문지 양식을 보내드리겠습니다.
>
> Anthony Vanderfell,
> 마케팅 지원 전문가

5. 어휘 - 부사

해설 빈칸은 현재 진행형의 동사 구문 are distributing을 수식하는 부사 자리이다. 문맥상 '현재 설문지를 배포하고 있다'는 내용이 되어야 자연스러우므로 (B)가 정답이다.

✚ Key word

We are currently distributing questionnaires to athletes and physical education teachers so that we can better understand their consumer behavior for both online and offline shopping.

6. 복합명사

해설 빈칸은 명사 habits를 수식하는 자리이다. 빈칸 앞 문장의 '온라인과 오프라인 쇼핑 모두에서 소비자 행동을 더 잘 파악하기 위해'라는 내용을 고려할 때, '구매 습관에 영향을 미치는 요소들을 조사하고 싶다'는 내용으로 이어져야 자연스러우므로 (A)가 정답이다.

✚ Key word

We are currently distributing questionnaires to athletes and physical education teachers **so that we can better understand their consumer behavior for both online and offline shopping**. We want to **examine the elements that affect buying habits**.

7. 동사의 태 / 시제

해설 빈칸은 주어 you에 대한 동사 자리이다. 빈칸 앞 부분의 '현재 운동선수와 체육교사에게 설문지를 배부 중'이라는 내용을 고려할 때, 문맥상 '귀하는 〈Boynton Fitness Enthusiast〉의 구독자라서 (설문대상자로) 선정되었다'는 내용으로 이어져야 자연스러우므로 현재 완료 수동태 (D)가 정답이다.

✚ Key word

We are currently distributing questionnaires to athletes and physical education teachers so that we can better understand their consumer behavior for both online and offline shopping. We want to examine the elements that affect buying habits. **You have been selected because you are a subscriber to Boynton Fitness Enthusiast.**

8. 문장 선택

(A) 유감스럽게도, 이것이 이 잡지의 마지막 호가 될 것입니다.
(B) 참가 장소의 리스트는 뒷면에 인쇄되어 있습니다.
(C) 우리는 다양한 분야의 일류 기업에 조언을 제공합니다.
(D) 설문은 15분을 초과하지 않을 것입니다.

해설 빈칸 앞 문장의 '(설문 대상으로) 선정되었다'는 내용과 빈칸 뒷문장의 '설문 참여시 쿠폰을 제공한다'는 내용을 고려할 때, 문맥상 설문조사와 관련된 내용이 들어가야 자연스러우므로 (D)가 정답이다.

✚ Key word

You have been selected because you are a subscriber to *Boynton Fitness Enthusiast*. The questionnaire should take no more than 15 minutes. Should you

take part, we will provide you with a $50 coupon for a meal at a restaurant in your area.

CASE 실전훈련
본서 p.46

| 1. (C) | 2. (D) | 3. (B) | 4. (B) | 5. (B) | 6. (B) |
| 7. (A) | 8. (C) | 9. (C) | 10. (B) | 11. (D) | 12. (A) |

1. 사람 명사 vs. 사물 / 추상 명사

About 50 percent of our streaming service's **subscribers** reside overseas.
우리 스트리밍 서비스 구독자의 약 50%는 해외에 거주한다.

해설 빈칸은 our streaming service's의 수식을 받는 명사 자리이다. 문맥상 '우리 스트리밍 서비스 구독자의 약 50%는 해외에 거주한다'라는 의미가 되어야 자연스러우므로 사람 명사 (C)가 정답이다.

어휘 streaming service 스트리밍 서비스 | reside 거주하다 | overseas 해외에

✚ Key point

명사 subscriber vs. subscription: subscriber는 '구독자'를, subscription은 '구독, 구독료'를 의미한다.

2. 복합명사

Urban scholars predict more population **growth** in the Sun Belt due to its well-developed infrastructure.
잘 발달된 기반 시설로 인해 도시학자들은 Sun Belt 내 더 많은 인구 증가를 예견한다.

해설 빈칸은 명사와 in 전치사구 사이의 자리이다. 문맥상 '발달된 기반 시설로 인해 인구 증가를 예견한다'는 의미가 되어야 자연스러우므로, 명사 population과 함께 복합명사를 이루는 명사 (D)가 정답이다.

어휘 urban 도시의 | scholar 학자 | predict 예견하다 | population 인구 | well-developed 잘 발달된 | infrastructure 기반 시설

✚ Key point

① 명사 growth vs. grower: 불가산 명사 growth는 '증가, 성장'을, 가산 명사 grower는 '재배자'를 의미한다.
② population growth(인구 증가)는 자주 출제되는 복합명사이므로 기억해 두자.

3. 사람 명사 vs. 사물 / 추상 명사

While Cherryville Growers is a well-known **producer** of fruit and vegetables, its market share is lower than its main competitor's.
Cherryville Growers는 유명한 철과물 생산업체인 반면, 시장 점유율은 주요 경쟁업체보다 낮다.

해설 빈칸은 well-known의 수식을 받는 명사 자리이다. while 종속절과 주절의 관계를 고려할 때, 'Cherryville Growers는 유명 생산업체인데, 시장 점유율은 낮다'라는 의미가 되어야 문맥상 자연스러우므로 '생산업체'를 의미하는 명사 (B)가 정답이다.

어휘 well-known 유명한, 잘 알려진 | market share 시장 점유율 | main 주된 | competitor 경쟁자

✚ Key point

명사 produce vs. producer vs. production: produce는 '농산물'을, producer는 '생산자'를, production은 '생산'을 의미한다.

4. 복합명사

Ms. Wu at the facility **management** office announced to us that the fire alarm system will be inspected at 10:00 A.M. today.

시설 관리 사무실 소속인 Wu 씨는 우리에게 화재 경보 장치가 오늘 오전 10시에 점검될 것이라고 알렸다.

해설 빈칸은 명사 facility, office와 함께 복합명사를 이루는 명사 자리이다. 문맥상 '시설 관리 사무실에 있는 Wu 씨'라는 의미가 되어야 자연스러우므로 명사 (B)가 정답이다.

어휘 facility 시설, 기관 | announce 알리다, 발표하다 | fire alarm system 화재 경보 장치 | inspect 검사하다, 점검하다

✦ Key point

복합명사는 「명사 + 명사」, 또는 「명사 + 명사 + 명사」로 구성된다.

5. 어휘 - 명사

Glenwood Electronics expects to finish the fiscal year with a budget **surplus** of 800,000 dollars.

Glenwood 전자는 80만 달러의 예산 흑자로 회계 연도를 마무리할 것으로 기대한다.

해설 빈칸은 a budget과 연결되는 명사 자리이다. 문맥상 '80만 달러의 예산 흑자로 회계 연도를 마무리한다'는 의미가 되어야 자연스러우므로 (B)가 정답이다. budget surplus는 '예산 흑자'라는 뜻의 복합명사이다.

어휘 finish 끝내다, 마무리하다 | fiscal year 회계 연도 | budget 예산

✦ Key word

Glenwood Electronics expects to **finish the fiscal year with a budget surplus of 800,000 dollars**.

6. 관용 표현

The Legend's third album, "Come on Now," sold well on the **strength** of the band's hit single.

The Legend의 세 번째 앨범인 'Come on Now'는 밴드의 히트곡에 힘입어 잘 팔렸다.

해설 빈칸은 the의 수식을 받는 명사 자리이다. '히트곡 덕분에 세 번째 앨범이 잘 팔렸다'는 의미가 되어야 문맥상 자연스러우므로 'on the strength of ~(~에 힘입어, 덕분에)'라는 관용 표현을 완성하는 명사 (B)가 정답이다.

어휘 sell 팔리다 | band 밴드 | hit single 히트곡

✦ Key word

The Legend's **third album**, "Come on Now," **sold well on the strength of** the band's **hit single**.

7. 어휘 - 명사

Potential candidates must complete and submit a personal **statement** before their interview.

잠재 지원자는 면접 전 자기 소개서를 작성해 제출해야 한다.

해설 빈칸은 형용사 personal의 수식을 받는 명사 자리이다. 문맥상 '지원자는 면접 전 자기소개서를 제출해야 한다'는 의미가 되어야 자연스러우므로 '자기소개서'라는 표현을 완성하는 명사 (A)가 정답이다.

어휘 potential 잠재적인 | candidate 지원자 | complete 완료하다, 작성하다 | submit 제출하다 | personal 개인적인

✦ Key word

Potential **candidates must** complete and **submit a personal statement before their interview**.

8. 어휘 - 명사

The Office of Public Roads has employed supplementary **contractors** so that motorways are quickly removed of any icy buildup.

도로공사는 얼음이 쌓인 고속도로가 빠르게 치워질 수 있도록 추가 하청업체들을 고용했다.

해설 빈칸은 형용사 supplementary의 수식을 받는 목적어 자리이다. so that 부사절과의 관계를 고려할 때 문맥상 '고속도로에 쌓인 얼음이 빠르게 제거될 수 있도록 추가 하청업체들을 고용했다'라는 의미가 되어야 자연스러우므로 (C)가 정답이다.

어휘 public 공공의 | employ 고용하다 | supplementary 추가의 | motorway 고속도로 | quickly 빠르게 | remove 제거하다 | icy 얼음이 덮인 | buildup 축적

✦ Key word

The Office of Public Roads has **employed supplementary contractors so that motorways are quickly removed of any icy buildup**.

9-12번은 다음 회람에 관한 문제입니다.

수신: 4영업팀

발신: Marcus Stone, 상품 관리자

날짜: 2월 3일

제목: 4분기 결과

환상적인 4분기 실적에 대해 팀 전체에 축하의 말씀부터 전합니다. 제가 상품별 매출 내역을 살펴봤을 **9때**, 놀라움을 금치 못했습니다. 저희가 월요일에 만나 조사 결과를 자세히 **10분석하는** 것을 제안드립니다.

특히, 가정 자동화 장비의 급격한 증가에 주목하고 싶습니다. **11작년에는 실적이 저조한 부문이었어요**. 무엇이 대중의 갑작스러운 관심을 불러 일으켰을까요? 저희 경쟁업체에서도 유사한 추세를 보이고 있나요? 올해 어디에 주목해야 할지 알아보려면 저희와 경쟁업체들의 결과치를 **12비교**해봐야 할 것 같습니다. 제가 안건 목록을 준비해서 내일까지 보내드리도록 하겠습니다.

어휘

product manager 상품 기획에서 판매까지 담당하는 직무 | quarter 분기 | result 결과 | preface ~로 서두를 떼다, 말문을 열다, 축하하다 | breakdown 내역 | astound 몹시 놀라게 하다 | propose 제안하다 | finding (조사) 결과 | in detail 자세히 | in particular 특히 | focus on ~에 주목하다 | sharp 급격한 | increase 증가 | home automation 가정 자동화 | equipment 장비 | spur 자극하다 | sudden 갑작스러운 | interest 관심 | public 대중

9. 접속사

해설 빈칸은 두 개의 완전한 절을 연결하는 부사절 접속사 자리이다. '상품별 매출 내역을 살펴봤을 때, 놀라움을 금치 못했다'는 의미가 되어야 문맥상 자연스러우므로 (C)가 정답이다.

10. 어휘 - 동사

해설 빈칸 앞 문장의 '상품별 매출 내역을 살펴봤을 때, 놀라움을 금치 못했다'는 내용을 고려할 때, 다같이 만나 조사 결과를 자세히 분석하자고 제안하는 내용으로 이어져야 문맥상 자연스러우므로 (B)가 정답이다.

+ **Key word**

In particular, I want to focus on the sharp increase in home automation equipment. **Last year, it was an underperforming category.** What spurred the sudden interest among the public? Are our competitors also seeing similar trends? I think we should do a comparison between our results and our competitors' to see where we should focus on for this year.

11. 문장 선택

(A) 회의는 20분 이상 걸리지 않을 거예요.
(B) 우리 브랜드를 개선하기 위해 몇 가지 제안을 해야 해요.
(C) 그에 따라 일정을 수정했어요.
(D) 작년에는 실적이 저조한 부문이었어요.

해설 빈칸 앞 문장의 '특히, 가정 자동화 장비의 급격한 증가에 주목하고 싶다'는 내용과 빈칸 뒷문장의 '무엇이 대중의 갑작스러운 관심을 불러일으켰을까?'라는 내용을 고려할 때, 작년에는 해당 부문의 실적이 저조했다는 내용이 들어가야 문맥상 자연스러우므로 (D)가 정답이다.

+ **Key point**

In particular, I want to focus on the sharp increase in home automation equipment. Last year, it(= home automation equipment) was an underperforming category. What spurred the sudden interest among the public?

12. 관용 표현

해설 빈칸은 a의 수식을 받는 명사 자리이므로 'do a comparison(비교하다)'라는 관용 표현을 완성하는 (A)가 정답이다. comparability는 '비교 가능성'이라는 뜻이다.

CHAPTER 03 대명사

CASE 집중훈련
본서 p.49

1. (C) **2.** (D) **3.** (B) **4.** (A) **5.** (D) **6.** (B)
7. (D) **8.** (C)

1. 주격 대명사

Customers have plenty of time to take advantage of the store discount, as **it** lasts until the end of the year.

상점 할인이 연말까지 지속되기 때문에, 고객들은 그것을 이용할 수 있는 시간이 충분하다.

해설 단수 동사 lasts에 수 일치되는 단수 대명사로, 앞의 명사 the store discount를 받는 3인칭 단수 대명사 (C)가 정답이다.

어휘 plenty of 충분한 | take advantage of ~을 이용하다 | last 지속되다

2. 주격 대명사

Mr. Barton promised Ms. Alvarez that **he** can complete the assignment with the assistance of his team members.

Barton 씨는 팀원들의 도움으로 그가 업무를 완수할 수 있다고 Alvarez 씨에게 약속했다.

해설 빈칸 뒤에 동사가 있으므로 빈칸은 주어 자리이다. 또한 문맥상 'Barton 씨가 업무를 완수할 수 있다고 약속했다'는 의미가 되어야 하므로 (D)가 정답이다.

어휘 complete 완료하다, 끝내다 | assignment 업무 | assistance 도움

3. 주격 대명사

Ms. Kimura was busy this morning, so **she** needs to be informed about the policy changes that were announced.

Kimura 씨가 오늘 아침에 바빴기 때문에 그녀는 발표된 정책 변화에 관하여 통지받아야 한다.

해설 빈칸은 동사 needs의 주어 자리이고 Ms. Kimura를 가리키므로 (B)가 정답이다.

어휘 inform 통지하다, 알리다 | policy 정책

4. 주격 대명사

Here at Parker's Learning Institute, **we** help underprivileged students master subjects they struggle to understand.

이곳 Parker 교육 기관에서, 우리는 혜택을 받지 못하는 학생들이 이해하기 어려워하는 과목들을 익히도록 돕습니다.

해설 Here at Parker's Learning Institute는 부사구이며, 빈칸은 동사 help 앞에 들어가는 주어 자리이므로 주격 대명사 (A)가 정답이다.

어휘 underprivileged 혜택을 못 받는 | master ~을 완전히 익히다 | subject 과목 | struggle 부단히 애쓰다, 힘겹게 하다

5-8번은 다음 웹페이지에 관한 문제입니다.

www.earlwin.edu/connect

모든 학생과 교수진은 지문 하나로 행사 및 수업 일정에서 카페테리아 메뉴에 이르기까지 모든 필요한 캠퍼스 정보를 제공하는 새로운 Earlwin Connect 앱을 사용해 볼 수 있습니다. 앱을 사용하려면, 학생들과 교수진은 우선 Earlwin Connect 계정에 가입해야 합니다. **⑤과정은 몇 가지 간단한 단계로 이루어져 있습니다.** (555) 462-9201번으로 '설치'라는 문자메시지를 보내거나, 제목 칸에 '설치'라고 작성해서 connectapp@earlwin.edu로 보내주세요. 몇 분 후, **⑥당신은** 아이디와 임시 비밀번호를 받을 것입니다. 받고 나서 스마트기기로 Connect 앱에 접속하고, 메시지가 나타나면 적절한 자격사항을 입력하세요.

통신망 보호를 위해, 일회성 비밀번호는 하루가 지나면 **⑦만료되오니**, 반드시 즉시 사용해 주세요. 등록 과정에서 발생하는 **⑧문제를** 해결하려면, IT부서에 (555) 462-2000번으로 연락주십시오.

어휘
faculty 교수진 | invite 초대하다 | app 앱(application의 약어) | resource 자원 | relevant 관련 있는, 적절한 | information 정보 | event 행사 | schedule 일정 | cafeteria 카페테리아, 식당 | fingerprint 지문 | sign up for 등록하다, 신청하다 | account 계정 | set up 설치하다 | subject 제목 | header 헤더 | thereafter 그 후 | temporary 임시의 | password 비밀번호 | access 접속하다 | device 기기, 장치 | enter 입력하다 | appropriate 적절한 | credential 자격 | prompt 메시지를 표시하다 | in the interest of ~를 위하여 | protect 보호하다 | network 통신망, 네트워크 | one-time 일회성의 | promptly 즉시 | clear up ~를 해결하다 | come up 발생하다, 생기다 | registration 등록 | procedure 과정, 절차

5. 문장 선택

(A) 당사의 온라인 포털은 정기적인 유지 보수를 받을 것입니다.

(B) 학생의 프라이버시를 보호하기 위해 일부 일정 정보가 삭제되었습니다.

(C) 설치에는 최신 버전의 Campus Messenger가 필요합니다.

(D) 과정은 몇 가지 간단한 단계로 이루어져 있습니다.

해설 빈칸 앞 문장의 '앱을 사용하려면, 우선 계정에 가입해야 한다'는 내용을 고려할 때, 가입 절차와 관련된 내용이 이어져야 자연스러우므로 (D)가 정답이다.

＋ Key word

To start using the app, **students and faculty** first need to sign up for an Earlwin Connect account. The process consists of several simple steps.

6. 주격 대명사

해설 빈칸은 문장의 주어 자리이다. 빈칸 앞 문장이 명령문이므로, 문맥상 '문자메시지 또는 이메일을 보내면, 몇 분 후 당신은 아이디와 임시 비밀번호를 받게 될 것'이라는 의미가 되어야 자연스러우므로 (B)가 정답이다.

＋ Key word

Send a text message reading "set up" to (555) 462-9201, **or write** "set up" in the subject header to connectapp@earlwin.edu. A few minutes thereafter, **you will be sent an ID and temporary password.**

7. 동사의 시제

해설 빈칸은 password를 주어로 하는 문장의 동사 자리이다. 접속사 so로 연결된 이어지는 문장이 현재 시제인 명령문 형태임을 고려할 때, 문맥상 '일회성 비밀번호는 하루 뒤 만료되니, 즉시 사용해 주세요'라는 내용으로 이어져야 자연스러우므로 일반적 사실을 전달하는 현재 시제 (D)가 정답이다.

＋ Key word

In the interest of protecting our network, **the one-time password expires after one day, so make sure to use it promptly.**

8. 어휘 - 명사

해설 빈칸은 구동사 clear up의 목적어이자, that 주격 관계절의 수식을 받는 명사 자리이다. 문맥상 '등록과정에서 발생하는 문제를 해결하려면'이라는 의미가 되어야 자연스러우므로 (C)가 정답이다.

＋ Key word

To clear up issues that come up during the registration procedure, call IT at (555) 462-2000.

CASE 집중훈련
본서 p.51

1. (C) **2.** (B) **3.** (D) **4.** (D) **5.** (A) **6.** (B)
7. (D) **8.** (A)

---

1. 소유격 대명사

This economic forecast relies on the assumption that all firms will be minimizing **their** costs.

이 경기 예측은 모든 회사들이 그들의 비용을 최소화할 것이라는 가정에 의존한다.

해설 빈칸은 동사 will be minimizing의 목적어인 명사 costs를 수식 및 한정해줄 대명사가 들어갈 자리이다. 명사를 수식 및 한정해줄 수 있는 것은 소유격 대명사이므로 (C)가 정답이다.

어휘 economic forecast 경기 예측 ｜ rely on ~에 의존하다 ｜ assumption 가정, 가설 ｜ firm 회사 ｜ minimize 최소화하다 ｜ cost 비용

＋ Key point

소유격 대명사는 한정사이므로 항상 명사 앞에 위치한다.

---

2. 소유격 대명사

Ms. Raina dealt with **her** clients' requests promptly and with professionalism.

Raina 씨는 그녀의 고객의 요구들을 전문성을 가지고 지체 없이 처리했다.

해설 빈칸은 명사 앞의 소유격 대명사 자리이므로 (B)가 정답이다.

어휘 deal with 처리하다, 다루다 ｜ request 요구 ｜ promptly 지체 없이, 즉시 ｜ professionalism 전문성

---

3. 소유격 대명사

There are numerous power tools available for **our** citizens to borrow for a nominal fee.

우리 주민이 아주 적은 수수료로 빌릴 수 있는 전동 공구가 많다.

해설 빈칸은 명사 citizens를 수식하는 자리이므로 소유격 대명사 (D)가 정답이다.

어휘 numerous 많은 ｜ power tool 전동 공구 ｜ available 이용할 수 있는 ｜ citizen 시민, 주민 ｜ borrow 빌리다 ｜ nominal 아주 적은, 명목상의 ｜ fee 수수료, 요금

---

4. 부사 자리

Included in the lease agreement to Whittingham Apartments is exclusive use of our **attractively** designed rooftop.

Whittingham 아파트의 임대 계약서에는 멋지게 설계된 루프탑의 독점 사용권이 포함되어 있다.

해설 빈칸은 형용사 역할을 하는 과거분사 designed를 수식하는 부사 자리이므로 (D)가 정답이다. 소유격 대명사와 명사 사이에 「부사＋형용사」가 들어온 구조이다.

어휘 lease 임대 ｜ agreement 계약(서) ｜ exclusive 독점적인 ｜ use 사용 ｜ design 설계하다 ｜ rooftop 옥상, 루프탑

> **5-8번은 다음 이메일에 관한 문제입니다.**
>
> 수신: Veronica Humphrey ⟨v.humphrey@corpsol.com⟩
> 발신: Darla Weimer ⟨darla.w@xcoindustries.com⟩
> 날짜: 6월 2일
> 제목: 5월 20일 세미나
>
> Humphrey 씨께,
>
> 이 이메일은 저희 사무실 건물에서 5월 20일에 Benjamin Morey가 진행했던 세미나에 대한 **⑤감사**를 표현하기 위한 것입니다. 몇몇 직원들이 이런 종류의 세미나가 필요하다는 데 대한 관심을 **⑥제기했습니다.** 이 직원들이 세미나에서 가장 열정적인 참가자들이었으며 비슷한 행사를 미래

에 주최할 수 있을지 문의했습니다. 참가자들은 **7 그 뒤에** 세미나의 유용함을 평가하기 위해 피드백 설문조사를 작성하도록 요청받았습니다. 대부분의 반응이 긍정적이었고 거의 85%의 참석자들이 이제 대중 연설 능력에 더 자신감을 느낀다고 밝혔습니다. **8 소수의 참가자들은 직접 해보는 활동을 원했다고 밝혔습니다.** 만약 직접 결과를 확인하는 데 관심이 있으시면 저에게 연락주십시오.

진심으로,

Darla Weimer

어휘

concern 우려, 관심사 | enthusiastic 열광적인 | participant 참가자 | host 주최하다 | attendee 참가자 | fill out 작성하다 | survey 설문 조사 | evaluate 평가하다 | usefulness 유용함 | majority 대다수 | response 반응 | positive 긍정적인 | indicate 나타내다 | confident 자신감 있는 | public speaking 공석에서 말하기 | result 결과

5. 명사 자리

해설 빈칸은 소유격 대명사의 수식을 받는 명사 자리이므로 (A)가 정답이다.

+ Key word

This e-mail is to show **our appreciation** for the seminar Benjamin Morey gave on May 20 at our office building.

6. 동사의 시제

해설 앞 문장의 내용을 고려할 때, 직원들이 5월 20일의 세미나 이후로 그러한 종류의 세미나의 필요성을 제기해왔다는 내용으로 이어져야 문맥상 자연스럽다. 메일을 보낸 시점이 6월 2일이고, 세미나는 5월 20일에 열렸으며, 세미나가 열리기 이전에 세미나의 필요성을 제기한 것이므로 빈칸에는 과거 완료 시제가 나와야 한다. 따라서, (B)가 정답이다.

+ Key word

This e-mail is to show our appreciation **for the seminar Benjamin Morey gave on May 20 at our office building.** Several staff members **have raised concerns about the need for this type of seminar.**

7. 어휘 – 부사

해설 빈칸 앞에서 완전한 문장이 끝나므로, 빈칸 이후는 to부정사의 부사적 용법으로 쓰인 수식어구이며 빈칸은 수식어인 부사 자리이므로 (C)는 소거한다. to부정사구의 내용을 고려하면, '세미나의 유용함으로 평가하기 위해 그 후(세미나가 끝난 후) 설문조사 작성을 요청받았다'는 내용이 문맥상 자연스러우므로 (D)가 정답이다.

+ Key word

Attendees were asked to fill out a feedback survey **afterwards to evaluate the usefulness of the seminar.**

8. 문장 선택

(A) 소수의 참가자들은 직접 해보는 활동을 원했다고 밝혔습니다.
(B) 시간 관리에 관한 다른 세미나가 수시로 개최될 것입니다.
(C) 청구 명세서가 곧 이메일 주소로 발송됩니다.
(D) 세미나는 다음 주로 연기되었습니다.

해설 앞 문장에서 설문조사 결과에 대한 다수의 의견을 설명하고 있으므로, 문맥상 소수의 의견을 알려주는 문장으로 이어지는 것이 자연스럽다. 따라서 (A)가 정답이다.

+ Key word

Attendees were asked to fill out **a feedback survey afterwards to evaluate the usefulness of the seminar. The majority of responses** were positive; nearly 85 percent of the attendees indicated that they were more confident in their public speaking abilities now. **A small number of attendees stated they wanted more hands-on activities.**

CASE 집중훈련
본서 p.53

1. (C) **2.** (B) **3.** (D) **4.** (D) **5.** (D) **6.** (B)
7. (A) **8.** (C)

1. 목적격 대명사

Mr. Howard promised to send **us** a confirmation e-mail by 5 this afternoon.

Howard 씨가 오늘 오후 5시까지 우리에게 확인 이메일을 보내준다고 약속했다.

해설 빈칸은 4형식 동사 send의 간접 목적어 자리이다. 'Howard 씨가 우리에게 답변을 보내준다고 약속했다'라는 의미가 되어야 자연스러우므로 목적격 대명사 (C)가 정답이다.

어휘 promise to do ~하기로 약속하다 | confirmation 확인

+ Key point

수여 동사 give, offer, send 등의 구조는 다음과 같다.
① 수여 동사 + sb + sth '~에게 ~를 주다'
② 수여 동사 + sth + to sb '~를 ~에게 주다'

2. 목적격 대명사

There are several books on public speaking at our store that will help **you** to improve your communication skills.

저희 매장에는 당신이 의사소통 기술을 향상시키는 데 도움을 줄 공개연설 도서들이 여럿 있습니다.

해설 public speaking을 선행사로 하는 주격 관계절(that will help ~) 및 준 사역 동사 help의 문장 구조 「help + 목적어(------) + 목적격 보어(=원형 부정사/to부정사)」를 확인하면, 빈칸은 목적어 자리임을 알 수 있으며, 주격 관계절의 동사 help의 의미상 주어가 public speaking인데, 주어와 빈칸에 들어갈 목적어가 일치하지 않으므로 목적격 대명사 (B)가 정답이다.

어휘 public speaking 공개연설, 공석에서 말하기 | improve 개선하다, 향상시키다 | communication 의사소통

3. 소유대명사

An employee of **mine** will be attending the global trade conference in Germany.

제 직원 중 한 명이 독일에서 열리는 국제 무역 학회에 참석할 것입니다.

해설 문맥상 '내 직원들 중 한 직원'이란 의미(An employee of my employees)이므로 「소유격 + 명사(my employees)」를 대신하는 소유대명사 (D)가 정답이다. 「a(n) + 명사 + of + ------」 구조가 보이고 해석이 '~중 한 명사'이면 무조건 소유대명사가 정답이다.

어휘 attend 참석하다 | global 세계적인 | trade 무역

4. 소유대명사

Your duties as a project manager are essentially the same as **his**.
프로젝트 매니저로서 당신의 직무는 기본적으로 그의 것과 동일합니다.

해설 빈칸은 전치사 as의 목적어 역할을 하는 대명사 자리이다. '당신의 직무는 기본적으로 그의 것과 동일합니다'라는 의미가 되어야 자연스러우며, his는 소유격 대명사 '그의'와 소유대명사 '그의 것'의 의미를 동시에 가진다. 여기서는 문맥상 '그의 것(his duties)'을 의미하므로 (D)가 정답이다.

어휘 duty 직무 | essentially 기본적으로

5-8번은 다음 회람에 관한 문제입니다.

수신: 주방 전 직원
발신: Rachel Wong, 인사 담당자
날짜: 2월 11일
제목: 새로운 보건 규정

3월 1일부로 건물 내에서 뜨거운 음식 보관에 관한 새로운 규정을 **⑤지켜야** 합니다. 음식용 온도계를 구입해 주방에 비치해 놓았습니다. **⑥정기적으로 온도를 기록하는데** 사용해 주세요. 온도를 기록하면서 정해진 지침 아래로 내려간 음식은 모두 버려주세요. 또한, 지난 점검 때 최신 건강 지침을 출력해 놓으라는 경고를 받았습니다. 이제 구 지침은 우리 레스토랑에 **⑦적용되지** 않습니다. 공유해 드렸던 내용과 관련하여 **⑧문의사항**이 있으면 무엇이든, 저에게 알려주세요.

어휘

regulation 규정 | as of ~부로 | rule 규칙 | regarding ~에 관하여 | premises 부지, 구내 | purchase 구입하다 | thermometer 온도계 | record 기록하다 | temperature 온도 | throw out 버리다 | fall 내려가다 | below ~ 아래로 | given 정해진 | guideline 가이드라인, 지침 | warn 경고하다 | check-up 점검 | print out 출력하다 | updated 최신의 | share 공유하다

5. 어휘 - 동사

해설 빈칸은 to부정사를 완성하는 동사 자리이다. 새로운 규칙에 순응해야 한다는 의미가 되어야 문맥상 자연스러우므로 (D)가 정답이다.

✦ **Key word**
As of March 1, **we will be required to accommodate new rules** regarding keeping hot food on our premises.

6. 문장 선택

(A) 검증자들은 그들의 직업을 위해 공부하는 데 몇 년을 보냅니다.
(B) 정기적으로 온도를 기록하는 데 사용해 주세요.
(C) 인증 프로세스는 웹 사이트에서 확인할 수 있습니다.
(D) 영상은 불일치에 대해 설명합니다.

해설 빈칸 앞 문장의 음식용 온도계를 구입해 주방에 비치해 놓았다는 내용을 고려할 때, 온도계를 사용해서 온도를 기록해 달라는 내용으로 이어져야 문맥상 자연스러우므로 (B)가 정답이다. 나머지는 전치사 없이 바로 목적어를 취하는 타동사이다.

✦ **Key word**
We have **purchased some food thermometers** to keep in the kitchen. **Use them to periodically record temperatures.**

7. 어휘 - 형용사

해설 지난 점검 때 최신 건강 지침을 출력해 놓으라고 경고받았다는 빈칸 앞 문장의 내용과 뒤에 for our restaurant가 있음을 고려할 때, 이제 구 지침은 우리 레스토랑에 적용되지 않는다는 내용으로 이어져야 문맥상 자연스러우므로 (A)가 정답이다. 지침이 게시되지 않는다는 의미가 되기 위해서는 뒤에 장소를 나타내는 전치사가 필요하다.

✦ **Key word**
Also, **we were warned** in our last check-up **to print out the updated health guidelines**. The **old one is no longer applicable for** our restaurant.

8. 단수 명사 vs. 복수 명사

해설 빈칸은 any의 수식을 받는 명사 자리이다. 명사 query는 가산 명사이므로 복수형 (C)가 정답이다. 참고로 "If you have any ~" 뒤의 명사는 불가산 명사나 가산 복수 명사만 가능하다는 점을 기억해두자.

✦ **Key point**
any 뒤에 가산 명사가 올 때는 복수형이 되어야 한다.

CASE 집중훈련
본서 p.55

1. (B) **2.** (A) **3.** (C) **4.** (D) **5.** (D) **6.** (B)
7. (B) **8.** (A)

1. 재귀대명사

Katrina Ling, Director of International Sales, chose to conduct the interview **herself**.
해외영업이사인 Katrina Ling은 면접을 그녀가 직접 하기로 결정했다.

해설 동사와 목적어 뒤 문장의 수식어 자리이다. 대명사 중 수식어 자리에 들어갈 수 있는 것은 강조 용법으로 쓰이는 재귀대명사이므로 (B)가 정답이다.

어휘 choose to do ~하기로 결정하다 | conduct 수행하다

✦ **Key point**
재귀대명사에는 2가지 용법이 있다.
① 재귀 용법-목적어 자리
② 강조 용법-수식어 자리

2. 재귀대명사

When visiting ABC Cosmetics' booth at the convention, remember to help **yourself** to a free sample.
컨벤션에서 ABC 화장품 부스를 방문하시면, 잊지 말고 무료 샘플을 받아보시기 바랍니다.

해설 빈칸은 동사 help의 목적어 자리이다. 소유격 대명사 your는 목적어 역할을 할 수 없으므로 제거한다. 재귀대명사 oneself는 목적어 자리에서 행위의 주체와 일치하는 경우 쓸 수 있는데, 명령문의 주어는 you가 생략된 것으로 행위의 주체인 you와 일치하므로 빈칸은 재귀대명사 자리이다. 'help oneself to'는 '마음껏 하다'를 의미하므로 (A)가 정답이다.

어휘 cosmetics 화장품 | free 무료의

✦ **Key point**
재귀대명사의 재귀 용법 vs. 강조 용법:
[재귀 용법] 주어와 목적어가 동일한 대상을 지칭할 때, 목적어 자리에 온다 - 생략불가.

[강조 용법] 주어나 목적어를 강조할 때, 수식어 자리에 온다 - 생략가능.

3. 재귀대명사

Vice President Harley has an impressive background in finance and so has appointed **himself** to fill the vacant finance director position.

Harley 부사장은 재무 분야에서 인상적인 경력을 보유했기에 비어 있는 재무이사 직위를 채우기 위해 자기 자신을 임명했다.

해설 빈칸은 동사 has appointed의 목적어 역할을 하는 대명사 자리이다. 'Harley 부사장은 비어 있는 재무이사 직위를 채우기 위해 자기 자신을 임명했다'라는 의미가 되어야 자연스러우며, 주어와 목적어가 동일할 때는 목적어 자리에 재귀대명사를 쓸 수 있으므로 (C)가 정답이다.

어휘 impressive 인상적인 | background 경력, 배경 | finance 재무, 금융 | appoint 임명하다 | vacant 비어 있는

4. 재귀대명사

Ms. Kimura assured the executives that she would complete the budget report **herself** by the end of the day.

Kimura 씨는 경영진에게 오늘까지 그녀가 직접 예산보고서를 완료할 것이라고 장담했다.

해설 빈칸은 문장의 목적어인 that절 내 목적어와 전명구 사이에서 강조 용법으로 쓰인 재귀대명사 자리이다. 문맥상 '그녀가 직접 오늘까지 보고서를 완료할 것'이라는 의미가 되어야 자연스러우므로 주어인 she를 지칭하는 (D)가 정답이다.

어휘 assure 장담하다, 보장하다 | executive 경영진, 간부 | budget 예산, 비용

5-8번은 다음 이메일에 관한 문제입니다.

수신: 전 직원 (listserv@wiztech.com)
발신: Lance Hughes ⟨lhuges@wiztech.com⟩
날짜: 9월 15일
제목: 아침식사 환급

여러분, 안녕하세요.

전 직원 여러분께 신나는 소식을 알려드리고 **⑤싶습니다.** 다음달부터 WizTech에서는 전 직원에게 아침식사를 변제해 드릴 예정입니다. 이는 새로운 직원 복지 프로그램의 일환이며, 첫 번째 단계는 전 직원이 매일 영양가 있는 아침 식사를 하도록 하는 것입니다. 환급 **⑥자격을 얻으려면,** 구입 영수증을 보관해 매달 말에 비용을 청구해야 합니다. 금액은 부서 예산에서 지급됩니다. **⑦대체로 구매액은 20달러 미만으로 유지해 주시기 바랍니다.** 저희의 신규 프로그램에 대해 문의사항이 있으시면, **⑧저나 인사팀 다른 직원에게 언제든지 연락해 주십시오.**

감사합니다.

Lance

어휘
reimbursement 상환, 변제 | greeting 인사 | share 공유하다 | reimburse 상환하다, 변제하다 | well-being 웰빙 | step 단계 | ensure 보장하다 | nutritious 영양가 높은 | receipt 영수증 | purchase 구입(한 것) | file 제출하다 | expense 비용 | budget 예산 | feel free to 언제든지 ~하다 | reach out to ~에게 접근하다 | human resources 인사

5. 동사의 시제

해설 빈칸은 주어 I에 대한 동사 자리이다. 다음 문장의 내용을 고려할 때, '신나는 소식을 알려드리고 싶다'라는 내용이 되어야 문맥상 연결이 자연스러우므로 (D)가 정답이다. would like to V는 '~하고 싶다'라는 뜻의 숙어 표현이다.

✛ Key word

I would like to share some **exciting news** with all employees. **Starting next month, WizTech will now be reimbursing all employees for breakfast meals.**

6. 어휘 - 동사

해설 빈칸은 to부정사구를 완성하는 동사 자리이다. 문맥상 '지원받을 자격을 얻으려면, 영수증을 보관해야 한다'라는 의미가 되어야 하며, 빈칸 뒤에 전치사 for가 있음을 고려할 때, '자격을 얻다'라는 의미의 동사구 'qualify for'를 완성하는 동사 (B)가 정답이다.

✛ Key word

To qualify for the reimbursement, you will need to keep the receipt for your purchase and file your expenses at the end of the month.

7. 문장 선택

(A) 자세한 영양 정보는 인터넷을 통해 확인할 수 있습니다.
(B) 대체로 구매액은 20달러 미만으로 유지해 주시기 바랍니다.
(C) 많은 직원들이 현재 아침을 먹지 않습니다.
(D) 맞은편 건물에 식당이 하나 문을 열었습니다.

해설 빈칸 앞 문장에서 금액에 대한 내용을 다루고 있음을 고려할 때, 문맥상 금액과 관련된 내용으로 이어져야 자연스러우므로 (B)가 정답이다.

✛ Key word

The money will come out of your team budget. As a rule, please try to keep purchases below $20.

8. 목적격 대명사

해설 빈칸은 동사구 reach out to의 목적어 자리이다. 접속사 or로 연결된 명사구를 고려할 때, 저(메일 발송인)나 다른 인사팀원에게 언제든지 연락해 달라는 내용이 되어야 문맥상 자연스러우므로 (A)가 정답이다.

✛ Key point

If you have any questions about our new program, please feel free to **reach out to myself or anyone else from the human resources team.**

CASE 집중훈련   본서 p.57

1. (B) **2.** (D) **3.** (D) **4.** (B) **5.** (B) **6.** (B)
7. (D) **8.** (A)

1. 지시대명사

If the conference time changes, **those** who register early will be informed by phone.

회의 시간이 변경될 경우, 일찍 등록한 사람들은 전화로 연락받을 것이다.

해설 빈칸은 관계사절 who 이하의 수식을 받으며 주어 역할을 하는 대명사 자리이다. 「those + who + 동사」는 '~하는 사람들'을 의미하므로 (B)

가 정답이다.

어휘 register 등록하다 | inform 알리다

✚ Key point

those '사람들'은 주로 「those who/-ing/p.p./with ~」의 구조로 관계사절, 분사, 전치사구의 수식을 받으며 '~하는 사람들'이라는 뜻으로 사용된다. 인칭대명사 they/them은 수식어의 꾸밈을 받을 수 없는 것이 문법 규칙이다.

---

2. 지시대명사

Those who are interested in participating in the clinical trial should contact Prof. Lee from the Molly Medical Research Institute.

임상실험에 참가하는 데 관심 있는 사람들은 Molly 의료기관의 Lee 교수에게 연락해야 한다.

해설 빈칸은 관계사절 who 이하의 수식을 받으며 주어 역할을 하는 명사 또는 대명사 자리이다. 'Those who ~'는 '~하는 사람들'로 복수 취급되며 'Anyone who ~'는 '~하는 누구든지'로 Anyone이 단수 취급됨을 고려할 때, who 뒤의 동사가 are이므로 (D)가 정답이다.

어휘 participate in ~에 참가하다 | clinical trial 임상실험

---

3. 어휘 - 동사

Vault Systems will **waive** its installation fee for anyone who purchases an air purifier this week.

Vault Systems는 이번 주에 공기청정기를 구입하는 사람들에게 설치비를 면제해줄 것이다.

해설 빈칸은 주어와 목적어 사이의 동사 자리이다. 문맥상 '이번 주에 공기청정기를 구입하는 사람들에게 설치비를 면제해 줄 것'이라는 의미가 되어야 자연스러우므로 (D)가 정답이다.

어휘 installation fee 설치비 | purchase 구입하다 | air purifier 공기청정기

✚ Key word

Vault Systems will **waive** its **installation fee** for anyone who purchases an air purifier this week.

---

4. 어휘 - 동사

Customers enrolled in our mailing list may receive rewards, such as gift cards, if they **acquire** a certain number of points.

저희 우편물 수신자 명단에 등록된 고객들은 일정 포인트를 획득할 경우 상품권과 같은 보상을 받게 됩니다.

해설 빈칸은 if 종속절 내의 주어와 목적어 사이의 동사 자리이다. 주절과의 관계를 고려할 때 일정 포인트를 획득할 경우 상품권과 같은 보상을 받게 된다는 의미가 되어야 문맥상 자연스러우므로 (B)가 정답이다.

어휘 enroll 등록하다 | mailing list 우편물 수신자 명단 | receive 받다 | reward 보상 | certain 일정한, 특정한

✚ Key point

Customers enrolled in our mailing list **may receive rewards, such as gift cards, if they acquire a certain number of points**.

5-8번은 다음 기사에 관한 문제입니다.

감세 원리

부유층을 대상으로 한 감세는 침체된 경제에 빠른 해결책으로 자주 **⑤촉진된다**. 본질적으로, 부유층 감세는 수혜자의 지출을 늘리려는 것이다. **⑥감세는 침체된 경기를 자극해 활성화할 수 있다.**

경기 침체는 미래에 대한 불확실성으로 사람들이 지출을 중단하면서 발생한다. 사람들이 소비를 멈추면, 많은 상점은 수익 감소를 **⑦겪게 된다**. 이는 점포 폐쇄뿐만 아니라 실직으로 이어진다.

감세를 뒷받침하는 **⑧근거**는 부유층 소비를 증진하는 것이다. 부유층이 돈을 더 많이 쓰면, 기업에 수익을 창출해, 더 많은 일자리로 이어진다. 따라서 감세는 경기 침체의 영향을 반전시킬 수 있다.

어휘
tax cut 감세 | a quick fix 빠른 해결책, 응급조치 | stagnant 침체된 | economy 경제 | at its core 본질적으로 | intend 의도하다 | increase 늘리다, 증가시키다 | spending 지출 | recipient 수신자, 수혜자 | slow economy 경기 침체 | occur 발생하다 | uncertainty 불확실성 | cause 야기하다 | decline 하락, 감소 | revenue 수익, 수입 | lead to ~로 이어지다 | closing 폐쇄 | loss 상실 | generate 발생시키다 | reverse 뒤집다 | effect 효과

---

5. 동사의 태

해설 빈칸은 be동사 뒷자리이다. 문맥상 '부유층 대상 감세는 침체된 경제에 빠른 해결책으로 자주 촉진된다'는 의미가 되어야 문맥상 자연스러우므로 수동태 동사 구문을 완성하는 과거분사 (B)가 정답이다.

✚ Key point

be동사 뒤에는 보어 역할을 하는 형용사/명사, 'be + p.p.'의 형태로 수동태 구문을 완성하는 과거분사, 'be + Ving'의 형태로 진행형 구문을 완성하는 현재분사가 올 수 있으므로, 주어진 보기에 여러가지 선택이 가능한 경우, 문맥상 적합한 형태를 선택한다. promotional '홍보의', promotion '홍보(활동), 승진'

---

6. 문장 선택

(A) 감세에는 많은 숨겨진 단점이 있습니다.
(B) 감세는 침체된 경기를 자극해 활성화할 수 있습니다.
(C) 경기 침체기에 일자리를 잃는 경우가 많습니다.
(D) 최근의 감세는 계획대로 되지 않았습니다.

해설 빈칸 앞 쪽의 '부유층 대상 감세는 침체된 경제에 빠른 해결책으로 자주 촉진된다. 본질적으로, 부유층 감세는 수혜자의 지출을 늘리려는 것이다'라는 내용을 고려할 때, 문맥상 앞 내용을 정리한 감세 효과에 관한 내용으로 이어져야 자연스러우므로 (B)가 정답이다.

✚ Key word

Tax cuts for the wealthy are often promote as a quick fix to a stagnant economy. At its core, tax cuts for the wealthy are intended to increase spending by the recipients. Tax cuts can stimulate slow economies into action.

---

7. 어휘 - 동사

해설 빈칸은 many stores를 주어로, a decline을 목적어로 하는 동사 자리이다. 빈칸 앞 부분의 '경기 침체는 미래에 대한 불확실성으로 사람들이 지출을 중단하면서 발생한다'는 내용을 고려할 때, '사람들이 소비를 멈추면, 많은 상점은 수익 감소를 겪게 된다'는 의미가 되어야 문맥상 자연스러우므로 (D)가 정답이다.

✦ **Key word**

A slow economy occurs when uncertainty about the future causes people to stop spending money. When people stop spending money, many stores experience a decline in their revenues.

8. 어휘 – 명사

해설 빈칸은 문장의 주어 자리이다. 빈칸 뒷부분에 '부유층이 돈을 더 많이 쓰면, 기업에 수익을 창출해, 더 많은 일자리로 이어진다. 따라서 감세는 경기 침체의 영향을 반전시킬 수 있다'는 내용이 이어지므로, '어떤 행동이나 조치를 실시하는/뒷받침하는 근거, 이유'의 의미를 갖는 (A)가 정답이다.

✦ **Key word**

The **rationale** behind a tax cut is to increase spending by the wealthy. If the wealthy spend more money in the economy, it will generate more revenue for businesses, leading to more jobs. Thus, tax cuts can reverse the effects of a slow economy.

CASE 집중훈련
본서 p.59

1. (C) **2.** (A) **3.** (B) **4.** (D) **5.** (C) **6.** (D)
7. (C) **8.** (B)

1. 부정대명사

Dr. Hanks will personally call **everyone** who was chosen to participate in the clinical trial for the allergy medication.

알레르기 약물 치료를 위한 임상 실험에 참가하기 위해 선정된 모든 사람들에게 Hanks 씨가 직접 전화할 것이다.

해설 빈칸은 관계절의 수식을 받는 선행사 자리이다. 문맥상 '임상 실험에 참가하기 위해 선정된 모두에게 Hanks 씨가 직접 전화할 것이다'라는 의미가 자연스러우므로 (C)가 정답이다. 주격 관계대명사 who는 사람 선행사를 취하는 것도 단서가 된다.

어휘 personally 직접, 개인적으로 | participate in ~에 참가하다 | clinical trial 임상 실험 | medication 약물

2. 부정대명사

All of the applicants are so well-qualified that **anyone** the CEO hires will be a good fit with the department.

모든 지원자들이 자격이 충분해서 CEO가 채용하는 누구든 부서에 잘 맞을 것이다.

해설 빈칸은 목적격 관계절(the CEO hires)의 꾸밈을 받으면서 that절의 주어 역할을 하는 명사 또는 대명사 자리이다. other은 한정사 '다른'이란 뜻으로 대명사로 쓰이기 위해서는 another, others, the other(s)의 형태를 띠어야 하므로 제거한다. '모든 지원자들이 자격이 충분해서 CEO가 채용하는 누구든 부서에 잘 맞을 것이다'라는 의미가 되어야 자연스러우며, 대명사 anyone은 '누구나, 누구든'을 의미하므로 (A)가 정답이다.

어휘 well-qualified 자격이 충분한 | hire 채용하다 | good fit 적임자

3. 부정대명사

The Kubeo Pro X200 laser printer is the most expensive **one** in the store at the moment.

현재 매장에서 가장 비싼 것은 Kubeo Pro X200 레이저 프린터이다.

해설 빈칸은 형용사 expensive의 수식을 받는 자리로 another, each, all은 형용사의 수식을 받지 않으므로 제거한다. '현재 매장에서 가장 비싼 것은 Kubeo Pro X200 레이저 프린터이다.'라는 의미가 되어야 자연스러우며, 대명사 one은 앞에 언급된 명사의 반복을 피할 때 쓰고, 정해지지 않은 가산 단수 명사를 대신할 수 있으며, 형용사의 수식을 받을 수 있으므로 (B)가 정답이다.

어휘 at the moment 지금, 현재

4. 부정대명사

We were previously unable to purchase additional computers for the office because our usual supplier has **none** in stock.

전에 우리는 거래하던 납품업체에 재고가 하나도 없어서, 사무용 컴퓨터를 추가로 구매할 수 없었다.

해설 빈칸은 타동사 has의 목적어 역할을 하는 명사 자리이다. '납품업체에 재고가 하나도 없었기 때문에, 컴퓨터를 추가로 구매할 수 없었다'라는 의미가 되어야 자연스러우며, 대명사 none은 '하나도[아무도] ~없다[않다]'로 부정문을 만들 수 있으므로 (D)가 정답이다.

어휘 previously 전에 | purchase 구매하다 | additional 추가의 | supplier 납품업체 | in stock 비축되어, 재고로

5-8번은 다음 이메일에 관한 문제입니다.

수신: Yvonne Reeves <yreeves@gkbank.com>
발신: Ian Day <iday@greenshoesoft.com>
날짜: 7월 14일
회신: 업데이트 중 오류

Reeves 씨께,

당신이 겪고 있는 소프트웨어 오작동에 대한 문의를 제출해 주셔서 감사합니다. 연락이 늦어진 점 사과드립니다. 문제가 복잡하여 저희가 문제를 **5**진단하는데 평소보다 오래 걸렸습니다. 저희 수석 엔지니어들 중 **6**한 명이 현재 휴가 중이어서 상황이 더 힘들어졌습니다. 문의하신 내용에 대해 고객 정보를 업데이트할 수 없는 이유를 확인했습니다. **7**설명해 드리기에는 문제가 복잡하지만, 해결방안이 적용되었습니다. 다음에 로그인하시면, 귀하께서 업데이트를 요청하는 **8**메시지를 보게 되실 겁니다. 화면에 나타나는 안내를 따르시면 업데이트가 올바르게 적용됩니다.

불편을 끼쳐드린 점 다시 한번 사과 드립니다.

감사합니다,

Ian Day
고객 서비스, GreenShoe 소프트웨어 그룹

어휘

error 오류 | submit 제출하다 | regarding ~에 관해서 | glitch 사소한 문제, 장애 | experience 경험하다 | apologize 사과하다 | delay 지연 | get back to ~에게 다시 연락하다 | issue 문제 | longer than usual 평소보다 오래 | complexity 복잡성 | compound 악화시키다, 더 심각하게 만들다 | senior 선임의 | currently 현재 | on leave 휴가중인 | return 돌아가다 | determine 알아내다, 밝히다 | log in 로그인하다 | follow 따르다 | on-screen 화면의 | instruction 설명, 지시 | correctly 정확하게 | apply 적용하다 | inconvenience 불편

5. 명사 자리

해설 빈칸은 목적어 the issue를 이끌고 문장의 주어 역할을 해야 하므로 동사와 명사의 역할을 동시에 할 수 있는 동명사 (C)가 정답이다.

6. 부정대명사

해설 빈칸은 that절 내의 주어자리로, 'of 복수 명사'의 수식을 받고 있으며, 동사 자리에는 단수 동사 is가 있으므로 「one of + 복수 명사(~ 중 하나)」의 표현을 완성하는 부정대명사 (D)가 정답이다.

✛ Key word

This has been compounded by the fact that **one of our senior engineers is** currently on leave.

7. 문장 선택

(A) 보안 위반의 가능성이 있기 때문에 소프트웨어의 갱신은 필수입니다.
(B) 모든 혜택을 받으려면 직장 이메일을 사용하여 가입해야 합니다.
(C) 그 문제는 설명하기 복잡하지만, 다행히도 해결되었습니다.
(D) 새로운 정보가 들어오면 저희 팀이 업데이트할 것입니다.

해설 빈칸 앞 문장의 '귀하께서 고객 업데이트를 하지 못하신 이유를 알아냈다'는 내용을 고려할 때, '설명하기에는 문제가 복잡하지만, 해결방안이 적용되었다'는 내용으로 이어져야 문맥상 자연스러우므로 (C)가 정답이다.

✛ Key word

To return to your ticket, we have determined why you have been unable to update the client. The issue is complicated to explain, but the fix has been deployed.

8. 어휘 - 명사

해설 뒤에 나온 'Following the on-screen instructions ~'에서 화면에 나온 안내를 따르라고 하므로 이를 가리키는 '(사용자에게 보내지는) 메시지'라는 뜻의 (B)가 정답이다.

✛ Key word

Next time you log in, you should see a prompt asking you to update. Following the on-screen instructions will correctly apply the update.

CASE 집중훈련 본서 p.61

1. (B) **2.** (D) **3.** (A) **4.** (D) **5.** (D) **6.** (A)
7. (C) **8.** (B)

---

1. 부정대명사

Neither of the two invoices sent to the accounting office was accepted on account of inadequate billing details.
계산서의 불충분한 정보로 인해 회계 사무소에 발송된 두 청구서 모두 받아들여지지 않았다.

해설 빈칸 뒤의 of 전치사구를 동반하여 '(둘 중) 어느 쪽도 ~이 아니다'라는 뜻의 대명사 (B)가 정답이다. '회계 사무소에서 발송된 두 청구서 어느 쪽도 받아들여지지 않았다'는 의미를 완성한다. Those는 '저것들'이란 뜻의 지시대명사로 앞에 대상이 나와야 하며, 뒤에 two와도 어

울리지 않는다. 「Neither of + 복수 명사」 뒤에는 단수 동사가 와야 하므로 단수 동사 was가 나왔다.

어휘 invoice 청구서, 송장 | accept 받아들이다, 수락하다 | on account of ~때문에 | inadequate 불충분한 | billing 계산서, 청구서 | details 정보

✛ Key word

Nether of the two invoices sent to the accounting office **was** accepted on account of inadequate billing details.

---

2. 인칭대명사

Though Zoom Fitness Center offers a cash discount, most of **its** members choose to pay with a credit card.
Zoom 피트니스센터에서는 현금 할인을 제공하지만, 그곳의 회원 대부분은 신용카드로 지불하는 것을 선택한다.

해설 빈칸은 명사 members를 수식하는 자리이다. 접속사 though로 연결된 두 절의 내용을 고려할 때, 문맥상 member는 Zoom 피트니스센터 회원을 가리킨다는 것을 알 수 있으므로 Zoom Fitness Center를 지칭하는 인칭대명사 (D)가 정답이다.

어휘 offer 제공하다 | discount 할인 | choose 선택하다 | pay 지불하다

---

3. 부정대명사

J&J Global Blog has **one** of the largest number of subscribers in Korean news media.
J&J 글로벌 블로그는 한국 뉴스 미디어에서 가장 많은 구독자들 중 하나를 보유하고 있다.

해설 빈칸은 of 이하의 전치사구의 수식을 받는 명사 또는 대명사 자리이므로 부사 (B), (D)는 제거한다. 'J&J 글로벌 블로그가 가장 많은 구독자들 중 하나를 보유하고 있다'라는 의미가 되어야 자연스러우며, 「one of + 복수 명사」는 '~ 중 하나'를 의미하므로 (A)가 정답이다.

어휘 subscriber 구독자

---

4. 부정대명사

Even though most supermarkets in the area offer delivery services, **few** provide the extensive list of grocery items that we do.
이 지역 대부분의 수퍼마켓이 배달 서비스를 제공하지만, 우리처럼 다양한 식료품을 제공하는 곳은 소수이다.

해설 빈칸은 주절의 주어 역할을 하는 대명사 자리이다. '대부분의 수퍼마켓이 배달 서비스를 제공하고 있지만, 우리처럼 다양한 식료품을 제공하는 곳은 거의 없다'라는 부정의 의미가 되어야 자연스럽다. few는 대명사 또는 형용사로 '적은 (수)'를 의미하며 긍정의 a few와 달리 부정의 의미를 갖고 가산 복수 명사를 가리킬 때 사용되므로 복수 동사 provide와도 수 일치가 맞아 (D)가 정답이다.

어휘 extensive 아주 많은, 폭넓은 | grocery 식료품

5-8번은 다음 공지에 관한 문제입니다.

Lincoln시 교통당국 정책 최신소식

Lincoln시 대중교통을 이용할 때 자전거를 가지고 오고 싶었던 적이 있나요? 최근의 업그레이드 덕분에, 모든 버스들은 이제 귀하의 자전거를 수용할 수 있는 ⑤설비를 가지게 되었습니다. 버스에 탑승하기 전, 운전기사에게 알려 주세요. 여러분과 여러분의 자전거를 위한 특별한 버스 티

켓이 **⑥요구된다는** 것을 명심하세요. 자전거를 위한 자리를 **⑦일찍** 예약해 주세요. 각 버스는 2대의 자전거만 들일 수 있습니다. 탑승 전에 자전거가 제대로 적재되었는지 확인하십시오. **⑧또한 안전한 자물쇠를 사용하는 것을 추천합니다.** 탑승시 개인 재산은 전적으로 여러분의 책임입니다.

어휘
transportation 교통 | authority 당국, 권한 | policy 정책 | update 최신 정보 | public transit 대중교통 | accommodate 수용하다 | board 탑승하다 | inform 알려주다 | keep in mind 명심하다 | book a place 장소를 예약하다 | confirm 확인하다 | properly 적절하게 | load 적재하다 | solely 단독으로, 오로지 | property 재산, 자산 | ride 타다

5. 어휘 - 명사
해설 빈칸 앞 문장의 자전거를 가지고 대중교통을 이용하고 싶었던 적이 있었는지를 묻는 내용을 고려할 때, 자전거를 실을 수 있는 설비가 버스에 설치되었다는 내용이 들어가야 자연스러우므로 (D)가 정답이다.

✦ **Key word**
Have you ever wanted to bring a bike with you when using Lincoln City Public Transit? Thanks to recent **upgrades**, all of our buses now have the **equipment to accommodate your bike**.

6. 동사의 태 / 시제
해설 빈칸은 ticket을 주어로 하는 동사 자리이다. 빈칸 뒤에 목적어가 없고 보기는 타동사이므로 수동태 자리이며, 규칙을 설명하고 있으므로 현재 시제 (A)가 정답이다.

7. 어휘 - 부사
해설 빈칸 뒷문장의 버스에 2대의 자전거만이 들어갈 수 있다는 내용을 고려할 때, 자전거를 위한 자리를 일찍 예약하라는 내용이 들어가야 자연스러우므로 (C)가 정답이다.

✦ **Key word**
Book a place for your bike **early. Each bus can only fit two bikes.**

8. 문장 선택
(A) 교통카드로 결제가 가능합니다.
(B) 또한 안전한 자물쇠를 사용하는 것을 추천합니다.
(C) 버스 시간표는 역에 게시되어 있습니다.
(D) 접이식 자전거가 요즘 더 인기가 있습니다.

해설 빈칸 뒷문장의 탑승 시에 개인 재산이 본인의 책임이라는 내용을 고려할 때, 자물쇠 사용을 권장한다는 내용이 앞에 들어가야 자연스러우므로 (B)가 정답이다.

✦ **Key word**
We also recommend using a secure lock. You are solely responsible for your personal property when riding with us.

CASE 실전훈련
본서 p.62

1. (B)	**2.** (D)	**3.** (D)	**4.** (C)	**5.** (B)	**6.** (B)
7. (B)	**8.** (A)	**9.** (C)	**10.** (C)	**11.** (D)	**12.** (A)

1. 소유격 대명사
Mr. Tanaka was awarded 'Employee of the Year' for **his** contribution to the advertising campaign.
Tanaka 씨는 광고캠페인에 대한 그의 기여로 '올해의 직원상'을 수상했다.

해설 빈칸은 명사 contribution을 수식하는 자리이므로 소유격 대명사 (B)가 정답이다.

어휘 award (상 등을) 수여하다 | employee 직원 | contribution 기여 | advertising campaign 광고 캠페인

2. 부정대명사
Mr. Salazar showed his appreciation that **all** of his many colleagues filled in for him while he was on holiday.
Salazar 씨는 자신이 휴가 중인 동안 많은 동료들 모두가 자신의 빈자리를 대신해준 것에 감사를 표했다.

해설 빈칸은 that 명사절 내 주어 자리이다. 전치사구 of his many colleagues가 빈칸을 수식하고 있으므로, '많은 동료들 모두가 자신의 빈자리를 대신해 준 것에 감사를 표했다'라는 의미가 되어야 문맥상 자연스러우므로 부정대명사 (D)가 정답이다.

어휘 appreciation 감사 | colleague 동료 | fill in for ~를 대신[대리]하다 | on holiday 휴가 중인

3. 목적격 대명사
Mr. Cole was not available to work on Wednesday due to personal reasons, so Ms. Hanson substituted for **him**.
Cole 씨는 개인적인 이유로 수요일에 근무할 수 없어서, Hanson 씨가 그를 대신했다.

해설 빈칸은 전치사 for의 목적어 자리이다. 문맥상 Hanson 씨가 Cole 씨를 대신해 수요일에 근무했다는 의미가 되어야 하므로 Cole 씨를 지칭하는 목적격 대명사 (D)가 정답이다.

어휘 personal 개인적인 | reason 이유 | substitute for ~을 대신하게 되다

✦ **Key point**
인칭대명사 문제는 빈칸의 자리에 들어갈 수 있는 대명사의 형태를 거른 후, 가능한 보기가 여러 개인 경우, 문맥을 통해 빈칸에 들어갈 대상을 파악한다.

4. 재귀대명사
Ms. Nichols will respond to all e-mails **herself** while Mr. Morris is on vacation.
Morris 씨가 휴가 간 동안, Nichols 씨가 직접 모든 이메일에 답할 것이다.

해설 빈칸은 주절과 종속절 사이의 자리이다. 주절에서 빠진 필수 문장성분이 없기 때문에, 빈칸은 수식어 자리이므로 대명사 중 수식어 자리에서 강조 역할을 하는 재귀대명사 (C)가 정답이다.

어휘 respond to ~에 답하다 | on vacation 휴가 중

+ **Key point**

재귀대명사가 주어나 목적어를 강조하는 강조용법으로 쓰일 때, 강조하는 대상 바로 뒤 또는 절의 끝에서 수식어처럼 쓸 수 있다.

5. 부정대명사

Palmer mayor Patricia Craig thanked **each** of the volunteers with a delicate handshake.

Palmer 시장인 Patricia Craig는 정중한 악수로 자원봉사자들 각각에게 감사를 표했다.

해설 빈칸은 동사 thank의 목적어 자리이다. 빈칸을 후치 수식하는 of 전치사구의 내용을 고려할 때, '자원봉사자들 각각에게 악수로 감사를 표했다'는 의미가 되어야 하므로 부정대명사 (B)가 정답이다. each 대신 every를 쓰고 싶으면 「every one of + 복수 명사」의 형태로 써야 한다.

어휘 mayor 시장 | volunteer 자원 봉사자 | delicate 섬세한, 품위 있는 | handshake 악수

+ **Key point**

부정대명사 「each of + 복수 명사」는 '~들 각각'을, 「either of + 복수 명사」는 '~중 어느 하나'를 의미한다. 이 때, either의 경우, '두 가지 중 어느 하나'라는 의미를 전달하기에, 복수 명사 자리에는 두 개를 나타내는 표현이 온다.

6. 목적격 대명사

Instead of throwing away expired ingredients and food waste, Green Eating composts **them** at our local farm.

유통기한이 지난 재료와 음식물 쓰레기를 버리는 대신, Green Eating에서는 그것들을 지역 농장에서 퇴비로 만든다.

해설 빈칸은 동사 composts의 목적어 자리이다. 문맥상 expired ingredients and food waste를 가리키는 대명사가 필요하므로 복수 대상을 지칭하는 목적격 인칭대명사 (B)가 정답이다.

어휘 throw away 버리다 | expire 만료하다 | ingredient 재료 | waste 쓰레기 | compost 퇴비를 만들다 | local 지역의 | farm 농장

+ **Key point**

부정대명사 ones vs. 인칭대명사 them: one은 앞서 언급된 명사와 같은 종류이되 불특정한 대상을, them은 앞서 언급한 바로 그 대상을 가리킬 때 사용된다.

7. 지시대명사

Dr. Moreno will experiment with different types of plastic that are less environmentally damaging than **those** used today.

Moreno 박사는 요즘 사용되는 것보다 환경에 덜 해로운 다른 종류의 플라스틱으로 실험을 할 것이다.

해설 빈칸은 비교급 구문에 해당하는 than의 목적어인 명사 자리이다. 해석상 '~한 것'의 의미를 가지며 과거분사구가 빈칸을 뒤에서 수식하고 있으므로 지시대명사 (B)가 정답이다.

어휘 experiment 실험하다 | type 유형 | plastic 플라스틱 | environmentally 환경적으로 | damaging 해로운

+ **Key point**

지시대명사 those는 앞에서 언급된 명사와 같은 종류·성질의 나타낼 때 사용되며, 「those + who~」, 「those + 전치사구」, 「those + 분사구」의 형태로 쓰여 '~한 것[사람]들'이라고 해석된다.

8. 부정대명사

None of the photos submitted by Mr. Wang were sold at the art fair.

Wang 씨가 제출한 사진 중 아무것도 아트 페어에서 팔리지 않았다.

해설 빈칸은 문장의 주어 자리이다. 문맥상 '사진 중 어떤 것도 팔리지 않았다'는 의미가 되어야 하며, of 전치사구의 후치 수식을 받고 있으므로 (A)가 정답이다.

어휘 photo 사진 | submit 제출하다 | sell 팔다 | fair 전시회, 박람회

+ **Key point**

부정대명사 none vs. nothing: 둘 다 '아무것도 ~않다'는 의미를 갖지만, none만이 뒤에 'of (대)명사'를 취할 수 있다.

9-12번은 다음 초대에 관한 문제입니다.

Glen 공원 혁신 센터에서는 5월 12일 **9 연간** 친목도모 행사에 여러분을 초대합니다. 올해의 행사는 자신의 사업을 운영하는 데 관심 있는 사람들이 지역 내 같은 뜻을 가진 사람들과 만나 **10 자신의** 아이디어를 논의할 수 있는 특히 좋은 기회가 올 것입니다. 저희는 사업 운영 경험에 대해 이야기를 나눠주십사 지역 내 성공한 사업가분들을 모셨습니다. **11 참석자**는 명함을 가져오셔야 하는데, 인적 네트워크는 초창기에 사업의 성패를 좌우할 수 있기 때문입니다. 행사 티켓 가격은 50달러이며, 이 가격에는 다과와 주차공간이 포함됩니다. **12 티켓이 한정되어 있으니, 티켓을 일찍 구입하세요.**

어휘
innovation 혁신 | invite 초대하다 | network 인맥을 형성하다 | entrepreneur 기업가 | interested in ~에 관심 있는 | run 운영하다 | likeminded 생각[뜻]이 비슷한 | area 지역 | successful 성공적인 | business owner 사업주, 경영주 | bring 가져오다 | business card 명함 | break 깨다 | early 초기의 | stage 단계 | cost 비용 | parking space 주차 공간 | refreshments 다과

9. 어휘 - 형용사

해설 빈칸은 명사구 networking event를 수식하는 형용사 자리이다. 빈칸 뒷문장의 'this year's event'를 통해 매년마다 열리는 행사임을 유추해 볼 수 있고, '5월 12일 연간 친목도모 행사에 초대한다'는 내용이 되어야 문맥상 자연스러우므로 (C)가 정답이다.

+ **Key word**

The Glen Park Center for Innovation invites you to its **annual networking event** on May 12.

10. 소유격 대명사

해설 빈칸은 명사 ideas를 수식하는 자리이므로 소유격 대명사 (C)가 정답이다.

11. 어휘 - 명사

해설 빈칸은 문장의 주어 자리이다. 'networking event에 지역기업가들을 초대한다는 글로 행사에서 마음이 맞는 기업가들의 경험을 들을 수 있다'는 내용을 고려할 때, '인적 네트워크는 초창기에 사업의 성패를 좌우할 수 있기 때문에 행사에 참석하시는 분들은 명함을 가져오라'는 내용이 되어야 문맥상 자연스러우므로 (D)가 정답이다.

+ **Key word**

The Glen Park Center for Innovation **invites you to its annual networking event** on May 12. **The event is for entrepreneurs who are interested in running their own businesses to meet and discuss their**

ideas with likeminded people from the area. We have invited successful businessowners from the area to talk about some of their experiences in running a business. **Attendees should bring business cards with them, as networking can make or break your business in the early stages.**

12. 문장 선택

(A) 티켓이 한정되어 있으니, 당신의 것을 일찍 구입하세요.
(B) 사업주는 작업 샘플을 가져와야 합니다.
(C) 이 행사는 참석자 수에 따라 내년에 취소될 수도 있습니다.
(D) 대학 학위는 기업가들에게 소지하기에 좋은 자격증입니다.

해설 빈칸 앞 부분의 '행사 티켓 가격은 50달러이며, 이 가격에는 다과와 주차공간이 포함된다'는 내용을 고려할 때, 티켓 구입과 관련된 내용으로 이어져야 문맥상 자연스러우므로 (A)가 정답이다.

✚ Key word
The cost of a ticket for the event is $50, and this price includes parking space as well as refreshments. Tickets are limited, so make sure you purchase yours early.

CHAPTER 04 형용사

CASE 집중훈련
본서 p.65

1. (A)   2. (C)   3. (D)   4. (D)   5. (C)   6. (D)
7. (A)   8. (A)

1. 형용사 자리

Increasing employee productivity at Kruger Consulting will require a **creative** modification of the current workflow.

Kruger 컨설팅사에서 직원 생산성을 늘리는 데는 현재 작업 흐름에 건설적인 수정을 필요로 할 것이다.

해설 빈칸은 관사 뒤 명사를 수식하는 자리이다. 문맥상 '건설적인 수정이 필요하다'는 내용이 되어야 자연스러우므로 형용사 (A)가 정답이다.

어휘 increase 증가하다, 늘리다 | employee productivity 직원 생산성 | modification 수정 | current 현재의 | workflow 작업 흐름

2. 형용사 자리

Ms. Fowler has a reputation for being overly aggressive in business deals, but her colleagues describe her as fairly **cautious** in other areas of her work.

Fowler 씨는 사업 거래에서 지나치게 공격적인 것으로 유명하지만, 그녀의 동료들은 다른 업무분야에서는 그녀가 꽤 신중하다고 설명한다.

해설 빈칸은 부사 fairly의 수식을 받는 자리이다. 접속사 but으로 연결된 두 문장의 관계를 고려할 때, '그녀는 거래에서는 지나치게 공격적인 걸로 유명하지만, 동료들이 그녀가 다른 업무분야에서는 꽤 신중한 사람이라고 설명한다'라는 의미가 되어야 문맥상 자연스러우므로 형용사 (C)가 정답이다.

어휘 reputation 명성 | overly 너무, 지나치게 | aggressive 공격적인 | colleague 동료 | fairly 꽤 | area 분야

✚ Key point
동사-전치사 관용 표현 'describe A as B(A를 B라고 묘사하다)'에서 A의 상태를 설명하는 B자리에는 형용사 또는 명사가 올 수 있으므로, 문맥 또는 주변 구조파악을 통해 빈칸에 올 적절한 품사를 파악한다.

3. 형용사 자리

Please keep in mind that **supplementary** materials are optional, but will be used in evaluating your application.

보충 자료는 선택사항이지만, 지원서를 평가하는데 쓰일 것임을 잊지 마세요.

해설 빈칸은 뒤의 명사 materials를 수식하는 형용사가 들어가야 하므로 순수 형용사인 (D)가 정답이다.

어휘 keep in mind 명심하다 | material 자료 | optional 선택적인 | evaluate 평가하다

✚ Key point
보기에서 현재분사(supplementing)와 과거분사(supplemented)도 형용사 역할을 하지만, 순수 형용사와 의미상 차이가 없다면 순수 형용사를 우선해야 한다.

4. 어휘 - 형용사

Social media marketers spend an **excessive** amount of time browsing the Web every day.

소셜 미디어 마케터들은 매일 인터넷을 돌아다니는 데 과도한 시간을 소비한다.

해설 빈칸은 명사 amount를 수식하는 형용사 자리이다. 문맥상 '과도한/지나친'이라는 의미가 되어야 자연스러우므로 (D)가 정답이다.

어휘 spend 쓰다, 소비하다 | amount 총액 | browse 돌아다니다

✚ Key word
Social media marketers **spend an excessive amount of time** browsing the Web every day.

5-8번은 다음 공지에 관한 문제입니다.

Luton 축구단은 Sandown 해변을 가로지르는 10킬로미터 걷기 행사를 매년 개최할 예정입니다. 행사는 이번 주말에 열리며, 일반인에게 공개됩니다. **⑥참가자**는 Luton 축구단 기념품과 더불어 무료 티셔츠를 받게 됩니다. 등록비는 15달러이며, 행사 전 웹 사이트로 **⑥지불되어야** 합니다. 모든 수익금은 Christchurch 지진 구호 기금에 쓰입니다. **⑦걷기 행사는 작년과 동일한 경로가 될 것입니다.** 주말에 비 예보가 있으니, **⑧따뜻한 옷을 입으시기** 바랍니다. 이번 주말에 좋은 일에 지원하면서 운동도 해보세요!

어휘
hold 개최하다, 열다 | annual 연간의 | walk 걷기 | take place 개최되다, 일어나다 | public 대중, 일반인 | goody 매력적인 물건 | cost 비용 | registration 등록 | proceeds 수익금 | go towards ~에 쓰이다 | earthquake 지진 | relief fund 구호 기금 | be sure to 반드시 ~하다 | wear 입다 | clothing 옷, 의복 | exercise 운동 | support 지원하다 | good cause 대의

5. 어휘 - 명사

해설 빈칸은 문장의 주어 자리이다. 앞 문장의 걷기 행사를 주관하고 이 행사가 일반인에게 공개된다는 내용을 고려할 때, (일반) 참가자는 기념품과 더불어 무료 티셔츠를 받게 된다는 내용으로 이어져야 문맥상 연결이 자연스러우므로 (C)가 정답이다.

The event will take place this weekend, and it **is open to the public. Participants** will **receive a free t-shirt as well as some Luton football club goodies.**

6. 동사의 태 / 시제

해설 빈칸은 조동사 뒤의 동사 자리이다. 문장의 주어는 this, 즉, 등록비를 의미하며, 등록비가 행사 전에 지불되어야 한다는 의미가 되려면 수동 태 동사가 필요하다. 'should have (been) p.p.'는 과거에 이루지 못 한 가정법 과거 완료로 문맥에 맞지 않고, 행사비 지불의 단순의무를 나 타내려면 'should be p.p.'의 단순 시제로 연결하는 것이 적절하므로, 현재 시제 수동태인 (D)가 정답이다.

+ **Key word**

The cost for registration is $15, and this should be paid through the Web site **before the event.**

7. 문장 선택

(A) 걷기 행사는 작년과 동일한 경로가 될 것입니다.
(B) 스포츠 선수들은 큰 이점을 얻을 것입니다.
(C) 뉴스는 운동의 이점에 대한 기사를 실을 것입니다.
(D) 내년에는 행사 가격이 인상될 수도 있습니다.

해설 뒷문장의 주말에 비가 올 예정이라는 내용을 고려할 때, 걷기 행사와 관 련된 내용이 앞 문장에 들어가야 문맥상 연결이 자연스러우므로 (A)가 정답이다.

+ **Key word**

The walk will take the same route as last year. Some **rain is expected over the weekend,** so be sure to wear warm clothing.

8. 형용사 자리

해설 빈칸은 명사 clothing을 수식하는 형용사 자리이므로 (A)가 정답이다.

+ **Key point**

최상급 앞에는 정관사 the나 소유격이 필요하다.

CASE 집중훈련   본서 p.67

1. (B)   **2.** (A)   **3.** (C)   **4.** (D)   **5.** (C)   **6.** (A)
7. (D)   **8.** (A)

1. 형용사 자리

The plant manager, Mr. Phuong revised the production record template because the language in it is too **repetitive**.

공장 관리자인 Phuong 씨가 그 안에 문구가 너무 반복적이어서 생산 기록 템플릿을 수정했다.

해설 빈칸은 종속절의 be동사 뒤의 보어 자리이다. 문맥상 주어인 the language가 '너무 반복적이어서'라는 의미로 전개되는 것이 자연스 러우므로 일반 형용사인 (B)가 정답이다. too가 부사이므로 형용사만 가능하고 명사는 올 수 없다.

어휘 plant 공장 | revise 수정하다, 개정하다 | production 생산 | template 템플릿 | repetitive 반복적인, 되풀이되는 | repetition 되풀이, 반복 | repeat 반복하다

+ **Key word**

The plant manager, Mr. Phuong **revised** the production record **template because the language in it is too repetitive**.

2. 형용사 자리

Customer service employees should not be **critical** of customers who call with complaints about our products.

고객 서비스 직원들은 우리 제품에 관해 항의 전화를 하는 고객들에게 비판적이면 안 된다.

해설 빈칸은 주어의 성질을 나타낼 수 있는 be동사 뒤의 주격 보어 자리로 형용사 (A)가 정답이다. '고객 항의 전화에 비판적이면 안 된다'는 의 미이다. 명사 (C)도 be동사의 보어로 올 수 있으나, '비평가'라는 의미 로 여기에 맞지 않으며, 관사도 없어서 탈락이다. be critical of는 동사 criticize와 같은 말이다.

어휘 complaint 항의

+ **Key word**

Customer service employees should not **be critical of** customers who call with complaints about our products.

3. 형용사 자리

Luxury watch maker Feltam reported its profits remained **steady** in the third quarter.

고급 시계 제조사 Feltam은 3분기 수익이 변함없이 유지되었다고 발 표했다.

해설 빈칸은 동사 remain 뒤의 주격 보어인 형용사 자리이다. 문맥상 '수익 이 변함없이 유지되었다'라는 의미가 되어야 자연스러우므로 (C)가 정 답이다.

어휘 luxury 고급의 | maker 제조사 | report 알리다, 발표하다 | profit 수익 | remain 계속 ~이다 | quarter 분기

+ **Key point**

동사 remain은 주격 보어로 형용사를 취한다.

4. 어휘 - 동사

The Market Times **keeps** its readers informed about business and the economy with its in-depth reporting.

Market Times는 심층 보도로 구독자에게 비즈니스와 경제에 대해 많 은 내용을 알고 있게 한다.

해설 빈칸은 주어와 목적어 사이의 동사 자리이다. 빈칸 뒤에 과거분사 구문 이 있음을 고려할 때, 「keep + 목적어 + 목적격 보어(~가 …한 상태를 유지하다)」의 5형식 문장을 완성하는 동사 (D)가 정답이다.

어휘 reader 구독자 | informed about ~에 대해 잘 알고 있는 | economy 경제 | in-depth 심도 있는 | reporting 보도

+ **Key word**

The Market Times **keeps its readers informed** about business and the economy with its in-depth reporting.

5-8번은 다음 기사에 관한 문제입니다.

비즈니스 뉴스

1월 10일 (Sacramento) — San Francisco에 본사를 둔 건설회사인 Zhang and Patel 기업은 멕시코의 Ensenada에 새 Playa de las Americas 비치 리조트 작업을 완공하는 30억 달러규모의 계약을 땄다고 확인했다. **5**리조트에는 고급 호텔과 3개의 레스토랑, 놀이동산이 포함될 것이다. **6**프로젝트는 완공하는 데 5년이 소요될 예정이다. Zhang and Patel의 공동소유자인 Zhang Xiao-Jun에 따르면, 작업이 더 일찍 마무리되면, 회사는 거액의 금융 인센티브를 **7**받게 될 것이다.

"저희가 이 목표를 달성할 거라 **8**자신합니다,"라고 Zhang이 말했다. "우리는 이전에도 비슷한 인센티브를 받았어서 분명 다시 해낼 수 있습니다."

어휘

corporation 기업 | based -를 기반으로 한 | construction 건설 | firm 회사 confirm 확인하다 | win 이기다, 따내다 | billion 10억 | contract 계약 | complete 완료하다 | predict 예상하다 | finish 끝내다 | co-owner 공동 소유자 | financial 금융의, 재정적인 | incentive 인센티브 | earlier 더 일찍 | confident 자신 있는, 확신하는 | accomplish 성취하다 | goal 목표 | award 상을 주다 | definitely 절대적으로

5. 문장 선택

(A) San Francisco에는 몇 개의 다른 유명 건설 회사들이 있다.
(B) Zhang and Patel은 최근 몇 년간 크게 성장했다.
(C) 리조트에는 고급 호텔과 3개의 레스토랑, 놀이동산이 포함될 것이다.
(D) 멕시코 관리들은 지난 주 그 시설을 둘러보았다.

해설 빈칸 앞 문장의 '신규 리조트 건설 작업의 계약을 땄다'는 내용을 고려할 때, 리조트의 규모에 대해 설명하는 문장으로 이어져야 자연스러우므로 (C)가 정답이다.

✦ **Key point**

Zhang and Patel Corporation, the San Francisco-based construction firm, confirmed that **they have won a $3-billion contract to complete work on the new** Playa de las Americas **beach resort** in Ensenada, Mexico. **The resort will house a luxury hotel, three restaurants, and an amusement park.**

6. 어휘 - 명사

해설 빈칸은 문장의 주어 자리이다. 빈칸 앞 문장의 '신규 리조트 건설 작업 계약을 따냈다'라는 내용을 고려할 때, '(리조트 건설) 프로젝트가 5년이 걸릴 예정'이라는 내용으로 이어져야 자연스러우므로 (A)가 정답이다.

✦ **Key word**

Zhang and Patel Corporation, the San Francisco-based construction firm, confirmed that **they have won a $3-billion contract to complete work on the new** Playa de las Americas **beach resort** in Ensenada, Mexico. The **project is predicted to take five years to finish.**

7. 동사의 시제

해설 빈칸은 주어와 목적어 사이 문장의 동사 자리이다. If 조건절의 시제가 현재(can be)이므로, 주절에는 미래 시제 (D)가 정답이다. 주절이 미래일 때 시간이나 조건의 부사절은 현재 시제를 쓴다.

✦ **Key word**

their company **will get** a large financial incentive **if it can be** completed earlier.

8. 어휘 - 형용사

해설 빈칸은 주어 we에 대한 주격 보어 자리이다. 빈칸 뒷문장의 '비슷한 인센티브를 받은 적이 있기에, 이번에도 달성할 수 있다'는 내용을 고려할 때, 문맥상 '저희가 이 목표를 성취할거라고 자신한다'는 의미가 자연스러우므로 (A)가 정답이다. 「사람 주어 + be confident that」 구문은 기억해 둔다.

✦ **Key word**

"We are confident that we can accomplish this goal," Zhang explained. **"We were awarded similar incentives before, so it's definitely possible to do it again."**

CASE 집중훈련

본서 p.69

1. (A) **2.** (C) **3.** (C) **4.** (B) **5.** (B) **6.** (C)
7. (A) **8.** (A)

1. 복수 명사를 취하는 수량형용사

Many advertisers distribute USB memories instead of **other** promotional items because of their portability.

많은 광고주들이 휴대성 때문에 다른 판촉 물품들 대신 USB 메모리를 나누어 준다.

해설 빈칸은 전치사 of의 목적어인 복수 명사 items를 수식해줄 형용사 자리이다. 보기 중에 every, another, each는 모두 단수 명사 앞에 올 수 있으므로, 복수 명사를 한정 및 수식해줄 수 있는 (A)가 정답이다.

어휘 advertiser 광고주 | distribute 나누어 주다, 배포하다 | instead of ~대신에 | promotional 판촉의, 홍보의 | portability 휴대성, 이동성

✦ **Key point**

형용사 other는 가산 복수 명사 또는 불가산 명사를 수식한다.

2. 어휘 - 형용사

This morning we received numerous **positive** messages from viewers about yesterday's episode.

오늘 아침 우리는 시청자들로부터 어제의 에피소드에 관한 수많은 긍정적인 메시지들을 받았다.

해설 빈칸은 messages를 수식하는 형용사 자리이다. 문맥상 '시청자들로부터 긍정적인 메시지들을 받았다'라는 의미가 되어야 자연스러우므로 (C)가 정답이다.

어휘 numerous 수많은 | viewer 시청자

✦ **Key word**

This morning **we received** numerous **positive messages from viewers** about yesterday's episode.

3. 복수 명사를 취하는 수량형용사

All product **inquiries** must be forwarded to the customer support team.

모든 제품 문의는 고객지원부서로 전송되어야 한다.

해설 빈칸은 명사 product와 복합명사를 이루는 명사 자리이다. 문맥상 '모든 제품문의는 고객지원부서로 보내져야 한다'는 의미가 되어야 자연스러우며, 한정사 all의 수식을 받고 있으므로 명사의 복수형 (C)가 정답이다.

어휘 forward 다시 보내주다; 앞으로 가는; 앞으로 | customer support 고객지원

+ Key point
복합명사는 명사＋명사로 구성되며, 두 번째 명사를 기준으로 단/복수가 결정된다.

----

4. 복수 명사를 취하는 수량형용사
Kwik Logistics truck drivers are required to comply with all local traffic **regulations** while making long-distance deliveries.
Kwik 물류트럭 운전사는 장거리 배송을 할 때, 모든 현지 교통규정을 지켜야 한다.

해설 빈칸은 명사 traffic과 함께 복합명사를 완성하는 명사 자리이다. 문맥상 '모든 교통 규정을 지켜야 한다'는 의미가 되어야 자연스러우므로 (B)가 정답이다.

어휘 logistics 물류 | require 요구하다 | comply with 지키다, 준수하다 | local 현지의, 지역의 | traffic 교통 | long-distance 장거리의 | delivery 배송

+ Key point
명사 regulation vs. regulator: 명사 regulation은 '규정'을, regulator는 '조절장치, 규제기관'을 의미한다.

5-8번은 다음 편지에 관한 문제입니다.

Rebecca Judy
HR부서
IMF Design Solutions
Sunnyvale, CA 91967

Judy 씨께,

저는 지난 7년간 LeetTech에서 소프트웨어 엔지니어로 제 밑에서 근무한 Chuck Bousculer를 위하여 이 추천서를 드립니다. 그의 매니저로서, 저는 Mr. Bousculer의 업무를 정기적으로 평가하였습니다. 그는 엄청난 창의성과 리더십에의 소질을 보였습니다. **⑤그는 다른 엔지니어들과 협업을 할 때 항상 뛰어났습니다.** 이번 6월, 그는 저의 부재 기간 동안 개발팀을 이끌었는데, 역할을 매우 **⑥능숙하게** 수행했습니다. 저는 그가 IMF Design Solutions에서 수석 엔지니어로서의 역할을 잘 할 것이라고 믿습니다. 그는 기량이 뛰어나고 야심이 있으며, 항상 추가 **⑦업무**를 자원해서 맡습니다. 저는 그를 귀사에 추천하는 데 **⑧아무런** 거리낌이 **없다**고 말씀드릴 수 있습니다.

감사합니다.

Basil Cleese
LeetTech Software

어휘
recommendation 추천 | on behalf of ~를 위해, ~를 대신하여 | in charge of ~를 담당하여 | evaluate 평가하다 | regularly 정기적으로 | show 보여주다 | tremendous 거대한, 엄청난 | creativity 창조성, 독창력 | aptitude 적성, 소질 | leadership 리더십, 지도력 | lead 이끌다(lead-led-led), 선두 | development team 개발팀 | absence 부재, 결석 | role 역할 | perform 수행하다 | accomplished 재주 많은, 기량이 뛰어난 | ambitious 야심 있는 | volunteer 자원하다 | take on (일을) 맡다 | reservation 의구심, 거리낌, 예약

5. 문장 선택
(A) 그는 7월에 귀사에 입사할 수 있을 것입니다.
(B) 그는 다른 엔지니어들과 협업을 할 때 항상 뛰어납니다.
(C) 그는 분야 전환에 관심을 표명했습니다.
(D) 그는 가을에 대학원 과정에 등록할 것입니다.

해설 빈칸 앞 문장의 '그는 리더십에 소질을 보였다'는 내용을 고려할 때, '다른 사람들과 협업할 때 항상 뛰어났다'는 내용으로 이어져야 자연스러우므로 (B)가 정답이다.

+ Key word
He showed tremendous creativity and an aptitude for leadership. **He always excels when collaborating with other engineers.**

6. 부사 자리
해설 빈칸은 동사 perform을 수식하며, 부사 very의 수식을 받고 있으므로 부사 (C)가 정답이다.

7. 어휘 - 명사
해설 빈칸은 동사 take on의 목적어인 명사 자리이다. 문맥상 '추가 업무를 자원해서 맡는다'는 의미가 자연스러우므로 (A)가 정답이다.

+ Key word
He is accomplished and ambitious, and always **volunteers to take on added duties**.

8. 문맥상 어울리는 수량형용사
해설 빈칸은 명사 reservations를 수식하는 한정사 자리이다. 빈칸 앞 문장에서 그의 장점들을 나열하고 있으므로, 문맥상 '그를 추천하는 데 그 어떤 거리낌도 없다'는 의미가 되어야 자연스러우므로 (A)가 정답이다.

+ Key word
He is accomplished and ambitious, and always volunteers to take on added duties. I can say that I have **no reservations about recommending him** to your company.

CASE 집중훈련 본서 p.71
1. (A) 2. (A) 3. (D) 4. (C) 5. (D) 6. (B)
7. (B) 8. (D)

1. 일반 형용사 vs. 분사 형용사
It is not an **exhaustive** list, but these are some of the many responsibilities of the managerial position at Bethlehem University Hospital.
그것이 완전한 목록은 아니지만, Bethlehem 대학병원 관리직의 많은 업무들 중 일부이다.

해설 빈칸은 명사 list를 수식하는 형용사 자리이다. 접속사 but으로 연결된 내용을 고려할 때, 문맥상 '완전한 것은 아니지만, 직무의 일부를 보여주는 목록'이라는 의미가 되어야 자연스러우므로 (A)가 정답이다. exhausted는 '기진맥진한, 다 써버린, 고갈된'이라는 뜻이다.

어휘 responsibility 책임, 의무 | managerial 관리의 | position 자리, 직위

+ Key point
① 명사 앞 자리에는 형용사, 형용사 역할을 하는 분사, 복합명사를 이

루는 명사가 올 수 있다.

② 형용사와 분사가 보기에 함께 있을 때, 특수한 경우를 제외하고 항상 형용사가 정답이다.

2. 일반 형용사 vs. 분사 형용사

Roh Agriculture negotiated an agreement with Yanjing Logistics and can now ship their merchandise internationally at very **reasonable** prices.

Roh 농업은 Yanjing 물류와 계약을 합의하여, 이제 아주 합리적인 가격으로 물품을 해외 배송할 수 있다.

해설 빈칸은 명사 prices를 수식하는 자리이다. '이제 합리적인 가격에 해외배송을 할 수 있다'는 의미가 되어야 문맥상 자연스러우므로, 'at a reasonable price/at reasonable prices(합리적인 가격에)'라는 관용 표현을 완성하는 형용사 (A)가 정답이다.

어휘 agriculture 농업 | negotiate 협상하다 | agreement 합의 | logistics 물류 | ship 보내다 | merchandise 상품 | internationally 국제적으로

✛ Key point
명사를 수식하는 자리에는 형용사, 분사, 명사 모두 올 수 있으므로, 보기에 해당 품사가 모두 있는 경우 문맥을 통해 파악한다. 참고로, 보통 형용사가 보기에 함께 있는 경우, 형용사가 정답인 경우가 대부분이다.

3. 혼동하기 쉬운 형용사

Please be **considerate** and refrain from using mobile phones while driving to guarantee the safety of other road users.

운전하는 동안 다른 도로 사용자들의 안전을 보장하기 위해 사려 깊게 행동하고 휴대폰 사용을 삼가 주세요.

해설 빈칸은 be동사 뒤의 보어 자리이다. 문맥상 '운전하는 동안에 사려 깊게 행동하고 휴대폰 사용을 삼가 주세요'라는 의미가 되어야 자연스러우므로 (D)가 정답이다.

어휘 refrain from ~하는 것을 삼가다 | guarantee 보장하다 | considerable 상당한, 꽤 | consider 고려하다 | consideration 고려, 숙고 | considerate 사려 깊은, 신중한

✛ Key word
Please **be considerate and refrain from using mobile phones while driving** to guarantee the safety of other road users.

4. 혼동하기 쉬운 형용사

Since survey takers described Galaway Resort's present logo as **forgettable**, the company wants to design a new one.

설문조사 응시자들은 Galaway 리조트의 현재 로고가 잊어버리기 쉽다고 하기에, 회사는 새로운 로고를 디자인하기를 원한다.

해설 빈칸은 'describe A(명사) as B(명사/형용사) (A를 B라고 묘사하다)'의 구조에서 B의 자리이다. 문맥상 주절에서 새 로고를 디자인하고 싶다고 하므로, 이유를 나타내는 부사절에서는 '현재 로고가 잊혀지기 쉽다고 하므로'라는 의미가 되어야 자연스러우므로 (C)가 정답이다.

어휘 survey 설문조사 | taker 응시자 | describe 묘사하다, 서술하다 | present 현재의; 제시하다, 보여주다; 선물 | logo 로고 | design 디자인하다, 설계하다

✛ Key point
형용사 forgetful vs. forgettable: forgetful은 '잘 잊어버리는', forgettable은 '쉽게 잊혀질, 별로 특별할 게 없는'을 의미한다.

5-8번은 다음 이메일에 관한 문제입니다.

수신: Esther Carter
발신: Tabitha Palinski
날짜: 6월 7일
제목: 선임 소프트웨어 기술자 지원

Carter 씨께,

오늘 아침 저와 만나주셔서 감사합니다. 저희가 나눈 논의는 정말 흥미로 **5왔습니다.** 저는 여전히 선임 소프트웨어 기술자 직무에 관심이 있습니다. 추가 **6면접**을 보게 되길 바랍니다.

저는 언급하셨던 프로젝트들에 필요한 다양한 능력을 갖추고 있다고 생각합니다. 지난 15년 간 저는 근무했던 회사들에서 이루었던 몇몇 주요 성공작들에 기여했으며, **7상당한** 경험을 쌓았습니다. 우리 업계에서 제조부문용 고급 보안 소프트웨어를 제작 및 개선하는 데 더 많은 세월을 몸 담은 사람은 별로 없습니다.

제 근무 시작 시기를 논의하면서 합의한 바와 같이 제 일정을 확정했습니다. **8저는 이번 달 27일 후라면 언제든지 시작할 수 있습니다.** 빠른 시일 내 연락 주시길 기다리겠습니다.

어휘
senior 선임의 | application 지원 | additional 추가의 | round 한 차례, 회전 (어떤 코스 전체를 한 바퀴 도는 것) | skill set 다양한 능력 | mention 언급하다 | contribute 기여하다 | employer 고용주 | acquire 얻다 | industry 산업, 업계 | refine 개선하다 | high-end 고급의 | security 보안 | manufacturing 제조 | sector 부문 | confirm 확인해주다 | agree 동의하다 | at one's earliest convenience 빠른 시일 내에

5. 동사의 시제

해설 빈칸은 주어와 목적어 사이의 동사 자리이다. 빈칸 앞 문장의 '오늘 아침 만나 주셔서 감사하다'는 내용을 고려할 때 과거 시제가 되어야 문맥상 자연스러우므로 (D)가 정답이다.

✛ Key word
Thank you for meeting with me this morning. I **found** our discussion very interesting.

6. 어휘 – 명사

해설 빈칸은 an additional round of의 수식을 받는 명사 자리이다. 빈칸 앞부분의 '오늘 아침 만나 주셔서 감사하고, 여전히 수석 소프트웨어 엔지니어직에 관심이 있다'는 내용을 고려할 때, 문맥상 '추가 인터뷰를 보게되길 바란다'는 의미가 되어야 자연스러우므로 (B)가 정답이다.

✛ Key word
Thank you for meeting with me this morning. I found our discussion very interesting. I'm **still interested in the job** as a senior software engineer. I **would be very happy to come in for an additional round of interviews.**

7. 혼동하기 쉬운 형용사

해설 빈칸은 관사와 명사 사이의 형용사 자리이다. 문맥상 '상당한 양의 경험'이라는 의미가 되어야 자연스러우므로 (B)가 정답이다.

✛ Key point
형용사 considerate vs. considerable: considerate은 '사려 깊은'을, considerable은 '상당한'을 의미한다.

8. 문장 선택

(A) 당신의 제안에 감사드리며, 기꺼이 검토해 보겠습니다.

(B) 제 배경이 제가 그 일에 적임이라고 생각합니다.

(C) 하지만 몇 가지 질문이 더 있습니다.

(D) 저는 이번 달 27일 후면 언제든지 시작할 수 있습니다.

해설 빈칸 앞 문장의 '근무 시작 시기에 대해 논의한 대로 일정을 확정했다'는 내용을 고려할 때, 근무시작일과 관련된 구체적인 내용으로 이어져야 문맥상 자연스러우므로 (D)가 정답이다.

✦ Key word

I have confirmed my schedule, as we agreed while discussing when I could begin work. I would be able to start any time after the 27th of the month. I hope to hear back from you at your earliest convenience.

CASE 실전훈련   본서 p.72

1. (B)	2. (D)	3. (A)	4. (D)	5. (A)	6. (B)
7. (C)	8. (C)	9. (D)	10. (A)	11. (D)	12. (B)

---

1. 형용사 자리

Bukhara Restaurant serves **authentic** cuisine from northern India.

Bukhara 레스토랑은 정통 인도 북부 요리를 제공한다.

해설 빈칸은 명사 cuisine을 수식하는 자리이므로 형용사 (B)가 정답이다.

어휘 serve (음식을) 제공하다 | cuisine 요리 | northern 북부의

---

2. 문맥상 어울리는 수량형용사

Nutri Health will be giving out complimentary supplement samples at local pharmacies on **each** Sunday in July.

Nutri Health에서는 7월의 매 일요일에 지역 약국에서 무료 보충제 샘플을 나눠줄 것이다.

해설 빈칸은 Sunday를 수식하는 자리이다. 문맥상 '7월의 매주 일요일에'라는 의미가 되어야 자연스러우므로 한정사 (D)가 정답이다.

어휘 give out ~를 나눠주다 | complimentary 무료의 | supplement 보충제 | pharmacy 약국

✦ Key point

한정사 several 뒤에는 복수 가산 명사만 올 수 있다.

---

3. 형용사 자리

Though Ella Dunn's team helped design the company's new electric car, she alone came up with the **original** concept.

Ella Dunn의 팀에서 회사의 신규 전기 자동차 설계를 돕긴 했지만, 그녀가 혼자서 최초 구상안을 제안했다.

해설 빈칸은 명사 concept을 수식하는 형용사 자리이므로 (A)가 정답이다.

어휘 electric 전기의 | alone 혼자, 단독으로 | come up with ~를 생각해내다 | concept 발상, 구상, 개념

---

4. 형용사 자리

The financial auditor suggests removing some **descriptive** wording from the statements for the yearly report in order to remain objective and factual.

재무 감사관은 객관적이고 사실적이게 유지하기 위해 연례 보고서의 진술에서 몇몇 서술적인 표현을 빼라고 제안한다.

해설 빈칸은 명사 wording을 수식하는 자리이다. 문맥상 '객관성과 사실성을 유지하기 위해 연례 보고서에서 몇몇 서술적인 표현을 없애라고 제안했다'는 의미가 되어야 자연스러우므로 형용사 (D)가 정답이다.

어휘 financial 재무의 | auditor 회계감사관 | suggest 제안하다 | remove 제거하다 | wording 표현 | statement 진술, 서술 | objective 객관적인 | factual 사실적인

---

5. 어휘 - 형용사

According to the system, you are **overdue** for your annual dental appointment with Dr. Herrera.

시스템에 따르면, 귀하의 Herrera 의사의 연례 치과 진료 예약 기한이 지났습니다.

해설 빈칸은 주어 you의 보어인 형용사 자리이다. 문맥상 '매년 하는 치과 진료 시기가 지났다고 시스템에 나와있다'는 의미가 되어야 자연스러우므로 (A)가 정답이다.

어휘 annual 연례의 | dental 치과의 | appointment 예약, 약속

✦ Key word

According to the system, you are overdue for your **annual dental appointment** with Dr. Herrera.

---

6. 어휘 - 형용사

Web Watch is the **leading** provider of on-demand streaming media for a worldwide audience.

Web Watch는 전세계 관객을 대상으로 한 주문형 스트리밍 미디어의 주요 제공업체다.

해설 빈칸은 정관사 the와 명사 provider 사이 형용사 자리이다. 명사를 후치 수식하는 of 전치사구의 내용을 고려할 때, 문맥상 '전세계 관객을 대상으로 주문형 스트리밍 미디어를 제공하는 주요 업체'라는 의미가 되어야 자연스러우므로 (B)가 정답이다.

어휘 provider 제공기관 | on-demand 주문형 | streaming media 스트리밍 미디어 | worldwide 전 세계적인 | audience 관객

✦ Key word

Web Watch is **the leading provider of on-demand streaming media for a worldwide audience**.

---

7. 어휘 - 형용사

Because of the reduced number of patrons, it is no longer **profitable** for Lumen Art Gallery to open for admissions every day of the week.

고객 수 감소로 인해, Lumen 미술관에서 더 이상 매일 입장객을 받는 일이 수익이 나지 않게 되었다.

해설 빈칸은 be동사 뒤의 문장의 보어 자리이다. Because of 전치사구와 빈칸 뒤에 이어지는 의미상 주어 및 진주어의 내용을 고려할 때, '고객 수 감소로, 미술관이 매일 문을 여는 것이 수익이 나지 않게 되었다'는 의미가 되어야 문맥상 자연스러우므로 (C)가 정답이다.

어휘 reduce 감소하다 | patron 고객 | no longer 더 이상 ~않다 | admission 입장

+ **Key word**

Because of reduced number of patrons, it is **no longer profitable for Lumen Art Gallery to open** for admissions every day of the week.

....

8. 어휘 - 형용사

The **likely** recipient of the promotion is the current manager of the Marketing Department.
승진의 유력한 수혜자는 현재 마케팅 부서의 매니저이다.

해설 빈칸은 명사 recipient를 수식하는 형용사 자리이다. 문맥상 '승진의 유력한 수혜자는 현재 마케팅 부서의 매니저'라는 의미가 되어야 자연스러우므로 (C)가 정답이다.

어휘 recipient 수혜자 | promotion 승진

+ **Key point**

명사에 -ly가 붙으면 형용사, 형용사에 -ly가 붙으면 부사가 된다.

9-12번은 다음 안내문에 관한 문제입니다.

Business Minds 계간지

공유할 이야기가 있으신가요?

최근 저희는 업종을 변경하는 방법에 관해 문의하는 독자 이메일을 많이 받았습니다. 장기화된 경기 침체로 많은 **⑨일자리**가 공석인 상태입니다. **⑩그 결과**, 많은 전문가들이 실직상태에 처하게 되었습니다. 하지만 이는 새로운 진로를 걸을 기회를 열어줍니다.

최근 업종을 변경하셔서 이야기를 공유하고 싶으시다면, 저희는 여러분의 이야기를 듣고 싶습니다. 여러분의 사연을 750자 미만으로 작성해 보내 주시되, 특히 **⑪어떤** 기술이 가장 도움이 되었는지 명시해 주세요. editorial@businessquarterly.com으로 여러분의 사연을 보내주세요. **⑫모든 이메일은 4월 23일까지 발송되어야 합니다**. 마감일이 지나면, 아쉽지만 이야기를 실어드릴 수 없습니다.

어휘
recently 최근 | reader 독자 | go about ~ing ~를 시작하다 | industry 업계, 업종 | vacant 비어 있는, 결원의 | prolonged 오래 계속되는 | economic downturn 경기 침체 | professional 전문직 종사자 | out of a job 실직 상태인 | opportunity 기회 | career path 진로 | share 공유하다 | in particular 특히 | state 명시하다 | deadline 마감일 | miss 놓치다 | unfortunately 아쉽게도 | include 포함시키다

9. 어휘 - 명사

해설 '장기화된 경기 침체로 많은 일자리가 공석인 상태'라는 의미가 되어야 문맥상 자연스러우므로 (D)가 정답이다.

+ **Key point**

Many **positions** have been **made vacant due to the prolonged economic downturn**.

10. 접속부사

해설 빈칸 앞 문장의 '장기화된 경기 침체로 많은 일자리가 공석인 상태'라는 내용과 빈칸 뒷부분의 많은 전문가들이 실직상태에 처하게 되었다'는 내용을 고려할 때, 두 문장이 인과관계로 연결되어야 문맥상 자연스러우므로 (A)가 정답이다.

+ **Key word**

Many positions have been made vacant due to the prolonged economic downturn. As a result,

many professionals have found themselves out of a job.

11. 의문사

해설 빈칸은 뒤에 이어지는 절을 동사 state의 목적어인 명사절로 만들어 줄 의문사 자리이다. 문맥상 '어떤 기술이 가장 도움이 되었는지 명시하세요'라는 의미가 되어야 자연스러우며, 빈칸이 수식하는 대상이 skills 이므로 의문형용사 (D)가 정답이다.

+ **Key point**

의문 형용사 which는 '어느, 어떤'을, whose는 '누구의'를 의미한다.

12. 문장 선택

(A) 면접 팁에 대한 기사도 요청되었습니다.
(B) 모든 이메일은 4월 23일까지 발송되어야 합니다.
(C) 우편함을 자주 확인하시기를 요청드립니다.
(D) 다음 판은 이 새로운 디자인을 선보일 것입니다.

해설 빈칸 앞 문장의 'editorial@businessquarterly.com으로 사연을 보내달라'는 내용과 빈칸 뒷문장의 '마감일이 지나면 이야기를 실어 줄 수 없다'는 내용을 고려할 때, 제출 마감일에 관한 내용이 들어가야 문맥상 자연스러우므로 (B)가 정답이다.

+ **Key word**

Send your story to editorial@businessquarterly.com. **All e-mails must be sent in by April 23. If the deadline is missed, we unfortunately cannot include your story.**

CHAPTER 05 부사

CASE 집중훈련   본서 p.75

1. (D)   2. (C)   3. (B)   4. (A)   5. (C)   6. (B)
7. (B)   8. (D)

1. 부사 자리

The inquiry revealed that the resort staff had handled the guest's complaints **appropriately**, and that their actions did not go against resort policy.
조사에서 리조트 직원들은 고객 불만을 적절하게 처리했다고 밝혀졌으며, 그러한 그들의 행동은 리조트 정책에 위배되지 않았다.

해설 빈칸은 명사 the guest's complaints의 뒤에 있으므로 형용사인 (A)와 (B)는 들어갈 수가 없다. 복합명사 형태도 아니므로 명사인 (C)도 제거한다. 빈칸 앞의 일반 동사인 had handled를 수식하는 부사가 들어가서 '적절하게 다뤘다'는 의미가 자연스러우므로 정답은 (D)이다.

어휘 inquiry 조사, 연구, 탐사 | reveal 밝히다

....

2. 어휘 - 부사

An agreement was **finally** signed after a lengthy negotiation between two corporations.
두 기업간의 긴 협상 후에 마침내 계약서에 서명이 되었다.

해설 빈칸은 be동사와 일반 동사 사이의 부사 자리이다. 문맥상 '마침내 서명되었다'는 의미가 되어야 자연스러우므로 (C)가 정답이다.

어휘 agreement 계약서, 협정서 | lengthy 너무 긴 | negotiation 협상 | corporation 기업

+ **Key word**

An agreement was **finally signed** after a lengthy negotiation between two corporations.

· ·

3. 부사 자리

Residents of the town must be consulted **individually** before making any changes to the current transportation system.

현재의 수송 체계를 변경하기 전에 반드시 지역 주민들과 개별적으로 상의되어야 한다.

해설 빈칸이 없어도 완벽한 문장이므로 빈칸은 앞의 수동태 동사 must be consulted를 수식하는 부사 자리이다. 따라서 (B)가 정답이다.

어휘 resident 주민 | consult 상의하다, 상담하다 | make a change 변경하다, 바꾸다 | current 현재의 | transportation system 수송 체계

· ·

4. 부사 자리

Motorists on the Brisbane Bridge are asked to drive **cautiously** during September due to the continuing street repairs.

Brisbane 대교 위의 운전자들은 9월 동안 계속되는 도로 보수로 인해 조심해서 운전하도록 요청된다.

해설 빈칸은 준동사 to drive를 수식하는 부사 자리이므로 (A)가 정답이다.

어휘 motorist 운전자 | continuing 계속적인

+ **Key point**

(준)동사를 수식할 수 있는 품사는 부사이다.

5-8번은 다음 이메일에 관한 문제입니다.

수신: Collette Snead

발신: Ayrton de Silva ⟨asilva@sarbaevents.com⟩

날짜: 9월 22일

제목: 창립기념일

Snead 씨께,

다음 달 있을 귀하의 파티를 위해 Sarba를 이용하는 것에 관심을 가져주셔서 감사드립니다. 저희의 이용 가능한 공간들에 대한 세부내용을 알려드리겠습니다.

⑤저희는 다양한 규모의 단체에 맞춤 환경을 제공해 드립니다. 이를테면, 저희 연회장은 최대 150명까지 수용할 수 있고 라이브 공연용 무대를 갖추고 있습니다. 이 공간은 회사 차원의 모임에 **⑥이상적**입니다. 전용 루프탑 라운지는 공식 **⑦행사**에 적합합니다. 또한, Eastwood Pavilion은 50-70명을 수용할 수 있는 공간으로, 경치가 좋고 공기가 맑습니다. 저희는 귀하의 필요와 일정에 따라 손님들을 위한 주차와/또는 지상교통수단을 **⑧쉽게** 마련해 드릴 수 있습니다.

더 궁금하신 점이 있으시면 바로 답장해 주시기 바랍니다. 저희는 언제나 제안에 열려 있습니다.

감사합니다.

Ayrton de Silva

어휘

appreciate 감사해하다 | interest 관심, 흥미 | details 세부내용 | space 공간 | at one's disposal ~의 마음대로 사용할 수 있게 | ballroom 연회장 | host (행사를) 주최하다 | up to 최대 ~까지 | stage 무대 | live 생중계의, 생방송의 | entertainment 오락, 유흥 | area 구역, 지역 | company-wide 회사 차원의 | gathering 모임 | exclusive 전용의, 독점적인 | rooftop 옥상, 루프탑 | lounge 라운지 | suitable 적합한 | formal 공식적인 | scenic 경치가 좋은 | room 공간 | party goer 파티 참석자 | arrange for 준비하다 | ground transportation 지상 교통 | in accordance with ~에 따라 | scheduling 일정 계획 | consideration 고려사항 | as well 또한 | reply 답장을 보내다 | directly 직접, 즉시 | open to (생각, 의견에) 열려있는, 귀 기울이는 | suggestion 제안, 의견

5. 문장 선택

(A) 추가 정보를 이메일로 보내드릴 수 있습니다.
(B) 시간을 내어 간단한 설문에 응해 주시면 감사하겠습니다.
(C) 저희는 다양한 규모의 단체에 맞춤 환경을 제공해 드립니다.
(D) 원하시는 장르의 음악 그룹을 예약해드릴 수 있습니다.

해설 빈칸 앞 문장의 '저희의 이용 가능한 공간들에 대한 세부내용을 알려드리겠다'는 내용과 빈칸 뒷문장에서 for example이라 하며 공간 중 한 곳의 예를 들어 설명하고 있음을 고려할 때, 문맥상 '다양한 규모의 단체에 맞춤 환경을 제공한다'는 내용이 들어가는 것이 자연스러우므로 (C)가 정답이다.

+ **Key point**

I'd be **happy to let you know some details about the spaces** at our disposal. **We provide custom settings suited to groups of varying sizes. Our ballroom, for example,** can host a group of up to 150 and has a stage for live entertainment.

6. 어휘 – 형용사

해설 빈칸은 be동사 뒤 주격 보어 자리이다. 빈칸 앞 문장에 '연회장은 최대 150명까지 수용할 수 있고 라이브 공연용 무대를 갖추고 있다'는 내용이 있으므로, 문맥상 '이 공간은 회사 차원의 모임에 이상적'이라는 내용으로 이어져야 자연스러우므로 (B)가 정답이다.

+ **Key word**

Our ballroom, for example, **can host a group of up to 150 and has a stage for live entertainment. This area is ideal for a company-wide gathering.**

7. 어휘 – 명사

해설 빈칸은 전치사 for의 목적어인 명사 자리이다. 문맥상 '루프탑 라운지는 공식 행사에 적합하다'는 의미가 되어야 자연스러우므로 (B)가 정답이다.

+ **Key word**

The more **exclusive rooftop lounge** is **suitable for formal occasions.**

8. 부사 자리

해설 빈칸은 조동사와 동사 사이의 부사 자리이므로 (D)가 정답이다.

CASE 집중훈련
본서 p.77

1. (C) **2.** (D) **3.** (B) **4.** (C) **5.** (B) **6.** (B)
7. (C) **8.** (D)

1. 명사를 수식하는 부사

Only films that have been released within the past year will be shown in the CineGlobe Film Festival.

지난해 개봉되었던 영화들만 CineGlobe 영화제에서 상영될 것이다.

해설 빈칸은 문맥상 '지난해 개봉되었던 영화들만 상영될 것이다'라는 의미가 되어야 자연스러우므로 (C)가 정답이다. only는 부사이지만 명사를 수식하는 특수한 쓰임새를 갖는다.

어휘 film 영화 | release 개봉하다 | show 상영하다 | film festival 영화제

+ Key point

〈명사(구)를 수식하는 부사〉
only, just, simply 단지, ~만
once 한때

2. 부사 자리

We offer free tours of the **historically** significant Gooseberry Porte to the public every Saturday.

저희는 매주 토요일 역사적으로 중요한 Gooseberry Porte에 대한 무료 투어를 대중에게 제공합니다.

해설 빈칸은 형용사 significant를 수식하는 자리이므로 부사 (D)가 정답이다.

어휘 significant 중요한, 특별한 | public 대중

3. 부사 자리

Perhaps the most important step in the hiring process is determining a fair pay and benefits package for the potential employee.

아마도 채용 과정에서 가장 중요한 단계는 잠재 직원을 위한 공정한 급여와 복리후생 제도를 결정하는 것이다.

해설 절이 하나이므로 부사절 접속사인 (A)는 제거한다. each는 한정사 the/a(n) 앞에 올 수 없으므로 (D)는 제거한다. 빈칸은 완전한 절의 앞이므로 부사 자리이고, 문맥상 '아마도 채용과정에서 가장 중요한 단계는~이다'라는 내용이 자연스러우므로 (B)가 정답이다.

어휘 step 단계 | hiring 고용 | process 과정, 절차 | determine 결정하다 | fair 공정한 | benefits package 복리후생 제도

+ Key point

부사는 문장 맨 앞에서 문장 전체를 수식할 수 있다.

4. 부사 자리

Moving operations to another country is **understandably** a challenging undertaking, but it can increase revenue.

다른 나라로 사업을 이전하는 것은 당연히 어려운 일이지만, 그것이 수익을 증가시킬 수 있다.

해설 빈칸은 be동사와 주격 보어 a challenging undertaking 사이의 부사 자리이므로 (C)가 정답이다.

어휘 operation 운영, 사업 | challenging 힘든, 도전적인 | undertaking 일, 프로젝트 | revenue 수익

+ Key point

부사는 문장 내에서 가장 다양한 위치에 올 수 있는 품사로, 부사가 be동사와 명사구 형태의 주격 보어 사이에 등장하는 경우,「be동사 + 주격 보어」인 동사구 전체를 수식 및 강조하는 역할을 한다. 이는 문두에서 부사가 문장 전체를 수식하는 또 다른 형태라고 생각하면 된다.

5-8번은 다음 공지에 관한 문제입니다.

Cano 센터 수도공급 임시중단

6월 27일 수요일에 정비직원들이 오전 8시부터 오후 8시까지 Cano센터 내 수도 공급을 중단할 예정입니다. 건물은 하루 종일 **5폐쇄될 것입니다.** 수도공급이 중단되는 동안, 배관 시스템이 점검될 것입니다. **6구체적으로는,** 모든 개수대가 보다 효율적인 모델로 업그레이드되고 구형 배관이 교체될 것입니다.

화요일에 사무실과 강의실을 떠나기 **7전,** 배관 담당 직원들에게 방해가 되는 것들을 만들지 않도록 모든 장비와 자재가 제대로 보관되어 있는지 확인하십시오. 또한, 휴게실에서 모든 음식과 개인 소지품을 치우는 것을 기억하십시오. **8남겨진 물건들은 모두 처분될 것입니다.** 질문이 있으시면, 555-948-1982번으로 캠퍼스 운영팀에 문의하십시오.

어휘
temporary 임시의 | shutdown 폐쇄 | maintenance (건물, 기계 등의) 유지보수, 정비 | turn off 끄다 | whole 전체의 | plumbing 배관 | overhaul 점검하다 | sink 싱크대, 개수대 | efficient 효율적인 | piping 관 | replace 교체하다 | equipment 장비 | material 재료 | store 보관하다 | properly 적절히 | avoid 피하다 | create 만들다 | obstruction 장애물 | clear 치우다 | belongings 소지품 | operation 운영, 사업

5. 동사의 태 / 시제

해설 빈칸은 주어 뒤 동사 자리이다. 빈칸 앞 문장의 '수도 공급이 중단될 예정'이라는 내용과 주어가 사물 명사 the building이고 목적어가 없는 것을 고려할 때, 미래 시제 수동태 문장을 완성하는 (B)가 정답이다.

+ Key point

동사의 형태는 '태', '수의 일치', '시제'를 고려해야 한다.

6. 어휘 - 부사

해설 빈칸 앞 문장의 '배관 시스템이 점검될 것'이라는 내용과 빈칸 뒷부분의 '개수대가 업그레이드되고 구형 배관이 교체될 것'이라는 내용을 고려할 때, 빈칸 뒷부분에서 점검되는 내용을 구체적으로 설명하고 있으므로 (B)가 정답이다.

+ Key word

While the water is off, **the plumbing system will be overhauled. Specifically, all the sinks will be upgraded to more efficient models and older piping will be replaced.**

7. 전치사 자리

해설 문맥상 '사무실을 떠나기 전, 모든 장비와 자재가 제대로 보관되어 있는지 확인하세요'라는 내용이 되어야 자연스러우므로 (C)가 정답이다.

+ Key word

Before leaving your offices and class rooms on Tuesday, **check to make sure that all equipment and materials are stored properly** to avoid creating obstructions for the plumbing staff.

8. 문장 선택

(A) 식품에는 보관 날짜를 표시해야 합니다.
(B) 사무실 직원들은 정규 근무 시간에 근무하도록 예상됩니다.
(C) 보충수업은 6월 30일로 예정되어 있습니다.
(D) 남겨진 물건들은 모두 처분될 것입니다.

해설 빈칸 앞 문장의 '휴게실에서 모든 음식과 개인 소지품을 치우라'는 내용을 고려할 때, 문맥상 '남겨진 물건들은 모두 처분될 것'이라는 내용으로 이어져야 자연스러우므로 (D)가 정답이다.

✛ **Key word**

Also, remember to clear all food and personal belongings from the break rooms. All items left behind will be disposed of.

CASE 집중훈련

본서 p.79

1. (A) **2.** (B) **3.** (D) **4.** (D) **5.** (D) **6.** (A)
7. (A) **8.** (C)

---

1. 시간부사

There were **already** 100 people attending the seminar when Ms. Nunez invited 10 of the current interns.
Nunez 씨가 현 인턴 10명을 초대했을 때에는 세미나 참석자가 이미 100명이었다.

해설 빈칸은 「There be ~」 구문에 해당하는 명사구 사이의 자리이다. 접속사 when으로 연결된 두 문장의 관계를 고려할 때, 문맥상 'Nunez 씨가 10명의 인턴을 초대했을 시점에 세미나에 참석하기로 한 사람들이 이미 100명이나 있었다'라는 의미가 되어야 자연스러우므로 부사 (A)가 정답이다.

어휘 attend 참석하다 | current 현재의

✛ **Key point**

부사는 문장 내에서 가장 다양한 위치에 올 수 있는 품사로, 부사가 be동사와 명사구 사이에 등장하는 경우, 동사구 전체를 수식 및 강조하는 역할을 한다.

---

2. 어휘 - 동사

The site for August's charity auction is yet to be **decided**.
8월 달 자선 경매 장소는 아직 정해지지 않았다.

해설 빈칸은 be동사와 함께 수동태 구문을 완성하는 과거분사 자리이다. 문맥상 '자선 경매 장소가 아직 정해지지 않았다'는 의미가 되어야 자연스러우므로 (B)가 정답이다.

어휘 site 장소 | charity auction 자선 경매 | be yet to 아직 ~하지 않다

✛ **Key word**

The **site** for August's charity auction **is yet to be decided**.

---

3. 시간부사

Although Janice Langdon was going to leave Kyro Inc., she **still** has a seat on the board of directors.
Janice Langdon은 Kyro 사를 퇴사하려고 했지만, 여전히 이사회에 자리를 갖고 있다.

해설 빈칸은 주어와 동사의 완전한 구조 사이의 부사 자리이다. 문맥상 'Janice Langdon은 퇴사하려고 했지만, 여전히 이사회에 자리를 갖고 있다'라는 의미가 되어야 자연스러우며, 부사 still은 양보 접속사, 양보 전치사 등과 쓰여 '~에도 불구하고, 여전히 ~한다'라는 의미로 자주 쓰이므로 (D)가 정답이다.

어휘 board of directors 이사회

---

4. 시간부사

The companies listed in this directory are first grouped by category and **then** alphabetized.
이 안내책자에 나와있는 회사들은 우선 카테고리별로 분류된 후 알파벳순으로 배열된다.

해설 수동태 동사 구문 「be + p.p.」 2개가 접속사 and로 연결된 구조로, 빈칸은 두 번째 과거분사를 수식하는 부사 자리이다. 첫 번째 동사 구문을 부사 first가 수식하고 있음을 고려할 때, 문맥상 '우선 카테고리별로 분류되고, 그리고 나서 알파벳순으로 배열된다'는 의미가 되어야 문맥상 자연스러우므로 (D)가 정답이다.

어휘 list 목록으로 만들다 | directory 안내 책자 | group (그룹으로) 나누다 | alphabetize 알파벳순으로 배열하다

✛ **Key word**

The companies listed in this directory are **first grouped by category and then alphabetized**.

5-8번은 다음 기사에 관한 문제입니다.

MONTPELIER — Sunflower 리조트 내 프렌치 레스토랑 Chez Les Rois가 25년 간의 영업을 마무리하고 다음 주 **⑤문을 닫는다**. 오너 겸 매니저인 Jean Bisset이 작년 말 은퇴하면서, 주요 변화에 대한 논의를 촉발시켰다. 리조트 대변인에 따르면, 식당은 여름 동안 리모델링은 거쳐, 새로운 운영진과 새로운 **⑥주제로** 다시 문을 열 예정이다. **⑦전체 메뉴가 채식으로 구성될 것이다**. 신규 레스토랑이 어떻게 불릴지는 **⑧아직** 정해지지 않았다.

어휘

resort 리조트 | century 세기, 100년 | in operation 운용 중인 | owner 주인, 소유주 | retire 떠나다 | spark 촉발시키다 | eatery 음식점 | undergo 겪다 | remodeling 개조, 리모델링 | ownership 소유(권) | representative 대표자, 대리인 | decide 결정하다

---

5. 동사의 시제

해설 빈칸은 주어와 목적어 사이의 동사 자리이다. 문장 내 미래 시제 표현 next week이 있으므로 미래 진행 시제 (D)가 정답이다.

✛ **Key word**

Chez Les Rois, **the French restaurant** in the Sunflower Resort, **will be closing its doors next week** after a quarter of a century in operation.

---

6. 어휘 - 명사

해설 빈칸은 전치사 with의 목적어이자, a new의 수식을 받는 명사 자리이다. 접속사 and로 연결된 두 문장의 관계를 고려할 때, 문맥상 '식당이 여름 동안 리모델링을 거쳐, 새로운 운영진과 새로운 주제로 다시 문을 열 것'이라는 의미가 되어야 자연스러우므로 (A)가 정답이다.

✛ **Key word**

The eatery is due to undergo remodeling over the summer, and will reopen under new ownership

---

with a new theme according to a representative from the resort.

7. 문장 선택

(A) 전체 메뉴가 채식으로 구성될 것입니다.
(B) 최근 몇 년 사이에 지출이 증가했습니다.
(C) Montpelier에는 다양한 식사 선택권이 있습니다.
(D) 근처에 다른 식당들이 있습니다.

해설 빈칸 앞 문장의 '식당은 여름 동안 리모델링을 거쳐, 새로운 운영진과 새로운 주제로 다시 문을 열 예정'이라는 내용을 고려할 때, 해당 내용에 대한 부가 설명으로 이어지는 것이 자연스러우므로 (A)가 정답이다.

✛ Key word

The **eatery** is due to undergo remodeling over the summer, and will reopen under new ownership with a new **theme** according to a representative from the resort. **The entire menu will be vegetarian.**

8. 관용 표현

해설 빈칸은 be동사와 주격 보어인 to부정사 사이의 자리이다. 빈칸 앞 부사 still과 접속사 though가 있음을 고려할 때, 문맥상 '신규 레스토랑이 어떻게 불릴지는 여전히 아직 정해지지 않았다'는 의미가 되어야 자연스러우므로 'be yet to do(아직 ~하지 않다)'의 관용 표현을 완성하는 (C)가 정답이다.

✛ Key word

What the new restaurant will be called, though, is still yet to be decided.

CASE 집중훈련
본서 p.81

1. (C) **2.** (C) **3.** (C) **4.** (A) **5.** (B) **6.** (D)
7. (C) **8.** (A)

1. 빈도 부사

The IT Department should **always** be consulted when there is an increase in server errors.
서버 오류가 증가하면, 항상 IT 부서와 상의해야 한다.

해설 빈칸은 완전한 동사구 사이에서 이를 수식하는 부사 자리이다. 문맥상 '서버 오류가 증가하면, 항상 IT 부서와 상의해야 한다.'라는 의미가 되어야 자연스러우므로 (C)가 정답이다.

어휘 consult 상의하다, 상담하다 ㅣ error 오류

2. 빈도 부사

Mr. Lee couldn't be here today, but he **usually** comes to all monthly meetings.
Lee 씨는 오늘 이곳에 올 수 없었지만, 그는 보통 모든 월례 회의에 참석한다.

해설 빈칸은 주어와 동사 사이에서 동사를 수식하는 부사 자리이다. 'Lee 씨는 오늘 이곳에 올 수 없었지만, 그는 보통 모든 월례 회의에 참석한다.'라는 의미가 되어야 자연스러우며, usually와 같은 빈도 부사는 습관적인 사실을 나타내는 현재 시제와 잘 쓰이므로 (C)가 정답이다.

어휘 monthly 매월의, 한 달에 한 번의

✛ Key point

부사 formerly '이전에, 예전에'는 과거 시제와 어울린다.

---

3. 부정부사

Ms. Mavis noted that Mr. Kasim is **seldom** late for appointments.
Mavis 씨는 Kasim 씨가 좀처럼 약속에 늦지 않는다고 언급했다.

해설 문맥에 어울리는 부사를 고르는 문제는 의미 파악이 우선되어야 한다. 'Kasim 씨가 좀처럼 약속에 늦지 않는다'는 의미가 적절하므로 '거의 ~않다'는 의미의 부정부사이면서 빈도를 나타내는 (C)가 정답이다.

어휘 note 언급하다, 주목하다 ㅣ late for ~에 늦은 ㅣ appointment 약속

✛ Key point

부정부사는 그 자체에 부정의 의미를 포함하고 있어 not과 같은 부정어와 함께 쓰지 않는다.
거의 ~않다: hardly (ever), seldom, rarely, barely, scarcely
절대 ~않다: never

---

4. 부정부사

Alan Yovich often played video games as a hobby but **never** thought he would make a fortune by joining a professional league.
Alan Yovich는 종종 취미로 비디오게임을 했지만 프로리그에 합류해서 돈을 벌 거라고는 절대 생각하지 못했다.

해설 Alan Yovich를 주어로 하는 두 개의 문장이 접속사 but으로 연결된 구조로, 빈칸은 접속사와 동사 사이에서 동사 thought를 수식하는 부사 자리이다. 접속사 but으로 연결된 두 문장의 관계를 고려할 때, 문맥상 '취미로 비디오게임을 했지만, 프로리그에서 돈을 벌 거라고는 결코 생각지 못했다'는 의미가 되어야 자연스러우므로 (A)가 정답이다.

어휘 make a fortune 재산을 모으다 ㅣ join 합류하다 ㅣ professional league 프로리그

5-8번은 다음 기사에 관한 문제입니다.

DUBLIN (9월 10일) — 다음 주는 신발 브랜드 Ida의 새로운 시대를 상징한다. 잉글랜드 전역에 매장을 두고 있는 이 프랜차이즈는 Wicklow 거리에 첫 아일랜드 지점을 **5열 것이다.** 2층짜리 이 지점은 **6유명한** Grafton 거리 쇼핑 아케이드와 Trinity 대학교에서 한 블록도 안 된다. "이 지역에는 쇼핑객, 학생, 관광객들의 엄청난 인파가 있습니다,"라고 개장을 위해 방문한 Ida의 임원인 Justin Mann은 설명했다. **7그는 지역 주민들과 방문객들 사이에서 이 지역의 인기가 Ida의 판매에 도움이 될 것이라고 덧붙였다.** Kilpatrick 빌딩의 상층에 있는 개조된 공간에는 커피숍과 어린이 놀이 공간뿐만 아니라 근처 공원의 **8경치가** 보이는 커다란 창문이 있다. Mann은 "Dublin 매장은 우리에게 좋은 기회이며 이미 인기 있는 지역에 또 다른 주요 명소가 되어 줄 것입니다."라며 덧붙였다.

어휘

represent 보여주다, 상징하다 ㅣ footwear 신발 ㅣ story 층 ㅣ arcade 아케이드 (양쪽에 상점들이 늘어서 있는 통로) ㅣ tremendous 엄청난 ㅣ foot traffic 도보 인파 ㅣ renovated 개조된 ㅣ nearby 근처의 ㅣ attraction 매력, 명소 ㅣ district 구역

5. 동사의 시제

해설 빈칸은 The franchise를 주어로 하는 동사 자리이다. 빈칸 앞 문장의 '다음 주가 신발 브랜드 Ida의 새로운 시대를 상징한다'라는 내용을 고려할 때, 문맥상 '이 프랜차이즈는 Wicklow 거리에 첫 아일랜드 지점을 열 것이다'라는 내용이 되어야 자연스러우므로 미래 시제 (B)가 정답이다.

+ **Key word**

Next week represents a new era for the footwear brand Ida. The franchise, which has stores across England, **will open** its first Irish location on Wicklow Street.

6. 어휘 – 형용사

해설 빈칸 뒷부분의 '이 지역에는 쇼핑객, 학생, 관광객들의 엄청난 인파가 있습니다'라는 내용을 고려할 때, 문맥상 '이 지점은 유명한 Grafton 거리 쇼핑 아케이드와 Trinity 대학에서 한 블록도 안된다'라는 내용이 되어야 자연스러우므로 (D)가 정답이다.

+ **Key word**

The two-story location is less than a block from the prominent Grafton Street Shopping Arcade and Trinity College. "There is tremendous foot traffic in the neighborhood, with shoppers, students, and tourists," explained Justin Mann, an Ida executive here for the opening.

7. 문장 선택

(A) 오히려 이 회사는 홍보를 위해 소셜 미디어 캠페인을 계획하고 있다.
(B) 건축가들이 이 공간의 독특한 디자인에 대해 토론하기 위해 참석할 것이다.
(C) 지역 주민들과 방문객들 사이에서 이 지역의 인기가 Ida의 판매에 도움이 될 것이라고 덧붙였다.
(D) 그 대학의 새 학기는 다음 달에 시작될 예정이다.

해설 빈칸 앞 문장의 이 지역에는 쇼핑객, 학생, 관광객들의 엄청난 인파가 있다며 Justin Mann이 인터뷰한 내용을 고려할 때, 문맥상 지역 주민들과 방문객들 사이에서 이 지역의 인기가 Ida의 판매에 도움이 될 것이라고 덧붙였다는 내용이 이어져야 자연스러우므로 (C)가 정답이다.

+ **Key word**

"There is tremendous foot traffic in the neighborhood, with shoppers, students, and tourists," explained Justin Mann, an Ida executive here for the opening. He added that Ida's sales will be helped by the area's popularity among locals and visitors to the city.

8. 어휘 – 명사

해설 빈칸은 전치사 with의 목적어 역할을 하는 명사 자리이다. 문맥상 '근처 공원의 경치가 보이는 커다란 창문'이라는 내용이 되어야 자연스러우므로 (A)가 정답이다.

+ **Key word**

The renovated space on the top floors of the Kilpatrick Building has **large windows with views of nearby parks**, as well as a coffee shop and children's play area.

CASE 집중훈련

본서 p.83

1. (B) 2. (B) 3. (C) 4. (C) 5. (B) 6. (C)
7. (D) 8. (D)

1. 전치사구 앞에 오는 강조부사

The Human Resources Department requires employees to hand in their travel plans **soon** after reserving tickets for a trip.

인사부는 직원들이 출장을 위해 티켓을 예약한 뒤 곧 출장 계획을 제출하기를 요구한다.

해설 빈칸은 전명구를 수식하는 부사 자리이다. 문맥상 '티켓을 예매한 후 곧'이라는 의미가 적합하므로 (B)가 정답이다.

어휘 require 요구하다 | hand in 제출하다 | reserve 예약하다

2. 명사구 앞에 오는 강조부사

Formerly the assistant sales manager, Mr. Cochran has just been appointed Director of Marketing at GP Corp.

전에 영업 대리였던 Cochran 씨는 이제 막 GP 사에서 마케팅 이사로 임명되었다.

해설 빈칸은 명사구 the assistant sales manager 전체를 수식하는 부사 자리이다. 주절의 내용을 고려할 때, 문맥상 '예전에 영업 대리였던 Cochran 씨가 이제 막 마케팅 이사로 임명되었다'는 의미가 되어야 자연스러우므로 (B)가 정답이다.

어휘 assistant 부-, 보조 | sales manager 판매관리자 | appoint 임명하다

+ **Key word**

Formerly the **assistant** sales manager, Mr. Cochran **has just been appointed Director** of Marketing at GP Corp.

3. 명사구 앞에 오는 강조부사

After your meeting is finished, please leave **just** five tables in the room and put the rest of them back into the storage room.

회의가 끝나고, 회의실에 단 다섯 개의 테이블만 남기고 나머지는 창고로 다시 갖다 놓으세요.

해설 빈칸은 형용사 five를 수식하는 부사 자리이다. '테이블을 5개만 남기고 다시 갖다 놔 달라'는 내용이 자연스러우므로 (C)가 정답이다.

어휘 rest 나머지 | put ~ back ~을 다시 제자리에 갖다 놓다 | storage room 창고

4. 어휘 – 부사

The management had **originally** planned to open a new branch by the end of the year, but it was deemed too costly.

경영진은 원래 연말까지 신규 지점을 열 계획이었으나, 비용이 너무 많이 드는 것으로 여겨졌다.

해설 빈칸은 과거 완료 동사 구문을 수식할 부사 자리이다. 접속사 but으로 연결된 두 문장 관계를 고려할 때, 문맥상 '원래는 연말까지 신규 지점을 열 계획이었지만, 비용이 너무 많이 드는 것으로 여겨졌다'는 의미로 연결되어야 자연스러우므로 (C)가 정답이다.

어휘 management 경영진, 관리진 | plan 계획하다 | branch 지점 | end 끝, 말 | deem 여기다, 생각하다 | costly 비싼

+ **Key word**

The management had **originally planned to open a new branch by the end of the year, but it was deemed too costly.**

5-8번은 다음 기사에 관한 문제입니다.

자신만의 마케팅 대행사 개업하기

새 마케팅 대행사를 여는 것은 흥미로운 벤처 사업일 수 있다. 하지만, 이러한 사업은 많은 난관을 동반한다. **⑤무엇**이 필요한지 알고 그런 다음 그에 맞게 행동하는 것이 중요하다. 첫째, 창업 비용을 충당하기 위해 사업 대출을 받아야 할 것이다. 현재의 연구는 7,000달러에서 20,000달러 사이의 금액이 필요할 것으로 나타난다. 다음으로, 숙련된 직원들을 고용해야 할 것이다. 이에는 비서와 적어도 한 명의 마케팅 보조원, 아마도 **⑥심지어** 최고 재무 관리자도 포함될 수도 있다. 물론, 일부 사무용 장비와 더불어 사업을 할 장소도 필요할 것이다. **⑦적절한 사무실은 소중한 자원**이 될 수 있다. 그리고 사업이 아주 잘 **⑧운영되도록** 유지해 줄 복사기, 파일 캐비닛 등과 같은 필요한 어떠한 용품들도 모두 빠뜨리지 않도록 해야 한다.

어휘
agency 대행사, 업체 | venture 벤처 사업, (모험적) 사업 | undertaking 사업, 일 | come with 동반되다, 딸려 있다 | obstacle 난관, 장애물 | crucial 중요한 | be aware of ~을 알고 있다 | accordingly 그에 맞게 | loan 대출 | cover (비용 등을) 충당하다 | current 현재의 | indicate 나타내다 | hire 고용하다 | skilled 숙련된 | include 포함하다 | at least 적어도, 최소한 | conduct 실시하다 | as well as ~에 더하여, ~뿐만 아니라 | equipment 장비 | leave out ~을 빠뜨리다, 제외하다 | supplies 용품

5. 명사절 접속사

해설 빈칸은 전치사 of의 목적어로서 뒤에 명사절을 이끌어줄 명사절 접속사 자리이다. 동사 need 뒤에 목적어가 빠진 불완전한 절이 제시되어 있으므로 불완전한 명사절을 이끄는 명사절 접속사인 (B)가 정답이다. when과 that은 완전한 절이 이끌고, whose는 소유격으로 쓰여 완전한 절을 이끈다.

+ **Key point**

전치사의 목적어로 명사와 명사구, 명사절, 동명사구가 올 수 있는데, 의문사로 시작되는 명사절의 경우 그 절의 주어/목적어 등이 빠져 있는지 확인해야 한다.

6. 명사구 앞에 오는 강조부사

해설 빈칸 뒤에는 명사구(a chief financial officer)가 나온다. 보통 명사구가 나오면 전치사를 생각하게 되지만 뒤의 명사구가 타동사 include의 목적어 중 하나이므로 전치사는 모두 답이 될 수 없고, 명사 앞에 강조를 위해 쓰일 수 있는 초점 부사인 (C)가 정답이다.

+ **Key point**

부사 even은 품사에 상관없이 강조를 원하는 단어 앞에 쓰일 수 있다.

7. 문장 선택

(A) 그들은 심지어 친구들과 함께 이 프로젝트를 할 수도 있다.
(B) 다음은 웹 사이트의 좋은 이름을 선택하기 위한 몇 가지 기준이다.
(C) 하지만 작업은 2주 안에 끝나야 할 것이다.
(D) 적절한 사무실은 소중한 자원이 될 수 있다.

해설 빈칸 앞 문장에서 사무용 장비 및 사업을 할 장소 등이 필요하다고 말하

는 내용을 고려할 때, 이어지는 내용으로 적절한 사무실의 중요성을 말하는 문장이 오는 게 알맞으므로 (D)가 정답이다.

+ **Key word**

Of course, you will also need a location to conduct business, as well as some office equipment. Suitable offices can be a valuable resource.

8. 어휘 – 형용사

해설 빈칸은 5형식 동사 keep의 목적어 뒤에 목적격 보어 자리이다. 문맥상 복사기, 파일 캐비닛 등과 같은 필요한 어떠한 용품들도 모두 빠뜨리지 않도록 해야 한다는 내용을 고려할 때, '사업이 아주 잘 운영되도록 유지해 줄'이라는 의미가 되어야 자연스러우므로 (D)가 정답이다.

+ **Key word**

And don't leave out any needed supplies such as copy machines, filing cabinets, etc., to keep business running very well.

CASE 집중훈련
본서 p.85

1. (A) **2.** (C) **3.** (B) **4.** (A) **5.** (C) **6.** (A)
7. (B) **8.** (C)

1. 접속사 자리

Enrollment at private universities is declining, **whereas** public universities are enjoying steady growth.
사립대학 등록은 줄어들고 있는 반면에 공립대학은 꾸준한 증가를 누리고 있다.

해설 빈칸은 앞뒤로 주어, 동사가 각각 포함된 절을 연결하는 접속사가 들어가야 하는 자리이므로, 보기에서 유일한 접속사인 (A)가 정답이다. 나머지 보기들은 모두 부사이다.

어휘 enrollment 등록, 입학 | decline 줄어들다 | enjoy 누리다, 향유하다 | steady 꾸준한 | growth 성장

+ **Key point**

접속사와 접속부사 차이를 묻는 문제는 매회 출제되니, 반드시 암기해야 한다.

2. 접속부사

Although material costs for our line of personal computers have been increasing, we will **nevertheless** maintain the current prices.
우리 PC 라인의 자재비가 증가하고 있지만, 그럼에도 불구하고 우리는 현재의 가격을 유지할 것이다.

해설 빈칸은 조동사와 동사 원형 사이의 부사 자리이다. 문맥상 '우리 PC 라인의 자재비가 증가하고 있지만, 그럼에도 불구하고 우리는 현재의 가격을 유지할 것이다.'라는 의미가 되어야 자연스러우므로 (C)가 정답이다.

어휘 material 재료 | maintain 유지하다 | current 현재의

+ **Key word**

Although material costs for our line of personal computers have been increasing, we will nevertheless maintain the current prices.

3. 접속사 자리

Over half of the committee must sign the agreement, **or** it will not be valid.

위원회의 절반 이상이 합의서에 서명하지 않으면 그것은 유효하지 않을 것이다.

해설 빈칸은 두 개의 완전한 문장을 연결하는 접속사 자리이다. 문맥상 '절반 이상이 합의서에 서명을 해야 한다, 그렇지 않으면 유효하지 않을 것이다'라는 의미가 자연스러우므로 (B)가 정답이다.

어휘 committee 위원회 | sign 서명하다 | agreement 합의(서) | valid 유효한

✛ Key point

접속부사는 문장 사이에서 연결어 역할을 하며, 콤마(,) 및 접속사 and 또는 세미콜론(;)과 함께 사용된다: 「문장1. 접속부사, 문장2.」, 「문장1; 접속부사, 문장2.」, 「문장1 and 접속부사, 문장2.」

....

4. 어휘 – 부사

As our usual supplier did not have the materials we required available, we ordered from a local distributor **instead**.

평소 이용하는 업체에 우리에게 필요한 재료가 없어서, 우리는 대신 현지 판매점에서 주문했다.

해설 빈칸은 문장 동사를 수식하는 부사 자리이다. 접속사 as로 연결된 두 문장의 관계를 고려할 때, 문맥상 '평소 이용하는 업체에 필요한 재료가 없어서, 대신 현지 판매점에서 주문했다'는 의미가 되어야 자연스러우므로 (A)가 정답이다.

어휘 usual 평상시의, 보통의 | supplier 공급업자[체] | material 재료, 물질 | require 요구하다 | local 현지의, 지역의 | distributor 유통업자[회사], 배급업자

✛ Key word

As our **usual supplier** did **not have** the **materials** we **required** available, we **ordered from a local distributor instead.**

5-8번은 다음 광고에 관한 문제입니다.

연말 Exham Sportswear 할인

연례 연말 행사 기간 동안 대폭 절약할 수 있는 이번 기회를 절대 놓치지 않도록 여러분께 급히 **⑤알립니다.** 노란색 태그가 있는 옷은 20퍼센트 할인되는 반면 분홍색 태그가 **⑥달린** 옷은 반값 할인됩니다. 우리의 가장 인기 있는 의류를 거의 모두 역대 최저 가격으로 구입할 수 있습니다. 절대 놓치지 마세요!

⑦추가로 매주 토요일 매장에 방문한 첫 고객 백 명은 매장 적립금 100 달러를 받습니다. **⑧제한사항이 일부 적용됩니다.** 매장 적립금은 이를 받는 매장에서만 사용할 수 있으며, 4월 말에 만료됩니다. 이 혜택에 대해 더 알고 싶거나 물품 목록을 확인하고 싶거나 저희 리워드 프로그램에 가입하고 싶다면 Exham-sports.co.uk에 방문해 주세요. 또는 가까이에 계시다면 지역 매장에 들러서 우리 직원에게 직접 물어보실 수 있습니다.

어휘
year-end 연말의 | savings 절약한 금액 | urgently 긴급히 | advise 알리다, 권고하다 | miss 놓치다 | save 절약하다 | clothing 옷 | label 라벨을 붙이다 | tag 꼬리표 | apparel 의류 | unbeatable 더 이상 좋을 수 없는, 무적의 | in-store 매장 내의 | credit 적립금 | limitation 제한 | apply 적용되다 | expire 만료되다 | offer 제안, 할인 | check out 확인하다 | inventory 재고 | reward 보상 | neighborhood 근처, 인근 | stop by 들르다 | associate (직장) 동료 | in person 직접

---

5. 동사 자리

해설 빈칸은 We를 주어로 하는 동사 자리이므로 (C)가 정답이다.

6. 어휘 – 형용사

해설 문맥상 '분홍색 태그가 붙여진 옷'이라는 내용이 되어야 자연스러우므로 (A)가 정답이다.

✛ Key word

Any piece of clothing labeled with a pink tag is half off, while those with yellow tags are discounted 20 percent.

7. 접속부사

해설 빈칸 앞 부분의 '우리의 가장 인기 있는 의류를 거의 모두 역대 최저 가격으로 구입할 수 있습니다.'라는 내용과 빈칸 뒷부분의 '매주 토요일 매장에 방문한 첫 고객 백 명은 매장 적립금 100달러를 받습니다'라는 내용을 고려할 때, 문맥상 '역대 최저 가격으로 구입할 수 있는데다 추가로 적립금도 받을 수 있다'라는 내용으로 이어져야 자연스러우므로 (B)가 정답이다.

✛ Key word

Almost all of our most popular apparel is available at unbeatable prices. Don't miss out! Additionally, our first 100 customers in the store each Saturday will win $100 in in-store credit.

8. 문장 선택

(A) 우리는 새 입고 상품을 위한 공간을 마련해야 합니다.
(B) 이것은 당사의 웹 사이트에서 이용할 수 있습니다.
(C) 제한사항이 일부 적용됩니다.
(D) 이 정도 규모의 다음 세일은 7월에나 있을 것입니다.

해설 빈칸 앞 문장의 '매주 토요일 매장에 방문한 첫 고객 백 명은 매장 적립금 100달러를 받습니다'라는 내용과 빈칸 뒷문장의 '매장 적립금은 이를 받는 매장에서만 사용할 수 있으며, 4월 말에 만료됩니다'라는 내용을 고려할 때, 문맥상 적립금이 제한적으로 사용된다라는 내용이 들어가야 자연스러우므로 (C)가 정답이다.

✛ Key word

Some limitations do apply. In-store credit may only be used at the store location where it was received, and will expire at the end of April.

CASE 집중훈련　　　　　　　　본서 p.87

1. (B)　**2.** (C)　**3.** (D)　**4.** (D)　**5.** (D)　**6.** (A)
7. (D)　**8.** (C)

1. 주의해야 할 부사

Since the writer did not submit the article early **enough**, it could not be revised in time for the autumn issue.

작가가 기사를 충분히 일찍 제출하지 않았기 때문에, 그것은 가을 발간호의 시기에 맞춰 수정될 수 없다.

해설 빈칸은 부사 early 뒤 종속절 내 문장의 수식어 자리이다. 접속사 since로 연결된 두 문장의 관계를 고려할 때, '충분히 일찍 기사를 제출

하지 않아서 제때 수정될 수 없다'는 의미가 자연스러우므로 (B)가 정답이다.

어휘 submit 제출하다 ᅵ article 기사 ᅵ revise 수정하다 ᅵ in time for ~의 시간에 맞춰 ᅵ issue (간행물의) 호

+ Key word
Since the writer **did not submit** the article **early enough**, **it could not be revised in time** for the autumn issue.

....

2. 관용 표현

Hansen Dining was hired to cater the office party because Ms. Marina spoke so **highly** of their services.
Hansen Dining은 Marina 씨가 그들의 서비스를 극구 칭찬했기 때문에 사무실 파티에 음식을 공급하도록 고용되었다.

해설 관용 표현 'speak highly of(~을 극구 칭찬하다)'를 알고 있어야 해결 가능한 문제로 (C)가 정답이다.

어휘 hire 고용하다 ᅵ cater 음식을 공급하다

....

3. 주의해야 할 부사

Jericho Fitness's beginner CrossFit courses have been in great demand **lately**.
Jericho 피트니스의 초급 크로스핏 과정이 최근 수요가 많았다.

해설 「have been in great demand -------.」에서 「동사 + 보어」의 2형식 구조가 완성되었으므로 빈칸은 부사가 들어갈 자리이며, 문장의 시제가 현재 완료이므로 (D)가 정답이다.

어휘 in demand 수요가 많은

....

4. 숫자를 수식하는 부사

Windsor Cleaning Company has been offering affordable service to local residents for **nearly** three decades.
Windsor 청소업체는 거의 30년 동안 지역 주민들에게 알맞은 가격의 서비스를 제공해왔다.

해설 빈칸은 숫자 형용사 three를 수식하는 부사 자리이다. '거의 30년 동안'이라는 의미가 되어야 자연스러우므로 (D)가 정답이다.

어휘 affordable 가격이 알맞은 ᅵ resident 주민 ᅵ decade 10년

+ Key point
approximately, about, around, nearly, just, up to, at least와 같은 부사는 숫자나 수사를 수식할 수 있다.

5-8번은 다음 회람에 관한 문제입니다.

수신: 전 직원
발신: Irene Turner, 인사부장
날짜: 9월 5일
제목: 건강 검진

이곳 Wilbur Communications에서 건강과 신체 관리를 증진하기 위한 지속적인 노력을 뒷받침하기 위해, 우리는 전 직원 및 가족들을 위해 무료로 건강 검진을 제공할 예정입니다. 누구도 의무적으로 검진을 **⑤받을** 필요는 없습니다. 전적으로 **⑥자발적인** 것입니다. 검진은 A동에서 진행될 것입니다. 검진마다 1인당 **⑦약** 20분의 시간을 감안해 주시기 바랍니다. 우리의 1차 검진은 9월 26일 토요일에 열릴 것입니다. 예약 일정을

잡으시려면, 우리 웹 페이지상의 '인사' 탭을 클릭하시기 바랍니다. 주저하지 마시고 건강 검진 일정을 잡으십시오. **⑧우선 예약에 따라 이용 가능한 시간대가 다를 수 있습니다.**

어휘
physical examination 건강 검진 ᅵ support 뒷받침하다, 지원하다 ᅵ effort 노력 ᅵ fitness 신체 관리, 건강 관리 ᅵ offer 제공하다 ᅵ at no charge 무료로 ᅵ required 필요한, 필수인 ᅵ undergo (시험 등을) 받다, 거치다 ᅵ strictly 전적으로 ᅵ take place 진행되다, 발생되다 ᅵ allow 감안하다 ᅵ hold 열리다, 개최되다 ᅵ appointment 예약, 약속 ᅵ personnel 인사(부) ᅵ hesitate to do ~하기를 주저하다

5. 어휘 - 동사

해설 목적어인 an examination과 호응을 이루어 '검사를 받다'라는 의미가 되어야 하므로 undergo '(시험 등을) 받다, 거치다'는 뜻의 동사인 (D)가 정답이다.

6. 어휘 - 형용사

해설 앞 문장의 '누구도 의무적으로 검진을 받을 필요는 없습니다'라는 내용을 고려할 때, '전적으로 자발적인 것입니다'라는 내용으로 이어져야 자연스러우므로 (A)가 정답이다.

+ Key word
No one is required to undergo an examination. They are strictly **voluntary**.

7. 숫자를 수식하는 부사

해설 빈칸 뒤에 수사인 twenty가 있으므로 숫자 표현 앞에 사용하는 부사인 (D)가 정답이다.

+ Key point
approximately, about, around 등은 숫자 표현 앞에 사용하는 부사이다.

8. 문장 선택

(A) 그 건물은 지난 금요일에 문을 닫았습니다.
(B) 체육관 회원권은 또 다른 옵션입니다.
(C) 우선 예약에 따라 이용 가능한 시간대가 다릅니다.
(D) 참석은 필수입니다.

해설 빈칸 앞 문장의 '주저하지 마시고 건강 검진 일정을 잡으십시오'라는 내용을 고려할 때, '우선 예약에 따라 이용 가능한 시간대가 다를 수 있습니다'라는 내용으로 이어져야 자연스러우므로 (C)가 정답이다.

+ Key word
Please do not hesitate to schedule your physical examination. Available times may vary based on prior reservations.

CASE 실전훈련   본서 p.88

| 1. (C) | 2. (D) | 3. (A) | 4. (D) | 5. (A) | 6. (A) |
| 7. (B) | 8. (D) | 9. (A) | 10. (D) | 11. (C) | 12. (C) |

1. 부사 자리

Moravia Inc.'s recent merger **firmly** established the company as an industry leader.

Moravia 사의 최근 합병은 회사를 업계 선두로 굳건히 자리잡게 했다.

해설 빈칸은 주어와 동사 사이 수식어 자리이므로 부사 (C)가 정답이다.

어휘 recent 최근 | merger 합병 | establish 확립하다, 자리 잡게 하다 | industry 산업(계) | leader 선두, 지도자

+ Key point
주어와 동사 사이에 올 수 있는 품사는 부사이다.

---

2. 부사 자리

The renowned business tycoon Brianna Warden's autobiography **openly** explains the monetary struggles she surmounted at the beginning of her career.

유명한 재계의 거물 Brianna Warden의 자서전에는 그녀가 경력 초반 극복한 금전 문제에 악전고투한 내용이 숨김없이 설명되어 있다.

해설 빈칸은 주어와 동사 사이 부사 자리이므로 (D)가 정답이다.

어휘 renowned 유명한 | tycoon 거물 | autobiography 자서전 | explain 설명하다 | monetary 금전상의, 재정상의 | struggle 투쟁, 분투 | surmount 극복하다 | career 경력

+ Key point
주어와 동사 사이에 올 수 있는 품사는 부사이다.

---

3. 부사 자리

Platforms 5 and 6 are **periodically** out of service for repair work at Gold Acres Station.

Gold Acres 역의 5번과 6번 승강장은 보수공사를 위해 정기적으로 이용이 중단됩니다.

해설 빈칸은 be동사와 형용사구 사이 부사 자리이므로 (A)가 정답이다.

어휘 platform 승강장, 플랫폼 | out of service 사용할 수 없는 | repair 수리

+ Key point
형용사(구)를 수식할 수 있는 품사는 부사다.

---

4. 부사 자리

Travis Webb's seminar suggests new perspectives about farming irrigation systems and **also** includes recommendations for further research.

Travis Webb의 세미나에서는 농업 관개시설에 대한 새로운 관점을 제시하고, 또한 추가 연구에 필요한 권장사항을 알려준다.

해설 Travis Webb's seminar를 주어로 하는 두 문장이 접속사 and로 연결된 구조로, 빈칸은 and와 두 번째 문장의 동사 사이의 수식어 자리이다. and로 연결된 두 문장의 관계를 고려할 때, 문맥상 '새로운 관점을 제시하고 추가 연구에 필요한 권장사항을 알려준다'는 의미가 되어야 자연스러우므로 (D)가 정답이다.

어휘 suggest (아이디어 등을) 제안하다 | perspective 견해, 관점, 시각 | farming 농업 | irrigation system 관개 시설 | recommendation 추천 | further 추가의 | research 연구, 조사

+ Key point
등위 접속사로 연결된 두 문장의 주어가 동일한 경우, 두 번째 문장에서는 주어를 생략한다.

---

5. 어휘 - 부사

Ms. Watts **normally** uses an outside consultant, but he recently employed an internal auditor to evaluate the company.

Watts 씨는 보통 외부 자문을 쓰지만, 최근 회사를 감정할 내부 감사를 고용했다.

해설 빈칸은 동사 uses를 수식하는 부사 자리이다. 접속사 but으로 연결된 두 절의 관계를 고려할 때, '보통은 외부 자문을 쓰는데, 최근 내부 감사를 고용했다'는 의미가 되어야 문맥상 자연스러우므로 (A)가 정답이다.

어휘 outside 외부의 | consultant 자문, 컨설턴트 | recently 최근 | employ 고용하다 | internal 내부의 | auditor 회계 감사인 | evaluate 감정하다, 평가하다

+ Key word
Ms. Watts **normally uses an outside** consultant, **but he recently employed an internal** auditor to evaluate the company.

---

6. 어휘 - 부사

Momma's Little Bakery had to **temporarily** stop its production for a week because its permits expired.

Momma's Little Bakery는 허가증이 만료돼서 생산을 일주일간 임시로 중단해야 했다.

해설 빈칸은 동사 stop을 수식하는 부사 자리이다. 뒤에 오는 because 종속절의 내용을 고려할 때, 문맥상 '허가증이 만료돼서 생산을 일주일간 임시 중단해야 했다'는 의미가 되어야 자연스러우므로 (A)가 정답이다.

어휘 production 생산 | permit 허가증 | expire 만료되다

+ Key word
Momma's Little **Bakery had to temporarily stop its production for a week because its permits were expired.**

---

7. 어휘 - 부사

With a week of extra showings, *The Midnight Song* will **now** play through July 28 at CMC Cinemas.

일주일 추가 상영으로, 〈The Midnight Song〉은 이제 CMC Cinemas에서 7월 28일까지 공연됩니다.

해설 빈칸은 동사구 will play를 수식하는 부사 자리이다. 문두의 with 전명구 내용을 고려할 때, '일주일 추가 상영으로, 이제 7월 28일까지 공연된다'는 의미가 되어야 문맥상 자연스러우므로 (B)가 정답이다.

어휘 extra 추가의 | showing 상영 | play 공연되다

---

8. 어휘 - 부사

At Friday's show, one fortunate Sarolah Theater Group fan will be **randomly** selected via a raffle to dine with the troupe.

금요일 공연에서는 운 좋은 Sarolah Theater Group의 팬 한 명이 극단과 함께 식사하는 자리에 추첨을 통해 무작위로 선정될 것이다.

해설 빈칸은 미래 시제 수동태 동사구를 수식하는 부사 자리이다. '추첨을 통해 무작위로 선정될 것'이라는 의미가 되어야 문맥상 자연스러우므로 (D)가 정답이다.

어휘 fortunate 운 좋은 | select 선정하다, 선택하다 | via ~를 통해 | raffle 추첨 | dine with ~와 식사를 하다 | troupe 공연단, 극단

+ Key word
At Friday's show, **one fortunate** Sarolah Theater Group fan will be **randomly selected via a raffle** to dine with the troupe.

9–12번은 다음 추천글에 관한 문제입니다.

Alice Holt는 매니저라면 누구나 공감할만한 문제로 씨름하고 있었는데, 시간 효율적인 방식으로 **9 채용**을 다루는 방법이었다. 우연히 동료 한 명이 Ms. Holt에게 중역 채용담당자를 소개해줬다. "제가 채용담당자를 써봐야 한다는 건 알고 있었어요. 이력서를 너무 많이 받아서 **10 그것들**을 검토하는데 하루 종일 걸렸거든요. Buff Recruiters의 Mr. Sok에게 연락해보기로 결심한 건 그때였습니다." Mr. Sok은 자신이 회사들이 알맞은 직원을 더 빠르게 찾는 걸 도와준다고 설명했다. 우선, 그는 기업체에서 찾고 있는 직원 유형을 **11 정확하게** 파악한다. 그리고 나서, 자신의 인적 네트워크를 이용해 해당 능력을 가진 전문가에게 연락한다. **12 그는 이런 방식으로 수백 개의 사업체에 도움을 줬다.** "결국, 사업에서 중요한 것은 사람이고, Buff Recruiters와 함께라면 저만의 드림팀을 꾸릴 수 있습니다"라고 Ms. Holt는 말한다.

어휘

grapple with 씨름하다, 고심하다 | relate to 공감하다 | handle 다루다, 처리하다 | time-efficient 시간 효율적인 | colleague 동료 | happen to 우연히 ~하다 | refer A to B A에게 B를 소개하다 | highly touted 아주 칭찬받는 | executive 관리직의, 경영의 | recruiter 채용담당자 | give ~ a go ~를 한번 해보다 | take up (시간 등을) 쓰다 | entire 전체의 | go through 살펴보다, 검토하다 | ensure 반드시 ~하다 | look for 찾다 | network 관계망, 네트워크 | get in touch with ~와 연락하다 | professional 전문직 종사자 | corresponding 해당[상응]하는 | skillset 다양한 능력

9. 어휘 – 명사

해설 빈칸은 동사 handle의 목적어 자리이다. 뒷문장의 '동료 한 명이 Holt 씨에게 간부 채용담당자를 소개해줬다'는 내용을 고려할 때, '시간 효율적인 방식으로 채용을 다루는 방법'이라는 의미가 되어야 문맥상 자연스러우므로 (A)가 정답이다.

+ **Key word**

Alice Holt had been grappling with a problem every manager can relate to, **which was how to handle recruitment in a time-efficient manner. A colleague** happened to **refer Ms. Holt to** a highly touted **executive recruiter.**

10. 인칭대명사 / 수 일치

해설 빈칸은 현재분사구 going through의 목적어 자리이다. 문맥상 '이력서를 검토하는 데 하루 종일 걸린다'는 의미가 되어야 자연스러우므로 résumés를 가리키는 인칭대명사 (D)가 정답이다.

+ **Key point**

앞서 언급된 특정한 대상을 지칭할 때에는 인칭대명사를 사용하며, 이 때 대명사가 들어가는 자리에 알맞은 격과 가리키는 대상에 맞는 수 일치를 반드시 이뤄야 한다.

11. 부사 자리

해설 빈칸은 동사와 목적어 사이 수식어 자리이므로, 부사 (C)가 정답이다.

12. 문장 선택

(A) 그는 그 업계에 각 입문했지만, 지금까지는 즐기고 있습니다.
(B) 그는 언젠가 Buff Recruiters를 맡고 싶어한다.
(C) 그는 이런 방식으로 수백 개의 사업체에 도움을 줬다.
(D) 그는 또한 미술관을 관리하는 것을 돕는다.

해설 빈칸 앞 부분의 'Sok 씨는 회사가 알맞은 직원을 더 빠르게 찾도록 도와준다'고 하면서 그 방법을 2단계로 설명하는 내용을 고려할 때, '이런 방식으로 수백 개의 사업체에 도움을 줬다'는 내용이 이어져야 문맥

상 자연스러우므로 (C)가 정답이다.

+ **Key word**

Mr. Sok explained that he helps companies find the right employees faster. First, he ensures that he understands precisely the kind of employee a business is looking for. Then, he uses his network to get in touch with professionals with the corresponding skillset. **He has helped hundreds of businesses this way.**

CHAPTER 06 동사

CASE 집중훈련   본서 p.91

1. (D)   **2.** (D)   **3.** (C)   **4.** (C)   **5.** (A)   **6.** (D)
7. (B)   **8.** (C)

1. 주어 – 동사 수 일치

Kelter's most popular photocopier **features** a document compiling system.

Kelter의 가장 인기 있는 복사기는 문서 편집 시스템을 특징으로 한다.

해설 빈칸은 주어와 목적어 사이의 동사 자리이다. 주어가 단수이고 목적어가 있으므로 (D)가 정답이다.

어휘 feature ~를 특별히 포함하다, 특징으로 하다 | compiling 편찬, 엮음

+ **Key point**

보기에 동사와 준동사가 있다면 빈칸의 동사 자리 여부를 먼저 확인해야 한다.

2. 어휘 – 동사

Visitors will be glad to know that Dartmoor Furniture now provides free delivery service, but this option **does** mean a later arrival date.

방문객들은 Dartmoor Furniture에서 지금 무료 배송서비스를 제공한다는 것을 알면 기뻐할 것이지만, 이 옵션은 늦은 배송일을 의미한다.

해설 빈칸은 주어와 동사 사이의 자리이다. 주어가 3인칭 단수(this option)이므로 동사 역시 3인칭 단수형이어야 하는데 동사 원형이 있으므로, 주어-동사 간 수 일치가 필요하다는 것을 고려할 때 대동사 (D)가 정답이다.

어휘 provide 제공하다 | delivery 배달 | later 나중의, 뒤의 늦은, 나중에 | arrival 도착

+ **Key point**

① 문장은 동사를 중심으로 이루어지며, 적절한 접속사 없이 한 문장에 두 개 이상의 동사가 올 수 없다.
② 주어-동사 간에는 항상 수 일치가 이루어져야 한다: 3인칭 단수 주어-3인칭 단수 동사
③ 대동사 do/does/did: 동사를 강조하고 싶을 때, 문장 내 동사에서 do동사를 분리하여 표현할 수 있다: This option means ~. → This option does mean ~.

3. 동사의 태

The revised spring issue **must be reviewed** by the

editor-in-chief before it is printed.

봄 개정판은 인쇄되기 전에 편집장에게 검토되어야 한다.

해설 빈칸은 문장의 주어 뒤 동사 자리이다. 주어 자리에 사물 명사가 있고, 빈칸 뒤 전치사 by가 있음을 고려할 때, '개정판은 편집장에 의해 검토되어야 한다'라는 의미가 되어야 적합하므로 수동태 문장을 완성하는 동사 (C)가 정답이다. (A)는 능동태 동사이므로 주어와 의미가 통하지 않고, (B)는 동사 자리에 올 수 없으며, (D)는 주어가 단수인 점에서 수 일치에 어긋난다.

어휘 revise 개정하다 I issue (정기 간행물의) 호 I editor-in-chief 편집장 I print 인쇄하다, 찍다

. . . .

4. 주어-동사 수 일치

During her two decades working at Shimmer Engineering & Construction, Ms. O'Driscoll **operated** the crane at numerous construction sites.

Shimmer Engineering & Construction에서 근무한 20년간, O'Driscoll 씨는 여러 공사 현장에서 크레인을 조작했다.

해설 빈칸은 주어와 목적어 사이의 동사 자리이므로 동사가 아닌 (B), (D)를 제거한다. 주어가 3인칭 단수 O'Driscoll 씨이므로 복수 동사 (A)를 제거한다. 보기 중 동사 형태로 적절한 것은 과거동사 operated 뿐이므로 (C)가 정답이다.

어휘 decade 10년 I numerous 수많은 I construction site 공사 현장

+ Key point

현재 시제는 주어와의 수 일치를 고려해야 한다.

5-8번은 다음 기사에 관한 문제입니다.

COPENHAGEN (6월 10일) — 오늘 아침, 기자간담회에서 Schmitt Aeronautics는 에너지 회사인 Nimbus의 **⑤매입**을 발표했다. Nimbus가 개발한 신 기술은 바닷물을 비행기 연료로 사용될 수 있는 MNV라 불리는 강력한 연료로 **⑥전환한다**. 인수는 Schmitt가 자사의 자원들 **⑦중** 이 최첨단 기술을 포함시킬 수 있음을 의미한다. "모두가 Nimbus팀과 협업할 수 있는 기회에 떠떠어요."라고 Schmitt의 대리인인 Torry Glass가 말했다. "MNV는 비싸고 환경을 파괴하는 석유기반의 연료에 대안을 제공해줄 겁니다." **⑧MNV 시스템으로 변환하는 비용은 놀라우리만큼 낮다.** MNV는 또한 현재의 연료자원들만큼이나 강력한데, 이는 현재 항공기 설계가 연료 자원을 사용하기 위해 변경될 필요가 없을 것임을 의미한다.

어휘

press conference 기자 간담회 I aeronautics 항공학 I announce 발표하다, 공지하다 I seawater 해수, 바닷물 I fuel 연료 I aircraft 항공기 I acquisition 인수 I count 세다, 포함시키다, 인정하다 I cutting-edge 최첨단의 I technology 과학기술 I asset 자원 I collaborate with ~와 협력하다 I representative 대리인, 대표자 I alternative 대안 I costly 비싼 I environment 환경 I damaging 피해를 주는, 해로운 I petroleum-based 석유를 원료로 한 I source 자원 I alter 바꾸다

---

5. 어휘-명사

해설 빈칸은 관사 the와 of 전명구의 수식을 받는 명사 자리이다. 뒤에 나온 The acquisition에서 인수와 동의어를 나타내고, '에너지 회사의 구입을 발표했다'는 의미가 되어야 자연스러우므로 (A)가 정답이다.

+ Key word

At a press conference this morning, Schmitt Aeronautics **announced** the **purchase of the**

---

energy company, Nimbus. The acquisition means Schmitt can count this cutting-edge technology among its assets.

6. 동사의 시제

해설 빈칸은 주어 a new technology와 목적어 seawater 사이 동사 자리이다. 주어가 3인칭 단수 명사이고 문장 후반부의 which 주격 관계절의 시제(can be used)가 현재임을 고려할 때, 주절 역시 현재 시제 동사 (D)가 정답이다.

+ Key word

A new technology created by Nimbus **converts seawater** into a powerful fuel called MNV which **can be used** to power aircrafts.

7. 전치사 자리

해설 빈칸은 명사 its assets를 목적어로 하는 전치사 자리이다. 문맥상 '이 최첨단 기술을 자사 자원들 중 하나로 포함시킬 수 있음을 의미한다'는 의미가 되어야 자연스러우므로 (B)가 정답이다. 전치사 among은 보통 셋 이상의 사물[사람]의 경우에 쓰이므로 목적어는 복수 명사가 나온다.

+ Key word

The acquisition means Schmitt can **count this cutting-edge technology among its assets**.

8. 문장 선택

(A) 안타깝게도, 이 기술은 내년이 되어서야 시중에 선보일 것으로 보인다.
(B) MNV로 움직이는 자동차는 상당히 많은 오염을 일으킨다.
(C) MNV 시스템으로 변환하는 비용은 놀라우리만큼 낮다.
(D) 현재 MNV는 소량만 생산될 수 있다.

해설 빈칸 앞 문장의 'MNV는 값비싼 연료에 대한 대안을 제공해줄 것'이라는 내용을 고려할 때, MNV로의 전환비용에 대한 우호적인 내용으로 이어져야 자연스러우므로 (C)가 정답이다.

+ Key word

"**MNV will provide an alternative to costly** and environment damaging petroleum-based **fuels.**" **The cost of switching to MNV systems is surprisingly low.**

CASE 집중훈련
본서 p.93

1. (C) **2.** (B) **3.** (D) **4.** (D) **5.** (D) **6.** (B)
7. (C) **8.** (A)

---

1. 어휘-명사

A **panel** of business and community leaders will be discussing SDK Laboratory's plans to build their headquarters in the city.

비즈니스 및 공동체 지도자들로 구성된 패널은 도시에 본사를 건설하고자 하는 SDK Laboratory의 계획에 대해 논의할 것이다.

해설 빈칸은 관사 a 뒤의 명사 자리이다. 문맥상 '비즈니스 및 공동체 지도자들로 구성된 패널(전문가 집단)'이라는 의미가 되어야 자연스러우므로 (C)가 정답이다. 문장의 동사가 will be discussing이므로 주어 자리

에 논의 주체인 사람을 가리키는 어휘가 와야 한다. 나머지 명사는 모두 사물을 가리킨다.

어휘 discuss 논의하다 ㅣ headquarter 본사

+ **Key word**

A panel of business and community leaders will be discussing SDK Laboratory's plans to build their headquarters in the city.

---

2. 부사 자리

The stock market analyst, Daniel Glutzer, **correctly** predicted last week's economic upswing.

주식 시장 분석가 Daniel Glutzer가 지난주의 경기 상승을 정확하게 예측했다.

해설 빈칸은 주어 뒤에 동사를 수식해줄 부사 자리이다. 뒤에 동사 predicted를 수식하여 '정확하게 예측했다'라는 의미를 완성해줄 부사인 (B)가 정답이다.

어휘 stock market 주식 시장 ㅣ analyst 분석가 ㅣ predict 예측하다, 예상하다 ㅣ upswing 증가, 상승 ㅣ correct 맞는, 정확한 ㅣ correctly 정확하게, 올바르게 ㅣ corrective 바로잡는, 수정하는 ㅣ correctness 정확함

+ **Key point**

부사가 동사를 수식할 때 동사 앞뒤 또는 목적어 뒤에 위치한다.

---

3. 어휘 – 명사

An **application** to build a storage shed was presented to the homeowners' association.

보관 창고를 짓기 위한 신청서가 주택 소유자 협회에 제출되었다.

해설 수동태를 능동태로 바꾸면 빈칸에 들어갈 명사는 present(제출하다)의 목적어로 호응을 이룰 수 있어야 한다. 문맥상 '신청서가 제출되었다'라는 의미가 되어야 자연스러우므로 (D)가 정답이다.

어휘 storage shed 저장실, 보관창고 ㅣ present 제출하다 ㅣ association 협회

+ **Key word**

An application to build a storage shed **was presented** to the homeowners' association.

---

4. 어휘 – 형용사

Mr. Perault, the **previous** head accountant, has provided comprehensive documentation that his replacement should find beneficial.

이전 수석 회계사인 Perault 씨는 후임자가 유익하다고 여길만한 종합적인 문서를 제공했다.

해설 빈칸은 명사구 head accountant를 수식하는 형용사 자리이다. 문맥상 '이전 수석 회계사인 Perault 씨'라는 의미가 되어야 자연스러우므로 (D)가 정답이다.

어휘 accountant 회계사 ㅣ comprehensive 종합적인, 포괄적인 ㅣ documentation 서류 ㅣ replacement 대체자 ㅣ find 알다 ㅣ beneficial 유익한, 유리한

+ **Key word**

Mr. Perault, the previous head accountant, has provided comprehensive documentation that his replacement should find beneficial.

5-8번은 다음 고객 후기에 관한 문제입니다.

첫 주문이었는데, 완전 그럴만한 가치가 있었습니다. 저는 의류 사업을 위해 신규 직물 공급업체를 찾고 있었어요. 이 지역 업체들과 좋지 않은 경험이 있었어요. **⑤그래서** Systema에 대해 큰 기대를 하지 않았습니다. 제가 주문한 걸 받았을 때, 결과물을 보고 깜짝 놀랐습니다. **⑥사양**은 제가 주문한 대로 정확했고, 배송은 놀라울 정도로 빨랐습니다. Systema에서 견적 내준 가격을 고려하면, 저는 품질이 받아들일만한지 확신이 서지 않았죠. 하지만 고객들에게 샘플을 몇 점 보내 봤어요. **⑦그들 모두 바로 차이를 알아보더군요.** 훌륭한 피드백을 바탕으로 저는 제 사업에 **⑧오직** Systema만 다시 이용할 예정입니다.

Cesar Bowers

어휘
order 주문하다 ㅣ absolutely 완전히 ㅣ worth ~의 가치가 있는 ㅣ fabric 직물 ㅣ supplier 공급업체 ㅣ clothing 의복 ㅣ area 지역 ㅣ hope 기대, 희망 ㅣ blow away 감명을 주다 ㅣ result 결과 ㅣ exactly 정확하게 ㅣ delivery 배송 ㅣ surprisingly 놀랍도록 ㅣ given ~을 고려해볼 때 ㅣ price 가격 ㅣ quote 견적을 내다 ㅣ acceptable 받아들일 수 있는 ㅣ client 고객 ㅣ based on ~을 바탕으로 ㅣ excellent 우수한, 훌륭한 ㅣ feedback 피드백

5. 접속부사

해설 빈칸은 두 의미를 연결하는 접속부사 자리이다. 빈칸 앞 문장의 '지역 내의 공급업체와 좋지 않은 경험이 있다'는 내용과 'Systema에 대한 기대가 크지 않았다'는 내용을 고려할 때, 두 문장이 인과관계로 이어져야 문맥상 연결이 자연스러우므로 (D)가 정답이다.

+ **Key word**

I have had bad experiences with suppliers in this area. Therefore, I didn't have high hopes for Systema.

6. 어휘 – 명사

해설 빈칸은 문장의 주어 자리이다. 빈칸 앞 문장과 접속사 and로 연결된 뒷 문장의 내용을 고려할 때, 주문한 사양 그대로 정확하게 결과물이 나왔다는 내용이 들어가야 문맥상 자연스러우므로 (B)가 정답이다.

+ **Key word**

When I received my order, I was blown away by the results. The specifications were exactly what I ordered, and the delivery was surprisingly fast.

7. 문장 선택

(A) 발송이 불가피하게 지연되었을 수 있습니다.
(B) 몇 가지 제안을 하고 싶습니다.
(C) 그들 모두 바로 차이를 알아보더군요.
(D) 비교는 매우 유용했을 것입니다.

해설 자신은 견적 대비 품질에 대해 확신이 서지 않았지만 고객에게 샘플을 보내봤다는 빈칸 앞 부분의 내용과 훌륭한 피드백을 바탕으로 Systema를 다시 이용할 거라는 내용을 고려할 때, 고객들은 바로 차이를 알아봤다는 내용이 들어가야 문맥상 자연스러우므로 (C)가 정답이다.

+ **Key word**

Given the price Systema quoted, **I wasn't sure if the quality would be acceptable. However, I sent out some samples to my clients. They could all immediately tell the difference. Based on the excellent feedback**, I will exclusively be using

Systema again for my business.

8. 부사 자리

해설 빈칸은 will be using 동사 구문을 수식하는 부사 자리이므로 (A)가 정답이다.

CASE 집중훈련

1. (D)　2. (D)　3. (B)　4. (A)　5. (A)　6. (D)
7. (B)　8. (C)

1. 수량 표현의 수 일치

The number of mobile phone **manufacturers** has decreased sharply in the past five years due to competition.

핸드폰 제조사들은 경쟁으로 인해 지난 5년동안 급격히 감소하고 있다.

해설 빈칸은 「the number of + 복수 명사 + 단수 동사」의 형태에 들어가야 하는 복수 명사 자리이므로 (D)가 정답이다.

어휘 decrease 감소하다 | sharply 급격하게 | competition 경쟁

+ Key point
「A number of + 복수 명사 + 복수 동사」 형태도 기억하자.

2. 소유격 대명사

The Hawthorne Times is planning to interview the president of Morrilton Textile Company regarding **its** recent announcement that it will soon lay off up to 100 employees.

Hawthorn Times는 Morrilton 직물 회사가 곧 최대 100명의 직원들을 해고할 거란 최근 발표에 대해 그 회사 대표를 인터뷰할 계획이다.

해설 문맥상 빈칸 뒤 that절의 주어인 it은 Hawthorne Times를 가리키는 대명사로, 이 회사가 100명의 직원들을 곧 해고할 거라는 의미이므로 that 이하의 최근 발표는 Hawthorne Times가 한 발표임을 알 수 있다. 따라서 소유격 대명사 (D)가 정답이다.

어휘 regarding ~에 관하여 | announcement 발표 | lay off 해고하다 | up to 최고 ~까지

+ Key word
The Hawthorne Times is planning to interview the president of Morrilton Textile Company **regarding its recent announcement that it will soon lay off up to 100 employees**.

3. 주어 자리 / 수량 표현의 수 일치

Each one of Harriet Solomon's performances was filmed for a documentary about the dancer.

Harriet Solomon의 각 공연은 그 댄서에 대한 다큐멘터리를 위해 촬영되었다.

해설 빈칸은 주어 역할을 하면서 of Harriet Solomon's performances의 수식을 받는 대명사 자리이다. 「All of the[one's] + 복수 명사」는 복수 동사와 어울리는데 동사가 단수 동사 was이므로 제거한다. 소유 대명사 Theirs는 전치사구 of의 수식을 받을 수 없고 Her own은 소유격으로 전치사 of가 아닌 명사 앞에 써야 하므로 제거한다. Each one은 '각 개, 각각의 것'을 의미하는 대명사임을 고려할 때, 'Harriet

Solomon의 공연 각각은'이라는 의미가 되어 자연스러우므로 (B)가 정답이다.

어휘 performance 공연 | film 촬영하다

---

4. 관계절의 주어 자리 / 수량 표현의 수 일치

The recent issue of *Politics Monthly Magazine* contains fifteen articles, **several** of which are about the upcoming election.

〈Politics Monthly Magazine〉의 최신호는 15개의 기사를 다루고 있는데, 그중 몇 개는 곧 있을 선거에 관한 것이다.

해설 빈칸은 of which의 수식을 받으며 복수 동사 are의 주어 역할을 하는 명사 또는 대명사 자리이다. which가 선행명사 'fifteen articles'를 수식함을 고려할 때, 문맥상 '15개의 기사 중에서 몇 개가 곧 있을 선거에 관한 것이다'라는 의미가 되어야 자연스러우므로 (A)가 정답이다.

어휘 issue (정기 간행물의) 호 | upcoming 다가오는, 곧 있을 | election 선거

5-8번은 다음 안내문에 관한 문제입니다.

〈Huber's Poetry Monthly〉의 대부분의 **5기고가들은** 수년간 우리와 긴밀하게 일해 온 노련한 작가들입니다. **6그렇지만,** 저희는 항상 새로운 인재를 찾고 있습니다. 매 발행본마다, 독자들을 새로운 시인에게 소개하기 위해 최선을 다하고 있긴 하지만, 잡지에서의 공간을 얻기 위한 경쟁은 매우 치열합니다. 이에, 저희가 저희의 출판물에 포함시키고자 하는 작품의 종류에 대해 감을 잡으시려면, www.huberpoetry.org/guidelines에 게시된 지침들을 주의 깊게 살펴봐 주십시오. **7이는 귀하의 제출작이 선택될 가능성을 높여줄 것입니다.**

저희는 가능한 한 빨리 문의에 답변하고자 노력하지만, 답변을 늦게 받을 때도 있을 것입니다. 이러한 이유로, 저희는 귀하가 조금만 **8인내해** 주시길 요청 드립니다.

어휘
majority 대다수 | seasoned 노련한 | closely 긴밀하게, 밀접하게 | search for ~를 찾다 | talent 재능, 재능 있는 사람(들) | issue (간행물의) 호 | do one's best 최선을 다하다 | introduce 소개하다 | poet 시인 | competition 경쟁 | intense 치열한 | get a feel 감을 잡다 | publication 출간(물) | strive 분투하다 | reply to ~에 답하다 | inquiry 문의

5. 명사 자리 / 주어 - 동사의 수 일치

해설 빈칸은 정관사 the 뒤의 명사 자리이다. 동사 자리에 복수 동사 are가 있으므로 가산 복수 명사 (A)가 정답이다. 또한 보어가 seasoned writers와 같이 사람을 가리키므로 주어에 동격 관계를 이루는 사람 명사가 와야 하는 것도 단서이다.

+ Key point
'the majority of ~(~의 대다수)'는 of 뒤에 오는 명사의 단/복수가 동사의 단/복수를 결정한다.

6. 접속부사

해설 빈칸 앞 부분의 '잡지사의 기고가들 대부분이 노련한 작가'라는 내용과 빈칸 뒷부분의 '언제나 새로운 인재들을 찾고 있다'는 내용을 고려할 때, 두 문장이 다소 대비되므로 '그렇지만, 그렇긴 해도'라는 역접의 의미를 가진 접속부사 (D)가 정답이다.

+ Key word
The majority of the contributors to *Huber's Poetry Monthly* **are seasoned writers** who have worked closely with us for years. **With that said, we**

are always searching for new talent.

7. 문장 선택

(A) 그래서, 출판사는 새로운 편집자를 뽑을 것입니다.
(B) 이는 귀하의 제출작이 선택될 가능성을 높여줄 것입니다.
(C) 유감스럽게도, 이번 호에서는 귀하의 작품을 사용할 수 없습니다.
(D) 이것은 입문 작가들을 선보이는 잡지를 찾는 데 좋은 자료입니다.

해설 빈칸 앞 부분의 '출판물에 포함될 만한 작품에 대한 감을 잡기 위해 지침을 살펴보라'는 내용을 고려할 때, '이렇게 함으로써 제출작이 선택될 가능성을 높일 수 있다'는 내용이 이어져야 자연스러우므로 (B)가 정답이다.

+ Key word

Therefore, **make sure to look carefully at the guidelines** posted on www.huberpoetry.org/guidelines **to get a feel for the kind of work we hope to include in our publication. This will make your submission more likely to be selected.**

8. 어휘 – 형용사

해설 빈칸 앞 부분의 '답변이 늦을 때가 있을 수 있다'는 내용을 고려할 때, '그러한 이유로 지원자들에게 인내해 줄 것을 요청한다'는 내용이 되어야 자연스러우므로 (C)가 정답이다.

+ Key word

Although we strive to reply to inquiries as quickly as possible, **there will be times where you may receive a slow response. Because of this, we must ask for you to be patient.**

CASE 집중훈련
본서 p.97

1. (A)　2. (D)　3. (B)　4. (A)　5. (C)　6. (B)
7. (B)　8. (C)

1. 동사의 태

Royale House will **be renovated** to include a library that contains videos and audiobooks related to the solar system.
Royale House는 태양계와 관련된 비디오와 오디오북들을 포함하는 도서관을 마련하기 위해 개조될 것이다.

해설 빈칸은 앞에 조동사 will이 있고 타동사인 renovate의 목적어가 없이 to 부정사가 왔으므로 수동태가 들어가야 자연스러우므로 (A)가 정답이다.

어휘 include 포함하다 | library 도서관 | contain 가지다, 포함하다

+ Key point

보기에 동사의 여러 형태가 있다면 수 일치/태/시제를 순서대로 확인해야 한다.

---

2. 동사의 태

Auditors' reports will be submitted only to the management and should not be **publicized** under any circumstances.
회계 감사관들의 보고서는 경영진에게만 제출될 것이며 어떠한 상황에서도 공개되어서는 안 된다.

해설 빈칸은 be동사 뒷자리로, 주어를 서술하는 형용사나 주어와 동격인 명사 또는 수동태를 완성하는 과거분사가 들어갈 수 있는데, 문맥상 '회계 감사관들의 의견이 어떠한 상황에서도 공개되어서는 안 된다'라는 의미가 자연스러우므로 '공개하다'라는 뜻의 동사 publicize의 과거분사인 (D)가 정답이다.

어휘 auditor 회계감사관 | management 경영진 | circumstance 상황, 환경 | publicity 홍보, 광고 | publicly 공개적으로 | publication 출판, 발행 | publicize 알리다, 공개하다

+ Key word

Auditors' reports will be submitted only to the management and **should not be publicized under any circumstances**.

---

3. 동사의 태

Job opportunities for part-time editors **are anticipated** to be posted on Ottawa Publishing's Web site on April 10.
시간제 편집자들을 위한 취업 기회들이 4월 10일에 Ottawa 출판사의 웹사이트에 게시될 것으로 예상된다.

해설 빈칸은 복수 주어 뒤 본동사 자리이다. 주어 opportunities가 복수이고 빈칸 뒤에 목적어가 없으며, 문맥상 '웹사이트에 게시될 것으로 예상된다'는 수동의 의미가 자연스러우므로 복수 주어에 수 일치되는 수동태 동사인 (B)가 정답이다.

어휘 job opportunity 취업 기회 | editor 편집자 | post 게시하다 | anticipate 예상하다, 기대하다

+ Key word

Job opportunities for part time editors **are anticipated to be posted** on Ottawa Publishing's Web site on April 10.

---

4. 동사의 태

Mr. Zhang will **be coordinating** the data transfer to the cloud with the service provider.
Zhang 씨는 클라우드로 데이터를 전송하는데 서비스 제공업체와 협력할 것이다.

해설 빈칸은 조동사 will 뒤 동사 원형 자리이다. 빈칸 뒤 명사구가 있으므로, 목적어를 취할 수 있는 능동태 동사 구조를 완성하는 (A)가 정답이다.

어휘 data transfer 데이터 전송 | service provider 서비스 제공업체

5-8번은 다음 기사에 관한 문제입니다.

SAN FRANCISCO (10월 4일) — Trifecta는 오늘 아침 Mayflower 사와 합작으로 생산된 새로운 액션 카메라, T6 모델의 곧 있을 출시를 발표했다. T6 모델은 Trifecta의 혁신적인 디자인과 Mayflower 사의 **⑤우수한 소재**가 조화를 이룬 것이다. Mayflower가 자사의 독창적인 기술을 이용하여 T6의 터치 스크린을 개발했는데, 사실상 깨지지 않도록 **⑥만들어진** 유리 같은 물질이다. 이것은 원래 현미경 렌즈용으로 의도된 것이었지만, 아주 높은 곳에서 떨어져도 산산조각 나지 않고 견딜 수 있는 능력이 다른 제품들에도 완벽하게 쓰일 수 있는 특성으로 Mayflower의 제품 개발부에 의해 **⑦즉각** 인정을 받았다. Trifecta의 대표인 Vivian Washington은 T6의 개발에 대한 귀중한 공헌에 대해 Mayflower 사의 연구 직원들에게 그 공을 돌렸다. **⑧두 회사는 그 프로젝트에 있어서 자신들의 제휴에 대해 아주 만족하고 있다.**

5. 어휘 - 형용사

해설 빈칸은 전치사 with의 목적어인 명사 materials를 수식해줄 형용사 자리이다. virtually unbreakable, to withstand drops from great heights without shattering 등을 통해 Mayflower 사의 우수한 소재가 조화를 이루고 있다는 의미가 되어야 자연스러우므로 (C)가 정답이다.

+ Key word

The T6 model blends Trifecta's innovative designs with superior materials by Mayflower, Inc. Mayflower developed the T6's touch screen using its original technique, a glasslike substance that ~ to be virtually unbreakable.

6. 동사의 태

해설 빈칸은 앞의 선행사 glasslike substance를 수식하는 that절의 동사 자리이다. 빈칸 뒤에 목적어 없이 to부정사만 있는 것으로 볼 때 타동사 create의 수동태 동사가 들어가야 함을 알 수 있으므로 (B)가 정답이다.

+ Key point

빈칸이 동사 자리인지 먼저 확인한 후, '태', '수의 일치', '시제'를 따져 봐야 한다.

7. 부사 자리

해설 빈칸은 수동태 동사 was recognized 사이에 동사를 수식해줄 부사 자리이다. 'Mayflower의 제품 개발부에 의해 즉각 인정을 받았다'라는 의미를 완성해줄 부사인 (B)가 정답이다.

+ Key point

수동태 동사를 이루는 'be동사+p.p.' 사이나 현재 완료 동사를 이루는 'have+p.p.' 사이에 빈칸은 동사를 수식하는 부사 자리이다.

8. 문장 선택

(A) 고객들은 전액 지불에 책임이 있습니다.
(B) 현재 Mayflower 사는 새로운 경영 하에 있습니다.
(C) 두 회사는 그 프로젝트에 있어서 자신들의 제휴에 대해 아주 만족하고 있습니다.
(D) 소비자들은 항상 최신 첨단 기기를 원하는 것은 아닙니다.

해설 앞서 Trifecta의 대표가 T6의 개발에 대한 가치 있는 공헌에 대해 Mayflower 주식회사의 연구 직원들에게 그 공을 돌렸다는 내용이 제시되어 있는 것으로 볼 때, 그 연장선상에서 두 회사가 함께한 프로젝트에 대해 아주 만족한다는 내용의 문장이 이어지는 것이 자연스러우므로 (C)가 정답이다.

+ Key word

A representative for Trifecta, Vivian Washington, credited the research staff at Mayflower, Inc., with

---

valuable contributions to the T6's development. Both companies are very delighted with their partnership in the project.

1. 부사 자리

Balmer Industries has responded **favorably** to Komplet Automotive's offer to jointly develop a forecasting system.

Balmer 산업은 예측 시스템을 합작해서 개발하자는 Komplet 자동차의 제의에 호의적으로 응답했다.

해설 빈칸은 자동사 respond를 수식하는 부사 자리이므로 (A)가 정답이다.

어휘 respond 응답하다 | offer 제의; 제의하다 | jointly 함께, 공동으로 | forecasting system 예측 시스템 | favorably 호의적으로 | favor 호의 | favorable 호의적인

+ Key point

respond는 '~에 응답하다'라는 뜻의 자동사로 뒤에 명사구를 이끌 때 전치사 to를 동반한다. (respond to: ~에 응답하다)

2. 어휘 - 동사

The board of directors will **convene** next month to approve the two-year strategic business plan for international activities.

이사회가 국제적인 활동을 위한 2년 간의 전략적인 사업 계획을 승인하기 위해 다음 달에 회합할 것이다.

해설 빈칸은 조동사 뒤, 문장의 본동사 자리이다. 빈칸 뒤에 목적어가 없는 것으로 볼 때 자동사가 들어가야 하고, 문맥상 '이사회가 ~을 승인하기 위해 다음 달에 회합할 것이다'라는 의미가 되어야 자연스러우므로 (D)가 정답이다.

어휘 the board of directors 이사회 | approve 승인하다 | strategic 전략적인 | business plan 사업 계획 | confide 비밀을 털어놓다; 신뢰하다 | acquire 얻다, 인수하다 | accompany 동행하다 | convene 회합하다, 모이다

+ Key word

The board of directors will convene next month **to approve the two-year strategic business plan** for international activities.

3. 어휘 - 부사

Ms. Kobayashi and her team worked **diligently** for weeks to land the profitable federal contract.

Kobayashi 씨와 팀원들은 수익성 있는 연방 계약을 따내려고 몇 주 동안 열심히 일했다.

해설 빈칸은 동사 worked를 수식하는 부사 자리이다. '계약을 따내려고 몇 주 간 열심히 일했다'는 의미가 되어야 문맥상 자연스러우므로 (C)가 정답이다.

어휘 land (노력의 결과로) 획득하다; 착륙하다 | profitable 수익성 있는 | federal 연방의 | contract 계약(서)

+ Key word

Ms. Kobayashi and her team **worked diligently for weeks to land** the profitable federal **contract**.

---

4. 어휘 – 형용사

Stock prices for Oceania Airlines will go back up when investors feel **confident** about the future.

투자자가 미래에 대해 확신을 가질 때 Oceania 항공공사 주가는 다시 올라갈 것이다.

해설 빈칸은 동사 feel의 보어 자리이다. 주절과 when 종속절의 관계를 고려할 때, 문맥상 '투자자가 미래에 대해 확신을 가질 때 주가가 다시 올라갈 것'이라는 의미가 되어야 자연스러우므로 (D)가 정답이다. feel confident about이 술어 표현이다.

어휘 stock price 주가 | go up 올라가다 | back (이전의 상태로) 다시, 돌아가서 | investor 투자자 | future 미래

+ Key word

Stock prices for Oceania Airlines **will go back up when investors feel confident about the future.**

5-8번은 다음 공지에 관한 문제입니다.

6월 21일, Middlesbrough 교통위원회(MTC)는 Hammock 터널과 도심지역 사이 105번 고속도로 구간에서 **⑤공사**를 시작합니다. 이 프로젝트는 도로재포장 및 **⑥현재** 4개에서 5개 차선으로의 노선 확장을 포함합니다. 프로젝트의 목적은 도로를 더 안전하게 만들고 혼잡시간 동안 교통 정체를 줄이는 것에 있습니다. MTC는 언제나 지역 내 모든 사람에게 효율적인 이동수단을 제공해 드리려 노력하며, 저희는 이 프로젝트가 정규 서비스에 혼란을 초래할 것임을 인지하고 있습니다. 프로젝트는 9월에 **⑦완료될** 예정입니다. **⑧그동안, 대중교통의 이용이 권장됩니다.** 최신 정보를 알아보시려면, mtc-connect.co.uk에서 확인해주세요.

어휘

transportation 교통, 수송 | commission 위원회 | stretch (특히 길게 뻗은) 구간, 지역 | highway 고속도로 | undertaking (중요한, 힘든) 일, 사업 | repave (도로를) 재포장하다 | expand 확장하다 | route 노선, 경로 | lane 차선, 도로 | reduce 줄이다 | peak 절정, 최고점 | ensure 보장하다 | efficient 효율적인, 능률적인 | transport 수송(수단) | recognize 인정[인식]하다 | disruption 혼란, 중단

---

5. 명사 자리

해설 빈칸은 동사 begin의 목적어인 명사 자리이므로 (C)가 정답이다.

6. 어휘 – 형용사

해설 빈칸은 명사구 four (driving lanes)를 수식하는 형용사 자리이다. 문맥상 '현재의 4개 차선에서 늘려 5개 차선으로 확장'이라는 의미가 되어야 자연스러우므로 (D)가 정답이다.

+ Key word

This undertaking will include repaving and **expanding** the **route to five** driving **lanes**, **up from** its **current four** (driving lanes).

7. 어휘 – 동사

해설 빈칸은 to부정사구를 완성하는 동사 자리이다. 지문 첫 문장의 '6월 21일에 공사를 시작할 것'이라는 내용을 고려할 때, 문맥상 '프로젝트는 9월에 완료될 예정'이라는 의미가 되어야 자연스러우므로 (C)가 정답이다.

+ Key word

On 21 June the Middlesbrough Transportation Commission (MTC) **will begin construction** on the long stretch of Highway 105 between Hammock Tunnel and the downtown area. The **project is set to conclude in September.**

8. 문장 선택

(A) 그동안, 대중교통의 이용이 권장됩니다.
(B) 그 사이에, 운용비를 삭감할 방법을 찾아보세요.
(C) 6월부터 9월까지, 통행료 지불 시스템이 업그레이드 될 것입니다.
(D) 많은 주민들이 MTC의 최신 모바일 앱에 대해 불만을 표하고 있습니다.

해설 빈칸 앞 부분의 '이 프로젝트는 정규 서비스에 혼란을 야기할 것이고, 9월에 완료될 예정'이라는 내용을 고려할 때, '그 기간 동안 대중교통 이용이 권장된다'는 내용으로 이어져야 자연스러우므로 (A)가 정답이다.

+ Key word

and we recognize that **this project will create some disruptions to regular service**. **The project is set to conclude in September. In the interim, the use of public transportation is recommended.** Check mtc-connect.co.uk for the latest updates.

CASE 집중훈련   본서 p.101

1. (B)   2. (C)   3. (D)   4. (C)   5. (D)   6. (B)
7. (C)   8. (D)

---

1. 동사의 태

Café Celeste **will be offering** patrons a complimentary dessert now through the end of June.

Café Celeste는 단골 손님에게 지금부터 6월 말까지 무료 디저트를 제공할 것이다.

해설 빈칸은 문장에서 동사 역할을 하면서 뒤에 2개의 목적어가 있는 능동태가 되어야 하므로 (B)가 정답이다.

어휘 patron 단골 손님 | complimentary 무료의

+ Key point

보기에 동사와 준동사가 있다면 빈칸의 동사 자리 여부를 먼저 확인해야 한다.

---

2. 명사 자리

Those without a permit will not be granted **entry** to the employee parking lot.

허가증이 없는 사람들은 직원주차장 출입이 승인되지 않을 것이다.

해설 문장 내에 동사 will not be granted가 있으므로 접속사 없이 동사 is entering은 제거한다. 동사 grant는 능동태로 목적어를 두 개 받으며 「grant + 간접 목적어 + 직접 목적어」로 쓰이며 '~에게 ~를 승인[허가]하다'로 쓰일 수 있고 수동태로 전환되면 「be granted + 직접 목적어」로 '~를 승인[허가]받다'로 쓰여 목적어가 남을 수 있으므로 명사 (C)가 정답이다.

어휘 permit 허가증 | grant 승인하다, 허락하다 | entry 출입, 입장 | parking lot 주차장

✦ Key point

[4V + I.O + D.O] '~에게 ~를 주다'의 4형식 동사로는 give, offer, send, bring, award, grant 등이 있다.

---

3. 동사의 태

Please be **assured** that every complaint from our clients will receive immediate attention.

저희 고객들의 모든 불만에 즉각적인 주의 조치가 이루어질 것을 보장합니다.

해설 be동사 뒤에 동사 원형이 이어질 수 없으므로 assure은 제거한다. assure '보증하다, 확신하다'는 능동태일 때 「assure + 목적어(사람) + that절」로 '~에게 ~할 것을 장담[확약]하다'를 의미하고 수동태로 바뀌어 'be assured that절' '~할 것을 장담[확약]받다'로 쓰일 수 있으므로 과거분사 (D)가 정답이다.

어휘 assure 보장하다 | complaint 불만 | immediate 즉시의, 즉각적인 | attention 주의

---

4. 어휘 - 형용사

The realtor will show Mr. Grant suitable **commercial** office spaces for the new accounting firm he is going to open.

부동산업자는 Grant 씨가 개업할 새 회계사무소에 적합한 상업용 사무실 자리들을 보여줄 것이다.

해설 '적합한 상업용 사무실 자리들'이 자연스러운 구문이므로 (C)가 정답이다.

어휘 realtor 부동산업자 | accounting firm 회계사무소

5-8번은 다음 이메일에 관한 문제입니다.

수신: Anna Badmaeva 〈ABadmaeva@starsupply.eu〉
발신: David Deehan 〈DDeehan@walkerengineering.co.uk〉
날짜: 8월 28일
제목: 주문

저는 Walker Engineering의 **⑤고정적인** 주문에 대한 변경을 요청하고 싶습니다. 요새 곰팡이를 막는 표면 작업을 요구하는 프로젝트가 줄었기 때문에 AF2713 살균 광택제를 훨씬 덜 사용하고 있습니다. **⑥그에 맞춰** 다음 달부터 주문 개수를 일곱 캔으로 줄이고 싶습니다. 또한 매달 LX 8757 내열 코팅도 10캔이 추가로 필요합니다.

어느 시점에 저희는 AF2713 광택제 사용을 필요로 하는 모든 프로젝트를 마무리하게 될 것입니다. 하지만 사전에 충분히 공지해 **⑦드리도록 하겠습니다.** 수정 사항을 반영하는 청구서를 저에게 보내주십시오. **⑧회계 부서에서 그것을 요청했습니다.**

감사합니다.

David Deehan
Walker Engineering

어휘
request 요청하다 | order 주문 | require 요구하다 | fungus-proof 곰팡이를 막아주는 | surfacing 표면의 마무리 재료 | fungicidal 살균제의 | varnish 광택제 | reduce 줄이다 | quantity 양 | additional 추가의 | heat-resistant 내열의, 열을 막아주는 | coating 코팅 | wrap up 마무리하다 | sufficient 충분할 만큼의 | notice 공지, 알림 | invoice 청구서 | reflect 반영하다 | revision 수정, 정정

---

5. 어휘 - 형용사

해설 다음 문장에서 제품에 대한 수요가 달라졌다는 내용을 알리고 있으므로 고정(적으로 하고 있는) 주문에 대한 내용을 변경하고 싶다는 내용이 되어야 자연스럽다. 따라서 (D)가 정답이다.

✦ Key word

I'd like to request a change to Walker Engineering's **standing** order. **Fewer of our projects require fungus-proof surfacing these days, so we are using much less AF2713 fungicidal varnish.**

---

6. 접속부사

해설 빈칸을 중심으로 앞, 뒤 문장의 관계를 살펴보면, '제품을 더 적게 사용하므로 주문량을 줄이고 싶다'는 인과관계로 연결되어야 자연스럽다. 따라서 (B)가 정답이다.

✦ Key word

Fewer of our projects require fungus-proof surfacing these days, so **we are using much less AF2713 fungicidal varnish. Accordingly, I'm hoping to reduce the order quantity** to just seven cans, starting next month.

---

7. 동사의 태 / 시제

해설 해당 제품을 사용하는 모든 프로젝트를 마무리할 예정이지만, 미리 알려주겠다는 내용으로 이어져야 하므로, 앞 문장과 같이 미래 시제 동사가 필요하다. 또한 목적어가 2개 있으므로 능동태 문장을 완성하는 (C)를 선택한다.

✦ Key word

we will wrap up all projects requiring the use of AF2713 varnish. But **I will give you** sufficient **notice** in advance.

---

8. 문장 선택

(A) 그 회사는 해안 지역에서 많은 프로젝트를 해 왔습니다.
(B) 우리는 필요하게 될 정확한 액수를 확신할 수 없습니다.
(C) 어제 제 동료로부터 그것을 받았어야 합니다.
(D) 회계 부서에서 그것을 요청했습니다.

해설 청구서를 보내달라는 앞 문장의 내용에 이어 그것(invoice)을 요청하는 이유를 언급하는 것이 문맥상 자연스러우므로 (D)가 정답이다.

✦ Key word

Please **send me an invoice** that reflects the revisions. **Our Accounting Department has requested it.**

CASE 집중훈련   본서 p.103

1. (A)   **2.** (D)   **3.** (A)   **4.** (B)   **5.** (A)   **6.** (A)
7. (D)   **8.** (D)

---

1. to부정사를 취하는 5형식 동사의 태

All factories currently operating in Texas are expected to **conform** to the stringent safety guidelines issued by the government.

Texas에서 현재 운영 중인 모든 공장들은 정부에서 공표한 엄격한 안전 지침에 따를 것으로 예상된다.

해설 빈칸 앞의 expect는 「expect + 목적어 + to do」의 형태로 to부정사를 목적격 보어로 취하는 5문형 동사이다. to부정사를 목적격 보어로 취하는 동사들은 수동의 형태로도 자주 쓰이는데, 이때 목적격 보어인 to부정사가 동사의 바로 뒤에 따라온다. 따라서 빈칸에는 동사 원형인 (A)와 (D)가 정답 후보인데, conform은 자동사로 수동태가 될 수 없기 때문에 (A)가 정답이다.

어휘 currently 현재 | stringent 엄격한, 엄중한 | safety guidelines 안전 지침 | issue 공표하다, 발표하다

---

2. 어휘 - 명사

Defects in its newest line of audio devices caused Kisaki Electronics to adopt higher **standards** for inspecting products.

최신 오디오 장비 라인의 결함이 제품을 검사하는 것에 대해 Kisaki 전자가 더 높은 기준을 채택하도록 만들었다.

해설 문맥상 제품 결함으로 인해 '제품을 검사하는 것에 대해 더 높은 기준을 채택하다'라는 의미가 자연스러우므로 (D)가 정답이다.

어휘 defect 결함 | device 장치 | cause 유발하다 | adopt 채택하다 | inspect 검사하다

+ Key word

Defects in its newest line of audio devices caused Kisaki Electronics to **adopt higher standards** for inspecting products.

---

3. 관용 표현

The fire sprinkler system must be kept clean at **all** times.

스프링클러 설비는 항상 깨끗이 유지되어야 한다.

해설 빈칸 앞, 뒤에 각각 at과 times가 있으므로, 'at all times(항상)'라는 관용 표현을 완성하는 (A)가 정답이다.

어휘 fire sprinkler system 스프링클러 설비 | keep 유지하다 (keep-kept-kept) | clean 깨끗한, 깔끔한

+ Key word

The fire sprinkler system must be kept clean **at all times**.

---

4. 5형식 동사의 태

Dr. Ryo was **appointed** the sales director due to his impressive credentials.

Ryo 박사는 그의 인상적인 자격으로 인해 영업 이사로 임명되었다.

해설 'Ryo 박사는 영업 이사로 임명되었다'라는 의미가 되어야 자연스러우며, 동사 appoint는 5형식 「appoint + 목적어 + 목적격 보어(~를 …로 임명하다)」로 쓰이며, 수동태로는 「be appointed + 목적격 보어(~로 임명되다)」의 형태이므로 (B)가 정답이다. 목적어와 목적격 보어가 동격 관계이므로 수동태 뒤에 명사가 나오는 것에 유의한다.

어휘 impressive 인상적인 | credential 자격 증명서

+ Key word

Dr. Ryo was appointed the sales director due to his impressive credentials.

5-8번은 다음 회람에 관한 문제입니다.

수신: Robert Green
발신: July Dench
날짜: 6월 29일
제목: 감사의 표시

안녕하세요, Robert 씨,

지난 달에 있었던 우리 설문조사에 관여하신 모든 분들, 특히 Indira Joseph 씨에게 제 감사의 인사를 전해 주시기 바랍니다. **⑤그분께서 제가 중요한 문제들에 관심을 갖도록 해주셨습니다.** 첫째, 몇몇 질문들이 너무 모호했다는 점을 저에게 알려주셨습니다. 실은 제가 설문지를 만들었을 때 아주 촉박한 상황이었습니다. **⑥게다가**, 그분께서는 자발적으로 전체적인 표현들을 수정하도록 저를 도와주시기도 했습니다.

Joseph 씨께서는 그 설문지가 배포되기 전에 완벽한 상태가 되도록 우리를 돕기 위한 대단한 **⑦헌신**과 의지를 보여주셨습니다. 그분의 성실함과 노력, 그리고 현명함으로 인해 설문조사가 제때 **⑧실시될** 수 있었습니다. 저는 다음 프로젝트를 위해 그분이 저희 팀에 합류할 수 있기를 바랍니다. 어쨌든, 모든 분에게 제 감사의 인사를 전해주십시오.

안녕히 계십시오.

July Dench
마케팅 부장
F&N Consultant

어휘
token 표시, 징표 | gratitude 감사, 감사의 뜻 | get involved in ~에 관여하다 | survey 설문조사 | vague 모호한 | indeed 실은, 정말로 | in a rush 급한 | create 만들다 | questionnaire 설문지 | revise 수정하다 | entire 전체의 | wording 표현, 단어 선택 | on one's own initiative 자발적으로 | willingness 의지, 의향 | ensure that ~임을 보장하다 | distribute 배부하다 | diligence 성실함 | effort 노력 | brightness 현명함 | allow A to do A가 ~할 수 있게 해주다 | on time 제때

---

5. 문장 선택

(A) 그분께서 제가 중요한 문제들에 관심을 갖도록 해주셨습니다.
(B) 설문지를 배포할 준비가 되었습니다.
(C) 응답자는 이미 선택되었습니다.
(D) 저는 모든 것을 준비했습니다.

해설 빈칸 앞 문장의 '특히 Indira Joseph 씨에게 제 감사의 인사를 전해 주시기 바랍니다'라는 내용을 고려할 때, '그분께서 제가 중요한 문제들에 관심을 갖도록 해주셨습니다'라는 내용으로 이어져야 자연스러우므로 (A)가 정답이다.

+ Key word

Please send my gratitude to everyone who got involved in our survey last month, especially to Ms. Indira Joseph. She brought important matters to my attention.

---

6. 접속부사

해설 빈칸 앞 문장의 '몇몇 질문들이 너무 모호했다는 점을 저에게 알려주셨습니다'라는 내용과 빈칸 뒷부분의 '그분께서는 자발적으로 전체적인 표현들을 수정하도록 저를 도와주시기도 했습니다'라는 내용을 고려할 때, 빈칸 뒷부분에 도움을 받은 일을 추가로 언급하고 있으므로 (A)가 정답이다.

+ Key word

First, **she let me know that some questions were**

too vague to ask. I indeed was in a rush when I created the questionnaire. **In addition, she also helped me to revise the entire wordings on her own initiative.**

7. 어휘 – 명사

해설 앞 단락의 '그분께서는 자발적으로 전체적인 표현들을 수정하도록 저를 도와주시기도 했습니다'라는 내용을 고려할 때, '우리를 돕기 위해 대단한 헌신과 의지를 보여주셨습니다'라는 내용이 되어야 자연스러우므로 (D)가 정답이다.

✦ Key word

In addition, **she also helped me to revise the entire wordings on her own initiative. Ms. Joseph showed a great dedication and willingness to help us in ensuring that the questionnaire was perfect before it got distributed.**

8. to부정사 / 동사의 태

해설 문장 내에 이미 동사 allowed가 있으므로 빈칸은 준동사 자리이다. 또한, conduct는 원래 목적어를 필요로 하는 타동사이므로 to부정사로 쓰여도 목적어가 있어야 하는데, 빈칸 뒤에 목적어 없이 전치사구만 있으므로 수동태 to부정사인 (D)가 정답이다.

✦ Key point

한 동사의 여러 형태가 보기에 제시될 때, 빈칸이 동사 자리인지 먼저 확인한 후, '수의 일치', '태', '시제'를 고려해 알맞은 것을 고른다.

CASE 집중훈련
본서 p.105

1. (B) **2.** (D) **3.** (C) **4.** (D) **5.** (D) **6.** (C)
7. (D) **8.** (A)

---

1. 동사의 태 / 시제

Mega Construction's safety managers meet monthly with employees to make sure that regulations **are being followed** properly.

Mega 건설의 안전 관리자들은 규정이 적절히 지켜지고 있는지 확인하기 위해 직원들과 매월 만남을 갖는다.

해설 빈칸은 명사절인 that절 내에서 regulations를 주어로 하는 동사 자리이므로 to부정사 (C)는 제거한다. 빈칸 뒤에 목적어가 없고 규정은 적절히 지켜진다라는 수동태가 되어야 하므로 능동태 (A)도 제거한다. 과거 완료 had p.p는 과거 시제와 함께 쓰여 더 이전 시점을 나타내는데 문장 내에 과거 시제가 없으므로 (D)를 제거한다. '규정이 적절히 지켜지고 있는 중인지를 확인한다'라는 의미가 되어야 자연스러우므로 (B)가 정답이다.

어휘 make sure 반드시 ~하다 ǀ regulation 규정 ǀ follow 지키다, 따르다 ǀ properly 제대로, 적절히

✦ Key point

동사 자리에 알맞은 동사구를 고르기 위해서는 '능동태/수동태'와 '주어와의 수의 일치', '시제'를 고려해야 한다.

---

2. 동사의 수 / 태

The annual pass **covers** admission to the amusement park and one free snack per day.

연간 패스는 놀이공원의 입장과 하루 한 번의 무료 간식을 포함한다.

해설 문장 내에 동사가 없는 것으로 보아 빈칸은 동사 자리이므로 준동사 covering은 제거한다. 주어가 단수이므로 복수 동사 cover도 제거한다. 빈칸 뒤에 목적어 admission이 있는 것으로 보아 수동태가 아닌 능동태가 정답이 되어야 하므로 (D)가 정답이다.

어휘 annual 연례의 ǀ pass 패스, 출입증 ǀ admission 입장 ǀ amusement park 놀이공원 ǀ free 무료의 ǀ snack 간식, 스낵

✦ Key point

동사 자리의 형태 문제는 '주어와 동사의 수의 일치'와 '능동태/수동태 여부', '시제'를 고려해야 한다.

---

3. 동사의 태

The mobile app developed by Weylan Solutions has been **customized** to meet your company's needs.

Weylan Solutions에서 개발된 모바일 앱은 귀의 요구에 맞추기 위해 주문 제작되었습니다.

해설 빈칸 앞에 be동사가 있고 빈칸 뒤에 목적어가 없으므로 빈칸은 수동태 be p.p의 형태를 완성하는 과거분사 자리이다. '모바일 앱이 주문 제작되었다'라는 의미가 되어야 자연스러우므로 (C)가 정답이다.

어휘 meet 맞추다, 충족시키다 ǀ needs 요구

---

4. 동사의 시제

The sales contracts the Legal Department had asked for **arrived** by express mail last Friday.

법무 부서가 요청했던 영업 계약서가 지난 금요일에 속달 우편으로 도착했다.

해설 명사 뒤에 「주어+동사」가 바로 올 경우 목적격 관계대명사 that이 생략되어 명사를 수식하는 구조임을 파악해야 풀 수 있는 문제이다. 즉, the Legal Department had asked for가 명사 the sales contracts를 수식하는 구조로 주어 the sales contracts에 이어지는 동사가 빈칸에 와야 하므로 (A)와 (B)는 오답이고, 주어가 복수이므로 (C)도 오답이다. 과거 시점을 나타내는 last Friday를 통해 과거 동사 (D)가 정답이다.

어휘 contract 계약(서) ǀ ask for 요청하다

5-8번은 다음 기사에 관한 문제입니다.

HOBART — 제 4회 연례 Hobart 문학 콘퍼런스가 7월 10일에 시작해 21일까지 **5지속됩니다.** 올해 콘퍼런스에서는 호주 작품 이상을 선보입니다. 유럽 및 북미판 **6소설** 또한 다룰 것입니다. 대중의 요구로 인해, 올해는 스타 작가 및 최고 편집자와 함께 하는 패널토론이 돌아옵니다. 이러한 **7흥미로운** 행사 입장권을 일찍 구입하시기 바랍니다. 꽤 일찍 매진될 것으로 예상됩니다. **8티켓은 6월 1일 월요일부터 판매됩니다.** Hobart 시민들은 입장권을 할인받을 수 있습니다. 입장권을 구입하시려면, 저희 핫라인 491-555-110으로 전화하시거나 웹사이트 www. hobartliteraryfestival.au를 방문해 주세요.

어휘

literary 문학의 ǀ national (특정 국가의) 국민 ǀ feature 특징으로 삼다 ǀ popular 대중들의, 대중적인 ǀ demand 요구, 수요 ǀ bring 가져오다 ǀ panel discussion 공개 토론회 ǀ author 작가 ǀ pass 출입증 ǀ sell out 다 팔리다 ǀ far 훨씬 ǀ in advance 미리, 사전에 ǀ citizen 시민 ǀ eligible for ~의 자격이 있는 ǀ discounted 할인된

5. 동사의 시제

해설 빈칸은 주어 The Fourth Annual Hobart Literary Conference에 대해 두 개의 동사가 접속사 and로 연결된 구조이다. 앞에 나온 동사 starts의 시제가 현재임을 고려할 때, '콘퍼런스가 7월 10일에 시작해 21일까지 계속될 것'이라는 의미가 되어야 자연스러우므로 미래 시제 동사 (D)가 정답이다.

+ Key word

The Fourth Annual Hobart Literary **Conference starts 10 July and will continue until the 21st.**

6. 어휘 - 명사

해설 빈칸은 동사 feature의 목적어 자리이다. 빈칸 앞 부분의 '올해 문학 콘퍼런스에서는 호주 작품 이상을 선보인다'는 내용과 빈칸을 후치 수식하는 from 전명구를 고려할 때, '올해는 유럽 및 북미 소설 또한 다룬다'는 내용이 되어야 문맥상 자연스러우므로 (C)가 정답이다.

+ Key word

The Fourth Annual Hobart **Literary Conference** starts 10 July and will continue until the 21st. **The Conference this year will offer more than just work by Australian nationals. We will also be featuring novels from Europe and North America.**

7. 어휘 - 형용사

해설 빈칸은 명사 event를 수식하는 형용사 자리이다. 빈칸 뒷문장의 '꽤 일찍 매진될 것으로 예상된다'는 내용을 고려할 때, 문맥상 '이러한 흥미로운 행사 입장권을 일찍 구입하라'는 내용이 되어야 자연스러우므로 (D)가 정답이다.

+ Key word

Be sure to get your pass for this exciting event early. It is **expected to sell out far in advance.**

8. 문장 선택

(A) 티켓은 6월 1일 월요일부터 판매됩니다.
(B) 행사장의 수용 인원이 확대되었습니다.
(C) 인터뷰는 Teri Schultz가 진행합니다.
(D) 그날 저녁 폐막 행사에는 많은 사람들이 참석했습니다.

해설 빈칸 앞 부분의 '행사 입장권을 일찍 구입하시기 바란다. 꽤 일찍 매진될 것으로 예상된다'라는 내용과 빈칸 뒷문장의 '시민들은 입장권을 할인받을 수 있다'는 내용을 고려할 때, 행사 입장권 판매 관련 내용이 들어가야 문맥상 자연스러우므로 (A)가 정답이다.

+ Key word

Be sure to get your pass for this exciting event early. It is expected to sell out far in advance. Tickets go on sale on Monday, 1 June. Citizens of Hobart are eligible for discounted passes. To get your pass, call our hotline at 491-555-110, or visit our Web site: www.hobartliteraryfestival.au.

CASE 집중훈련

본서 p.107

1. (B) **2.** (A) **3.** (D) **4.** (A) **5.** (B) **6.** (D)
7. (B) **8.** (A)

1. 미래 시제 시간 표현

The sales report will be discussed at the **next** weekly meeting.

판매 보고서는 다음 주간 회의에서 논의될 것이다.

해설 미래 시제 will be discussed와 어울릴 수 있는 (B)가 정답이다. soon도 미래 시제와 어울리지만 부사이고 이 문장처럼 명사구를 수식하지 못한다.

어휘 discuss 논의하다 | weekly 주간의

+ Key word

The sales report will be discussed **at the next weekly meeting.**

2. 미래 시제 시간 표현

Mr. Routhier will **soon** have the opportunity to visit the office in San Jose.

Routhier 씨는 San Jose에 있는 사무실을 방문할 기회를 곧 가질 것이다.

해설 문맥상 '사무실에 방문할 기회가 곧 있을 것이다'라는 의미가 자연스러우므로 (A)가 정답이다.

어휘 opportunity 기회 | soon 곧 | even 심지어, ~조차 | simply 단순히, 간단히 | yet 아직

+ Key word

Mr. Routhier will soon have the opportunity to visit the new office in San Jose.

3. 현재 시제 시간 표현

Paulson Law Firm started as a small, six-person firm and **now** provides services to prominent celebrities and politicians across the country.

Paulson 법무 법인은 6명의 직원이 있는 작은 회사로 시작했으며, 지금은 국내 전역의 저명한 유명 인사와 정치인들에게 서비스를 제공한다.

해설 등위 접속사 and 뒤에 주어 Paulson Law Firm이 생략된 형태로 주어와 동사 사이에서 동사 provides를 수식하는 부사 자리이다. Paulson Law Firm은 작은 회사로 시작했으며, 지금은 ~를 제공한다'라는 의미가 되어야 자연스러우며, 부사 now는 현재 시제와 잘 쓰이므로 (D)가 정답이다.

어휘 prominent 저명한 | celebrity 유명 인사 | politician 정치인

4. 현재 시제 시간 표현

The monthly payments charged by Amazing Prime Videos are **periodically** updated depending on changes in taxes and inflation.

Amazing Prime Videos 사에서 청구하는 월 요금은 세금과 물가 상승률의 변화에 따라 정기적으로 업데이트된다.

해설 동사 are updated를 수식하는 부사 자리이다. '세금과 물가 상승률의 변화에 따라 월 요금이 정기적으로 업데이트된다'는 의미가 자연스러

우며, 동사의 시제가 단순 현재 시제임을 고려할 때 빈도부사 (A)가 정답이다.

어휘 payment 요금, 납부액 | charge 청구하다 | depending on ~에 따라 | inflation 인플레이션, 물가 상승률

✦ Key point
recently는 현재 완료 또는 과거 시제와, formerly는 과거 시제와 함께 쓰일 수 있다.

5-8번은 다음 기사에 관한 문제입니다.

Mondale-Sterling, 지역 의료기관과 협력하다

Hamilton (8월 11일) — 지난 주, Mondale-Sterling의 Gerard Mondale 사장은 Hamilton 병원시스템과의 제휴를 **5발표했다**. 이 회사는 North Island의 최고 냉난방 계약업체로, 더 높은 효율과 낮은 에너지 소비로 작동할 수 있게 냉난방 시스템을 최적화하는 작업에 필요한 장비를 잘 갖추고 있다. 신규 **6선풍기**, 감지기, 그리고 스마트 온도조절장치를 특징으로 하는 이 업그레이드는 비효율적인 냉난방으로 발생하는 비용을 최대 50%까지 줄여서 전력비용을 낮출 것이라고 Mondale은 말한다. "저희는 **7평소의** 3분의 1가격으로 이러한 개선책들을 제공해 드릴 수 있어 기쁩니다. Mondale-Sterling에서는 새로운 VulcanMax 시스템의 기능을 증명하면서 동시에 시에 좋은 일을 하게 되어 기대됩니다. **8Mondale-Sterling의 HVAC 서비스에 대해 더 알아보려면, MondaleSterling.co.nz를 방문해보세요.**

어휘
team up with ~와 협력하다 | health provider 의료기관 | alliance 동맹, 제휴 | heating 난방 | air conditioning 에어컨 | contractor 도급업자 | firm 회사 | well-equipped 잘 갖추어진 | optimize 최적화하다 | cooling system 냉각 장치 | run 작동하다 | efficiency 효율성 | consumption 소비 | upgrade 업그레이드 | feature 특징으로 삼다, 특별히 포함하다 | sensor 감지기, 센서 | smart 스마트한, 컴퓨터로 조정되는 | thermostat 온도조절장치 | reduce 줄이다 | power bill 전력 비용 | eliminate 제거하다 | generate 발생시키다 | inefficient 비효율적인 | provide 제공하다 | improvement 개선, 향상 | prove 증명하다 | capability 능력, 역량 | at the same time 동시에

5. 동사의 시제

해설 빈칸은 주어와 목적어 사이 동사 자리이다. 문두에 과거 시점을 가리키는 표현 Last week이 있으므로 과거 시제 동사 (B)가 정답이다.

✦ Key point
시간부사(구)와 시제 일치: last week, yesterday, ago 등 과거 시점을 나타내는 부사(구)는 과거 시제와 함께 쓰일 수 있다.

6. 어휘 – 명사

해설 빈칸은 which 주격 관계절 내 동사 feature의 목적어 중 하나인 명사 자리이다. 빈칸 앞 문장의 '이 회사는 최고 냉난방 계약업체로, 냉난방 시스템을 최적화하는 작업에 필요한 장비를 잘 갖추고 있다'는 내용과 콤마(,)로 나열된 다른 명사들을 고려할 때, 문맥상 '신규 선풍기, 감지기, 그리고 스마트 온도조절장치를 특징으로 하는 이 업그레이드는 전력비용을 낮출 것'이라는 내용이 되어야 자연스러우므로 (D)가 정답이다.

✦ Key word
As the North Island's top **heating and air conditioning contractor, the firm is well-equipped to do the work necessary to optimize heating and cooling systems** to run with greater efficiency and lower energy consumption. The upgrades, which feature new **fans**, sensors, and smart thermostats, will

reduce power bills by eliminating as much as 50 percent of the cost generated by inefficient heating and cooling, says Mondale.

7. 어휘 – 형용사

해설 빈칸은 명사 price를 수식하는 형용사 자리이다. 빈칸 앞 문장의 '이 업그레이드는 전력비용을 낮출 것'이라는 내용을 고려할 때, 문맥상 '평소의 3분의 1가격으로 이러한 개선책들을 제공해 드릴 수 있어 기쁘다'는 내용으로 이어져야 자연스러우므로 (B)가 정답이다.

✦ Key word
The upgrades, which feature new fans, sensors, and smart thermostats, **will reduce power bills** by eliminating as much as 50 percent of the cost generated by inefficient heating and cooling, says Mondale. **We're happy to provide these improvements at a third of the usual price.**

8. 문장 선택

(A) Mondale-Sterling의 HVAC 서비스에 대해 더 알아보려면, MondaleSterling.co.nz를 방문해보세요.
(B) 일부 병원 시스템은 25년 동안 업그레이드되지 않았다.
(C) 병원 네트워크는 다음에 에어컨들을 교체할 계획이다.
(D) 자격이 있는 경우, 직접 Waikato구 보건국에 신청하도록 한다.

해설 빈칸 앞 문장의 'Mondale-Sterling에서는 새로운 VulcanMax 시스템의 기능을 증명하면서 동시에 시에 좋은 일을 하게 되어 기대됩니다'는 내용을 고려할 때, 빈칸에는 Mondale-Sterling 웹사이트에서 서비스에 대한 더 자세한 내용을 볼 수 있다는 내용으로 이어져 기사가 마무리되어야 문맥상 자연스러우므로 (A)가 정답이다.

✦ Key word
"We're happy to provide these improvements at a third of the usual price. **Mondale-Sterling is excited to prove the capabilities of our new VulcanMax system and do some good for the city at the same time." To learn more about Mondale-Sterling's HVAC services, visit MondaleSterling. co.nz.**

CASE 집중훈련
본서 p.109

1. (C) **2.** (A) **3.** (D) **4.** (D) **5.** (C) **6.** (A)
7. (C) **8.** (D)

1. 어휘 – 부사

A local burger BBX **recently** announced that it will no longer serve French fries with its burgers.
지역 햄버거 BBX는 최근에 프렌치 프라이를 더 이상 햄버거와 함께 제공하지 않겠다고 발표했다.

해설 빈칸은 과거 동사 announced를 수식하는 부사 자리이다. 문맥상 '더 이상 프렌치 프라이를 햄버거와 함께 제공하지 않겠다는 사실을 최근에 발표했다'라는 의미가 되어야 자연스러우므로 (C)가 정답이다.

어휘 announce 발표하다, 알리다 | no longer 더 이상 ~이 아닌 | serve 제공하다 | entirely 완전히, 전적으로 | kindly 친절하게 | recently 최근에 | fully 완전히, 충분히

+ **Key word**

A local burger BBX **recently announced that it will no longer serve French Fries fries with its burgers**.

---

2. 접속사 자리

Excessive spending by government officials has decreased **since** new policies were introduced last year.

작년에 새로운 정책이 도입된 이후 공무원의 과도한 지출이 감소했다.

해설 빈칸은 두 개의 문장을 연결하는 접속사 자리이다. '새로운 정책 도입 후, 과도한 지출이 감소했다'는 의미가 되어야 문맥상 자연스러우므로 (A)가 정답이다.

어휘 excessive 과도한 | spending 지출 | government official 공무원 | decrease 감소하다 | policy 정책 | introduce 소개하다, 도입하다

+ **Key point**

시점을 나타내는 since는 주절에 현재 완료 시제와 주로 함께 쓰인다.

---

3. 어휘 - 명사

Crosston's economy has been improving recently thanks to an **influx** of new businesses.

신규 사업체들의 유입덕분에 최근 Crosston의 경제가 좋아지고 있다.

해설 빈칸은 thanks to 전치사구의 목적어 자리이다. 주절과의 관계를 고려할 때, 문맥상 '신규 사업체들의 유입 덕분에 경제가 좋아지고 있다'는 의미가 되어야 자연스러우므로 (D)가 정답이다.

어휘 economy 경제 | recently 최근 | business 사업(체)

+ **Key word**

Crosston's **economy** has been **improving** recently **thanks to an influx of new businesses**.

---

4. 동사의 시제

Over the last three decades, Mr. Drake **has climbed** quickly up the corporate ladder at an international consulting firm.

Drake 씨는 지난 30년에 걸쳐 국제 컨설팅 회사에서 빠르게 승진 가도를 달렸다.

해설 문장에 동사가 없으므로 빈칸에는 동사가 필요하다. 준동사인 (B) climbing과 주어가 3인칭 단수이므로 (A) climb은 답에서 제외시킨다. 「over [for/in] the last [past] + 기간」이 보이면 현재 완료 시제가 정답이므로 (D)가 정답이다.

어휘 decade 10년 | climb up the corporate ladder 회사에서 승진 가도를 달리다

5-8번은 다음 이메일에 관한 문제입니다.

발신: 경영진
날짜: 2월 12일
제목: Chris Searle
수신: 전 직원

전 직원 여러분께,

Chris Searle이 신임 인수 합병 담당 책임자가 되어 달라는 우리의 제안을 **⑤수락했음**을 여러분 모두에게 알리고 싶습니다. 그의 근무 첫날은 3월 19일로 예정돼 있습니다. Searle 씨는 전략적 기업 활동에 있어 20년

간의 경험을 가지고 있는데 마지막 5년은 주로 은행 **⑥분야**였습니다. 그의 첫 번째 업무는 Quad City Mutual의 인수 가능성에 관해 우리 이사회에 저에게 자문하게 될 것입니다. 그의 근무 첫날에 환영 파티가 계획되어 있습니다. **⑦오후 6시부터 Barney's Grill에서 열릴 것입니다. ⑧ 참석**을 원하신다면 이메일을 보내 주세요.

어휘
management 경영진 | inform 알려주다 | accept 수락하다 | merger 합병 | acquisition 인수 | decade 10년 | strategic 전략적인 | corporate 기업의 | action 조치, 활동 | banking 은행업무 | task 업무 | board of directors 이사회 | welcome party 환영 파티

---

5. 동사의 태 / 시제

해설 빈칸은 명사절 that의 동사 자리이다. 빈칸 뒷부분의 '그의 근무 첫날은 3월 19일로 예정돼 있습니다.'라는 내용과 빈칸 뒤 목적어 our offer이 있어 능동태가 돼야 함을 고려할 때, 'Chris Searle이 신임 책임자가 되어달라는 제안을 수락했다'라는 내용이 들어가야 자연스러우므로 현재 완료 능동태 (C)가 정답이다.

+ **Key point**

동사의 형태는 '태', '수의 일치', '시제'를 고려해야 한다.

---

6. 어휘 - 명사

해설 문맥상 'Searle 씨는 전략적 기업 활동에 있어 20년간의 경험을 가지고 있는데 마지막 5년은 주로 은행 분야였습니다'라는 내용이 되어야 자연스러우므로 (A)가 정답이다.

+ **Key word**

Mr. Searle has two decades of experience in strategic corporate actions, **the last five mainly in the banking sector**.

---

7. 문장 선택

(A) 이번 주에 날짜를 확정하고 싶습니다.
(B) Searle 씨는 여러분의 통찰력에 감사할 것입니다.
(C) 오후 6시부터 Barney's Grill에서 열릴 것입니다.
(D) 그때 추가 상담이 있을 것입니다.

해설 빈칸 앞 문장의 '그의 근무 첫날에 환영 파티가 계획되어 있습니다'라는 내용을 고려할 때, 문맥상 환영 파티 일정에 대한 내용으로 이어져야 자연스러우므로 welcome party를 It으로 받는 (C)가 정답이다.

+ **Key word**

A welcome party is being planned on his first day. It will take place at Barney's Grill starting at 6 P.M.

---

8. 어휘 - 명사

해설 빈칸 앞 문장의 '그의 근무 첫날에 환영 파티가 계획되어 있습니다. 오후 6시부터 Barney's Grill에서 열릴 것입니다.'라는 내용을 고려할 때, 문맥상 '참석을 원하신다면 이메일을 보내 주세요'라는 내용으로 이어져야 자연스러우므로 (D)가 정답이다.

+ **Key word**

A welcome party is being planned on his first day. It will take place at Barney's Grill starting at 6 P.M. Please email me if you'd like to attend.

1. (C)   2. (B)   3. (A)   4. (B)   5. (A)   6. (B)
7. (D)   8. (D)

1. 동사의 태 / 시제

Excelsior Dentistry allows a 10-minute grace period for late arrivals after which the patient **is rescheduled**.

Excelsior Dentistry에서는 늦게 도착하는 경우 10분의 유예시간을 주고, 그 후 환자는 일정이 재조정된다.

해설 빈칸은 the patient를 주어로 하는 동사 자리이다. 두 개의 문장이 관계절로 연결된 구조로, 주절의 시제가 현재이고 문맥상 '10분의 유예시간이 지난 후, 그 (늦은) 환자는 일정이 재조정된다'는 의미가 되어야 자연스러우므로 현재 시제 수동태 (C)가 정답이다.

어휘 dentistry 치과학 | allow 허용하다, 허락하다 | grace period 유예기간 | arrival 도착 | patient 환자

2. 동사의 수 일치

After acquiring OneClick Money, Milton Ltd. **offered** a broad selection of online financial services.

Milton 사는 OneClick Money 사를 인수한 이후에 엄선된 온라인 금융 서비스를 제공했다.

해설 주절에 동사가 없는 것으로 보아 빈칸은 동사 자리이므로 준동사 (C), (D)는 제거한다. 주어가 Milton Ltd.인 단수 명사이므로 수 일치에 어긋나는 (A)도 제거한다. 과거 시제는 주어와의 수의 일치에 영향을 받지 않으므로 (B)가 정답이다.

어휘 acquire 인수하다 | broad 폭넓은, 다양한 | a selection of 엄선된

+ Key point

동사 자리에 알맞은 동사 형태를 고르기 위해서는 '능동태/수동태'와 '주어와의 수의 일치', '시제'를 고려해야 한다.

3. 동사의 시제

All job applicants are required to state what key skills they **possess** before their interviews.

모든 구직자들은 면접 전에 그들이 가지고 있는 핵심 기량이 무엇인지를 명시하라고 요청받는다.

해설 빈칸은 명사절 접속사 what이 이끄는 절의 동사 자리이므로 (C)는 오답이며, 선택지들이 수 일치를 모두 충족하고 모두 능동태이므로 알맞은 시제를 파악해야 한다. 일반적인 사실에 해당하는 내용[그들이 소유하고 있는 핵심 기량이 무엇인지]을 나타내므로 현재 시제 (A)가 정답이다.

어휘 job applicant 구직자 | state 명시하다 | key 핵심적인

4. 동사의 태 / 시제

By the end of this quarter, the plant in Texas **will have built** at least 10,000 air conditioning units.

이번 분기 말까지 Texas에 있는 그 공장은 적어도 일만 개의 에어컨을 만들게 될 것이다.

해설 빈칸 뒤에 목적어가 있으므로 수동태 동사인 (A) will be built와 (D) has been built는 제외시킨다. 도입부에 「by + 미래 시점」이라는 단서가 있으므로 미래 완료 시제 동사인 (B)가 정답이다.

어휘 plant 공장 | at least 적어도, 최소한

5-8번은 다음 이메일에 관한 문제입니다.

수신: Omar Radcliffe ⟨oradcliffe@yelcot.com⟩
발신: LY Sports Equipment ⟨orders@lysportsequipment.com⟩
날짜: 10월 2일
제목: 주문번호 3862

Radcliffe 씨께,

조절 가능한 기둥으로 된 Louisville 농구 골대에 대한 귀하의 주문에 감사드립니다. 저희는 이 농구 골대가 이렇게 인기 있는 제품이 되어 아주 빨리 품절될 것이라고 **5 예견하지** 못했습니다. 안타깝게도, 저희는 지금 바로 귀하의 주문 사항을 이행할 수 없습니다. 하지만, 저희 공장에서 추가 골대에 대한 빠른 배송을 저희에게 약속해 주었습니다. 저희는 귀하의 제품이 약 3주 후에 배송될 것으로 **6 예상합니다.** 귀하께서는 트럭이 **7 가는 대로** 이메일을 하나 받으시게 됩니다. **8 불편을 끼쳐 드린 데 대해 사과드립니다.** 주문품을 취소하시기로 결정하시는 경우, 기꺼이 전액 환불해 드리겠습니다.

안녕히 계십시오.

LY Sports Equipment

어휘
order 주문(품) | adjustable 조절 가능한 | pole 기둥 | popular 인기 있는 | sell out 품절되다, 매진되다 | unfortunately 안타깝게도 | be unable to do ~할 수 없다 | fulfill 이행하다 | promise 약속하다 | additional 추가적인 | about 약, 대략 | receive 받다 | on one's way 가는 중인, 오는 중인 | decide 결정하다 | cancel 취소하다 | issue 지급하다 | full refund 전액 환불

5. 어휘 - 동사

해설 빈칸 뒤의 '안타깝게도, 저희는 지금 바로 귀하의 주문 사항을 이행할 수 없습니다'라는 내용을 고려할 때, 문맥상 '저희는 이 농구 골대가 이렇게 인기 있는 제품이 되어 아주 빨리 품절될 것이라고 예견하지 못했습니다'라는 내용이 되어야 자연스러우므로 (A)가 정답이다.

+ Key word

We did not **foresee this basketball goal becoming such a popular item and selling out so quickly. Unfortunately, we are unable to fulfill your order right now.**

6. 동사의 태 / 시제

해설 빈칸 뒤에 목적어가 있으므로 빈칸은 능동태 동사 자리이다. 빈칸 앞 문장의 '저희 공장에서 추가 골대에 대한 빠른 배송을 저희에게 약속해 주었습니다'라는 내용을 고려할 때, 약 3주 후에 배송될 것으로 현재 예상하고 있다는 내용이 되어야 자연스러우므로 현재 시제인 (B)가 정답이다.

+ Key point

동사의 형태는 '태', '수의 일치', '시제'를 고려해야 한다.

7. 접속사 자리

해설 빈칸 앞뒤에 위치한 '이메일을 하나 받을 것이다'와 '트럭이 가다'라는 내용을 고려할 때 '트럭이 가는 대로 이메일을 하나 받을 것이다'와 같은 내용이 되어야 자연스러우므로 (D)가 정답이다. 또한, 이 문장은 주절은 미래 시제인데 종속절은 현재 시제가 나왔다. 시간의 부사절 접속사가 주절이 미래일 때 현재 시제를 쓰는 것도 정답을 찾는 단서가 된다.

✦ **Key word**

You will receive an e-mail as soon as the truck is on its way.

8. 문장 선택

(A) 사실, 농구 골대는 다양한 크기로 나옵니다.
(B) 배송비는 꾸준히 증가하고 있습니다.
(C) 저희 카탈로그는 다양한 제품군을 갖추고 있습니다.
(D) 불편함을 끼쳐 드린 데 대해 사과드립니다.

해설 빈칸 앞 문장의 '저희는 귀하의 제품이 약 3주 후에 배송될 것으로 예상합니다. 귀하께서는 트럭이 가는 대로 이메일을 하나 받으시게 됩니다'라는 내용을 고려할 때, '불편을 끼쳐 드린 데 대해 사과드립니다.'라는 내용으로 이어져야 자연스러우므로 (D)가 정답이다.

✦ **Key word**

We expect your item to ship in about three weeks. You will receive an e-mail as soon as the truck is on its way. Please accept our apologies for the inconvenience.

CASE 집중훈련

본서 p.113

1. (D) **2.** (A) **3.** (B) **4.** (A) **5.** (C) **6.** (D)
7. (A) **8.** (C)

1. 시간 / 조건절의 시제

As soon as the warehouse **is examined** for fire hazards, you may resume your normal business operations.

화재 위험에 대비한 창고 조사가 완료되는 대로, 일반 영업 활동을 재개할 수 있다.

해설 빈칸은 접속사 As soon as(~하자마자)가 이끄는 부사절의 동사 자리이다. examine은 '~을 조사하다'라는 뜻의 타동사로 빈칸 뒤에 목적어가 없다는 점에서 수동형이 들어가야 하므로 (A)는 답에서 제외시키며, 주절이 미래를 나타낼 때(may resume), 시간/조건의 부사절에서는 미래 시제 대신 현재 시제나 현재 완료 시제를 쓴다는 점에서 (D)가 정답이다.

어휘 as soon as ~하자마자 | warehouse 창고 | fire hazard 화재 위험 | resume 재개하다 | normal 보통의, 일반적인 | business operation 영업 활동

✦ **Key point**

시간이나 조건의 부사절에서는 미래의 일을 나타낼 때 현재 시제나 현재 완료 시제를 쓴다.

2. 시간 / 조건절의 시제

After the trial period **expires**, users have the option of paying for the software or deleting it from their servers.

무료 체험 기간이 만료된 후, 사용자는 소프트웨어를 구입하거나 서버에서 그것을 삭제하는 선택권을 갖는다.

해설 빈칸은 the trial period를 주어로 하는 부사절의 동사 자리이다. 주절의 시제가 일반적인 사실을 나타내는 현재 시제이므로, 시간 접속사 after가 이끄는 부사절의 시제 역시 현재 시제가 되어야 하므로 (A)가 정답이다.

어휘 trial period 시험 기간, 사용 기간 | expire 만료하다, 만기하다 | option 선택(권) | delete 삭제하다

✦ **Key point**

시간·조건의 접속사(after, before, if 등)가 이끄는 부사절에서는 현재 시제가 미래 시제를 대신한다.

3. 시간 / 조건절의 시제

If an employee **wishes** to take a leave of absence, they must first speak to their manager.

직원이 휴가를 내고자 할 경우, 관리자에게 먼저 알려야 한다.

해설 빈칸은 if 조건절 내 주어 an employee에 대한 동사 자리이다. 주어가 3인칭 단수 명사이며, 주절의 must speak '알려야만 한다'는 미래의 의미인데 주절이 미래 시제일 때 시간/조건 부사절의 시제는 미래 시제 대신 현재 시제를 사용해야 하므로 (B)가 정답이다.

어휘 a leave of absence 휴가

4. 요구 동사가 이끄는 that절의 시제

To validate yesterday's results, Dr. Kim is asking that the test **be repeated** today by a different research laboratory.

어제의 결과를 입증하기 위해, Kim 박사는 테스트가 다른 연구소에 의해 오늘 반복되어야 한다고 요청하고 있다.

해설 빈칸은 명사절 that절 내의 동사 자리이다. ask와 같은 제안 동사가 목적어로 that절을 이끌 때, that절의 동사는 should가 생략된 동사 원형이 와야 하며 빈칸 뒤에 목적어가 없으므로 수동태로 써야 한다. 따라서 「ask + that + 주어 (should) 동사 원형~」의 형태를 완성하는 (A)가 정답이다.

어휘 validate 입증하다

✦ **Key point**

다음의 타동사들은 목적어로 that절을 받을 때, that절의 동사에 조동사 should가 생략되며 동사 원형이 와야 한다:
주장(insist, claim), 명령(order), 요구(ask, request, require, demand), 제안(suggest, propose)

5-8번은 다음 이메일에 관한 문제입니다.

수신: laura.lewis@tnet.com
발신: WeightLossManagementHelp@wlm.net
날짜: 11월 28일
제목: 업데이트

고객 여러분께,

저희 체중 감량 관리 회사가 올해 세 배가 넘는 고객 숫자를 기록했다는 점을 알려 드리게 되어 기쁩니다. 이러한 증가 때문에, 저희는 회원 자격 갱신 선택권에 대한 절차의 변화를 포함해 저희 정책에 몇 가지 업데이트를 ⑤시행할 것입니다. 저희는 자동 납부 기능을 추가할 예정입니다. ⑥이 변화들은 12월 16일부터 효력이 발생될 것입니다. 하지만, 여러분께서는 현재 계속해서 여러분의 회원 계정에 접속하셔서 저희 '회원 자격 갱신' 페이지에서 이러한 업데이트에 관한 ⑦상세 정보를 읽어보실 수 있습니다. 저희 홈페이지에 접속하실 때, 로그인 상자 하단에 성함의 첫 글자들을 입력하셔서 새로운 업데이트에 동의하신다는 점을 ⑧인증하셔야 합니다.

저희는 여러분의 체중 감량 여정에 있어 도움을 드리도록 신뢰해 주시는 데 감사드리며, 목표에 도달하시도록 행운을 빌어 드립니다.

Weight Loss Management 고객 지원팀

어휘

announce 알리다 | weight loss 체중 감량 | management 관리 | more than triple ~의 세 배를 넘다 | due to ~ 때문에 | increase 증가 | policy 정책 | procedure 절차 | renewal 갱신 | feature 기능, 특징 | sign into ~에 접속하다 | account 계정 | initial 이름의 첫 글자 | bottom 하단, 아래 | verify 인증하다 | agree 동의하다 | reach 도달하다

5. 어휘 – 동사

해설 빈칸 뒤에 언급된 '회원 자격 갱신 선택권에 대한 절차의 변화를 포함해'라는 말을 고려할 때, '몇몇 업데이트를 시행할 것이다'라는 내용이 되어야 자연스러우므로 (C)가 정답이다.

+ Key word

Due to this increase, we will be **implementing some updates to our policies, including a change in procedure for membership renewal options**.

6. 문장 선택

(A) 고객님께 위반 통지서를 발송하겠습니다.
(B) 최근 경험을 평가하려면 피드백 링크를 클릭하십시오.
(C) 고객들은 이것이 성공적인 다이어트 계획이라고 보고합니다.
(D) 이 변화들은 12월 16일부터 효력이 발생될 것입니다.

해설 앞 단락의 '회원 자격 갱신 선택권에 대한 절차의 변화를 포함해 저희 정책에 몇몇 업데이트를 시행할 것입니다'라는 내용을 고려할 때, '이 변화들은 12월 16일부터 효력이 발생될 것입니다'라는 내용으로 이어져야 자연스러우므로 (D)가 정답이다.

+ Key word

we will be implementing some updates to our policies, including a change in procedure for membership renewal options. ~ The changes will go into effect on December 16.

7. 어휘 – 형용사

해설 information을 수식해 '회원 자격 갱신' 페이지에서 읽을 수 있는 정보로서 '업데이트에 관한 상세 정보'라는 의미가 되어야 자연스러우므로 (A)가 정답이다.

+ Key word

However, you can go ahead and sign into your membership account now to **read detailed information about these updates on our Membership Renewal page**.

8. 시간 / 조건절의 시제

해설 빈칸 뒤에 목적어가 없으므로 타동사 require가 수동태로 쓰여야 하며, when절의 동사가 현재 시제일 때 주절의 동사는 미래 시제로 쓰여야 하므로 (C)가 정답이다.

+ Key point

「When + 주어 + 현재 시제 동사」, 「주어 + 미래 시제 동사」

CASE 실전훈련
본서 p.114

1. (B) **2.** (D) **3.** (D) **4.** (D) **5.** (A) **6.** (C)
7. (C) **8.** (B) **9.** (A) **10.** (C) **11.** (B) **12.** (A)

1. 동사 자리

The Center for National Health's recent report **concludes** that the amended rules and regulations have been successful.
국립 보건센터의 최신 보고서에서는 개정된 규칙 및 규정이 성공적이라고 결론짓는다.

해설 빈칸은 주어와 목적어인 that 명사절 사이 문장의 동사 자리이므로 (B)가 정답이다.

어휘 amended 개정된 | regulation 규정 | successful 성공적인

---

2. 동사의 태

Gershwin Theater Group **will debut** its latest musical *The Midnight Sky* on December 10.
Gershwin 연극부는 12월 10일 최신 뮤지컬 〈The Midnight Sky〉를 초연할 것이다.

해설 빈칸은 주어와 목적어 사이 문장의 동사 자리이므로 능동태 문장을 완성하는 (D)가 정답이다.

어휘 theater 연극 | latest 최신의 | musical 뮤지컬

+ Key point
동사 뒤 목적어가 있으면 능동태 문장이다.

---

3. 동사의 태

The floor plan of the apartment complex **was found** to be in accordance with all the codes stipulated in the building regulation.
아파트 단지 평면도는 건물 규정에 명시된 모든 법규를 따른 것으로 나타났다.

해설 빈칸은 주어 The floor plan에 대한 동사 자리이다. 문맥상 '평면도는 모든 규칙에 따른 것으로 발견되었다'는 의미가 되어야 자연스러우므로 수동태 동사 구문을 완성하는 (D)가 정답이다. find는 5형식 동사로서 목적격 보어에 to부정사가 오거나 to be를 생략하고 형용사가 바로 쓰이기도 한다.

어휘 floor plan 평면도 | apartment complex 아파트 단지 | in accordance with ~에 따라서 | code 규칙, 관례 | stipulate 규정하다, 명기하다 | regulation 규정

---

4. 명사 자리 / 단수 명사 vs. 복수 명사

Camping gear from Norseland Outdoors are manufactured with an innovative synthetic **substance** that resists harsh weather conditions.
Norseland Outdoors의 캠핑 장비는 혹독한 기상 상황을 견디는 혁신적인 합성물질로 생산된다.

해설 빈칸은 an innovative synthetic의 수식을 받는 명사 자리이다. 부정관사 an이 있으므로 단수 명사 (D)가 정답이다. 아니면 that절 이하 동사가 resists인 것도 단서가 된다.

어휘 gear 장비 | outdoors 야외 | manufacture 생산[제조]하다 | innovative 혁신적인 | synthetic 합성의, 인조의 | resist 견디다 | harsh 혹독한 |

---

weather conditions 기상 조건

+ Key point
가산 명사는 단수일 때는 관사와 함께 오거나 그렇지 않은 경우 복수형으로 올 수 있다.

----

5. 어휘 – 동사

When Ms. Patterson checked her credit card statement, she **noticed** a discrepancy in the billed cost.

Patterson 씨가 신용카드 명세서를 확인했을 때, 청구된 비용에 차이가 있음을 알아챘다.

해설 빈칸은 주어 she와 목적어 a discrepancy 사이 동사 자리이다. when 종속절의 내용을 고려할 때, '카드 명세서를 확인해보니, 청구비용과 차이가 있음을 알아차렸다'는 의미가 되어야 문맥상 자연스러우므로 (A)가 정답이다.

어휘 check 확인하다 | statement 명세서 | discrepancy 차이, 불일치 | bill 청구서를 보내다 | cost 비용

+ Key word
When Ms. Patterson checked her **credit card statement**, she **noticed a discrepancy** in the billed cost.

----

6. 동사의 시제

At present, Costsave Supermarket **is working** to implement a long-awaited home delivery service through their Web site.

현재 Costsave 슈퍼마켓은 웹사이트를 통해 고대하던 가정 배달 서비스를 시행하려고 노력하고 있다.

해설 빈칸은 주어 Costsave Supermarket의 동사 자리이다. 문두에 부사구 At present가 있으므로 현재 진행 시제 (C)가 정답이다.

어휘 at present 현재 | implement 시행하다 | long-awaited 오래 기다려온 | delivery 배달

+ Key point
부사구 at present는 현재의 상태를 나타내는 표현이므로 현재 또는 현재 진행 시제와 함께 사용된다.

----

7. 어휘 – 동사

For the last two years, Vunder Partners has persistently **offered** the lowest commission rates on commercial real estate.

지난 2년 간 Vunder Partners는 지속적으로 상업용 부동산에 최저 수수료율을 제공해왔다.

해설 빈칸은 has와 함께 현재 완료 동사 구문을 이루는 과거분사 자리이다. 문맥상 '지난 2년간 지속적으로 최저 수수료율을 제공해왔다'는 의미가 되어야 자연스러우므로 (C)가 정답이다.

어휘 persistently 집요하게, 지속적으로 | commission 수수료 | rate 비율 | commercial 상업의 | real estate 부동산

+ Key word
For the last two years, Vunder Partners **has persistently offered the lowest commission rates on commercial real estate**.

----

8. 어휘 – 동사

Ms. Berretta amended the company's hiring policy to **grant** new recruits higher base salaries.

Berretta 씨는 신입 사원에게 더 높은 기본급을 주기 위해 사내 고용 정책을 수정했다.

해설 빈칸은 to부정사구를 완성하는 동사 자리이다. 빈칸 뒤 목적어에 해당하는 명사구가 2개 있으며 주절과의 관계를 고려할 때, '신입 사원에게 더 높은 기본급을 주기 위해'라는 의미가 되어야 문맥상 자연스러우므로 (B)가 정답이다.

어휘 amend 수정하다 | hiring policy 고용 정책 | recruit 신입 사원 | base salary 기본급

+ Key point
수여 동사는 목적어를 2개 필요로 하며, 대표적인 동사는 다음과 같다: grant, give, offer, show 등

9-12번은 다음 공지에 관한 문제입니다.

우리 시에서 진행 중인 친환경 계획의 일환으로, 올해 Greenbriar 국제 푸드 페스티벌에서는 플라스틱 사용이 전면 중지될 것입니다. 따라서 모든 ⑨소모품은 종이접시에만 제공됩니다. 이는 마찬가지로 커트러리에도 적용되는데, 방문객은 각자 본인 것을 챙겨오거나 제공되는 나무 집게를 이용하게 됩니다.

Greenbriar 국제 푸드 페스티벌은 5월 16일 토요일 오전 9시부터 오후 4시까지 Highland Fields에서 열립니다. 올해 판매자이신 경우, 가판을 준비할 수 있도록 최소 1시간 전에는 ⑩도착하시길 요청 드립니다. ⑪상품 수송에 도움이 필요하신 경우, 저희에게 알려주세요.

행사에 필요한 자금과 ⑫허가를 제공해주신 시의회에 감사의 말씀을 전하고 싶습니다. 올해 축제에 온 가족과 함께 오시기를 바랍니다.

어휘
ongoing 진행 중인 | green 환경 친화적인 | initiative 계획 | completely 완전히 | plastic-free 플라스틱이 없는 | apply to ~에 적용되다 | cutlery (식탁용) 날붙이, 커트러리 | utilize 활용하다 | wooden 나무로 된 | utensil (가정용) 도구, 기구 | provide 제공하다 | vendor 노점상, 행상인 | at least 최소한, 적어도 | prior 사전의 | prepare 준비하다 | stall 가판대 | extend one's thanks 감사의 인사를 전하다 | provide A with B A에게 B를 제공하다 | city council 시의회 | fund 자금

----

9. 어휘 – 명사

해설 빈칸 앞 문장과 인과관계를 전달하는 접속부사 therefore로 연결되어 있으며, '올해 Greenbriar 국제 푸드 페스티벌에서는 플라스틱 사용이 전면 중지될 것'이라는 내용을 고려할 때, '따라서 모든 소모품은 종이접시에만 제공될 것'이라는 내용으로 이어져야 문맥상 자연스러우므로 (A)가 정답이다. 또한 뒷문장이 지시대명사로 시작되는 'This also applies to cutlery ~'로 연결되고 cutlery, utensils라는 단어를 통해서도 빈칸에 들어갈 어휘를 유추할 수 있다.

+ Key word
As part of our city's ongoing green initiative, the Greenbriar International Food Festival will be completely plastic-free this year. **Therefore, all consumables will only be offered on paper plates.**

----

10. 요구 동사가 이끄는 that절의 시제

해설 빈칸은 문장의 목적어인 that 명사절 내 주어 you에 대한 동사 자리이다. 주절의 동사 자리에 ask가 있으므로 동사 원형 (C)가 정답이다.

✦ Key point

주절에 [추천/제안/주장/요구/명령] 동사(recommend/suggest/ask/request/demand...)가 올 때, 목적어인 that절에는 '(should)+동사 원형'이 온다.

11.

(A) 판매자가 되려면, 신청서를 작성해야 합니다.
(B) 상품 수송에 도움이 필요하신 경우, 저희에게 알려주세요.
(C) 우리는 녹색 정책이 더 많은 가정용 재활용으로 이어지길 바랍니다.
(D) 작년 축제에서는 다양한 나라의 음식을 선보였습니다.

해설 빈칸 앞 문장의 '올해 판매자인 경우, 가판을 준비할 수 있도록 최소 1시간 전에는 도착해달라'는 내용을 고려할 때, 판매자에게 전하는 내용으로 이어지는 것이 문맥상 자연스러우므로 (B)가 정답이다.

✦ Key word

If you are a vendor this year, we ask that you arrive at least an hour early in order to prepare your stalls. If you require help with transporting your goods, please let us know.

12. 명사 자리

해설 빈칸은 the necessary funds와 접속사 and로 연결된 명사 자리이다. '행사에 필요한 자금과 허가를 제공해주신 시의회에 감사의 말씀을 전하고 싶다'는 의미가 되어야 문맥상 자연스러우므로 '허가'를 의미하는 (A)가 정답이다.

✦ Key point

명사 permit는 '허가(증)'을, permittance '허가하는 행위'를, permittee '허가를 받은 사람'을 의미한다.

CHAPTER 07 준동사

CASE 집중훈련 　　　　　　본서 p.117

1. (D)　**2.** (C)　**3.** (D)　**4.** (C)　**5.** (D)　**6.** (B)
7. (C)　**8.** (A)

1. to부정사 자리

Bellefontaine District Council officials have drafted a proposal **to attract** additional businesses to the newly opened office complex.
Bellefontaine 지역 의회 관계자는 새로 문을 연 사무 단지에 추가 업체를 유치하기 위해 제안서 초안을 작성했다.

해설 빈칸 앞에서 주어, 동사, 목적어를 갖춘 완전한 문장이 끝나고 빈칸 뒤에는 명사구가 있어, 빈칸은 준동사 자리이므로 to부정사 (D)가 정답이다.

어휘 District Council 지역 의회 | official 관계자 | draft 초고를 작성하다 | proposal 제안(서) | additional 추가의 | business 사업체 | newly 새롭게 | complex 복합 건물

✦ Key point

하나의 문장에는 적절한 형태의 접속사 또는 연결어 없이 한 개 이상의 동사가 올 수 없다.

2. to부정사의 형태

The chef will demonstrate how to **prepare** some of his most popular meals, and then audience members will be given samples to taste.
그 요리사가 자신의 가장 인기 있는 요리의 일부를 준비하는 방법을 시연할 것이고, 그런 다음 청중들은 맛볼 시식용 샘플을 제공받을 것이다.

해설 빈칸은 to부정사를 완성해줄 동사 원형 자리이다. 「how to V」는 명사구로서 '~하는 방법'이라는 뜻으로 to부정사를 완성해줄 동사 원형인 (C)가 정답이다.

어휘 chef 요리사 | demonstrate 시연하다 | meal 식사, (한끼) 요리 | audience member 청중, 관객 | taste 맛보다

✦ Key point

why를 제외한 의문사가 명사절을 이끄는 접속사로 쓰일 때, 뒤에는 문장뿐만 아니라 이를 축약한 〈의문사+to부정사〉 형태도 올 수 있다.
how+완전한 절 → how to부정사: 어떻게 ~하는지, ~하는 방법

3. 어휘 - 동사

Teowool Travel Services will match the price from any other major ticketing agencies to **ensure** that they remain competitive.
Teowool Travel Services는 가격경쟁력이 있음을 보장하기 위해 다른 주요 티켓팅 업체들의 가격에 맞춰줄 것이다.

해설 빈칸은 to부정사구를 완성하는 동사 자리이다. 문맥상 '여행사가 가격경쟁력이 있음을 보장하기 위해 다른 업체들의 가격에 맞춰준다'는 의미가 되어야 자연스러우며, that절을 목적어로 취할 수 있어야 하므로 (D)가 정답이다.

어휘 match 맞추다, 대등하게 만들다 | remain ~로 남다 | competitive 경쟁력 있는

✦ Key word

Teowool **Travel Services will match the price** from any other major ticketing agencies **to ensure that they remain competitive**.

4. to부정사의 의미상 주어

In order **for** Dr. Garth to contact you regarding your next therapy session, he will need your e-mail address.
다음 치료 세션에 관해서 의사 Garth가 연락을 할 수 있도록, 그는 당신의 이메일 주소가 필요할 것이다.

해설 빈칸은 in order to do '~하기 위해서'라는 to부정사구 사이에서 의미상의 주어를 이어주는 전치사 자리이다. to부정사의 의미상의 주어를 나타낼 때 to부정사 앞에 전치사 for을 사용할 수 있으므로, 「for+의미상의 주어+to do ~」형태를 완성하는 (C)가 정답이다. 'It was kind of you to offer'와 같이 사람의 성질을 나타내는 형용사 보어가 나올 때는 to V의 의미상 주어는 of N을 쓴다.

어휘 contact 연락하다 | regarding ~에 관해서 | therapy 치료, 요법

✦ Key point

'in order to do'는 '~하기 위해서'라는 to부정사 구문이고 to부정사의 의미상의 주어를 나타내기 위해서는 「in order for+명사+to do」의 형태로 쓸 수 있다.

5-8번은 다음 공지에 관한 문제입니다.

6월 21일 교통 주의보: 예정된 폐쇄 알림

Hollow Glade 지역이 오늘 폐쇄될 예정임을 시민 여러분께 알려드립니다. 지난주 폭풍으로 인한 피해를 ⑤**복구하기 위해** 오전 9시부터 오후 4시까지 Whitwell Street와 Binhamy Road가 폐쇄됩니다.

또한, 6월 25일에는 Bowden Dale의 대학교 바로 아래 지역이 매우 혼잡할 수 있습니다. 대학에서 개최하는 ⑥**특별** 행사로 인한 것이며, 하루 종일 진행될 예정입니다. 주민 여러분께서는 Cotswold Cross를 거치는 우회로를 이용하시길 권장드립니다.

Southview Gate로 이어지는 Gipsy Street가 6월 30일과 31일 오전 9시부터 폐쇄됩니다. 농민 협회에서 낮 ⑦**동안** 연례 파머스 마켓을 개최합니다. ⑧**그 거리는 오후 4시에 다시 개방될 예정입니다.**

어휘

traffic 교통 | advisory 주의보, 권고 | notification 알림 | upcoming 다가오는, 곧 있을 | disruption 지장, 중단 | notify 알리다 | public 대중 | area 지역 | close off 차단하다, 폐쇄하다 | directly 바로 | below ~아래에 | highly 매우, 대단히 | congest 혼잡하게 하다 | run 진행되다, 계속되다 | entire 전체의 | resident 주민 | advise 권고하다 | alternative 대안의 | route 길, 경로 | via ~를 경유하여, 거쳐 | lead to ~로 이어지다 | farmer 농부 | association 협회

5. to부정사 자리

해설 빈칸은 완전한 문장과 명사구를 연결하는 준동사 자리이다. 문맥상 '태풍 피해를 복구하기 위해 도로를 폐쇄한다'는 의미가 되어야 자연스러우므로 to부정사의 부사적 용법을 완성하는 (D)가 정답이다.

✚ **Key word**

Whitwell Street and Binhamy Road will be closed from 9 A.M. to 4 P.M. **to repair damages from last week's storm.**

6. 어휘 – 형용사

해설 빈칸은 명사 event를 수식하는 형용사 자리이다. 빈칸 앞 문장의 '대학가가 혼잡할 수 있다'는 내용을 고려할 때, '대학에서 주최하는 특별 행사 때문'이라는 내용으로 이어져야 문맥상 자연스러우므로 (B)가 정답이다.

✚ **Key word**

Additionally, **areas directly below the university on Bowden Dale may be highly congested** on June 25. **This is due to a special event held by the university,** which will run for the entire day.

7. 전치사 자리

해설 빈칸은 the day를 목적어로 취하는 전치사 자리이다. 빈칸 앞 부분의 '파머스 마켓을 개최한다'는 내용과 빈칸 뒤에 기간을 나타내는 명사가 있음을 고려할 때, 낮 동안이라는 의미가 되어야 문맥상 자연스러우므로 기간 전치사 (C)가 정답이다. by(~까지)는 시점 명사와 어울리고 이 문장처럼 동사에 지속(will be hosting) 동사가 아닌 finish 등의 완료 동사가 나오게 된다.

✚ **Key word**

Gipsy Street leading to Southview Gate **will be closed on June 30 and June 31 from 9 A.M.** The Farmer's Association will be **hosting their annual farmer's market for the day.**

8. 문장 선택

(A) 그 거리는 오후 4시에 다시 개방될 예정입니다.
(B) 초대장이 곧 발송될 것입니다.
(C) 우리는 새 토지에 대한 제안을 받고 있습니다.
(D) 매월 내역을 이메일로 요청하실 수 있습니다.

해설 빈칸 앞 부분의 'Gipsy 가는 6월 30일과 31일에 오전 9시부터 폐쇄되며, 농민 협회에서 낮 동안 파머스 마켓을 개최한다'는 내용을 고려할 때, '그 거리가 오후 4시에 다시 개방된다'는 도로 이용 가능 정보를 알려주는 내용으로 이어져야 문맥상 자연스러우므로 (A)가 정답이다.

✚ **Key word**

Gipsy Street leading to Southview Gate **will be closed on June 30 and June 31 from 9 A.M.** The Farmer's Association will be **hosting their annual farmer's market for the day. The street is expected to reopen around 4 P.M.**

CASE 집중훈련
본서 p.119

1. (B) **2.** (A) **3.** (B) **4.** (A) **5.** (C) **6.** (A)
7. (C) **8.** (B)

1. to부정사의 명사 역할

Ms. Bowen would like **to organize** a training session about the new accounting software within this month.
Bowen 씨는 이번 달 중으로 신규 회계 소프트웨어에 관한 연수를 마련하고 싶어한다.

해설 빈칸은 would like이 있으므로, 'would like to V(V하고 싶다)'의 관용 표현을 완성하는 (B)가 정답이다.

어휘 training session 교육, 연수 | accounting 회계

2. to부정사의 명사 역할

Trolley Consulting has failed to **maintain** positive relationships with its clients.
Trolley 컨설팅은 고객들과 긍정적인 관계를 유지하는 데 실패했다.

해설 'fail to do(~하는 데 실패하다, ~하지 못하다)' 구문을 묻는 문제로서, 빈칸은 to부정사를 완성하는 동사 원형 자리이므로 (A)가 정답이다.

어휘 fail to do ~하는 데 실패하다, ~하지 못하다 | positive 긍정적인, 낙관적인 | relationship 관계

✚ **Key point**

to부정사를 목적어로 취하는 타동사들은 hope, wish, aim, promise, offer, refuse, agree, try, strive, expect, fail 등이 있다.

3. to부정사의 가주어 – 진주어 구문

The Medical Doctors Association announced that maintaining indoor humidity at 50 percent will undoubtedly diminish the time it takes **to recover** from respiratory illnesses.
Medical 의사협회는 실내 습도를 50퍼센트로 유지하는 것이 확실히 호흡기질환에서 회복하는 데 걸리는 시간을 줄여줄 것이라고 발표했다.

해설 빈칸은 동사 take와 from 전명구 사이의 자리이다. It ~ illnesses까지 명사 the time을 수식하는 목적격 관계절에 해당하며, 관계절 내 동사 takes가 있으므로 빈칸은 준동사 자리이다. '호흡기질환에서 회

복하는 데 걸리는 시간'이라는 의미가 되어야 하므로 'recover from (~로부터 회복하다)'의 표현을 완성하는 능동형의 to부정사구 (B)가 정답이다.

어휘 association 협회 | announce 발표하다, 알리다 | maintain 유지하다 | indoor 실내의 | humidity 습도 | undoubtedly 의심할 여지없이, 확실히 | diminish 줄이다 | respiratory 호흡기의 | illness 병

+ Key point
① 'It takes 시간 (for 사람) to V'는 '(사람이) V하는데 (시간이)~이 걸린다'를 의미한다.
② 목적격 관계대명사절에서 관계사는 생략 가능하다.

....

4. 어휘 – 동사

Mr. Woodworth emphasized that it is important to **establish** explicit policies regarding telecommuting.
Woodworth 씨는 재택근무와 관련한 명백한 정책을 수립하는 것이 중요하다고 강조했다.

해설 빈칸은 to부정사구를 완성하는 동사 자리이다. 목적어 자리에 policies가 있으므로 문맥상 '정책을 수립하는 것'이라는 의미가 되어야 자연스러우므로 (A)가 정답이다.

어휘 emphasize 강조하다 | explicit 분명한, 명백한 | policy 정책 | regarding ~에 관하여 | telecommuting 재택근무

+ Key word
Mr. Woodworth emphasized that it is important to **establish** explicit **policies** regarding telecommuting.

5-8번은 다음 보도기사에 관한 문제입니다.

CARDIFF (2월 1일) — 캐나다의 주요 스포츠 의류업체인 Doonesbury는 영국에 진출하려고 **⑤계획하고 있다.** 오늘 오후, 회사는 투자자들에게 다음 달 Cardiff를 기반으로 하는 매장의 개장을 시작으로, 10개의 Doonesbury 매장이 잉글랜드와 웨일스 전역에서 문을 열 것이라고 말했다. **⑥나머지는 앞으로 6개월 이내 오픈할 것이다.** Doonesbury의 **⑦전략**은 업계 최고 최저가 보장뿐만 아니라, 다양한 아웃도어 및 스포츠 의류를 제공하는 거대한 교외 아웃렛 매장의 개장을 포함한다. "이사회는 저희의 사업을 영국 고객들에게 제공하고 저희의 훌륭한 브랜드와 고객서비스를 함께 나누고 **⑧싶어합니다.**"라고 회사의 부회장 Christina Maddow는 말했다.

어휘
major 주요한 | apparel 의류, 의복 | retailer 소매업체 | presence 존재 | investor 투자자 | location 위치, 지점 | involve 포함하다 | sprawling 제멋대로 퍼져나가는 | suburban 교외의 | outlet 아웃렛, 할인점 | offer 제공하다 | variety 다양성 | outdoor 아웃도어의 | as well as 뿐만 아니라 | industry-leading 업계 최고의 | price match guarantee 최저 가격 보장 | board 이사회 | business 사업(체) | share 공유하다 | incredible 믿어지지 않는, 놀라운 | explain 설명하다 | firm 회사

---

5. 동사의 시제

해설 빈칸은 주어와 목적어인 to부정사 사이 동사 자리이다. 빈칸 뒷문장의 '10개의 매장이 문을 열 것'이라는 내용을 고려할 때, '영국에 진출하려고 계획 중에 있다'는 의미가 되어야 자연스러우므로 현재 진행 시제 (C)가 정답이다.

+ Key word
Major Canadian sports apparel retailer **Doonesbury is planning to make its presence known in the UK**. This afternoon, the company told investors that **10 Doonesbury locations will be opened across England and Wales, with a Cardiff-based store opening first next month**.

6. 문장 선택

(A) 나머지는 앞으로 6개월 이내에 오픈할 것입니다.
(B) Doonesbury는 기존 매장을 업그레이드할 계획입니다.
(C) 곧 유명한 운동선수가 방문할 것입니다.
(D) 제안된 시내 위치는 충분한 공간을 제공하지 못했습니다.

해설 빈칸 앞 문장의 '다음 달 최초로 개장하는 Cardiff 매장을 기점으로, 10개 매장이 문을 열 것'이라는 내용을 고려할 때, 나머지 매장들의 개장 일정으로 이어져야 자연스러우므로 '나머지는 6개월 내 문을 열 것'이라는 내용의 (A)가 정답이다.

+ Key word
This afternoon, the company told investors that **10 Doonesbury locations will be opened across England and Wales, with a Cardiff-based store opening first next month. The rest will open within the next six months**.

7. 어휘 – 명사

해설 빈칸은 Doonesbury's의 수식을 받는 문장의 주어 자리이다. 빈칸 뒤 이어지는 내용을 고려할 때, 문맥상 'Doonesbury의 전략은 최저가보장 및 아웃렛 매장개장을 포함한다'는 의미가 되어야 자연스러우므로 (C)가 정답이다.

+ Key word
Doonesbury's **strategy involves opening** sprawling suburban **outlet stores** which offer a wide variety of outdoor and sports apparel, **as well as an industry-leading price match guarantee**.

8. 어휘 – 형용사

해설 빈칸은 be동사 뒤 주어 The board의 보어 자리이다. 빈칸 뒤 to부정사가 있으며, 바로 앞 부분의 'Doonesbury의 전략은 거대한 교외 아울렛 매장을 개장하는 것'이라는 내용을 고려할 때, 문맥상 '이사회는 저희의 사업을 영국고객들에게 제공하고 싶어한다'는 의미가 자연스러우므로, 'be eager to V(V하고 싶어하다)'의 표현을 완성하는 (B)가 정답이다.

+ Key word
Doonesbury's **strategy involves opening sprawling suburban outlet stores** which offer a wide variety of outdoor and sports apparel, as well as an industry-leading price match guarantee. "**The board is eager to bring our business to UK customers and to share** our incredible brands and customer service,"

CASE 집중훈련   본서 p.121

1. (B) **2.** (B) **3.** (C) **4.** (D) **5.** (C) **6.** (D)
7. (A) **8.** (C)

---

1. to부정사의 형용사 역할

Marriage counselor Jordan Mitchell advises people

to find a partner who has similar life goals.

결혼 카운슬러 Jordan Mitchell은 사람들에게 비슷한 인생 목표를 가진 파트너를 찾으라고 권고한다.

해설 빈칸은 5형식동사 advise의 목적격 보어 자리이다. 'advise + 목적어 + to부정사'는 '~에게 ~하라고 충고[권고]하다'를 의미하므로 (B)가 정답이다.

어휘 counselor 카운슬러, 상담역 | advise 권하다

+ Key point
to부정사를 목적격 보어로 받는 5형식 「5V + O + to do」가 수동태로 쓰이면 「be p.p + to do」의 형태로 쓰일 수 있는데 이러한 동사로는 advise, urge, persuade, tell, allow, permit, expect, encourage 등이 있다.

---

2. to부정사의 형용사 역할

The security system in the plant allows managers to **monitor** the manufacturing processes via cameras.

공장의 보안 체계는 관리자들로 하여금 제조 과정을 카메라로 감시할 수 있게 한다.

해설 빈칸은 allow의 목적격 보어인 to부정사를 완성하는 동사 원형 자리이다. 「allow + 목적어 + to 부정사」는 '~에게 ~할 것을 허용하다'를 의미하므로 (B)가 정답이다.

어휘 security system 보안 체계 | plant 공장 | allow 허용하다

+ Key point
목적격 보어로 to부정사를 받으며 「5V + O + to do」의 구조로 쓰이는 동사로는 advise, urge, persuade, tell, allow, permit, expect, encourage 등이 있다.

---

3. to부정사의 형용사 역할

Vella Beverage's board of directors cited the numerous customer complaints as the main reason for the decision **to discontinue** production of all sugary drinks marketed to children.

Vella 음료의 이사회는 아이들을 대상으로 내 놓은 모든 설탕이 들어간 음료의 생산을 중단하기로 한 결정에 대한 주된 이유로 많은 고객 불만을 들었다.

해설 명사 decision을 뒤에서 수식하는 자리이므로 형용사 역할을 하는 to부정사 (C)가 정답이다.

어휘 board of directors 이사회 | cite (예를) 들다, 인용하다 | sugary 설탕이 들어간 | market 시장에 내놓다

+ Key point
to부정사의 형용사적 용법 「명사 + to부정사」은 명사를 뒤에서 수식하는 형용사 역할을 한다.

---

4. to부정사의 형용사 역할

The first viewer **to call** this number and accurately identify the creator of this artwork will win a free trip for two to the Metropolitan Museum of Art.

이 번호로 전화해 이 미술품을 정확하게 맞히는 첫 번째 시청자는 Metropolitan 미술관 2인 무료 방문권을 타게 됩니다.

해설 문장의 동사가 이미 존재하므로(will win), 빈칸은 문장의 주어 the first viewer를 후치 수식하는 준동사 자리이다. 문맥상 '이 번호로 전화해 이 미술품을 정확하게 맞히는 첫 번째 시청자'라는 의미가 되어야 자연스러우므로 to부정사의 형용사적 용법을 완성하는 (D)가 정답이

다. 아니면 and 뒤에 to가 생략된 동사 원형(identify)이 나오므로 앞에 to V 형태가 와야 하는 것도 단서가 된다. for ~ing는 목적을 나타낸다.

어휘 viewer 시청자 | accurately 정확하게 | identify (신원 등을) 알아보다 | creator 창조자 | artwork 미술품 | win (경기 등에서 이겨서 무엇을) 타다, 이기다

+ Key point
접속사 등으로 연결되지 않는 한, 하나의 문장에는 하나의 동사만 올 수 있다.

5-8번은 다음 기사에 관한 문제입니다.

RICHMOND (7월 13일) — Portsmith 주식회사가 자사의 Epicurious 앱에 대한 업데이트를 완료했다고 어제 발표했다. Epicurious는 사용자들에게 인근의 레스토랑 위치를 **5찾고**, 쿠폰을 이용하고, 고객 후기들도 읽을 기회를 제공한다. 사용자들이 Epicurious에 로그인하면, 반경 5마일 이내의 모든 식당들을 정확히 찾은 위치가 표시된 지도를 보여줄 것이다. 사용자들은 요리 종류와 가격 **6범위**로 검색할 수 있고, 좋은 한 곳을 찾기 위해 평점으로 레스토랑들을 분류할 수 있다. **7그리고 이제**, 가장 최신의 업데이트로, Epicurious는 사용자들에게 쿠폰과 예정된 프로모션에 관한 알림도 보낼 것이다. **8따라서, 이 모든 즐거움을 놓칠 이유가 없다.**

어휘
announce 발표하다 | completion 완료 | provide A with B A에게 B를 제공하다 | nearby 인근의, 근처의 | access 이용하다 | review 후기, 평가 | sign in to ~에 로그인하다 | pinpoint 정확히 찾아내다 | location 위치 | eating establishment 식당 | radius 반경 | cuisine 요리 | sort 분류하다 | rating 평점, 등급 | alert 알림 | scheduled 예정된 | promotion 프로모션, 판촉 행사

---

5. to부정사 자리

해설 빈칸은 앞에 명사 opportunity를 수식하는 형용사적 용법의 to부정사 자리이다. 앞에 명사를 수식하여 '~을 찾고, ~을 이용하고, ~을 읽을 기회를 제공한다'라는 의미가 되어야 자연스러우므로 이를 완성해줄 준동사인 (C)가 정답이다.

+ Key point
to부정사의 수식을 받는 명사로 effort, ability, chance, way, plan, right 등이 토익에 자주 등장한다.

---

6. 어휘 – 명사

해설 빈칸은 앞의 명사 price와 함께 복합명사를 완성해줄 명사 자리이다. 문맥상 '사용자들은 요리 종류와 가격 범위로 검색할 수 있고 ~'라는 의미가 되어야 자연스러우므로 (D)가 정답이다.

+ Key word
They can search by cuisine type and **price range** and can sort restaurants by ratings to find a good one.

---

7. 접속부사

해설 빈칸은 앞뒤에 완전한 두 문장을 의미적으로 연결해줄 접속부사 자리이다. 앞에서는 Epicurious로 요리 종류와 가격대로 검색이 가능하다고 했고, 뒤에서는 최신 업데이트로 쿠폰관련 정보도 받을 수 있다고 한다. 앱의 업데이트 기능이 여러 개 나열되는 문맥이므로 순접이 포함된 (A)가 정답이다.

+ Key word
They can search by cuisine type and price range, **and** can sort restaurants by ratings to find a

---

good one. And now, with the most recent update, Epicurious will send users alerts about coupons and scheduled promotions.

8. 문장 선택

(A) 자세한 내용은 계약이 체결되고 나서야 공개될 것이다.
(B) 최근에는 앱 마켓에 매우 인기가 있다.
(C) 따라서, 이 모든 즐거움을 놓칠 이유가 없다.
(D) 따라서, 이 기능은 더 이상 사용할 수 없다.

해설 앞서 가장 최신 업데이트로 고객들이 누릴 수 있는 추가적인 혜택을 알리는 내용이 제시되어 있는 것으로 볼 때, 그와 관련하여 '따라서, 이 모든 즐거움을 놓칠 이유가 없다'라는 내용으로 마무리짓는 것이 자연스러우므로 (C)가 정답이다.

✛ Key word
And now, with the most recent update, Epicurious will send users alerts about coupons and scheduled promotions. Therefore, there is no reason to lose out on all the excitement.

CASE 집중훈련
본서 p.123

1. (D) **2.** (D) **3.** (C) **4.** (D) **5.** (B) **6.** (C)
7. (A) **8.** (D)

---

1. to부정사의 부사 역할

The institute requires its researchers to provide it with the written evidence needed **to support** the financing of their projects.
그 기관은 연구원들에게 그들의 프로젝트에 대한 융자를 지원하기 위해 필요한 증거 서류를 제공할 것을 요구한다.

해설 문맥상 '융자를 지원하기 위해 필요한 증거 서류를 제공하다'라는 의미이므로 목적을 나타낼 수 있는 품사가 필요한데 보기 중 부사 역할을 하면서 목적을 나타내는 것은 to부정사이므로 (D)가 정답이다.

어휘 institute 기관, 협회 | written evidence 증거 서류 | financing 융자, 자금 조달 | support 지원하다; 지원

✛ Key point
to부정사는 부사처럼 다른 품사나 문장 전체를 수식하여 목적, 결과, 이유 등을 의미하기도 한다.

---

2. to부정사 관용 표현

All authorized staff must enter a personal identification number **in order to** enter the laboratory.
승인 받은 직원들은 모두 실험실에 들어가기 위해 개인 식별번호를 입력해야 한다.

해설 빈칸은 주어, 동사, 목적어를 갖춘 완전한 문장과 동사구 사이의 자리이므로 빈칸 뒤 동사구를 수식어인 부사구로 만들어주는 to부정사의 관용 표현 (D)가 정답이다.

어휘 authorized 공인된, 권한을 부여 받은 | enter ~에 들어가다, (내용 등을) 입력하다 | personal identification 개인 식별 | laboratory 실험실

✛ Key point
① 한 개의 문장 안에는 접속사 없이 두 개 이상의 동사가 올 수 없다.
② 목적을 나타내는 to부정사의 관용 표현 'in order to V'는 'V하기 위하여'로 해석된다.

---

3. 어휘 – 형용사

Given the present real estate market, Cristobal Investments is **hesitant** to acquire new property.
현재 부동산 시장을 고려해, Cristobal Investments는 새 부동산을 매입을 주저하고 있다.

해설 hesitant '주저하는, 망설이는'은 서술형으로 쓰일 때 to부정사와 동반하여 be hesitant to V '~하기를 주저하다'라고 자주 쓰이므로 기억해두자. 따라서 (C)가 정답이다.

어휘 given ~를 고려해볼 때 | present 현재의 | real estate 부동산 | acquire 얻다, 취득하다 | property 부동산, 자산

---

4. 어휘 – 형용사

After evaluating each applicant interested in the sales representative position, we are **pleased** to inform you that you have been selected for the job.
영업사원 자리에 관심 있는 각 지원자를 평가한 뒤, 우리는 당신에게 그 직책에 선정되었음을 알려드리게 되어 기쁩니다.

해설 빈칸은 be동사 뒤 보어 자리이다. 빈칸에 들어갈 형용사는 뒤에 to부정사와 연결 되는데, 'be pleased to V(~하게 되어 기쁘다)'라는 숙어 표현을 이루고 문맥상 '그 직책에 선정되었음을 알려드리게 되어 기쁘다'라는 의미가 되어야 자연스러우므로 (D)가 정답이다.

어휘 evaluate 평가하다 | each 각각의 | applicant 지원자 | interested in ~에 관심 있는 | sales representative 영업 사원 | position 자리, 직책 | inform 알리다

✛ Key word
After evaluating each applicant interested in the sales representative position, **we are pleased to inform you that you have been selected for the job**.

5-8번은 다음 이메일에 관한 문제입니다.

수신: All@TarkingtonAccounting.co.uk
발신: Philippa Houston
날짜: 12월 16일
제목: 직원 매뉴얼 세미나

Tarkington Accounting은 직원 매뉴얼의 내용을 일부 변경했습니다. **⑤이는 5년 만에 처음 변경된 것입니다.** 대부분의 정책과 절차들은 그대로지만, 주요 변경사항이 몇 가지 있습니다. 매뉴얼에는 이제 온라인 데이터 저장, 암호화된 통신, 그리고 특별 경비 보고서에 대한 지침이 수록됩니다. 휴가신청 절차 또한 **⑥개정되었습니다.** 새로운 절차는 모두에게 더욱 쉽고 공정할 것입니다.

각 직원은 이 지침에 대해 살펴보는 회의에 참석할 것이 예상됩니다. 회의는 이번 달 말까지 회의실 D에서 매주 화요일과 목요일 오후 5시부터 6시까지 진행됩니다. **⑦그 후,** 직원들은 매뉴얼 사본을 수령했고 그 내용을 이해했음을 증명하는 서류에 서명하게 됩니다. 이들 회의 중 하나의 **⑧참석을 위해** 부서장과 일정을 잡으시기 바랍니다.

Philippa Houston,
인사팀

어휘
accounting 회계 | the majority of 대다수의 | policy 정책 | procedure 절차 | unchanged 바뀌지 않은 | key 핵심적인, 필수적인 | adjustment 수정, 조정 | guidelines 지침, 가이드라인 | storage 저장 | encrypted 암호화된 | expense 비용 | process 과정 | request 신청[요청]하다 | time off 휴가 |

straightforward 간단한, 복잡하지 않은 | fair 공평한, 공정한 | go over 검토하다 | conduct (활동을) 하다 | sign 서명하다 | certify 증명하다 | content 내용 | make arrangements with 일정을 잡다, 약속을 정하다 | department head 부서장

5. 문장 선택

(A) 새로운 디자인 변경은 1월 1일부터 시행됩니다.
(B) 이는 5년 만에 처음 변경된 것입니다.
(C) 사내 변호사가 새로운 규칙을 만들었습니다.
(D) 이 사안에 대해 협조해 주셔서 감사합니다.

해설 빈칸 앞 문장에서 'Tarkington Accounting은 직원 매뉴얼의 내용을 일부 변경했다'고 했으므로, some changes를 지시대명사 These로 받고 문맥상 '이는 5년 만에 처음 변경된 것'이라는 내용으로 이어져야 자연스러우므로 (B)가 정답이다.

+ Key word

Tarkington Accounting has made **some changes** to its employee manual. **These are the first alterations to be made in 5 years.**

6. 어휘 - 동사

해설 빈칸은 현재 완료 수동태 동사 구문을 완성하는 과거 분사 자리이다. 빈칸 앞 부분의 '주요 변경사항이 몇 가지 있다'는 내용과 문장 내 부사 also가 있음을 고려할 때, 문맥상 '휴가신청 절차 또한 개정되었다'는 내용이 되어야 자연스러우므로 (C)가 정답이다.

+ Key word

Though the majority of policies and procedures are unchanged, **a few key adjustments have been made**. The manual now features guidelines on online data storage, encrypted communications, and special expense reports. **The process for requesting time off has also been updated.**

7. 접속부사

해설 빈칸은 앞뒤 문장의 의미를 연결하는 접속부사 자리이다. 빈칸 앞 부분의 '각 직원은 이 지침에 대해 살펴보는 회의에 참석하게 된다'는 내용과 빈칸 뒷부분의 '직원들은 매뉴얼 사본을 수령했고 그 내용을 이해했음을 증명하는 서류에 서명하게 된다'는 내용을 고려할 때, 일의 순서상 회의에 참석한 후 서류에 서명하게 될 것임을 알 수 있으므로 (A)가 정답이다.

+ Key word

Each employee will be expected to attend a meeting to go over these guidelines. Meetings will be conducted from 5 to 6 P.M. every Tuesday and Thursday until the end of the month in Conference Room D. **Afterwards, employees will be expected to sign a document certifying that they've gotten a copy of the manual and understand its contents.**

8. to부정사 자리

해설 빈칸은 명령문 형태의 완전한 문장과 명사구 사이의 자리이다. 빈칸 앞 부분의 '각 직원은 이 지침에 대해 살펴보는 회의에 참석하게 된다'는 내용을 고려할 때, 문맥상 '회의 참석을 위해 부서장과 일정을 잡으라'는 내용으로 이어져야 자연스러우므로 목적의 부사구를 만들어주는 to 부정사 (D)가 정답이다. 나머지 형태들은 수식어로서 빈칸에 구조적

으로는 가능하지만 문맥에 맞지 않아 오답이다.

+ Key word

Each employee will be expected to attend a meeting to go over these guidelines. **Make arrangements with your department head to attend one of these meetings.**

CASE 집중훈련   본서 p.125

1. (D)   **2.** (B)   **3.** (B)   **4.** (C)   **5.** (D)   **6.** (A)
7. (C)   **8.** (B)

1. 원형 부정사를 취하는 help

My manager highly recommended taking the training course on the new marketing automation system because it will help **improve** work efficiency.
우리 매니저는 그것이 업무 효율성을 증대시키는 데 도움을 줄 것이기 때문에 새 마케팅 자동화 시스템에 대한 교육 과정을 이수하는 것을 적극 권장했다.

해설 동사 help는 목적어나 목적격 보어 자리에 원형 부정사를 목적어로 취하므로 (D)가 정답이다.

어휘 automation 자동화 | work efficiency 업무 효율성

2. 접속사

Many stores provide free gifts to customers who share their social media posts **because** they help build the company's online presence.
업체의 온라인 입지를 구축하는 데 도움이 되기 때문에 많은 상점에서 소셜 미디어 게시물을 공유하는 고객에게 사은품을 제공한다.

해설 빈칸은 두 개의 완전한 문장을 연결하는 접속사 자리이므로 (B)가 정답이다.

어휘 provide 제공하다 | share 공유하다 | social media 소셜 미디어 | post 게시물 | build 구축하다 | company 회사 | presence 존재

3. 원형 부정사를 취하는 help

According to the employee survey, flexible work hours help employees **strengthen** relationships with their family.
직원 설문에 따르면, 유연 근무 시간은 직원들이 가족과의 관계를 강화시키는 데 도움을 준다.

해설 빈칸은 동사 help의 목적격 보어 역할을 하는 원형 부정사 또는 to부정사 자리이다. help는 5형식으로 쓰일 때 「help+목적어+원형 부정사/to부정사」 '~가 ~하는 것을 돕다'로 목적격 보어로 원형 부정사 또는 to부정사를 취하므로 (B)가 정답이다.

어휘 according to ~에 따르면 | flexible 유연한 | relationship 관계

4. 어휘 - 동사

Mr. Parker in the lost and found department is tired of his job helping people **locate** their lost phones.
분실물 안내 부서의 Parker 씨는 사람들이 잃어버린 전화기를 찾아주는 업무에 싫증이 나 있다.

해설 Parker 씨가 the lost and found department(분실물 안내 부서)
소속이라고 했으므로 '~의 위치를 찾다'라는 의미의 locate가 의미상
가장 적절하다. 따라서 (C)가 정답이다.

어휘 lost and found 분실물 보관소 ǀ be tired of ~에 실증이 나다

5-8번은 다음 이메일에 관한 문제입니다.

수신: Jody Triesch
발신: Gerald Ko
날짜: 11월 11일
제목: 온라인 전기
첨부: 요약본

Jody,

시간 있을 때, 저희 새로운 CEO이신 Heidecker 씨에 관해 전기를 작
성해서 웹사이트에 올려주세요. 저희 회사에서의 그녀의 많은 **5업적**
을 작성한 요약본을 함께 보내드렸어요. 그녀가 한 일에 대해 추가 정보
가 필요하시면, Rebecca Stevens와 이야기를 나눠보시길 추천드려요.
**6Stevens 씨와 Heidecker 씨는 다양한 프로젝트에서 자주 함께 작업
하셨어요.** 가능하다면, 전기를 잡지 프로필처럼 **7보이게** 만들어 주세요.
언론매체나 소셜 미디어 사이트에서 기사거리로 이용한다면 좋을 거예
요. **8바라건대,** 더 많은 언론에서 유능한 인재들을 회사로 유치할 가능
성을 높여줄 것입니다. 수요일 퇴근 전까지 완성된 초안을 저에게 보내주
세요.

감사합니다.

Gerald Ko

어휘
biography 전기 ǀ upload 업로드하다 ǀ regarding ~에 관하여 ǀ include
포함하다 ǀ summary 요약, 개요 ǀ detail 열거하다 ǀ require 필요로 하다, 요구하다 ǀ
additional 추가의 ǀ recommend 추천하다 ǀ magazine 잡지 ǀ profile
프로필, 개요 ǀ news outlet 언론매체[기관] ǀ press 언론 ǀ improve 개선하다 ǀ
attract 끌어들이다 ǀ talented 재능 있는 ǀ complete 완료하다 ǀ draft 초안, 원고 ǀ
business day 영업일

---

5. 어휘 - 명사

해설 빈칸은 현재분사 detailing의 목적어인 명사 자리이다. 빈칸 앞 문장의
'새로운 CEO에 관한 전기를 작성해달라'는 내용을 고려할 때, '회사에
서 이룬 그녀의 많은 업적에 대해 요약한 내용을 함께 보냈다'는 내용으
로 이어져야 자연스러우므로 (D)가 정답이다.

✚ **Key word**
When you get a chance, please **write** and upload a
biography to our Web site **regarding our new CEO**,
Ms. Heidecker. I included a **summary detailing her
many achievements at our company**.

6. 문장 선택

(A) Stevens 씨와 Heidecker 씨는 다양한 프로젝트에서 자주 함께
    작업하셨어요.
(B) 저는 웹사이트의 새로운 디자인에 매우 감명받았습니다.
(C) 저는 오늘 오후에 Heidecker 씨를 만날 것입니다.
(D) 그 축하 행사는 수요일에 열릴 것입니다.

해설 빈칸 앞 문장의 '추가 정보가 필요하면 Rebecca Stevens에게 의견을
구하라'는 내용을 고려할 때, 문맥상 'Stevens 씨와 Heidecker 씨가
자주 함께 작업했었다'는 부연설명으로 이어지는 것이 자연스러우므로
(A)가 정답이다.

✚ **Key word**
**If you require additional information about what
she has done**, I'd **recommend speaking with
Rebecca Stevens. Ms. Stevens and Ms. Heidecker
have often worked together on various projects.**

7. 사역 동사

해설 빈칸은 사역동사 make의 목적격 보어 자리이므로 동사 원형 (C)가 정
답이다.

✚ **Key point**
사역동사(have, let, make)의 목적격 보어 자리에는 동사 원형이 온
다.

8. 어휘 - 부사

해설 빈칸은 조동사와 동사 사이 부사 자리이다. 문장의 시제가 미래이고,
빈칸 앞 문장의 '더 많은 언론에서 새로운 CEO에 대한 전기를 기사로
이용하면 좋을 것'이라는 내용을 고려할 때, '바라건대, 더 많은 언론에
서 더 많은 인재를 회사로 유치할 기회를 높여줄 것이다'는 내용으로 이
어져야 자연스러우므로 (B)가 정답이다.

✚ **Key word**
**It would be great if we can get some news outlets
or social media sites to use it for a story.** More press
will **hopefully** improve our chances of attracting
other talented individuals to the company.

CASE 집중훈련
본서 p.127

1. (B) **2.** (D) **3.** (C) **4.** (D) **5.** (B) **6.** (C)
7. (B) **8.** (A)

1. 동명사 자리

Scheduling sales meetings is one of the secretary's
most important responsibilities.
영업 회의의 예약 일정을 잡는 일은 비서의 가장 중요한 직무 중 하나이다.

해설 과거분사가 들어가면, 문장의 주어는 복수 명사인 sales meetings
가 되어 수 일치상 복수 동사 are가 와야할 뿐만 아니라 전체 문맥도 어
색해지므로 과거분사 Scheduled는 제외시킨다. 빈칸은 뒤의 명사구
'sales meetings'를 목적어로 취하며 주어 역할을 하면서 단수 취급
하는 동명사 자리이다. '영업회의의 예약 일정을 잡는 일은 ~ 중 하나
이다.'라는 의미가 되어야 자연스러우므로 동명사 (B)가 정답이다.

어휘 secretary 비서 ǀ responsibility 직무

✚ **Key point**
동명사와 to부정사 모두 명사적 용법이 가능하지만, 동명사는 실재적
인 내용을, to부정사는 비실재적이거나 미래의 일을 내포한다.

2. 동명사 자리

At Ivanhoe Rental Properties, all tenants are responsible
for **maintaining** their own apartments.
Ivanhoe Rental Properties에서, 모든 세입자들은 그들의 아파트를
유지보수할 책임이 있다.

해설 빈칸은 전치사 for의 목적어 자리로, 보기 중 전치사 뒤에 목적어로 올
수 있는 것은 동명사뿐이므로 (D)가 정답이다.

어휘　tenant 세입자 | responsible for ~에 책임이 있는 | maintain 유지하다

+ Key point

동명사는 명사와 마찬가지로 문장에서 주어, 목적어, 보어뿐만 아니라 전치사의 목적어로도 쓰이며, '~하기, ~하는 것'으로 해석된다.

---

3. 어휘 - 부사

Because of her education at an award-winning culinary institute in Rome, Maria Espinoza is **especially** skilled at preparing tasty pasta dishes.

수상경력에 빛나는 Rome의 요리학교에서 받은 교육으로 인해, Maria Espinoza는 맛있는 파스타 요리를 하는 것에 특히 능숙하다.

해설　빈칸은 보어인 형용사 skilled를 수식하는 부사 자리이다. Because of 전명구와 주절의 관계를 고려할 때, '요리학교에서 받은 교육으로, 파스타 요리를 하는 것에 특히 능숙하다'는 의미가 되어야 자연스러우므로 (C)가 정답이다.

어휘　award-winning 수상한, 상을 받은 | culinary 요리의 | institute 기관, 협회 | skilled 능숙한, 숙련된 | prepare 준비하다 | tasty 맛있는 | dish 요리

+ Key word

Because of her education at an award-winning culinary institute in Rome, Maria Espinoza **is especially skilled at** preparing tasty **pasta dishes.**

---

4. 어휘 - 동사

The video *From Mansion to Inn* guides viewers in **developing** old homes into successful bed and breakfasts.

비디오 〈From Mansion to Inn〉은 오래된 집을 성공적인 숙박시설로 개발하는 데 있어 시청자들을 안내한다.

해설　빈칸은 전치사 in의 목적어인 동명사 자리이다. 빈칸 뒤 이어지는 내용을 고려할 때, '오래된 집을 숙박시설로 개발하는 것'이라는 의미가 자연스러우므로 'develop ~ into ...(~를 …로 개발하다)'의 형태를 완성하는 (D)가 정답이다.

어휘　guide 안내하다, 보여주다 | viewer 시청자 | successful 성공적인 | bed and breakfast 아침식사를 제공하는 숙박시설(B&B)

+ Key word

The video *From Mansion to Inn* guides viewers in **developing old homes into successful bed and breakfasts.**

5-8번은 다음 공지에 관한 문제입니다.

LCK Ventures와의 계약이 무산되어 유감스럽습니다. 하지만 Baratic 기업과의 새로운 거래를 **⑤공개하게 되어** 아주 기쁘게 생각합니다. Baratic은 기술 스타트업에 자금을 제공하는 회사로 잘 알려져 있지만, 그곳 경영진은 자사 포트폴리오를 **⑥다각화**할 필요가 있다고 보았습니다. 지원 자금으로 새로운 지역으로 진출하려는 올해 계획을 계속해서 진행할 수 있습니다. 높은 수익을 올릴 수 있는 기회가 될만한 **⑦몇몇** 지역을 추천받았으며, 조만간 어디로 진출할지 결정할 것입니다. **⑧도시 북부 지역이 유망해 보였습니다.** 결정이 마무리되면 다음 분기 세부 계획이 게시될 예정입니다.

어휘

regrettable 유감스러운 | deal 거래 | fall through 실패로 돌아가다, 불발되다 | pleasure 기쁨 | be known for ~로 알려져 있다 | provide 제공하다 | funding 재정 지원 | tech 기술상의 | start-up 스타트업 | management 경영, 관리 | portfolio (특정 회사의) 서비스 범위, 포트폴리오 | proceed with ~를 계속 진행하다 | plan 계획 | expand into ~확장하다 | area 지역 | suggest

추천하다, 제안하다 | lucrative 수익성 좋은 | opportunity 기회 | decision 결정 | shortly 곧 | detailed 상세한 | quarter 분기 | post 게시하다 | finalize 마무리하다, 완결하다

5. 동사의 시제

해설　빈칸은 주어 we에 대한 동사 자리이다. LCK Ventures와의 계약이 무산되어 유감이라는 빈칸 앞 문장의 내용을 고려할 때, 하지만 새로운 거래를 공개하게 돼 기쁘다는 내용으로 이어져야 문맥상 연결이 자연스러우므로 현재 시제 (B)가 정답이다.

+ Key word

It is **regrettable that the deal with LCK Ventures fell through. However, it is with great pleasure we reveal a new deal** with Baratic Corporation.

6. 어휘 - 명사

해설　빈칸은 전치사 for의 목적어 자리이다. for 전치사구가 앞에 있는 the need를 수식하며 접속사 while로 연결된 두 절의 내용을 고려할 때, 새로운 거래를 맺게 된 기업은 주로 기술 스타트업에 자금을 지원하지만 경영진이 포트폴리오 다각화가 필요하다고 판단하면서 이 같은 결정으로 이어졌다는 내용으로 연결되어야 문맥상 자연스러우므로 (C)가 정답이다.

+ Key word

While Baratic is a company best known for providing funding for tech start-ups, the management team there saw the need for diversification in the firm's portfolio.

7. 한정사

해설　빈칸은 문장의 주어인 areas의 앞 자리이다. 빈칸에는 명사 areas를 앞에서 수식하거나 areas를 목적어로 취하는 동사 주어가 올 수 있다. 접속사 and로 연결된 두 문장의 내용을 고려할 때, 몇몇 지역을 추천 받았으며 조만간 결정할 것이라는 내용으로 이어져야 문맥상 연결이 자연스러우므로 명사 areas를 수식하는 한정사 (B)가 정답이다.

+ Key word

Several areas have been suggested as lucrative opportunities, **and we will make a decision** regarding the location of our expansion shortly.

8. 문장 선택

(A) 도시 북부 지역이 유망해 보였습니다.
(B) 우리는 최근에 규모를 줄여야만 했습니다.
(C) 이러한 회의에서는 좀처럼 제안이 받아들여지지 않습니다.
(D) 기술 업계는 최근에 자금이 부족했습니다.

해설　빈칸 앞 문장의 조만간 어디로 진출할지 결정할 것이라는 내용을 고려할 때, 진출 지역 선정과 관련된 내용으로 이어져야 문맥상 연결이 자연스러우므로 (A)가 정답이다.

+ Key word

Several areas have been suggested as lucrative opportunities, and we will make a decision regarding the location of our expansion shortly. The northern parts of the city have looked promising.

CASE 집중훈련

본서 p.129

1. (B) **2.** (C) **3.** (B) **4.** (C) **5.** (B) **6.** (A)
7. (A) **8.** (D)

1. 형용사 자리

The HR Department decided that Friday's reception will require **additional** seating.

인사부는 금요일에 있을 환영회에 추가적인 좌석배치가 필요하다고 결정했다.

해설 빈칸은 'seating (좌석배치)'이란 명사를 수식하는 형용사 자리이므로 (B)가 정답이다.

어휘 reception 환영행사, 리셉션 | require ~를 필요로 하다, 요구하다 | seating 좌석, 좌석배치

✦ Key point

-ing로 끝나는 명사는 다음과 같다:
marketing 마케팅, seating 좌석배치, pricing 가격책정, funding 재정지원, ticketing 발권, etc.

2. 동명사 자리

Felrafel Enterprises is interested in **exploring** new business models as part of an ongoing effort to expand its production lines.

Felrafel Enterprises는 생산 라인을 확대하기 위한 지속적인 노력의 일환으로 새로운 비즈니스 모델을 탐험하는 데 관심이 있다.

해설 빈칸은 전치사 in의 목적어 자리이다. 전치사 in의 목적어가 되면서 뒤에 명사구 new business models를 목적어로 가질 수 있는 것은 동명사이므로 (C)가 정답이다.

어휘 be interested in ~에 관심이 있다 | ongoing 지속적인, 계속되는 | expand 확대하다, 확장하다 | production line 생산 라인 | explore 개척하다, 탐구하다 | exploration 개척, 탐구

✦ Key point

동명사와 명사는 그 쓰임이 비슷하지만, 동명사는 동사의 기능을 가지고 있어 뒤에 목적어를 취할 수 있다는 것이 명사와 다른 점이다.

3. 동명사 자리

After **assessing** the product specifications, Ms. Nunez decided not to upgrade the refrigeration system in her factory.

제품 사양을 살펴본 후, Nunez 씨는 자신의 공장에 있는 냉장 시스템을 업그레이드하지 않기로 결정했다.

해설 빈칸은 전치사이자 접속사인 after와 명사구를 연결하는 자리이다. 뒤에 오는 명사구를 목적어로 취하되, 전치사 after의 목적어 역할을 해야 하므로 동명사 (B)가 정답이다.

어휘 specification 사양, 설명서 | refrigeration 냉장, 냉각 | factory 공장

✦ Key point

① after가 전치사일 때는 뒤에 명사구를, 접속사일 때는 뒤에 절을 취할 수 있다.
② 명사 역할을 하면서 명사(구)를 목적어로 취할 수 있는 것은 동명사이다.

4. 명사 자리

The temporary **closing** of schools in the area was unavoidable due to the inclement weather conditions.

악천후로 인해 지역의 학교들은 임시 폐쇄를 피할 수 없었다.

해설 빈칸은 The temporary의 수식을 받는 명사 자리이므로 (C)가 정답이다.

어휘 temporary 임시의 | unavoidable 피할 수 없는 | inclement 좋지 못한

✦ Key point

closing은 '폐쇄, 폐점'을 의미한다.

5-8번은 다음 회람에 관한 문제입니다.

수신: all@davidwallaceuniversity.edu
발신: 대표 Doug Benson
날짜: 1월 2일
제목: 공용 공간

새로 단장한 Foster-Allen Hall이 이번 학기에 다시 개방될 것임을 발표하게 되어 매우 기쁩니다. 강좌 진행뿐만 아니라, 이 건물은 이제 회의 또는 활동들을 위한 몇몇 공용 공간들을 포함하게 될 것입니다. 이 모든 용도실은 Foster-Allen 중앙 로비에서 **⑤입장 가능합니다.**

공간들은 10명에서 25명 규모의 게스트들을 수용할 수 있도록 크기가 다양하며, 학생과 교직원 모두가 사용할 수 있습니다. **⑥공간들 중 하나를 이용하기 위해선 사전 예약이 요구됩니다.** Patrick Lucas가 2월 15일까지는 용도실 예약을 담당하게 될 것입니다. **⑦그때, 그는 입학 부서로 복귀해 근무할 것입니다.** 저희는 현재 정규직 캠퍼스 행사담당자로 근무할 지원자들을 인터뷰하고 있습니다. 이 직원이 새 용도실 예약의 **⑧감독**을 맡게 될 것입니다.

어휘

common 공통의, 흔한 | refurbish 새로 꾸미다 | semester 학기 | host 주최하다, 진행하다 | vary 다르다 | anywhere from A to B (수량·시간·가치 따위) A와 B 사이의 어딘가(에서) | A and B alike A와 B 모두 | in charge of ~를 담당하는 | admission 입학, 입장 | serve 근무하다, 복무하다 | permanent 영구적인, 정규직의

5. 어휘 – 형용사

해설 accessible은 '이용[접근] 가능한' 외에도 '입장 가능한'이란 의미가 있으므로 새로 개방되는 공간을 로비에서 입장할 수 있다라는 것이 해석상 적절하다. 따라서 (B)가 정답이다.

✦ Key word

All of these **rooms are accessible from** the Foster-Allen central **lobby.**

6. 문장 선택

(A) 공간들 중 하나를 이용하기 위해선 사전 예약이 요구됩니다.
(B) Lucas 씨가 그 회의의 개회를 이끌 것입니다.
(C) 리모델링 프로젝트는 여름까지 연기되었습니다.
(D) Butler 도서관에도 더 많은 용도실이 추가되었습니다.

해설 앞의 내용을 살펴보면 새로운 공간들을 학생과 교직원들이 사용할 수 있다고 하였으므로 이 공간 이용에 관한 내용이 계속 이어지는 것이 자연스럽다. 따라서 (A)가 정답이다.

✦ Key word

The spaces vary in size, holding anywhere from 10 to 25 guests, and **they may be used by students and staff alike. Advance booking is required to use one of the spaces.**

7. 접속부사

해설 Patrick Lucas가 2월 15일까지만 예약을 담당할 것이라고 했으므로 그가 입학 부서에 복귀해 근무하는 것은 2월 15일 이후임을 알 수 있다. 따라서 앞의 날짜를 지칭하며 '그때, 그즈음에'라는 부사구가 들어가는 것이 가장 자연스러우므로 (A)가 정답이다.

+ Key word

Patrick Lucas will be in charge of room reservations **until February 15. At that time**, he will go back to work in the Admissions Department.

8. 동명사 자리

해설 앞에 전치사가 있으므로 supervise '감독하다'를 동명사로 바꾸어 '예약을 감독하는 것'이라고 쓰는 것이 문법/해석상 가장 적절하므로 (D)가 정답이다.

+ Key word

This employee will be in charge **of supervising reservations** of the new rooms.

CASE 집중훈련
본서 p.131

1. (B) **2.** (C) **3.** (C) **4.** (D) **5.** (D) **6.** (B)
7. (C) **8.** (A)

---

1. 동명사를 목적어로 취하는 동사

The designer suggested **chainging** the font to enhance the readability of the brochure.
그 디자이너는 책자의 가독성을 향상시키기 위해 폰트를 바꿀 것을 제안했다.

해설 빈칸은 타동사 suggest의 목적어 자리이다. suggest '제안하다'는 뜻으로 동명사를 목적어로 취할 수 있으므로 동명사 (B)가 정답이다.

어휘 font 서체, 폰트 | enhance 향상시키다 | readability 가독성, 읽기 쉬움

+ Key point

동명사를 목적어로 받을 수 있는 타동사로는 consider, mind, include, avoid, suggest, recommend, quit, discontinue, give up 등이 있다.

---

2. 동명사를 목적어로 취하는 동사

It would be better for Fabulous Footwear to discontinue **producing** sandals and focus on hiking boots instead.
Fabulous Footwear는 샌들 생산을 중단하고, 대신에 등산화에 중점을 두는 것이 더 나을 것이다.

해설 '~을 그만두다'라는 뜻의 타동사 discontinue는 동명사를 목적어로 취하므로 (C)가 정답이다.

어휘 discontinue 중단하다 | focus on ~에 중점을 두다 | hiking boots 등산화 | instead 그 대신

---

3. 동명사 관용 표현

Upon arriving at the main building, all visitors must sign in at the reception desk and obtain an identification tag.
본관에 도착하는 대로, 모든 방문객들은 접수 데스크에서 서명하고 신

분 배지를 받아야만 한다.

해설 빈칸은 뒤의 동명사를 목적어로 갖는 전치사 자리이다. 문맥상 도착하는 대로 해야 할 것을 알려주는 내용으로 전개되는 것이 자연스러우므로 'upon ~ing(~하는 대로, ~하자마자)'라는 관용 표현을 완성해줄 (C)가 정답이다.

어휘 arrive 도착하다 | sign in 도착 서명을 하다 | reception desk 접수 데스크 | obtain 받다, 얻다 | identification tag 신분 배지, 인식표 | out of ~밖으로, ~에서 벗어나서 | within ~이내에 | upon ~하는 대로 | up to 최고 ~까지

+ Key word

Upon arriving at the main building, all visitors must sign in at the reception desk and obtain an identification tag.

---

4. 어휘 - 동사

The spike in interest in Pavilion Tech can be **attributed** to the variety of projects the company has undertaken over the past few months.
Pavilion Tech에 급등한 관심은 지난 몇 개월동안 회사가 착수해 온 프로젝트들의 다양성 덕으로 보여진다.

해설 attribute는 attribute A to B 'A를 B의 덕(탓)으로 보다(돌리다)'로 쓰인다. 해당 문장은 수동태로 바뀌어있지만 빈칸 뒤에 여전히 전치사 to가 있고 '급등한 관심이 ~덕으로 여겨진다'라는 것이 문맥상 적절하므로 (D)가 정답이다.

어휘 spike 급등 | interest in ~에 대한 관심 | variety 다양성 | undertake 착수하다

+ Key word

The spike in **interest** in Pavilion Tech can be **attributed to** the variety of projects the company has undertaken over the past few months.

5-8번은 다음 이메일에 관한 문제입니다.

수신: Ronald Kuba
발신: Piper Keurig
날짜: 11월 16일
제목: 화요일 만남

Kuba 교수님께,

생물학 대학원 과정에 대해 이야기하는데 시간을 내주셔서 감사합니다. 교수님의 **⑤통찰력**은 매우 도움이 되었고, 저는 이제 지원하기 전에 유급 조교 직책에 대해 몇몇 대학에 이메일을 쓸 계획입니다. 언급하셨던 학교로 시작할 거예요.

또한 제안하셨던 대로, 저는 생물과학 대학원 협회(BSGS) 온라인 포럼에 회원자격을 **⑥고려해볼 겁니다. ⑦또래** 동료들과 함께 문제를 논의하는 것이 도움이 될 것입니다. 이런 종류의 재원을 웹에서 얻을 수 있다는 것을 알게 되어 좋습니다.

다시 한번, 교수님의 **⑧관대한** 조언에 매우 감사드립니다.

감사합니다.

Piper Keurig

어휘
appreciate 고마워하다 | graduate 대학원생, 졸업자 | biology 생물학 | extremely 극도로 | helpful 도움이 되는 | regarding ~에 대해 | paid 유급의 | teaching assistant 조교, 보조교사 | apply 지원하다, 적용하다 | per ~에 따라, ~마다 | suggestion 제안 | forum 포럼, 토론회 | issue 문제, 사안 | fellow 동료, 동년배 | peer 또래 | resource 자원, 재원

5. 어휘 - 명사

해설 빈칸은 문장의 주어 자리이다. 빈칸 앞 문장의 대학원 프로그램에 대해 이야기하는데 시간을 내줘서 감사하다는 내용을 고려할 때, 문맥상 교수님의 조언해준 내용, 즉, 통찰력이 도움이 되었다는 내용이 되어야 자연스러우므로 (D)가 정답이다. per your suggestion, your advice 등도 단서이다.

+ Key word

I appreciate you making time to discuss graduate programs in Biology. Your **insights** were extremely **helpful**, …

6. 어휘 - 동사

해설 문맥상 교수의 조언에 따라 협회 포럼에 회원으로 가입하는 것을 고려해볼 것이라는 내용이 되어야 자연스러우므로 (B)가 정답이다.

+ Key word

Also, **per your suggestion**, I will **consider a membership** in the Biological Sciences Graduates Society's (BSGS) online forum.

7. 문장 선택

(A) 곧 채용 공고가 꽉 차게 될 겁니다.
(B) 다음 달에 멤버십을 연장할 수 있을지 모르겠어요.
(C) 또래 동료들과 함께 문제를 논의하는 것이 도움이 될 것입니다.
(D) 저는 그녀의 최신 연구에 대한 강의에 참석하는 것을 기대하고 있습니다.

해설 빈칸 앞 문장의 '대학원생 협회 온라인 포럼에 가입하는 것을 고려해보겠다는 내용을 고려할 때, 협회에 있는 또래의 동료들과 포럼에서 문제들에 대해 논의하는 것이 도움이 될 것이라는 내용으로 이어지는 것이 자연스러우므로 (C)가 정답이다.

+ Key word

I will **consider a membership in the Biological Sciences Graduates Society's (BSGS) online forum**. It will be helpful discussing issues with my fellow peers.

8. 형용사 자리

해설 빈칸은 명사 advice를 수식하는 형용사 자리이므로 (A)가 정답이다.

CASE 집중훈련
본서 p.133

1. (B) **2.** (B) **3.** (D) **4.** (D) **5.** (A) **6.** (D)
7. (A) **8.** (C)

---

1. 현재분사 vs. 과거분사

Ms. Whitlock is examining the bids to choose the company best **qualified** for the project.
Whitlock 씨는 그 프로젝트에 가장 적격인 회사를 선정하기 위한 입찰을 검토하고 있다.

해설 'best ~ project'까지 앞의 명사 the company를 후치 수식하는 분사 구문으로, 문맥상 '그 프로젝트에 가장 적격인 회사'라는 의미가 되어야 자연스러우므로 과거분사 (B)가 정답이다.

어휘 examine 검토하다, 조사하다 | bid 입찰 | choose 선택하다, 고르다 | qualified for ~에 적합한, 적격인

+ Key point

① 과거분사는 수동, 현재분사는 능동의 의미를 갖는다.
② 주격 관계절을 구성하는 「관계사 + be동사」는 생략 가능하다: ~ the company (which is) best qualified for the project

---

2. 현재분사 vs. 과거분사

Mobile Meals has customizable catering menus to satisfy all clients' **entertaining** needs.
Mobile Meals는 모든 고객의 접대 수요를 충족시키기 위해 맞춤식 케이터링 메뉴를 제공한다.

해설 빈칸은 명사 needs를 수식하는 자리이다. 문맥상 '접대 수요를 충족시키기 위해'라는 의미가 되어야 자연스러우므로 현재분사 (B)가 정답이다.

어휘 customizable 맞춤형의 | catering 음식공급 | satisfy 만족시키다 | need 필요, 요구

+ Key point

현재분사 vs. 과거분사: 현재분사는 수식하는 대상과 의미상 능동 관계를, 과거분사는 수식하는 대상과 의미상 수동 관계를 갖는다.

---

3. 현재분사 vs. 과거분사

The executives of Morton Fragrances sent an e-mail to the staff members **commending** them for the exceptional sales revenue this quarter.
Morton Fragrances의 임원진은 직원들에게 이번 분기 뛰어난 판매 실적을 칭찬하는 이메일을 보냈다.

해설 빈칸은 완전한 문장과 목적격 대명사 사이의 자리이다. 빈칸 앞에 완전한 문장이 있고 별도의 접속사가 없으므로, 빈칸은 문장과 빈칸 뒤 이어지는 부분을 연결하는 준동사 자리이다. 빈칸 뒤 목적격 대명사 them이 있으므로 현재분사 (D)가 정답이다.

어휘 executive 임원 | exceptional 예외적인, 뛰어난 | sales 판매 | revenue 수익 | quarter 분기

+ Key point

타동사의 현재분사는 목적어를 가질 수 있다.

---

4. 어휘 - 형용사

Because of the **impending** typhoon, ferry services will be suspended for the next two days.
임박한 태풍으로 인해, 페리 운행이 앞으로 2일간 중단될 것이다.

해설 빈칸은 명사 typhoon을 수식하는 형용사 자리이다. 문맥상 '태풍이 임박하여 페리 운행이 중단될 것'이라는 의미가 자연스러우므로 (D)가 정답이다.

어휘 typhoon 태풍 | ferry 페리 | suspend 중단하다

+ Key word

Because of the impending typhoon, ferry services will be suspended for the next two days.

5-8번은 다음 이메일에 관한 문제입니다.

수신: 제품 디자인팀
발신: Brandon Conner
날짜: 7월 12일
제목: 축하 저녁식사

팀원 여러분께,

팀 **5**전원의 노고를 치하하고자, 다음주 팀 회식을 제안하고 싶습니다. Bell 영업부장님께 근사한 이탈리안 레스토랑 **6**추천을 받았습니다. 이 일대 좋은 레스토랑은 다 알고 계신 것 같더군요. 식이요법 중이신 분들이 계신 걸로 알고 있습니다. **7**그곳에서 일반 채식주의자 및 완전한 채식주의자를 위한 음식을 제공한다는 것을 제가 확인했습니다. 그 자리에 Ellis Holt도 초대하고 싶은데요. 아시다시피, 다음 달에 저희 팀에 합류할 예정입니다. **8**소개는 우리 팀에 익숙해지는데 크게 도움을 줄 거예요.

감사합니다.

Brandon Conner, 제품 디자인부장

KD 제조사

어휘
celebration 기념, 축하 | celebrate 축하하다, 기념하다 | hard work 노고 | propose 제안하다 | head 책임자 | area 지역, 일대 | dietary 식이요법의 | restriction 제한, 규제 | acclimatize 익숙해지다, 적응하다 | greatly 크게, 대단히 | manufacturing 제조

5. 부정 대명사

해설 빈칸은 전치사 from의 목적어인 대명사 자리이다. 팀 회식을 제안한다는 주절의 내용을 고려할 때, '팀 전원의 노고를 치하하고 싶다'는 의미가 되어야 문맥상 자연스러우므로 (A)가 정답이다.

6. 명사

해설 빈칸은 동사 have 뒤의 자리이다. 동사 recommend는 목적어를 필요로 하는 타동사임을 고려할 때 빈칸 뒤에 for 전치사구가 있어 빈칸에는 recommend의 동사형이 올 수 없으므로, 동사 have의 목적어에 해당하는 명사 (D)가 정답이다.

7. 문장 삽입

(A) 그곳에서 일반 채식주의자 및 완전한 채식주의자를 위한 음식을 제공한다는 것을 제가 확인했습니다.
(B) 저희가 조금만 일찍 도착하면 주말에 일하는 것을 피할 수 있습니다.
(C) 새 프로젝트는 이번 분기에 시작될 것입니다.
(D) 다른 팀들은 이미 월 예산을 초과했습니다.

해설 빈칸 앞 문장의 '식이요법 중이신 분들이 계신 걸로 알고 있다'는 내용을 고려할 때, '식당에서 그곳에서 일반 채식주의자 및 완전한 채식주의자를 위한 음식을 제공한다는 것을 확인했다'는 내용으로 이어져야 문맥상 자연스러우므로 (A)가 정답이다.

+ **Key word**
I understand there are people with dietary restrictions. I confirmed that it does cater to vegetarians and vegans.

8. 어휘 – 명사

해설 빈칸은 문장의 주어 자리이다. 빈칸 앞 부분에서 '다음 달 팀에 합류할 Ellis Holt도 초대하고 싶다'는 내용을 고려할 때, '서로 소개하며 안면을 트면 팀에 적응하는데 크게 도움이 될 것'이라는 의미로 이어져야 문맥상 자연스러우므로 (C)가 정답이다.

+ **Key word**
I would like to also invite Ellis Holt to join us. As you know, he will be joining our team next month. Introductions will help him acclimatize to our team greatly.

CASE 집중훈련

본서 p.135

1. (A) 2. (A) 3. (D) 4. (C) 5. (C) 6. (B)
7. (D) 8. (A)

1. 감정 동사의 분사

I am **pleased** to announce that our advertising campaign was a huge success.
우리의 광고 캠페인이 큰 성공이었음을 알려드리게 되어 기쁩니다.

해설 빈칸은 be동사 뒤에서 주어 I의 보어 역할을 하는 형용사 자리이다. please는 감정 동사로 주체가 사람일 때 과거분사를 사용함을 고려할 때, 문맥상 '~를 알려드리게 되어 저는 기쁩니다'라는 의미가 되어야 자연스러우므로 (A)가 정답이다.

어휘 announce 알리다, 발표하다 | huge 큰, 엄청난

+ **Key point**
현재분사는 능동(~한 상태를 유발시키는), 과거분사는 수동(~한 상태가 된)의 의미를 갖는다.

---

2. 감정 동사의 분사

Analysis of the sales data revealed some **surprising** information about the spending habits of customers in their 20's.
매출 자료의 분석은 20대 소비자의 소비습관에 대해 상당히 놀라운 정보를 드러냈다.

해설 빈칸은 명사 information을 꾸미는 형용사 자리이다. 보기의 감정분사 surprising '놀라운'과 surprised '(사람이) 놀란' 중 고려할 때, '놀라운 정보'라는 의미가 되어야 자연스러우므로 (A)가 정답이다.

어휘 analysis 분석 | reveal 드러내다 | spending habit 소비습관

+ **Key point**
감정동사의 현재분사는 능동(~한 감정을 유발시키는), 과거분사는 수동(~한 감정을 느끼는)의 의미를 갖는다.

---

3. 감정 동사의 분사

Although the latest Blaze tablet PC has received largely positive reviews for its affordable price point, its sales have thus far been **disappointing**.
최신 Blaze 태블릿 PC가 알맞은 소매가에 주로 긍정적인 평가를 받았지만 지금까지의 매출은 실망스럽다.

해설 be동사 뒤의 보어 자리에 오는 감정동사 disappoint의 알맞은 분사 형태를 묻는 문제이다. 감정동사 disappoint와 주어의 수동/능동 관계를 해석해 보면 매출은 실망스러운 감정을 유발하는 요인이므로 현재분사인 (D)가 정답이다.

어휘 latest 최신의 | largely 주로 | affordable 알맞은 가격의 | price point 기준 소매가 | thus far 이제까지는, 여태까지

---

4. 어휘 – 명사

Sherman Inc. now provides assistance of tuition for personnel interested in the **completion** of certification programs.
Sherman 주식회사는 인증프로그램 수료에 관심이 있는 직원들에게 현재 수업료 지원을 제공한다.

해설 빈칸은 of 전명구의 수식을 받는 명사 자리이다. 문맥상 '자격증 프로그램 수료에 관심이 있는 직원'이라는 의미가 되어야 자연스러우므로 (C)가 정답이다.

어휘 provide 제공하다 | assistance 보조, 지원 | tuition 수업(료) | personnel 직원 | certification 증명, 인증

✦ Key word
Sherman Inc. now **provides assistance of tuition for personnel interested in the completion of certification programs**.

5-8번은 다음 이메일에 관한 문제입니다.

수신: Christian Shelton
발신: web@eatingbetter.com
날짜: 8월 2일
제목: EatingBetter Foods

Shelton 씨께,

세계 최고의 식단 및 운동 전문가, EatingBetter Foods를 소개해 드리게 되어 **⑤매우 기쁩니다**. 저희는 개인별 건강 목표에 맞춰 최고의 영양관리 및 운동 조언만을 제공해 드리기 위해 최선을 다합니다. 웹사이트를 둘러보시면, 저희가 제공하는 전체 서비스 목록을 보실 수 있습니다. **⑥개인별 운동 프로그램뿐만 아니라 식사 계획도 포함됩니다**. 저희는 보다 건강한 식사와 생활을 통해 사람들의 삶을 향상시키는데 전념하고 있으며, 오늘 귀하의 인생을 변화시키는데 도움을 드리고 싶습니다.

무료 상담을 **⑦잡으시려면** 030-555-9712로 오늘 저희에게 연락주세요. 이달 안에 등록하는 **⑧고객** 모두 2달 동안 30퍼센트 개점 할인을 받게 됩니다.

감사합니다.

EatingBetter Foods 일동

어휘
foremost 가장 유명[중요]한 | exercise 운동 | expert 전문가 | cater 음식을 공급하다 | nutritional 영양상의 | be committed to ~에 전념하다, 헌신하다 | better 개선하다 | transform 변형시키다 | complimentary 무료의 | consultation 상담 | sign up 등록하다 | grand opening 개장

---

5. 감정 동사의 분사

해설 빈칸은 be동사 뒤 보어 자리이다. 주어가 we이고 빈칸 뒤 to부정사가 있으며 문맥상 '저희는 EatingBetter Foods를 소개해드리게 되어 너무 기쁘다'는 의미가 되어야 자연스러우므로, 'be thrilled to V(V하게 되어 매우 기쁘다)'의 표현을 완성하는 과거분사 (C)가 정답이다.

✦ Key point
① 감정을 나타내는 분사형 형용사: 과거분사는 사람을, 현재분사는 사물을 주어로 취할 수 있다.
② 보어 자리에 명사가 오는 경우, 주어와 의미상 동격 관계가 되어야 한다.

6. 문장 선택

(A) EatingBetter Foods는 다른 사람들의 삶을 개선하려는 욕구에서 탄생했습니다.
(B) 개인별 운동 프로그램뿐만 아니라 식사 계획도 포함됩니다.
(C) 또한 직원 명단과 자격증도 요청할 수 있습니다.
(D) 그것들은 추가 비용이 들 수 있습니다.

해설 빈칸 앞 문장의 웹사이트에 제공하는 서비스 목록이 있다는 내용을 고

려할 때, 빈칸에는 services를 They로 받으면서 해당 서비스와 관련된 내용이 들어가야 자연스러우므로 (B)가 정답이다.

✦ Key word
If you take a look at our Web site, you can **see the full list of services we can provide. They include eating plans as well as personalized workout programs.**

7. to부정사의 태

해설 빈칸은 완전한 문장과 명사구를 연결하는 준동사 자리이다. 빈칸 뒤 목적어에 해당하는 명사구가 있으며, 문맥상 '상담을 잡으려면'이라는 목적의 의미를 전달해야 자연스러우므로 능동형 to부정사 (D)가 정답이다.

8. 어휘 - 명사

해설 빈칸 앞 문장의 무료 상담을 잡으려면 연락달라는 내용을 고려할 때, '이번 달 안에 등록하는 고객 모두 할인을 받게 된다'는 내용이 되어야 문맥상 자연스러우므로 (A)가 정답이다.

✦ Key word
Contact us today at 030-555-9712 **to arrange a complimentary consultation. All customers who sign up within the month will receive** our grand opening **discount** of 30 percent off for two months.

CASE 집중훈련 본서 p.137

1. (B) **2.** (C) **3.** (B) **4.** (A) **5.** (B) **6.** (B)
7. (C) **8.** (D)

---

1. 형용사로 굳어진 분사

The **following** e-mail is the summary of the order that we are currently processing for you.
다음의 이메일은 저희가 귀하를 위해 현재 처리하고 있는 주문에 관한 개요입니다.

해설 빈칸은 문장의 주어인 명사 e-mail을 수식해줄 형용사 자리이다. 문맥상 '다음의 이메일은 ~'이라는 의미를 완성해줄 현재분사 형용사인 (B)가 정답이다.

어휘 summary 개요, 개괄, 요약본 | currently 현재의 | process 처리하다

2. 형용사로 굳어진 분사

GL Optical Center will be open during the holiday season with **limited** hours.
GL Optical Center에서는 연휴기간 동안 제한된 영업시간으로 개방될 것입니다.

해설 빈칸은 명사 hours를 수식하는 자리이다. 제한된 시간만 개방된다는 의미가 되어야 문맥상 자연스러우므로 과거분사 (C)가 정답이다.

어휘 optical 시각적인 | hours 영업시간

✦ Key point
과거분사 vs. 현재분사: 수식 받는 명사를 기준으로, 과거분사는 수동(~한 상태가 된), 현재분사는 능동(~한 상태를 유발시키는)의 의미를 갖는다.

3. 어휘 – 형용사

At Harrison Technical College only **renowned** instructors will be teaching your classes.

Harrison 전문 대학에서는 오직 유명 강사들만 여러분의 수업을 가르칠 것입니다.

해설 빈칸은 명사 instructors를 수식하는 형용사 자리이다. 유명한 강사라는 의미가 되어야 문맥상 자연스러우므로 (B)가 정답이다.

어휘 instructor 강사

+ **Key word**

At Harrison Technical College **only renowned instructors will be teaching your classes.**

....

4. 형용사로 굳어진 분사

According to the Department of Transportation, the addition of the new bus routes should reduce traffic congestion in the **surrounding** area.

교통국에 따르면, 새 버스 노선의 추가가 주변 지역의 교통 혼잡을 감소시켜줄 것이다.

해설 명사 앞 빈칸이므로 형용사의 역할을 하는 분사 (A) surrounding 또는 (D) surrounded가 정답 후보인데, '인근의, 주위의'라는 뜻은 surrounding이 순수 형용사로 쓰이므로 (A)가 정답이다.

어휘 according to ~에 따르면 | addition 부가 | traffic congestion 교통 혼잡

5-8번은 다음 이메일에 관한 문제입니다.

수신: 회계팀 직원
발신: Donna Cutler
날짜: 12월 1일
제목: Ronald Kaepernick

여러분, 안녕하세요.

여러분 모두에게 알려드릴 아쉬운 소식이 있습니다: Ronald Kaepernick이 우리 회사를 떠나 Douglass 금융에 수석 분석가로 합류하게 되었습니다. 그의 **5마지막** 근무일은 다음 주 수요일인 12일이 될 것입니다.

그가 우리와 함께 하는 동안, Ronald는 회계팀에서 매우 중요한 역할을 맡아왔습니다. 지난 몇 년간, 그는 가장 민감한 대형 프로젝트들을 리드하며 탁월함을 보여주었습니다. 그러면서도, 그는 회사 내에서 만나게 되는 모든 사람들과 강하고 지속적인 유대관계를 **6발전시켰습니다.** 훌륭한 업무를 옳은 방법으로 행하는 그의 신념은 우리에게 엄청나게 도움을 주었습니다. **7우리 모두는 Ronald의 긍정적인 태도뿐만 아니라 그의 유머감각을 그리워할 것입니다.**

Ronald가 앞으로 하는 일이 잘 되길 바라고, 그의 새로운 직장에서도 **8계속된** 성공을 기원합니다.

행운을 빌며,

Donna Cutler, 부사장

어휘

bittersweet 시원섭섭한 | leave 떠나다 | financial 재정의, 금융의 | analyst 분석가 | crucial 중대한 | accounting 회계 | several 몇몇의 | excel 뛰어나다, 탁월하다 | lead 이끌다 | sensitive 민감한 | lasting 지속적인, 오랜 | bond 유대 | in contact with ~과 연락하는 | commitment 헌신, 약속, 견념 | tremendously 엄청나게 | go forward 전진하다, 진행시키다

5. 어휘 – 형용사

해설 빈칸은 소유격 대명사 his와 함께 명사 day를 수식하는 자리이다. 빈칸 앞 문장의 '우리 회사를 떠나게 되었다'는 내용을 고려할 때, '그의 마지막 날은 다음주 수요일이 될 것'이라는 내용으로 이어져야 자연스러우므로 (B)가 정답이다.

+ **Key word**

I have some bittersweet news to share with you all: Ronald **Kaepernick will be leaving our company** to join Douglass Financial as a senior analyst. **His last day here will be next Wednesday,** the 12th.

6. 동사의 시제

해설 빈칸은 주어 he와 목적어 bonds 사이 동사 자리이다. 문장 후반부 everyone을 수식하는 관계절의 시제가 과거(came)임을 고려할 때, 주절의 시제 역시 과거가 되어야 하므로 (B)가 정답이다.

+ **Key word**

While doing so, **he developed** strong and lasting **bonds with** just about **everyone he came in contact with** at the company.

7. 문장 선택

(A) 그는 Middleton 대학교에서 수학 석사 학위를 취득했습니다.
(B) 인터뷰는 다음 주 목요일에 동부 회의실에서 진행됩니다.
(C) 우리 모두는 Ronald의 긍정적인 태도뿐만 아니라 그의 유머감각을 그리워할 것입니다.
(D) 그의 프로젝트 작업은 올해 3/4분기에 기록적인 이익을 가져왔습니다.

해설 빈칸 앞 문장의 '훌륭한 업무를 옳은 방법으로 행하는 그의 신념은 우리에게 엄청나게 도움을 주었다'는 내용을 고려할 때, 그가 재직하는 동안 보여준 장점들을 이어서 소개하는 내용으로 이어져야 자연스러우므로 '우리 모두 그의 유머와 긍정적인 태도를 그리워할 것'이라는 내용의 (C)가 정답이다.

+ **Key word**

His commitment to doing excellent work the right way helped us tremendously. All of us will miss Ronald's sense of humor as well as his positive attitude.

8. 형용사로 굳어진 분사

해설 빈칸은 명사 success를 수식하는 자리이므로 (D)가 정답이다. continued는 '지속적인'이라는 뜻의 순수 형용사이다.

+ **Key point**

분사(현재분사, 과거분사)는 형용사처럼 명사를 앞에서 수식할 수 있다.

CASE 집중훈련

1. (A)　2. (D)　3. (D)　4. (C)　5. (D)　6. (A)
7. (D)　8. (B)

1. 분사 구문

Ms. Liam, a talk show host, recently secured an exclusive interview with a world-famous pop star, **making** it her most celebrated guest yet.

토크쇼 호스트, Liam 씨는 최근 세계적으로 유명한 팝스타와 독점 인터뷰를 확보했는데, 그것이 이제껏 자신의 가장 유명한 게스트였다.

해설 「접속사+주어+동사」 구조의 종속절에서 접속사와 주어 생략 후 분사 구문으로 전환한 것으로, 뒤에 목적어 it이 있으므로 능동의 의미를 나타내는 현재분사 (A)가 정답이다.

어휘 secure 확보하다 | exclusive 독점적인 | celebrated 유명한

---

2. 분사 구문

When **consistently** used, Tia Skincare Device rejuvenates your face by toning and lifting your skin.
꾸준히 사용하면, Tia 스킨케어 기기는 피부를 탄력 있고 탱탱하게 만들어 활기를 되찾아줍니다.

해설 빈칸은 when 종속절 내 과거분사를 수식하는 자리이므로 부사 (D)가 정답이다.

어휘 device 기구, 장치 | rejuvenate 활기를 되찾게 하다 | tone (피부를) 탄력 있게 만들다 | lift 들어올리다; 주름살을 펴다

✦ Key point
① 시간 접속사 when이 이끄는 종속절에서 주절과 주어가 동일한 경우, 종속절 내 「주어+be동사」는 생략될 수 있다.
② 분사나 동사를 수식할 수 있는 품사는 부사이다.

---

3. 어휘 - 부사

Utilizing high-quality wood will lower the chance of warping, **consequently** increasing the structural integrity.
품질이 좋은 목재를 사용하는 것은 휘어질 가능성을 낮춰주어, 결과적으로 견고함을 높여줄 것이다.

해설 빈칸은 분사 구문을 수식하는 부사 자리이다. 주절과 분사 구문의 관계를 고려할 때, 문맥상 '휘어질 가능성을 낮춰주어, 결과적으로는 견고함을 높인다'는 의미가 되어야 자연스러우므로 (D)가 정답이다. 이 문장처럼 분사 앞에 consequently, then, thus 등을 묻는 문제가 종종 출제된다.

어휘 utilize 이용하다 | high-quality 고품질의 | lower 낮추다 | warp 휘다, 틀어지다 | structural 구조적인 | integrity 온전함, 완전성

✦ Key word
Utilizing high-quality wood will **lower the chance of warping, consequently increasing** the **structural integrity**.

---

4. 분사 구문

Staff members who take public transportation to work will be eligible for travel reimbursement **starting on** Monday.
대중교통으로 출근하는 직원들은 월요일부터 교통비를 환급받을 자격을 얻을 것이다.

해설 빈칸은 문장과 Monday를 연결하는 자리이다. 문맥상 '대중교통으로 출근하는 직원들은 월요일부터 교통비를 환급 받을 자격을 얻을 것이다.'는 의미가 되어야 자연스러우므로 현재분사 구문을 완성하는 (C)가 정답이다.

어휘 public transportation 대중교통 | be eligible for ~할 자격이 있다 | reimbursement 환급, 상환

---

5. 어휘 - 명사

해설 빈칸은 문장의 목적어인 명사 자리이다. 빈칸 앞 문장의 '실제로 세금은 겉으로 보이는 것처럼 복잡하지 않다'는 내용을 고려할 때, '대부분의 사람들이 그저 과정을 모르는 것일 뿐'이라는 내용으로 이어져야 문맥상 자연스러우므로 (D)가 정답이다. 뒤에서 책을 통해 하루만에 세무 처리를 할 수 있다는 내용도 단서가 된다.

✦ Key word
Taxes really aren't as complicated as they seem. Most people simply don't know the process," said Carter.

6. 동사의 시제

해설 빈칸은 you를 주어로 하는 문장의 동사 자리이다. 빈칸 뒷문장의 '게다가 돈도 많이 절약하게 된다'는 내용과 시제가 미래임을 고려할 때, '안내서를 참고하면, 하루 만에 세금을 처리할 수 있다'는 의미가 되어야 문맥상 자연스러우므로 (A)가 정답이다.

✦ Key word
Using my guide, you can be done with your taxes in a day. Plus, you'll save yourself a lot of money by not hiring a tax expert every year."

7. 문장 선택

(A) 세율 인상은 새로운 정책 때문이다.
(B) Carter는 최근 회사에서 새로운 역할을 맡게 되었다.
(C) 회계 부서에 자리가 날 지도 모른다.
(D) 책에는 법인세에 관한 내용도 포함되어 있다.

해설 빈칸 앞 부분에서 책을 보면 얻게 되는 이점에 대해 소개하고 있으므로, 문맥상 책과 관련된 내용이 이어져야 자연스러우므로 (D)가 정답이다.

✦ Key word
"Using my guide, you can be done with your taxes in a day. Plus, you'll save yourself a lot of money by not hiring a tax expert every year." The book also includes sections on corporate taxes.

8. 어휘 – 동사

해설 빈칸은 명사 your copy를 목적어로 하는 명령문 문장의 동사 자리이다. 접속사 and로 연결된 문장 앞 부분의 내용을 고려할 때, '오늘 서점에 가서 책을 구입하라'는 내용으로 연결되어야 문맥상 자연스러우므로 (B)가 정답이다.

+ Key word

Head on down to your local bookstore and purchase your copy today!

CASE 실전훈련

본서 p.140

1. (A) 2. (D) 3. (D) 4. (D) 5. (C) 6. (D)
7. (B) 8. (D) 9. (B) 10. (C) 11. (B) 12. (A)

---

1. 동명사 자리

All visitors must show valid identification at the reception desk before **entering** the office building.

모든 방문객은 사무실 건물에 들어가기 전 접수처 안내 데스크에서 유효한 신분증을 보여줘야 한다.

해설 빈칸은 전치사 before의 목적어 자리이자, 명사구 the office building을 목적어로 취해야 하는 자리이므로 동명사 (A)가 정답이다.

어휘 show 보여주다 | valid 유효한 | identification 신분증 | reception desk 접수처

---

2. 동사의 시제

The slides for Mr. Neal's board of directors meeting **will be included** in our team's annual strategy packet next week.

Neal 씨의 이사회 회의용 슬라이드는 다음 주 우리 팀의 연간 전략 자료집에 포함될 것이다.

해설 빈칸은 주어 The slides에 대한 동사 자리이다. 주어가 사물 명사이며 뒤에 목적어가 없으므로 수동태 구문이 필요하며, 문장 내 미래 시점을 나타내는 표현이 있으므로 미래 시제 수동태 (D)가 정답이다.

어휘 slide 슬라이드 | board of directors 이사회 | annual 연간의 | strategy 전략 | packet (서류 등의) 꾸러미, 뭉치

---

3. 관용 표현

Arrow Assurance assigns office workspaces to employees **depending** on their seniority.

Arrow 보험사는 연공서열에 따라 직원에게 사무실 자리를 배정한다.

해설 빈칸이 완전한 문장과 「on + 명사구」 사이의 자리이며, 문맥상 '연공서열에 따라 사무실 자리를 배정한다'는 의미가 되어야 자연스러우므로, 구전치사 표현 'depending on(~에 따라)'을 완성하는 (D)가 정답이다.

어휘 assurance 보험 | assign 할당하다, 지정하다 | workspace 작업공간 | seniority 연공서열

---

4. 분사 구문 자리

Having entered the contest past the due date, Ms. Chen was surprised to be admitted.

마감일을 지나 대회에 참가했기에, Chen 씨는 등록돼서 깜짝 놀랐다.

해설 빈칸은 뒤에 이어지는 명사구를 주절과 연결하는 분사 자리이다. 빈칸 뒤 목적어에 해당하는 명사구가 있음을 고려할 때, 현재분사가 필요하므로 완료형 현재분사 (D)가 정답이다.

어휘 contest 대회, 시합 | past 지나서 | due date 마감일 | surprised 놀란 | admit 받아들이다

+ Key point

분사 구문은 주절과 종속절의 주어가 동일한 경우, 종속절의 「접속사 + 주어」를 생략하고 동사를 분사로 전환한 형태이다: As she had entered the contest ~ → Having entered the contest ~

---

5. 어휘 – 부사

It was **entirely** fitting for the company to invite its owner, Mr. Regal, to the reopening of its premises following the devastating earthquake.

강력한 지진이 있은 후 부지 재개장에 회사가 소유주인 Regal 씨를 초대한 것은 완전히 적절한 일이었다.

해설 빈칸은 형용사 fitting을 수식하는 부사 자리이다. 「for + 의미상 주어」, 「to + 진주어」 형태의 문장 구조로, 문맥상 '지진 후 회사 부지 재개장에 소유주를 초대한 일은 완전히 적절했다'는 의미가 되어야 자연스러우므로 (C)가 정답이다.

어휘 fitting 알맞은, 적절한 | invite 초대[초청]하다 | owner 소유주, 주인 | reopening 재개장 | premises (한 사업체가 소유하는 건물 딸린) 부지 | following ~후에 | devastating 파괴적인, 강력한 | earthquake 지진

+ Key word

It was **entirely fitting for the company to invite its owner**, Mr. Regal, **to the reopening of its premises following** the devastating **earthquake**.

---

6. 어휘 – 부사

The Mikku Automatic Vacuum has many convenient features, but **above all**, it is easy to use.

Mikku Automatic Vacuum에는 편리한 기능이 많지만, 무엇보다도 사용이 편리하다.

해설 빈칸은 뒤에 이어지는 문장 전체를 수식하는 부사 자리이다. 접속사 but으로 연결된 두 문장 관계를 고려할 때, '편리한 기능이 많지만, 무엇보다도 사용이 편리하다'는 내용으로 연결되어야 문맥상 자연스러우므로 (D)가 정답이다. as well은 '~도 또한'이라는 뜻인데 문미에 쓰인다.

어휘 automatic 자동의 | vacuum 진공 청소기 | convenient 편리한 | feature 기능

+ Key word

The Mikku Automatic Vacuum **has many convenient features, but above all, it is easy to use.**

---

7. 부사 자리

By utilizing more energy-efficient processors, we could reduce our monthly power bills by **roughly** 6 percent in the long run.

더 에너지 효율이 좋은 프로세서를 사용해서 우리는 월간 전력요금을 장기적으로 대략 6퍼센트까지 낮출 수 있다.

해설 빈칸은 수를 나타내는 표현 6 percent를 수식하는 부사 자리이므로 (B)가 정답이다.

어휘 utilize 이용하다 | energy-efficient 에너지 효율이 좋은 | processor 프로세서, 처리기 | reduce 낮추다, 줄이다 | monthly 월간의 | power 전력 | bill 고지서 | in the long run 결국에는, 장기적으로는

✦ Key point

수치, 양을 나타내는 표현 앞에 주로 사용되는 부사는 다음과 같다: about, approximately, roughly(대략), nearly, almost(거의) 등

· ·

8. 명사 자리

This experimental eye drop will provide much needed **relief** from itchiness and dryness.

이 실험적인 안약은 매우 필요한 가려움과 건조함의 완화를 제공해 줄 것이다.

해설 빈칸은 동사 provide의 목적어인 명사 자리이므로 (D)가 정답이다.

어휘 experimental 실험적인 | eye drop 안약 | provide 제공하다 | itchiness 가려움 | dryness 건조함

9-12번은 다음 보도자료에 관한 문제입니다.

AZWELL (8월 3일) — Chorevic은 오늘 **9** 매우 기대를 모아온 자사의 StreetWiFi 시스템을 핸드폰 이용자에게 무료로 배포한다고 발표했다.

도시에 있는 수많은 핫스팟에 비해, 교외에서 와이파이를 수신하는 것은 녹록치 않을 수 있다. Chorevic의 새로운 WiShare 프로그램은 인근 Chorevic 라우터에서 와이파이 신호를 **10** 모아서 작동한다. Chorevic 휴대폰은 결합된 신호를 이용해 와이파이에 접속할 수 있다. **11** 그렇게 하면 네트워크가 지역 전체를 포괄할 수 있다. 더 많은 사람들이 Chorevic 라우터로 변경할수록, 네트워크는 계속해서 더 확대될 것이다. 회사에서는 앞으로 몇 달 안에 자사 네트워크 **12** 범위가 모든 서비스 제공업체를 앞설 것으로 기대한다.

새로운 WiShare 프로그램이나 Chorevic의 제품군에 관한 더 자세한 정보는 웹사이트 www.chorevicglobal.com에서 확인할 수 있다.

어휘

announce 발표하다 | anticipate 기대하다, 고대하다 | release 출시 | at no charge 무료로 | compared to ~과 비교하여 | abundant 많은, 풍부한 | the number of ~의 수 | hotspot 핫스팟 | suburb 교외 | challenging 도전적인 | nearby 인근의 | router 라우터 | combine 결합하다 | signal 신호 | have access to ~에 접근할 수 있다 | continue 계속하다 | grow 커지다, 늘어나다 | wider 더 넓은 (wide의 비교급) | expect 기대하다 | lead 이끌다, 선두를 달리다 | service provider 서비스 제공업체 | in the coming months 다음 몇 달 동안

---

9. 부사 자리

해설 빈칸은 형용사 자리에 있는 과거분사 anticipated를 수식하는 부사 자리이다. 문맥상 '대단히 기대를 모아온'이라는 의미가 되어야 자연스러우므로 (B)가 정답이다.

10. 동명사 자리

해설 빈칸은 전치사 by의 목적어 자리이다. '새로운 프로그램이 와이파이 신호를 모아서 작동한다'는 의미가 되어야 문맥상 자연스러우므로 동명사 (C)가 정답이다.

✦ Key point

전치사 by는 'by ~ing'의 형태로 쓰여 '~함으로써'라는 '수단, 방법'을 나타낸다.

11. 문장 선택

(A) 이전 시스템이 최신 시스템과 호환되지 않을 수 있다.
(B) 그렇게 하면 네트워크가 지역 전체를 포괄할 수 있다.
(C) 사용되는 기술은 그 분야의 최근 발전된 기술이다.
(D) 그 지역의 평균 인터넷 속도는 기하급수적으로 빨라졌다.

해설 빈칸 앞 부분의 '새로운 WiShare 프로그램은 인근 Chorevic 라우터에서 와이파이 신호를 모아서 작동한다. Chorevic 핸드폰은 결합된 신호를 이용해 와이파이에 접속할 수 있다.'는 내용을 고려할 때, 와이파이 네트워크가 구성되는 원리에 대한 설명이 이어져야 문맥상 자연스러우므로 '그렇게 하면 네트워크가 지역 전체를 포괄한다'는 내용의 (B)가 정답이다.

✦ Key word

Chorevic's new WiShare program works by pooling WiFi signals from nearby Chorevic routers. Using the combined signal, Chorevic mobile phones will have access to WiFi. The network can then span entire neighborhoods.

12. 어휘 – 명사

해설 빈칸은 문장의 목적어 자리이자, network와 복합명사를 이루는 명사 자리이다. 빈칸 앞 문장의 '네트워크는 계속해서 더 확대될 것'이라는 내용을 고려할 때, 문맥상 '회사는 자사 네트워크 범위가 모든 서비스 제공업체를 앞설 것으로 기대한다'는 내용으로 이어져야 자연스러우므로 (A)가 정답이다. coverage는 여기서 서비스 이용이 가능한 지역범위(the area in which a particular sevice is available) 정도를 뜻한다.

✦ Key word

As more people change to Chorevic routers, the network will continue to grow wider. **The company expects its network coverage to lead all service providers** in the coming months.

CHAPTER 08 전치사

CASE 집중훈련   본서 p.143

1. (D) **2.** (C) **3.** (A) **4.** (D) **5.** (A) **6.** (D)
7. (A) **8.** (A)

1. 시간 전치사

Customers who visited La Belle Bakery **on** opening day received special cookies to celebrate.

La Belle 제과점의 개점일에 방문한 고객들은 기념하는 특별 쿠키를 받았다.

해설 빈칸 뒤의 명사구 opening day를 목적어로 갖는 전치사 자리이다. 뒤에 특정 일을 나타내는 명사구 opening day가 있으므로 요일 등 특정 일 앞에 쓸 수 있는 전치사인 (D)가 정답이다.

어휘 opening day 개점일, 개장일 | celebrate 축하하다, 기념하다

✦ Key point

시점 전치사 '~에'
① in: 계절, 연도, 월, 아침/점심/저녁(in winter, in 2020, in June, in the morning 등)
② at: 시각, 시점(at 3 o'clock, at noon 등)
③ on: 요일, 날짜(on Sunday, on June 12 등)

· ·

2. 시간 전치사

All personnel must upload their work to the shared

folder **before** leaving for the day.

모든 직원들은 일과를 마치고 가기 전 공유 폴더에 작업물을 업로드해야 한다.

해설 문맥상 '퇴근하기 전에 작업한 내용을 업로드 해야 한다'는 내용이 자연스러우므로 (C)가 정답이다. within은 기간 명사와 어울리는데, leaving for the day는 기간이 아닌 시점 표현이므로 within은 어울리지 않는다.

어휘 personnel 직원, 인원 | shared folder 공유 폴더

---

3. 시간 전치사

The Accounting Department will pay employees only by direct deposit **from** October 1 onward.

회계 부서는 10월 1일부터 계좌 입금으로만 직원들에게 급여를 지급할 것이다.

해설 빈칸은 명사구 October 1를 목적어로 하는 전치사 자리이다. 목적어 자리에 시점에 해당하는 표현이 있으므로, 문맥상 '10월 1일부터'라는 의미를 완성하는 (A)가 정답이다.

어휘 accounting department 회계부 | pay 지불하다 | direct deposit (급여의) 계좌 입금 | onward 앞으로

+ Key point

전치사 from vs. during: from은 '시점'을 나타내는 표현과 함께 쓰여 '~부터'를 의미하고, during은 '기간'을 나타내는 표현과 함께 쓰여 '~동안에'를 의미한다.

---

4. 시간 전치사

The 13-inch laptop from IJM Electronics is currently out of stock and will not be available **until** November 7.

IJM 전자의 13인치 노트북은 현재 재고가 없어 11월 7일까지 구할 수 없을 것이다.

해설 빈칸은 시점을 나타내는 표현을 목적어로 하는 전치사 자리이다. 문맥상 '현재 품절되어 11월 7일까지 구할 수 없을 것'이라는 의미가 되어야 자연스러우므로 (D)가 정답이다

어휘 laptop 노트북 | currently 현재 | out of stock 재고가 없는, 품절된 | available 구할[이용할] 수 있는

+ Key point

시간 접속사 until vs. since: until은 '~까지', since는 '~부터, ~이래'를 의미한다.

5-8번은 다음 초대장에 관한 문제입니다.

관계자께,

World Peace Committee는 시청에서 열리는 연례 Global Introduction Day 행사에 여러분의 참석을 정중히 요청드립니다. 매년, 저희는 이 연례 행사에 대표자들을 5보내 기여해 주십사 각 지역 사회에 요청드리고 있습니다. 대표자들께서는 행사 중에 세계 평화를 구축하는 방법에 관해 아이디어를 공유하도록 요청 받으시게 될 것입니다. 저희는 모든 참가자들께 최소 2시간 동안 저희 토론회에 참석하시도록 요청드릴 것입니다. 6이 토론회는 오직 하루 동안만 진행됩니다.

저희에게 75월 31일 전까지 답변해 주시면 감사하겠습니다. 모든 참가자들로부터 답변을 듣는 대로 이 행사의 추가 7세부 사항을 공유해 드릴 것입니다. 토론회 의제는 86월 4일 8당일에 또는 그 전에 공유될 것입니다. 시간을 내 주신 모든 참가자들께 진심으로 감사드립니다.

안녕히 계십시오.

Mario Hill, World Peace Committee 회장

어휘
cordially 정중하게 | invite A to do A에게 ~하도록 요청하다 | annual 연례의 | local community 지역 사회 | representative 대표자 | contribute 기여하다, 제공하다 | be asked to do ~하도록 요청받다 | require A to do A에게 ~하도록 요청하다 | participant 참가자 | join 참석하다, 함께 하다 | discussion 토론회 | at least 최소한 | appreciate 감사하다 | respond to ~에게 답변하다 | share 공유하다 | agenda 의제 | grateful 감사하는

---

5. 어휘 - 동사

해설 빈칸 앞 문장의 'World Peace Committee는 시청에서 열리는 연례 Global Introduction Day 행사에 여러분이 참석하시도록 정중히 요청드립니다'라는 내용을 고려할 때, '매년, 저희는 이 연례 행사에 대표자들을 보내 기여하도록 각 지역 사회에 요청드리고 있습니다'라는 내용으로 이어져야 자연스러우므로 (A)가 정답이다.

+ Key word

We at the World Peace Committee **cordially invite you to attend our annual Global Introduction Day at the City Hall**. Every year, **we invite local communities to send their representatives to contribute toward this annual event**.

---

6. 문장 선택

(A) 귀하의 사회에 따라 참가가 확인되었습니다.
(B) 그곳에는 주차장이 충분합니다.
(C) 시청은 무료라서 선정되었습니다.
(D) 이 토론회는 오직 하루 동안만 진행됩니다.

해설 앞서 참가자 전원에게 최소 2시간 동안 토론에 참가해 주실 것을 요청드릴 것이라고 하므로, 토론회와 관련된 또 다른 정보로서 '이 토론회는 오직 하루 동안만 지속됩니다.'라는 내용으로 이어져야 자연스러우므로 (D)가 정답이다.

+ Key word

We would **require all participants to join our discussion for at least two hours**. **The discussion will only last for one day**.

---

7. 어휘 - 명사

해설 빈칸 뒷부분의 '토론회 의제는 6월 4일에 또는 그 전에 공유될 것입니다'라는 내용을 고려할 때, '모든 참가자들로부터 답변을 듣는 대로 이 행사의 추가 세부 사항을 공유해 드리겠습니다'라는 내용이 되어야 자연스러우므로 (A)가 정답이다.

+ Key word

We will **share more details about the event once we have heard from all participants**. **The discussion agenda will be shared** on or before August 4.

---

8. 전치사 자리

해설 '------- (June 4) or before June 4'와 같이 공동 목적어인 June 4가 등위접속사 or 앞에서 생략된 형태이므로 빈칸에 들어갈 전치사는 특정일 앞에 오는 전치사가 필요하다. 문맥상 '토론회 의제는 6월 4일 당일에 또는 그 전에 공유될 것입니다'라는 내용이 되어야 자연스러우므로 날짜 앞에 사용하는 전치사 (A)가 정답이다.

✦ Key word

The discussion agenda will be shared **on or before June 4**.

CASE 집중훈련
본서 p.145

1. (C)   **2.** (C)   **3.** (B)   **4.** (A)   **5.** (B)   **6.** (D)
7. (A)   **8.** (C)

---

1. 기간 전치사

Design Enthusiast Magazine features articles written by experts who have worked in the interior design industry **for** several years.

〈Design Enthusiast Magazine〉은 수년 동안 인테리어 디자인 업계에서 일해 오고 있는 전문가들이 쓴 기사가 특징이다.

해설 several years를 수식하는 기간과 어울리는 전치사인 (C)가 정답이다.

어휘 feature 특징이다 | expert 전문가

✦ Key word

Design Enthusiast Magazine features articles written by experts who have worked in the interior design industry **for several years**.

---

2. 기간 전치사

The newly renovated Shocker Stadium, scheduled to open **in** about five weeks, has 100,000 seat capacity.

새롭게 단장된 Shocker 스타디움은 약 5주 뒤에 개장할 예정이며, 10만석의 수용력을 갖추고 있다.

해설 빈칸은 뒤의 명사구를 이끄는 전치사 자리이다. 문맥상 '약 5주 뒤에 문을 열 예정이다'라는 의미가 자연스러우므로 기간 명사(구)를 이끌어 '~뒤에[후에]'라는 뜻으로 쓰이는 (C)가 정답이다. about은 여기서 전치사가 아닌 수사 five를 꾸미는 부사로서 '약, 대략'이라는 뜻이다.

어휘 renovate 수리하다, 개조하다 | scheduled to do ~할 예정인 | capacity 수용력

✦ Key word

The newly renovated Shocker Stadium, **scheduled to open in about five weeks**, has 100,000 seat capacity.

---

3. 기간 전치사

Marie's Alpine Café has already opened three new branches **within** its first five years of operation.

Marie's Alpine 카페는 사업 첫 5년 이내에 이미 3개의 신규 지점들을 오픈했다.

해설 빈칸은 기간을 나타내는 표현 its first five years를 목적어로 하는 전치사 자리이다. 문맥상 '첫 5년 내 3개의 신규 지점을 오픈했다'라는 의미가 되어야 자연스러우므로 (B)가 정답이다.

어휘 branch 지점 | operation 운영

✦ Key point

within은 기간, 장소, 범위, 한도를 의미하는 명사 앞에 쓰이며 '~이내'를 의미한다.

---

4. 기간 전치사

The Home Improvement Emporium's employee manual states that all mobile devices must be turned off **during** work hours.

Home Improvement Emporium의 직원 매뉴얼에는 근무시간 중에는 반드시 모든 모바일 기기를 꺼야 한다고 명시한다.

해설 빈칸은 수동태 동사 구문 must be turned off와 명사 work hours 사이의 자리이다. 수동태 문장에는 목적어가 올 수 없으므로, 빈칸은 work hours를 목적어로 하는 전치사 (A)가 정답이다.

어휘 manual 매뉴얼 | state 명시하다 | electronic device 전자기기

✦ Key point

수동태 문장에서는 동사 뒤 수식어구(ex. 부사, 전명구 등)만이 자리할 수 있다.

5-8번은 다음 이메일에 관한 문제입니다.

수신: Carrie Ann Richardson
발신: Rikard 시력 관리 센터
날짜: 2월 15일
제목: 고객님의 시력

Richardson 씨 귀하,

저희에게 고객님의 시력은 **⑤중요합니다**. 고객님께서는 검진 예약을 하실 때입니다. 저희 센터의 최근 방문이 16개월 **⑥이상** 지났습니다. Rikard 시력 관리 센터에서는 **⑦정기적인** 시력 검사를 12개월마다 받으실 것을 권해 드립니다. 고객님을 곧 뵙고 고객님의 시력 관리의 필요성에 도움을 드리기를 기대합니다. **⑧질문이나 궁금한 사항이 있으시면 저희에게 전화해 주세요.**

진심으로,

Barbara Ong
Rikard 시력 관리 센터
4587 Jaunty 로, Suite B
Singapore 168938
전화번호: 65 6323 0112

어휘
eyesight 시력 | make an appointment 예약하다 | checkup 건강 진단 | look forward to ~하기를 고대하다

---

5. 어휘 - 형용사

해설 해당 문장의 주어(Your eyesight)와 빈칸 뒷문장의 '고객님께서는 검진 예약을 하실 때입니다.'라는 내용을 고려할 때 고객의 시력이 중요하다는 의미가 되어야 자연스러우므로 (B)가 정답이다.

✦ Key word

Your eyesight is important to us. It is time for you to make an appointment for a checkup.

---

6. 기간 전치사

해설 빈칸 뒤에 과거 시점(16 months ago)이 연결되어 있고, 마지막 방문한 시점이 16개월이 넘었다는 의미가 적절하므로 '~이상'의 의미를 뜻하는 (D)가 정답이다.

✦ Key word

Your last visit with us was over 16 months ago.

---

7. 어휘 - 형용사

해설 복합명사 eye exam(시력검사)을 수식하는 자리로 이 센터에서는 정기적인 시력 검사를 매 12개월마다 받을 것을 권한다는 내용이 자연스러우므로 (A)가 정답이다.

+ Key word

At Rikard Eye Care Center, **we suggest that you get a routine eye exam every 12 months.**

8. 문장 선택

(A) 귀사의 대리점과 거래하게 되어 즐거웠습니다.
(B) 이번이 마음을 바꿀 수 있는 마지막 기회입니다.
(C) 질문이나 궁금한 사항이 있으시면 저희에게 전화해 주세요.
(D) 유감스럽게도, 진료에 신규 환자를 받을 수 없습니다.

해설 빈칸 앞 문장의 '고객님을 곧 뵙고 고객님의 시력 관리의 필요성에 도움을 드리기를 기대합니다.'란 내용과 안내문 말미에 들어가기에 적절한 문장을 고려할 때, 질문이나 궁금한 사항이 있으시면 전화해 달라는 내용으로 이어져야 자연스러우므로 (C)가 정답이다.

+ Key word

We look forward to seeing you and serving your eye care needs. Please give us a call if you have any questions or concerns.

CASE 집중훈련

본서 p.147

1. (A) **2.** (D) **3.** (A) **4.** (A) **5.** (D) **6.** (B)
7. (B) **8.** (B)

1. 장소 전치사

The mission of our outreach program is to develop cooperation and understanding **between** groups.
저희 봉사 프로그램의 사명은 집단 간의 이해와 협력을 발달시키는 것이다.

해설 빈칸은 명사를 목적어로 하는 전치사 자리이다. 문맥상 '집단 간 (서로서로)'의 의미가 되어야 자연스러우므로 (A)가 정답이다.

어휘 mission 임무, 사명 | outreach 봉사 활동 | develop 발달시키다 | cooperation 협력, 협조

+ Key point

전치사 between은 'between A and B'의 형태로 가장 많이 쓰이나, 두 개 이상의 여러 개체들을 대상으로 하면서도 각 개체 간의 관계에 보다 초점을 맞추고자 할 때 'between 복수 명사(~간[사이]에)'의 형태로 쓸 수 있다.

---

2. 장소 전치사

The board of directors approved the installation of cell phone charging stations to be located **throughout** the student center.
이사회는 학생회관 전역에 위치하게 될 충전소의 설치를 승인했다.

해설 빈칸 뒤에 특정 장소(the student center)가 나왔고, 문맥상 '학생회관 전역에 위치하게 될 충전소'라는 의미가 자연스러우므로 '~전역에'라는 뜻의 (D)가 정답이다.

어휘 board of directors 이사회 | approve 승인하다 | installation 설치 | cell phone 휴대폰 | charging station 충전소 | student center 학생회관

+ Key point

전치사 throughout은 기간을 나타내는 명사(구)를 받을 때는 '~내내'라는 뜻으로 쓰이지만, 장소 명사(구)를 받을 때는 '~전역에'라는 의미로 쓰인다.

---

3. 장소 전치사

Falkland Island is located near Norminton City, just a short drive **across** the Chesapeake Bay Bridge.
Falkland 섬은 Chesapeake Bay Bridge를 가로질러 짧게 운전해 가면 되는, Norminton 시 인근에 위치해 있다.

해설 빈칸은 뒤의 명사구를 목적어로 갖는 전치사 자리이다. 문맥상 'Chesapeake Bay Bridge를 가로질러 짧게 운전해 가면 되는 ~'이라는 의미가 되어야 자연스러우므로 (A)가 정답이다.

어휘 be located 위치해 있다 | near 인근에, 근처에 | bridge 다리, 교각 | across ~을 가로질러 | between ~사이에 | outside ~의 밖에 | about ~에 관하여

+ Key word

Falkland Island is located near Norminton City, **just a short drive across the Chesapeake Bay Bridge.**

---

4. 장소 전치사

Museum visitors can enjoy a spectacular view of the sunset **through** the west-facing windows.
박물관 입장객은 서쪽으로 난 창을 통해 장엄한 일몰을 즐길 수 있다.

해설 빈칸은 명사구 the west-facing windows를 목적어로 하는 전치사 자리이다. 문맥상 '서쪽 창을 통해 일몰을 즐길 수 있다'는 내용이 되어야 자연스러우므로 전치사 (A)가 정답이다.

어휘 enjoy 즐기다 | spectacular 눈부신, 장관을 이루는 | face 향하다 | west-facing 서쪽을 향하는

+ Key word

Museum visitors can **enjoy** a spectacular **view** of the sunset **through** the west-facing **windows**.

5-8번은 다음 편지에 관한 문제입니다.

7월 15일

Gretchen Cunningham
12 Washington Street
San Antonio, TX 78213

Cunningham 씨께,

7월 12일에 출발 예정이었던 Highgate Escape 유람선 이용과 관련하여 귀하의 경험을 저희에게 알려주셔서 감사드립니다. 이 여행이 **⑤취소되어** 유감스럽게 생각합니다. 저희 정책에 따라, **⑥불편을** 끼쳐드린 것에 대해 보상을 제공해드릴 것입니다. 미사용하신 750달러 티켓은 환불 처리해 드렸습니다. 또한 저희는 취소 **⑦로** 인해 귀하께서 지불하신 추가 여행경비에서 발생한 500달러를 부담해 드리겠습니다. **⑧이해해 주셔서 대단히 감사드립니다.** 각 금액 이체는 처리되는데 최대 72시간까지 소요될 수 있다는 점을 유의해 주십시오.

감사합니다.

Terry Clare
Coleridge Cruises

어휘

cruise ship 유람선 | schedule 예정하다 | depart 출발하다 | regret 유감스럽게 생각하다 | voyage 여행 | in keeping with ~와 일치하여, ~에 따라 | policy 정책 | provide 제공하다 | compensation 보상 | refund 환불(금) | unused 미사용한 | amount 총액 | cover (돈을) 대다 | incur (비용을) 발생시키다 | additional 추가의 | travel expense 출장비 | disruption 혼란, 중단 | aware 알고 있는 | transfer 이체, 이동 | up to ~까지 | process 처리하다

5. 동사의 태 / 시제

해설 빈칸은 주어 this voyage에 대한 동사 자리이다. 7월 15일에 작성된 서신에서, 빈칸 앞 문장의 '7월 12일에 출발 예정이었던 Highgate Escape 유람선 이용과 관련한 경험'이라는 내용을 고려할 때, 문맥상 '이 여행이 취소되어 유감스럽게 생각한다'는 내용으로 이어져야 자연스러우므로 과거 시제 수동태 동사 (D)가 정답이다.

+ **Key word**

Thank you for letting us know about **your experience with the cruise ship Highgate Escape, which was scheduled to depart on July 12. We regret that this voyage was canceled.**

6. 어휘 - 명사

해설 빈칸은 전치사 for의 목적어 자리이다. 빈칸 앞 문장의 '여행이 취소되어 유감스럽게 생각한다'는 내용을 고려할 때, '정책에 따라, 불편을 끼친 것에 대해 보상을 제공하겠다'는 내용으로 이어져야 문맥상 자연스러우므로 (B)가 정답이다.

+ **Key word**

We regret that this voyage was canceled. In keeping with our policy, we will **provide compensation for** the **inconvenience**.

7. 전치사

해설 빈칸은 명사 the disruption을 목적어로 하는 전치사 자리이다. 빈칸 앞 현재분사 resulting과 함께 result from(~의 결과로 발생하다)의 표현을 완성하여 '취소로 인해 발생한 추가 여행경비'라는 의미를 전달하는 (B)가 정답이다. result in은 '(결과적으로) ~을 낳다[야기하다], 그 결과 ~이다'라는 뜻이다.

+ **Key word**

We are also happy to cover the $500 you incurred in **additional travel expenses resulting from the disruption**.

8. 문장 선택

(A) Coleridge Cruises를 선택해 주셔서 감사합니다.
(B) 이해해 주셔서 대단히 감사드립니다.
(C) 두 금액 모두 이미 잔액에 표시되어 있을 것입니다.
(D) 말씀하신 문제를 조사하겠습니다.

해설 빈칸 앞 문장들의 '불편에 대한 보상으로 미사용 티켓 환불 및 추가 지불 경비의 일부를 부담하겠다'는 내용과 빈칸 뒷문장의 '각 금액 이체는 처리에 72시간까지 소요될 수 있다'는 내용을 고려할 때, '(이러한 상황 및 처리를) 이해해 주셔서 감사드린다'는 내용이 들어가야 문맥상 자연스러우므로 (B)가 정답이다.

+ **Key word**

In keeping with our policy, **we will provide compensation for the inconvenience. We have sent a refund for your unused ticket in the amount**

of $750. We are also happy to cover the $500 you incurred in additional travel expenses resulting from the disruption. Your understanding is greatly appreciated. Be aware that each transfer may take up to 72 hours to process.

CASE 집중훈련
본서 p.149

1. (A) 2. (B) 3. (C) 4. (D) 5. (A) 6. (A)
7. (D) 8. (A)

1. 주제 전치사

Some managers may have heard **about** the database program that the company has been working on for the past year.
몇몇 관리자들은 회사가 지난해 동안 작업하고 있었던 데이터 프로그램에 관하여 들었을지도 모른다.

해설 문맥상 '데이터베이스 프로그램에 관하여 들었을지도 모른다'는 의미가 자연스러우므로 '~에 관하여'라는 뜻의 주제를 나타내는 전치사 (A)가 정답이다.

어휘 look for ~을 찾다 | about ~에 관하여 | from ~부터 | before ~전에 | inside ~안에

+ **Key point**

주제 전치사 '~에 관하여'
about, on, over, as to, as for, regarding, concerning, in [with] regard to, with respect to, pertaining to

2. 추가 전치사

Besides requiring a large capital investment, these projects will need a more highly trained workforce.
많은 자본 투자를 요구하는 것 이외에도, 이 프로젝트들은 고도로 숙련된 노동력이 필요할 것이다.

해설 빈칸은 뒤의 명사구를 이끄는 전치사 자리이므로 (A)와 (C)는 답에서 제외시킨다. 문맥상 '많은 자본 투자 외에도 노동력도 필요하다'는 의미가 자연스러우므로 추가를 나타내는 (B)가 정답이다.

어휘 capital 자본 | investment 투자 | workforce 노동력

+ **Key word**

Besides requiring a large capital investment, these projects will need a more highly trained workforce.

3. 관용 표현

Bleifer Solutions plays a vital role **in** ensuring our company has the best personnel for each project.
Bleifer Solutions는 우리 회사가 각 프로젝트를 위한 최적의 인력을 갖추는데 있어 중요한 역할을 한다.

해설 빈칸은 명사와 동명사구를 연결하는 전치사 자리이다. 문맥상 '최적의 인력을 갖추는 데 있어 중요한 역할을 한다'는 의미가 되어야 자연스러우므로 'a role in(~에 있어서의 역할)'이라는 표현을 완성하는 전치사 (C)가 정답이다.

어휘 play a role 역할을 맡다 | ensure 반드시 ~하게 하다, 보장하다 | personnel 인원, 직원들

+ Key word

Bleifer Solutions **plays a** vital **role in ensuring** our company has the best personnel for each project.

4. 고려 전치사

Given her exceptional computer skills, Katja Goldstein was made Head of IT at Parker Industries.

그녀의 뛰어난 컴퓨터 실력을 고려해, Katja Goldstein은 Parker Industries에서 IT 책임자가 되었어.

해설 빈칸은 명사구와 주절을 연결하는 전치사 자리이다. 문맥상 '그녀의 뛰어난 컴퓨터 실력을 고려해, Katja Goldstein은 Parker Industries에서 IT 책임자가 되었다.'는 의미가 되어야 자연스러우므로 (D)가 정답이다.

어휘 exceptional 이례적인, 특출한 | head (조직의) 책임자

+ Key point

since의 특징: 전치사 since는 '~이래'를 의미하고, 접속사 since는 '~이래'와 '~때문에'라는 두 가지 의미를 갖는다.

5-8번은 다음 광고에 관한 문제입니다.

La View Catering Services

파티 또는 특별 행사를 위한 음식이 필요하신가요? **⑤저희는 전문 출장 요리 서비스를 제공합니다.** 대규모 결혼식에서부터 소규모 휴일 파티에 이르기까지 어떤 종류의 행사를 계획하시든, La View가 도와 드릴 수 있습니다.

저희는 모든 종류의 훌륭한 요리를 전문으로 하는 숙련된 직원을 보유하고 있습니다. 여기에는 케이크를 비롯한 기타 디저트와 멕시코 음식, 이탈리아 파스타, 중국 및 태국 요리, 그리고 전통적인 애피타이저가 포함됩니다. 대부분의 다른 출장 요리 제공업체들**⑥과 달리,** 저희 직원들은 전문적으로 교육 받은 요리사들로 모두 구성되어 있습니다. 이러한 특별함으로 인해 저희가 다른 어떤 **⑦경쟁사**들이 제공할 수 있는 것보다 더 맛있는 음식을 여러분께 제공해 드릴 수 있습니다.

La View Catering Services는 여러분의 파티 음식이 제 시간에 전달되도록 한다는 점을 확신하셔도 됩니다. 저희는 여러분께서 여러분의 손님들에게 **⑧다시 집중하기**를 원합니다!

어휘 whatever ~하는 무엇이든 | plan 계획하다 | skilled 숙련된 | specialize in ~을 전문으로 하다 | cuisine 요리 | include 포함하다 | traditional 전통적인 | cater 출장 요리 제공업체 | consist of ~로 구성되다 | entirely 모두, 완전히 | trained 교육 받은 | specialization 특별함 | allow A to do A에게 ~할 수 있게 하다 | provide A with B A에게 B를 제공하다 | confident 확신하는 | on time 제 시간에 | focus on ~에 집중하다

5. 문장 선택

(A) 저희는 전문 출장 요리 서비스를 제공합니다.
(B) 장식이 포함되어 있습니다.
(C) 가격은 전액 보상됩니다.
(D) La View는 개인 소유의 회사입니다.

해설 빈칸 앞 문장의 '파티 또는 특별 행사를 위한 음식이 필요하신가요?'라는 내용을 고려할 때, '저희는 전문 출장 요리 서비스를 제공합니다'라는 내용으로 이어져야 문맥상 자연스러우므로 (A)가 정답이다.

+ Key word

Need food for a party or special event? We provide

---

professional catering services.

6. 전치사 자리

해설 문맥상 '대부분의 다른 출장 요리 제공업체들과 달리, 저희 직원들은 전문적으로 교육 받은 요리사들로 모두 구성되어 있습니다'라는 내용이 되어야 자연스러우므로 (A)가 정답이다.

+ Key word

Unlike most other caters, our staff consists entirely of professionally trained chefs.

7. 어휘 - 명사

해설 앞에 나온 other caters를 받을 수 있는 competitors가 들어가 '이러한 특별함으로 인해 저희가 다른 어떤 경쟁사들것보다 더 맛있는 음식을 여러분께 제공해 드릴 수 있습니다'라는 내용이 되어야 자연스러우므로 (D)가 정답이다.

+ Key word

Unlike most **other caters**, our staff consists entirely of professionally trained chefs. This specialization allows us to provide you with food that is more delicious than any of **our competitors** can provide.

8. to부정사

해설 빈칸 앞에 이미 문장의 동사 want가 있으므로 빈칸은 준동사 자리이다. 동사 want는 'want to do' 또는 「want + 목적어 + to do」의 구조로 쓰이므로 목적어 뒤에 위치한 빈칸에 필요한 것으로 to부정사인 (A)가 정답이다.

+ Key point

동사 want는 「want to do」 또는 「want + 목적어 + to do」의 구조로 쓰인다.

CASE 집중훈련
본서 p.151

1. (A) **2.** (C) **3.** (D) **4.** (D) **5.** (A) **6.** (C)
7. (B) **8.** (B)

1. 대상 전치사

The prime minister commended HCO Hospital **for** its assistance in developing the nation's physical activity guidelines.

수상은 국가 신체활동 지침 개발을 지원한 것에 대해 HCO 병원을 칭찬했다.

해설 commend, praise 등 '칭찬하다'와 같은 동사는 「commend [praise] + A + for B」 'A에게 B에 대해 칭찬하다'로 전치사 for와 함께 쓰므로 (A)가 정답이다.

어휘 prime minister 수상 | commend 칭찬하다 | assistance 도움 | develop 개발하다 | physical 신체의 | guideline 가이드라인, 지침

---

2. 자격 전치사

Though her résumé was short, Theresa Lim made the most convincing arguments for hiring her **as** our sales manager.

이력서 내용이 짧긴 했지만, Theresa Lim은 그녀를 영업부장으로 채

용하는 것에 대한 가장 설득력 있는 주장을 펼쳤다.

해설 빈칸은 명사구 our sales manager를 목적어로 하는 전치사 자리이다. 문맥상 '그녀를 영업부장으로 채용하는 것'이라는 의미가 되어야 자연스러우므로 (C)가 정답이다.

어휘 though ~이긴 하지만 | convincing 설득력 있는 | argument 논거, 주장, 논쟁 | hire 채용하다

✚ Key word
Though her résumé was short, Theresa Lim made the most convincing arguments for **hiring her as our sales manager**.

---

3. 대비 전치사

Executives should compare the company's financial as well as historical performance **against** industry norms.
경영진은 회사의 재정 및 과거 실적을 업계 표준에 대비해 비교해야 한다.

해설 빈칸은 명사구 industry norms를 목적어로 하는 전치사 자리이다. '회사의 실적을 업계 표준에 대비해 비교해야 한다'는 의미가 되어야 자연스러우므로 '~ 대비'라는 의미를 가진 전치사 (D)가 정답이다.

어휘 executive 경영진 | compare 비교하다 | financial 금융의 | historical 역사상의 | performance 실적, 성과 | industry norm 산업 표준

✚ Key word
Executives should **compare the company's** financial as well as historical **performance against industry norms**.

---

4. 어휘 - 명사

In the last year, manufacturing at the Gilman facility has nearly tripled in **volume**.
작년에 Gilman 시설에서의 생산량이 거의 3배 가까이 증가했다.

해설 빈칸은 전치사 in의 목적어인 명사 자리이다. 문장의 내용을 고려할 때, 생산량이 거의 3배가 되었다'는 의미가 되어야 자연스러우므로 (D)가 정답이다. 'in volume'은 주로 증가/감소를 의미하는 동사와 함께 쓰여 '양이 증가/감소하다'의 의미를 나타낸다.

어휘 manufacture 제조하다, 생산하다 | nearly 거의 | triple 3배가 되다

✚ Key word
In the last year, **manufacturing** at the Gilman facility has nearly **tripled in volume**.

5-8번은 다음 광고에 관한 문제입니다.

Dagabe 체육관에서 새로운 **5**플랜인 '연휴 스페셜'에 등록하셔서 새해를 건강하게 시작하세요. **6**변화를 주기에 더 나은 때는 없습니다. 월 30달러의 저렴한 요금으로, 새로운 스파 룸을 **7**포함해 체육관 기구 및 수영장을 이용하게 됩니다. 이번 시즌에는 자격을 보유한 수많은 저희 트레이너의 도움을 받아 건강을 가꿔보세요. **8**저희 트레이너의 실력을 보증하는 고객들이 수백 명 있습니다. 더 자세한 내용은 www.dagabe.com.au/newyear에서 확인해 주세요.

어휘
sign up 등록하다 | gym 체육관 | There's no better time to ~하기에 더 좋은 때는 없다 | low 낮은 | rate 요금 | per ~당 | gain access to ~에 접근하다 | equipment 장비 | swimming pool 수영장 | get in shape 건강하게 몸을 단련하다 | qualified 자격을 갖춘 | trainer 트레이너

---

5. 명사 자리

해설 빈칸은 our new의 수식을 받는 명사 자리이다. '연휴 스페셜'이라는 체육관의 새로운 프로그램, 운동 플랜이라는 의미가 되어야 문맥상 자연스러우므로 (A)가 정답이다.

✚ Key point
명사 plan vs. planning vs. planner: plan은 '계획, 제도'를, planning은 '계획(세우기)'를, planner는 '계획자, 일정 계획표(수첩·컴퓨터 프로그램 등)'를 의미한다.

---

6. 어휘 - 명사

해설 빈칸은 동사 make의 목적어 자리이다. 체육관에 등록해 새해를 건강하게 시작하라는 빈칸 앞 문장의 내용을 고려할 때 변화를 주기에 더 나은 때는 없다는 내용으로 이어져야 문맥상 자연스러우므로 (C)가 정답이다.

✚ Key word
Start the New Year by signing up at Dagabe Gym for our new plan: the Holiday Special. **There's no better time to make a change.**

---

7. 전치사 자리

해설 빈칸은 명사구 our new spa room을 목적어로 하는 전치사 자리이다. 주절의 내용을 고려할 때 새로운 스파 룸을 포함해 체육관 기구 및 수영장을 이용하게 된다는 내용이 나와야 문맥상 자연스러우므로 (B)가 정답이다.

✚ Key word
For a low rate of $30 per month, you will **gain access to our gym equipment and swimming pool including our new spa room**.

---

8. 문장 선택

(A) 체육관은 가끔 청소를 위해 문을 닫을 수 있습니다.
(B) 저희 트레이너들과 함께 성공적으로 일해온 수백 명의 고객들이 있습니다.
(C) 작업 안전에 대한 우려가 제기되어야 합니다.
(D) 현재 프로모션 이벤트가 진행 중입니다.

해설 자격을 보유한 수많은 트레이너의 도움을 받아 건강을 가꾸라는 빈칸 앞 문장의 내용을 고려할 때, 트레이너에 대한 내용으로 문장이 이어져야 문맥상 자연스러우므로 (B)가 정답이다.

✚ Key word
Get in shape this season **with the help of our many qualified trainers. We have hundreds of clients who can vouch for our trainers.**

CASE 집중훈련   본서 p.153

1. (C)   **2.** (B)   **3.** (C)   **4.** (B)   **5.** (A)   **6.** (B)
7. (B)   **8.** (B)

---

1. 특정 전치사를 동반하는 동사

Farmers in cotton production and its by-products have suffered heavy losses **resulting** from high operating costs.

목화 생산과 부산물 업계의 농부들은 높은 운영비로 비롯된 많은 손실에 고통받았다.

해설 빈칸 앞 명사 losses를 수식하는 형용사 자리이다. 문맥상 '높은 운영비로 비롯된 많은 손실'이라는 의미가 자연스러우며, 빈칸 뒤 전치사 from을 동반하여 '~에서 비롯되다'라는 뜻의 (C)가 정답이다.

어휘 cotton 목화, 면직물 | production 생산 | by-product 부산물 | suffer 고통받다, 시달리다 | heavy 많은, 심한 | loss 손실 | operating cost 운영비

---

2. 특정 전치사를 동반하는 형용사

For recruitment purposes, three years of relevant work experience is **equivalent** to having a degree.
채용 목적상, 관련된 업무경력 3년은 학위를 가진 것과 상응한다.

해설 빈칸은 be동사 뒤 문장의 보어 자리이다. 빈칸 뒤 전치사 to와 어울리면서 문맥상 '업무경력 3년은 학위를 가진 것과 상응한다'라는 의미를 완성하는 (B)가 정답이다.

어휘 recruitment 채용 | relevant 관련 있는 | degree 학위

＋ Key word

For recruitment purposes, three years of relevant work experience **is equivalent to** having a degree.

---

3. 관용 표현

Ms. Tanaka was **close to** resigning when the vice president asked her to manage the IT team at the new data center.
Tanaka 씨가 거의 사임하려던 찰나 부사장이 그녀에게 신설 자료센터에서 IT팀을 맡아달라고 요청했다.

해설 빈칸은 be동사와 -ing형태 사이의 자리이다. 주절과 when 종속절의 관계를 고려할 때, 문맥상 '부사장이 팀을 맡아달라고 요청했을 당시, 그녀는 사임하려는 상황에 있었다'는 의미로 연결되어야 자연스러우므로 'be close to N(~의 상태가 되다, ~에 근접하다)'의 관용 표현을 완성하는 (C)가 정답이다.

어휘 resign 사임하다, 물러나다 | vice president 부사장 | manage 운영하다, 관리하다 | data 자료, 정보

＋ Key point

to부정사 관용 표현 be about to V는 '막 V하려는 참이다'를 의미한다.

---

4. 특정 전치사를 동반하는 명사

Every branch of Third Dimension Custom Printing keeps at least 5,000 kilograms of raw materials in **storage**.
Third Dimension Custom Printing의 모든 지점은 적어도 5천 킬로그램의 원료를 창고에 보관한다.

해설 빈칸은 전치사 in의 목적어 역할을 하는 명사 자리이다. 문맥상 '5천 킬로그램의 원료를 창고에 보관한다'라는 의미가 되어야 자연스러우므로 (B)가 정답이다.

어휘 branch 지점 | raw material 원료, 원자재

＋ Key word

Every branch of Third Dimension Custom Printing **keeps at least 5,000 kilograms of raw materials in storage**.

5-8번은 다음 회람에 관한 문제입니다.

수신: 회계 직원들, Prodio Bank
발신: Isaac O'Reilly, 부사장
날짜: 6월 15일
제목: 공지

Tom Harris가 이 은행에 온 것을 저와 함께 **⑤환영해** 주세요. 공인 회계 감사관으로, 그의 주된 직무들 중 하나는 주와 연방 **⑥법률에 따라** 적절한 법적 조치가 취해지도록 보장하기 위해 세무 사건들에 은행의 선임 파트너들을 돕는 일이 될 것입니다. Tom은 11년의 경력 동안 아주 많은 수의 사건을 다뤄본 상당한 경험을 가지고 있습니다. **⑦이전의** 은행에서, 그는 성장 전략 및 구조 조정 계획에 관해 아주 다양한 고객들에게 조언을 해주었습니다. **⑧Tom이 이 분야에 직접 체험으로 얻은 지식을 전수해줄 것입니다.** 그의 첫 근무 일자는 6월 20일이 될 것입니다.

어휘

accounting 회계 | announcement 공지, 안내 | join 함께하다 | certified 공인된 | auditor 회계 감사관 | responsibility 책무, 책임 | assist 돕다 | case 사건, 소송 | ensure that ~임을 보장하다 | appropriate 적절한 | take legal action 법적 조치를 취하다 | federal 연방의 | a great deal of 상당한, 아주 많은 | a large number of 아주 많은 수의 | advise 조언하다 | a wide variety of 아주 다양한 | growth 성장 | strategy 전략 | restructuring 구조 조정, 재편성

---

5. 어휘 – 동명사

해설 빈칸은 전치사 in의 목적어가 될 동명사 자리이다. 문맥상 다음 문장에 회계 감사관으로서 Tom Harris의 주된 책무들 중 하나를 설명하는 내용을 고려할 때, 'Tom Harris가 이 은행에 온 것을 저와 함께 환영해 주세요'라는 의미가 되어야 자연스러우므로 (A)가 정답이다.

＋ Key word

Kindly **join** me in welcoming Tom Harris to the bank. As a certified auditor, one of his main responsibilities will be to assist the bank's senior partners ~.

---

6. 구전치사

해설 빈칸은 앞의 절에 뒤에 명사구를 연결해줄 전치사 자리이다. 문맥상 '~ 주와 연방 법률에 따라 적절한 법적 조치가 취해지도록'이라는 의미가 되어야 자연스러우므로 (B)가 정답이다. in accordance with는 '~에 부합되게, (규칙·지시 등에) 따라'라는 뜻이다.

＋ Key word

~ appropriate legal action is taken **in accordance with** state and federal laws

---

7. 어휘 – 형용사

해설 빈칸은 뒤에의 명사를 수식해줄 형용사 자리이다. 뒤이어 '그는 성장 전략 및 구조 조정 계획에 관해 아주 다양한 고객들에게 조언을 해주었습니다'라는 과거 경험이 제시되어 있는 것으로 볼 때, '이전의 은행에서'라는 의미가 되어야 자연스러우므로 (B)가 정답이다.

＋ Key word

At his **previous** bank, he has advised on a wide variety of clients on their growth strategies and restructuring plans.

---

8. 문장 선택

(A) 저희는 5월 12일부터 간단한 시스템을 사용하고 있습니다.
(B) Tom이 이 분야에서 직접 체험으로 얻은 지식을 전수해줄 것입니다.

(C) 당 은행은 새로운 모바일 뱅킹 서비스를 시작할 것입니다.
(D) 최근 대규모 자금 조달 프로그램이 승인되었습니다.

해설 앞에 Tom Harris의 이전 경험이 구체적으로 제시되어 있는 것으로 볼 때, 그 연장선상에서 'Tom이 이 분야에 직접 체험으로 얻은 지식을 전수해줄 것입니다'라는 내용의 문장이 삽입되는 것이 자연스러우므로 (B)가 정답이다.

＋ Key word

At his previous bank, he has advised on a wide variety of clients on their growth strategies and restructuring plans. Tom will bring firsthand knowledge in this field.

CASE 실전훈련

1. (D)	2. (C)	3. (A)	4. (C)	5. (A)	6. (C)
7. (C)	8. (B)	9. (A)	10. (D)	11. (A)	12. (C)

1. 시간 전치사

Restaurant visitors can enjoy a jazz performance every evening **at** 7 P.M.
식당 방문객은 매일 저녁 7시에 재즈공연을 즐길 수 있다.

해설 빈칸은 특정 시간을 나타내는 표현 앞 전치사 자리이다. '매일 저녁 7시에'라는 의미가 되어야 자연스러우므로 시각 앞에 쓰이는 (D)가 정답이다.

어휘 visitor 방문객 I enjoy 즐기다, 누리다 I jazz performance 재즈공연

＋ Key point

시간 전치사 at vs. on vs. in: at은 '특정 시각' 앞에, on은 '요일, 날짜' 앞에, in은 '월, 연도' 앞에 자리한다.

2. 기간 전치사

Attendees are welcome to bring snacks and beverages and enjoy it **during** the training session.
참석자는 교육 시간 동안 스낵과 음료를 가져와 즐길 수 있습니다.

해설 빈칸 뒤 명사구 the training session이 있으므로 전치사 (C)가 정답이다.

어휘 attendee 참석자 I training 교육

＋ Key point

전치사는 명사(구/절) 앞에, 접속사는 「주어+동사」를 갖춘 문장 앞에 올 수 있다.

3. 방향 / 위치 전치사

Pixel Design Studio is situated **along** Moorcroft Street, near its junction with Arden Terrace.
Pixel 디자인 스튜디오는 Moorcroft 가에 위치하는데, Arden Terrace의 교차로 근처이다.

해설 빈칸은 Moorcroft Street를 목적어로 하는 전치사 자리이다. '디자인 스튜디오가 Moorcroft 가에 있다'는 의미가 되어야 자연스러우므로 (A)가 정답이다.

어휘 situate 위치시키다 I near ~근처에 I junction 교차로

＋ Key point

장소 전치사 along vs. under vs. within: along은 '~를 따라',

under는 '~바로 밑에', within은 '(범위) 안에'를 의미한다.

4. 전치사 자리

Vacancies at the Alkyna Hotel are generally affordable, **considering** its quality and reputation.
Alkyna 호텔의 객실은 품질과 평판을 고려하면, 대체로 가격이 저렴하다.

해설 빈칸 앞 콤마, 빈칸 뒤 명사구 its quality and reputation이 있음을 고려할 때, 빈칸은 명사구를 목적어로 하는 전치사 자리이다. 문맥상으로도 '품질과 평판을 고려하면, 객실 가격이 대체로 저렴하다'는 의미가 되어야 자연스러우므로 (C)가 정답이다.

어휘 vacancy 빈 방, 공석 I generally 일반적으로, 대체로 I affordable (가격이) 알맞은 I quality 품질 I reputation 평판, 명성

5. 구전치사

Ms. Nguyen spoke **on behalf of** her entire division when receiving the Outstanding Design Award at the annual conference last month.
지난달 연례 총회에서 디자인 우수상을 받았을 때, Nguyen 씨가 부서 전체를 대신해 말했다.

해설 빈칸 뒤 명사구가 있으므로 전치사 자리이다. 접속사 when으로 연결된 두 절의 관계를 고려할 때, '지난달 상을 받는 자리에서 전체 부서를 대신해 Ms. Nguyen이 소감을 말했다'는 의미가 되어야 문맥상 자연스러우므로 구전치사 (A)가 정답이다.

어휘 entire 전체의 I division 부서 I outstanding 뛰어난, 우수한 I award 상 I annual 연례의

＋ Key point

구전치사의 경우, 구를 구성하는 가장 끝 단어의 품사에 따라 뒤에 올 목적어의 종류가 결정된다.
under the condition that ~(~라는 조건 하에)의 경우, 마지막 단어가 접속사 that이므로 뒤에 절(문장)의 형태가 와야 한다.

6. 특정 전치사와 어울리는 명사

The strategic announcement of the Acaru XC70 automobile was propelled by a decline **in** sales of the XC60 model.
Acaru XC70 자동차의 전략적 발표는 XC60 모델 매출에서의 감소로 인해 추진되었다.

해설 빈칸은 명사 a decline과 sales 사이 전치사 자리이다. 'XC60 모델의 매출 감소로'라는 의미가 되어야 자연스러우므로 'a decline in ~ (~에서의 감소[하락])'의 「명사+전치사」 관용 표현을 완성하는 (C)가 정답이다.

어휘 strategic 전략적인 I announcement 발표 I automobile 자동차 I propel (어떤 상황으로) 몰고 가다, 추진하다 I decline 감소, 하락 I sale 매출(량)

＋ Key word

The strategic announcement of the Acaru XC70 automobile was propelled by **a decline in sales** of the XC60 model.

7. 특정 전치사와 어울리는 동사

The Bard Theater Group invites the local residents **to** a free play at Fuller Amphitheater this weekend.
Bard Theater Group은 이번 주말 Fuller 원형극장에서 열리는 무료 공연에 지역 주민을 초대한다.

84 파고다 토익 종합서 RC

해설 빈칸은 a free play를 목적어로 취하는 전치사 자리이다. 동사 자리에 invite가 있으며 문맥상 '지역 주민을 무료 공연에 초대한다'는 의미가 되어야 자연스러우므로, 「invite A to B(A를 B에 초대하다)」의 구문을 완성하는 전치사 (C)가 정답이다.

어휘 invite 초대하다, 초청하다 | local resident 지역 주민 | amphitheater 원형 극장

+ Key word

The Bard Theater Group **invites the local residents to a free play** at Fuller Amphitheater this weekend.

---

8. 전치사 자리

Mr. Joseph is the most qualified person in the accounting department **after** Ms. Sims.

Joseph 씨는 회계부서에서 Sims 씨 다음으로 가장 적임자다.

해설 빈칸은 명사구 Sims 씨를 목적어로 하는 전치사 자리이므로 (B)가 정답이다.

어휘 qualified 자격이 있는 | accounting 회계 | department 부서

+ Key point

after는 전치사와 접속사 역할을 모두 할 수 있으며, 시간이나 순서상 '~의 뒤에, 다음에, 후에'를 의미한다.

9-12번은 다음 이메일에 관한 문제입니다.

수신: employees@eastgate.com
발신: jwillis@eastgate.com
날짜: 7월 16일
제목: 직무능력 개발 계획

전 직원 여러분께,

Eastgate에서는 8월 11일에 시작해 9월 8일까지 **9 내내** 계속해서 Strathfield Collective와 협력해 전 직원에게 직업 개발 계획을 제공할 예정입니다. 여러분 모두 배정된 날짜와 시간 목록을 이메일로 받게 됩니다. 여러분의 부서장 또한 이메일을 받게 됩니다. **10 따라서 사전에 보고하지 않아도 됩니다.**

대단히 **11 존경 받는** 컨설턴트인 Dr. Miranda Conner께서 세션을 진행합니다. 그 분께서는 여러분이 경력 **12 발달**을 개선하는 것을 지도해 줄 것입니다. 다른 부서나 역할로 진출해볼 아주 좋은 기회입니다. Dr. Conner께서는 여러분이 해낼 수 있도록 여러분의 개발 계획 작성을 도와줄 예정입니다.

세션에서 최대한으로 얻어갈 수 있도록, www.strathfield.com/about 에 올라온 소개 영상을 시청해 주시기 바랍니다.

감사합니다.

Joe Willis, 인사팀

어휘
professional 직업의, 전문적인 | development 개발 | planning 계획 | in partnership with ~와 제휴 [협력]하여 | assigned 할당된, 배정된 | session 세션, 수업 | run (강좌 등을) 운영하다 | guide 인도하다, 지도하다 | improve 개선하다 | career 경력 | opportunity 기회 | try 시도하다 | branch out into (새로운 분야로) 진출하다 | role 역할 | write out 자세히 작성하다 | ensure 보장하다 | get the most out of ~을 최대한 활용하다 | view 보다 | introduction 소개 | get there (목표 등을) 달성하다, 해내다

9. 전치사 자리

해설 빈칸은 현재분사 continuing과 until 전치사구 사이의 자리이다. 보기가 모두 전치사로 이루어져 있으므로, 빈칸 뒤 전치사 until과 함께 쓰여 'through until ~(~까지 줄곧, 내내)'를 의미하는 (A)가 정답이다.

+ Key word

Starting on 11 August and continuing through until 8 September, in partnership with Strathfield Collective, Eastgate will be providing professional development planning for all employees.

10. 문장 선택

(A) 추가적으로 통신 회선을 개선하기 위한 제안도 환영합니다.
(B) 이전 회의는 이미 취소되었습니다.
(C) 자세한 것은 Web 사이트를 참조해 주세요.
(D) 따라서, 사전에 보고하지 않아도 됩니다.

해설 빈칸 앞 부분의 '여러분 모두 배정된 날짜와 시간 목록을 이메일로 받게 된다. 여러분의 부서장 또한 이메일을 받게 된다'는 내용을 고려할 때, '따라서 (부서장에게) 사전에 보고하지 않아도 된다'는 내용으로 이어져야 인과관계로 문맥상 자연스럽게 연결되므로 (D)가 정답이다.

+ Key word

You will all have received an e-mail with a list of your assigned dates and times. Your team leaders will have also received the e-mails. Therefore, you do not need to give advance notice.

11. 과거분사

해설 빈칸은 부사 highly의 수식을 받으며, 명사 consultant를 수식하는 자리이다. 문맥상 '대단히 존경 받는 컨설턴트'라는 의미가 되어야 자연스러우므로 (A)가 정답이다.

+ Key point

considering은 전치사 및 접속사로, '~를 고려하면'을 의미한다.

12. 어휘 – 명사

해설 빈칸은 career와 복합명사를 이루는 명사 자리이다. 뒤에 나온 opportunity to try and branch out into different teams or roles에서 타 팀이나 역할로 진출할 기회라고 하므로 이를 받을 수 있는 말로 경력 발달이 적절하다. 따라서 (C)가 정답이다.

+ Key word

She will guide you in improving your career progression. This is a great opportunity to try and branch out into different teams or roles.

CHAPTER 09 접속사

CASE 집중훈련 본서 p.157

1. (B)	2. (C)	3. (D)	4. (A)	5. (B)	6. (B)
7. (B)	8. (C)				

1. 시간 접속사

Since he joined our group in January, Mr. Kang has

worked to raise Chevoir's brand awareness in the global marketplace.

1월에 그룹에 합류한 이후로, Kang 씨는 전 세계 시장에서 Chevoir의 브랜드 인지도를 높이기 위해 일해왔다.

해설 빈칸은 「주어+동사, 주어+동사」를 연결하는 접속사가 들어가야 한다. 종속절의 동사는 과거 시제이고 주절은 현재 완료이며 문맥상 '그룹에 합류한 이후로, 브랜드 인지도를 높이기 위해 일해왔다'는 의미가 되어야 하므로 시간의 부사절 접속사인 (B)가 정답이다. As much as는 보통 원급 표현(~만큼)이고, 접속사이면 양보의 의미(~이지만)로 쓰인다.

어휘 awareness 인식 | global 전 세계의 | marketplace 시장

✚ Key point
Since는 접속사로 쓸 때는 '~이래로, ~때문에'의 두 가지 뜻이 있고, 전치사로 쓰일 때는 '~이래로'라는 한 가지 뜻으로만 쓰인다.

---

2. 조건 접속사

This warranty is valid **only if** the product is used in the country in which it was purchased.

이 품질 보증서는 그 제품이 그것이 구매된 나라에서 사용되는 경우에만 유효하다.

해설 빈칸은 앞뒤의 두 절을 연결해줄 접속사 자리이다. 문맥상 '그 제품이 그것이 구입된 나라에서 사용되는 경우에만 유효하다'라는 의미가 되어야 자연스러우므로 (C)가 정답이다.

어휘 warranty 품질 보증서 | valid 유효한 | purchase 구입하다 | whenever ~할 때마다 | within ~이내에 | only if ~인 경우에만 | even though 비록 ~이긴 하지만

---

3. 조건 접속사

Weekly meetings generally take place in the 19th floor conference room **unless** otherwise noted on the company Web site.

회사 웹사이트에 달리 언급이 없는 한 주간 회의는 일반적으로 19층 회의실에서 열린다.

해설 빈칸은 분사 구문 noted를 이어주는 부사절 접속사 자리이다. 부사절 접속사 'unless'는 과거분사 구문 p.p.와 함께 쓰여, 'unless (otherwise) p.p. (달리 ~되지 않는 한)'을 의미하므로 (D)가 정답이다.

어휘 generally 일반적으로 | otherwise 달리, 그렇지 않다면 | note 언급하다

✚ Key point
분사 구문은 부사절의 「접속사+(주절과 동일한) 주어」를 생략하고 동사를 분사로 전환한 형태이다. 이때, 부사절의 동사와 주절의 주어와의 능동/수동 의미관계에 따라 분사 구문 내 현재/과거분사의 종류가 결정된다.

---

4. 조건 접속사

The corporation's profits over the next fiscal year will escalate, **assuming that** the lucrative merger with Shrader Financial can be concluded before the end of the quarter.

Shrader 금융과의 수익성 높은 합병이 분기말 전에 마무리될 수 있다고 가정하면, 다음 회계 연도에 기업이윤이 증가할 것이다.

해설 빈칸은 두 개의 절을 연결하는 부사절 접속사 자리이다. 두 절의 내용관계를 고려할 때, '분기말 전에 합병이 마무리될 수 있다고 가정하면, 다음 회계 연도에 기업이윤이 증가할 것'이라는 의미가 되어야 자연스러우므로 가정, 조건의 의미를 갖는 접속사 (A)가 정답이다.

어휘 corporation 기업 | profit 이윤 | fiscal 회계의 | escalate 증가되다 | lucrative 수익성이 좋은 | merger 합병 | conclude 결론을 내리다 | quarter 분기

5-8번은 다음 편지에 관한 문제입니다.

3월 14일
Amy Blanche 씨
4421 Council 가
Seattle, WA 98123

Blanche 씨께,

이 편지는 3월 9일자 귀하의 문의에 대한 **⑤답변**입니다. 저는 귀하께서 여름 동안 Denali 국립공원에서 투어 가이드로 일할 예정이고, 타주외 거주자 요금을 내지 않고 낚시 면허증을 발급받기를 원하는 걸로 알고 있습니다. 실은, 이곳에서 일하거나 공부를 하는 알래스카 이외 주민들을 위한 면제권이 있습니다. **⑥이에**, 귀하께서는 표준 요금으로 면허증을 받을 수 있는 경우에 해당됩니다. 고용 증명을 제공하는 한, 주내 면허증을 **⑦신청할 수 있습니다**. **⑧야생동물 위원회 사무실로 서류를 가져오시면 됩니다**. 저희가 고용주와 귀하의 신분을 확인한 후, 주내(州內) 가격으로 면허증이 부여될 것입니다.

안부를 전하며,

Douglas Jefferson 드림
야생동물 위원회, Anchorage 지사

어휘
inquiry 질의 | obtain 얻다, 획득하다 | license 자격증 | incur (비용을) 발생시키다, 물게 되다 | out-of-state 다른 주의 | resident 거주자 | fee 요금 | indeed 실은, 사실 | waiver 면제, 포기 | qualify 자격을 얻다 | standard rate 표준 요금 | in-state 주내의 | proof 증거(물), 증명 | employment 고용 | confirm 확인하다 | status 신분, 지위 | employer 고용주 | be eligible for ~의 자격이 있다 | wildlife 야생동물

---

5. 관용 표현

해설 빈칸은 전치사 in과 to사이 명사 자리이므로 'in response to(~에 답하여)'의 관용 표현을 완성하는 (B)가 정답이다.

6. 접속부사

해설 빈칸 앞 문장의 '이곳에서 일하거나 공부를 하는 비알래스카인들을 위한 면제권이 있다'는 내용과 빈칸 뒷부분의 '귀하께서는 표준 요금으로 자격증을 받을 수 있는 경우에 해당된다'는 내용을 고려할 때, 문맥상 두 문장이 인과관계로 연결되어야 자연스러우므로 (B)가 정답이다.

✚ Key word
There is indeed a waiver for non-Alaskans who work or study here. Accordingly, you do qualify to receive a license at the standard rate.

7. 동사의 시제

해설 빈칸은 주어 you에 대한 동사 자리이다. as long as 종속절의 시제가 현재임을 고려할 때, 주절의 시제 역시 현재가 되어야 문맥상 자연스러우므로 (B)가 정답이다.

✚ Key word
You **may apply** for an in-state license **as long as** you **provide** proof of employment.

8. 문장 선택

(A) 이번 시즌의 생선은 특히 신선합니다.
(B) 안타깝게도 Anchorage 지점은 현재 보수 공사를 위해 문을 닫았습니다.
(C) 야생동물 위원회 사무실로 서류를 가져오시면 됩니다.
(D) 라이선스를 갱신하려면 25달러의 수수료를 내야 합니다.

해설 빈칸 앞 문장의 '고용상태를 증명하면 주내 자격증을 신청할 수 있다'는 내용을 고려할 때, 문맥상 '사무실로 (고용상태를 증명하는) 서류를 가져오면 된다'는 내용으로 이어져야 자연스러우므로 (C)가 정답이다.

+ **Key word**

You may apply for an in-state license as long as you provide proof of employment. Simply bring your documents to the Wildlife Commission office.

CASE 집중훈련

본서 p.159

| 1. (A) | 2. (A) | 3. (C) | 4. (C) | 5. (A) | 6. (C) |
| 7. (B) | 8. (A) |

---

1. 이유 접속사

Because attendance at monthly book club meetings has been declining, the club leader decided that the group would select a different book.

월간 북클럽 회의의 참석률이 감소하고 있어서, 그룹이 다른 책을 고르는 걸로 클럽 리더는 결정했다.

해설 '------- 절1, 절2'의 구조로, 빈칸은 두 개의 절을 이어주는 접속사 자리이다. 문맥상 '북클럽 회의의 참석률이 감소하고 있어서, 그룹이 다른 책을 고르기로 했다'라는 의미가 되어야 자연스러우므로 '~이기 때문에'의 이유 접속사인 (A)가 정답이다.

어휘 attendance 출석률, 참석자 수 | monthly 월례의 | declining 기우는, 쇠퇴하는 | select 선정하다

---

2. 양보 접속사

Many stores are still demanding cash payments **even though** there are now lots of other alternatives.

많은 대안들이 있다고는 하지만, 여전히 많은 상점들이 현금 지급을 요구하고 있다.

해설 빈칸은 두 개의 절을 이어주는 접속사 자리이다. even though를 제외한 나머지는 부사 기능이므로 모두 소거된다. 문맥상 '많은 상점들이 여전히 현금 지급을 요구한다'는 것과 '많은 대안들이 있다'는 것은 대조되는 내용이므로 '비록 ~이지만'이란 뜻의 양보를 나타내는 접속사 (A)가 정답이다.

어휘 demand 요구하다, 따지다 | cash payment 현금 지급 | alternative 대안

+ **Key point**
양보를 나타내는 접속사
although, though, even though 비록 ~이지만
while ~하는 반면에
whereas ~한 반면에

---

3. 이유 접속사

Now that Eagle Sporting Goods has found a more suitable commercial space, it will start negotiating the lease agreement.

Eagle 스포츠용품점에서 보다 적합한 상업부지를 찾았으니, 임대 계약 협상을 시작할 것이다.

해설 빈칸은 두 개의 절을 연결하는 부사절 접속사 자리이다. 두 절의 내용을 고려할 때 원인과 결과로 이어지는 것이 자연스러우므로 (C)가 정답이다.

어휘 suitable 적합한 | commercial 상업의 | space 공간 | negotiate 협상하다 | lease agreement 임대 계약

+ **Key point**
① '------- 문장1, 문장2'의 구조에서 빈칸은 부사절 접속사 자리이다.
② 접속사 'now that(이제 ~이므로, ~이기 때문문)'은 인과, 'although (~지만, ~에도 불구하고)'는 양보의 의미를 전달한다.

---

4. 한정사

Mr. Campanella will develop training courses for the new design software, since **few** employees are familiar with the program.

프로그램에 익숙한 직원들이 거의 없기 때문에, Campanella 씨는 신규 디자인 소프트웨어용 교육과정을 개발할 것이다.

해설 빈칸은 명사 employees를 수식하는 자리이다. 접속사 since로 연결된 두 문장의 관계를 고려할 때, '신규 소프트웨어를 잘 다루는 직원이 거의 없기 때문에, 해당 교육과정을 개발할 것'이라는 의미가 되어야 자연스러우므로 '거의 ~ 없는'의 부정의 의미를 갖는 한정사 (C)가 정답이다.

어휘 develop 개발하다 | training course 교육과정 | be familiar with ~에 친숙하다, 익숙하다

+ **Key word**

Mr. Campanella **will develop training courses** for the new design software, **since few employees are familiar** with the program.

5-8번은 다음 이메일에 관한 문제입니다.

수신: Nick Peralta 〈nperalta@theorymail.com〉
발신: Libbie Sweeney 〈lsweeney@bruno.us〉
날짜: 9월 12일
제목: 오리엔테이션

Peralta 씨께,

올해 Bruno 아카데미의 견습 프로그램에 귀하의 자리를 확정해 드리게 되어 기쁩니다. 아시다시피, 프로그램은 월요일부터 수요일까지는 **⑤출석하는** 수업이 포함되는 반면 목요일과 금요일에는 자택에서 학습이 가능하다. 로그인이 의무사항은 아니 **⑥지만**, 전화로는 연락이 닿을 수 있어야 합니다.

수업은 Brighton 캠퍼스에서 10월 30일에 **⑦시작됩니다.** 앞으로 며칠 내 우편함을 확인해 주세요. **⑧상세한 일정과 지도를 받아보실 겁니다.** 곧 만나 뵙길 고대하겠습니다!

감사합니다.

Libbie Sweeney
채용담당관

어휘
delighted 기쁜 | confirm 확정하다 | position 자리 | intake 입학[채용] 인원수 | apprenticeship 견습, 수습 | aware 알고 있는 | entail 수반하다 | sign in 서명하(고 들어가)다 | reachable 닿을 수 있는, 도달 가능한 | in the coming days 며칠 내, 곧 | recruitment 채용

5. 동명사 자리

해설 빈칸은 동사 entail과 명사 classes 사이의 자리로, 동사의 목적어 역할을 하되, 뒤에 이어지는 명사를 자신의 목적어로 취해야 하므로 준동사 자리이다. 동사 entail은 동명사만을 목적어로 취할 수 있으므로 (A)가 정답이다.

6. 양보 접속사

해설 빈칸은 절과 절을 연결하는 부사절 접속사 자리이다. 문맥상 '로그인할 필요는 없지만, 전화로는 연락이 닿아야 한다'라는 의미가 되어야 자연스러우므로 '비록 ~지만'을 의미하는 부사절 접속사 (C)가 정답이다.

✛ Key point
'------- 문장1, 문장2'의 구조에서 빈칸은 부사절 접속사 자리이다.

7. 동사의 시제

해설 빈칸은 주어 The classes에 대한 동사 자리이다. 편지 발송일이 9월 12일이므로, '10월 30일에 수업이 시작될 것'이라는 의미를 완성하는 미래 시제 동사 (B)가 정답이다.

8. 문장 선택

(A) 상세한 일정과 지도를 받아보실 겁니다.
(B) 신청서를 처리하려면 먼저 서명하셔야 합니다.
(C) 새로운 견습생들은 업무용 전화를 받을 것입니다.
(D) 새로운 혜택을 곧 이용하실 수도 있습니다.

해설 빈칸 앞 문장의 '수업이 10월 30일에 시작됩니다. 앞으로 며칠 내 우편함을 확인해 주세요'라는 내용을 고려할 때, '(우편으로) 상세한 일정과 지도를 받을 것'이라는 내용으로 이어져야 자연스러우므로 (A)가 정답이다.

✛ Key word
The classes will commence on 30 October at the Brighton Campus. **Please check your mail in the coming days. You will receive a detailed schedule and map.**

CASE 집중훈련 본서 p.161

1. (D) **2.** (C) **3.** (C) **4.** (B) **5.** (D) **6.** (C)
7. (D) **8.** (B)

1. 고려 접속사

Considering the time allocated for this project is extremely short, it is important to prioritize speed at each phase of the project.

이 프로젝트에 할당된 시간이 매우 짧다는 점을 고려해 볼 때, 그 프로젝트의 각 단계의 속도에 우선순위를 두는 것이 중요하다.

해설 빈칸 뒤에 '주어 + 동사'의 절이 왔으므로 접속사 자리이며, 시간이 짧다는 점을 고려할 때 각 단계의 속도에 우선순위를 둬야 한다는 문맥에 적절한 (D)가 정답이다.

어휘 allocate 할당하다 | extremely 극도로 | prioritize 우선순위를 매기다 | phase 단계, 국면

---

2. 대비 접속사

In the event that the renovation of the lobby is incomplete, please use the garage entrance.

로비 개조작업이 미완성인 경우, 주차장 입구를 이용해 주시기 바랍니다.

해설 빈칸 뒤 두 개의 완전한 문장이 있으므로, 빈칸은 바로 뒤 이어지는 문장을 부사절로 만들어줄 접속사 (C)가 정답이다.

어휘 renovation 보수, 개조 | incomplete 불완전한, 미완성의 | garage 주차장, 차고 | entrance 입구

✛ Key point
① In the event that은 접속사 that으로 끝나므로 절(문장)이 뒤에 와야 하며, As a result of는 전치사 of로 끝나므로 명사 형태가 이어진다.
② 접속부사는 두 개의 문장 사이에서 의미적인 연결어 역할을 한다.

---

3. 결과 접속사

The spring sale last year was **so** profitable that it will take place again this April.

작년 봄 판매가 너무 수익이 좋아서, 올해 4월 다시 열릴 것이다.

해설 빈칸은 형용사 profitable을 수식하는 부사 자리이다. 형용사 뒤 that 절이 있음을 고려할 때, 'so ~ that ...(너무 ~해서 …하다)'의 구문을 완성하는 (C)가 정답이다.

어휘 profitable 수익성이 있는 | take place 개최되다, 일어나다

✛ Key point
결과를 나타내는 부사절 접속사 「~ so + 형용사/부사 + that」 문장은 '너무 ~해서 …하다'를 의미한다.

---

4. 어휘 - 부사

The intelligent guidance system is specially designed so that all workers can perform complex tasks **efficiently**.

모든 직원들이 복잡한 일을 효율적으로 실행하기 위해 지능적인 안내 시스템이 특별히 고안되었다.

해설 빈칸은 동사 perform을 수식하는 부사 자리이다. '복잡한 일을 효과적으로 수행할 수 있게'라는 내용이 되어야 자연스러우므로 (B)가 정답이다.

어휘 intelligent 영리한, 똑똑한 | guidance 지도(안내) | perform 시행하다 | complex 복잡한 | task 일, 과업

✛ Key word
The intelligent guidance system is specially designed so that all workers can **perform complex tasks efficiently**.

5-8번은 다음 공지에 관한 문제입니다.

3월 1일부터 오래 기다려온 Metro Wheels가 마침내 운행을 시작합니다. 이 셔틀 서비스는 도움없이 걷지 못하는 Jacobson의 고령층 시민들에게 **⑤제공될 것입니다.** 모든 Metro Wheel 버스는 휠체어 경사로와 온도조절이 되는 내부를 갖추고 있습니다. **⑥승객들은 승차 지점에서 20km 내 어디서든 하차할 수 있습니다.** 셔틀 서비스는 월요일부터 토요일, 오전 8시부터 오후 6시까지 운행할 예정입니다.

이용 일정을 잡으려면, 저희가 적절한 준비를 할 수 **⑦있도록**, 최소 3일 전 Metro Wheels 고객센터(555-3494)로 연락해 주세요. Metro Wheels 서비스는 무료이나, 재정 **⑧기부는** 권장됩니다. 온라인으로 지불하시거나 버스기사 우측에 놓인 수금함에 현금을 넣어주시면 됩니다.

---

5. 동사의 시제

해설 빈칸은 This shuttle service를 주어로 하는 동사 자리이다. 빈칸 앞 문장의 'Metro Wheels가 3월 1일부터 마침내 운행을 시작할 것'에서 미래 시제가 쓰이므로 이어지는 문장에서도 미래의 의미가 포함되어야 한다. 예정된 미래는 Will V 대신 현재 또는 현재 진행으로 쓸 수 있고 빈칸 뒤에 목적어없이 전명구가 나오므로 현재 진행 수동태인 (D)가 정답이다.

+ Key word
Starting 1 March, the long-awaited Metro Wheels will finally be ready for action. This shuttle service is being provided to Jacobson **senior citizens** who are unable to walk unassisted.

6. 문장 선택

(A) 주민들은 저렴한 요금으로 인해 대중 버스를 타는 경향이 있습니다.
(B) 오늘 Metro Wheels 서비스를 이용해 주셔서 감사합니다.
(C) 승객들은 승차 지점에서 20km내 어디든 하차할 수 있습니다.
(D) 운전자는 앞으로 20분 이내에 안내방송을 할 것입니다.

해설 빈칸 앞 문장의 모든 버스는 휠체어 경사로와 온도조절 내부를 갖추고 있다는 내용과 빈칸 다음 문장의 셔틀 서비스의 운행일정에 대한 설명을 고려할 때, 셔틀서비스를 안내하는 내용이 들어가야 자연스러우므로 '승객들은 승차지점 20km 내 어디서든 하차할 수 있다'는 내용의 (C)가 정답이다.

+ Key word
All Metro Wheel buses are equipped with wheelchair ramps and temperature-controlled interiors. Passengers can be dropped off anywhere within 20 kilometers of their departure point. The shuttle service will run from Monday – Saturday, 8 A.M. – 6 P.M.

7. 부사절 접속사

해설 빈칸은 완전한 두 문장을 연결하는 부사절 접속사 자리이다. 빈칸 뒷문장에 can이 있으므로 '저희가 적절한 준비를 할 수 있도록 최소 3일전 연락해 주세요'라는 의미를 만들어주는 'so that ~ can …(~가 …할 수 있도록)이라는 구문을 완성하는 (D)가 정답이다.

+ Key word
To schedule a trip, please **contact** the Metro Wheels guest center (555-3494) at least three days beforehand **so that we can make** the proper arrangements.

8. 사람 명사 vs. 사물 / 추상 명사

해설 빈칸은 financial의 수식을 받는 주어 자리이다. 접속사 but으로 연결된 두 문장의 관계를 고려할 때, '서비스는 무료이지만, 기부금은 권장된다'는 의미가 자연스러우므로 (B)가 정답이다.

+ Key point
명사 contributions vs. contributors: 명사 contribution은 '기부금'을, contributor는 '기부자'를 의미한다.

CASE 집중훈련   본서 p.163

1. (A) **2.** (A) **3.** (D) **4.** (B) **5.** (C) **6.** (B)
7. (D) **8.** (B)

---

1. 접속사 vs. 전치사

Given that there has been a 70 percent increase in sales, four new managers have been hired to deal with urgent matters.

판매량에서 70퍼센트의 증가가 있었다는 점을 감안하여, 긴급한 문제를 처리하기 위해 네 명의 매니저들이 고용되었다.

해설 '------ 절1, 절2'의 구조로, 빈칸은 두 개의 절을 이어주는 접속사 자리이므로 전치사인 (B), (D)는 먼저 소거하여 답을 고를 수 있는 문제이다. 문맥상 '판매량에서 70퍼센트의 증가가 있었다는 점을 감안해서, 새 매니저들이 고용되었다'는 의미가 자연스러우므로 '~을 감안하여'라는 뜻의 접속사 표현인 (A)가 정답이다.

어휘 sales 판매량, 매출액 | hire 고용하다 | deal with ~을 처리하다 | urgent 긴급한 | matter 사안, 문제 | given that ~을 감안하여[고려하여] | beyond ~을 넘어서 | as long as ~하는 동안, ~하는 한 | except for ~을 제외하고는, ~이 없으면

---

2. 접속사 vs. 전치사

Preventive maintenance of elevators in your building guarantees that minor problems can be resolved **before** they become major ones.

건물 내 엘리베이터의 예방용 유지보수는 사소한 문제가 심각해지기 전에 해결되는 것을 보장한다.

해설 빈칸 뒤 주어와 동사를 갖춘 완전한 문장이 있으므로 접속사 (A)가 정답이다.

어휘 preventive 예방의 | maintenance 유지보수 | guarantee 보장하다 | minor 사소한 | resolve 풀다, 해결하다 | major 심각한, 주요한

+ Key point
① 전치사 뒤에는 명사구가, 접속사 뒤에는 문장 형태를 갖춘 절이 올 수 있다.
② before는 전치사와 접속사 역할을 모두 할 수 있다.

---

3. 이유 접속사

Since Wes Chamberlain has now retired, Yumiko Fujihara will take over as our sales representative.

Wes Chamberlain이 이제 퇴직했기 때문에, Yumiko Fujihara가 우리의 영업 담당자로서 인계받을 것이다.

해설 빈칸은 앞뒤의 두 절을 연결해줄 접속사 자리이다. 문맥상 'Wes Chamberlain이 이제 퇴직했기 때문에, Yumiko Fujihara가 우리의 영업 담당자로서 인계받을 것이다'라는 인과관계의 의미로 전개되는 것이 자연스러우므로 이를 나타내 줄 이유 접속사인 (D)가 정답이다.

어휘 retire 퇴직하다, 은퇴하다 | take over 인계 받다 | sales representative 영업 담당자 | while ~하는 동안 | unless ~하지 않는다면 | though 비록 ~일지라도 | since ~이기 때문에; ~이후로

✦ **Key point**

이유 접속사: because, as, since, now that

....

4. 접속사 vs. 전치사

California Recycling Systems announced to its workers that all types of aluminum materials **except** aerosol cans should first be processed with hydraulic presses.

California Recycling Systems는 직원들에게 연무통을 제외한 모든 종류의 알루미늄 물체는 먼저 유압 프레스로 처리되어야 한다고 공지했다.

해설 빈칸은 that 명사절 내 주어 자리에 있는 명사구 2개를 연결하는 전치사 자리이다. 문맥상 '연무통을 제외한 모든 종류의 알루미늄 물체'라는 의미가 되어야 자연스러우므로 (B)가 정답이다.

어휘 recycling 재활용 | announce 알리다, 발표하다 | aluminum 알루미늄 | material 재료, 물질 | aerosol 연무제, 에어로졸 | process 처리하다 | hydraulic press 유[수]압 프레스

✦ **Key word**

California Recycling Systems announced to its workers that **all types of aluminum materials except aerosol cans** should first be processed with hydraulic presses.

5-8번은 다음 회람에 관한 문제입니다.

수신: Penasquitos 이사진
발신: 이사회 의장 Daniel Winokur
날짜: 5월 15일
제목: 회의

Penasquitos 사는 5월 22일 목요일 오후 5시에 본사에서 이사회 회의를 개최할 예정입니다. ⑤화상회의 시스템을 통해 참여하실 수도 있습니다.

일정상의 첫 업무는 다음 분기 운영비 목록을 ⑥승인하는 일이 될 것입니다. 이중 상당수는 ⑦정례적이기 때문에, 확정 절차는 그리 오래 걸리지 않을 것입니다. 그 확정 절차 ⑧이후에는, 제안된 본사 이전 건에 관하여 심도 있는 논의가 있을 것입니다.

어휘
executive 경영[운영] 간부[이사/중역] | executive board 중역[이사]회 | main office 본사 | via 통하여 | videoconferencing 화상 회의 | operating expenses 운영비 | routine 정례적인 | relocation 이전 | headquarters 본사

---

5. 문장 선택

(A) 가능한 한 빨리 강좌에 등록해 주세요.
(B) 그 공사 프로젝트는 지난주에 마무리되었습니다.
(C) 화상회의 시스템을 통해 참여하실 수도 있습니다.
(D) 이 문제는 이사회에 의해 시기적절하게 처리될 것입니다.

해설 회의 일정을 알리는 앞 문장에 대한 부연설명이 되는 (C)가 정답이다.

✦ **Key word**

Penasquitos Industries will hold an executive board meeting at 5:00 P.M. on Thursday, May 22 at our main office. You also have the option of participating via our videoconferencing system.

---

6. 동사의 태 / 시제

해설 미래에 있을 회의의 주제를 알려주고 있으므로 미래 시제 동사인 (B)가 정답이다.

✦ **Key word**

Penasquitos Industries will hold an executive board meeting at 5:00 P.M. on Thursday, May 22 at our main office. You also have the option of participating via our videoconferencing system. The first task on our schedule will be to approve the list of operating expenses for next quarter.

7. 어휘 – 형용사

해설 회의 시간이 길지 않은 이유는 회의 주제가 정례적인 것이어야 자연스러우므로 (D)가 정답이다.

✦ **Key word**

Since many of these are routine, the confirmation process should not take too long.

8. 접속사 vs. 전치사

해설 빈칸은 먼저 that confirmation라는 명사를 목적어로 취하는 전치사 자리이고, 문맥상 회의 진행 순서를 설명하고 있으므로 (B)가 정답이다.

✦ **Key word**

Since many of these are routine, the confirmation process should not take too long. After that confirmation, we'll have a serious talk about the proposed relocation of our headquarters.

CASE 집중훈련   본서 p.165

1. (B)   **2.** (A)   **3.** (D)   **4.** (B)   **5.** (A)   **6.** (C)
7. (C)   **8.** (C)

---

1. 어휘 – 동사

Senior employees are required to have regular meetings with interns while **assessing** their progress.

선임 직원들은 인턴들의 진행과정을 평가하면서 그들과 정기적인 면담을 해야 한다.

해설 빈칸은 their progress를 목적어로 하는 동사 자리이다. 접속사 while로 연결된 두 문장의 관계를 고려할 때, '인턴들의 진행과정을 평가하면서 정기적으로 면담을 해야 한다'는 의미가 자연스러우므로 (B)가 정답이다.

어휘 senior 상급의, 고위의 | employee 직원 | require 요구하다 | regular 정기적인, 규칙적인 | progress 진행, 진척

✦ **Key word**

Senior employees are required to **have regular meetings with interns while assessing their progress**.

....

2. 접속사 자리

Visitors must keep their phones on silent mode at all times **while** on the studio grounds.

방문객은 스튜디오 구역에 있는 동안 휴대폰을 항상 무음으로 해놓아야 합니다.

해설 빈칸은 완전한 문장과 on 전명구 사이의 자리이다. 문맥상 '스튜디오 구역에 있는 동안 휴대폰을 무음으로 해놓아야 한다'는 의미가 되어야 자연스러우므로 접속사 (A)가 정답이다.

어휘 silent 조용한 | mode 방식, 모드 | at all times 항상 | grounds (특정용도를 위한) 장

✛ Key point

접속사 while의 특징: 「while + (주어 + be동사) + 전명구」의 구조에서 종속절과 주절의 주어가 동일한 경우, 「주격 인칭대명사(he, it, they) 등 + be동사」는 생략 가능하다: Visitors must keep their phones on silent mode at all times **while (they are) on the studio grounds**.

---

3. 부사 자리

The deposit is **definitely** reimbursable as indicated so long as the following requirements are met.

보증금은 명시된 대로 다음의 필요 조건을 맞추는 한 분명히 상환받을 수 있다.

해설 빈칸은 형용사 reimbursable를 수식하는 부사 자리이므로 (D)가 정답이다.

어휘 deposit 보증금 | as indicated 명시된 대로 | reimbursable 상환받을 수 있는 | so long as ~하는 한 | requirement 필요 조건

---

4. 명사 자리

To avoid leakage, users should exercise **caution** when replacing the toner cartridge.

새지 않도록 하려면, 이용자들은 토너 카트리지를 교체할 때 주의해야 한다.

해설 빈칸은 동사 exercise와 when 부사절 사이의 자리이다. 문맥상 '주의를 해야 한다'는 의미가 되어야 자연스러우므로 타동사 exercise의 목적어인 명사 (B)가 정답이다.

어휘 avoid 피하다 | leakage 누출 | exercise 행사하다, 발휘하다 | replace 대체하다, 대신하다 | toner cartridge 토너 카트리지

✛ Key point

① 자동사면서 타동사인 동사의 경우, 문장 내에서 어떤 역할/의미인지 문맥을 통해 파악한다:
동사 exercise는 자동사-'운동하다', 타동사-'행사하다, 발휘하다'를 의미한다.
② 관용 표현 exercise caution은 '주의하다, 조심하다'를 의미한다.

5-8번은 다음 보도자료에 관한 문제입니다.

즉시 배포용
연락 담당자: Shirley Frazier, (188) 555-7996

(3월 5일) — Tulare의 북부지역과 도심을 연결하는 대교가 정식으로 개통될 예정임을 Merrill 교통국에서 알려드리게 되어 영광입니다. Tulare 주민 여러분은 3월 11일 오후 12시 30분부터 2시 30분까지 열리는 개통식에 **⑤참여해** 주시길 권장드립니다. 행사에서는 최근 **⑥추가된** 버스 전용 차선도 공개될 예정입니다. 이 대교는 Brightwater Limited에서 설계했으며 교통 혼잡을 완화시켜줄 것으로 예상됩니다. **⑦실제로**, 이동 시간을 최대 30분까지 줄여줄 것입니다. 이 공사 프로젝트는 3년 만에 마침내 완공됐습니다. **⑧노동자 파업과 관련한 지연이 몇 번 있었습니다.** 개통식에서 모든 분을 뵐 수 있길 바랍니다.

어휘

immediate 즉각적인 | release 배포, 발표 | transportation 수송 (기관) | announce 발표하다 | bridge 다리 | connect 연결하다 | northern 북부의 | part 지역, 부분 | officially 공식적으로 | resident 주민 | unveil 발표하다 | recently 최근에 | design 설계하다 | reduce 줄이다, 축소하다 | congestion 혼잡 | travel time 이동 시간 | construction 건설, 공사 | finally 마침내 | complete 완료된 | in progress 진행 중인 | ceremony 식, 의식

---

5. to부정사 자리

해설 빈칸은 수동태 동사구와 전치사구를 연결하는 자리이다. 동사 자리에 encourage가 있으며 수동태 형태임을 고려할 때 to부정사 자리임을 알 수 있으므로 (A)가 정답이다.

✛ Key point

동사 encourage는 목적격 보어 자리에 to부정사를 취하는 대표적인 5형식 동사로, 다음과 같은 문장 구조를 취한다: [능동태] 「S + encourage + O + to부정사」 → [수동태] 「O + be encouraged + to부정사 + (by S)」

---

6. 현재분사 vs. 과거분사

해설 빈칸은 부사 recently의 수식을 받으면서, 복합명사 bus lanes를 수식하는 자리이다. 버스 전용 차선이 추가되었다는 수동의 의미가 되어야 문맥상 자연스러우므로 과거분사 (C)가 정답이다.

✛ Key point

additive는 명사 '첨가물'의 의미로 주로 사용되며, 형용사 '부가적인'의 의미일 때에는 부가적인 성질을 갖는다는 의미를 내포한다.

---

7. 접속부사

해설 빈칸은 두 문장의 의미를 연결하는 접속부사 자리이다. 앞 문장의 '다리는 교통 혼잡을 줄여줄 것으로 예상된다'는 내용과 빈칸 뒷부분의 '이동 시간을 최대 30분까지 줄여줄 것'이라는 내용을 고려할 때 뒷문장에서 교통 혼잡 개선 정도를 구체적으로 제시하며 강조하고 있음을 알 수 있으므로, 방금 한 말에 대해 자세한 내용을 덧붙일 때 쓰이는 접속부사 (C)가 정답이다.

✛ Key word

The **bridge** was designed by Brightwater Limited and **is expected to reduce congestion**.
In fact, it will reduce travel times by up to 30 minutes.

---

8. 문장 선택

(A) 그 도시에 대한 분석 결과 몇 가지 놀라운 추세가 드러났습니다.
(B) 전기자동차가 가까운 미래에 선도할 수 있습니다.
(C) 노동자 파업과 관련한 지연이 몇 번 있었습니다.
(D) 새 계획이 대중에게 공개되었습니다.

해설 빈칸 앞 문장의 3년 만에 공사 프로젝트가 완료됐다는 내용을 고려할 때, 그 이유를 설명하는 내용으로 이어져야 문맥상 연결이 자연스러우므로 (C)가 정답이다.

✛ Key word

The construction project is finally complete after having been in progress for three years. There were several delays relating to worker strikes.

CASE 집중훈련

본서 p.167

1. (B) **2.** (B) **3.** (D) **4.** (C) **5.** (A) **6.** (D)
7. (C) **8.** (D)

---

1. 등위 접속사

Both full-time and part-time business programs have advantages, **so** prospective students should weigh each option carefully against the other.

전일제와 시간제 비즈니스 프로그램들 둘 다 이점이 있어, 예비 학생들은 각 옵션을 다른 것에 견주어 주의 깊게 따져봐야 한다.

해설 빈칸은 앞뒤의 두 절을 연결해줄 접속사 자리이다. 앞뒤의 두 절이 서로 인과관계의 의미로 전개되는 것이 자연스러우므로 이를 나타내 줄 등위 접속사인 (B)가 정답이다.

어휘 advantage 이점 | prospective student 예비 학생, 입학 희망자 | weigh 따져보다, 견주다, 판단하다 | carefully 주의 깊게

✛ Key point

등위 접속사는 앞뒤로 동일한 문장 성분을 병치 구조로 연결하여 중복된 부분은 생략할 수 있으며, 문두에 올 수 없다는 점에서 부사절 접속사와 구분된다.

---

2. 어휘 - 명사

Many personal trainers find working with trainees to be a rewarding **aspect** of the job, but the overall satisfaction is relatively low.

많은 개인 트레이너들은 교육생들과 일하는 것이 그 일의 보람 있는 면이라는 것을 알지만 전반적인 만족도는 비교적 낮다.

해설 빈칸은 형용사 rewarding의 수식을 받는 명사 자리이다. 문맥상 '교육생들과 일하는 것이 그 일의 보람 있는 면이다'라는 의미가 되어야 자연스러우므로 (B)가 정답이다.

어휘 rewarding 보람이 있는 | overall 전반적인 | relatively 비교적, 상대적으로 | overview 개관, 개요 | aspect 측면

✛ Key word

Many personal trainers **find working with trainees to be a rewarding aspect of the job**, but the overall satisfaction is relatively low.

---

3. 등위 접속사

The new sleeping bags by Wildling Provisions have more space than the previous designs, **but** they are not comfortable.

Wilding Provisions가 만든 새 침낭은 이전 디자인보다 공간은 더 넓지만, 편하지는 않다.

해설 빈칸 앞뒤의 절을 병렬 관계로 연결해주는 접속사를 찾는 문제이다. 문맥상 '새 침낭이 공간은 더 넓지만, 편하지는 않다'란 의미가 자연스러우므로 '역접'의 의미를 지닌 등위 접속사 (D)가 정답이다.

어휘 sleeping bag 침낭 | space 공간, 자리 | previous 이전의 | comfortable 편한, 편안한

✛ Key point

등위 접속사는 문법적 특성이 동등한 단어, 구, 절을 연결하며 중복된 부분은 생략할 수 있다.
and 그리고 or 또는 but 그러나 yet 그러나 so 그래서 for 왜냐하면

---

4. 어휘 - 부사

Pontchartrain Supermarket has expanded **considerably**, and its Baton Rouge location now has a baked goods section as well as a pharmacy.

Pontchartrain 슈퍼마켓은 상당히 규모가 커져서, Baton Rouge 지점에는 이제 약국뿐만 아니라 제과 구역도 있다.

해설 빈칸은 동사 expanded를 수식하는 부사 자리이다. 접속사 and로 연결된 문장의 내용을 고려할 때, '슈퍼마켓의 규모가 상당히 커졌다'는 의미가 자연스러우므로 (C)가 정답이다.

어휘 expand 확대하다, 확장하다 | location 지점 | baked goods 제과 | section 구역, 섹션 | as well as ~뿐만 아니라 | pharmacy 약국

✛ Key word

Pontchartrain Supermarket has **expanded considerably**, **and its** Baton Rouge **location now has a baked goods section** as well as a pharmacy.

5-8번은 다음 정보에 관한 문제입니다.

Pelmont 교육협회(PEA)는 연례 기금마련 행사의 20주년을 기념하게 되어 **⑤자랑스럽습니다.**

이 행사에서는 교육자, **⑥기부자**, 그리고 관심 있는 주민들이 모여 PEA가 지역 교육 프로그램을 개선하는 데 이뤄낸 진전을 인정하는 자리를 가질 것입니다. **⑦기념행사는 4월 8일 금요일에 열립니다.** Lavantino's에서 준비한 저녁식사는 오후 6시 정각에 시작됩니다.

오후 8시 30분에는 추첨행사가 있을 예정입니다. 손님들은 오후 10시 30분에 행사가 **⑧끝날** 때까지 머물며 어울리실 수 있습니다.

어휘

education 교육 | association 협회 | mark 기념하다, 표시하다 | annual 연례의, 연간의 | fundraiser 기금모금 행사 | allow 허용하다, 허락하다 | educator 교육자 | resident 거주자, 주민 | recognize 알아보다, 인정하다 | progress 진척, 진전 | improve 개선하다, 향상시키다 | cater 음식을 공급하다 | promptly 정각에, 즉시 | raffle (기금 모금을 위한) 복권, 래플 | permit 허용하다, 허락하다 | stick around 가지않고 있다 | mingle (사람들과) 어울리다

---

5. 어휘 - 형용사

해설 빈칸은 be동사 뒤 주격보어 자리이다. 빈칸 뒤 to부정사구의 내용을 고려할 때 '20주년을 기념하게 되어 자랑스럽다'는 내용이 되어야 자연스러우므로, 'be proud to V(~하게 되어 자랑스럽다)'의 표현을 완성하는 (A)가 정답이다.

✛ Key word

The Pelmont Education Association (PEA) is **proud to mark the 20th year of its annual fundraiser**.

---

6. 사람 명사 vs. 사물 / 추상 명사

해설 동사 allow의 목적어 자리에 3개의 명사가 나열된 구조이므로, 빈칸은 명사 자리이다. 빈칸 앞, 뒤에 자리한 명사들이 모두 사람 명사임을 고려할 때, 문맥상 '교육자, 기부자, 관심있는 사람들이 모이는 자리가 될 것'이라는 내용이 되어야 자연스러우므로 사람 명사 (D)가 정답이다.

✛ Key point

명사 donor vs. donation: 명사 donor는 '기부자'를, 명사 donation은 '기부'를 의미한다.

---

7. 문장 선택

(A) PEA 본사는 수리로 인해 다음 주에 문을 열지 않을 것입니다.
(B) PEA는 현재 회원 신청을 받고 있지 않습니다.
(C) 기념행사는 4월 8일 금요일에 열릴 것입니다.
(D) 작년 행사에는 소수의 손님이 몰렸습니다.

해설 빈칸 뒷문장의 '저녁식사가 오후 6시 정각에 시작된다'는 내용을 고려할 때, 기념행사 일정을 알려주는 내용이 앞에 들어가야 자연스러우므로 (C)가 정답이다.

+ Key word

The celebration will take place on Friday, April 8. Dinner, catered by Lavantino's, **will begin promptly at 6:00 P.M.**

8. 어휘 - 동사

해설 빈칸은 주어 the event에 대한 동사 자리이다. 빈칸 앞 부분의 '오후 6시에 저녁식사, 오후 8시 30분에 추첨행사가 있을 것'이라는 내용과 접속사 until로 연결된 주절과 종속절의 관계를 고려할 때, 문맥상 '오후 10시 30분에 행사가 끝날 때까지 손님들은 머무르는 것이 허용된다'는 내용이 되어야 자연스러우므로 (D)가 정답이다.

+ Key word

Dinner, catered by Lavantino's, will **begin** promptly at 6:00 P.M.
There will be **a raffle at 8:30 P.M. Guests are permitted to stick around** and mingle **until the event concludes at 10:30 P.M.**

CASE 집중훈련
본서 p.169

1. (B) 2. (D) 3. (B) 4. (D) 5. (A) 6. (C)
7. (A) 8. (B)

1. 상관 접속사

Mountainview Hotel offers **both** valet parking and complimentary breakfasts to all VIP guests.
Mountainview 호텔에서는 모든 VIP 고객들에게 대리 주차와 무료 아침식사를 둘 다 제공한다.

해설 동사 offer의 목적어 자리에 명사구가 등위 접속사 and로 연결된 구조이므로, 빈칸은 상관 접속사 both A and B 'A, B 둘 다'를 완성시키는 (B)가 정답이다.

어휘 valet parking 대리 주차 | complimentary 무료의

+ Key word

Hillside Condos **offers both private parking and wireless internet service** to short-term lease residents.

---

2. 상관 접속사

Greenery Architecture specializes in sustainable design that is affordable **as well as** environmentally friendly.
Greenery 건축회사는 환경친화적일 뿐만 아니라 합리적인 비용의 지속 가능한 설계를 전문으로 한다.

해설 빈칸 앞, 뒤로 형용사가 나란히 있으므로 서로 동등한 대상을 연결해주는 상관 접속사 (D)가 정답이다.

어휘 architecture 건축 | specialize in ~를 전문으로 하다 | sustainable 지속 가능한 | affordable (비용이) 합리적인 | environmentally friendly 환경친화적인

+ Key point

'A as well as B'는 'B뿐만 아니라 A도'라는 부가의 의미로 사용되며, A와 B를 병렬시킨다.

---

3. 상관 접속사

Rather than laying off employees, the CEO decided to reduce executive travel privileges.
직원들을 해고하는 대신, CEO는 임원들의 출장 특혜를 줄이기로 결정했다.

해설 문맥상 '직원해고 대신, 임원 출장 특혜 줄이기'라는 내용이 자연스러우므로, 빈칸은 동명사구를 목적어로 취하는 자리이다. 따라서 (B) Rather than이 정답이다. rather than의 중심으로 서로 상반되는 내용이 온다는 점을 기억하자.

어휘 lay off 해고하다 | decide 결정하다 | reduce 줄이다 | executive 임원 | privilege 특전, 특혜

---

4. 상관 접속사

The Hannam Library is seeking volunteers between the hours of 9 **and** 6 for its summer program.
Hannam 도서관은 여름 프로그램을 위해 9시에서 6시 사이에 자원봉사자들 구하고 있다.

해설 빈칸은 시간을 나타내는 표현 9과 6사이에 올 접속사 자리이다. 빈칸 앞 부분에 between이 있으므로 'between A and B(A와 B 사이에)'의 관용 표현을 완성하는 (D)가 정답이다.

어휘 seek 찾다, 구하다 | volunteer 자원봉사자

+ Key word

The Hannam Library is seeking volunteers **between** the hours of **9 and 6** for its summer program.

5-8번은 다음 이메일에 관한 문제입니다.

수신: Jessie Reyes
발신: Wade Morton
날짜: 11월 24일
제목: 파티 출장요리

Jessie께,

저희 송년회 때 Benson Caterers를 이용하기로 했습니다. 그래서 이제 파티**⑤**를 위해 필요한 모든 계획이 확정됐습니다.

기술지원 팀에서 행사장에 카메라, 모니터, 음향 장비 설치를 **⑥도와줄 겁니다.** 하지만 음식, 음료, 선물용 가방을 준비해 줄 팀이 더 필요합니다. 또한, **⑦행사가** 끝난 후 청소를 담당할 팀도 필요할 거예요. 제품 디자인팀에서 늦게까지 있을 거라고 들었어요. **⑧그 일에 자원해 달라고 요청드려야겠어요.** 확인을 받으면 알려드릴게요. 혹시 모르니, 대안을 마련해 놔야 해요.

감사합니다.

Wade

5. 전치사

해설 빈칸은 명사구 the party와 함께 전명구를 이룸, 앞의 명사 plans를 수식하는 전치사 자리이다. 파티를 위한 계획이라는 의미가 되어야 문맥상 자연스러우므로 목적을 나타내는 (A)가 정답이다.

+ Key word

This means that all of the necessary **plans for the party** are now confirmed.

6. 동사의 시제

해설 빈칸은 주어 Our technical support team에 대한 동사 자리이다. 다가올 행사에 대해 이야기하고 있으며, 뒤에 오는 문장들이 모두 미래 시제이므로 동사의 미래 시제 (C)가 정답이다.

7. 어휘 - 명사

해설 빈칸은 전치사 after의 목적어 자리이다. 송년회 준비사항에 대해 이야기를 전개하고 있으므로 송년회가 끝난 후 정리를 담당할 부서가 필요하다는 내용으로 이어져야 문맥상 연결이 자연스러우므로 송년회를 의미하는 (A)가 정답이다.

+ Key word

I have decided to go with Benson Caterers **for our end-of-year party**.
Additionally, we will need a team to clean up after the ceremony.

8. 문장 선택

(A) 팀들은 그에 따라 서로 다른 시간대에 도착할 거예요.
(B) 그 일에 자원해 달라고 요청드려야겠어요.
(C) 이맘때면 다른 팀과의 소통이 느려져요.
(D) 그 장소는 모두에게 너무 작을 수도 있어요.

해설 빈칸 앞 부분의 행사가 끝난 후 청소를 담당할 팀도 필요한데, 제품 디자인팀에서 늦게까지 있을 거라고 들었다는 내용과 빈칸 뒷부분의 확인 후 알려주겠다는 내용을 고려할 때, 그 일을 맡아달라고 요청해야겠다는 내용으로 이어져야 문맥상 연결이 자연스러우므로 (B)가 정답이다.

+ Key word

Additionally, we will need a team to clean up after the ceremony. I heard that the product design team will stay late. We should ask them to volunteer to do that. I will receive confirmation and let you know.

CASE 집중훈련

본서 p.171

1. (B) **2.** (D) **3.** (C) **4.** (C) **5.** (C) **6.** (C)
7. (A) **8.** (A)

1. 명사절 접속사 자리

The goal of probationary period is to figure out **whether** the skills and performances of the employee matches their résumé.

수습 기간의 목표는 직원의 기량과 성과가 이력서에 부합하는지의 여부를 알아보기 위한 것이다.

해설 빈칸은 타동사 figure out의 목적어 역할을 하면서 빈칸 뒤의 완전한 절을 이끄는 명사절 접속사 자리이다. 보기 중 명사절 접속사는 whether '~인지 아닌지' 뿐이며, '직원의 기량과 성과가 이력서와 부합하는지를 알아보기 위한 것이다'라는 의미가 되어야 자연스러우므로 (B)가 정답이다.

어휘 goal 목표 | probationary period 견습 기간 | figure out 알아내다 | performance 성과 | match 부합하다 | résumé 이력서

+ Key point

명사절 접속사는 명사 자리에서 절을 이끄는 접속사로 that, whether, when, where, why, how 등이 있다.

---

2. 명사절 접속사 자리

What needs to be determined is the date for the company's upcoming charity fundraiser.

결정되어야 하는 것은 곧 있을 회사 자선 모금 행사를 위한 날짜이다.

해설 빈칸은 본동사 is 앞에서 명사절을 이끄는 명사절 접속사 자리이다. 빈칸 뒤에 needs to be determined라는 주어가 빠진 불완전한 절이 왔으며, 명사절 접속사 what은 불완전한 절을 이끌며 '것, 무엇'을 의미함을 고려할 때, '결정되어야 하는 것'이라는 의미가 되어야 자연스러우므로 (D)가 정답이다.

어휘 determine 알아내다, 결정하다 | upcoming 다가오는, 곧 있을 | charity fundraiser 자선 모금 행사

+ Key point

명사절 접속사 what은 불완전한 절을 이끌며, 문장에서 주어·목적어·보어 역할을 한다.

---

3. 어휘 - 동사

Mr. Heath was **flattered** that his landscape photographs were used on the company's official Web site.

Heath 씨는 그의 풍경 사진이 회사의 공식 웹사이트에 사용되어서 으쓱해졌다.

해설 빈칸은 주어의 기분/상태를 설명하는 보어 자리이다. 문맥상 '자신이 찍은 사진이 웹사이트에 사용되어서 으쓱해졌다'는 내용이 되어야 자연스러우므로 (C)가 정답이다.

어휘 landscape 풍경, 경치 | official 공식의

---

4. 어휘 - 동사

Sterlington Supermarket sent an e-mail to its frequent customers **confirming** that it now provides free same-day shipping.

Sterlington 슈퍼마켓은 현재 무료 당일 배송을 제공한다는 확인 이메일을 단골 고객들에게 발송했다.

해설 빈칸은 an e-mail을 수식하는 현재분사 자리이다. 빈칸은 뒤에 that 명사절을 목적어로 취하고 있으며, 문맥상 that절 이하의 내용이 사실이라고 확인하는 이메일, 즉, 현재 무료 당일 배송 행사를 진행한다고 알려주는 이메일을 단골 고객에게 보냈다는 의미가 되어야 문맥상 자연스러우므로 (C)가 정답이다. 이 문장처럼 분사구나 관계절이 명사를 수식할 때 수식하는 명사 바로 뒤에 오지 않을 수 있음을 기억하자.

어휘 frequent customer 단골 고객 | provide 제공하다 | free 무료의 | same-day 당일의 | shipping 배송

✛ Key word

Sterlington **Supermarket sent an e-mail** to its frequent customers **confirming that** it now provides free same-day shipping.

5-8번은 다음 이메일에 관한 문제입니다.

수신: TeriKim@globobiz.com
발신: Frieda.Juarez@DBZTech.com
날짜: 10월 30일
제목: 회신: 소프트웨어 문제

Kim 씨께,

귀하의 부서가 그룹웨어 파일 시스템에 접속하지 못해 불편을 끼쳐드린 점 사과드립니다. 다른 부서들도 동일한 불만을 표하고 있습니다. 로그인 정보 변경을 **⑤시도했었는지**를 아는 것이 도움이 됩니다.

저희는 아직 이 문제의 원인을 조사하는 중입니다. **⑥대개는**, 서버 결함 문제나 호환되지 않는 이전 버전의 소프트웨어로 인해 발생합니다. **⑦잠시 시간을 내어 최신 소프트웨어 업데이트를 다운받았는지 확인해 주시기 바랍니다.** 저희 팀에서는 그 문제에 대해 조사하는 중이고, 앞으로 24시간 **⑧내로** 문제가 해결될 것 같습니다. 해결되면, 모든 분께 이메일을 발송해드리겠습니다.

감사합니다.

Frieda Juarez
Digital Solutions 애널리스트

어휘

apologize 사과하다 | inconvenience 불편, 애로 | cause 야기하다 | department 부서 | inability 무능 | access 접속하다 | groupware 그룹웨어 | complaint 불평, 항의 | helpful 도움이 되는 | investigate 조사하다 | source 근원, 원천 | trouble 문제 | faulty 결함이 있는, 잘못된 | server 서버 | incompatible 호환성이 없는 | look into ~를 살펴보다 | issue 문제 | sort out ~를 정리하다 | analyst 분석가, 애널리스트

5. 동사의 시제

해설 빈칸은 that명사절 내 주어 you에 대한 동사 자리이다. 빈칸 앞 부분에서 '그룹웨어 파일 시스템에 접속하지 못해 불편을 끼쳐드린 점'이라고 했으므로, 문맥상 '로그인 정보 변경을 시도했었는지를 아는 것은 도움이 된다'는 내용으로 이어져야 자연스러우므로 과거 시제 동사 (C)가 정답이다.

✛ Key word

I apologize for **the inconvenience caused by your department's inability to access the groupware file system**. Others have been making the same complaint. It is **helpful to know that you attempted to change your login information**.

---

6. 접속부사

해설 빈칸은 문장 수식 부사 자리이다. 빈칸 앞 문장의 '아직 문제 원인을 조사하는 중'이라는 내용을 고려할 때, 문맥상 '대개 이런 문제는 서버 결함이나 호환되지 않는 이전 버전의 소프트웨어로 인해 발생한다'는 내용으로 이어져야 자연스러우므로 (C)가 정답이다.

✛ Key word

We're **still investigating the source of this trouble. Ordinarily, it is caused by a faulty server or an incompatible older version of the software.**

7. 문장 선택

(A) 잠시 시간을 내어 최신 소프트웨어 업데이트를 다운받았는지 확인해 주시기 바랍니다.
(B) 파일 공유를 통해 부서 간 협업을 강화할 수 있습니다.
(C) 현재 로그인 정보가 작동하지 않는 것 같습니다.
(D) IT 전문가 분들이 각 부서를 개별적으로 교육할 것입니다.

해설 빈칸 앞 문장의 '대개는 서버 결함 문제나 호환되지 않는 이전 버전의 소프트웨어로 인해 발생한다'는 내용을 고려할 때, '소프트웨어가 최신버전인지 확인해보라'는 내용으로 이어져야 문맥상 자연스러우므로 (A)가 정답이다.

✛ Key word

Ordinarily, it is caused by a faulty server or an incompatible older version of the software. **Take a moment to verify that you have downloaded the latest software update.**

8. 전치사 자리

해설 빈칸은 수동태 문장과 명사구 사이의 자리이므로, 기간 명사구를 목적어로 하는 전치사 (A)가 정답이다.

✛ Key point

수동태 문장에는 목적어가 있을 수 없으며 동사 뒤에는 수식어구만이 올 수 있다.

CASE 집중훈련 본서 p.173

1. (C) **2.** (B) **3.** (D) **4.** (A) **5.** (D) **6.** (B)
7. (A) **8.** (A)

---

1. 명사절 접속사 that

The manager requests **that** all interns submit their monthly progress reports by 3 P.M. on April 30.

관리자는 모든 인턴들이 그들의 월간 경과 보고서를 4월 30일 오후 3시까지 제출할 것을 요청한다.

해설 동사 request의 목적어 자리이다. 빈칸 뒤 완전한 문장이 이어지므로, 문장을 명사절로 만들어주는 명사절 접속사 (C)가 정답이다. if도 명사절 접속사로 쓰이지만 '~인지'는 문맥에 맞지 않는다.

어휘 submit 제출하다 | monthly 매월의 | progress report 경과 보고

2. 명사절 접속사 that

The fact **that** celebrity endorsements can cause both positive and negative publicity is an important aspect of advertising.

유명인 광고가 긍정적인 홍보와 부정적인 홍보에 모두 영향을 줄 수 있는 사실은 광고의 중요한 측면이다.

해설 주어와 동사 사이에서 주어 The fact를 수식하며 완전한 절을 이끄는 접속사 자리이다. the fact '사실'을 수식하는 동격절 that은 완전한 절을 이끌며 선행사를 수식할 수 있으므로 (B)가 정답이다.

어휘 celebrity endorsement 유명인 광고 | cause 야기시키다 | publicity 홍보, 광고 | aspect 면, 측면

✛ Key point
동격절 that은 완전한 절을 이끌며 선행사를 수식할 수 있으며 자주 쓰이는 표현으로는 the fact[truth] that '~라는 사실', the belief that '~라는 믿음', the decision that '~라는 결정', the news that '~라는 뉴스', the rumor that '~라는 소문' 등이 있다.

---

3. 명사 자리

Ms. Poole emailed yesterday afternoon for **confirmation** that the job application she sent on Friday had been accepted.
Poole 씨는 어제 오후에 자신이 금요일에 보낸 입사지원서가 수령되었음을 확인하는 이메일을 받았다.

해설 빈칸은 전치사 for의 목적어인 명사 자리이다. 빈칸 뒤 that절 내 완전한 문장이 있음을 고려할 때, 'confirmation that ~ (~에 대한 확인)'이라는 구조를 완성하는 명사 (D)가 정답이다.

어휘 job application 입사지원서 | accept 받아들이다

✛ Key point
동격의 that 명사절은 앞에 나온 명사의 내용을 보충설명하는 역할을 한다. 「confirmation that S+V~ (~라는 확인)」, 「rumor that S+V~ (~라는 소문)」, 「fact that S+V~ (~라는 사실)」, 「news that S+V~ (~라는 소식)」

---

4. 형용사 자리

The organizers are **hopeful** that the weather will clear up for the festival.
주최측은 축제 때 날씨가 갤 것으로 기대하고 있다.

해설 빈칸은 주어 the organizers에 대한 주격보어 자리이다. 빈칸 뒤 that 명사절이 있으므로, 'be hopeful that ~ (~에 대해 희망적이다, ~를 기대하고 있다)'의 구조를 완성하는 형용사 (A)가 정답이다.

어휘 organizer 주최자, 조직자 | clear up (날씨가) 개다

5-8번은 다음 편지에 관한 문제입니다.

5월 5일

Frances Moon
BBD 건설
Goose Bay, Labrador

Moon 님,

Goose Bay 학교 시스템에서 귀사를 Tommy Prince 초등학교의 새 부속 건물 건설사로 ⑤**선택했다**는 점을 알려드리게 되어 기쁩니다. 귀사의 직원들은 7월 1일부터 ⑥**현장**에 출입하실 수 있습니다.

입찰 과정에서 논의한 바와 같이, BBD 건설은 학교 내에서 일어나기 마련인 모든 피해와 부상에 법적 책임이 있습니다. 제가 최신 일정을 담고 있는 학군의 종합 계획을 함께 넣었습니다. ⑦**추가로**, 그 서류는 다른 중요 관계자들의 연락처를 포함하고 있습니다. 질문이나 궁금한 사항이 있

으실 경우 저에게 직접해 주십시오. ⑧**시기적절하게 문제를 다룰 수 있도록 최선을 다하겠습니다.**

인사를 드리며,

Virginia Jayne, 감독관
Goose Bay 학군

어휘
construction 건설 | pleased 만족하는 | announce 알리다, 공지하다 | wing 부속 건물 | elementary school 초등학교 | crew 팀 | enter 들어가다, 출입하다 | effective 시행되는, 발효되는 | discuss 논의하다 | bidding process 경매 과정 | liable 법적 책임이 있는 | incidental -에 따르기 마련인 | damage 피해, 손상 | injury 부상, 상처 | occur 발생하다 | property 건물 구내 | school district 학군 | master plan 종합 계획 | up-to-date 최근의, 최신의 | stakeholder 관계자, 이해 당사자 | directly 직접 | concern 우려, 걱정 | superintendent 관리자, 감독관

---

5. 동사의 시제

해설 '귀사를 건설사로 선택했다는 것을 알리게 되어 기쁘다'는 내용이 되어야 하며, 과거 어느 시점에 결정된 사항을 현재 시점에서 전달하고 있으므로 현재 완료 시제 (D)가 정답이다.

✛ Key word
We are pleased to announce that the Goose Bay School System **has selected** your company for the construction of the new wing of Tommy Prince Elementary School.

---

6. 어휘 – 명사

해설 앞 문장에서 단서를 포착하면, 초등학교 부속 건물 건설사로 귀사가 선택되었고, 직원들은 7월 1일부터 현장에 들어갈 수 있다는 내용이 문맥상 자연스러우므로 (B)가 정답이다.

✛ Key word
We are pleased to announce that the Goose Bay School System has selected your company for the construction of **the new wing** of Tommy Prince Elementary School. Your crew may enter the site effective 1 July.

---

7. 접속부사

해설 빈칸을 중심으로 앞, 뒤 문장의 관계를 살펴보면, '종합 계획서에는 최신 일정이 들어있고, 또한 주요 관계자들의 연락처도 포함되어 있다'는 내용이 되어야 문맥상 자연스럽다. 따라서 부가의 의미를 갖는 접속부사 (A)가 정답이다.

✛ Key word
I've included the School District's **master plans, which contain our up-to-date schedule. Additionally, the document includes the contact information of other key stakeholders** in the project.

---

8. 문장 선택

(A) 시기적절하게 문제들을 다룰 수 있도록 최선을 다하겠습니다.
(B) 프로젝트를 시작하기 전에 이 정보를 작성해야 합니다.
(C) 한 달 안에 알려드리겠습니다.
(D) 다시 한번 저희 회사를 선택해 주셔서 감사합니다.

해설 바로 앞 문장의 내용을 살펴보면, '질문이나 궁금한 사항에 대해 전화 주시면, 시기적절하게 문제를 다룰 수 있도록 최선을 다하겠다'는 내용

으로 이어지는 것이 문맥상 자연스러우므로 (A)가 정답이다.

+ Key word

Give me a call directly if you have questions or concerns. I will do my best to address them in a timely manner.

CASE 집중훈련
본서 p.175

1. (B) **2.** (D) **3.** (B) **4.** (A) **5.** (C) **6.** (A)

7. (A) **8.** (B)

---

1. 명사절 접속사 whether

Please tell us **whether** you would like to use a credit card or pay cash once you have chosen the item you would like to purchase.

일단 구매하고자 하는 품목을 선택하셨으면, 신용 카드로 결제하기를 원하는지 현금으로 지불하기를 원하는지 말씀해 주세요.

해설 빈칸은 4형식동사 tell '~에게 ~를 말하다'의 직접 목적어 역할을 하며 절을 이끄는 명사절 접속사 자리이다. whether A or B는 '~인지 아닌지, ~인지 ~인지'라는 상관 접속사로 '신용 카드로 결제하기를 원하는지 현금으로 지불하기를 원하는지 말씀해 주세요'라는 의미가 되어야 자연스러우므로 (B)가 정답이다.

어휘 once 일단 ~하면

+ Key point

접속사 whether은 불확실한 상황을 나타낼 때 사용되며 or이 뒤따라오는 경우가 많다.

---

2. 명사절 접속사 whether

The CEO has reviewed Mr. Reilly's qualifications and will decide **whether** to appoint him as the new marketing director.

CEO가 Reilly 씨의 자격을 검토하고 그를 새 마케팅 책임자로 임명할지를 결정할 것이다.

해설 빈칸은 decide의 목적어 역할을 하는 명사 자리이다. whether '~인지 아닌지'는 명사절 접속사로 완전한 절을 이끌거나 주어가 주절의 주어와 같을 때 주어를 생략하고 to부정사 구문을 이끌 수 있다는 점을 고려할 때, '그를 이사회 임원으로 임명할지 (말지)를 결정할 것이다'라는 의미가 되어야 자연스러우므로 (D)가 정답이다.

어휘 review 검토하다, 평가하다 | qualification 자격 | appoint 임명하다

+ Key point

명사절 접속사 whether '~인지 아닌지'는 완전한 절을 이끌거나 또는 주절의 주어와 같을 때 주어를 생략하고 to부정사를 이끌 수 있다.

I don't know whether I should go (or not).
= I don't know whether to go (or not).

---

3. 명사절 접속사 whether

The HR department is still having a discussion about **whether** it is necessary to increase the number of monthly staff training sessions.

HR부는 월례 직원 교육 세션의 수를 늘리는 것이 필요한지에 대해서 여전히 논의 중이다.

해설 전치사의 목적어 역할을 하는 완전 구조의 명사절을 이끌 접속사가 필요하므로 (B)가 정답이다. (A)와 (C)는 의문 대명사로서 불완전 구조의 명사절을 이끌며 경우에 따라 의문형용사 역할이 되면 뒤에 명사가 와야 하므로 답이 될 수 없으며 (D)는 부사절을 이끄는 부사절 접속사이므로 전치사의 목적어 자리에 올 수 없다.

어휘 necessary 필요한 | monthly 월례의

---

4. 명사절 접속사 whether

Panther Manufacturing has not decided **whether** or not to upgrade its safety equipment at its factory.

Panther Manufacturing은 공장의 안전 장비를 업그레이드할지 여부를 결정하지 않았다.

해설 명사절 접속사 whether는 완전한 절 앞에 쓰이면서 or이 뒤따라오는 구조로 잘 쓰이는데, whether 뒤의 주어가 생략되면 whether (or not) to do '~할지 아닐지'로도 쓰일 수 있으므로 (A)가 정답이다.

어휘 safety equipment 안전 장비

+ Key point

whether뒤의 주어가 주절의 주어와 같거나 명시할 필요가 없을 때, whether (or not) to do의 구조로 쓰일 수 있다.

5-8번은 다음 광고에 관한 문제입니다.

Lenexa 은행이 새 사업개발 매니저를 찾고 있습니다. 매니저는 Toledo 지점에서 사업개발 활동을 **5**감독합니다. 다른 무엇보다도, 이 자리는 영업 캠페인 준비, 잠재고객 및 기존 고객의 만남 및 신규 거래처 담당자의 활동과 결과 평가를 해야 합니다. 이 업무에는 잦은 고객 기밀 데이터 처리가 포함되기 때문에, 합격자는 모든 자료에 대해 **6**신중하고 조심스러워야 합니다. 지원자는 개인 은행거래 업무에 사전 경력이 있어야 하며, 되도록 SalesHorse 잠재고객 추적 소프트웨어에 대한 풍부한 지식이 있는 것이 좋습니다. **7**그렇기는 하지만, 다른 업계에서의 풍부한 영업 경력이 있는 분이라면 또한 지원하시기 바랍니다. 심사를 위해 이력서와 최근 사진을 이메일 HR@Lenexabank.com으로 보내시기 바랍니다. **8**반드시 메시지에 조회번호 504번을 적어주시기 바랍니다.

어휘

among other things 다른 무엇보다도 | organize 조직하다, 준비하다 | prospect 잠재고객 | existing 기존의 | evaluate 평가하다 | account 거래처 | confidential 기밀의 | successful candidate 합격자 | discreet 분별 있는, 신중한 | preferably 되도록이면 | nonetheless 그렇지만 | industry 업계 | cv(curriculum vitae) 이력서 | reference number 조회번호

---

5. 동사의 시제 / 수 일치

해설 3인칭 단수 주어와 맞지 않는 (A)와 동사 자리에 들어갈 수 없는 (D)는 제외시킨다. 공석이 있음을 광고하면서 업무내역을 설명하는 데는 현재 시제가 알맞으므로 (C)가 정답이다.

+ Key word

Bank of Lenexa is looking for a new Business Development Manager. The manager supervises the business development activity in our Toledo branch.

6. 어휘 - 형용사

해설 and 뒤에 나온 careful과 의미적 순접을 이루고 기밀 데이터를 다루는 태도를 나타내는 형용사가 필요하므로 (A)가 정답이다.

+ Key word

This work includes frequent handling of confidential client data, so the successful candidate must be discreet and careful with all materials.

7. 접속부사

해설 앞 문장에서 설명한 자격요건을 갖추지 못한 사람도 지원할 수 있다는 내용이므로 (A)가 정답이다.

+ Key word

Applicants should have prior experience in personal banking, and preferably, a good knowledge of the SalesHorse prospect tracking software. Nonetheless, applicants with strong sales backgrounds in other industries are also encouraged to apply.

8. 문장 선택

(A) 우리는 75년 동안 중서부에서 은행 서비스를 제공해 왔습니다.
(B) 반드시 메시지에 조회번호 504번을 적어주시기 바랍니다.
(C) 우리는 Garrington에 또 다른 지점을 열 계획입니다.
(D) 지원서는 여러분이 계신 지점에서 작성하셔야 합니다.

해설 이메일 발송을 지시하는 앞 문장에 대한 자연스러운 부연 설명이 되는 (B)가 정답이다.

+ Key word

For consideration, please e-mail your CV and a recent photograph to HR@Lenexabank.com. Make sure to mention reference number 504 in your message.

CASE 집중훈련   본서 p.177

1. (A) 2. (B) 3. (C) 4. (B) 5. (A) 6. (C)
7. (B) 8. (D)

---

1. 의문사 자리

LAC Auto executives met this afternoon to discuss **how** to increase sales of its new pickup trucks.
LAC 자동차의 임원들은 오늘 오후에 만나서 새 픽업 트럭의 판매를 늘리는 방법을 논의했다.

해설 동사 discuss의 목적어로 명사 (B) trial을 사용하려면 관사가 필요하므로 제외시킨다. 전치사의 목적어로 to 부정사를 사용할 수 없으므로 (C) for도 제외하고 (D) later를 넣으면 동사 discuss의 목적어가 없게 되므로 제외시킨다. '판매를 늘리는 방법을 논하다'가 자연스러운 구문이므로 (A)가 정답이다.

어휘 executive 경영 간부 | pickup truck 픽업 트럭, 소형 오픈 트럭

---

2. 사람 명사 vs. 사물 / 추상 명사

The Internet survey asks **residents** how they prefer to learn about upcoming community events.
인터넷 설문조사는 주민들에게 다가올 지역 행사에 대해 어떻게 접하고 싶은지 묻는다.

해설 빈칸은 동사 ask의 목적어인 명사 자리이다. 문맥상 '설문조사는 주민

들에게 묻는다'는 의미가 자연스러우므로 (B)가 정답이다.

어휘 survey 설문조사 | prefer 선호하다 | learn about ~에 대해 알다[접하다] | upcoming 곧 있을, 다가올 | community 커뮤니티, 지역사회

+ Key point

명사 residence vs. resident vs. residency: residence는 '거주지'를, resident는 '거주자, 주민'을, residency는 '전속기간, 관저'를 의미한다.

---

3. 의문사 자리

Ms. Patel asked us to explain to her **which** of the three mobile phones was most user-friendly.
Patel 씨는 우리에게 휴대폰 3개 중 어떤 게 가장 사용자 친화적인지 그녀에게 설명해달라고 요청했다.

해설 빈칸 이하는 타동사 explain의 목적어로 「주어(------ of the three mobile phones) + 동사(was) + 보어(most user-friendly)」의 완전한 문장이 연결되므로, 빈칸은 완전한 문장을 이끌며, 주어 역할을 하는 명사절 접속사가 필요한 자리이다. 주어가 빈칸 뒤의 of the three mobile phones의 수식을 받는 자리임을 고려할 때 '핸드폰 세 개 중 어느 것'이라는 의미가 적절하므로 (C)가 정답이다.

어휘 explain 설명하다 | user-friendly 사용하기 쉬운

+ Key point

의문사는 명사절을 이끌어, 문장 내에서 주어, 목적어, 보어 자리에 올 수 있다.

---

4. 의문 형용사 자리

Having only three days until the presidential race, eligible voters must soon decide **which** contender has the most attractive policies.
대통령 선거까지 3일밖에 남지 않았기에, 유권자들은 어떤 후보가 가장 매력적인 정책을 가지고 있는지 조만간 결정해야 한다.

해설 빈칸은 동사 decide와 빈칸 뒤 이어지는 문장을 연결하는 자리이다. 동사 decide는 목적어를 취하는 타동사임을 고려할 때, 빈칸 뒤 문장을 동사 decide의 목적어인 명사절로 만들어주는 의문형용사 자리이다. 이때 '(여러 후보들 중) 어떤 후보의 정책이 가장 마음에 드는지를 결정해야 한다'는 의미가 되어야 문맥상 자연스러우므로 (B)가 정답이다.

어휘 presidential race 대통령 선거 | eligible ~할 수 있는 | voter 유권자 | contender 도전자, 경쟁자 | attractive 매력적인 | policy 정책

+ Key point

의문형용사(which, whose, what)는 「의문사 + 명사 + 동사~」의 형태로, 명사절을 이끄는 접속사 역할을 할 수 있으며, which는 '어느, 어떤'을, whose는 '누구의'를 의미한다.

5-8번은 다음 회람에 관한 문제입니다.

수신: 전 직원
발신: Landon Donovan, 대표이사, Advanced Technologies
날짜: **7** 2월 7일
제목: Sanvit Tech 인수

우리 회사의 사보 잡지에서 읽어 보셨을 수도 있겠지만, 협상이 어느새 이미 최종 단계에 접어들고 있기 때문에, 우리가 Sanvit Tech를 인수하는 데 가까워지고 있다는 사실을 틀림없이 알고 계실 겁니다. 이 합의는 시장 전반에 걸쳐 우리의 경쟁 우위를 한층 더 강화할 수 있는 **5**능력을 제공해줄 것입니다.

여러분 중 일부는 이번 인수가 회사에서 자신의 자리에 ⑥**어떻게** 영향을 미칠 수 있을지에 관해 분명 의문을 갖고 계신 분들이 있을 거라 생각합니다. 저는 여러분 모두가 각자의 직책을 ⑦**유지하게 될 것이라는** 점을 확실히 말씀드립니다. ⑧**우리는 심지어 여러분의 업무를 도울 직원을 추가로 고용할 계획도 갖고 있습니다.** 따라서, 여러분은 다가오는 변화에 대해 걱정하실 필요가 없습니다.

어휘

acquisition 인수, 매입 ㅣ internal 내부의 ㅣ be aware that ~임을 알다 ㅣ acquire 인수하다, 매입하다 ㅣ negotiation 협상 ㅣ phase 단계 ㅣ deal 합의, 거래 ㅣ further 더욱, 한층 더 ㅣ enhance 강화하다 ㅣ competitive 경쟁 우위 ㅣ question 의문을 갖다 ㅣ impact 영향을 미치다 ㅣ position 직책, 일자리 ㅣ convince A that ~라고 A를 확신시키다 ㅣ thus 따라서 ㅣ upcoming 다가오는

5. 어휘 – 명사

해설 빈칸 앞 문장의 '우리가 Sanvit Tech를 인수하는 데 가까워지고 있다는 사실을 틀림없이 알고 계실 것입니다'라는 내용을 고려할 때, '이 합의는 시장 전반에 걸쳐 우리의 경쟁 우위를 더욱 강화할 수 있는 능력을 제공해줄 것입니다'라는 내용이 되어야 자연스러우므로 (A)가 정답이다.

✚ **Key word**

As you may have read on our internal magazine, you must be aware that **we are closing in to acquire Sanvit Tech, as the negotiations are already in the final phase. This deal will give us the capability to further enhance our competitive edge over the market.**

6. 의문사 자리

해설 전치사 about 뒤로 주어와 동사가 포함된 절이 이어져 있으므로 이 절은 about의 목적어로 쓰일 명사절이 되어야 하며, 빈칸 뒤에 위치한 절이 「주어＋동사＋목적어＋전치사구」로 되어 있어 빠진 요소 없이 완전한 구조이므로 완전한 명사절을 이끄는 (C)가 정답이다.

✚ **Key point**

동사나 전치사 바로 뒤에 위치하는 명사절을 이끌 접속사를 고를 때, 그 절이 빠진 요소가 있는 불완전한 절인지 또는 빠진 요소 없이 완전한 절인지 확인해 알맞은 명사절 접속사를 고른다. that은 동사의 목적어로 쓰이는 명사절만 이끌 수 있고, what과 which는 불완전한 명사절을 이끈다.

7. 동사의 시제

해설 앞 단락에 '이 합의는 시장 전반에 걸쳐 우리의 경쟁 우위를 더욱 강화할 수 있는 능력을 제공해줄 것입니다'라는 내용을 고려할 때, '모두가 각자의 직책을 유지하게 될 것'이라는 미래의 의미가 되어야 자연스러우므로 미래 시제인 (B)가 정답이다.

✚ **Key point**

동사의 형태는 '수의 일치', '태', '시제'를 고려해야 한다. 특히 파트 6에서 '시제'를 정할 때 지문의 다른 문장에 단서가 제시될 수 있으므로 관련된 문장의 동사 시제를 참고해야 한다.

8. 문장 선택

(A) 그 결과, 직원 회의는 취소되었습니다.
(B) 그렇게 느낀다면 정상입니다.
(C) 게다가, 여러분은 아직 할 일이 있습니다.
(D) **우리는 심지어 여러분을 도울 직원을 추가로 고용할 계획도 갖고 있습니다.**

해설 빈칸 앞 문장의 '저는 여러분 모두가 각자의 직책을 유지하게 될 것이라는 점을 확신시켜 드릴 수 있습니다.'라는 내용을 고려할 때, 일자리를 잃지 않게 된다는 점과 관련해 '우리는 심지어 여러분을 도울 추가 직원도 고용할 계획입니다.'라는 내용으로 이어져야 자연스러우므로 (D)가 정답이다.

✚ **Key word**

I can convince you that all of you will retain your position. **We even plan to hire additional staff to help you out.**

CASE 실전훈련
본서 p.178

1. (A) **2.** (A) **3.** (D) **4.** (A) **5.** (A) **6.** (B)
7. (A) **8.** (D) **9.** (C) **10.** (A) **11.** (B) **12.** (C)

1. 부사절 접속사

Before summer arrives, stagnant bodies of water must be drained to repel mosquitoes.
여름이 오기 전에 모기를 쫓으려면 고인 물이 배출되어야 한다.

해설 빈칸 뒤 주어와 동사 구조가 이어지므로 빈칸은 부사절 접속사 자리이다. 주절과의 관계를 고려할 때, '여름이 오기 전에 모기를 쫓으려면 고인 물이 배출되어야 한다'는 의미가 되어야 문맥상 자연스러우므로 (A)가 정답이다.

어휘 stagnant 고여 있는, 정체된 ㅣ body 많은 양 ㅣ drain 빼내다, 배수하다 ㅣ repel 쫓아 버리다, 물리치다 ㅣ mosquito 모기

✚ **Key word**

Before summer arrives, stagnant bodies of **water must be drained to repel mosquitoes.**

2. 상관 접속사

Both the director and the assistant director are authorized to make remuneration for the staff.
감독과 조감독 모두 스태프에게 보수를 줄 권한이 있다.

해설 빈칸 뒤 명사 and 명사 구조가 있으므로, 상관 접속사 'both A and B(A와 B 모두)'를 완성하는 (A)가 정답이다.

어휘 assistant 부, 조 ㅣ authorize 권한을 부여하다 ㅣ remuneration 보수

3. 부사절 접속사

Exchanges on purchases will not be approved **unless** a tax invoice or receipt is presented.
세금계산서나 영수증이 제시되지 않으면 구입품 교환은 승인되지 않습니다.

해설 빈칸은 완전한 두 개의 절을 연결하는 부사절 접속사 자리이다. 두 절이 조건과 결과로 이어져야 문맥상 자연스러우므로 접속사 (D)가 정답이다. 종속절은 현재 시제인데 주절은 미래 시제인것도 빈칸에 조건의 부사절 접속사가 필요함을 확인시켜준다.

어휘 exchange 교환 ㅣ purchase 구매(한 것) ㅣ approve 승인하다 ㅣ tax invoice 세금계산서 ㅣ present 제시하다

✚ **Key point**

전치사 뒤에는 명사 형태가(명사구, 명사절), 접속사 뒤에는 문장 형태가 올 수 있다.

4. 부사절 접속사

Until Marketing Insights hires a replacement for its chief financial officer, Kaitian Guan will assume the position.

Marketing Insights에서 최고 재무 책임자 자리에 앉을 후임자를 구할 때까지, Kaitian Guan이 그 자리를 맡을 것이다.

해설 빈칸 뒤로 두 개의 완전한 절이 콤마로 이어져 있으므로, 빈칸은 두 개의 절을 연결하는 부사절 접속사 자리이다. 문맥상 '후임자를 구할 때까지 Kaitian Guan이 그 자리를 맡을 것'이라는 의미가 되어야 자연스러우므로 시간 접속사 (A)가 정답이다.

어휘 hire 고용하다 | replacement 후임자 | chief financial officer 최고 재무 책임자(CFO) | assume 맡다 | position 직위, 일자리

＋ Key point

'------- 문장1, 문장2'의 구조에서 빈칸은 부사절 접속사 자리이다.

---

5. 의문사

Ms. Boyd will make an announcement to the department members **when** the company-wide meeting will take place.

Boyd 씨는 언제 전사 회의가 열릴지 부서원에게 알릴 것이다.

해설 빈칸은 뒤에 오는 절을 명사절로 만들어주는 의문사 자리이다. 빈칸 뒤 완전한 문장이 있으므로 (A)가 정답이다. 참고로, 여기서 when은 시간의 부사절 접속사가 아닌 명사절 접속사로 쓰였다. 명사절 접속사로 쓰일 때는 when 이하가 미래 내용일 때 미래 시제와 어울림을 파악해 둔다.

어휘 announcement 공고, 발표 | department 부서 | company-wide 전사의 | take place 일어나다, 발생하다

＋ Key point

의문사가 명사절 접속사 역할을 하는 경우, who/what/which/whose 뒤에는 불완전한 절이, when, where, whose, why, how 뒤에는 완전한 절이 자리한다.

---

6. 등위 접속사

The discount is no longer valid online, **but** other offers may be available at the physical store.

이제 더 이상 온라인 할인은 유효하지 않지만, 다른 할인은 매장에서 이용하실 수 있습니다.

해설 빈칸 양쪽에 주어, 동사를 갖춘 완전한 절이 있으므로, 빈칸은 접속사 자리이다. 문맥상 두 절의 내용이 서로 상반되므로 등위 접속사 (B)가 정답이다.

어휘 valid 유효한 | offer 할인 | available 이용 가능한 | physical store 오프라인 매장

---

7. 동사의 시제

Chairman Silvia conveyed dissatisfaction that CPO Industries **lost** market share compared to last year.

Silvia 회장은 CPO Industries가 작년에 비해 시장점유율을 잃은 것에 불만을 전했다.

해설 빈칸은 종속절인 that 명사절 내 주어 CPO Industries에 대한 동사 자리이다. 주절의 시제가 과거이고 주어 자리에 3인칭 단수 명사가 있으므로 과거 시제 동사 (A)가 정답이다.

어휘 chairman 회장, 의장 | convey 전달하다 | dissatisfaction 불만 | market share 시장 점유율 | compared to ~과 비교하여

＋ Key point

동격의 that 명사절은 앞에 나온 명사의 내용을 보충 설명하는 역할을 하며, 접속사 that 뒤에는 완전한 절이 온다.

---

8. 등위 접속사

Mordring, Inc. carpeting may be coordinated with the conference room's wallpaper, obtainable in contrasting **or** complementary colors.

대비되는, 즉 보색으로 구할 수 있어, Mordring 사 카펫은 회의실 벽지와 어울릴 수도 있다.

해설 빈칸은 명사 colors를 수식하는 대등한 두 형용사를 연결하는 자리이다. '대비되는 즉 보색'이라는 의미가 되어야 문맥상 자연스러우므로 (D)가 정답이다.

어휘 carpeting 카펫류 | coordinate 조화를 이루다 ~와 조화시키다 | wallpaper 벽지 | obtainable 구할 수 있는 | contrasting 대비를 이루는 | complementary 상호보완적인

＋ Key point

① 등위 접속사는 단어, 구, 절 등을 대등하게 연결해준다: and, but, yet, or 등
② 접속사 or은 2개 이상 중 하나를 선택할 때 '또는', 동격의 어구를 설명할 때 '즉' 등의 의미를 갖는다.

9-12번은 다음 공지에 관한 문제입니다.

Ellsworth 시립 도서관은 추후 통지가 있을 때까지 폐쇄될 예정입니다. 최근 해당 지역에 폭풍우가 **9점점 더** 거세져, 건물 내 누수가 발생하고 있습니다. 현 상황에서 저희는 **10수리를** 받을 수 밖에 없습니다. 계획은 지붕 손상부터 수리하는 것입니다. **11도서관 바닥도 새로 해야 할지 모릅니다.**

도서관에 책 반납이 불가능하여, 외부에 도서 반납함을 설치했습니다. 하지만 이미 도서를 대출하신 이용자는 도서관이 다시 개관할 때 **12까지** 이용하실 수 있도록 할 예정입니다.

어휘
until further notice 추후 통지가 있을 때까지 | prevalence 널리 퍼짐 | storm 폭풍우 | area 지역 | recently 최근 | experience 경험하다 | water leak 누수 | have no choice but to ~할 수 밖에 없다 | undergo 겪다, 받다 | repair 수리하다 | roof 지붕 | damage 손상, 피해 | unavailable 이용할 수 없는 | return 반납하다 | set up 설치하다 | deposit 보관 | outside 밖에 | allow 허용하다 | patron 고객, 이용자 | check out 대출하다

---

9. 현재분사

해설 빈칸은 관사 the와 명사 prevalence 사이 명사를 수식하는 자리이므로, 형용사 역할이 가능한 현재분사 (C)가 정답이다.

---

10. 어휘 - 명사

해설 빈칸은 동사 undergo의 목적어인 명사 자리이다. 빈칸 앞 문장의 '건물 내 누수가 발생하고 있다'는 내용을 고려할 때, '현재로서는 수리를 받을 수 밖에 없다'는 내용으로 이어져야 문맥상 자연스러우므로 (A)가 정답이다.

＋ Key word

we are experiencing water leaks throughout the building. **At this point, we have no choice but to undergo renovations.**

---

11. 문장 선택

(A) 도서관은 30년 넘게 있어 왔습니다.
(B) 도서관 바닥도 새로 해야 할지 모릅니다.
(C) 도서관은 오로지 자원봉사자들에 의해서 운영됩니다.
(D) 도서관은 곧 새 책을 받을 것입니다.

해설 빈칸 앞 문장의 '계획은 지붕 손상부터 수리하는 것'이라는 내용을 고려할 때, 건물 수리와 관련된 내용으로 이어져야 문맥상 자연스러우므로 '도서관 바닥도 새로 해야 할지 모른다'는 내용의 (B)가 정답이다.

✛ Key word

The plan is to repair the roof for any damages first. The library may also need new flooring.

12. 접속사 vs. 전치사

해설 빈칸 뒤 주어와 동사로 이루어진 절이 자리하고 있으므로 빈칸은 뒤에 오는 절을 앞의 문장과 연결해주는 접속사 자리이다. 문맥상 '도서관이 다시 개관할 때까지 이미 도서를 대출하신 이용자가 책을 보유하고 있을 수 있도록 할 예정'이라는 의미가 되어야 자연스러우므로 (C)가 정답이다.

✛ Key point

전치사 뒤에는 명사 형태가(명사구, 명사절), 접속사 뒤에는 문장 형태가 올 수 있다.

CHAPTER 10 관계사

CASE 집중훈련
본서 p.181

1. (B) **2.** (C) **3.** (C) **4.** (B) **5.** (D) **6.** (C)
7. (C) **8.** (A)

1. 주격 관계대명사

A meeting will be held for the delegates from the two academic research institutions, **which** will work collaboratively.

협력해서 일할 두 학문 연구 기관에서 오는 대표들을 위한 회의가 열릴 것이다.

해설 빈칸은 앞의 명사를 수식하는 형용사절의 주어 자리이다. 앞에 사물 선행사인 research institutions가 있고 뒤에 동사 will work가 연결되어 있으므로, 사물 선행사를 수식하며 주어 자리에 올 수 있는 주격 관계대명사인 (B)가 정답이다.

어휘 delegate 대표자, 대리인 | academic 학문적인 | research institution 연구 기관 | collaboratively 협력해서

✛ Key word

A meeting will be held for the delegates from the two academic **research institutions, which will work** collaboratively.

2. 주격 관계대명사

First-time users are strongly encouraged to read the operation manual that **accompanies** their product.

첫 사용자들은 제품에 딸려 오는 사용 설명서를 읽도록 강력히 권장된다.

해설 주격 관계대명사 that이 이끄는 관계사절에 동사가 없으므로 빈칸은 동사 자리이다. 따라서 동사 형태인 (A) accompany와 (C) accompanies가 정답 후보인데, 관계사절의 동사는 선행사에 수와 태를 일치시켜야 한다. 선행사 operation manual이 단수 명사이므로 단수 동사인 (C)가 정답이다.

어휘 first-time 처음의, 첫 번째의 | strongly 강력히 | encourage 권하다, 장려하다 | operation manual 사용 설명서

✛ Key word

First-time users are strongly encouraged to read the **operation manual that accompanies their product**.

3. 소유격 관계대명사

The sales director congratulated all employees whose **collective** effort led to a 30 percent increase in annual revenue.

영업 이사는 모든 직원들을 축하했는데, 그들의 공동의 노력이 연간 수익의 30퍼센트 증가로 이끌었다.

해설 빈칸은 명사 effort를 수식하는 형용사 자리이므로 (C)가 정답이다.

어휘 congratulate 축하하다 | lead to ~을 이끌다 | annual 연례의, 매년의 | revenue 수익, 수입

✛ Key point

collective는 '집단의, 공동의'라는 의미의 형용사이다.

4. 목적격 관계대명사

The user manual contains solutions to any problems you may **encounter** with the product.

사용자 설명서는 여러분이 제품에 대해 부딪칠 수 있는 문제들에 대한 해결책들을 담고 있습니다.

해설 빈칸은 problems를 선행사로 하는 목적격 관계절의 동사 자리로, '제품에 대해 부딪칠 수 있는 문제들'이란 의미가 적절하므로 (B)가 정답이다.

어휘 user manual 사용자 설명서 | solution to ~에 대한 해결책 | qualify 자격을 갖추다 | encounter 직면하다, 맞닥뜨리다 | embrace 안다, 받아들이다 | reside 살다, 거주하다

5-8번은 다음 기사에 관한 문제입니다.

DUBROVNIK — Marko Gligorov가 Dubrovnik의 Old Town에서 고급 거리 음식을 제공하는 푸드트럭 Boskarin Kolica를 운영하기 시작한 것은 불과 4년 전 여름이었다. 원래의 운영은 Gligorov가 직접 요리를 하고 음식을 제공하는 것에 불과했지만 현재는 상당히 성장했다. **5**이제 Boskarin Kolica는 두 명의 요리사와 소셜 미디어 매니저를 고용하고 있다.

Boskarin Kolica를 창업하기 전에 Gligorov는 정기적으로 유럽 전역을 가는 **6**조직에서 일했다. 그는 그 일을 좋아했지만 집이 그리웠다고 말한다. "여행은 **7**고단했어요. 저는 거의 매일 밤 새로운 도시에 있었고, 영원히 그러고 싶지는 않다는 것을 깨달았어요."라고 Gligorov가 말했다.

그래서 Gligorov는 시의 미래 기업가 계획의 지원을 받아 자신의 사업을 시작하기로 결정했다. "저는 작은 사업을 창업하는 사람들을 위한 많은 **8**도움이 있다는 것을 알게 되었어요."라고 그는 말했다. "그들이 제게 준 안내가 없었다면, 저는 이런 일을 전혀 할 수 없었을 거예요."

Boskarin Kolica는 화요일부터 일요일까지 Old Town에서 영업한다. 트럭의 당일 위치는 BoskarinKolica.hr를 참조하면 된다.

5. 문장 선택

(A) 그는 그 식당을 위해 상설 지점을 열 계획이 없습니다.
(B) 푸드트럭 바깥의 줄은 보통 짧습니다.
(C) Gligorov는 요리학원을 다니기 위해 Dubrovink로 이사했습니다.
(D) 이제 Boskarin Kolica는 두 명의 요리사와 소셜 미디어 매니저를
고용하고 있습니다.

해설 빈칸 앞 문장의 원래는 Gilgorov가 직접 요리하고 음식을 제공했지만
상당히 성장했다는 내용을 고려할 때, 문맥상 푸드트럭이 성장하여 요
리사와 매니저를 고용했다라는 내용이 이어져야 자연스러우므로 (D)
가 정답이다.

✛ Key word

**Though the original operation was just Gligorov
cooking and serving food by himself, it has
grown substantially. Now Boskarin Kolica
employs two cooks and a social media manager.**

6. 명사 자리

해설 빈칸은 부정관사 an이 한정하는 명사 자리이므로 (C)가 정답이다.

7. 어휘 - 형용사

해설 빈칸은 주어 The travel을 서술하는 주격보어 역할을 하는 형용사 자
리이다. 빈칸 뒷문장의 거의 매일 밤 새로운 도시에 있었고 영원히 그러
고 싶지 않았다라는 내용을 고려할 때, 문맥상 '여행은 고단했다'라는
내용이 되어야 자연스러우므로 (C)가 정답이다.

✛ Key word

**"The travel was exhausting. I found myself in a
new city almost every night, and realized I didn't
want to keep doing that forever,"**

8. 어휘 - 명사

해설 빈칸 앞 문장의 시의 지원을 받아 사업을 시작했다라는 내용과 빈칸 뒷
문장의 그들이 준 도움 없이는 이런 일을 할 수 없었을 것이라는 내용을
고려할 때, 문맥상 '저는 작은 사업을 창업하는 사람들을 위한 많은 도
움이 있다는 것을 알게 되었어요'라는 내용이 되어야 자연스러우므로
(A)가 정답이다.

✛ Key word

**That's why Gligorov decided to start his own
venture, with the support of the city's Entrepreneurs
for the Future Initiative. "I found there was plenty
of assistance out there for people starting small
businesses," he said. "Without the guidance they
gave me, I wouldn't have been able to do any of
this.**

CASE 집중훈련
본서 p.183

1. (D) **2.** (A) **3.** (D) **4.** (A) **5.** (A) **6.** (D)
7. (C) **8.** (C)

1. 관계대명사 that vs. what

What is particularly remarkable about Mega Express
Market is its one-day delivery option.

Mega Express 마켓이 특히 주목할 만한 것은 하루 배송 옵션이다.

해설 빈칸에는 'is ~ Mega Express Market'을 전체 문장의 주어로 만들
어 주는 명사절 접속사이면서, 동시에 명사절 내 주어 역할을 할 수 있
는 단어가 필요하다. 따라서 The thing which를 나타내는 (D)가 정
답이다.

어휘 particularly 특히 | remarkable 주목할 만한

---

2. 관계대명사 that vs. what

The HR department requests **that** all employees
submit their monthly expense reports by 2 P.M. on
April 25.

인사부는 모든 직원들이 그들의 월간 경비 보고서를 4월 25일 오후 2
시까지 제출할 것을 요청한다.

해설 빈칸은 동사 request의 목적어 자리이다. 빈칸 뒤 완전한 문장이 이어
지므로, 문장을 명사절로 만들어주는 명사절 접속사 (A)가 정답이다.

어휘 request 요청하다 | submit 제출하다 | monthly 월례의, 매월의 | expense
report 경비 보고서

---

3. 관계대명사 that vs. what

The online employee training video explains **what**
new employees need to know regarding workplace
safety regulations.

온라인 직원 교육 영상은 새 직원들이 작업장 안전 규정에 관해 알아야
할 것들을 설명해준다.

해설 빈칸은 타동사 explain의 목적어 역할을 하면서 절을 이끄는 명사절
접속사 자리이다. 보기의 명사절 접속사들 중 what '~것, 무엇'이나
which '어느 것'은 불완전한 절을 이끌 수 있는데 빈칸 뒤의 절에서 to
know가 목적어를 받지 않는 불완전한 절이며, 문맥상 '신입직원들이
작업장 안전 규정에 관해 알아야 할 것들을 설명해준다'라는 의미가 되
어야 자연스러우므로 (D)가 정답이다.

어휘 regarding ~에 관하여 | workplace 작업장 | safety regulations 안전 규정

✛ Key point

의문사 when, where, why, how는 완전한 절을 이끌며 명사절로 쓰
일 수 있다.

---

4. 어휘 - 부사

If you need to improve your public speaking ability,
a course at Toronto Business Academy may be
exactly what you are looking for.

대중 연설능력을 향상시켜야 한다면, Toronto Business Academy
의 수업이 바로 당신이 찾는 것입니다.

해설 빈칸은 주절의 보어인 what 명사절을 수식하는 부사 자리이다. 문맥
상 '당신이 찾고 있는 바로 그것'이라는 의미가 되어야 자연스러우므로
(A)가 정답이다.

어휘 improve 향상시키다, 개선하다 | public 공공의, 대중의 | look for 찾다

+ **Key word**

If you need to improve your public speaking ability, **a course at Toronto Business Academy** may **be exactly what you are looking for**.

5-8번은 다음 기사에 관한 문제입니다.

Da Nang (2월 12일) — Bien Dong 기업은 지역에 세계 최대 수준의 워터파크를 개장할 계획이다. 회사는 금요일 지방당국에 워터파크 제안서를 **⑤제출했다**. 정부관료는 그 계획에 "호의적인 인상"을 받은 것으로 알려졌다.

그 공원의 명물에는 상급 수준의 서퍼들에게조차 도전이 될 특별 파도풀장이 포함될 것이다. 하지만 심한 모험은 주저하는 방문객들을 위해, 대형풀장으로 **⑥천천히** 내려가는 재밌는 워터 슬라이드도 있다. 지역의 해양 생물에 대한 **⑦실제적인** 학습 경험을 제공하는 데 기여할 대형 수족관 또한 있을 것이다. "저희는 방문객들에게 바다의 경이로움에 빠져들 기회를 선사하고 싶어요,"라고 최고 기획자인 Dao Viet Ha가 말한다. 공원은 Hoi An 시에서 잠깐 보트를 타면 갈 수 있는 Hon Kho Lon 섬에 위치할 것이다. **⑧그곳에서 바다의 멋진 전망을 모든 방향에서 볼 수 있다.**

어휘
enterprise 기업, 회사 | plan 계획 | world-class 세계 최고수준의 | area 구역, 지역 | proposal 제안 | local authority 지방당국, 지방정부 | official 공무원, 정부관료 | favorably 호의적으로 | impress 깊은 인상을 주다 | attraction 명소, 명물, 매력 | wave 파도 | challenge 도전의식을 북돋우다, 도전하다 | advanced 상급의, 고급의 | surfer 서퍼, 파도타기하는 사람 | less 더 적은 | adventurous 모험을 즐기는, 모험심이 강한 | pleasant 기분 좋은, 즐거운 | water slide 워터슬라이드 | flow 흐르다 | enormous 거대한 | aquarium 수족관, 아쿠아리움 | devote 전념하다, 바치다 | provide 제공하다 | marine 해양의 | immerse 담그다, ~에 몰두하다 | wonder 경탄, 경이 | ocean 대양, 바다 | ride 타기, (차 등을 타고 가는) 여정

5. 동사의 시제

해설 빈칸은 주어 the firm과 목적어 its proposal 사이 동사 자리이다. 빈칸 다음 문장의 '정부관료가 계획에 대해 호의적인 인상을 받았다'는 내용을 고려할 때 회사가 제안서를 이미 제출했음을 알 수 있고, 문장 내 시점을 나타내는 표현(on Friday)이 있으므로 과거 시제 동사 (A)가 정답이다.

+ **Key word**

The firm submitted its proposal for the water park to local authorities on Friday. Officials are said to have been "favorably impressed" with the plans.

6. 부사 자리

해설 빈칸은 동사 flow와 부사 down 사이 동사를 수식하는 부사 자리이므로 (D)가 정답이다.

7. 어휘 – 형용사

해설 빈칸은 learning experience를 수식하는 형용사 자리이다. 뒤에서 방문객들에게 바다의 경이로움에 빠져들 기회를 선사하고 싶다고 하므로 문맥상 '해양 생물에 대한 실제적인 학습 경험을 제공하는 아쿠아리움'이라는 의미가 자연스러우므로 (C)가 정답이다.

+ **Key word**

There will also be a large aquarium devoted to **providing a realistic learning experience about**

---

the area's **marine life**. "We want to give visitors a chance to **immerse themselves in the wonders of the ocean**," says Chief Planner Dao Viet Ha.

8. 문장 선택

(A) Bien Dong 기업은 과거에도 여러 성공적인 프로젝트를 진행해왔다.
(B) Dao는 이전에 Nha Trang에 있는 해양학 연구소의 소장이었다.
(C) 그곳에서 바다의 멋진 전망을 모든 방향에서 볼 수 있다.
(D) 베트남에서는 관광이 늘면서 서핑이 인기를 끌고 있다.

해설 빈칸 앞 문장의 '공원이 Hon Kho Lon 섬에 위치할 것'이라는 내용을 고려할 때, '공원에서 바다의 멋진 뷰를 모든 방향에서 볼 수 있다'는 내용이 이어져야 자연스러우므로 (C)가 정답이다.

+ **Key word**

The park will be located on Hon Kho Lon Island, just a short boat ride from Hoi An City. 142. **It has a stunning view of the ocean on all sides.**

CASE 집중훈련   본서 p.185

1. (A)   **2.** (B)   **3.** (B)   **4.** (C)   **5.** (C)   **6.** (C)
7. (A)   **8.** (D)

---

1. 전치사+관계대명사

Mr. Garfield needs more training for the new project, **in which** he will be in charge of data management.

Garfield 씨는 새로운 프로젝트를 위해 교육이 더 필요한데, 거기서 그는 데이터 관리를 담당하게 될 것이다.

해설 빈칸은 절과 절을 이어주는 접속사 자리이므로 전치사 along with와 instead of는 제거한다. not only는 'not only ~ but (also) ~' '~뿐만 아니라 ~도'라는 구문으로 쓰여야 하므로 제거한다. 목적관계대명사 which가 선행명사를 수식하는 [~ which he will be in charge of data management in the new project]의 구조에서 전치사 in이 앞으로 나오면서 「전치사+which」가 선행명사를 수식하며 수식절을 이끌 수 있으므로 (A)가 정답이다.

어휘 in charge of ~을 담당하는 | data management 데이터 관리

+ **Key point**

「선행명사+목적격관계대명사 which/whom+주어+동사 ~+전치사」의 구문에서 전치사가 앞으로 이동하면서 「선행명사+전치사+목적격관계대명사 which/whom+주어+동사 ~」의 구조로 쓰일 수 있다.

---

2. 전치사+관계형용사

Résumés and cover letters may be submitted via the company's recruitment website, in **which** case the documents should be uploaded as a single file.

이력서와 자기소개서는 회사 채용 웹사이트를 통해 제출할 수 있으며, 이 경우 서류들은 한 개의 파일로 업로드되어야 합니다.

해설 빈칸은 콤마 뒤의 문장을 주절과 이어주면서 명사 case를 수식하는 관계형용사 자리이다. 문맥상 which가 앞의 절의 내용을 받으며 '이러한 경우에'라는 의미가 되어야 자연스러우므로 (B)가 정답이다.

어휘 resume 이력서 | cover letter 자기소개서 | submit 제출하다 | recruitment 채용 | single 단 하나의, 한 개의

✛ Key point
관계형용사는 선행사를 수식하는 수식절을 이끄는 관계사와 명사를 수식하는 형용사의 역할을 동시에 한다.

---

3. 수량 표현의 관계대명사

Ten photographs, five of **which** were over 100 years old, were recently found on the property.

최근 그 건물에서 10장의 사진이 발견되었는데, 그 중 다섯 장은 100년 이상 된 것들이었다.

해설 주어 Ten photographs와 본동사 were recently found 사이에서 수식절을 이끌 수 있는 관계사 자리이므로 수식절을 이끌 수 없는 대명사 (C), (D)는 제거한다. what은 선행사를 수식할 수 없으므로 (A)도 제거한다. 수식절이 '10장의 사진들 중 다섯 장이 백 년 이상 되었다'라는 의미가 되어야 자연스러우며, 관계대명사 which가 ten photographs를 받으며 「선행사, 수량표현+of which+동사 ~」의 형태로 수량표현과 쓰일 수 있으므로 (B)가 정답이다.

어휘 recently 최근에 | property 건물, 부지

✛ Key point
관계대명사 which는 수량표현 all, most, some, half, 숫자 등과 함께 선행사를 수식하며 「선행사, 수량표현+of which+동사 ~」의 형태로 쓰일 수 있다.

---

4. 수량 표현의 관계대명사

Lately, Greenville Hospital has received a number of large donations, **most of which** are from members of former patients and local charities.

최근에 Greenville 병원이 많은 고액 기부금을 받았는데, 그 중 대부분이 이전 환자들과 지역 자선단체 회원들로부터 온 것이다.

해설 빈칸 앞에 완전한 절이 있고, 빈칸 뒤에 동사가 있으므로 동사를 이어줄 수 없는 the reason for, due to them은 제거한다. considering that '~를 고려하면'에서 that 뒤에는 완전한 절이 따라와야 하는데 빈칸 뒤는 주어가 빠진 동사만 있으므로 제거한다. 전치사 of 뒤에서 목적격관계대명사 which가 선행사 donations를 받아 '그것들(고액 기부금) 대부분이 이전 환자들과 지역 자선단체 회원들로부터 온 것이다'라는 의미가 되어야 자연스러우므로 (C)가 정답이다.

어휘 donation 기부(금) | former 이전의 | charity 자선단체

✛ Key point
「수량표현(all/some/most/one/two …)+of+목적격 관계대명사+동사 ~」가 선행사를 수식하며 선행사 뒤에 올 수 있다.

5-8번은 다음 기사에 관한 문제입니다.

Birdie's, 손을 내밀다

(6월 24일) — Arlington 내 주요 생수 공급업체인 Birdie's에서 대담한 약속을 했다. 국제 원조 기구(UAO)와 제휴를 맺은 Birdie's는 아시아 내 빈곤 국가에 깨끗한 식수를 공급할 계획이다. CEO인 Sinead Legge는 이들 국가에서 직면하는 상황을 더 잘 이해하고자 아시아를 둘러보는 데 작년 한 해를 **5바쳤다. 6상황은** 그녀가 조치를 취하게 만들었다. 그 후 Legge 씨는 UAO 직원들과 회의하는 데 시간을 보냈고, **7거기서** 이들 지역을 도울 최선의 방법에 의견을 같이 했다. 또한 Legge 씨는 그녀의 **8경쟁사들**에도 똑같이 할 것을 촉구했다. 그녀는 "우리는 도울 수 있는 위치에 있습니다,"라며 "뭘 기다리는 거죠?"라고 말한다.

어휘
lend a hand 도움을 주다 | leading 선두적인 | supplier 공급업체 | bottled water 생수 | bold 대담한 | promise 약속 | provide 제공하다 | partner with ~와 제휴하다 | aid 원조, 지원 | organization 기관 | impoverished 빈곤한 | gain 얻다 | condition 상황, 환경 | agree on ~에 합의하다 | strategy 전략, (목표 달성을 위한) 방법 | region 지역 | challenge (상대방에게 도전이 될 일을) 요구하다 | do the same 똑같이 하다 | in a position ~의 입장[위치]에

---

5. 동사의 시제

해설 빈칸은 주어 CEO Sinead Legge에 대한 동사 자리이다. 명백한 과거 시점을 나타내는 표현 last year가 있으므로 과거 시제 (C)가 정답이다.

---

6. 문장 선택

(A) Legge 씨는 자신의 역할에서 물러날 것을 고려했다.
(B) UAO는 아시아 각지에 여러 사무소를 두고 있다.
(C) 그녀가 본 것이 그녀를 행동에 옮기게 했다.
(D) 향후 다른 지역도 고려할 수 있다.

해설 빈칸 앞 문장의 '이들 국가에서 직면하는 상황을 더 잘 이해하고자 작년 한 해 아시아를 둘러봤다'는 내용과 빈칸 뒷문장의 '그 후 Legge 씨는 직원들과 회의하는 데 시간을 보냈다'는 내용을 고려할 때, 빈칸에는 상황을 두 눈으로 직접 보고 행동으로 옮기게 되었다는 내용이 들어가야 문맥상 자연스러우므로 (C)가 정답이다.

✛ Key word
CEO Sinead Legge **dedicated last year to traveling in Asia to gain a better understanding of the conditions these countries face. What she saw compelled her to take action.** Ms. Legge then spent time meeting with employees from UAO, ~

---

7. 관계부사

해설 빈칸은 완전한 두 문장을 연결하는 자리이다. '회의를 하는데 시간을 보냈다'는 앞 문장과 '이들 지역을 돕는 방법에 합의했다'는 뒷문장의 내용을 고려할 때, '회의를 하는 자리에서 이들 지역을 돕는 방법에 합의했다'는 내용으로 문장이 연결되어야 문맥상 자연스럽다. 따라서 장소를 나타내는 부사구를 대체하는 관계부사 (A)가 정답이다.

---

8. 어휘 - 명사

해설 빈칸은 its의 수식을 받는 명사 자리이자 문장의 목적어 자리이다. 빈칸 앞 문장의 '이들 지역을 돕기로 했다'는 내용과 빈칸 뒷문장의 '우리는 도울 수 있는 위치에 있다'는 내용을 고려할 때, 비슷한 위치에 있는 경쟁사들에도 자신처럼 하라고 촉구했다는 의미가 되어야 문맥상 자연스러우므로 (D)가 정답이다.

✛ Key word
Ms. Legge then spent time meeting with employees from UAO, where **they agreed on the best strategy to help these regions. Ms. Legge has also challenged her competitors to do the same.** "**We are in a position to lend a hand,**" she says, "So what are we waiting for?"

CASE 집중훈련

본서 p.187

1. (D) **2.** (A) **3.** (D) **4.** (B) **5.** (C) **6.** (D)
7. (A) **8.** (C)

---

1. 관계대명사의 생략

To appeal to a younger audience, Channel 12 has created more shows **appropriate** for children.

더 어린 시청자의 관심을 끌기 위해, Channel 12는 어린이에게 적절한 프로그램을 더 많이 만들었다.

해설 빈칸 앞에 「주격 관계대명사＋be동사 (which are)」가 생략된 형태로, 빈칸은 문장의 목적어 more shows를 후치 수식하는 형용사 자리이다. 문두의 to부정사구와 주절의 관계를 고려할 때, 문맥상 '어린이들에게 적절한 더 많은 프로그램'이라는 의미가 되어야 자연스러우므로 (D)가 정답이다.

어휘 appeal 관심을 끌다, 호소하다 | audience 청중, 시청자

＋ **Key word**

To appeal to a younger audience, Channel 12 has created more **shows appropriate for children**.

....

2. 관계대명사의 생략

The HR manager could not start the employee orientation because the conference room **he** usually used was no longer available.

인사팀 매니저는 그가 보통 사용했던 회의실이 더 이상 이용할 수 없게 되어서 직원 오리엔테이션을 시작할 수 없었다.

해설 「선행사＋목적격 관계대명사＋주어＋동사」의 구조를 묻는 문제이다. 이때 목적격 관계대명사는 생략 가능하므로 주어에 해당하는 (A)가 정답이다.

어휘 no longer 더 이상 ~않은 | available 이용할 수 있는

....

3. 관계대명사의 생략

The revised manuscript contains information Mr. Rogers **will correct**.

수정된 원고는 Rogers 씨가 수정할 정보를 포함하고 있다.

해설 목적격관계대명사 that이 생략되면서 「명사＋(that)＋주어＋동사」의 구조로 「주어＋능동동사」가 선행명사 information을 수식해야 하며, 문맥상 'Rogers 씨가 수정할 정보'라는 의미가 되어야 자연스러우므로 능동태 미래 시제 (D)가 정답이다.

어휘 revised 수정된, 개정된 | manuscript 원고 | correct 고치다, 수정하다

＋ **Key point**

목적격관계대명사 whom, which 또는 that은 생략될 수 있고, 생략되면서 「선행명사＋(that) 주어＋동사」의 형태로 쓰일 수 있다.

....

4. 관계대명사의 생략

There is sensitive information **relevant** to all aspects of the company and its clients in a secure server at the company's headquarters.

그 회사 본사에 있는 보안 서버에는 그 회사와 고객들의 모든 것과 관련된 민감한 정보가 있다.

해설 문맥상 '회사와 고객들의 모든 것과 관련된 민감한 정보'라는 의미가 되어야 자연스러우며, 빈칸 앞에 information을 수식하는 which is가 생략되었다고 보아 [information (which is) relevant to all aspects]의 형태를 완성시키는 형용사 (B)가 정답이다.

어휘 sensitive 민감한 | aspect 면, 측면 | secure server 보안 서버 | headquarters 본사

＋ **Key point**

형용사가 전치사구 등을 동반하며 서술적 용법으로 쓰였을 경우 「주격 관계대명사＋be동사」가 생략되며 명사 뒤에서 수식할 수 있다.
I met a person (who is) resposible for the job.
나는 그 일을 담당하는 사람을 만났다.

5-8번은 다음 안내문에 관한 문제입니다.

Chastain 전자는 자사 제품이 구매일로부터 최소 2년 간은 광고된 대로 **5작동할** 것임을 보증합니다. **6특별한 경우에,** 일부 제품을 대상으로 기간이 연장될 수도 있습니다. 이 보증은 Chastain 전자제품 매장과 그 밖의 허가 받은 다른 소매점에서 **7판매된** 제품들에만 적용됩니다. 손상된 것으로 보이는 제품들은 수리나 교환을 위해 저희 주소로 반송하실 수 있습니다. 가능한 한 **8결함**으로 인해 반품되는 제품들은 처음에 배송해드린 상자에 담아서 저희에게 운송해주셔야 한다는 것을 알고 계십시오.

어휘
guarantee 보증하다 | at least 적어도, 최소한 | apply 적용하다 | licensed 인가 받은, 허가 받은 | retailer 소매상, 소매업체 | damaged 파손된, 피해를 입은 | exchange 교환; 교환하다

5. 어휘 - 명사

해설 전자제품점이 특정 기간 동안 보증하는 것과 주어가 제품(products)이라는 점을 고려할 때, '제 기능을 하다'는 뜻의 (C)가 정답이다.

＋ **Key word**

Chastain Electronics guarantees that its products will function as advertised **for at least two years** from the purchase date.

6. 문장 선택

(A) Chastain 전자 매장은 4개국에 있습니다.
(B) 그때 고객님에게 디지털 영수증이 발송되었습니다.
(C) 상품 샘플은 저희 매장에서 이용 가능합니다.
(D) 특별한 경우에, 일부 제품을 대상으로 기간이 연장될 수도 있습니다.

해설 빈칸 앞 문장에서 '자사 제품을 최소 2년간 보증한다'는 내용을 고려할 때, 문맥상 '일부 제품에 대해서는 보증 기간을 연장해 줄 수 있다'는 내용으로 이어져야 자연스러우므로 (D)가 정답이다.

＋ **Key word**

Chastain Electronics guarantees that its products will function as advertised for at least two years from the purchase date. Under specific cases, this period may be extended for some products.

7. 현재분사 vs. 과거분사

해설 빈칸 문장의 동사는 applies이고, 접속사가 없으므로 빈칸에는 동사가 들어갈 수 없다. 따라서, 보기에서 동사인 (C)는 우선 제외한다. 빈칸 뒤에 동사 sell의 목적어가 없으므로 능동태인 (D)도 제외한다. 빈칸 앞에 동사 applies의 목적어가 나오므로 명사 (B)도 제외한다. 빈칸 앞에 which were가 생략된 과거분사인 (A)가 정답이다.

+ **Key word**

This warranty applies only to items sold at Chastain Electronics stores and other licensed retailers.

8. 어휘 - 명사

해설 빈칸 앞에서 파손된 경우 수리를 위해 반환하라고 했고 빈칸이 포함된 문장을 고려할 때 '결함' 때문에 반품되는 제품들을 원래 보낸 상자에 담아서 보내야 한다는 내용이 자연스러우므로 (C)가 정답이다.

+ **Key word**

Items that are found to be **damaged** may be mailed back to our address for repair or exchange. Please be aware that, whenever possible, items that are being returned due to **defect** should be mailed to us in the original box.

CASE 집중훈련

본서 p.189

1. (A) **2.** (D) **3.** (B) **4.** (D) **5.** (A) **6.** (B)
7. (B) **8.** (C)

1. 복합 관계대명사 자리

We only have a few reference sources, so remember to quickly return **whichever** ones you signed out.
저희에게 참고자료가 몇 개밖에 없으니, 대출받으신 것들 중 어느 것이든 빨리 돌려주셔야 한다는 걸 기억해 주시기 바랍니다.

해설 빈칸 뒤의 ones를 수식하면서 '어떤 것들이든 대출받은 것을 돌려달라'는 의미로 동사 return의 목적어를 완성하는 (A)가 정답이다.

어휘 reference 참고, 참조 | source 자료 | return 돌려주다 | sign out 서명하고 (책 등을) 대출받다

2. 복합 관계부사 자리

Please email me the transcript of the meeting with Mr. Torres **whenever** it is possible for you.
Torres 씨와의 회의 기록본을 가능할 때마다 저에게 이메일로 보내주세요.

해설 빈칸 앞, 뒤로 주어와 동사를 갖춘 완전한 문장이 있으므로 완전한 문장을 연결하는 접속사 (D)가 정답이다. whatever는 접속사 기능이 있지만 불완전한 절을 이끈다.

어휘 transcript (구술된 내용을) 글로 옮긴 기록

+ **Key point**

복합관계부사(whenever/wherever/however)는 완전한 문장을 이끌며, 부사절을 이끌 수 있다.

3. 복합 관계대명사 자리

Whoever accesses company files on public computers should make sure to delete them when finished.
공용 컴퓨터로 회사 파일에 접속하는 사람은 누구든지 마치면 반드시 삭제해야 한다.

해설 문장에 동사가 2개(accesses, should make sure)가 있으므로, 빈칸은 복합관계대명사 자리이다. 빈칸부터 두 번째 동사 전까지 문장

의 주어인 명사절로 묶여야 하며, '공용 컴퓨터로 회사 파일에 접속하는 사람은 누구든지 마치면 파일을 반드시 삭제해야 한다'는 의미가 되어야 문맥상 자연스러우므로 사람 선행사를 포함하는 복합관계대명사 (B)가 정답이다.

어휘 access 접속하다 | make sure 반드시 ~하다 | delete 삭제하다 | finish 끝내다

+ **Key point**

① 적절한 접속사 없이 한 문장에 두 개 이상의 동사가 올 수 없다.
② 문장에서 명사절 또는 부사절을 이끌 수 있는 복합관계대명사는 그 자체에 선행사를 포함하고 있다. 명사절일 때에는 문장의 주어 또는 목적어 자리에 올 수 있으며, whoever는 'anyone who ~ (~하는 사람이면 누구나)'로, whatever는 'anything that ~ (~하는 것은 무엇이나)'을 의미한다.

4. 복합 관계대명사 자리

The e-mail sent by the director stated that employees may discuss **whatever** they like at the upcoming all-hands meeting.
이사가 발송한 이메일은 직원들이 다가오는 전체 회의에서 그들이 원하는 것은 무엇이든 논의할 수 있다고 명시했다.

해설 '------ they like'가 동사 may discuss의 목적어인 명사절이 되도록 명사절을 이끄는 복합관계대명사 (D)가 정답이다.

어휘 state 명시하다, 진술하다 | upcoming 다가오는, 곧 있을 | all-hands 전원, 총원

5-8번은 다음 메모에 관한 문제입니다.

수신: 전 유지보수부 직원
발신: Ricardo Strauss
날짜: 1월 8일, 화요일
제목: 차량 점검

여러분,

어제 유지보수 부서회의에서 언급된 것처럼, 관리부에서 전 활주로로 차량에 대해 정밀 점검을 **⑤실시할 예정입니다.** 그 부서의 목표는 **⑥어떤** 차량 및 화물취급차량에 교체가 필요한지 결정하는 것입니다.

이 **⑦일**에 대해 도움을 주시면 감사하겠습니다. 차량을 운행하면서 경험한 기계 결함이나 반복적인 문제들을 반드시 알려주세요. 여러분의 관리자에게 RV100 양식을 제출해 주시면 됩니다. **⑧자세한 내용을 알려주실 필요는 없습니다.** 단지 차량 모델번호 및 해당 문제를 간략히 요약한 내용을 포함해 주시면 됩니다. 항상 여러분의 노고에 감사드립니다.

어휘

maintenance 유지보수 | personnel 직원 | management 경영, 관리 | detailed 상세한, 자세한 | inspection 점검, 검사 | runway 활주로 | vehicle 차량, 탈 것 | aim 목적 | determine 결정하다 | transport 차량, 수송 | luggage-handling 화물 취급 | replace 대체하다, 대신하다 | appreciate 고마워하다 | assistance 지원 | be sure to 반드시 ~하다 | indicate 나타내다, 보여주다, 명시하다 | mechanical 기계적인 | defect 결함 | persistent 끊임없이 지속되는 | issue 문제, 이슈 | encounter 맞닥뜨리다, 부딪히다 | operate 가동하다, 운용하다 | submit 제출하다 | supervisor 관리자 | summary 요약 | explain 설명하다

5. 동사의 시제

해설 빈칸은 주어 the management team과 목적어 inspection 사이 동사 자리이다. 빈칸 앞 부분의 '어제 회의에서 논의된 것처럼'이라는 내용을 고려할 때, '관리부에서 정밀점검을 실시할 예정'이라는 의미가 되어야 자연스러우므로 미래진행시제 (A)가 정답이다.

+ **Key word**

As discussed at yesterday's Maintenance Department **meeting, the management team will be conducting a** detailed **inspection** of all runway vehicles.

6. 의문 형용사 자리

해설 빈칸 뒤 주어 및 동사를 갖춘 완전한 문장이 이어진다는 것을 고려할 때, 빈칸은 뒤에 이어지는 문장을 동사 determine의 목적어인 명사절로 만들어주는 접속사 자리인데 transport and luggage-handing vehicles라는 명사구를 수식하게 되므로 의문형용사인 (B)가 정답이다. whom은 뒤에 연결되는 절에 목적어가 없는 불완전한 문장이 올 때 쓸 수 있다.

+ **Key word**

Their aim is to **determine which transport and luggage-handling vehicles need to be replaced.**

7. 어휘 – 명사

해설 빈칸은 this의 수식을 받는 명사 자리이다. this가 가리키는 내용을 앞 단락에서 찾으면, '관리부에서 실시하는 차량 정밀점검'이라는 것을 알 수 있으므로, 문맥상 '이 일에 도움을 주시면 감사하겠습니다'라는 의미가 되어야 자연스러우므로 (B)가 정답이다.

+ **Key word**

the management team will be conducting a detailed inspection of all runway vehicles. We would appreciate your assistance on this matter.

8. 문장 선택

(A) 회의 일정은 아직 확정되지 않았습니다.
(B) 유지보수 직원이 되고 싶은 사람이 있으면 알려주세요.
(C) 자세한 내용을 알려주실 필요는 없습니다.
(D) 문제의 원인을 아직 밝히는 중입니다.

해설 빈칸 뒷문장의 '차량 모델번호 및 문제에 대한 간략한 설명만 포함해주면 된다'는 내용을 고려할 때, 문맥상 '자세하게 설명할 필요가 없다'는 내용이 앞에 들어가야 자연스러우므로 (C)가 정답이다.

+ **Key word**

It is unnecessary to provide comprehensive details. You only need to include the vehicle's model number and a short summary explaining the problem.

CASE 집중훈련
본서 p.191

1. (A)　2. (C)　3. (B)　4. (D)　5. (D)　6. (B)
7. (A)　8. (C)

1. 관계부사

Every year, the university holds a free seminar **where** mental health professionals discuss topics on clinical depression.

그 대학은 매년 정신 건강 전문가들이 임상 우울증과 같은 토픽들에 대해 논의하는 무료 세미나를 개최한다.

해설 장소를 선행사로 뒤에 완전한 문장이 와 있으므로 관계부사 (A)가 정답이다. 관계대명사 (D) which 뒤에는 주어나 목적어가 빠진 불완전

한 구조가 와야 하므로 오답이며, 부사 (B)와 대명사 (C)는 접속사 역할을 하지 못한다.

어휘 hold 열다, 개최하다 | mental health 정신 건강 | professional 전문가 | such as ~와 같은 | clinical 임상의 | depression 우울증

2. 전치사+관계대명사

Calwell Financial Services puts all new employees through a training period during **which** exams for several professional licenses are taken.

Calwell Financial Services는 모든 신입 사원들에게 여러 전문 자격증 시험을 치르는 훈련 기간을 부여한다.

해설 사물 선행사와 쓰이며 전치사 during 뒤에 오는 목적격 관계대명사인 (C)가 정답이다.

어휘 put A through ~에게 (교육 등을) 받게 하다 | professional license 전문 자격증

3. 관계부사

The CEO of Blitz International moved to Hong Kong, **where** he founded a data analytics company called Nomad Analysis.

Blitz International의 CEO는 홍콩으로 이동하여, Nomad Analysis라는 이름의 데이터 분석 회사를 설립했다.

해설 앞에 선행사가 나와서 what은 소거하고, which는 완전한 문장 앞에 쓰지 못하므로 소거한다. while은 '~동안에'나 '~반면에'라는 뜻이므로 문맥상 적절하지 않다. where는 장소를 나타내는 선행사 Hong Kong을 받아주는 관계부사로서 문법적으로나 문맥상으로나 빈칸에 들어가기에 적합하다. 따라서 (B)가 정답이다.

어휘 found 설립하다 | analytics 분석 | called ~라는 이름의

4. 전치사+관계대명사

The Temple Tower Building, **in** which OBW Logistics has resided for the last nine years, will undergo renovations this June.

OBW Logistics가 지난 9년 간 머물고 있는 Temple Tower 빌딩은 올해 6월에 수리를 할 것이다.

해설 관계대명사 목적격 앞의 전치사를 묻는 문제이다. 빈칸 뒤의 동사 reside와 선행사 building을 연결해보면 그 건물 안에 거주한다는 의미가 되어야 하므로 (D)가 정답이다.

어휘 reside 머물다, 거주하다 | undergo (변화 등을) 겪다, 받다

5-8번은 다음 안내문에 관한 문제입니다.

저희 Carver 자동차는 차량 내구성에 대해 자부하며, 그렇기 때문에 모든 차량에 단 몇 달러만 더 내면 ⑤**연장될 수 있는** 5만 마일 완전 보증서를 제공합니다. 그럼에도 귀하의 차나 트럭이 수리가 필요한 경우라면 아래 양식을 작성하여 우리 본사로 보내주십시오. 모든 수리는 공인된 Carver 자동차 정비사가 수행해야 합니다. ⑥**그렇지 않으면** 수리비 전액을 부담하게 될 것입니다. 정비사 자격을 확인하기 ⑦**위하여** 청구와 함께 상세한 송장을 반드시 동봉해 주십시오.

환불은 수표 형식으로 보내질 것입니다. ⑧**상환받는 데 2주에서 4주가 걸릴 것입니다.** 이 과정을 빨리 진행하려면 서류를 저희에게 팩스 또는 이메일로 보내주십시오.

어휘
take pride in 자랑하다 | durability 내구성 | come with ~이 딸려있다 | guarantee 보증, 보장 | extend 연장하다 | just in case ~한 경우에 한해서 | in need of ~가 필요한 | fill out 기입하다 | perform 수행하다 | approved 공인된 | mechanic 정비공 | enclose 동봉하다 | detailed 상세한 | invoice 송장 | claim 청구 | verify 확인하다, 입증하다 | certification 증명, 자격 | check 수표 | expedite 신속히 처리하다 | process 과정 | paperwork 서류

5. 동사의 태

해설 빈칸은 관계사절의 동사 자리이다. 선행사가 a full 50,000-mile guarantee이며 빈칸 뒤에 목적어가 없음을 고려할 때, 보증서가 몇 달러만 내면 연장될 수 있다라는 내용이 되어야 자연스러우므로 수동태 동사구 (D)가 정답이다.

+ Key word

At Carver Auto, we take pride in our vehicles' durability, and that's why **every one of them comes with a full 50,000-mile guarantee, which may be extended for just a few dollars more.**

6. 접속부사

해설 빈칸 앞 문장의 '모든 수리는 공인된 Carver 자동차 정비사가 수행해야 합니다'는 내용과 빈칸 뒷부분의 '수리비 전액을 부담하게 될 것입니다'라는 내용을 고려할 때, 문맥상 '공인된 Carve 자동차 정비사가 수리하지 않는다면 수리비를 전액 부담할 것이다'라는 내용으로 이어져야 자연스러우므로 (B)가 정답이다.

+ Key word

All repairs must be performed by an approved Carver Auto mechanic. **Otherwise, you will be responsible for the full cost of the repairs.**

7. 관용 표현

해설 빈칸 뒤에 동사 원형 verify가 있고 나머지 보기들은 모두 전치사구로 동사 원형이 뒤따라올 수 없음을 고려할 때, in order to만이 to부정사구로 동사 원형이 따라오며 '~하기 위해'라는 목적의 의미로 쓰일 수 있으므로 (A)가 정답이다.

+ Key point

in order to 뒤에는 동사 원형이 따라오며 '~하기 위해서'를 뜻한다.

8. 문장 선택

(A) Carver 자동차의 차량은 신뢰성 면에서 1위로 평가됩니다.
(B) 구입해 주셔서 다시 한 번 감사드리며 안전운전 부탁드립니다.
(C) 상환받는 데 2주에서 4주가 걸릴 것입니다.
(D) 공인 딜러를 찾으려면 당사 웹 사이트를 방문하십시오.

해설 빈칸 앞 문장의 '환불은 수표 형식으로 보내질 것입니다'라는 내용을 고려할 때, 문맥상 환불을 받는데 걸리는 기간에 대한 내용으로 이어져야 자연스러우므로 (C)가 정답이다.

+ Key word

A refund will be sent in the form of a check. **It will take 2 to 4 weeks to receive your reimbursement.**

CASE 집중훈련

본서 p.193

1. (B) **2.** (B) **3.** (C) **4.** (A) **5.** (A) **6.** (C)
7. (C) **8.** (D)

1. 복합 관계부사

However carefully the accountant goes through the figures, there is always a possibility of an error being made.
그 회계사가 수치를 아무리 주의해서 살펴본다고 하더라도, 오류가 발생할 가능성은 항상 존재한다.

해설 「-------+주어+동사, 주어+동사」의 구조이므로 쉼표 앞이 부사절이 되도록 빈칸에 부사절 접속사가 필요하다. 부사절을 이끌 수 있는 것은 보기 중 However뿐이므로 (B)가 정답이다. However는 뒤에 나온 부사 carefully를 수식해 '아무리 ~하더라도'의 의미로 쓰였다.

어휘 accountant 회계사 | go through 검토하다, 살펴보다 | figure 수치 | possibility 가능성 | error 오류

2. 복합 관계부사

Whenever a national holiday falls on a Saturday, Finley Ltd. allows its employees to take an extra day off the following week.
국경일이 토요일이 될 때마다, Finlay 법인에서는 직원들이 그 다음주에 하루 더 휴가를 낼 수 있도록 허가한다.

해설 빈칸은 주절 앞에 부사절을 이어주는 부사절 접속사 자리이다. 보기 중 절을 이끌 수 있는 접속사는 Whenver '~할 때는 언제든지, ~할 때마다'뿐이므로 (B)가 정답이다.

어휘 national holiday 국경일 | fall on (어떤 날이) ~에 해당되다, ~에 있다 | allow 허용하다 | take a day off 하루 휴가 내다 | following 그 다음의

+ Key point

whenever은 no matter when으로 바꿔 쓸 수 있다.

3. 어휘 – 부사

Whenever customers are lined up outside the restaurant, we must offer them free beverages **promptly**.
손님들이 식당 밖에 줄을 설 때마다, 그들에게 무료 음료를 즉시 제공해야 한다.

어휘 line up 줄 서다 | free 무료의

해설 빈칸은 동사 must offer를 수식하는 부사 자리이다. 문맥상 '손님들에게 무료 음료를 즉시 제공해야 한다'라는 의미가 되어야 자연스러우므로 (C)가 정답이다.

+ Key word

Whenever customers are lined up outside the restaurant, **we must offer them free beverages promptly.**

4. 복합관계 부사

No matter how inconvenient it may be, visitors to the Wakeville College Dormitories must provide an acceptable form of identification.
아무리 불편하더라도, Wakeville 대학 기숙사 방문객들은 반드시 허

용 가능한 신분증을 제공해야 한다.

해설 빈칸은 절과 절을 이어주는 부사절 접속사 자리이므로 접속부사 Nonetheless와 전치사 Notwithstanding은 제거한다. how는 절을 이끌 때 '어떻게'라는 의미 외에도 「how+형용사/부사+주어+동사」 '얼마나 ~하는지'의 패턴으로 쓰일 수 있고 no matter how도 마찬가지로 '아무리[얼마나] ~ 하더라도'라는 의미로 형용사/부사와 함께 부사절을 이끌 수 있으므로, 「No matter how+형용사/부사+주어+동사~,」의 부사절의 형태를 완성하는 (A)가 정답이다. In order that은 목적의 부사절 접속사로 이 뒤에 이 문장처럼 부사나 형용사가 바로 오지 않고 「주어+동사」의 완전한 절 형태가 와야 한다.

어휘 inconvenient 불편한 | dormitory 기숙사 | acceptable 받아들여지는, 허용할 수 있는 | identification 신분 증명(서)

✦ **Key point**
No matter how(=However) '아무리 ~하더라도'가 절을 이끄는 구조는 다음과 같다.
「No matter how+형용사/부사+S1 +V1 ~, S2 +V2 ~.」 형용사가 올지, 부사가 올지는 뒤따르는 동사가 결정한다. 동사가 be동사 계열로 보어가 필요하면 형용사가, 완전한 형태이면 부사가 쓰이게 된다.

5-8번은 다음 이메일에 관한 문제입니다.

수신: Blackwell 오케스트라 〈orchestra@bwcommunity.com〉
발신: Gladys Phelps 〈gphelps@bwcommunity.com〉
날짜: 3월 25일
제목: 공연일

단원 여러분께,

제가 방금 우리의 연례 여름 공연 확정 소식을 들었습니다. **5장소는** 오페라하우스가 될 것이고, 6월 19일에 공연할 예정입니다. **6우리는** 작년 12월 Bennett에 방문했을 때의 것과 동일한 프로그램으로 공연할 예정입니다. 동일한 프로그램을 쓰는 이유는 휴가철로 인해 함께 연습할 시간이 많지 않기 때문입니다. 저 **7역시도** 4월에 해외에 갈 예정입니다. 제 생각에는 우리에게 이미 익숙한 것으로 공연하면 더 수월할 것 같습니다. 여러분이 잃어버렸을 경우에 대비해서 제가 악보를 다시 올려놨습니다. **8다음 주 월요일 항상 하는 시간에 첫 번째 리허설을 할 예정입니다.** 안 가져올 경우에 대비해 제가 복사본을 몇 부 챙겨가겠습니다. 거기서 모두 보게 되길 바랍니다.

감사합니다.

Gladys Phelps, 지휘자

어휘
performance 공연 | confirmation 확인, 확정 | annual 연례의, 연간의 | schedule 일정을 잡다, 예정하다 | perform 공연하다 | reason 이유 | rehearse 연습하다, 리허설을 하다 | together 함께 | overseas 해외의 | in my opinion 내 생각에는, 내가 보기에는 | already 이미, 벌써 | be familiar with ~에 익숙하다 | score 악보 | in case ~에 대비해서 | copy 복사본, 한 부 | bring 가져오다 | conductor 지휘자

5. 어휘 – 명사

해설 빈칸은 문장의 주어 자리이다. be동사 뒤 보어 자리에 장소를 나타내는 표현이 나오며, 빈칸 앞 문장의 여름 공연이 확정되었다는 내용과 접속사 and로 연결된 빈칸 뒷부분에는 시간 정보에 해당하는 공연 일정 내용이 있으므로 공연 장소라는 의미를 전달하는 (A)가 정답이다.

✦ **Key word**
I have just received confirmation for our annual summer performance. The **venue will be the Opera House, and we are scheduled to perform on 19 June**.

6. 인칭대명사

해설 빈칸은 문장의 주어 자리이다. 빈칸 앞 부분의 '우리의 연례 여름 공연 확정 소식을 들었다'는 내용과 '우리는 6월 19일에 공연할 예정'이라는 내용을 고려할 때, 공연을 하는 주체가 '우리'라는 것을 알 수 있으므로 (C)가 정답이다.

✦ **Key word**
I have just received confirmation for **our annual summer performance**. The venue will be the Opera House, and **we are scheduled to perform on 19 June. We will be performing the same program as we did when we visited Bennett in December last year**.

7. 부사 자리

해설 빈칸은 문장 끝에서 문장을 수식하는 부사 자리이다. 빈칸 앞 문장의 '휴가철로 인해 연습할 시간이 많지 않다'는 내용을 고려할 때, 문맥상 '저도 4월에 해외에 갈 예정'이라는 의미가 되어야 문맥상 자연스러우므로 '역시, 또한'의 의미를 갖는 부사구 (C)가 정답이다. 부사로서 since가 문미에 위치할 수는 있는데 이 경우 주절의 동사는 현재 완료 시제가 쓰이게 된다.

✦ **Key word**
The reason for using the same program is because we haven't had much time to rehearse together due to the holiday season. I will be going overseas in April **as well**.

8. 문장 선택

(A) 그 전에 프로그램이 변경될 것 같습니다.
(B) 필요하시면 저에게서 직접 한 부 구매하셔도 됩니다.
(C) 새로운 멤버들도 함께 하는 것을 환영합니다.
(D) 다음 주 월요일 항상 하는 시간에 첫 번째 리허설을 할 예정입니다.

해설 빈칸 앞 문장의 '악보를 올려놨다'는 내용과 빈칸 뒷문장의 '안 가져올 경우에 대비해서 복사본 몇 부를 챙겨가겠다. 거기서 보자'는 내용을 고려할 때, 공연 연습을 위한 모임을 알리는 내용이 들어가야 문맥상 연결이 자연스러우므로 (D)가 정답이다.

✦ **Key word**
I have uploaded the score again in case you lost your copy. **We'll have our first rehearsal next Monday at our usual time.** I will bring some copies in case you don't bring yours. I hope to see everyone there.

CASE 실전훈련　　　　　　　본서 p.194

1. (A)　**2.** (B)　**3.** (B)　**4.** (D)　**5.** (D)　**6.** (A)
7. (B)　**8.** (B)　**9.** (D)　**10.** (B)　**11.** (A)　**12.** (C)

1. 의문사

The directors will gather on Tuesday to see **who** will be appointed Chief Finance Officer.
임원들은 누가 최고 재무책임자로 임명되는지 보기 위해 화요일에 모일 것이다.

해설 빈칸은 동사 see의 목적어 자리이다. 빈칸 뒤 동사 구문 will be appointed가 있음을 고려할 때, 빈칸은 뒤에 오는 주어가 빠진 불완전한 절을 동사 see의 목적어로 만들어주면서 동시에 해당 절의 주어 역할을 하는 의문사 자리이다. 문맥상 '누가 최고 재무책임자로 임명되는지 보기 위해'라는 의미가 되어야 자연스러우므로 (A)가 정답이다.

어휘 director 임원, 이사 | gather 모이다 | appoint 임명하다 | Chief Finance Officer 최고 재무책임자(CFO)

＋ Key point
의문사 who/what/which는 '의문사＋동사~'구조로 명사절의 주어이자 명사절 접속사 역할을 할 수 있으며, 문장 속에서 주어, 목적어, 보어 자리에 올 수 있다.

----

2. 주격 관계대명사

Having a subway station **that** is within walking distance from your home is a practical choice.
집에서 걸어갈 수 있는 거리 내에 지하철역이 있는 것은 현실적인 선택이다.

해설 빈칸 뒤 동사가 두 개(is, is) 있으므로, 빈칸은 문장의 주어인 동명사구를 선행사로 하는 관계대명사절 자리이다. 빈칸 앞에는 명사구, 뒤에는 동사가 있음을 고려할 때, 빈칸은 주격 관계대명사 자리이므로 (B)가 정답이다.

어휘 within walking distance 도보 거리 내에 | practical 현실적인

＋ Key point
① 적절한 접속사 없이 한 문장에 두 개 이상의 동사가 올 수 없다.
② 주격 관계대명사 앞에는 명사(선행사), 뒤에는 동사가 온다.

----

3. 소유격 관계대명사

Ida Manning is a renowned tapestry artist **whose** products are unparalleled in their exquisite designs and impeccable quality.
Ida Manning은 정교한 디자인과 흠잡을 데 없는 품질에 있어 비할 데 없는 제품으로 유명한 태피스트리 예술가다.

해설 문장 내 동사가 두 개 있으므로(is, are), 빈칸은 두 개의 절을 연결하는 접속사 자리이다. 빈칸을 중심으로 두 개의 절이 '정교한 디자인과 흠잡을 데 없는 품질에 있어 비할 데 없는 제품으로 유명한 태피스트리 예술가'라는 내용으로 연결돼 뒤의 절이 앞의 명사구 tapestry artist를 수식하는 형태가 되어야 문맥상 연결이 자연스러우므로 소유격 관계대명사 절을 완성시켜주는 관계대명사 (B)가 정답이다.

어휘 renowned 유명한 | tapestry 태피스트리 | product 상품 | unparalleled 비할 데 없는 | exquisite 정교한 | design 디자인 | impeccable 흠잡을 데 없는 | quality 품질

＋ Key point
부사절 접속사 as는 이유, 시간, 양태 등의 다양한 뜻으로 쓰이는데 여기서는 어떠한 문맥도 어울리지 않아 빈칸에 올 수 없다.

----

4. 명사 자리

Artists who care about **consistency** in the quality of their work paint with Worchester brand brushes.
자기 작품의 품질에 있어 일관성에 신경 쓰는 예술가는 Worchester 브랜드의 브러쉬를 이용해 그린다.

해설 빈칸은 구동사 care about의 목적어인 명사 자리이다. 작품 품질의 일관성에 신경 쓰는 예술가라는 의미가 되어야 문맥상 자연스러우므로 (D)가 정답이다.

어휘 care about ~에 마음을 쓰다 | quality 품질 | work 작품 | paint 그리다

----

5. 주격 관계대명사

ParkPlace Industries' employees **who** have signed the new employment contracts may work from their homes once a week.
새로운 고용 계약서에 서명한 ParkPlace Industries의 직원들은 주 1회 재택 근무를 할 수 있다.

해설 문장에 동사가 2개(have signed, may work) 있으나 적절한 접속사가 없으므로, 빈칸은 접속사 역할을 하는 품사 자리이다. 보기 중 접속사 역할을 하는 것은 관계대명사뿐이므로 (D)가 정답이다.

어휘 sign 서명하다 | employment contract 고용 계약서 | work from home 재택 근무하다

＋ Key point
① 관계대명사 who는 형용사절 접속사 역할을 해, 앞에 오는 선행사를 수식해 준다.
② 주격 관계대명사 앞에는 명사(선행사), 뒤에는 동사가 온다.

----

6. 목적격 관계대명사의 생략

Mr. Barry is printing the documents **he** prepared for this week's meeting.
Barry 씨는 이번 주 회의를 위해 자신이 준비한 서류를 인쇄하고 있다.

해설 빈칸은 완전한 문장과 동사구 사이의 자리이다. 빈칸 뒤 동사가 있음을 고려할 때 빈칸은 the documents를 선행사로 하는 관계절 내 주어 자리임을 알 수 있으며, 문맥상 Barry 씨가 준비한 서류라는 의미가 되어야 자연스러우므로 (A)가 정답이다. his가 '그의 것'이라는 뜻의 소유대명사이면 주어 자리에 올 수 있지만 여기서는 문맥에 맞지 않다. 재귀대명사는 주어 자리에 올 수 없다.

어휘 print 인쇄하다 | document 서류 | prepare 준비하다

＋ Key point
목적격 관계대명사는 문장 내에서 생략 가능하다.

----

7. 어휘 - 명사

In their application, prospective students should state only those portions of their education **history** that pertain to the degree they are pursuing.
지원서에서 예비 학생들은 지원서에 자신이 추구할 학위와 관련된 학력 부분만 작성해야 한다.

해설 빈칸은 their education의 수식을 받는 명사 자리이다. 문맥상 '자신이 추구할 학위와 관련된 학력 부분만 지원서에 작성해야 한다'는 의미가 되어야 자연스러우므로 (B)가 정답이다. that 뒤의 동사가 pertain이라는 복수 동사이므로 선행사는 those portions를 가리킨다.

어휘 application 신청서 | prospective 장래의, 유망한 | state 명시하다 | portion 부분, 일부 | education 교육 | pertain to ~와 관련되다 | degree 학위 | pursue 추구하다

＋ Key word
In their application, prospective students should state only those portions of their education history that pertain to the degree they are pursuing.

----

8. 어휘 - 명사

A critical **shortcoming** of the new electrical vehicle was the high price point, which discouraged many potential buyers.

새 전기차의 결정적인 단점은 높은 가격대였고, 이로 인해 많은 잠재 구매자들을 낙담시켰다.

해설 빈칸은 앞, 뒤로 각각 관사와 형용사, of전명구의 수식을 받는 명사 자리이다. be동사의 보어로 명사구가 나오므로 the high price point라는 부정의 의미를 내포하는 단어가 빈칸에 필요하다. 문맥상 '새 전기차의 결정적인 단점은 높은 가격대'라는 의미가 되어야 자연스러우므로 (B)가 정답이다.

어휘 critical 결정적인, 중대한 | electrical vehicle 전기 자동차 | price point 기준 소매 가격, 가격대 | discourage 낙담하게 하다 | potential 잠재적인 | buyer 구매자

+ **Key word**
A critical shortcoming of the new electrical vehicle was the high price point, which discouraged many potential buyers.

9-12번은 다음 기사에 관한 문제입니다.

GENOA (9월 21일) — Lincoln County 동물원이 마침내 9월 25일 토요일 대중에게 다시 문을 연다. 2월부터 보수공사를 위해 문을 닫았던 동물원은 방문객에게 업그레이드된 시설을 제공할 것이다. 보수공사로 사파리 존이 추가됐고, 거기에 어린이 구역 또한 생겨났다. **⑨후자는 새로운 카페 옆에 편리하게 위치한다.**

Lincoln County의 Rose Erickson 시장은 오전 9시에 기념 리본을 자른 후, 이어서 개막 연설을 할 예정이다. **⑩전체적으로, 개관식은 한 시간 동안 진행될 예정이다.** 보수 프로젝트의 촉매제 역할을 **⑪한** 시장은 Lincoln County에 더 많은 관광객을 유치할 필요성에 대해 예전에 이야기했었다. 또한, 동물원은 아이들에게 **⑫상당한** 학습경험을 제공하는 것으로도 여겨지고 있다. Erickson은 동물에 대해 더 많이 알아두면 미래에 동물과의 더 나은 소통을 위한 기틀을 마련하게 될 것이라고 강조한다.

어휘
county 자치주, 카운티 | zoo 동물원 | re-open 재개하다, 다시 문을 열다 | public 대중 | close 문을 닫다 | renovation 보수, 수리 | offer 제공하다 | experience 경험 | addition 추가 | safari 사파리 | zone 구역 | mayor 시장 | cut 자르다 | ceremonial 의식의 | ribbon 리본 | follow (순서상) 뒤를 잇다 | opening speech 개막 연설 | opening ceremony 개관식 | expect 예상하다 | run 진행되다 | catalyst 촉매(제) | attract 유치하다, 끌다 | tourist 관광객 | note 주목하다; 언급하다 | pave the way for ~를 위해 길을 열다, 기틀을 마련하다 | conversation 대화 | effort 노력 | in the future 미래에

9. 문장 선택
(A) 일부 멤버십 패스는 재개장 시 유효하지 않을 수 있다.
(B) 앞으로 몇 달 동안 공사가 진행 중일 수도 있다.
(C) 다음 단계의 수리 계획이 곧 발표될 것이다.
(D) 후자는 새로운 카페 옆에 편리하게 위치한다.

해설 빈칸 앞 문장의 '보수공사로 사파리 존이 추가됐고, 거기에 어린이 구역 또한 생겨났다'는 내용을 고려할 때, 이에 대한 추가 정보를 제공하는 내용으로 이어지는 것이 문맥상 자연스러우므로 (D)가 정답이다.

+ **Key word**
The renovations saw the addition of a safari zone as well as a children's area. The latter is conveniently located next to a new café.

10. 접속부사

해설 빈칸은 뒤에 오는 내용을 앞 문장과 의미적으로 연결해주는 접속부사 자리이다. 빈칸 앞 문장의 '시장은 오전 9시에 기념 리본을 자른 후, 개

막 연설을 할 예정'이라는 내용을 고려할 때, 빈칸 뒤에서 행사 진행 예정 시간을 정리해서 제시하고 있으므로 문맥상 '전체적으로, 개관식은 한 시간 동안 진행될 예정'이라는 내용으로 이어져야 자연스러우므로 (B)가 정답이다.

+ **Key word**
Lincoln County **mayor Rose Erickson will be cutting the ceremonial ribbon at 9 A.M., followed by an opening speech. In all, the opening ceremony is expected to run for one hour.**

11. 주격 관계대명사

해설 빈칸은 콤마와 함께 문장 중간에 삽입된 절을 문장의 주어인 the mayor와 연결해주는 관계대명사 자리이다. 선행사가 사람이고, 빈칸 뒤 be동사인 was가 있으므로 빈칸은 주격 관계 대명사 자리로서 (A)가 정답이다.

+ **Key point**
① 주격 관계대명사 앞에는 명사, 뒤에는 동사가 온다.
② 관계대명사 that은 콤마(,) 뒤에 오지 않는다.

12. 형용사 자리

해설 빈칸은 명사구 educational value를 수식하는 형용사 자리이므로 (C)가 정답이다.

CHAPTER 11 특수 구문

CASE 집중훈련 　　　　　　　　　본서 p.197
1. (C) 　**2.** (C) 　**3.** (A) 　**4.** (C) 　**5.** (C) 　**6.** (D)
7. (D) 　**8.** (B)

1. 형용사의 원급
Marlena Stewart's newest article is a **thoughtful** and revealing analysis of stock market trends.
Marlena Stewart의 최신 기사는 주식 시장 동향에 대한 사려깊고 흥미로운 분석이다.

해설 빈칸은 등위 접속사 and 뒤의 형용사 revealing과 병렬구조를 이루며 명사 analysis를 수식하는 형용사 자리이다. '사려깊고 흥미로운 분석'이라는 의미가 되어야 자연스러우므로 (C)가 정답이다.

어휘 revealing 흥미로운 | analysis 분석 | stock market 주식시장 | trend 동향, 추세

+ **Key point**
형용사의 최상급은 정관사 the 또는 소유격 뒤에 와야 한다.

2. as + 형용사 + as
No previous client was as **responsive** to our feedback as Mr. Newman.
이전의 어떤 고객도 Newman 씨처럼 우리의 피드백에 반응하지 않았다.

해설 as와 as 사이에는 형용사나 부사 원급이 들어가야 하므로 (C) responsive나 (D) responsively 중에, be동사 was의 보어 자리에 들어갈 수 있는 형용사 (C)가 정답이다.

---

3. as many + 복수 명사 + as

Advertising on **as many** social media platforms as possible can be expensive, but it is the most effective in reaching a younger demographic.

가능한 한 많은 소셜미디어 플랫폼상의 광고는 비쌀 수 있지만, 젊은층에 다다르는 데 있어서 가장 효과적이다.

해설 뒤의 as possible과 결합하여 「as ~ as possible」의 원급 구문을 이루어야 하며 「as many[much] + 명사 as」는 '~만큼 많은 ~'을 의미하고 빈칸 뒤의 platforms는 복수 명사이므로 many가 와야한다. 따라서, 「as many + 복수 명사 as possible」 '가능한 한 많은 ~'의 형태를 완성하는 (A)가 정답이다.

어휘 effective 효과적인 | reach 닿다. 미치다 | younger demographic 젊은 층

✦ Key point
「as many[few] + 복수 명사 as ~」는 '~만큼 많은[적은] ~'으로 복수 명사와 함께 쓰이며 'as much[little] + 불가산 명사 as ~'는 '~만큼 많은[적은] ~'이란 뜻으로 불가산 명사와 쓰이는 원급표현이다.

---

4. 원급 비교 구문 as~as

Few of the dehumidifiers tested for their capacity turned out to be as impressive **as** their manufacturers claimed.

성능에 대해 실험된 제습기들 중에서 그 제품들의 제조업체가 주장했던 것만큼 인상적이라 판명된 것은 거의 없었다.

해설 빈칸 앞에 'as 형용사'가 쓰인 것으로 봐서 「as~as 원급」이므로 동급 비교를 만드는 (C)가 정답이다.

어휘 dehumidifier 제습기 | capacity 성능 | turn out 판명되다 | impressive 인상적인 | manufacturer 제조업체 | claim 주장하다

5-8번은 다음 고객 후기에 관한 문제입니다.

저는 최근 Westbrook 씨의 컴퓨터 수리 서비스를 받아볼 기회가 있었습니다. 제 컴퓨터가 작동을 멈췄는데, 이번 달 생활비가 얼마 안 남은 저는 최대한 **⑤저렴하게** 수리를 받아야 하는 절실한 상황이었어요. 제가 Westbrook 씨의 가게에 들어섰을 때, 그분은 저를 따뜻하게 맞아주셨어요. 제가 미리 예약을 하지 않았음 **⑥에도**, 바로 문제를 살피고 설명해주셨지요. 그리고 나서 제 예산 내에서 컴퓨터가 다시 제대로 작동할 수 있게 만들어주셨고, 심지어 컴퓨터에 있는 바이러스도 제거해주시고 먼지까지 닦아주셨어요. **⑦이제 예전보다 속도가 훨씬 빠릅니다.**

컴퓨터 문제에 다들 Westbrook 씨를 추천하는 것이 당연합니다. 그는 **⑧비교 불가한** 서비스를 제공하기에, 저는 단연코 모두에게 그를 추천하겠습니다.

Sander Evans, Christchurch

어휘
recently 최근 | opportunity 기회 | try out 시도해보다 | repair 수리 | work 작동하다 | leave 남기다 | desperately 필사적으로 | fix 고치다 | greet 인사하다 | warmly 따뜻하게, 다정하게 | book 예약하다 | ahead of time 사전에 | immediately 즉시 | diagnose 진단한다 | explain 설명하다 | proceed 진행하다 | up and running 잘 작동하는 | budget 예산 | go out of one's way 굳이 ~하다 | clear out 치우다 | dust 먼지 | remove 제거하다 | It's no wonder ~하는 게 놀랄 일도 아니다/당연하다 | recommend 추천하다

---

5. 부사 자리

해설 빈칸은 분사 fixed를 수식하는 부사 자리이므로 (C)가 정답이다.

✦ Key point
원급 관용 표현 as ~ as possible(가능한 한 ~한/하게)은 형용사 또는 부사와 함께 올 수 있으며, as ~ as possible을 걷어내고 어떤 품사를 수식하는 자리인지 판단해 빈칸에 들어갈 품사를 알 수 있다.

6. 부사절 접속사 자리

해설 빈칸은 두 개의 절을 연결하는 부사절 접속사 자리이므로 (D)가 정답이다.

✦ Key point
문장과 문장을 연결하려면 반드시 접속사가 필요하다. 접속부사는 앞뒤 의미만을 연결할 뿐이다.

7. 문장 선택

(A) 그 가게에는 손님이 많았습니다.
(B) 새 부품을 몇 개 샀습니다.
(C) 귀하께서는 미리 예약해야 합니다.
(D) 이제 예전보다 속도가 훨씬 빠릅니다.

해설 빈칸 앞 문장의 예산을 초과하지 않는 비용으로 컴퓨터를 수리해줬을 뿐만 아니라 컴퓨터에 있는 바이러스 제거 및 먼지까지 닦아줬다는 내용을 고려할 때, 빈칸에는 그가 제공한 컴퓨터 수리 서비스에 대한 결과 문장으로 이어지는 것이 자연스러우므로 (D)가 정답이다.

✦ Key word
He then proceeded to **get my computer up and running again** within my budget, **and he even went out of his way to clear out some dust as well as remove some viruses** from my computer! **It runs even faster than before.**

8. 어휘 - 형용사

해설 빈칸은 service를 수식하는 형용사 자리이다. 접속사 and로 연결된 내용을 고려할 때, '비교 불가한 서비스를 제공하기에, 그 분을 강력히 추천한다'는 의미가 되어야 문맥상 자연스러우므로 (B)가 정답이다.

✦ Key word
He provides **unparalleled service**, and I would certainly recommend him to everybody.

CASE 집중훈련
본서 p.199

1. (C) **2.** (B) **3.** (D) **4.** (B) **5.** (A) **6.** (D)
7. (A) **8.** (C)

---

1. 비교급 형용사 + than

According to new figures, the statewide production of tomatoes is **lighter** than expected.

새로운 수치에 따르면, 주 전체의 토마토 생산량이 기대보다 많지 않다.

해설 빈칸 뒤의 than은 비교급과 함께 쓰이므로 비교급 형태인 (C)가 정답이다.

어휘 statewide 주 전체의 | production 생산

---

2. 부사 + 비교급 형용사

The new Robomark washing machines are **significantly** more efficient than the existing models, saving you money on both electricity and water.

Robomark 세탁기가 전기료와 수도세 모두에서 돈을 절감해준다는 점에서 기존 모델들보다 훨씬 더 효율적이다.

해설 빈칸은 비교급 형용사 more efficient를 강조하는 부사 자리이므로 (B)가 정답이다.

어휘 efficient 경제적인, 능률적인 | standard model 표준 모델 | save 절약하다, 아끼다 | electricity 전기

✛ Key point
비교급 강조 부사
even, much, a lot, far, still + significantly, substantially, considerably

----

3. 비교급 강조부사

The updated banking app makes it much **simpler** for customers to track their spending.

업데이트된 은행 앱은 고객들이 자신의 지출을 추적하는 것을 훨씬 더 간단하게 만들어준다.

해설 빈칸은 5형식 동사 make의 목적격 보어인 형용사 자리이다. 빈칸 앞에 비교급 강조 부사 much가 있는 것으로 보아 빈칸은 형용사의 비교급이 되어야하므로 (D)가 정답이다.

어휘 app 앱, 응용프로그램(=application) | track 추적하다 | spending 지출, 소비

✛ Key point
목적격 보어 자리에 주로 형용사나 명사를 받는 [동사 + 목적어 + 목적격 보어]의 구조를 취하는 5형식 동사들로는 make, keep, find, consider, deem 등이 있다.

----

4. 어휘 – 형용사

Salespeople at Crater Publishing offer their textbooks for **lower** prices than the competition.

Crater 출판사의 영업 사원들은 경쟁사보다 더 낮은 가격에 교과서를 제공한다.

해설 빈칸은 명사 prices를 수식하는 형용사 자리이다. 문맥상 '경쟁사보다 더 낮은 가격에 교과서를 제공한다'라는 의미가 되어야 자연스러우므로 (B)가 정답이다.

어휘 textbook 교과서 | competition 경쟁, 경쟁사

✛ Key word
Salespeople at Crater Publishing **offer their textbooks for lower prices than the competition.**

5-8번은 다음 광고에 관한 문제입니다.

인도의 아름다운 전원 지역을 보고 싶으시면 최고의 방법은 기차에서 보시는 겁니다. 그리고 만약 멀리 넓은 지역을 여행하실 계획이라면 인도 기차 여권(IRP)을 사용하십시오. 이 티켓 한 장으로 인도의 주된 기차 노선 대부분을 무제한으로 이용하실 수 있습니다. 그래서 더 멀리 **5여행할 수록**, 더 많은 돈을 아끼실 수 있습니다. **6이 특별 패스는 해외 관광객에게만 제공됩니다.** 본국을 떠나시기 전 IRP 웹사이트에서 티켓을 주문하셔야 하며, 티켓은 인도에 도착하는 즉시 사용 가능합니다. IRP는 6주 동안 **7유효합니다.** 티켓 가격에는 고급 기념 지도와 전용 할인 쿠폰 **8또한** 포함되어 있습니다.

어휘
countryside 시골 지역, 전원 지대 | unlimited 제한 없는 | major 주된 | farther 더 멀리, 더 먼 | order 주문하다 | depart 출발하다, 떠나다 | deluxe 고급의 | commemorative 기념하는, 기념의 | exclusive 전용의, 독점적인

----

5. 동사의 시제

해설 「the 비교급 + 주어 + 동사」, 「the 비교급 + 주어 + 동사」의 구문으로, 빈칸은 주어 뒤 동사 자리이다. 문맥상 현재 시제가 되어야 하므로 (A)가 정답이다.

✛ Key word
So **the farther** you travel, **the more** you **will save**.

----

6. 문장 선택

(A) 특정 여행사만 개별 투어를 제공합니다.
(B) 여름철에는 기차가 종종 붐빕니다.
(C) 비행기 여행은 더 비싼 옵션입니다.
(D) 이 특별 패스는 해외 관광객에게만 제공됩니다.

해설 앞서 언급된 Indian Rail Passport, This single ticket에 관한 내용이 연결되고 있으므로 이를 This special pass로 받는 (D)가 빈칸에 들어가야 한다. 이어지는 문장에서도 Tickets 내용이 나오므로 앞뒤 자연스러운 흐름을 확인할 수 있다.

✛ Key word
This special pass is only offered to international tourists. Tickets should be ordered through the IRP Web site **before departing from your own country**

----

7. 어휘 – 형용사

해설 '티켓이 6주간 유효하다'는 내용이 되어야 자연스러우므로 (A)가 정답이다.

✛ Key word
The IRP will remain valid for six weeks.

----

8. 부사 자리

해설 빈칸은 주어와 동사 사이 부사 자리이므로 (C)가 정답이다.

✛ Key word
The price (of the ticket) **also includes** a deluxe commemorative map and exclusive discount coupons.

CASE 집중훈련
본서 p.201

1. (D)   **2.** (D)   **3.** (B)   **4.** (A)   **5.** (C)   **6.** (A)
7. (D)   **8.** (A)

----

1. 소유격 + 최상급 형용사

The success of the project will bring new life to the city park, which was once one of Millville's **most popular** recreation spots.

이 프로젝트의 성공은 한때 Millville에서 가장 인기가 좋았던 레크리에이션 장소였던 도시 공원에 새로운 활기를 불러 일으킬 것이다.

해설 빈칸은 소유격 뒤에서 뒤의 명사를 수식하는 형용사가 들어가야 할 자리이며, 앞의 「one of + 소유격」이 최상급 표현의 힌트가 되어서 정답은 (D)이다.

어휘 once 한때 | spot 장소

✦ Key point
최상급은 '가장 ~한'이라는 의미로 셋 이상을 비교할 때 쓰며, 최상급 표현 앞에서 명사를 꾸밀 때 반드시 the나 소유격이 있어야 한다.

....

2. 어휘 - 형용사

Among the likely candidates for the job, Ms. Wang is the most **qualified**.
그 일자리에 가능성 있는 지원자들 중에, Wang 씨가 가장 자격이 있다.

해설 빈칸은 주절의 최상급 표현을 완성해줄 보어 자리이며, 문맥상 '~ 지원자들 중에, Wang씨가 가장 자격이 있다'라는 의미가 되어야 자연스러우므로 (D)가 정답이다.

어휘 likely 가망 있는, 유력한 | candidate 지원자, 후보자 | conditional 조건부의 | requisite 필요한, 필수의 | secured 확보된 | qualified 자격이 있는

✦ Key word
Among the likely candidates for the job, **Ms. Wang is the most qualified**.

....

3. the + 최상급

Ms. Yun plans to purchase the **brightest** shade of green curtains for the employees' offices.
Yun 씨는 직원들의 사무실을 위해 녹색 커튼 중에서 가장 밝은 톤을 구매할 계획이다.

해설 빈칸 뒤의 명사 shade를 수식하는 형용사이면서, 정관사 the를 동반하고 뒤에 전치사 of로 대상을 한정하고 있으므로 빈칸은 형용사 최상급 자리임을 알 수 있다. 따라서 (B)가 정답이다.

어휘 purchase 구매하다 | shade 색조, 음영

✦ Key point
형용사 최상급은 앞에 반드시 정관사 the나 소유격이 오고, 보통 뒤에 범위를 나타내는 전치사구나 절을 동반한다.

....

4. 최상급 강조부사

At Midian Investments, **even** the most successful stock market brokers must attend weekly training seminars.
Midian 투자사에서는 가장 능력 있는 주식 중개인조차도 주간 교육세미나에 참석해야 한다.

해설 빈칸은 전명구와 문장 사이의 자리이다. 빈칸 뒤 최상급 표현이 있으므로 최상급 강조부사 (A)가 정답이다.

어휘 investment 투자 | successful 성공적인 | stock market 주식시장 | broker 중개인, 브로커 | attend 참석하다 | weekly 매주의 | training seminar 교육 세미나

✦ Key point
부사 even(~조차)은 최상급 문장에서 「even + 최상급」의 형태로 쓰여 그 의미를 강조하는 역할을 한다.

────────────────────────────

5-8번은 다음 이메일에 관한 문제입니다.

수신: 전 직원
발신: Daniel Harris
날짜: 8월 9일
제목: 축하 행사

────────────────────────────

직원 여러분께,

오늘 Flora Norton을 영업부분 신임 사장으로 **⑤발표하게** 되어 기쁩니다. Norton 씨는 15년간 우리 회사에 재직했고, 그녀의 실적은 설명이 필요없습니다. Jensza에서 가장 성공적인 프로젝트의 일부는 Norton 씨께서 쏟은 노고의 결과물이었습니다. **⑥가장 주목할만한 그녀의 업적은 StateCom 계약입니다.** 그리하여 기쁜 마음으로 Norton 씨께 축하 인사를 드립니다.

Norton 씨의 **⑦인상적인** 승진을 축하하기 위해 8월 15일 오후 3시에 A 회의장에서 기념식을 열고자 합니다. 모두 참석해 주시길 바랍니다. 또한 Norton 씨로부터 직접 재임기간 중 Jensza의 **⑧비전**에 대해 듣게 될 것입니다.

안부를 전하며,

Daniel Harris
인사팀

어휘
promotion 승진 | track record 실적 | speak for itself 설명이 필요 없다 | result 결과 | hard work 노고 | pleasure 기쁨 | extend one's congratulation to ~에게 축하인사를 하다 | hold 개최하다 | ceremony 의식 | in honor of ~를 기념하여 | accomplishment 업적 | join 함께 하다 | tenure 재임(기간)

5. 어휘 - 동사

해설 이메일 제목이 승진 행사이므로, '오늘 Flora Norton을 영업부분 신임 사장으로 발표하게 되어 기쁘다'는 내용이 되어야 문맥상 자연스러우므로 (C)가 정답이다.

✦ Key word
It is with **pleasure today that we can announce Flora Norton as our new President of Sales**.

6. 문장 선택

(A) 가장 주목할만한 그녀의 업적은 StateCom 계약입니다.
(B) 내년은 그녀가 Jensza에서 16년째가 됩니다.
(C) 내년에는 해외 프로젝트가 우선입니다.
(D) 저희 웹사이트에는 최근에 달성한 많은 성과들이 나열되어 있습니다.

해설 빈칸 앞 부분에서 '그녀의 실적은 설명이 필요 없습니다. Jensza에서 가장 성공적인 프로젝트의 일부는 Norton 씨께서 쏟은 노고의 결과물이었습니다'라는 내용이 있으므로 Norton 씨의 인상적인 업무성과와 관련된 내용으로 이어져야 문맥상 자연스러우므로 (A)가 정답이다.

✦ Key word
Ms. Norton has been with our company for 15 years, and **her track record speaks for itself. Some of Jensza's most successful projects have been the result of Ms. Norton's hard work**. **The most notable was her work on the StateCom deal.**

7. 일반 형용사 vs. 부사 형용사

해설 빈칸은 명사 accomplishments를 수식하는 자리이며, 문맥상 'Norton 씨의 인상적인 업적'이라는 의미가 되어야 자연스러우므로 형용사 (D)가 정답이다.

8. 어휘 - 명사

해설 빈칸은 her의 수식을 받는 명사 자리로, 문맥상 '기념식에서 Norton 씨가 재임 중 Jensza의 비전에 대해 직접 말하는 것을 듣게 될 것'이라는 의미가 되어야 자연스러우므로 '비전, 미래상'을 의미하는 (A)가 정

답이다.

+ **Key word**

We would like to hold a ceremony at 3:00 P.M. on 15 August in Conference Hall A **in honor of Ms. Norton's** for her impressive accomplishments. We hope everyone joins us. **We will also be hearing from Ms. Norton herself about her vision for Jensza during her tenure.**

CASE 집중훈련
본서 p.203

1. (A) 2. (B) 3. (D) 4. (B) 5. (C) 6. (D)
7. (B) 8. (C)

1. 어휘 – 부사

During the monsoon season, staff members are permitted to work **remotely** rather than commuting to headquarters.

우기 동안에, 직원들은 본사로 통근하는 대신 원격으로 근무하도록 허가받았다.

해설 문맥상 '본사로 통근하는 대신 원격으로 근무하는 것을 허가받았다'는 내용이 적합하므로 (A)를 선택한다.

어휘 monsoon 우기, 장마 | permit 허가하다 | commute 통근하다 | headquarters 본사

2. 비교급 관용 표현

The Greene Art Museum is **all the more** spectacular when you realize that it was constructed over hundreds of years ago.

Greene 미술관이 100년 전에 지어졌다는 것을 알게 되면 더욱더 대단하다.

해설 빈칸은 be동사 뒤 문장의 주격보어인 형용사 spectacular를 수식하는 부사(구) 자리이다. 접속사 when으로 연결된 두 문장관계를 고려할 때, 문맥상 '미술관이 지어진 지 100년도 더 됐다는 것을 알면 (미술관이) 더욱더 대단하다'는 의미가 되어야 자연스러우므로 의미를 강조하는 부사구 (B)가 정답이다.

어휘 spectacular 굉장한, 대단한 | realize 깨닫다, 알게 되다 | construct 건설하다

+ **Key point**
① by far는 '훨씬'을 의미하며, 최상급 표현을 강조할 때 사용된다.
② at most는 '많아 봐야, 기껏해야'를 의미한다.

3. 비교급 관용 표현

It is necessary that every job applicant submit their résumé **no later than** June 30.

모든 지원자들은 늦어도 6월 30일까지 이력서를 제출해야 한다.

해설 문맥상 '늦어도 6월 30일까지 이력서를 제출해야 한다'는 의미가 되어야 자연스러우므로 (D)가 정답이다.

어휘 necessary 필요한, 필수적인 | job applicant 구직자 | submit 제출하다 | resume 이력서

+ **Key point**
① 「no later than + 시간」 '늦어도 ~까지'는 「before [by] + 시간」 '~전에 [까지]'로 의미상 대체될 수 있다.

② 주절에 necessary라는 형용사가 나와 that절에 주어가 3인칭 단수여도 동사 자리에 should가 생략되어 원형 형태를 쓴 것에 주의한다.

4. 비교급 관용 표현

Given the steady increase in the popularity of healthy foods, Cheap-O Burgers is **no longer** the number one restaurant in the country.

건강식 인기의 꾸준한 증가를 고려해 볼 때, Cheap-O Burgers는 더 이상 국내 제일의 식당이 아니다.

해설 비교의 관용 표현 중 'no longer (더 이상~아니다)'를 묻는 문제이므로 (B)가 정답이다. 문장에 부정어가 있다면 anymore도 정답일 수 있으나 부정어가 없기 때문에 오답이다.

어휘 given ~을 고려해 볼 때 | steady 꾸준한 | popularity 인기

5-8번은 다음 공지에 관한 문제입니다.

5-8번은 다음 공지에 관한 문제입니다.

Sanderson 사무용품 웹사이트는 현재 유지보수로 인해 **5 이용하실 수 없습니다.** 새롭고 향상된 사이트는 오늘 저녁 6시 이후에 이용 가능합니다. 여러분의 데이터를 보호하기 위해 강화된 보안을 제공 **6 하는 것 외에도,** 저희 온라인 상점은 Sanderson에서의 주문을 과거 어느 때보다 더 간단하게 해드리는 특징이 포함될 것입니다. 이들은 더 사용하기 쉬운 네비게이션 장치와 여러분의 이전 주문 **7 에 근거한** 상품 추천 기능을 포함합니다. **8 이 시간 동안 여러분의 인내에 감사드립니다.** 업데이트된 기능들은 앞으로 더 편리한 거래를 제공할 것입니다.

어휘
currently 현재 | maintenance 유지보수 | improved 향상된, 개선된 | heightened 강화된 | security 보안 | user-friendly 사용하기 쉬운 | transaction 거래

5. 어휘 – 동사

해설 빈칸 뒷문장의 '새롭고 향상된 사이트는 오늘 저녁 6시 이후에 이용 가능합니다.'라고 한 내용을 고려할 때, 현재 이 웹사이트가 유지보수로 인해 이용이 불가하다는 내용이 자연스러우므로 '이용할 수 없는'이란 뜻의 (C)가 정답이다.

+ **Key word**

The Sanderson Office Supplies **Web site is currently inaccessible due to maintenance. The new and improved site can be used after 6 P.M. this evening.**

6. 비교급 관용 표현

해설 빈칸은 동명사구 providing ~을 취하면서 주절과 연결되어야 하는 전치사(구)이며, 내용상 강화된 보안을 제공하는 것뿐만 아니라 주문을 간소화시키는 특징을 포함할 것이라는 내용이 적절하므로 부가 설명의 기능을 하는 '~외에도, ~뿐만 아니라'라는 뜻의 (D)가 정답이다. despite는 동명사(구)를 목적어로 취하지 않는다.

+ **Key point**
other than
1) ~이외에도 (=in addition to)
2) ~을 제외하고 (=besides, aside from, apart from)

7. 어휘 – 형용사

해설 빈칸 뒤 전치사 on을 동반하면서 '이전 주문에 근거한 상품 추천 기능을 포함한다'는 의미를 완성하는 (B)가 정답이다.

해설서 **115**

+ Key word

These include more user-friendly navigation tools and item recommendations based on your past orders.

8. 문장 선택

(A) 유효 주문은 오후 6시 이전에 해야 합니다.
(B) 신상품은 종종 사이트에서 빠르게 팔립니다.
(C) 이 시간 동안 여러분의 인내에 감사드립니다.
(D) 참여해 주셔서 감사합니다.

해설 지문 맨 앞에서 웹사이트의 유지보수로 얼마간 이용할 수 없다고 했으며, 빈칸 뒷문장의 업데이트된 기능들이 앞으로 더 편리한 거래를 제공할 거라는 내용을 고려할 때, 문맥상 이 유지보수 기간 동안 참고 기다려준 데 대한 감사의 의미를 담은 문장이 자연스러우므로 (C)가 정답이다.

+ Key word

The Sanderson Office Supplies Web site is currently inaccessible due to maintenance. The new and improved site can be used after 6 P. M. this evening. ~ We appreciate your patience during this time. The updates should provide easier transactions in the future.

CASE 집중훈련   본서 p.205

1. (D) **2.** (D) **3.** (C) **4.** (B) **5.** (A) **6.** (C)
7. (D) **8.** (C)

1. 가정법 과거 완료

Mr. Gruber would have attended the meeting if his flight **had arrived** as scheduled.
Gruber 씨는 비행기가 예정대로 도착했다면 회의에 참석했을 것이다.

해설 빈칸은 his flight를 주어로 하는 if 종속절의 동사 자리이다. 주절의 시제(would have attended)를 고려할 때 가정법 과거 완료의 문장이므로, if절에는 「had + p.p.」의 형태를 완성하는 (D)가 정답이다.

어휘 attend 참석하다 | flight 비행, 항공편

+ Key point

가정법 과거 완료 구조는 다음과 같다: 「If S1 + had p.p. ~, S2 + 조동사 have p.p. ~.」

2. 가정법 과거 완료

If Ms. Chung had remained with the company longer, she **could have revised** the company's strategic business plan.
만약 Chung 씨가 회사에 더 오래 남아있었다면, 회사의 전략 사업 계획을 수정할 수 있었을 텐데.

해설 빈칸은 가정법 과거 완료 주절의 동사 자리이다. If절의 동사가 과거 완료 had p.p.일 때, 주절의 동사는 'would/might/could have p.p.'를 써서 과거의 반대되는 상황을 나타낼 수 있으므로, 「If + S + had p.p. ~, S + would [could/should/might] have p.p. ~.」의 형태를 완성하는 (D)가 정답이다.

어휘 remain 남다, 계속 ~이다 | revise 수정하다 | strategic 전략적인 | business plan 사업 계획

+ Key point

가정법 과거 완료 구조는 다음과 같다.
「S + would [could/should/might] have p.p. ~ + if + S + had p.p. ~.」
「If + S + had p.p. ~, S + would [could/should/might] have p.p. ~.」

3. 가정법 과거 완료의 도치

Had hotel reservations **been made** sooner, we might have been able to eat at the hotel buffet tonight.
호텔을 좀 더 일찍 예약했더라면, 우리는 오늘 밤 호텔 뷔페를 먹을 수 있었을텐데.

해설 주절의 시제가 'might have p.p.'가 나온 것으로 보아 해당 문장은 가정법 과거 완료 「If + S + had p.p. ~, S + would [should/might/could] have p.p. ~」 구조인데 If가 생략되고 had가 주어 앞으로 도치되면서 빈칸은 「Had + S + p.p.」의 형태를 완성하는 과거분사 p.p. 자리이다. 빈칸 뒤에 목적어가 없고 '예약되었다'라는 수동의 의미가 들어가야 하므로 (C)가 정답이다.

어휘 make a reservation 예약하다

+ Key point

가정법 과거 완료 구조는 다음과 같다. If가 생략되면 had가 주어 앞으로 도치될 수 이다.
「If + S + had p.p. ~, S + would [should/might/could] have p.p. ~」
「Had + S + p.p. ~, S + would [should/might/could] have p.p. ~」
'~했었더라면, ~했었을텐데.'

4. 가정법 미래의 도치

Should the quality of our products not meet your expectations, contact our customer service center to notify us of any issues.
제품의 품질이 귀하의 기대를 충족시키지 못할 경우, 고객서비스 센터에 연락하셔서 어떠한 문제든 알려 주십시오.

해설 빈칸 뒤의 동사 원형 not meet을 통해, 가정법 미래 시제 구문 If the quality of our products should not meet your expectations가 도치된 것임을 알 수 있으므로 조동사인 (B)가 정답이다.

어휘 meet 충족시키다 | expectation 기대 | notify 알리다, 통지하다 | issue 문제, 사안

5-8번은 다음 광고에 관한 문제입니다.

Polinar Place 58번지에 위치한 Highpoint Cleaners는 Oklahoma시 인근의 낙서 제거를 **5전문으로 합니다.** 저희는 다른 업체에서 낙서 제거 시 사용하는 일반인 화학물질이나 물 분사제를 쓰지 않습니다. 대신, 저희는 드라이아이스로 낙서를 없애는 새로운 기법을 사용합니다. **6따라서** 저희는 가장 깨끗하고, 안전하며, 환경친화적인 낙서 제거 해결책을 제공해 드립니다. **7저희는 최저가를 보장함을** 자신합니다. 저희보다 저렴한 가격을 발견하시면, 거기에 맞춰드리겠습니다. 여전히 확신이 없으신가요? 저희에게 전화해 주시면, 저희 서비스를 무료로 **8시연해** 드립니다. 한번 보시면, 분명 확신이 드실 겁니다.

어휘

locate (장소에) 두다, 차리다 | graffiti (공공장소에 한) 낙서, 그래피티 | removal 제거 | traditional 전통적인 | chemical 화학물질 | blaster 발파공 | remove 제거하다 | technique 기술 | dry ice 드라이 아이스 | blast away 없애다 | offer 제공하다 | environmental-friendly 환경 친화적인 | solution 해법, 해결책 | cheap 저렴한 | match 맞추다 | convinced 확신하는 | provide 제공하다 | guarantee 보장하다

5. 동사의 시제

해설 빈칸은 주어 Highpoint Cleaners에 대한 동사 자리이다. 광고라는 지문의 특성과 뒤에 이어지는 문장이 모두 현재 시제로 이루어져 있음을 고려할 때, 일반적 사실에 해당하는 업체의 주요 특징을 설명하는 문장이 되어야 하므로, Highpoint Cleaners는 낙서 제거를 전문으로 한다'는 내용을 완성하는 현재 시제 (A)가 정답이다.

6. 접속부사

해설 빈칸은 이어지는 문장을 앞 문장과 의미적으로 접속부사 자리이다. 빈칸 앞쪽의 '타사에서 쓰는 화학물질 등을 쓰지 않으며, 드라이아이스를 이용한 새로운 기법을 사용한다는 내용과 빈칸 뒷부분의 가장 깨끗하고, 안전하며, 환경친화적인 낙서 제거 해결책을 제공한다는 내용을 고려할 때, 두 문장이 인과관계로 연결되어야 문맥상 자연스러우므로 (C)가 정답이다.

✛ Key word

We do not traditional chemicals or water blasters other companies use to remove graffiti. **Instead, we use a new technique** that uses dry ice to blast away any graffiti. **Therefore, we offer the cleanest, safest, and most environmental-friendly graffiti removal solution.**

7. 문장 선택

(A) 세정제를 사용하여 낙서를 지울 것을 권장합니다.
(B) 저희는 사업을 운영한 지 10년이 넘었습니다.
(C) 저희는 최근에 지역 의회와 제휴했습니다.
(D) 저희는 최저가를 보장함을 자신합니다.

해설 빈칸 다음 문장의 '더 저렴한 가격을 발견하면, 거기에 맞춰주겠다'는 내용을 고려할 때, 자사 가격이 최저가임을 자신한다는 내용의 문장이 들어가야 문맥상 자연스러우므로 (D)가 정답이다.

✛ Key word

We are confident we have the lowest prices. If you find a cheaper price than us, we will match it.

8. 어휘 – 명사

해설 빈칸은 a free의 수식을 받는 명사 자리이다. 빈칸 뒷문장의 '한번 보면, 확신이 들 것을 보장한다'는 내용을 고려하면, 서비스를 무료로 시연해 주겠다는 의미가 되어야 문맥상 자연스러우므로 (C)가 정답이다.

✛ Key word

Give us a call, and we will **provide a free demonstration of our service. Once you see it**, we guarantee you will be convinced.

CASE 집중훈련
본서 p.207

1. (A) 2. (B) 3. (B) 4. (D) 5. (A) 6. (C)
7. (C) 8. (B)

1. 도치 구문

Never should any personal data about clients or coworkers be shared outside the company through any social media platform.

고객과 동료에 관한 어떠한 개인 데이터도 소셜미디어 플랫폼을 통해 회사 밖으로 공유되어서는 안 된다.

해설 부정의 부사가 문장의 맨 앞에 오는 경우 주어 동사의 어순이 바뀌는 도치 구문이 가능하기 때문에 부정의 부사 (A)가 정답이다.

어휘 client 고객 ǀ coworker 동료 ǀ share 공유하다

2. 도치 구문

Only recently has the company's marketing director **assessed** the proposed changes for the new advertising campaign.

최근에야 비로소 그 회사의 마케팅 책임자는 새 광고 캠페인에 대한 변경안을 평가했다.

해설 「Only + 부사(구)」가 문두에 나오는 경우 뒷부분이 도치되어야 하며, 도치되는 문장의 동사가 완료시제 형인 경우 「have/has/had + 주어 + p.p.」 형태가 되므로 (B)가 정답이다.

어휘 director 책임자 ǀ proposed 제안된 ǀ advertising campaign 광고 캠페인

3. 도치 구문

As the number of visitors visiting the Wakeville Gallery increases, **so** does the need for curators.

Wakeville 미술관을 방문하는 관광객들의 숫자가 증가함에 따라, 큐레이터의 필요성도 증가한다.

해설 빈칸 뒤에 주어와 조동사가 도치된 구문이 나왔고, 부사 so 〈역시〉가 문두에 올 경우 주어와 동사의 도치가 일어나며 '~도 그러하다'를 나타낼 수 있으므로, 「so + do동사/be동사/조동사 + 주어 ~」의 형태를 완성하는 (B)가 정답이다.

어휘 visitor 방문객 ǀ curator 큐레이터, 전시 담당자

4. 도치 구문 / 어휘 – 형용사

Primary among the qualifications the company is seeking is the ability to fluently communicate in several different languages.

회사가 찾고 있는 자격요건 중 가장 중요한 것은 여러 다른 언어들로 유창하게 의사소통할 수 있는 능력이다.

해설 문장의 주어는 the ability to fluently communicate in several different languages이고 빈칸은 is의 보어역할로 도치 구문이 쓰였다. 문맥상 '회사가 찾고 있는 자격요건 중 가장 중요한 것은 ~이다'라는 의미가 되어야 자연스러우므로 (D)가 정답이다.

어휘 qualification 자격, 자질 ǀ seek 찾다, 구하다 ǀ ability 능력 ǀ fluently 유창하게

✛ Key word

Primary among the qualifications the firm is seeking **is the ability** to manage staff in several different countries.

5-8번은 다음 이메일에 관한 문제입니다.

수신: aharmon@coolmail.com.au
발신: ddrake@diamondrealty.co.au
날짜: 1월 11일
제목: Lyndale가 505번지

Lyndale가 101번지에 있는 가구를 매입할 수 있는지에 관해 문의해 주셔서 감사합니다. 오늘 아침 저희 온라인 시스템에서 막 찾아봤는데, **5 보아하니** 부동산이 이미 매입된 듯 하네요.

귀하께서 구매에 관심있는 사양을 저에게 알려주시면, 다른 적합한 선택들을 확인하는데 귀하께 **6 도움을 드릴 수 있습니다**. 이메일로 위치, 평수 및 가용 예산에 관해 귀하가 선호하는 바를 저에게 알려주시기만 하면 됩니다. **7 이것이 저에게 귀하의 필요에 맞는 아파트를 찾도록 해줄 것입니다.**

귀하는 또한 **8 알림**을 등록할 수도 있습니다. 그렇게 함으로써, 신규 부동산 목록이 게시되자마자 귀하는 문자 메시지를 받을 수 있습니다.

안부 전합니다,

Daniel Drake
수석 부동산 중개인, Diamond 부동산

어휘
inquire about ~에 관하여 묻다 | availability 유용성, 입수 가능성 | unit 단위, (주택의 한) 가구 | look up (참고자료, 컴퓨터 등에서 정보를) 찾아보다 | property 부동산, 자산 | specification 사양 | in the market for ~의 구입에 관심이 있는 | identify 확인하다, 알아보다, 식별하다 | suitable 적합한 | preference 선호 | in regard to ~에 관해 | floor space 바닥 면적, 평수 | via ~를 통해 | register for ~에 등록하다

5. 어휘 – 부사

해설 apparently는 '분명하게'란 뜻 외에도 '보아하니, 보기에, 외관상 (…인 듯하다)'란 뜻도 있다. 빈칸 앞의 내용을 보면 온라인 시스템에 부동산을 확인해 보았다고 했으므로 온라인에서 보기엔 이미 매입된 것 같다라는 것이 의미상 자연스럽기 때문에 (A)가 정답이다.

+ Key word
I just **looked it up in our online system** this morning, and **apparently, the property has already been purchased**.

6. 동사의 시제

해설 고객이 앞으로 원하는 사양을 알려준다면, 고객을 도와줄 수 있다는 것이 가장 자연스러우므로 (C)가 정답이다. 나머지는 현재 도와주고 있는 것이 아니므로 오답이 된다.

+ Key word
If you let me know the specifications of what you're in the market for, **I can help you** in identifying other suitable options.

7. 문장 선택

(A) 그것은 다가오는 부동산 컨벤션의 주제가 될 것이다.
(B) 서류에 귀하의 서명이 필요하니 참고하시기 바랍니다.
(C) 이것이 저에게 귀하의 필요에 맞는 아파트를 찾도록 해줄 것입니다.
(D) 오픈하우스는 8월 8일 오후 8시에 열립니다.

해설 빈칸 앞의 내용에서 고객에게 선호하는 부동산 내용을 알려달라고 했으며 그 내용으로 고객의 요구에 맞는 부동산을 찾을 수 있을 것이라는 내용이 이어지는 것이 적절하므로 (C)가 정답이다.

+ Key word
Simply **let me know what your preferences are** in regards to location, floor space, and your available budget via e-mail. **This will allow me to find an apartment that meets your needs.**

8. 어휘 – 명사

해설 빈칸 뒤의 내용을 살펴보면 앞에서 지시한 바대로 한다면 부동산 목록이 게시될 때마다 문자메시지를 받을 수 있을 것이라고 하였으므로 문자메시지 '알림'에 등록할 수 있다는 것이 가장 적절하다. alert는 '기민한'이란 뜻 외에도 '경보, 알림'이란 뜻이 있으므로 (B)가 정답이다.

+ Key word
You can also **register for alerts**. By doing so, **you will get a text message** as soon as a new property listing is posted.

CASE 실전훈련   본서 p.208

1. (B) **2.** (D) **3.** (C) **4.** (C) **5.** (A) **6.** (A)
7. (A) **8.** (A) **9.** (B) **10.** (D) **11.** (D) **12.** (A)

1. 비교급 형용사

The grape-flavored beverage received **higher** ratings in the focus group than the orange-flavored one.
포도 맛 음료가 오렌지 맛 음료보다 포커스 그룹에서 더 높은 평가를 받았다.

해설 빈칸은 명사 ratings를 수식하는 형용사 자리이다. 빈칸 뒷부분에 비교급 관용 표현 than이 있으므로 비교급 구문을 완성하는 형용사의 비교급 (B)가 정답이다.

어휘 flavored ~의 맛이 나는 | beverage 음료 | rating 순위, 평가 | focus group 포커스 그룹

+ Key point
than은 항상 비교급 표현과 함께 쓰인다.

---

2. 최상급 형용사

Selecting an ideal location is the **most important** aspect to consider when expanding overseas.
이상적인 장소를 선정하는 일은 해외 진출 시 고려할 가장 중요한 면이다.

해설 빈칸은 정관사 the와 명사 aspect 사이의 형용사 자리이므로 형용사 최상급 (D)가 정답이다.

어휘 select 선택하다 | ideal 이상적인 | location 위치 | aspect 측면 | consider 고려하다 | expand 확대되다, 발전하다 | overseas 해외로

+ Key point
최상급 앞에는 반드시 정관사 the가 온다.

---

3. 비교급 구문

This year's materials science conference will showcase more innovations in sustainable fabrics **than** in previous years.
올해의 재료과학 콘퍼런스에서는 예년보다 지속 가능한 직물에 더 많은 혁신을 선보일 것이다.

해설 빈칸은 완전한 문장과 전명구를 연결하는 자리이다. 빈칸 앞 부분에 비교급 부사 more이 있으므로, 비교급 구문을 완성하는 (C)가 정답이다.

어휘 materials science 재료 과학 | showcase 소개하다 | innovation 혁신, 획기적인 것 | sustainable 지속 가능한 | fabric 직물 | previous 이전의

4. 원급 구문

No one can clean and organize your office as **efficiently** as Marty Cleaners.

누구도 Marty Cleaners만큼 효율적으로 사무실을 청소 및 정리하지 못합니다.

해설 빈칸 양 옆으로 as가 있으므로 원급 비교 구문 문장이다. 첫 번째 as앞에서 주어, 동사, 목적어를 갖춘 완전한 문장요소를 갖추고 있으므로 빈칸은 부사 자리이다. 원급 비교 구문을 완성해야 하므로 (C)가 정답이다.

어휘 clean 청소하다 | organize 정리하다

✚ Key point
① 원급 비교 구문은 'A ~ as 형용사/부사 as B(A는 B만큼 ~하다)'의 형태를 취한다. as 원급 비교 구문 내 품사문제는 as 비교 구문을 제외한 후 문장 구조를 파악하여 결정한다.
② as ~ as는 원급, than은 비교급 구문을 나타내는 대표적인 표현이다.

5. 전치사 자리

The yearly bake sale has been pushed back **because of** uncertain weather conditions.

연례 베이크 세일은 불확실한 기상 상황으로 인해 연기되었다.

해설 빈칸은 명사구 uncertain weather conditions를 목적어로 하는 전치사 자리이므로 (A)가 정답이다.

어휘 yearly 연간의 | bake sale 베이크 세일(기금 마련을 위해 가정에서 제과를 만들어 파는 행사) | push back 미루다 | uncertain 불확실한 | weather conditions 기상 조건

6. 어휘 – 부사

Senior employees **seldom** work on Mondays except when they show up to meet with executives.

고위급 직원은 임원을 만나러 모습을 드러낼 때 외에는 월요일에는 거의 일하지 않는다.

해설 빈칸은 주어와 동사 사이 부사 자리이다. 두 개의 절이 except when으로 연결되어 있으므로, 문맥상 '임원을 만나러 모습을 드러낼 때 외에는 월요일에 거의 일하지 않는다'는 의미가 되어야 자연스러우므로 (A)가 정답이다.

어휘 senior 고위의 | employee 직원 | except when ~할 때를 제외하고, ~이외에는 | show up 나타나다, 눈에 띄다 | executive 임원

✚ Key word
Senior employees **seldom** work on Mondays **except when** they show up to meet with executives.

7. 관용 표현

Students may borrow books and media from libraries **other than** their own university's if they are unavailable.

학생들은 구할 수 없는 경우 자신의 대학도서관 외의 도서관에서 책과 미디어 자료를 빌릴 수 있다.

해설 빈칸은 their own university's를 목적어로 하는 자리이다. 구할 수 없는 경우 자기 학교 도서관 외에 다른 도서관에서 빌릴 수 있다는 의미가 되어야 문맥상 자연스러우므로 (A)가 정답이다.

어휘 borrow 빌리다 | own 자신의 | university 대학교 | unavailable 손에 넣을 수 없는

8. 어휘 – 명사

Should anyone require a **consultation** with Mr. Cruz, make sure to do so after the board meeting.

Cruz 씨와 협의가 필요한 사람이 있으면, 반드시 이사회가 끝난 후 진행하세요.

해설 종속절과 주절의 관계를 고려할 때, 'Cruz 씨와 협의가 필요한 사람이 있으면, 이사회가 끝나고 반드시 하라'는 의미가 되어야 문맥상 자연스러우므로 '협의, 상담'을 의미하는 명사 (A)가 정답이다.

어휘 require 요구하다, 필요로 하다 | board meeting 이사회

✚ Key word
Should anyone require a **consultation with Mr. Cruz**, make sure to do so after the board meeting.

9~12번은 다음 이메일에 관한 문제입니다.

수신: Ellen Park ⟨e.park@commercemail.com⟩
발신: Adam Harrison ⟨aharrison@duskshine.net⟩
날짜: 9월 28일
제목: 환영합니다
첨부: 사전 고용 서류

Park 씨, 안녕하세요.

Duskshine Finance 입사를 환영합니다! 귀하가 합류하게 되어 매우 기쁩니다.

시작하기 전에, 작성해 주셔야 할 서류가 있습니다. 첨부 문서에서 고용 제안서와 건강 문진서가 들어 있습니다. 살펴보시고 입사일 **9**전에 저희에게 이메일로 보내주시기 바랍니다. 또한 궁금한 점이 있으시면 언제든지 **10**회신해 주시기 바랍니다.

11저희 계약에 따라, 귀하의 입사일은 10월 12로 정해졌습니다. 직원으로서의 권리와 혜택, 필수 업무, 사무실 내 적절한 **12**행동에 대해 아주 상세하게 다루는 신입 교육 과정이 마련되어 있습니다. 후자에는 일부 문화 규범과 외국인 신입 사원은 알지 못할 것으로 예상되는 내용이 포함됩니다.

어휘
employment 취업, 고용 | greeting 인사 | on board 탑승한, 합류한, 참여한 | document 서류 | complete 작성하다 | questionnaire 질문지 | thorough 철저한 | onboarding 신입 직원 교육 | process 과정 | right 권리 | benefit 혜택 | required 필수의 | duties 업무 | appropriate 적절한 | cultural norms 문화적 규범 | latter 후자 | expectation 예상(되는 것) | recruit 신입 사원 | unaware ~을 알지 못하는

9. 전치사 자리

해설 빈칸은 완전한 문장과 명사구 your start date를 연결하는 전치사 자리이므로 (B)가 정답이다.

10. to부정사

해설 빈칸 앞 feel free가 있으므로 관용 표현 'feel free to V(언제든지~하다)'를 완성하는 to부정사 (D)가 정답이다.

11. 문장 선택

(A) 우리 시설에는 업계에서 가장 진보된 도구가 준비되어 있습니다.
(B) 귀하의 급여 기대치를 고려했습니다.
(C) 레크리에이션 구역은 전 직원이 무료로 즐길 수 있습니다.
(D) 저희 계약에 따라, 귀하의 입사일은 10월 12로 정해졌습니다.

해설 빈칸 뒷문장의 신입 교육 과정이 마련되어 있다는 내용을 고려할 때, 입사일에 대한 내용이 들어가야 문맥상 자연스러우므로 (D)가 정답이다.

✚ **Key word**

As per our agreement, your start date has been set for October 12. We have a very thorough onboarding process planned which covers your rights and benefits as an employee, your required duties, and appropriate conduct in the office.

12. 어휘 - 명사

해설 빈칸은 형용사 appropriate의 수식을 받는 명사 자리이다. 동시에 동사 cover의 목적어 자리로, 병렬 연결된 다른 목적어(your rights and benefits as an employee, your required duties)를 고려할 때, '사무실 내 적절한 행동'이라는 의미가 되어야 문맥상 자연스러우므로 (A)가 정답이다.

✚ **Key word**

We have a very thorough onboarding process planned which covers your rights and benefits as an employee, your required duties, and appropriate conduct in the office.

CHAPTER 12 어휘

CASE 집중훈련

1. (B) **2.** (D) **3.** (C) **4.** (D) **5.** (D) **6.** (B)
7. (A) **8.** (C)

1. 어휘 - 명사

All subsidiaries are expected to conduct an in-house **audit** and subsequently submit full reports on the findings before March.
모든 자회사들이 내부 감사를 수행하고 그 뒤에 그 결과에 대해 전체 보고서를 3월 전에 제출할 것으로 예상된다.

해설 빈칸은 앞의 형용사 in-house의 수식을 받는 명사 자리이며, conduct의 목적어 역할을 해야 하므로 특정 활동 관련 명사가 나와야 한다. 문맥상 '모든 자회사들이 내부 감사를 수행할 것으로 예상된다'는 의미가 자연스러우므로 (B)가 정답이다.

어휘 subsidiary 자회사 | conduct 수행하다 | in-house 내부의 | subsequently 그 뒤에 | submit 제출하다 | finding 결과

✚ **Key word**

All subsidiaries are expected to conduct an in-house audit and subsequently submit full reports on the findings before March.

2. 어휘 - 명사

Delegation of duties can reduce a supervisor's workload and enable other staff members to try new assignments.
업무의 위임은 상사의 업무량을 줄이고 다른 직원들이 새로운 임무를 시도하는 것을 가능케 한다.

해설 문맥상 '업무의 위임이 업무량을 줄여준다'라는 의미가 되어야 자연스러우므로 (D)가 정답이다.

어휘 delegation 위임, 대표단 | duty 업무 | reduce 줄이다 | workload 작업량 | enable 가능하게 하다 | assignment 배정, 임무

✚ **Key word**

Delegation of duties can reduce a supervisor's workload and enable other staff members to try new assignments.

3. 어휘 - 명사

Ms. Van Tassel wants to see her team members take more **initiative** and follow through with their annual goals.
Van Tassel 씨는 팀원들이 보다 주도권을 쥐고 자신들의 연간 목표를 끝까지 해내는 걸 보길 원한다.

해설 빈칸은 동사 take의 목적어 자리이다. 두 동사구가 접속사 and로 연결되어 있음을 고려할 때, 문맥상 '직원들이 보다 주도권을 쥐고 연간 목표를 끝까지 달성하는 것'이라는 의미가 되어야 자연스러우므로 'take the initiative(주도권을 쥐다)'의 표현을 완성하는 명사 (C)가 정답이다.

어휘 follow through 끝까지 해내다 | annual 연간의 | goal 목표

✚ **Key point**

① 지각동사(see, watch, hear, feel 등)는 5형식 문장에서 목적격 보어 자리에 to부정사가 아닌 원형 부정사(동사 원형)가 와야 한다.
② 명사 initiation vs. initiative: initiation은 '가입, 시작'을, initiative는 '주도권, 계획'을 의미한다.

4. 어휘 - 명사

Please send the information requested to the address listed above at your earliest **convenience**.
형편이 닿는 대로 요청된 정보를 위에 열거된 주소로 보내주세요

해설 빈칸은 전치사 at의 목적어로 형용사의 최상급 earliest의 수식을 받는 명사 자리이다. 문맥상 'at one's earliest convenience(형편이 닿는 대로, 되도록 빨리)'라는 관용 표현을 완성해줄 명사가 들어가야 하므로 (D)가 정답이다.

어휘 information 정보 | requested 요청된 | listed 열거된 | at one's earliest convenience 형편이 닿는 대로, 가급적 빨리

✚ **Key word**

Please send the information requested to the address listed above at your earliest convenience.

5-8번은 다음 광고에 관한 문제입니다.

Dawson 음료회사에서는 오직 가장 신선한 유기농으로 재배한 과일만이 주스에 이용된다고 **5보장드립니다**. 10년 전 설립한 순간부터 저희의 사명이었습니다. 그때 **6이후로**, 저희는 전국의 신뢰할 수 있는 농부들과 제휴를 맺어 매 순간 동일한 고품질의 주스를 제공해 드렸습니다. 저희 베스트셀러는 아보카도 바나나 주스와 딸기 자두 주스입니다. **7이것들은 시즌 상품이니, 계속 있지는 않을 겁니다.**

오늘 저희 매장에 방문하셔서 저희 신규 스무디 제품의 특별한 **8샘플을** 받아보세요. 재고가 있을 때까지만 유효하니, 오늘 받아보세요!

어휘
fresh 신선한 | organically 유기농으로 | grown 재배된 | fruit 과일 | mission 사명 | founding 설립, 창립 | partner with ~와 제휴를 맺다 | trusted 신뢰받는 | farmer 농부 | ensure 보장하다 | high quality 고품질 | plum 자두 | offer 제의, 제안 | good 유효한 | stock 재고(품) | last 지속하다

5. 동사의 시제

해설 빈칸은 주어 we에 대한 동사 자리이다. 빈칸 뒷문장들의 내용을 고려할 때 현재 시제가 되어야 문맥상 자연스러우므로 (D)가 정답이다.

6. 전치사 자리

해설 빈칸은 시점을 나타내는 표현 then을 목적어로 하는 전치사 자리이다. 주절의 시제가 현재 완료이며, '그때 이후로 농부들과 제휴를 맺어왔다'는 의미가 되어야 문맥상 자연스러우므로 (B)가 정답이다.

+ Key point

시점을 나타내는 전치사 since는 현재 완료 시제와 함께 쓰인다.

7. 문장 선택

(A) 이것들은 시즌 상품이니, 계속 있지는 않을 겁니다.
(B) 주스를 냉장고에 보관하면 유통기한을 보존할 수 있습니다.
(C) 웹사이트에는 우리 농부들이 어디에 있는지 자세히 나와 있습니다.
(D) 모든 과일은 철저한 세척 과정을 거칩니다.

해설 빈칸 앞 문장의 '베스트셀러는 아보카도 바나나 주스와 딸기 자두 주스'라는 내용을 고려할 때, our avocado banana juice and our strawberry plum juice를 These으로 받으면서 이것들은 시즌 상품이니, 계속 있지 않는다는 내용으로 이어져야 문맥상 자연스러우므로 (A)가 정답이다.

+ Key word

Our best sellers include our avocado banana juice and our strawberry plum juice. These are seasonal products, so they won't be here forever.

8. 어휘 - 명사

해설 빈칸은 동사 receive의 목적어인 명사 자리이다. 빈칸을 앞, 뒤에서 수식하는 표현을 고려할 때 '신규 스무디 제품의 특별한 샘플을 받아보라'는 내용이 되어야 문맥상 자연스러우므로 (C)가 정답이다.

+ Key word

Visit any one of our stores today to **receive a special sample of our new smoothie line**.

CASE 집중훈련
본서 p.213

1. (A) **2.** (B) **3.** (A) **4.** (D) **5.** (A) **6.** (B)
7. (C) **8.** (C)

---

1. 어휘 - 동사

This accommodation also provides area information and a coupon to **obtain** a discount at the outlet mall.
이 숙박 시설은 또한 지역 정보와 아울렛 쇼핑몰에서 할인을 받을 수 있는 쿠폰을 제공한다.

해설 빈칸은 a discount을 목적어로 취하는 타동사 자리이며, 문맥상 '할인을 받을 수 있는 쿠폰'이라는 의미가 되어야 자연스러우므로 (A)가 정답이다.

어휘 accommodation 숙박 시설 | provide 제공하다

+ Key word

This accommodation also provides area information and **a coupon to obtain a discount** at the outlet mall.

2. 어휘 - 동사

Monsoi Toy Company amended the contract with its shipper, so complaints about late deliveries should **diminish** in the near future.
Monsoi Toy Company는 해운 회사와의 계약을 수정했기 때문에, 지연 배송들에 대한 불만 사항은 가까운 미래에 줄어들 것이다.

해설 빈칸은 동사 자리인데, 뒤에 전치사구(in the near fure)만 있으므로, 자동사가 들어가야 간다. 또한 배송이 늦는 것에 대한 불만들이 '약해지다, 줄어들다'는 뜻이 가장 적절하므로 자동사인 (B)가 정답이다.

어휘 amend 수정하다 | shipper 해운 회사

+ Key word

Monsoi Toy Company amended the contract with its shipper, **so complaints about late deliveries should diminish in the near future.**

3. 어휘 - 동사

Mayflower Foundation **pledged** to donate 3,000 books to a local library in honor of National Literacy Week.
Mayflower 재단은 전국 독서 주간을 기념하여 지역 도서관에 3,000권의 도서를 기부하기로 약속했다.

해설 문맥상 '재단이 3,000권의 책을 기부하기로 서약했다'는 의미가 자연스러우므로 (A)가 정답이다. warrant는 보통 물건의 품질을 보증한다고 할 때 쓴다.

어휘 foundation 재단 | donate 기부하다 | in honor of ~을 축하하여 | literacy 읽고 쓰는 능력 | pledge 약속하다, 서약하다 | warrant 보증하다

4. 어휘 - 동사

Following the introduction of a new menu at Shin-U Restaurant a month ago, the number of customers has almost **tripled**.
한 달 전 Shin-U 레스토랑에서 새 메뉴를 도입하고 나서, 고객들의 수가 거의 세 배가 되었다.

해설 빈칸은 문장의 본동사 자리이다. 문맥상 '새로운 메뉴를 도입하고 나서, 고객들의 수가 거의 세 배가 되었다'는 의미가 자연스러우므로 (D)가 정답이다.

어휘 following ~이후에 | introduction 도입 | almost 거의

+ Key word

Following the introduction of a new menu at Shin-U restaurant a month ago, the number of customers has almost tripled.

5-8번은 다음 이메일에 관한 문제입니다.

수신: JCI 전 회원
발신: Richard White
날짜: 7월 11일, 금요일
제목: 워크숍 장소 변경

JCI 회원 여러분,

올해 열리는 연례 JCI 워크숍 행사가 통제 불가능한 일들로 인해 장소가 **⑤이전될** 것이라는 사실을 알려 드리기 위해 이메일을 드립니다. 저희는 이번 워크숍 장소를 JCI California의 본관에서 New York에 위치한 JCI

본사로 옮길 것입니다. 이 워크숍이 종료되는 데 분명 많은 시간이 **⑥소요될** 것이므로, 여러분께서는 이번 기회를 통해 New York 시 곳곳을 둘러보시고 다양한 장소들도 방문해 보세요. **⑦그곳들은 진정으로 숨이 막히게 놀랍습니다.** 거리를 따라 거닐며 길거리의 상인들이 판매하는 맛있는 음식들도 즐겨보세요. 인근에 명소들이 있어 아침이나 또는 야간에 산책하기에도 **⑧안성맞춤입니다.** 저희는 추가 의류 및 신발을 여유 있게 소지해 오시길 권해 드립니다.

다음 달에 여러분을 만나 뵐 수 있기를 고대합니다.

안녕히 계십시오.

Richard White, 워크숍 진행 책임담당자
JCI

어휘
relocation (위치) 이전, 이동 | inform A that A에게 ~라고 알리다 | annual 연례적인 | due to ~로 인해 | uncontrollable 통제 불가능한 | occasion 일, 때, 경우, 기회 | complete 끝내다, 완료하다 | take this opportunity to do 이번 기회에 ~하다 | browse 둘러보다 | as well 또한, ~도 | merchant 상인 | nearby 근처의 | attraction 명소 | extra 추가의, 별도의 | look forward to -ing ~하기를 고대하다

---

5. 동사의 태

해설 조동사 will 다음에 위치한 빈칸은 동사 원형이 필요한 자리이다. 동사 relocate은 타동사와 자동사로 모두 쓰이는데, 빈칸이 속한 that절의 주어 JCI Workshop은 스스로 이전할 수 있는 것이 아니라 사람에 의해 이전되는 대상이므로 수동의 의미를 나타내는 수동태 동사 (A)가 정답이다.

✦ Key word
I am writing to inform you that **the annual JCI Workshop this year will be relocated** due to uncontrollable occasions.

6. 어휘 - 동사

해설 빈칸 바로 뒤에 위치한 목적어 much time을 고려할 때, '이 워크숍이 종료되는 데 분명 많은 시간이 소요될 것이므로'와 같은 의미가 되어야 자연스러우므로 (B)가 정답이다.

✦ Key word
As it will surely **consume much time for the workshop to be completed,** you can take this opportunity to browse around the city of New York and visit various places as well.

7. 문장 선택
(A) 그들은 새로운 사업을 유치하고 있습니다.
(B) 그것들은 지역 주민들을 위해 남겨져 있습니다.
(C) 그곳들은 진정으로 숨이 멎을 듯 놀랍습니다.
(D) 그들은 식사와 음료를 제공해야 합니다.

해설 빈칸 앞 문장의 '이번 기회를 통해 New York 시 곳곳을 둘러보시고 다양한 장소들도 방문하실 수 있습니다'라는 내용을 고려할 때, 그 장소들의 특징과 관련해 '그곳들은 진정으로 숨이 멎을 듯 놀랍습니다'라는 내용으로 이어져야 자연스러우므로 (C)가 정답이다.

✦ Key word
As it will surely consume much time for the workshop to be completed, you can **take this opportunity to browse around the city of New York and visit**

---

various places as well. **They are truly breathtaking.**

8. 어휘 - 형용사

해설 문장의 주어 '근처의 명소들'과 목적을 나타내는 전치사구 '아침 또는 야간 산책을 위해'라는 말들을 고려할 때, '아침 또는 야간 산책에 최적입니다'와 같은 의미가 되어야 자연스러우므로 (C)가 정답이다.

✦ Key word
The **nearby attractions** are **perfect for a morning or night walk,** too.

CASE 집중훈련
본서 p.215

1. (D)　2. (C)　3. (C)　4. (C)　5. (D)　6. (B)
7. (B)　8. (A)

---

1. 어휘 - 형용사

Due to privacy reasons, the clients' current **postal** address cannot be displayed until their consent is given.
프라이버시의 이유로, 고객들의 현 우편 주소는 그들의 동의가 있을 때까지 표시될 수 없다.

해설 빈칸은 명사 address를 수식하는 형용사 자리이며, 문맥상 '고객들의 현 우편 주소가 그들이 동의할 때까지 표시될 수 없다'라는 의미가 되어야 자연스러우므로 (D)가 정답이다.

어휘 due to ~때문에 | privacy 프라이버시, 사생활 | current 현재의 | display 표시하다, 나타내다 | consent 동의 | global 세계적인 | arrival 도착 | essential 필수의 | postal 우편의

---

2. 어휘 - 형용사

Many people are opening bank accounts with the Yolo Bank following its **unconditional** offer to grant account holders fixed interest.
계좌 소지자들에게 고정 이자를 주겠다는 무조건적인 제의를 하고 나서 많은 사람들이 Yolo 은행의 은행 계좌를 개설하고 있다.

해설 명사 offer를 수식하는 형용사 자리이며, '계좌 소지자들에게 고정 이자를 주겠다는 무조건적인 제의를 한 후에 많은 사람들이 해당 은행의 계좌를 개설하고 있다'는 의미가 자연스러우므로 (C)가 정답이다.

어휘 open a bank account 은행 계좌를 개설하다 | following ~이후에 | offer 제의, 제공 | grant 주다, 승인하다 | account holder 계좌 소지자 | fixed 고정된 | interest 이자 | diminished 감소된 | invaluable 매우 귀중한 | unconditional 무조건의 | farthest 가장 먼

---

3. 어휘 - 형용사

The CEO was **skeptical** of the proposed new product ranges but he gave in after an impressive presentation by the sales team.
CEO는 제안된 새 제품군에 대해 회의적이었지만 영업팀의 인상적인 발표가 끝나고 마지못해 받아들였다.

해설 빈칸은 주어의 상태를 나타내는 주격 보어 자리이다. 보기 모두 전치사 of를 동반할 수 있으므로 해석해서 답을 골라야 한다. 문맥상 'CEO가 제안된 새 제품군 안에 대해 회의적이었지만 인상적인 발표 후에 마지못해 받아들였다'라는 의미가 자연스러우므로 (C)가 정답이다.

어휘 proposed 제안된, ~안 | product range 제품군 | give in (마지못해) 받아들이다 | impressive 인상적인 | be proud of ~을 자랑스러워하다 | be capable of ~할 수 있다 | be skeptical of ~에 회의적이다 | be aware of ~을 알고 있다

✦ Key word

The CEO was skeptical of the proposed new product ranges but he gave in after an impressive presentation by the sales team.

....

4. 어휘 - 형용사

Nina Tom won her 4th **consecutive** businesswoman-of-the-year award after her company earned $30,000 more in profits ahead of Emmy Baker's company, her closest competitor.

Nina Tom은 그녀의 가장 강력한 경쟁자인 Emmy Baker's 사를 수익 면에서 3만 달러 이상 앞지르면서, 올해의 여성 사업가 상을 네 번 연속해서 수상했다.

해설 빈칸은 뒤의 명사구 businesswoman-of-the-year award를 수식하는 형용사 자리이다. 문맥상 'Nina Tom이 경쟁사를 3만 달러 이상 앞지르면서 네 번 연속 상을 수상했다'라는 의미가 되어야 자연스러우므로 (C)가 정답이다.

어휘 win (상을) 수상하다 | award 상 | earn 얻다, 벌다 | profit 수익 | ahead of ~에 앞서는 | competitor 경쟁업체 | constant 지속적인, 끊임없는 | following 다음의 | consecutive 연속적인, 연속되는 | repeated 되풀이되는

5-8번은 다음 편지에 관한 문제입니다.

Rubinstein 교장선생님께,

귀교의 저희 박물관 견학에 관심을 보여주심에 감사드립니다. 문의주신 내용에 대해 답변을 드리면, 저희 박물관 입장가능 최소연령은 7세입니다. **5**이는 엄격히 시행되는 규칙입니다. 추가로, 박물관에서 제공하는 **6**학구적인 활동 목록을 제공해 드립니다. 여기 있는 **7**전시 중 일부는 날씨로 인해 이용 불가능할 수도 있음에 유의해 주시기 바랍니다. 특히, 가장 인기 있는 장소인, 전망 데크와 식물원은 폐쇄될 수도 있습니다.

일정이 어떻게 되는지 다음주까지 **8**저희에게 알려주시기 바랍니다. 조만간 모두 뵙게 되길 고대하겠습니다!

감사합니다.

Paul Costello, 코디네이터
Eagle Harbor 박물관

어휘
principal 교장 | express 표현하다 | interest 관심 | in response to ~에 응하여, 답하여 | minimum 최소 | entry 입장 | additionally 추가로 | note 주목하다 | in particular 특히 | popular 인기 있는 | attraction 명소, 볼거리 | namely 즉 | observatory deck 전망 데크 | botanical garden 식물원 | close off 차단하다, 폐쇄시키다 | coordinator 담당자, 진행자

5. 문장 선택

(A) 박물관은 휴일 동안 많은 행사를 엽니다.
(B) 이는 날씨에 따라 일시적으로 변경될 수 있습니다.
(C) 어린 학생은 추가 비용 없이 입장할 수 있습니다.
(D) 이는 엄격히 시행되는 규칙입니다.

해설 빈칸 앞 문장의 박물관 입장가능 최소연령이 7세라는 내용을 고려할 때, 빈칸에는 이 규칙과 관련된 내용이 들어가야 자연스러우므로 (D)가 정답이다.

✦ Key word

In response to your questions, **the minimum age for entry into our museum is seven years old. This is a rule that is enforced strictly.**

6. 어휘 - 형용사

해설 빈칸은 activities를 수식하는 형용사 자리이며 앞 부분에서 학교의 박물관 견학에 관심주어 감사하다는 내용을 고려할 때, 박물관에서 제공하는 학구적인 활동 목록을 제시하는 것이 문맥상 자연스러우므로 (B)가 정답이다.

✦ Key word

Thank you for **expressing interest in having your school visit our museum**. In response to your questions, the minimum age for entry into our museum is seven years old. This is a rule that is enforced strictly ~. Additionally, here is a list of some of the **academic activities we offer here at the museum**.

7. 어휘 - 명사

해설 빈칸은 these의 수식을 받는 명사 자리로, 앞 문장에서 these가 가리키는 대상이 academic activities이고 뒷문장에서 활동의 예로 전망 데크와 식물원을 언급하고 있으므로 (B)가 정답이다.

✦ Key word

Additionally, here is a list of some of the **academic activities we offer here at the museum**. Please note that **some of these exhibits may be unavailable due to weather** conditions. **In particular, our most popular attractions, namely the observatory deck and the botanical garden, may be closed off.**

8. 인칭대명사

해설 빈칸은 동사 keep의 목적어 자리이다. 'keep 사람 updated'는 사람에게 '최신 소식을 알려주다'의 의미이므로 '저희, 즉, 박물관 측에 학교에서 박물관 견학에 대한 계획을 알려달라는 의미가 되어야 하며, 편지에서 박물관 측을 we라고 지칭하고 있으므로 (A)가 정답이다.

✦ Key word

Please **keep us updated about** what **your plans** are by next week. **We are looking forward to seeing you** all soon!

CASE 집중훈련 본서 p.217

1. (A) **2.** (B) **3.** (D) **4.** (B) **5.** (B) **6.** (A)
7. (D) **8.** (D)

---

1. 어휘 - 부사

This vending machine will deliver reliable quality service to the user as long as maintenance checks are performed **regularly**.

이 자판기는 유지 점검이 정기적으로 실시되는 한, 사용자에게 믿을 수 있는 품질의 서비스를 제공할 것이다.

해설 빈칸은 앞의 동사 are performed를 수식해줄 부사 자리이며, 문맥상 '유지 점검이 정기적으로 실시되는 한'이라는 의미가 되어야 자연스러

우므로 (A)가 정답이다.

어휘 vending machine 자판기, 자동 판매기 | reliable 믿을 수 있는 | as long as
~하는 한 | maintenance 유지 | perform 실시하다, 수행하다 | widely 널리,
광범위하게 | brightly 밝게

+ Key point

recently는 주로 현재 완료/과거 시제 동사와 함께 쓰는 부사이다.

....

2. 어휘 - 부사

Adams said that he **fondly** remembered his first visit
to India to perform in a charity concert.

Adams는 자선 콘서트에서 공연하기 위해 처음 방문했던 인도를 애정
어리게 기억한다고 말했다.

해설 빈칸은 that절의 동사를 수식하는 부사 자리이다. 문맥상 '자신의 첫
인도 방문을 애정 어리게 기억한다고 말했다'라는 의미가 되어야 자연
스러우므로 (B)가 정답이다.

어휘 perform 공연하다 | charity concert 자선 콘서트 | curiously 호기심에서 |
fondly 애정 어리게, 애틋하게 | punctually 시간을 엄수하여 | equally 똑같이,
마찬가지로

+ Key word

Adams said that **he fondly remembered his first
visit** to India to perform in a charity concert.

....

3. 어휘 - 부사

Despite adopting different marketing approaches,
both Comms Global & PM Wireless have **similarly**
gained thousands of new subscribers.

다른 마케팅 접근 방식을 채택했음에도 불구하고, Comms Global과
PM Wireless 둘 다 수천 명의 신규 구독자를 비슷하게 얻었다.

해설 빈칸은 동사 gained를 수식하는 부사 자리이며, 문맥상 '두 회사가 다
른 마케팅 방식을 채택했음에도 불구하고, 신규 구독자 수를 비슷하게
얻었다'는 의미가 되어야 자연스러우므로 (D)가 정답이다.

어휘 despite ~에도 불구하고 | adopt 채택하다 | approach 접근법 | gain
얻다 | thousands of 수 천의 | subscriber 구독자 | moreover 더욱이 |
namely 즉 | nevertheless 그럼에도 불구하고 | similarly 비슷하게, 마찬가지로

+ Key word

**Despite adopting different marketing approaches
during the first quarter, both Comms Global &
PM Wireless have similarly gained thousands of
new subscribers.**

....

4. 어휘 - 부사

Flexible work hours would **significantly** improve the
efficiency of our managerial staff.

유연한 근무시간은 관리직 직원의 능률을 상당히 향상시켜줄 것이다.

해설 빈칸은 동사 improve를 수식하는 부사 자리이며, '능률을 상당히 향
상시켜줄 것'이라는 의미가 되어야 문맥상 자연스러우므로 (B)가 정
답이다. 부사 significantly는 증가, 감소 또는 향상을 나타내는 동사
increase, decrease, improve 등과 주로 함께 쓰인다.

어휘 flexible 유연한 | work hour 근무시간 | improve 향상하다 | efficiency
능률, 효율(성) | managerial staff 관리직원

+ Key word

Flexible work hours would **significantly improve**
the **efficiency** of our managerial staff.

5-8번은 다음 편지에 관한 문제입니다.

독자 여러분께,

이 편지는 여행할 때나 읽지 못한 잡지들이 쌓일 수도 있는 여타 상황에서
주간 배송 중지에 관한 저희 잡지사의 정책 변경을 귀하께 **⑤알려 드리기**
위함입니다.

7일 전 저희에게 알려주시면, 추가요금 없이 최대 30일 동안 배송을 중
단할 수 있습니다. **⑥그 이후 정기 배송이 재개될 것입니다.**

또한 귀하의 구독에는 저희 온라인 심층 뉴스 **⑦보도**의 무제한 이용도 포함되
어 있다는 것을 잊지 마세요. WeeklyInquirer.com/Digitalsubscription
에서 계정 정보를 입력하여 디지털용 자격 증명을 신청하시면, 한 번에
최대 5대의 기기로 이용할 수 있습니다.

잡지 배송을 **⑧일시적으로** 중단하시려면, 저희에게 customerservice
@weeklyinquirer.com으로 이메일을 보내주시거나 555 991-2313
으로 전화주세요.

어휘

modification 수정 | policy 정책 | pause 잠시 멈추다 | occasion 상황,
경우 | issue (정기 간행물의) 호 | otherwise 달리, 그렇지 않다면 | pile up 쌓이다 |
notice 통지 | suspend 중단하다 | additional 추가적인 | fee 요금, 수수료 |
subscription 구독(료) | unlimited 무제한의 | access 이용, 접근 | in-depth
심층적인 | register for 등록하다 | credential 자격증명 | account 계정 |
device 장비 | at once 한 번에

5. 어휘 - 동사

해설 빈칸은 to부정사구를 완성하는 동사 자리이다. 빈칸 뒷부분의 구조를
고려할 때, 'inform A of B'로 'A에게 B에 관해 알려주다'의 형태를 완
성하는 (B)가 정답이다.

+ Key word

This letter is to inform you of a modification to
our magazine's policy on pausing weekly delivery
when you travel, or on other occasions when unread
issues might otherwise pile up.

6. 문장 선택

(A) 그 이후, 정기 배송이 재개될 것입니다.
(B) 할인은 디지털 계정에 적용될 것입니다.
(C) 당사의 품질 보고는 여러분과 같은 독자 분들에 의해 가능합니다.
(D) 이 결정은 비용 증가 때문에 내려졌습니다.

해설 빈칸 앞 문장의 '최대 30일동안 정기 배송을 중단할 수 있다'는 내용을
고려할 때, 문맥상 '30일 이후에는 정기 배송이 재개된다'는 내용으로
이어져야 자연스러우므로 (A)가 정답이다.

+ Key word

**If you give us 7 days notice, we can suspend
delivery for up to 30 days without an additional fee.
Subsequently, regular delivery will resume.**

7. 어휘 - 명사

해설 빈칸은 our in-depth online news의 수식을 받는 명사 자리이므로
news와 함께 복합명사를 이뤄 'news coverage(뉴스 보도)'를 완성
하는 (D)가 정답이다.

+ Key point

coverage가 복합명사로 쓰이는 경우는 다음과 같다: news
coverage(뉴스 보도), media coverage(매스컴 보도), insurance

coverage(보험 보장범위) 등

8. 어휘 – 부사

해설 빈칸은 to부정사인 동사 suspend를 수식하는 부사 자리이다. '잡지 배송을 최대 30일 동안 중단할 수 있다'는 두 번째 단락의 내용을 고려할 때, 문맥상 '잡지 배송을 일시적으로 중단하시려면'이라는 내용이 되어야 자연스러우므로 (D)가 정답이다.

+ Key word

If you give us 7 days notice, we can suspend delivery for up to 30 days without an additional fee. ~
To temporarily suspend print delivery, email us at customerservice@weeklyinquirer.com **or call us** at 555 991-2313.

CASE 실전훈련
본서 p.218

1. (B) 2. (A) 3. (D) 4. (C) 5. (B) 6. (D)
7. (C) 8. (C) 9. (B) 10. (D) 11. (C) 12. (B)

1. 어휘 – 부사

Medellin Industries grew **rapidly** in its first five years of operations, increasing its annual growth rate by 50 percent.
Medellin Industries는 영업 초반 5년 만에 빠르게 성장해, 연간 성장률이 50%까지 상승했다.

해설 빈칸은 동사 grew를 수식하는 부사 자리이다. 빈칸 뒤 내용을 고려할 때, 문맥상 '영업 초반 5년 만에 빠르게 성장해, 연간 성장률이 50%까지 상승했다'는 의미가 되어야 자연스러우므로 (B)가 정답이다.

어휘 grow 성장하다, 발달하다 | operation 영업, 사업 | increase 증가시키다 | annual 연간의 | growth rate 성장률

+ Key word

Medellin Industries **grew rapidly in its first five years of operations, increasing its annual growth rate by 50 percent.**

---

2. 어휘 – 명사

Six vendors submitted construction bid **proposals** for the new hospital building.
업체 6곳에서 신규 병원 건물을 위한 공사 입찰 제안서를 제출했다.

해설 빈칸은 construction bid의 수식을 받고 동사 submitted의 대상이 될 수 있는 명사 자리이다. '신규 병원 건물을 위한 공사 입찰 제안서를 제출했다'는 의미가 되어야 문맥상 자연스러우므로 (A)가 정답이다.

어휘 vendor 행상인, 판매자 | submit 제출하다 | construction 공사 | bid 입찰

+ Key word

Six vendors **submitted construction bid proposals** for the new hospital building.

---

3. 어휘 – 동사

Once orders are placed on our Website, they are **fulfilled** within 24 hours.
웹사이트로 주문이 들어오면, 24시간 이내 이행된다.

해설 빈칸은 수동태 동사 구문(be p.p.)을 완성하는 과거분사 자리이다. once 종속절과 주절의 관계를 고려할 때, they는 orders를 받고 '주문을 이행하다'라는 표현이 되어야 하므로 '이행[실행]하다'를 의미하는 (D)가 정답이다.

어휘 once 일단 ~하면 | order 주문 | place (주문을) 하다

+ Key word

Once orders are placed on our Website, they are fulfilled within 24 hours.

---

4. 어휘 – 동사

This afternoon's presentation will **examine** best practices for communicating with our clients to see how we can improve our services.
오늘 오후 프레젠테이션에서는 서비스 개선 방법을 알아보기 위해 고객과 소통하는 모범 사례에 대해 살펴볼 것입니다.

해설 빈칸은 문장의 동사 자리이다. '오늘 프레젠테이션에서는 고객과 소통하는 모범 사례에 대해 살펴볼 것'이라는 의미가 되어야 문맥상 자연스러우므로 (C)가 정답이다.

어휘 best practice 모범 사례 | communicate 소통하다 | client 고객 | improve 향상시키다

+ Key word

This afternoon's **presentation** will **examine best practices for communicating with our clients** to see how we can improve our services.

---

5. 어휘 – 동사

Mr. Medina will not be able to attend the seminar this afternoon because she is **stuck** in traffic.
교통 체증에 갇혀 있어, Medina 씨는 오늘 오후 세미나에 참석하지 못할 것이다.

해설 빈칸은 be동사와 함께 수동태 동사 구문을 완성하는 과거분사 자리이다. 빈칸 뒤 in traffic이 있음을 고려할 때, 'stuck in traffic(교통체증에 갇힌)'이라는 관용 표현을 완성하는 (B)가 정답이다.

어휘 attend 참석하다 | traffic 교통(량)

+ Key word

Mr. Medina will not be able to attend the seminar this afternoon because she **is stuck in traffic.**

---

6. 어휘 – 형용사

Blue Lode Solutions remunerates its software developers with some of the most **competitive** salaries in all of Comobabi.
Blue Lode Solutions는 Comobabi를 통틀어 소프트웨어 개발자에게 가장 경쟁력 있는 급여를 지급한다.

해설 빈칸은 명사 salaries를 수식하는 형용사 자리이다. '개발자에게 경쟁력 있는 급여를 지급한다'는 의미가 되어야 문맥상 자연스러우므로 (D)가 정답이다.

어휘 remunerate 보수를 지불하다 | developer 개발자 | salary 급여

+ Key word

Blue Lode Solutions **compensates its software developers with** some of the most **competitive salaries** in all of Comobabi.

7. 어휘 - 명사

Stabilo Corporation compensates high-earning sales representatives with weekend **stays** at the finest hotels.

Stabilo Corporation에서는 고수익을 올리는 영업사원들에게 최고급 호텔에서의 주말 숙박으로 보상해 준다.

해설 빈칸은 weekend와 함께 명사구를 이루는 명사 자리이다. 문맥상 '최고급 호텔에서의 주말 숙박'이라는 의미가 되어야 자연스러우므로 (C)가 정답이다.

어휘 corporation 기업 | compensate 보상하다 | high-earning 고소득의 | sales representative 영업 사원 | fine 질 높은, 괜찮은

✦ Key word
Stabilo Corporation compensates high-earning sales representatives with **weekend stays at the finest hotels.**

----

8. 어휘 - 형용사

Although the government supports first-time home buyers, it may take time before **meaningful** changes to policies are passed.

정부가 생애 첫 주택구입자를 지지하지만, 정책에 유의미한 변경사항이 통과되기까지는 시간이 걸릴 수 있다.

해설 빈칸은 before 종속절의 주어인 명사 changes를 수식하는 형용사 자리이다. '정부가 생애 첫 주택구입자를 지지하지만, 정책에 유의미한 변경사항이 통과되기까지는 시간이 걸릴 것'이라는 의미가 되어야 문맥상 자연스러우므로 (C)가 정답이다.

어휘 government 정부 | support 지원하다 | first-time 처음으로 하는 | home buyer 주택 구입자 | change 변경사항 | policy 정책 | pass 통과시키다

✦ Key word
Although the government supports supporting first-time home buyers, **it may take time before meaningful changes to policies are passed.**

> **9-12번은 다음 기사에 관한 문제입니다.**
>
> GRENVILLE (4월 23일) — 미국의 패션 거물 StackRack이 영국으로의 진출 계획을 ⑨**밝혔다.** StackRack의 대변인 Ivan Palmer는 최근 Grenville을 첫 번째 지점으로 하는 자사의 유럽 진출 계획을 공개했다.
>
> ⑩**StackRack은 신규 지점을 단계적으로 열기로 결정했다.** 최초 출시에서는 인상적인 의류 제품군을 선보일 예정인데, 단순하지만 ⑪**최신 유행하는** 디자인으로 언론에서 화제가 됐다. 첫 출시 이후, 회사는 시기를 특정할 수는 없지만 자사의 상징적인 라운지와 스파를 열고 싶어한다. ⑫**개발은** 9월 중 시작될 예정이다.
>
> **어휘**
> giant 거대 기업 | expansion 확장, 확대 | make public 공개[공표]하다 | location 지점 | initial 처음의 | launch 개시, 착수 | impressive 인상적인 | clothing 옷, 의복 | range 범위 | buzz 열광, 흥분 | open up 열다 | iconic 상징이 되는 | lounge 휴게실, 라운지

9. 어휘 - 동사

해설 빈칸 뒷문장의 'StackRack의 대변인이 회사의 유럽 진출 계획을 공개했다'는 내용을 고려할 때, '회사에서 영국 진출 계획을 밝혔다'는 의미가 되어야 문맥상 자연스러우므로 (B)가 정답이다.

✦ Key word
American fashion giant StackRack **revealed plans on its expansion into the United Kingdom.** StackRack's spokesperson Ivan Palmer recently made public the plans for its expansion into Europe, with Grenville being its first location.

10. 문장 선택

(A) StackRack은 그 지점이 성공할 것으로 낙관하고 있습니다.
(B) StackRack의 확장 전략은 위험하다고 간주되어 왔습니다.
(C) StackRack은 최근 아시아 시장에도 진출했습니다.
(D) StackRack은 신규 지점을 단계적으로 열기로 결정했습니다.

해설 빈칸 앞 단락에서 'Grenville을 첫 번째 지점으로 하는 자사의 유럽 진출 계획을 공개했다'는 내용에 이어, 빈칸 뒷부분의 '최초 출시에서는 인상적인 의류 제품군을 선보일 예정이고, 첫 출시 이후에는 자사의 상징적인 라운지와 스파를 열고 싶어한다'는 내용을 고려할 때, 첫 지점을 단계적으로 열 계획이라는 내용이 앞에 제시된 후, 각 단계에 대한 내용을 구체적으로 설명하는 것이 문맥상 자연스러우므로 (D)가 정답이다.

✦ Key word
StackRack's spokesperson Ivan Palmer recently made public the **plans for its expansion into Europe, with Grenville being its first location. StackRack has elected to open the new location in phases. The initial launch will offer its impressive clothing range,** which has created media buzz for its simple yet fashionable designs. **Following the initial launch, the company hopes to also open up its iconic lounge and spa,** although the company could not specify the time frame.

11. 형용사 자리

해설 빈칸은 명사 designs를 수식하는 자리이다. '인상적인 의류 제품군을 선보일 예정인데, 단순하지만 최신 유행하는 디자인으로 언론에서 화제가 됐다'는 의미가 되어야 문맥상 자연스러우므로 형용사 (C)가 정답이다.

✦ Key word
The initial launch will offer its impressive **clothing range, which has created media buzz for its simple yet fashionable designs.**

12. 어휘 - 명사

해설 빈칸 앞 문장의 '시기를 특정할 수는 없지만 자사의 상징적인 라운지와 스파를 열고 싶어한다'는 내용을 고려할 때, 라운지와 스파 개발작업이 9월 중 시작될 예정이라는 내용으로 이어져야 문맥상 자연스러우므로 (B)가 정답이다.

✦ Key word
Following the initial launch, **the company hopes to also open up its iconic lounge and spa, although the company could not specify the time frame. Development is due to start in September.**

PART 6

CHAPTER 13 파트 6 문제 유형

본서 p.225

CASE 집중훈련

1. (D) **2.** (C) **3.** (B) **4.** (C) **5.** (D) **6.** (C)
7. (A) **8.** (B)

---

1. 어휘 - 형용사

After a **favorable** review in the online food blog, profits at Gigi's Café increased last week.

온라인 음식 블로그에 호의적인 후기가 올라온 후, 지난주 Gigi's 카페의 수익이 증가했다.

해설 빈칸은 명사 review를 수식하는 형용사 자리이다. 호의적인 후기가 올라온 후 수익이 증가했다는 주절의 내용으로 연결되어야 문맥상 자연스러우므로 (D)가 정답이다.

어휘 review 후기 | profit 수익 | increase 증가하다

➕ **Key word**

After a **favorable review** in the online food blog, **profits** at Gigi's Café **increased** last week.

---

2. 어휘 - 명사

All factory floor workers must print and keep a copy of workplace safety tips close at hand for quick **reference**.

모든 작업 현장 근로자들은 업무환경 안전수칙 가이드 사본을 출력하여 빠르게 참고할 수 있도록 가까운 곳에 보관해야 한다.

해설 빈칸은 전치사 for의 목적어 자리이다. 문맥상 '업무환경 안전수칙 사본을 출력해 빠르게 참고할 수 있도록 가까운 곳에 보관해야 한다'는 의미가 되어야 자연스러우므로 (C)가 정답이다.

어휘 factory 공장 | workplace 업무 현장 | safety 안전 | close at hand 쉽게 손 닿는 곳에

➕ **Key word**

All **factory floor workers must print and keep** a copy of **workplace safety tips close at hand for** quick **reference**.

---

3. 어휘 - 부사

Regrettably, both domestic and international travel to industry conventions are discouraged due to budget cuts.

안타깝게도, 국내와 해외 모두 예산 삭감으로 인해 업계 컨벤션 출장이 좌절되고 있다.

해설 빈칸은 문장 전체를 수식하는 부사 자리이다. 예산 삭감으로 인해 국내든 해외든 산업 컨벤션 참석을 하지 말라고 권하는 내용을 고려할 때, 전반적으로 부정적인 내용을 전하고 있으므로 (B)가 정답이다.

어휘 domestic 국내의 | industry 산업 | recommend 권하다 | budget 예산 | cut 삭감

➕ **Key word**

Regrettably, both domestic and international travel to industry conventions are discouraged due to budget cuts.

---

4. 어휘 - 동사

While each of the accountants **performed** well during their final interviews, Ga-In Lee stood out from everyone else.

최종 면접 동안 각 회계사들이 잘 하긴 했지만, Ga-In Lee는 다른 모든 사람들 중에 가장 돋보였다.

해설 빈칸은 주어 each of the accountants에 대한 동사 자리이다. 접속사 while로 연결된 두 문장관계를 고려할 때, 문맥상 '각각의 회계사들이 면접에서 잘 하긴 했지만, Ga-In Lee가 가장 돋보였다'는 의미로 이어져야 자연스러우므로 (C)가 정답이다. perform well(좋은 활약을 하다)이 숙어 표현이다.

어휘 authority 권한 | allow ~할 수 있도록 한다, 허락하다 | ability 능력

➕ **Key word**

While each of the accountants performed well during their final interviews, **Ga-In Lee stood out from everyone else.**

5-8번은 다음 회람에 관한 문제입니다.

수신: 15 Quarry Oval 주민
발신: Willie Ingram, 시설 관리자
날짜: 3월 16일

주민 여러분께,

3월 23일과 24일에는 저희 작업반이 이곳에 거주하는 주민 몇 분께서 요청하신 필수 조정 작업을 **5할 예정입니다.** 주된 작업은 출입구 전자 보안시스템 설치입니다. **6이는** 건물에 들어갈 수 있는 사람을 제한해 보안을 대폭 강화할 것입니다. 설치의 일환으로, 전자문을 자동으로 잠그는 것뿐만 아니라 주 출입구에 카드 리더기를 설치할 예정입니다. **7해당 기간 동안 주 출입구는 폐쇄됩니다.** 뒷문은 이용 가능하지만, 폭이 상당히 좁습니다. 따라서 양일간 부피가 큰 **8배송** 계획을 세우지 마시기 바랍니다. 설치가 완료되면, 모든 주민분께 건물 출입용 카드를 2장 발급해드릴 예정입니다.

감사합니다.

Willie Ingram

어휘
facility 시설 | resident 주민 | crew 작업반 | adjustment 조정 | request 요청하다 | reside 거주하다 | chief 주된, 주요한 | installation 설치 | electronic 전자의 | security 보안 | entrance 입구 | drastically 급격히 | limit 제한하다 | card-reader 카드 리더기 | automatically 자동적으로 | lock 잠그다 | narrow 좁은 | plan 계획하다 | complete 완료된 | issue 발급하다 | grant 주다

---

5. 동사의 시제

해설 빈칸은 주어와 목적어 사이 능동태 동사 자리이다. 회람 발송 날짜가 3월 16일임을 고려할 때, 미래 시제가 되어야 문맥상 자연스러우므로 미래진행 시제 (D)가 정답이다.

6. 지시대명사

해설 빈칸은 문장의 주어 자리이다. 빈칸 앞 문장의 '출입구 전자 보안시스템 설치가 주된 작업'이라는 내용을 고려할 때 출입구 전자 보안시스

템 설치로 보안이 대폭 강화될 것이라는 의미가 되어야 문맥상 자연스러우므로 '출입구 전자 보안시스템 설치'를 의미할 수 있는 지시대명사 (C)가 정답이다.

+ Key word

Chief among those is **the installation of an electronic security system at the entrance. This will drastically increase security by limiting who can enter the building.**

7. 문장 선택

(A) 해당 기간 동안 주 출입구는 폐쇄됩니다.
(B) 날씨 때문에 일정이 늦어질 수 있습니다.
(C) 추가 수리가 이루어질 수 있지만, 일부 수리 비용이 발생할 수 있습니다.
(D) 창문이 세심하게 관리되어야 합니다.

해설 빈칸 앞 문장의 '주 출입구에 카드 리더기를 설치할 예정'이라는 내용과 뒷문장의 '뒷문은 이용 가능하지만'이라는 내용을 고려할 때, 출입구와 관련된 내용이 들어가야 문맥상 연결이 자연스러우므로 (A)가 정답이다.

+ Key word

As part of the installation, **we will be installing a card-reader at the main entrance** as well as automatically locking electronic doors. **The main entrance will be closed off for the duration.** The backdoor will be available, but it is quite narrow.

8. 어휘 – 명사

해설 빈칸은 any large의 수식을 받는 명사 자리이다. 빈칸 앞 문장의 '뒷문은 이용 가능하지만, 폭이 상당히 좁다'는 내용을 고려할 때, '양일간 부피가 큰 배송 계획을 세우지 말라는 내용으로 이어져야 문맥상 자연스러우므로 (B)가 정답이다.

+ Key word

The backdoor will be available, but it is quite narrow. Therefore, please do not plan for any large deliveries on either day.

CASE 집중훈련
본서 p.227

1. (A) 2. (A) 3. (D) 4. (A) 5. (D) 6. (A)
7. (B) 8. (A)

1. 어휘 – 명사

Education experts predict that AI programs that are designed to personalize students' learning progress will continue increasing in **popularity**.
교육 전문가들은 학생의 학습 진도를 개인화하도록 설계된 인공지능 프로그램이 계속하여 인기가 증가할 것이라고 예측한다.

해설 빈칸은 전치사 in의 목적어인 명사 자리이다. 문맥상 'AI 프로그램의 인기가 계속하여 증가할 것으로 예상한다'는 의미가 되어야 자연스러우므로 (A)가 정답이다.

어휘 education 교육 | expert 전문가 | predict 예상하다 | AI 인공지능(Artificial Intelligence) | design 설계하다 | personalize (개인의 필요에) 맞추다 | progress 진전, 진척 | continue 계속하다 | increase 증가하다

+ Key word

Education experts predict that **AI programs that are designed to personalize students' learning progress** will **continue increasing in popularity**.

2. 어휘 – 동사

Following the resignation of Ms. Tsang, the department **launched** a search for a new director of operations.
Tsang 씨의 사임 후에, 그 부서는 새로운 영업 책임자 탐색을 시작했다.

해설 빈칸은 주어와 목적어 사이 타동사 자리이다. 문맥상 '새로운 책임자 찾기를 시작했다'라는 의미가 자연스러우므로 (A)가 정답이다.

어휘 following ~후에 | resignation 사임 | search 찾기, 수색 | operations 영업 활동

+ Key word

Following the resignation of Ms. Tsang, the department **launched a search for a new director** of operations.

3. 어휘 – 동사

The new division of We Build For You mainly **focuses** on roofing supplies and installations for both residential and commercial properties.
We Build For You의 새 분과는 주로 주거용과 상업용 건물 모두를 대상으로 지붕 공사 물품 공급과 설치에 주력한다.

해설 빈칸은 문장의 본동사 자리로 빈칸 뒤 전치사 on을 동반하여 '~에 집중하다'란 뜻의 자동사 (D)가 정답이다. (B)는 전치사 to(→ belong to ~의 것이다), (C)는 전치사 with(→ cooperate with ~와 협력하다)를 동반한다.

어휘 division 분과, 국 | mainly 주로 | roofing 지붕공사 | supplies (공급) 물품 | installation 설치 | residential 주거의 | commercial 상업의 | property 건물, 부동산

+ Key word

The new division of We Build For You mainly **focuses on roofing supplies and installations** for both residential and commercial properties.

4. 접속사 자리

National Public Transport will convert its subway trains to be completely automated **only if** the technology improves the reliability of the system.
전국 대중 교통 공사는 기술이 시스템의 신뢰도를 향상해야만 지하철 열차를 전면 자동화되도록 전환할 것이다.

해설 빈칸은 주어와 동사를 갖춘 완전한 두 문장을 연결하는 접속사 자리이므로 (A)가 정답이다.

어휘 convert 전환하다 | completely 완전히 | automate 자동화하다 | technology 기술 | improve 향상시키다 | reliability 신뢰도

+ Key point

no longer, moreover는 부사구, prior to는 구전치사이므로 문장을 연결할 수 없다.

5-8번은 다음 기사에 관한 문제입니다.

CANTERBURY (2월 15일) — 집안 행사로 시작한 일이 Glasgow 대학교의 연례 행사가 되었다. 오늘날, 🅱방문객은 대학교 정문에서부터 펼

처지는 50미터 길이의 거대한 히아신스 정원을 즐길 수 있다. **ⓕ아마도 세계 최대의 히아신스 정원일 것이다.** 히아신스를 심는 전통이 왜 지역사회의 관심을 얻게 되었는지는 아무도 **ⓖ정확하게** 모른다. 우리가 아는 내용은 그것이 적어도 70년 동안 지속되어온 전통이라는 것이다.

ⓗ다행히도, 그 전통은 변함없는 인기를 누릴 것으로 보인다. 대학의 학생들은 자원해서 일년 내내 물과 흙을 제공하고, 해충을 없애면서 정원을 돌본다. 히아신스는 계속 남아 여러 세대가 즐길 수 있을 것이다.

어휘
start out as ~로 시작하다 | tradition 전통 | turn into ~로 바뀌다[변하다] | yearly 연례의 | massive 거대한 | hyacinth 히아신스 | run 이어지다 | along ~를 따라 | main entrance 정문 | plant 심다 | catch on with ~에게 인기를 얻다 | community 지역사회 | ongoing 계속 진행중인 | at least 적어도, 최소한 | enjoy 즐기다, 누리다 | consistent 변함없는, 한결 같은 | popularity 인기 | volunteer 자원하다 | take care of 보살피다 | provide 제공하다 | soil 흙 | clear out 없애다 | pest 해충 | around 주변에 있는 | generation 세대

5. 사람 명사 vs. 사물 / 추상 명사

해설 빈칸은 문장의 주어인 명사 자리이다. 문맥상 '방문객은 히아신스 정원을 즐길 수 있다'는 의미가 되어야 자연스러우므로 사람 명사 (D)가 정답이다.

✦ **Key point**
명사 visit vs. visitor: visit은 '방문'을, visitor는 '방문객'을 의미한다.

6. 문장 선택

(A) 아마도 세계 최대의 히아신스 정원일 것이다.
(B) 다른 꽃 종들은 관리하기 더 쉬울 수 있다.
(C) 히아신스는 보통 봄 중순쯤에 꽃을 피운다.
(D) 히아신스는 인기 때문에 비싼 값에 팔린다.

해설 빈칸 앞 부분의 '오늘날, 방문객은 거대한 히아신스 정원을 즐길 수 있다'는 내용을 고려할 때, 히아신스 정원의 규모에 대해 언급하는 내용으로 이어져야 문맥상 자연스러우므로 (A)가 정답이다.

✦ **Key word**
Today, visitors can enjoy a massive 50-meter hyacinth garden that runs along the main entrance to the university. **It may be the biggest hyacinth garden in the world.**

7. 부사 자리

해설 빈칸은 문장의 동사와 목적어인 why 의문사 명사절 사이의 자리이므로 동사를 수식하는 부사 (B)가 정답이다.

✦ **Key point**
부사는 부사(구), 형용사, 동사, 문장 등을 수식하며, 문장 내 가장 다양한 위치에 올 수 있는 품사이다.

8. 접속부사

해설 빈칸은 문장 도입부의 접속부사 자리이다. 빈칸 앞 부분의 '히아신스 정원이 최소 70년 동안 지속되어온 전통'이라는 내용을 고려할 때, '다행히도 변함없는 인기를 누릴 예정'이라는 내용으로 이어져야 문맥상 자연스러우므로 (A)가 정답이다.

✦ **Key word**
What we do know is that **it has been an ongoing tradition for at least 70 years.**
Fortunately, the tradition looks to be enjoying consistent popularity.

CASE 집중훈련

본서 p.229

1. (C) 2. (B) 3. (A) 4. (B) 5. (C) 6. (D)
7. (D) 8. (A)

1. 어휘 – 부사

Dr. Cheng designed detailed charts to record the factory's energy needs **precisely**.
Cheng 박사는 공장의 에너지 수요를 정확하게 기록하기 위해 상세한 차트를 고안했다.

해설 빈칸은 동사 record를 수식하는 부사 자리이다. 문맥상 '정확하게 기록하기 위해서'라는 의미가 되어야 자연스러우므로 (C)가 정답이다. detailed charts 때문에 broadly는 문맥에 어울리지 않는다.

어휘 design 고안하다 | record 기록하다

✦ **Key word**
Dr. Cheng designed detailed charts to **record** the factory's energy needs **precisely**.

2. 어휘 – 동사

Even though admission to the Kenville Nature Museum is free, tourists are encouraged to **donate** to the exhibition fund.
비록 Kenville 자연 박물관의 입장료가 무료이기는 하지만, 관광객은 전시회 기금에 기부하도록 장려된다.

해설 빈칸은 to부정사를 완성해줄 동사 원형 자리이다. 문맥상 '~의 입장료가 무료이기는 하지만, 관광객들은 전시회 기금에 기부하도록 장려된다'라는 의미가 되어야 자연스러우므로 (B)가 정답이다.

어휘 admission 입장(료) | encourage 장려하다, 격려하다 | exhibition 전시(회) | fund 기금, 자금 | apply 적용하다 | donate 기부하다 | dedicate 전념하다 | support 지원하다

✦ **Key word**
Even though admission to the Kenville Nature Museum **is free, tourists are encouraged to donate to the exhibition fund.**

3. 어휘 – 명사

Passengers aboard Pacific Air aircrafts will appreciate traveling alongside an **expert** group of flight attendants.
Pacific 항공의 여객기 탑승객들은 전문가 승무원들과 함께 여행하는 것에 감사해할 것이다.

해설 빈칸은 명사 group을 수식하는 형용사 자리이다. 문맥상 '전문가로 구성된 승무원들'이라는 의미가 되어야 자연스러우므로 (A)가 정답이다.

어휘 passenger 승객 | aboard 탑승한 | aircraft 항공기 | appreciate 감사해하다 | alongside ~와 함께 | flight attendant 승무원

✦ **Key word**
Passengers aboard Pacific Air aircrafts will **appreciate traveling alongside an expert group of flight attendants.**

4. 어휘 – 형용사

Haldane Industry released some **optimistic** forecast

in its latest financial report.
Haldane Industry에서 최신 재무 보고서에 낙관적인 예측을 발표했다.

해설 빈칸은 명사 forecast 를 수식하는 형용사 자리이다. 재무 보고서에 대한 낙관적인 예측을 발표했다는 의미가 되어야 문맥상 의미가 자연스러우므로 (B)가 정답이다.

어휘 release 공개하다, 발표하다 | forecast 예측 | latest 최신의 | financial report 재무 보고서

+ **Key word**
Haldane Industry **released** some **optimistic forecast in its latest financial report**.

5-8번은 다음 편지에 관한 문제입니다.

10월 17일

직원 여러분께,

Gamst Partners와의 합병이 공식적으로 이루어졌습니다. 오늘은 Kristin & Gamst라는 새로 합병된 회사의 첫 날입니다. **5** 이제 Kristen & Gamst 국내 최대 법률 사무소가 되었습니다. 합병에 이어, 우리는 공동 자원을 활용해 해외시장에 공격적으로 진출할 **6** 계획입니다. Gamst Partners가 가진 조세법 관련 전문지식과 우리의 계약법 관련 지식이 있기에, 성공가능성은 매우 높습니다.

합병 이후 생겨나는 가장 큰 변화는 신규 경영진 **7** 발표가 될 것입니다. 이는 Gamst Partners 측과 이미 사전에 협의된 것이며, 여러분께 세부 내용에 대해 알려드리게 되어 기쁩니다. 회사는 오늘 오후 2시 길 건너편에 있는 Conference Hall에서 모일 예정이며, 그곳에서 행사를 축하할 것입니다. **8** 또한 다가오는 새해에 저희가 계획한 것을 공개할 예정입니다. 그곳에서 뵙게 되길 바랍니다.

감사합니다.

Damon Sandoval
인사 담당자
Kristin기업

어휘
merger 합병 | officially 공식적으로 | go through 성사되다 | combined 결합된 | following ~후에 | aggressively 공격적으로, 적극적으로 | expand 확장하다 | overseas 해외로 | pooled 공동의 | resource 자원 | expertise 전문지식 | tax law 조세법 | knowledge 지식 | contract law 계약법 | chance 가능성 | success 성공 | take place 일어나다 | management 경영 [관리] (진) | pre-negotiate 사전 협상하다 | fill ~ in on the details ~에게 상세한 내용을 알려주다 | convene 모이다, 회합하다 | reveal 드러내다, 밝히다

---

5. 문장 선택
(A) 오늘날 기업의 법률 서비스는 수요가 높습니다.
(B) 직원들은 문의 사항이 있을 경우 담당자에게 이메일을 보내야 합니다.
(C) 이제 Kristen & Gamst는 국내 최대 법률 사무소가 되었습니다.
(D) 그 지역은 경쟁이 치열하기 때문에 어떤 장점이든 환영합니다.

해설 빈칸 앞 문장의 '오늘은 Kristin & Gamst라는 새로 합병된 회사의 첫 날'이라는 내용을 고려할 때, 문맥상 '이제 Kristen & Gamst가 국내 최대 법률 사무소'라는 내용으로 이어져야 자연스러우므로 (C)가 정답이다.

+ **Key word**
Today is the first day of our new combined company, Kristin & Gamst. Kristen & Gamst is now one of the country's largest law firms.

---

6. 동사의 시제

해설 빈칸은 주어 we에 대한 동사 자리이다. 빈칸 뒷문장의 'Gamst Partners가 가진 조세법 관련 전문지식과 우리의 계약법 관련 지식이 있기에, 성공가능성은 매우 높다'는 내용을 고려할 때, '합병에 이어, 공동 자원을 활용해 해외시장에 공격적으로 진출할 계획'이라는 의미가 되어야 문맥상 자연스러우므로 (D)가 정답이다.

+ **Key word**
Following the merger, we are planning to aggressively **expand overseas using our pooled resources. With Gamst Partners' expertise in tax law and our knowledge of contract law, our chances of success are very high.**

7. 어휘 - 명사

해설 빈칸은 주어 The biggest change에 대한 주격 보어 자리이다. 빈칸을 후치 수식하는 of 전명구 내용을 고려할 때, '신규 경영진 발표'라는 의미가 되어야 문맥상 자연스러우므로 (D)가 정답이다. we are excited to fill you in on the details에서 세부정보를 알려준다고 하므로 추측(speculation)은 문맥에 맞지 않다.

+ **Key word**
The biggest change taking place following the merger **will be the announcement of the new management team**.

8. 접속부사

해설 빈칸 앞 문장의 '오늘 Conference Hall에서 모여 축하할 것'이라는 내용과 빈칸 뒷부분의 '다가오는 새해에 저희가 계획한 것을 공개할 예정'이라는 내용을 고려할 때, 빈칸 뒷부분에서 행사 때 일어날 일을 추가로 제시한다는 것을 알 수 있으므로 부가의 의미를 갖는 접속부사 (A)가 정답이다.

+ **Key word**
The company will be convening in the Conference Hall across the street at 2 P.M. this afternoon, **where we will celebrate the occasion. Additionally, we will reveal what we have planned for this coming year.**

CASE 집중훈련   본서 p.231

1 (A)   **2.** (A)   **3.** (D)   **4.** (A)   **5.** (B)   **6.** (A)
7. (A)   **8.** (C)

---

1. 어휘 - 동사

COMED Corporation **enforces** its dress code only for staff that work in the laboratory.
COMED 기업은 실험실에서 근무하는 직원에 한해 복장 규정을 시행한다.

해설 빈칸은 주어와 목적어 사이 동사 자리이다. 문맥상 '실험실 근무직원에 한해 복장규정을 시행한다'는 의미가 되어야 자연스러우므로 (A)가 정답이다.

어휘 dress code 복장 규정 | staff (전체) 직원 | laboratory 실험실

+ Key word

COMED Corporation **enforces** its **dress code only for staff that work in the laboratory**.

------

2. 어휘 - 형용사

To determine which caterer would be the most affordable, Gretchen Kim requested bids from **numerous** services.

어떤 출장뷔페 업체가 가장 저렴할지를 알아내기 위해, Gretchen Kim은 많은 서비스업체들로부터 가격제시를 요청했다.

해설 빈칸은 명사 services를 수식하는 형용사 자리이다. 문두의 to부정사구와 주절의 내용관계를 고려할 때, 문맥상 '어떤 출장 뷔페 업체가 가장 저렴할지를 알아내기 위해, 많은 서비스 업체들로부터 가격 제시를 요청했다'라는 의미가 되어야 자연스러우므로 (A)가 정답이다.

어휘 determine 결정하다, 알아내다 I caterer (행사의) 음식공급사 I affordable (가격이) 알맞은 I request 요청하다 I bid 입찰, 가격 제시 I service 서비스 (회사)

+ Key word

To determine which caterer would be the most affordable, Gretchen Kim requested bids from numerous services.

------

3. 어휘 - 명사

Lassiter Hardware generally does not offer refunds, but for certain items it will make an **exception**.

Lassiter Hardware는 일반적으로 환불을 제공하지 않지만, 특정 품목에 대해서는 예외로 할 것이다.

해설 빈칸은 타동사 make의 목적어인 명사 자리이다. 접속사 but으로 연결된 두 문장관계를 고려할 때, 문맥상 '특정 품목에 대해서는 예외로 한다'는 의미가 되어야 자연스러우므로, 'make an exception(예외로 하다)'이라는 관용 표현을 완성하는 명사 (D)가 정답이다.

어휘 hardware 철물 I generally 일반적으로 I refund 환불 I certain 특정한

+ Key word

Lassiter Hardware **generally does not offer refunds, but for certain items** it will **make an exception**.

------

4. 어휘 - 부사

The merger agreement draft must be completed this week so that the lawyers will have the opportunity to review it **thoroughly**.

변호사들이 철저히 검토할 수 있는 기회를 갖도록 합병 합의서 초안은 이번 주에 마무리되어야 한다.

해설 빈칸은 동사 review를 수식하는 부사 자리이다. 문맥상 '그것을 철저히 검토할 수 있는 기회'라는 의미가 되어야 자연스러우므로 (A)가 정답이다.

어휘 merger 합병 I agreement 계약, 합의 I review 검토하다

+ Key word

The merger agreement draft must be completed this week so that the lawyers will have the opportunity to **review it thoroughly**.

5-8번은 다음 공지에 관한 문제입니다.

UD 복장규정 업데이트

최근 직원 설문조사 결과를 바탕으로, Ubiquitous Designs에서는 직원들이 현재 복장규정 정책에 자신들의 패션 **⑤선호도**가 더 많이 반영되기를 바란다는 것을 인지했습니다.

따라서 다음달부터 정책에 다음의 변경사항을 적용할 예정입니다. **⑥이제 목걸이와 팔찌를 포함한 귀금속이 허용될 것입니다.** 또한, 직원은 사무실에서 오픈토 신발을 **⑦자유롭게** 신을 수 있습니다. 마지막으로, '캐주얼 프라이데이'에 대한 요청이 많아, 다른 변경사항과 더불어 시행할 예정임을 알려드리게 되어 기쁩니다.

⑧일터의 변화에 만족하시길 바랍니다. 궁금하신 점이 있으면, 인사팀으로 연락 주시면 됩니다.

어휘
recognize 인식하다, 알아보다 I accommodate 수용하다 I current 현재의 I dress code 복장규정 I policy 정책 I adjustment 수정, 조정 I additionally 추가로 I allow 허용하다 I wear 입다 I open-toed 발가락 부분이 트인 I announce 알리다, 발표하다 I come into effect 시행되다 I alongside ~과 함께 I reach out to ~에게 접근하다

5. 명사 자리

해설 빈칸은 명사 fashion과 함께 복합명사를 이루는 명사 자리이다. 문맥상 '현재 복장규정 정책에 자신들의 패션 선호도가 더 많이 반영되기를 바란다'는 의미가 되어야 자연스러우므로 (B)가 정답이다.

+ Key point

would like A to V는 'A가 V하기를 바라다'를 의미한다.

6. 문장 선택

(A) 이제 목걸이와 팔찌를 포함한 귀금속이 허용될 것입니다.
(B) 최근에 드레스는 많은 변화를 겪고 있습니다.
(C) 복장 규정은 2년 전에 마지막으로 갱신되었습니다.
(D) 직원들은 고용과 동시에 두 벌의 유니폼을 지급 받습니다.

해설 빈칸 앞 문장의 '다음의 변경사항을 적용할 예정'이라는 내용과 빈칸 뒷문장의 '직원은 사무실에서 오픈토 신발을 신을 수 있다'는 내용을 고려할 때, 빈칸에는 복장 규정의 변경사항에 해당하는 내용이 들어가야 자연스러우므로 (A)가 정답이다.

+ Key word

Therefore, starting next month, we will be making the **following adjustments to the policy. Jewelry, including necklaces and bracelets, will now be allowed. Additionally, employees will be allowed to wear open-toed shoes freely** around the office.

7. 어휘 - 부사

해설 빈칸은 동사구 wear open-toed shoes를 수식하는 부사 자리이다. 문맥상 '사무실에서 오픈토 신발을 자유롭게 신을 수 있다'는 내용이 되어야 자연스러우므로 (A)가 정답이다.

+ Key word

Additionally, employees **will be allowed to wear open-toed shoes freely around the office**.

8. 어휘 - 명사

해설 빈칸은 명사 changes를 수식하는 자리이다. 빈칸 앞 단락에서 복장규정의 변경사항에 대해 언급하고 있음을 고려할 때, '일터의 변화에 만

족하길 바란다'는 내용으로 이어져야 문맥상 자연스러우므로 (C)가 정답이다.

＋ Key word

Therefore, starting next month, **we will be making the following adjustments to the policy. Jewelry**, including necklaces and bracelets, will **now be allowed. Additionally, employees will be allowed to wear open-toed shoes freely around the office. Finally, Casual Fridays** have been much requested, so we are happy to announce that **they will be coming into effect alongside the other changes. We hope you are happy with the workplace changes.**

CASE 실전훈련

본서 p.232

1. (A) 2. (C) 3. (A) 4. (B) 5. (B) 6. (B)
7. (D) 8. (C) 9. (B) 10. (C) 11. (C) 12. (A)
13. (B) 14. (D) 15. (A) 16. (B)

1-4번은 다음 채용 공고에 관한 문제입니다.

H2Go Games에서 게임 개발팀에 합류할 재능 있는 작가를 구합니다. H2Go Games는 게임 산업의 선두주자로, 현재 자사의 최신 게임은 지난 10년을 ❶**상징하는** 게임으로 여겨지고 있습니다. 저희는 Gamma2 신규 게임을 출시하며 변함없이 훌륭한 게임 경험을 제공해 드리고자 합니다. 작가들은 몰입감 있는 세상을 ❷**설계하고** 게이머들을 저희가 만든 세상 속으로 끌어들이는 깊이 있는 스토리라인을 창조하는 작업을 합니다. 저희는 스토리텔링에 소질 있고 비디오게임 업계 경력이 있는 분들을 찾고 있습니다. ❸**하지만**, 저희는 업계 경력보다는 비전을 훨씬 더 중요하게 생각합니다. 저희는 경쟁력 있는 급여와 유연한 근무시간, 경력 개발 기회를 충분히 보장하는 훌륭한 기업 문화를 제공합니다. ❹**직원 만족도 점수가 높은 이유를 직접 눈으로 확인해 보세요.** 오늘 www.h2gogames.com/recruit에서 지원하세요.

어휘

seek 찾다 ｜ talented 재능 있는 ｜ join 합류하다 ｜ development 개발 ｜ leader 선두주자 ｜ decade 10년 ｜ release 출시 ｜ gaming 컴퓨터게임을 하기 ｜ experience 경험, 체험 ｜ immersive 몰입 형의 ｜ deep 깊은 ｜ storyline 줄거리 ｜ have a knack for ~에 대한 재능이 있다 ｜ value 가치 있게 생각하다 ｜ vision 비전, 미래상 ｜ far 훨씬 ｜ offer 제공하다 ｜ competitive 경쟁력 있는 ｜ salary 급여 ｜ flexible 유연한 ｜ hours 근무 시간 ｜ work culture 기업 문화 ｜ plenty of 많은 ｜ room 공간, 여지 ｜ career development 경력 개발 ｜ apply 지원하다

1. 어휘 - 형용사

해설 빈칸은 명사 games를 수식하는 형용사 자리이다. 빈칸 뒷문장의 '신규 게임을 출시하며 변함없이 훌륭한 게임 경험을 제공해 드리려 한다'는 내용을 고려할 때, 게임산업의 선두주자인 자사의 게임이 지난 10년의 상징이 되는 게임으로 여겨진다는 의미가 되어야 문맥상 자연스러우므로 (A)가 정답이다.

2. 동명사 자리

해설 빈칸은 전치사 by의 목적어 자리이다. 빈칸 뒤 명사구가 있으므로, 명사를 목적어로 취하면서 전치사의 목적어 역할을 할 수 있는 동명사 (C)가 정답이다.

3. 접속부사

해설 빈칸 뒤 콤마가 있음을 고려할 때, 빈칸은 접속부사 자리이다. 빈칸 앞 문장의 '스토리텔링에 소질 있고 비디오게임 업계 경력이 있는 분들을 찾고 있다'는 내용과 빈칸 뒤 이어지는 '업계 경력보다는 비전을 훨씬 더 중요하게 생각한다'는 내용을 고려할 때, 두 가지 요소를 갖춘 사람을 찾고 있지만 경력보다는 비전을 더 중요시한다는 내용으로 이어져야 문맥상 자연스러우므로 (A)가 정답이다.

＋ Key point

① 접속부사 However vs. Otherwise: However는 '하지만, 그러나'를, Otherwise는 '그렇지 않으면, 반면에'를 의미한다.
② 접속사는 절 형태 없이, 전치사는 목적어 없이 단독으로 쓰일 수 없기에, 바로 뒤 콤마가 올 수 없다.

4. 문장 선택

(A) 인터뷰는 3개의 섹션으로 구성됩니다.
(B) 직원 만족도 점수가 매우 높은 이유를 직접 눈으로 확인해 보세요.
(C) 과거 작품 포트폴리오를 꼭 포함시키세요.
(D) H2Go Games는 5년 안에 시장의 선두주자가 되는 것을 목표로 하고 있습니다.

해설 빈칸 앞 문장의 '경쟁력 있는 급여와 유연한 근무시간, 경력 개발 기회를 충분히 보장하는 훌륭한 기업 문화를 제공한다'는 내용과 빈칸 뒷문장의 '오늘 지원하세요'라는 내용을 고려할 때, 앞에서 제시한 항목들을 직접 경험해보라는 의미의 문장이 들어가야 문맥상 연결이 자연스러우므로 (B)가 정답이다.

＋ Key word

We offer a competitive salary, flexible hours, and a great work culture with plenty of room for career development. See for yourself why our employee satisfaction scores are so high. Apply today at www.h2gogames.com/recruit.

5-8번은 다음 보도 자료에 관한 문제입니다.

GULF HILLS — DMP Media는 두 달 전 Jackson 지사에서 새로운 인턴십 프로그램을 ❺**시작했다.** 그때부터 회사에서는 50명이 넘는 학생들에게 귀중한 직업 ❻**체험**을 제공해왔으며, 그 중 다수는 미디어 분야에서의 경력을 추구하고 있다.

프로그램은 Jackson 지역 학생들에게 더 많은 기회가 필요하다고 여긴 CEO Jana Thomas의 노력 덕분에 시작되었다. ❼**또한 회사는 지역사회에 기여하기를 원한다.** 인턴십 프로그램은 사무 업무, 편집, 이메일 작성하기를 포함해 사무실 내 소소한 역할을 고등학생들에게 부여한다.

프로그램 내 자리에 ❽**지원하려면**, 고등학생은 DMP Media의 웹사이트 (www.dmpmedia.com/intern)에 있는 양식을 작성해야 한다. 인턴십 기간은 세 달이지만, 연장될 수 있다.

어휘

media 대중 매체 ｜ valuable 귀중한 ｜ pursue 추구하다 ｜ career 경력 ｜ opportunity 기회 ｜ provide 제공하다 ｜ minor 사소한, 가벼운 ｜ role 역할, 임무 ｜ deskwork 책상에서 하는 일, 사무 ｜ edit 편집하다 ｜ spot 자리 ｜ fill out 작성하다, 기입하다 ｜ form 양식 ｜ extend 연장하다

5. 동사의 시제

해설 빈칸은 문장의 동사 자리이다. 문장 내 명백한 과거 표현 two months ago가 있으므로 과거 시제 (B)가 정답이다.

✦ **Key point**

ago, yesterday, then 등 명백한 과거 시점을 나타내는 표현은 과거 시제 문장에서만 쓰일 수 있다.

6. 어휘 - 명사

해설 빈칸은 valuable work의 수식을 받는 문장의 목적어 자리이다. 인턴 십 프로그램을 시작했다는 앞 문장의 내용을 고려할 때, 그때부터 학생 들에게 직업 체험을 제공해왔다는 내용으로 이어져야 문맥상 자연스러 우므로 (B)가 정답이다.

✦ **Key word**

DMP **Media launched** its new **internship program** at its Jackson office two months ago. **Since then, the company has provided valuable work experience to** over 50 **students**, many of whom are pursuing careers in media.

7. 문장 선택

(A) 학생들은 종종 직무에 전념할 시간이 부족합니다.
(B) 내년에 그 지역에 새 사무실이 문을 열 것으로 예상됩니다.
(C) 법적 요건 때문에, 직급은 보통 무급입니다.
(D) 또한 회사는 지역사회에 기여하기를 원합니다.

해설 지역 학생들에게 기회가 필요해 인턴십 프로그램을 시작했다는 빈칸 앞 문장의 내용을 고려할 때, 회사에서 지역사회에 기여하고 싶어한다 는 내용이 들어가야 문맥상 연결이 자연스러우므로 (D)가 정답이다.

✦ **Key word**

The program was launched thanks to the efforts of its CEO, Jana Thomas, who thought Jackson students needed more opportunities. The company also hopes to give back to the community.

8. 어휘 - 동사

해설 빈칸은 to부정사구를 완성하는 동사 자리이다. 빈칸 뒤 전치사 for가 있으며, '프로그램 내 자리에 지원하려면'이라는 의미가 되어야 문맥상 자연스러우므로 'apply for ~(~에 지원하다)'라는 의미를 완성하는 (C)가 정답이다.

✦ **Key word**

To apply for a spot in the program, high school students should fill out the form on DMP Media's Web site (www.dmpmedia.com/intern).

9-12번은 다음 기사에 관한 문제입니다.

BIGLER (10월 12일) — 내년부터 Arbiter Collective의 전기 자동차 는 Minassi의 배터리로 작동 **9**될 것이다. Minassi는 이전에 다른 **10**자 동차 회사들과 함께 일해왔지만, Arbiter Collective와 독점 계약을 체결 했다. Minassi의 CEO, Ross Norman이 자신의 사업을 지역 회사들에 더 집중시키는 데 관심을 갖게 된 후, **11**파트너십이 생겼났다. **12**배터 리 수출 비용이 크게 올랐다. "Arbiter Collective의 팀을 만나본 후, 그들이 우리에게 딱 들어맞는 대상이란 걸 알았습니다. 우리는 같은 목표 를 가지고 있었고, 목표를 이루기 위해서라면 얼마든지 열심히 일할 겁니 다,"라고 Mr. Norman이 말했다. Arbiter Collective의 입장은 듣지 못 했다.

어휘

electric vehicle 전기 자동차 | power 동력을 공급하다, 작동시키다 | previously 이전에 | sign 서명하다 | exclusive 독점적인 | agreement 계약 | arise 생기다, 발생하다 | focus 집중하다 | local 현지의 | have ~ in mind ~을 염두에 두다 | be willing to 기꺼이[흔쾌히] ~하다 | available 이용할 수 있는

9. 동사의 시제

해설 빈칸은 문장의 동사 자리이다. 빈칸 뒤 과거분사 powered가 있으며, 문두에 명백한 미래 시제를 나타내는 표현 From next year가 있음을 고려할 때, 미래 시제 수동태 구문을 완성하는 (B)가 정답이다.

10. 어휘 - 형용사

해설 빈칸은 명사 companies를 수식하는 형용사 자리이다. Arbiter Collective의 전기 자동차에 배터리를 공급한다는 빈칸 앞 문장의 내용을 고려할 때, 다른 자동차 회사들과 함께 일해왔지만, Arbiter Collective와 독점 계약을 체결했다는 내용으로 이어져야 문맥상 자연 스러우므로 vehicles와 호응이 되는 (C)가 정답이다.

✦ **Key word**

From next year, electric **vehicles** from Arbiter Collective will be powered by Minassi batteries. Minassi has previously worked with other **automotive** companies, but it has signed an exclusive agreement with Arbiter Collective.

11. 어휘 - 명사

해설 빈칸은 문장의 주어 자리이다. 빈칸 앞 문장의 독점 계약을 체결했다는 내용을 고려할 때, 파트너십이 생겼났다는 내용으로 이어져야 문맥상 자연스러우므로 (C)가 정답이다.

✦ **Key word**

Minassi has previously worked with other automotive companies, but **it has signed an exclusive agreement with Arbiter Collective**. The partnership arose after Minassi's CEO, Ross Norman, became interested in focusing his business more on local companies.

12. 문장 선택

(A) 배터리 수출 비용이 크게 올랐습니다.
(B) 그 배터리는 시장에서 가장 효율적인 것으로 나타났습니다.
(C) 그 차량들은 가격이 인상될 것으로 예상됩니다.
(D) 그 산업은 최근 몇 년 동안 침체되어 있었습니다.

해설 빈칸 앞 문장의 'Minassi의 CEO가 더 많은 현지 업체를 대상으로 한 사업에 집중하고 싶어한다'는 내용을 고려할 때, 현지 업체에 집중하려 는 이유로 배터리 수출 비용이 크게 올랐다는 내용과 연결 지을 경우 문맥상 연결이 자연스러워지므로 (A)가 정답이다.

✦ **Key word**

The partnership arose after Minassi's CEO, Ross Norman, became interested in focusing his business more on local companies. **The costs of exporting batteries had risen sharply.**

13-16번은 다음 이메일에 관한 문제입니다.

수신: kreed@sporacle.co.uk
발신: omurphy@callaghantours.com
날짜: 9월 17일
제목: 제안

Reed 씨께,

지난주 시간 내어 저희와 만나 주셔서 감사합니다. 제공해 주실 수 있는 요금 **13**으로 저희는 저희 설계 필요를 처리하는 일에 Sporacle Partners를 고용하고 싶습니다. 저희에게 보여주신 컨셉 사진은 **14** 분명하게 표현되어 있고 저희의 시장 요구에 명확하게 맞춰져 있었습니다. **15** 그것들이 젊은 층에 강력하게 어필할 거라 확신합니다.

저희는 CEO의 승인도 필요합니다. 회의에 참석하지 않으셔서, 귀하께서 저희에게 보여주셨던 샘플을 보여드리고 싶습니다. 가급적 빨리 이메일로 사본을 보내주실 수 있으신가요?

마지막으로, 일정표 관련 세부 사항 **16** 명확히 하고 싶습니다. 저희는 12월이나 1월에 광고 캠페인을 시작하는 것 사이에서 의견이 나뉘어 있었습니다. 그런데 저희가 현재 제품 라인을 몇 가지 변경하고 있어서 2월로 연기하고 싶습니다.

감사합니다, 연락 기다리겠습니다.

Orlando Murphy

어휘
proposal 제안 | rate 요금 | provide 제공하다 | hire 고용하다 | handle 처리하다 | design 디자인하다, 설계하다 | need 요구, 필요 | approval 승인 | absent from ~에 빠지다, 결석하다 | possible 가능한 | at one's earliest convenience 가급적 빨리 | detail 세부사항 | regarding ~에 관하여 | timeline 일정표 | split 의견이 갈라지다 | launch 시작하다 | hold off 미루다 | last-minute 막바지의, 최후의 | product 제품

13. 전치사 자리

해설 빈칸은 the rate을 목적어로 하는 전치사 자리이므로 (B)가 정답이다.

+ Key point
명사(구)를 목적어로 취할 수 있는 품사는 전치사다.

14. 형용사 자리

해설 빈칸은 be동사 뒤 자리이다. 문장의 주어가 The concept pictures이고 등위 접속사 and로 연결된 내용을 고려할 때, '컨셉 사진이 분명하게 표현되어 있고 저희의 시장 요구에 명확하게 맞춰져 있다'는 의미가 되어야 문맥상 자연스러우므로 be동사 뒤 주격 보어 역할을 하는 형용사 (D)가 정답이다.

15. 문장 선택

(A) 그것들이 젊은 층에 강력하게 어필할 거라 확신합니다.
(B) 승인하기 전에 청구서를 갱신해야 합니다.
(C) 제 연락처는 명함에 기재되어 있습니다.
(D) 신제품은 비용이 많이 들 것 같습니다.

해설 빈칸 앞 문장의 '보여주신 컨셉 사진은 분명하게 표현되어 있고 저희의 시장 요구에 명확하게 맞춰져 있었다'는 내용을 고려할 때, The concept pictures를 they로 받으며 이어서 '젊은 층에 강력하게 어필할 거라 확신한다'는 내용으로 이어져야 문맥상 연결이 자연스러우므로 (A)가 정답이다.

+ Key word
The concept pictures you showed us were articulate and clearly tailored for our market needs. I'm sure they will strongly appeal to our younger demographic.

16. 어휘 - 동사

해설 빈칸은 문장의 동사 자리이다. 빈칸 뒤 이어지는 내용을 고려할 때, 일정상 세부사항을 명확하게 정리하고 싶다는 내용이 앞에 제시되어야 문맥상 자연스러우므로 (B)가 정답이다.

+ Key word
Finally, **I would like to clarify a detail regarding the timeline. We were split between launch the advertising campaign in December or January. However, we would like to hold off until February** because we are making some last-minute changes to our product line.

PART 7

CHAPTER 14 파트 7 문제 유형

CASE 집중훈련
본서 p.242

1. (A)	**2.** (A)	**3.** (A)	**4.** (A)	**5.** (A)	**6.** (C)
7. (D)	**8.** (D)	**9.** (A)	**10.** (B)	**11.** (B)	**12.** (A)
13. (B)	**14.** (C)	)**15.** (A)	**16.** (C)		

1-3번은 다음 기사에 관한 문제입니다.

LONDON (11월 5일) — ❶Birkstein Media가 공식적으로 Juniper 스튜디오를 인수했다. Juniper는 현재 다수 방송에서 8개의 TV프로그램을 제작한다. —[1]—. 스튜디오는 최근 TV 제작의 우수성을 인정받아 Tremon 상을 수상했다. —[2]—.

Birkstein CEO인 Robert Segor는 성명을 통해 "저희는 Juniper Studios를 Birkstein 가족으로 맞이하여 모두가 즐길 수 있는 프로그램 제작을 위해 함께 일할 수 있게 되어 매우 기쁩니다"라고 견해를 밝혔다. ❷Bill Lorrie는 25년 전 동료 Gail Bonds와 함께 Juniper를 창립했다. —[3]—. 회사를 오늘날 대기업으로 성장시킨 후, Lorrie는 다음 단계로 넘어갈 때라고 판단된다. "회사를 돕기 위해 제가 할 수 있는 모든 걸 했습니다. 회사가 다음 단계로 나아가려면, 이것이 올바른 방향이라고 생각합니다." —[4]—.

어휘
officially 공식적으로, 정식으로 | acquire 인수하다 | multiple 다수의, 많은 | network 네트워크, 방송망 | award 수여하다 | excellence 뛰어남, 탁월함 | production 생산 | thrilled 아주 흥분한 | produce 생산하다 | comment 견해를 밝히다 | statement 성명서 | powerhouse 유력기관, 실세 집단 | move on 넘어가다, 이동하다 | move 조치, 행동, 이동

1. 주제 / 목적 / 대상

기사의 목적은 무엇인가?
(A) 회사 인수를 발표하려고
(B) 텔레비전 일정에 대해 논의하려고
(C) 신규 프로그램을 홍보하려고
(D) 수상자를 공개하려고

해설 첫 번째 단락에서 'Birkstein Media has officially acquired Juniper Studios.'라고 했으므로 (A)가 정답이다.

2. 사실 확인

Juniper 스튜디오에 관하여 언급된 것은?
(A) 두 명의 동업자에 의해 시작되었다.
(B) 주로 다큐멘터리를 제작한다.
(C) 25년간 8개의 프로그램을 제작했다.
(D) 새로운 장소로 이사했다.

해설 두 번째 단락에서 'Bill Lorrie founded Juniper 25 years ago with his colleague, Gail Bonds.'라고 했으므로 (A)가 정답이다.

3. 문장 삽입

[1], [2], [3], [4]로 표시된 곳 중, 다음 문장이 들어갈 위치로 가장 적절한 곳은?

"각각의 장르에서 많은 시청자들을 끌어들인다."

(A) [1]
(B) [2]
(C) [3]
(D) [4]

해설 첫 번째 단락에서 'Juniper currently produces eight television shows across multiple networks.'라며 제작 프로그램에 대한 부가설명을 제공하고 있어, 주어진 문장이 이어지기에 eight television shows를 They로 받을 수 있는 (A)가 정답이다.

4-6번은 다음 이메일에 관한 문제입니다.

수신: C팀
발신: Amanda Yazzy
날짜: 10월 15일
제목: 회사 발급폰 업그레이드

❹Resolute 보험은 자사 보상 부서원 전원에게 회사에서 발급한 스마트폰을 제공해드리는 것을 자랑스럽게 생각합니다. 저희 서류에 따르면, 이 이메일을 받으신 분들은 11월 말까지 업그레이드를 받으셔야 합니다. —[1]—. 회사 정책에 따라, 귀팀의 전화는 24개월 후 서비스가 종료되어야 합니다.

❺제 동료인 Timothy Sullivan에게 (555) 891-2855로 문자를 보내셔서, 귀하의 폰을 신규 모델로 교환 가능한 일정을 알려주세요. 11월 첫째 주에 받고 싶으시면, 내일 퇴근시간 전까지 반드시 그에게 연락주세요. —[2]—. ❺그가 귀하의 업그레이드 시간을 잡아줄 겁니다.

❻과정이 원활하게 진행될 수 있도록, 약속된 시간 전에 모든 개인정보를 삭제해 주시고 백업해 주시기 바랍니다. —[3]—. 서류를 처리하고, 현재 폰을 반납한 후 새로운 기기를 설치하는 데에는 약 30분 정도 소요될 것입니다. —[4]—.

어휘
company-issued 회사에서 발급한 | resolute 단호한, 확고한 | insurance 보험 | Claims Department 보험보상 부서 | take pride in ~를 자랑스럽게 여기다 | equip ~를 갖추다 | due ~하기로 되어 있는, ~을 받아야 | as per ~에 따라 | retire 은퇴하다 | colleague 동료 | availability 유용성, 용이성 | exchange 교환하다 | reach out to 연락하다 | set 정하다 | in the interest of ~을 위하여 | run 작동하다, 기능하다 | smoothly 순조롭게 | delete 삭제하다 | personal 개인적인 | backup 백업파일 | ahead of ~보다 빨리 | appointed 정해진, 약속된 | file (문서를 정리하여) 보관하다, 철하다 | turn in 반납하다 | set up 설치하다 | device 기기

4. 주제 / 목적 / 대상

이메일은 누구를 대상으로 하는가?
(A) Resolute 보험사 보상부서 직원
(B) 최근 채용된 직원
(C) Ms. Yazzy 팀의 IT 전문가
(D) 전화기에 수리가 필요한 직원

해설 '첫 번째 단락에서 Resolute Insurance takes pride in equipping everyone in its Claims Department with company-issued smartphones.'라고 했으므로 (A)가 정답이다.

5. 상세 정보

스마트폰 반납절차에 관하여 언급된 것은?
(A) Sullivan 씨와 일정을 잡아야 한다.
(B) 직원들은 관리자 승인을 받아야 할 것이다.
(C) 10월 16일까지 준비되어야 한다.
(D) 백업되지 않은 정보는 삭제될 것이다.

해설 두 번째 단락에서 Please send a text message to my colleague Timothy Sullivan at (555) 891-2855 about your availability to exchange your phone for a new model.(제 동료인 Timothy Sullivan에게 (555) 891-2855로 문자를 보내셔서, 귀하의 폰을 신규 모델로 교환 가능한 일정을 알려주세요.)라고 하면서 He will set a time for your upgrade.(그가 귀하의 업그레이드 시간을 잡아줄 겁니다.)라고 했으므로 (A)가 정답이다.

6. 문장 삽입

[1], [2], [3], [4]로 표시된 곳 중, 다음 문장이 들어갈 위치로 가장 적절한 곳은?

"또한 첨부된 회사 스마트폰 약관 서류를 꼼꼼히 읽고 서명해 주십시오."

(A) [1]
(B) [2]
(C) [3]
(D) [4]

해설 세 번째 단락에서 'In the interest of making the process run smoothly, please delete any personal data and make a backup ahead of your appointed time.'라고 하여 주어진 문장이 이어지기에 자연스러우므로 (C)가 정답이다.

7-11번은 다음 기사와 일정표에 관한 문제입니다.

Lakewood 오페라 하우스 주요 소식
Leia Mansoori, 전속기자

LAKEWOOD (12월 15일) — **[7]**작년에 Lakewood 오페라 하우스가 문을 닫게 되면서, 이 마을에 라이브 뮤지컬 공연을 위한 적절한 공간이 없어지게 되었다. 이웃의 인기 있는 Buzz Jazz Diner도 동시에 문을 닫았다. 하지만 이제, Patrick Crosby는 그것들을 다시 주목 받게 하려고 한다.

[11]Crosby 씨는 음악업계에서 오랫동안 성공적인 경력을 누려왔다. 실력 있는 음악가로 인정받은 후, 그는 약 7년 전 지휘에 집중했다. Chicago 출신인 그는 친구들을 만나러 왔다가 버려진 Lakewood 오페라 하우스를 발견했다. 바로 그 때, 그는 부지를 매입하고 40년 된 건물을 복구하기 위해 돈을 마련하기로 결정했다. 몇 가지 사고에도 불구하고, 개조된 센터는 곧 방문객들로 공연장을 가득 채울 것이다.

1월 5일, 리모델링된 센터는 데뷔 무대를 갖는 특별 게스트 바이올리니스트 Mina Song이 출연하며, Austin Summers가 지휘하는 〈Letters from Louis〉라는 첫 번째 공연을 주최할 것이다. 이 공연은 3주 동안 계속될 것이다.

[8]12월 26일에는 새롭게 보수된 Buzz Jazz Diner 역시 대중에게 공개된다. 고객들은 새로 추가된 채식 항목들을 포함한 다양한 음식을 즐기면서 라이브 음악을 들을 수 있을 것이다. Crosby씨는 "음악은 인생의 중요한 부분이며, 그 일부를 이 지역사회에 다시 도입할 수 있어서 기쁩니다"고 말했다.

어휘
staff writer 전속 기자 | force 강요하다, (어쩔 수 없이) ~하게 하다 | shut down (가게의) 문을 닫다 | leave ~한 상태로 두다 | proper 적절한 | performance 공연 | neighboring 인근의 | at the same time 동시에 | look to do ~할 예정이다 | spotlight 스포트라이트, 주목 | industry 산업, 업계 | recognition 인정 | skilled 숙련된 | attention 관심, 주의 | conduct 지휘하다 | originally 원래 | notice 알아차리다 | abandoned 버려진 | raise (자금을) 모으다 | acquire 얻다, 획득하다 | lot 부지 | restore 복구하다 | mishap 작은 사고 | revamp 개조하다, 개량하다 | auditorium 강당, 객석 | remodel 보수하다, 개조하다 | host 주최하다 | violinist 바이올리니스트 | debut 데뷔, 첫 출연 | run for (일정 기간 동안) 계속되다 | renovate 개조하다 | open ~ to the public ~를 대중에게 공개하다 | vegetarian 채식주의자 | reintroduce 재도입하다

Lakewood 오페라 하우스 행사

현재 공연 중: 〈Letters From Louis〉

[9]대중의 요구로, 이 공연은 일주일 더 이어질 것입니다! 지금 티켓을 구입하세요. 왜 모두가 이 놀라운 공연에 대해 이야기하는지 오셔서 알아보세요. 티켓은 여전히 10달러부터 시작합니다.

다음 공연: 〈Growing Up My Way〉

유명 여배우 Margaret Yeldon의 삶을 바탕으로 한, 영감을 주는 이야기가 〈Growing Up My Way〉에서 오페라로 전해집니다. **[10]**Yeldon은 이 자전적 작품을 쓰고 편곡했는데, 이 작품은 비평가의 격찬을 받았습니다. **[11]**Patrick Crosby가 지휘하는, 이 연출은 분명히 숨을 죽이고 더 많은 것을 원하게 할 것입니다. 〈Growing Up My Way〉는 매일 밤 쇼와 함께 2월 22일에 시작합니다. 티켓은 15달러에서 50달러까지 다양합니다.

더 많은 내용은 www.lakewoodoperahouse.com/events 웹 사이트에서 확인하십시오.

어휘
stage 무대 | popular demand 대중의 요구 | find out 알아내다 | amazing 놀라운 | production 제작, 연출 | inspirational 영감을 주는 | renowned 유명한 | actress 여배우 | arrange 편곡하다 | autobiographical 자서전의 | piece 작품 | critical acclaim 비평가의 격찬 | leave ~하게 두다 | hold one's breath 숨을 죽이다 | range from A to B A에서 B의 범위에 이르다

7. 주제/목적/대상

기사는 왜 작성되었는가?
(A) 지역 음악 축제에 관한 정보를 제공하기 위해
(B) 은퇴하는 예술가의 업적을 강조하기 위해
(C) 최근 음악 공연들을 논평하기 위해
(D) 지역 시설의 재개장을 알리기 위해

해설 첫 번째 지문[기사], 첫 번째 단락에서 'Last year, the Lakewood Opera House was forced to shut down, leaving the town without a proper space for live musical performances. The neighboring and popular Buzz Jazz Diner also closed its doors at the same time. But now, Patrick Crosby looks to bring them back to the spotlight.'라고 했으므로 (D)가 정답이다.

8. 암시/추론

Buzz Jazz Diner에 관하여 알 수 있는 것은?
(A) 저렴한 가격에 제공한다.
(B) 녹음실이 있다.
(C) 평판이 좋은 요리사를 고용한다.
(D) 메뉴를 늘렸다.

해설 첫 번째 지문[기사], 네 번째 단락에서 'On 26 December, the newly renovated Buzz Jazz Diner will also be open to the public. Customers will be able to listen live music while enjoying various dishes, including newly added vegetarian items.'라고 했으므로 (D)가 정답이다.

✦ Paraphrasing

added vegetarian items → expanded its menu

9. 상세 정보

〈Letters From Louis〉의 어떤 부분이 달라졌는가?
(A) 공연의 수
(B) 공연 감독
(C) 사운드 장비
(D) 입장료

해설 두 번째 지문 [일정표], 첫 번째 단락에서 'Currently on Stage: Letters From Louis / Due to popular demand, this performance will run for one extra week!'라고 했으므로 (A)가 정답이다.

10. 상세 정보

Margaret Yeldon은 누구인가?
(A) 오페라 가수
(B) 작곡가
(C) Crosby 씨의 학생
(D) 연예 기획사의 매니저

해설 두 번째 지문 [일정표], 두 번째 단락에서 'Yeldon wrote and arranged this autobiographical piece'라고 했으므로 (B)가 정답이다.

11. 사실 확인 - 연계 질문

〈Growing Up My Way〉의 지휘자에 관하여 사실인 것은?
(A) Lakewood 출신이다.
(B) Lakewood 오페라 하우스를 소유하고 있다.
(C) Mina Song을 가르쳤다.
(D) 작품을 같이 썼다.

해설 첫 번째 지문 [기사], 두 번째 단락에서 'Mr. Crosby has enjoyed a long and successful career in the music industry. After gaining recognition as a skilled musician, he focused his attention on conducting about seven years ago. Originally from Chicago, he noticed the abandoned Lakewood Opera House while visiting some friends. Right then, he decided to raise money to acquire the lot and restore the four-decade-old building.'라고 했고, 두 번째 지문 [일정표], 두 번째 단락에서 'Next Up: Growing Up My Way / Conducted by Patrick Crosby'라고 하여, 〈Growing Up My Way〉의 지휘자인 Patrick Crosby가 자금을 마련해 Lakewood를 샀음을 알 수 있으므로 (B)가 정답이다.

12-16번은 다음 웹페이지, 이메일, 설문조사에 관한 문제입니다.

http://cscglobalcon.com/thisyear

| 홈 | 올해 | 전시 | 컨벤션 등록 | 로그인 |

제 8회 화장품 및 스킨케어 글로벌 컨벤션이 9월 4일부터 6일까지 Seoul에서 개최됩니다.

화장품 및 스킨케어 글로벌(CSG) 컨벤션에서 전시자 및 연사, 방문객이 서로 교류하고 개인 관리 산업의 새로운 기술과 트렌드에 대해 배울 수 있는 장을 마련합니다. 대한민국에서 주최하는 이번 컨벤션에서는 ⑮Dr. Kim Hyo-won이 기조연설자로 나섭니다. 미용업 아시아지부장인 Dr. Kim께서 업계 내에 증가하는 환경친화적인 방식에 대한 수요를 알아봅니다. 또한, Anita Praznik, Song-ran Ma, Irene Zaric, Bernard Lee를 비롯해 유명 전문가분들이 강연을 할 예정입니다. 이들 연사 및 기타 프레젠테이션에 대한 더 자세한 정보는 '전시' 부문에서 확인하실 수 있습니다.

올해 컨벤션 장소는 Continental 호텔입니다. ⑫저희가 일부 객실을 예약해놓았는데, CSG 회원은 할인가에 이용하실 수 있습니다. 객실 예약 시, 회원번호와 코드 CSG를 입력하십시오.

등록기간은 7월 3일부터입니다. 조기등록 할인 마지막 날은 8월 3일입니다. 프레젠테이션 티켓은 매진될 확률이 높으니, '컨벤션 등록' 페이지에서 오늘 등록하세요.

어휘

exhibit 전시회 | cosmetics 화장품 | prepare 준비하다 | schedule 일정을 잡다 | exhibitor 전시자[업체] | educate 교육하다 | personal 개인적인, 직접 한 | care 관리, 케어 | industry 산업, 업계 | host 주최하다 | keynote speaker 기조연설자 | Director-General 단체장 | cosmetology 미용술 | examine 조사하다, 검토하다 | environmentally friendly 환경친화적인 | practice 관행, 지침, 습관 | lineup 정렬 | distinguished 유명한 | professional 전문가 | fixed 고정된 | book 예약하다 | early bird 일찍 일어나는[하는] 사람을 위한 | be sure to 반드시 ~하다 | sell out 다 팔리다

수신: Irene Zaric (izaric@zaricresearch.hr)
발신: Seth Lim (slim@cscglobalcon.com)
날짜: 9월 8일
제목: 보고서
첨부: 설문결과

Zaric 씨께,

드디어 직접 만나 뵙고 말씀 나눌 수 있어 좋았습니다. 시간 내서 한국에 오셔서, 귀하의 사업에 대한 통찰을 제공해 주셔서 감사드립니다. ⑯피부타입이 서로 다른 고객들에게 개별 스킨케어 루틴을 만들어주기 위해 빅데이터를 이용하는 귀하의 연구는 유익하고 통찰력이 있었습니다. ⑭이것이 앞으로 수년 간 어떻게 업계에 영향을 미칠지 보는 건 흥미로울 것입니다. ⑬아시다시피, 저희는 참석자들에게 각 강연 후에 설문지를 작성해 달라고 요청드립니다. 귀하의 세션에 참석하셨던 Jung-min Ko 님의 카드를 함께 보내 드립니다. 그분의 답변은 많은 참석자들이 귀하의 강연을 어떻게 받아들였는지를 대표해서 보여줍니다.

감사합니다.

Seth Lim, CSC 준비 위원회

어휘

in person 직접 | insight 통찰력, 이해 | business 사업(체) | individualize 개별화하다 | skincare 피부관리 | routine 규칙적으로 하는 일의 통상적인 순서와 방법, 루틴 | informative 유익한 | insightful 통찰력 있는 | shape 형성하다 | attendee 참석자 | complete 작성하다 | talk 연설, 강연 | response 대답, 반응 | represent 대표하다, 대변하다 | the majority of 대다수의 | organizing committee 준비 위원회

화장품 및 스킨케어 글로벌 컨벤션 설문조사

	우수	보통	미흡
장소	X		
전시자	X		
준비			X
숙박	X		

의견: 컨벤션에 체크인하는 게 골치 아팠습니다. 확인증을 가지고 있었지만, 제 세부정보가 시스템에 없었습니다. 결국에는 상황이 해결됐지만, ⑮이로 인해 기조연설을 놓쳤습니다. 하지만 나머지 행사는 순조롭게 진행됐습니다. ⑯특히 데이터 분석에 관한 프레젠테이션이 돋보였습니다. 아주 흥미로워서, 저는 이제 스킨케어 산업 기술에 대해 새롭게 인식하게 되었습니다.

Jung-min Ko

어휘

venue 장소 | preparation 준비 | accommodations 숙박시설 | remark 말, 발언 | confirmation 확인 | situation 상황 | eventually 궁극적으로 | resolve 해결하다 | cause 야기하다 | miss 놓치다 | smoothly 순조롭게 | in particular 특히 | stand out 두드러지다 | analysis 분석 | educational 교육적인 | newfound 새로 얻은 | appreciation 인식, 감상

12. 사실 확인

컨벤션에 관하여 언급된 것은?

(A) 자격이 되는 참석자들은 숙박요금을 할인받을 수 있다.
(B) 매년 같은 장소에서 개최된다.
(C) 모든 참가자들은 8월 3일까지 등록해야 한다.
(D) 업계 전문가들만 참석하도록 초대된다.

해설 첫 번째 지문 [웹페이지], 세 번째 단락에서 'We have reserved a fixed number of rooms, which will be available to CSG members at a discount.'라고 했으므로 (A)가 정답이다.

13. 주제/목적/대상

이메일의 목적은 무엇인가?

(A) 컨퍼런스 토론에 등록하려고
(B) 세션에 관한 의견을 제공하려고
(C) 설문조사 작성을 요청하려고
(D) 프레젠테이션 주제를 제안하려고

해설 두 번째 지문 [이메일]에서 'As you know, we asked attendees to complete a survey after each talk. I've included a card from Jung-min Ko,'라고 했으므로 (B)가 정답이다.

+ **Paraphrasing**

talk → session

14. 동의어

이메일에서 첫 번째 단락, 네 번째 줄의 단어 "shapes"와 의미상 가장 가까운 것은?

(A) 윤곽을 만들다
(B) 생산하다
(C) 영향을 미치다
(D) 손으로 만들다

해설 두 번째 지문 [이메일]의 'It'll be interesting to see how this shapes the industry over the next few years.'에서 'shape'은 '중요한 영향을 미쳐서 형성하다'라는 의미로 쓰였으므로 보기 중 같은 의미를 갖는 (C)가 정답이다.

15. 암시/추론 - 연계 문제

Ko 씨에 관하여 알 수 있는 것은?

(A) Kim 씨의 프레젠테이션에 참석할 수 없었다.
(B) 체크인 과정에 감명받았다.
(C) 일부 강연이 더 길었으면 한다.
(D) 행사 장소가 불편했다고 생각한다.

해설 첫 번째 지문 [웹페이지], 두 번째 단락에서 'Dr. Kim Hyo-won as the keynote speaker. Dr. Kim, the Director-General of Cosmetology Asia, will examine the need for more environmentally friendly practices within the industry.'라고 했는데, 세 번째 지문 [Jung-min Ko가 작성한 설문조사], Remarks(의견)에서 'it caused me to miss the keynote speech.'라고 하여 Mr. Ko가 Dr. Kim의 기조연설 프레젠테이션을 놓쳤다는 것을 알 수 있으므로 (A)가 정답이다.

+ **Paraphrasing**

miss → not attend

16. 상세 정보 - 연계 문제

Ko 씨가 특히 맘에 들어 한 연사는 누구인가?

(A) Anita Praznik
(B) Song-ran Ma
(C) Irene Zaric

(D) Bernard Lee

해설 두 번째 지문 [Ms. Zaric에게 보낸 이메일]에서 'Your research on using big data to create individualized skincare routines for customers with different skin types was informative and insightful.'라고 했는데, 세 번째 지문 [Jung-min Ko가 작성한 설문조사], Remarks(의견)에서 'One presentation in particular stood out—the one about data analysis.'라고 하여 Ko 씨가 Zaric씨의 프레젠테이션을 좋아했다는 것을 알 수 있으므로 (C)가 정답이다.

CASE 집중훈련
본서 p.250

1. (D) **2.** (B) **3.** (B) **4.** (C) **5.** (A) **6.** (C)
7. (A) **8.** (B) **9.** (B) **10.** (B) **11.** (D) **12.** (A)
13. (D) **14.** (B) **15.** (B)

1-2번은 다음 광고에 관한 문제입니다.

Kitsap Solution

❶Kitsap Solution은 수년 동안 국내 최고의 가정 수리 서비스를 제공해 온 것을 자랑스럽게 생각합니다. 이 기간 동안, 저희는 배관 문제, 천장 누수, 잘못된 배선 등 필요하실 수 있는 수리를 포함시키도록 서비스 목록을 지속적으로 확대해왔습니다. 필요한 집 수리에 업계 최저 요금과 수상 경력을 보유한 전문가 팀으로 구성된 Kitsap Solution을 선택하는 건 아주 쉬운 결정입니다! ❷오늘 저희 팀에 전화 주셔서 무료 진단을 받아보세요. 저희는 항상 작업시작 전 전체 견적을 제공해 드리기 때문에, 저희가 문제에 대한 진단을 완전히 마칠 때까지 아무 것도 결제하실 필요가 없습니다.

어휘
repair 수리 | continuously 계속해서 | expand 확장하다 | plumbing 배관 (작업) | leaky 새는 | ceiling 천장 | faulty 잘못된 | wiring 배선 | award-winning 수상 | coupled with ~와 결합된 | rate 요금 | industry 산업, 업계 | choose 선택하다 | no-brainer 쉬운 결정[일] | issue 문제 | diagnose 진단하다 | pay for 지불하다 | quote 견적

1. 상세 정보

Kitsap Solution은 무엇을 제공하는가?

(A) 건강관리 상담
(B) 기계 수리
(C) 건축 설계
(D) 주택 개조

해설 첫 번째 줄에서 'Kitsap Solution is proud to have offered the very best home repair service in the country.'라고 했으므로 (D)가 정답이다.

+ **Paraphrasing**

home repair service → home improvement

2. 사실 확인

Kitsap Solution에 관하여 언급된 것은?

(A) 작년에 운영을 시작했다.
(B) 무료로 견적을 제공할 것이다.
(C) 직원들의 업적으로 수상했다.
(D) 지불을 받아야 작업을 시작할 수 있다.

해설 다섯 번째 줄에서 'Call our team and have your issue diagnosed for free today. And don't worry about paying for anything until we have fully diagnosed the issue because we will always provide a full quote before we start on any work.'라고 했으므로 (B)가 정답이다.

✛ Paraphrasing

for free → free of charge

LifeCoach를 이용해 온라인에서 새로운 기술을 배워 보세요!

- **③**지금 등록하시고 경력을 신장시켜줄 새로운 기술을 배워보세요. 사전 경험이나 대학 학위는 필요 없습니다!
- 프로그래밍, 그래픽 디자인, 시장 조사를 비롯해 저희가 마련한 수백 가지 과정들을 이용하세요.
- **④**저희 전문 강사 팀에게 과제에 대한 개인별 피드백을 받아보세요.
- 달성한 진도와 성과를 확인하십시오.

한 달에 단 16.99달러로 경력을 다음 단계로 끌어올리십시오. 오늘 등록하시고, 첫 3개월 간 50%를 할인받을 수 있는 한정 특가를 누려보세요. **⑤**제공 내용에 대해 더 자세히 알고 싶으시면, 주저하지 마시고 저희 고객서비스 번호 0800-555-1352로 연락해 주시기 바랍니다.

지금 등록하시고, LifeCoach로 경력을 완전히 바꿔보세요!

어휘

sign up 등록하다 | boost 신장시키다 | career 경력, 직업 | prior 사전의 | degree 학위 | necessary 필요한 | access 접근하다, 이용하다 | selection 선택, 선정 | personalize 개인의 필요에 맞추다 | assignment 과제 | expert 전문가 | instructor 강사 | view 보다 | achievement 업적, 성과 | earn 얻다 | take advantage of ~를 기회로 이용하다 | limited 한정된 | offer 할인 | hesitate 망설이다 | transform 완전히 바꿔놓다

---

3. 암시 / 추론

LifeCoach에 관하여 알 수 있는 것은?
(A) 비교적 신생 기업이다.
(B) 사전 지식을 필요로 하지 않는다.
(C) 많은 회사와 협력을 맺고 있다.
(D) 실황 수업을 제공할 것이다.

해설 첫 번째 단락에서 'Sign up now and learn new skills to boost your career—no prior experience or university degrees necessary!'라고 했으므로 (B)가 정답이다.

✛ Paraphrasing

prior experience → prior knowledge

---

4. 상세 정보

LifeCoach 이용자는 무엇을 할 수 있는가?
(A) 강사를 자신이 선택할 수 있다
(B) 자신의 진도를 다른 이용자와 비교할 수 있다
(C) 등급별 평가를 볼 수 있다
(D) 구독을 업그레이드할 수 있다

해설 첫 번째 단락에서 'Receive personalized feedback on assignments from our team of expert instructors'라고 했으므로 (C)가 정답이다.

---

5. 상세 정보

웹페이지에 따르면, 고객은 고객서비스 번호로 왜 연락하겠는가?

(A) 정보를 요청하려고
(B) 구독을 취소하려고
(C) 카탈로그를 받으려고
(D) 요금에 이의를 제기하려고

해설 두 번째 단락에서 'If you wish to find out more about what we can offer you, please do not hesitate to contact our customer service line at 0800-555-1352.'라고 했으므로 (A)가 정답이다.

---

http://www.divible.com/help/support_ticket

티켓을 제출하세요.
아래 양식을 작성하고 "제출"을 클릭하세요. 그러면 수령을 확인하는 이메일을 받게 됩니다. 담당자가 귀하의 사례를 검토한 후 답변해 드릴 것입니다.

고객명: Kristoph Becker
회사명: Propic 사
이메일 주소: kbecker@propic.com
제목: 공유문서 동기화

귀하의 문제를 자세히 설명해 주십시오.

⑦저희 회사는 8월에 귀사의 온라인 문서공유 시스템으로 옮겼고, 사용하기 좋았습니다. 하지만 어제 저희가 서비스를 이용하던 중, 동기화 문제를 겪었습니다. 저희가 중요 문서를 공동작업하고 있을 때, "Divible에서 보수작업을 진행 중입니다"라는 메시지가 뜨면서 업데이트가 중단됐습니다. 많은 직원들이 원격으로 근무하는데, 이 일로 인해 저희는 마감일을 놓쳤습니다. **⑥**보수작업이 예정되어 있을 때 사전 알림을 받을 수 있나요? **⑧⑩**그럴 수 없다면, 저는 저희 요금제를 취소해야 합니다. 저희는 이런 일이 다시 발생한다는 두려움 없이 서비스를 이용할 수 있어야 합니다.

제출

어휘

fill out 작성하다 | form 양식 | submit 제출하다 | confirm 확인해주다 | receipt 수령, 인수; 영수증 | agent 대리인 | review 검토하다 | case 사례 | share 공유하다 | document 문서 | syncing 동기화, (작업 등이 속도를 맞춰) 동시에 이뤄지는 것 | description 서술, 기술 | switch over to ~로 바꾸다 | run into 우연히 마주치다 | collaborate on 공동으로 일하다, 협동하다 | state 언급하다 | undergo 겪다 | maintenance 유지 | remotely 원격으로, 멀리서 | miss 놓치다 | deadline 기한, 마감일 | prior 사전의 | notification 알림 | schedule 일정을 잡다 | take place 개최되다, 일어나다 | fear 두려움 | happen 일어나다, 발생하다

수신: Kristoph Becker ⟨kbecker@propic.com⟩
발신: Divible 헬프데스크 ⟨help@divible.com⟩
날짜: 12월 4일
제목: 지원 티켓 1249058 - 공유문서 동기화

Becker 씨께,

지난주 화요일 귀하께서 겪으신 불편에 대해 회사를 대표해 사과의 말씀을 드립니다. 저희 서버 시설의 정전으로 인해 문제가 발생했습니다. 물론, 이것은 예상치 못한 일이었습니다. 따라서 저희는 미리 고객들께 알려드릴 수 없었습니다. 평소대로라면 비상 전원시스템이 자동으로 켜지는데, 이번에는 그렇지 못했습니다.

⑨귀하의 의견을 고려한 후, 저희 경영진은 대화상자 문구를 "보수작업 진행 중"에서 "기술문제 발생"으로 수정하기로 했습니다. 이는 사용자들

에게 문제가 예상치 못한 것이고 사전에 계획되지 않은 것이라는 것을 명확히 알려줄 것입니다. 저희가 유지보수 점검과 업그레이드를 수행할 때 저희 서버가 꺼지는 일은 드물다는 것을 말씀드리고 싶습니다.

다시 한번, 저희 서비스 이용중단과 이로 인해 귀하의 부서에 문제를 발생시켜드린 것에 대해 진심으로 사과드립니다. 귀하의 의견과 성원은 저희에게 매우 중요합니다. **⑩ 감사의 표시로, 저희는 이번 달 요금을 귀하의 기업계정에 넣어드렸습니다.**

정말 감사드립니다.

Vernon Enunwa, Divible 지원부서

어휘

help desk 업무 지원 센터 | support 지원 | on behalf of ~를 대신하여 | inconvenience 불편 | experience 겪다 | power outage 정전 | unexpected 예상 밖의, 예기치 않은 | inform 알리다 | ahead of time 미리 | normally 대개, 보통 | turn on 켜다 | emergency 비상[응급] (사태) | automatically 자동으로 | consider 고려[숙고]하다 | executive 임원 | rephrase 바꾸어 말하다 | face 직면하다 | technical 기술적인 | clarify 명확하게 하다 | unanticipated 예상하지 않은 | perform 수행하다 | rarely 드물게 | offline 오프라인의 | sincerely 진심으로 | disruption 혼란, 방해 | as a token of ~의 표시로 | appreciation 감사 | credit 입금하다

6. 상세 정보

Becker 씨는 온라인 양식에서 무엇을 요청하는가?
(A) IT 기술자의 방문
(B) 새로운 문서 업로드 방법
(C) 유지보수 일정
(D) 지불금 환불

해설 첫 번째 지문 [온라인 양식], 세 번째 단락에서 'Is it possible to get prior notifications when maintenance is scheduled to take place?'라고 했으므로 (C)가 정답이다.

7. 암시/추론

Becker 씨에 관하여 알 수 있는 것은?
(A) 온라인에서 문서를 작업한다.
(B) 8월에 Propic에 입사했다.
(C) Divible에 입사 지원했다.
(D) 매주 화요일에 마감일이 있다.

해설 첫 번째 지문 [온라인 양식], 세 번째 단락에서 'My company switched over to your online shared document system in August,'라고 하여 그가 온라인으로 문서작업을 한다는 것을 알 수 있으므로 (A)가 정답이다.

8. 상세 정보

Divible의 문서 공유 시스템에 대한 Becker 씨의 불만은 무엇인가?
(A) 일부 문서를 열 수 없다.
(B) 안정적이지 않다.
(C) 재택근무직원들이 이용할 수 없다.
(D) 찾기가 어렵다.

해설 첫 번째 지문 [온라인 양식], 세 번째 단락에서 'If not, I'll have to cancel our plan. We need to be able to use your service without fear of this happening again.'이라고 했으므로 (B)가 정답이다.

9. 상세 정보

Enunwa 씨는 Divible에서 무엇이 바뀔 거라고 하는가?
(A) 사용자 매뉴얼

(B) 오류 알림
(C) 회원 혜택
(D) 전력원

해설 두 번째 지문 [이메일], 두 번째 단락에서 'After considering your feedback, our executives have agreed to rephrase our dialog box from "undergoing some maintenance" to "facing technical problems."'라고 했으므로 (B)가 정답이다.

10. 사실 확인 – 연계 문제

Propic 사에 관하여 언급된 것은?
(A) 구독 옵션을 업그레이드했다.
(B) Divible의 월요금제를 이용한다.
(C) 서버를 매일 점검한다.
(D) 전세계에서 직원들을 고용한다.

해설 첫 번째 지문 [온라인 양식], 세 번째 단락에서 'If not, I'll have to cancel our plan. We need to be able to use your service without fear of this happening again.'이라고 했고, 두 번째 지문 [이메일], 세 번째 단락에서 'As a token of our appreciation, we have credited your business account for this month's fees.'라고 하여 Propic 사에서 월간 요금제로 Divible의 서비스를 이용하고 있다는 것을 알 수 있으므로 (B)가 정답이다.

11-15번은 다음 기사와 이메일, 그리고 양식에 관한 문제입니다.

지역사회 프로젝트에 전시된 Freddington 예술가들
Shelby de Mello 작성

Freddington (9월 3일) — 어제 Freddington 시민회관에서 열린 중소기업 컨벤션에서 Freddington 상공회의소는 공공예술을 통해 중소기업을 육성하는 새로운 캠페인을 발표했습니다. Drawing Inspiration이라는 이름의 **⑪ 이 계획은** 도시의 상점들을 재설계하기 위해 지역 예술가들을 지역사회의 자영업자들과 연결시켜줍니다.

관심 있는 사업주들은 현 위치에서 3년 이상 영업했음을 증명하는 기록과 지역사회에 대한 업체의 참여 내용을 포함한 신청서를 작성해 주시면 됩니다. 캠페인에 참여하기를 원하는 예술가들은 자신의 작품 견본과 함께, Freddington과의 연관성을 설명하는 상세 신청서를 제출해야 합니다.

모든 신청서를 늦어도 10월 1일까지 kosmough@freddingtoncoc.org로 Kathleen Osmough에게 보내주세요. **⑬ Freddington은 예술가들에게 최고 100달러의 필요한 물품비용을 지원해 드립니다.**

어휘

on display 전시된, 진열된 | chamber of commerce 상공회의소 | announce 발표하다 | promote 장려하다, 촉진하다 | via 통하여, 거쳐 | public art 공공 미술 | call 부르다 | initiative (특정한 목적 달성을 위한 새로운) 계획 | match 연결시키다 | area 지역, 구역 | redesign 재설계하다 | storefront 가게 앞에 딸린 공간, 상점 | involvement 관련, 관여 | record 기록 | in operation 운영[영업] 중인 | current 현재의 | get involved with ~와 연관되다 | detailed 상세한 | connection 연결 | artwork 미술품 | no later than 늦어도 ~까지 | compensate 보상하다 | supply 물품 | up to ~까지

수신: Kathleen Osmough
발신: Tae-kyung Lim
날짜: 10월 7일
제목: Drawing Inspiration 신청
첨부: 스케치_ver. 2

Osmough 씨께,

이번 주 시간 내어 Mali Bakery에서 저와 만나 Drawing Inspiration

재설계 프로젝트 아이디어에 대해 논의해 주셔서 감사드립니다. 그 빵집은 제가 어렸을 때 가장 좋아하던 곳이었고, 지금도 그곳의 유명한 애플파이가 땡길 때마다 정기적으로 그곳을 방문합니다. 실은 제가 그곳에 너무 자주 가서 사장님이 가게 벽에 제 그림을 걸어놓으실 정도입니다.

15 추천해 주신대로, Mali Bakery의 인테리어에 어울리게 색상 패턴을 수정했습니다. **12** 살펴보시고, 다른 변경사항을 원하시면 알려 주세요.

감사드립니다.

Tae-kyung Lim

어휘

drawing 그림, 도면, 도안 | inspiration 영감 | favorite 좋아하는 것 | grow up 자라다, 성장하다 | regularly 정기적으로 | have a craving for ~가 먹고 싶다 | put up 올리다 | per ~에 대하여, ~당 | recommendation 추천 | modify 수정하다, 변경하다 | match 어울리다; 일치하다

Freddington 상공회의소 환급 신청서

14 양식을 작성하고 구매 항목별 서류를 제출해 주세요. 일주일 내로 처리될 것입니다.

날짜: 10월 8일
이름: Tae-kyung Lim
목적: Drawing Inspiration
내용: Drawing Inspiration 프로젝트에 필요한 재료. 모든 상품은 Freddington's Art Box에서 구입하였습니다. 영수증이 첨부되었습니다.

항목	항목당 가격	항목수	총 금액
15 카나리아 노란색 아크릴 물감, 32 oz	25.99달러	1	25.99달러
15 머스타드 노란색 아크릴 물감, 18 oz	15.99달러	1	15.99달러
물감용 칼세트	9.99달러	1	9.99달러
아크릴 스프레이 광택제, 11 oz	10.99달러	2	21.98달러
		13 총계(세금포함)	76.53달러
승인자: K. Osmough		승인일: 10월 15일	

어휘

reimbursement 상환, 환급 | provide 제공하다 | itemized 항목별로 적은 | documentation 서류; 문서화 | processing 과정, 처리 | no longer than 더 이상 ~않은 | goods 상품 | invoice 송장, 청구서 | canary yellow 카나리아빛 노란색 | acrylic paint 아크릴 물감 | painting knife 물감용 칼 | acrylic 아크릴로 만든 | varnish spray 스프레이 광택제 | grand total 총계 | approve 승인하다

---

11. 상세 정보

기사에 따르면, 예술가들은 자신의 작품을 어디에 전시할 것인가?
(A) 상공 회의소
(B) 공원
(C) Freddington 시민회관
(D) 지역 사업체

해설 첫 번째 지문[기사], 첫 번째 단락에서 'this initiative matches area artists with business owners in the community to redesign storefronts in the city.'라고 했으므로 (D)가 정답이다.

12. 주제/목적/대상

이메일의 목적은 무엇인가?
(A) 설계에 대해 확인을 받으려고
(B) 회의 장소를 예약하려고

(C) 예산 인상을 요청하려고
(D) 일자리 제의를 수락하려고

해설 두 번째 지문[이메일], 두 번째 단락에서 'Please take a look and let me know if you'd like to see any other changes.'라고 했으므로 (A)가 정답이다.

13. 사실 확인 – 연계 문제

Lim 씨가 구입한 물품에 관하여 언급된 것은?
(A) 온라인으로 구매되었다.
(B) Freddington에서 구할 수 없다.
(C) 승인이 확정되지 않았다.
(D) 비용이 전액 환급될 것이다.

해설 첫 번째 지문[기사], 세 번째 단락에서 'Freddington will compensate artists for necessary supplies of up to $100.'라고 했는데, 세 번째 지문[양식], 표에서 'Grand Total (tax incl.)'이 '$76.53'로 100 달러를 초과하지 않아 신청액이 전액 환급될 것임을 알 수 있으므로 (D)가 정답이다.

14. 상세 정보

양식에 무엇이 포함되어야 하는가?
(A) 프로젝트 완료 사진
(B) 판매 영수증
(C) 사업체 주소
(D) 은행 계좌번호

해설 세 번째 지문[양식], 첫 번째 단락에서 'Please fill out the form and provide itemized documentation of the purchase.'라고 했으므로 (B)가 정답이다.

+ Paraphrasing
documentation of the purchase → a sales receipt

15. 암시/추론 – 연계 문제

Mali Bakery에 관하여 무엇이 사실이겠는가?
(A) Lim 씨가 디자인한 새로운 로고를 사용할 것이다.
(B) 인테리어가 노란색이다.
(C) 3년 전에 문을 열었다.
(D) 지역 예술가들을 위해 모금을 한다.

해설 두 번째 지문[이메일], 두 번째 단락에서 'Per your recommendation, I have modified the color pattern to match the interior of Mali Bakery.'라고 했는데, 세 번째 지문[양식], 표의 항목에 'Canary yellow acrylic paint, 32 oz'와 'Mustard yellow acrylic paint, 18 oz'라고 되어 있어 빵집 인테리어가 노란색으로 되어있음을 알 수 있으므로 (B)가 정답이다.

CASE 집중훈련
본서 p.258

1. (D) 2. (B) 3. (A) 4. (B) 5. (A) 6. (A)
7. (A) 8. (A) 9. (C) 10. (D) 11. (B) 12. (C)
13. (A) 14. (D) 15. (D) 16. (D)

1–3번은 다음 송장에 관한 문제입니다.

Gryseld Allied Workforce

Tresa Maddox
49 Austin Hill
Glenmora, Louisiana 71433

송장 번호: 197-914

내용: ❶진입로에 움푹 파인 곳이 많다는 것을 나타내는 심각한 손상 흔적이 보입니다. 진입로를 파내어 물을 먼저 빼는 것을 권해드립니다. 그러고 나서 아스팔트로 재작업이 이루어져야 합니다. ❷진입로에는 정문까지 이어지는 16 x 10 피트 크기의 벽돌 길이 포함되어 있습니다. 총 비용에는 이 길을 교체하는 비용이 포함됩니다.

❸처음 이용하시는 모든 고객들에게 10퍼센트 할인을 제공해 드립니다.

서비스 및 자재 비용:

내용	금액
진입로 파낸 후 배수	2,400달러
신규 진입로 설치	1,750달러
자재비 (아스팔트, 벽돌)	950달러
인건비	1,200달러
총 요금	36,300달러 – 10% = 5,670달러 작업 전 25퍼센트에 해당하는 계약금 1,417.50달러를 요합니다.

모든 작업에는 시작 전 25퍼센트에 해당하는 계약금이 필요합니다. 금액은 신용카드로 지불 가능합니다.

어휘
driveway 진입로 I sign 흔적 I severe 심각한 I damage 피해, 손상 I evidence 증거가 되다, 증명하다 I abundance 풍부 I pothole 도로에 움푹 파인 곳 I recommendation 추천, 권고 I dig up 파내다 I drain 액체를 빼내다 I redo 다시 하다 I asphalt 아스팔트 I brick 벽돌 I measure (치수 등이) ~이다 I replace 갈다, 교체하다 I discount 할인 I first-time 처음으로 하는 I install 설치하다 I labor cost 인건비 I charge 요금 I down payment 계약금 I require 요구하다 I ahead of ~ 전에 I via ~를 통해

1. 동의어
첫 번째 단락, 첫 번째 줄의 단어, "evidenced"와 의미상 가장 가까운 것은?
(A) 반대된
(B) 확인된
(C) 촉진된
(D) 반영된

해설 Description에서 'The driveway shows signs of severe damage evidenced by the abundance of potholes.'에서 evidenced는 '증거가 되는, 나타내는'의 의미로 쓰였으므로 보기 중 '반영된'을 뜻하는 (D)가 정답이다.

2. 사실 확인
길에 관하여 언급된 것은?
(A) 거의 이용하지 않는다.
(B) 집으로 통한다.
(C) 수리할 예정이다.
(D) 최근 만들어졌다.

해설 Description에서 'The driveway includes a brick path to the front door which measures 16 x 10 feet.'이라고 했으므로 (B)가 정답이다.

3. 암시 / 추론
Maddox 씨에 관하여 알 수 있는 것은?
(A) 그 업체를 처음으로 이용한다.
(B) 수표로 지불하려고 한다.
(C) 더 낮은 작업 비용을 기대했다.
(D) 최근 이 지역으로 이사했다.

해설 Description에서 'We provide a 10 percent discount to all first-time clients.'라고 했는데, Costs for services and materials에 나온 표의 Total charge를 보면 10퍼센트 할인을 적용받은 첫 이용 고객임을 알 수 있으므로 (A)가 정답이다.

4-6번은 다음 회람에 관한 문제입니다.

회람

수신: 지점장들
발신: Dalia Kay, 최고 재무 책임자
날짜: 4월 29일
제목: 분기별 보고서

❹5월 4일까지 분기별 보고서를 제출해야 한다는 점을 다시 한번 친히 알려드립니다. 전 지점장에게는 고용 상황에 따라 보고서를 작성해야 할 의무가 있으며, 이는 저희가 특별히 중요시하는 책임입니다. ❺ⓐ저희는 지점들이 주에서 정한 보건 안전 기준을 잘 따르고 있다는 것을 보여줘야 할 법률상의 의무가 있기 때문입니다. ❺ⓑ하지만 보고서는 저희 식품 중 어떤 것이 잘 팔리는 지도 나타냅니다. 이는 보통 저희가 메뉴를 조정할 필요가 있는지의 여부를 결정하는 방법입니다. ❺ⓒ보고서는 매 분기 말에 취합되며, 주주총회 때 저희가 결과를 발표합니다.

편리하시도록 보고서 양식을 이메일에 첨부해 드렸습니다. 다시 한번 말씀드리면, 보고서 작성 방법을 변경했습니다. ❻이제부터는 순 수익뿐만 아니라 영업 수익도 알려주셔야 합니다. 이는 곧 있을 세제 변경이 저희 수익에 미칠 영향을 살펴보는 데 도움이 될 것입니다.

어휘
Chief Financial Officer 최고 재무 책임자(CFO) I branch 지점 I quarterly 분기별의 I friendly 우호적인, 선의의 I reminder 상기시켜주는 것 I submit 제출하다 I duty 의무 I fill out 작성하다 I as per ~에 따라 I employment conditions 고용 조건 I responsibility 책임, 책무 I place emphasis on ~를 중요시[강조]하다 I legal obligation 법률상의 의무 I show 보여주다 I conform to ~에 따르다 I safety 안전 I standard 기준 I prescribe 지시하다, 규정하다 I province (행정 단위) 주, 지방 I sell 팔리다 I typically 보통, 일반적으로 I determine 결정하다 I adjust 조정하다 I compile (자료를) 엮다, 모으다 I present 제시하다, 보여주다 I result 결과 I shareholder 주주 I template 양식, 템플릿 I attach 첨부하다 I operating revenue 영업 수익 I net income 순수익 I effect 영향 I upcoming 다가오는 I tax 세금 I bottom line (계산된) 순이익

4. 주제 / 목적 / 대상
회람의 목적은 무엇인가?
(A) 관리자에게 새로운 시스템을 소개하는 것
(B) 관리자에게 마감일을 상기시키는 것
(C) 회사의 향후 전망에 대해 언급하는 것
(D) 신규 고용계약서를 송부하는 것

해설 첫 번째 단락에서 'This is a friendly reminder that your quarterly reports must be submitted by 4 May. Every branch manager has a duty to fill out the report as per his or her employment conditions, and it is a responsibility we place special emphasis on.'이라고 했으므로 (B)가 정답이다.

5. 사실 확인

보고서의 가능한 용도로 언급되지 않은 것은?
(A) 경쟁사와 비교하는 것
(B) 필요한 변경사항을 계획하는 것
(C) 현재 및 미래 투자자에게 공유하는 것
(D) 요구되는 기준을 준수하는 것

해설 지문의 단서와 보기를 매칭 시키면, 첫 번째 단락의 'This is because we have a legal obligation to show that our branches are conforming to the health and safety standards as prescribed by the province.'는 (D)와, 'However, the reports also reflect which of our food items are selling well. This is typically how we determine whether we need to adjust our menus.'는 (B)와, 'The reports are compiled at the end of every quarter, and we present the results at our shareholder meetings.'는 (C)와 일치하지만, 경쟁사와 비교한다는 내용은 언급된 바가 없으므로 (A)가 정답이다.

✚ **Paraphrasing**

conform to → comply with

6. 상세 정보

회람에 따르면, 올해 보고서는 예년 분기와 어떻게 다른가?
(A) 추가 재무 정보가 요구될 것이다.
(B) 독립 기관의 감사를 받아야 할 것이다.
(C) 새로운 시스템을 통해 제출되어야 할 것이다.
(D) 목적에 따라 경비가 분류되어야 한다.

해설 두 번째 단락에서 'We are now requiring that you provide your operating revenue as well as your net income.'이라고 했으므로 (A)가 정답이다.

7-11번은 다음 이메일과 안건목록에 관한 문제입니다.

수신: Klaus DSI 제조사 관리자들
7 발신: Paul Kleber 사장
날짜: 6월 27일, 오전 9시 12분
제목: 운영위원회 회의
첨부: 안건목록

여러분, 안녕하세요.

7 오늘 오후 3시로 있을 운영위원회 회의에 변동사항이 있습니다. 이 이메일에 업데이트된 안건목록을 첨부했습니다.

8 이번 주에 있었던 Stockholm 콘퍼런스에 대한 내용은 참석자였던 기계 엔지니어 Michael Becker가 기상문제로 귀국행 비행기에 타지 못해, 듣지 못하게 되었습니다. 그는 내일 저녁 Berlin에 도착할 예정입니다. 콘퍼런스 관련 내용은 다음 회의에서 보고될 것입니다.

Becker 씨 자리에 발표자를 2명을 넣었습니다. 먼저, Julian Hodges 이사가 저희 최신 3D프린터를 시연해주실 겁니다. 저희가 보유한 가장 효율적인 모델이 될 것으로 기대됩니다. **9** 그리고 나서 부서장 중 한 명이 Edetta Greco 부서장의 업적에 대해 알려 드릴 예정인데, 그녀는 임원 승진 대상입니다. 그녀의 실적에 대해 평가하는 시간을 가진 후, 그녀의 지위에 대해 투표하도록 하겠습니다.

회의록에 추가하고 싶은 게 있으시면, 제 비서 Chadwick Peters에게 오늘 정오까지 알려주시면 저희가 포함 가능 여부를 살펴보겠습니다.

11 Paul Kleber 사장

어휘

adjustment 수정, 조정 | operating committee 운영 위원회 | schedule 일정을 잡다, 예정하다 | take place 일어나다 | mechanical engineer 기계 공학자, 기계 기사 | in attendance 참석한 | flight 항공기, 비행 | inclement weather 악천후 | slot 자리, 시간, 틈 | executive director 이사 | demonstration 시연 | latest 최신의 | efficient 효율적인 | department head 부서장 | accomplishment 업적 | eligible for 자격이 있는 | promotion 승진 | evaluate 평가하다 | performance 실적 | vote 투표하다 | status (사회적) 지위 | add 추가하다 | minutes 회의록

Klaus DSI 제조사

운영위원회 회의 안건목록
6월27일, 오후 3시 — 오후 5시 30분

오후 3시 — 오후 3시20분	**10** Chadwick Peters 씨 (연금정책 및 회의실 유지보수)
오후 3시20분 — 오후 3시 50분	Gemma Schneider 씨 (고객 커뮤니케이션)
오후 3시 50분 — 오후 4시 20분	Lina Jacobs 씨 (연구조사 및 개발, 혁신)
오후 4시 20분 — 오후 5시 15분	Bailey Hodges 씨 (시연)
	9 Ian Thys 씨 (소개 및 평가, 투표)
오후 5시 15분 — 오후 5시 30분	**11** Paul Kleber 씨 (마무리 발언)

어휘

pension 연금 | policy 정책 | maintenance 유지보수 | client research 고객 조사 | development 개발 | innovation 혁신 | demonstration 시연 | evaluate 평가하다 | final 최종의, 마무리의 | remark 발언

7. 주제 / 목적 / 대상

이메일의 목적은 무엇인가?
(A) 안건목록에 변경사항을 설명하려고
(B) 직원들에게 콘퍼런스에 대해 알리려고
(C) 직원들에게 직원의 승진에 대해 알려주려고
(D) 프레젠테이션 장소를 공개하려고

해설 첫 번째 지문 [이메일], 첫 번째 단락에서 'Adjustments have been made to the operating committee meeting that is scheduled for today at 3 P.M. You can find the updated agenda attached to this e-mail.'이라고 했으므로 (A)가 정답이다.

✚ **Paraphrasing**

adjustments → revisions

8. 사실 확인

이메일에서 Becker 씨에 관해 무엇을 언급하는가?
(A) 회의에 참석하지 않을 것이다.
(B) 온라인으로 투표했다.
(C) 휴가 중이다.
(D) 승진 대상이다.

해설 첫 번째 지문 [이메일], 두 번째 단락에서 'We will not be hearing a summary on the Stockholm Conference that took place this week because Michael Becker, our mechanical engineer who was in attendance, was unable to get on a flight back due to inclement weather. He will be arriving in Berlin tomorrow evening. His report on the conference will be given at our next meeting.'이라고 했으므로 (A)가 정답이다.

9. 상세 정보 – 연계 문제

누가 Greco 씨의 업적에 관해 이야기할 것인가?

(A) Hodges 씨
(B) Jacobs 씨
(C) Thys 씨
(D) Schneider 씨

해설 첫 번째 지문 [이메일], 세 번째 단락에서 'Then, one of our department heads will introduce the accomplishments of senior manager Edetta Greco, who is eligible for a promotion to an executive position. We will take a moment to evaluate her performance and vote on her status.'라고 했는데, 두 번째 지문 [안건목록]에서 오후 4시 20분 안건에 'Ian Thys' 씨가 'Introduce, Evaluate, and Vote'한다고 되어 있어 Thys 씨가 Greco 씨의 업적에 대해 발표할 예정임을 알 수 있으므로 (C)가 정답이다.

10. 암시/추론

무엇이 Peters 씨의 업무에 해당하겠는가?

(A) 혁신적인 제품을 개발하는 것
(B) 프린터를 제조하는 것
(C) 커뮤니케이션하는 것
(D) 사무실 공간을 관리하는 것

해설 두 번째 지문 [안건목록]에서 오후 3시에 'Chadwick Peters' 씨가 'Pension Policy and Meeting Room Maintenance'에 관해 이야기한다고 되어 있는 것으로 보아 그가 사무공간 유지보수를 담당하고 있음을 알 수 있으므로 (D)가 정답이다.

11. 상세 정보 – 연계 문제

누가 마무리 발언을 할 것인가?

(A) 이사회 의장
(B) 회사 사장
(C) 기계 엔지니어
(D) 행정보조

해설 두 번째 지문 [안건목록]에서 오후 5시 15분에 'Paul Kleber' 씨가 'Final Remarks'를 한다고 되어 있는데, 첫 번째 지문 [이메일]에서 발신인에 'Paul Kleber, President'라고 하여 Paul Kleber 씨가 회사 사장임을 알 수 있으므로 (B)가 정답이다.

✛ Paraphrasing

final remarks → closing remarks

12-16번은 다음 두 이메일과 웹페이지에 관한 문제입니다.

수신: Rima Albert ⟨r.albert@lbjdesigns.com⟩
발신: Tracey Emerson ⟨t.emerson@iccity.com⟩
날짜: 6월 28일
제목: 인터넷 옵션

Albert 씨께,

12 귀하의 디자인 회사에 적합한 인터넷 옵션에 대한 추천에 대해 문의해 주셔서 감사합니다. 가능한 최선의 추천을 제공하고자 다음 질문들에 대한 답을 알아야 합니다.

1. **14A** 예산이 얼마나 유연하고 예산에 설치 비용이 포함되어 있나요? **13** 계약 기간에 따라 다른 요금을 제공할 수 있습니다. 일반적으로 계약 기간이 길수록 좋습니다.

2. **14B** 연결 상태가 얼마나 안정적이어야 하나요? 안정적인 연결은 흔치 않고 일반적으로 더 비쌉니다.

3. **14C** 광범위한 인터넷 사용이 필요한 귀사의 주요 활동은 무엇인가요? 이메일 및 웹 검색과 같은 보통의 사무실에서의 사용은 빠른 연결을 필요로 하지는 않지만, 디지털 미디어 등과 같은 접속은 가능합니다.

4. 귀사에서 업로드가 얼마나 중요한가요? 인터넷 공급자들은 빠른 다운로드 속도를 제공하지만 일반적으로 요청되는 기능이 아니기 때문에 업로드 속도를 무시하는 경우가 많습니다.

5. **14** 향후에 인터넷 사용 확대가 예상되나요?

가능한 한 빠른 시일 내에 회신해 주시면 기꺼이 추천해 드리겠습니다.

진심으로,

Tracey Emerson

어휘

inquire 문의하다 | flexible 유연한 | budget 예산 | depending on ~에 따라 | contract 계약(서) | in general 일반적으로 | stable 안정적인 | extensive 광범위한 | access 접속하다, 이용하다 | neglect 무시하다, 하지 않다 | anticipate 고대하다, 예상하다 | get back to ~에 나중에 다시 연락하다 | at one's earliest convenience 되도록 일찍 | make a recommendation 추천하다

수신: Tracey Emerson ⟨t.emerson@iccity.com⟩
발신: Rima Albert ⟨r.albert@lbjdesigns.com⟩
날짜: 6월 29일
제목: 회신: 인터넷 옵션

Emerson 씨께,

현재, 업로드와 다운로드 모두에 대한 저희의 인터넷 요구는 높습니다. **14C 15** 저희는 많은 국제 회사들과 함께 일하는 디자인 회사이기 때문에 미디어 파일들의 업로드와 다운로드를 매 시간마다 합니다. **14B** 요즘 온라인 미팅이 많은 만큼 안정성 또한 저희에게 큰 요소입니다. **16** 저희는 최소한의 작업 중단을 경험하고 싶습니다. 저희 사무실의 경우, 계약을 무기한 연장하기 위해 최선을 다하고 있다고 생각합니다.

14A 16 어제 사장님과 예산 문제를 상의했는데, 사장님께서는 우리가 일을 더 효율적으로 할 수 있는 한 비용이 우선이 아니라고 말씀하셨습니다. 따라서 이 점에 대해서는 걱정하지 않아도 될 것 같습니다. 저희에게 가장 적합한 패키지를 찾으시는 데 이 답변들이 도움이 되기를 바랍니다.

Rima Albert

어휘

needs 요구 | every single hour 매 시간마다 | stability 안정성 | factor 요인, 요소 | experience 겪다, 경험하다 | disruption 중단 | as for ~에 관해서라면 | be committed to ~에 전념하다 | renew 연장하다, 갱신하다 | lease (대여 등의) 계약 | indefinitely 무기한 | priority 우선 사항, 우선권 | so long as ~하는 한, ~하기만 하면 | aspect 측면, 양상

---

http://www.consumerwatch.com

지난 주 이용 가능한 다양한 인터넷 옵션에 대한 최신 조사를 바탕으로 가장 적합한 인터넷 서비스 공급업체들을 추렸습니다.

회사	전문 분야	의견
Limitless Networks	가정	저렴하지만 연결이 고르지 못할 수 있음
Spark	홈 오피스	저렴하면서도 일반 용도로 적합함
WorldNet	기업	비싸지만 설치 비용은 들지 않음
16 TrustPower	**16** 기업	**16** 매우 비싸지만 매우 신뢰할 수 있음

upload and download media files every single hour.'라고 했으므로 (D)가 정답이다.

16. 암시/추론 – 연계 문제

Emerson 씨가 가장 추천할 만한 회사는?
(A) Limitless Networks
(B) Spark
(C) WorldNet
(D) TrustPower

해설 두 번째 지문 [이메일]에서, Albert 씨가 'We would like to experience minimal disruptions.'와 'I discussed the budget issue with my boss yesterday, and he has said that cost is not a priority for us, so long as we can get our job done more efficiently.'를 언급했는데, 세 번째 지문 [웹페이지]에서 Emerson 씨가 선정한 공급업체 명단을 보면 이 두 가지 조건에 부합하는 업체가 'TrustPower (Enterprise, Very high cost but extremely reliable)'이므로 (D)가 정답이다.

CASE 집중훈련
본서 p.266

1. (A)	2. (B)	3. (C)	4. (A)	5. (B)	6. (C)
7. (B)	8. (A)	9. (D)	10. (C)	11. (A)	12. (A)
13. (D)	14. (A)	15. (D)	16. (A)	17. (A)	

1-3번은 다음 이메일에 관한 문제입니다.

수신: RobinSimeon@simeonmoss.com
발신: VLatowski@simeonmoss.com
날짜: 8월 22일
제목: 새로운 소식
첨부: Latowski_file

Robin께,

저의 앞으로의 계획에 대해 알려 드리고자 이메일을 보냅니다. 말씀 드렸듯이, 이번 주 목요일부터 한 주 동안 저는 Stockholm 회의에 있을 것입니다. —[1]—. **①**저와 함께 일하는 고객 명단과 연락처 정보와 함께, 그들의 사건 요약 및 다가오는 재판 날짜를 보내드립니다. —[2]—. 당신이 이 사무실의 선임 파트너로써 아주 바쁘다는 것을 알고 있으므로 저는 동료에게 저의 부재 기간 동안 이 고객들을 맡아달라고 요청했었습니다.

Natalia Dubrovsky와 저는 지난 1년의 대부분 시간 동안 계약과 인수에 대해 협력해서 일해와서, 그녀는 고객과 친숙하고 일들을 제대로 유지하기 위해 무엇을 해야 할지 알 것입니다. 우리는 세부 내용들을 논의하기 위해 오늘 아침 Diane's Bakery에서 아침식사를 하러 만났습니다. —[3]—. **②**제가 지시했던 대로, Natalia는 전화로 긴급한 조언을 필요로 하는 고객들에게 연락할 것입니다. 또한, 제가 머무는 호텔에 믿을만한 와이파이 서비스가 있지는 않지만, 제가 부재중인 동안 내내, 저는 매일의 진행상황을 전해드릴 것입니다. —[4]—.

잘 지내세요,
Virginia Latowski

어휘
keep ~ informed ~에게 계속해서 알려주다 | upcoming 곧 있을, 다가오는 | along with ~와 함께 | summary 요약 | case 사건, 소송 사건 | court 법정 | have one's hands full 아주 바쁘다 | associate 동료 | look after 맡다, 돌보다

어휘
based on ~에 근거하여 | investigation 조사 | compile 엮다, 편집하다 | spotty 고르지 못한, 매끄럽지 않은 | extremely 매우, 극도로 | reliable 믿을 수 있는, 신뢰할 수 있는

12. 암시/추론

Emerson 씨의 직업은 무엇이겠는가?
(A) 신문기자
(B) 고객서비스
(C) 기술 상담역
(D) 토목기사

해설 Tracey Emerson이 Rima Albert에게 보낸 첫 번째 지문 [이메일]에서 'Thank you for inquiring about recommendations for which internet plan is right for your design company.'라고 했으므로 (C)가 정답이다.

13. 사실 확인

인터넷 옵션에 관하여 Emerson 씨가 언급하는 것은?
(A) 계약 기간이 길어질수록 대개 가격은 낮아진다.
(B) 인터넷 가격이 최근 몇 년간 오름세를 보였다.
(C) 해외 사이트로의 통신은 추가 비용이 발생할 수 있다.
(D) 설치 수수료는 보통 인터넷 서비스 공급자에 의해 면제된다.

해설 첫 번째 지문 [이메일]의 1번 항목에서 'Different companies may offer different rates depending on how long the contract is. In general, the longer the better.'라고 했으므로 (A)가 정답이다.

14. 사실 확인

Emerson 씨의 질문 중 Albert 씨가 대답하지 못하는 것은?
(A) 1번
(B) 2번
(C) 3번
(D) 5번

해설 Tracey Emerson과 Rima Albert가 주고 받은 앞의 두 이메일에서 Emerson 씨의 질문과 Albert 씨의 답변을 매칭하면, 'How flexible is your budget, and does your budget include the installation fees? → I discussed the budget issue with my boss yesterday, and he has said that cost is not a priority for us, so long as we can get our job done more efficiently. → (A), 'How stable do you require your connection to be? → Stability is also a big factor for us as we have many of our meetings online these days. → (B), 'What are the main activities of your company that would require extensive internet use? → As we are a design company working with many international companies, we upload and download media files every single hour. → (C)'에 해당하지만, 5번의 'Do you anticipate expanding your internet usage in the future?'란 질문에는 답한 내용이 없으므로 (D)가 정답이다.

15. 암시/추론

두 번째 이메일에 따르면, 디자인 회사에 관하여 알 수 있는 것은?
(A) 최근에 사무실을 이전했다.
(B) 올해 들어 사업이 급증했다.
(C) 주로 광고를 다룬다.
(D) 빠른 업로드 및 다운로드 속도가 필요하다.

해설 두 번째 지문 [이메일], 첫 번째 단락에서 'As we are a design company working with many international companies, we

1. 암시 / 추론

Latowski 씨는 어디서 일하겠는가?

(A) 법률 사무소
(B) 부동산
(C) 호텔
(D) 빵집

해설 두 번째 줄에서 'I'm sending over a list of clients I'm working with and their contact information along with summaries of their cases and upcoming court dates.'라고 했으므로 (A)가 정답이다.

2. 상세 정보

Latowski 씨는 Dubrovsky 씨가 무엇을 할 것이라고 하는가?

(A) 조찬 회의를 준비할 것이다
(B) 전화 몇 건을 할 것이다
(C) 호텔 객실을 예약할 것이다
(D) 인터넷 연결을 고칠 것이다

해설 본문의 아홉 번째 줄에서 'As I've directed, Natalia will reach out to clients who require urgent advice over the phone.'이라고 했으므로 (B)가 정답이다.

3. 문장 삽입

[1], [2], [3], [4]로 표시된 곳 중, 다음 문장이 들어갈 위치로 가장 적절한 것은?

"우리가 거기 있는 동안, 고객들 명단을 마무리 짓고 그녀의 다음 업무들을 검토했습니다."

(A) [1]
(B) [2]
(C) [3]
(D) [4]

해설 여덟 번째 줄에서 'We met for breakfast at Diane's Bakery this morning to discuss the details.'라고 하여 Diane's Bakery를 there로 받으며 주어진 문장이 이어지기에 자연스러우므로 (C)가 정답이다.

4-7번은 다음 기사에 관한 문제입니다.

Norfolk Unlimited

BERRINGTON (12월 3일) — ❹**Norfolk Unlimited는 Berrington Bears 여자 하키팀의 공식 후원사를 맡는 것에 동의했다.** Norfolk는 이전에 Colt Active가 맡았던 역할을 맡을 것이다. Colt Active는 올해 11월에 그들의 이전 계약이 만료된 후 팀을 후원하지 않기로 결정했다. ❺**그 이후로 Colt Active는 하키 스틱과 스케이트 라인을 중단했고,** 레저활동용 장비를 홍보하기 위해 회사의 재원을 이전시켰다.

Norfolk의 홍보이사 Terry Greene에 따르면, 이 회사는 고급 카본 스틱을 제공할 것이라고 한다. 또한 Norfolk는 팀에 향상된 보호복을 제공하는데 동의했다. ❻**연습용 링크장을 임대하는 비용에 관한 한, 저희는 여**

전히 경기 참관에서 발생하는 수입에 의존해야 할 것입니다."라고 수석 코치 Ellen Smythe는 말했다.

Smythe 씨는 팀의 장비 책임자의 도움을 받아 Norfolk Unlimited와의 계약을 준비했다. ❼Smythe 씨는 Malton 대학교에서 물리치료를 전공했고, 여러 전문 하키팀들에 고용되어 부상당한 선수들을 돕는 치료 계획들을 고안했다. 그 기간 동안, 그녀는 코치가 되는 데 필요한 기술들을 발전시켰고, 결국 Berrington Bears를 맡게 되었다. 그녀는 이번 거래에 대해 "이러한 기회를 얻게 되어 매우 신납니다. 이는 우리와 Norfolk Unlimited 모두에게 생산적인 관계가 될 것입니다."라고 말했다.

4. 주제 / 목적 / 대상

기사는 주로 무엇에 대해 논하고 있는가?

(A) 팀의 새로운 후원사
(B) 경기 일정 변경
(C) 최근 경기 결과
(D) 수석코치의 은퇴

해설 첫 번째 단락에서 'Norfolk Unlimited has agreed to take over as the official supporter of the Berrington Bears Women's Hockey Team.'이라고 했으므로 (A)가 정답이다.

5. 암시/추론

Colt Active에 관하여 알 수 있는 것은?

(A) Norfolk Unlimited가 인수했다.
(B) 일부 스포츠 장비 판매를 중단했다.
(C) 상점 몇 개를 폐쇄했다.
(D) 최근에 경영진을 바꿨다.

해설 첫 번째 단락에서 'Since then, Colt Active has discontinued its line of hockey sticks and skates,'라고 했으므로 (B)가 정답이다.

+ Paraphrasing

discontinued its line of hockey sticks and skates → stopped selling certain sports gear

6. 상세 정보

Berrington Bear 예산의 어느 부분이 사람들의 경기 참관으로 조달되는가?

(A) 해외여행
(B) 보호장비
(C) 훈련시설
(D) 선수 연봉

해설 두 번째 단락에서 'As far as the cost of renting a rink for practice, we will still have to rely on revenue generated by attendance at our games'라고 했으므로 (C)가 정답이다.

+ **Paraphrasing**

a rink for practice → training facilities

7. 암시/추론

Smythe 씨의 이전 직업은 무엇이겠는가?

(A) 회계 전문가

(B) 물리치료사

(C) 장비 담당자

(D) 이벤트 플래너

해설 세 번째 단락에서 'Ms. Smythe majored in physical therapy at the University of Malton and was employed by various professional hockey teams, designing treatment plans to help injured athletes.'라고 했으므로 (B)가 정답이다.

8-12번은 다음 이메일과 기사에 관한 문제입니다.

수신: Jose Romero 〈jromero@centennialtech.org〉
발신: Lynne Osborne 〈losborne@centennialtech.org〉
날짜: 5월 20일
회신: 기념일 축하행사

Romero 씨께,

다음주 있을 전사 행사에 대해 알려주셔서 감사합니다. 🔟저는 회사의 주요 구성원이 연설한다는 아이디어가 너무 마음에 듭니다. 연설 초대를 받은 것을 영광스럽게 생각하며, 수락하고 싶습니다.

일정을 검토하니 제가 오후 2시에 강연을 하는 걸로 되어 있네요. 그런데 제가 오후 2시 15분에 그곳에 도착할 수 있을 거라서 시간이 너무 빠듯할 것 같습니다. 🔢🔢Cox 씨가 제 다음 순서로 되어 있는데요. 제 시간을 Cox 씨의 시간과 바꿔서 제가 그녀 다음에 연설하는 게 가능할까요? 🔢 그러면 제가 일정에 맞출 수 있을 거에요.

🔟이런 훌륭한 행사를 준비해 주신 것에 칭찬의 말씀 드리고 싶습니다. 답변 주시면, 필요한 준비를 해 놓겠습니다.

감사드립니다.

Lynne Osborne

어휘

anniversary 기념일 | celebration 축하 행사 | company-wide 회사 전반의 | absolutely 전적으로 | key 주요한 | give a speech 연설하다 | accept 수용하다 | review 검토하다 | appear 나타나다 | timing 시간, 시기 | tight (여유 없이) 빠듯한 | fit into ~에 들어맞다 | commend 칭찬하다, 추천하다 | put together 준비하다, 만들다 | preparation 준비

Centennial Tech 기념일

CLEARMONT (5월 29일) — 🔢Clearmont에 본사를 둔 급성장 기업 Centennial Tech가 5월 27일 1주년 기념 행사를 가졌다. 기업은 주식 회사로 화려한 첫 해를 보내며 Clearmont가 유명세를 타는 데 일조했다. 최근에는 활동 영역을 넓혀 남서부 지역 대부분을 관장하며, 가까운 미래에는 해외로 진출할 계획이다.

기념행사에는 많은 직원이 참석해, 거의 500명에 육박했다. 🔟🔢저녁에는 고급 음식과 더불어, CEO Warren Miller, COO Linda Cox, CFO Lynne Osborne, CTO Harry Ford 등 회사 창립자들의 연설이 포함됐다. 🔢저녁 행사는 Four Men 사중창의 공연으로 마무리되었다.

어휘

fast-growing 급성장하는 | headquarter ~에 본사를 두다 | public company 주식 공개 기업, 주식회사 | put ~ on the map ~를 유명하게 만들다 | recently 최근 | expand 확대[확장]하다 | operation 영업[사업]활동 | cover 다루다, 포함시키다 | attendance 참석 | approach 다가가다 | fine 질 높은, 좋은 | CEO 최고 경영자 | COO 최고 운영 책임자 | CFO 재무담당 최고 책임자 | CTO 최고 기술 책임자 | founder 설립자 | round off with ~로 마무리하다 | performance 공연 | quartet 사중창

8. 주제/목적/대상

Osborne 씨는 왜 Romero 씨에게 글을 썼는가?

(A) 일정 변경을 요청하려고

(B) 행사에 관해 문의하려고

(C) 초대를 거절하려고

(D) 문서를 검토하려고

해설 첫 번째 지문[Ms. Osborne이 보낸 이메일], 두 번째 단락에서 'I see that Ms. Cox is scheduled to speak after me. Would it be possible to switch my position with Ms. Cox's position so that I speak after her? I will then be able to fit it into my schedule.'라고 했으므로 (A)가 정답이다.

9. 동의어

이메일에서 세 번째 단락, 첫 번째 줄의 단어 "commend"와 의미상 가장 가까운 것은?

(A) 통제하다

(B) 견디다

(C) 알아보다

(D) 갈채를 보내다

해설 첫 번째 지문[이메일], 세 번째 단락, 첫 번째 줄의 'I would like to commend you for putting together this fantastic event.'에서 'commend'는 '칭찬하다'의 의미로 쓰였으므로 보기 중 '갈채를 보내다'를 뜻하는 (D)가 정답이다.

10. 사실 확인

Osborne 씨에 관하여 언급된 것은?

(A) 해외에서 일한 적이 있다.

(B) Clearmont에 살지 않는다.

(C) 회사 창립에 기여했다.

(D) 인사팀에 근무한다.

해설 첫 번째 지문[Osborne 씨가 보낸 이메일], 첫 번째 단락에서 'I absolutely love the idea of having the key members of the company give speeches. I am honored to have received an invitation to speak, and I would love to accept.'라고 했는데, 두 번째 지문[기사], 두 번째 단락에서 'The night included fine food as well as speeches from company founders including Warren Miller, the CEO; Linda Cox, the COO; Lynne Osborne, the CFO; and Harry Ford, the CTO.'라고 하여 Osborne 씨가 회사 창립의 주요 일원이라는 것을 알 수 있으므로 (C)가 정답이다.

11. 상세 정보

기사에 따르면, 5월 27일에는 무슨 일이 있었는가?

(A) 공연이 있었다.

(B) 경영진의 변화가 발표됐다.

(C) 잡지가 출간됐다.

(D) 회사에서 해외진출 계획을 발표했다.

해설 두 번째 지문[기사], 첫 번째 단락에서 'Centennial Tech, a fast-growing company headquartered in Clearmont, held their one-year anniversary celebration on May 27.'라고 하면서, 두 번째 단락에서 'The night was rounded off with a performance by The Four Men Quartet.'라고 했으므로 (A)가 정답이다.

12. 암시/추론 – 연계 문제

기념 행사에 관하여 알 수 있는 것은?
(A) Osborne 씨가 연설을 했다.
(B) Miller 씨가 자리에서 물러났다.
(C) Cox 씨가 병으로 힘들어했다.
(D) Ford 씨가 일찍 자리를 떠야 했다.

해설 첫 번째 지문[Ms. Osborne이 보낸 이메일], 두 번째 단락에서 'I see that Ms. Cox is scheduled to speak after me. Would it be possible to switch my position with Ms. Cox's position so that I speak after her? I will then be able to fit it into my schedule.'라고 했는데, 두 번째 지문[기사], 두 번째 단락에서 'The night included fine food as well as speeches from company founders including Warren Miller, the CEO; Linda Cox, the COO; Lynne Osborne, the CFO; and Harry Ford, the CTO.'라고 하여 Osborne 씨가 연설을 했다는 것을 알 수 있으므로 (A)가 정답이다.

13-17번은 다음 이메일, 티켓, 그리고 일정에 관한 문제입니다.

수신: Thomas Bradford <tbradford@orthocare.au>
발신: Winnie Hawkins <whawkins@orthocare.au>
날짜: 2월 10일
제목: **13** 회신: 치과교정술 회의

Bradford 의사님께,

이메일을 보내주셔서 감사합니다. 저 또한 올해 치과교정 회의에 참석하게 되어 너무 기쁩니다. 그곳에 함께 가면 즐거웠을 텐데, 아쉽게도 **15** 저는 2월 22일 오후 4시까지 약속된 일정이 있습니다. 그래서 저는 첫날 있을 행사에 모두 참석하지 못할 거예요. 하지만 그날 밤 그리고 그 다음 3일 동안은 그곳에 있습니다.

혹시 저녁에 하루 함께 식사할 시간이 있으신가요? **13** Ozan Demirel께서 두 분이 새로운 3D 디지털 기술을 연구하신다고 말씀하셨는데요, 이 수단에 대해 더 듣고 싶습니다.

답장 기다리고 있겠습니다.

감사합니다.

Winnie Hawkins, DDS

어휘
orthodontic 치과교정의 | congress 회의, 의회 | attend 참석하다 | enjoy 즐기다 | travel 여행하다 | sadly 슬프게도, 아쉽게도 | appointment 약속 | schedule 일정을 잡다 | perhaps 아마, 혹시 | research 연구 조사하다 | digital technologies 디지털 기술 | tool 도구, 수단

JOW Air		**16** 상용고객번호: 029580059
날짜		항공편
2월 22일		MLA401
탑승객	등급	좌석
Thomas Bradford	이코노미 플러스	**14** 미지정

출발지	왕복여행	적립 마일리지
Queensland	해당 없음	**16** 0마일리지

목적지	식사	탑승시간
Melbourne	채식	오전 5시

2월 11일에 예약됨

어휘
frequent flyer (비행기의) 상용 고객, 단골 고객 | flight 항공편 | passenger 승객 | seat 자리 | unassigned 지정되지 않은 | origin 기원, 출신 | return trip 왕복여행 | N/A 해당 없음(not applicable의 약어) | boarding 탑승 | priority 우선 | destination 목적지 | meal 식사 | vegetarian 채식주의자

Townsville 공항 출발 일정
17 Queensland발 Melbourne행

항공편명	게이트	출발시각	도착시각	기간
MLA 401	24	05:25	07:20	1시간 55분
JOW 723	41	08:00	10:00	2시간
MLA 258	12	11:15	13:25	2시간 10분
JOW 194	38	12:45	14:50	2시간 5분
MLA 326	12	14:25	16:15	1시간 50분
15 JOW 590	41	**15** 18:45	21:00	2시간 15분

16 상용고객 마일리지로 구입한 티켓에는 마일리지가 발급되지 않습니다. 상용고객 프로그램에 가입한 탑승객은 전용 우선탑승을 누리실 수 있습니다. 식사는 모든 항공편에서 제공되며, 메뉴는 http://www.jowair.com/mealplan에서 확인하실 수 있습니다.

어휘
departure 출발 | arrival 도착 | duration 기간 | issue 지급하다, 발행하다 | purchase 구입하다 | exclusive 독점적인 | serve (음식을) 제공하다

13. 암시/추론

Ozan Demirel은 누구겠는가?
(A) 엔지니어
(B) 사무보조
(C) 회의 대표
(D) 치과의사

해설 첫 번째 지문[이메일], 두 번째 단락에서 'Ozan Demirel mentioned that the two of you were researching new 3D digital technologies,'라고 하여 그가 Thomas Bradford, Winnie Hawkins와 동종업계에 있는 사람임을 알 수 있고, 이메일 제목이 'RE: Orthodontic Congress'인 것으로 미루어 그가 치과의사라는 것을 알 수 있으므로 (D)가 정답이다.

14. 사실 확인

티켓은 Bradford 의사의 여행에 관해 무엇을 나타내는가?
(A) 그는 어디에 앉을 지 선택할 수 있다.
(B) 그는 비즈니스 클래스로 업그레이드되었다.
(C) 그는 2시간 경유를 할 것이다.
(D) 그에게 식사가 제공되지 않을 것이다.

해설 두 번째 지문[티켓], 'Seat' 항목에 'Unassigned'라고 되어 있어 Bradford 의사의 좌석이 아직 지정되지 않았음을 알 수 있으므로 (A)가 정답이다.

15. 암시/추론 - 연계 문제

그녀의 가능시간을 고려할 때, Hawkins 의사는 어떤 비행기를 타겠는가?
(A) MLA 401
(B) MLA 258
(C) JOW 194
(D) JOW 590

해설 첫 번째 지문[이메일], 첫 번째 단락에서 'I have an appointment scheduled until 4 P.M. on February 22.'라고 했는데, 세 번째 지문[일정], 표에서 오후 4시 이후에 출발하는 항공편은 18시 45분에 출발하는 JOW 590편 밖에 없으므로 (D)가 정답이다.

16. 암시/추론 - 연계 문제

Bradford 의사에 관하여 알 수 있는 것은?
(A) 항공사 마일리지로 표를 구입했다.
(B) 여행사를 통해 표를 예약했다.
(C) Melbourne에 가족이 있다.
(D) 동료와 함께 여행할 것이다.

해설 두 번째 지문[티켓]에서 'Frequent Flyer #(상용고객 번호)'가 0295 800590이고 Miles Earned'가 '0 mi'로 되어 있는데, 세 번째 지문[일정], 표에서 'Mileage will not be issued for tickets purchased with frequent flyer miles.'라고 하여 그가 마일리지로 표를 구매했다는 것을 알 수 있으므로 (A)가 정답이다.

17. 사실 확인

일정에 따르면, 항공기 노선에 관하여 사실인 것은?
(A) 동일한 목적지에 도착한다.
(B) 동일한 시간이 소요된다.
(C) 동일한 게이트에서 출발한다.
(D) 동일한 항공사에서 운항한다.

해설 세 번째 지문[일정], 표의 제목에서 'Queensland to Melbourne'이라고 하여 모든 항공편의 목적지가 Melbourne이라는 것을 알 수 있으므로 (A)가 정답이다.

CASE 집중훈련
본서 p.274

1. (D) 2. (A) 3. (D) 4. (C) 5. (A) 6. (A)
7. (D) 8. (C) 9. (A) 10. (B) 11. (D) 12. (B)
13. (C) 14. (D) 15. (D) 16. (D) 17. (A) 18. (A)

1-4번은 다음 기사에 관한 문제입니다.

〈The Long Distance〉, 감독의 재기를 보여주다

OHIO (11월 21일) — Dianne Bush의 최신 연극 〈The Long Distance〉가 젊은 층에 인기가 많은 것으로 밝혀졌다. ❶수용규모가 1,500석에 달하는 Cincinnati 극장은 공연 종료를 앞두고 관람하려는 팬으로 가득 찼다.

❷공연에는 Randall Parker와 Beatrice Riley라는 두 명의 친숙한 배우가 주연으로 출연하는데, 둘 다 Bush의 이전 공연에서 주연을 맡았다.

하지만 Bush는 작품에 새로운 배우를 참여시키고 싶다는 바램을 강조해 왔다. 이러한 이유로, 관객은 Jeanette Griffith와 Gustavo Graves라는 새로운 배우 2명을 보게 됐다.

❸연극의 설정은 관객, 특히 젊은 관객을 사로잡았는데, 공감대를 형성하는 설정이기 때문이다. "연극이 마음 따뜻해지는 사랑이야기여서 확실히 젊은층에게 반향을 불러일으켰어요."라고 극단 관리자 Kathryn Harmon이 말했다. "연애의 기복을 정확하게 그려낸 사랑 이야기거든요."

❹"연극은 처음에는 관객이 많지 않았지만, 곧 입소문을 타고 퍼져나갔어요. 하지만 갑작스럽게 인기가 치솟은 거죠? 그건 저희도 놀라울 따름이에요."라고 Harmon 씨는 이어 말했다. "저희는 공연이 화제가 될 줄은 예상하지 못했어요."

Bush는 지난 두 번의 연극에서 시큰둥한 반응을 얻고 극작가로서의 경력에 침체기를 경험했다. 다시 집중하기 위해 작년 일년간 휴식을 취한 후, 그녀는 〈The Long Distance〉로 극작가 순위에서 상위권에 재진입하게 됐다.

어휘

mark 보여주다, 표시하다 | director 감독 | comeback 복귀, 재기 | crowd (특정) 집단, 사람들 | theater 극장 | capacity 수용력 | reach ~에 닿다, 이르다 | packed with ~로 가득한 | eager 열렬한 | performance 공연 | run 상영 | feature 주연하다, ~를 특징으로 하다 | familiar 익숙한, 친숙한 | previous 이전의 | emphasize 강조하다 | desire 바램, 소망 | bring in 참여하게 하다 | production (영화, 연극 등의) 제작 | to this end 이를 위하여 | audience 관중 | treat 대접하다 | newcomer 신입 | premise 전제 | relatable 공감대를 형성하는 | definitely 확실히 | resonate with ~에게 반향을 불러일으키다 | heartwarming 마음이 따뜻해지는 | accurately 정확하게 | depict 묘사하다 | highs and lows 고저, 기복 | debut 첫 선을 보이다 | word of mouth 입소문 | spread 퍼져나가다 | sudden 갑작스러운 | spike 상승 | popularity 인기 | anticipate 예상하다 | buzz 열광, 흥분 | generate 만들어내다, 발생시키다 | downturn 하락, 침체 | playwright 각본가, 극작가 | lukewarm 미적지근한, 시큰둥한 | reception 반응, 평판 | take off ~동안을 쉬다 | re-focus 다시 집중하다 | echelon 계급, 계층 | push up 밀어 올리다

1. 사실 확인

Cincinnati 극장에 관하여 언급된 것은?
(A) Ohio에서 가장 오래된 극장이다.
(B) Bush가 자주 선택하는 극장이다.
(C) 도심에 위치한다.
(D) 관객을 1,500명 수용할 수 있다.

해설 첫 번째 단락에서 'The Cincinnati Theater, whose capacity reaches 1,500 seats, was packed with fans, eager to see the performance before the end of its run.'이라고 했으므로 (D)가 정답이다.

2. 사실 확인

Parker 씨에 관하여 언급된 것은?
(A) Bush의 이전 공연에 출연했다.
(B) 작년에 상을 탔다.
(C) 경력 있는 배우와 함께 일하는 것을 선호한다.
(D) 공연에서 주연을 맡는다.

해설 두 번째 단락에서 'The play features two familiar names in Randall Parker and Beatrice Riley, both of whom featured in Bush's previous play.'라고 했으므로 (A)가 정답이다.

3. 동의어

세 번째 단락, 첫 번째 줄의 단어 "captivated"와 의미상 가장 가까운 것은?
(A) 배치했다

(B) 영향을 미쳤다
(C) 몰아넣었다
(D) 사로잡았다

해설 세 번째 단락의 'The premise of the play captivated audiences, particularly the young, because of its relatable premise.'에서 "captivated"는 '사로잡았다'는 의미로 쓰였으므로 보기 중 같은 의미를 갖는 (D)가 정답이다.

4. 상세 정보

무엇이 Harmon 씨를 놀라게 했는가?
(A) 극장의 규모
(B) 배우의 반응
(C) 수요 증가
(D) 관객 소리

해설 네 번째 단락에서 'The play didn't debut to a big audience, but word of mouth soon spread. But the sudden spike in popularity? That was surprising for us," continued Ms. Harmon. "We did not anticipate the buzz the play generated.'라고 했으므로 (C)가 정답이다.

5-8번은 다음 안내문에 관한 문제입니다.

Marietta Jam House

Marietta Jam House의 주문은 최대 7일까지 소요될 수 있습니다. ⑤만약 이러한 과정이 너무 긴 것 같다면, 이는 오직 신선한 잼만을 보내 드리는 저희의 정책 때문입니다. 잼에 들어가는 과일은 주문이 들어가고 우리의 시스템이 그것을 처리한 후에 선택됩니다.

주문을 받으면, 저희는 직원을 보내 고객님의 주문에 가장 잘 익은 과일만을 수확합니다. 그 다음, 과일은 깨끗하게 세척된 후, 공장으로 수송됩니다. 그곳에서 저희 잼 기계로 투입되며, 그 단계에서 저희는 펙틴을 비롯해 약간의 설탕을 가미합니다. 그 상태로 12시간 넘게 조리된 후, 병에 담겨 발송됩니다. ⑥품질 보증을 위해, 저희 공장 관리자는 이 모든 과정 내내 분주하게 작업합니다. 과일이 익었는지 확인하고, 잼이 만들어지면 맛을 보며, 잘 포장되어 고객님의 장소에 발송되는 것까지 확인합니다.

⑦저희 월간 잼 클럽 회원들께 드리는 특별 혜택으로, 저희는 '이달의 잼'이라는 신규 서비스를 시작할 예정인데, 일년에 단 50달러로 매달 비 판매용 특별 잼을 보내 드립니다.

저희 잼은 계절에 크게 영향을 받는다는 것을 유념해 주시기 바랍니다. ⑧일부 잼은 연중 내내 구입 가능하지만, 대부분은 어떤 계절인지에 따라 달려 있습니다. 잼 전체 목록과 구입 가능한 시기를 알고 싶으시면, 705-555-9715로 저희에게 전화 주셔서 무료 카탈로그를 받아보세요. 또는 www.mariettajam.com/jams로 가셔서 디지털 버전을 이용하시기 바랍니다.

어휘

order 주문 | take 걸리다 | up to ~까지 | process 과정, 절차 | sound ~처럼 들리다 | excessively 지나치게 | policy 정책 | send 보내다 | fresh 신선한 | pick 따다 | place (주문을) 하다 | process 처리하다 | ripest 익은, 숙성한 | thoroughly 철저히 | wash 세척하다 | transport 운송하다 | factory 공장 | place 놓다 | jam 잼으로 만들다 | machine 기계 | add 추가하다 | a bit of 약간의 | sugar 설탕 | as well as 뿐만 아니라 | pectin 펙틴 | leave 놓다 | cook 요리[준비]되다 | bottle 병에 담다 | send out 발송하다 | guarantee 보장 | quality 품질 | taste 맛보다 | ensure 보장하다 | well-packaged 잘 포장된 | head 향하다 | location 장소 | launch 출시하다, 시작하다 | not-for-sale 판매용이 아닌 | note 유념하다 | highly 대단히 | seasonal 계절에 따라 다른 | year-round 연중 계속되는 | alternatively 그 대신 | access 이용하다, 접속하다

5. 상세 정보

Marietta Jam House의 긴 배송 시간의 이유는 무엇인가?
(A) 신선도 유지의 필요성
(B) 가용 직원 부족
(C) 배송 서비스의 불확실성
(D) 공장의 외진 위치

해설 'If this process sounds excessively long, it is because of our policy to only send fresh jam. The fruit that goes into your jam is not picked until your order has been placed and our system has processed it.'라고 했으므로 (A)가 정답이다.

6. 사실 확인

공장 관리자가 완수하는 업무로 언급되지 않은 것은?
(A) 위생 기준을 유지하는 것
(B) 잼을 맛보는 것
(C) 사용되는 과일을 점검하는 것
(D) 포장이 적절한지 확인하는 것

해설 지문의 단서와 보기를 매칭시키면, 두 번째 단락의 'As a guarantee of our quality, our factory manager is busy at work throughout this entire process. He is making sure the fruit is ripe, tasting the jam once made, and ensuring that it is well-packaged and headed to your location.' → (B), (C), (D)'와 일치하지만, 위생기준을 유지한다는 내용은 언급된 바 없으므로 (A)가 정답이다.

7. 상세 정보

어떤 서비스가 클럽 회원에게만 제공되는가?
(A) 특별 할인
(B) 익일 배송
(C) 주문 제작용 사이즈
(D) 독점 제공되는 잼

해설 'As a special offer to our Monthly Jam Club members, we are launching a new service called Jam of the Month, where we send out a special, not-for-sale jam to you every month for just $50 a year.'라고 했으므로 (D)가 정답이다.

+ **Paraphrasing**
special, not-for-sale jam → exclusive jam

8. 동의어

네 번째 단락, 두 번째 줄의 단어, "contingent"와 의미상 가장 가까운 것은?
(A) 주관적인
(B) 뿌리 깊은
(C) 의존하는
(D) 변함없는

해설 네 번째 단락의 'Although some jams are available year-round, most are contingent on what season it is.'에서 contingent는 '~에 의존하는, ~의 여하에 달린'이라는 의미로 쓰였으므로 보기 중 같은 의미를 가진 (C)가 정답이다.

9-13번은 다음 이메일과 보고서에 관한 문제입니다.

수신: g.mack@calmelon.com
발신: t.fisher@calmelon.com
날짜: 4월 19일
제목: 회신: 저녁식사 장소

Mack 씨께,

아시다시피, Wayford 여관에서 식당에 심각한 누수가 발생한 걸 확인했습니다. **13**문제가 4월 23일 금요일 전에 해결되지는 않을 것 같습니다. 그래서 우리가 고객들을 다른 곳으로 모시는 게 최선인 것 같습니다. 실례를 무릅쓰고 제가 여러 장소들을 살펴봤습니다. 제 제안은 이렇습니다.

10Wayford 여관과 같은 거리에 위치한 Grand Harbor가 가장 실행 가능한 옵션입니다. 그들은 우리 일행을 수용할 수 있는 위층이 있습니다. 하지만 서비스 관련해서 걸리는 부분이 있긴 합니다. 대규모 행사 주최로 유명한 시설을 선택하고 싶었습니다. 하지만 아쉬운 대로 이용 가능한 수준에서 만족해야 할 겁니다.

11Wayford에서 다시 한번 자기들 문제에 대해 솔직하지 않았다는 데 용납할 수 없었다는 당신 의견에 전적으로 동의합니다. 과거에 그곳과 있었던 경험을 고려하면, 다시는 그곳을 고려해선 안될 것 같습니다. **9**심지어 우리가 행사장만 사용하고 저희 음식을 가져가도 되는지 물어봤어요. 그런데, 그쪽에서는 우리를 도울 의지가 없었습니다. 저는 가능한 빨리 보증금 환불을 요청할 예정이고, 다시는 그쪽과 거래하지 않을 거라고 알릴 겁니다.

안부를 전하며,

Tricia Fisher

어휘

venue 장소 | experience 겪다, 경험하다 | major 심각한, 주요한 | leaking 누수 | issue 문제 | unlikely ~할 것 같지 않은 | resolve 해결하다 | take the liberty to do 무례하게도 ~하다 | look around (결정하기 전에) 이것저것 고려하다 | locate 위치시키다 | viable 실행 가능한 | option 선택권 | upper floor 층 | reserve 예약하다 | accommodate 수용하다 | party 단체 | reservation 거리낌, 의구심 | choose 선택하다 | establishment 시설, 기관 | be known for ~로 알려져 있다 | host 주최하다 | make do with (아쉬운 대로) ~로 만족하다, 견디다 | unacceptable 받아들일 수 없는 | upfront 솔직한 | function 행사 | request 요청하다 | refund 환불 | deposit 보증금

Harrell Brothers
Commercial Plumbing

고객: Wayford 여관 163 Tavistock Strand Parnell, Illinois 61842	메모: 급수 기반시설은 튼튼해 보임. 건물은 작년에 점검한 결과 양호한 상태로 나옴

사건 보고

4월 19일 월요일에 총괄 주방장이 호출했고, 주방 쪽 수압이 너무 낮다고 언급했습니다. 물이 똑똑 떨어지는 소리도 들렸다고 합니다. 4월 20일 화요일에 배관공 2명이 파견을 나갔습니다. 문제는 수도관 파열로 확인되었습니다. 누수된 물이 벽에도 광범위하게 손상을 입혔습니다. 임시로 파이프를 때웠습니다. **12**이는 일시적인 해결책으로, 파이프 전체를 교체해야 할 것입니다. 부품이 다음주 초에 도착할 겁니다. **13**수리가 완료될 때까지 Wayford 측에 부지를 폐쇄하라고 권고했습니다.

전기기사에게 배선을 점검해야 한다고도 권고할 예정입니다.

어휘

commercial 상업적인 | plumbing 배관 공사 | water supply 상수도, 급수시설 | infrastructure 기반시설 | sound 견고한, 튼튼한 | standing 평탄, 지위 | incident 사고 | call in 부르다 | note 언급하다 | dripping 물이 똑똑 떨어지는 | plumber 배관공 | dispatch 보내다, 파견하다 | identify 확인하다 | burst pipe 수도관 파열 | cause 야기하다 | extensive 광범위한 | damage 손상 | temporarily 임시로 | patch 덧대다, 때우다 | recommendation 권고, 추천 | wiring 배선 | check 확인하다 | electrician 전기기사

---

9. 동의어

이메일에서 세 번째 단락, 4번째 줄의 단어, "help"와 의미상 가장 가까운 것은?

(A) 공간을 제공하다
(B) 상담하다
(C) 유익하다
(D) 조언하다

해설 첫 번째 지문 [이메일], 세 번째 단락의 However, they were not willing to help us.에서 help는 '(행사장을 제공하는 방법으로) 도와줄'이라는 의미로 쓰였으므로 보기 중 '공간을 제공하다'를 뜻하는 (A)가 정답이다.

10. 상세 정보

Fisher 씨에 따르면, Grand Harbor는 왜 받아들일 만한가?
(A) 행사 주최 경험이 있다.
(B) 편리한 곳에 위치한다.
(C) 후기가 좋다.
(D) 최저가를 제공한다.

해설 첫 번째 지문 [이메일], 두 번째 단락에서 The Grand Harbor, which is located on the same street as the Wayford Inn, is our only viable option.이라고 했으므로 (B)가 정답이다.

11. 암시 / 추론

Fisher 씨는 Wayford 여관에 관하여 무엇을 암시하는가?
(A) 직원을 더 채용할 필요가 있다.
(B) 만찬 파티 주최를 계획해 놓지 않았다.
(C) 경영진 교체 기한이 지났다.
(D) 적절한 서비스를 제공하지 못하고 있다.

해설 첫 번째 지문 [이메일], 세 번째 단락에서 I do agree with your comment that it was unacceptable for Wayford to, once again, not be upfront about their issues. Given our past experiences with them, I don't think we should consider them again.이라고 했으므로 (D)가 정답이다.

12. 상세 정보

보고서에 따르면, Wayford 여관 주방에 무엇이 문제인가?
(A) 물이 오염되었다.
(B) 배관을 교체해야 한다.
(C) 장비 배선을 새로 해야 한다.
(D) 벽에 곰팡이 흔적이 있다.

해설 두 번째 지문 [보고서]에서 This is only a temporary solution as we will need to fully replace the pipe. The parts should be arriving early next week.라고 했으므로 (B)가 정답아다.

13. 암시 / 추론 - 연계 문제

Wayford 여관에 관하여 암시된 것은?
(A) Parnell에서 가장 오래된 식당이다.
(B) Fisher 씨에게 행사장을 대여해줄 것이다.
(C) 4월 23일에 만찬을 주최할 수 없다.
(D) 최근 부지를 개조했다.

해설 첫 번째 지문 [이메일], 첫 번째 단락에서 I think it's unlikely the issue will be resolved before Friday, 23 April. Therefore, I think it's best we bring our clients elsewhere.라고 했는데, 두 번째 지문 [보고서]에서 Wayford is advised to close its premises until the repairs are done.이라고 했으므로 (C)가 정답이다.

http://www.hawkeyegardeners.com

[홈]　　**[갤러리]**　　**[후기]**　　**[연락처]**　　**[소식]**

Hawkeye Gardeners에서 귀하의 잔디를 업그레이드하십시오!

저희는 20년 넘게 Phoenix 대역에서 서비스를 제공해온 정원관리업체입니다. 저희 전문 디자이너들이 야외 공간을 완벽하게 설계하고 만들 수 있도록 함께 작업해 드립니다. **14**기본 정비든 전체 정비든, 귀하의 정원에 필요한 관리로 처리해 드리니 저희에게 믿고 맡기세요.

16현재 시간당 요금은 다음과 같습니다:

정원사 1명=70달러, 정원사 2명=125달러, 정원사 3명=170달러, 정원사 4명=225달러

예약시간 24시간 내 취소 시 요금이 부과됩니다.

모든 프로젝트는 각각 특징이 다르기 때문에, 추가 요금이 부과될 수 있습니다. 보다 정확한 견적을 받아 보시려면 저희 작업 요청서를 작성해 주시되, 가능한 한 자세하게 내용을 적어주세요. 아니면 (602) 555-1953번으로 저희에게 전화주셔도 됩니다.

17봄맞이 이벤트: 5월 한 달간 월요일에서 금요일 중 예약을 잡으시고, 〈정원 디자인〉 잡지 구독료 25% 할인코드를 받으세요.

어휘

upgrade 업그레이드하다 l lawn 잔디 l gardener 정원사 l gardening 원예 l serve (상품, 서비스를) 제공하다 l expert 전문가 l design 설계하다 l build 짓다 l outdoor 야외의 l space 공간 l basic 기본적인 l maintenance 유지관리 l complete 완전한 l overhaul 점검, 정비 l count on 의지하다 l deserve ~를 해야 마땅하다, ~할 자격이 있다 l current 현재 l hourly 시간당 l rate 요금 l incur (비용이) 발생시키다 l cancellation 취소 l characteristic 특징 l charge 청구하다 l estimate 견적서 l fill out 작성하다 l spring 갑자기 나타나다 l subscription 구독

Hawkeye Gardeners
작업요청서

날짜:	4월 28일 화요일
고객명:	Hunter Blue
연락정보:	이메일: hblue@inet.com 전화: (602) 555-7438
작업지 주소:	1855 Elmwood Avenue, Tempe, AZ 85283
작업 요청일:	5월 18일 월요일
요청 작업	**15**건물 구역 내 화단 10곳의 꽃(난초, 라벤더, 라일락 등), 유칼립투스 나무 15그루, 중국느릅나무 7그루, 각종 관목과 수풀 가지치기 및 일반 관리
메모	저희는 쇼핑몰 주변 조경을 관리해주실 정원사를 구하고 있습니다. **15**꽤나 큰 프로젝트라서, 가지치기를 도와주실 분이 최소 3분이 필요할 것 같습니다. 지금 계신 정원사분이 최근 퇴직하셔서 후임자를 구하고 있습니다. **17**제가 우선 시작일을 임시로 5월 18일로 적어 놨는데, 온라인에 나와있는 프로모션 자격에만 해당된다면, 더 빠른 날짜를 선호합니다.

어휘

work site 작업 장소 l pruning 가지치기 l general 일반적인 l care 관리 l flowerbed 화단 l orchid 난초 l lavender 라벤더 l lilac 라일락 l eucalyptus 유칼립투스 l elm 느릅나무 l bush 관목, 덤불 l shrub 관목 l property 건물, 부동산 l maintain 유지하다 l landscape 풍경 l prune 가지치기를 하다 l recently 최근에 l retire 은퇴하다 l replacement 대체, 후임자 l initially 처음에는 l potential 잠재적인 l prefer 선호하다 l so long as ~하는 한 l qualify for ~의 자격을 갖추다

수신: Hunter Blue 〈hblue@inet.com〉
발신: Leslie Perkins 〈leslie@hawkeyegardeners.com〉
날짜: 4월 29일
제목: 쇼핑몰 조경작업
첨부: 견적서 #91824.xls

Blue 씨께,

Hawkeye Gardeners에 연락해 주셔서 감사합니다!

저희는 최근 인근 아파트단지에서 비슷한 규모의 프로젝트를 진행했는데, 그 경험으로 미뤄볼 때 작업을 하는데 3명으로는 부족할 겁니다. **16**정원사 4명 및 기계류, 기타 관리작업이 들어간 전체 인건비가 포함된 견적서를 이메일에 첨부해드렸습니다. 철거비는 견적서에 포함되어 있지 않으나, 필요한 경우 부과될 수 있다는 점 유의해 주시기 바랍니다.

18저희 일정을 확인해보니, 양식에 요청하신 날짜에서 정확히 일주일 전에 비는 날이 있습니다. 그러면 여전히 저희 봄맞이 이벤트에 참여하실 수 있습니다.

저희 서비스를 이용하고 싶으시거나 견적서에 관한 문의사항이 있으면, (602)555-2359로 전화주시기 바랍니다. 시간 내주셔서 감사드리며, 연락 주시길 기다리고 있겠습니다.

감사합니다.

Leslie Perkins
Hawkeye Gardeners

어휘

landscaping 조경 l judging from ~로 판단하건대 l nearby 근처의 l apartment complex 아파트단지 l complete 완료하다 l attach 첨부하다 l quotation sheet 견적서 l labor cost 인건비 l machinery 기계류 l removal 제거 l opening 빈자리, 공석 l prior to ~전에 l participate in ~에 참여하다 l continue 계속하다

---

14. 동의어

웹 페이지에서 첫 번째 단락, 세 번째 줄의 단어 "treat"와 의미상 가장 가까운 것은?
(A) 지켜보다
(B) 만족시키다
(C) 지불하다
(D) 처리하다

해설 첫 번째 지문 [웹페이지], 첫 번째 단락의 'Whether it is basic maintenance or a complete overhaul, you can count on us to treat your garden with the care it deserves.'에서 'treat'는 '다루다, 처리하다'라는 의미로 쓰였으므로 보기 중 같은 의미를 갖는 (D)가 정답이다.

15. 사실 확인

Blue 씨는 정원에 대하여 뭐라고 언급하는가?
(A) 이전에 관리 받은 적이 없다.
(B) 특수 장비가 필요할 것이다.
(C) 완료하는데 수일이 걸릴 것이다.
(D) 다양한 식물이 있다.

해설 두 번째 지문[Blue 씨가 작성한 작업요청서]에서 'Work to be Done'에서 'Pruning and general care of the flowers in our 10 flowerbeds (including orchids, lavenders, and lilacs, and others), 15 eucalyptus trees, 7 Chinese Elm trees, and various bushes and shrubs on our property.'라고 하면서, 'Notes'에서 'It's quite a big project, so I think we need at least

3 people to help prune.'이라고 하여 식물이 많아 작업이 방대하다는 것을 알 수 있으므로 (D)가 정답이다.

16. 암시/추론 – 연계 문제

Blue 씨가 Hawkeye Gardeners를 이용한다면, 표준요금으로 시간당 얼마를 지불하겠는가?
(A) 70달러
(B) 125달러
(C) 170달러
(D) 225달러

해설 첫 번째 지문 [웹페이지], 두 번째 단락에서 'Our current hourly rates are as follows: 1 gardener = $70; 2 gardeners = $125; 3 gardeners = $170; 4 gardeners = $225'라고 했는데, 세 번째 지문 [이메일], 두 번째 단락에서 'Attached to this e-mail you will find a quotation sheet which includes all labor costs, including four gardeners.'라고 하여 Blue 씨가 정원사 4명에 해당하는 금액을 지불할 것임을 알 수 있으므로 (D)가 정답이다.

17. 암시/추론 – 연계 문제

Blue 씨에 관하여 알 수 있는 것은?
(A) 평일로 예약을 잡길 원한다.
(B) 최근 쇼핑몰에서 퇴직했다.
(C) 이전에 정원을 많이 만들어봤다.
(D) 경험이 있는 정원관리업체를 고용하고 싶어한다.

해설 첫 번째 지문 [웹페이지], 네 번째 단락에서 '**Spring Has Sprung Event: Schedule an appointment Monday through Friday within the month of May to receive a 25 percent off code for a subscription to *Garden Designs* magazine.'라고 했는데, 두 번째 지문 [작업요청서], 'Notes'에서 'I initially wrote down May 18 as a potential start date, but I would prefer something earlier—so long as I qualify for the promotion that's listed on your online page.'라고 하여 그가 이벤트 혜택을 받기 위해 평일로 예약을 잡았음을 알 수 있으므로 (A)가 정답이다.

✛ Paraphrasing

schedule → set up,
Monday through Friday → weekday

18. 상세 정보

Perkins 씨에 따르면, 그녀 회사에서 무엇을 할 수 있는가?
(A) 예상보다 빨리 정원 작업을 할 수 있다
(B) 이전에 작업한 사진들을 제공할 수 있다
(C) 철거비를 제외할 수 있다
(D) 화단을 설치할 수 있다

해설 세 번째 지문 [Perkins 씨가 보낸 이메일], 두 번째 단락에서 'Upon checking our schedule, we have an opening exactly one week prior to the date you requested on the form.'이라고 했으므로 (A)가 정답이다.

CASE 집중훈련   본서 p.282

1. (C)   2. (C)   3. (C)   4. (A)   5. (B)   6. (B)
7. (D)   8. (B)   9. (D)   10. (C)   11. (A)   12. (A)
13. (D)   14. (B)   15. (C)   16. (C)   17. (C)   18. (B)

1-3번은 다음 공지에 관한 문제입니다.

전 Umi 직원 주목

—[1]—. Umi Sushi에서 네 번째 Umi Sushi 지점 개장을 알려드리게 되어 자랑스럽습니다. 특히 Auckland 교외 신개발 지역에서 저희 음식에 대한 고객 수요가 늘어나, 경영진은 Whangaparaoa에 지점을 열기로 결정했습니다. —[2]—. 개장 후 몇 달 간 Monique Jacobs가 총주방장 자리에 있을 것입니다. Jacobs 씨가 신규 직원 교육으로 바쁠 시간을 보낼 테니, 가능한 한 많이 도와주시기 바랍니다.

지점은 10월 8일에 문을 열 예정입니다. —[3]—. 행사에 관한 더 자세한 정보는 저희 웹사이트 www.umisushi.co.nz에서 확인하실 수 있습니다. —[4]—.

어휘

location 지점 | growing 늘어나는 | particularly 특히 | newly-developed 신개발의 | suburb 교외 | management 경영진, 운영진 | designate 지명하다 | head chef 수석 요리사, 총 주방장 | train 교육시키다 | assist 돕다 | due ~하기로 되어 있는, 예정된

1. 주제 / 목적 / 대상

공지의 목적은 무엇인가?
(A) 이름 변경을 제안하는 것
(B) 직원에게 도움을 요청하는 것
(C) 회사의 최신소식을 알려주는 것
(D) 상품에 대한 피드백을 요구하는 것

해설 첫 번째 단락에서 'Umi Sushi is proud to be announcing the opening of our fourth Umi Sushi location.'이라고 했으므로 (C)가 정답이다.

2. 사실 확인

지점에 관하여 언급된 것은?
(A) 보수공사를 거쳤다.
(B) Auckland에 위치한다.
(C) 신규 직원이 있다.
(D) Jacobs 씨가 소유한다.

해설 첫 번째 단락에서 'Ms. Jacobs will have a busy time training new staff members, so please assist her as much as you can.'이라고 했으므로 (C)가 정답이다.

3. 문장 삽입

[1], [2], [3], [4]로 표시된 곳 중, 다음 문장이 들어갈 위치로 가장 적절한 것은?

"개장 기념식이 있을 예정입니다."

(A) [1]
(B) [2]
(C) [3]
(D) [4]

해설 주어진 문장의 to commemorate the opening과 호응을 이루려면 두 번째 단락 'The location is due to open on 8 October.' 뒤에 들어가야 is due to open과 연결될 수 있다. 따라서, (C)가 정답이다.

4-6번은 다음 이메일에 관한 문제입니다.

수신   Silva Solutions 직원
발신   Harrison Studebaker
날짜   1월 12일

제목   중요 공지

직원 여러분께,

❹저는 출장비 보고서에 관한 개정된 정책을 다시 살펴보고 싶습니다. —[1]—. 2월 1일부터, 연료 구입 영수증에는 업체별 마일리지 추정치가 포함되어야 합니다. ❻그 어떤 개인적인 용도로의 차량 사용은 보고서를 제출하기 전 총 마일리지에서 차감해 주세요. —[2]—. ❺마지막으로, IT 부서에서 재무 프로그램을 업그레이드해서, 여러분의 총 환급액을 자동으로 빠르게 계산할 수 있도록 했습니다. 시스템에 영수증 사진만 올려주시면 됩니다.

문의사항이 있으시면 저에게 알려주세요. —[3]—. 저는 이번 주 Wellington으로 출장을 가서, 메시지에 바로 답변을 드리지 못할 수도 있음을 유념해 주세요. —[4]—.

진심을 담아,

Harrison Studebaker
Silva Solutions 회장

어휘
notice 통지, 알림 | go over 점검하다, 검토하다, 거듭 살피다 | revise 개정하다, 수정하다 | policy 정책 | travel expense 여행경비 | receipt 영수증 | fuel 연료 | purchase 구매 | include 포함하다 | estimate 견적서, 추정(치) | specific 특정한 | ensure 반드시 ~하게 하다, 보장하다 | subtract 빼다 | turn in 돌려주다, 반납하다 | lastly 마지막으로 | upgrade 업그레이드하다 | calculate 계산하다 | reimbursement 상환, 변제, 배상 | amount 양, 액수 | inquiry 문의 | keep in mind 명심하다, 유념하다 | respond 응답하다, 반응하다 | right away 바로, 즉시

4. 사실 확인

Silva Solutions에 관하여 알 수 있는 것은?
(A) 출장비 보고에 관한 개정된 정책을 실시할 것이다.
(B) 기름 구입에 할당된 예산을 줄였다.
(C) 신규 IT직원을 채용할 것이다.
(D) 지역 내 여러 개의 지점이 있다.

해설 첫 번째 단락에서 'I want to go over some revised policies about company travel expense reports. Starting 1 February, receipts for fuel purchases must include an estimate of business-specific mileage.'라고 하여 개정된 정책을 2월 1일부터 시행할 것임을 알 수 있으므로 (A)가 정답이다.

+ Paraphrasing

revised policies about company travel expense reports → updated policies for reporting business trip expenses

5. 상세 정보

재무 프로그램은 왜 언급되는가?
(A) 계속되는 오류에 대해 사과하려고
(B) 특별한 기능 중 하나를 언급하려고
(C) 직원들에게 다운로드하도록 권하려고
(D) 곧 업그레이드될 것임을 직원들에게 상기시키기 위해

해설 첫 번째 단락에서 'Lastly, IT has upgraded our finance program so that it can automatically and quickly calculate your total reimbursement amount. All you have to do is enter photos of the receipts into the system.'이라고 했으므로 (B)가 정답이다.

6. 문장 삽입

[1], [2], [3], [4]로 표시된 곳 중, 다음 문장이 들어갈 위치로 가장 적절한 것은?

"이 가이드라인을 준수함으로써, 저희는 여러분께 적시에 상환해드릴 수 있을 겁니다."

(A) [1]
(B) [2]
(C) [3]
(D) [4]

해설 주어진 문장의 these guidelines는 receipts for fuel purchases must include an estimate of business-specific mileage와 any personal use of your vehicle is subtracted from the report's total mileage를 가리킨다. 따라서, (B)가 정답이다.

7-10번은 다음 이메일에 관한 문제입니다.

수신: kburns@fissionmail.com
발신: mwillis@nwpublishings.co.nz
날짜: 8월 7일
제목: 인터뷰 가능성

Burns 씨께,

저는 May Willis이고, 작고하신 Leroy Mendez 작가의 전기를 쓰고 있습니다. 그 분의 일대기에 대해 작업하도록 미망인께 권한을 위임 받았습니다. —[1]—. 미망인께서 지금까지 저희에게 말씀해주신 내용에 따르면, 귀하께서는 Mendez 씨께서 작가가 되기로 결심하는데 아주 상당한 영향을 미치셨습니다. —[2]—. ❽이 주제에 대해 제가 조사한 바로는, Mendez 씨께서 주로 비공개 생활을 하셔서, 제가 이 부분에 대해 많은 정보를 찾을 수 없었습니다.

❼❿이에, 제가 귀하께 방문해 몇 가지 질문을 드려도 괜찮을지 요청 드리고 싶습니다. —[3]—. 언제라도 가능하실 때 연락주신다면, 아주 좋을 것 같습니다.

전기에 관해서라면, 저희는 가능한 한 많은 일화를 포함하고 싶습니다. ❾그의 가까운 친지 분들께서 책의 일부를 작성할 예정입니다. 공유하실 좋은 일화가 있으시면, 귀하께도 이 제의는 열려 있습니다. —[4]—. 관심 있으신 경우에 대비해 알려드리면, 저희 책의 마감일은 10월 31일입니다.

진심을 담아,

May Willis
수석 작가

어휘
possibility 가능성 | biography 전기 | late 고인이 된, 작고한 | author 작가 | right 권리 | widow 미망인 | significant 상당한 | influence 영향 | research 조사 | largely 대체로, 주로 | private 사적인, 비공개의 | stop by 들르다 | prefer 선호하다 | instead 대신에 | get back to (회신을 위해) 연락해 주다 | as for ~에 대해서는 | anecdote 일화 | close 가까운 | relative 친척 | invitation 초청, 초대 | in case ~할 경우에 대비해서 | deadline 마감일 | head 수석

7. 주제 / 목적 / 대상

Willis 씨는 왜 Burns 씨에게 연락했는가?
(A) 전기 작가를 추천하려고
(B) 세미나 일정을 잡으려고
(C) 계약을 확인하려고
(D) 인터뷰를 요청하려고

해설 두 번째 단락에서 'Therefore, I would like to ask whether you would be open to me stopping by and asking you a few questions.' 했으므로 (D)가 정답이다.

8. 사실 확인

Willis 씨의 조사에 관하여 언급된 것은?
(A) 하루에 실시되었다.
(B) 결론을 내지 못했다.
(C) 팀에서 수집했다.
(D) 부정확하다고 간주되었다.

해설 첫 번째 단락에서 'From my research into this topic, I couldn't find much information on this, as Mr. Mendez largely led a private life.'라고 했으므로 (B)가 정답이다.

9. 사실 확인

전기에 관하여 언급된 것은?
(A) 10월에 출간될 것이다.
(B) Mr. Burns의 서문이 포함될 것이다.
(C) 영화로 만들어질 것이다.
(D) 다수의 사람들이 저술할 것이다.

해설 세 번째 단락에서 'Some of his close friends and relatives will write some sections of the book. This invitation is also open to you if you have a great anecdote to share.'라고 했으므로 (D)가 정답이다.

➕ Paraphrasing

write → author

10. 문장 삽입

[1], [2], [3], [4]로 표시된 곳 중, 다음 문장이 들어갈 위치로 가장 적절한 것은?

"원하신다면, 전화통화로 대신할 수 있습니다."

(A) [1]
(B) [2]
(C) [3]
(D) [4]

해설 주어진 문장에 instead가 나오므로 전화 대신 이 앞에 다른 선택지가 제시되어야 한다. 'Therefore, I would like to ask whether you would be open to me stopping by and asking you a few questions.'라고 하여 주어진 문장이 이어지기에 자연스러우므로 (C)가 정답이다.

11-14번은 다음 안내책자에 관한 문제입니다.

Feilong Business Movers (FBM)

—[1]—. **11 14** 회사를 중국시장으로 진출시키려고 계획하시나요? 그러려면, 중국에서의 사업 운영의 법률적, 문화적 측면에 대한 광범위한 지식을 가지고 있어야 합니다. 전문가로 구성된 FBM팀이 이 국가로의 이주가 순조롭고 성공적이 되도록 보장해 드립니다. —[2]—.

법률 문서
해외 근무에서 가장 중요한 부분은 아마도 모든 필수 서류가 준비되었는지 확인하는 것입니다. 필요한 비자 및 허가증을 받는 것은 부담이 클 수 있습니다. 게다가 지방정부는 자국 내 외국인에 대한 절차를 지속적으로 개정하고 있습니다. **12** 다행히, 저희 법률 전문가들은 매년 **최신 법률개정에 관한 최신정보를 얻기 위해 세미나에 참석합니다.** 저희와 함께라면, 서류작업은 전혀 신경쓰지 않으셔도 됩니다. —[3]—.

부동산 관리
FBM은 중국 내 부동산을 전담하는 부서를 두고 있습니다. 담당 직원이 필요에 맞는 사무실 공간을 찾을 수 있게 도와줄 것입니다. 또한, **13** 저희 시설 관리자는 귀하의 초과 물품들을 보관할 최상의 임대 창고에 대한 조언을 제공할 것입니다.

문화 교육
또한 FBM은 귀하께서 새로운 환경에 적응할 수 있게 도와드릴 것입니다. 관심 있는 분들은 언어 수업 및 예절 교육을 받을 수 있습니다. 이들 수업은 귀하와 다른 직원들이 해당 국가에 적응하는 것을 돕기 위해 고안되었습니다. —[4]—.

어휘

expand 확대[확장]시키다 | presence 존재, 있음 | extensive 폭넓은, 광범위한 | knowledge 지식 | legal 법률과 관련된, 법적인 | cultural 문화의 | aspect 측면, 양상 | run 운영하다 | business 사업, 장사 | professional 전문적인 | ensure 반드시 ~하게 하다, 보장하다 | smooth 매끄러운, 순조로운 | documentation 서류 | perhaps 아마도 | abroad 해외에[로] | make sure 반드시 ~하다 | prepare 준비하다 | obtain 얻다, 획득하다 | permit 허가증 | overwhelming 압도적인, 엄청난 | local 지역의, 현지의 | government 정부 | constantly 끊임없이 | revise 수정하다, 개정하다 | procedure 절차, 방법 | foreigner 외국인 | fortunately 다행히도 | specialist 전문가 | attend 참석하다 | up-to-date 최신의 | latest 최신의 | law 법 | change 변화 | paperwork 서류작업 | be the last thing on somebody's mind 전혀 생각하지 않는다 | property 재산 | management 경영(진), 관리 | dedicate 전념하다, 헌신하다 | deal with 처리하다 | real estate 부동산 | designate 지정하다, 지명하다 | match 일치하다, (필요에) 맞추다 | need 필요, 요구 | facility 시설, 기관 | offer 제공하다 | advice 조언, 충고 | storage unit 임대창고 | excess 초과한 | item 항목, 물품 | culture 문화 | training 교육, 훈련 | get acclimated to ~에 적응하다 | surroundings 환경 | etiquette 에티켓, 예의 | design 설계하다, 고안하다 | relevant 관련 있는 | adjust to ~에 적응하다

11. 주제 / 목적 / 대상

안내책자는 누구를 대상으로 작성되었는가?
(A) 성장하는 글로벌 회사
(B) 중국의 이사업체
(C) 중국 공무원
(D) 부동산 소유자

해설 첫 번째 단락에서 'Do you plan on expanding your company's presence into the Chinese market? In order to do so, you must have extensive knowledge about the legal and cultural aspects of running a business in China. FBM's team of professionals can ensure that your move into this country will be smooth and successful.'이라고 했으므로 (A)가 정답이다.

➕ Paraphrasing

company → firm

12. 상세 정보

안내책자에 따르면, 어떤 FBM 직원들이 연간 교육을 받는가?
(A) 법률 전문가
(B) 문서 정리원
(C) 부동산 중개인
(D) 언어 교사

해설 두 번째 단락에서 'our legal specialists attend seminars every year to stay up-to-date on the latest law changes.'라고 했으므로 (A)가 정답이다.

➕ Paraphrasing

legal specialists → legal experts, receive annual training → attend seminars every year

13. 상세 정보

안내책자에 따르면, FMB 시설 관리자는 어떤 조언을 제공하는가?
(A) 작업구역을 정리하는 방법
(B) 조명을 설치하는 방법
(C) 구입할 사무용가구 항목
(D) 이용할 임대창고

해설 세 번째 단락에서 'our facility managers will offer you advice on the best unit for storing your excess items.'라고 했으므로 (D)가 정답이다.

14. 문장 삽입

[1], [2], [3], [4]로 표시된 곳 중, 다음 문장이 들어갈 위치로 가장 적절한 것은?

"저희가 제공하는 서비스에 대해 더 자세히 알아보시려면, 아래를 읽어 보세요."

(A) [1]
(B) [2]
(C) [3]
(D) [4]

해설 첫 번째 단락에서 'FBM's team of professionals can ensure that your move into this country will be smooth and successful.'이라고 하며 다음 단락에서 서비스를 분야별로 설명하고 있어, 주어진 문장이 이어지기에 자연스러우므로 (B)가 정답이다.

15-18번은 다음 웹페이지에 관한 문제입니다.

EXJ 산업의 경영진은 팀원들이 발전하길 바랍니다. —[1]—. **¹⁸자사 조언 프로그램은 각 직원이 곤경에 처했을 때 믿고 의지하며 조언을 구할 사람이 곁에 있도록 보장해 드립니다.** —[2]—.

¹⁶조언을 주고 받는 관계는 관련된 사람들 모두에게 도움이 됩니다. 조언을 받는 자는 경험 많은 동료에게 배움을 얻습니다. 조언을 주는 자는 동료의 신뢰를 얻으면서, 의사소통 기술도 연마합니다. 결국, 기업은 더 많이 알고 보다 단합된 노동력을 보유할 때, 더욱 더 성장합니다. —[3]—.

현재 진행 중인 조언 프로그램 목록은 아래와 같습니다. —[4]—.

¹⁸신입 사원 조언: 모든 신입 사원은 각자의 지점에서 해당 분야에 경험이 많은 조언자를 배정받습니다. 조언자는 조언을 받는 자와 직접적으로 일하지 않으며, 정해진 일정에 맞춰 만날 필요도 없습니다. 그럼에도, 많은 사람들이 이 관계의 진가를 인정하며, 일부는 수십 년 간 생산적인 동반자 관계를 이어가기도 합니다.

사무실 간 조언: EXJ의 다른 지점 동료들에게 배울 수 있는 기회입니다. **¹⁷경력 수준에 관계없이 팀원들에게 열려 있습니다.**

¹⁵국제 조언: 직원이 해외 지사로 전근 갈 때, 해당 지역을 잘 아는 현지 조언자를 배정받습니다. 이 관계는 6개월 정도 지속됩니다.

경력 매칭 조언: 이 연간 프로그램은 1월에 시작됩니다. 선발된 지점의 팀원들이 인턴과 짝을 맺는데, 이들은 다양한 부서에 대해 알아볼 기회를 얻게 됩니다.

이들 프로그램에 대해 알아보고 싶으시면, Stewart Browning에게 555-931-2394로 전화주세요.

어휘
thrive 번창하다 | advise 조언하다 | initiative (특정 목적 달성을 위한) 계획 | ensure 보장하다 | confide in 비밀을 털어놓다 | input 조언; 투입 | run into 만나다, 겪다 | difficulty 어려움, 곤경 | advisor 조언자 | advisee 조언을 받는

사람 | relationship 관계 | beneficial 유익한 | involve 관련시키다, 포함하다 | seasoned 경험 많은 | coworker 동료 | gain 얻다 | trust 신뢰 | hone 기술을 연마하다 | firm 회사 | grow 자라다, 커지다 | informed (특정 주제에 대해) 잘 아는 | cohesive 결합하는 | workforce 노동력 | currently 현재 | ongoing 계속 진행 중인 | hire 신입 사원 | branch 지점 | field 분야 | necessarily 꼭, 반드시 | set 정해진, 계획된 | appreciate 진가를 알아보다, 고마워하다 | productive 생산적인 | partnership 동반자관계 | last 지속되다 | decade 10년 | inter-office 사내의, 사무실 간 | peer 동료 | overseas 해외의 | assign 배정하다 | region 지역 | career 경력 | match 연결시키다 | year-long 일년 내내 계속되는 | select 선발된 | pair 짝을 짓다

15. 암시/추론

EXJ 산업에 관하여 알 수 있는 것은?
(A) 본사를 이전할 계획이다.
(B) 최근 직원을 대규모로 채용했다.
(C) 다양한 국가에 지점이 있다.
(D) 최근 10년 내 설립되었다.

해설 여섯 번째 단락에서 'International Advising: When staff members are relocated to an overseas office,'라고 하여 여러 국가에 지점이 있음을 알 수 있으므로 (C)가 정답이다.

16. 암시/추론

웹페이지에서는 조언 프로그램에 대해 무엇을 암시하는가?
(A) EXJ 산업에 새로 생긴 프로그램이다.
(B) 일부 지점 직원들만 이용할 수 있다.
(C) 회사 전체에 유익하다.
(D) 전 직원에게 의무사항이다.

해설 두 번째 단락에서 'The advisor-advisee relationship is beneficial for everyone involved. Advisees learn from their seasoned coworkers. Advisors gain the trust of their colleagues, while honing their communication skills. After all, a firm grows more when it has a better informed and more cohesive workforce.'라고 하여 결국 회사 전체에 유익하다는 것을 알 수 있으므로 (C)가 정답이다.

17. 사실 확인

현 조언 프로그램에 관하여 언급된 것은?
(A) 최대 6개월간 지속된다.
(B) 일부 부서에만 제공된다.
(C) 다양한 경력의 직원들이 이용할 수 있다.
(D) 이용할 수 있는 프로그램은 하나뿐이다.

해설 다섯 번째 단락에서 'Open to team members with any level of experience.'라고 했으므로 (C)가 정답이다.

✛ Paraphrasing
team members with any level of experience employees
→ with any experience level

18. 문장 삽입

[1], [2], [3], [4]로 표시된 곳 중, 다음 문장이 들어갈 위치로 가장 적절한 것은?

"조언자는 전문적인 조언을 제공할 뿐만 아니라, 업무 외적으로도 돈독한 관계를 맺습니다."

(A) [1]
(B) [2]
(C) [3]
(D) [4]

해설 첫 번째 단락에서 'Our advising initiative ensures that each employee has someone to confide in and offer input when they run into difficulty.'라고 하여 주어진 문장이 이어지기에 자연스러우므로 (B)가 정답이다.

CASE 집중훈련

본서 p.290

1. (A) **2.** (C) **3.** (B) **4.** (C) **5.** (D) **6.** (C)
7. (D) **8.** (A) **9.** (B) **10.** (C) **11.** (C) **12.** (D)
13. (C) **14.** (B) **15.** (D) **16.** (B)

1-2번은 다음 문자 메시지 대화에 관한 문제입니다.

Gilda Oshea (오전 9시 41분)
안녕하세요, Mai. 제가 방금 사장님께 연락 받았는데요. 저희가 새로운 팀원을 뽑는걸 정식 승인하셨어요. 생각했던 분 있으세요?

Mai Holman (오전 9시 43분)
잘됐어요. 때가 왔네요. 관심을 많이 보이는 예전 직장동료가 한 명 있어요. 당신과 나머지 팀원들에게 그에 대해서 의견을 묻고 싶어요. ■오늘이 수요일이니까, 저희 팀 회의 때 하는 거 어때요?

Gilda Oshea (오전 9시 46분)
좋은 생각이에요. 그런데 저희 팀에 관리자가 너무 많아서 보조급으로만 채용할 수 있다는 걸 유념해 주세요. ■그러니 당신 동료가 당신만큼 자격을 갖춘 분이라면, 아주 끌리는 직무는 아닐 수 있어요.

Mai Holman (오전 9시 52분)
■아, 그렇네요. 네, 저도 그에게 직무에 대해 잘못된 생각을 심어주고 싶진 않아요. 그가 보조직에 대해 아주 좋아할 것 같진 않아요. 다시 생각해봐야겠어요.

Gilda Oshea (오전 9시 54분)
그렇다면, 저희가 온라인에 구인광고를 올리거나 전에 이용했던 채용 대행업체와 함께 할 수도 있어요.

Mai Holman (오전 9시 58분)
제가 채용업체에 전화해볼게요. 과거에 그들과 함께 일하는 게 만족스러웠거든요.

Gilda Oshea (오전 10시 02분)
좋아요. 해줘서 고마워요.

어휘
officially 공식적으로, 정식으로 | approval 승인 | hire 고용하다 | have ~ in mind ~을 염두에 두다 | former 이전의 | colleague 동료 | run by (의중을 알아보기 위해) 말하다 | rest 나머지 | given ~을 고려해볼 때 | bear in mind 명심하다 | assistant 조수, 보조 부-, 조- | qualified 자격이 있는 | re-consider 재고하다 | in that case 그렇다면 | post up 게시하다, 올리다 | job advertisement 구인 광고 | recruitment 채용

1. 암시 / 추론
Oshea 씨와 Holman 씨에 관하여 알 수 있는 것은?
(A) 수요일마다 만난다.
(B) 연예기획사에서 근무한다.
(C) 저녁 약속이 있다.
(D) 함께 출퇴근한다.

해설 오전 9시 43분에 Mai Holman이 'Given that it's Wednesday,

how about we do it during our team meeting?'라고 했으므로 (A)가 정답이다.

2. 화자 의도 파악
오전 9시 52분에, Holman 씨가 "다시 생각해봐야겠어요"라고 할 때 무엇을 의미하는가?
(A) 인사팀과 이야기할 것이다.
(B) 사장과 회의를 마련할 것이다.
(C) 동료에게 일자리를 권하지 않을 것이다.
(D) 다음 회사 회의에 참석하지 않을 것이다.

해설 오전 9시 46분에 Gilda Oshea가 'Therefore, if your colleague is as qualified as you are, it may not be an very attractive position.'라고 한 말에, Mai Holman이 'I don't think he would be very happy with an assistant position. I guess I'll have to re-consider.'라고 한 것이므로 (C)가 정답이다.

3-4번은 다음 문자메시지 대화에 관한 문제입니다.

Heather Hartley (오후 2시 02분)
Jonas, 제가 보내드린 파일 확인하셨나요? 제가 교과서 표지 디자인을 보내드렸어요.

Jonas Kask (오후 2시 05분)
봤어요. ■스타일에 대해 생각을 좀 해봤는데요. 미리보기에는 다른 요소들이 너무 많이 들어가지 않으면서, 좀 더 심플하고 깔끔해야 해요.

Heather Hartley (오후 2시 06분)
그렇군요. 제가 예전 지침을 참조한 것 같네요. ■제가 오늘 오후에 처음부터 다시 할 시간이 됩니다.

Jonas Kask (오후 2시 07분)
■실은, 잘 모르겠어요. 선택하신 이미지도 아주 좋고, 서체도 잘 어울리는 것 같거든요. 제 생각엔 몇 부분만 편집하면 될 것 같아요.

Heather Hartley (오후 2시 08분)
알겠습니다. 그건 두어 시간 정도면 할 수 있어요.

Jonas Kask (오후 2시 09분)
좋습니다. 제가 지금 회의에 가야 하는데, 어떻게 만드실지 너무 궁금하네요.

어휘
check 확인하다 | submit 제출하다 | text book 교과서 | cover 표지 | thought 생각 | element 요소 | thumbnail 미리보기, 섬네일 | base ~에 근거지를 두다 | guidelines 지침 | start over 다시 시작하다 | from scratch 처음부터 | choose 선택하다 | appealing 매력적인, 흥미로운 | typeface 서체 | work 효과가 나다, 영향을 미치다 | component (구성)요소 | edit out ~를 잘라내다 | eager 열렬한, 간절히 바라는 | come up with 내놓다, 제안하다

3. 상세 정보
Hartley 씨는 어떤 실수를 했는가?
(A) 부적절한 이미지를 사용했다.
(B) 그녀가 적용한 스타일이 너무 복잡했다.
(C) 프로젝트에 시간을 충분히 쓰지 않았다.
(D) 표지 형식이 잘못됐다.

해설 오후 2시 05분, Jonas Kask의 메시지에서 'I saw it. I had some thoughts about the style. We need something simpler and cleaner, without so many different elements for the thumbnail.'이라고 말했으므로 (B)가 정답이다.

PART 7 CHAPTER 14

4. 화자 의도 파악

오후 2시 07분에, Kask 씨가 "실은, 잘 모르겠어요"라고 할 때 무엇을 의미하겠는가?
(A) Hartley 씨가 디자인을 제출해선 안 된다.
(B) Hartley 씨가 일정을 변경하지 않아도 된다.
(C) Hartley 씨가 디자인 작업을 완전히 다시 할 필요가 없다.
(D) Hartley 씨가 회의 일정을 다시 잡으면 안 된다.

해설 오후 2시 06분 ~ 2시 07분 대화에서 Heather Hartley가 'I have time this afternoon to start over from scratch.'라고 한 말에 Jonas Kask가 'Actually, I'm not so sure. I think you chose an appealing image and the typeface works well. I think some of the features just need to be edited out.'이라고 말한 것이므로 (C)가 정답이다.

✚ **Paraphrasing**

start over from scratch → completely redo

5-8번은 다음 온라인 채팅 대화문에 관한 문제입니다.

Anthony Collier (오후 2시 42분)
Lacy, Tran, 안녕하세요. 이 미팅을 위해 몇 분간 시간을 내주셔서 감사합니다. ⑤두 분의 각 전시회에 대한 현황 정보를 알고 싶어요. 관심을 모으기 위해 저희가 홍보 자료를 내기 시작하려고 합니다.

Lacy Segura (오후 2시 45분)
⑤저는 제가 보여주고 싶은 거의 모든 작품들을 큐레이션했습니다. ⑥지난 몇 년 동안 총 6개의 작품을 완성했고요.

Anthony Collier (오후 2시 47분)
정말 멋지네요. 얘기한 것 중에 몇 개는 본 것 같습니다.

Tran Williford (오후 2시 50분)
저도 마찬가지예요. ⑥이제 막 마지막 작품을 완성하고 있는데, 2년이란 시간을 아우르는 작품을 보여드리고 싶어서요.

Anthony Collier (오후 2시 53분)
대단하시네요. ⑦⑧두 분 중에 화랑까지 작품을 운반해 오실 수 있도록 준비하신 분 계신가요?

Lacy Segura (오후 2시 55분)
⑦아, 죄송합니다. 그걸 알아볼 시간이 없었네요.

Tran Williford (오후 2시 56분)
저도 같은 처지입니다.

Anthony Collier (오후 2시 59분)
걱정하지 마세요. ⑧전에 같이 일했던 회사들 몇 곳에 연락해 보겠습니다. 우리가 필요한 걸 그들에게 알려주고, 그들이 두 분께 연락하도록 하겠습니다. 감사합니다!

어휘
status (진행 과정의) 상황 | respective 각각의 | exhibition 전시회 | promotional materials 홍보자료 | generate 발생시키다, 만들어 내다 | curate 큐레이션하다 (자료를 수집, 분류, 구조화하는 행위) | art piece 예술 작품 | in total 통틀어 | likewise 마찬가지야, 동감이야 | finish up 끝내다 | span 시간, 기간 | look into ~을 주의 깊게 살피다, 조사하다 | get in touch with ~와 연락을 취하다

5. 암시 / 추론

Collier 씨는 누구이겠는가?
(A) 물류 직원
(B) 학교 교사
(C) 프로 운동선수

(D) 미술 큐레이터

해설 오후 2시 42분 ~ 2시 45분 대화에서 Anthony Collier가 'I just wanted to get status updates on your respective exhibitions.'라고 말했고, Lacy Segura가 'I have curated nearly all of the art pieces I would like to show.'라고 한 점을 토대로 Collier가 미술관 큐레이터임을 짐작할 수 있으므로 (D)가 정답이다.

6. 사실 확인

Segura 씨와 Williford 씨의 작품에 관하여 알 수 있는 것은?
(A) 현대미술의 영향을 받았다.
(B) 이전에 전시된 적이 있다.
(C) 최근 몇 해에 걸쳐 완성되었다.
(D) 앞으로 나흘 안에 배송될 것이다.

해설 Lacy Segura의 오후 2시 45분 대화문 'I have, in total, six pieces I have completed over the past few years.'와 Tran Williford의 오후 2시 50분 대화문 'I am just finishing up one last art piece, as I would like to show my works covering a two-year span.'을 토대로 이들 모두 몇 년에 걸쳐 작품을 완성해왔다는 사실을 알 수 있으므로 (C)가 정답이다.

7. 화자 의도 파악

오후 2시 56분에, Williford 씨가 "저도 같은 처지입니다"라고 말할 때 그가 의미한 것은 무엇이겠는가?
(A) 현재 해외여행 중이다.
(B) 실수에 대한 책임을 진다.
(C) Ms. Segura에게 실망하고 있다.
(D) 운송수단을 마련하지 않았다.

해설 오후 2시 53분 ~ 2시 56분 대화에서 'Anthony Collier가 Have either of you arranged transportation of your works to the gallery?'라고 묻자, Lacy Segura가 'Oh, I'm sorry. I haven't had the time to look into that.'라고 대답했고, 이에 Tran Williford가 'I'm in the same boat.'라고 말한 것이므로 Williford 씨가 자신도 작품을 운반할 운송수단을 마련하지 않았음을 나타낸 것이다. 따라서 (D)가 정답이다. in the same boat는 '같은 상황에 있는, 같은 문제를 안고 있는'이란 뜻이다.

8. 암시 / 추론

Collier 씨는 다음에 무엇을 하겠는가?
(A) 운송 회사와 얘기한다.
(B) 몇몇 작품들을 운반한다.
(C) 몇몇 광고를 낸다.
(D) 작가들에게 마감일을 상기시킨다.

해설 Anthony Collier의 2시 53분 대화에서 'Have either of you arranged transportation of your works to the gallery?'라고 물었고, 두 작가 모두 운송수단을 준비하지 않았다고 하자, Collier 씨가 2시 59분에 'I'll get in touch with some of the companies we've worked with in the past.'라고 말했으므로 (A)가 정답이다.

9-12번은 다음 온라인 채팅 대화문에 관한 문제입니다.

10월 12일 수요일

Penelope Everdeen 오후 7시 16분
금요일 오후에 Tranchford에서 하청업자들이 Alton사를 방문해 주차장 일부를 파고 배관 교체작업을 실시할 예정임을 다시 한번 알려드립니다. 저희 직원들이 주차장 전체를 막을 예정이니, 여러분과 각자 팀에서는 대체 교통수단을 마련하거나 인근 주차장을 이용해야 한다는 걸 기억해 주세요.

Mohamed Khoury 오후 7시 17분

Salford 산업에서 Kenneth Davis가 금요일 오후 5시에 하는 프레젠테이션에 참석하러 차를 몰고 올 예정이에요. 그 분은 어떡하죠? **⁹건물 관리부에 연락해야 할까요?**

Lucinda Dubuque 오후 7시 18분

¹²제가 방금 일기예보를 보고 있었는데, 강풍이 있을 확률이 높네요. 그래도 굴착작업이 가능한가요?

Penelope Everdeen 오후 7시 19분

⁹맞아요. ¹⁰Davis 씨께 제 연락처를 알려주세요. 제가 그 분한테 Baker 가에 있는 주차장 주소를 알려드리고 자리를 마련해 놓을게요.

Penelope Everdeen 오후 7시 20분

¹²알겠습니다. Tranchford에서는 자사 팀에서 제 때 완료하려고 상황이 좋든 안 좋든 작업하게 할 거예요.

Beatrice Ianucci 오후 7시 21분

¹¹그리고, 금요일에는 직원들이 원격근무를 선택할 수 있다는 걸 명심하세요. 전원이 회사 메신저에 로그인하게만 하면 됩니다.

Penelope Everdeen 오후 7시 23분

좋은 말씀이에요. 모두 저녁시간 잘 보내세요.

어휘

reminder 상기시켜주는 메모, 편지 | contractor 계약자, 하청업자 | excavate 파다 | portion 일부, 부분 | replace 교체하다 | pipe 배관, 파이프 | block off 차단하다 | arrange 마련하다 | alternative 대체 가능한 | transportation 차편 | garage 주차장 | nearby 인근에 | reach out to ~에 연락하다 | excavation 발굴, 땅파기, 굴착 | reserved spot 지정자리 | through thick and thin 좋을 때나 안 좋을 때나, 한결같이 | on time 정시에 | keep in mind 명심하다 | work remotely 원격 근무하다 | log on to ~에 접속하다

9. 암시 / 추론

Everdeen 씨는 누구겠는가?
(A) 굴착 작업반원
(B) 건물 관리자
(C) 민간 배관공
(D) 타지 고객

해설 오후 7시 17분 ~ 오후 7시 19분 대화에서 Mohamed Khoury가 'Should he reach out to building management?'라고 한 말에, Penelope Everdeen가 'That's right. You can give Mr. Davis my contact information.'이라고 말한 것으로 보아 Everdeen 씨가 건물 관리자임을 알 수 있으므로 (B)가 정답이다.

✚ **Paraphrasing**

building management → building supervisor

10. 상세 정보

Davis 씨는 왜 Everdeen 씨에게 연락할 것인가?
(A) 대체 교통수단을 추천하려고
(B) 사무실 가는 길을 알려주려고
(C) 주차 지원을 마련하려고
(D) 프레젠테이션 일정을 변경하려고

해설 Wednesday, October 12에서 날짜와 요일을 확인할 수 있고, 14일은 금요일이다. 오후 7시 19분, Penelope Everdeen의 메시지에서 'You can give Mr. Davis my contact information. I'll give him the address of the lot on Baker Street and reserve a spot.'이라고 말했으므로 (C)가 정답이다.

11. 암시/추론

10월 14일에 무슨 일이 있겠는가?
(A) Alton사가 문을 닫을 것이다.
(B) Davis 씨가 Khoury 씨와 저녁식사를 할 것이다.
(C) 일부 Alton사 직원들이 재택근무를 할 것이다.
(D) Ianucci 씨가 소프트웨어를 설치할 것이다.

해설 Wednesday, October 12에서 날짜와 요일을 확인할 수 있고, 14일은 금요일이다. 오후 7시 21분, Beatrice Ianucci의 메시지에서 'Also, keep in mind that we do have the option of letting staff members work remotely on Friday.'라고 하여 Alton사에서 자율적으로 재택근무를 실시할 것임을 알 수 있으므로 (C)가 정답이다.

✚ **Paraphrasing**

work remotely → work from home

12. 화자 의도 파악

오후 7시 20분에, Everdeen 씨가 "자사 팀에서 제 때 완료하려고 상황이 좋든 안 좋든 작업하게 할 거예요"라고 할 때 무엇을 의미하는가?
(A) Tranchford는 직원들이 유능한 것으로 유명하다.
(B) Alton사 직원들은 날씨가 굿을 때조차도 제 시간에 와야 한다.
(C) 일기예보가 맞지 않을 수 있다.
(D) 야외 작업 일정은 변경되지 않을 것이다.

해설 오후 7시 18분 ~ 오후 7시 20분 대화에서 Lucinda Dubuque가 'I was just watching the weather report and there's a high chance of severe winds. Is the excavation still possible?'이라고 한 말에, Penelope Everdeen이 'And yes. Tranchford makes sure their teams work through thick and thin to finish on time.'이라고 대답한 것이므로 (D)가 정답이다. through thick and thin은 '좋을 때나 안 좋을 때나[어떤 고난이 있어도]'라는 뜻이다.

13-16번은 다음 온라인 채팅 대화문에 관한 문제입니다.

Kirsten Holland 오후 2시 37분

오늘 오후에 4층에 올라와보신 분 있으세요? **¹³거기 냉방장치가 작동하지 않는 것 같아요.**

Beverly Alvarado 오후 2시 38분

저요. **¹³확실히 덥고 답답해요.**

Kirsten Holland 오후 2시 40분

맞아요, 어제 밤 천둥번개가 칠 때 콘덴서가 나간 거 같아요. 이번 주말 일기예보에서 너무 덥지 않다고 해서 다행이에요. 수리할 부품이 없거든요. 어쨌든, 제가 전문 수리팀에 연락할 거예요.

Beverly Alvarado 오후 2시 41분

객실 할증료를 지불한 고객들은 기분이 좋지 않을 거 같아요. 내일 대규모 컨퍼런스가 있고, 좌석이 모두 팔렸다는 걸 기억하세요. **¹⁴저희 설비실에 휴대용 냉방장치가 있지 않나요?**

Jamal Salamanca 오후 2시 42분

우리는 더 이상 나쁜 후기를 받으면 안 돼요.

Kirsten Holland 오후 2시 43분

¹⁴다른 지점에만요. Salamanca 씨가 승인해 주시면, 제가 트럭을 몰고 Toledo 지점에 다녀올 수 있어요. 그쪽에서 아마 5, 6개 정도 나눠줄 수 있을 거예요. **¹⁵제가 밤 9시 30분이나 10시는 되어야 돌아오겠지만요.**

Jamal Salamanca 오후 2시 44분

Kirsten, **¹⁵¹⁶당장 영향을 받을 것 같은 객실 전체에 선풍기를 구입하도록 제가 법인카드 사용을 승인할게요.** 몇 개 필요한지 확인하고, 비용

효율이 좋은 모델이 뭔지 찾아 보세요. 반드시 품목별 영수증으로 받아오세요.

Kristen Holland 오후 2시 45분
네, **16** 제가 할게요.

Jamal Salamanca 오후 2시 46분
지역 가전매장에 없으면, Henderson Valley몰로 가보세요.

어휘
cooling system 냉방장치 | work 작동하다 | definitely 확실히 | stuffy (공간에 환기가 안되어) 답답한 | capacitor 콘덴서 | go down (작동이) 중단되다 | thunderstorm 뇌우, 천둥번개 | forecast 일기예보 | part 부품 | fix 수리하다 | in any case 어쨌든 | contact 연락하다 | professional 전문적인 | repair 수리 | pay 지불하다 | premium 할증료 | completely 완전히 | sell out 다 팔리다 | portable 휴대용의 | AC unit 냉방장치 | maintenance 유지보수 | afford 여유가 되다 | a batch of 한 묶음의 | location 지점, 위치 | authorize 승인하다 | branch 지점 | spare (시간 등을) 할애하다 | permission 허가 | company credit card 법인카드 | electric fan 선풍기 | affect 영향을 미치다 | immediately 즉시 | cost-effective 효과적인 | itemized 항목별로 작성한 | receipt 영수증 | appliance (전자)기기

13. 주제 / 목적 / 대상

작성자들은 주로 어떤 문제에 대해 이야기하고 있는가?
(A) 주말에 기온이 높을 것으로 예상된다.
(B) 콘덴서 교체하는 게 너무 비싸다.
(C) 온도 조절장치가 고장 났다.
(D) 회사차량에 수리가 필요하다.

해설 오후 2시 37분 ~ 오후 2시 38분 대화에서 Kristen Holland가 'Has anyone been up on the fourth floor this afternoon? It doesn't feel like the cooling system is working up there.'라고 한 말에, Beverly Alvarado가 'I have. It's definitely getting hot and stuffy.'라고 대답한 것이므로 (C)가 정답이다.

+ Paraphrasing
cooling system → climate control system

14. 화자 의도 파악

오후 2시 43분에, Holland 씨가 "다른 지점에만요."라고 할 때 무엇을 의미하겠는가?
(A) 지역 손님들이 불평하지 않을 것 같다.
(B) 현장에 휴대용 장치가 보관되어 있지 않다.
(C) 호텔에 설비실이 없다.
(D) 그녀는 조치를 취할 필요가 없다고 생각한다.

해설 오후 2시 41분 ~ 오후 2시 43분 대화에서 Beverly Alvarado가 'Don't we have some portable AC units in the maintenance office?'라고 물었을 때, Kristen Holland가 'Only at other locations.'라고 대답한 것이므로 (B)가 정답이다.

15. 암시 / 추론

Salamanca는 왜 Toledo에 있는 장치를 사용하는 것에 반대하는 결정을 하겠는가?
(A) 아주 빨리 반납되어야 해서
(B) 지역매장에서 구할 수 있어서
(C) 효과적으로 운송될 수 없어서
(D) 도착하는 데 너무 오래 걸릴 거라서

해설 오후 2시 43분 ~ 오후 2시 44분 대화에서 Kristen Holland가 'I wouldn't be back until 9:30 or 10:00 P.M., though.'라고 하자, Jamal Salamanca가 'I'm giving you permission to use the company credit card to buy electric fans for all the guest

rooms likely to be affected immediately.'라고 한 것이므로 (D)가 정답이다.

16. 암시 / 추론

다음에 무슨 일이 있겠는가?
(A) Salamanca 씨가 가격 몇 가지를 비교할 것이다.
(B) Hollnd 씨가 구매를 할 것이다.
(C) 설비팀에서 교체부품을 찾아볼 것이다.
(D) 선풍기가 호텔로 배달될 것이다.

해설 오후 2시 44분 ~ 오후 2시 45분 대화에서 Jamal Salamanca가 'I'm giving you permission to use the company credit card to buy electric fans for all the guest rooms likely to be affected immediately.'라고 한 말에 Kristen Holland가 I'm on it.'이라고 하여 그녀가 선풍기를 사러 갈 것임을 알 수 있으므로 (B)가 정답이다. be on it은 actively dealing with a problem, job, etc.의 의미이다.

+ Paraphrasing
buy → make a purchase

CASE 집중훈련
본서 p.298

1. (A)　2. (A)　3. (A)　4. (D)　5. (A)　6. (A)
7. (A)　8. (C)　9. (B)　10. (D)　11. (D)　12. (B)
13. (A)　14. (D)　15. (A)　16. (B)　17. (C)　18. (B)
19. (D)　20. (C)

1-5번은 다음 이메일과 직원 안내서에 관한 문제입니다.

수신: Lulwa Hamdi
발신: Randy O'Neal
날짜: **3** 7월 3일
제목: 정보
첨부: 안내서

Hamdi 씨, 안녕하세요.

AttoTech Industries에 오신 것을 환영합니다. **2** 근무환경을 쾌적하다는 것을 알게 되실 거라 확신합니다.

1 회사 규칙 및 지침에 대한 정보를 첨부해 드렸습니다. 잠시 시간 내셔서 살펴봐 주세요. **4** 그리고 한정된 주차공간으로 인해, 이 곳 직원들에게 카풀 프로그램에 참여하실 것을 권장드립니다. 참여하시려면, 오전 9시에서 오후 7시 사이 아무 때나 시설과 사무실에 들러주세요.

또한, 다른 지점을 방문하는 여정을 위해 적절한 출장준비를 하는 것을 잊지 마세요. **3** 첫 번째 가실 곳은 다음주 월요일 본사 사무실입니다. 그후, 월말에 지점으로 복귀하기 전 다른 지점들을 가게 될 거에요. 도움이 필요하시면, Ned Ewing에게 newing@attotech.ca로 연락하세요.

문의사항이 있으시면, 언제든지 저에게 연락해 주세요.

진심을 담아,

Randy O'Neal

어휘
environment 환경 | pleasant 쾌적한 | attach 붙이다, 첨부하다 | regarding ~에 관하여 | rule 규칙 | guidelines 지침, 가이드라인 | look over 살펴보다 | encourage 권장하다, 장려하다 | participate in 참여하다 | carpool 카풀

[승용차 함께 타기]을 하다 | **join** 참여하다 | **facility** 시설 | **proper** 적절한, 올바른 | **arrangement** 준비 | **head** 향하다, 가다 | **branch** 지점, 지사 | **assistance** 도움, 지원

AttoTech Industries
정책 및 절차 안내서

전자기기 정책

❸전자기기의 사용은 사무실 위치에 따라 다릅니다. Toronto 본사 및 Detroit 지점 직원들은 근무시간에 회사 발급 기기를 사용해야 합니다. Syracuse와 Ontario 지점 직원들은 매 교대 전에 기기를 반납해야 합니다. 비상 시, 시설 전체에서 유선전화가 이용 가능합니다.

교통

AttoTech는 환경친화적 회사가 되기 위해 노력합니다. 이에, 저희는 통근방법에 따라 직원들에게 다양한 인센티브를 제공합니다.

Toronto 근무자들은 할인 교통권을 받을 수 있는데, 도시 전역의 지하철 및 버스에서 사용 가능합니다. 구입하시려면, 해당 시설과를 방문해주세요.

버스, 자전거, 또는 도보로 통근을 하는 Syracuse와 Ontario 지점 직원들은 통근거리에 따라 금전적 보상을 받을 수 있습니다. 또한, 업무 관련 출장 시 회사차량 이용 권한을 받게 됩니다. 등록하려면, HR 부서로 문의하세요.

❹Detroit 지점은 카풀 계획을 장려합니다. 운전자에게는 주유비와 더불어, 출입구 근처 자리가 제공됩니다. 더 많은 정보를 알아보려면, 시설과 담당자에게 문의해 주세요.

어휘
policy 정책 | procedure 절차 | manual 설명서, 안내서 | electronic device 전자기기 | depend on ~에 달려있다 | require 요구하다 | issue 발표하다, 교부하다 | turn in 반납하다, 돌려주다 | shift 교대근무 | In the case of ~의 경우에는 | emergency 비상 | landline 일반전화 | transportation 교통, 수송 | strive 분투하다 | eco-friendly 친환경적인 | offer 제공하다 | various 다양한 | incentive 장려책, 인센티브 | commute 통근하다 | be eligible for ~할 자격이 있다 | discounted transit 수송, 교통체계 | pass 출입증, 탑승권 | purchase 구매 | choose 선택하다 | monetary 금전적인 | reward 보상 | additionally 또한, 추가로 | grant 주다 | access 입장, 접근 | vehicle 차량 | promote 촉진하다, 홍보하다 | initiative 계획, 주도권 | entrance 입구 | stipend 급료 | representative 대표자, 대리인

1. 주제 / 목적 / 대상

이메일의 목적은 무엇인가?
(A) 회사 파일을 제공하려고
(B) 교육 워크숍을 공지하려고
(C) 휴가 일정을 살펴보려고
(D) 개정 절차를 설명하려고

해설 O'Neal 씨가 Hamdi 씨에게 보낸 첫 번째 지문 [이메일], 두 번째 단락에서 'I have attached information regarding the company's rules and guidelines.'라고 했으므로 (A)가 정답이다.

✛ Paraphrasing

company → corporate

2. 동의어

이메일에서 첫 번째 단락, 첫 번째 줄의 밑줄 친 단어 "find"와 의미상 가장 가까운 것은?
(A) 발견하다

(B) 위치를 찾아내다
(C) 드러내다
(D) 얻다

해설 O'Neal 씨가 Hamdi 씨에게 보낸 첫 번째 지문 [이메일], 첫 번째 단락의 'I am certain that you'll find your work environment to be pleasant.' 에서 'find'는 '알게 되다, 발견하다'라는 의미로 쓰였으므로 보기 중 같은 의미를 갖는 (A)가 정답이다.

3. 암시/추론

Hamdi 씨에 관하여 알 수 있는 것은?
(A) 7월 달 내내 출장을 가게 될 것이다.
(B) 회사 안내서를 편집했다.
(C) Ewing 씨가 그녀의 면접을 봤다.
(D) 지하철을 타고 출근한다.

해설 O'Neal 씨가 Hamdi 씨에게 보낸 첫 번째 지문 [이메일], 세 번째 단락에서 'Your first stop will be to the main office next Monday. After that, you will head to our other locations before returning to your branch at the end of the month.'라고 했는데, 메일을 보낸 날짜가 'July 3'인 걸로 미루어 그녀가 7월 말까지 다른 지점들을 돌아본다는 것을 알 수 있으므로 (A)가 정답이다.

4. 암시/추론 – 연계 문제

Hamdi 씨는 어디서 일하겠는가?
(A) Toronto
(B) Syracuse
(C) Ontario
(D) Detroit

해설 O'Neal 씨가 Hamdi 씨에게 보낸 첫 번째 지문 [이메일], 세 번째 단락에서 'In addition, due to limited parking spaces, we encourage employees here to participate in our carpool program.'이라고 했는데, 두 번째 지문 [안내서]의 'Transportation'의 네 번째 단락에서 'The Detroit branch promotes a carpool initiative.'라고 하여 그녀가 Detroit 지점에서 근무한다는 것을 알 수 있으므로 (D)가 정답이다.

5. 상세 정보

안내서에 따르면, AttoTech 전 지점의 공통점은 무엇인가?
(A) 직원들은 특정 전자기기 정책을 따라야 한다.
(B) 회사 차량이 대여 가능하다.
(C) 휴대폰은 근무 전에 따로 보관되어야 한다.
(D) 직원들이 지점에 가려면 대중교통만 이용할 수 있다.

해설 두 번째 지문 [안내서], 'Electronic Device Policy'에서 'The use of electronics depends on the location of your office. The main office in Toronto and our Detroit location require employees to use company issued devices during working hours. Employees at our Syracuse and Ontario locations are required to turn in their devices before each shift.'라고 했으므로 (A)가 정답이다.

6-10번은 다음 편지와 이메일에 관한 문제입니다.

Firstrate Realtors • 715 Leigh Crest • Christchurch NZ 1250

10월 9일

Geneva Boone
6 Overdale 가

Fendalton NZ 1279

Webb 씨께,

귀하의 Andover Point 127번지에 대한 임대차 계약이 12월 31일에 만료될 예정임을 안내드립니다.

임대 갱신을 원하시면, 다음 변경사항에 유념해 주시기 바랍니다. 귀하께 동일한 요금으로 드리고 싶으나, 불가피하게 임대료를 인상하게 되었습니다. **7**이곳의 인상된 물가를 잘 알고 계시리라 생각합니다. **6**이에 저희 5년 표준 월 임대료는 이제 3,000달러입니다. 이는 내년 1월 1일부터 적용될 새로운 요금입니다.

10임대 갱신에 관심 있으시면, 저희 쪽에 알려주시면 관련 서류를 준비하게 됩니다. 임차 종료를 원하시는 경우에도 가급적 빨리 저에게 알려주시기 바랍니다. 감사합니다.

Morris Green

어휘

realtor 부동산 중개인 | notice 공지, 안내문 | lease 임대차 계약 | due 예정된 | expire 만료되다 | renew 갱신하다 | note 주목하다, 유념하다 | following 다음의 | amendment 수정, 개정 | rate 요금 | force 어쩔 수 없이 ~하게 만들다 | increase 증가하다, 인상하다 | be aware of ~를 알다 | monthly 월간의 | standard 일반적인, 표준의 | price of goods 물가 | accordingly 그래서, 그런 이유로 | prepare 준비하다 | relevant 관련된 | paperwork 서류 (작업) | end 끝내다 | tenancy 임차 (기간) | at one's earliest convenience 가급적 빨리

수신: Morris Green 〈m.green@firstrate.co.nz〉
발신: Simon Webb 〈s.webb@hayleys.co.nz〉
날짜: 10월 14일
제목: 임대 계약

Green 씨께,

9우선, 지난 5년간 너무 훌륭한 임대인이셨던 데 대해 Firstrate께 감사 드리고 싶습니다. **7 8**가격을 인상하기로 한 Firstrate의 결정을 충분히 이해합니다. 저희는 상승하는 물가에 맞추느라 전 지점의 가전제품 가격을 인상해야 했습니다. **8 9**그럼에도 불구하고 저희 매장, 특히 Andover Point 지점은 개장 이래 최고 매출을 기록했습니다. **8**실은 저희 가전제품이 너무 잘 팔려서 이 지역 근방에 두 번째 지점을 내려고 알아보고 있습니다.

10본론으로 다시 돌아가서, 저희는 새로운 임대 요금을 수락하기로 했습니다. 금액이 저희가 지불하고자 하는 것보다 높지만, Andover Point가 저희 주력 지점이라 그곳에 건물을 그대로 유지하는 게 더 중요한 것 같습니다. **10**새로운 임대계약서를 보내주시면, 서명하도록 하겠습니다.

다시 한번 여러 가지로 감사 드립니다.

Simon Webb

어휘

agreement 계약(서) | first off 우선 | landlord 임대인, 주인 | completely 완전히 | home appliance 가전 제품 | location 지점 | keep up with 시류에 따르다 | rise 오르다, 증가하다 | record 기록하다 | inception 개시, 시작 | look into 주의 깊게 살피다, 조사하다 | open up 시작하다, 개업하다 | area 지역 | sell 팔리다 | accept 받아들이다, 수락하다 | pay 지불하다 | flagship 주력 상품[서비스] | premises 부지, 지역 | sign 서명하다

6. 상세 정보

편지에 따르면, Andover Point 127번지의 임대 요금은 어느 날짜에 인상되는가?
(A) 1월 1일

(B) 10월 9일
(C) 10월 14일
(D) 12월 31일

해설 첫 번째 지문 [편지], 두 번째 단락에서 'Accordingly, our monthly rate for our standard five-year lease is now $3,000. This will be the new rate going into next year on 1 January.'라고 했으므로 (A)가 정답이다.

7. 상세 정보 – 연계 문제

Green 씨와 Webb 씨 둘 다 무엇에 동의하는가?
(A) 수년간 물가가 상승했다는 것
(B) 광고가 지나치게 비싸다는 것
(C) 상업 부지 공급이 줄어들었다는 것
(D) 지역이 신규 사업체로 포화상태라는 것

해설 첫 번째 지문 [편지], 두 번째 단락에서 'I am sure you are aware of the increasing price of goods here.'라고 했고, 두 번째 지문 [이메일], 첫 번째 단락에서 'We have had to increase prices of our home appliances across our locations to keep up with the rising costs of goods.'라고 했으므로 (A)가 정답이다.

+ Paraphrasing

costs of goods → costs for things

8. 상세 정보

이메일에 따르면, Andover Point 사무공간에는 어떤 종류의 사업체가 있는가?
(A) 상업용 부동산 중개소
(B) 시장조사 기관
(C) 가전제품 매장
(D) 장비 제조업체

해설 두 번째 지문 [이메일], 첫 번째 단락에서 'We have had to increase prices of our home appliances across our locations to keep up with the rising costs of goods. Despite this, our stores, and especially our location at Andover Point, recorded our highest sales since our inception. We have actually been looking into opening up a second location around this area as our home appliances have been selling so well.'라고 했으므로 (C)가 정답이다.

9. 사실 확인

Webb 씨의 사업체에 관하여 이메일에서 언급하는 것은?
(A) 신문에 소개됐다.
(B) 5년간 운영해왔다.
(C) 다른 회사의 자회사다.
(D) 해외 진출을 고려 중이다.

해설 두 번째 지문 [이메일], 첫 번째 단락에서 'First off, I would like to thank Firstrate so much for being such excellent landlords over the past five years.'라고 하며, 'Despite this, our stores, and especially our location at Andover Point, recorded our highest sales since our inception.'라고 했으므로 (B)가 정답이다.

10. 상세 정보 – 연계 문제

Webb 씨는 Firstrate Realtors의 요청에 어떻게 대응하는가?
(A) 가격 비교를 위해 다른 부동산 중개인을 찾는 것으로
(B) 확장할 새로운 지점을 제안하는 것으로
(C) 부동산 가격에 대해 조사를 실시하는 것으로
(D) 새로운 임대 가격 갱신에 동의하는 것으로

해설 첫 번째 지문 [편지], 세 번째 단락에서 'If you are interested in renewing your lease, please let us know and we will prepare the relevant paperwork.'라고 했는데, 두 번째 지문 [이메일], 두 번째 단락에서 'To bring us back on topic, we have decided to accept the lease at the new price.'라고 하며 'If you could send the new lease over, we will be happy to sign it.'이라고 했으므로 (D)가 정답이다.

+ Paraphrasing

accept the lease at the new price → agree to renew the lease at the new price

---

11-15번은 다음 안내책자, 이메일, 광고에 관한 문제입니다.

Juniper 그룹

인터넷 마케팅 필요에 관한 모든 것을 원스톱으로 해결해줄 The Juniper 그룹을 통해 광고가 원하는 타깃층에 닿을 수 있게 하세요. **11** **15**저희는 Amsterdam에 본사를 두고 10년 넘게 운영해왔으며, 저희 실적이 모든 걸 말해줍니다. 저희는 소셜 미디어 마케팅, 검색엔진 최적화를 비롯해 다양한 서비스를 제공합니다. **12**junipergroup.com에서 저희 예전 작업들을 살펴보시거나 137-555-9485로 저희에게 전화주세요. 필요하신 사항을 바탕으로, 저희가 제공하는 전체 서비스 목록을 제공해 드립니다. **14**지금 등록하세요, 첫 고객이시라면 전체 금액에서 10퍼센트를 할인해 드립니다.

어휘
advertisement 광고 | reach 닿다, 미치다 | audience 관객 | one-stop 원스톱, 한 곳에 다 할 수 있는 | headquarter ~에 본사를 두다 | in business 영업 중인 | track record 실적 | speak for itself 자명한 | a range of 다양한 | search engine 검색 엔진 | optimization 최적화 | browse through ~를 훑어보다, 살펴보다 | previous 이전의 | sign up 등록하다 | knock off (값을) 인하하다

수신: jbarton@sbmerch.com
발신: services@junipergroup.com
날짜: 4월 21일
제목: 회신: 업데이트

Barton 씨께,

13회신이 늦어져 진심으로 죄송한 말씀을 드립니다. 저희가 사무실 이사로 정신이 없어서, 업무가 지연되었습니다. 귀하의 대금을 수령하였고 최대한 빨리 주문을 처리해 드릴 예정임을 알려드리고자 합니다.

14또한 이것은 저희의 통상적인 기준이 전혀 아니라는 것을 알아주시길 바라며, 이로 인해 저희 회사와의 첫 번째 경험이 훼손되지 않기를 바랍니다. 이후의 경험은 흠잡을 데 없도록 최선을 다하겠습니다.

정말 감사드립니다.

Lora Wong

어휘
sincerely 진심으로 | delay 지연 | out of one's mind 제정신이 아닌 | move 이사하다 | fall behind 뒤쳐지다 | reassure 안심시키다 | payment 지불, 결제 | fulfill 이행하다 | usual 평상시의, 통상의 | standard 기준 | mar 훼손하다, 망치다 | impeccable 흠잡을 데 없는

모집 중

15The Juniper 그룹에서는 Amsterdam 팀에 합류할 재능 있는 인턴을 찾고 있습니다. 정규직 전환이 가능한 사내 유급 인턴십입니다. **15**인

턴이 되면, 직원 행정업무를 지원하게 됩니다. 또한 이메일로 저희 팀과 고객 간 원활한 커뮤니케이션을 담당하게 됩니다. 적임자는 서비스 마인드가 있고, 소셜 미디어를 자주 하거나 이에 친숙해야 합니다. 관심 있는 지원자는 Lora Wong에게 137-555-9485로 연락하거나 lwong@junipergroup.com으로 직접 문의하시면 됩니다.

어휘
seek 찾다, 구하다 | talented 재능 있는 | crew (같은 일에 종사하는) 팀, 조 | in-house (조직) 내부의 | paid internship 유급 인턴십 | possibility 가능성 | lead to ~로 이어지다 | full-time position 정규직 | administrative support 행정 지원 | be responsible for ~에 책임이 있다 | ensure 보장하다 | smooth 순조로운, 매끄러운 | via ~을 통해 | ideal 이상적인 | service-oriented 서비스 지향적인 | frequent 잦은, 빈번한 | be familiar with ~에 익숙하다 | applicant 지원자 | contact ~에게 연락하다 | inquire 문의하다 | directly 직접

---

11. 상세 정보

안내책자에서는 Juniper 그룹의 사업 중 어떤 측면을 강조하는가?
(A) 중요 고객
(B) 수익 증가
(C) 낮은 가격
(D) 높은 명성

해설 첫 번째 지문 [안내책자]에서 'we have been in business for over 10 years, and our track record speaks for itself.'라고 했으므로 (D)가 정답이다. speak for itself는 '분명한 의미를 갖는다, 그 이상의 설명을 필요로 하지 않다'는 뜻이다.

12. 암시/추론

안내책자에 따르면, Juniper 그룹에 관하여 알 수 있는 것은?
(A) 국제적인 회사다
(B) 온라인에 작업 샘플이 올려져 있다.
(C) 신문광고를 만든다.
(D) 고객에게 보증금 지불을 요구한다.

해설 첫 번째 지문 [안내책자]에서 'Browse through some of our previous work at junipergroup.com'이라고 했으므로 (B)가 정답이다.

13. 상세 정보

이메일에 따르면, 왜 Wong 씨로부터 연락이 늦어졌는가?
(A) 회사가 사무실을 이전했다.
(B) 회사가 직원감축을 겪었다.
(C) 회사에 업무가 너무 많았다.
(D) 회사가 문을 닫았다.

해설 두 번째 지문 [Wong 씨가 Barton 씨에게 보낸 이메일], 첫 번째 단락에서 'I am sincerely sorry for the delay in getting back to you. We have been out of our minds due to moving offices, so things have fallen behind.'라고 했으므로 (A)가 정답이다.

+ Paraphrasing

move → relocate, fall behind → slow

14. 암시/추론 - 연계 문제

Barton 씨의 광고 주문에 관하여 무엇이 사실이겠는가?
(A) 새로운 사업을 광고하고 있다.
(B) 아주 성공적이었다.
(C) 실수로 삭제되었다.
(D) 할인가에 구입되었다.

해설 첫 번째 지문 [안내책자]에서 'Sign up now and if you are a first-time customer, we'll knock 10 percent off your price.'라고 하

였는데, 두 번째 지문[Wong씨가 Barton씨에게 보낸 이메일], 두 번째 단락에서 'I also want you to know that this is not at all our usual standards, and I hope this doesn't mar your first experience with us.'라고 하여 Barton 씨가 첫 이용 고객으로 10퍼센트 할인을 받았을 것을 알 수 있으므로 (D)가 정답이다.

+ Paraphrasing

price → rate

15. 상세 정보 – 연계 문제

인턴의 업무는 무엇인가?

(A) 회사 본사 직원을 지원하는 것
(B) 고객을 직접 만나러 해외로 출장 가는 것
(C) 온라인 마케팅 캠페인을 만드는 것
(D) 해외 시장조사를 실시하는 것

해설 첫 번째 지문[안내책자]에서 'Headquartered in Amsterdam, we have been in business for over 10 years, and our track record speaks for itself.'라고 했고, 세 번째 지문[광고]에서 'The Juniper Group is seeking talented interns to join our crew in Amsterdam.'라고 하면서 'As an intern, you will provide administrative support for our employees.'라고 하여 본사인 Amsterdam 직원의 행정지원 업무를 하게 된다는 것을 알 수 있으므로 (A)가 정답이다.

+ Paraphrasing

provide support for → assist

16-20번은 다음 기사, 웹 페이지, 일정에 관한 문제입니다.

앞서가기 위해 후원하기

오늘날처럼 광고로 가득한 세상에서 기업은 눈에 띄면서 고객에게 메시지를 전달하려고 다양한 방법을 찾고 있다. 후원이 바로 그러한 방법을 제공하는데, 대상 인구층에 돋보이는 방법이 된다. 그렇다면 후원은 어떻게 작용할까?

상업 후원은 특정한 행사, 활동, 단체를 지원하기 위해 기업에서 지불하는 현금을 가리킨다. 이것은 주로 기업에서 지역 사회를 돕거나 특별한 대의에 지지를 표현하려는 목적으로 행해진다.

후원이 기업의 자산을 낭비하는 것처럼 보일 수 있으나, 많은 혜택을 가져다 줄 수 있다. **16중요한 것은, 회사가 대중의 인기를 얻게 된다는 것이다.** 회사가 자선행사를 후원하는 경우, 대중은 회사를 긍정적으로 바라볼 수 있다. **17이는 더 많은 사람들이 상품을 구입하게 되면서 기업의 사업 증대로 이어질 수도 있다.** 게다가 사람들이 기업의 제품을 다른 사람들에게 추천할 가능성도 더 높아질 수 있다.

후원은 많은 기업에서 이익을 증대시키면서 지역 사회를 이롭게 하는 귀중한 도구가 될 수 있다.

어휘

sponsor 스폰서가 되다, 후원하다 | get ahead 성공하다, 앞서다 | advertisement 광고 | saturated 포화된 | business 사업(체) | offer 제공하다 | stand out 눈에 띄다 | demographic 인구통계학 | sponsorship 후원, 협찬 | commercial 상업적인 | refer to ~를 가리키다, 나타내다 | cash 현금 | specific 특정한 | organization 조직, 기관 | particular 특정한, 특별한 | cause 이유, 대의명분 | help out 도와주다 | community 지역 사회 | appear ~처럼 보이다 | drain 유출, 고갈, 낭비 | resources 자원, 자산 | confer 수여[부여]하다 | benefit 이득, 혜택; ~에게 이롭다 | importantly 중요하게 | gain 얻다 | favor 인기 | public 대중 | instance 사례, 경우 | charity 자선 | view 보다 | positive 긍정적인 | lead to ~로 이어지다 | increase 증가하다 | additionally 게다가 | valuable 소중한, 귀중한 | tool 도구, 수단 | profit 수익, 이윤

---

www.holbrookcounty.gov

홈	행사	티켓 구입	후원하기

모든 행사는 자치주에서 운영하며, 모든 수익금은 지역 사회를 돕는데 사용됩니다. 저희의 모든 행사에 후원할 수 있으며 몇 가지 큰 혜택을 받을 수 있습니다. 다가오는 행사에 대해 아래와 같이 제공해 드립니다:

18노숙자 지원' 음악 축제 5월 18일	**기업가와의 만남 6월 6일**	**연례 나무 심기 행사 6월 18일**
1 주요 후원사 10,000달러 3 공동 후원사 7,000달러	3 후원사 7,000달러	2 후원사 3,000달러
- **18주요 후원사의 이름을 딴 메인 무대** - **17상호가 들어간 대형 표지판 2개** - 행사 뒤풀이 저녁파티 입장권 - 마케팅 및 홍보 자료에 포함	- 행사장 내 회사명이 적힌 현수막 - **17상호가 들어간 대형 표지판 1개** - 직원 주차장 이용 - 마케팅 및 홍보 자료에 포함	- 회사에 바치는 나무 1그루 - **17상호가 들어간 표지판 1개** - 마케팅 및 홍보 자료에 포함

어휘

run 운영하다 | county 자치주, 카운티 | proceeds 수익금 | go towards ~에 쓰이다 | following 다음 | upcoming 다가오는 | the homeless 노숙자 | main 주요한 | co-sponsors 공동 후원자 | stage 무대 | name 명명하다 | sign 표지판 | access 입장 | inclusion 포함 | promotional material 홍보 자료 | entrepreneur 기업가 | Meet and Greet (유명인을) 만나는 행사 | banner 현수막 | carpark 주차장 | annual 연간의 | tree-planting 나무심기 | dedicate to ~에 바치다

**'노숙자 지원' 음악 축제
행사 일정
4월 29일, 토요일**

무대로 찾아오는 방법은 첨부된 지도를 참고해 주십시오. **20홀마다 최대 수용인원이 있으며 선착순으로 운영됩니다. 작년에 저희가 일부 참석자를 돌려보내야 했다는 점을 유념하셔서, 일찍 도착해 주시기 바랍니다.**

시간	행사	장소
오후 4시 30분	Yeonwoo Kim 피아노 연주회	**19"DreamIns" 공연장**
오후 4시 30분	록 그룹 "Yellow Glasses"	**19"A&E Partners" 무대**
오후 7시	**18스타 R&B 가수 "Hugo Monte"**	**1819"Reach Services" 메인 무대**
오후 10시	재즈 그룹 "Kilo Davis"	**19"Pylo Vendors" 무대**
오후 10시	R&B 가수 "Shona Veronica"	**19"DreamIns" 공연장**
오후 11시 30분	폐회사	**19"Reach Services" 메인 무대**

*비고: 날씨가 좋으면, Hugo Monte가 "DreamIns" 공연장에서 공연할 수 있습니다.

16. 상세 정보

기사에 따르면, 행사를 후원하는 기업에게 주어지는 주요 혜택은 무엇인가?

(A) 자격을 충족하는 지원자 수 증가
(B) 기업의 사회적 입지 향상
(C) 기업에 대한 세금 인하
(D) 여러 장소로 진출할 폭넓은 기회

해설 첫 번째 지문 [기사], 세 번째 단락에서 'Importantly, the company gains favor with the public.'이라고 했으므로 (B)가 정답이다.

17. 사실 확인

웹 페이지에서 언급된 것은?

(A) 후원사는 할인을 받을 수 있다.
(B) 음악 축제에 후원하면 무료 티켓도 제공한다.
(C) 모든 후원사는 상호가 들어간 표지판을 받는다.
(D) 나무 헌정은 후원사 1곳으로 한정된다.

해설 두 번째 지문 [웹 페이지], 표에서 모든 행사에 각각 'Two large signs posted with your business name', 'One large sign posted with your business name', 'One sign posted with your business name' 이 들어 있으므로 (C)가 정답이다.

18. 상세 정보 – 연계 문제

일정에 나와있는 어떤 회사가 음악 축제의 주요 후원사인가?

(A) Dreamins
(B) Reach Services
(C) A&E Partners
(D) Pylo Vendors

해설 두 번째 지문 [웹 페이지], 표의 'Help the Homeless' Music Festival'에서 후원 혜택 중 하나가 'Main stage named for the main sponsor'라고 했는데, 세 번째 지문 [일정], 표의 Location(장소)에서 메인 무대명이 '"Reach Services" Main Stage'임을 알 수 있으므로 (B)가 정답이다.

19. 상세 정보 – 연계 문제

기업들은 기사에서 어떤 조언을 따랐는가?

(A) 다른 회사와 제휴해 행사를 함께 후원했다.
(B) 후원하기 전 행사 계획 단계에 참여했다.
(C) 후원에 대한 추가 특혜를 요청했다.
(D) 이미지 향상에 도움이 될 수 있게 자선 행사를 후원했다.

해설 첫 번째 지문 [기사], 세 번째 단락에서 'In instances where a company sponsors a charity event, the public may view the company in a favorable light. This may lead to increased business for the company as more people may buy their products. Additionally, people may be more likely to recommend their products to other people.'이라고 했는데, 세 번째 지문 [일정], 표의 'Location'의 "DreamIns" Theater', '"A&E Partners" Stage', '"Reach Services" Stage', '"Pylo Vendors" Stage'에서 많은 기업이 자선행사를 후원했음을 알 수 있으므로 (D)가 정답이다.

20. 암시/추론

일정을 보고 무엇을 결론지을 수 있는가?

(A) 폐회사는 시간을 초과해 진행될 수 있다.
(B) 주차 자리는 티켓의 일부로 포함되지 않는다.
(C) 축제는 보통 수용인원을 초과한다.
(D) Hugo Monte가 작년에 축제에서 공연했다.

해설 세 번째 지문 [일정]에서 'Each hall has a maximum capacity and will operate on a 'first come, first serve' basis. Please remember that we had to turn away some attendees last year, so make sure to arrive early.'라고 했으므로 (C)가 정답이다.

CASE 실전훈련

본서 p.306

1. (B)   2. (C)   3. (D)   4. (A)   5. (C)   6. (C)
7. (B)   8. (B)   9. (C)   10. (A)   11. (A)   12. (D)
13. (D)   14. (B)   15. (C)   16. (A)   17. (D)   18. (C)
19. (A)   20. (C)   21. (C)   22. (D)

1-2번은 다음 채팅 대화에 관한 문제입니다.

Bart Townsley (오전 11시 08분)
Ashberg Power Tools에 연락해 주셔서 감사합니다. 제 이름은 Bart입니다. 무엇을 도와 드릴까요?

Larry Davis (오전 11시 09분)
🏵안녕하세요, Bart 씨. 제가 8주 전에 제품 하나를 되돌려 보냈는데, 제 계정 페이지의 주문 상태가 여전히 "미완료"라고 나와서요.

Bart Townsley (오전 11시 09분)
제가 기꺼이 대신 확인해 드리겠습니다. 배송 추적 번호 또는 거래내역서 번호를 알려주시겠습니까?

Larry Davis (오전 11시 10분)
거래내역서 번호는 10395830이고, 배송 추적 번호는 IG3145입니다.

Bart Townsley (오전 11시 10분)
감사합니다. 제가 저희 컴퓨터를 확인하는 동안 잠시만 기다려 주시기 바랍니다. 잠깐이면 됩니다.

Bart Townsley (오전 11시 13분)
여전히 "미완료"라고 되어 있기는 하지만, 저희가 반품된 제품을 받았고 귀하의 United 신용카드로 입금되었습니다. 제가 지금 수동으로 "환불 완료" 상태로 업데이트하겠습니다. 종종 저희 컴퓨터 프로그램이 자동으로 업데이트되는 데 며칠 걸립니다.

Larry Davis (오전 11시 16분)
정말 감사합니다. 🏵비용 입금이 처리되었는지 확실히 할 수 있게 제 신용카드 명세서를 확인해 볼게요.

Bart Townsley (오전 11시 17분)
🏵말씀하실 필요도 없습니다. 고객님의 이메일 수신함에 이 채팅 대화 사본을 받으시게 됩니다. 다른 어떤 질문이나 문제라도 있으시면 주저하지 마시고 저희에게 다시 연락 주십시오.

Larry Davis (오전 11시 18분)
도와 주셔서 감사합니다!

어휘

contact 연락하다 | assist 돕다 | order status 주문 상태 | account 계정 | incomplete 완료되지 않은 | tracking number 배송 추적 번호 | invoice 거래내역서 | patient 참을성 있는 | receive 받다 | returned 반품된 | credit 입금하다 | manually 수작업으로 | refunded 환불된 | on its own (기계 등이) 자동으로 | statement 명세서 | make sure ~임을 확실히 하다 | process 처리하다 | transcript 사본, 필사본 | session (특정 활동에 대한) 시간 | hesitate to do ~하기를 주저하다 | appreciate 감사하다

어휘

on sale 판매 중인 | intermission (연극 등의) 중간 휴식 시간 | hold 개최하다, 열다 | promptly 정각에, 즉시 | in residence 전속의 | rotating 번갈아 가며 하는 | strive 애쓰다 | bring 소개하다 | talent 인재 | addition 추가, 추가되는 것 | regular 정규의 | troupe 공연단, 극단 | matinee performance 낮 공연 | celebrate 축하하다 | next generation 차세대 | field 분야 | feature 특징으로 하다 | an assortment of 여러 가지의 | favorite 선호하는 것 | select 선정하다 | perform 공연하다

1. 상세 정보

Davis 씨는 왜 Ashberg Power Tools에 연락했는가?
(A) 환불 규정에 관해 문의하기 위해
(B) 반품 상태를 확인하기 위해
(C) 신용카드 명세서 사본을 검토하기 위해
(D) 주문 사항에서 빠진 제품을 알리기 위해

해설 11시 09분 메시지에서 Davis 씨가 'Hello, Bart. I sent back an item eight weeks ago, but the order status on my account page still says "incomplete."'라고 했으므로 (B)가 정답이다.

2. 화자 의도 파악

오전 11시 17분에, Townsley 씨가 "말씀하실 필요도 없습니다"라고 한 것은 무엇을 의미하겠는가?
(A) 나중에 Davis 씨에게 연락할 것이다.
(B) Davis 씨가 불만스러워한다는 것을 알아차리고 있다.
(C) Davis 씨의 반응을 이해하고 있다.
(D) Davis 씨를 돕게 되어 기뻐하고 있다.

해설 오전 11시 16분 메시지에서 Davis 씨가 'I'll check my credit card statement to make sure the credit was processed.'라고 말하자, Townsley 씨가 'Needless to say.'라고 답변하고 있으므로 (C)가 정답이다. Needless to say는 'very likely or obvious, self-evident'라는 뜻이다.

3-5번은 다음 뉴스 게시판에 관한 문제입니다.

Evansville 발레 뉴스

현재 판매 중인 시즌 입장권
지금 www.evansvilleballet.com/seasontickets에서 시즌 입장권을 주문하십시오.
4월 3일-11일: 〈The Tea Dance〉 (1시간 30분, 중간 휴식 시간 1회)
5 6월 5일-13일: 〈Mirage〉 (2시간 30분, 중간 휴식 시간 1회)
3 8월 13일-21일: 〈Titan's Curse〉 (1시간, 중간 휴식 시간 없음)
10월 29일 – 11월 7일: 〈Peter Pan〉 (3시간, 중간 휴식 시간 2회)
공연은 Tatiana Theater에서 오후 7시 정각에 시작됩니다.

전속 무용수 시리즈
번갈아 가며 진행되는 저희 '전속 무용수' 프로그램에서는 전 세계에서 온 새로운 인재를 저희 정규 발레단 공연의 추가 무용수로 소개해 드리기 위해 애쓰고 있습니다. **4** 그들은 많은 상을 받았고, 국제적으로 명성이 있습니다. 이 무용수들에 의해 진행되는 오후 1시 낮 공연 특별 시리즈에 함께 하셔서 발레 분야에 입성하는 차세대 인재를 축하할 수 있도록 도와주십시오. 각 공연은 저희 전속 무용수들 중 한 명이 가장 선호하는 발레를 선택해서 연기하는 것이 특징입니다.

4월 3일: Elaine Thomas
5 6월 5일: Luis Ruiz
8월 13일: Daniela Hedenheim
10월 29일: Olga Cieminski

3. 상세 정보

어느 발레가 휴식 없이 공연될 것인가?
(A) The Tea Dance
(B) Mirage
(C) Peter Pan
(D) Titan's Curse

해설 첫 단락에 'August 13-21: *Titan's Curse* (1 hour with no intermission)'라고 쓰여 있으므로 (D)가 정답이다.

+ Paraphrasing

without a break → no intermission

4. 암시/추론

'전속 무용수'에 관해 무엇이 사실일 것 같은가?
(A) 모두 전 세계적으로 잘 알려져 있다.
(B) 전에 Evansville에서 공연한 적이 있다.
(C) 정규 무용수들보다 나이가 더 많다.
(D) 배우로서 전문적으로 교육받았다.

해설 두 번째 단락에 'They've received many awards and much international recognition.'이라고 쓰여 있으므로 (A)가 정답이다.

+ Paraphrasing

much international recognition → all well-known around the globe

5. 암시/추론

누가 Mirage에서 공연하겠는가?
(A) Thomas 씨
(B) Hedenheim 씨
(C) Ruiz 씨
(D) Cieminski 씨

해설 상단에 'June 5-13: *Mirage* (2 1/2 hours with 1 intermission).'라고 되어 있고, 하단에 June 5: Luis Ruiz라고 했으므로 (C)가 정답이다.

6-8번은 다음 기사에 관한 문제입니다.

베트남, HANOI, 10월 13일 — **6B** 스튜디오는 현재 최신 프로젝트인 Street Footballers의 12월 출시를 준비하고 있다고 Blue Games가 오늘 막 성명을 발표했다. —[1]—. 약 300명의 행운의 프로 플레이어들이 다음 주에 베타 버전을 써볼 기회를 가지게 될 것이다. —[2]—. Street Footballers 자체가 거리 축구 경기의 방식을 택하고 있고, 거기서 플레이어들은 5명이 한 그룹으로 경기한다. —[3]—. **7A** 플레이어들은 온라인 경기에 참여하고 다른 플레이어들과 함께 그룹을 만든다. 그들은 시스템에 의해 그룹이 자동으로 분류된다. **7C** 플레이어들이 각자의 아바타를 만드는 것에는 무한한 가능성이 있다. —[4]—. **7D** 플레이어들은 또한 우리 오프라인 매장에서 아주 다양한 스포츠용품도 구입할 수 있다.

어휘

release 발표하다, 공개하다 | statement 성명 | currently 현재 | prepare for ~을 준비하다 | launch 출시, 공개 | around 약, 대략 | get the chance to ~할 기회를 가지다 | format 방식, 유형 | be able to ~할 수 있다 | join 참여하다, 함께하다 | automatically 자동으로 | group 그룹을 이루다 | limitless 무제한의 | possibility 가능성 | a wide range of 아주 다양한 | sporting goods 스포츠 용품

6. 암시 / 추론

Street Footballers는 무엇이겠는가?
(A) 스포츠 행사
(B) 교육 프로그램
(C) 비디오 게임
(D) TV 프로그램

해설 도입부에 'Blue Games just released a statement today that the studio is currently preparing for the launch of its latest project, Street Footballers, in December.'라고 한 후, 'Around 300 lucky professional players will get the chance to try the beta version next week.'라고 제시되어 있으므로 (C)가 정답이다.

7. 사실 확인

Street Footballers에 관해 언급되지 않은 것은 무엇인가?
(A) 플레이어들이 온라인 경기에 참여할 수 있다.
(B) 플레이어들이 자신들의 아이템을 교환할 수 있다.
(C) 플레이어들이 캐릭터를 만들 수 있다.
(D) 플레이어들이 상품을 구입할 수 있다.

해설 중반부에 'Players will be able to join an online match and group with other players.'라고 한 것에서 (A), 'There are limitless possibilities for players in building their avatars.'라고 한 것에서 (C), 'Players could also buy a wide range of sporting goods in our offline store.'라고 한 것에서 (D)는 모두 언급된 내용으로 확인되므로 (B)가 정답이다.

8. 문장 삽입

[1], [2], [3] 그리고 [4]로 표시된 곳 중, 다음 문장이 들어갈 가장 적절한 것은?

"그들은 게임이 정식으로 출시되기 전에 개발업체에 의견을 제공할 것이다."

(A) [1]
(B) [2]
(C) [3]
(D) [4]

해설 주어진 문장에 They가 가리키는 것은 초반부의 'Around 300 lucky professional players will get the chance to try the beta version next week.'라고 제시된 문장에서 Around 300 lucky professional players일 것이므로, 그 문장 바로 뒤인 (B)가 정답이다.

9-12번은 다음 공지에 관한 문제입니다.

GREENVIEW PARK

제안서 요청

Greenview Park는 공원의 일일 유지 관리를 위해 현재 평판 좋은 청소 용역 업체를 찾고 있습니다. [9]업체들은 9월 29일부터 10월 31일까지 Timlin Avenue 33번지, 공원 관리 사무소에 제안서를 제출하실 수 있습니다. 지연된 제출물은 수락하지 않습니다.

[10D]모든 제안서에는 업체의 영업 허가증, 연혁, 자격 사항, 그리고 장점들이 담겨 있어야 합니다. [10C]제안서 4부가 필요합니다. [10B]그 제안서에는 또한 지난 6개월 이내에 업체의 고객들로부터 받은 추천서를 적어도 두 통 포함해야 합니다. [12]질문이 있으시면 위 주소에 있는 Ms. Jessica Roberts에게 보내시면 됩니다. 질문은 반드시 서면으로 제출되어야 하고, 그에 맞게 답변될 것입니다.

[11]제안서들은 공원 위원회에 의해 평가될 것입니다. 다섯 곳의 최종 후보로 선정되는 업체들은 11월 4일에 위원회 앞에서 각자의 제안서를 발표해야 할 것입니다. 통과된 회사는 우편으로 통보받을 것입니다. 최종 결정은 업체의 적합성 및 전문 기술을 바탕으로 이루어질 것입니다.

어휘

call for ~에 대한 요청 | proposal 제안, 제안서 | currently 현재 | look for ~을 찾다 | reputable 평판 좋은 | vendor 공급업체, 판매자 | maintenance 유지 관리 | submit 제출하다 | accept 받다 | submission 제출, 제출되는 것 | include 포함하다 | qualification 자격 사항, 자격 요건 | advantage 장점 | required 필요한, 필수의 | at least 최소한, 적어도 | reference letter 추천서 | be directed to ~로 보내지다 | respond 응답하다 | accordingly 그에 따라 | assess 평가하다 | shortlisted 최종 후보 명단에 오른 | present 발표하다 | notify ~에게 통보하다 | make a final decision 최종 결정을 내리다 | based on ~을 바탕으로 | suitability 적합성 | expertise 전문 기술, 전문 지식

9. 상세 정보

10월 31일 이후에 무슨 일이 있을 것인가?
(A) 유지 관리가 실시될 것이다.
(B) 프로젝트들이 재배정될 것이다.
(C) 제안서들이 평가될 것이다.
(D) 어떤 팀이 구성될 것이다.

해설 첫 번째 단락에 'Businesses may submit their proposals starting from September 29 to October 31 to the Park Management Office, 33 Timlin Avenue.'라고 제시되어 있는 것에서 제출이 끝난 10월 31일 이후에는 제안서들이 평가될 것임을 알 수 있으므로 (C)가 정답이다.

10. 사실 확인

제안서 제출에 요구되지 않은 것은 무엇인가?
(A) 샘플 사진들
(B) 추천서 2통
(C) 제안서의 사본
(D) 강점에 대한 설명

해설 두 번째 단락에 'Every proposal must include the vendor's business license, history, qualifications, and advantages.'에서 (D), 'Four copies of the proposal are required.'라고 한 것에서 (C), 'The proposal shall also include at least two reference letters from the vendor's clients within the past six months.'라고 한 것에서 (B)는 모두 요구되는 사항으로 확인되므로 (A)가 정답이다.

11. 암시/추론

공원 위원회에 관해 알 수 있는 것은?
(A) 제출된 제안서들을 고려할 것이다.
(B) 계획된 프로젝트를 온라인으로 게시한다.
(C) 잔디를 관리하는 일에 중점을 둔다.
(D) 방문객 센터를 운영할 계획이다.

해설 세 번째 단락에 'Proposals will be assessed by the Park's Committee.'라고 제시되어 있으므로 (A)가 정답이다.

✦ Paraphrasing

Proposals will be assessed → consider submitted proposals

12. 암시/추론

Ms. Roberts에 관해 알 수 있는 것은?
(A) 곧 자신의 진로를 변경할 것이다.
(B) 뛰어난 행정 능력을 지니고 있다.
(C) 회사 담당자에게 이메일을 보냈다.
(D) 업체들에게 답변을 제공할 것이다.

해설 두 번째 단락 후반부에 'Any questions should be directed to Ms. Jessica Roberts at the address above.'라고 한 후, 'They must be submitted in writing and will be responded to accordingly.'라고 제시되어 있으므로 (D)가 정답이다.

13-17번은 다음 두 이메일에 관한 문제입니다.

수신: customersupport@topride.com
발신: cgupta@fivestar.com
날짜: 7월 28일, 화요일, 오전 11:17
제목: 도움 문의

고객 서비스 담당자께,

귀사의 웹 페이지를 통해 예약하는 데 계속 실패했음을 알려 드리고자 이 메일을 씁니다. 계속 반복해도 페이지가 뜨지 않는 걸보니 예약 화면이 먹통인 것 같습니다.

13 저와 제 친척들은 2주 뒤 New Mexico로 7일간 여행을 갈 계획이며, 그곳에 있는 동안 렌트할 차가 필요합니다. **14** 6인승에, 대형 배낭 6개를 넣을 수 있는 널찍한 트렁크가 있고 하루에 비용이 120달러를 넘지 않는 자동차를 원합니다.

저는 작년에 귀사의 서비스를 이용해본 경험이 있는데, 그때 당시 우산 세트 외에 추가 서비스를 제공해 주셨던 걸로 알고 있었습니다. 지금도 그런 추가 서비스를 제공해 주시나요? 아니면 제가 혜택을 받을 있는 다른 서비스가 있나요?

곧 답변 주실 수 있기를 고대합니다.

Chandra Gupta

어휘
inquiry 문의 | assistance 도움, 지원 | inform A that A에게 ~라고 알리다 | fail to do ~하는 데 실패하다, ~하지 못하다 | make a booking 예약하다 | It seems that ~인 것 같다 | broken 망가진, 고장 난 | load 화면에 띄우다 | over and over again 계속 반복해서 | relative 친척 | for rent 대여용의, 임대용의 | contain 포함하다 | spacious 널찍한 | no more than ~을 넘지 않는, ~이내의 | notice that ~임을 알게 되다, ~임에 주목하다 | offer 제공하다 | extra 별도의 | including ~을 포함해 | benefit from ~로부터 혜택을 보다 | look forward to -ing ~하기를 고대하다

수신: cgupta@fivestar.com
발신: ianrich@topride.com
날짜: 7월 28일, 화요일, 오후 2:25
제목: 회신: 도움 문의

Gupta 씨께,

저희 웹 사이트에 접속하려 하셨을 때 겪으셨던 좋지 못한 경험에 대해 사과의 말씀드립니다. 귀하의 우려를 저희 IT팀에 전달했으며, 그쪽에서 두어 시간 후에 문제가 해결될 것이라고 합니다. 오후 5시경 다시 예약을 진행해보시길 바랍니다

14 16 귀하의 요건과 관련하여 제가 제안해 드릴 수 있는 것은 HR-V Uniq입니다. 이 자동차는 귀하의 모든 요건을 완벽히 충족합니다. 이메일에서 언급하셨던 추가 서비스와 관련해서는, 추가 비용을 내시면 이용 가능합니다. **15** 또한 저희 Business Reference Program에 참여하는 호텔 중 한 곳에 숙박하시는 경우, 15퍼센트 할인을 받으실 수 있다는 소식을 알려 드리게 되어 대단히 기쁘게 생각합니다.

추가 문의사항이 있으시면, 555-374-7774번으로 전화하셔서 저희 고객 서비스 직원과 이야기하실 수 있습니다. **17** 또한 최근 출시된 저희 앱을 다운받으셔서 예약하실 수 있습니다.

제 답변이 만족스러우셨기를 바랍니다.

Ian Richardson, 고객 서비스 담당자

Top Ride

어휘
apologize for ~에 대해 사과하다 | access 접속하다, 이용하다 | forward 전달하다 | concern 우려, 걱정 | fix 바로잡다 | retry to do ~하는 것을 다시 해보다 | in regard with ~와 관련해 | requirement 요건, 필요 조건 | suggestion 제안, 의견 | meet 충족하다 | regarding ~와 관련해 | refer to ~를 언급하다 | available 이용 가능한 | at an additional fee 추가 요금을 내고 | let A know that A에게 ~라고 알리다 | take part in ~에 참여하다 | further 추가적인 | representative 직원 | recently 최근에 | launch 출시하다 | response 답변, 반응 | satisfy 만족시키다

13. 사실 확인

첫 번째 이메일은 Gupta 씨에 관해 무엇을 언급하는가?
(A) New Mexico에 거주하고 있다.
(B) Top Ride의 서비스를 이용해 본 적이 없다.
(C) 막 새로운 차량을 구입했다.
(D) 일주일 동안 대여할 자동차가 필요하다.

해설 첫 번째 지문[이메일] 두 번째 단락에서 'I and my relatives are planning to fly to New Mexico in two weeks for a 7-day trip, and we would need a car for rent for our time there.'라고 했으므로 (D)가 정답이다.

✦ Paraphrasing

for a 7-day trip → for one week

14. 사실 확인 - 연계 문제

HR-V Uniq에 관해 무엇이 사실인가?
(A) Gupta 씨에게 너무 비싸다.
(B) 최대 6명까지 태울 수 있다.
(C) Top Ride의 베스트셀러이다.
(D) 트렁크가 넓지 않다.

해설 첫 번째 지문[이메일] 두 번째 단락에서 'I would love to have a car that can contain six people with a spacious trunk for six large backpacks.'라고 했고, 두 번째 지문[이메일] 두 번째 단락에서 'In regard with your requirements, my suggestion would be HR-V Uniq. The car meets all of your requirements perfectly.'라고 했으므로 (B)가 정답이다.

15. 상세 정보

Richardson 씨는 Gupta 씨에게 무엇을 제안하는가?
(A) 무료 우산 세트
(B) 여행 가이드북
(C) 호텔 예약에 대한 할인 프로그램
(D) 자동차 대여 예약에 대한 단골고객 프로그램

해설 두 번째 지문 [이메일] 두 번째 단락에서 'I am also more than pleased to let you know that you can get 15% discount if you stay at one of the hotels that take part in our Business Reference Program.'라고 했으므로 (C)가 정답이다.

16. 동의어

두 번째 이메일에서, 두 번째 단락, 첫 번째 줄의 단어 "meets"와 의미상 가장 가까운 것은?

(A) 충족하다
(B) 위치를 찾다
(C) 제공하다
(D) 알리다

해설 두 번째 지문 [이메일] 두 번째 단락에서 'In regard with your requirements, my suggestion would be HR-V Uniq. The car meets all of your requirements perfectly.'에서 meets는 '충족하다'라는 의미로 쓰였으므로 보기 중 같은 의미를 갖는 (A)가 정답이다.

17. 사실 확인

두 번째 이메일은 Top Ride에 관해 무엇을 언급하는가?

(A) New Mexico에서 최고의 렌터카 업체이다.
(B) 자사의 웹 사이트에 대한 정해진 유지 보수 일정을 갖고 있다.
(C) 최근에 여러 다른 도시로 서비스를 확장했다.
(D) 예약을 하는 새로운 방법을 추가했다.

해설 두 번째 지문 [이메일] 세 번째 단락에서 'You may also download our recently launched app for your booking needs.'라고 했으므로 (D)가 정답이다.

✛ Paraphrasing

our recently launched app for your booking needs → has added a new way to make reservations

---

18-22번은 다음 기사, 이메일, 평면도에 관한 문제입니다.

DeLillo 복합 타워

EAST ORANGE (3월 11일) — **18 20** O'Malley Properties(OP)는 자사의 야심찬 복합타워 건설을 중단해야 할지도 모른다. 시의회 관계자는 공사로 인해 지역사회의 환경에 미칠지 모르는 영향에 대해 깊은 우려를 표현했다. OP의 계약 조건에서는 에너지 순 제로 등급을 달성하는 태양전지판을 사용하는 것 외에도, 인근 공영주차장과 녹지도 개선해야 한다고 규정했다. 시의원들은 업체에서 두 가지 사항을 모두 지키지 못할 것을 우려한 나머지 OP의 건축허가를 동결하겠다고 위협하고 있다.

프로젝트를 지지하는 사람들은 이러한 새로운 국면에 대해 언짢아한다. "이 프로젝트는 다른 상업 기업을 East Orange 도심으로 끌어들이는 자석 역할을 해줄 겁니다. OP가 앞으로 나아갈 수 있도록 우리가 의견을 모아야 합니다. **19** 국회의원은 OP가 지역사회에 랜드 마크로 자리매김하는 아름다운 건물을 설계하고 건설하는 일에 흠잡을 데 없이 완벽한 기록을 보유하고 있다는 걸 떠올릴 필요가 있습니다."라고 Mark Carlsen 시장 비서실장이 말했다.

어휘
force 강요하다 | halt 멈추다 | construction 건설 | ambitious 야심적인, 어마어마한 | source 소식통, 정보원 | city council 시의회 | express 표현하다 | major 중요한, 주요한 | concern 우려, 걱정 | environmental 환경의 | impact 영향 | terms (계약 등의) 조건, 조항 | contract 계약서 | solar panel 태양열 전지판 | achieve 달성하다 | net-zero (특정물질의 손실잉여나 부족 어느 것도 내지 않는) 순 제로 | rating 순위, 평가 | nearby 근방의 | fall short on 부족하다, ~에 미치지 못하다 | count 사항 | threaten 위협하다 | freeze

---

동결하다, 정지시키다 | permit 허가증 | backer 후원자 | uncomfortable 불편한 | development 개발 | mayor 시장 | development 새로이 전개된 국면 | chief of staff 비서실장 | promise 약속하다 | serve as ~의 역할을 하다 | magnet 자석 | attract 끌어들이다 | commercial enterprise 영리 기업 | come to an agreement 합의를 보다 | legislator 입법자, 국회의원 | unimpeachable 의심할 여지없는 | record 기록 | landmark 주요 지형지물, 랜드마크

수신: "Danielle Henderson" 〈Henderson@omalleyproperties.com〉
발신: DRoth@Pfeifferandpfeiffer.com
날짜: 12월 3일
제목: 이용 가능한 사무 공간

Henderson 씨께,

저는 Pfeiffer and Pfeiffer 법률사무소 선임 파트너입니다. 저희는 이곳에서 10년 넘게 운영해왔는데, 저희 사무실을 업그레이드하기 위해 알아보고 있습니다. DeLillo 복합 타워는 저희 주요 후보지 중 한 곳입니다. **20** 내년 여름 개장하는 걸로 알고 있는데, 저희 회사에는 딱 좋은 시기입니다. 저희는 시내에 있다는 것과, 도시 한가운데라는 점, 근방에는 녹지가 있다는 점에서 관심이 아주 많습니다. 아직 사무 공간을 임대 중이신가요? **22** 저희 회사에서는 4,000평방피트가 넘는 곳이 필요할 거에요. **21** 그리고, 건물에서 입주민에 고속 와이파이를 제공하나요? 건물에 대해 더 많이 알고 싶습니다.

정말 감사드립니다.

Donald Roth

어휘
senior 선임의 | attorney 변호사 | operate 운영하다 | locally 현지에서, 근방에서 | decade 10년 | prime 주요한, 최고의 | neighborhood 인근, 주위 | lease 임대하다 | square feet 제곱피트, 평방피트 | tenant 임차인, 세입자 | property 부동산, 건물

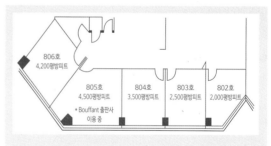

어휘
publishing 출판(업) | occupy 차지하다, 사용하다

18. 주제 / 목적 / 대상

기사의 주요 목적은 무엇인가?

(A) 현지 부동산 개발업체의 프로필을 알려주는 것
(B) 새로운 도시 규정에 대해 보고하는 것
(C) 프로젝트의 진행과정을 논의하는 것
(D) 친환경 시공방법에 대해 논의하는 것

해설 첫 번째 지문 [기사], 첫 번째 단락에서 'O'Malley Properties (OP) may be forced to halt construction of its ambitious DeLillo Tower complex. A source within the city council has expressed major concerns about the possible environmental impact construction could have on the rest of the community.'라고 했으므로 (C)가 정답이다.

19. 상세 정보

Carlsen 씨는 DeLillo 복합타워의 어떤 장점에 대해 언급하는가?

(A) 건축물의 기대가치
(B) 에너지 효율
(C) 이용 가능한 상업용지 규모
(D) 중심 위치

해설 첫 번째 지문 [기사], 두 번째 단락에서 'Our legislators need to remember OP's unimpeachable record in designing and constructing beautiful buildings that become community landmarks.'라고 했으므로 (A)가 정답이다.

20. 암시/추론 – 연계 문제

Roth 씨의 이메일에서 OP에 관하여 암시하는 것은?

(A) 10년 넘게 영업해왔다.
(B) East Orange로 이전할 계획이다.
(C) 잠재적 갈등을 해결했다.
(D) 소매점용 공간만을 제공한다.

해설 첫 번째 지문 [기사], 첫 번째 단락에서 'O'Malley Properties (OP) may be forced to halt construction of its ambitious DeLillo Tower complex. A source within the city council has expressed major concerns about the possible environmental impact construction could have on the rest of the community.'이라고 했는데, 두 번째 지문 [이메일]에 'I understand that it will open by next summer, which is perfect timing for my firm.'라고 하여 건설이 중단되지 않아 OP의 복합타워 건설과 관련하여 생길 수 있는 갈등이 해결되었다는 것을 알 수 있으므로 (C)가 정답이다.

21. 상세 정보

Roth 씨는 Henderson 씨에게 복합건물에 관한 어떤 정보를 요청하는가?

(A) 복합건물 입점 업체
(B) 복합건물 개관일
(C) 인터넷 연결 이용 가능성
(D) 인근 공원과의 거리

해설 두 번째 지문 [Roth 씨가 Henderson 씨에게 보낸 이메일]에서 'Also, does the complex offer a high-speed WiFi to tenants?'라고 물었으므로 (C)가 정답이다.

✦ Paraphrasing

WiFi → Internet connection

22. 암시/추론 – 연계 문제

Pfeiffer and Pfeiffer에서는 어떤 장소를 임대하기로 선택하겠는가?

(A) 802호
(B) 803호
(C) 804호
(D) 806호

해설 두 번째 지문 [Roth 씨가 Henderson 씨에게 보낸 이메일]에서 'Our firm would need something over 4,000 square feet.'라고 했는데, 세 번째 지문 [평면도]에서 비어있는 공간 중 4,000 평방피트가 넘는 곳은 806호뿐이므로 (D)가 정답이다.

ACTUAL TEST

ACTUAL TEST 01

본서 p.316

101. (D)	102. (C)	103. (B)	104. (D)	105. (A)
106. (B)	107. (C)	108. (B)	109. (D)	110. (B)
111. (D)	112. (B)	113. (D)	114. (C)	115. (A)
116. (B)	117. (B)	118. (C)	119. (A)	120. (B)
121. (B)	122. (B)	123. (B)	124. (D)	125. (C)
126. (C)	127. (B)	128. (B)	129. (D)	130. (C)
131. (B)	132. (A)	133. (D)	134. (D)	135. (C)
136. (B)	137. (D)	138. (B)	139. (D)	140. (C)
141. (A)	142. (C)	143. (D)	144. (B)	145. (D)
146. (A)	147. (D)	148. (C)	149. (B)	150. (B)
151. (B)	152. (B)	153. (C)	154. (B)	155. (D)
156. (C)	157. (C)	158. (D)	159. (B)	160. (D)
161. (D)	162. (A)	163. (B)	164. (B)	165. (A)
166. (B)	167. (C)	168. (D)	169. (A)	170. (A)
171. (B)	172. (B)	173. (C)	174. (D)	175. (B)
176. (D)	177. (B)	178. (D)	179. (B)	180. (B)
181. (A)	182. (B)	183. (A)	184. (B)	185. (D)
186. (D)	187. (B)	188. (C)	189. (C)	190. (B)
191. (B)	192. (A)	193. (C)	194. (B)	195. (B)
196. (D)	197. (D)	198. (B)	199. (B)	200. (B)

101. 등위 접속사

The cafeteria will be closed on Wednesday for renovations, **so** please make other arrangements for lunch.

구내식당이 수리를 위해 수요일에 문을 닫을 것이니 점심 식사 약속은 다른 곳으로 잡아주세요.

해설 빈칸 앞뒤로 두 개의 문장이 연결되어 있으며, 문맥상 구내식당이 문을 닫을 테니 다른 곳으로 약속을 잡아 달라는 의미가 되어야 자연스러우므로 (D)가 정답이다.

어휘 cafeteria 구내식당 | renovation 수리 | make an arrangement 약속을 정하다

✦ Key point

등위 접속사 so는 「원인절, so 결과절」의 문장을 연결한다.

102. 사람 명사 vs. 사물 / 추상 명사

Mr. Cech earned the trust of his clients when he delivered his **report** two days ahead of schedule.

Cech 씨가 자신의 보고서를 일정에 이틀 앞서 전달했을 때, 고객들의 신뢰를 얻었다.

해설 빈칸은 소유격 대명사 his의 수식을 받는 명사 자리이다. 보기의 명사 (C) report와 (D) reporter 중에 Cech 씨가 전달한 대상이 될 수 있는 것으로는 '보고서'가 자연스러우므로 (C)가 정답이다.

어휘 earn 받다, 얻다 | trust 신뢰 | deliver 전달하다 | ahead of ~보다 앞선, 일찍 | schedule 일정

✛ Key point

보기에 사람 명사와 사물 명사가 함께 있을 경우, 먼저 관사나 소유격이 있는지 확인하고 그런 다음 의미를 따져봐야 한다.

---

103. 어휘 – 동사

McCullough Corporation is often **perceived** as a company that hires employees of all ages.

McCullough 기업은 흔히 모든 연령대의 직원을 채용하는 회사로 여겨진다.

해설 빈칸은 수동태 동사 구문을 완성하는 과거분사 자리이다. 빈칸 뒤에 전치사 as가 있으며, 문맥상 '기업은 자주 모든 연령대의 직원을 채용하는 회사로 여겨진다'는 의미가 되어야 자연스러우므로, 'perceive A as B(A를 B로 여기다)'의 표현을 완성하는 (B)가 정답이다.

어휘 hire 고용하다 | employee 직원 | age 연령, 나이

✛ Key word

McCullough **Corporation** is often **perceived as a company that hires employees of all ages**.

---

104. 형용사 자리

The Maitre Hotel chain employs a strict set of regulations to ensure a **consistent** guest experience.

Maitre 호텔 체인은 일관된 고객 경험을 보장하기 위해 엄격한 규정을 적용한다.

해설 빈칸은 복합명사 guest experience를 수식하는 자리이다. 문맥상 '일관된 고객 경험을 보장하기 위해'라는 의미가 되어야 자연스러우므로 형용사 (D)가 정답이다.

어휘 employ 고용하다, (방법 등을) 쓰다 | strict 엄격한 | regulation 규정 | ensure 보장하다

✛ Key point

명사 앞자리에는 형용사, 분사, 명사가 올 수 있으며, 문맥을 통해 적합한 어휘를 파악한다. 참고로, 형용사와 분사가 보기에 함께 있는 경우, 대부분 형용사가 정답이다.

---

105. 어휘 – 명사

To our **knowledge**, a new system for monitoring waste has been implemented in seven cities.

우리가 알기로는, 쓰레기를 감시하는 새로운 시스템이 일곱 개의 도시에서 행해지고 있다.

해설 숙어 표현을 알아야 쉽게 풀 수 있는 문제이다. 'to one's knowledge'는 '~가 아는 바로는'이란 뜻으로, 여기서는 '우리가 알기로는'이라는 내용이므로 (A)가 정답이다.

어휘 monitor 감시하다 | waste 쓰레기 | implement 시행하다 | ability 능력 | competence 능숙함

---

106. 소유격 대명사

Since we installed an energy-saving central air conditioner, expect **your** utility fee to be reduced.

에너지 절약형 중앙 냉방장치를 설치했으니 귀하의 공과금이 절감되기를 기대하세요.

해설 빈칸은 복합명사 utility fee를 수식하는 자리이므로 소유격 대명사 (B)가 정답이다.

어휘 install 설치하다 | energy saving 에너지를 절약하는 | central 중앙의 | air conditioner 냉난방장치 | expect 기대하다, 예상하다 | utility fee 공과금 | reduce 감소하다

✛ Key point

① 동사 expect는 목적어와 목적격 보어를 취할 수 있으며, 목적격 보어 자리에는 to부정사가 올 수 있다.

② 명령문에서는 주어 you가 생략된다.

---

107. 어휘 – 형용사

The Filmmakers Association urges viewers not to blindly accept **biased** reviews about a movie.

영화 제작자 협회는 관객에게 영화에 대한 편향된 비평을 맹목적으로 받아들이지 말라고 충고한다.

해설 빈칸은 명사 reviews를 수식하되, 빈칸 앞 문맥과 잘 어울릴 수 있는 형용사 자리이다. '편향된 비평을 맹목적으로 받아들이지 말라'라는 것이 적절하므로 (C)가 정답이다.

어휘 filmmaker 영화 제작자 | association 협회 | urge 충고하다 | viewer 시청자, 보는 사람 | blindly 맹목적으로 | review 비평, 평가

---

108. 어휘 – 동사

Monthly maintenance costs **vary** depending on the location and size of the apartment unit rented.

월 관리비는 임대한 아파트의 위치와 크기에 따라 다르다.

해설 빈칸 뒤에 목적어 없이 전명구가 나오므로 빈칸에 자동사가 필요하다. 문맥상으로 '관리비는 아파트 위치 및 크기에 따라 달라진다'는 내용이 되어야 적합하므로 (B)가 정답이다.

어휘 monthly 매월의 | cost 비용 | rent 임대하다

---

109. 부사절 접속사

Given that he has experience and expertise in the field, Mr. Walker is an ideal candidate for the position.

그 분야에 경험과 전문 지식을 가지고 있다는 점을 고려하면, Walker 씨가 그 직책에 이상적인 지원자이다.

해설 빈칸은 앞뒤의 두 절을 연결해줄 접속사 자리이다. 문맥상 '그 분야에 경험과 전문 지식을 가지고 있다는 점을 고려하면 ~'이라는 의미가 되어야 자연스러우므로 (D)가 정답이다. Rather than과 Owing to는 뒤에 (동)명사 계열이 목적어로 오게 된다.

어휘 experience 경험 | expertise 전문 지식 | field 분야 | ideal 이상적인 | candidate 후보자 | if so 만일 그렇다면 | rather than ~보다는 차라리 | owing to ~때문에 | given that ~을 고려하면

---

110. 어휘 – 형용사

Marketing Department staff must be **punctual** with regard to client meeting starting times.

마케팅 부서 직원들은 고객회의 시작시간에 관해서는 시간을 엄수해야 한다.

해설 빈칸은 be동사 뒤의 보어 자리이다. 뒤에 오는 전치사의 내용을 고려할 때, '회의 시작시간에 관해서는 시간을 엄수해야 한다'는 의미가 되어야 자연스러우므로 (B)가 정답이다.

어휘 marketing 마케팅 | department 부서 | staff 직원 | with regard to ~에 관해 | client 고객

+ Key word

Marketing Department staff must be **punctual with regard to** client **meeting starting times**.

111. 어휘 – 명사

Ms. Park is evaluating the **scope** of the partnership agreement with Sauber GmbH.

Park 씨는 Sauber GmbH와의 파트너십 계약의 범위를 평가하고 있다.

해설 문맥상 '파트너십 계약의 범위'라는 의미가 되어야 자연스러우므로 (D)가 정답이다.

어휘 evaluate 평가하다 | partnership 파트너십 | agreement 계약, 협정 | scope 범위

+ Key word

Ms. Park is evaluating the **scope of the** partnership **agreement** with Sauber GmbH.

112. 일반 형용사 vs. 분사 형용사

Mr. Jalah has submitted a **conservative** estimate of the expenses of opening a new store location.

Jalah 씨는 신규매장의 개장 비용에 대해 적게 잡은 견적을 제출했다.

해설 빈칸은 명사를 수식하는 형용사 자리이므로 (B)가 정답이다. '보존하다'를 뜻하는 동사 conserve의 과거분사인 conserved(보존된)로 명사를 수식할 수 있으나 의미상 어울리지 않는다.

어휘 submit 제출하다 | expense 비용 | conservative 보수적인, (실제 수나 양보다) 적게 잡은

+ Key point

형용사는 명사 앞에서 명사를 수식할 수 있다.

113. 부사 자리

While growth was **admittedly** slow in the early years, it gave Pavicen Construction a chance to thoroughly learn the business.

초창기 몇 해 동안은 성장이 명백히 느렸지만, Pavicen 건설이 사업을 철저히 배울 수 있는 기회를 주었다.

해설 빈칸은 형용사 slow를 수식하는 부사 자리이므로 (D)가 정답이다.

어휘 growth 성장 | thoroughly 철저히

+ Key point

부사는 문장 내에서 가장 다양한 위치에 올 수 있는 품사로, 주로 형용사를 수식한다.

114. 어휘 – 동사

Last month, the council **issued** 76 fines to companies that violated the regulation.

지난달, 의회는 규정을 위반한 회사들에게 76회의 과태료를 발행했다.

해설 빈칸은 주어와 목적어 사이의 타동사 자리이다. 문맥상 '과태료를 부과했다'라는 내용이 되어야 자연스러우므로 (C)가 정답이다.

어휘 council 의회 | issue 발행하다, (선언, 명령 등을) 내리다, 발하다 | fine 벌금 | violate 위반하다 | regulation 규정

+ Key word

Last month, the **council issued 76 fines** to companies that violated the regulation.

115. 형용사 자리

When you remove a price tag label, great care should be taken to avoid leaving a **sticky** residue.

가격 라벨을 제거할 때, 끈적한 잔류물이 남지 않도록 많은 주의가 필요하다.

해설 빈칸은 명사 residue를 수식하는 형용사 자리로, 문맥상 '가격표를 뗄 때, 끈적한 잔류물이 남지 않도록 많은 주의가 필요하다'라는 의미가 자연스러우므로 (A)가 정답이다. 형용사의 최상급은 앞에 정관사나 소유격이 와야 쓰일 수 있다.

어휘 price tag label 가격 라벨 | avoid 피하다 | residue 잔류 | sticky 끈적한 | stick 막대기; 고수하다

116. 전치사

Warren Brothers employees are entitled to negotiate their salary figure **after** six months of working at the company.

Warren Brothers 직원들은 회사에서 6개월간 근무한 후에 봉급을 협상할 자격이 주어진다.

해설 '회사에서 6개월간 근무한 후에 봉급을 협상할 자격이 주어진다'는 의미가 자연스러우므로 (B)가 정답이다.

어휘 be entitled to V ~할 자격이 주어지다

117. 명사 자리

With its production facilities in Mexico and Argentina nearing **completion**, RK Automobiles is now concentrating its efforts on entering the local market.

멕시코와 아르헨티나의 생산시설이 완료되어 가면서, RK 자동차는 이제 현지 시장에 진입하려는 노력에 집중할 것이다.

해설 빈칸은 현재분사 nearing의 목적어 자리이다. 문맥상 '생산시설이 완공되어 가면서'라는 의미가 되어야 자연스러우므로, 'near completion(끝나간다, 완료되어간다)'의 관용 표현을 완성하는 (B)가 정답이다.

어휘 production 생산 | facility 시설 | near 가까워지다; 가까운; 가까이 | automobile 자동차 | concentrate 집중하다 | effort 노력 | local 현지의, 지역의

+ Key point

독립분사 구문 「with + 목적어 + 분사」는 주된 상황(주절)에 부수적으로 일어나는 상황을 설명하며, 목적어와 분사의 의미 관계에 따라 현재/과거분사가 올 수 있다.

118. 어휘 – 부사

According to the consumer research held two years ago and **again** this year, younger customers are more likely to make purchases online rather than at physical stores.

2년 전과 올해 다시 실시한 소비자 조사에 따르면, 더 젊은 고객들은 실제 매장보다 온라인에서 더 구매를 하려고 한다.

해설 빈칸은 부사구 this year를 수식하는 부사 자리이다. 접속사 and

로 연결된 two years ago와 this year가 모두 과거분사 held를 수식하고 있음을 고려할 때, '2년 전에 (실시)하고 올해 다시 실시한 소비자 조사에 따르면'이라는 의미가 되어야 문맥상 자연스러우므로 (D)가 정답이다.

어휘 consumer 소비자 | research 조사 | customer 고객 | make purchases 구매하다 | rather than ~보다는 | physical 물리적인

✚ Key word

According to the **consumer research held two years ago and again this year**, younger customers are more likely to make purchases online rather than at physical stores.

---

119. 부사 자리

The feature about Maarsden Corp. was **easily** Marilyn Carter's best article of the year.
Maarsden 사에 관한 특집기사는 아마 틀림없이 올해의 Marilyn Carter의 최고의 기사였다.

해설 빈칸 뒤에 주어와 일치하는 명사구 보어가 있어 이미 완전한 문장 구조를 이루고 있으므로 빈칸은 보어를 포함하여 동사구 전체를 강조, 수식하는 부사 자리이다. easily는 '쉽게'라는 뜻 외에도 '필시, 아마 틀림없이'라는 의미도 있어서 문맥상 '~에 관한 특집기사가 아마 틀림없이 올해의 최고의 기사였다'라는 의미가 되어야 자연스러우므로 (A)가 정답이다.

어휘 feature 특집(기사, 방송) | easily 아마 틀림없이, 필시, 쉽게 | article 기사

✚ Key point

부사는 문장 내에서 가장 다양한 위치에 올 수 있는 품사로, 부사가 be동사와 명사구 보어 사이에 등장하는 경우, 「be동사＋명사구 보어」인 동사구 전체를 수식 및 강조하는 역할을 한다.

---

120. 전치사

Companies should improve their products' quality **instead of** committing more resources to the marketing of poor-quality products to gain a bigger market share.
기업들은 더 큰 시장 점유율을 얻기 위해 형편없는 품질의 제품 홍보에 자원을 더 쓰는 대신, 그들의 제품 품질을 개선해야 한다.

해설 빈칸은 뒤의 명사구를 이끄는 전치사 자리이다. 문맥상 '형편없는 품질의 제품들에 자원을 더 쓰는 대신, 제품의 품질을 개선해야 한다'는 의미가 되어야 자연스러우므로 (B)가 정답이다.

어휘 improve 개선하다 | commit (돈, 시간을) 쓰다 | resource 자원, 재원 | poor-quality 형편없는 품질 | gain 얻다 | market share 시장 점유율 | according to ~에 따르면 | instead of ~대신에 | in regard to ~에 관해서 | as to ~에 관해서

✚ Key word

Companies should **improve their products' quality instead of committing more resources to the marketing of poor-quality products** to gain a bigger market share.

---

121. 어휘 – 형용사

Marder Studios creates **compelling** short films that are often intended to highlight the pros and cons of business strategies.
Marder 스튜디오는 종종 기업전략의 장단점을 강조하도록 의도된 강렬한 단편영화를 제작한다.

해설 빈칸은 명사구 short films를 수식하는 자리이다. 뒤에 이어지는 that 관계절의 내용을 고려할 때, '기업전략을 강조하려고 만든 강렬한 단편영화를 제작한다'는 의미가 자연스러우므로 (B)가 정답이다.

어휘 intend 의도하다 | highlight 강조하다 | pros and cons 장단점 | strategy 전략

✚ Key word

Marder Studios creates **compelling short films that are often intended to highlight the pros and cons of business strategies**.

---

122. 부사절 접속사

Although the two models of wireless earphones feature different options, they look nearly identical.
무선 이어폰의 두 가지 모델은 다른 옵션을 가지고 있음에도 불구하고, 보기에는 거의 동일해 보인다.

해설 빈칸은 두 개의 완전한 문장을 이끄는 접속사 자리이다. 두 문장의 내용이 different options와 look nearly identical로 상반된다는 점을 고려할 때, 문맥상 '옵션은 다르지만 보기에는 동일해 보인다'는 의미로 이어져야 자연스러우므로 부사절 접속사 (B)가 정답이다.

어휘 feature 특별히 포함하다 | identical 동일한

✚ Key point

등위 접속사인 but과 yet은 문두에 올 수 없다.

---

123. 상관 접속사

Please provide your receipts **as well as** your travel reimbursement forms by September 15.
9월 15일까지 출장비 상환양식뿐만 아니라 영수증을 제출해 주세요.

해설 빈칸은 your receipts와 your travel reimbursement forms라는 두 개의 명사구를 연결하는 자리이다. '출장비 상환양식뿐만 아니라 영수증을 제출해 주세요'라는 의미가 되어야 자연스러우므로 (D)가 정답이다. in addition은 부사이고 in addition to의 형태가 되면 빈칸에 쓰일 수 있다.

어휘 receipt 영수증 | reimbursement 상환, 배상

✚ Key point

'A as well as B'는 'B뿐만 아니라 A도'라는 부가의 의미로 사용되며, A와 B를 병렬시킨다.

---

124. 관용 표현

Next to the Shinhwa Resort is an extravagant entertainment area, complete **with** a golf course and temperature-regulated outdoor spa.
Shinhwa 리조트 옆에는 골프코스와 온도가 조절되는 야외 스파를 완비한 최고급 엔터테인먼트 구역이 있다.

해설 빈칸은 형용사 complete와 명사 구문을 연결하는 전치사 자리이다. 문맥상 '골프코스와 야외 스파를 완비한 엔터테인먼트 구역'이라는 의미가 되어야 자연스러우므로, 빈칸 앞 complete와 함께 'complete with(~를 포함하여, ~이 완비된)'라는 관용 표현을 완성하는 (D)가 정답이다.

어휘 next to ~옆에 | extravagant 화려한, 사치스러운 | entertainment 오락, 여흥 | temperature-regulated 온도가 조절되는 | outdoor 야외의

Next to the Shinhwa Resort is an extravagant **entertainment area, complete with a golf course and** temperature-regulated outdoor **spa**.

125. 어휘 - 형용사

Many people find the wait before receiving the results from their physical checkup almost **unbearable**.

많은 사람은 건강검진 결과를 받기 전에 기다림을 거의 참을 수 없어 한다.

해설 빈칸은 부사 almost의 수식을 받는 형용사 자리이다. 동사 자리에 find가 있으므로, 빈칸은 동사 find의 목적격 보어 자리이므로 목적어를 서술적으로 설명할 수 있는 어휘가 들어가야 한다. 문맥상 '검진 결과를 기다리는 시간을 견디기 힘들어한다'는 의미가 되어야 자연스러우므로 (C)가 정답이다.

어휘 wait 기다림 | result 결과 | physical checkup 건강검진

+ Key word

Many **people find** the **wait** before receiving the results from their physical checkup almost **unbearable**.

126. 어휘 - 형용사

Frank Harwood created a cash flow chart technique, which is now used by many **other** investors all over the world.

Frank Harwood가 전 세계의 많은 다른 투자자들에 의해 사용되고 있는 현금 흐름도 기법을 만들었다.

해설 명사 investors를 수식하는 형용사 자리이므로 부사 (A)는 오답으로 제외한다. 문맥상 '그 밖의 다른 많은 투자자들'이라는 의미가 되어야 자연스러우므로 (C)가 정답이다. else 역시 '그 밖의, 다른'이란 뜻으로 쓰이지만 이 때는 부정대명사 뒤에 위치한다는 점에 주의한다. (someone else 다른 사람[누군가], anyone else 다른 사람 누구든지, anything else 그 밖의 다른 것)

어휘 cash flow chart 현금 흐름도 | technique 기법 | investor 투자자 | also 또한, 역시 | extra 추가의, 여분의 | other 또 다른, 그 밖의 | else 그 밖의, 다른

127. 어휘 - 부사

The entire team at FM Finance is ready to provide any assistance, and we hope our cooperation will be **mutually** beneficial for now and in the long run.

FM Finance의 모든 팀은 모든 지원을 제공할 준비가 되어 있으며, 우리의 협업이 당분간, 그리고 장기적으로 상호 간에 이익이 되기를 바랍니다.

해설 빈칸은 뒤의 형용사 beneficial을 수식하기에 알맞은 부사 자리이다. 문맥상 '우리의 협업이 상호 간에 이익이 되기를 바란다'는 의미가 되어야 자연스러우므로 (B)가 정답이다. 참고로 '각자, 각각'을 의미하는 (C) respectively는 앞에 언급된 둘 이상의 대상을 언급할 때 사용되는데, 언급된 대상이 하나(The entire team)이므로 (C)는 의미상 어색하다.

어휘 entire 모든, 전체의 | ready to do ~할 준비가 된 | assistance 지원 | cooperation 협력 | beneficial 이로운 | for now 당분간은 | in the long run 장기적으로 | punctually 늦지 않게 | mutually 상호 간에 |

respectively 각각, 각자 | precisely 정확히

+ Key word

The entire team at FM Finance is ready to provide any assistance, and **we hope our cooperation will be mutually beneficial** for now and in the long run.

128. 어휘 - 명사

The president's address will be recorded in its **entirety** and uploaded to our Web site for staff who could not attend the meeting.

대표의 연설은 전부 기록될 것이고 회의에 참석할 수 없는 직원들을 위해 웹사이트에 업로드될 것입니다.

해설 빈칸은 전치사 in의 목적어인 명사 자리이다. 문맥상 '연설은 전부 기록될 것'이라는 의미가 되어야 자연스러우므로 관용 표현 'in its entirety(완전히, 전부)'를 완성하는 (B)가 정답이다.

어휘 address 연설 | record 기록하다 | upload 업로드하다 | attend 참석하다

+ Key word

The president's **address will be recorded in its entirety** and uploaded to our Web site for staff who could not attend the meeting.

129. 동사의 태

The total cost of the manufacturing process should be **calculated** before proposing the production of a new item.

제조 공정의 총비용은 새로운 상품의 생산을 제안하기 전에 계산되어야 한다.

해설 빈칸은 be동사 뒤의 보어 자리이므로 형용사 역할을 하는 분사 자리이다. 빈칸 뒤에 목적어가 없는 것으로 보아 수동태를 완성시키는 과거분사 (D)가 정답이다.

어휘 manufacturing 제조 | process 공정, 과정 | propose 제안하다 | production 생산

130. 어휘 - 부사

Many wholesalers of fresh fruit **purposely** base their operations near the growers' orchards.

많은 신선과일 도매상들은 의도적으로 재배자의 과수원 근처에 자신들의 사업 근거지를 둔다.

해설 빈칸은 주어와 동사 사이의 부사 자리이다. 문맥상 '과일 도매상들이 의도적으로 과수원 근처에 근거지를 둔다'는 의미가 되어야 자연스러우므로 (C)가 정답이다.

어휘 wholesaler 도매업자 | base ~에 근거지를 두다 | operation 활동, 사업 | grower 재배자 | orchard 과수원

+ Key word

Many **wholesalers of fresh fruit purposely base** their operations **near** the **growers' orchards**.

131-134번은 다음 공지에 관한 문제입니다.

다음 주 주말은 시간을 비워 놓으세요, Norman Sparks가 방문하니까요. Sparks 씨는 자신의 **131 노래**로 유명해졌는데, 그 곡으로 올해의 최고 데뷔상을 탔습니다. 그는 형편이 어려운 아동을 돕는 모금 행사의 일환으로 Voci Arena에서 콘서트를 개최합니다. 콘서트는 다음 주말인 3월 22일에 열립니다. 모든 분이 나오셔서 대의를 **132 지지해** 주시길 바랍니다. 또한 구매되는 모든 티켓은 무대 뒤에서 Sparks 씨를 직접 만나볼 수 있는 **133 한** 추첨 행사에 응모됩니다. **134 친필 사인이 들어간 상품도** 있을 예정입니다. 또한 그와 대화를 나눌 기회도 갖게 됩니다. 일생에 한 번뿐인 기회이니, 반드시 놓치지 마세요! 더 자세한 내용을 알아보시려면, www.vociarena.com/events를 방문해 주세요.

어휘

save 남겨두다, 아껴 두다 | make headlines 화제가 되다, 유명해지다 | earn (이익 따위를) 받게 하다 | award 상 | hold 개최하다 | arena 경기장 | fundraiser 모금 행사 | in need 어려움에 처한 | take place 개최되다 | a good cause 대의(명분) | additionally 또한, 뿐만 아니라 | purchase 구입하다 | enter 들어가다 | raffle 경품 추첨 | backstage 무대 뒤에서 | in person 직접 | chat with ~와 대화하다 | once-in-a-lifetime 생애 한 번뿐인 | opportunity 기회 | miss out 좋은 기회 를 놓치다 | head on over to ~로 가다

131. 어휘 – 명사

해설 빈칸 뒷부분의 '올해의 최고 데뷔상을 탔다'는 내용과 다음 문장의 '콘서트를 개최한다'는 내용을 고려할 때, '노래로 유명해졌다'는 의미가 되어야 문맥상 자연스러우므로 (B)가 정답이다.

✚ **Key word**

Mr. Sparks has been **making headlines for his song, which earned him the award for Best Debut of the Year. He will be holding a concert** at the Voci Arena as part of his fundraiser to help kids in need.

132. 어휘 – 동사

해설 빈칸 앞부분의 '형편이 어려운 아동을 돕는 모금 행사의 일환으로 콘서트를 개최한다'는 내용을 고려할 때, '모두 참석해 대의를 지지해 달라'는 의미가 되어야 문맥상 자연스러우므로 (A)가 정답이다.

✚ **Key word**

He will be holding a concert at the Voci Arena **as part of his fundraiser to help kids in need.** The concert will take place next weekend, March 22. **We hope everyone comes out to support a good cause.**

133. 관사 자리

해설 빈칸은 단수 명사 raffle을 수식하는 자리이다. '구매되는 모든 티켓은 무대 뒤에서 Sparks 씨를 직접 만나볼 수 있는 추첨 행사에 응모된다'는 내용이 되어야 문맥상 자연스러우므로 '어떤, 하나의'라는 의미로 부정관사 (D)가 정답이다.

✚ **Key word**

Additionally, **every ticket purchased will enter you into a raffle** where you can meet Mr. Sparks backstage in person.

134. 문장 선택

(A) 경기장은 만원이 될 것으로 예상됩니다.
(B) 새로운 콘서트 날짜가 발표될지도 모릅니다.
(C) 시상식은 다음 주에 있을 것입니다.

(D) 친필 사인이 들어간 상품도 있을 예정입니다.

해설 빈칸 앞 문장의 '구매되는 모든 티켓은 무대 뒤에서 Sparks 씨를 직접 만나볼 수 있는 한 추첨 행사에 응모된다'는 내용과 빈칸 뒤 문장의 '또한 그와 대화를 나눌 기회도 갖게 된다'는 내용을 고려할 때, 콘서트에 참석해서 얻을 수 있는 혜택과 관련된 내용이 나와야 문맥상 연결이 자연스러우므로 (D)가 정답이다.

✚ **Key word**

Additionally, **every ticket purchased will enter you into a raffle** where you can meet Mr. Sparks backstage in person. **There will be some autographed goodies. You'll also have a chance to chat with him.**

135-138번은 다음 회람에 관한 문제입니다.

수신: Grunsfield Spa 전 직원
발신: Vicki Farmer
날짜: 9월 7일
제목: 최신 보고서

135 곧 속상한 소식을 듣게 될 겁니다. 최근 조사에 따르면, 고객들이 우리 평판을 상당히 부정적으로 평가하고 있습니다. 실은, **136 자신들의** 경험에 대해 이야기하는 데 주력하는 온라인 그룹이 존재합니다. 울적해하기보다는 이걸 기회로 삼아야 합니다. **137 조사를 해서 개선할 수 있는 방법을 알아봅시다.** 우리가 팀을 나눠서, 불만 있는 고객을 인터뷰해봐도 좋을 것 같습니다. 많은 시간이 드는 다른 업무를 진행하고 계신 점 잘 알고 있습니다. **138 하지만** 이 일이 더 중요합니다. 다른 모든 일보다 우선으로 해야 합니다.

어휘

spa 스파 | upsetting 속상한 | rate 평가하다 | reputation 명성, 평판 | quite 꽤, 상당히 | negative 부정적인 | dedicated to ~에 전념하는, 헌신하는 | rather than ~보다는, 대신에 | opportunity 기회 | divide into ~로 나누다 | disgruntled 불만을 품은, 언짢은 | take up (시간을) 차지하다 | take priority over ~에 우선하다

135. 부사 자리

해설 빈칸은 동사 hear를 수식하는 부사 자리이며, 고객들의 부정적 평가에 대한 문장이 뒤따르고 있으므로 '이제 속상한 소식을 듣게 될 겁니다'라는 의미가 자연스럽다. 따라서 '이제, 지금'이라는 뜻의 부사 (C)가 정답이다.

✚ **Key word**

You will now hear some upsetting news. According to the latest surveys, customers rate our reputation to be quite negative.

136. 명사 – 대명사 일치

해설 빈칸은 명사 experiences를 수식하는 자리이다. 앞 문장의 고객들이 우리에 대해 부정적으로 평가한다는 내용을 고려할 때, 우리 서비스를 이용한 고객들의 경험이라는 의미가 되어야 문맥상 자연스러우므로 복수 명사 customers를 지칭하는 소유격 대명사 (D)가 정답이다.

✚ **Key word**

According to the latest surveys, **customers rate our reputation to be quite negative.** In fact, there are online groups dedicated to **talking about their experiences with us.**

해설서 **175**

137. 문장 선택

(A) 최근 몇 년 동안 우리의 수입이 줄었습니다.
(B) 다음 프로젝트를 위한 아이디어가 필요합니다.
(C) 우리는 다른 팀들을 초대해서 그들의 의견을 듣는 것을 고려할 수 있습니다.
(D) 조사를 해서 개선할 수 있는 방법을 알아봅시다.

해설 빈칸 앞 문장의 이걸 기회로 삼아야 한다는 내용과 뒷문장의 팀을 나눠 불만 고객을 인터뷰해보자는 내용을 고려할 때, 현재 상황을 개선할 방안에 대해 조사를 해보자는 내용이 들어가야 문맥상 연결이 자연스러우므로 (D)가 정답이다.

✛ Key word

Rather than feeling sad, we should take this as an opportunity. **Let's do some research to find out how we can do better.** I want us to divide into teams and maybe interview some disgruntled customers.

138. 접속부사

해설 빈칸 뒤에 콤마가 있으므로 접속부사 자리이다. 다른 업무를 하느라 많은 시간이 든다는 점 잘 알고 있다는 앞 문장의 내용과, 이 일이 더 중요하며 다른 모든 일보다 우선해야 한다는 빈칸 뒤 내용을 고려할 때 상반되는 내용을 연결하는 (B)가 정답이다. 참고로 (D) In contrast(~에 반해서)은 둘 사이의 차이를 기술할 때 쓰이므로 문맥상 부적절하다.

✛ Key word

I know we have other work going on that is taking up a lot of your time. **However, this is more important. It should take priority over everything else.**

139-142번은 다음 이메일에 관한 문제입니다.

수신: TBW 독자들
발신: customerservice@tbw.com
날짜: 3월 31일
제목: 장애

저희 Tavermont 비즈니스 주간지(TBW)는 독자 여러분께 양질의 콘텐츠를 제공하는 데 **139 전념합니다**. 그러나 최근에는 그러한 기준에 부합되지 못했던 것으로 보입니다. 최근호에 많은 편집상의 오류가 있었음을 알아차리셨을 것으로 압니다. **140 유감스럽지만, 저희는 몇몇 큰 인사 문제를 처리하고 있었습니다.** 이 때문에 4월호는 다음 주 평소의 날짜에 출간되지 못할 겁니다. 이것은 **141 일시적인** 상황입니다. 문제를 완전히 해결하기 위한 계획이 진행 중입니다. **142 사실**, 최종 결과로 출판물의 품질이 상당히 개선될 것이라고 믿습니다. 지연에 대해 매우 죄송하며, 양해에 감사드립니다.

고맙습니다.

Calvin Lo
TBW 고객서비스 매니저

어휘
interruption 중단, 방해 | issue (잡지·신문 같은 정기 간행물의) 호 | regrettably 유감스럽게(도), 애석하게(도) | personnel 인사의 | release (레코드·책 따위)를 발매하다 | temporary 일시적인, 임시의 | in place 가동 중인 | address (문제·상황 등에 대해) 고심하다[다루다] | publication 출판물

139. 동사의 시제

해설 관용 표현 'be dedicated to/dedicated oneself to(~에 헌신[전념]하다)'를 묻는 문제이므로 (D)가 정답이다.

140. 문장 선택

(A) 유감스럽게도, 전액 환불해 드릴 수 없었습니다.
(B) 유감스럽게도, 우리는 구독료를 인상할 수밖에 없습니다.
(C) 유감스럽지만, 저희는 몇몇 큰 인사 문제를 처리하고 있습니다.
(D) 안타깝게도, 구독료 지불이 제대로 처리되지 않았습니다.

해설 뒷문장 Because of this, April's issue will not be released on its usual date next week.에서 4월호 출간이 지연될 것이라고 하므로 이 앞으로 이에 대한 원인이 나와야 한다. 따라서 인사상의 문제를 겪고 있다는 (C)가 정답이다.

✛ Key word

I'm sure you noticed that **there were many editing errors** in our most recent issue. **Regrettably, we have been dealing with some major personnel issues.** Because of this, April's issue **will not be released on its usual date** next week.

141. 어휘 - 형용사

해설 뒷문장에서 영구적인 해결책이 있음을 알려주고 있으므로 '일시적인 상황'이라는 의미가 되어야 적절하다. 따라서 (A)가 정답이다.

✛ Key word

This is a temporary situation. We have plans in place to fully address the problem.

142. 접속부사

해설 뒷문장이 앞 문장에 대한 부연 설명이므로 (C)가 정답이다. 참고로 (D) On one side(한쪽에서, 한편으로)는 보통 두 개의 대조적인 관점 중 첫 번째를 소개할 때 사용되므로 문맥상 어울리지 않는다.

✛ Key word

We have plans in place to fully address the problem. As a matter of fact, **we believe that the final result will be a significant improvement in the quality of our publication.**

143-146번은 다음 기사에 관한 문제입니다.

Fernbrook 사, Kangley 물류와 제휴 맺다

Fernbrook, 잉글랜드 — 컴퓨터 부품을 주로 취급하는 신생 업체인 Fernbrook 사가 Kangley 물류와 파트너십을 **143 발표했다**. 이번 파트너십으로 Kangley 물류가 Fernbrook 사의 국제 수송 건을 모두 처리할 것으로 기대된다.

"Kangley 물류를 저희에게 더할 나위 없는 **144 협력사**로 보기 때문에, 이는 중대한 결정입니다"라고 Fernbrook의 소유주 Frankie Watson이 말했다. "저희 국제 배송이 엄청나게 늘어나고 있습니다. 이제 Kangley 물류와 함께하게 되어 너무 좋습니다. **145 그들은 해외 배송에 있어 전문가입니다.**"

또한 Watson 씨는 Kangley 물류의 유통센터가 아주 **146 체계적**이라며 찬사를 보냈다. "센터에 들어서면 모두가 자기 업무에 정통하다는 걸 바로 알 수 있어요. 모든 게 아주 세세하게 짜여 있었고, 그곳 직원은 저희가 묻는 모든 질문에 답을 알고 있었어요. 모두가 Kangley 물류를 추천하는 데는 이유가 있습니다."

어휘

partner with ~와 협력하다, 합작하다 | logistics 물류 | up-and-coming 전도유망한, 떠오르는 | deal in (상품을) 취급하다 | primarily 주로 | computer parts 컴퓨터 부품 | partnership 동반자 관계, 동업 | handle 처리하다 | shipping 수송, 배송 | momentous 중대한 | decision 결정 | owner 소유주 | pick up 더 강해지다 | side 편, 쪽 | praise 칭찬하다 | distribution centre 유통센터 | meticulously 꼼꼼하게, 세심하게 | arrange 정리하다, 배열하다 | recommend 추천하다

143. 동사의 시제

해설 빈칸은 주어 Fernbrook Co.에 대한 동사 자리이다. 빈칸 다음 문장에서 '이번 파트너십으로 Kangley 물류가 Fernbrook 사의 국제 수송 건을 모두 처리할 것으로 기대된다'라고 하여 파트너십을 이미 체결했음을 알 수 있으므로 현재 완료 시제 (D)가 정답이다.

✦ **Key word**

Fernbrook Co., an up-and-coming business dealing primarily in computer parts, **has announced a partnership with Kangley Logistics. Under this partnership, it is expected that Kangley Logistics will handle all of Fernbrook Co.'s international shipping orders.**

144. 어휘 - 명사

해설 빈칸은 주어 Kangley Logistics에 대한 보어 자리이자, the perfect의 수식을 받는 명사 자리이다. 빈칸 앞 문장의 '이번 파트너십으로 Kangley 물류가 Fernbrook 사의 국제 수송건을 모두 처리할 것으로 기대된다'는 내용을 고려할 때, 'Kangley 물류를 저희에게 더할 나위 없는 협력사로 본다'는 내용이 들어가야 문맥상 자연스러우므로 (B)가 정답이다.

✦ **Key word**

~, a partnership with Kangley Logistics. Under this partnership, it is expected ~. This is a momentous decision for us because **we feel that Kangley Logistics is the perfect ally for us**

145. 문장 선택

(A) 우리는 해외 판매를 시작하려고 합니다.
(B) 국내 배송은 문제가 되지 않습니다.
(C) 주문이 아직 이루어지지 않았습니다.
(D) 그들은 해외 배송에 있어 전문가입니다.

해설 빈칸 앞 문장의 '저희 국제 배송이 엄청나게 늘어나고 있습니다. 이제 Kangley 물류와 함께하게 되어 너무 좋습니다'라는 내용을 고려할 때, 그 업체가 해외 배송에 있어 전문가라는 내용으로 이어져야 문맥상 자연스러우므로 (D)가 정답이다.

✦ **Key word**

"Our international orders have been picking up a lot. It's great that we have Kangley Logistics on our side now. They are experts in overseas shipping."

146. 어휘 - 형용사

해설 빈칸은 의문사 how의 수식을 받아 how 명사절을 완성하는 형용사 자리이다. Kangley 물류의 유통센터를 묘사하는 형용사가 들어갈 자리로, 빈칸 뒷부분의 '모든 게 아주 세세하게 조직되어 있었고, 그곳 직원은 저희가 묻는 모든 질문에 답을 알고 있었어요'라는 내용을 고려할 때, '유통센터가 아주 체계적이라고 찬사를 보냈다'

라는 내용이 되어야 자연스러우므로 (A)가 정답이다.

✦ **Key word**

Mr. Watson also praised Kangley Logistics on **how systematic their distribution centre is.** "You can just tell when you walk into their centre that they know what they're doing. **Everything was meticulously arranged**, and their employees knew the answers to all of the questions we had.

147-148번은 다음 공지에 관한 문제입니다.

Sun King Suites는 귀하의 이용에 감사드립니다.

귀하의 체류가 더 즐거울 수 있도록, **147 148** 구시가지 내 모든 역에서 이용하실 수 있는 경전철 패스를 무료로 제공해 드립니다. 경전철 시스템은 역사박물관, 대통령궁, MPX몰을 포함해 시내 가장 인기 있는 많은 명소들과 연결되어 있습니다. **148** 이들 장소에 도보로 갈 수 있지만, 특히 더운 여름철에는 경전철이 훨씬 더 편리할 것입니다. 여행객과 지역민 모두에게 사랑받는 경전철은 또한 중앙역까지 연결되는데, 거기서 지방열차를 타실 수 있습니다.

호텔 웹사이트에서 전체 시간표를 보실 수 있습니다. 로열티 클럽 회원은 위에 언급된 장소들에서 할인을 받으실 수 있습니다. 자세한 내용은 프론트 데스크에 문의해 주세요.

어휘

appreciate 감사하다 | business 이용; 사업 | enjoyable 즐거운 | light rail 경전철 | pass 탑승권, 출입증 | station 역 | neighborhood 인근, 근처 | connect 연결되다, 이어지다 | popular 인기 있는 | landmark 명소 | location 장소 | accessible 접근할 수 있는 | on foot 도보로, 걸어서 | convenience 편리 | especially 특히 | favor 좋아하다, 찬성하다 | tourist 관광객 | local 지역주민 | alike 비슷한; 비슷하게 | catch 잡다, 타다 | regional 지역의 | complete 완전한, 전체의 | timetable 시간표 | eligible for ~할 자격이 있는 | discount 할인 | site 장소 | mention 언급하다 | above 위에 | ask 물어보다 | detail 세부 사항

147. 상세 정보

무엇이 제공되는가?
(A) 대통령궁 입장권
(B) 지방열차 특별 요금
(C) 신규 로열티 클럽 회원권
(D) 무료 교통편

해설 첫 번째 단락에서 'we provide a free light rail pass that can be used at all stations in the Old Town neighborhood'라고 했으므로 (D)가 정답이다.

✦ **Paraphrasing**

free → complimentary

148. 암시 / 추론

Sun King Suites에 관하여 알 수 있는 것은?
(A) 출장 여행객들에게 평가가 좋다.
(B) 구시가지 인근에 있다.
(C) 관광객들에게 인기 있다.
(D) 유명한 지역 명소이다.

해설 첫 번째 단락에서 'we provide a free light rail pass that can be used at all stations in the Old Town neighborhood. The light rail system connects to many of the city's most popular landmarks,'라고 하면서 'these locations are accessible on foot,'이라고 하여 Sun King Suites가 구시가지에서 멀지 않다는 것을 알 수 있으므로 (B)가 정답이다.

149-150번은 다음 광고에 관한 문제입니다.

Mondegreen 무술 체육관

149 여러분의 일상에 저희의 입증된 운동요법을 더해 건강을 유지하세요.

지금부터 11월 30일까지, 모든 6개월짜리 회원 패키지는 33% 할인합니다.

또한, **150** 귀하의 추천으로 체육관에 등록하는 추가 한 명당, 회원 패키지에서 10% 추가 할인을 받으세요.

회원 혜택에는 다음이 포함됩니다:
- 전문 트레이너의 개인지도
- 등급별 수업: 초급부터 마스터까지
- 샤워실 및 사우나 완비
- 24시간 이용 가능한 운동 장비

어휘

martial arts 무술, 무예 | gym 체육관 | fit 건강한 | proven 증명된, 입증된 | workout regimen 운동 관리 | daily routine 일상 | recommendation 추천 | earn 얻다, 받다 | extra 추가의 | advantage 이점, 강점 | personal 개인적인 | instruction 설명, 지시 | skilled 숙련된, 전문적인 | on-site 현장의, 현지의 | exercise equipment 운동 장비 | 24/7 연중무휴의, 언제나

149. 상세 정보

광고에 따르면, 체육관에 왜 등록해야 하는가?
(A) 야외에서 운동하기 위해
(B) 무술 지도자가 되기 위해
(C) 전문 네트워크를 구축하기 위해
(D) 건강한 습관을 만들기 위해

해설 첫 번째 단락에서 'Stay fit by adding our proven workout regimen to your daily routine.'이라고 했으므로 (D)가 정답이다.

150. 상세 정보

고객은 어떻게 할인을 받을 수 있는가?
(A) 초급반 수업에 등록해서
(B) 또 다른 고객을 소개해서
(C) 연간 회원권을 구입해서
(D) 12월에 체육관에 등록해서

해설 세 번째 단락에서 'for each additional person to join the gym on your recommendation, earn extra 10 percent off your membership package.'라고 했으므로 (B)가 정답이다.

+ Paraphrasing

each additional person → another customer

151-152번은 다음 이메일에 관한 문제입니다.

수신: Schmieg 사업 개발팀
발신: Jason Herrera
날짜: 2월 13일
제목: Wu 씨

직원 여러분께,

Schmieg Industries에서는 당사 사업 개발부장이신 Yabin Wu께서 Business Digest의 '올해의 여성 기업가' 후보에 올랐음을 알려드리게 되어 자랑스럽습니다. Schmieg를 국제적인 기업으로 변모시킨 그녀의 업적을 고려하면, 이건 놀라운 일이 아닙니다. **152** 5년 전, Schmieg는 3천 명의 고객을 모셨습니다. 5년이 지난 후, Wu 씨께서 전체 팀을 지휘

하고 있는 현재, 5만 명의 고객을 모시고 있습니다. **151** 따라서 저희는 그녀의 업적을 축하하는 시간을 가지려 합니다.

151 이번 주 금요일 Chandelier Room이라는 레스토랑을 예약했습니다. 정확한 인원수를 파악할 수 있도록 참석 여부를 저희에게 알려주시기 바랍니다. 또한 사무실에서 Wu 씨를 뵙게 되면, 그분에게 뛰어난 업적에 대해 축하해 주시기 바랍니다.

안부를 전하며,

Jason Herrera, 인사팀
Schmieg Industries

어휘

announce 발표하다 | head 책임자 | nominate 지명[추천]하다 | businesswoman 여성 기업인 | come as no surprise 놀라운 일이 아니다 | given ~을 고려해 볼 때 | accomplishment 업적, 성취 | serve (상품, 서비스를) 제공하다 | at the helm 책임지고 있는, 배의 키를 잡고 있는 | international 국제적인 | firm 회사, 기업 | reserve 예약하다 | attend 참석하다 | accurate 정확한 | head count 인원수 | be sure to 반드시 ~하다 | congratulate 축하하다 | excellent 탁월한, 훌륭한

151. 주제 / 목적 / 대상

Herrera 씨는 왜 이메일을 보냈는가?
(A) 직원의 퇴사를 알리려고
(B) 직원의 성과를 축하하려고
(C) 최근 결정 사항에 대한 최신 소식을 전하려고
(D) 직원들에게 경영진 변화에 대해 알려주려고

해설 첫 번째 단락에서 'Therefore, we would like to take this time to celebrate her accomplishment.'라고 했으므로 (B)가 정답이다.

+ Paraphrasing

accomplishment → achievement

152. 암시 / 추론

Wu 씨에 관하여 알 수 있는 것은?
(A) 5년간 회사에 재직 중이다.
(B) 최근 회사 내에서 역할이 바뀌었다.
(C) 처음에 Herrera 씨에게 고용되었다.
(D) 한동안 해외에서 근무했다.

해설 첫 번째 단락에서 'Five years ago, Schmieg served 3,000 customers. Five years later, with Ms. Wu at the helm the entire time, we are now serving 50,000 customers.'라고 했으므로 (A)가 정답이다.

153-154번은 다음 문자 메시지 대화에 관한 문제입니다.

Daniela Brasco [오후 6:02]
퇴근하셨나요? **153** 테라스에 있는 꽃들을 덮지 않은 게 막 생각났는데, 오늘 밤에는 폭설이 내릴 예정이에요.

Ryan Bing [오후 6:07]
막 하려던 참이었어요. 그리고 네, 눈송이가 내리는 게 보이기 시작하네요.

Daniela Brasco [오후 6:08]
153 밤 동안 그걸 덮어둘 천 좀 찾아주실 수 있나요?

Ryan Bing [오후 6:12]
그런 걸 찾지 못하겠네요. 주방에 있는 비닐랩을 사용하는 건 어떨까요?

Daniela Brasco [오후 6:13]
내일 오찬에 사용될 거라서요. 계속 찾아봐 주실래요?

Ryan Bing [오후 6:18]
154 휴게실에 담요가 있는데, 먼지가 꽤 많아요.

Daniela Brasco [오후 6:19]
그건 문제가 아니에요. 꽃들을 얼리게 두느니 닦아주는 것이 훨씬 낫겠어요.

Ryan Bing [오후 6:20]
알았어요.

어휘
leave 떠나다 | cover 덮다 | patio 파티오, 집 뒤의 테라스 | heavy snowfall 폭설 | be about to 막~하려던 참이다 | snowflake 눈송이 | fabric 천, 직물 | plastic wrap 비닐 랩 | luncheon 오찬 | blanket 담요 | dusty 먼지투성이인 | wipe off 닦아내다 | freeze 얼다, 얼리다

153. 상세 정보

Brasco 씨는 Bing 씨에게 무엇을 하라고 요청하는가?
(A) 파티오 가구를 옮기라고
(B) 휴게실을 정리하라고
(C) 식물을 보호하라고
(D) 일기예보를 보라고

해설 오후 6시 2분 Daniela Brasco의 메시지에서 'I just remembered I didn't cover the flowers on the patio, and there's going to be heavy snowfall tonight.'이라고 했고, 오후 6시 8분 메시지에서 'Could you find some fabric to put over them for the night?'이라고 했으므로 (C)가 정답이다.

✛ Paraphrasing

flowers → plants, put over → protect

154. 화자 의도 파악

오후 6시 19분에 Brasco 씨가 "그건 문제가 아니에요."라고 할 때 그녀가 의미한 것은?
(A) 그녀는 원예 도구를 구입할 것이다.
(B) 그녀는 먼지를 개의치 않아 한다.
(C) 그녀는 Bing 씨가 오찬을 주최하길 원한다.
(D) 그녀는 Bing 씨가 휴가를 사용하는 것이 괜찮다.

해설 오후 6시 18분 ~ 6시 19분 대화에서 Ryan Bing 씨가 'There's a blanket in the break room, but it's pretty dusty.'라고 했고, Daniela Brasco 씨가 'That's not a problem. I'd much rather wipe off the flowers than have them freeze.'라고 했으므로 (B)가 정답이다.

155-157번은 다음 기사에 관한 문제입니다.

MANCHESTER, 7월 15일 — 155 Manchester 소유의 Cinco 사는 Eindhoven에 본사를 둔 AJX Electronik과의 합병에 합의했다. —[1]—. Cinco는 고급 텔레비전을 생산 판매한다. 지난 10년 동안, Cinco는 AJX에게 LED 패널을 구입해왔는데 AJX의 부품은 업계 표준으로 널리 알려져 있다. —[2]—. 157 다른 제조사들의 AJX LED 패널에 대한 높은 수요로 인해 패널이 때때로 부족했고, 이로 인해 Cinco는 일부 제품 설계를 절충할 수밖에 없었다. —[3]—. AJX CEO인 Wout Van Der Poel은 156 AJX가 이제 Utrecht에 두 번째 제조 공장을 열 수 있을 것이라고 단언했다. —[4]—. Van Der Poel은 "의심할 여지가 없습니다. 이 거래는 진정한 윈윈입니다."라고 말했다.

어휘
agree 동의하다 | produce 생산하다 | high-end 고급의 | component 부품 | widely 널리 | consider 여기다 | standard 표준 | demand 수요 | manufacturer 제조사 | occasionally 가끔 | shortage 부족 | force 어쩔 수 없이 ~하게 만들다 | compromise 타협, 절충 | assert 주장하다 | doubt 의심

155. 주제 / 목적 / 대상

기사의 목적은 무엇인가?
(A) 인수에 대한 문제를 논의하기 위해
(B) 고해상도 TV의 새로운 모델을 공개하기 위해
(C) 향후 공장 개설에 대한 일정을 제공하기 위해
(D) 합의 결과를 발표하기 위해

해설 첫 번째 줄에서 'Manchester's own Cinco Corporation has agreed to a merger with the Eindhoven-based AJX Electronik.'이라고 했으므로 (D)가 정답이다.

156. 암시 / 추론

기사는 어떤 일이 일어날 것이라 나타내는가?
(A) TV 가격이 계속 오를 것이다.
(B) LED 패널이 더 많은 제품에 포함될 것이다.
(C) LED 패널이 새로운 장소에서 생산될 것이다.
(D) TV 제작이 늘어날 것이다.

해설 여섯 번째 줄에서 'AJX would now be able to open a second manufacturing plant in Utrecht.'라고 했으므로 (C)가 정답이다.

157. 문장 삽입

[1], [2], [3], [4]로 표시된 곳 중에서 다음 문장이 들어갈 위치로 가장 적절한 곳은?

"하지만 이 변화는 Cinco의 독점적 이용을 보장해 준다."

(A) [1]
(B) [2]
(C) [3]
(D) [4]

해설 주어진 문장이 But으로 시작하므로 이 앞뒤로 대조되는 내용이 나와야 하고, Cinco's exclusive access를 뒷받침 할 수 있는 문장을 찾아야 한다. 네 번째 줄에서 'High demand for AJX LED panels from other manufacturers occasionally created shortages, forcing Cinco to make compromises on the design of some products.'라고 하여 주어진 문장이 이어지기에 자연스러우므로 (C)가 정답이다.

158-160번은 다음 기사에 관한 문제입니다.

SAN JOSE (9월 14일) — 오늘 아침, 이곳 San Jose에 본사를 둔 JBXL은 Pingguo 사를 인수하는 것에 합의했다고 밝혔다. 158 159 텔레비전 및 가정용 오디오 제조업체는 이 거래가 JBXL로 하여금 휴대용 프로젝터 시장에서 입지를 구축할 수 있게 할 뿐만 아니라, 새로운 대륙으로 확장할 수 있게 해줄 것이라고 말한다. Pingguo 제품들은 원산지인 대만에서 잘 팔리는데, 그곳에서 가장 인기 있는 홈시어터 솔루션 중 하나이다.

"Pingguo는 비교적 신생회사임에도 불구하고 세계에서 최첨단 제조기술을 보유하고 있어, 저희가 대만에서 발판을 마련하는 데 도움이 될 것입니다,"라고 CEO Hope Chun이 발표를 위해 모인 기자들에게 말했다. "그리고 저는 JBXL과 Pingguo에 계신 모든 분들께 저희가 태평양 양쪽에서 사업을 키우려고 한다는 것만 확실하게 말씀드리고 싶습니다."라며 합병이 인력 감축으로 이어질 거라는 소문에 답하여 덧붙였다.

160 "Pingguo 인수는 텔레비전 및 가정용 오디오, 프로젝터 판매에서 글로벌 리더가 되려는 전략에 매우 중요합니다."라고 Chun은 설명했다. "저희는 훌륭한 제품에 대해 저희와 생각을 같이하는 일류 제조업체 및 디자이너와의 협력을 통해 새로운 시장에 진출하는 것을 목표로 합니다."

어휘

reveal 밝히다, 드러내다 | reach 도달하다 | agreement 합의 | deal 거래, 합의 | expand 확장하다 | continent 대륙 | presence 입지, 존재 | portable 휴대용의 | native 원산지의 | relatively 비교하여 | cutting-edge 최첨단의 | foothold 발판 | assure 장담하다, 확인하다 | intend 의도하다 | grow 키우다 | operation 사업, 영업 | Pacific 태평양 | in response to ~에 답하여 | merger 합병 | loss 손실 | strategy 전략 | aim 목표하다 | collaboration 협동 | leading 선두적인, 주요한 | commitment 헌신, 약속, 책무

158. 상세 정보

JBXL은 Pingguo 사를 왜 인수했는가?
(A) JBXL은 더 저렴한 공급업체를 찾고 있었다.
(B) Pingguo는 주요 경쟁사였다.
(C) Pingguo는 오랜 성공 실적을 가지고 있다.
(D) JBXL은 새로운 지역에 진출하길 원했다.

해설 첫 번째 단락에서 'The television and home audio maker says the deal will allow JBXL to expand to a new continent as well as build its presence in the portable projector market.'이라고 했으므로 (D)가 정답이다.

✛ Paraphrasing

expand to a new continent → enter a new region

159. 사실 확인

Pingguo 사가 제조하는 상품에 관하여 사실인 것은?
(A) San Jose에서 조립된다.
(B) 영화에 종종 사용된다.
(C) 곧 새로운 제품을 출시할 것이다.
(D) 용이하게 운반될 수 있다.

해설 첫 번째 단락에서 'The television and home audio maker says the deal will allow JBXL to expand to a new continent as well as build its presence in the portable projector market.'이라고 했으므로 (D)가 정답이다.

✛ Paraphrasing

portable → carried easily

160. 암시 / 추론

기사에 따르면, JBXL은 향후 무엇을 하겠는가?
(A) 대만으로 본사를 이전할 것이다
(B) San Jose에 있는 인원을 감축할 것이다
(C) 새로운 임원을 임명할 것이다
(D) Pingguo같은 회사들과 더 많이 협력할 것이다

해설 세 번째 단락에서 '"Purchasing Pingguo is essential in our strategy to become a global leader in television, home audio, and projector sales," "We aim to enter new markets through collaborations with leading manufacturers and designers who share our commitment to great products."'라고 했으므로 (D)가 정답이다.

✛ Paraphrasing

collaborations with → partner with,
manufacturers → companies

161-163번은 다음 고용 계약서에 관한 문제입니다.

> **Florence 호텔 그룹**
>
> **고용 계약서**

1. Florence 호텔 그룹과 Jordan Abbas 간 계약

2. 고용 시작일: 3월 1일

3. 업무: **161** 직무는 다음의 업무들로 구성됩니다:
   - ◆ 전화로 예약 처리하기
   - ◆ 고객에게 인사 및 친근한 관계 구축하기
   - ◆ 방문객을 위해 버스 및 택시 서비스 예약하기
   - ◆ 호텔 편의시설 관련 불만 사항 해결하기
   - ◆ 지역 관광명소 및 관광지 추천하기
   - ◆ 교대 관리자에게 일일 수익 보고하기

4. 기타 업무: 직원은 3개월 수습 기간 동안 필수교육에 참여해야 합니다.

5. 보수: 직원은 연간 급여를 받게 되는데, 매년 38,000달러의 금액이 월 단위로 지급됩니다. **162** 성과 평가는 4/4분기에 진행됩니다. 급여는 평가 결과를 바탕으로 인상될 수 있습니다.

6. **163** 표준 연차휴가: **163** 회사의 표준 연차 휴가(SAL) 정책에 따라, 직원들에게는 매년 **163D** 20일의 유급 휴가, **163C** 5일의 병가 및 **163A** 10일의 공휴일이 부여됩니다. 의학적 이유로 5일 이상 휴가를 써야 하는 직원은, 이러한 경우 SAL 정책에 의해 보장되지 않기 때문에, 회사의 연장 휴가 정책을 참조해야 합니다.

어휘

employment 고용 | contract 계약 | agreement 합의, 동의 | period 기간 | duties 업무 | position 직위, 일자리 | consist of ~로 구성되다 | following 그다음의 | responsibility 책임 | process 처리하다 | reservation 예약 | greet 인사하다 | build 쌓다 | rapport (친밀한) 관계 | schedule 일정을 잡다 | visitor 방문객 | address 처리하다 | complaint 불만 | regarding ~에 관하여 | amenity 생활 편의시설, 호텔 편의용품 | recommend 추천하다 | local 현지의, 지역의 | tourist attraction 관광지 | site 장소 | report 보고하다 | daily 매일의 | earnings 소득, 수입 | shift 교대 조 | manager 관리자 | partake in ~에 참가하다 | mandatory 필수인 | training session 교육, 연수 | probationary 시험적인, 수습의 | remuneration 보수 | annual 연례의 | salary 월급 | payable 지불할 수 있는, 지불해야 하는 | monthly 매월의 | installment 분할 불입금 | performance 성과 | evaluation 평가 | quarter 4분의 1 | be subject to ~의 대상이다 | increase 증가 | result 결과 | assessment 평가 | standard 일반적인, 표준의 | leave 휴가 | in accordance with ~에 따라 | policy 정책 | entitle 자격을 주다 | paid vacation day 유급 휴가 | sick day 병가 | public holiday 공휴일 | medical 의학적인 | refer to ~에게 문의하다, ~를 참조하다 | extended 늘어난, 길어진 | absence 결석 | case 경우, 사례 | cover 포함시키다, 보장하다

161. 암시 / 추론

Abbas 씨의 직업은 무엇이겠는가?
(A) 여행 가이드
(B) 기업 트레이너
(C) 객실 관리 직원
(D) 프론트 데스크 보조

해설 '3. Duties' 항목에서 'Processing reservations over the phone, Greeting and building rapport with guests, Scheduling bus and taxi services for visitors, Addressing complaints regarding hotel amenities, Recommending local tourist attractions and sites, Reporting daily earnings to the shift manager'라고 했으므로 (D)가 정답이다.

162. 암시 / 추론

Abbas 씨의 급여는 언제 조정되겠는가?

(A) 4/4분기 동안
(B) 3개월 수습기간 마지막에
(C) 내년 3월
(D) 내년 1월

해설 '5. Remuneration' 항목에서 'Performance evaluations are held during the fourth quarter of the year. Salary is subject to increases based on the results of the assessment.'라고 했으므로 (A)가 정답이다.

163. 사실 확인

Florence 호텔 그룹의 SAL 정책에 의해 보장되지 않는 것은?

(A) 공휴일
(B) 연장 휴가
(C) 병가
(D) 개인 휴가

해설 '6. Standard Annual Leave' 항목에서 지문의 단서와 보기를 매칭시키면, 'In accordance with the company's standard annual leave (SAL) policy, employees are entitled to 20 paid vacation days, 5 sick days, and 10 public holidays every year.'는 (A), (C), (D)와 일치하며, 'Staff members who need to take more than 5 days off due to medical reasons must refer to the company's extended leave of absence policy, as this kind of case is not covered by the SAL policy.'라고 하여 연장 휴가는 SAL 정책으로 보장되지 않는다는 것을 알 수 있으므로 (B)가 정답이다.

+ Paraphrasing

vacation days → personal vacations,
sick days → sick leave,
extended leave of absence → extended time off

164-167번은 다음 편지에 관한 문제입니다.

11월 27일

Timothy Ng
3543 Rue Levy
Montreal, Quebec

Ng 씨께,

164 11월 25일 저희에게 보내주신 편지에서의 귀하의 의견에 감사드립니다. **165** Bello Ristorante를 대신하여, 11월 21일 귀하의 졸업파티 중 저희 식당에서 겪으신 불쾌한 경험에 대해 사과드립니다. —[1]—. 안타깝게도, 그날 저희 요리사 중 2명이 병가를 내서 평소보다 음식이 늦게 나왔습니다. 불편을 끼쳐드려 대단히 죄송합니다. 시간 내어 불만사항에 대해 알려주셔서 감사드립니다. 고객 만족은 저희에게 최우선으로 중요합니다. 그래도, 식사를 즐기셨다니 다행입니다. —[2]—.

167 귀하의 이용에 감사드리며, 무료 식사권을 보내드립니다. —[3]—. 이 이용권은 Bello Ristorante나 Greenhouse가 22번지에 있는 저희 자매 레스토랑 Garden Opera에서 사용 가능합니다. **166A** Garden Opera는 Bello Ristorante보다 좌석 수는 적지만, 더 분위기가 있습니다. **166D** 게다가, Garden Opera는 독특한 메뉴로 몇몇 요리 잡지에 소개된 바 있습니다. **166C** 또한, 레스토랑의 자연 그대로의 실내장식은 다른 어느 곳에서도 얻을 수 없는 식사 경험을 선사합니다. —[4]—.

다시 한번 사과드리며, 저희에게 시간 내어 편지를 보내주셔서 감사드립니다. 제가 해드릴 수 있는 것이 있다면, 주저 말고 저에게 연락해 주세요.

진심을 담아,

Esther Lyons

Esther Lyons, 총지배인

동봉물 재중

어휘

appreciate 고마워하다 | on behalf of ~를 대신하여 | apologize 사과하다 | unpleasant 불쾌한 | graduation 졸업 | call in sick 병가를 내다 | inconvenience 불편함 | voice 목소리를 내다 | frustration 불만, 좌절 | upmost 가장 중요한, 가장 위의 | relieve 안도하게 하다 | patronage (상점, 식당에서 고객의) 애용, 후원 | entrée 주요리, 앙트레 | voucher 할인권, 쿠폰 | valid 유효한 | intimate (장소가) 분위기 있는, (사람이) 친밀한 | feature 특징, 특색 | culinary 요리의 | natural 자연의, 천연의 | décor 실내장식 | hesitate 망설이다, 주저하다

164. 상세 정보

Ng 씨는 처음에 왜 Lyons 씨에게 연락했는가?

(A) 예약 일정을 잡으려고
(B) 서비스에 관해 불만을 제기하려고
(C) 메뉴에 관해 문의하려고
(D) 새로운 소유권을 지지하려고

해설 첫 번째 단락에서 'I appreciate your comments from the letter you sent us on November 25. On behalf of Bello Ristorante, I want to apologize for your unpleasant experience at our restaurant during your graduation party on November 21.'라고 했으므로 (B)가 정답이다.

165. 상세 정보

Ng 씨는 언제 Bello Ristorante를 방문했는가?

(A) 11월 21일
(B) 11월 22일
(C) 11월 25일
(D) 11월 27일

해설 Ng 씨에게 보낸 편지의 첫 번째 단락에서 'On behalf of Bello Ristorante, I want to apologize for your unpleasant experience at our restaurant during your graduation party on November 21.'라고 했으므로 (A)가 정답이다.

166. 사실 확인

Lyons 씨가 Garden Opera에 관하여 언급하지 않은 것은?

(A) Bello Ristorante만큼 많은 좌석을 보유하지 않는다.
(B) 주로 채식주의자용 메뉴를 판매한다.
(C) 실내장식이 모두 자연적이다.
(D) 출간물에서 다뤄진 적이 있다.

해설 두 번째 단락에서 지문의 단서와 보기를 매칭시키면, 'The Garden Opera has fewer seating areas than Bello Ristorante has, but is more intimate.'는 (A)와, 'Not to mention, Garden Opera has been featured in several culinary magazines for its unique menu.'는 (D)와, 'In addition, the all-natural décor of the restaurant'은 (C)와 일치하지만, 채식주의자용 메뉴를 판매한다는 내용은 언급된 바 없으므로 (B)가 정답이다.

+ Paraphrasing

seating areas → seats, magazines → publications,

décor → decorations

167. 문장 삽입

[1], [2], [3], [4]로 표시된 곳 중에서 다음 문장이 들어갈 위치로 가장 적절한 곳은?

"일 년 이내에 사용되어야 합니다."

(A) [1]
(B) [2]
(C) [3]
(D) [4]

해설 주어진 문장의 It이 가리키는 대상이 나온 문장을 찾아야 한다. 두 번째 단락에서 'Because we appreciate your patronage, I have sent you a voucher for a free entrée.'라고 하여 주어진 문장이 이어지기에 자연스러우므로 (C)가 정답이다.

168-171번은 다음 문자메시지 대화에 관한 문제입니다.

Igor Malkin (오전 8시 22분)
모두 안녕하세요. 우리가 오늘 처리해야 할 중요한 문제가 있어요. 시작하려면, **168 169** 저희 Merst 지점에 와서 줄뿌림 작물 트랙터를 살펴볼 전문가가 필요해요. **171** 또한, 시 공무원이 곧 저희 Salvern 지점의 농산물을 검사하러 올 거예요.

Katie Gareth (오전 8시 24분)
169 전문가가 언제 필요하죠? 보통 사전 공지를 줘야 해요.

Igor Malkin (오전 8시 27분)
169 빠를수록 좋아요. 트랙터 전기시스템에 문제가 있어요.

Katie Gareth (오전 8시 30분)
169 알았어요. 제가 준비할게요.

Samantha Brown (오전 8시 31분)
저기, 여러분. **170** 제가 방금 Calvin's Vehicle and Machinery의 광고를 봤는데요. 신규 고객은 최초 수리서비스에서 최대15%까지 할인을 받을 수 있어요. 저희의 다른 시설에서의 서비스 이용을 고려해봐도 되겠어요.

Igor Malkin (오전 8시 33분)
저도 그 광고 봤어요. 제가 맞게 기억한다면, **170** 할인은 일요일까지 유효해요.

Katie Gareth (오전 8시 36분)
제가 전화해볼게요. Merst 지점에만 해당되는 거 맞죠?

Igor Malkin (오전 8:39분)
네, 지금은요. Samantha, **171** Erikson 씨에게 전화해서 그녀가 언제 Salvern 지점에 방문할 계획인지 알아봐요.

Samantha Brown (오전 8시 42분)
지금 할게요.

어휘
address 다루다, 처리하다 | specialist 전문가 | come by 오다 | check out 살펴보다, 확인하다 | row crop 줄뿌림 작물 | tractor 트랙터 | location 위치, 지점 | expect 예상하다, 기대하다 | city official 시 공무원 | inspect 검사하다, 점검하다 | produce 농산물 | branch 지점 | prior 사전의 | notice 공지 | wrong 잘못된 | electrical 전기의 | arrange 마련하다, (일을) 처리하다 | advertisement 광고(ad) | vehicle 탈 것 | machinery 기계(류) | first-time 처음으로 해보는 | client 고객 | up to ~까지 | repair 수리 | consider 고려하다 | service 점검 [정비]하다, (서비스를) 제공하다 | facility 시설, 공장 | correctly 올바르게, 맞게 | offer 할인, 제안 | valid 유효한

---

168. 암시 / 추론

글쓴이들이 종사하는 사업에 관하여 알 수 있는 것은?

(A) 최근 새로운 지점을 오픈했다.
(B) 재고관리 시스템을 업그레이드했다.
(C) 기계 부품을 판매한다.
(D) 농장을 운영한다.

해설 오전 8시 22분, Igor Malkin의 메시지에서 'we need a specialist to come by and check out one of our row crop tractors at our Merst location. Also, we're expecting a city official to inspect the produce at the Salvern branch soon.'이라고 했으므로 (D)가 정답이다.

169. 화자 의도 파악

오전 8시 30분에, Gareth 씨가 "제가 준비할게요."라고 할 때 무엇을 의미하겠는가?

(A) 그녀가 정비사에게 연락할 것이다.
(B) 그녀가 Salvern 지점을 방문할 것이다.
(C) 그녀가 계약서 양식을 준비할 것이다.
(D) 그녀가 몇몇 고객들에게 이메일을 보낼 것이다.

해설 오전 8시 22분 ~ 8시 30분 대화에서 Igor Malkin 씨가 'we need a specialist to come by and check out one of our row crop tractors'라고 한 말에 Katie Gareth가 'When do we need the specialist?'라고 물었고, 이에 Igor Malkin이 'The sooner, the better.'라고 하자, Katie Gareth가 'Alright. I'll have it arranged.'라고 한 것이므로 (A)가 정답이다.

+ Paraphrasing

specialist → mechanic

170. 사실 확인

Calvin's Vehicle and Machinery에 관하여 언급된 것은?

(A) 시간한정 할인을 제공하고 있다.
(B) 일요일에는 문을 닫는다.
(C) 15년간 영업해왔다.
(D) 국제배송을 제공한다.

해설 오전 8시 31분 ~ 8시 33분 대화에서 Samantha Brown이 'I just saw an advertisement from Calvin's Vehicle and Machinery. First-time clients can receive up to 15 percent off their first repair service.'라고 한 말에, Igor Malkin이 'the offer is valid until the end of the day Sunday.'라고 했으므로 (A)가 정답이다.

171. 암시 / 추론

Erikson 씨는 누구겠는가?

(A) 시 검사관
(B) 슈퍼마켓 주인
(C) 판매직원
(D) 차량 디자이너

해설 오전 8시 39분, Igor Malkin의 메시지에서 'call Ms. Erikson and see when she plans on visiting the Salvern location.'이라고 하였는데, 오전 8시 22분, Igor Malkin의 메시지에서 'Also, we're expecting a city official to inspect the produce at the Salvern branch soon.'이라고 하여 Salvern 지점에 방문하는 시 공무원이 Erikson 씨라는 것을 알 수 있으므로 (A)가 정답이다.

+ Paraphrasing

a city official → a city inspector

172-175번은 다음 이메일에 관한 문제입니다.

수신: 전 직원
발신: Robert Upton
날짜: 5월 25일
제목: IBA 컨벤션
첨부: 컨벤션 시간표

모든 분들께,

172 173 올해 국제 바리스타협회 컨벤션이 8월 마지막 주간에 이곳 Kona에서 열립니다. 주최 책임자 Jake Hu의 초청을 받아, 제가 2개의 세미나를 진행하게 된 것을 알려드리게 되어 영광입니다. 이렇게 수상한 바리스타에게 인정받는 것은 성과인데, 그는 Hawaii 고유의 커피 전통에 관한 다큐멘터리 시리즈 수상작 〈Finding Black Gold〉의 감독이기도 합니다. 무엇보다도, 이것은 Upton's 카페가 세계 수준의 품질을 더 많은 사람들에게 광고할 수 있는 굉장한 기회입니다.

첫 번째 세미나는 커피콩을 평가하는 감별 기술에 관한 것이 될 것입니다. 174 우리 수석 로스터인 Cindy Hong이 이것에 뛰어나서, 저는 그녀에게 워크숍을 함께 이끌어 달라고 요청했습니다. 두 번째 세미나에서는 단골고객 기반을 구축하고 유지하는 것의 어려움에 대해 이야기할 예정입니다. 174 Jim Plunkett은 부매니저로서 대중의 관심을 끌기 위한 행사 준비를 언제나 잘 해왔기 때문에, 그에게 도움을 요청했습니다.

일정 중에 시간을 낼 수 있으시면, 적어도 한 세션에는 오시면 좋을 것 같습니다. 하지만 가게에 수요가 꽤 많아질 것이므로, 컨벤션 내내 커피숍에 전 직원이 필요합니다. 175 파악할 수 있게, 모든 팀원들은 컨벤션이 시작하는 8월 23일에서 최소 2주 전에 어떤 세션에 참석하고 싶은지 저에게 알려주시겠어요? 참고하시라고 전체 시간표를 첨부해 드렸습니다.

안부를 전하며,
Robert Upton

어휘
association 협회 | honored 영광스러운 | share 공유하다, 나누다 | put on (쇼 등을) 무대에 올리다 | achievement 업적, 성취 | recognize 인정받다 | decorated 훈장을 받은, 장식된 | barista 바리스타 | unique 고유의, 특유의 | tradition 전통 | market 시장에 출시하다, 광고하다 | cupping 커핑 (커피의 맛을 감별하는 것) | evaluate 평가하다 | bean 콩 | excel 뛰어나다 | be supposed to ~하기로 되어있다 | build 쌓다, 구축하다 | maintain 유지하다 | loyal 충성스러운 | organize 조직하다, 준비하다 | engage (주의, 관심을) 끌다 | make time 시간을 내다 | strong (수효가) 아주 많은 | keep track of ~를 파악하다, 알고 있다 | attach 첨부하다 | time table 시간표 | reference 참조

172. 주제 / 목적 / 대상

이메일의 목적은 무엇인가?
(A) 상에 관한 세부 내용을 공개하는 것
(B) 행사 참가에 관해 논의하는 것
(C) 곧 있을 판촉행사를 홍보하는 것
(D) 직원 휴가에 관한 변경 사항을 발표하는 것

해설 첫 번째 단락에서 'This year's convention of the International Baristas' Association will be held here in Kona during the last week of August.'라고 했고 뒤이어 몇 가지 관련 일정을 소개하므로 (B)가 정답이다.

+ Paraphrasing

convention → event

173. 사실 확인

Hu 씨에 관하여 언급된 것은?
(A) Hawaii에 기반을 두고 있다.

(B) 기조연설을 할 것이다.
(C) 다수의 영화를 감독했다.
(D) 8월에 Upton 카페에 올 것이다.

해설 첫 번째 단락에서 'I am honored to share that I've been invited by Jake Hu, the chief organizer, to put on two seminars. It is an achievement ~, who is also the director of the award-winning documentary series on Hawaii's unique coffee traditions, *Finding Black Gold*.'라고 했으므로 (C)가 정답이다.

174. 암시 / 추론

Hong 씨와 Plunkett 씨에 관하여 알 수 있는 것은?
(A) 자신들의 일에 능숙하다.
(B) 워크숍을 이끈 경험이 있다.
(C) 커피 로스팅 전문가이다
(D) 가장 오래 근무한 직원들이다.

해설 두 번째 단락에서 'As our chief roaster, Cindy Hong, excels at this, I've asked her to co-lead the workshop.'이라고 했고, 'As assistant manager, Jim Plunkett has always done fine work organizing events to engage the public'이라고 하여 두 사람 모두 자신의 일에 능숙함을 알 수 있으므로 (A)가 정답이다.

+ Paraphrasing

excel, fine work → proficient

175. 상세 정보

직원들은 무엇을 하라고 요청받는가?
(A) 컨벤션 티켓을 예약하라고
(B) 어떤 정보를 제출하라고
(C) 첨부된 양식을 작성하라고
(D) 추가 시간을 더 근무하라고

해설 세 번째 단락에서 'To keep track of this, could all team members let me know which sessions they'd like to attend at least two weeks before the convention starts on August 23?'라고 했으므로 (B)가 정답이다.

176-180번은 다음 편지와 주문서에 관한 문제입니다.

Emperor 엔터테인먼트 사
1797 Edsel 로, Los Angeles, CA, 90017

2월 19일

Isabelle Frankel 씨
Tuttgarter Platz 33
Berlin, 독일

176 Frankel 씨께,

176 〈Walking to the Moon〉으로 귀하께 누적된 저작권료를 입금해 드렸습니다. 177 귀하의 앨범 및 디지털 판매로 받게 될 저작권 지급액 뿐만 아니라 판매수치를 분류한 이메일이 귀하께 발송되었습니다.

178 저희는 Emperor 엔터테인먼트가 지난 12월 미국 음악위원회에서 선정한 올해의 음반사로 선정되었음을 알려드리게 되어 기쁩니다. 이는 8년 전 설립 이래 저희와 함께 작업해온 훌륭한 아티스트분들 덕분입니다.

감사를 전하기 위해, 179 Emperor 엔터테인먼트 음반사 소속 모든 아티스트들은 저희 온라인 스토어의 모든 상품에 대해 반값 할인을 받게 됩니

다. 결제하실 때 코드 LOY983을 입력해 주세요.

도움이 필요하시면 저에게 연락해 주시기 바랍니다.

진심을 담아,

Marshall Benson
Marshall Benson

어휘
deposit 넣다, 두다, 예치하다; 예(치)금 | royalty 저작권 사용료, 수익금, 로열티 | accrue 누적되[하]다 | break down 분류하다, 나누다 | sales 판매, 매출 | as well as ~뿐만 아니라 | owe 빚지고 있다 | establish 설립하다 | appreciation 감사, 감상 | label 상표, 음반사 | merchandise 물품, 상품 | enter 입력하다, 들어가다 | checkout 계산대 | get in touch with ~와 연락하다 | assist 돕다

---

https://www.emperorent.com/confirmationpage

귀하의 주문이 접수되었습니다!

[180] 2월 한 달 동안 50달러를 초과하는 모든 구매에 대해 무료 포스터를 받으세요.

결제자:	Pamela Coutee
확인 이메일:	pam.coutee@allmail.com
[180] 처리일:	2월 23일
배송지:	Pamela Coutee 3927 Mesa Drive Las Vegas, NV 89101

1. Turning Point 후드 티셔츠 (M)	60.00달러
2. Henry James의 〈Sounds of the Night〉 서명본	50.00달러
[179] 쿠폰 (LOY983)	-55.00달러
[180] 총액	55.00달러

*카드번호 끝자리 3247로 결제

일부 상품은 재고부족으로 이용 가능하지 않을 수 있습니다. 귀하의 주문에 변동사항이 생기면 알림을 받을 것입니다.

어휘
place 주문하다, 두다, 배치하다 | confirmation 확인 | process 과정, 절차 | hood 모자 | sign 서명하다 | payment 지불(금) | available 이용할 수 있는 | inventory 물품 목록, 재고(품) | notify 알리다, 통지하다

---

176. 주제 / 목적 / 대상

편지는 왜 보내졌는가?
(A) 음악을 추천하려고
(B) Frankel 씨를 기념행사에 초대하려고
(C) 계약서 변경 사항을 알리려고
(D) Frankel 씨에게 입금에 대해 알려주려고

해설 첫 번째 지문[편지], 첫 번째 단락에서 'We have deposited the royalties you have accrued for *Walking to the Moon*.'이라고 했으므로 (D)가 정답이다.

177. 상세 정보

Frankel 씨에게 별도의 메시지로 무엇이 전송되었는가?
(A) 수정된 앨범 로고
(B) 상품권

(C) 판매 수치에 대한 설명
(D) 투어 달력

해설 첫 번째 지문[편지], 첫 번째 단락에서 'An e-mail was sent to you breaking down the number of sales as well as the royalty payments you will be receiving for the physical and digital copies of your album.'이라고 했으므로 (C)가 정답이다.

✦ **Paraphrasing**
the number of sales → sales figures

178. 사실 확인

Benson 씨는 Emperor 엔터테인먼트에 대하여 무엇을 언급하는가?
(A) 8주년 기념 콘서트를 개최할 것이다.
(B) 12월에 새로운 밴드를 모집했다.
(C) 영화 제작을 시작할 것이다.
(D) 인정을 받았다.

해설 Benson 씨가 Frankel 씨에게 보낸 첫 번째 지문[편지], 두 번째 단락에서 'We are pleased to inform you that Emperor Entertainment was named Record Label of the Year by the American Music Committee last December.'라고 했으므로 (D)가 정답이다.

✦ **Paraphrasing**
was named Record Label of the Year → received recognition

179. 암시 / 추론 - 연계 문제

Coutee 씨에 관하여 암시되는 것은?
(A) 〈Sounds of the Night〉을 제작했다.
(B) Emperor 엔터테인먼트의 아티스트이다.
(C) Frankel 씨와 같은 대학을 나왔다.
(D) 전에 Emperor 엔터테인먼트에서 상품을 구매한 적이 있다.

해설 Benson 씨가 Frankel 씨에게 보낸 첫 번째 지문[편지], 세 번째 단락에서 'To show our appreciation, every artist under the Emperor Entertainment label will be given an artist discount of half off all merchandise from our online store. Enter code LOY983 during checkout.'이라고 했는데, 두 번째 지문[주문서]에서 쿠폰번호 'LOY983'를 입력한 걸로 미루어 Emperor 엔터테인먼트에 소속된 아티스트임을 알 수 있으므로 (B)가 정답이다.

✦ **Paraphrasing**
artist under the Emperor Entertainment label → Emperor Entertainment artist

180. 암시 / 추론

주문에 관하여 알 수 있는 것은?
(A) 몇 가지 의류 상품을 포함한다.
(B) 무료 포스터와 함께 온다.
(C) 할부로 결제될 것이다.
(D) 익일 배송이 이루어질 것이다.

해설 두 번째 지문[주문서]에서 'Receive a free poster on all purchases over $50 during the month of February.'라고 했는데, 'Process Date'가 'February 23'이고, 'TOTAL'이 55달러인 걸로 미루어 무료 포스터를 받는 조건에 해당함을 알 수 있으므로 (B)가 정답이다.

+ **Paraphrasing**
  free → complimentary

181-185번은 다음 이메일과 정보에 관한 문제입니다.

수신: cs@travelbuddy.com
발신: agruskin@kmail.com
날짜: 9월 3일
제목: 다가오는 여행

안녕하세요.

저는 12월이나 1월에 중미로 가족여행을 계획하고 있는데, 귀사의 여행 패키지에 관심이 있습니다. **185** 총 8명이 될 것입니다(모두 성인). 따뜻하면서 물가인 곳으로 가려고 알아보고 있습니다(저희는 스노클링에도 관심이 있습니다). **181** 그런데 안정적인 무선인터넷 제공하는 숙소를 잡는 것이 중요합니다. **182** 저는 휴가 중에 매우 중요한 전화 회의를 진행해야 해서, 안정적인 연결이 필요합니다.

답장을 기다리겠습니다.

진심을 담아,

Abraham Gruskin

어휘
upcoming 곧 있을, 다가오는 | organize 조직하다, 준비하다 | package 패키지, 일괄 프로그램 | snorkeling 스노클링 | book 예약하다 | accommodation 숙박 | provide 제공하다 | steady 꾸준한, 안정된 | wireless service 무선 서비스 | lead 이끌다, 지휘하다 | conference call 전화 회의 | stable 안정적인 | connection 연결, 접속 | eagerly 간절히 | await 기다리다 | response 대답, 회신

Travel Buddy 여행 패키지 안내 책자 모든 패키지는 콘퍼런스 센터, 24시간 무선인터넷 연결, 수상 경력이 있는 레스토랑을 갖춘 4성급 이상 호텔에서의 숙박을 포함합니다.	패키지 코드
코스타리카: 12월 14일-22일 **183** 이 코스타리카 여행에서 산부터 해변까지 가보세요. 이 여행은 해수면 3,432미터 위 Volcán Irazu로 데려갈 것입니다. 근처 국립공원에서 잠시 시간을 보내세요. 그러고 나서 물가로 이동하여, 해변에서 지척에 있는 Manuel Antonio라는 작은 마을에 머무를 것입니다.	325
멕시코: 12월 22일-31일 Playa Del Carmen을 그 자체로 즐기세요: **183** 흰 모래 해변에서의 휴식과 청록빛 바다에서의 수영. **184** 고대 마야 문명지 Chichén Itzá로 당일치기 여행 하시는 걸 잊지 마세요. 그곳은 고대 구조물에 대해 알고 싶은 분들에게 이상적인 곳입니다.	**185** 166
벨리즈: 12월 28일-1월 3일 San Ignacio에서 최고의 자연을 경험하세요. 주변 정글은 다양한 야생동물과 폭포, 동굴의 안식처로, 보다 흥미로운 경험을 찾는 사람들에게 완벽한 여행을 만들어줍니다. 그러고 나서, 벨리즈의 해안가 섬 Caye Caulker로 이동하여 카리브해가 선사하는 **183** 가장 아름다운 해변가에서 간절히 필요했던 휴식을 취해보세요.	290

185 파나마: 1월 5일-15일
185 태양 아래에서의 재미를 찾으신다면, 더 찾아볼 것도 없습니다. Bocas del Toro에서 최고의 카리브해를 경험해 보세요. 수정같이 맑은 바다에서 스노클링을 하고 산호초를 코앞에서 만나보거나, **183** 해변에서 편히 쉬며 선탠을 해보세요. 또한 사람들과 어울리는 것을 즐긴다면, Bocas del Toro는 파나마의 최고 밤 문화를 경험하게 해줍니다. 이 패키지는 아이가 없는 단체에게 안성맞춤입니다.

185 789

어휘
include 포함하다 | lodging 숙박 | above ~보다 위에 | conference center 회의장, 컨퍼런스 센터 | 24/7 항상, 연중무휴의 | wireless internet 무선 인터넷 | award-winning 상을 받은, 수상한 | excursion 소풍 | journey 여행 | nearby 근처의 | head 향하다 | just a stone's throw away 가까운 거리 | turquoise 청록색 | day trip 당일 여행 | ancient 고대의 | ideal 이상적인 | structure 구조(물) | experience 경험하다 | nature 자연 | at its best 한창때 | surrounding 인근의, 주위의 | wildlife 야생동물 | waterfall 폭포 | cave 동굴 | coast 해안 | relaxation 휴식 | the Caribbean 카리브해 지역 | further 더 | crystal clear 수정같이 맑은 | coral reef 산호초 | up close 바로 가까이에서 | tan 선탠 | socialize (사람들과) 어울리다, 사귀다 | nightlife 밤에 하는 유흥[오락] | perfect 완벽한

181. 암시 / 추론

Gruskin에 관하여 알 수 있는 것은?
(A) 여행하는 동안 일을 할 것이다.
(B) 사업을 시작하기 위해 중미로 이주할 것이다.
(C) 전에 Travel Buddy로 패키지여행을 예약했었다.
(D) 프로 수영선수였다.

해설 첫 번째 지문 [Gruskin 씨가 보낸 이메일]에서 'It is important, however, that we book an accommodation that provides steady wireless service. I will need to lead some very important conference calls while on vacation, and I need to have a stable connection.'이라고 했으므로 (A)가 정답이다.

+ **Paraphrasing**
  while on vacation → during his trip

182. 동의어

이메일에서 첫 번째 단락, 다섯 번째 줄의 단어 "lead"와 의미상 가장 가까운 것은?
(A) 관리하다
(B) 능가하다
(C) 영향을 미치다
(D) 초래하다

해설 첫 번째 지문 [Gruskin 씨가 보낸 이메일]에서 'I will need to lead some very important conference calls while on vacation, and I need to have a stable connection.'에서의 'lead'는 '이끌다'라는 의미로 쓰이므로 보기 중 같은 의미를 갖는 (A)가 정답이다.

183. 상세 정보

모든 투어들에 공통적인 한 가지는 무엇인가?
(A) 해변에서의 시간을 포함한다.
(B) 운동선수를 대상으로 한다.
(C) 아이가 있는 가족을 위해 만들어졌다.
(D) 정확히 일주일간 지속된다.

해설 두 번째 지문 [정보]에서, 'Costa Rica: December 14-22'의

'Go from the mountain to the beach in this Costa Rican excursion.', 'Mexico: December 22-31'의 'relaxing on the white-sand beaches', 'Belize: December 28-January 3'의 'relaxation at one of the most beautiful beaches', 'Panama: January 5-15'의 'just relax on the beach and get your tan on.'을 통해 모든 투어에 해변에서의 시간이 포함되어 있음을 알 수 있으므로 (A)가 정답이다.

184. 상세 정보

건축에 관심 있는 사람들에게 최고인 여행지는 어디인가?

(A) 코스타리카
(B) 멕시코
(C) 벨리즈
(D) 파나마

해설 두 번째 지문[정보]에서, 'Mexico: December 22-31'의 'Don't forget to take a day trip to the ancient Mayan site Chichén Itzá, which is ideal for those wanting to learn about old structures.'을 통해 멕시코가 유명함을 오래된 건축물로 알 수 있으므로 (B)가 정답이다.

✚ **Paraphrasing**

old structures → architecture, ideal → best

185. 암시 / 추론 - 연계 문제

Gruskin 씨는 무슨 투어를 선택하겠는가?

(A) 325
(B) 166
(C) 290
(D) 789

해설 첫 번째 지문[Gruskin 씨가 보낸 이메일]에서 'There will be a total of eight people (all adults). We're looking to go somewhere warm and near the water (we're also interested in snorkeling).'이라고 했는데, 두 번째 지문[정보], 'Panama: January 5-15'에서 'Snorkel in the crystal clear waters, and see coral reefs up close, or just relax on the beach and get your tan on. This package is perfect for groups without children.'이라고 하여 Gruskin 씨가 제시한 조건을 모두 충족하고 있으므로 (D)가 정답이다.

186-190번은 다음 공지, 이메일, 배치도에 관한 문제입니다.

모든 고객 여러분께

186 지난주 시 건축 검사관들로부터 세 번째 평가를 받은 즉시, Shelby County 공원 협회(SCPA)는 4월 11일 Wayne 공원 온실의 문을 닫아야 합니다. 실내관에서 대다수의 식물을 보존할 수 있었으나, 1월 21일 있었던 지진은 건물에 심각한 손상을 입힌 것으로 보입니다. 애석하게도, 저희 기관은 백 년된 이 역사적인 건축물의 복원을 감당할 자금이 충분치 않습니다. 190 하지만, 감사하게도 Wellington 인근의 Unity 수목원에서 저희의 가장 사랑받는 식물들 대다수를 받아주겠다고 제안해 주셨습니다. 식물은 Unity 수목원의 새로 개조된 구역에 새로운 보금자리를 갖게 될 것인데, 5월 25일 개장할 예정입니다. 188 SCPA는 현재 4월 13일에 다음 식물 운송 또는 창고 정리 업무들 중 하나를 도와 자원봉사하실 분을 구하고 있습니다: 또한 다양한 식물이 관심 있는 개인 및 기관에 경매로 판매될 것입니다.

어휘

patron 후원자, 고객 | evaluation 평가 | inspector 검사관, 감독관 | shut down 문을 닫다 | conservatory 온실 | preserve 지키다, 보존하다 | plant

---

식물 | indoor 실내의 | earthquake 지진 | irreparable 회복할 수 없는 | damage 손해, 피해 | structure 구조(물) | sadly 애석하게도, 슬프게도 | organization 조직 | sufficient 충분한 | fund 자금 | cover (돈을) 대다 | restoration 복원, 복구 | landmark 역사적인 건물, 랜드마크 | nearby 인근의 | graciously 고맙게도, 자비롭게 | beloved 사랑하는 | renovate 개조하다, 보수하다 | section 부분, 구역 | currently 현재 | seek 찾다, 구하다 | volunteer 자원 봉사를 하다 | duties 업무 | transport 수송하다 | organize 정리하다 | storage 저장, 보관 | auction off 경매로 처분하다 | organization 조직, 단체

수신: DeanNewton@lwmail.com
발신: GeorgeB@scpa.org
날짜: 3월 17일
제목: Golden Barrel 선인장

Newton 씨,

메시지를 주셔서 감사드립니다. 저희의 최근 결정으로 여전히 마음이 아프지만, 저희 식물 대부분이 새로운 거처를 찾게 되어 기쁩니다.

문의주신 내용과 관련하여, 저희 golden barrel 선인장은 구입 가능합니다. 경매기간(4월 8일-11일)동안 이 식물 및 다른 물품들을 보실 수 있습니다. 189 하지만 물품을 구입하시려면 www.scpa.org/auction_event에 로그인하셔야 합니다. 물품 수령자는 4월 15일에 발표됩니다. 187 거실에 활기를 불어넣을 많은 장식품도 있을 것입니다.

188 식물 이동을 도와주시겠다는 제안에 대해서는 555-984-1987번으로 Mikhail Gabbert에게 메시지를 보내주세요. 그가 자원봉사 배정을 담당하고 있습니다.

안부를 전하며,

George Blanche
Shelby County 공원 협회, 부회장

어휘

cactus 선인장 | grieve 슬퍼하다 | inquiry 문의 | purchase 구입, 구매 | view 보다 | auction 경매 | on offer 살 수 있는, 제공되는 | recipient 수신인, 수령인 | announce 알리다, 발표하다 | decorative 장식용의 | liven up 활기를 불어넣다 | relocate 이동시키다 | text 문자를 보내다 | in charge of ~를 맡은, 담당하는 | coordinate 조정하다, 편성하다 | volunteer 자원봉사자 | effort 노력, 수고

Unity 수목원 배치도

Rothman 숲
웅장한 조경이 늘어서 있는 우아한 산책로

190 Juniper 온실 (5월 25일 재개장)

양치류 실	Woodward 식물센터	야자수 온실	토란 컬렉션

Hillside 정원
봄철 꽃과 현지 식물 종을 위한 최적의 장소

Stevenson 난초원
전 세계 희귀 표본 보유

어휘

arboretum 수목원 | layout 배치, 레이아웃 | elegant 우아한 | walkway 통로, 보도 | lined with 늘어서 있는 | spectacular 장관을 이루는, 굉장한 |

186. 주제 / 목적 / 대상

공지의 목적은 무엇인가?

(A) 식물 관리 팁에 대해 논의하려고
(B) 새로운 공원을 홍보하려고
(C) 기부금을 요청하려고
(D) 폐업을 알리려고

해설 첫 번째 지문 [공지], 첫 번째 줄에서 'Upon receiving the third evaluation from city building inspectors last week, the Shelby County Park Association (SCPA) has no choice but to shut down the Wayne Park Conservatory on 11 April.' 이라고 했으므로 (D)가 정답이다.

187. 암시 / 추론

Newton 씨에 관하여 알 수 있는 것은?

(A) 다수의 물품을 기부하는 것에 관심이 있다.
(B) 자신의 집을 장식할 만한 것을 찾고 있다.
(C) 수많은 선인장을 보유하고 있다.
(D) Shelby County 공원 협회의 회원이다.

해설 두 번째 지문 [Newton 씨에게 보낸 이메일], 두 번째 단락에서 'There will be plenty of decorative items to liven up your living room.'이라고 하여 그가 자신의 거실에 놓을 장식품을 찾고 있음을 알 수 있으므로 (B)가 정답이다.

188. 암시 / 추론 – 연계 문제

Newton 씨는 언제 Wayne 공원 온실에서 자원 봉사를 하겠는가?

(A) 4월 8일
(B) 4월 11일
(C) 4월 13일
(D) 4월 15일

해설 첫 번째 지문 [공지], 여덟 번째 줄에서 'The SCPA is currently seeking people to volunteer on 13 April for either of the following duties: transporting plants ~'라고 했는데, 두 번째 지문 [Newton 씨에게 보낸 이메일], 세 번째 단락에서 'As for your offer to help with relocating plants,'라고 하여 그가 식물 운송 봉사를 할 것임을 알 수 있으므로 (C)가 정답이다.

✚ Paraphrasing

transporting plants → relocating plants

189. 상세 정보

이메일에 따르면, 고객들은 협회 웹사이트에서 무엇을 할 수 있는가?

(A) 자원봉사자로 등록할 수 있다
(B) 소식지를 신청할 수 있다
(C) 물품에 입찰할 수 있다
(D) 글을 올릴 수 있다

해설 두 번째 지문 [이메일], 두 번째 단락에서 'To make an offer on an item, though, you'll have to log in to www.scpa.org/auction_event.'라고 했으므로 (C)가 정답이다.

190. 상세 정보 – 연계 문제

Wayne 공원 온실의 일부 물품은 어디에 보관될 것인가?

(A) Rothman 숲
(B) Juniper 온실
(C) Hillside 정원
(D) Stevenson 난초원

해설 첫 번째 지문 [공지], 여섯 번째 줄에서 'However, Unity Arboretum in nearby Wellington has graciously offered to accept many of our most beloved plants. They will have a new home in the newly renovated section of Unity Arboretum, set to open on 25 May.'라고 했는데, 세 번째 지문 [배치도]에서 'Juniper Greenhouse (reopening May 25)'라고 하여 Juniper 온실에 보관될 것임을 알 수 있으므로 (B)가 정답이다.

191-195번은 다음 문자 메시지, 일정, 그리고 이메일에 관한 문제입니다.

192 수신: Terrell Elway
발신: Lupita Monroe
191 시간: 7월 10일 오후 2시 14분

Terrell께,

Chester's World에서 다음 달 있을 Music on the Rocks에서 공연을 할 수 없다고 저희에게 알려왔어요. **192** 그래서 오후 4시 45분 Littleton 무대에 빈자리가 생깁니다. 이 자리에 관심 있으시면, 저에게 바로 연락 주세요. **191** 홍보용 포스터가 내일 오후에 인쇄에 들어가야 하거든요.

어휘
notify 알리다, 통지하다 | perform 공연하다 | spot (특정한) 장소, 자리 | promotional poster 홍보용 포스터 | print 인쇄하다

Music on the Rocks

공연 라인업: 8월 15일, 일요일

	오후 12시	**195** 오후 2시 15분	**192** 오후 4시 45분	오후 6시
Copperton 무대		**195** Jubilee Crew		The Counters
192 Littleton 무대	Marsha Payne		**192** The Writing	Angelus
Brandly 무대	Vince Clip	Social System	Reignmen	

최초 입장고객 100명은 모든 구입 기념품에 적용되는 20% 할인권을 받게 됩니다. **193** 모든 참석자는 입장 시 무료 티셔츠를 받습니다. 외부 음식 및 음료는 엄격히 금지됩니다. 행사장이 고도가 높은 곳에 있으므로, 여분의 옷을 챙겨오시길 권장 드립니다. 쇼는 날씨에 관계없이 진행됩니다. 공연장 및 공연자에 대해 더 알아보시려면, www.musicontherocks.com을 방문해 주세요.

어휘
performance 공연 | lineup 정렬, 라인업, (행사 등의) 예정표 | gate 문 | voucher 할인권, 쿠폰 | souvenir 기념품 | purchase 구입하다 | attendee 참석자 | complimentary 무료의 | entry 입장 | strictly 엄격히, 절대적으로 | prohibit 금지하다 | bring 가져오다 | extra 추가의 | layer (표면을 덮는) 층, 겹 | clothing 옷, 의복 | venue 장소 | locate (특정한 위치에) 두다 | altitude 고도 | go on (공연을) 시작하다 | rain or shine 날씨와 관계 없이 | performer 공연 (연주)자

수신: lupitam@musicontherocks.com
발신: chadwick@lockstudios.com
날짜: 8월 28일
제목: 사진
첨부: 산 사진

Lupita, 안녕하세요.

콘서트 촬영 기회를 주셔서 감사합니다! 제가 지금 사진들을 살펴보는 중인데, 195제 눈길을 사로잡은 사진 한 장을 첨부해 드려요. 이 사진은 Jubilee Crew가 무대 위로 올라오는 순간 촬영됐어요. 저는 이 사진이 배경에 Pike 산맥과 전체 관중이 나와서 정말 마음에 들어요. 웹사이트 홈페이지에 이 사진을 사용하는 걸 고려하셨으면 해요. 194제가 사진들을 살펴보면서 〈Music Today〉의 다음 달 호에 넣기에 괜찮아 보이는 몇 장을 따로 빼놓을게요.

곧 연락드릴게요.

Chadwick Lock
Lock 스튜디오

어휘

opportunity 기회 | shoot 촬영하다 | currently 현재 | go through 살펴보다, 검토하다 | attach 첨부하다 | catch my eye 눈길을 사로잡다 | stage 무대 | shot 사진 | entire 전체의 | crowd 군중, 무리 | mountain range 산맥 | background 배경 | continue 계속하다 | look through ~을 살펴[훑어]보다 | set aside ~를 한쪽으로 치워 놓다 | issue (정기 간행물의) 호

---

191. 상세 정보

문자 메시지에 따르면, 7월 11일에 무슨 일이 있을 것인가?
(A) Chester's World가 투어를 할 것이다.
(B) Monroe 씨가 콘서트에서 노래를 할 것이다.
(C) 공연 무대가 설치될 것이다.
(D) 광고가 인쇄될 것이다.

해설 첫 번째 지문[7월 10일에 발송한 문자 메시지]의 Time: 02:14 P.M., July 10에서 메시지를 보낸 날짜를 확인할 수 있고, 'The promotional posters must be printed tomorrow afternoon.'이라고 했으므로 (D)가 정답이다.

+ **Paraphrasing**

promotional posters → an advertisement

192. 상세 정보 - 연계 문제

Elway 씨의 밴드명은 무엇인가?
(A) The Writing
(B) Reignmen
(C) The Counters
(D) Angelus

해설 첫 번째 지문[Elway 씨에게 보낸 문자 메시지]에서 'This means that there is an opening on the Littleton Stage at 4:45 P.M. If you'd like to take this spot,'이라고 했는데, 두 번째 지문[일정 표에서] '4:45 P.M.', 'Littleton Stage'의 공연자가 'The Writing'임을 알 수 있으므로 (A)가 정답이다.

193. 사실 확인

일정에 관하여 언급된 것은?
(A) 행사장에서 음식이 제공될 것이다.
(B) 기념품을 온라인으로 구입할 수 있다.
(C) 무료 상품이 참석자들에게 제공될 것이다.
(D) 우천 시 콘서트가 연기될 것이다.

해설 두 번째 지문[일정]에서 'All attendees will receive a complimentary T-shirt upon entry.'라고 했으므로 (C)가 정답이다.

+ **Paraphrasing**

complimentary → free

194. 암시 / 추론

Lock 씨의 사진에 관하여 알 수 있는 것은?
(A) 웹사이트에서 구입 가능하다.
(B) 출판물에 실릴 것이다.
(C) 공연자들의 사인이 실려있었다.
(D) Pike 산맥에서 촬영되었다.

해설 세 번째 지문[이메일]에서 'As I continue to look through the photos, I'll set aside a few that I think will look good in next month's issue of *Music Today*.'라고 했으므로 (B)가 정답이다.

195. 상세 정보 - 연계 문제

Lock 씨는 이메일에 첨부한 사진을 언제 찍었는가?
(A) 오후 12시
(B) 오후 2시 15분
(C) 오후 4시 45분
(D) 오후 6시

해설 세 번째 지문[이메일]에서 'I have attached one that caught my eye. This picture was taken just as the Jubilee Crew was walking onto the stage.'라고 했는데, 두 번째 지문[일정 표]에서, 'Jubilee Crew'의 공연시간이 '2:15 P.M.'임을 알 수 있으므로 (B)가 정답이다.

196-200번은 다음 웹페이지, 이메일, 그리고 기사에 관한 문제입니다.

http://www.chet.com

홈	소식	갤러리	프로필	연락처

직업적으로 Chet이라는 예명으로 알려져 있는 Chester Foles는 Sunderland를 잉글랜드 집이라고 불렀습니다. Foles 씨는 어렸을 때, 독서와 음악 연주하는 것을 좋아했습니다. 그는 기타 치는 법을 독학했고, 18세가 되었을 때는 196지역 음반사 High Notes에서 그에게 아티스트 계약을 제의했습니다. 하지만 Foles 씨는 이를 거절했고, 대신 사회학 학사학위를 따는 걸 선택했습니다. 학위를 취득한 후, Foles 씨는 마침내 꿈을 쫓기로 결심하고 음반사와 계약을 맺었습니다.

Foles 씨는 다재다능한 기타리스트이자 재능 있는 작곡가이지만, 자선활동에 헌신하는 것으로도 유명합니다. 투어 중이 아닐 때는, 종종 자신의 재단 Physical Feats에서 일하는 모습이 포착됩니다. 197그 재단은 사람들에게 전반적인 행복에 미치는 영향을 포함하여 신체건강의 중요성에 대해 교육합니다. 또한 저소득층 가정에 영양가 있는 유기농 식사를 제공합니다.

어휘

professionally 직업적으로, 전문적으로 | teach oneself 독학하다 | record label 음반사 | contract 계약 | turn down 거절하다 | instead 대신 | opt 선택하다 | earn 얻다, 획득하다 | bachelor's degree 학사학위 | sociology 사회학 | pursue 추구하다 | sign 계약하다, 서명하다 | record 음반 | versatile 다재 다능한 | talented 재능 있는 | commitment 헌신, 전념 | philanthropy 자선활동 | on tour 순회공연 중인 | foundation 재단, 토대 | educate 교육시키다 | importance 중요성 | physical fitness 신체 건강 | impact 영향 | overall 전반적인 | nutritious 영양가가 높은 | organic 유기농의 | meal 식사 | low-income 저소득의

수신: Olga Mazur ⟨omazur@raltut.com⟩
발신: Kenny Uma ⟨kuma@raltut.com⟩
날짜: 7월 22일
제목: 새로운 홍보자

Olga 씨께,

논의 드린 것처럼, 저는 우리가 영국 시장에 진출 시 모델이 될 유명 인사를 구하고 있었어요. 잉글랜드 Sunderland의 뮤지션인 Chester Foles라는 사람을 우연히 알게 됐는데, 제가 보기엔 그가 우리 프로필에 맞는 것 같아요. **197** 그의 비영리단체는 웰빙에 중점을 두고 있는데, 우리 Raltut 제품과 자연스럽게 연결됩니다. 그의 웹사이트 www.chet.com에서 그에 대해 더 알아보실 수 있어요. 그가 적임자라는 생각이 드시면, 제가 그의 팀에 연락해서 관심도를 알아볼게요.

198 199 그리고 오늘 오후에 Sakic 씨와 통화했는데요. 마케팅 캠페인이 연기됐다고 했습니다. 그녀는 저희가 11월까지 홍보자를 찾는 한, 괜찮을 거라고 했습니다.

진심을 담아,

Kenny

어휘

endorser 지지[홍보]자 | candidate 지원자, 후보자 | celebrity 유명 인사 | spokesperson 대변인 | come across 우연히 발견하다 | musician 음악가 | profile 개요, 프로필 | non-profit organization 비영리 단체 | focus on ~에 주력하다 | well-being 행복, 웰빙 | natural 자연스러운 | connection 연관(성) | fit ~하게 맞는 것 | gauge 알아내다, 판단하다 | level 수준 | interest 관심, 흥미 | mention 언급하다 | put on hold 연기하다, 보류하다

Raltut, 대서양을 건너다

Sunderland (**199** 9월 3일) — **197** 미국의 유기농 과자 제조업체인 Raltut는 Sunderland 출신 예술가 Chester "Chet" Foles를 회사의 새로운 얼굴로 내세워 영국 시장에 진출했다. **199** 화요일에 예고 영상이 공개돼, 시청자들은 Foles 씨와 출시될 제품들을 일부 엿볼 수 있었다. 광고 캠페인은 다음 주부터 단계적으로 시작될 것이다.

200 Colorado의 Boulder에 본사를 둔 이 유기농 과자 회사는 Rhonda Faulk 신임 CEO가 취임한 이래 성공 가도를 달리고 있다. 이 회사는 거의 10년 전 일본에 진출한 후, 이제 지구 반대편에서 다시 성공의 역사를 쓰려고 한다.

어휘

cross 가로지르다, 횡단하다 | pond 연못, 대서양 | snack 과자 | manufacturer 제조[생산]업체 | make one's way 나아가다 | marketplace 시장 | raise 자라다, 키우다 | teaser video 예고 영상 | release 출시하다, 공개하다 | viewer 시청자 | glimpse 잠깐 봄 | launch 시작하다 | advertising campaign 광고 캠페인 | kick off 시작하다 | in stages 단계적으로 | based in ~에 기반을 둔 | success 성공 | take over 인계 받다 | expand 확대하다 | nearly 거의 | decade 10년 | repeat 반복하다

196. 상세 정보

웹페이지에 따르면, Foles 씨는 음반사에 합류하기 전 무엇을 받았는가?
(A) 노래 수업
(B) 운동 장비
(C) 새 기타
(D) 학사 학위

해설 첫 번째 지문 [웹페이지], 첫 번째 단락에서 'Mr. Foles, however, turned it down and instead opted to earn a bachelor's degree in sociology. After receiving his degree, Mr. Foles

decided to finally pursue his dream and signed with the record company.'라고 했으므로 (D)가 정답이다.

+ Paraphrasing

a bachelor's degree → an undergraduate degree, sign with → join

197. 상세 정보 – 연계 문제

Uma 씨는 왜 Foles 씨를 적합한 유명인 홍보자로 고려하는가?
(A) Raltut가 악기를 만들기 때문에
(B) Raltut가 Sunderland를 기반으로 활동하기 때문에
(C) 그의 가창력이 널리 인정받기 때문에
(D) 그의 재단이 건강한 식생활을 장려하기 때문에

해설 첫 번째 지문 [웹페이지], 두 번째 단락에서 'The foundation educates people on the importance of physical fitness, including its impact on overall happiness. In addition, it provides nutritious organic meals to low-income families.'라고 했는데, 두 번째 지문 [이메일], 첫 번째 단락에서 'His non-profit organization focuses on well-being, which has a natural connection to our products at Raltut.'라고 하였고, 세 번째 지문 [기사], 첫 번째 단락에서 'Raltut, the American organic snack manufacturer'라고 했으므로 (D)가 정답이다.

198. 암시 / 추론

이메일에서는 Sakic 씨에 대해 무엇을 시사하는가?
(A) Foles 씨의 매니저이다.
(B) Uma 씨와 Mazur 씨의 동료이다.
(C) Raltut의 현 홍보자이다.
(D) Foles 씨의 웹페이지를 방문했다.

해설 두 번째 지문 [Kenny Uma가 Olga Mazur에게 보낸 이메일], 두 번째 단락에서 'I also spent some time on the phone with Ms. Sakic this afternoon. ~ She said that as long as we find an endorser by November, we will be fine.'이라고 하여 세 사람이 동료 사이라는 것을 알 수 있으므로 (B)가 정답이다.

199. 사실 확인 – 연계 문제

Foles 씨에 관하여 언급된 것은?
(A) Raltut에 돈을 투자했다.
(B) 계획보다 빨리 캠페인에 합류했다.
(C) 수익금 전액을 기부할 예정이다.
(D) 신규 앨범을 최근 출시했다.

해설 두 번째 지문 [이메일], 두 번째 단락에서 'She said that as long as we find an endorser by November, we will be fine.'이라고 했는데, 세 번째 지문 [9월 3일자 기사], 첫 번째 단락에서 'A teaser video was released on Tuesday, giving viewers a glimpse of Mr. Foles and some of the products that will be launched. The advertising campaign will kick off in stages starting next week.'이라고 하여 Foles 씨가 11월보다 이른 9월에 이미 캠페인에 합류했다는 것을 알 수 있으므로 (B)가 정답이다.

200. 상세 정보

Raltut에 관한 어떤 정보가 기사에 포함되어 있는가?
(A) 업계에 있었던 기간
(B) 소재지
(C) 회사 설립자
(D) 가장 인기 있는 상품 종류

해설 세 번째 지문 [기사], 두 번째 단락에서 'The organic snack company, based in Boulder, Colorado,'라고 했으므로 (B)가 정답이다.

+ **Paraphrasing**
based in → located

ACTUAL TEST 02

본서 p.346

101. (C)	102. (C)	103. (C)	104. (C)	105. (C)
106. (D)	107. (D)	108. (C)	109. (B)	110. (D)
111. (B)	112. (A)	113. (D)	114. (B)	115. (B)
116. (B)	117. (C)	118. (D)	119. (D)	120. (C)
121. (A)	122. (C)	123. (D)	124. (D)	125. (D)
126. (A)	127. (D)	128. (A)	129. (B)	130. (C)
131. (C)	132. (B)	133. (D)	134. (B)	135. (B)
136. (D)	137. (A)	138. (A)	139. (D)	140. (B)
141. (B)	142. (A)	143. (C)	144. (A)	145. (D)
146. (A)	147. (B)	148. (D)	149. (C)	150. (A)
151. (B)	152. (D)	153. (D)	154. (D)	155. (A)
156. (B)	157. (A)	158. (D)	159. (D)	160. (D)
161. (A)	162. (B)	163. (B)	164. (B)	165. (C)
166. (D)	167. (C)	168. (D)	169. (A)	170. (B)
171. (C)	172. (B)	173. (B)	174. (D)	175. (C)
176. (C)	177. (A)	178. (D)	179. (A)	180. (B)
181. (A)	182. (A)	183. (D)	184. (C)	185. (D)
186. (A)	187. (A)	188. (D)	189. (D)	190. (C)
191. (D)	192. (B)	193. (D)	194. (A)	195. (D)
196. (C)	197. (D)	198. (B)	199. (D)	200. (D)

101. 어휘 - 명사

Liberty Fashion makes their **line** of summer clothing with the highest quality fabric.

Liberty Fashion은 여름 의류 라인을 최고 품질의 옷감으로 만든다.

해설 line은 제품과 함께 자주 쓰이며 제품의 종류를 나타낸다. '여름 의류 라인'이라는 말이 가장 적절하므로 (C)가 정답이다.

어휘 clothing 의복, 옷 | fabric 옷감

102. 관용 표현

A group of marine scientists will be brought **together** to try to increase tuna farm yields.

해양 과학자 한 그룹이 참치 농장 생산량을 늘리기 위해 합쳐지게 될 것이다.

해설 bring together이 '~를 합치다, 묶다'란 뜻이고 이것이 수동태로 쓰여 together이 뒤따라야 했다. 문맥상 '해양 과학자 한 그룹이 ~를 위해 합쳐지게 될 것'이란 의미가 되어야 자연스러우므로 (C)가 정답이다.

어휘 marine 해양의 | tuna 참치 | farm 농장 | yield 생산량, 산출량

103. 어휘 - 동사

After the parade **circles** Huber Park, the town will conduct its tree lighting ceremony.

가두 행진이 Huber 공원 주위를 돌고 난 후, 마을은 나무 점등식을 시행할 것이다.

해설 빈칸은 the parade에 대한 동사 자리이다. 가두 행진을 묘사해야 하는데, spin은 '제자리에서 빙빙 돈다'는 의미로, circle과는 구분된다. 문맥상 'Huber Park 주위를 돌고 난 후'라는 의미로 이어져야 자연스러우므로 (C)가 정답이다.

어휘 parade 가두 행진 | conduct 시행하다, 실시하다 | lighting ceremony 점등식

+ **Key word**
After the parade circles Huber Park, the town will conduct its tree lighting ceremony.

104. 형용사 자리

Keitel's Cleaners provides clients with discrete document disposal service at an **affordable** price.

Keitel's Cleaners는 저렴한 가격에 별도의 문서 폐기 서비스를 고객들에게 제공한다.

해설 빈칸은 뒤의 명사를 수식하는 형용사 자리이다. affordable price는 '저렴한 가격, 알맞은 가격'으로 자주 쓰이므로 기억해두자. 따라서 (C)가 정답이다.

어휘 provide 제공하다 | discrete 별개의 | disposal 폐기

105. 복합명사

The high cost of comprehensive employee health **insurance** poses a financial burden to small-sized businesses.

직원 종합 건강 보험의 높은 요금은 소규모 사업체들에게 재정 부담을 야기한다.

해설 빈칸은 전치사 of의 목적어이자, employee health와 함께 복합명사를 완성하는 명사 자리이므로 (C)가 정답이다.

어휘 cost 요금, 비용 | comprehensive 종합적인, 포괄적인 | employee 직원 | pose (문제 등을) 제기하다 | financial 금융의, 재정의 | burden 짐, 부담 | business 사업(체)

+ **Key point**
복합명사는 두 개 이상의 명사가 「명사+명사」의 형태로 하나의 단어처럼 쓰이며, 마지막 명사를 기준으로 복합명사의 성격이 결정된다.

106. 전치사

After selling five hundred thousand shares in a month, Kopac Mining is now **among** Warsaw's fastest-growing companies.

한 달에 50만 주를 매각한 후, Kopac Mining은 현재 Warsaw에서 가장 빠르게 성장하는 회사들 중 하나이다.

해설 빈칸은 명사구 Warsaw's fastest-growing companies를 목적어로 하는 전치사 자리이다. 문맥상 'Kopac Mining은 현재 Warsaw에서 가장 빠르게 성장하는 회사들 중 하나'라는 의미가 되어야 자연스러우므로 (D)가 정답이다.

어휘 sell 팔다 ㅣ share 주, 주식 ㅣ growing 커지는, 성장하는

+ **Key point**

전치사 among은 셋 이상을 의미하는 복수 명사와 함께 쓰여 '~들 중 하나, ~들 사이에 있는'을 의미한다.

---

107. 어휘 - 명사

A built-in red light serves as an **alert** to users when the cord is left plugged in.

내장되어 있는 빨간 빛은 선이 여전히 전기 코드에 연결되었을 때 이용자들에게 경고로 쓰일 수 있다.

해설 빈칸은 관사 an 뒤의 명사 자리이다. 문맥상 선이 여전히 전기 코드에 연결되었을 때 '이용자들에게 경고한다'는 의미가 되어야 자연스러우므로 (D)가 정답이다.

어휘 built-in 내장된 ㅣ serve 쓰일 수 있다

+ **Key word**

A built-in **red light serves as an alert to users** when the cord is left plugged in.

---

108. 부사절 접속사

Employees traveling for business will share accommodations **unless** they request prior approval for a private room.

출장을 떠나는 직원들은 개인 객실을 사전에 승인 신청하지 않는다면 숙소를 공유하게 된다.

해설 빈칸 앞뒤로 「주어+동사」를 갖춘 절이 있으므로, 빈칸은 절과 절을 연결하는 접속사 자리이다. 두 개의 절이 조건과 결과의 의미로 연결되어야 문맥상 자연스러우므로 (C)가 정답이다.

어휘 share 공유하다 ㅣ accommodations 숙박시설 ㅣ request 요청하다 ㅣ prior 이전의 ㅣ approval 승인

+ **Key point**

부사절 접속사 unless는 'if ~ not'으로 바꿔 쓸 수 있으며, '~하지 않는다면'이라는 조건의 의미를 전달한다. 또한 주절이 미래일 때 조건의 부사절은 현재 시제를 쓴다.

---

109. 형용사 자리

In July, a shopping mall will be opening in the vicinity, offering convenient eating options with a **charming** atmosphere.

7월에는 인근에 쇼핑몰이 개장할 예정으로, 멋진 분위기와 함께 편리한 식사 옵션을 제공할 것이다.

해설 빈칸은 관사와 명사 사이의 형용사 자리이므로 (B)가 정답이다.

어휘 vicinity 부근, 인근 ㅣ convenient 편리한 ㅣ eating 식사 ㅣ option 선택권 ㅣ atmosphere 분위기

---

110. 어휘 - 부사

The Johannesburg Daily News is broadcast **simultaneously** on television and their Web site.

Johannesburg Daily News는 텔레비전과 웹사이트에서 동시에 방송된다.

해설 빈칸은 수동태 동사 구문과 전치사구 사이의 부사 자리이다. 문맥상 '텔레비전과 웹사이트에서 동시에 방송된다'는 의미가 되어야 자연스러우므로 (D)가 정답이다.

어휘 broadcast 방송하다 (broadcast-broadcast-broadcast)

+ **Key word**

The Johannesburg Daily **News is broadcast simultaneously on television and their Web site**.

---

111. 부사 자리

The wardrobe for the cast of the musical *The Emperor Dragonfly* has been **clearly** labeled.

뮤지컬 〈The Emperor Dragonfly〉의 출연진용 의상은 확실하게 라벨로 분류되었다.

해설 빈칸은 현재 완료 수동태 동사 구문 has been labeled 사이의 자리이므로, 동사를 수식하는 부사 (B)가 정답이다.

어휘 wardrobe 옷(장) ㅣ cast 출연진 ㅣ label 라벨을 붙여 분류하다, 라벨을 붙이다

+ **Key point**

동사를 수식할 수 있는 품사는 부사이다.

---

112. 어휘 - 명사

The company contracted by the city council has used a stone wall to create a strict **boundary** for the town.

시의회와 계약한 업체는 마을에 엄격한 경계를 만들기 위해 돌담을 사용했다.

해설 빈칸은 to부정사 to create의 목적어이자, a strict의 수식을 받는 명사 자리이다. 주절과 to부정사구의 관계를 고려할 때, '마을에 엄격한 경계를 만들기 위해 돌담을 사용했다'는 의미가 되어야 자연스러우므로 (A)가 정답이다.

어휘 contract 계약하다 ㅣ stone wall 돌담 ㅣ strict 엄격한, 엄한

+ **Key word**

The company contracted by the city council has **used a stone wall to create a strict boundary for the town**.

---

113. 어휘 - 부사

Traffic on Summit Boulevard **nearly** comes to a standstill when major sports competitions are held at Jefferson Stadium.

Jefferson 경기장에서 주요 스포츠 대회가 열릴 때면 Summit 가의 교통은 거의 멈춰버린다.

해설 'Summit 가의 교통은 거의 멈춰버린다.'가 자연스러운 구문이므로 (D)가 정답이다. '정지하다, 꼼짝도 못하다'라는 뜻의 동사 관용 표현 come to a standstill을 수식하기에 알맞은 부사를 고르는 문제이다. 주요 대회가 있을 때 'Summit 가의 교통이 거의 멈춰버린다'라는 의미가 자연스러우므로 '거의'라는 뜻의 (D)가 정답이다.

어휘 come to a standstill 멈추다, 정지하다

---

114. 전치사

Markham Supermarket delivers groceries at no charge **within** a 10-kilometer radius.

Markham 슈퍼마켓은 반경 10킬로미터 이내에서는 식료품을 무료로 배달해 준다.

해설 빈칸은 명사구 a 10-kilometer radius를 목적어로 하는 전치사 자리이다. 목적어 자리에 장소와 관련한 범위를 나타내는 표현이

있음을 고려할 때, 문맥상 '반경 10킬로미터 이내에서는 식료품을 무료로 배달해준다'는 의미가 되어야 자연스러우므로 (B)가 정답이다.

어휘 deliver 배달하다 | grocery 식료품 | at no charge 무료로 | radius 반경

➕ Key point
전치사 within은 '기간, 범위, 장소'를 나타내는 표현을 목적어로 취하며, '~이내에'라는 의미를 갖는다. 전치사 during은 특정한 기간 동안에 관하여 쓰고 장소 표현과는 어울리지 않는다.

---

115. 어휘-동사

Shwester Medical Group never **discloses** patient data to other parties without the individual's official permission.

Shwester 의료그룹은 개인의 공식적인 허가 없이 환자 정보를 다른 사람에게 절대 공개하지 않습니다.

해설 빈칸은 주어와 목적어 사이 동사 자리이다. 문맥상 '허가 없이 환자 정보를 다른 사람에게 절대 공개하지 않는다'는 의미가 되어야 자연스러우므로 (B)가 정답이다.

어휘 patient 환자 | data 자료, 정보 | party 당사자 | individual 개인 | official 공식적인 | permission 허가

➕ Key word
Shwester Medical Group **never discloses patient data to other parties without** the individual's official **permission**.

---

116. 어휘-부사

Researchers at DRI Medical announced outcomes much like those published **elsewhere**.

DRI Medical의 연구원들은 다른 곳에서 출판된 것들과 매우 유사한 결과를 발표했다.

해설 빈칸 앞의 (which are) published를 수식할 부사를 골라야 하는데 문맥상 '다른 곳에서 출판된 것들'이 적절하므로 (B)가 정답이다.

---

117. 부사 자리

Ms. Yamato's budget estimate is **certainly** too low now, given the alterations to the building plans.

건축 계획의 변경을 고려해 볼 때, Yamato 씨의 예산 견적은 현재 확실히 너무 낮다.

해설 빈칸은 be동사와 주격 보어 사이의 수식어 자리이므로 부사 (C)가 정답이다.

어휘 budget 예산 | estimate 추정(치), 견적서 | given ~를 고려해 볼 때 | alteration 변경 | building plan 건축 계획

➕ Key point
부사는 형용사(구), 부사(구), 동사(구), 문장 등을 수식하며, 문장 내 가장 다양한 위치에 올 수 있는 품사이다.

---

118. 관용 표현

Ms. Lang suggested sending a text message to clients **immediately** after their monthly payment is received.

Lang 씨는 월 요금이 수령된 직후 고객들에게 문자메시지를 발송하는 것을 제안했다.

해설 빈칸은 주어, 동사, 목적어의 완전한 문장으로 이루어진 주절과 after 종속절 사이의 부사 자리이다. 문맥상 '월 요금 납부 직후 문자를 발송하는 것'이라는 의미가 되어야 자연스러우므로 'immediately after ~ (~한 직후)'라는 표현을 완성하는 부사 (D)가 정답이다.

어휘 suggest 제안하다 | monthly 매월의 | payment 지불(금)

---

119. 동사의 태

Due to increasing demands for sustainability, the solar energy market is **projected** to grow over the next few years.

지속 가능성에 대한 증가하는 수요 증가로, 태양 에너지 시장은 향후 몇 년간 성장할 것으로 예상된다.

해설 빈칸은 be동사와 to부정사 사이의 자리이다. 문장의 주어가 the solar energy market임을 고려할 때, '태양 에너지 시장이 성장할 것으로 예상된다'는 의미가 되어야 적합하므로 수동태 동사 구문을 완성하는 과거분사 (B)가 정답이다.

어휘 due to ~로 인해 | increasing 증가하는 | demand 수요 | sustainability 지속 가능성 | solar energy 태양 에너지 | grow 성장하다

---

120. 어휘-형용사

The renovated wing of the museum will feature a more spacious food court, a second gift shop, more exhibit halls, and **improved** parking.

새로 개조되는 박물관 부속건물에는 보다 넓은 푸드코트와 새로운 기념품점, 더 많은 전시관, 그리고 개선된 주차 공간이 갖춰질 것이다.

해설 빈칸은 명사 parking을 수식하는 형용사 자리이다. parking과 함께 나열된 다른 특징들을 고려할 때, '새로 개조되는 박물관 부속건물에 개선된 주차 공간이 갖춰질 것'이라는 의미가 되어야 문맥상 자연스러우므로 (C)가 정답이다.

어휘 renovate 개조하다 | wing 별관, 부속건물 | feature ~을 특징으로 하다 | spacious (공간이) 널찍한 | exhibit hall 전시관

➕ Key word
The **renovated wing** of the museum **will feature a more spacious food court, a second gift shop, more exhibit halls, and improved parking.**

---

121. 전치사

Despite increased admission fees, every show of Alexia Montez's new musical for the entire summer season has sold out.

인상된 입장료에도 불구하고, 여름 시즌 내내 Alexia Montez의 새로운 뮤지컬 쇼는 모두 매진되었다.

해설 빈칸은 명사구를 목적어로 취하는 전치사 자리이다. 문맥상 '인상된 입장료에도 불구하고, 쇼가 모두 매진되었다'라는 내용이 자연스러우므로 (A)가 정답이다.

어휘 admission fee 입장료 | entire 전체의 | sell out 다 팔리다

➕ Key word
Despite increased admission fees, every show of Alexia Montez's new musical for the entire summer season **has sold out.**

---

122. 어휘-부사

The high amount of risk linked with investing

in the stock market **surely** justifies a thorough studying of the company's performance using financial statements.

주식 투자와 관련된 높은 수준의 위험은 재무제표를 이용해 회사 실적을 철저하게 분석하는 것을 확실히 정당화한다.

해설 빈칸은 동사 justifies를 수식하는 부사 자리이다. 문맥상 '주식 투자는 위험도가 높으므로 회사 실적을 철저하게 분석하는 것을 확실히 정당화한다'는 의미가 되어야 자연스러우므로 (C)가 정답이다.

어휘 risk 위험 | linked with ~과 연관된 | invest in ~에 투자하다 | stock 주식 | justify 정당화하다 | thorough 철저한 | performance 실적, 성과 | financial statement 재무제표

✦ Key word

The **high amount of risk** linked with **investing in the stock** market **surely justifies a thorough studying of** the **company's performance** using financial statements.

123. 분사 자리

The marketing team recently surveyed customers to ensure our products work as **intended**.

마케팅 팀은 당사의 제품이 의도된 대로 작동하도록 최근 고객들을 대상으로 설문조사를 실시했다.

해설 빈칸은 as와 함께 분사 구문을 완성하는 자리이므로 과거분사 (D)가 정답이다.

어휘 recently 최근 | survey 조사하다 | customer 고객 | ensure 보장하다 | product 제품

✦ Key point

분사 구문 관용 표현 'as p.p.'는 '~된 대로'를 의미한다: as intended (의도된 대로), as planned (계획된 대로), as scheduled (예정된 대로)

124. 명사 자리

Ms. Bernal was pleased to get a **notification** that her firm soon will appear on the Top Ten Canadian Companies list.

Bernal 씨는 그녀의 회사가 곧 상위 10개의 캐나다 기업 목록에 나올 것이라는 통보를 받고 기뻐했다.

해설 빈칸은 동사 get의 목적어이자 that 동격절의 수식을 받는 명사 자리이므로 (D)가 정답이다.

어휘 be pleased to do ~하게 되어 기뻐하다 | appear 나오다

✦ Key point

명사 뒤에 나온 that절이 완전한 절이면 동격의 명사절로 쓰인다. 불완전 절이 나오면 관계대명사 역할이다.

125. 어휘 - 형용사

When writing your self-evaluation report, make sure to record only the significant accomplishments and disregard **incidental** details.

본인 평가 보고서를 작성할 때는 중요한 업적만 기록하고 부수적인 세부 내용은 무시하세요.

해설 빈칸은 명사 details를 수식하는 형용사 자리이다. to부정사구가 and로 연결된 구조로, '중요한 업적만 기록하고 부수적인 내용은 무시하라'는 의미가 되어야 문맥상 자연스러우므로 (D)가 정답이다.

어휘 self-evaluation 본인 평가 | record 기록하다 | significant 중요한, 의미 있는 | accomplishment 성취 | disregard 무시하다 | details 세부 사항

✦ Key word

When writing your self-evaluation report, make sure **to record only the significant accomplishments and disregard incidental details**.

126. 어휘 - 명사

Academic dissertations must be handed in by this Thursday and should include an outline and a one-page **abstract**.

학위논문은 이번 주 목요일까지 제출되어야 하고, 반드시 개요 및 한 페이지 분량의 초록을 포함해야 한다.

해설 빈칸은 one-page의 수식을 받는 명사 자리이다. 문맥상 '학위논문에는 개요와 한 페이지 분량의 초록이 포함되어야 한다'는 의미가 되어야 자연스러우므로 (A)가 정답이다.

어휘 academic 학업의 | dissertation 논문 | hand in 제출하다 | outline 개요

✦ Key word

Academic dissertations must be handed in by this Thursday and **should include an outline and a one-page abstract**.

127. 어휘 - 명사

Travel Africa Magazine hails Mangaluru Hotel as surprisingly inexpensive considering its exceptional **amenities** and central location.

〈Travel Africa Magazine〉은 뛰어난 편의시설과 중심적인 위치를 고려할 때, Mangaluru 호텔을 놀랄 만큼 저렴한 곳으로 열렬히 지지한다.

해설 빈칸은 전치사 considering의 목적어로 형용사 exceptional의 수식을 받는 명사 자리이다. 문맥상 '뛰어난 편의시설과 중심적인 위치를 고려할 때'라는 의미가 되어야 자연스러우므로 (D)가 정답이다.

어휘 hail 열렬히 지지하다, 갈채를 보내다 | surprisingly 놀랄 만큼 | inexpensive 저렴한, 값이 싼 | exceptional 뛰어난, 특출한 | testimony 증언, 증거 | subsidy 보조금, 지원금 | remedy 치료, 구제 | amenity 편의시설

128. 부사절 접속사

Please explain your concern with the accommodation **so that** we can address it promptly.

저희가 즉시 처리해드릴 수 있도록 숙소에 대한 우려 사항을 설명해 주세요.

해설 빈칸은 두 개의 절을 연결하는 접속사 자리이다. 문맥상 '즉시 처리해드릴 수 있도록 우려 사항을 설명해 달라'는 의미로 연결되어야 자연스러우므로 목적을 나타내는 부사절 접속사 (A)가 정답이다.

어휘 explain 설명하다 | concern 걱정, 우려 | accommodation 숙소, 거처 | address 처리하다 | promptly 즉시

✦ Key point

접속사 'so that (~할 수 있도록, ~하기 위해서)'은 주로 조동사 can과 함께 「문장 + so that + 주어 + can ~.」의 구문으로 사용된다.

129. 어휘 - 형용사

Mr. Hwang is **doubtful** that a replacement for a receptionist can be found by Monday.

Hwang 씨는 월요일까지는 접수원의 후임자를 구할 수 있다는 것에 회의적이다.

해설 문맥상 '접수원의 후임자를 월요일까지 구할 수 있다는 것에 회의적이다'라는 의미가 되어야 자연스러우므로 (B)가 정답이다.

어휘 replacement 후임자 | receptionist 접수원 | remote 원격의, 먼 | doubtful 회의적인, 의심스러운 | hesitant 망설이는 | exemplary 모범적인

+ Key word

Mr. Hwang is doubtful that a replacement for a receptionist can be found by Monday.

130. 어휘 - 명사

Ms. Bryant will be invited to interview for the open position first because she has the best **credentials**.

Bryant 씨는 최고의 자격을 갖췄기 때문에, 공석에 가장 먼저 면접을 보도록 초대될 것이다.

해설 빈칸은 because 종속절 내의 목적어 자리이다. 두 문장이 인과관계를 나타내는 접속사 because로 연결되어 있음을 고려할 때, 문맥상 '최고의 자격을 갖춰서 가장 먼저 면접을 보게 될 것'이라는 의미로 이어져야 자연스러우므로 (C)가 정답이다.

어휘 invite 초대하다 | interview 인터뷰하다, 면접을 보다 | open position 공석, 빈자리

+ Key word

Ms. Bryant **will be invited to interview** for the open position **first because she has the best credentials**.

131-134번은 다음 기사에 관한 문제입니다.

JAKARTA (11월 5일) — 세계 **131** 패션산업의 선두 주자인 Lorenzen 그룹은 오늘 아침 자사 웹사이트에의 주요 업데이트를 발표했다. 웹사이트 LorenzenLook.com은 Morales Design과 제휴하여 **132** 재설계되었고 화요일 저녁 늦게 공개되었다. LorenzenLook.com은 이제 고객들에게 다음 시즌 제품 미리보기부터 할인된 캐쥬얼 의류에 이르기까지 자사 의류 전체 **133** 를 둘러볼 기회를 제공한다. 사이트를 이용하는 고객은 독점 할인 기회를 얻고 일부 상품을 조기에 주문할 수 있게 된다. **134** LorenzenLook.com은 이러한 할인이 있을 때 알림 또한 보내준다. 이는 Lorenzen의 온라인 고객이 누구보다 먼저 가장 좋은 혜택을 알기 쉽게 해줄 것이다.

어휘

announce 발표하다 | major 주요한, 중대한 | update 최신 정보, 업데이트 | in partnership with ~와 제휴하여 | launch 시작하다, 출시하다 | browse 훑어보다, 둘러보다 | clothing 옷, 의복 | preview 미리보기, 프리뷰 | offering 제공된 것 | exclusive 독점적인 | access 접근, 입장 | certain 어떤, 확실한 | deal 거래, 합의

131. 복합명사

해설 빈칸은 명사 industry를 수식하는 자리이다. 빈칸 뒷부분의 '고객들에게 다음 시즌 제품 미리보기부터 할인된 캐쥬얼 의류에 이르기까지 자사 의류 전체를 둘러볼 기회를 제공한다'는 내용을 고려할 때, 문맥상 '세계 패션산업의 선두 주자'라는 의미가 되어야 자연스러우므로 명사 industry와 함께 복합명사를 이루는 명사 (C)가 정답이다.

+ Key word

Lorenzen Group, a leader in the international **fashion industry**, announced a major update to its Web site this morning. **LorenzenLook. com now gives customers a chance to browse through all of the company's clothing, from previews of next season's offerings to discounted casual wear.**

132. 동사의 시제

해설 빈칸은 주어 the Web site에 대한 동사 자리이다. and launched late Tuesday evening에서 과거 시제를 써서 공개되었다고 하므로 내용을 고려할 때, 웹사이트가 이미 재설계되었음을 알 수 있으므로 과거 시제 수동태 (B)가 정답이다.

+ Key word

Lorenzen Group, a leader in the international fashion industry, **announced a major update to its Web site this morning. The Web site, LorenzenLook.com, was redesigned** in partnership with Morales Design **and launched** late Tuesday evening.

133. 전치사

해설 빈칸은 동사와 목적어인 명사 사이의 전치사 자리이다. 동사 browse와 함께 구동사 'browse through(~를 훑어보다)'를 완성하는 (D)가 정답이다.

+ Key word

LorenzenLook.com now gives customers a chance to **browse through all of the company's clothing**, from previews of next season's offerings to discounted casual wear.

134. 문장 선택

(A) 그 세일은 앞으로 2주간 계속될 예정이다.
(B) LorenzenLook.com은 이러한 할인이 있을 때 알림을 또한 보내준다.
(C) 겨울 컬렉션은 언론으로부터 널리 찬사를 받아왔다.
(D) 로열티 클럽 회원은 대부분의 주요 소매점에서 포인트를 사용할 수 있다.

해설 빈칸 뒤 문장의 '이는 Lorenzen의 온라인 고객이 누구보다 먼저 가장 좋은 혜택을 알기 쉽게 해줄 것'이라는 내용을 고려할 때 '이것'이 가리키는 내용이 앞 문장에서 등장해야 하므로, 문맥상 'LorenzenLook.com은 할인이 있을 때 미리 알림을 보내준다'는 내용이 앞에 들어가야 자연스러우므로 (B)가 정답이다.

+ Key word

LorenzenLook.com even sends reminders when these offers become available. This will make it easy for Lorenzen's online customers to learn about the best deals before anyone else.

135-138번은 다음 회람에 관한 문제입니다.

회람

수신: Starzone 전 직원

발신: Sara Jordan
날짜: 7월 12일
제목: 고객 정보 업데이트

7월 24일부로 고객 정보 저장에 관한 새로운 규정이 **135** 시행된다는 점을 유의해 주시기 바랍니다. 고객으로부터 **136** 수집된 모든 정보는 새로운 보호 방법을 이용해 안전하게 저장되어야 합니다. 또한 행여 위반이 발생한다고 하더라도 어떠한 식별 정보도 누출되지 않도록, 고객 정보는 가능하면 항상 익명으로 처리되어야 합니다. **137** 이런 일이 일어날 가능성은 낮지만, 그래도 대비되어 있어야 합니다. 새로운 설명과 규정을 이 메일로 보내드렸으니, 이번 주말에 시간 내셔서 자세히 읽어주시기 바랍니다. **138** 변경 사항이 완전히 이해되지 않으면, 문의사항을 저희에게 답장으로 보내주십시오.

감사합니다.

Sara Jordan
IT 팀

어휘

note 유의하다 | as of ~부로 | regulation 규정 | storage 저장 | information 정보 | store 저장하다 | securely 안전하게 | protection 보호 | method 방법 | anonymize 익명으로 하다 | whenever possible 가능하면 항상 | breach 위반 | take place 일어나다 | identifying information 식별 정보 | leak 유출하다 | instruction 지시, 설명 | read through 쭉읽다, 통독하다 | carefully 신중하게 | unclear 완전히 이해하지 못한

135. 관용 표현

해설 빈칸은 전치사 into의 목적어 자리이다. 문맥상 '새로운 규정이 시행된다'는 의미가 되어야 하므로, 'come into effect(시행되다)'라는 관용 표현을 완성하는 명사 (B)가 정답이다.

➕ **Key point**

전치사는 명사를 목적어로 취할 수 있다.

136. 어휘 – 동사

해설 빈칸 앞 문장의 '고객 정보 저장에 관한 새로운 규정이 시행된다'는 내용을 고려할 때, '고객으로부터 수집된 모든 정보는 안전하게 저장되어야 한다'는 의미가 되어야 문맥상 자연스러우므로 (D)가 정답이다.

➕ **Key word**

Please note that as of July 24, **new regulations on the storage of customer data will come into effect. All information collected from customers** must be stored securely using the new protection methods.

137. 문장 선택

(A) 이런 일이 일어날 가능성은 작지만, 그래도 대비되어 있어야 합니다.
(B) 원한다면 새로운 제안을 할 수 있습니다.
(C) 국회의원들은 이 주제에 대해 계속 토론하고 있습니다.
(D) 다음 주에 투표가 있을 것입니다.

해설 빈칸 앞 문장의 '행여 위반이 발생한다고 하더라도 어떠한 식별 정보도 누출되지 않도록, 고객 정보는 가능하면 항상 익명으로 처리되어야 한다'는 내용을 고려할 때, '이런 일이 일어날 가능성은 낮지만, 그래도 대비되어 있어야 한다'는 내용으로 이어져야 문맥상 연결이 자연스러우므로 (A)가 정답이다.

➕ **Key word**

Customer data should also be anonymized whenever possible so that even if a breach does take place, no identifying information is leaked. While this is unlikely, we should still be prepared.

138. 어휘 – 명사

해설 빈칸은 the의 수식을 받는 명사 자리이다. 빈칸 앞 문장의 '이메일로 발송한 새로운 설명과 규정을 자세히 읽어달라'는 내용을 고려할 때, 변경 내용이 잘 이해되지 않는다면 문의해달라'는 의미가 되어야 문맥상 자연스러우므로 (A)가 정답이다.

➕ **Key word**

We have sent an e-mail with the new instructions and regulations, so please take some time this weekend to read through it carefully. If you are unclear about the changes, please e-mail us back with any questions.

139–142번은 다음 이메일에 관한 문제입니다.

수신: 모든 영업사원
발신: Ray Tran
날짜: 9월 1일
제목: 새 잠재고객 추적 소프트웨어
첨부파일: 시간표.doc

9월 15일부터 Bakersfield 보험은 PC 기반의 잠재고객 추적 시스템에서 ProTrac이라는 새 스마트폰 애플리케이션으로 **139** 전환합니다. 이 **140** 편리한 애플리케이션으로, 우리 영업 컨설턴트들은 어디서든 필요한 만큼 모든 고객 및 잠재고객 정보를 이용하고 갱신할 수 있는 능력을 갖추게 될 것입니다. 이것을 새 거래처 프로필을 작성하는 데도 사용할 수 있습니다.

영업사원들은 이 애플리케이션을 사용하여 모든 활동을 기록해야 하며 데이터는 지점장에 의해 검토되어 직원 분기별 평가에 사용될 것입니다.

9월 둘째 주에 교육 수업이 제공됩니다. **141** 추가 정보는 첨부된 파일을 참조하시기 바랍니다. 지정된 **142** 시간대에 오실 수 없다면, 저에게 연락하시기 바랍니다.

이만 줄입니다.

Ray Tran

어휘

prospect 잠재고객 | attachment 첨부파일 | application 응용 프로그램 | access 접속하다 | update 갱신하다 | as needed 필요한 대로 | account 거래처 | review 검토하다 | quarterly 분기별의 | evaluation 평가 | refer to ~을 참조하다 | attach 첨부하다 | make it to ~에 이르다[도착하다] | designated 지정된 | time slot 시간대 | track 추적하다

139. 동사의 시제

해설 이메일이 작성된 날짜는 9월 1일이고 9월 15일은 미래이므로 (D)가 정답이다.

➕ **Key word**

Date: September 1
Starting on September 15, Bakersfield Insurance Company **is going to switch** from

using a personal computer-based prospect tracking system to a new smartphone application called ProTrac.

140. 어휘 - 형용사

해설 어느 장소에서든 데이터에 접속하여 갱신할 수 있는 기능은 편리하다고 묘사하는 것이 알맞으므로 (B)가 정답이다.

✚ **Key word**

With this convenient application, our sales consultants will have the ability to access all client and prospect information and update it as needed from any location.

141. 문장 선택

(A) 이것이 비용을 절감하는 가장 좋은 방법이었습니다.
(B) 추가 정보는 첨부된 파일을 참조하시기 바랍니다.
(C) 이번 주말까지 제출해 주시기 바랍니다.
(D) 지금까지의 결과는 훌륭했습니다.

해설 교육 일정을 알리는 문장에 이어지기에 가장 자연스러운 (B)가 정답이다.

✚ **Key word**

Training classes will be offered in the second week of September. Refer to the attached file for more information.

142. 어휘 - 명사

해설 교육이 있을 것임을 알리는 문장에 이어지는 부분에서는 '지정된 시간대에 오실 수 없다면'이 문맥상 자연스러우므로 (B)가 정답이다.

✚ **Key word**

Training classes will be offered in the second week of September. Refer to the attached file for more information. If you cannot make it to your designated time slot, please contact me.

143-146번은 다음 공고에 관한 문제입니다.

LEXINGTON (2월 13일) — 겨울 시즌이 143 빠르게 끝나감에 따라, Expediters 사는 훌륭한 여행 상품들과 조언들로 가득한 무료 뉴스레터를 배포할 것이다. 뉴스레터에는 도시 내 숨겨진 보석 같은 곳뿐만 아니라 올해 방문할 가장 인기 있는 장소에 관한 144 제안을 실었다.

무료 뉴스레터를 받아보려면, 웹사이트에서 신청하고 몇 가지 기본적인 질문에 답변만 하면 된다. 145 설문은 익명으로 안전하게 저장된다. 신청하고 질문에 답변을 완료한 이용자는 이메일로 뉴스레터를 146 받게 된다. 뉴스레터에는 여행 시 할인 혜택을 제공하는 특별 쿠폰도 들어있다.

어휘
reach ~에 이르다, 도달하다 | expediter 홍보[보도] 담당자 | release 공개하다, 배포하다 | free 무료의 | newsletter 소식지, 뉴스레터 | filled with ~로 가득 찬 | hot 인기 있는 | place 지역, 장소 | as well as ~뿐만 아니라 | hidden 숨겨진 | gem 보석 | sign up 신청하다 | complete 완료하다, 작성하다

143. 어휘 - 부사

해설 빈칸은 현재분사 reaching을 수식하는 부사 자리이다. 문맥상 '겨울 시즌이 빠르게 끝나감에 따라'라는 의미가 되어야 자연스러우므로 (C)가 정답이다.

144. 어휘 - 명사

해설 빈칸은 동사 include의 목적어인 명사 자리이다. '뉴스레터에 도시 내 숨겨진 보석 같은 곳뿐만 아니라 올해 방문할 가장 인기 있는 장소에 관한 제안을 실었다'는 의미가 되어야 문맥상 자연스러우므로 (A)가 정답이다.

✚ **Key word**

In the newsletter, we have included **suggestions on the hottest places to visit this year as well as some hidden gems located in the city.**

145. 문장 선택

(A) 해외여행은 인기 있는 선택이 아닐 수도 있다.
(B) 뉴스레터는 TravelGate에서 후원한다.
(C) 우리는 앞으로 웹 사이트를 업데이트할 예정이다.
(D) 설문은 익명으로 안전하게 저장된다.

해설 빈칸 앞 문장의 '무료 뉴스레터를 받아보려면, 웹사이트에서 신청하고 몇 가지 기본적인 질문에 답변만 하면 된다'는 내용을 고려할 때, 문맥상 해당 질문에 대한 부가 설명을 제공하는 내용이 이어져야 자연스러우므로 (D)가 정답이다.

✚ **Key word**

To receive our free newsletter, **all you have to do is sign up on our Web site and answer a few basic questions. The survey will be anonymous and securely stored.**

146. 동사의 시제

해설 빈칸은 주어 users에 대한 문장의 동사 자리이다. 빈칸 앞, 뒤 문장이 모두 미래 시제임을 고려할 때, 문맥상 '질문에 답변을 완료한 이용자는 이메일로 뉴스레터를 받게 될 것'이라는 의미가 되어야 문맥상 자연스러우므로 미래 시제 (A)가 정답이다.

✚ **Key word**

The survey **will be anonymous and securely stored.** Users who sign up and complete the questions **will receive the newsletter** via e-mail. The newsletter **will also have special coupons** that will provide discounts for your travels.

147-148번은 다음 공지에 관한 문제입니다.

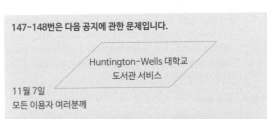

Huntington-Wells 대학교
도서관 서비스

11월 7일
모든 이용자 여러분께

148 저희의 출력 정책이 개정되었습니다. 아래의 내용을 참고해 주세요:

- HWU 도서관 카드를 소지한 이용자는 이제 매주 50 출력 포인트를 받습니다.
- 컬러 출력은 페이지당 3 출력 포인트에 이용할 수 있습니다.
- 포인트는 더 이상 차주로 이월되지 않습니다.
- 모든 컴퓨터는 이제 기본으로 양면 출력됩니다.
- 더 이상 직원이 개별 맞춤 출력 프로젝트를 위해 용지를 교체해 드리지 않습니다.

의견이나 문의 사항은 2층의 참고문헌 데스크로 연락주세요.

협조해 주셔서 감사합니다.

Huntington-Wells 대학교
도서관 서비스

어휘

guest 손님 | printing 인쇄 | policy 정책, 방침 | revise 개정하다 | note 주목하다, 주의하다 | following 그다음의, 다음에 나오는 | allot 할당하다, 배당하다 | credit 공제액 | per ~당, 마다 | available 이용할 수 있는 | transfer 이동하다, 이전하다 | double-sided 양면의 | by default 자동적으로, 기본적으로 | staff (전체) 직원 | no longer 더 이상 ~ 아니다 | custom 주문 제작한 | direct ~로 향하다 | comment 논평, 언급 | reference 참고(문헌) | appreciate 고마워하다 | cooperation 협조, 협력

147. 암시 / 추론

공지는 어디에 게시되겠는가?
(A) 기숙사에
(B) 컴퓨터실에
(C) 상품 설명서에
(D) 수업 카탈로그에

해설 첫 번째 줄에서 'Our printing policies have been revised. Please note the following:'이라고 하여 개정된 출력 정책에 대한 내용을 다루고 있는 것으로 미루어 보아 대학교 도서관 서비스 중 컴퓨터실에 게시될만한 공지임을 알 수 있으므로 (B)가 정답이다.

148. 주제 / 목적 / 대상

공지의 목적은 무엇인가?
(A) 몇 가지 개정된 지침을 알려주려고
(B) 설문 참여를 독려하려고
(C) 몇 개의 새로운 프린터 구매를 알리려고
(D) 공사 프로젝트의 진행 상황에 대해 알리려고

해설 첫 번째 줄에서 'Our printing policies have been revised. Please note the following:'라고 했으므로 (A)가 정답이다.

✚ **Paraphrasing**

policies → guidelines, revised → updated

149-150번은 다음 설명서에 관한 문제입니다.

Wronken Home Store의 신제품 Trappa 의자 (MZDA 323) 조립 방법

1. 의자 등받이가 아래를 향하고 팔걸이가 위쪽을 향하도록 하여 의자 본체를 평평한 표면에 놓으십시오.
2. 제공된 공구를 사용하여 **149** 의자 등받이에 짧은 볼트로 알루미늄 시트 프레임을 연결해 주시고 너무 조이지 않도록 주의해 주십시오.
3. 시트 프레임 하단의 구멍에 의자 다리를 삽입하고, 각 슬라이더가 알맞은 구멍에 들어가도록 하십시오 **150** (참고: 앞쪽 왼쪽 다리에 노란색 글자로 "Wronken"이라고 적혀있음).
4. 긴 볼트를 조여 다리를 고정하십시오.
5. 의자를 똑바로 놓고 좌석 쿠션을 프레임 위에 놓으십시오.

어휘

build 만들다 | body 본체, 중심부 | flat 평평한 | surface 표면 | face down 엎어 두다 | armrest 팔걸이 | tool 도구 | connect 연결하다 | frame 틀 | take care 조심하다 | overtighten 너무 조이다 | insert 삽입하다 | slot 구멍 | appropriate 알맞은 | label 적다, 라벨 붙이다 | lettering 글자 | tighten 조이다 | secure 고정하다 | upright 똑바로

149. 상세 정보

설명서에 따르면, 조립하는 사람은 의자 등받이에 어떤 부분을 부착해야 하는가?
(A) 팔걸이
(B) 다리
(C) 시트 프레임
(D) 쿠션

해설 2번에서 'connect the chair back to the aluminum seat frame with the shorter bolts'라고 했으므로 (C)가 정답이다.

✚ **Paraphrasing**

connect → attach

150. 상세 정보

부품 중 하나에 무엇이 표시되었는가?
(A) 브랜드 이름
(B) 회사 로고
(C) 제품 가격
(D) 모델 번호

해설 제목의 'How to build your brand-new Trappa Chair (MZDA 323) from Wronken Home Store'와 3번의 'note: the front left leg is labeled "Wronken" in yellow lettering'으로 미루어 의자 다리에 브랜드 이름인 Wronken이 적혀있음을 알 수 있으므로 (A)가 정답이다.

✚ **Paraphrasing**

labeled → marked, the front left leg → one of the parts

151-152번은 다음 일정에 관한 문제입니다.

안녕하세요 Angie,

아래에 있는 제 일정을 검토해 주세요. David가 저에게 Hammersted 해변 근처에 있는 호텔 객실을 예약해줬습니다. 빨리 도시에서 떠나고 싶네요! **151** 저는 막 Hammersted 컨벤션 홀에서 제가 진행하고 있는 워크숍 슬라이드 쇼를 만드는 것을 마쳤습니다. 월요일에 사무실로 출근할 거예요. Anderson 박사를 위한 설계도를 작업할 시간이 좀 필요해서, 가능하다면 이번 주 초에는 제 스케줄을 비워 주세요.

Brent O'Keefe의 일정 5월 1일 금요일	
오전 8:15	개발팀의 Jana Abernathy와 진행 상황 업데이트
오전 **152** 9:30	Hamilton 프로젝트를 위한 새로운 디자인 발표, Todd Chen
오전 10:45	Joaquin Berry와의 직원 평가
오후 2:00	Q2 예산안 요약, Sven Torbjorn
오후 4:00	퇴근
오후 7:00	Hammersted에 있는 호텔 체크인

Brent

어휘

review 검토하다 | below 아래에 | book 예약하다 | get out of ~에서 나가다, 떠나다 | lead 이끌다 | clear 분명한, 아무것도 없는 | blueprint 설계도, 청사진 | progress 진척, 진행 상황 | evaluation 평가 | summary 요약 | budget 예산(안) | leave 떠나다

151. 상세 정보

O'Keefe 씨는 Hammersted에서 무엇을 할 것인가?

(A) 여행을 할 것이다
(B) 세미나를 진행할 것이다
(C) 설계도를 만들 것이다
(D) 수영 수업에 등록할 것이다

해설 첫 번째 단락에서 'I just finished making the slide show for the workshop I'm leading at Hammersted Convention Hall.'이라고 했으므로 (B)가 정답이다.

+ Paraphrasing

lead the workshop → conduct a seminar

152. 암시 / 추론

누가 새로운 아이디어를 소개하겠는가?

(A) Abernathy 씨
(B) Chen 씨
(C) Berry 씨
(D) Torbjorn 씨

해설 표에서 '9:30 A.M. New design presentation for Hamilton project, Todd Chen'이라고 했으므로 (B)가 정답이다.

153-154번은 다음 문자메시지 대화에 관한 문제입니다.

Natalie Bardet (오전 9시 31분)
Quincy, 안녕하세요. 제가 지하실을 정리하려고 하는데요. 153 "마케팅"이라고 적힌 보관함이 몇 개 있는데, 당신 것인지 궁금해서요.

Quincy Pondexter (오전 9시 33분)
153 네, 제 예전 고객 서류예요. 거의 대부분이 버려도 되는 것들일 텐데, 154 제가 다시 확인차 살펴봐야 할 거예요. 제가 지금 들를까요? 전화회의 전에 30분 정도 시간이 있어요.

Natalie Bardet (오전 9시 34분)
당신이 결정하면 돼요. 시간이 더 필요하면, 구석으로 치워놓을게요.

Quincy Pondexter (오전 9시 36분)
그렇게 해주시면 감사합니다. 내일 오전에 시간 내서 살펴볼게요.

어휘
clear 치우다 | space 공간, 자리 | basement 지하실 | notice 의식하다, 알다 | storage 저장, 보관 | bin 통 | wonder 궁금해하다 | throw away 버리다 | double check 재확인하다 | drop by 들르다 | conference call 전화회의 | set aside 한쪽으로 치워 놓다 | appreciate 고마워하다

153. 상세 정보

Bardet 씨는 왜 Pondexter 씨에게 연락했는가?

(A) 지하실을 정리하는 데 도움을 요청하려고
(B) 추가 보관 공간이 필요한지 알아보려고
(C) 열쇠 위치를 알아내려고
(D) 몇몇 문서가 그의 것인지 알아보려고

해설 오전 9시 31분 ~ 9시 33분 대화에서 Natalie Bardet가 'I noticed a few storage bins with "Marketing" written on them, and I was wondering if they were yours.'라고 하자, Quincy Pondexter가 'Yes, those are my old client files.'라고 말한 것이므로 (D)가 정답이다.

+ Paraphrasing

files → documents

154. 화자 의도 파악

오전 9시 34분에, Bardet 씨가 "당신이 결정하면 돼요."라고 할 때 무엇을 의미하는가?

(A) 그녀는 Pondexter 씨를 위해 고객 기록을 정리할 수 있다.
(B) Pondexter 씨는 어떤 통을 사용할지 선택할 수 있다.
(C) 그녀는 전화회의용 장비를 설치할 수 있다.
(D) Pondexter 씨가 문서를 언제 살펴볼지 결정할 수 있다.

해설 오전 9시 33분 ~ 9시 34분 대화에서 Quincy Pondexter가 'I would need to go through them to double-check. Should I drop by now?'라고 물었을 때 Natalie Bardet가 'That's your call.'이라고 대답한 것이므로 (D)가 정답이다.

155-157번은 다음 웹페이지에 관한 문제입니다.

www.bombaygarden.com

홈	소개	메뉴	케이터링

Bombay Garden
인도의 맛을 경험해 보세요.

155 Vikas Jaffey가 Davenport에 작은 음식점을 열면서 요리 여정을 시작한 이래, 열정적으로 최고급 정통 카레를 제공해왔습니다. 20년째 156 그의 친척들이 저희의 유명한 카레 요리를 위해 예로부터 전해 내려오는 조리법과 최고급 재료를 이용하여 전통을 이어오고 있습니다.

저희는 4곳의 지점 외에도, 가장 인기 있는 배달앱과 제휴를 맺고 중소규모 행사장에 케이터링을 제공합니다.

157D 모든 카레 요리는 마늘 또는 플레인 난 빵과 157B 사모사나 파코라 중 선택하신 에피타이저, 157C 저희 인기 디저트 Gulab Jamun과 함께 제공됩니다.

*채식주의 옵션을 이용할 수 있습니다.
*모든 난은 특수 탄두르 오븐에서 신선하게 만들어집니다.

더 자세한 내용을 알아보시거나 지금 온라인으로 주문하시려면, 아래에서 지점을 선택하세요.

Moline	Rock Island	Bettendorf	Davenport

어휘
catering 음식 공급, 출장 연회 | passion 열정 | finest 질 높은 | authentic 정통의, 진짜의 | curry 카레 | embark on ~에 착수하다, 시작하다 | culinary 요리의 | journey 여행 | eatery 음식점 | relative 친척 | carry on ~을 계속하다 | time-honored 예로부터의, 유서 깊은 | recipe 조리법, 레시피 | ingredient 재료 | collaborate with ~와 협력[합작]하다 | garlic 마늘 | plain 꾸미지 않은, 무지의 | samosas 사모사(삼각형 튀김만두 같은 남아시아 요리) | pakora 파코라(고기나 채소를 넣은 튀김 같은 동남아시아 음식) | beloved 인기 많은 | vegan 엄격한 채식주의자(의) | tandoor 탄두르(숯불을 밑바닥에 놓는 원통형의 인도 화덕)

155. 사실 확인

Bombay Garden의 Davenport 지점에 관하여 무엇이 사실인가?

(A) 최초로 문을 열었다.
(B) 케이터링을 제공하지 않는다.
(C) 주인이 새로 바뀌었다.
(D) 확장 중이다.

해설 첫 번째 단락에서 'Our passion has been offering the finest and most authentic curry ever since Vikas Jaffey embarked on this culinary journey by opening a small eatery in Davenport.'라고 했으므로 (A)가 정답이다.

156. 사실 확인

Bombay Garden의 카레 요리에 관하여 언급된 것은?
(A) 인도에서 수입된다.
(B) 가족 조리법으로 만들어진다.
(C) 가격이 비싸지 않다.
(D) 특수 오븐에서 만들어진다.

해설 첫 번째 단락에서 'his relatives carry on the tradition of using time-honored recipes and the finest ingredients for our famous curry dishes.'라고 했으므로 (B)가 정답이다.

157. 사실 확인

카레 주문에 포함되지 않는 것은?
(A) 음료
(B) 애피타이저
(C) 디저트
(D) 난 빵

해설 지문의 단서와 보기를 매칭시키면, 세 번째 단락에서 'Each curry comes with garlic or plain naan bread, your choice of samosas or pakoras as an appetizer, and our beloved Gulab Jamun for dessert.'는 (D), (B), (C)와 일치하지만, 음료를 제공한다는 내용은 언급된 바가 없으므로 (A)가 정답이다.

158-160번은 다음 메모에 관한 문제입니다.

고객님께,

Ridgemont 리조트에 숙박하시게 된 것을 환영합니다. —[1]—. 귀하를 고객으로 맞이하게 되어 영광입니다. 158 159A **보통 투숙객이 많기 때문에, 저희는 고객 여러분께서 지켜주셨으면 하는 몇 가지 규칙을 알려드리려고 합니다.**

159D **수영장과 체육관 같은 저희 리조트 시설은 추가 비용 없이 누구나 이용하실 수 있습니다.** —[2]—. 하지만 다른 고객에 방해가 되지 않도록 지나친 소음은 삼가 주시길 요청 드립니다. 159C **또한, 리조트 후문 근처에는 식물원이 있습니다.** —[3]—. 개방 되는 동안에는 경로를 이탈하지 말아 주시기 바랍니다. 160 **마지막으로, 12세 미만 아이와 함께 투숙하시는 경우, 항상 관리 감독해 주시기를 요청 드립니다.** —[4]—. 감사드리며, 즐거운 숙박 되시길 바랍니다.

어휘
stay 숙박 | honor 영광을 주다 | generally 대개, 보통 | share 공유하다 | rule 규칙 | adhere to ~를 고수하다 | facility 시설 | pool 수영장 | gym 체육관 | at no additional charge 추가 요금 없이 | excessive 지나친 | noise 소음 | avoid 피하다 | disturb 방해하다 | additionally 또한 | botanical garden 식물원 | locate ~에 위치시키다 | entrance 입구 | refrain from ~를 삼가다 | veer off 이탈하다, 벗어나다 | path 진로 | finally 마지막으로 | supervise 지도하다, 감독하다 | at all times 항상

158. 주제 / 목적 / 대상

메모의 목적은 무엇인가?
(A) 신규 서비스를 홍보하려고
(B) 가격을 명확하게 설명하려고
(C) 몇몇 활동을 추천하려고
(D) 몇몇 규칙에 대해 알려주려고

해설 첫 번째 단락에서 'Due to the high number of guests we generally have, we would like to share some rules we expect our guests here to adhere to.'라고 했으므로 (D)가 정답이다.

✦ Paraphrasing

share → inform on

159. 사실 확인

Ridgemont 리조트에 관하여 언급되지 않은 것은?
(A) 평소 고객들로 붐빈다.
(B) 호숫가에 위치한다.
(C) 후문이 있다.
(D) 무료로 사용할 수 있는 시설을 제공한다.

해설 지문의 단서와 보기를 매칭시키면, 첫 번째 단락의 'Due to the high number of guests we generally have,'은 (A)와, 두 번째 단락의 'The facilities at our resort, such as the pool and gym, are open for all to use at no additional charge.'은 (D)와, 'Additionally, there is a botanical garden located near the back entrance of the resort.'은 (C)와 일치하지만, 호숫가에 위치한다는 내용은 언급된 바가 없으므로 (B)가 정답이다.

✦ Paraphrasing

generally → normally, at no additional charge → free

160. 문장 삽입

[1], [2], [3], [4]로 표시된 곳 중에서 다음 문장이 들어갈 위치로 가장 적절한 곳은?

"기타 문의사항이 있으시면, 555-1837번으로 프런트 데스크로 전화해 주십시오."

(A) [1]
(B) [2]
(C) [3]
(D) [4]

해설 주어진 문장에서 그 밖에 궁금한 사항을 문의해 달라고 하므로 모든 전달 내용이 나온 후 마지막에 들어가야 한다. 따라서 (D)가 정답이다.

161-163번은 다음 기사에 관한 문제입니다.

옛것을 새롭게
Sandra Lim

Bristol (10월 10일) — 어제 있었던 합동 기자회견에서, 161 **시장은 오래된 전화부스를 활용하여 도시 내 여러 장소에 스마트 충전소를 짓는 3자 협력을 발표했다.** 각 충전소는 초고속 와이파이의 접속 지점의 역할을 하면서, 전기 자전거 및 스쿠터, 162D **스마트폰 충전,** 162A **관광 정보 제공과** 162C **인근 상점 및 레스토랑 이용 쿠폰 제공과 같은 많은 기능을 수행할 것이다.** 등록된 사용자는 무료로 한 번에 30분간 이 서비스를 이용할 수 있다.

협력에는 Newport에 본사를 둔 Shenk Communications뿐만 아니라, 아일랜드 기술회사 O'Rourke Enterprises와 현지 건축회사 JFC Designs가 참여한다. O'Rourke와 JFC는 기술, 설계, 건설 분야에서 협력하고, Shenk Communications에서 인터넷 연결을 제공할 것이다. 광고 및 이용료를 활용하여 프로젝트에서 최소의 비용만을 납세자에게 부담할 것이다.

충전소는 12월에 서비스를 시작하는 25개 역과 내년 여름까지로 예정된 추가 75개로, 앞으로 몇 달에 걸쳐 선보일 것이다. 163 **O'Rourke는 유럽에서 유사한 프로젝트를 맡았던 경험이 있다.** 3년 전 출시된 Dublin 스마트 충전소는 매일 5천 대의 차량에 연료를 공급하며, 수천 명의 사람이 방전된 스마트폰 배터리를 충전하는 데 도움을 주었다.

어휘

joint 공동의, 합동의 | press conference 기자회견 | mayor 시장 | announce 발표하다 | collaboration 공동 작업, 협력 | charging station 충전소 | location 장소, 위치 | metro area 도시권 | make use of ~를 이용 [활용]하다 | outdated 구식인 | function 기능 | allow 허용하다 | electric bicycle 전기 자전거 | scooter 스쿠터 | charge 충전하다: 요금 | nearby 인근의 | access point (네트워크 접속 중계점) 접속점 | registered 등록한 | regional 지역의 | architecture 건축 | partner 파트너가 되다 | construction 건설 | connectivity 연결(성) | advertising 광고 | subscription 구독 | fee 요금 | ensure 보장하다 | minimum 최저의 | taxpayer 납세자 | debut 데뷔하다, 첫 선을 보이다 | due 예정된 | go into service 봉사하다, 근무하다 | comparable 비교할만한 | launch 시작하다, 출시하다 | fuel 연료를 공급하다 | vehicle 차량 | top up ~를 보충하다, 가득 채우다 | deplete 격감[고갈]시키다

161. 사실 확인

프로젝트에 관해서 언급된 것은?

(A) 오래된 전화부스를 활용할 것이다.
(B) 인상된 세금으로 비용 처리될 것이다.
(C) 12월에 끝내는 것으로 일정이 잡혔다.
(D) 지역 방문자 수를 증가시켰다.

해설 첫 번째 단락에서 'the mayor announced a three-way collaboration to build smart charging stations in a number of locations in the metro area by making use of outdated telephone booths.'라고 했으므로 (A)가 정답이다.

➕ **Paraphrasing**

make use of outdated telephone booths → utilize obsolete telephone booths

162. 사실 확인

기사에서 충전소의 특징으로 언급하지 않은 것은?

(A) 지역 정보
(B) 무한한 인터넷 서비스
(C) 레스토랑 쿠폰
(D) 휴대폰 충전

해설 지문의 단서와 보기를 매칭시키면, 첫 번째 단락에서 'smartphone charging'은 (D)와, 'providing tourist information'은 (A)와 'offering coupons to nearby shops and restaurants'는 (C)와 일치하지만, 무제한 인터넷 서비스를 제공한다는 내용은 언급된 바가 없으므로 (B)가 정답이다.

➕ **Paraphrasing**

smartphone → cellphone, coupons → vouchers

163. 사실 확인

O'Rourke Enterprises에 관하여 언급된 것은?

(A) JFC Designs에 인수됐다.
(B) 과거에 유사한 충전소를 지었다.
(C) 인터넷 서비스가 널리 이용된다.
(D) 본사가 Bristol에 있다.

해설 세 번째 단락에서 'O'Rourke has experience with comparable projects in Europe. Its smart charging stations in Dublin,'이라고 했으므로 (B)가 정답이다.

164-167번은 다음 온라인 채팅 대화문에 관한 문제입니다.

Crispin Adams (3:04 P.M.)
안녕하세요. 164 Shelly McSteel의 제작자가 방금 마지막 곡의 새로운 믹스를 보냈는데, 곡들이 아주 훌륭해요. 이 앨범을 출시할 때가 왔어요!

Devon Carter (3:05 P.M.)
아주 좋은 소식이에요. 164 팬들이 언제 구입할 수 있을까요?

Crispin Adams (3:07 P.M.)
늦봄에요. 164 5월 3째 주요. 우선, 법무부에 몇몇 샘플을 승인 받고, 커버 디자인을 할 그래픽 디자이너를 채용하고, 언론 인터뷰 일정을 잡아야 해요. 아, 그리고 홍보 사진도 몇 장 필요해요. 빨리 끝냅시다.

Devon Carter (3:08 P.M.)
그렇고 말고요. 제 기억으로는, 그녀가 사진 촬영을 Great Basin 공원에서 하고 싶어했어요.

Crispin Adams (3:09 P.M.)
165 Mina, 다음 주에 Great Basin 공원에서 McSteel 씨 촬영을 진행할 수 있으세요?

Mina Doan (3:10 P.M.)
165 그럼요. 그녀가 만나기를 원하는 장소만 저에게 정확히 알려주세요. 목요일이 좋을 것 같아요.

Devon Carter (3:12 P.M.)
방금 그녀에게 메시지를 받았는데요. 금요일이 제일 좋다고 하네요.

Crispin Adams (3:13 P.M.)
167 Mina, McSteel 씨 일정에 맞춰주실 수 있으신가요? 166 그리고 Devon, McSteel 씨에게 진행 상황을 알려주세요.

Devon Carter (3:14 P.M.)
알겠습니다. 166 정리되면 그녀에게 연락할게요.

Mina Doan (3:15 P.M.)
167 맞출 수 있어요.

Crispin Adams (3:16 P.M.)
좋습니다. 다 된 것 같네요. 고마워요, 여러분.

어휘

producer 제작자 | mix 혼합 | track (음악) 한 곡 | put out 출간하다, 발표하다 | record 음반 | authorize 인가하다, 권한을 부여하다 | hire 고용하다 | cover 표지 | press 언론 | shoot 사진 촬영 | shot 사진 | message 메시지를 보내다 | schedule around ~에 맞춰 일정을 잡다 | keep ~ updated ~에게 진행 상황을 알려주다 | work 작동하다, 효과가 있다

164. 상세 정보

5월에 무슨 일이 있을 것인가?

(A) 인터뷰가 있을 것이다.
(B) 앨범이 발매될 것이다.
(C) 노래가 녹음될 것이다.
(D) 전시가 열릴 것이다.

해설 오후 3시 04분 ~ 3시 07분 대화에서 Crispin Adams가 'Shelly McSteel's producer just submitted a new mix of the last few tracks, and they sound great. It's time to put this record out!'이라고 한 말에, Devon Carter가 'When are the fans going to be able to buy it?'이라고 하자, Crispin Adams 가 'Third week of May.'라고 대답한 것이므로 (B)가 정답이다.

➕ **Paraphrasing**

record → album

165. 암시 / 추론

Doan 씨는 누구겠는가?

(A) 그래픽 아티스트
(B) 언론인

(C) 사진작가

(D) 가수

해설 오후 3시 09분 ~ 3시 10분 대화에서 Crispin Adams가 'Mina, would you be able to take some shots of Ms. McSteel next week in Great Basin Park?'라고 한 말에, Mina Doan이 'Definitely. Just let me know where she wants to meet exactly.'라고 대답한 것으로 미루어 그녀가 사진작가임을 알 수 있으므로 (C)가 정답이다.

166. 암시 / 추론

Carter 씨는 다음에 무엇을 하겠는가?

(A) 새 앨범을 편집할 것이다

(B) 인터뷰를 할 것이다

(C) 법무부에 연락할 것이다

(D) 진행 상황을 확인할 것이다

해설 오후 3시 13분 ~ 3시 14분 대화에서 Crispin Adams가 'And Devon, please keep Ms. McSteel updated.'라고 한 말에, Devon Carter가 'Certainly. I'll call her when we're done.' 이라고 말한 것이므로 (D)가 정답이다.

167. 화자 의도 파악

오후 3시 15분에, Doan 씨가 "맞출 수 있어요"라고 할 때 무엇을 의미하는가?

(A) 출시일을 조정할 것이다.

(B) 장비를 가져올 수 있을 것이다.

(C) 자신의 일정을 조정할 것이다.

(D) 음악 몇 곡을 들을 것이다.

해설 오후 3시 13분 ~ 3시 15분 대화에서 Crispin Adams가 'Mina, do you mind scheduling around Ms. McSteel?'이라고 한 말에, Mina Doan이 'I can make it work.'라고 답한 것이므로 (C)가 정답이다.

168-171번은 다음 기사에 관한 문제입니다.

CHENNAI TIMES

(3월 10일) — 현재, 〔168〕2곳의 유명 소셜 미디어 업체가 인도에서 가장 많은 사용자를 확보하려는 경쟁을 하고 있다. 소셜 미디어 거물인 Instabook과 Chidiya는 그들이 국내 최고자리를 놓고 겨루고 있음을 분명히 했다. —[1]—.

지난여름, Silicon Valley에 본사를 둔 기술업체인 Instabook은 마침내 인도에서 모바일 앱을 출시했다. —[2]—. 그 회사는 이미 전 세계 수천만의 사용자를 보유한 선두 업체였다. 반면, Chidiya는 아대륙 밖에서는 거의 알려지지 않았지만, 인도에서는 엄청난 사용자 기반을 확보했다. Chidiya의 도달 범위는 이미 인상적이고, 국가에서 가장 신뢰받는 정보 출처 중 하나가 되었다.

〔171〕—[3]—. Seoul 소재의 Murmur를 포함한 소셜 미디어 기업들은 특히 정부가 공유 컨텐츠에 가하는 제약이 글로벌 플랫폼에 변화를 야기하면서 이러한 제약에 대해 불만을 표시해왔다. 〔169〕결과적으로, Murmur는 현지 지점을 폐쇄했고, 인도에서 활동한 지 1년 만에 인도의 유명 앱스토어에서 서비스를 중단했다.

반면, Chidiya는 다른 업체들에 비해 우위를 점하고 있다. —[4]—. 〔170A〕이 회사는 사이트에 게시되는 콘텐츠의 정확성을 확인하는 데 힘을 쏟고 있다. 〔170C〕또한 Chidiya는 민족적으로 다양한 사용자층의 니즈를 잘 반영하여, 자사 앱에 8가지의 언어 선택권을 제공한다. 게다가, 이 회사는 〔170D〕팝 음악 협찬과 음악 독점 배포를 통해 젊은 사용자층에 어필

한다. Instabook은 더 많은 글로벌 사용자를 보유했지만, Chidiya와 같은 기존 브랜드를 넘어서기 어려울 것이다.

Salmaan Reddy

어휘

currently 현재 | firm 회사 | engage (주의, 관심을) 끌다 | competition 경쟁, 대회 | acquire 얻다, 획득하다 | giant 거대한; 거물 | vie for 겨루다, 경쟁하다 | spot 장소, 자리 | launch 시작하다, 착수하다 | in contrast 그에 반해서, 반면 | mostly 대개 | subcontinent 아(亞)대륙 | attract 끌어들이다, 끌어모으다 | reach 접근; 닿다, 도달하다 | source 원천, 근원 | restriction 제한 | platform 플랫폼, 발판 | consequently 그 결과, 따라서 | pull 끌다, 끌어당기다 | have an edge over ~보다 우위를 점하다, 유리하다 | dedicate 전념하다, 헌신하다 | accuracy 정확(성) | post 게시하다, 공고하다 | adapt 맞추다, 적응하다 | ethnically 민족적으로 | diverse 다양한 | provide 제공하다 | option 옵션, 선택(권) | app 앱(application의 준말) | additionally 또한, 게다가 | appeal 관심을 끌다, 호소하다 | sponsorship 후원, 협찬 | exclusive 독점적인 | release 출시, 발표, 공개 | overcome 이기다, 극복하다 | established 인정받는, 확실히 자리를 잡은

168. 주제 / 목적 / 대상

기사는 주로 무엇에 관해 이야기하고 있는가?

(A) 혁신적인 마케팅 기법들

(B) 공학 직무의 부상

(C) 인도의 유명 전자회사들

(D) 회사들 간 경쟁

해설 첫 번째 단락에서 'two popular social media firms are engaged in a competition to acquire the most users in India.'라고 했으므로 (D)가 정답이다.

✦ **Paraphrasing**

firms → companies, a competition → a rivalry

169. 암시 / 추론

Murmur에 관하여 알 수 있는 것은?

(A) 잠시 인도 고객들을 대상으로 사업을 했다.

(B) 젊은 사용자들에게 인기가 있다.

(C) 1년 전에 설립되었다.

(D) 최근 실리콘밸리로 본사를 옮겼다.

해설 세 번째 단락에서 'Consequently, Murmur closed its local offices and pulled its service from popular Indian app stores after only one year of activity in the country.'라고 했으므로 (A)가 정답이다.

170. 사실 확인

Chidiya의 강점으로 언급되지 않은 것은?

(A) 온라인 게시물의 정확성을 확인한다.

(B) 여러 국가에 지점이 있다.

(C) 다양한 언어로 프로그램을 제공한다.

(D) 독점 음악 이용권을 제공한다.

해설 네 번째 단락에서 지문의 단서와 보기를 매칭시키면, 'The firm is dedicated to checking the accuracy of content posted on its site.'는 (A)와, 'Chidiya has also adapted well to the needs of its ethnically-diverse users, providing eight different language options on its app.'은 (C)와, 'pop music sponsorships and exclusive music releases.'는 (D)와 일치하지만, 여러 국가에 지점이 있다는 내용은 언급된 바가 없으므로 (B)가 정답이다.

✦ **Paraphrasing**

check the accuracy of content posted on its site

→ confirm the accuracy of online posts,
provide eight different language options → offer a program in multiple languages,
exclusive music releases → access to exclusive music

171. 문장 삽입

[1], [2], [3], [4]로 표시된 곳 중에서 다음 문장이 들어갈 위치로 가장 적절한 곳은?

"엄격한 규제가 큰 장애물이 되었다."

(A) [1]
(B) [2]
(C) [3]
(D) [4]

해설 주어진 문장의 a major obstacle이 가리킬 수 있는 내용이 나와야 한다. 세 번째 단락에서 'Social media firms, including Seoul-based Murmur, have been unhappy with restrictions the government has placed on content that can be shared, especially as these restrictions created changes in their global platforms.'라고 하여 주어진 문장에 이어지기에 자연스러우므로 (C)가 정답이다.

172-175번은 다음 편지에 관한 문제입니다.

10월 12일

174 Carolyn Carter 씨
Oasis Architecture
5 Kimberly Leys
Carleton, OH 33022

Carter 씨께,

172 Carleton 대학교의 건축 및 설계 대학에서는 저희 신규 건물인 Osman Building의 개관식에 귀하를 연사 중 한 분으로 초대합니다. **174** 건물 설계에 기여해주셨을 뿐만 아니라, **173** 우리 학교의 성공한 동문 자격으로 귀하를 연사로 모시게 되면 영광이겠습니다. **174** 설계 단계에서 귀사의 지원이 없었더라면, Osman Building은 절대 가능하지 않았을 것입니다.

개관식은 10월 24일 토요일에 열리며, 행사는 오전 10시에 시작합니다. **175D** 초청 인사의 연설로 일정을 시작한 후, 개관식을 시작할 것입니다. 현지 신문사에서 행사를 취재할 예정으로, 이때 사진 촬영도 있을 것입니다. **175B** 또한 Papermoon 카페에서 제공하는 점심 식사도 마련되어 있습니다. **175A** 학과장이신 Suzanne Park 교수의 폐회사로 일정이 마무리됩니다.

10월 24일 기념식에 함께해 주시면 영광스러울 것입니다. 궁금하신 점이 있으시면, 197-555-4682로 저에게 연락해 주십시오. 참석 여부를 가능한 한 빨리 확정해 주시면, 대단히 감사하겠습니다.

진심을 전하며,

Lance Luna
부교수, 건축 및 설계 대학원
Carleton 대학교

어휘
architecture 건축학 | planning 계획 | extend an invitation 초대하다 | opening ceremony 개관식 | distinguished 유명한, 성공한 | alumnus 동문 | contribution 기여 | firm 회사 | assistance 지원 | due 예정된

---

take place 일어나다 | commence 시작하다 | ribbon-cutting ceremony 개관식 | cover 취재[보도]하다 | photoshoot 사진 촬영 | paid-for 지불된 | cater 음식을 공급하다 | round out 마무리하다 | closing speech 폐회사 | reach 연락하다 | confirm 확인해 주다 | availability 이용가능성 | at your earliest convenience 가능한 한 빨리 | appreciate 고마워하다 | senior lecturer 부교수

172. 주제 / 목적 / 대상

편지의 목적은 무엇인가?
(A) Carter 씨에게 새로운 프로젝트에 대해 지원을 요청하려고
(B) Carter 씨를 개관 행사에 초대하려고
(C) Carleton 대학교에 관한 오해를 바로 잡으려고
(D) 제휴 가능성에 대해 문의하려고

해설 첫 번째 단락에서 'The School of Architecture and Planning at Carleton University would like to extend an invitation for you to be one of our speakers at the opening ceremony of our new building, the Osman Building.'이라고 했으므로 (B)가 정답이다.

173. 사실 확인

Carter 씨에 관하여 언급된 것은?
(A) 건축학을 강의한다.
(B) Carleton 대학교를 다녔다.
(C) 자기 사업을 시작했다.
(D) 학교에 정기적으로 기부한다.

해설 첫 번째 단락에서 'We would be honored to have you as a speaker as a distinguished alumnus of our school,'이라고 했으므로 (B)가 정답이다.

174. 사실 확인

Oasis Architecture에 관하여 사실인 것은?
(A) Carleton 대학교 학생에게 인턴십을 제공한다.
(B) 조만간 본사를 이전할 것이다.
(C) 신문에 실린 적이 있다.
(D) Osman Building의 설계에 컨설팅을 제공했다.

해설 첫 번째 단락에서 'as well as your contributions to the design of the building'이라고 하며, 'Without your firm's assistance during the planning stages, the Osman Building would never have been possible.'이라고 했으므로 (D)가 정답이다.

175. 사실 확인

편지에서 기념식의 일환으로 언급되지 않은 것은?
(A) 폐회사
(B) 사진 촬영
(C) 뒤풀이 파티
(D) 게스트 연설

해설 두 번째 단락에서 'We will start the day with speeches from invited guests and then commence with the ribbon-cutting ceremony.'는 (D)와, 'A local newspaper will be covering the event, so we will be having a photo shoot as well.'는 (B)와, 'The day will be rounded out with a closing speech by Professor Suzanne Park, the Head of School.'은 (A)과 일치하지만, 뒤풀이 파티는 언급된 바가 없으므로 (C)가 정답이다.

176-180번은 다음 웹페이지와 이메일에 관한 문제입니다.

Millennium Rockets

저희는 지금 내년 발사 때의 공유 공간에 대한 예약을 받고 있습니다. 저희와 함께하시면, 업계 최저 요금뿐만 아니라 최고의 서비스도 받게 됩니다. 아래 일정표를 확인하시고 저희가 곧 있을 귀하의 노력에 도움을 드릴 수 있을지 알아보세요.

발사 번호	176 발사일	궤도 높이	위성 발사지	중량 제한
1	1분기	3,800km	인도	250kg
2	1분기	37,000km	중국	50kg
3	176 2분기	3,000km	176 미국	50kg
4	3분기	5,400km	러시아	175kg
178 5	178 3분기	178 37,000km	중국	250kg
6	4분기	3,000km	노르웨이	175kg

어휘

accept 받다 | booking 예약 | shared 공유된 | space 공간 | launch 발사 | rate 요금 | industry 업계 | upcoming 곧 있을, 다가오는 | endeavor 노력, 시도 | quarter 사분기, 4분의 1 | orbit 궤도 | height 높이, 고도 | weight 무게, 중량 | limit 제한

수신: Garrett Hampton ⟨ghampton@spinstitute.com⟩
발신: Brenda Lowe ⟨blowe@spinstitute.com⟩
날짜: 12월 2일
제목: 위성 발사일

Hampton 씨께,

추천해 주신 내용을 바탕으로, 저는 Millennium의 내년 발사 일정표를 받았습니다. 날짜가 확정되지는 않았지만, 그쪽에서 대략적인 발사일을 보내줬습니다. 178 저희에게 필요한 사항을 고려하면, 그쪽에서 발사하는 위성 중 2개만 저희 요건에 충족할 정도로 높습니다. 하지만, 그 중 하나는 1분기에 발사되는데, 그건 저희에게 너무 이를 수도 있습니다. 다른 하나는 3분기에 발사됩니다. 저희가 최대한 빨리 발사를 원한다는 건 알지만, 1사분기에 발사하면 저희가 세부 사항을 서둘러 검토하게 될 수도 있습니다. 177 178 그래서, 저는 SKY 위성 발사일을 늦추는 일이 조금이라도 가능한지 알고 싶습니다.

179 제가 선호하는 옵션은 저희가 모든 위험요인을 가능한 최소화할 수 있도록 발사를 3분기로 연기하는 것입니다. 이렇게 하면 저희 방송이 위성 안테나로 정확하게 수신되도록 구성요소를 세부 조정할 시간이 충분할 겁니다. 위의 계획이 실행 가능한지 알려주시면, 제가 거기에 맞춰 Millennium 측에 연락하겠습니다.

진심을 담아,

Brenda Lowe, SP협회, SKY 프로젝트팀

어휘

recommendation 추천 | set in stone 확정된, 개략적인, 대충의 | rush 급히 서두르다, 경솔하게 하다 | detail 세부내용 | delay 연기하다, 미루다 | on the cards 발생 가능성이 있는 | preferred 바람직한 | mitigate 줄이다 | risk 위험 (요인) | finetune 세부 조정하다 | component 요소, 부품 | broadcast 방송 | correctly 정확하게 | satellite dish 위성방송 수신용 안테나 | viable 실행 가능한 | accordingly 그에 맞춰 | institute 기관, 협회

176. 상세 정보

Millennium Rockets는 2분기에 어느 나라에서 로켓을 발사할 것인가?

(A) 인도
(B) 노르웨이
(C) 미국
(D) 중국

해설 첫 번째 지문 [웹페이지], 표에서 2분기에 발사하는 나라는 the United States (미국)임을 알 수 있으므로 (C)가 정답이다.

177. 주제 / 목적 / 대상

이메일의 목적은 무엇인가?

(A) 기존의 계획을 연기하는 것
(B) 추가 자금을 요청하는 것
(C) 새로운 상품을 제안하는 것
(D) 회사의 정책을 설명하는 것

해설 두 번째 지문 [이메일], 첫 번째 단락에서 'Therefore, I would like to know whether delaying the launch date for the SKY satellite is at all on the cards.'라고 했으므로 (A)가 정답이다.

+ Paraphrasing

delay → postpone

178. 상세 정보

Lowe 씨는 어느 발사 번호에 맞춰 준비해야 한다고 권장하는가?

(A) 발사 번호 2
(B) 발사 번호 3
(C) 발사 번호 4
(D) 발사 번호 5

해설 두 번째 지문 [이메일], 첫 번째 단락에서 'Based on our needs, only two of the satellites they are launching are high enough for our requirements. However, one of them launches in the first quarter, which may be too early for us. The other launches in the third quarter.'이라고 하면서 'Therefore, I would like to know whether delaying the launch date for the SKY satellite is at all on the cards.'라고 했으므로 (A)가 정답이다.

179. 암시 / 추론

이메일에서 SKY 위성의 기능으로 암시하는 것은?

(A) 텔레비전 편성
(B) 기상 예보
(C) 비행기 통신
(D) 우주 탐험

해설 두 번째 지문 [이메일], 두 번째 단락에서 'This will give us enough time to finetune our components so that our broadcasts are correctly received by the satellite dishes.'라고 했으므로 (A)가 정답이다.

180. 동의어

이메일에서 두 번째 단락, 두 번째 줄의 단어, "mitigate"와 의미상 가장 가까운 것은?

(A) 부담을 주다
(B) 낮추다
(C) 충족시키다
(D) 나누다

해설 두 번째 지문 [이메일], 두 번째 단락의 'My preferred option would be to delay our launch until the third quarter so that we can mitigate any risks possible.'에서 'mitigate'은 '최소화하다'라는 의미로 쓰였으므로 보기 중 '낮추다'를 뜻하는 (B)가 정답이다.

181-185번은 다음 이메일과 일정에 관한 문제입니다.

수신: Epic Industries 부서 관리자들
발신: Justin Sherman
날짜: 12월 2일
제목: 회의
첨부: 최종_일정

안녕하세요,

내일 오전 10시에 관리자 회의가 있으니 기억해 주시기 바랍니다. 최종 회의 일정을 첨부해 드립니다. **181 182** 초기 일정에서 다른 항목이 추가되었음을 보게 되실 거예요. 저희 판매 관리자 Phan Nguyen이 신상품 출시에 대한 정보를 논의할 것입니다. 그의 발표는 약 30분 정도 걸릴 것입니다.

회의 전에, 회사의 다음 분기 사업 계획을 반드시 검토해 주시길 바랍니다. **183** 또한, 여러분의 다음 분기 최신 예산보고서 및 예상 비용의 사본을 준비해 주세요.

문의 사항이 있으시면, 저에게 연락해 주세요.

Justin Sherman

어휘
finalize 마무리를 짓다 | include 포함하다 | initial 초기의 | discuss 논의하다 | detail 세부 사항 | latest 최신의 | launch 출시 | run (기간 동안) 계속되다 | prior to ~ 이전에 | look over 살펴보다 | business 사업 | plan 계획 | quarter 4분의 1 | prepare 준비하다 | recent 최근의 | budget 예산, 비용 | estimated 견적의, 추측의 | expense 비용 | following 다음의

Epic Industries 관리자 회의

장소: 5층 회의실
날짜: 12월 3일
시간: 오전 10시

발표자	주제	내용
182 Phan Nguyen	**182** 차량 내비게이터	•**185** 모바일 앱의 판매수치 분석
Patrick Bell	회사 경비	•예상비용과 현재 예산 검토
Justin Sherman	진행 상황 업데이트	•발생 문제들 제시 •타임라인 및 정시 프로젝트 완료가 가능한지 검토
Amber Vessel	마케팅 전략	•**185** 앱을 홍보할 최상의 플랫폼 논의
184 Michelle Finney, Work Together 주식회사 공동 창업자	이용자층 확대	•타킷 시장 이외 대상층을 사로잡는 방법

어휘
analyze 분석하다 | figure 수치 | mobile application 모바일 앱 | review 검토하다 | progress 진행, 진전 | emerge 생겨나다, 나오다 | timeline 시각표, 타임라인 | complete 완료하다 | on time 제시간에 | discussion 토론, 논의 | platform 플랫폼(사용기반이 되는 컴퓨터 시스템, 소프트웨어) | advertise 광고하다 | app 앱(application의 약어) | co-founder 공동 설립자 | expand 확장시키다 | demographic 인구, 인구구조 | capture 사로잡다 | target 목표

---

181. 암시 / 추론

이메일에서, Sherman 씨는 회의에 관하여 무엇을 암시하는가?
(A) 예상보다 더 오래 걸릴 것이다.

(B) 케이터링 식사가 포함할 것이다.
(C) 일부 투자자들이 참석할 것이다.
(D) 새로 고용된 관리자가 진행할 것이다.

해설 Sherman 씨가 보낸 첫 번째 지문[이메일], 첫 번째 단락에서 'You'll see that another item has been included in the initial schedule. Our sales manager, Phan Nguyen, will discuss the details of our latest product launch. His talk will run for about half an hour.'이라고 하여 원래 일정보다 30분이 더 걸릴 것임을 알 수 있으므로 (A)가 정답이다.

182. 상세 정보 - 연계 문제

안건에서 새로운 항목은 무엇인가?
(A) 차량 내비게이터
(B) 진행 상황 업데이트
(C) 마케팅 전략
(D) 이용자층 확대

해설 Sherman 씨가 보낸 첫 번째 지문[이메일], 첫 번째 단락에서 'You'll see that another item has been included in the initial schedule. Our sales manager, Phan Nguyen, will discuss the details of our latest product launch.'라고 했는데, 두 번째 지문[일정], 표의 Subject에서 Phan Nguyen의 발표 주제가 'Car Navigator'이라고 하여 새롭게 추가된 항목임을 알 수 있으므로 (A)가 정답이다.

183. 상세 정보

Sherman 씨는 회의 참석자들에게 무엇을 준비하라고 요청하는가?
(A) 고객 연락 정보
(B) 수정된 일정
(C) 자격을 갖춘 지원자 목록
(D) 최신 재무파일

해설 Sherman 씨가 보낸 첫 번째 지문[이메일], 두 번째 단락에서 'In addition, please prepare copies of your most recent budget report and estimated expenses for the following quarter.'라고 했으므로 (D)가 정답이다.

+ Paraphrasing
most recent budget report and estimated expenses
→ Updated financial files

184. 암시 / 추론

일정에서 Finney 씨에 관하여 무엇을 알 수 있는가?
(A) 금융관리 전문가이다.
(B) 화상회의를 통해 회의에 참여할 것이다.
(C) 본인의 회사를 차렸다.
(D) Sherman 씨의 동료이다.

해설 두 번째 지문[일정], 표의 Speaker 항목에서 'Michelle Finney, Co-founder of Work Together, Inc.'라고 했으므로 (C)가 정답이다.

185. 암시 / 추론

Epic Industries는 무엇을 판매하겠는가?
(A) 소형차량
(B) 전자기기
(C) 가정용품
(D) 소프트웨어 프로그램

해설 두 번째 지문[일정], 표의 Details에서 'Analyze the sales figures of the mobile application', 'Discussion of the best platforms to advertise apps on'이라고 하여 모바일 앱을 판매하는 회사임을 알 수 있으므로 (D)가 정답이다.

186-190번은 다음 제안서 양식들과 이메일에 관한 문제입니다.

186 Precision Painters 제안서

고객:	Elio Marketing
주소:	39 Mt. Taylor Drive St. Heliers, Auckland, NZ 6022
날짜:	2월 6일

Precision Painters는 계약서에 명시되고 제조사 규격에 적용되는 모든 벽을 칠, 코팅, 마감합니다. **190** 벽과 선반 위에 있는 물품들은 주의해서 상자 안에 담았다가 완료후 원상 복귀시켜드립니다. **188** 당사의 작업은 1년 간 보증됩니다 (전체 품질보증서 세부내용은 당사 웹사이트에 있습니다).

서비스 요금: 7,450 달러 + 세금 (추천 할인 포함)
이 금액은 프로젝트 완수 즉시 지불되어야 합니다.

186 작성자:	Denise Nel
배송지:	
날짜:	

어휘
proposal 제안 | indicate 명시하다, 표시하다 | contract 계약 | apply 적용하다, 바르다 | per ~에 따라 | specification 사양, 규격 | shelf 선반 | original 원래의 | position 위치 | completion 완성 | guarantee 보증하다 | complete 완전한 | warranty 품질 보증서 | detail 세부 사항 | charge 요금 | referral 소개, 추천 | prepare 준비하다

제안서

계약자	고객
Handy Painters	Elio Marketing
32 Robina Court	39 Mt. Taylor Drive
Burswood, Manukau, NZ 2105	St. Heliers, Auckland, NZ 6022

작업 범위
- 모든 표시된 구역에 페인트 준비 및 도포
- 페인트가 **190** 칠해질 표면 위의 철물, 부속물과 이와 유사한 품목들은 고객이 치워야 합니다.
- 책상을 덮을 시트와 테이프가 제공됩니다.
- *참고: **188** 모든 도장된 벽 마감을 포함하여 전체 작업은 6개월간 보증됩니다.

회사 제안
- Handy Painters는 세금, 페인트, 인건비를 포함하여 6,350달러의 가격으로 상기 작업을 완료할 것을 제안합니다.
- **187** 페인트 작업 완료 7일 이내에 대금이 지불되어야 합니다.
- 이 제안은 1개월간 유효합니다.

제출자: Janice Hart
날짜: 2월 9일

고객 서명: _____
날짜: _____

어휘
contractor 계약자, 도급업자 | scope 범위 | preparation 준비 | application 적용, 도포, 바르기 | hardware 철물 | accessory 부속물, 액세서리 | similar 유사한 | surface 표면 | remove 제거하다, 치우다 | cover 덮다, (보험으로) 보장하다 | finish 마감칠 | propose 제안하다 | labor fee 인건비 | due ~하기로 예정된, (돈을) 지불해야 하는 | valid 유효한 | signature 서명

수신: all@eliomarketing.com
발신: Renée Young, 대표
날짜: 3월 1일
제목: 실내 페인트칠

대부분 아시겠지만, 다음 주 월요일부터 벽을 다시 페인트칠할 예정입니다. 작업이 완료되는데 약 일주일이 걸릴 것입니다. **189** 그 결과, 우리는 몇 가지를 준비해야 합니다. 우선, 여러분은 페인트로 인해 손상되지 않도록 여러분의 소지품을 보호해야 합니다. 저희가 책상 위에 덮을 천을 제공해 드릴 것입니다. **190** 벽에 걸린 그림들은 걱정하지 마십시오. 계약자가 그것들을 처리할 것입니다. 도장공들이 여기 있는 동안에는 우리가 사무실에서 일을 할 수 없을 것이기 때문에, 다음 주 업무를 위한 공간을 임대했습니다(자세한 내용은 곧 발송될 예정입니다). 이해해 주셔서 감사합니다.

어휘
approximately 대략 | protect 보호하다 | belongings 소유물 | damage 손상시키다 | drape 덮는 천, 드레이프 | handle 다루다, 처리하다 | rent 임대하다

---

186. 암시 / 추론

Nel 씨는 누구겠는가?

(A) Precision Painters의 직원
(B) Elio Marketing의 관리자
(C) Young 씨의 친구
(D) 프리랜서 도장공

해설 첫 번째 지문 [제안서], 제목에서 'Precision Painters PROPOSAL'이라고 했고, 세 번째 단락에서 'Prepared by: Denise Nel'이라고 하여 Nel 씨가 Precision Painters의 직원임을 알 수 있으므로 (A)가 정답이다.

187. 상세 정보

고객들은 Handy Painters에 서비스에 대한 요금을 언제 지불해야 하는가?

(A) 프로젝트 완료 일주일 이내에
(B) 전자 청구서를 받자마자
(C) 제안서를 받고 한 달 후에
(D) 제안서 양식에 서명한 날

해설 두 번째 지문 [제안서], 세 번째 단락에서 'Payment is due within seven days of finishing the paint job.'이라고 했으므로 (A)가 정답이다.

188. 상세 정보 - 연계 문제

두 회사가 고객들에게 제공하는 것은?
(A) 몇몇 안전 장비
(B) 서비스 품질 보증서
(C) 대금 할부 선택
(D) 다양한 페인트 색깔

해설 첫 번째 지문 [제안서], 두 번째 단락에서 'Our work is guaranteed for one year.'라고 했고, 두 번째 지문 [제안서], 두 번째 단락에서 'All work comes with a six-month warranty that covers all painted wall finishes.'라고 하여 두 회사 모두 품질 보증을 제공하는 것을 알 수 있으므로 (B)가 정답이다.

189. 상세 정보

Young 씨는 모든 직원들에게 무엇을 하라고 요청하는가?

(A) 월요일에 원격 근무를 하라고
(B) 제안서를 선택하라고
(C) 벽에서 물품들을 제거하라고
(D) 그들의 작업 공간을 덮으라고

해설 세 번째 지문 [이메일], 두 번째 줄에서 'First, you'll need to protect your belongings from being damaged by the paint. We will provide drapes to place over your desks.'라고 했으므로 (D)가 정답이다.

✦ Paraphrasing

place over → cover, desks → workstations

190. 암시 / 추론 - 연계 문제

Elio Marketing에 관하여 알 수 있는 것은?

(A) 최근에 새로운 건물로 이주했다.
(B) Handy Painters와 이전에 작업했다.
(C) Precision Painters를 고용했다.
(D) 한 주 동안 문을 닫을 것이다.

해설 첫 번째 지문 [제안서], 두 번째 단락에서 'Items on walls and shelves will be carefully placed in boxes and returned to their original positions after completion.'이라고 했는데, 세 번째 지문 [이메일], 네 번째 줄에서 'Don't worry about the pictures on the wall — the contractor will handle those.'라고 하여 Elio Marketing이 Precision Painters를 고용했다는 것을 알 수 있으므로 (C)가 정답이다.

191-195번은 다음 광고, 양식, 이메일에 관한 문제입니다.

혁신을 위한 Trinchera Innovation 무역 박람회가 돌아옵니다!
192 **7월 5-6일, 토요일과 일요일**
Trinchera 경기장

Trinchera Innovation 무역 박람회가 올해 다시 열리며, 다시 돌아온 올해 행사는 이제껏 분명 최고가 될 것입니다. 우선, 저희는 아주 중요한 초청 연사를 몇 분 모셨습니다. 저희가 전체 연사 목록을 확정하는 중이나, Pantomime의 CEO이신 Darnell Sutton이 참석하시는 것은 확실히 말씀드릴 수 있습니다. 193 **언제나 그렇듯이, 작년 행사에 참여하셨던 업체는 25퍼센트의 할인을 받을 수 있습니다.**

Trinchera Innovation 무역 박람회는 중소기업에서 자사의 제품과 서비스를 대중에게 선보일 최고의 방법입니다. 191 **매년 그렇듯이, 15인 미만의 소규모 사업체만이 부스를 구입할 수 있습니다.** 이는 Trinchera에서 기업가 정신을 고취하려는 저희의 목표와 일맥상통합니다. 192 **행사 시작 전날 밤에는 모든 업체를 위한 환영 연회가 있습니다.** 뜻이 맞는 기업가가 모여 인적 네트워크를 형성하고 파트너십을 구축할 아주 좋은 기회입니다.

어휘
innovation 혁신 | trade fair 무역 박람회 | stadium 경기장 | iteration 반복 | be sure to 반드시 [분명] ~하다 | invite 초청하다 | speaker 초청 연사 | confirm 확정하다 | be in attendance 참석하다 | as always 언제나처럼 | vendor 노점상인, 행상인 | participate in ~에 참여하다 | be eligible for ~의 자격이 있다 | discount 할인 | showcase 소개하다 | public 대중 | small-sized 소규모의 | less than ~보다 적은 | enterprise 기업 | allow 허용하다 | purchase 구입하다 | booth 부스 | in line with ~와 함께, ~에 따라, ~에 발맞춰 |

goal 목표 | promote 촉진하다, 고취하다 | entrepreneurship 기업가 정신 | reception 환영 연회 | opportunity 기회 | like-minded 생각이 비슷한 | build 짓다 | network 관계망 | forge 구축하다 | partnership 동반자 관계

Trinchera Innovation 무역 박람회 판매 부스 신청 양식

회사명: Coolair 사
담당자 이름: Anthony Porter
날짜: 5월 29일
이메일: aporter@coolair.com

193 **작년에 참석하셨나요? ☑ 예 □ 아니요**
선호 전시 공간이 있으신가요? 최대 4개까지 선택해 주세요. 첫 번째 선택에 우선순위를 두도록 노력하겠습니다.
첫 번째 선택: 75A
두 번째 선택: 67D
194 **세 번째 선택: 57C**
네 번째 선택: 73C

전체 부스 공간의 지도를 보시려면, 저희 웹사이트 www.trincheracouncil.com/ITF/map을 방문해 주세요.

어휘
application form 신청서 | attend 참석하다 | previous 이전의 | preferred 선호하는 | exhibit 전시 | space 공간, 자리 | list 작성하다, 열거하다 | up to ~까지 | choice 선택 | prioritize 우선적으로 처리하다 | map 지도 | head on over to ~로 향하다, 가다

수신: Anthony Porter, Coolair 사
발신: Kayla Abbott, Trinchera Innovation 무역 박람회
날짜: 6월 12일
제목: 신청 관련 최신 소식

Porter 씨께,

Trinchera Innovation 무역 박람회에 다시 한번 참여해 주셔서 감사합니다. 194 **아쉽지만, 귀하의 신청서를 늦게 전달받아, 귀하께서 선택하신 상위 선택 2가지를 예약해드릴 수 없었습니다.** 이에, 세 번째 선택으로 예약해 드렸습니다.

195 **이 행사에서 최대한 많이 얻어 가실 수 있도록, 연설 중간 광고에 주목해 주셨으면 합니다.** 저희는 연설 중간중간 업체 광고를 게재할 예정이며, 이는 귀하의 사업체로 관심을 불러 모을 아주 좋은 방법이 될 수 있습니다. 가격에 대한 자세한 정보를 원하시면, 저에게 알려주시기 바랍니다.

남은 한주 잘 보내시고, 행사 때 뵙겠습니다.

안부를 전하며,

Kayla Abbott
행사 담당자

어휘
regret to 유감스럽게도 ~하다 | inform 알려주다 | receive 받다 | reserve 예약하다 | maximize 극대화하다, 최대한 활용하다 | attention 주의집중, 관심 | advertising 광고 | advertisement 광고 | in between 중간에, 사이에 | attract 끌어들이다 | detail 세부 사항 | pricing 가격 책정 | coordinator 진행자, 코디네이터

191. 암시 / 추론

광고에서는 올해 행사와 관련해 무엇이 변하지 않을 것이라고 제시하는가?

(A) 초청 연사 목록

(B) 행사 장소
(C) 부스 가격
(D) 업체 자격

해설 첫 번째 지문[광고], 첫 번째 단락에서 'Like every year, only small-sized (less than 15 employees) enterprises will be allowed to purchase booths.'라고 했으므로 (D)가 정답이다.

192. 사실 확인

환영 연회에 대해 광고에서 언급하는 것은?
(A) 참석하려면 티켓이 필요하다.
(B) 7월 4일에 열릴 것이다.
(C) 참석자 수에 따라 일정이 조정될 수 있다.
(D) 저녁 식사가 포함된다.

해설 첫 번째 지문[광고]에서 무역 박람회가 'July 5-6'에 열린다고 했는데, 두 번째 단락에서 'There will be a reception for all vendors the night before the event begins.'라고 했으므로 바로 전날인 7월 4일에 환영 연회가 열린다는 것을 알 수 있으므로 (B)가 정답이다.

193. 상세 정보 – 연계 문제

Porter 씨에 대하여 내릴 수 있는 결론은 무엇인가?
(A) 행사 주최자 중 한 명이다.
(B) 최근 Trinchera로 옮겼다.
(C) 부스에 대해 할인을 받을 것이다.
(D) 전에 Sutton 씨를 만난 적이 있다.

해설 첫 번째 지문[광고], 첫 번째 단락에서 'As always, vendors who participated in last year's event will be eligible for a 25 percent discount.'라고 했는데, 두 번째 지문[양식]에서 'Attended Previous Year?'에 Y(예)에 체크하여 25퍼센트 할인 대상임을 알 수 있으므로 (C)가 정답이다.

✛ Paraphrasing

last year → previous year

194. 상세 정보 – 연계 문제

Coolair 사는 자사 제품을 어디에 전시할 것인가?
(A) 57C
(B) 67D
(C) 73C
(D) 75A

해설 세 번째 지문[이메일], 첫 번째 단락에서 'Therefore, we have reserved your third choice.'라고 했는데, 두 번째 지문[양식]에서 'Third choice'가 57C임을 알 수 있으므로 (A)가 정답이다.

195. 상세 정보

이메일에 따르면, Abbott 씨는 Porter 씨에게 무엇을 하라고 권하는가?
(A) 더 일찍 행사에 신청하라고
(B) 제품 샘플을 보내라고
(C) 부스에 협력사를 초대하라고
(D) 광고 시간을 구입하라고

해설 세 번째 지문[이메일], 두 번째 단락에서 'To maximize what you can get out of this event, I want to call your attention to the advertising during the speeches. We will be playing advertisements from our vendors in between speeches, and this can be a great way to attract attention to your business.'라고 했으므로 (D)가 정답이다.

196-200번은 다음 이메일들과 메모에 관한 문제입니다.

수신: Joseph Han
발신: Kelly Owens
날짜: 5월 13일
제목: 제안

Han 씨께,

고객서비스 부서가 우리 사무실로 이사한 이후로, 근무하기 너무 시끄럽습니다. **196** 그들이 고객과 대화를 해야 한다는 것은 알고 있지만, 소리가 너무 방해가 되서 저희 부서원들은 업무를 마무리하려고 빈 회의실이나 다른 공간을 찾고 있습니다. 이는 생산성에 부정적인 영향을 미쳤고, 반감을 불러일으켰습니다.

197C 한 가지 해결책은 저희 팀을 3층 회의실로 이동시키는 것입니다. 저희 직원들이 주로 그곳을 사용하기는 합니다. **197D** 그게 곤란하다면, 저희는 소음을 차단하는 데 도움이 될 칸막이를 설치할 수 있습니다. **197A** 또 다른 옵션은 저희 점심시간을 변경해서 저희가 다른 시간대에 사무실 밖에 있는 것입니다. 또한, **197B** 일부 직원들은 원격근무가 가능한지를 물었습니다. 이는 비용 절감과 생산성 향상으로 이어질 수 있습니다.

가급적 빨리 답변 부탁드립니다.

감사합니다.

Kelly Owens
회계 관리자, Nirvana 기업

어휘
noisy 시끄러운 | client 고객 | distract 집중이 안 되게 하다 | empty 텅 빈 | assignment 과제, 임무 | affect 영향을 미치다 | productivity 생산성 | create 창조하다, 불러일으키다 | animosity 반감, 적대감 | solution 해결책 | inconvenient 불편한, 곤란한 | set up 세우다, 놓다 | several 몇명의 | partition 칸막이 | block out 가리다, 차단하다 | remotely 멀리서, 원격으로 | lead to ~로 이어지다, 초래하다 | cost 비용 | saving 절약 | increase 증가하다

메모

수신: 회계 및 고객서비스
발신: Joseph Han, 인사 임원
날짜: 5월 18일
제목: 사무실 문제

199 Gio 건설은 2층의 사용하지 않는 미디어센터를 새로운 회계팀 사무실로 전환하는 중입니다. 작업이 마무리되는 6월 8일에 이동이 있을 것입니다.

197 그동안, 유지보수팀은 두 부서를 분리할 칸막이를 설치했습니다. 이는 양 팀에서 발생하는 소리를 줄이는 데 도움이 될 것입니다.

또한, 저는 사무실 내 직원 대다수가 점심을 싸 온다는 것을 알았습니다. 이는 가능하나, **198** 일부 음식은 냄새가 강해서 사무실에 냄새가 나게 할 수 있다는 점에 유의해 주세요. 따라서 점심을 싸 올 때는 이 점을 명심해 주시기 바랍니다.

어휘
accounting 회계 | construction 건설, 공사 | in the process of ~하는 과정에서 | transform 변형시키다, 탈바꿈시키다 | unused 사용하지 않는 | maintenance 유지 | install 설치하다 | divider 칸막이 | separate 분리하[되]다 | department 부서 | reduce 줄이다, 축소하다 | generate 발생시키다 | majority 다수 | tend to ~하는 경향이 있다 | pack 싸다 | acceptable 받아들일 수 있는, 용인되는 | odor 냄새

수신: jhan@nirvana.co.uk
발신: **199** fcristafno@gioconstruction.co.uk
제목: 사무실 변환
날짜: 6월 14일

Han 씨, 안녕하세요.

직원들이 새로운 공간을 즐기고 있기를 바랍니다. 저희는 2년마다 제공하는 점검과 함께, 5년 보증을 제공합니다. **199** 최초 점검은 프로젝트 완료 6개월 후에 있을 것입니다. 그 전에 문제가 생기면, 언제든지 저희에게 연락해 주세요. 저희가 바로 직원을 보내드리겠습니다.

사무실을 더 매력적으로 만들려고 하시나요? **200** 저희 Spruce Up 서비스를 살펴보세요. 합리적인 가격에, 저희 전문가 중 한 명이 방문해 근무공간을 꾸미는 방법에 대한 팁을 제공해 드립니다. 관심이 있으시면, 언제든지 저에게 연락주시기 바랍니다.

진심을 전하며,

Frank Cristafano
고객 관계 관리자, Gio 건설

어휘

transformation 탈바꿈, 변신 | guarantee 품질보증 | bi-yearly 연 2회의 | inspection 점검, 검토 | check 점검 | take place 일어나다, 열리다 | complete 완료하다 | encounter 맞닥뜨리다, 마주치다, 접하다 | hesitate 망설이다 | right away 즉시, 바로 | affordable 가격이 알맞은 | rate 요금 | specialist 전문가 | come by 잠깐 들르다 | tip 정보, 조언 | decorate 장식하다, 꾸미다 | workspace 업무 공간 | interest 관심을 끌다

196. 상세 정보

첫 번째 이메일에 따르면, 일부 직원들은 어떻게 문제에 대처했는가?
(A) 고품질의 헤드폰을 사용함으로써
(B) 사무실에 늦게 남음으로써
(C) 자신의 자리가 아닌 곳에서 근무함으로써
(D) 추가 직원을 채용함으로써

해설 Owens 씨가 Han 씨에게 보낸 첫 번째 지문[이메일], 첫 번째 단락에서 'We understand that they need to speak with clients, but the noise has gotten so distracting that my team members are trying to find empty meeting rooms and other areas to complete their assignments.'라고 했으므로 (C)가 정답이다.

197. 상세 정보 – 연계 문제

Owens 씨의 어떤 아이디어를 Han 씨가 실행했는가?
(A) 점심시간을 변경하는 것
(B) 직원들에게 재택근무를 허용하는 것
(C) 회의실을 사용하는 것
(D) 공간 내 칸막이를 설치하는 것

해설 Owens 씨가 Han 씨에게 보낸 첫 번째 지문[이메일], 두 번째 단락의 내용과 보기를 매칭시키면, 'One solution would be to move our team into the third-floor meeting room — it's mostly used by our employees anyway.'는 (C)에, 'If that's inconvenient, we can set up several partitions to help block out the noise.'는 (D)에, 'Another option is to change our lunch schedule, so we are out of the office at different times.'는 (A)에 'Also, some of the employees asked if it would be possible to work remotely.'는 (B)에 해당하는데, Han 씨가 보낸 두 번째 지문[메모], 두 번째 단락에서 'In the meantime, the maintenance team has installed

some dividers to separate the two departments.'라고 하여 Owens 씨의 아이디어 중 칸막이 설치를 실행에 옮긴 것을 알 수 있으므로 (D)가 정답이다.

+ Paraphrasing

set up → place

198. 상세 정보

메모에 따르면, 일부 음식과 관련된 문제는 무엇인가?
(A) 값비싼 재료를 사용한다.
(B) 불편한 환경을 조성한다.
(C) 준비하는 데 시간이 오래 걸린다.
(D) 특정한 방법으로 포장되어야 한다.

해설 두 번째 지문[메모], 세 번째 단락에서 'please note that certain dishes produce strong odors and can make the room smell.'이라고 하여 강한 냄새로 불편함을 야기할 수 있음을 알 수 있으므로 (B)가 정답이다.

199. 사실 확인 – 연계 문제

새로운 회계 사무실에 관하여 사실인 것은?
(A) 회사 내에서 가장 규모가 큰 곳이다.
(B) 보안 잠금 기능을 포함한다.
(C) 가구를 사용했다.
(D) 12월 8일에 점검될 것이다.

해설 두 번째 지문[메모], 첫 번째 단락에서 'Gio Construction is in the process of transforming the unused media center on the second floor into a new office for the accounting team. The move will take place on June 8, when the work is finished.'라고 했는데, Cristafano 씨가 Han 씨에게 보낸 세 번째 지문[이메일], 첫 번째 단락에서 'The first check will take place six months after the project completion date.'라고 하여 작업이 완료된 6월 8일로부터 6개월 후인 12월 8일에 점검이 있을 것이므로 (D)가 정답이다.

200. 상세 정보

Spruce Up 서비스는 무엇을 제공하는가?
(A) 주말 사무실 청소
(B) 컴퓨터 시스템 업그레이드
(C) 정기적인 장비 유지보수
(D) 실내장식 상담

해설 Cristafano 씨가 Han 씨에게 보낸 세 번째 지문[이메일], 두 번째 단락에서 'Look into our Spruce Up service. At an affordable rate, one of our specialists will come by and provide tips on how to decorate your workspace.'라고 했으므로 (D)가 정답이다.

+ Paraphrasing

how to decorate your workspace → interior decoration

101. (C)	102. (B)	103. (C)	104. (D)	105. (B)
106. (C)	107. (A)	108. (B)	109. (C)	110. (C)
111. (C)	112. (C)	113. (B)	114. (C)	115. (D)
116. (C)	117. (D)	118. (D)	119. (B)	120. (B)
121. (D)	122. (C)	123. (A)	124. (완비)	125. (C)
126. (A)	127. (B)	128. (A)	129. (B)	130. (B)
131. (A)	132. (C)	133. (B)	134. (A)	135. (B)
136. (B)	137. (D)	138. (C)	139. (C)	140. (A)
141. (D)	142. (C)	143. (A)	144. (D)	145. (B)
146. (D)	147. (D)	148. (A)	149. (A)	150. (B)
151. (C)	152. (A)	153. (C)	154. (C)	155. (A)
156. (C)	157. (A)	158. (C)	159. (C)	160. (B)
161. (C)	162. (D)	163. (B)	164. (A)	165. (C)
166. (D)	167. (B)	168. (A)	169. (D)	170. (A)
171. (C)	172. (B)	173. (C)	174. (A)	175. (B)
176. (B)	177. (A)	178. (B)	179. (D)	180. (B)
181. (D)	182. (B)	183. (D)	184. (B)	185. (B)
186. (C)	187. (A)	188. (B)	189. (C)	190. (B)
191. (A)	192. (D)	193. (A)	194. (D)	195. (A)
196. (B)	197. (D)	198. (D)	199. (A)	200. (C)

101. 형용사 자리

During his time as Vice President, Mr. Harper demonstrated many **admirable** traits.

부회장으로 재직하는 동안, Harper 씨는 많은 훌륭한 자질들을 보여주었다.

해설 빈칸은 명사 traits를 수식하는 자리이다. 문맥상 '많은 훌륭한 자질들을 보여주었다'는 의미가 되어야 자연스러우므로 형용사 (C)가 정답이다.

어휘 demonstrate 입증하다, 보여주다 | trait 특성, 특징

+ Key point
명사 앞자리에는 형용사, 형용사 역할을 하는 분사, 복합명사를 이루는 명사가 올 수 있다.

102. 소유격 대명사

The owner of FamChem Pharmaceutical Company is proud of **her** business role in the industry.

FamChem 제약 회사의 소유주는 그 업계에서 그녀의 비즈니스 역할을 자랑스럽게 여긴다.

해설 빈칸은 뒤에 오는 명사 business role을 수식해 주는 한정사 역할을 한다. 소유격 인칭대명사 her가 명사 앞에서 한정사 역할을 하므로 (B)가 정답이다.

어휘 owner 주인, 소유주 | pharmaceutical 제약 | be proud of ~을 자랑스럽게 여기다 | role 역할 | industry 업계, 산업

+ Key point
소유격 대명사는 한정사이므로 항상 명사 앞에 위치한다.

103. 어휘 - 형용사

Although it is rare to find fully **furnished** condominiums in Bridgeton, dining tables and chairs are occasionally provided.

Bridgeton에서 가구가 완비된 아파트를 찾는 것은 드물지만, 식탁과 의자는 간혹 제공된다.

해설 빈칸은 명사 condominiums를 수식하는 형용사 자리이다. 문맥상 '가구가 완비된 아파트'라는 의미가 되어야 자연스러우므로 (C)가 정답이다.

어휘 rare 드문 | fully 완전히 | condominium 아파트 | dining table 식탁 | occasionally 때때로 | provide 제공하다

+ Key word
Although it is **rare to find fully furnished condominiums** in Bridgeton, **dining tables and chairs** are occasionally **provided**.

104. 어휘 - 형용사

The remodeled Montaine Resort contains an **immense** water park with many refreshment stands and shaded seating.

개조된 Montaine 리조트에는 스낵 판매점들과 차양이 있는 좌석들이 많은 거대한 워터파크가 있다.

해설 빈칸은 명사구 water park를 수식하는 형용사 자리이다. 명사구를 수식하는 with 전치사구를 고려할 때, 문맥상 '많은 스낵 판매점들과 차양 좌석이 있는 거대한 워터파크'라는 의미가 되어야 자연스러우므로 (D)가 정답이다.

어휘 remodel 개조하다 | contain 포함하다 | refreshment stand 다과 판매점 | shaded 그늘진, 차양을 씌운 | seating 좌석, 자리

+ Key word
The remodeled Montaine Resort contains **an immense water park with many refreshment stands and shaded seating**.

105. 어휘 - 명사

For such a big company, the key **elements** that determine profitability entail proper management of the human resource.

그렇게 큰 회사에서, 수익성을 결정하는 핵심 요소는 인적 자원의 적절한 관리를 필요로 한다.

해설 빈칸은 주격 관계사절(that determine profitability)의 수식을 받는 명사 자리이다. 문맥상 '수익성을 결정하는 핵심 요소'라는 의미가 되어야 자연스러우므로 (B)가 정답이다.

어휘 key 핵심적인, 필수적인 | determine 결정하다, 확정하다 | profitability 수익성 | entail ~를 필요로 하다 | proper 적절한 | management 관리, 경영 | human resource 인적 자원

+ Key word
For such a big company, the **key elements that determine profitability entail proper management of the human resource**.

106. 어휘 - 명사

Before the improved version can go into **production**, the software has to be updated.

개선된 버전이 생산을 시작하기 전에, 소프트웨어가 업데이트되어야 한다.

해설 빈칸은 전치사 into의 목적어인 명사 자리로, 'go into production (생산을 시작하다)'이라는 관용 표현을 완성하는 명사 (C)가 정답이다.

어휘 improve 개선하다 | update 갱신하다, 업데이트하다

+ Key point
명사 produce vs. product vs. production: produce는 '농작물'을, product는 '상품'을, production은 '생산'을 의미한다.

107. 어휘 - 부사

Sunday's heavy rainfall **temporarily** disrupted power service at Sculper, Ltd.'s assembly plant.

일요일 폭우가 Sculper 사의 조립 공장의 전력에 일시적으로 지장을 주었다.

해설 빈칸은 주어와 동사 사이의 부사 자리이다. 문맥상 '일요일 폭우가 전력에 일시적으로 지장을 주었다'라는 의미가 되어야 자연스러우므로 (A)가 정답이다.

어휘 heavy rainfall 폭우 | disrupt 방해하다, 지장을 주다 | power service 전력 | assembly 조립

+ Key word
Sunday's heavy rainfall temporarily disrupted power service at Sculper, Ltd.'s assembly plant.

108. 관계대명사

A sports-club member **who** wishes to cancel must give 30 days' notice without exception.

취소를 원하는 스포츠 센터 회원은 예외 없이 반드시 30일 전에 통지를 해야 한다.

해설 빈칸은 관계대명사가 들어가야 할 자리이다. 사람 명사를 수식할 수 있으면서 wishes 동사 앞에 위치해 주어 역할을 하는 주격 관계대명사 (B)가 정답이다.

어휘 wish 바라다 | notice 통지, 통보 | without exception 예외 없이

+ Key point
whoever는 anyone who와 같아서 앞에 중복이 되는 선행사가 오지 못한다.

109. 전치사

The Accord Building features uniquely designed sand curtains, which can turn windows **from** clear to opaque at the press of a button.

Accord 빌딩에는 독특하게 설계된 모래 커튼이 있는데, 버튼만 누르면 창문을 투명에서 불투명으로 바꿀 수 있다.

해설 빈칸은 '버튼만 누르면 창문을 투명에서 불투명으로 바꿀 수 있다'는 의미를 만드는 'from A to B(A에서 B로)'이 들어가야 자연스러우므로 전치사 (C)가 정답이다.

어휘 feature 특징으로 하다 | uniquely 독특하게, 특별하게 | design 설계하다 | sand 모래 | curtain 커튼 | turn 돌리다, 바꾸다 | window 창문 | clear 투명한 | opaque 불투명한 | press 누름

+ Key word
The Accord Building features uniquely designed sand curtains, which can **turn windows from clear to opaque** at the press of a button.

110. 어휘 - 명사

Jazz guitarist Mila Foreman enjoys performing in smaller venues because they give her a **connection** with the entire audience.

재즈 기타리스트 Mila Foreman은 소규모 장소가 그녀로 하여금 전체 관객과 교감할 수 있게 하기 때문에 보다 작은 장소에서 연주하는 것을 즐긴다.

해설 빈칸은 동사 give의 직접 목적어인 명사 자리이다. 빈칸 뒤에 전치사구가 있음을 고려할 때, '보다 작은 장소가 그녀에게 전체 관객과의 교감을 주기 때문'이라는 의미가 되어야 자연스러우므로 (C)가 정답이다.

어휘 guitarist 기타 연주자 | perform 연주하다 | venue 장소 | entire 전체의 | audience 관객

+ Key word
Jazz guitarist Mila Foreman enjoys performing in smaller venues because they **give her a connection with the entire audience.**

111. 부사 자리

These economical insect repellants from Buzz Removal are **unbelievably** potent.

이 Buzz Removal의 경제적인 벌레 퇴치제는 믿을 수 없을 정도로 효능이 강력하다.

해설 빈칸은 형용사를 수식하는 자리이므로 부사 (C)가 정답이다.

어휘 economical 실속 있는, 경제적인 | insect repellant 벌레 퇴치제 | potent (효능이) 강력한

+ Key point
형용사를 수식할 수 있는 품사는 부사이다.

112. 어휘 - 형용사

To bring in fresh ideas, the Harrisburg City Council is organizing an **external** search for an innovative architect.

참신한 아이디어를 유치하기 위해, Harrisburg 시의회는 혁신적인 건축가를 구하는 데 외부 탐색을 준비하고 있다.

해설 빈칸은 명사 search를 수식하는 형용사 자리이다. 문맥상 '참신한 아이디어를 얻기 위해 건축가를 외부에서 찾을 것'이라는 의미가 되어야 자연스러우므로 (C)가 정답이다.

어휘 bring in 도입하다, 유치하다 | fresh 신선한, 참신한 | City Council 시의회 | organize 준비하다, 조직하다 | search 탐색, 검색; 찾다 | innovative 혁신적인 | architect 건축가

+ Key word
To bring in fresh ideas, the Harrisburg City Council is organizing an **external search for an innovative architect.**

113. 어휘 - 동사

Gemini Motors CEO confirmed that its new line

of electric cars would be ready to **launch** by February 22.

Gemini 자동차 회사 CEO는 2월 22일이면 자사 신규 전기 자동차 라인이 출시 준비가 될 것이라고 확인했다.

해설 빈칸은 'be ready to V(~할 준비가 되다)'의 표현을 완성할 동사 자리이다. '신규 전기 자동차 라인이 출시 준비가 될 것이라고 확인했다'라는 의미가 되어야 문맥상 자연스러우므로 (B)가 정답이다.

어휘 confirm 확인해주다, 공식화하다 | line (상품의) 종류 | electric car 전기 자동차 | ready 준비가 된

+ Key word

Gemini Motors CEO confirmed that its **new line** of electric **cars** would be **ready to launch** by February 22.

114. 부사 자리

The Contemporary Art Museum is allocating its funds on **extensively** renovating the sculpture garden.

현대 미술관은 조각 공원을 대대적으로 보수하는데 자금을 할당할 것이다.

해설 빈칸은 동명사 renovating을 수식하는 자리이므로 부사 (C)가 정답이다.

어휘 allocate 할당하다 | fund 자금 | renovate 수리하다, 보수하다 | sculpture 조각

+ Key point

동명사를 수식할 수 있는 품사는 부사이다.

115. 어휘 - 형용사

Unless otherwise indicated, all instructional videos on this Web page are the **exclusive** property of Youngstown Clinic.

달리 명시되지 않는 한, 이 웹페이지에 있는 모든 교육용 비디오는 Youngstown 클리닉의 독점 자산이다.

해설 빈칸은 명사 property를 수식하는 형용사 자리이다. 문맥상 '달리 명시되지 않는 한, 모든 교육용 비디오는 클리닉의 독점 자산'이라는 의미가 되어야 자연스러우므로 (D)가 정답이다.

어휘 unless otherwise indicated 달리 명시되지 않는 한 | instructional 교육상의 | property 재산 | clinic 병원

+ Key word

Unless otherwise indicated, all instructional videos on this Web page are **the exclusive property of Youngstown Clinic.**

116. 어휘 - 동사

New company policies implemented last week **mandate** all visitors wear identification badges issued at the information desk upon arrival.

지난주에 실시된 새로운 회사 정책은 모든 방문객이 도착하면 안내 데스크에서 발급하는 신분증을 착용하는 것을 의무화한다.

해설 빈칸은 완전한 문장을 목적어로 하는 동사 자리이다. 문맥상 '새로운 정책에서는 모든 방문객이 발급받은 신분증을 착용하는 것을 의무화한다'는 의미가 되어야 자연스러우므로 (C)가 정답이다.

어휘 policy 정책, 방침 | implement 실행하다 | wear 착용하다 | identification

신원 확인 | badge 명찰, 배지 | issue 발급하다 | information desk 안내 데스크 | upon ~하자마자 | arrival 도착

+ Key word

New company policies implemented last week **mandate all visitors wear identification badges** issued at the information desk upon arrival.

117. 전치사

The e-mail was sent to all staff members **across** multiple branches.

그 이메일은 다수 지사 전역에 있는 모든 직원들에게 보내졌다.

해설 빈칸은 위치 명사를 목적어로 하는 전치사 자리로, 문맥상 '다수 지사 전역에 있는 모든 직원들'이라는 의미가 되어야 적합하므로 (D)가 정답이다.

어휘 multiple 다수의 | branch 지점

118. 어휘 - 동사

Industry Insider magazine **credits** its rising subscription rate to the quality of its editorial staff.

〈Industry Insider〉 잡지는 구독률 상승이 편집 직원들 자질의 덕이라 여긴다.

해설 빈칸은 주어와 목적어 사이의 동사 자리이다. 'credit A to B'는 'A를 B의 공이라 여기다'를 의미하므로 (D)가 정답이다.

어휘 subscription 구독 | quality 자질 | editorial 편집의

+ Key word

Industry Insider magazine **credits** its rising subscription rate **to** the quality of its editorial staff.

119. 어휘 - 명사

For the past three years, net cocoa **output** from the Cacao Coast has fallen due to drought.

지난 3년간, 가뭄으로 인해 Cacao Coast의 순 코코아 생산량이 줄어들었다.

해설 빈칸은 net cocoa의 수식을 받는 명사 자리이다. 문맥상 '가뭄으로 인해 순 코코아 생산량이 줄어들었다'는 의미가 되어야 자연스러우므로 (B)가 정답이다.

어휘 past 지난 | net 순, 실 | cocoa 코코아 | fall (수량 등이) 줄다, 내려가다 | drought 가뭄

+ Key word

For the past three years, **net cocoa output from the Cacao Coast has fallen due to drought.**

120. 전치사

Applicants must have at least three years of management experience to qualify **for** this position.

이 직무에 자격을 갖추려면 지원자는 최소 3년의 관리 경험이 있어야 한다.

해설 빈칸은 동사 qualify와 명사구 this position 사이의 자리이므로, 'qualify for ~(~의 자격을 얻다)'의 표현을 완성하는 전치사 (B)가 정답이다.

어휘 applicant 지원자 | at least 적어도, 최소한 | management 관리 | experience 경험 | qualify 자격을 얻다

✛ Key word

Applicants must have at least three years of management experience to **qualify for this position**.

---

121. 어휘 – 동사

Reyes Grocers recently **expanded** its organic produce section to offer a wider variety of fruits and vegetables.

Reyes Grocers는 최근 다양한 과일과 채소를 제공하기 위해 유기농 농산물 코너를 확장했다.

해설 빈칸은 문장의 동사 자리이다. '과일 및 채소를 더 많이 선보이기 위해 유기농 농산물 코너를 확장했다'는 의미가 되어야 문맥상 자연스러우므로 (D)가 정답이다.

어휘 recently 최근 | organic 유기농의 | produce 농산물 | offer 제공하다 | a wide variety of 매우 다양한 | vegetable 채소

✛ Key word

Reyes Grocers recently **expanded its organic produce section to offer a wider variety of fruits and vegetables**.

---

122. 부사절 접속사

Because heavy snow is so common in Kashkingrad, the city council approved a plan to connect all buildings downtown.

Kashkingrad에서는 폭설이 자주 오기 때문에, 시 의회에서는 시내 모든 건물들을 연결하는 기획안을 승인했다.

해설 빈칸은 두 문장을 연결하는 접속사 자리이다. 문맥상 '폭설이 흔하기 때문에, 시내 모든 건물들을 연결하는 기획안에 승인했다'는 의미가 되어야 자연스러우므로 (C)가 정답이다.

어휘 heavy snow 폭설 | common 흔한 | approve 승인하다 | plan 기획 | connect 연결하다 | downtown 시내에

✛ Key word

Because heavy snow is so common in Kashkingrad, the city council **approved a plan to connect all buildings downtown**.

---

123. 관용 표현

City residents may now choose to purchase electricity from a private company **other than** the federal energy agency.

도시 주민은 이제 연방 에너지 기구 외에 사기업에서 전기를 구입하는 것을 선택할 수 있다.

해설 빈칸은 완전한 문장과 명사구를 연결하는 자리이다. 연방 에너지 기구 외에 사기업에서 전기를 구입하도록 신청할 수 있다는 의미가 되어야 문맥상 자연스러우므로 (A)가 정답이다.

어휘 resident 주민, 거주자 | choose 선택하다 | purchase 구입하다 | electricity 전기 | federal 연방 정부의

---

124. 어휘 – 명사

The city government has voted unanimously to renovate some of the city's oldest **structures** in the downtown area, including the West Street Postal Office.

시 정부는 West Street 우체국을 포함하여, 도심지에 있는 시에서 가장 오래된 건축물들 일부를 수리하는 데 만장일치로 찬성했다.

해설 최상급 형용사 oldest의 수식을 받는 명사 자리이다. 문맥상 'West Street 우체국을 포함하여, 시에서 가장 오래된 건축물 일부를 수리하다'라는 의미가 되어야 자연스러우므로 (C)가 정답이다.

어휘 vote (찬성[반대]에) 투표하다 | unanimously 만장일치로 | renovate 수리하다 | downtown area 도심지 | including ~을 포함하여

✛ Key word

The city government has voted unanimously to **renovate** some of **the city's oldest structures in the downtown area, including the West Street Postal Office**.

---

125. 부정 대명사

The house went back on the market since **neither** of our clients' final offers was accepted by the owner.

그 집은 고객들의 최종 제안들 중 아무것도 주인이 수락하지 않았기 때문에 다시 시장에 나왔다.

해설 빈칸은 since 종속절 내의 주어 자리이다. 빈칸을 수식하는 of 전치사구의 내용과 주절과 종속절의 관계를 고려할 때 문맥상 '고객들의 최종 제안들 중 아무것도 수락되지 않았기 때문에 집이 다시 시장에 나왔다'는 의미가 되어야 자연스러우므로 (C)가 정답이다. neither of our clients' final offers was accepted ~처럼 neither 뒤에 복수 명사가 나와도 동사는 단수로 받을 수 있다.

어휘 on the market (상품이) 시장에 나와 있는 | client 고객 | final 최종의 | offer 제안 | accept 수락하다 | owner 주인

---

126. 어휘 – 형용사

After receiving **favorable** reviews in literary magazines, Umberto Ello's latest novel was nominated for several awards.

문학잡지에서 호의적인 평가를 받은 후, Umberto Ello의 최신 소설은 몇몇 상에 후보로 올랐다.

해설 빈칸은 명사 reviews를 수식하는 형용사 자리이다. 주절과의 관계를 고려할 때, 문맥상 호의적인 평가를 받은 후 상에 후보로 올랐다는 의미로 연결되어야 자연스러우므로 (A)가 정답이다.

어휘 review 평론 | literary 문학의 | nominate 후보로 지명하다 | several 몇몇의 | award 상

✛ Key word

After receiving favorable reviews in literary magazines, Umberto Ello's latest **novel was nominated for** several **awards**.

---

127. 어휘 – 명사

In light of unexpected **circumstances**, the Ballet Focus Group was obligated to cancel its play last night at the King Edward's Hall.

예상치 못한 상황을 고려해, Ballet Focus 그룹은 어젯밤 King

Edward 홀에서의 연극을 취소해야만 했다.

해설 빈칸은 unexpected의 수식을 받는 명사 자리이다. 주절의 내용을 고려할 때, 문맥상 '예상치 못한 상황으로 어젯밤 공연을 취소할 수밖에 없었다'는 의미가 되어야 자연스러우므로 (B)가 정답이다.

어휘 in light of ~을 고려하여, 감안하여 | unexpected 예상치 못한 | obligate 강요하다 | cancel 취소하다 | play 연극

+ **Key word**

In light of unexpected circumstances, the Ballet Focus Group **was obligated to cancel** its play last night at the King Edward's Hall.

---

128. 부사절 접속사

Since Dr. Valdez is occupied with reviewing the employee assessments, she will attend this Friday's conference **only if** no other executive is able to.

Valdez 박사는 직원 평가 검토로 바빠서, 참석 가능한 다른 임원이 아무도 없는 경우에만 이번 금요일에 있을 콘퍼런스에 참석할 것이다.

해설 빈칸 앞뒤로 주어, 동사를 갖춘 절이 있으므로, 빈칸은 두 문장을 연결하는 접속사 자리이다. 문두의 since 종속절의 내용을 고려할 때, 문맥상 '평가 검토를 하느라 바쁘기 때문에, 다른 임원 중 참석할 수 있는 사람이 없는 경우에만 콘퍼런스에 갈 것'이라는 의미가 되어야 자연스러우므로 (A)가 정답이다.

어휘 be occupied with ~하느라 바쁘다 | review 검토하다 | employee 직원 | assessment 평가 | attend 참석하다 | conference 콘퍼런스 | executive 임원

+ **Key point**

접속사 so that은 주로 조동사 can(could)과 함께 쓰여 목적의 의미를 전달한다.

---

129. 전치사 자리

As part of its effort to innovate its product and user experience, Gellar Electronics has hired a new Head of Design.

제품 및 사용자 경험을 혁신하려는 노력의 일환으로, Gellar 전자에서는 신규 디자인 임원을 고용했다.

해설 빈칸은 명사구를 목적어로 하는 전치사 자리이므로 (B)가 정답이다.

어휘 effort 노력 | innovate 혁신하다 | product 상품 | user 사용자 | experience 경험

+ **Key point**

to부정사의 관용 표현인 In order to 뒤에는 동사 원형이, 부사절 접속사인 even though와 in case 뒤에는 절이 와야 한다.

---

130. 어휘 - 형용사

Passengers for the Caledonia Resort's complimentary shuttle service must be at the lobby five minutes before the bus's **anticipated** departure time.

Caledonia 리조트의 무료 셔틀서비스 승객은 버스의 출발 예정시간보다 5분 일찍 로비에 있어야 한다.

해설 빈칸은 before 전치사구의 목적어인 명사구 departure time을 수식하는 자리이다. 주절과의 관계를 고려할 때, 문맥상 '버스의 예

정된 출발시간보다 5분 전에'라는 의미가 되어야 자연스러우므로 (B)가 정답이다.

어휘 passenger 승객 | complimentary 무료의 | departure 출발

+ **Key word**

Passengers for the Caledonia Resort's complimentary shuttle service must be at the lobby **five minutes before the bus' anticipated departure time**.

131-134번은 다음 공지에 관한 문제입니다.

제3회 연례 Bruger Partners 가족 피크닉이 9월 12일에 개최됩니다. 작년에 직원들 사이에 **131그것의** 높은 인기로 인해, 저희는 Dazai 호수에서 행사를 열기로 결정했습니다. 더 넓은 **132공간**은 모든 가족과 친구를 수용할 수 있음을 의미합니다. 게다가, 스포츠 게임과 보물찾기 같은 활동을 더 많이 할 가능성을 열어둘 것입니다. 올해엔 보너스로 유명 가수 Roy Mills의 서비스도 어렵게 마련했습니다. 그가 짧은 콘서트를 **133선보일 것입니다.** 그의 팬들은 CD나 포스터를 가져오세요. **134이는 사인을 받을 아주 좋은 기회입니다.** 행사에 관한 자세한 정보는 회사 웹사이트를 확인해 주세요.

어휘

third 세 번째의 | annual 연례의 | take place 개최되다 | popularity 인기 | among 사이에 | employee 직원 | hold 개최하다, 열다 | event 행사 | larger 더 큰 | mean 의미하다 | accommodate 수용하다 | additionally 또한, 게다가 | open up 열다, ~을 가능하게 하다 | possibility 가능성 | activity 액티비티, 활동 | such as ~과 같은 | treasure hunt 보물찾기 | bonus 보너스 | secure 확보하다, 획득하다 | prominent 유명한 | bring 가져오다 | poster 포스터 | detailed 상세한

---

131. 명사 - 대명사 일치

해설 빈칸은 명사구 high popularity를 수식하는 소유격 대명사 자리이다. 빈칸 앞 문장에서 '가족 피크닉이 개최된다'고 했으므로, 피크닉의 인기가 높았다는 내용으로 이어져야 문맥상 자연스러우므로 family picnic을 지칭하는 (A)가 정답이다.

+ **Key word**

The third annual Bruger Partners **family picnic** will take place on September Due to **its** high popularity among employees last year, we have decided to hold the event by Dazai Lake.

---

132. 어휘 - 명사

해설 빈칸은 The larger의 수식을 받는 문장의 주어 자리이다. 빈칸 앞 문장의 '행사를 Dazai 호수에서 열기로 했다'는 내용과 빈칸 뒤에 이어지는 '가족과 친구를 모두 수용할 수 있다'는 내용을 고려할 때, 더 큰 공간이라는 의미가 되어야 문맥상 자연스러우므로 (C)가 정답이다.

+ **Key word**

Due to its high popularity among employees last year, we have **decided to hold the event by Dazai Lake. The larger space means we will be able to accommodate all of our families and friends.**

---

133. 동사의 시제

해설 빈칸 앞 문장에서 '올해 행사에서는 유명 가수의 서비스도 어렵게 마련했다'고 했으며, 올해 행사는 미래에 일어날 예정이므로, 그가

짧은 콘서트를 선보일 것이라는 미래 시제의 문장이 되어야 문맥상 연결이 자연스러우므로 (B)가 정답이다.

+ **Key word**

As a bonus this year, **we have also secured the services of prominent singer** Roy Mills. He **will perform** a short concert.

134. 문장 선택

(A) 이는 사인을 받을 아주 좋은 기회입니다.
(B) 그는 최근 해외여행에서 돌아왔습니다.
(C) 비가 오면 그 행사는 실내에서 열어야 할 것입니다.
(D) 자리가 한정되어 있어 사전 예약이 필요할 수 있습니다.

해설 빈칸 앞 문장의 '그의 팬들은 CD나 포스터를 가져오라'는 내용을 고려할 때, 'CD나 포스터에 가수의 사인을 받을 아주 좋은 기회'라는 내용으로 이어져야 문맥상 자연스러우므로 (A)가 정답이다.

+ **Key word**

Fans of his should bring any CDs or posters. This is a great chance to get them autographed.

135-138번은 다음 안내문에 관한 문제입니다.

오늘날의 비즈니스 세계에서는 강력한 지도자가 변화를 가져올 수 있습니다. Velimas Life Coaching (VLC)의 사명은 간단합니다. 저희는 사람들을 진정한 지도자로 **135 성장시키기**를 원합니다. VLC에서는 유능한 지도자가 되는 역량을 갖추게 하기 위해 리더십 **136 강좌**와 코칭 서비스를 제공합니다. 각자 성공적인 경력을 가진 비즈니스 리더가 강좌를 가르칩니다. **137 또한,** VLC에는 여러분에게 귀중한 직장 경험을 제공해 드리기 위해 고안된 인턴십 프로그램도 있습니다. **138 많은 유명 기업에서 매년 참여합니다.** 이는 자신의 리더십 기술을 시험하면서 인맥도 만들 아주 좋은 방법이 됩니다.

어휘
strong 강한 | difference 차이, 변화 | life coaching 인생 코칭 | mission 임무, 사명 | ensure 반드시 ~하게 하다, 보장하다 | be equipped with ~를 갖추다 | skill 기량, 기술 | effective 효과적인, 유능한 | of one's own 자기 자신의 | valuable 귀중한 | workplace 직장 | experience 경험 | test 시험하다 | network 인맥, 망, 네트워크

135. to부정사

해설 빈칸은 동사 want의 목적어 자리이다. 빈칸 앞에 to가 있으므로 함께 to부정사구를 이루는 동사 원형 (B)가 정답이다.

136. 어휘 - 명사

해설 빈칸은 leadership과 함께 복합명사를 이루는 명사 자리이다. 복합명사가 동사 provide의 목적어 역할을 하고 있으며, 접속사 and로 연결된 또 다른 목적어와의 관계를 고려할 때, 'VLC에서 리더십 강좌와 코칭 서비스를 제공한다'는 의미가 되어야 문맥상 자연스러우므로 (B)가 정답이다.

+ **Key word**

At VLC, we provide leadership courses and coaching services to ensure you are equipped with the skills to become an effective leader.

137. 접속부사

해설 빈칸은 문장의 도입부에 들어갈 접속부사 자리이다. 앞 문장의 '강

좌는 성공적인 경력을 가진 비즈니스 리더가 가르친다'는 내용과 빈칸 뒷부분의 'VLC에는 인턴십 프로그램도 있다'는 내용을 고려할 때, VLC에서 제공하는 프로그램을 덧붙여 소개하고 있으므로 부가의 의미를 전달하는 (D)가 정답이다.

+ **Key word**

Our courses are taught by business leaders who have had successful careers of their own. **Additionally, VLC also has an internship program** designed to give you some valuable workplace experience.

138. 문장 선택

(A) 전 세계 각지에서 저희 커리어 코치들을 모십니다.
(B) 이 강좌는 1년에 한 번만 수강할 수 있습니다.
(C) 많은 유명 기업에서 매년 참여합니다.
(D) 수강료 할인을 받을 수 있습니다.

해설 빈칸 뒤에 나온 지시대명사가 This가 가리킬 수 있는 내용이 빈칸에 들어가야 한다. '리더십 기술을 시험하면서 인맥도 만들 아주 좋은 방법이 된다'는 내용을 고려할 때, '많은 유명 기업에서 (인턴십 프로그램에) 매년 참여한다'는 내용이 들어가야 문맥상 자연스러우므로 (C)가 정답이다.

+ **Key word**

Additionally, VLC also has an internship program designed to give you some valuable workplace experience. Many prestigious businesses participate every year. This is a great way to test your leadership skills while also creating your own network.

139-142번은 다음 광고에 관한 문제입니다.

Freeport 더 나은 미래 프로젝트
11월 4일 수요일부터 11월 6일 금요일까지

Griswold 카운티는 Freeport **139 에서** 차로 20분 거리에 위치하며, 친환경을 실천하는데 맡은 바 역할을 다하고 있습니다. Griswold **140 주민**들은 합심하여 연간 친환경 목표를 이미 거의 달성했습니다. 그리고 올해 말까지 이 목표치를 뛰어넘으 **141 려고 합니다.** 비결이 궁금하신가요? **142 카운티**를 소개하는 저희 독점 텔레비전 다큐멘터리에서 확인해보세요. 프로그램은 다음 주 Channel One에서 방송됩니다. 많은 시청 바랍니다!

어휘
county 자치주, 카운티 | drive (자동차로 가는) 노정 | part 역할 | go green 환경친화적이 되다 | nearly 거의 | reach 닿다, 도달하다 | annual 연례의 | sustainability 지속 가능성 | goal 목표 | already 이미 | exceed 초과하다 | end 말, 끝 | wonder 궁금해하다 | secret 비밀, 비결 | air 방송되[하]다 | tune in 시청하다

139. 전치사

해설 빈칸은 장소를 나타내는 지명 Freeport를 목적어로 하는 전치사 자리이다. 전치사구가 빈칸 앞 명사구 'a 20-minute drive'를 수식하는 구조로, 'Freeport에서 운전해서 20분 걸리는 거리'라는 의미가 되어야 자연스러우므로 (C)가 정답이다.

+ **Key word**

Griswold County is just **a 20-minute drive from Freeport**

---

140. 사람 명사 vs. 사물/추상 명사

해설 빈칸은 문장의 주어인 명사 자리이다. 문맥상 'Griswold 주민이 합심하여 연간 친환경 목표를 이미 거의 달성했다'는 내용이 되어야 문맥상 자연스러우므로 사람 명사 (A)가 정답이다.

+ Key point

명사 resident vs. residence, residency: 사람 명사 resident는 '거주자'를, 사물 명사 residence는 '거주지를', residency는 '(대사 등의) 공관, 관저'를 의미한다.

141. 어휘 - 동사

해설 빈칸은 주어 they에 대한 동사 자리이다. they는 Griswold 주민들을 지칭한다는 것을 알 수 있으며, 빈칸 앞 문장의 'Griswold 주민들이 합심하여 연간 친환경 목표를 이미 거의 달성했다'는 내용을 고려할 때 '올해 말까지 이 목표치를 뛰어넘으려고 한다'는 내용으로 이어져야 자연스럽다. 또한 빈칸 뒤의 구조를 고려할 때 'intend to(V하려고 한다)'의 표현을 완성하는 (D)가 정답이다.

+ Key word

The **residents from Griswold** have come together and **nearly reached their annual sustainability goal already**. And **they intend to exceed this goal by year's end**.

142. 문장 선택

(A) 소식지에 가입하시면 특별 할인을 받으실 수 있습니다.
(B) 카운티로 내려가는 여행에 참여하시고 직접 체험해 보세요.
(C) 카운티를 소개하는 저희 독점 텔레비전 다큐멘터리에서 확인해보세요.
(D) 지침에 따라 저희에게 질문을 제출해 주세요.

해설 빈칸 뒤 문장의 '프로그램은 다음 주 Channel One에서 방송됩니다'라는 내용을 고려할 때, '저희 독점 텔레비전 다큐멘터리에서 확인해보세요'라는 내용이 들어가야 문맥상 자연스러우므로 (C)가 정답이다.

+ Key word

Find out in our exclusive television documentary covering the county. The show will be airing next week on Channel One.

143-146번은 다음 도서 후기에 관한 문제입니다.

Franchesca Thurman의 최신 도서 〈Kitchen Masterpieces〉는 올해 조금 더 건강하게 먹고 싶은 사람들에게 확실히 관심을 끌 것이다. 이 책은 매일 쇼핑하러 갈 시간이 없는 직장인을 염두에 두고 **143** 쓰여 있다. **144** 조리법은 대부분의 주방에서 손쉽게 구할 수 있는 재료만을 사용한다. 게다가 이 책은 요즘 온라인에서 으레 볼 수 있는, 조리법에 덧붙여 **145** 일상의 개인적인 이야기를 하지 않는데, 이는 Thurman이 격렬히 반대하는 트렌드다. Thurman은 모든 조리법은 빠르고 이해하기 쉬워야 한다고 주장한다. 〈Kitchen Masterpieces〉에는 Thurman의 유명한 크리스마스 쿠키를 포함해 주요 **146** 연휴용 조리법도 들어 있다. 책은 2월에 출간될 예정이다.

어휘
be sure to 반드시 ~하다 | appeal 관심[흥미]을 끌다 | adult 성인 | in mind 염두에 둔 | moreover 게다가 | forgo 포기하다, 무시하다 | personal 개인적인 | typically 보통, 일반적으로 | accompany 동반하다 | vehemently 격렬히, 맹렬히 | be opposed to ~에 반대하다 | insist 주장하다 | contain ~이 들어있다 | hit the shelves (서점 등에) 나오다

143. 동사의 태 / 시제

해설 빈칸은 주어 the book 뒤의 동사 자리이다. 주어 자리에 사물 명사가 있으니 수동태 구문이 필요하며, 앞 문장의 내용을 고려할 때 책의 특징을 소개하는 내용이 되어야 문맥상 자연스러우므로 현재 시제 (A)가 정답이다.

144. 문장 선택

(A) 그 책에는 그 지역의 저렴한 레스토랑들에 대한 섹션이 포함되어 있다.
(B) 그 요리법은 채식주의자들에게 우호적임을 보장하지 않는다.
(C) 그 책은 또한 몇 달 안에 디지털판으로 제공될 것이다.
(D) 조리법은 대부분의 주방에서 손쉽게 구할 수 있는 재료만을 사용한다.

해설 빈칸 앞 문장의 '매일 쇼핑하러 갈 시간이 없는 직장인을 염두에 두고 쓰여 있다'는 내용을 고려할 때, '조리법은 대부분의 주방에서 손쉽게 구할 수 있는 재료만을 사용한다'는 내용으로 이어져야 문맥상 자연스러우므로 (D)가 정답이다.

+ Key word

The **book is written with working adults in mind who may not have the time to go shopping every day**. **The recipes only use ingredients readily available in most kitchens**.

145. 어휘 - 형용사

해설 빈칸은 명사구 personal stories를 수식하는 형용사 자리이다. 빈칸 뒤 문장의 'Thurman은 모든 조리법은 빠르고 이해하기 쉬워야 한다고 주장한다'는 내용을 고려할 때, 문맥상 '요즘 온라인에서 흔히 볼 수 있는 조리법에 덧붙여 개인적인 일상의 이야기를 하는 것은 Thurman이 격렬히 반대하는 트렌드'라는 의미가 되어야 문맥상 자연스러우므로 (B)가 정답이다.

+ Key word

Moreover, the book forgoes the **mundane personal stories that typically accompany recipes found online in today's world, a trend Thurman is** vehemently **opposed to. Thurman insists that all recipes should be quick and easy to understand.**

146. 어휘 - 명사

해설 빈칸은 the major의 수식을 받는 명사 자리이다. '유명한 크리스마스 쿠키를 포함해 주요 연휴용 조리법도 들어 있다'는 내용이 되어야 문맥상 자연스러우므로 (D)가 정답이다.

+ Key word

Kitchen Masterpieces also **contains recipes for the major holidays including** Thurman's famous **Christmas cookies**.

147-148번은 다음 기사에 관한 문제입니다.

147 Rochester 리조트 채용을 위한 유력한 지원자를 모집하기 위해 Belwater 전시회장에서 이번 주말 오전 10시부터 오후 5시까지 직업 박람회를 개최합니다.

프론트 데스크 직원 및 안내원에서 보안요원과 청소직원에 이르기까지 다양한 분야의 직무가 나와 있어, 지원 가능한 일자리가 아주 다양합니

다. 행사 입장은 무료이고, 웹사이트를 통해 사전 등록한 분들은 박람회 전에 이력서를 검토받을 수 있습니다.

148 Belwater의 최고 정보 책임자인 Rita Logan은 전시회장을 대신하여 박람회 개최에 대한 기쁨을 표하는 성명을 발표했습니다. Naworld Inn에서 보조 행사기획자로 경력을 쌓기 시작한 그녀는 서비스업의 일이 어떻게 흥미로운 기회들로 이어지는지를 경험을 통해 알고 있습니다.

"이 업계의 일은 매우 만족스럽고 보람 있습니다,"라고 Logan 씨가 언급했습니다. "서비스산업에서 경력을 쌓는데 관심이 있는 분들은 박람회에 꼭 참석하세요."

어휘
host (행사를) 주최하다 | career 직업 | expo 엑스포 | recruit 채용하다 | potential 잠재적인 | candidate 지원자 | employment 취업, 고용 | position 일자리, 직위 | sector 분야, 부문 | representative 대표자, 대리인 | concierge 안내원, 컨시어지 | admission (료) | complimentary 무료의 | pre-register 사전 등록하다 | look over 살펴보다, 검토하다 | Chief Information Officer 최고 정보 책임자 | release 발표하다, 공개하다 | statement 성명(서), 진술(서) | on behalf of ~를 대신하여 | exhibition 전시(회) | express 표현하다 | delight 기쁨 | fair 박람회 | assistant 조수, 보조 | inn 여관 | firsthand 직접 (체험으로), 바로 | hospitality 접대, 환대 | industry 산업 | lead to ~로 이어지다, 초래하다 | opportunity 기회 | satisfying 만족스러운 | rewarding 보람 있는 | visible (눈에) 보이는, 뚜렷한 | attend 참석하다

---

147. 주제 / 목적 / 대상

기사의 목적은 무엇인가?
(A) 공사 프로젝트를 발표하려고
(B) 신규 오픈한 사업체를 검토하려고
(C) 임원 임명에 대해 논하려고
(D) 다가올 행사를 홍보하려고

해설 첫 번째 단락에서 'The Belwater Exhibition Center will host a career expo this weekend from 10 A.M. to 5 P.M. to recruit potential candidates for employment at the Rochester Resort.'라고 했으므로 (D)가 정답이다.

148. 사실 확인

Logan 씨에 관하여 언급된 것은?
(A) 호텔에서 근무한 경험이 있다.
(B) 이력서를 살펴볼 것이다.
(C) 직업을 바꾸고 싶어 한다.
(D) Rochester 인근에 살았었다.

해설 세 번째 단락에서 'Rita Logan, Chief Information Officer at Belwater, released a statement on behalf of the exhibition center expressing her delight in hosting the fair. Having started her career as an assistant event planner at Naworld Inn,'이라고 했으므로 (A)가 정답이다.

149-151번은 다음 기사에 관한 문제입니다.

Hyper 철도, 고속 선로를 놓다
Sherry Lee, 전속작가

BEIJING (5월 2일) — 오늘 아침 일찍, Hyper 철도는 더 길고, 더 빠른 열차를 수용하기 위해 현재 철로를 업그레이드하는 동시에 철도망을 확장하는 계획들을 발표했다. —[1]—. **149** 시속 400킬로미터까지 속도를 낼 수 있어, 승객들은 전보다 빨리 목적지에 도착할 수 있게 될 것이다. 서쪽으로 Xinjiang 지역까지 연장되는 6개의 신규 역사 구축이 이 개발에 포함된다. —[2]—.

"저희의 주된 목표는 최신 기술을 이용하여 고객들께서 원하는 곳에 도착하는 것을 좀 더 편리하게 만들어드리는 것입니다."라고 CEO이자 설립자인 Qiao Cai가 말했다.

150 또한, Hyper 철도는 10월 1일부터 이용 가능한, 할인 및 기타 혜택을 제공하는 새로운 리워드 카드를 선보였다. 충분한 리워드 포인트를 적립한 이용객은 좌석 업그레이드 선택권을 갖게 된다. **151** 하지만, 이들 좌석은 사전에 선택될 수 없다는 것에 유의한다. —[3]—. 가입에 관심 있는 개인들은 웹사이트 www.hyperrails.com/rewards에서 확인하면 된다. —[4]—.

어휘
railway 철도 | announce 발표하다 | plan 계획 | extend 연장하다, 확장하다 | railroad 철도 | network 통신망, 네트워크 | current 현재의 | track (기차) 선로, 트랙 | accommodate 수용하다 | capable of ~할 수 있는 | reach ~에 이르다, 도달하다 | passenger 승객 | destination 목적지 | include 포함하다 | development 개발 | creation 창조, 구축 | station 역 | province 지방, (행정단위의) 주, 도 | main 주요한 | goal 목표 | convenient 편리한 | founder 설립자 | unveil 발표하다 | reward 보상(금) | offer 제공하다 | discount 할인 | perk 특전 | accrue 축적하[되]다 | choose 고르다 | note 주의하다, 주목하다 | select 선택하다 | in advance 미리, 사전에 | individual 개인 | sign up 가입하다, 등록하다 | check out 확인하다

---

149. 사실 확인

Hyper 철도에 관하여 언급된 것은?
(A) 이동시간을 줄이는 것을 목표로 한다.
(B) 새로운 열차 좌석을 디자인했다.
(C) 다른 국가들에 노선을 만들었다.
(D) 본사를 Xinjiang으로 이전할 것이다.

해설 첫 번째 단락에서 'Capable of reaching speeds of 400 km/h, passengers will be able to arrive at their destinations quicker than ever before.'라고 했으므로 (A)가 정답이다.

+ Paraphrasing

arrive at their destinations quicker than ever before → reduce travel times

150. 상세 정보

10월에 무슨 일이 있을 것인가?
(A) Hyper 철도에서 직업박람회를 개최할 것이다.
(B) 멤버십 프로그램이 시작될 것이다.
(C) 승객들이 예매 앱을 다운받을 수 있게 될 것이다.
(D) Cai 씨가 은퇴를 발표할 것이다.

해설 세 번째 단락에서 'In addition, Hyper Railways unveiled a new rewards card, available from 1 October, that will offer discounts and other perks.'라고 했으므로 (B)가 정답이다.

151. 문장 삽입

[1], [2], [3], [4]로 표시된 곳 중에서 다음 문장이 들어갈 위치로 가장 적절한 곳은?

"그것들은 출발 당일에 지정될 것이다."

(A) [1]
(B) [2]
(C) [3]
(D) [4]

해설 주어진 문장의 They가 가리키는 것을 찾아야 하는데 세 번째 단락에서 'However, note that these seats cannot be selected in advance.'라고 하여 주어진 문장이 이어지기에 자연스러우므로 (C)가 정답이다.

152-153번은 다음 웹 페이지에 관한 문제입니다.

http://www.arcinternational.com/staff

Daryl Anderson, 재무 담당자

Anderson 씨는 ARC International에서 이제 5년째 근무 중입니다. 그의 10년간의 은행 업계에서의 경험은 저희가 재무 관리를 할 수 있도록 돕는데 매우 중요합니다. 이것은 저희가 기부자들의 후한 기부금을 더 잘 활용하고 소액 융자를 제공하는 ARC의 사명을 완수할 수 있도록 해줍니다.

152 ARC에 입사하기 전, Anderson 씨는 5년간 Lagos 소재의 Astorium 금융에서 근무했으며, 그곳에서 그는 이용하기 쉬운 대출 프로그램이 어떻게 경제적 성장을 촉진시킬 수 있는지를 직접 입증했습니다. 그는 Astorium 금융에 La Paz와 Quito에 여러 제조공장을 짓는 것에 대해 현명하게 투자하라고 권고했습니다. **153** 잠시 은퇴한 후, 그는 비영리 산업에 전념했는데, 이는 모든 사람들을 위한 소액 융자 및 개발 촉진에 도움을 주기 위해 ARC International에서 근무하러 Boston으로 이주하기로 한 그의 결정으로 이어졌습니다.

어휘

finance 재정, 재무 | coordinator 코디네이터, 책임자, 조정자 | decade 10년 | banking 은행업 | industry 산업, 업계 | crucial 중대한 | allow 허용하다, ~하도록 하다 | donor 기부자 | generous 관대한, 후한 | contribution 기여, 기부 | achieve 성취하다 | mission 임무 | micro loan 소액 융자 | directly 직접 | witness 목격하다, 입증하다 | accessible 이용[접근]하기 쉬운 | promote 촉진[고취]하다 | growth 성장 | wisely 현명하게 | invest in 투자하다 | construction 건설 | manufacturer 제조업체 | briefly 잠시 | retire 은퇴하다 | commit oneself to ~에 헌신하다 | nonprofit 비영리의 | lead to ~로 이어지다

152. 상세 정보

Anderson 씨의 이전 직장은 어디였는가?
(A) Lagos
(B) La Paz
(C) Quito
(D) Boston

해설 두 번째 단락에서 'Before joining ARC, Mr. Anderson was at Astorium Capital for five years in Lagos'라고 했으므로 (A)가 정답이다.

153. 암시 / 추론

ARC International에 관하여 알 수 있는 것은?
(A) 공장을 운영하고 있다.
(B) 투자은행과 협력한다.
(C) 비영리 기업이다.
(D) 여러 국가에 소재하고 있다

해설 두 번째 단락에서 'he committed himself to the nonprofit industry, which led to his decision to move to Boston to work for ARC International'이라고 했으므로 (C)가 정답이다.

154-155번은 다음 문자 메시지 대화에 관한 문제입니다.

Taurean Kingsbury [오후 3:21]
저기요, 제가 Farsight Books에 있는데요. **154** 이번 학기 강의에 인용문을 포함시키기 위해 책이 필요하다고 말하지 않았나요? 제가 한 부 찾아줄 수 있을 것 같은데요.

Donna Mejor [오후 3:22]
그러면 고맙죠. Durden Press에서 나온 〈문학 입문〉 5번째 판이에요. 최근에 나왔는데 저번에 가게에 마지막으로 갔을 때는 못 봤어요.

Taurean Kingsbury [오후 3:23]
제가 알아볼게요.

Taurean Kingsbury [오후 3:30]
알겠어요! **155** 금요일 전에 지출 보고서 제출만 꼭 해주세요, 그러지 않으면 제가 지불해야 해서요.

Donna Mejor [오후 3:31]
물론이죠! 감사드려요!

어휘

mention 언급하다 | include 포함하다 | quotation 인용 | lecture 강의 | semester 학기 | appreciate 감사하다 | edition 판 | expense 비용, 지출

154. 암시 / 추론

책에 관하여 알 수 있는 것은?
(A) Mejor 씨가 편집했다.
(B) Farsight Books에서 판매하지 않는다.
(C) 강의에 참고될 것이다.
(D) 강좌에 배정되었다.

해설 오후 3시 21분, Kingsbury 씨의 메시지에서 'Didn't you mention needing a book so you can include some quotations in your lectures this semester?'라고 했으므로 (C)가 정답이다.

155. 화자 의도 파악

오후 3시 31분에, Mejor 씨가 "당연하죠"라고 할 때 무엇을 의미하겠는가?
(A) 제때 서류를 제출할 것이다.
(B) 책값을 지불할 것이다.
(C) 책이 있는지 확인할 것이다.
(D) 금요일에 구입할 것이다.

해설 오후 3시 30분 ~ 3시 31분 대화에서 Kingsbury 씨가 'Just make sure you turn in an expense report before Friday'라고 하자, Mejor 씨가 'Of course!'라고 말한 것이므로 (A)가 정답이다.

✛ Paraphrasing

turn in an expense report → submit a document

156-157번은 다음 웹 페이지에 관한 문제입니다.

http://www.theseeker.com/search/murdo

The Seeker

골프 제품을 전문으로 하는 Luminosity Range에서 Murdo에 신규 지점을 개장합니다. 회사에서 현재 신규 지점을 관리할 시설 관리자를 구하고 있습니다.

역할 및 책임: 시설 관리자는 매장의 모든 측면을 감독하며 원활한 운영을 보장합니다. **157D** 업무에는 재고 모니터링하기, 필요에 따라 주문하기, 고객 관련 문제 해결하기, 월별 보고서 제출하기가 포함됩니다.

요건: **157C** 소매업 환경에서 시설 관리자로서 입증 가능한 최소 5년의 경력이 있어야 합니다. **157B** 시간관리 능력 및 세심함은 필수입니다. 가급적, 골프 및 골프 제품에 관심이 많으면 좋습니다.

Luminosity Range 소개: 고품질의 제품을 시장에 선보이고 싶었던 열정 넘치는 골퍼들 몇 명이 합심해 설립했습니다. **156** 그런 신생 기업이 지난 해 사상 유례없는 성장을 경험하면서, 공격적인 확장에 나서게 되었습니다. 저희와 함께 일하시면, 최고 수준의 급여, 넉넉한 휴가, 자기 계발 기회와 같은 훌륭한 혜택을 누리시게 됩니다.

어휘

specialize in ~를 전문으로 하다 | golf 골프 | product 제품 | location 지점 | facility 시설 | manage 관리하다 | oversee 감독하다 | aspect 부분 | ensure 보장하다 | smooth 순조로운 | operation 운용 | responsibility 업무 | monitor 추적 관찰하다 | inventory 재고 | place (주문을) 넣다 | order 주문 | as required 요청[요구]대로 | resolve 해결하다 | customer-related 고객 관련의 | issue 문제 | submit 제출하다 | requirement 요건 | a minimum of 최소한의 | proven 입증된 | retail 소매업, 소매의 | environment 환경 | attention to detail 꼼꼼함, 세심함 | punctuality 시간 엄수 | essential 필수적인 | preferably 가급적이면 | passion 열정 | found 설립하다 | passionate 열정적인 | golfer 골프 치는 사람 | high-quality 고품질의 | experience 경험하다 | unprecedented 전례 없는 | growth 성장 | expand 확장하다 | aggressively 공격적으로 | confer 주다 | benefit 혜택 | salary 급여 | generous 후한, 넉넉한 | vacation day 휴가 | opportunity 기회 | personal 개인적인 | development 발전

156. 암시 / 추론

Luminosity Range에 관하여 알 수 있는 것은?
(A) 국제적인 기업이다.
(B) 여러 직무를 채용하는 중이다.
(C) 비교적 신생 기업이다.
(D) 자사의 전 제품을 생산한다.

해설 네 번째 단락에서 'We experienced unprecedented growth last year for such a young company'라고 했으므로 (C)가 정답이다.

✚ **Paraphrasing**

young → relatively new

157. 사실 확인

시설 관리자 지원서에 포함될 것으로 예상되지 않는 것은?
(A) 경영 관련 학위
(B) 문서를 늦지 않게 제출하는 능력
(C) 소매 지점 관리 경험
(D) 소비자 불만 해결 능력

해설 지문의 단서와 보기를 매칭시키면, 두 번째 단락의 'resolving any customer-related issues,'는 (→ (D))와, 세 번째 단락의 'Requirement: Must have a minimum of five proven years as a facility manager in a retail environment.'는 (→ (C))와, 'Excellent attention to detail as well as punctuality is essential.'는 (→ (B))와 일치하지만, 경영 관련 학위에 관한 내용은 언급된 바 없으므로 (A)가 정답이다.

✚ **Paraphrasing**

resolve customer-related issues → settle consumer complaints

158-160번은 다음 기사에 관한 문제입니다.

Mutumobo에의 기대치가 강화되다

[160] 서아프리카 전역에 콩 판매가 증가하면서 이번 분기는 CTS 브랜드의 강세가 예상된다. [158] 유독 낮은 기온뿐만 아니라 홍수로 인해 지난 몇 년간 수확량이 감소해왔다. [159] 하지만 이러한 힘든 상황하에서도 CTS의 콩 작물은 수확 철에 기록을 세울 수 있었다.

[160] CTS는 나이지리아 Lagos에 있는 Mutumobo 사에 의해 고안되었다. 농부들은 전통적으로 저가 브랜드 구입을 선호해왔지만, CTS의 고유한 특성들은 대륙 전역에서 유명해졌다. 그 결과, 이번 분기 영업보고서에 대한 기대로 회사 주식이 상승했다.

어휘

projection 예상, 추정 | strengthen 강화하[되]다, 강력해지다 | quarter 4분의 1, 사분기 | project 예상[추정]하다, 기획하다 | increase 증가; 증가하다 | soybean 콩 | decline 감소하다 | yield 산출량, 수확량; 산출하다 | flooding 홍수 | as well as ~뿐만 아니라 | unusually 대단히, 몹시, 평소와 달리 | temperature 온도 | crop 농작물 | harvest 수확(기) | traditionally 전통적으로 | proper 적절한, 올바른 | continent 대륙 | as a result 그 결과 | stock 주식 | rise 오르다, 상승하다 | in anticipation of ~를 예상하고, 기대하여

158. 상세 정보

기사에 따르면, 콩 생산에 영향을 미친 한 가지 요인은 무엇인가?
(A) 지나친 강우
(B) 높은 기온
(C) 농작물 병충해
(D) 신규 수확 기법

해설 첫 번째 단락에서 'The last several years have seen declining yields due to flooding as well as unusually low temperatures.'라고 했으므로 (A)가 정답이다.

✚ **Paraphrasing**

flooding → excessive rainfall

159. 동의어

첫 번째 단락, 네 번째 줄의 단어 "set"과 의미상 가장 가까운 것은?
(A) 준비하다
(B) 추정하다
(C) 달성하다
(D) 일정을 잡다

해설 첫 번째 단락의 'But even under these difficult conditions, CTS soybean crops have been able to set records at harvest time.'에서 'set'은 '세우다, 달성하다'라는 의미로 쓰였으므로 보기 중 '성취하다, 해내다'를 뜻하는 (C)가 정답이다.

160. 상세 정보

기사에 따르면, Mutumobo 사는 무엇을 하였는가?
(A) 신규 임원을 채용했다
(B) 신종 콩을 개발했다
(C) Lagos에 연구개발 시설을 열었다
(D) CTS 브랜드를 다른 회사에 팔았다

해설 첫 번째 단락에서 'This quarter is projected to be a strong one for the CTS brand after an increase in its soybean sales across West Africa.'라고 했고, 두 번째 단락에서 'CTS was designed by Mutumobo Co. in Lagos, Nigeria.'라고 하여 Mutumobo 사에서 콩 브랜드를 만들었음을 알 수 있으므로 (B)가 정답이다.

161-163번은 다음 언론보도에 관한 문제입니다.

즉시 배포용

**최신 메이저 기업 Darnold Industries,
TAMOS의 수상 경력에 빛나는 서비스 채택**

Lagos (1월 10일) — 나이지리아의 주요 청정에너지 기업인 Darnold Industries는 보안을 강화하기 위해 안면인식 시스템을 설치할 예정이다. 스코틀랜드 업체 TAMOS가 설치 및 관리할 시스템은 직원들의 얼굴을 인식해서 공장에 출입할 수 있게 해줄 것이다.

161 Darnold의 회장 Sandra McGee는 안면인식이 이전 보안 방법들과 비교했을 때 도약이라고 말했다.

"**161** TAMOS에 투자함으로써, 저희가 굉장한 진보를 하게 될 것이라고 생각합니다."라고 McGee가 말했다. "예전에는 직원들이 공장에 출입하려면 사진 출입증을 사용해야 했습니다. **162** 하지만, 계속하여 신규 출입증을 만드는 것은 비용이 많이 드는 일이었습니다. 이러한 출입증을 이용하는 것이 항상 안전한 것도 아닙니다. 이를테면, 직원들이 출입증을 분실했을 때, 보안직원이 그 상황을 해결하기 위해 어떤 조치를 취해야 했습니다. 결국, 출입증은 재정과 보안 문제를 야기했습니다."

TAMOS는 5년 전 출범한 이래, 직장 보안 시스템의 혁신 자원이 되어왔다. **163** Edinburgh에 본사를 둔 이 회사는 자랑스럽게 전 세계 회사들에 제품을 제공한다. 그 회사의 최신 안면인식 시스템 상품에 대해 더 알아보려면, www.tamos.com을 방문하면 된다.

어휘

immediate 즉시의, 즉각적인 | release 배포 | adopt 채택하다 | award-winning 상을 받은 | install 설치하다 | facial recognition 안면인식 | bolster 강화하다, 개선하다 | security 보안 | maintain 유지하다 | Scottish 스코틀랜드 사람의 | allow 허용하다 | gain access to ~에 접근하다 | comment 견해를 밝히다 | leap forward 진보, 도약 | compared to ~과 비교하여 | previous 이전의 | solution 해결책 | invest in ~에 투자하다 | improvement 개선, 향상 | previously 이전에 | pass 출입증 | constantly 끊임없이 | prove 증명하다 | costly 비싼 | remedy 해결하다 | situation 상황 | ultimately 궁극적으로 | present 주다, 보여주다 | budget 예산, 비용 | issue 문제 | innovative 혁신적인 | source 근원, 원천, 출처 | workplace 직장 | launch 출시하다 | updated 업데이트된 | check out 확인하다

161. 암시 / 추론

McGee 씨에 관하여 알 수 있는 것은?
(A) 자신의 출입증을 여러 번 분실했다.
(B) 사이버 보안 전문가이다.
(C) 여러 공장들을 관리한다.
(D) 보통 Edinburgh에서 근무한다.

해설 두 번째 단락에서 'Darnold's President, Sandra McGee'라고 했는데, 세 번째 단락에서 "By investing in TAMOS, I really think we're going to see a big improvement," said McGee. "Previously, we required employees to use photo ID passes to enter our factories.'라고 하여, 그녀가 회장으로 있는 회사에 공장이 여러 개가 있다는 것을 알 수 있으므로 (C)가 정답이다.

+ **Paraphrasing**

factories → plants

162. 상세 정보

McGee 씨는 왜 과거 상품들보다 TAMOS의 상품을 선호하는가?
(A) 사용자가 출입코드를 입력할 수 있게 해준다.
(B) 사진 신분증을 필요로 한다.
(C) 잦은 유지보수를 필요로 하지 않는다.
(D) 결국에는 비용을 절약하게 될 것이다.

해설 세 번째 단락에서 'However, constantly making new IDs proved to be costly.'라고 했으므로 (D)가 정답이다.

163. 암시 / 추론

TAMOS에 관하여 암시되는 것은?
(A) 본사를 Lagos로 옮겼다.
(B) 많은 해외고객을 보유한다.
(C) 신규 공장 건설을 계획 중이다.

(D) Darnold Industries가 인수했다.

해설 네 번째 단락에서 'The company, based in Edinburgh, is proud to provide its products to companies around the world.'라고 했으므로 (B)가 정답이다.

164-167번은 다음 편지에 관한 문제입니다.

Timothy da Silva
276 Cedar 로
Dayton, Ohio 45406

Samantha Simmons
6061 Plainview Terrace
Beavercreek, OH 44831

Simmons 씨께,

164 Montgomery 자치주 웹사이트에서 부동산 기록을 살펴보던 중, 저는 귀하께서 현재 한 때 구 Pinegrove 극장이었던 복합건물을 소유하고 있다는 것을 알게 되었습니다. **165** 저는 그 복합건물이 수년 전 극장이 문을 닫은 이후로 비어있는 걸로 알고 있습니다. —[1]—. 저는 그 건물이 판매 중인지 알고 싶습니다.

저의 동업자와 저는 빈티지 옷가게 및 식당이 입점된 소매점을 개발하려고 알아보고 있습니다. 약간의 리모델링을 하면, 귀하의 건물이 이상적인 장소가 될 거라고 생각합니다. **167** 정확하게는, 그 복합건물의 원래 성격을 유지하는 것이 저희의 의도입니다. —[2]—. 단지 약간의 개선만 있을 것입니다.

166 시내에 더 많은 유동 인구를 끌 만한 다른 장소들이 있긴 하지만, 주민들은 그곳들에 동일한 애착을 갖고 있지 않습니다. —[3]—. 저는 그 극장을 얼마나 그리워하는지에 관해 이야기하고, 그 건물이 새롭게 다시 태어나는 것을 보고 싶어 하는 많은 현지인을 알고 있습니다. —[4]—. 저는 저희의 계획이 Dayton에서 인기가 있을 것이라고 확신합니다.

시간을 내어 이 제안을 고려해 주셔서 감사합니다. 이 건과 관련하여 만남을 갖고 싶으시면, dasilva@silverchairdevelopment.com으로 저에게 이메일을 보내주세요.

정말 감사드립니다.

Timothy da Silva

Timothy da Silva

어휘

look through 검토하다 | property 부동산, 재산 | record 기록 | county 자치주 | currently 현재 | own 소유하다 | complex 복합건물 | serve as ~의 역할을 하다 | empty 빈 | shell 껍데기 | theater 극장 | develop 개발하다 | retail 소매업 | property 부동산, 재산 | feature ~를 특징으로 하다 | vintage 고전적인, 오래된 | clothing 옷, 의복 | dining 식사 | option 옵션, 선택권 | remodel 리모델링하다 | ideal 이상적인 | spot 장소 | intention 의도 | preserve 지키다, 보존하다 | original 원래의 | character 특징, 특질 | slight 약간의, 조금의 | improvement 개선 | attract 끌다 | foot traffic 유동인구 | resident 거주자 | attachment 애착, 부착 | miss 그리워하다 | consider 고려하다 | proposal 제안

164. 암시 / 추론

Montgomery 자치주에 관하여 알 수 있는 것은?
(A) 부동산 정보를 온라인에 게시한다.
(B) 시내에 대형 의류 아울렛이 있다.
(C) 최근 신규 건축 규약을 도입했다.
(D) 주요 사무실이 극장 맞은편에 위치한다.

해설 첫 번째 단락에서 'While looking through property records on the Montgomery County Web site, I found out that you currently own the complex'라고 했으므로 (A)가 정답이다.

+ Paraphrasing

on the Web site → online

165. 암시 / 추론

Pinegrove 극장 복합건물에 관하여 암시되는 것은?
(A) 현재 방문객이 출입할 수 있다.
(B) 최근 리모델링되었다.
(C) 한동안 비어있었다.
(D) 여러 명의 다른 주인들에 의해 소유되었다.

해설 첫 번째 단락에서 'old Pinegrove Theater. From what I understand, the complex has been an empty shell since the theater closed years ago.'라고 했으므로 (C)가 정답이다.

+ Paraphrasing

an empty shell → unoccupied

166. 암시 / 추론

da Silva 씨는 왜 Simmons 씨의 부동산에 관심을 갖겠는가?
(A) 상업구역에 위치한다.
(B) 구매가가 협의 가능하다.
(C) 편의시설이 새것이다.
(D) 현지인들에게 잘 알려져 있다.

해설 세 번째 단락에서 'There are other spaces in the downtown area that would attract more foot traffic, but residents do not have the same attachment to them. I know many people in the area who tell stories about how much they miss the theater and would like to see it come back to life as something new.'라고 했으므로 (D)가 정답이다.

+ Paraphrasing

many people in the area → locals

167. 문장 삽입

[1], [2], [3], [4]로 표시된 곳 중에서 다음 문장이 들어갈 위치로 가장 적절한 곳은?

"이를테면, 아치형 입구에 있는 1950년대 스타일의 간판은 그곳의 고풍스러운 매력을 유지시켜줄 것입니다."

(A) [1]
(B) [2]
(C) [3]
(D) [4]

해설 두 번째 단락에서 'To be clear, it is our intention to preserve the original character of the complex.'라고 하여, 그 방법을 예를 들어 제시하는 주어진 문장이 이어지기에 자연스러우므로 (B)가 정답이다.

168-171번은 다음 회람에 관한 문제입니다.

회람

수신: 연구개발팀 직원
발신: Suha Mathur
날짜: 2월 16일
제목: 신상품 회의

---

168 제가 이번 주 목요일인 2월 19일 오전 9시에 회의실 B를 예약해서, 저희는 최신 영양바 FiBur의 개발을 시작할 수 있습니다. 이 회의에서 저희는 재료부터 포장디자인에 이르기까지 모든 것을 살펴볼 것입니다. **169** 또한, 저희는 헬스장에서 운동 후 먹을 간식거리를 찾는 고객들의 관심을 끌 수 있는 로고를 만들어야 합니다.

170 오후에는 소그룹으로 나뉘어 다른 나라에서 상품을 판매할 방안에 대해 심도 있게 논의할 것입니다. **171** 저는 Michak International 회사에서 실시한 시장조사 보고서를 여러분께 이메일로 보내드렸습니다. 여기에는 저희에게 분명 도움이 될 소비자 동향에 대한 데이터가 들어 있습니다. 모바일 기술과 앞으로의 사용에 관한 부분에 특히 집중해 주세요.

어휘

book 예약하다 | development 개발 | nutrition 영양 | ingredient 재료 | wrap 싸다, 포장하다 | catch 잡다 | attention 주의, 주목 | post-workout 운동 후 | split into (작은 부분들로) 나누다 | further 더 나아가(far의 비교급), 더 | firm 회사 | consumer 소비자 | surely 확실히, 분명히, 틀림없이, 의심의 여지 없이 | pay attention to ~에 주의 집중하다, 주목하다 | regarding ~에 관해

168. 암시 / 추론

Mathur 씨는 어떤 업종에 종사하겠는가?
(A) 식품 제조회사
(B) 광고 회사
(C) 스포츠 경기장
(D) 그래픽 디자인 회사

해설 첫 번째 단락에서 'I have booked Conference Room B for this Thursday, 19 February, at 9 A.M., so we can get started on the development of our latest nutrition bar, FiBur.'라고 했으므로 (A)가 정답이다.

169. 암시 / 추론

FiBar에 관하여 무엇이 사실이겠는가?
(A) 유기농 재료로 만들어질 것이다.
(B) Michak International에 의해 분석되었다.
(C) 여러 가지 다른 맛으로 나온다.
(D) 헬스장에서 구입할 수 있을 것이다.

해설 첫 번째 단락에서 'In addition, we'll need to create a logo that will catch the attention of customers who are looking to have a post-workout snack at the gym.'이라고 했으므로 (D)가 정답이다.

+ Paraphrasing

gym → fitness club

170. 상세 정보

회람에 따르면, 소그룹은 회의에서 무엇을 할 것인가?
(A) 사업 확장 전략을 논의할 것이다
(B) 설문 결과를 확인할 것이다
(C) 역할분담 활동에 참여할 것이다
(D) 새로운 모바일 기술을 시험할 것이다

해설 두 번째 단락에서 'In the afternoon, we'll split into small groups to further discuss how we can sell our products in other countries.'라고 했으므로 (A)가 정답이다.

171. 상세 정보

회람 수신자들은 무엇을 할 예정인가?
(A) 점심 선호 사항을 알려줄 것이다
(B) 고객에게 이메일을 보낼 것이다

(C) 조사 보고서를 살펴볼 것이다

(D) 경쟁사의 상품을 시식할 것이다

해설 두 번째 단락에서 'I have e-mailed you a market research paper by the firm, Michak International. It has data on consumer trends that will surely help us. Pay special attention to the section regarding mobile technology and its uses going forward.'라고 했으므로 (C)가 정답이다.

✦ Paraphrasing

pay attention to → review

172-175번은 다음 온라인 채팅 대화문에 관한 문제입니다.

Meryl Lindholm [오후 2시 08분]
여러분, 안녕하세요. 저는 여기 Klay & Field에서 팀을 이끌게 되어 영광입니다. 하지만 **172** 편집장 직위는 예상치 못했기에, 저는 여러분의 전문지식에 의지하게 될 거예요. 우선, 지적 재산으로 추가 수익을 창출하는 방안들을 저와 공유해 주세요.

Aaron Salters [오후 2시 10분]
173 저희는 오디오북의 품질을 개선하는 작업을 해왔고, 다음 주까지 결과물을 드릴 수 있습니다.

Ray Walters [오후 2시 11분]
흥미로운데요. 저희는 새로운 성우를 들이고, 고품질 오디오를 사용할 예정입니다. 그리고 저희는 모든 과거 자료를 웹사이트에 업로드해서, 무엇이든 쉽게 디지털 구매가 가능해질 거예요.

Meryl Lindholm [오후 2시 14분]
환영할 만한 변화이긴 한데요. 신규 고객의 관심을 끌 만한 뭔가를 할 필요가 있어요.

Julia Roglic [오후 2시 16분]
174 저는 신규 스마트폰 앱의 베타버전을 거의 마무리했어요. 한 달 요금으로 고객은 자료에 대한 무제한 이용권을 구입하게 됩니다. **172 174** 특수 알고리즘은 관심을 보인 작가나 장르, 주제를 기반으로 이용자들에게 뉴미디어를 추천해 줍니다.

Meryl Lindholm [오후 2시 17분]
174 느낌이 좋은데요. 진행 상황에 대해 최대한 많이 듣고 싶어요.

Julia Roglic [오후 2시 18분]
175 수요일까지 베타버전을 작동시킬 수 있어요.

Meryl Lindholm [오후 2시 19분]
좋습니다. **175** 저에게 사용법을 직접 보여줄 수 있나요? 우리 모두 목요일 이 시간에 제 사무실에서 만날까요?

어휘
honor 명예를 주다 | lead 이끌다 | head editor 편집장, 수석 편집자 | unexpected 예상치 않은, 뜻밖의 | rely on ~에 의존하다 | expertise 전문지식 | generate 발생[창출]시키다, 만들어내다 | additional 추가의 | revenue 수익, 수입 | intellectual property 지적 재산 | work on ~에 애쓰다, 노력을 들이다 | improve 개선하다, 향상시키다 | quality 질 | bring in 도입하다 | talent 재능 있는 사람 | high fidelity 고성능, 고품질 | entire 전체의 | back 과거의 | archive 기록 보관소 | digital 디지털 방식의 | charge 요금 | purchase 구입; 구입하다 | attention 주의(집중), 주목 | beta version 베타 버전 | unlimited 무제한의 | access 접근(권) | algorithm 알고리즘 | recommend 추천하다 | subscriber (서비스) 이용자, 가입자 | based on ~에 근거하여 | author 작가 | genre 장르 | promising 유망한, 조짐이 좋은 | progress 진척, 진행 | up and running 제대로 작동되는 | in person 직접

---

172. 암시 / 추론

글쓴이들은 어디서 일하겠는가?

(A) 통신사

(B) 소프트웨어 개발업체

(C) 회계 사무소

(D) 출판사

해설 오후 2시 08분, Meryl Lindholm의 메시지에서 'this position as Head Editor came unexpected,'라고 했고, 오후 2시 16분, Julia Roglic의 메시지에서 'A special algorithm would recommend new media to subscribers based on authors, genres, or subjects they've shown interest in.'이라고 했으므로 (D)가 정답이다.

173. 상세 정보

현재 무엇이 업그레이드되고 있는가?

(A) 특정 자원의 배분

(B) 광고예산 규모

(C) 오디오 음질

(D) 웹사이트 디자인

해설 오후 2시 10분, Aaron Salters의 메시지에서 'We've been working on improving the quality of our audiobooks and can have some results for you to hear by next week.'이라고 했으므로 (C)가 정답이다.

✦ Paraphrasing

improve → upgrade, audiobooks → audio files

174. 화자 의도 파악

오후 2시 17분에, Lindholm 씨가 "느낌이 좋은데요."라고 할 때 무엇을 의미하는가?

(A) Roglic 씨가 설계하는 프로그램을 맘에 들어 한다.

(B) 수익 보고서에 만족해한다.

(C) 변화가 필요하다는 것에 동의한다.

(D) 신규 채용 인력에 대해 기대하고 있다.

해설 오후 2시 16분 ~ 2시 17분 대화에서 Julia Roglic이 'I'm almost done with the beta version of a new smartphone app.'이라고 하며 'A special algorithm would recommend new media to subscribers based on authors, genres, or subjects they've shown interest in.'이라고 한 말에, Meryl Lindholm이 'That could be promising.'이라고 말한 것이므로 (A)가 정답이다.

175. 암시 / 추론

목요일에 무슨 일이 있겠는가?

(A) 시연

(B) 영업 회의

(C) HR 워크숍

(D) 상품 출시

해설 오후 2시 18분 ~ 오후 2시 19분 대화에서 Julia Roglic이 'I can have a beta version up and running by Wednesday.'라고 한 말에 Meryl Lindholm이 'Do you mind showing me how to use it in person? Can we all meet in my office around this time on Thursday?'라고 했으므로 (A)가 정답이다.

176-180번은 다음 광고와 이메일에 관한 문제입니다.

VIDALIA SOLUTIONS

Vidalia Solutions는 20년 넘게 Lauderdale 시에서 이사 서비스를 제공하는 업계 1위 업체입니다. 저희가 제공하는 서비스는 다음과 같습니다.
- 주택 또는 사무실 이사
- 대청소
- 물품 장기 보관
- 가구 및 쓰레기 처리

177 모든 서비스에는 환불을 보장해 드립니다. 저희 서비스에 만족스럽지 않으시면, 한 푼도 안 내셔도 됩니다.

179 그리고 한 해를 시작하며, 저희는 지금부터 2월까지 보관 서비스 비용에서 30퍼센트 할인을 제공해 드립니다. 저희의 모든 서비스에 대해 무료 견적을 받아 보시려면, 555-7375로 전화해 주시거나, bookings@vidalia.com으로 이메일을 보내주세요. **176** 또는 전에 없이 편리하게 예약하실 수 있는 새로운 앱이 이용 가능합니다. 오늘 받으세요!

어휘
provider 제공 기관 | moving service 운송업, 이사 서비스 | long-term 장기적인 | item 물품 | storage 저장(고) | furniture 가구 | rubbish 쓰레기 | disposal 처분, 처리 | money-back guarantee 환불 보장 | fully 전적으로 | satisfy 만족하다 | pay 지불하다 | kick off 시작하다 | quote 견적 | alternatively 대신에, 또는 | app 앱 | conveniently 편리하게 | like never before 전에 없이

수신: bookings@vidalia.com
발신: jkang93@deltalook.com
날짜: 1월 8일
제목: 견적서 요청

안녕하세요,

179 최근 우연히 귀사의 광고를 접했는데, 우연히도 제가 딱 필요로 하던 서비스에 할인을 제공하고 있더라고요! **178** 저는 최근 Lauderdale로 이사 가는 과정인데, 새 집이 수리 중이라 아직 준비가 안 되어 있어요. **179** 그래서 그동안 제 가구를 보관할 방법을 찾고 있습니다. 장기 보관을 제공하신다고 보았는데, 한 달 보관료가 어떻게 되는지 궁금합니다. **180** 제가 1월 21일에 제 주택 계약을 마무리하러 그쪽에 갈 예정이라, 그때까지 가구 보관 방법을 마련해놓고 싶습니다. 무엇이 가능한지 알려주시면, 연락드리겠습니다.

감사합니다.

Jisoo Kang

어휘
request 요청 | estimate 견적서 | recently 최근에 | come across 우연히 보다 | advertisement 광고 | as chance would have it 마침 다행히도, 우연히도 | ready 준비가 된 | renovate 개조[수리]하다 | in the meantime 그동안에 | rate 요금 | worth 가치 | finalize 마무리 짓다 | contract 계약 | arrange 마련하다 | as well 또한 | get in touch 연락하다

176. 주제 / 목적 / 대상
광고의 한 가지 목적에 해당하는 것은?
(A) 대중에게 가격 인상을 알리려고
(B) 새로운 앱 출시를 광고하려고
(C) 상 받은 것을 축하하려고
(D) 정책 변경 캠페인을 벌이려고

해설 첫 번째 지문[광고], 세 번째 단락에서 'Alternatively, we have a new app available that lets you conveniently book like never before.'라고 했으므로 (B)가 정답이다.

177. 사실 확인
광고에서 Vidalia Solutions에 관해 무엇을 언급하는가?
(A) 훌륭한 서비스 제공을 약속한다.
(B) 다른 도시에 지점이 더 있다.
(C) 주택 개조 서비스도 제공한다.
(D) 상장 기업이다.

해설 첫 번째 지문[광고], 두 번째 단락에서 'All services come with our money-back guarantee. If you're not fully satisfied with our service, you won't have to pay a cent.'라고 했으므로 (A)가 정답이다.

178. 사실 확인
Kang 씨에 관하여 언급된 것은?
(A) Lauderdale로 이사 갈 것이다.
(B) 생애 최초 주택 구입자다.
(C) 부동산 업계에서 일한다.
(D) 이전에 Vidalia Solutions를 이용한 적 있다.

해설 두 번째 지문[이메일]에서 'I am in the process of moving to Lauderdale, but the new house isn't ready yet as it is being renovated.'라고 했으므로 (A)가 정답이다.

179. 암시 / 추론 - 연계 문제
Kang 씨는 어떤 서비스를 준비하고 싶어 하겠는가?
(A) 주택 청소
(B) 물품 운송
(C) 쓰레기 처리
(D) 가구 보관

해설 첫 번째 지문[광고], 세 번째 단락에서 'And to kick off the year, we are offering a 30% discount on our storage service from now until February.'라고 했는데, 두 번째 지문[이메일]에서 'Therefore, I'm looking for some storage options for my furniture in the meantime. I saw that you offer long-term storage, but I was wondering what rates you offer for one month worth of storage.'라고 했으므로 (D)가 정답이다.

180. 상세 정보
이메일에 따르면, 1월 21일에 Kang 씨는 무엇을 할 계획인가?
(A) 사무실을 이사할 계획이다
(B) Lauderdale에 갈 계획이다
(C) Vidalia Solutions에 전화할 계획이다
(D) 예약을 확정할 계획이다

해설 Kang 씨가 쓴 두 번째 지문[이메일]의 날짜가 1월 8일(Date: January 8)이며, 두 번째 줄에서 'I am in the process of moving to Lauderdale, but the new house isn't ready yet as it is being renovated.'라고 하면서, 'I will be in town on January 21 to finalize my housing contract'라고 했으므로 (B)가 정답이다.

181-185번은 다음 양식과 이메일에 관한 문제입니다.

저희 직원에게 연락하시려면, 아래 양식을 작성해 주시기 바랍니다. 처리하는 데 2~3일 정도 고려해 주시기 바랍니다. Korgale LLC에 관심을 가져주셔서 감사합니다.

이름	Lois Hayes
전화	(143) 555-4992
이메일	lhayes@hazymornings.com
사업체명	Hazy Mornings
활동년수	7
지점	2

필요한 것을 간략하게 작성해 주세요.

181 저희는 공급사를 변경하려고 알아보고 있습니다. 현재는 아시아에 있는 공급업체에서 차를 얻고 있습니다. 그런데, 그쪽과 자꾸 마찰이 생기고 있습니다. 차라리 더 믿을 수 있고 경험이 풍부한 업체를 선택하고 싶습니다. **182** 과거 이용했던 경험에 비추어, 귀사에 연락하기로 했습니다. **183 184** 저는 미리 정해진 일정이 있는 월요일과 금요일을 제외하면 다음 주 중에 담당 직원과 만날 수 있습니다.

예상 주문 규모 및 빈도는 어떻게 되나요?

이상적이게는, 2주에 한 번씩 주문을 넣고 싶습니다. 저희는 2주마다 귀사의 찻잎 한 통을 사용했었습니다.

어휘
get in touch with ~와 연락하다 | fill in (서식을) 작성하다 | allow for ~을 감안하다 | process 처리하다 | supplier 공급업체 | currently 현재 | source 얻다 | reliable 신뢰할 수 있는 | experienced 경험이 풍부한 | prior 사전의, 우선하는 | obligation 의무, 일 | put in an order 주문하다 | tin 통

수신: lhayes@hazymornings.com
발신: shawndaniel@korgale.com
날짜: 8월 17일
제목: Hazy Mornings

Hayes 씨께,

Korgale LLC를 공급업체로 고려해 주셔서 감사합니다. 신뢰할 수 없는 공급업체로부터 느꼈을 좌절감을 이해합니다. 다행히도 저희가 도와드릴 수 있습니다. **183** 제 동료 Tanya Andrews가 연락을 드리도록 하겠습니다. 그녀는 Liane을 포함한 교외지역을 대표합니다. **184** 그녀는 보통 일요일부터 수요일까지 오전 9시부터 오후 5시까지 사무실에 있습니다. 하지만 이번 주 수요일에는 자리에 없을 예정이니 참고하세요. 저희와 마지막으로 함께하신 이후로, 저희는 신규 상품을 아주 광범위하게 추가했습니다. Andrews 씨에게 말해 차 시음 자리를 마련해 드리도록 하겠습니다.

Andrews 씨가 이번 주 내로 연락드릴 것입니다. **185** 다시 돌아오신 것을 환영하며, 첫 주문에 대해 할인 요금도 제공해드리고자 합니다.

관심 보내주셔서 감사드리며, Hazy Mornings와 다시 함께 하시길 바라겠습니다.

정말 감사합니다.

Shawn Daniel, 고객 관리
Korgale LLC

어휘
frustration 좌절 | unreliable 믿을 수 없는, 신뢰할 수 없는 | fortunately 다행스럽게도 | colleague 동료 | represent 대표하다 | area 지역 | add 추가하다 | set up 마련하다 | sample 시음[시식]하다 | session (특정 활동을 하는) 시간 | reduced 할인된 | rate 요금

181. 상세 정보

Hayes 씨는 왜 양식을 작성했는가?
(A) 배송 문제를 알리려고
(B) 서비스에 피드백을 제공하려고
(C) 광고에 관해서 문의하려고
(D) 공급업체와 만남을 요청하려고

해설 첫 번째 지문 [양식], 두 번째 상자에서 'We are looking to change suppliers.'라고 했으므로 (D)가 정답이다.

182. 사실 확인

Hazy Mornings에 관하여 언급된 것은?
(A) 현재 신규 매장을 열려고 한다.
(B) 작년에 공급업체를 바꿨다.
(C) 텔레비전에 소개된 적 있다.
(D) 과거에 Korgale을 공급업체로 이용했다.

해설 첫 번째 지문 [양식], 두 번째 상자에서 'Given our past experiences with you, I decided to contact you.'라고 했으므로 (D)가 정답이다.

183. 암시 / 추론 – 연계 문제

Andrews 씨는 누구겠는가?
(A) 회계사
(B) 매장 매니저
(C) 연구 분석가
(D) 판매 직원

해설 첫 번째 지문 [양식], 두 번째 상자에서 'I will be available to meet with a representative all of next week except Monday and Friday, as I have prior obligations.'라고 했는데, 두 번째 지문 [이메일], 첫 번째 단락에서 'I will get my colleague, Tanya Andrews, to contact you. She represents the greater Liane area.'라고 했으므로 (D)가 정답이다.

184. 암시 / 추론 – 연계 문제

Hazy Mornings에서의 차 시음은 언제 있을 것인가?
(A) 월요일에
(B) 화요일에
(C) 수요일에
(D) 목요일에

해설 첫 번째 지문 [양식], 두 번째 상자에서 'I will be available to meet with a representative all of next week except Monday and Friday,'라고 했는데, 두 번째 지문 [이메일], 첫 번째 단락에서 'She is She is normally in the office 9:00 A.M. to 5:00 P.M. from Monday to Wednesday. However, please note that she will not be in the office this Wednesday.'라고 하여 두 사람이 모두 시간이 되는 화요일에 만날 예정임을 알 수 있으므로 (B)가 정답이다.

185. 상세 정보

Daniel 씨는 Hazy Mornings에게 무엇을 제공하는가?

(A) 우선 배송
(B) 할인가격
(C) 업계 연락망
(D) 독점 상품

해설 두 번째 지문 [이메일], 두 번째 단락에서 'As part of our welcome back package, we would also like to offer you a reduced rate on your first order.'라고 했으므로 (B)가 정답이다.

✛ **Paraphrasing**

a reduced rate → a discounted price

186-190번은 다음 웹 페이지, 온라인 양식, 이메일에 관한 문제입니다.

Building Connections에서는 기관에서 팀워크를 쌓을 수 있는 창의적인 방법을 제공합니다. Building Connections에서는 다양한 사람들에게 적합한 각종 워크숍을 보유하고 있어, 각 워크숍은 3시간 동안 진행됩니다. 팀이 보다 잘 소통하고 더욱 효율적이 될 수 있도록 도와드립니다.

워크숍 종류:
· 보트 타기 · 나만의 도자기 만들기 · 단편영화 촬영하기 · 게임 설계하기
· 🔢186 벽화 칠하기(대중의 요구를 기반으로)

워크숍 가격표:

참가자 수	인당 요금
10인 미만	65달러
10-20인	60달러
🔢188 21-30인	55달러
31인 이상	50달러

어휘
promote 촉진하다 | team building 팀 빌딩, 단합 | organization 기관 | an array of 다수의 | workshop 워크숍 | suitable 알맞은, 적합한 | a range of 다양한 | communicate 소통하다 | efficient 효율적인 | last 지속되다 | sail 항해하다 | pottery 도자기 | shoot 촬영하다 | mural 벽화 | based on ~에 근거하여 | popular 대중의 | demand 수요, 요구 | pricing 가격 책정 | less than ~보다 적은

단체명: Canterbury 대학교
이름: Leonard Gaines
이메일: lgaines@canterbury.ac.nz
🔢188 **참가자 수:** 29
요청일 및 시간: 8월 11일 오전 10시

워크숍 종류: (선호하는 순서대로 적어주세요)
첫 번째 선택: 보트 타기
🔢189 **두 번째 선택: 벽화 칠하기**
세 번째 선택: 게임 설계하기
네 번째 선택: 단편영화 촬영하기

귀하의 단체에 대해 알려주세요.
🔢187 최근 대학교에서 주요 개편이 있었습니다. 그 결과, 완전히 새로운 팀으로 새로 구성되었습니다. 저는 저희 팀원들이 서로 친해지길 바라며, 뭔가 실제적인 행사가 기억에 남을 것 같습니다.

어휘
participant 참가자 | choice 선택 | list 열거하다 | preference 선호도 | restructure 구조 조정[개혁], 개편하다 | as a result 그 결과 | entirely 완전히 | get acquainted with 친해지다 | memorable 기억에 남는

수신: Leonard Gaines 〈lgaines@canterbury.ac.nz〉
발신: Maureen Crawford
〈mcrawford@buildingconnections.co.nz〉
날짜: 8월 5일
제목: 수락: 팀 빌딩 워크숍 요청

Gaines 씨께,

전액 송금해 주셔서 감사합니다. 저희가 자금을 받았기에, 이제 8월 11일 오전 10시로 확정되었습니다. 🔢189 일기 예보를 바탕으로, 제가 귀하의 단체에 대해 두 번째 선호 항목으로 일정을 잡아드렸습니다.

🔢190 행사는 3시간 동안 진행될 것입니다. 기본 다과 및 음료는 제공됩니다. 하지만 전체 케이터링 서비스 제공을 원하신다면, 그렇게 준비해 드릴 수 있습니다. 이 경우에는 추가 비용이 든다는 점을 유의해 주시기 바랍니다. 전원이 함께 드실 수 있는 구역이 있으니, 그 공간을 편안하게 이용하셔도 됩니다.

다음 주에 귀하와 귀하의 단체를 만날 날을 기다리고 있겠습니다. 변경 사항이 생기면, 최대한 빨리 저희에게 알려주시기 바랍니다.

마음을 담아,

Maureen Crawford
Building Connections

어휘
transfer 송금하다 | full amount 전액 | fund 자금, 돈 | forecast 예보[예측]하다 | schedule 일정을 잡다 | run 계속되다 | refreshment 다과 | beverage 음료 | catering service 음식 공급 서비스 | arrange 준비하다, 마련하다 | cost 비용이 들다 | extra 추가로 | entire 전체의 | make use of ~을 이용[활용]하다

---

186. 사실 확인

Building Connections에 관하여 첫 번째 웹 페이지에서 언급하는 것은?

(A) 지방 정부에서 운영한다.
(B) 고객 맞춤형 워크숍을 제공할 수 있다.
(C) 참가자의 피드백을 이용하여 워크숍 내용을 변경한다.
(D) 매달 새로운 워크숍을 하나씩 추가한다.

해설 첫 번째 지문 [웹 페이지], 'Workshop Options'에서 'Paint a Mural (based on popular demand)'라고 했으므로 (C)가 정답이다.

187. 암시 / 추론

Canterbury 대학교에 관하여 양식에서 알 수 있는 것은?

(A) 직원들이 새로운 팀으로 배치됐다.
(B) 지역내에서 가장 오래된 대학교이다.
(C) 그 직원들은 여러 워크숍에 참여하려고 한다.
(D) 경영진에 변화가 있었다.

해설 두 번째 지문 [온라인 양식], 'Please tell us about your group' 항목에서 'The university has recently gone through a major restructure. As a result, we've found ourselves in entirely new teams.'라고 했으므로 (A)가 정답이다.

188. 상세 정보 - 연계 문제

Canterbury 대학교의 워크숍의 인당 비용은 얼마이겠는가?

(A) 50달러
(B) 55달러
(C) 60달러
(D) 65달러

해설 두 번째 지문[온라인 양식], 'Number of participants' 항목에서 29라고 했는데, 첫 번째 지문[웹 페이지], 워크숍 가격표에서 21-30인인 경우 인당 가격이 55달러임을 알 수 있으므로 (B)가 정답이다.

189. 상세 정보 - 연계 문제

Crawford 씨는 어떤 워크숍의 등록을 확인해주는가?
(A) 단편영화 촬영하기
(B) 보트 타기
(C) 벽화 칠하기
(D) 게임 설계하기

해설 세 번째 지문[이메일], 첫 번째 단락에서 'Based on the forecasted weather, I have scheduled your group for your second preference.'라고 했는데, 두 번째 지문[온라인 양식], 'Workshop Options'에서 '2nd choice'가 'Paint a Mural'임을 알 수 있으므로 (C)가 정답이다.

190. 사실 확인

이메일에서 다과에 관하여 언급하는 것은?
(A) 현지 업체의 후원을 받는다.
(B) 추가 비용 없이 제공된다.
(C) 부지 내에서 먹을 수 없다.
(D) 일부 워크숍에서만 제공된다.

해설 세 번째 지문[이메일], 두 번째 단락에서 'We do provide basic refreshments and beverages.'라고 했으므로 (B)가 정답이다.

191-195번은 다음 예약 영수증, 규정, 그리고 이메일에 관한 문제입니다.

Hiro Rent-a-Car

대여인 성함: Nancy Ori
[193] **픽업일:** 7월 4일 오전 10시
[195] **반납일:** 7월 8일 오후 6시 (5일)
대여 장소: Nagasaki 공항

Hiro Rent-A-Car는 공항 터미널에서 셔틀버스로 짧은 거리에 위치해 있습니다. [191]결제 증빙으로, 반드시 이 영수증 사본을 서비스 카운터로 가지고 오십시오. 도착 즉시 귀하의 차량이 준비될 것입니다.

읽어주세요: [192]각 차량의 연료량은 상이합니다. 저희가 매일 대여 및 수령하는 차량수로 인해, 모든 연료탱크를 가득 채워놓는 것은 불가능합니다. 하지만 저희는 귀하가 근처 주유소까지 운전해서 갈 수 있도록 보장해 드립니다. 픽업일과 동일한 수준으로 차량에 연료를 다시 채우는 것은 대여자의 책임입니다. 같은 양의 연료로 차량을 반환하지 못하는 경우, 연료탱크를 가득 채우는 비용이 귀하의 신용카드로 부과될 것입니다.

어휘
renter 임대인 | return 반납 | receipt 영수증 | proof 증명 | vehicle 차량 | fuel 연료 | vary 다르다 | responsibility 책임 | refuel 재급유하다 | charge 부과하다 | completely 완전히 | refill 다시 채우다

Hiro Rent-A-Car — 고속도로 통행료 서비스

[195]일주일 이상 차를 빌리는 분들에게는, 통행료 스티커가 차량 앞 유리에 놓일 것입니다. 이 스티커는 통행료 징수구역의 맨 우측 차선에 있는 급행 요금소를 이용할 수 있게 하여 귀하의 시간을 절약해 줍니다. 통행료는 기록된 신용카드로 청구될 것입니다.

스티커가 없는 차량은 통행료를 현금으로 지불하기 위해 좌측 차선의 부스에 정차해야 합니다. 결제를 하지 못한 차량은 딱지를 끊고 원 통행료의 최고 10배까지 벌금이 부과된다는 것을 유념해 주십시오. 처리 수수료와 법정 비용도 발생할 수 있습니다.

어휘
toll 통행료 | windshield (자동차) 앞 유리 | save 절약하다 | express 고속의, 급행의 | lane 차선 | on file 기록이 보관되어 있는 | ticket 딱지를 발부하다 | fine 벌금을 물리다 | original 원래의 | process 처리하다 | court 법정 | incur (비용을) 발생시키다, 물게 되다

수신: Nancy Ori 〈nori@falcom.ca〉
발신: Hiro Rent-A-Car 〈help@hirocars.co.jp〉
날짜: 7월 5일
제목: 수신 메시지

Ori 씨께,

[193][195]저는 귀하가 여기서 첫날에 통행료를 내지 않고 실수로 7번 고속도로 급행 요금소를 통과했다는 내용의 메시지를 오늘 받았습니다. [194]이 문제를 해결하려면, 도시 고속도로 공사의 웹사이트(www.mepc.com)를 방문해 렌트 차량의 번호판 숫자와 이동 날짜를 입력하셔야 합니다. 귀하의 통행료가 계산될 것입니다. 정보를 재확인하고 진행하십시오. 그리고 나서, 결제 정보를 입력하셔야 합니다. 사건 발생 5일 이내에 요금을 정산하시면, 모든 추가 수수료가 면제됩니다.

진심으로,

Hiro Rent-A-Car 지원센터

어휘
explain 설명하다 | issue 문제 | accidently 우연히 | expressway 고속도로 | settle 처리하다, 정산하다 | matter 문제 | metropolitan 대도시의 | license plate 인가 번호판 | rental 임대, 대여 | calculate 계산하다 | confirm 확인하다 | charge 요금 | incident 사건 | waive 포기하다

191. 사실 확인

Ori 씨의 대여 계약에 관하여 언급된 것은?
(A) 차량이 이미 전액 결제되었다.
(B) GPS 시스템은 추가 비용이 들 것이다.
(C) 연료 효율이 좋은 차량에 대한 것이다.
(D) 그녀의 회사가 미리 준비했다.

해설 첫 번째 지문[예약 영수증], 첫 번째 단락에서 'Please be sure to bring a copy of this receipt to the service counter as proof of your payment.'라고 했으므로 (A)가 정답이다.

192. 상세 정보

예약 영수증에는 어떤 정보가 강조되어 있는가?
(A) 갑작스러운 통지로는 대여 기간을 연장할 수 없다.
(B) 일일 평균요금은 차량 반납일 아침에 계산된다.
(C) Hiro Rent-A-Car는 운전자 수를 2명으로 제한한다.
(D) 차량에 일정량의 연료가 남아 있어야 한다.

해설 첫 번째 지문[예약 영수증], 세 번째 단락에서 'It is the renter's responsibility to refuel the vehicle to the same level on the pickup date.'라고 했으므로 (D)가 정답이다.

✛ **Paraphrasing**
the same level → a certain amount

193. 상세 정보 – 연계 문제

Ori 씨는 어느 날짜에 7번 고속도로를 이용했는가?

(A) 7월 4일
(B) 7월 5일
(C) 7월 6일
(D) 7월 7일

해설 첫 번째 지문[예약 영수증], 첫 번째 단락에서 'Pickup Date: 4 July, 10:00 A.M.'이라고 했고, 세 번째 지문[Hiro Rent-A-Car가 Ori 씨에게 보낸 이메일], 첫 번째 단락에서 'I received the message you sent today explaining the issue of accidentally passing through the express toll booth on Expressway 7 without paying the toll on your first day here.'라고 하여 차량 대여 첫날인 7월 4일에 7번 고속도로를 이용했음을 알 수 있으므로 (A)가 정답이다.

194. 상세 정보

Ori 씨는 왜 Hiro Rent-A-Car의 지원센터로 메시지를 보냈는가?

(A) 자동차 사고에 대해 자세히 설명하려고
(B) 차량번호판을 확인하려고
(C) 새로운 반납일을 예약하려고
(D) 미지급된 요금을 해결하려고

해설 세 번째 지문[Hiro Rent-A-Car가 Ori 씨에게 보낸 이메일], 첫 번째 단락에서 'To settle this matter, you will need to visit the Metropolitan Expressway Public Corporation's Web site (www.mepc.com) and enter the license plate number of the rental vehicle and travel date.'라고 했으므로 (D)가 정답이다.

✛ Paraphrasing

settle the charge → resolve a payment

195. 암시 / 추론 – 연계 문제

Ori 씨에 관하여 알 수 있는 것은?

(A) 통행 요금소의 맨 오른쪽 차선을 이용했다.
(B) 최신 송장을 찾을 수 없다.
(C) 예약 영수증을 발급받지 못했다.
(D) 예상치 못한 우회를 해야 했다.

해설 두 번째 지문[규정], 첫 번째 단락에서 'This sticker will save you time by allowing you to use the express toll booths in the far-right lanes of the toll collection area.'라고 했고, 세 번째 지문[Hiro Rent-A-Car가 Ori 씨에게 보낸 이메일], 첫 번째 단락에서 'I received the message you sent today explaining the issue of accidentally passing through the express toll booth on Expressway 7 without paying the toll on your first day here.'라고 하여 통행 요금소 맨 오른쪽에 있는 급행 요금소를 지나갔음을 알 수 있으므로 (A)가 정답이다.

196-200번은 다음 프레젠테이션 슬라이드, 이메일, 그리고 보고서에 관한 문제입니다.

C-Cellular 고객서비스 담당자 전화응대 교육 매뉴얼	
현재: 스크립트 이용	**앞으로: 매뉴얼 이용**
■ 서비스 담당자는 스크립트를 이용하여 모든 고객 문제를 처리합니다.	■ 서비스 담당자는 매뉴얼에 따라 고객을 돕습니다.
■ 서비스 담당자는 스크립트에서 다루지 않는 문제를 관리자에게 이전합니다.	■ 서비스 담당자는 고객에게 보다 더 개별 맞춤의 지원을 제공합니다.

장점
▶ 통화 이전 감소
▶ **196** 신속한 해결
▶ 고객 경험 개선

어휘
customer service representative 고객서비스 담당자 | training manual 교육 매뉴얼 | handle 처리하다 | call 전화 통화 | script 대본, 원고 | issue 문제 | transfer 넘겨주다, 이동하다 | address (문제 등을) 다루다 | supervising manager 상사 | assist 돕다 | personalize (개인의 필요에) 맞추다 | support 지원, 도움 | advantage 이점, 장점 | fewer 보다 적은 [few의 비교급] | quicker 더 빠른 [quick의 비교급] | solution 해법, 해결책 | improved 향상된, 개선된

수신: C-Cellular 고객서비스 부서
발신: Renee Young, 교육이사
날짜: 2월 8일
제목: 초기 테스트 지침

고객서비스 부서 관리자들께,

저희가 고객서비스 상담전화를 업데이트 및 개선하는 동안 기다려주셔서 감사드립니다. **197** 여러분도 저희만큼이나 웹 기반의 라이브 교육을 즐기셨기를 바랍니다. 서로 간의 거리가 있음에도, 저희가 많은 공통 우려 사항들을 해결할 수 있는 기회가 되었습니다.

앞서 언급했듯이, 저희는 3월 4일부터 시작되는 한 달짜리 파일럿 프로그램을 위해 새로운 고객서비스 매뉴얼을 출시할 겁니다. 이 기간 동안, 저희가 실행 전에 프로세스를 재조정할 수 있게 프로그램의 효능에 대한 데이터가 수집될 것입니다.

199 200 파일럿 프로그램과 관련하여, 저희는 각 지점에서 다음 수에 해당하는 직원을 원합니다: Karachi와 Lagos에서 15명, Dhaka와 Edmonton에서 각 7명 이상입니다. **198** 이 직원들은 세부 조정을 위한 주 2회 평가 회의 참석과 함께, 모든 통화를 기록해야 합니다.

안부를 전하며,

Renee Young
교육이사, C-Cellular 운영부서

어휘
initial 초기의 | testing 테스트(하기) | patience 인내력, 참을성 | update 갱신하다 | improve 개선하다 | hotline 상담 전화, 핫라인 | live 실시간의, 생중계의 | Web-based 웹 기반의, 인터넷의 | training session 교육(과정) | distance 거리 | opportunity 기회 | resolve 해결하다 | common 공통의 | concern 우려, 걱정 | mention 언급하다 | roll out (신상품을) 출시하다 | pilot 시험 [실험]하는 | efficacy 효능, 능률 | collect 수집하다 | readjust 조정[변경]하다 | process 과정 | implementation 실행, 이행 | branch 지점 | participant 참가자 | a minimum of 최소 | keep a record of 기록하다 | attend 참석하다 | assessment 평가 | fine-tuning 세부 조정 | purpose 목적

신규 매뉴얼 파일럿 프로그램

3주 차 보고서

통화 시간은 조금 더 길어진 것으로 보이지만, 설문조사에 따르면 고객 평점은 향상되었음을 알 수 있습니다. 저희 직원들이 새로운 시스템을 배워가면서, 통화 시간도 감소할 것이라고 생각합니다.

지점	직원
Karachi	16
Lagos	15
200 Dhaka	5
Edmonton	7

어휘

report 보고(서) | duration 기간 | survey (설문) 조사 | rating 순위, 평가 |
decrease 감소하다, 줄다

196. 상세 정보

슬라이드에 따르면, C-Cellular는 왜 절차를 변경하는가?

(A) 이전되는 통화 수를 늘리기 위해
(B) 서비스 담당자의 통화 시간을 단축시키기 위해
(C) 교육과정의 효능을 향상시키기 위해
(D) 업데이트된 정부 프로토콜에 따르기 위해

해설 첫 번째 지문 [슬라이드], 'Moving Forward: Using a Manual'
의 'Advantages'에서 'Quicker solutions'라고 하여 고객통화
를 더 빨리 해결할 수 있음을 알 수 있으므로 (B)가 정답이다.

197. 사실 확인

이메일에서 언급된 교육에 관하여 사실인 것은?

(A) 사전에 녹음될 것이다.
(B) 한 달간 진행될 것이다.
(C) 3월 4일에 실시되었다.
(D) 원격으로 열렸다.

해설 두 번째 지문 [이메일], 첫 번째 단락에서 'We hope that you
enjoyed the live Web-based training session as much as
we did; despite the distance between us, it gave us an
opportunity to resolve a lot of common concerns.'라고 했
으므로 (D)가 정답이다.

198. 상세 정보

이메일에 따르면, 파일럿 참가자들은 무엇을 해야 하는가?

(A) 동료들에게 새로운 프로세스를 보여줘야 한다
(B) 통화하는 동안 관리자와 협력해야 한다
(C) 다른 C-Cellular 콜센터를 평가해야 한다
(D) 자신들이 받는 모든 통화를 기록해야 한다

해설 두 번째 지문 [이메일], 세 번째 단락에서 'These employees will
need to keep records of all the calls they take in addition
to attending assessment meetings twice a week for fine-
tuning purposes.'라고 했으므로 (D)가 정답이다.

✚ **Paraphrasing**

keep records of all the calls they take → log all of
the calls they answer

199. 암시 / 추론

파일럿 참가자는 누구겠는가?

(A) 고객서비스 직원
(B) 새로운 서비스 공급자
(C) 관리자
(D) C-Cellular 교육 담당자

해설 두 번째 지문 [이메일], 세 번째 단락에서 'As for the pilot
program, we would like the following numbers of
representatives from each branch: 15 participants from
Karachi and Lagos, and a minimum of seven each from
both Dhaka and Edmonton.'이라고 하여 지점별 고객서비스
직원들이 참여할 것임을 알 수 있으므로 (A)가 정답이다.

✚ **Paraphrasing**

representatives → agents

200. 상세 정보 - 연계 문제

어떤 서비스센터에서 필요한 파일럿 참가자 수를 제공하지 않았
는가?

(A) Karachi
(B) Lagos
(C) Dhaka
(D) Edmonton

해설 두 번째 지문 [이메일], 세 번째 단락에서 'As for the pilot
program, we would like the following numbers of
representatives from each branch: 15 participants from
Karachi and Lagos, and a minimum of seven each from
both Dhaka and Edmonton.'이라고 했는데, 세 번째 지문 [보고
서], 표에서 'Dhaka'에서 '5'명의 직원이 참여하여 7명 미만임을
알 수 있으므로 (C)가 정답이다.

MEMO

파고다
토익 RC
종합서 | 해설서